ENGLISH THEATRICAL LITERATURE

ENGLISH THEATRICAL LITERATURE

1559–1900

A BIBLIOGRAPHY

incorporating

ROBERT W. LOWE'S

A BIBLIOGRAPHICAL ACCOUNT
OF ENGLISH THEATRICAL LITERATURE

published in 1888

by

JAMES FULLARTON ARNOTT
and
JOHN WILLIAM ROBINSON

THE SOCIETY FOR THEATRE RESEARCH
London
1970

On behalf of
The Society for Theatre Research
this work is dedicated
to the memory of
IFAN KYRLE FLETCHER
1905–1969
Theatre Historian and Bookseller
by whose initiative the Society was founded

INTRODUCTION

It was at the end of 1953 that the Committee of the Society for Theatre Research decided to put in hand "as a long term project" a recension of Lowe's *Bibliographical Account of English Theatrical Literature*. This work, published in 1888, had long been regarded as a standard reference book in its own field and indispensable to any student of theatrical history. Published in a limited edition, it had been out of print for many years and was by then very scarce, second-hand copies commanding a high price. The Society had inaugurated its publishing programme three years previously with a bibliographical work, *The Theatre of the British Isles excluding London* compiled by Alfred Loewenberg, and felt justified in accepting the responsibility for what we knew would be a long and onerous undertaking. None of us realised at the time just how long and onerous it would prove to be.

Under the direction of the Chairman of the Publications Subcommittee, Miss Muriel St Clare Byrne, an editorial board was set up consisting of Miss A. M. C. Kahn as chairman and Mr George Speaight and Mr Bertram Shuttleworth as members. At an early stage the decision was made to extend the terminal date of the work to 1900, after which date bibliographical information from other sources was more easily available than for the earlier period; to check and revise Lowe's descriptions in the light of modern bibliographical practice; and to add titles that had been missed at the time of the original compilation.

For two or three years this editorial team set about their task, during which time we were greatly helped in various ways by Sir St. Vincent Troubridge, Mr George Nash of the Victoria and Albert Museum, Mr Ifan Kyrle Fletcher and Mr Peter Murray Hill. But the volume of the work proved too much for our part-time labours, and one by one we were forced to relinquish our posts. In 1958 it was announced that Mr Ian Gibb, a librarian at University College, would undertake the preparation of the new edition, assisted by the members of the London Group of the Society. But in his turn Mr Gibb was obliged to retire and in 1959 the Society invited applications for a new editor.

We were fortunate enough to receive an offer to undertake this work from Mr James Arnott, who brought with him, first as an assistant and then as joint editor, his past student, Mr John Robinson. Together these editors made an entirely fresh start and for ten years they have pursued their painstaking labours on both sides of the Atlantic, checking and double-checking, aiming at a perfection that continually eludes the perfectionist, until at last the result of their work is ready to be placed before the public. They make their own acknowledgement of those who have assisted them in their monumental task. The members of the Lowe Subcommittee have guided the progress of the work on the behalf of the Society; among its members I should particularly mention Mr Basil Francis who, as treasurer for many years, established the financing of this considerable undertaking upon firm foundations.

To those of our members, and other purchasers of this work, who have waited so long for it to appear, we offer our apologies for the delay, but we hope that the resultant volume will prove worth waiting for and will, indeed, prove to be the service to theatrical scholarship that we had envisaged when we put the work in hand seventeen years ago. To all those who have helped, at one stage or another, to bring this book into existence the Society for Theatre Research extends its grateful thanks.

GEORGE SPEAIGHT
General Editor of Publications,
The Society for Theatre Research

PUBLISHER'S ACKNOWLEDGEMENTS

The Society for Theatre Research extends its grateful thanks to the American Council of Learned Societies, to the British Academy and to the Carnegie Trust for Scotland for financial assistance towards the cost of printing this book, without which its publication would not have been possible.

TABLE OF CONTENTS

PREFACE

Our title "English Theatrical Literature 1559–1900: a bibliography" attempts to define the scope of the work; but if the scope is to be quite clear, several glosses on the words of the title should be offered. Since we were continuing the work of R. W. Lowe, it seemed best to use the terminology which he had made familiar. We have kept Lowe's "English", though, as he did, we include the Irish and the Scottish theatre; and the word also carries his further sense of "published in the British Isles". Unlike Lowe, we record American and other overseas editions, and also translations, though only in a brief note to the entry for the British edition or editions, which alone receive our full bibliographical description. "Theatrical", as with Lowe, excludes the purely literary aspects of the drama. This is a line which we have drawn rather more strictly than Lowe did. While Lowe excluded plays, prologues and epilogues, and recitations, he occasionally admitted works which we regard as literary criticism or literary history. These we have kept in, but we did not let them serve as a precedent when we were considering the claims for admission of new items of a purely literary character. These occasional anomalies have arisen from our giving priority to the rule that every item in Lowe should be found in our work, either in the main body of entries or in the Appendix. For a work to count with us as theatrical literature it must be mainly concerned with the theatre; incidental references, however important, are not enough. Our definition of the theatrical does not extend to all the arts of spectacle. Opera, pantomime and music hall are included, but not ballet or circus, except where these are closely linked with the legitimate drama. It should be added that, like Lowe, we exclude fiction dealing with theatrical life, except for one or two works of a strong documentary interest.

Our "literature" excludes manuscripts, but includes printed matter in all formats from the book to the broadside, except for playbills and programmes, though an exception has been made for a few souvenir programmes of special interest. A few engraved prints have also been included when the letter-press was of equal importance with the picture. The dates "1559–1900" refer, of course, not to events in the history of the theatre, but to the original publication of the works which we describe. Editions later than 1900 of works first published before that date are also included.

This is "a bibliography" primarily in the sense of a guide to printed sources. We could subscribe to the statement of Lowe in his preface: "My primary object has been to produce a handbook for the literary worker. . . . My principle of arrangement has been to give the full description of each book under the subject heading." Here, we think, we can claim to have improved on Lowe. His subject classification is very idiosyncratic. Many things which are said to be "not in Lowe" are merely hard to find in Lowe. Our subject classification will be found, we believe, more rational than Lowe's. There was never any possibility, of course, of our supplying a detailed subject bibliography. This limitation, however, is to some extent offset by the provision of numerous cross-references and of three indexes, of author, title, and place of publication. Another apparent limitation — that our bibliography stops at 1900 — is offset, not only by our recording later editions (as indicated in the preceding paragraph), but also by our providing in the notes to section headings and to individual works, references to some of the most important later studies of the pre-1900 theatre.

Lowe's notes, except for a few which seemed no longer of value, have been kept and reprinted as they stand, apart from the silent correction of minor errors in the light of more recent knowledge, and the omission of the auction sale prices which he occasionally supplies. Since our system of classification differs from his, it follows that his notes will not always be found in the original location. Most of his scattered biographical notes will be found under BIOGRAPHY: INDIVIDUAL. As for our own notes, we have indicated, as Lowe did, the content of a work when the classification or title do not make this clear. Otherwise, our notes reflect the advance in the study of theatrical history since Lowe's time. He went into considerable historical and biographical detail: we can give the bare facts and provide references to the host of new authorities.

Other users that we had in mind are the bibliographer, the bookseller, the collector and the librarian. We hope that the omission of the auction prices which Lowe occasionally gives will not be regarded as a serious loss: it seemed to us only of a very specialised historical interest. On the other hand, we have tried to do more for these users by moving farther than Lowe in the direction of critical bibliography. Lowe was perfectly clear about the limits of his objective: that is why he called his work, not a bibliography, but "a bibliographical account". Lowe, of course, worked on sound bibliographical principles; he writes in his preface, "I have examined the vast majority of the works I describe and have made myself acquainted with their contents as well as their title pages." We have at least been able to follow the first principle to the limit of our resources, if we could not always live up to the second. We made it our rule to examine and collate by gatherings as many of the copies available to us of a work as was necessary to recognise and find a perfect copy, which we then chose for description, recording its location. With our limited resources, there had to be exceptions to the rule. Sometimes we have had to be content with describing a copy which is imperfect, but the best available to us. Some periodicals with extremely long runs (e.g. *The Era*, 1838–1939; *The Stage*, 1880–in progress; *The Entr'acte*, 1869–1907) have not been collated volume by volume. We have included items which we have failed to examine ourselves (provided our source of information was reliable) so that our bibliography could also serve as a check-list; such items are preceded by an asterisk.

It will be seen from the description of our way of working that the fact that only one location is given is no indication of the number of copies we have examined, or of the rarity of a work; nor is the fact that a particular location may be a provincial library necessarily any indication that a copy of the work in question is not to be found in one of the great metropolitan libraries.

Our work embodies the results of a search, varying in thoroughness with the time available, of the libraries of the British Museum, the Garrick Club, the Society for Theatre Research, the Universities of Glasgow, Nebraska and Harvard, the Victoria and Albert Museum, the Folger Shakespeare Library, the National Library of Scotland, the Mitchell Library, Glasgow, and a few private libraries; of a random use of a large number of other libraries, large and small; and of a scrutiny of Lowe's and Loewenberg's bibliographies and of contributions from members of the Society for Theatre Research (the three sources which were our starting point), of the catalogue of the Brown Collection in the Boston Public Library and of many specialised bibliographies and bookseller's catalogues.

It would no doubt be helpful if we were to clarify our relationship to two bibliographies which already supplement the work of Lowe: Alfred Loewenberg's *The Theatre of the British Isles excluding London: a Bibliography* (London, 1950); and Carl Stratman's *A Bibliography of British Dramatic Periodicals* (New York, 1962). While we can claim to incorporate Lowe, we do not entirely replace Loewenberg in his field. His bibliography extends beyond 1900, and includes books and periodicals containing theatrical information, but not primarily theatrical, as well as collections of playbills, programmes, press cuttings and manuscript materials. Father Stratman's bibliography also extends beyond 1900, and includes a few periodicals with important theatrical sections but not meeting our criterion of being largely devoted to the theatre.

ORDER OF ENTRIES

1. Entries are classified by subject, the classes then being ordered by width of reference, the class with the wider reference taking precedence. The resulting system of classification is set out in the table of contents on pages ix–x. Information should be sought, not only under the particular subject-headings, but also under the more general preceding headings.

2. Within classes, entries are arranged according to the date of publication: the historical progress of theatrical literature can thus be observed. It should be noted that the doubtful comes before the firm date, e.g. 1888? before 1888.

3. For ease of reference, the system of subject-classification and chronological sequence has in certain cases been set aside either in favour of alphabetical order or by bringing together closely related entries.

(*a*) All later issues and editions of a work follow immediately after the first.

(*b*) A short series of announcements or of complaints and answers are arranged in order of their appearance.

(*c*) Contributions to a controversy are grouped together under a sub-heading, the end of the subsection being indicated by a rule. The work which started the controversy comes first, followed by the remaining entries arranged firstly by the year of publication, then in alphabetical order within years.

(*d*) Two or more works appearing in the same year, but not related as in (*a*), (*b*) or (*c*) above, are arranged in alphabetical order.

METHOD OF DESCRIPTION

A method of description should, as far as possible, explain and justify itself. In the hopeful belief that our method has achieved these ends, we do not reproduce the elaborate formulary from which as a practical necessity we had to work. There are however a few points which call for comment.

1. Each main entry, except for those in the appendix, is preceded by its number. In place of a number, cross-references have the sign ✖, and references to Acts, Bills and Parliamentary Papers, the sign ¶.

2. An asterisk ★ indicates that the editors or their immediate associates have not examined the item which follows. The source of the description is given in the library symbol or at the end of the entry in a note. The sign † indicates that the copy has some major imperfection. We have not considered the absence of a half-title page serious enough to require the use of this sign.

3. Main entries begin with a cataloguing element extracted from the title page, and printed in capitals, either the author's name (surname first), his pseudonym, or, if the work is anonymous, the title as far as is necessary to give a distinctive short title. An author's name is given in its full form, but with information not appearing on the title page in square brackets. When the author of an anonymous work is known, the entry begins with his name in square brackets, but is catalogued under the title.

4. A transcription of the title page follows, complete except for references to authors' other works, descriptions in general terms of illustrations, and mottoes. The capitalisation, line arrangement, and typography (except for italicisation of titles cited) of the original are not recorded. With regard to this italicisation, a *caveat* should be entered: our revised rule has been to follow the practice of the original, reproducing its roman, italics or quotation marks; but a few descriptions dating from an earlier period when we standardised the treatment of titles cited may have survived our revision. The punctuation is kept, and no additional punctuation is provided, except that the end of the transcription is always indicated by a full stop, whether that is present in the original or not.

5. The pagination recorded, which is based on a collation by gatherings, takes account of all pages in the book as published. It is expressed as a series. Wherever possible, unnumbered pages are incorporated in the series by giving them an inferred number which is printed in *roman* within square brackets. Numbers printed in *italics* within square brackets represent totals of unnumbered pages which are not incorporated in the series. The contents of unnumbered final leaves are noted; also, exceptionally, of a final unnumbered page. Bound-in advertisements are not recorded. Two exceptions should be mentioned. A very few early unnumbered or irregularly numbered works are described by collation of signatures; and single sheets printed on one side only are recorded as broadsides, abbreviated as "bs".

6. The abbreviation "illus." refers to illustrations, diagrams, plans and the like (but not ornaments) on the printed sheets. Inserted illustrations are described as plates; if they bear an indication of order, this is kept and recorded as a series, (e.g. front., II–X); if unnumbered, the designation is inferred for a frontispiece and the remaining plates recorded, not as a series but as a total, all within square brackets (e.g. [front., 6]). If not numbered by the printer as plates, insets printed from type, such as type-facsimile, genealogical tables, type-printed music, coloured advertisements, are distinguished as "insets". Engraved title pages, inserted errata slips and inserted spine labels are also recorded.

7. The introductory phrases "published by" and "sold for" in publisher's imprints are omitted, as are street addresses. If no place of publication is recorded, London is to be inferred. Dates are always given in arabic.

8. Periodicals are catalogued under the title. They may occasionally be described as issued in volume form, or in parts, if this is not clear from the collation. Lozenge-shaped brackets ⟨⟩ distinguish a passage found in the title of the volume, but not of the individual parts; double lozenge-shaped brackets ≪≫ a passage found in the title of the parts, but not of the volume.

9. The location of the copy described is recorded by a library symbol printed at the right-hand margin of the last line of the pagination. The symbols used are listed on p. xvi. When the copy is not in a library, the location or source of information is recorded in a note.

10. A printed rule introduces another issue or edition of the preceding item. It is to be assumed that the title pages are unchanged apart from any variations recorded.

11. The note beginning "Reprinted in . . ." refers not to the particular edition of a work which it follows, but to the work in general.

12. The sign ¶ introduces Parliamentary material, described as follows.

Acts: long title; regnal year, chapter number and category (if not Public General); source of preceding information (if not taken from King's or Queen's Printer's copies, *i.e.* if before George I); short title, calendar year, and page reference to *Chronological Table of the Statutes* or *Index of Local and Personal Acts* (according to category of the Act).

Bills, Reports of Committees, etc.: long title; year; short title (if needed) and reference to collected series of Parliamentary papers, the reference consisting of title and date of volume or volumes, and number of paper, followed by a further reference to the copy of the series in the British Museum State Paper Room cited by volume number (if more than one) and page number (added in manuscript to this copy). This further reference is not supplied for House of Lords papers, the British Museum set being incomplete.

Note: The rules listed above may not apply to entries preceded by an asterisk, which, it will be recalled, are descriptions of works we have not ourselves examined. Here our course was to follow the style of the source of our information.

CROSS REFERENCES AND INDEXES (*by Cathrine D. Aird*)

Two main types of cross-reference have been employed throughout the bibliography. The first is the short-title entry (distinguished from main entries by being preceded by the cross-reference symbol ✖ and followed by the formula "see no. . . ."); the second type, takes the form of headnotes to the individual sections (as at the beginning of the Opera section, p. 194).

The use of the first type of cross-reference arose from the desire to produce not only a bibliographer's manual, but also a study of the development of the British theatre as seen through the books and pamphlets of the period. As explained above, entries are arranged chronologically under subject headings; the function of the short-title cross-reference is normally to complete this chronological sequence by including at the appropriate date, a relevant item from another section.

The main function of the headnote cross-reference, on the other hand, is to group together references to related items in other sections. These latter references lay no claim to being exhaustive and are in fact intended only as a rough guide and signpost to researchers using the work as a broad subject bibliography. (In order to give some hint of the scope of these references, and to avoid long lists of unidentifiable numbers, the section heading as well as the entry number has been included.)

In practice, only in those sections where the chronological approach is particularly important are there internal short-title cross-references; extensive headnote references, on the other hand, occur mainly in those sections where the subject approach is more applicable.

The indexes have been utilised to try to solve in part the vexed question of the classification of books which belong to more than one subject field. Priority has, in some cases, been given to subject before place – *i.e.* a book published in Bath on the morality of the theatre will be found under *The Morality of the Theatre* and not under *Bath* — but a great many such local history items can be traced in the *Index of Places of Publication*. Similarly, works by lesser known actors, managers, etc. have often been classified by subject rather than by person — *i.e.* works written by Thomas Sheridan (as manager) will be found under *Ireland* and not under *Biography* — and these can be traced in the *Author Index*.

To avoid researchers looking up long strings of numbers in the indexes, semi-colons have been employed to break up the numbers into their subject sections — *e.g.* anyone interested solely in Government regulations, etc., morality of the theatre, need only check back on numbers within the groups 138–242, 243–679, etc.

In the *Title Index* books with title headings (*e.g.* "Covent Garden Theatre" or "Fairburn's edition") are entered normally under the title heading only, except that headings giving merely particulars of price, number of edition, *etc.*, are ignored. This may account for the apparent non-appearance of some titles in the index and it is wise to check either in the *Author Index* or in the relevant subject section for any book apparently not listed in the *Title Index*.

LIBRARY SYMBOLS

AP	Aberdeen Public Library.	LvP	Liverpool Public Library.
BP	Birmingham Public Library.	MP	Manchester Public Library.
BU	Birmingham University	MB	Boston Public Library, Boston, Massachusetts.
BdP	Bradford City Library.		
BhP	Municipal Library, Bath.	MH	Harvard University, Cambridge, Massachusetts.
BiP	Royal Pavilion Public Library, Brighton.		
BrP	Bristol Public Library.	MgP	Margate Public Library.
C	Cambridge University.	NP	Nottingham Public Library.
CP	Cambridge Public Library.	NIC	Cornell University, Ithaca, New York.
CLaU	University of California at Los Angeles, California.	NN	New York Public Library, New York, New York
CSmH	Henry E. Huntington Library, San Marino, California.	NNC	Columbia University, New York, New York.
CtY	Yale University, New Haven, Connecticut.	NNUQ	Queens College, City University of New York, New York.
D	Trinity College, Dublin.	NbU	University of Nebraska, Lincoln, Nebraska.
DA	Royal Irish Academy, Dublin.		
DP	Pearse Street Library, Dublin.	NjP	Princeton University, Princeton, New Jersey.
DN	National Library of Ireland, Dublin.		
DFo	Folger Shakespeare Library, Washington, D.C.	NoR	Rye Library of Local History, Norwich.
		NwP	Newcastle-upon-Tyne Public Library.
DLC	Library of Congress, Washington, D.C.	NwU	University of Newcastle.
E	National Library of Scotland, Edinburgh.	O	Bodleian Library, Oxford.
		OQ	Queen's College, Oxford.
EP	Edinburgh Public Library.	OWO	Worcester College, Oxford.
EU	Edinburgh University.	OCU	University of Cincinnati, Cincinnati, Ohio.
GM	Mitchell Library, Glasgow.		
GU	Glasgow University.	PP	Free Library, Philadelphia, Pennsylvania.
GrP	Gloucester City Library.	PPL	Library Company of Philadelphia, Pennsylvania.
IP	Ipswich Central Library.		
ICN	Newberry Library, Chicago, Illinois.	PU	University of Pennsylvania, Philadelphia, Pennsylvania.
ICU	University of Chicago, Chicago, Illinois.		
IEN	Northwestern University, Evanston, Illinois.	RdP	Richmond-upon-Thames, Borough Library.
L	British Museum, London.	ReP	Rochdale Central Library.
LDW	Dr Williams's Library, London	SP	Sheffield Public Library.
LE	British Library of Political and Economic Science, London School of Economics.	SdSC	Shakespeare Centre, Stratford-upon-Avon.
LGk	Garrick Club, London.	SptP	Atkinson Central Library, Southport, Lancashire.
LGU	Guildhall Library, London.		
LLib	London Library.	SwP	Swansea Public Library.
LRO	Public Record Office, London	SyP	Shrewsbury Public Library.
LSTR	Library of the Society for Theatre Research (in Senate House Library, University of London).	TnP	Taunton Public Library.
		TnSA	Somerset Archeological Society, Taunton.
LU	London University.	TxU	University of Texas, Austin, Texas.
LUC	University College, London.	WeP	Social Reference Library, Woodbridge.
LVA	Victoria and Albert Museum, London.	WmP	Westminister Public Libraries.
LdP	Leeds Public Library.	YP	York City Library.

ABBREVIATED REFERENCES

Accounts and Papers: The printed Parliamentary Papers collected under this title in the State Paper Room of the British Museum, London.

Acts and Ordinances of the Interregnum: *Acts and Ordinances of the Interregnum, 1642–60.* London, 1911.

Appleton: William W. Appleton. *Charles Macklin: An Actor's Life.* Cambridge, Mass., 1960.

Baker: Herschel C. Baker. *John Philip Kemble: The Actor in His Theatre.* Cambridge, Mass., 1942.

Barker: R. H. Barker. *Mr. Cibber of Drury Lane.* New York, 1939.

Belden: M. M. Belden. *The Dramatic Works of Samuel Foote.* (Yale Studies in English 80.) New Haven, 1929.

Bentley: Gerald Eades Bentley. *The Jacobean and Caroline Stage.* 7 vols. Oxford, 1941–68.

Bibliotheca Lindesiana: R. Steele. *A Bibliography of Royal Proclamations of the Tudor and Stuart Sovereigns. 1485–1714.* Vol. I, England and Wales. (Bibliotheca Lindesiana Vol. V.) Oxford, 1910.

Bibliotheca Somersetensis: Emanuel Green. *Bibliotheca Somersetensis.* 3 vols. Taunton, 1902.

BMC: Refers usually to the interleaved copy of the *British Museum General Catalogue of Printed Books* in the Reading Room of the British Museum, and to the card catalogue of newspapers at Colindale.

Boyce: B. Boyce. *Tom Brown of Facetious Memory.* Cambridge, Mass., 1939.

Brewer: Luther A. Brewer. *My Leigh Hunt Library: The First Editions.* Cedar Rapids, Iowa, 1932.

Brewster: Dorothy Brewster. *Aaron Hill.* New York, 1913.

Brown: *A Catalogue of the Allen A. Brown Collection of Books Relating to the Stage in the Public Library of the City of Boston.* Boston, 1919

BUCOP: J. D. Stewart and others, eds. *British Union-Catalogue of Periodicals.* 4 vols. London, 1955–62.

CBEL: F. W. Bateson, ed. *The Cambridge Bibliography of English Literature.* 5 vols. Cambridge, 1940–57.

Chambers, *Elizabethan:* E. K. Chambers. *The Elizabethan Stage.* 4 vols. Oxford, 1923.

Chambers, *Mediaeval:* E. K. Chambers. *The Mediaeval Stage.* 2 vols. Oxford, 1903.

Chambers, *Shakespeare:* E. K. Chambers. *William Shakespeare.* 2 vols. Oxford, 1930

Chase: Frank E. Chase's annotations in his copy of Lowe, *A Bibliographical Account of English Theatrical Literature* (1888), in the Harvard Theatre Collection.

Clark: Arthur M. Clark. "A Bibliography of Thomas Heywood," *Oxford Bibliographical Society Proceedings and Papers,* I (1927), [97]–153.

Clunes: Information from catalogues issued by Alec Clunes, Bookseller.

Cohn: Albert M. Cohn. *George Cruikshank. A Catalogue raisonné of the work executed during the years 1806–1877 with collations, notes, approximate values, facsimiles and illustrations.* London, 1924.

Colby: Elbridge Colby. *A Bibliography of Thomas Holcroft.* New York, 1922.

Collier: John Payne Collier. *The History of English Dramatic Poetry to the Time of Shakespeare: and Annals of the Stage to the Restoration.* 3 vols. London, 1831.

Courtney: William Prideaux Courtney. *Bibliography of Johnson.* (Oxford Historical and Literary Studies.) Oxford, 1915.

CTS: *Chronological Table of the Statues.* London, 1965.

Cunningham: R. N. Cunningham. "A Bibliography of the Writings of Peter Anthony Motteaux," *Oxford Bibliographical Society Proceedings and Papers,* III (1933), 317–36.

Davis: Thomas Davis. *Memoirs of the Life of David Garrick, Esq.* 2 vols. London, 1780.

Dibdin, *Annals:* James C. Dibdin. *The Annals of the Edinburgh Stage.* Edinburgh, 1888.

Dibdin, E. R.: Edward R. Dibdin. *A Charles Dibdin Bibliography.* Liverpool, 1937.

DLC Cat.: Catalogue of the Library of Congress, Washington, D.C.

DNB: *Dictionary of National Biography.*

Douglas: R. J. H. Douglas. *The Works of George Cruikshank.* London, 1903.

Eames: Wilberforce Eames's annotations in his copy of Lowe, *A Bibliographical Account of English Theatrical Literature* (1888), in Folger Shakespeare Library, Washington, D.C.

ECB: *The English Catalogue of Books, 1801—*. London, 1864—*in progress.*
Eckel: J. C. Eckel. *The First Editions of the Writings of Charles Dickens.* London, 1932.

Findlater: Richard Findlater. *Grimaldi, King of Clowns.* London, 1955.
Foxon: Information from David Foxon, Oxford.

Genest: [John Genest.] *Some Account of the English Stage, from the Restoration in 1660 to 1830.* 10 vols. Bath, 1832.
George: Mary Dorothy George. *Catalogue of Political and Personal Satires Preserved in the Department of Prints and Drawings in the British Museum.* Vols. 5–11. London, 1935–54. [See also Stephens.]
Grant: Douglas Grant, ed. *The Poetical Works of Charles Churchill.* Oxford, 1965.
Greg: W. W. Greg. *A Bibliography of the English Printed Drama to the Restoration.* 4 vols. London, 1939–59.
Griffith: Reginald Harvey Griffith. *Alexander Pope: A Bibliography.* Austin, Texas, 1922.
Grove: *Grove's Dictionary of Music and Musicians.* Fifth Edition, ed. Eric Blom. 10 vols. London, 1957–61.
GS: Information supplied by George Speaight, or from copy in his possession.

Hall: Lillian A. Hall. *Catalogue of Dramatic Portraits in the Theatre Collection of the Harvard College Library.* 4 vols. Cambridge, Mass., 1930–34.
H and L: Samuel Halkett and John Laing. *Dictionary of Anonymous and Pseudonymous English Literature.* New ed. by James Kennedy, W. A. Smith and A. F. Johnson. 9 vols. Edinburgh, 1926–62. Vols. 8 and 9 ed. Dennis E. Rhodes and Anna E. C. Simoni.
Hazlitt: William Carew Hazlitt. *The English Drama and Stage under the Tudor and Stuart Princes, 1534–1664.* London, 1889.
Herford and Simpson: C. H. Herford and P. and E. M. Simpson, eds. *Ben Jonson.* 11 vols. Oxford, 1925–52.
Hillebrand: Harold N. Hillebrand. *Edmund Kean.* New York, 1933.
Hooker: Edward Niles Hooker, ed. *The Critical Works of John Dennis.* 2 vols. Baltimore, 1939–43. With a list (I, 468–469) of "the more important and interesting items in the Collier controversy between 1698 and March, 1700". Items are dated by advertisements.
House of Lords Bills: Printed Parliamentary Papers collected under this title in the State Paper Room of the British Museum, London.
House of Lords Sessional Papers: Printed Parliamentary Papers collected under this title in the State Paper Room of the British Museum, London.
Hudson: *Dramatic Essays by John Dryden.* Introduction by W. H. Hudson. London, 1912.

IKF: Information supplied by Ifan Kyrle Fletcher, or taken from copy made available by him for examination.
ILPA: *Index of Local and Personal Acts 1801–1947.* London, 1949.
Irving: Lawrence Irving. *Henry Irving: the Actor and his World.* London, 1951.

Jaggard: William Jaggard. *Shakespeare Bibliography: A Dictionary of every known issue of the writings of our national poet and of recorded opinion thereon in the English language.* Stratford-on-Avon, 1911.
JEGP: *Journal of English and Germanic Philology.*
JFA: Information from J. F. Arnott's copy.
JWR: Information from J. W. Robinson's copy.

Kelly: John Alexander Kelly. *German Visitors to the English Theatres in the Eighteenth Century.* Princeton, 1936.
Ker: W. P. Ker, ed. *Essays by John Dryden.* 2 vols. Oxford, 1900.
Keynes: Geoffrey L. Keynes. *Bibliography of William Hazlitt.* London, 1931.
Knapp: Mary E. Knapp. *A Checklist of Verse by David Garrick.* Charlottesville, Virginia, 1955.
Krutch: J. W. Krutch. *Comedy and Conscience after the Restoration.* New York, 1924.

Lefèvre: Jean M. Lefèvre. "John Home. A Check List of Editions," *The Bibliothek*, 3 (1961).

Little and Kahrl: David M. Little and George M. Kahrl, eds. *The Letters of David Garrick*, 3 vols. London, 1963.

Loewenberg: Alfred Loewenberg. *The Theatre of the British Isles Excluding London. A Bibliography*. London, 1950.

Loftis, *Politics*: John Loftis. *The Politics of Drama in Augustan England*. Oxford, 1963.

London Stage: See LS.

Lowe: R. W. Lowe. *A Bibliographical Account of English Theatrical Literature*. London, 1888.

Lowe MS Cat: Manuscript catalogue of R. W. Lowe's library in Harvard Theatre Collection.

Lowndes: W. T. Lowndes. *The Bibliographer's Manual of English Literature*. Henry G. Bohn, ed. 4 vols. London, 1864.

LS: William Van Lennep, Emmett L. Avery, Arthur H. Scouten, George Winchester Stone Jr, Charles Beecher Hogan. *The London Stage 1660–1800*. 11 vols. Carbondale, Illinois, 1960–69.

Macdonald: Hugh Macdonald. *John Dryden. A Bibliography of Early Editions and of Drydeniana*. Oxford, 1939.

Martin: Burns Martin. *Bibliography of Allan Ramsay*. Glasgow, 1931.

Milford: R. T. Milford and D. M. Sutherland. "A Catalogue of English Newspapers and Periodicals in the Bodleian Library 1622–1800," *Oxford Bibliographical Society Proceedings and Papers*, IV (1936), [163]–344.

MLN: *Modern Language Notes*.

Moore: John R. Moore. *A Checklist of the Writings of Daniel Defoe*. Bloomington, Indiana, 1960.

Motley: Information from catalogues issued by Motley, Booksellers, London.

Nicoll: Allardyce Nicoll. *A History of English Drama 1600–1900*. 6 vols. Cambridge, 1952–59.

OCT: Phyllis Hartnoll, ed. *The Oxford Companion to the Theatre*. 3rd edn. London, 1967.

O'Neill: J. J. O'Neill. "A Bibliographical Account of Irish Theatrical Literature", *The Bibliographical Society of Ireland*, I, no. 6 (1920).

Page: Eugene R. Page. *George Colman the Elder: Essayist, Dramatist and Theatrical Manager 1732–1794*. (Columbia University Studies in English and Comparative Literature No. 120.) New York, 1935.

PBSA: *The Papers of the Bibliographical Society of America*.

Pforzheimer: *The Carl H. Pforzheimer Library English Literature 1475–1700*. [A Catalogue.] 3 vols. New York, 1940.

PH and KB: Information supplied by Philip Highfill and Kalman Burnim.

Pottle: F. A. Pottle. *The Literary Career of James Boswell, Esq*. Oxford, 1929.

Public Bills: Printed Parliamentary Papers collected under this title in the State Paper Room of the British Museum, London.

Reports Committee: Printed Parliamentary Papers collected under this title in the State Paper Room of the British Museum, London.

RES: *The Review of English Studies*.

Rhodes: R. Crompton Rhodes, ed. *The Plays and Poems of Richard Brinsley Sheridan*. 3 vols. Oxford, 1928.

Ringler: William Ringler. *Stephen Gosson. A Biographical and Critical Study*. (Princeton Studies in English Vol. 25.) Princeton, 1942. Bibliography, 139–51.

Rothschild: *The Rothschild Library. A Catalogue of the Collection of Eighteenth-Century Printed Books and Manuscripts Formed by Lord Rothschild*. 2 vols. Cambridge, 1954.

Rothwell: Information from catalogues issued by John Rothwell, Bookseller, London.

Sadleir, *Evolution*: Michael T. H. Sadleir. *The Evolution of Publishers' Binding Styles 1770–1900*. London, 1930.

Schultz: William E. Schultz. *Gay's* Beggar's Opera: *Its Content, History and Influence*. New Haven, 1923.

Searle: T. Searle. *A Bibliography of Sir William Schwenck Gilbert*. London, 1931.

Sheldon: Esther K. Sheldon. *Thomson Sheridan of Smock-Alley*. Princeton, NJ., 1796.

Smith: Joseph Smith. *A Descriptive Catalogue of Friends' Books, or Books written by Members of the Society of Friends, commonly called Quakers.* 2 vols. London, 1867.

Smithers: Peter Smithers. *The Life of Joseph Addison*. Oxford, 1954.

SP: *Studies in Philology*.

Speaight: George Speaight. *The History of The English Puppet Theatre*. London, 1955.

Spingarn: Joel E. Spingarn, ed. *Critical Essays of the Seventeenth Century*. 3 vols. Oxford, 1908–9.

SR: Information supplied by Sybil Rosenfeld.

Statutes of the Realm: *The Statutes of the Realm from Magna Carta to the end of the Reign of Queen Anne.* 11 vols. in 12. [London], 1810–28.

STC: A. W. Pollard and G. R. Redgrave, comps. *A Short-Title Catalogue of Books Printed in England, Scotland and Ireland and of English Books Printed Abroad 1475–1640*. London, 1926.

Stephens: [Frederick George Stephens.] *Catalogue of prints and drawings in the British Museum. Division I. Political and Personal Satires.* Vols. 1–4. London, 1870–83. See also George.

Stevenson: Thomas George Stevenson. *Bibliographical List of the Various Publications by J. Maidment from . . . 1817 to 1859*. Edinburgh, 1859.

Stott: R. Toole Stott. *Circus and Allied Arts: A World Bibliography 1500–1957*. 3 vols. Derby, 1958–62.

STR: Information from members of the Society for Theatre Research.

Stratman: Carl J. Stratman. *A Bibliography of British Dramatic Periodicals 1720–1960*. New York, 1962.

Stratman, *Play Lists:* Carl J. Stratman. *Dramatic Play Lists 1591–1963*. New York, 1966.

Stratman, *Tragedy:* Carl J. Stratman. *Bibliography of English Printed Tragedy 1565–1900*. Carbondale and Edwardsville, Illinois, 1966.

Straus: Ralph Straus. *The Unspeakable Curll*. London, 1927. A handlist 1706–46 (pp. 201–314).

TC: Edward Arber, ed. *The Term Catalogues, 1668–1709*. 3 vols. London, 1903–6.

Thorn-Drury: G. Thorn-Drury's annotations in his copy of Lowe, *A Bibliographical Account of English Theatrical Literature* (1888).

Times: *Tercentenary Handlist of English & Welsh Newspapers, Magazines & Reviews*. London, The Times, 1920.

TN: *Theatre Notebook. A Quarterly of Notes and Research*.

Tooley: R. V. Tooley. *English Books with Coloured Plates, 1790 to 1860*. London, 1954.

Trewin: J. C. Trewin. *Mr. Macready. A Nineteenth-Century Tragedian and his Theatre*. London, 1955.

ULS: Edna Brown Titus, ed. *Union List of Serials in Libraries of the United States and Canada*. Third Edition, New York, 1965.

Urwin: G. G. Urwin. "Bunn and His Influence in the Theatre." 1956. Unpublished thesis at Senate House Library, University of London.

Wade: Allan Wade. *A Bibliography of the Writings of W. B. Yeats*. (The Soho Bibliographies I.) London, 1951.

Watson: George Watson, ed. *Of Dramatic Poesy, and Other Critical Essays by John Dryden*. 2 vols. London, 1962.

Wiley: Autrey Nell Wiley, ed. *Rare Prologues and Epilogues 1642–700*. London, 1940.

Williams: Iolo A. Williams. *Seven XVIIIth Century Bibliographies*. London, 1924. Includes Charles Churchill and R. B. Sheridan.

Wing: Donald Wing, comp. *Short-Title Catalogue of Books Printed in England, Scotland, Ireland, Wales, and British America, and of English Books Printed in Other Countries 1641–1700*. 3 vols. New York, 1945–51.

Wise: T. J. Wise. *A Bibliography of the Writings in Verse and Prose of Byron*. 2 vols. 1932–33.

Zimansky: Curt A. Zimansky, ed. *The Critical Works of Thomas Rymer*. London, 1956.

AUTHORS' ACKNOWLEDGEMENTS

Our debt to Mrs Jan McDonald, of the Department of Drama of the University of Glasgow, and to Mrs Cathrine Aird, of the Library of the Royal Scottish Academy of Music and Drama, seems greater than can be adequately met by an acknowledgement, customarily the return for help at a particular stage in the writing of a book. Mrs Aird and Mrs McDonald have been our colleagues for a period of years. To Mrs McDonald we owe the bibliographical description of many items; but she also conducted much of our correspondence with librarians, organised teams of helpers, and undertook major tasks during the final assembly of our material for the printer and proof correction: her administration made an indispensable contribution to the completion of our work. Mrs Aird's contribution ranged far beyond the cross references and indexes with which she is credited elsewhere; in particular her advice as a professional librarian was always at our disposal.

The revision of Lowe, as Mr George Speaight writes in his Introduction, was begun by the Society for Theatre Research; and we should add that it has continued to be very much an enterprise of the Society as a whole: we are obliged to the many fellow members who have contributed ideas to the plan of the work, provided information about items, or undertaken administrative tasks. Over and above their help in these spheres, Mr George Speaight and Mr Jack Reading advised on layout and type, and negotiated with the printers for us; the late Ifan Kyrle Fletcher let us examine the many rarities which passed through his hands while our work was in progress; Miss O. E. B. Youngs rallied the London Group of the Society to our support in several critical stages of the operation; and the late C. B. Oldman, c.v.o., read the entire work in manuscript, a scrutiny which led to many improvements in scholarship and clarity. Other members of the Society who should be individually mentioned are Miss Kathleen Barker, Miss Toni Bunch, Miss Muriel St Clare Byrne, o.b.e., Mr V. C. Clinton-Baddeley, the late Mrs F. Anstey Cooke, Mr D. G. Corble, Mrs Allan Gomme, Mr William Kendall, Mr Tom Milne and Miss D. M. Moore.

We have also to acknowledge the generosity of Mr David Foxon who gave us descriptions of many poems which he had come across in his researches for his bibliography of early eighteenth-century poetical miscellanies; of Professor Phillip Highfill, of Professor Kalman Burnim, and of Professor Lucyle Hook who placed at our disposal the material collected for their biographical dictionary of seventeenth and eighteenth-century actors; and of Professor A. C. Sprague, who presented us with a unique item. Miss F. Angel sent us a photostat of the late G. Thorn-Drury's annotated copy of Lowe. We are proud to acknowledge that Professor Allardyce Nicoll and the late Peter Alexander and Howard Lowry have been our guides and sponsors.

The section on the Government Regulation of the Theatre owes a very great deal to the erudition and professional address of Miss Sheila Richards. For assistance in research and in the preparation of copy we are also indebted to Mrs Mary Begg, Miss Norma Campbell, Mrs Allison Fenwick, Mr B. M. Garton, and a team of students from the Department of Drama of the University of Glasgow: Miss Mary Brennan, Miss Muriel Ritchie, Mr Peter Easton, Mr Stuart Johnson, Mr Barry Nonweiler and Mr Finlay Welsh. We owe a similar debt to two students from the University of Nebraska: Mr Gilbert Kelly and Mr John Harwood. The exacting task of typing the entries was carried out by Mrs Ruth Pepper.

The full record of our debt to libraries and librarians is the list of Library Symbols. Most of our work was done in the British Museum where we were given many facilities by Mr H. M. Nixon and Mr Dennis Rhodes. At the Victoria and Albert Museum we had the guidance of Mr George Nash. The Committee of the Garrick Club gave us the privilege of regular access to the Club Library. Of British Libraries outside of London we have been most dependant on the hospitality of the National Library of Scotland and of the Library of the University of Glasgow and the Mitchell Library, Glasgow. Among American libraries our greatest obligations are to the Boston Public Library, the Folger Shakespeare

Library, the Widener and Houghton Libraries and the Theatre Collection of Harvard University, the New York Public Library and the library of the University of Nebraska. To Mr John Alden and Miss Ellen M. Oldham of Boston Public Library we are greatly obliged for permission to quote the descriptions in the Allan A. Brown Collection Catalogue of those items which time did not allow us to examine ourselves. Dr Louis B. Wright and Dr James G. MacManaway were our guides while we were working at the Folger and later Miss Dorothy E. Mason sent us information about a number of items. To Mr Philip A. Knachel we are obliged for permission to quote certain manuscript notes in Folger copies. The late William Van Lennep listed some Harvard items not in Lowe; to Miss Helen Willard we are obliged for answering many enquiries and for permission to quote from manuscript notes in Harvard Theatre Collection copies and for much other assistance and hospitality. At the New York Public Library we had the benefit of the late George Freedley's counsel.

Other librarians to whom we are obliged for sending us information about items in their keeping are Mrs Dorothy Anderson, the Garrick Club, London; Mr John Bebbington, Sheffield Central Library; Miss C. Bonfield, library of the Royal Irish Academy, Dublin; Mr A. B. Craven, Leeds Central Library; Mr W. E. G. Critchley, Aberdeen Public Library; Dr Levi Fox, O.B.E., The Shakespeare Centre, Stratford-upon-Avon; Mr R. J. Hayes, National Library of Ireland, Dublin; Dr K. W. Humphreys, Birmingham University Library; Mr Michael F. Messenger, Shrewsbury Public Library; Mr S. W. Musgrave, O.B.E. and Mr A. W. Ball, The Royal Pavilion, Museums, Art Gallery and Public Libraries, Brighton; Mr Peter Pagan, City of Bath Municipal Libraries and Victoria Art Gallery; Mr A. J. I. Parrott and Mr A. A. Hurst, M.C., Gloucester City Library; Mr M. Pollard, Trinity College Library, Dublin; Mr Paul Sykes and Mr George E. Thornber, Central Library and Art Gallery, Rochdale; Mr W. A. Taylor, M.C., City of Birmingham Public Libraries; Mr O. S. Tomlinson, York City Library; Mr E. G. Twigg, Atkinson Central Library, Southport; Miss Dorothy M. White, Ipswich Central Library.

All workers in our field will understand the extent of our debt to the enterprise and professional knowledge of booksellers, whether conveyed through their catalogues or at one's disposal in answer to specific enquiries: our debt to Ifan Kyrle Fletcher has already been acknowledged, but we should also mention Messrs. Alec Clunes, Percy Dobell and Son, Peter Murray Hill (Rare Books) Ltd, Motley Books Limited, and John Rothwell.

* * * *

On four occasions we were enabled to give our time almost entirely to the preparation of the work. For this most valuable contribution to our progress Mr Arnott is indebted to the University of Glasgow for twice granting him a term's leave of absence, to the Carnegie Trust for the Universities of Scotland for a research grant, and to the Folger Shakespeare Library for a Fellowship; Dr Robinson is indebted to the University of Nebraska, first for a Faculty Fellowship, which enabled him to spend one long vacation in London, and again for a year's leave of absence, made possible by a grant from the Woods Charitable Fund, Inc., of Lincoln and Chicago, to which foundation he is much indebted. To the University of Glasgow we are under a further debt, for a grant towards the cost of typing our manuscript.

* * * *

So far we have written of those who have contributed directly to our work. Under this heading we might have included our wives, Mrs Martha Arnott and Mrs Ann Robinson, who have helped with research and administration, especially in hours of crisis; but our chief debt to them, and to our families, has been for cheerfully foregoing so much over a whole decade so that our work could go forward.

Long as this list already is, other debts come to mind, more than can be recorded. It will long be our pleasure to recall them, as it will all the kindnesses here acknowledged.

BIBLIOGRAPHY

GENERAL

1 LOWE, ROBERT W[ILLIAM]. A bibliographical account of English theatrical literature from the earliest times to the present day by Robert W. Lowe.

pp. [i–vii] viii–x [xi–xii], [1] 2–384; t.p. in red and black
L

John C. Nimmo   1888 [for 1887]

"Three hundred and fifty copies printed for England, and one hundred and fifty for America". Copies numbered. The American copies have the imprint: New York: J. W. Bouton; London: J. C. Nimmo 1888.

2 ——[large paper issue].

pp. [i–vii] viii–x [xi–xii], [1] 2–384; t.p. in red and black
L

John C. Nimmo   1888 [for 1887]

Seventy-five copies for England, twenty-five for America, "fine deckle-edge royal 8vo paper". Copies numbered. The American copies have the imprint: New York: J. W. Bouton; London: J. C. Nimmo 1888.

——[American edition] Detroit: The Gale Research Company, 1966.

✖ Cameron, James. A bibliography of Scottish theatrical literature. Edinburgh. 1892. *See nos. 1845–1846.*

LISTS AND DICTIONARIES
Playlists and dictionaries of plays and persons.

See also ARTS OF THE THEATRE nos. 750, 809–810, 813; GENERAL HISTORY nos. 824, 839–841, 843, 851–853; MEDIEVAL AND RENAISSANCE STUDIES nos. 1031, 1038; THE AMATEUR THEATRE nos. 2195, 2198.

3 G[OFFE], T[HOMAS]. The careles shepherdess. A tragi-comedy acted before the King & Queen, and at Salisbury-Court, with great applause. Written by T. G. Mr. of Arts. With An alphabeticall catalogue of all such plays that ever were printed.

pp. [2] [1] 2–76 [77–82 (catalogue)]   L
Richard Rogers and William Ley   1656

Rogers and Ley's catalogue is edited with an introduction and notes in Greg, III, 1319–1327. Greg no. 761; Wing G 1005; Stratman, Play Lists 2.

4 MASSINGER, PHIL[LIP], THO[MAS] MIDDLETON and WILLIAM ROWLEY. The excellent comedy, called The old law: or a new way to please you. By Phil. Massinger. Tho. Middleton. William Rowley. Acted before the King and Queene at Salisbury House, and at severall other places, with great applause. Together with An exact and perfect catalogue of all the playes, with the authors names, and what are comedies, tragedies, histories, pastoralls, masks, interludes, more exactly printed then ever before.

pp. [2] 1–76 [16 (catalogue)]   L
Edward Archer   1656

The catalogue has the head-title: "An exact and perfect catalogue of all the plaies that were ever printed; together, with all the authors names; and what are comedies, histories, interludes, masks, pastorels, tragedies: and all these plaies you may either have at the Signe of the Adam and Eve, in Little Britain; or, at the Ben Johnson's Head in Thredneedlestreet, over against the Exchange." Archer's catalogue

is edited, with an introduction and notes, in Greg, III, 1328–1338. Greg no. 766; Wing M 1048; Stratman, Play Lists 3.

5 TOM TYLER and his wife. An excellent old play, as it was printed and acted about a hundred years ago. Together, with An exact catalogue of all the playes that were ever yet printed. The second impression.

pp. [2] 1–26, ²1–15 [16]   L
[Francis Kirkman]   1661

The catalogue has the head-title, on p. ²1: "A true, perfect, and exact catalogue of all the comedies, tragedies, tragi-comedies, pastorals, masques and interludes, that were ever yet printed and published, till this present year 1661. all which you may either buy or sell at the several shops of Nath. Brook at the Angel in Cornhil, Francis Kirkman at the John Fletchers Head, on the back-side of St. Clements, Tho Johnson at the Golden Key in St. Pauls Churchyard, and Henry Marsh at the Princes Arms in Chancery-lane near Fleetstreet. 1661" It is bibliographically independent of Tom Tyler, was advertised separately, and so may have been issued separately also: a copy without the play preceding it is at MB, and others are recorded in Wing T 2853 and K 637. There was another issue of Tom Tyler in 1661, without the catalogue. Kirkman's catalogue is edited with an introduction and notes in Greg, III, 1338–1356. Greg no. 820 (AII); Wing T 1792 A; Stratman, Play Lists 4.

6 ——[second edition of the catalogue] Nicomede. A tragi-comedy, translated out of the French of Monsieur Corneille, by John Dancer. As it was acted at the

Theatre-Royal in Dublin. Together with An exact catalogue of all the English stage-plays printed, till this present year 1671. Licensed Dec. 16. 1670. Roger L'estrange.

pp. [4] 1–56, ²1–16   L

Francis Kirkman   1671

> *This is the second edition of the catalogue. It has the head-title, on p. ²1: "A true, perfect, and exact catalogue of all the comedies, tragedies, tragi-comedies, pastorals, masques and interludes, that were ever yet printed and published, till this present year 1671. all which you may either buy or sell, at the shop of Francis Kirkman, in Thames-street, over-against the Custom House, London." It is bibliographically independent of Nicomede, and may also have been issued separately: a copy without the play preceding it is at MB, and others are recorded in Wing K 637 A. On p. ²16 there is a "very quaint" (Lowe) advertisement. Wing C 6315; Stratman, Play Lists 6.*

7 [LANGBAINE, GERARD.] AN EXACT CATA-LOGUE of all the comedies, tragedies, tragi-comedies, opera's, masks, pastorals and interludes that were ever yet printed and published, till this present year 1680.

pp. [2] 1–16   L

Oxon: Nicholas Cox   1680

> *A reprint of Kirkman's Catalogue (nos. 5 and 6), with additions. Wing L 373 A; Stratman, Play Lists 10.*

8 LANGBAINE, GERARD. Momus triumphans: or, the plagiaries of the English stage; expos'd in a catalogue of all the comedies, tragi-comedies, masques, tragedies, opera's, pastorals, interludes, &c. both ancient and modern, that were ever yet printed in English. The names of their known and supposed authors. Their several volumes and editions: with an account of the various originals, as well English, French, and Italian, as Greek and Latine; from whence most of them have stole their plots. By Gerard Langbaine Esq;

pp. [16] 1–32 [33–40 (index)]   L

N[icholas] C[ox] and are to be sold by Sam. Holford
                                          1688 [for 1687?]

> *Most copies of this edition have the imprint "London: Printed for Nicholas Cox, and are to be sold by him in Oxford." Langbaine's first list (no. 7 above), a reprint with additions of Kirkman's 1671 catalogue, had been published at Oxford by Nicholas Cox in 1680. Momus Triumphans was an unauthorised title (devised by Cox) for the 1688 list, and after 500 copies had been sold a new title-leaf was substituted, the work now being called A new catalogue of English plays (no. 9 below). See Greg, III, 1320. According to Lowe, Langbaine was supposed to be "a constant and critical theatre-goer". Wing L 377; Stratman, Play Lists 12.*

9 ——*[reissue] A new catalogue of English plays.
                                                      MH

Printed at London for Nicholas Cox in Oxford   1688

> *With variant imprints as no. 8. Wing L 377 A; Stratman, Play Lists 13.*

10 LANGBAINE, GERARD. An account of the English dramatick poets. Or, some observations and remarks on the lives and writings, of all those that have publish'd either comedies, tragedies, tragi-comedies, pastorals, masques, interludes, farces, or opera's in the English tongue. By Gerard Langbaine.

pp. [16] 1–556 [557–576 (index) 577–587 (appendix) 588 (bl.) 589 (errata) 590–591 (bl.) 592 (perpendicular short title)]   NbU

Oxford: George West, and Henry Clements   1691

> *Pforzheimer 577. See also Greg, III, 1319, and, for annotated copies, Essays and Studies (1936). Wing L 373; Stratman, Play Lists 14.*

11 LANGBAIN[E], [GERARD] [and CHARLES GILDON]. The lives and characters of the English dramatick poets. Also An exact account of all the plays that were ever yet printed in the English tongue; their double titles, the places where acted, the dates when printed, and the persons to whom dedicated; with remarks and observations on most of the said plays. First begun by Mr. Langbain, improv'd and continued down to this time, by a careful hand.

pp. [16] 1–150 *151–*152 151–182 [183–197 (index) 198–206 (advts.) 207–208 (bl.)] [=210]   L

Tho. Leigh and William Turner   [1698 or 1699]

> *Wing L375.*

12 ——[another issue]

pp. [16] 1–150 *151–*152 151–182 [183–197 (index) 198–206 (advts.)] [=208]   NbU

William Turner   1699

> *Wing L 376; Stratman, Play Lists 15 records a title page with imprint "for Nich. Cox, and William Turner", not in Wing.*

13 [MEARS, W.] A TRUE AND EXACT CATA-LOGUE of all the plays that were ever yet printed in the English tongue; with the authors names against each play (alphabetically digested) and continued down to October, 1713.

pp. 1–16; head-title   L

W. Mears. . . . Where may be had great variety of plays
                                                      1713

> *Stratman, Play Lists 17.*

14 ——*[another edition] Continu'd down to April, 1714   DLC

W. Mears   1714

> *DLC Cat.*

15 ——[another edition] continuation of the following Catalogue of plays to October, 1715. To which is prefix'd a Catalogue of plays, printed in 12mo with a neat Elziver letter.

pp. 1–2; head-title   L

Sold by W. Mears . . . of whom may be had about five hundred several sorts of plays, in 4to and 12mo   [1715]

Apparently prefixed to a reissue of A true and exact catalogue *(1713 or 1714). The list of "Plays printed in 12mo in a neat Elzevir letter" is on p. 2.*

16 ——[another edition] A compleat catalogue of all the plays that were ever yet printed in the English language.

pp. [1–3] 4–95 95 (engr. colophon) [96] 97–104; head-title   L

n.p.   [1718]

"The Appendix", pp. 97–104.

17 ——[another edition] A compleat catalogue of all the plays that were ever yet printed in the English language. Containing the dates, and the number of plays written by every particular author: an account of what plays were acted with applause, and of those which were never acted; and also of the authors now living. In two separate alphabets.

pp. [1–3] 4–104   GU

W. Mears   1719

"The Appendix", pp. 97–104. Stratman, Play Lists 19.

18 ——Continued to this present year, 1726. The second edition.

pp. [1–3] 4–104   L

W. Mears   1726

"The Appendix", pp. 97–104. Stratman, Play Lists 20.

19 [JACOB, GILES.] THE POETICAL REGISTER: or, the lives and characters of the English dramatick poets. With an account of their writings.

2 vols. pp. [4] [i] ii–vii [viii–xx], [1] 2–334 (misprinting 334 as "433") [335–356 ("Interments", errata, index of plays)]; pls. [front., 5] + pp. [i–iii] iv–xxvi [xxvii–xxxiv], [1] 2–328 [329–336 (index)]; pls. [front., 7]   L

E. Curll   [1719–1720]

The first volume concerns dramatists, the second poets. The second has the title: "An historical account of the lives and writings of our most considerable English poets, whether epick, lyrick, elegiack, epigramatists, &c." The plates also sold separately. That the work was intended to be in two volumes may be inferred from the Dedication, though it is not indicated on the title page. Straus states that the work was commissioned by Curll, and that the second volume was published on 16 July 1720. Stratman, Play Lists 18.

20 ——[another edition] The Poetical Register: or the lives and characters of all the English poets. With an account of their writings. Adorned with curious sculptures engraven by the best masters.

2 vols. pp. [2] [i] ii–vii [viii–xx], [1] 2–333 433 [2] 437–444 [445–464 (index)] [= 364]; pls. [front., 5] + pp. [i–iii] iv–xxvi [xxvii–xxxiv], [1] 2–328 [329–336 (index)]; pls. [front., 7]   L

Printed and Sold by A. Bettesworth, W. Taylor, and J. Batley; J. Wyat and C. Rivington; E. Bell and W. Meadows; J. Pemberton and J. Hooke   1723

A reissue of The poetical register *(1719–1720), with some additions to the first volume.*

21 ——*[third edition] An historical account of the lives and characters of the English dramatic poets, with an account of their writings.

2 vols.   MH

W. Mears   1724

✖ Weaver, John. The history of the mimes and pantomimes. . . . To which will be added, a list of the modern entertainments. 1728. *See no. 2105.*

22 [FEALES, W.] A TRUE AND EXACT CATALOGUE of all the plays and other dramatick pieces, that were ever yet printed in the English tongue, in alphabetical order: continued down to April, 1732.

pp. [1–2] 3–35 [36]   L

W. Feales   1732

Apparently reissued with additional final leaf in 1734, advertising The English Theatre.

23 ——[another issue of the catalogue] THE THREE CELEBRATED PLAYS of that excellent poet Ben Jonson. Viz. The Fox, a comedy. The Alchymist, a comedy. The Silent Woman, a comedy. To which is added, A compleat catalogue of all the plays that were ever printed in the English language to the year 1732.

pp. [2] ¹[1–3] 4–96, ²[1–3] 4–96, ³[1–3] 4–100, ⁴[1–2] 3–35 [36 (advt.)]   GU

W. Feales   1732

Head-title of Catalogue (p. ⁴[1]–[36]): "A true and exact catalogue of all the plays and other dramatick pieces, that were ever yet printed in the English tongue, in alphabetical order: continu'd down to April 1732." Stratman, Play Lists 21: Herford and Simpson, IX, 153.

24 THE DRAMATIC HISTORIOGRAPHER: or, the British theatre delineated, &c. Exhibiting the argument, conduct and chief incidents of the most celebrated plays; with an account of such previous circumstances as serve to illustrate each representation.

pp. [12] [1] 2–286 [287–288 (advts.)]; two t.pp., the second reading ". . . delineated; exhibiting. . . ."   L

F. Cogan; and J. Nourse   1735

A second volume completing the work is promised, but apparently was not published.

25 ——[reissue] A companion to the theatre: or, a key to the play. Containing the stories of the most celebrated dramatick pieces. The plan, character, and design of each performance is exhibited and explain'd; with remarks on each representation. The second edition.

pp. [*10*] [1] 2–286 [287–288 (advt.)]   L

F. Cogan; and J. Nourse   1740

26 ——[third edition] A companion to the theatre: or, a view of our most celebrated dramatic pieces: in which the plan, characters, and incidents of each are particularly explained. Interspers'd with remarks historical, critical and moral.

2 vols. pp. [*10*] [1] 2–286 + [*4*] [1] 2–355 [*356*]   MH

J. Nourse   1747

27 ——[another edition]

pp. [*6*] 1–272   L

Dublin: Sam. Price   1751

Incorporates a considerable part of the earlier editions but virtually a new work.

28 WHINCOP, THOMAS. Scanderbeg: or, love and liberty. A tragedy. Written by the late Thomas Whincop, Esq. To which are added A list of all the dramatic authors, and some account of their lives; and of all the dramatic pieces ever published in the English language, to the year 1747.

pp. [*12*] [i] ii–viii, ²[i] ii–xx, [1] 2–320 [321–350 (index)]; pls, front., [*5*]; vignettes   L

W. Reeve   1747

On p. [87] full title: "A compleat list of all the English dramatic poets, and of all the plays ever printed in the English language, to the year, M,DCC,XLVII." This list, pp. [87]–320, has been attributed to John Mottley, dramatist and compiler of Joe Miller's Jests (1739), on internal evidence. Dedication is signed 'M. Whincop'. Stratman, Play Lists 22.

29 THEATRICAL RECORDS: or, an account of English dramatic authors, and their works.

pp. [1–3] 4–135 [136 (bl.) 137–166 (indices) 167–168 (advts.)]   L

R. and J. Dodsley   1756

Apparently founded on Jacob's The Poetical Register —Lowe. Advertised as published "this day" 23 April 1757—LS. Variously atributed to W. R. Chetwood, and Robert Dodsley. Stratman, Play Lists 27.

30 [BAKER, DAVID ERSKINE and others.] THE COMPANION to the play-house: or, an historical account of all the dramatic writers (and their works) that have appeared in Great Britain and Ireland, from the commencement of our theatrical exhibitions, down to the present year 1764. Composed in the form of a dictionary, for the more readily turning to any particular author, or performance. Vol I. contains, a critical and historical account of every tragedy, comedy, farce, &c. in the English language. The respective merits of each piece; and of the actors who performed the principal characters, are particularly examined and pointed out. Vol II contains, the lives and productions of every dramatic writer for the English or Irish theatres, including not only all those memoirs that have been formerly written, but also a great number of new lives and curious anecdotes never before communicated to the public. — Also the lives of our most celebrated actors, who were likewise authors of any theatrical composition from Shakespear and Johnson, down to the present times.

2 vols. pp. [i–iv] v–xlii, [*326*] + [*374*]   GM

T. Becket and P. A. Dehondt; C. Henderson; T. Davies   1764

Stratman, *Play Lists 29.*

31 ——[REED, ISAAC, *ed.*] Biographia dramatica, or, a companion to the playhouse: containing historical and critical memoirs, and original anecdotes, of British and Irish dramatic writers, from the commencement of our theatrical exhibitions; amongst whom are some of the most celebrated actors. Also an alphabetical account of their works, the dates when printed, and occasional observations on their merits. Together with an introductory view of the rise and progress of the British stage. By David Erskine Baker, Esq. A new edition: carefully corrected; greatly enlarged; and continued from 1764 to 1782.

2 vols. pp. [i–iv] v [vi] vii–lii, 1–496; cancels, pp. 5–6, 183–184, 293–294, 357–358, 393–394 + pp. [*4*] [1] 2–442; cancels, pp. 35–36, 185–186, 247–250   MH

Mess. Rivingtons, T. Payne and Son, L. Davies, T. Longman and G. Robinson, J. Dodsley, J. Nichols, J. Debret, and T. Evans.   1782

In his interleaved copy, now at O, Malone preserved six of the cancelled leaves. They contain satirical articles by George Steevens. See L. F. Powell, "George Steevens and Isaac Reed's Biographia Dramatica" RES, V (1929), 289–293. Stratman, Play Lists 33.

32 ——[another edition]

2 vols. pp. [i–iv] v–li [lii], 1–496 + [*4*] [1] 2–442   GU

Dublin: W. and H. Whitestone, W. Sleater, J. Sheppard, T. Walker, J. Beatty, R. Burton, P. Byrne, T. Webb, and N. Cross   1782

33 ——[another edition] . . . also an alphabetical account, and chronological lists, of their works, the dates when printed, and observations on their merits: together with an introductory view of the rise and progress of the British stage. Originally compiled, to the year 1764, by David Erskine Baker. Continued thence to 1782, by Isaac Reed, F.A.S. And brought down to the end of November 1811, with very considerable additions and improvements throughout, by Stephen Jones. 3 vols. in 4 (vol. I in 2 pts.) pp. [i–v] vi–lxxv [lxxvi], [1] 2–384 + [2] 385–789 [790] + [4] [1] 2–404 + [4] [1] 2–478   GU

Longman, Hurst, Rees, Orme, and Brown, T. Payne, G. and W. Nicol, Nichols and son, Scatcherd and Letterman, J. Barker, W. Miller, R. H. Evans, J. Harding, J. Faulder, and Gale and Curtis   1812

Stratman, *Play Lists 43.*

———[Austrian edition] Graz: Akademische Druck und Verlagsanstalt, 1964 (*reprint of no. 33*)

34 FRIEND TO CANDOUR AND TRUTH, A, *pseud.* of Stephen Jones. Hypercriticism exposed: in a letter addressed to the readers of *The Quarterly Review,* respecting an article in the XIVth number of that publication, professing to be an examen of Mr. Stephen Jones's edition of the *Biographia Dramatica,* lately published. By a friend to candour and truth.

pp. [1–3] 4–43 [44 (note by Stephen Jones)]   L
J. Murray   1812

A reply to unfavourable criticism by Octavius Gilchrist.

35 THE PLAYHOUSE POCKET-COMPANION or theatrical vademecum: containing I. A catalogue of all the dramatic authors who have written for the English stage, with a list of their works, shewing the dates of representation or publication. II. A catalogue of anonymous pieces. III. An index of plays and authors. In a method entirely new, whereby the author of any dramatic performance, and the time of its appearance, may be readily discovered on inspection. To which is prefixed, A critical history of the English stage from its origin to the present time; with an inquiry into the causes of the decline of dramatic poetry in England.

pp. [9–13] 14–46 [47] 48–132 [133] 134–174 [180]   L
Richardson and Urquhart; J. Wenman; J. Southern 1779

Stratman, *Play Lists 31.*

36 THE THEATRICAL REMEMBRANCER, containing a complete list of all the dramatic performances in the English language; their several editions, dates, and sizes, and the theatres where they were originally performed: together with an account of those which have been acted and are unpublished, and a catalogue of such Latin plays as have been written by English authors, from the earliest production of the English drama to the end of the year MDCCLXXXVII. To which are added Notitia dramatica, being a chronological account of events relative to the English stage.

pp. [i–iii] iv–vi [vii–viii], [1] 2–354   PU
T. and J. Egerton   1788

Generally known as Egerton's Theatrical Remembrancer — Lowe. Stratman, *Play Lists 35.*

37 ———Oulton, Walley Chamberlain, *compiler.* Barker's continuation of Egerton's *Theatrical remembrancer,* Baker's *Biographia dramatica,* &c. Containing, a complete list of all the dramatic performances their several editions, dates and sizes, together with those which are unpublished, and the theatres where they were originally performed; from MDCCLXXXVII to MDCCCI. Including several omissions, additions and corrections, also a continuation of the *Notitia dramatica,* with considerable improvements. To which is added A complete list of plays, the earliest date, size, and author's name, (where known.) From the commencement to 1801. The whole arranged, &c. by Walley Chamberlain Oulton.

pp. [4] [1] 2–336   L
Barker & Son, Dramatic Repository   [1801]

Stratman, *Play Lists 38.*

38 ———[another edition] Barker's complete list of plays, exhibiting, at one view, the title, size, date, and author, from the commencement of theatrical performances, to 1803. To which is added A continuation to *The theatrical remembrancer,* designed to shew collectively each author's work.

pp. [4] [1] 2–350   L
Barker & Son, Dramatic Repository   [1803]

Preface signed by Oulton. Stratman, *Play Lists 40*

39 ———[another edition] The drama recorded; or, Barker's list of plays, alphabetically arranged, exhibiting at one view, the title, size, date, and author, with their various alterations, from the earliest period, to 1814; to which are added, Notitia dramatica, or, a chronological account of events relative to the English stage.

pp. [4] [1] 2–212   L
J. Barker (Dramatic Repository)   1814

Stratman, *Play Lists 44.*

40 [JOHNSON, RICHARD?] A NEW THEATRICAL DICTIONARY. Containing an account of all the dramatic pieces that have appeared from the commencement of theatrical exhibitions to the present time. Together with their dates when written or printed, where acted, and occasional remarks on their merits and success. To which is added, An alphabetical catalogue of dramatic writers, with the titles of all the pieces they have written, annexed to each name. And also a short sketch of the rise and progress of the English stage.

pp. [8] [1] 2–400   GU
S. Bladon   1792

Stratman, *Play Lists 36.*

41 LOWNDES, WILLIAM. *Theatrical list. Containing anecdotes, ballets, burlettas, comedies . . . Annexed, a catalogue of books and tracts principally consisting of dramatic authors and treatises relative to the stage sold by W. Lowndes.

pp. 24   MB

[London]   [18–?]

✘ Oulton, Walley Chamberlain, *compiler*. Barker's continuation of Egerton's *Theatrical remembrancer*, Baker's *Biographia dramatica*, &c. [1801]. *See no. 37.*

42 THE THESPIAN DICTIONARY; or, dramatic biography of the eighteenth century; containing sketches of the lives, productions, &c. of all the principal managers, dramatists, composers, commentators, actors, and actresses, of the United Kingdom: interspersed with several original anecdotes; and forming a concise history of the English stage.

pp. [*230*]; pls., [front., 6]; cancels, leaves T2 and T3   NbU

London: T. Hurst; Dublin: W. Porter, and J. Archer   1802

Stratman, *Play Lists 30.*

43 ——The Thespian dictionary; or, dramatic biography of the present age; containing sketches of the lives, lists of the productions, various merits, &c. &c. of all the principal dramatists, composers, commentators, managers, actors and actresses, of the United Kingdom: interspersed with numerous original anecdotes, forming a complete modern history of the English stage. Second edition with considerable improvements and additions. Illustrated by twenty-two elegant engravings.

pp. [i–iii] iv, [*396*]; added t.p., engr.; pls. [front., 19]

James Cundee   1805

JFA. Stratman, *Play Lists 41.*

✘ [Oulton, Walley Chamberlain, *compiler*.] Barker's complete list of plays . . . To which is added A continuation to *The theatrical remembrancer* . . . [1803]. *See no. 38.*

44 GILLILAND, THOMAS. The dramatic mirror: containing the history of the stage, from the earliest period to the present time; including a biographical and critical account of all the dramatic writers, from 1660; and also of the most distinguished performers, from the days of Shakspeare to 1807: and a history of the country theatres, in England, Ireland, and Scotland. Embellished with seventeen elegant engravings. By Thomas Gilliland.

2 vols. pp. [i–iii] iv–xii, [1] 2–622 629–630 (=624); pls. [front., 7] + pp. [2] [625] 626–1048; pls. [10]   L

C. Chapple   1808

Stratman, *Play Lists 42.*

✘ Baker, David Erskine, Isaac Reed and Stephen Jones. Biographia Dramatica; or a companion to the playhouse . . . brought down to the end of November, 1811. 1812. *See no. 33.*

✘ [Jones, Stephen] Hypercriticism exposed . . . respecting an article in the XIVth number of . . . [*The Quarterly Review*], professing to be an examen of Mr. Stephen Jones's edition of the *Biographica Dramatica* lately published. By a friend of candour and truth. 1812. *See no. 34.*

45 WEWITZER, RALPH. A theatrical pocket book, or brief dramatic chronology, from the earliest periods of history: with a list of British dramatists, and of actors, &c. on the London stage, from the introduction of theatrical entertainments into England. By Ralph Wewitzer.

pp. [i–iii] iv [v–viii], [1] 2–127 [128 (bl.) 129–130 (additional index)]   L

Printed for the Editor: and Sold by John Miller   1814

Pp. [109]–[112]: "Addenda"; pp. [113]–130: supplement, issued after the publication of the main work, with corrections and additions, "delivered to the Subscribers gratis".

46 ——A brief dramatic chronology of actors, &c. of the London stage, from the introduction of theatrical entertainments into England to the present time. A new edition, to which is added a miscellaneous appendix. By Ralph Wewitzer, of the Theatre Royal, Drury Lane.

pp. [1–3] 4–8, [1] 2–115 [116]   PU

John Miller   1817

Pp. [101]–[116]: "Addenda"; the imprint is on p. 99. Reprinted in Wewitzer, Dramatic reminiscences [185–?], no. 3631 below.
Mrs. Baron-Wilson, in her Memoirs of Miss Mellon (1886), says that this book is most inaccurate, and that Wewitzer used to ask his favourites, "What character would you like to have named as your first?" — Lowe.

47 vacant

48 FOOTE, HORACE. A companion to the theatres; and a manual of the British drama. By Horace Foote.

pp. [i–iii] iv–vi, [1] 2–148; pl. [front.]   LGk

Edward Philip Sanger   1829

49 ——second edition

pp. [i–iii] iv–vi, [1] 2–148; pl. [fold.]   L

William Marsh and Alfred Miller   1829

50 LITERARY AND GRAPHICAL ILLUSTRATIONS of Shakspeare, and the British drama: comprising an historical view of the origin and improvement of the English stage, and a series of critical and descriptive notices of upwards of one hundred of the most celebrated tragedies, comedies, operas, and farces. Embellished with more than two hundred engravings on wood, by eminent artists.

pp. [i–iv] v–xvi, [1] 2–204; illus. incl. [front.] GM

Printed by and for Maurice and Co and published by Hurst, Chance and Co; and Effingham Wilson 1831

51 ——[reissue] The dramatic souvenir: being literary and graphical illustrations of Shakespeare and other celebrated English dramatists. Embellished with upwards of two hundred engravings on wood, by eminent artists.

pp. [i–iv] v–xvi, [1] 2–204; illus., incl. [front.] L

Charles Tilt 1833

⌘ A return, specifying the number and name of each theatre . . . Also 2. A return of the number and title of each dramatic piece or song licensed . . . during the years 1829, 1830, and 1831 to the present time. 1832. *See below p. 30*

52 *BIBLIOTHECA HISTRIONICA, part 3. Catalogue of dramatic literature, comprising ancient and modern plays, Shakesperiana, theatrical biography and criticism, controversial works, history of theatres, play bills, now on sale by T. H. Lacy.

pp. 24 MB

Lacy [*ca.* 1860]

⌘ Catalogue of dramatic pieces, the property of the members of the Dramatic Authors' Society, brought down to September, 1865. [1865, 1866]. *See nos. 2134, 2135.*

⌘ Dramatic Authors' Society's tariff. [1881?]. *See no. 2137.*

Lists fees for performance.

⌘ [Hogg, Wentworth, *compiler.*] Guide to selecting plays; or manager's companion. Giving a complete description of 1,500 pieces. [1882?]. *See no. 813.*

CATALOGUES

Sale catalogues and catalogues of collections

THEATRES, INSTITUTIONS, EXHIBITIONS

Arranged alphabetically under name of theatre, institution or exhibition.

Covent Garden, Theatre Royal

53 THEATRE ROYAL COVENT GARDEN. Catalogue of the valuable properties of this splendid establishment, unquestionably the best, as well as the most extensive collection, in every department, that has ever been created for the purpose of scenic representations. The best efforts of Roberts, the Grieve's, Whitmore, Pugh, Phillips, and other celebrated artists, here abound in every variety of subject. Favorite panoramic views, exhibited in the recent pantomimes, and many grand drop scenes. The extraordinarily fine toned organ, built by Bishop, at an expence little short of £1000. The magnificent centre chandelier, those for the principal entrance, lobbies, dress and front circles. The wardrobe, embracing a most expensive, elegant, and general assemblage of dresses, and which cost, within a few years, upwards of £20,000. Eighteen brilliant glasses, in gilt frames, of the following dimensions, 79 in. by 68, 70 by 52, 50 by 45, 45 by 36, 42 by 36, 36 by 33, &c. Furniture and fittings of the principal dressing rooms; portrait of Mr. Harris, and other valuable effects; which will be sold by auction, by Mr. Thomas, in the saloon of the theatre, on Thursday, the 10th day of September, 1829, and several following days, at twelve for one very punctually. To be publicly viewed three days prior to the sale, and catalogues had, at 2s. 6d. each, (without one not a person will be admitted,) at Mr. Thomas's offices, 38, King Street, Covent Garden.

pp. [1–3] 4–65 [66 (bl.)]

J. T[homas]; printed by W. Smith [1829]

IKF.

54 †TO THEATRICAL MANAGERS. A catalogue of all the music (in score) of the numerous operas and plays produced at the Theatre Royal, Covent Garden, from the year 1809 to about the year 1846, including those of Dr. Arne, Shield, Dibden, Attwood, Davy, Sir Henry R. Bishop and C. M. von Weber. The adapted operas of Mozart, Spohr, Rossini, Meyerbeer, and other eminent composers, also of the melodramas and pantomimes, with the various plays, prompt books and play bills, from an early period, some of which are great curiosities from a variety of associations; numerous autographs, the pay ledgers, from 1776 to 1826, with the autograph receipts of the actors and actresses during these periods; manuscript dramas. Sir Wm. Davanant's original patent, with royal seal affixed; a capital large iron repository, a smaller ditto, some theatrical portraits, and sundry articles of furniture; which will be sold by auction, by Messrs. Robins, at their rooms, Piazza, Covent Garden, on Thursday, the 3rd day of July, 1856, and the following day, at twelve o'clock.

pp. [2]

Alfred Robins, printer [1856]

IKF.

Dramatic Authors' Society

✠ Catalogue of dramatic pieces, the property of the members of the Dramatic Authors' Society, brought down to September, 1865. [ca. 1866]. See nos. 2134–2135.

Dramatic Fine Art Gallery

55 *CATALOGUE

pp. 14   MB
Aubert   [1880]

Brown, which also has Illustrated notes *on the pictures, edited by W. G. Larkins [1880] and auction sale catalogue [1881.]*

Dulwich College

56 WARNER, GEORGE F[REDERIC]. Catalogue of the manuscripts and muniments of Alleyn's College of God's Gift at Dulwich by George F. Warner, M.A. of the Department of Manuscripts, British Museum.

pp. [i–v] vi–liv [lv (errata) lvi (bl.)], [1] 2–388   L
For the Governors by Longmans, Green, and Co. 1881

Contains a life of Alleyn, and notes on "Mr. Collier's much discussed emendations" (Lowe.) A supplement to the catalogue itself, edited by Francis Bickley, was published in 1903.

Her Majesty's Theatre, Haymarket

57 HER MAJESTY'S THEATRE, HAYMARKET. A catalogue of the first portion of the valuable properties of Her Majesty's Theatre, including the scenery, painted by first-rate artists; the fixed and moveable stage machinery, a splendid full compass organ, by Flight; the very extensive and superior wardrobe of ladies' and gentlemen's apparel, a large portion of which is of the most costly materials; a magnificent chandelier for the centre of the theatre; and numerous smaller chandeliers. The decorative furniture & fittings of the boxes, dressing rooms, committee rooms and offices. The very extensive collection of stage properties, the fittings of the National Concerts and all the fixtures throughout the building. Which will be sold by auction, by Mr. James Scott, on the premises, in the Haymarket, on Thursday, the 17th day of March, 1853, and several following days . . . by order of the mortgagee in possession . . .

pp. [1–4] 5–70 [71–72 (bl.)]   WmP
Alfred Robins, printer   [1853]

58 NO. 2696. Her Majesty's Theatre Haymarket. A catalogue of the excellent furniture including pedestal and other library tables, mahogany chairs, couches, settees, Ottomans, desks, a dial, noble glasses, of various dimensions, a 12-light chandelier, upwards of 700 chairs, 20 chandeliers, an immense quantity of damask, chints, and satin, lengths of drugget, 332 yellow satin curtains & draperies, sundry pieces of chints, worsted, and moreen, the fittings of Her Majesty's box compris-

ing nine glasses, pier table with marble slab, cabriole chairs, covered in satin, &c. A grand piano-forte, and numerous useful miscellanies. Which will be sold by auction by Messrs. Oxenham & sons on the premises, on Thursday, March 3rd, 1853, at 11 for 12 o'clock punctually, under distraint for rates.

pp. [1–2] 3–8.
[London]   [1853]
   IKF.

59 PARTICULARS AND CONDITIONS OF SALE of the valuable properties of Her Majesty's Theatre, Haymarket. Which will be sold by auction, by Mr. James Scott, on the premises, on Monday, the 14th day of March, 1853, at two for three o'clock, in one lot, by order of the mortgagee in possession.

pp. [4]
[London]   [1853]
   IKF.

King's Theatre

60 KING'S THEATRE, or opera house, to be sold by private contract, together with its extensive scenery, machinery, wardrobe, music, and other properties belonging thereto.

fold. doc., pp. [1–3] 4–7 [8 (filing-title: Particulars relative to the King's Theatre . . .)]   L
[London]   [1820]

Olympic

61 LORD CHAMBERLAIN'S LICENCE. Particulars of the Olympic Theatre, in Drury Lane: which will be sold by auction by Messrs. Robins, at the auction mart, opposite the Bank, on Tuesday, the 13th of June, 1820, at twelve o'clock.

fold. doc., pp. [4]; filing-title   L
[London]   [1820]

R. W. Elliston, proprietor.

Royal Aquarium & Summer & Winter Garden Society Ltd., London

62 DU PLAT, E. A. Catalogue of exhibition of mementoes of the national stage from Shakespeare to the present day. Compiled and arranged by Mr. E. A. du Plat, B.A., (St. John's College, Cambridge) who also organised the exhibition.

pp. [1–3] 4–48   MH
Royal Aquarium & Summer & Winter Garden Society, Ltd. J. Ritchie, Esq., chairman and managing director. J. W. Wilkinson, Esq., Secretary.   [1892]

The exhibition was held at the Royal Aquarium, Westminster, December 20th, 1892 to January 21st, 1893, according to printed paper cover of the catalogue. Irving and Bancroft were among the contributors.

Royal Dramatic College

63 *A CATALOGUE of the valuable and interesting collection of pictures, water-colour drawings and prints, books, manuscript plays, and a variety of items connected with the drama. The property of the trustees of the Royal Dramatic College, and others. Which will be sold by auction by Farebrother, Lye & Palmer, the 24th of February, 1881.

pp. 20   MB
[London]   1881

Stratford-upon-Avon Tercentenary

64 CATALOGUE of pictures and drawings exhibited at the Town Hall, Stratford-on-Avon, at the celebration of the tercentenary birthday of William Shakespeare.

pp. [1–5] 6–63 [64]   L
Stratford-on-Avon: Published by the Committee
                                    April 23 1864

65 *SHAKESPEARE TERCENTENARY, Stratford-upon-Avon. Catalogue of the very numerous and valuable fittings and effects supplied for the recent dramatic and musical performances, comprising the elegant proscenium, painted by Mr. O'Connor, of the Haymarket Theatre, new act drop, painted by Mr. Telbin, of Her Majesty's Theatre, stage machinery and appliances, new gas fittings . . ., the centre 320-light corona, the fittings of the dressing rooms . . . and 2300 new chairs of stained birchwood, cane seats, supplied expressly for the late festival. . . . the remaining copies of the illustrated official handbook . . . etc, etc. Which will be sold by auction . . . by Messrs. Puttick and Simp-son at the Pavilion, Stratford upon Avon, on Tuesday, May 31st, 1864 &c.

pp [ii] 12
[London]   [1864]
    Loewenberg.

Vauxhall Gardens

66 †VAUXHALL GARDENS. A catalogue of the whole of the valuable moveable property comprising the temple of arts; theatrical wardrobe; library of music; 25 dozen of wine; furniture; iron repository; pidometer; plate; linen; 4 lofty stages, on iron wheels; 2 organs, &c. which will be sold by auction, by Messrs. Ventom & Hughes, on the premises, the Royal Gardens, Vauxhall, on Tuesday, October 12th, 1841, at eleven o'clock, by order of the assignees of Messrs. Gye and Hughes. . . .

pp. [1–3] 4–15 [16]   MH
[London]   [1841]

Cut and mounted.

Wilson Street Dramatic Institution

67 *CATALOGUE of the complete and elegant wardrobe of theatrical dresses of the dramatic institution in Wilson Street, Gray's Inn Road; which will be sold by auction by Mr. Edmund Robins, 12th January 1847.

pp. 8

                                          1847

STR.

PRIVATE COLLECTIONS

Arranged alphabetically under name of owner.

Anonymous

✘ Valuable theatrical wardrobes of a distinguished amateur, and a celebrated comedian . . . [1819]. *See no. 114.*

68 EXTENSIVE AND UNCOMMON COLLECTION of theatrical portraits. A catalogue of a very curious collection of engravings of actors and actresses, from the earliest period to the present day, many of them after Hogarth, Sir Joshua Reynolds, Zoffany, and other artists of celebrity. In this series of portraits, will be found many proof impressions, & others of rare occurrence, formed from the collection of Bindley, Kemble, Sir M. M. Sykes, and others. The whole being the genuine property of a well-known theatrical connoisseur: which will be sold by auction, (without reserve) by Messrs. Robins, at their spacious rooms, piazza, Covent Garden, on Wednesday, the 8th of June, 1825, at twelve o'clock.

pp. [1–3] 4–14 [15–16 (bl.)]   LGk
[London]   [1825]

Priced.

✘ A catalogue of the portion of the dramatic library of a gentleman. 1899. *See no. 95.*

Irving's library.

Barrymore, *Earl of*

69 †A CATALOGUE of all the valuable materials of the theatre and several erections, at Wargrave, near Twyford, in the County of Berks; late the property of the Right Hon. Earl Barrymore; comprising . . . the entire fittings of the compleatest private theatre in the kingdom, with the scenes and machinery . . . which will be sold by auction by Mr. Christie, on the premises, on Monday, October 15, 1792 . . . A person attends at the theatre to shew the premises, of whom catalogues may be had; also at the Castle, Windsor; Sun, Maiden-

head . . . at the Rainbow Coffee House, Cornhill; and in Pall Mall, London. N.B. The extensive and elegant wardrobe of the above theatre . . . may be treated for, by application in Pall Mall.

pp. [1–3] 4–21 [22 (bl.)]   MH
[London]   [1792]

   Cut and mounted.

Blanchard, E. L.

See below no. 113.

Burgess, Frederick

70 †CATALOGUE of the valuable dramatic & miscellaneous library of Frederick Burgess, Esq. deceased, late of Burgess Hall, Finchley (to be sold by order of the executors), consisting of important works relating to the stage, &c.; a choice series of the original writings of Dickens, Thackeray, Ruskin, Leigh Hunt and Byron; additionally illustrated books; works of the dramatists, plays and play-bills; books illustrated by the Cruikshanks, and others; first editions of popular authors; standard works in general literature; autograph letters; sporting & theatrical engravings, &c. which will be sold by auction, by Messrs. Sotheby, Wilkinson & Hodge. . . . on Thursday, the 31st day of May, 1894, and three following days. . . .

pp. [2] [1] 2–66   L
[London]   [1894]

   Cut and mounted.

Daniel, George

The well-known poet and antiquary. His prefaces to Cumberland's editions of Plays, signed D——G., are valuable — Lowe.

71 CATALOGUE of the most valuable, interesting and highly important library of the late George Daniel, Esq. of Canonbury, together with his collection of original drawings and engraved portraits of distinguished actors and actresses, beautiful water-colour drawings, of the first quality . . . miscellaneous objects of art, interest & curiosity, beautiful pottery and porcelain of Chelsea manufacture, and other fine examples of art and vertu. Which will be sold by auction, by Messrs. Sotheby, Wilkinson & Hodge . . . on Wednesday, the 20th of July, 1864 . . .

pp. [2] [i–iii] iv–v [vi], [1] 2–164 [2] 165–222 [223–4 (bl.)]
                                              MB
J. Davy & Sons, printers   [1864]

   The leaf inserted after p. 164 describes an additional item, 1507★. With inserted invitation to private view. Priced.

Daniel, Henry

72 CATALOGUE of the select & valuable library of the late Henry Daniel, Esq. of St. Paul's Terrace,

Islington, comprising the best works of the English dramatists & poets, memoirs of popular actors & actresses, enriched with numerous and curious illustrations, dramatic biographies and miscellanies. . . . Which will be sold by auction, by Messrs. S. Leigh Sotheby & John Wilkinson . . . on Monday, 23rd of November, 1863, & following day. . . .

pp. [2] [1] 2–54   L
J. Davy and Sons, printers   [1863]

   Another copy at L is priced.

Dodd, James William

73 A CATALOGUE of the very curious and valuable library of the late Mr. James William Dodd, of the Theatre Royal, Drury-Lane. Consisting of a fine collection of old plays, old poetry, romances, history, belles lettres, miscellanies, comic and humorous books, &c. &c. which will be sold by auction, by Leigh and Sotheby, booksellers, at their house in York-Street, Covent Garden, on Thursday, January 19, 1797, and eight following days. . . .

pp. [2] 1–93 [94]   L
[London]: Catalogues to be had of the following booksellers: Walter; Beckett; Faulder; White; Sewell [1797]

Elliston, Robert William

74 ★CATALOGUE of the remaining household furniture, &c., of R. W. Elliston. The private and theatrical wardrobe of Mr. Elliston which will be sold by auction, by Geo. Robins, the 5th of September.

pp. 20   MB
[London]   [1831]

Field, John

75 BIBLIOTHECA HISTRIONICA. A catalogue of the theatrical and miscellaneous library of Mr. John Field, in which are contained several interesting specimens of the early drama . . . historical, critical, and controversial pieces on the subject of the stage; lives and memoirs of the celebrated performers, Betterton, Booth, Wilks, the Cibbers, Macklin, Garrick, Kemble, Siddons, &c.; with several scarce works relating to the Irish, Scottish, and English provincial theatres, including other places of public amusement; a singular volume of manuscript papers connected with the stage, written and collected by the Killigrew family, containing several interesting autographs; the largest collection of play bills ever submitted to public notice; an unique assemblage of checks and tickets of admission to the theatres, from the reign of Charles II to the present time; fine and scarce theatrical prints and portraits; several rare prints and caricatures relating to Hogarth; two original paintings of Quin in the character of Falstaff, and of Henderson in the character of Iago. The whole collected with a view to forming materials for a complete history of the British stage. Which will be sold by auction, by

Mr. Sotheby . . . on Monday, 22nd of January, 1827, and five following days, at twelve o'clock . . .

pp. [2] [1–3] 4–96 [97–98 (advts.)]   L
[London]   [1827]

76 CATALOGUE of the miscellaneous library of Mr. John Field, which includes . . . many works relating to the drama; a very interesting Shakespearean relic, being the snuff box ordered by Garrick for his friend Thos. Hull, to be made out of the wood of the mulberry tree planted by Shakespeare. . . . To which is added, a portion of the library of David Garrick. . . . Which will be sold by auction, by Messrs. S. Leigh Sotheby & Co. . . . July 25th, 1848, and two following days. . . .

pp. [1–3] 4–56   L
Compton and Ritchie, printers   [1848]

Priced.

Garrick, David

For further Garrickiana see especially nos. 76, 120, 129–130.

77 CATALOGUE of a miscellaneous assemblage of valuable property of Mrs. Garrick, dec^d. Comprehending in great variety, Dresden, Seve, Oriental, & Chelsea porcelaine. . . . Removed from the residence in the Adelphi Terrace and Hampton; which will be sold by auction, by Messrs. Robins. . . . Thursday, the 22nd. day of May, 1823 . . .

pp. [1–3] 4–8   MH
[London]   [1823]

78 A CATALOGUE of the library, splendid books of prints, poetical and historical tracts, of David Garrick, Esq. removed from his villa at Hampton, and house on the Adelphi Terrace, with the modern works added thereto by Mrs. Garrick. Which will be sold by auction, by Mr. Saunders, at his great room, "The poets' gallery", no. 39, Fleet Street, on Wednesday, April 23rd, 1823, and 9 following days . . .

pp. [4] [1] 2–90, ²[1] 2 (addenda)   L
[London]: Messrs. Longman and Co.; Mr. Triphook
                                               [1823]
Priced.

79 *——[another edition]
pp. [4] 1–90, ²1–2, ³1–90   MH
                                               1823
With printed lists of purchasers and prices.

80 A CATALOGUE of the small, but valuable collection, of Italian, French, Flemish, Dutch, and English pictures, the property of the late David Garrick, Esq. deceased, and brought from the mansion of Mrs.

Garrick, deceased, on the Adelphi Terrace, and from his villa at Hampton . . . To be sold by auction, by Mr. Christie, at his great room, in Pall Mall, on Monday, June the 23d, 1823, at one o'clock precisely.

pp. [1–3] 4–8   MH
[London]   [1823]

81 [DEAN, J.] GARRICK'S VILLA, Hampton. Observations on the printed particulars circulated for the sale of this property.

fold. doc., pp. [1] 2 [3–4]; filing-title   MH
T. Dolby, printer   1823

Signed and dated 7 June 1823.

82 GARRICK'S VILLA, temple, and pleasure grounds, at Hampton; and his mansion on the Adelphi terrace. In chancery. . . . Particulars and conditions of sale, of copyhold and leasehold estates, at Hampton, on the banks of the Thames, and on the terrace, in the Adelphi, consisting of . . . which will be sold, with the approbation of W. Alexander, Esq. one of the Masters of the High Court of Chancery, in pursuance of an order made in these causes, at the public sale room of the said court, in Southampton Buildings, Chancery Lane, on Wednesday, the 11th day of June, 1823 . . .

pp. [1–2] 3–4   MH
Printed by W. Molineaux   [1823]

83 HAMPTON, Middlesex. A catalogue of the valuable and curious effects of the late David Garrick, Esq. at Hampton, including the antique elbow chair, enriched with emblematical carved work, and a medallion of Shakespear, formed in the wood of the mulberry tree, by Hogarth. . . . To be sold by auction, by Messrs. Burrell & Sons, on the premises, at Hampton, Middlesex, on Monday, July 21, and two following days. . . .

pp. [1–3] 4–28   DFo
[J. Shuttleworth and Co, printers]   [1823]

Priced.

84 IN CHANCERY. Garrick v. Camden. Particulars of Garrick's villa, temple, and pleasure grounds, at Hampton; mansion on the Adelphi Terrace; which will be sold, in pursuance of an order from the High Court of Chancery, at the public sale room of the said Court, in Southampton Buildings, Chancery Lane, on Wednesday, the 11th of June, 1823, in two lots.

pp. [1] 2–5 [6–8]; title on p. [8]   DFo
[London]: W. Molineux, printer   [1823]

85 †MODERN FURNITURE, superior cabinet pianoforte, clock, china, glass, &c. Catalogue of modern household furniture, chimney-glass, superior cabinet piano-forte eight-day clock, handsome wardrobe, china service, cut glass, &c. Part removed from Bayswater, and some articles of cut glass, wardrobe, and eight-day clock, of the late Mrs. Garrick. . . . Which will be sold by auction, by Messrs. Robins. . . . on Friday, the 27th of June, 1823. . . .

pp. [1–3] 4–12   MH
London]   [1823]

Mounted

86 ROYAL ADELPHI TERRACE. A catalogue of the late David Garrick's effects, in the Adelphi. House-hold furniture, large pier glasses, and other property, the effects, comprise a general assortment of bed room articles, elegant satin wood. . . . To be sold by auction, by Messrs. Burrell & Sons, on the premises, No, 5, on the Royal Adelphi Terrace, on Thursday, July 3, and following day, at 12 o'clock, by direction of William Alexander, Esq. one of the Masters of the High Court of Chancery.

pp. [1–3] 4–16   MH
J. Shuttleworth and Co. Lithographic and Letter Press Printers   [1823]

87 A CATALOGUE of a valuable and highly interest-ing collection of engravings, consisting chiefly of English and foreign portraits . . . also a few antique cameos and intaglios, snuff-boxes, seals, rings, and medals, connected with Shakspeare, and the much famed cup, carved from Shakspeare's mulberry tree . . . which was presented to the great English Roscius, on the occasion of the Jubilee, at Stratford upon Avon; and five well-authenticated blocks from the same tree; also, a gold medal of the Jubilee, at Stratford, D. G. steward, and the gold repeater, the property of the late David Garrick, Esquire, which will be sold by auction, by Mr. Christie, at his great room, 8, King Street, St. James's Square. On Thursday, May the 5th, 1825 . . .

pp. [1–3] 4–12   DFo
[London]   [1825]

Priced.

Green, John

88 CATALOGUE of the miscellaneous and theatrical library of Mr. John Green, of Covent Garden, books and tracts relating to the drama, theatres, and places of amusement . . . collections relating to celebrated actors, D. Garrick, Edm. Kean, the Kembles, etc. . . . autograph letters, English sovereigns, actors . . . character portraits of J. Quick, etc. . . . which will be sold by auction, by Messrs. Puttick and Simpson. . . . No. 47, Leicester Square . . . on Monday, May 22nd, 1871. . . .

pp. [2] [1] 2–66   MH
[London]   [1871]

Grimaldi, Joe

See below no. 90.

Harley, J. P.

89 A CATALOGUE of the excellent furniture chimney glasses, horizontal semi-grand piano-forte, by Tomkison; oriental china vases and Chelsea and Dresden figures, a few articles of plate and souvenirs, table and bed linen, handsome services of china, cut glass, theatrical prints and portraits, framed and in portfolios; portraits of Mr. Harley, by Clint and De Wilde; the literary and dramatic library of books, elegantly bound . . . numerous manuscript plays and parts, a col-lection of interesting autograph letters, play bills, music and the private wardrobe of character dresses of the late J. P. Harley, Esq., the celebrated comedian, at No. 14, Upper Gower Street, Bedford Square. . . . Which will be sold by auction, by Mr. Robins, on the premises, on Tuesday, the 23rd of November, 1858, and two following days. . . .

pp. [1–3] 4–38   MH
Alfred Robins, printer   [1858]

Harris, Thomas

90 A CATALOGUE of a collection of theatrical portraits of a gentleman, deceased, formerly forming part of the gallery of the late Thomas Harris, Esq., including whole-lengths of Emery, Barry, Palmer, J. P. Kemble, Fawcett & Mathews by Clint, Hogarth and De Wilde; likewise the celebrated whole-length picture of Miss Foote, as Maria Darlington, by Clint, and other portraits of esteemed favourites. Also the following genuine property of the late inimitable Joe Grimaldi, several original character portraits, by De Wilde, Cawse, and W. Heath, of that talente [*sic*] pantomimist; pictures, manuscript songs & pantomimes, score music, trick models, and costume drawings, endorsed in his own writing; the identical watch alluded to in Boz's *Life*, handsome stage-jewels, fire arms, Covent Garden, Drury Lane and other play bills for many years, dressing and drawing boxes and various interesting items, sold by order of his residuary legatee; a model theatre with scenery and machinery; finger organ, suitable for a concert room or small chapel; and a capital Parisian billiard table, complete. Which will be sold by auction, by Messrs. Robins, at their rooms, in Covent Garden, on Tuesday, the 13th day of June, 1848, at twelve o'clock.

pp. [1–2] 3–10   L
[London]   [1848]

The date of sale corrected in MS in this copy to Wednes-day, 14 June.

Haslewood, Joseph

91 A CATALOGUE of a collection of books, the property of Mr. Haslewood, (with some addition.) Principally consisting of early printed books . . . A considerable number of old plays. — Shakespeare, 15 vol. with Geo. Steeven's MS notes. — A collection for theatrical biography, &c. Which will be sold by auction, by Messrs. King & Lochée. . . . on Monday, May 8, 1809, and two following days. . . .

pp. [1–3] 4–38   L

Printed by J. Barker   [1809]

Another sale of Haslewood's library was held by Evans, 16th December 1833; it included theatrical MSS, and the 29 volume collection of theatrical tracts now in the Barton Collection at Boston Public Library.

Henderson, John

92 A CATALOGUE of the library of John Henderson, Esq; (late of Covent Garden Theatre,) deceased, consisting of a well chosen collection of the most approved modern writers, many of the earliest editions of the old English poets, novels and romances, and the completest assemblage of English dramatic authors that has ever been exhibited for sale in this country; also some capital prints, mostly proofs, and in fine preservation which will be sold by auction by T. and J. Egerton, booksellers. . . . on Monday, the 20th of February, 1786, and the five following days. . . .

pp. [2] [1] 2–71 [72 (bl.)]   L

To be had of Mr. Sewell; Mr. Owen; and of Mess. Egerton.   [1786]

Herman, Henry

93 †CATALOGUE of a portion of the dramatic library of Henry Herman, Esq. consisting of many unique & rare dramatic works, including grand extra illustrated books, in which scarce prints, valuable autographs, play bills, and other interesting documents have been inserted; second and fourth folio Shakespeare; scarce dramatic memoirs & lives of actors. . . . which will be sold by auction, by Messrs. Sotheby, Wilkinson & Hodge. . . . on Friday, the 23rd day of January, 1885. . . .

pp. [1–3] 4–27 [28 (bl.)]   L

[Dryden Press: J. Davy & Sons]   [1885]

Mounted. On the high prices fetched, often recorded by Lowe, see Joseph Knight in DNB, First Supplement, II, 413.

Hull, Thomas

94 VALUABLE LIBRARY of books a catalogue of the excellent & valuable library of books, the property of Mr. Tho. Hull, late of Covent Garden Theatre, deceased. . . . Also, a quantity of music. Which (by order of the executrix) will be sold by auction by Mr. Fisher, at his rooms, No. 41, King Street, and No. 11, Hart Street, Covent Garden, on Monday, the 23d of May, 1808, and following day.

pp. [1–3] 4–12   MH

[Printed by J. & W. Smith]   [1808]

Priced.

Ireland, William Henry

See below no. 117.

Irving, *Sir* Henry

95 †CATALOGUE of a portion of the valuable library of a gentleman comprising the publications of the Villon Society; Transactions of the Bristol and Gloucestershire Archaeological Society, 1876–1891; Blake's Prologue and Characters of Chaucer's Pilgrims; Book of Job; Dante; and other works illustrated by this artist. The writings of R. and E. B. Browning, first editions; chap books. An extensive series of works illustrated by George and Robert Cruikshank. Autograph letters. Atkyns's Gloucestershire, and other books relating to the county; Dover's Annalia Dubrensia. A fine collection of old black-letter ballads. Cromwelliana, extra illustrated; Leigh Hunt's works, first editions; Chaucer's works, and other publications issued from the Kelmscott Press; Kipling's writings, first editions; Vertue's Catalogue of the works of Hollar, extra illustrated; Raymond's Memoirs of Elliston, extra illustrated; Combe's Tours of Dr. Syntax and other works, illustrated by Rowlandson; the writings of R. L. Stevenson, first editions. Sporting books. The works of Tennyson, Swinburne, Thackeray, Dickens, &c. first editions. Whitney's Choice of Emblemes, contemporary MS. Works on art, archaeology, music, history, biography, etc. which will be sold by auction, by Messrs Sotheby, Wilkinson & Hodge . . . on Thursday, the 23rd of March, 1899 . . .

pp. [2] [1] 2–61 [62]   L

[Printed by Dryden Press: J. Davy & Sons]   [1899]

Cut and mounted, with prices.

Kean, Charles

96 CATALOGUE of presentation silver plate, jewels, miniatures, snuff boxes, portraits & theatrical decorations, &c. formerly the property of, or relating to, the celebrated actor and actress, Mr. & Mrs. Charles J. Kean; and other jewellery . . . the property of the late Mrs. Mary Maria Logie, only daughter of Charles Kean and grand-daughter of Edmund Kean: which (by order of the executor) will be sold by auction by Messrs. Christie, Manson & Woods . . . 8 King Street, St. James's Square, on Monday, July 11, and Tuesday, July 12, 1898. . . .

pp. [1–3] 4–23 [24 (bl.)]   MH

[Printed by Wm. Clowes]   [1898]

97 CATALOGUE of the library of the late Charles Kean (the eminent actor), including valuable autograph letters, engravings and relics, of his father Edmund Kean. Sold by order of the executor of Mrs. Mary Logie, the only child of Charles Kean, who inherited the collections. Which will be sold by auction, (by order of the executors), by Messrs. Sotheby, Wilkinson & Hodge. . . . No. 13, Wellington Street, Strand, W.C. on Thursday, the 23rd day of June, 1898, and the following day, at one o'clock precisely. . . .

pp. [1–3] 4–44   MH

[Dryden Press: J. Davy & Sons]   [1898]

Kean, Edmund

98 A CATALOGUE of genuine furniture. . . . A variety of lots left uncleared at Mr. Kean's sale by Mr. Young, of Agar Street, Strand . . . which will be sold by auction, by Messrs. Robins, at their rooms, in Covent Garden, on Monday, the 8th day of July, 1833 . . .

pp. [1–2] 3–10   DFo

[London]: Alfred Robins, printer   [1833]

99 A CATALOGUE of the household furniture, and various effects, of the late celebrated Mr. Kean, at his residence at Richmond, adjoining the theatre, comprising . . . a few lots of books, including many interesting works, amongst which are 20 vols. of plays with Mr. Kean's favourite parts having written memoranda of the stage business. The theatrical wardrobe comprises 25 splendid character dresses, richly embroidered, composed of the most expensive materials, and presenting the correct costume of all the leading characters in the drama, so successfully pourtrayed by that mighty genius, whose early death all must deplore. Several suits of stage armour. Rich crimson and purple silk velvet cloaks, trimmed with ermine, and all paraphernalia connected with each character. A variety of beautiful stage swords, stars, ornaments, buttons, &c. several presented by the widow of David Garrick; also a few lots of stage dresses and properties . . . which will be sold by auction, by Mr. George Robins, on the stage of the Richmond Theatre, on Monday, the 24th of June, 1833, by direction of the administrator . . .

pp. [1–3] 4–15 [16]   DFo

[London]: Alfred Robins, printer   [1833]

Copy at MH priced.

100 A CATALOGUE of the following unique selection of valuables of the late Edmund Kean, Esq. culled especially from his cottage in the Isle of Bute, and removed for peremptory sale. . . . which will be sold by auction, by Mr. George Robins, . . . Tuesday, June the 17th, 1834. . . .

pp. [1–3] 4–12   MH

Alfred Robins, typ.   [1834]

Mounted and priced.

100.1 PARTICULARS of Wood End Cottage, the property of the late Edmund Kean, Esq. with its well adapted furniture, library of books, collection of prints, plate, linen, china and glass, near the town of Rothsay, in the Island & County of Bute. The domain includes twenty-four acres, which will be sold by auction, by Mr. Geo. Robins, at the Buck Inn, Argyll Street, Glasgow, on Thursday, May the 1st, 1834 . . . Geo. Robins, Covent Garden.

pp. [1–2] 3 [4]; title on p. 4   DFo

[London]: Alfred Robins, printer   [1834]

Kemble, Charles

101 A CATALOGUE of [a] most splendid theatrical wardrobe of an eminent actor, who has recently quitted the stage. Unrivalled for richness, correctness of costume and value, prepared during the several past years, regardless of expense and trouble, from the most authentic sources for character and costume, the wardrobe embraces almost all the dresses for the principal parts in the tragic and comic dramas, with a profusion of stage jewels and valuable swords, also, the celebrated standard of Napoleon . . . the late Sir Walter Scott's wardrobe with an interesting lyrical remembrance, addressed to it, by its late master in his own hand. Also a collection of beautiful stained glass. Which will be sold by auction, by Mr. Edmund Robins, at the Great Rooms, in Covent Garden, on Thursday, the 15th day of June, 1837, at twelve o'clock.

pp. [1–2] 3–10

Alfred Robins, typ.   [1837]

   IKF.

Priced. Lot 70 consisted of about one hundred of J. P. Kemble's prompt copies.

Kemble, John Philip

102 CATALOGUE of the excellent household furniture, pier and chi[m]ney glasses, mirrors, table services of Nankin and English china, cut glass, a few fine plaister busts, prints, a capital billiard-table, cellar of unusually fine wines, . . . and other effects, the property of J. P. Kemble, Esq. and removed from his late residence, in Great Russell-Street, Bloomsbury. . . . Which will be sold by auction, by Messrs. Robins, at their spacious rooms, Great Piazza, Covent-Garden, on Thursday, December 14, 1820, and following day. . . .

pp. [1–2] 3–16   MH

[London]   [1820]

103 A CATALOGUE of the valuable and extensive miscellaneous library, choice prints, and theatrical portraits, of John Philip Kemble, Esq. which will be sold by auction, by Mr. Evans, at his house, No. 93, Pall-Mall, on Friday January 26, and nine following days (Sunday excepted).

pp. [2] [1] 2–66 [67 (advt.) 68 (bl.)]   MH

[Printed by W. Bulmer and W. Nicol]   1821

Copy at L priced.

Lacy, T. H.

104 CATALOGUE of the extensive and valuable collection of portraits of Mr. T. H. Lacy, late of the Strand, deceased; comprising theatrical performers, dramatists, composers and others connected with the stage, including several in the finest state, and of great rarity; numerous water-colour drawings, illustrative of the plays of Shakespeare, by Wright, in his best manner; portraits of celebrated actors, by de Wilde and Wageman, and S. Harding, being fine drawings in watercolours, from life; paintings of actors & landscapes, finely executed in oil; framed drawings & engravings; a beautifully chased & enamelled gold box, with singing bird, &c. &c. Which will be sold by auction, (in special pursuance of the will) by Messrs. Sotheby, Wilkinson & Hodge, auctioneers of literary property & works illustrative of the fine arts, at their house, No. 13, Wellington Street, Strand, W.C., on Monday, 1st Decemrer [sic], 1873, and two following days. . . .

pp. [2] [1] 2–38   MH

Dryden Press: J. Davy and Sons   1873

Priced.

105 *CATALOGUE of the valuable theatrical & miscellaneous library of T. H. Lacy, which will be sold by auction, by Sotheby, Wilkinson & Hodge, 24th of November, 1873.

pp. (2), 111   MB
[London]   1873

Mackenzie, John Mansfield

106 CATALOGUE of the very choice dramatic & general library of John Mansfield Mackenzie, Esq. of Edinburgh; comprising an extensive and most valuable collection of biographies, histories, controversies, facetiae, &c. relating to the stage; a remarkable series of the original editions of the works of Dickens, Thackeray, Lever, Tennyson, Keats & other popular authors; an extensive and choice collection of the books illustrated by the inimitable George Cruikshank; rare books of jests, songs, drolleries, &c., old plays, play-bills, theatrical newspapers and periodicals; additionally illustrated books with rare portraits, including a fine copy of Bartolozzi and works, containing original drawings, very numerous portraits and plates, autograph letters, &c. important works by Scottish writers or relating to Scotland; best editions of the dramatists; privately printed books; illustrated works by Rowlandson, Leech, Phiz, Crowquill, and others; standard books in all classes of literature; all fine copies, in perfect condition, bound by the most eminent English binders; valuable theatrical portraits, including original drawings, autograph letters, &c. which will be sold by auction, by Messrs. Sotheby, Wilkinson & Hodge . . . on Monday, the 11th day of March, 1889, and seven following days, at one o'clock precisely. . . .

pp. [4] [1] 2–170   MH

Dryden Press: J. Davy and Sons   1889

Priced. In the Preface to his Bibliographical Account *Lowe acknowledges his indebtedness to Mackenzie. "His magnificent theatrical library, one of the finest in the world, was freely placed at my disposal; and most collectors would be surprised to learn how many of the rarest books in my list were seen by me in his collection."*

Macklin, Charles

107 *A CATALOGUE of the library of the late Mr. Charles Macklin, comedian, deceased: comprising a general assemblage of books in the various languages; among them are Nuict's de Straparole, 5 vol. on vellum; Harding's Shakspeare; Wood's Athenae, 2 vol. L.P. Chronicle History of King Lear and Richard II. by Shakspeare; with sundry old plays by Shirley, Glapthorne, Chapman, L. Batrey, &c. . . . which will be sold by auction by Mr. King, on the premises, no. 6, Tavistock-Row, Covent-Garden, on Tuesday, November 21, 1797, and four following days, at twelve o'clock.

pp. 21   DFo
[London]   [1797

Macready, William Charles

108 CATALOGUE of a valuable collection of engravings from the old and modern masters, being, for the most part, proofs before letters, collected by the tragedian, William Charles Macready, Esq. . . . also the following drawings, for the engravings made from them . . . also, some fine books of prints. Which will be sold by auction, by Messrs. Sotheby, Wilkinson & Hodge . . . on Friday, the 13th day of March, 1868 . . .

pp. [1–3] 4–12   LVA
J. Davy and Sons, printers   [1868]

109 CATALOGUE of the library of William Charles Macready, Esq. deceased; comprising. . . . Shakspeare's plays, marked for reading by Mr. Macready. Many of the books have Mr. Macready's autograph, and some contain his MS. notes: also, the collection of pictures, drawings, and engravings, sculpture, bronzes, and ornamental objects, and some decorative furniture: which will be sold by auction, by Messrs. Christie, Manson & Woods . . . on Tuesday, July 8, 1873, and following day . . .

pp. [1–3] 4–30 [31–32 (bl.)]   MH
[Printed by W. Clowes and Sons]   [1873]

Priced.

Maidment, James

110 CATALOGUE of the extensive, curious, and valuable library of the late James Maidment, Esq., advocate (editor of numerous publications) . . . The works in dramatic literature are very rare, and form two days' sale. Which will be sold by auction by Messrs. T. Chapman & Son, in their great rooms, No. 11 Hanover Street, Edinburgh, on Tuesday, April 27th, and fourteen following lawful days (excepting Saturdays, May 1st, 8th, and 15th), each day precisely at one o'clock . . .

pp. [4] [1] 2–288; ptd. covers   E
[Edinburgh]: Colston & Son, printers   [1880]

Malone, Edmond

III [BANDINEL, B.] Catalogue of early English poetry and other miscellaneous works illustrating the British drama, collected by Edmond Malone, Esq. and now preserved in the Bodleian Library.

pp. [i–iii] iv–viii, [1] 2–52   L
Oxford: at the University Press   1836

Mapleson, James Henry

112 TO OPERA AND THEATRICAL MANA-GERS, costumiers, and others. A catalogue of an extensive and valuable operatic wardrobe, lately the property of Colonel Mapleson, comprising principals' and subsidiary dresses, in fancy coloured silk, satin, velvet, and other expensive materials; ladies' and gentlemen's tan, patent, velvet, and other fancy boots and shoes; forty-one lots of new costumes, made for the opera Lohengrin; swords, shields, hats, tights, sashes, and numerous stage properties; also the library of music, with orchestral, chorus, and principals' parts, and scores; which will be sold by auction by Messrs. Debenham, Storr, and Sons . . . on Wednesday, the 20th day of July, 1898. . . .

pp. [1–2] 3–15 [16: "Approaching Sales"]; headed "[No. 22, 946."]   MH
Sweeting and Co., printers   [1898]

Marshall, Frank Albert

113 †CATALOGUE of the dramatic, Elizabethan and miscellaneous library of the late Frank A. Marshall, Esq. comprising an important collection of literature relating to the stage; works of the dramatists & rare old plays; Shakespeare and Shakespeariana. . . . To which is added the library of the late E. L. Blanchard, Esq. consisting of dramatic and general works. Which will be sold by auction, by Messrs. Sotheby, Wilkinson & Hodge . . . on Monday, the 30th of June, 1890, and five following days. . . .

pp. [2] [1] 2–134   L
Dryden Press J. Davy & Sons   [1890]

Mounted and priced.

Mathews, Charles (*the elder*)

114 VALUABLE THEATRICAL WARDROBES of a distinguished amateur, and a celebrated comedian, retiring. A catalogue of a valuable collection of theatrical dresses, stage ornaments, and properties, of the most costly and useful description; the property of an amateur, who spared no expence in their formation; some costly court dress suits, and the private dressess [sic] of a celebrated comedian, who has no further occasion for them, including thirty fine character wigs. The whole will be found well worthy the attention of amateurs, provincial managers, the profession in general, and the masquerade warehouses; which will be sold by

auction, by Messrs. Robins . . . on Wednesday, the 12th of May, 1819. . . .

pp. [1–3] 4–11 [12 (bl.)]   MH
[London]   [1819]

The "comedian" is implausibly identified in this copy in a nineteenth-century hand, as "Mr. Mathews".

115 [MATHEWS, CHARLES JAMES, *compiler*] CATALOGUE raisonée of Mr. Mathews's gallery of theatrical portraits, now exhibited for the first time, and forming a nearly complete dramatic record from the year 1659 down to the present time. Queen's Bazaar, Oxford Street.

pp. [1–3] 4–74 [75–78 (index) 79–80 (bl.)]   L
Printed by W. Clowes   1833

Compiled, according to a note (possibly by Anne Mathews) in this copy, by Charles James Mathews. Reprints Charles Lamb's essay "The Old Actors" from the London Magazine, 1822. The pictures were exhibited at the Queen's Bazaar in 1833, and acquired by the Garrick Club in 1852.

116 PARTICULARS OF MR. MATHEWS' ADMIRED VILLA and grounds, called Ivy Cottage . . . which will be sold by auction, by Mr. Geo. Robins . . . on Tuesday, April the 16th, 1833, at twelve o'clock.

fold. doc., pp. [4]; filing-title   LGk
Geo. Robins   [1833]

117 †CATALOGUE of the miscellaneous and dramatic library, engraved theatrical portraits, dramatic and literary autograph letters, and collection of theatrical relics, the property of the late Charles Mathews, Esq. The library is principally theatrical; it embraces the first four editions of the collected works of Shakespeare; a very complete collection of the play bills of the Theatres Royal, Drury Lane and Covent Garden, including the series formed by Mr. Fawcett and his father; numerous theatrical tracts and collections of critiques upon the dramatic performances during the last and present centuries; numerous plays; and the best editions of the collected works of the early dramatic authors. The engraved theatrical portraits are rendered peculiarly interesting, the late Mr. Mathews having devoted much time in enriching them with MS. observations, critical and biographical; a very interesting and extensive collection of all the various portraits and prints that have appeared tending to illustrate the life of David Garrick; also numerous documents, play bills, and, in short, every thing that could in any way throw light on his glorious career. Among the autograph letters will be found those of royal and illustrious persons, judges and statesmen, authors, actors and actresses, artists, and musical composers; including many of great rarity and interest. The theatrical relics include the cassolette made from the Shaksperian mulberry tree, and presented to Garrick, by the Corporation of Stratford-upon-Avon;

medals, miniatures, busts and other highly interesting curiosities, relating to Shakespeare, Garrick, J. P. Kemble, G. F. Cooke, and other eminent performers. At the end of the autograph letters are, with permission, added the unpublished writings and literary productions of the late Mr. William Henry Ireland, author of the Shaksperian forgeries, &c. Which will be sold by auction, by Mr. Sotheby and Son, Wellington Street, Strand, on Wednesday, August 19th, 1835, and three following days, at twelve o'clock.

pp. [1-3] 4-48, misprinting 48 as "47"; probably lacks an inset slip   L
[London]   [1835]

Mounted.

118 A CATALOGUE of all the elegant furniture, the greater portion was made by Messrs. Gillows, within the last few years, together with the tastefully selected appendages, the property of the late celebrated comedian, Charles Mathews, Esq. at no. 102, Great Russell Street, Bloomsbury; it includes a drawing room suite . . . which will be sold by auction, by Mr. Geo. Robins, on the premises, on Monday, the 21st of March, 1836, and two following days. . . .

pp. [1-3] 4-32   LGk
Alfred Robins, typ.   [1836]

Mathews, Charles James (Charles Mathews, *the younger*)

119 UNDER THE WILL OF THE LATE CHARLES MATHEWS, ESQ. Sale no. 2083. 59, Belgrave Road, S.W. A catalogue of the well-made modern furniture, comprising articles suited to the various appartments, elegant ornamental china, clocks, bronzes and decorative items, also a large collection of rare old engravings, etchings and sketches, by Sir E. Landseer, R. A. Pictures and drawings, by Chalon, R. A., Cosway, Bartolozzi, Charles Mathews and others. Several scrap books, with original sketches, 1,500 vols. of books, numerous miscellaneous and interesting effects connected with the career of the late Charles Mathews, Esq. Also the beneficial lease of the residence, which will be sold by auction, by Messrs. Robinson & Fisher, on the premises as above, on Monday, July 22nd, 1878, and following days, at one o'clock precisely each day.

pp. [1-5] 6-16, ²[1] 2-12, ³[1] 2-9 [10 (bl.)]   LGk
[Blakeman & Jagger, steam printers]   [1878]

Mitchell, William

120 CATALOGUE of an interesting collection of autograph letters, the collection of William Mitchell, Esq. including fine specimens of Beethoven . . . also several letters, poetry, etc., in the autograph of Edmund Kean, to which is added, forty-eight unpublished letters of David Garrick, of the highest interest . . . and an

undoubtedly original portrait of Margaret Woffington, by Hogarth, etc. etc. which will be sold by auction by Messrs. Puttick and Simpson . . . 191, Piccadilly, on Monday, Dec. 17, 1849. . . .

pp. [1-3] 4-28   MH
[London]   [1849]

Oldfield, Ann

121 *A CATALOGUE of all the rich furniture of Mrs. Oldfield, deceased . . . A cabinet of French and English books, etc. which will be sold by auction at her late dwelling house in Grosvenor Street, on Tuesday 9th of February, 1731.

                                                  1731

STR.

Phelps, Samuel

122 †BY ORDER OF THE EXECUTORS OF THE LATE SAMUEL PHELPS. Theatrical costumes. A catalogue of the theatrical wardrobe of the late eminent tragedian, Samuel Phelps; also a few volumes of interesting books, including authorities upon ancient costumes, and some engravings of R. W. Elliston, Charles Matthews, J. P. Kemble, Liston and others; a complete fitting up for a small stage; also a few lots of old choice wines. Another property. Which will be sold by auction, by Mr. George Robins at the Rooms, 13, High Holborn, on Friday, the 26th of September, 1879. . . . Catalogues at Mr. W. H. Griffiths' Dramatic, Musical and General Agency Offices, 30, Tavistock Street, Covent Garden, W.C. . . . and of Mr. George Robins, auctioneer and valuer, 5, Chancery Lane. . . .

pp. [1-2] 3-12; lacking 3-10   MH
T. Pettitt & Co. printers, &c.   [1879]

Mounted.

Raymond, J. G.

123 *A CATALOGUE of the library of books, more particularly as relates to theatricals, and about forty very fine original pictures, which will be sold by auction by Messrs. Robins, May 25th, 1818.

pp. 10
[London?]   1818

IKF.

Reed, Isaac

A most learned antiquary and authority upon all matters connected with the stage. His collection of books, which was sold in 1807, was one of the most valuable theatrical libraries ever brought together — Lowe.

124 BIBLIOTHECA REEDIANA. A catalogue of the curious & extensive library of the late Isaac Reed, Esq. of Staple Inn. deceased. Editor of the last edition of

Shakspeare. Comprehending a most extraordinary collection of books, in English literature; particularly relating to the English drama, and poetry, many of them extremely scarce, and enriched by his ms. notes, and observations. Together with his manuscripts, prints, books of prints, book cases, &c. Which will be sold by auction, by Messrs. King and Lochée, at their great room, No. 38, King Street, Covent-Garden, on Monday, Nov. 2, 1807, and 38 following days . . .

pp. [2] [1] 2–5 v ix–xii, ²[1] 2–405 [406] [=412], pagination irregular; pl. [front.]   E

J. Barker, printer   [1807]

   With a preface by Henry John Todd.

Rhodes, William Barnes

125 BIBLIOTHECA DRAMATICA. A catalogue of the entire, curious, and extensive dramatic library of William Barnes Rhodes, Esq. Containing a most rare and copious collection of plays . . . amounting in the whole to nearly 5,000 pieces; besides criticisms on Shakespeare and the drama; tracts and pamphlets on the history of the stage, including lives and memoirs of authors, actors, &c. &c. Which will be sold by auction, by Mr. Sotheby . . . on Monday, April 18, 1825, and nine following days, (Sunday excepted) at twelve o'clock . . .

pp. [1–3] 4–114 [115–6], [i] ii–iv (advt.)   L

                              [1825]

Richardson, John

126 A CATALOGUE of the whole of the travelling theatres, which for excellence and completeness, stand unrivalled. The scenery, wardrobe, carriages, and numerous effects, of the late Mr. John Richardson, the celebrated travelling comedian. Which will be sold by auction, by Taylor & Sons on the premises, Horsemonger Lane, Newington, on Monday, 19th of December, 1836, and following days. . . .

pp. [1–3] 4–20   MH

Southey & Cuthbert, printers   [1836]

   A printed poster (copy at MH) advertising the sale is dated 25 November 1836.

Saker, Horatio

See below no. 130.

Siddons, *Mrs.* Sarah

127 VERY EXCELLENT HOUSEHOLD FURNITURE, china, glass and plated articles, the property of the late Mrs. Siddons. A catalogue of the excellent household furniture . . . a small library of books, paintings, wines, and sundry effects; late the genuine property of Mrs. Siddons, deceased; which will be sold by auction, by Mr. Nixon, on the premises, No. 27, Upper Baker Street, on Wednesday, July 27, 1831. . . .

Printed particulars, and catalogues at 6d. each, to be had of Mr Nixon, 123, Great Portland Street. . . .

pp. [1–3] 4–18   MH

Howlett and Brimmer, printers   [1831]

Smith, Albert Richard

128 ★CATALOGUE of the dramatic library of A. R. Smith.

                              MH

[London]   [1882]

Smith, Richard John ("O. Smith")

129 CATALOGUE of the dramatic and miscellaneous library of Richard John Smith, Esq. (commonly known as 'O. Smith') of the Adelphi Theatre: including a large and well selected collection of books. . . . "Garrickiana" . . . collections for a history of the stage, in 20 quarto volumes, the formation of which is the result of many years indefatigable labour and research of the late Mr. Smith; the Haslewood collection upon the same subject . . . which will be sold by auction, by Messrs. Puttick and Simpson . . . Thursday, May 17th, 1855, and 2 following days. . . .

pp. [2] 7–55 [56 (advts.)]   L

[London]   [1855]

130 CATALOGUE of a collection of interesting and valuable books, including the library of an Indian official . . . also the dramatic collections of the late Mr. Horatio Saker, of the Princess's Theatre; the matchless "Garrickiana" formed by the late Mr. R. J. Smith, of the Adelphi, an extraordinary collection of upwards of 200 unpublished dramas, many being in the handwriting of the authors, the original MSS. of the "Rejected Addresses" . . . two costly medleys of dramatic portraits . . . which will be sold by auction, by Messrs. Puttick and Simpson . . . Monday, July 22nd, 1861, and four following days. . . .

pp. [2] [1] 2–89 [90 (bl.)]   L

[London]   1861

   Priced.

Southgate, J. W.

131 TO BE SOLD. A very unique collection of original letters of dramatic performers . . .

bs.   L

[J. W. Southgate]   [*ca.* 1835]

   An auctioneer's advertisement.

Stephens, Catherine, *Countess of Essex*

132 CATALOGUE of the choice collection of old French decorative furniture, and other objects of art, of the late Dowager Countess of Essex, removed from

Belgrave Square: which (by order of the executors of the late Miss Johnston) will be sold by auction, by Messrs. Christie, Manson & Woods, at their Great Rooms, 8 King Street, St. James's Square, on Tuesday, March 6, 1883, and the following day, at one o'clock precisely.

pp. [1–3] 4–22 [23–24 (bl.)]

[London]   [1883]

IKF.

Thornber, Harry

133 THORNBER, HARRY. *The Arts Club, Manchester. Catalogue of engravings of theatrical scenes and portraits. Lent and arranged by Harry Thornber.

pp. 17; pls. 16   MB

Bedford Press   [1888]

Vestris, *Madame*

134 CHESHAM PLACE, Belgrave Square. A catalogue of all the elegant household furniture noble glasses, console tables, a drawing room suite, in silk taberet and rose-wood, consisting of three sets of curtains, ottoman, sofas, fauteuils, loo, card and occasional tables, or-molu lustres. . . . Wilkie's prints; the Kemble family after Harlowe, theatrical portraits . . . the entire property of Madame Vestris, by whose direction they will be sold by auction by Messrs. Foster & Sons, on the premises, No. 2, Chesham Place, Belgrave Square, on Thursday, 22 June, 1837. . . .

pp. [1–3] 4–18   MH

[London: printed by J. Davy]   [1837]

Mounted.

Winston, James

135 BIBLIOTHECA DRAMATICA et histrionica. Catalogue of the extensive and highly valuable printed and manuscript library of Mr. James Winston, deceased, late proprietor of the Haymarket Theatre, and many years manager of Drury Lane Theatre, comprising very numerous autograph papers of dramatic authors and players, books of accounts, and other historical collections relative to the metropolitan and provincial theatres; and the biographies of past and present actors and actresses; Vice-Chamberlain Coke's papers, temp. Q. Anne, on the introduction of the Italian opera; the original manuscripts of the rejected addresses on the opening of Drury Lane Theatre, 1812; Colman and Elliston correspondence, a matchless collection relating to Edmund Kean, several thousand portraits, and graphic illustrations, Stanfield's model of his first diorama; and many other interesting items in dramatic history and literature, which will be sold by auction, by Messrs. Puttick and Simpson, auctioneers of literary property, at their great room, 191, Piccadilly, on Wednesday, December 13th, and two following days. . . .

pp. [1–3] 4–65 [66 (bl.)]   MH

[G. Norman, printer]   [1849]

Priced.

136 ——[large paper issue]

pp. [1–3] 4–65 [66 (bl.)]   MH

[G. Norman, printer]   [1849]

Twelve or thirteen copies printed. Priced.

Woodward, Henry

137 A CATALOGUE of all the elegant household furniture, pictures, and drawings, a neat library, china, rich silver brocaded silks, diamond rings, gold watch, &c. of Henry Woodward Esq. deceased, brought from his late house in Chapel-Street, Grosvenor-Place, consisting of beautiful cotton & other furniture in bedsteads and window curtains, cabriole chairs, capital pictures and drawings, by Rubens, Rembrandt, and other admired masters, a well chosen library containing about 400 volumes, &c. which will be sold by auction, by Mr. Pollard, at Mr. Hathwell's great auction room, in St. Alban's Street, on Monday, the 30th of June, 1777, and the three following days. . . .

pp. [1–2] 3–16   MH

[London]   [1777]

GOVERNMENT REGULATION OF THE THEATRE

Inserted in the numbered series, and preceded by the sign ¶, are the principal acts, bills and parliamentary papers dealing with the theatre from the accession of Elizabeth I. For the explanation of the style of these entries, see INTRODUCTION. In a few instances later printings of special interest are included in the numbered series.

The most important printed documents of government control before the reign of Elizabeth are the Act of 1543 "for the advancement of true religion" (34, 35 Henry VIII c.1) and the Proclamations of Edward VI of 6 August 1549 and 28 April 1551, and of Mary of 18 August 1553 (Bibliotheca Lindesiana 365, 395, 427). These are reprinted in W. C. Hazlitt, The English Drama and Stage under the Tudor and Stuart Princes, 1869 (no. 1045 below) and Glynne Wickham, Early English Stages, Vol II Part I, 1963.

See also THE THEATRE OUT OF LONDON: IRELAND, especially nos. 1771, 1795–6, 1800, 1830 (Dublin): SCOTLAND, especially nos. 1854–1859, 1916, 1924–1936, 1953, 1970–1972 (Edinburgh); no. 2011 (Glasgow). For banned plays see THEATRICAL CRITICISM: INDIVIDUAL PLAYS nos. 3811 passim.

138 ★BY THE QUEENE. Forasmuche as the time wherein common interludes in the English tongue are wont vsually to be played is now past vntill Allhallontyde. . . . Yeven at our Palayce of Westminster the. XVI. daye of Maye, the first yeare of oure raygne.

bs.   O

[London]: Jugge and Cawood   [1559]

  Bibliotheca Lindesiana 508, STC 7896.

139 ———[another edition] By the Quene. Forasmuche as the tyme . . .

bs.   L

Imprinted by Rychard Iugge and Iohn Cawood Printers to the Quenes Maiestie   [1559]

  Bibliotheca Lindesiana 509, STC 7897.

  Reprinted in Collier, I, 168–169; Hazlitt, pp. 19–20; Chambers, Elizabethan, IV, 263–264.

  Forbidding the performance of unlicensed plays.

¶ An Acte for the punishement of vacabondes and for relief of the poore & impotent (14 Eliz. I c. 5) (Statutes of the Realm).

  Vagabonds, etc. (1572), CTS *p. 59.*

  "Comon Players in Enterludes & Minstrels, not belonging to any Baron of this Realme or towardes any other honorable Personage of greater Degree" to be deemed rogues and vagabonds.

¶ An Acte for punyshment of rogues, vagabondes and sturdy beggars (39 Eliz. I c. 4) (Statutes of the Realm).

  Vagabonds (1597), CTS *p. 62.*

¶ An Acte for the continuance and explanation of the statute made in the 39 yeere of the raigne of our late Queene Elizabeth, intituled An acte for punishmente of rogues vagabondes and sturdie beggers (1 Ja. 1, c. 7) (Statutes of the Realm).

  Vagabonds (1603), CTS *p. 62.*

¶ An Acte to restrain abuses of players (3 Ja. 1, c. 21) (Statutes of the Realm).

  Plays (1605), CTS *p. 63.*

  "The great abuse of the Holy Name of God."

140 TAYLOR, JOHN. ★The true cause of the water-mens suit concerning players, and the reasons that their playing on London side is their extreame hindrances. With a relation how farre that suit was proceeded in, and the occasions that it was not effected.

        [1614]

A pamphlet evidently published in 1614, but no copy is known. "Probably written in the winter of 1614, and touched up before 1630" (Chambers, Elizabethan, II, 370 seq.) Reprinted in All the Workes of John Taylor the Water-Poet (1630 and 1869 for the Spenser Society), pp. ²171–176; with the above title in The Old Book Collector's Miscellany ed. Charles Hindley (1871–1873), II, [no.] 15.

¶ An Acte for punishing of divers abuses comitted on the Lorde[s] day called Sunday (1 Cha. 1, c. 1) (Statutes of the Realm).

Sunday Observance (1625), CTS *p. 65.*

  The abuses include "interludes" and "common plays".

141 THE STAGE-PLAYERS COMPLAINT. In a pleasant dialogue betweene Cane of the Fortune, and Reed of the Friers. Deploring their sad and solitary conditions for want of imployment. In this heavie and contagious time of the plague in London.

pp. [2] 1–6; illus.   L

Tho. Bates   1641

  Published in the autumn. With woodcuts on title-page probably intended to represent Andrew Cane and Timothy Reed — Bentley. Wing S 5126.

142 ———(Occasional Fac-Simile Reprints . . . under the direction of Mr. E. W. Ashbee. III.)

pp. [2] 1–6; ptd. covers   L

John Tuckett   1868

  Limited to 100 copies.

Reprinted in Collier, *II, 110–111;* Hazlitt, *pp. 253–258;* The Old Book Collector's Miscellany *ed. Charles Hindley (1871–1873), III, [no.] 14.*

Reed was a celebrated performer at the Blackfriars Theatre. Mr. Hindley quotes from "The Careless Shepherdess" the following lines regarding Reed:
  "*There is ne'er a part*
  About him but breaks jests.——
  I never saw Reade peeping through the curtain,
  But ravishing joy entered the heart." — Lowe.

The Suppression of Plays 1642–1660

¶ Order for stage-plays to cease (Interregnum 2 September 1642) (Acts and Ordinances of the Interregnum *I, 26*).

143 A DECLARATION of the Lords and Commons assembled in Parliament, for the appeasing and quietting of all unlawful tumults and insurrections. ... Also an Ordinance of both Houses, for the suppressing of stage-plays. Ordered by the Lords and Commons, that this order be forthwith printed and published. John Browne Cler. Parliament.

pp. [8]   L
John Wright   Septemb. 3 1642

A declaration *was first published, also on 3 September, without the "Order concerning stage-plays" on the last page of this edition. Wing E 1411(?) Reprinted in Hazlitt, p. 63, from Collier, II, 105; a facsimile reproduction on the last four leaves of Joseph Knight's reprint of "Roscius Anglicanus", 1886 (no. 827 below).*

144 THE ACTORS REMONSTRANCE, or complaint: for the silencing of their profession, and banishment from their severall play-houses. In which is fully set downe their grievances, for their restraint; especially since stage-plays, only of all publike recreations are prohibited; the exercise at the Beares Colledge, and the motions of puppets being still in force and vigour. As it was presented in the names and behalfes of all our London comedians to the great God Phoebus-Apollo, and the nine Heliconian sisters, on the top of Pernassus, by one of the Masters of Requests to the muses, for this present month. And published by their command in print by the Typograph Royall of the Castalian province. 1643.

pp. [1–2] 3–8   L
Edw. Nickson   Januar. 24. 1643

Wing A 453.

144.1 ——(Occasional Facsimile Reprints ... under the direction of Mr. E. W. Ashbee. IV.)

pp. [1–2] 3–8; ptd. covers   L
John Tuckett   1869

Limited to 100 copies.

Reprinted 1822 as supplement to The British Stage and Literary Cabinet *(no. 4112 below); in* Hazlitt, *pp. [259]–265; in* The Old Book Collector's Miscellany *ed. Charles Hindley (1871–1873), III, [no.] 19.*

¶ An Ordinance for the Lord Major and City of London, and the Justices of Peace to suppress stage-playes and interludes (Interregnum 22 October 1647) (Acts and Ordinances of the Interregnum *I, 1027*).

145 TWO ORDINANCES of the Lords and Commons assembled in Parliament one for the Lord Major of the City of London, and the Justices of the Peace for the City, and parts adjacent, to suppresse stage-playes, interludes, and common playes, and commit the actors to the gaole, to be tryed at the next Sessions, to be punished as rogues. The other for setling of the major ... for the City of Chester ...

pp. [2] 1–6   L
Printed by Robert Ibbitson   1647

Dated "die Veneris, Octob. 22. 1647." Wing E 2413. Reprinted in Collier, *II, 110–111;* Hazlitt, *p. 64.*

¶ An Ordinance for the utter suppression and abolishing of all stage-plays and interludes, within the penalties to be inflicted on the actors and spectators therein expressed. (Interregnum 11 February 1647/8) (Acts and Ordinances of the Interregnum *I, 1070*).

146 AN ORDINANCE of the Lords and Commons assembled in Parliament, for, the utter suppression and abolishing of all stage-playes and interludes. With the penalties to be inflicted upon the actors and spectators, herein exprest. Die veneris 11 Februarii. 1647. Ordered by the Lords assembled in Parliament, that this ordinance for the suppression of stage-playes, shall be forthwith printed and published. John Brown cler. Parliamentorum.

pp. [2] 1–5 [6 (bl.)]   L
John Wright   1647 [1648]

Wing E 2070.

147 ——(Mr. Ashbee's Occasional Fac-Simile Reprints ... ix).

pp. [2] 1–5 [6 (bl.)]; ptd. covers   L
Ashbee   1869

Limited to 100 copies.

Reprinted in A Collection of Several Acts of Parliament, *published in the Years 1648, 1649, 1650, and 1651, ed. by Henry Scobell, 1651, pp. 207–211;* Collier *II 114–17;* Hazlitt, *pp. 65–70;* The Old Book Collector's Miscellany *ed. Charles Hindley, (1871–1873), III, [no.] 20.*

148 THE DAGONIZING of Bartholomew Fayre, caused through the Lord Majors command, for the battering downe the vanities of the gentiles, comprehended in flag and pole, appertayning to puppet-play. The 23. of August being the day before the apostolicke fayre.

pp. [2]   L
[London]   [1647]

Eight stanzas, beginning
> *On August's foure and twentieth eve,*
> *The cities soveraigne and the shrieve*
> *To Smithfield came if you'l beleeve*
> *to see th'ungodly flagges.*

On p. [1] is the ballad "I thanke you twice" dated 1647. Wing D 109.

149 ——[another edition]
bs.   MH
[London?]   [1647?]

In title no hyphen in "Puppet-play"; without "I thanke you twice".

150 ——[another edition]
bs.   L
[London?]   1647 [*for 1820?*]

With the following variants in title: apostrophe in "Major's"; "puppet = play"; no stop after "23"; comma after "August".
On The Dagonizing of Bartholomew Fayre *see George Speaight*, The History of the English Puppet Theatre, 1955, pp. 70–71, 281–2, *and H. E. Rollins, "A Contribution to the History of the English Commonwealth Drama", SP XVIII (1921), pp. 267–333, where it is reprinted.*

150.1 [By the Commons.] ★Ordered by.
bs.
E. Husband   21 sept 1648

Includes order of 26 July for execution of Ordinances for Sunday observance and suppression of plays. Bibliotheca Lindesiana 2789.

151 ACTORS OF BLACKFRIERS, THE ★To the supream authoritie, the Parliament of the Commonwealth of England. The humble petition of diverse poor and distressed men, heretofore the actors of Black-Friers and the Cock-Pit.
bs.   OW
                         [1650]

Reprinted in Theatre miscellany. Six pieces connected with the seventeenth-century stage, *ed. by C[yril] H[ackett] Wilkinson (Luttrell Society Reprints No. 14) Oxford: published for the Luttrell Society by Basil Blackwell (1953), pp. 117–122.*

¶ An Ordinance for ejecting scandalous, ignorant and insufficient ministers and schoolmasters. (Interregnum

28 August 1654) (Acts and Ordinances of the Interregnum II, 977).

Countenancing plays to be deemed "scandalous".

151.1 [By the Lord Chamberlain.] ★To all maiors, sheriffs, justices.
bs.   LRO
n.p.   1661

Licences of travelling companies, if not issued by Master of Revels, to be confiscated. Dated Whitehall 31 July 1661 Bibliotheca Lindesiana 3316. Wing T 1325.

151.2 [By the King] ★WHEREAS COMPLAINT hath been made unto Us.
bs.   OQ
Assigns of Bill & Barker   1670

Against persons entering Theatre Royal without paying. Dated Whitehall 23 July 1670. Bibliotheca Lindesiana 3536. Wing C 3627

152 WHEREAS COMPLAINT hath often been made unto Us, that divers persons do rudely press, and with evil language and blows force their way into Our theatres.
bs., headed "Charles R.", with Royal Arms   L
Printed by the Assigns of John Bill and Christopher Barker   1673

Against persons entering the Theatres Royal without paying and their intruding on stage. Dated "Whitehall the Second day of February in the Twenty Sixth Year of Our Reign", i.e. February 1672/3. Bibliotheca Lindesiana 3588. Wing C 3628.

¶ An Act for settling and adjusting the proportion of fine silver silk for the better making of silver and gold thread and to prevent the abuses of wire-drawers. (9 Will. III, c. 39) (Statutes of the Realm).

Silver and Gold Thread (1697), CTS *p. 78.*

Allows the use of inferior metals in materials manufactured solely for theatrical costumes.

¶ An Act for the more effectuall punishment of vagrants and sending them whither by law they ought to be sent. (11 Will. III, c. 18) (Statutes of the Realm).

Vagrancy (1698), CTS *p. 79.*

¶ An Act for continuing and amending the act made in the ninth year of His late Majesties reign intituled An act for the settling and adjusting the proportions of fine silver and silk and for the better making of gold and silver thread and to prevent the abuses of wire-drawers. (1 Anne, c. 11) (Statutes of the Realm).

Gold and Silver Thread (1702), CTS *p. 80.*

See note to 9 Will. III, c. 39 (1697) above.

¶ An Act for the continuance of the laws for the punishment of vagrants and for making such laws more effectual. (5 Anne, c. 32) (Statutes of the Realm).

Vagrants (1706), CTS *p. 83.*

153 TO THE QUEEN'S MOST EXCELLENT MAJESTY in Council. The humble petition of Your Majesty's most loyal and dutiful subjects, the patentees and claimants under two royal grants for building theatres within the cities of London and Westminster, and the suburbs thereof, and for acting of plays, &c.

pp. [2]; filing title: Complaint of patentees and claimants
LGk

[1710]

Petitioning the Council to reach a decision on Christopher Rich's appeal of 18 February 1709 (O.S.) against the Lord Chamberlain's order barring him from further management of Drury Lane.

¶ An Act for reducing the laws relating to rogues vagabonds sturdy beggars and vagrants into one act of Parliament and for the more effectual punishing such rogues vagabonds sturdy beggars and vagrants and sending them whither they ought to be sent. (13 Anne, c. 26) (Statutes of the Realm).

Vagrants (1713), CTS *p. 89.*

The Revocation of Steele's Patent

A dispute arose between the Lord Chamberlain (the young Duke of Newcastle) and Steele as Governor of Drury Lane as to which of them should have jurisdiction over the players. Steele's claim was based on a licence issued by the King in 1714 and on a patent of 1715 valid for his lifetime and three years beyond; but the patent was revoked on 23 January 1719/20. See also Periodicals nos. 4068–4073.

154 [STEELE, *Sir* RICHARD.] THE STATE of the case between the Lord-Chamberlain of His Majesty's houshold, and the governor of the Royal Company of comedians. With the opinions of Pemberton, Northey, and Parker, concerning the theatre.

pp. [1–3] 4–31 [32 (advt.)]   L
W. Chetwood; J. Roberts; J. Graves; and Charles Lillie
1720

155 ——the second edition.

pp. [1–3] 4–31 [32 (advt.)]   MH
J. Roberts; J. Graves; and Charles Lillie   1720

Reprinted in The Theatre, *ed. J. Nichols (1791), pp. 446–467; Tracts and pamphlets by Richard Steele, ed. Rae Blanchard (Baltimore, 1944), pp. 591–608. Said by Blanchard to have been published in March 1720.*

156 THE STATE of the case, between the Lord Chamberlain of his Majesty's houshold, and Sir Richard Steele, as represented by that knight. Restated, in vindication of King George, and the most noble the Duke of Newcastle. With a true copy of King Charles's patent to Sir William D'avenant, for erecting a playhouse, &c.

pp. [4] [1] 2–35 [36 (bl.)]   L
Printed and sold by John Applebee; and A. Dod 1720

Reprinted in The Theatre, *ed. J. Nichols (1791), pp. 468–509. This is a reply to Steele's* The State of the Case *(no. 154 above).*

---

157 *CASE of Charles Lee, Master of the Revels.
Folio
London   1733

From Lowe, who adds: 'I have not seen this. Lee was Master of the Revels at the time of the Secession of 1735'. Possibly occasioned by Cibber's attempt to strengthen the legal position of the seceding actors by claiming that the Master of the Revels had equal authority with the Lord Chamberlain to license performances (See LS, pt. 3, p. xcii).

Goodman's Fields, Sir John Barnard's Bill of 1735 and the 1737 Act

158 CITIZEN, A, *pseud.* A letter to the Right Honourable Sir Richard Brocas, Lord Mayor of London. By a citizen.

pp. [1–3] 4–32   L
Printed by Thomas Reynolds   1730

An energetic protest against the new theatre in Goodman's Fields, which was opened by Odell on 31st October 1729 — Lowe.

159 GIFFARD, HENRY. *Proposals by Henry Giffard for erecting a theatre in or near Goodmans Fields
bs.   LGu
1731

To replace Odell's theatre. LS, pt. 3, p. xxiii, n. 12.

160 A PROPOSAL for the better regulation of the stage. With Some remarks on the state of the theatre among the ancient Greeks and Romans.

pp. [8] [1] 2–55 [56]   L
J. Peele   1732

Largely reprinted in the Weekly Register, *5 Feb 1732. See Loftis,* Politics, *p. 78. A (burlesque?) plan for a national academy of drama.*

161 TO HIS MAJESTY'S WORSHIPFUL JUSTICES OF THE PEACE for the County of Middlesex. Rules humbly proposed and submitted to your consideration by the proprietors of the house commonly called

Goodman's-Fields Wells, if so happy as to obtain your Worships licence and protection for the same.

bs.   MH
[London]   [1732?]

A note in an unidentified modern hand attached to the copy seen says that after he had opened his Goodman's Fields (2nd October 1732) Giffard endeavoured to satisfy the magistrates by submitting these rules to them.

162 A BILL for restraining the number of houses for playing of interludes, and for the better regulating common players of interludes.

fold. doc., pp. 1–7 [8]; filing-title   L
                                                                      [1735]

Introduced by Sir John Barnard, read for first time 3 April 1735, thrown out 30 April.

163 THE CASE of Benjamin Johnson, Josias Miller, Theophilus Cibber, John Harper, Benjamin Griffin, William Mills, William Milward, and Elizabeth Butler, lessees of the Theatre-Royal in Drury-Lane.

fold. doc., pp. [2]; filing-title (as head-title)
[London]   [1735]

164 vacant

165 THE CASE of Henry Giffard, proprietor of the Theatre in Goodman's-Fields, in relation to a bill now depending in Parliament, for restraining the number of play-houses, &c.

fold. doc., pp. [2]; filing-title   L
[London]   [1735]

166 THE CASE of John Mills, Benjamin Johnson, James Quin. . . . and Elizabeth Buchanan, in behalf of themselves and the rest of the comedians of the Theatres-Royal of Drury-Lane and Covent Garden.

fold. doc., pp. [1] 2–3 [4]; filing-title: The case of His Majesty's Company of Comedians, &c.   L
[London]   [1735]

167 THE CASE of the comedians, &c. belonging to the Theatre in Goodman's-Fields, in relation to a bill for restraining the number of play-houses.

fold. doc., pp. [2]; filing-title (same as head-title)   L
[London]   [1735]

168 THE CASE of the several persons upon whose subscription the Theatre at Goodman's-Fields hath been built, in relation to a bill now brought into Parliament to restrain the number of playhouses, &c.

fold. doc., pp. [2]; filing-title: The case of the subscribers who have built the Theatre in Goodman's-Fields.   L
[London]   [1735]

169 PHÆNIX, JOHN, COMMEDIAN, *pseud.* ★A song on the Bill prefered in Parliament for suppressing of players and playhouses. By John Phænix, commedian.

                                                                      1735

Advertised in Gentleman's Magazine, May 1735.

170 A SEASONABLE EXAMINATION of the pleas and pretensions of the proprietors of, and subscribers to, play-houses, erected in defiance of the Royal Licence. With some brief observations on the printed case of the players belonging to Drury-Lane and Covent-Garden Theatres.

pp. [1–2] 3–32   L
T. Cooper   1735

171 ★SOME THOUGHTS on the present state of the theatres, and the consequences of an act to destroy the liberty of the stage.

pp. 3   MH
[London]   [1735?]

Against the restriction of the number of playhouses with the resulting tyranny of managers; compares the freedom of the stage to the freedom of the press.

172 TO THE HONOURABLE HOUSE OF COMMONS. The case of the company of comedians, belonging to the Theatre in Goodman's Fields.

fold. doc., pp. [2]; filing-title (as head-title, but omitting 'To the Honourable House of Commons') L
[London]   [1735]

✠ Tony Aston's petition . . . before the hon[ble] H——se of C——ns in behalf of himself and the actors in town and country. 1735. *See no. 2395.*

Against the bill

¶ An Act for the more effectual preventing the unlawful playing of interludes within the precincts of the two Universities, in that part of Great Britain called England, and the places adjacent, and for explaining and amending so much of an act passed in the last session of Parliament, intituled, An act for laying a duty upon the retailers of spiritous liquors, and for licensing the retailers thereof, as may affect the privilege of the said Universities, with respect to licensing taverns, and all other publick houses within the precincts of the same (10 Geo. II, c. 19).

Plays and Wine Licences (1736), CTS *p. 103.*

¶ An Act to explain and amend so much of an act made in the twelfth year of the reign of Queen Anne, intituled, An act for reducing the laws relating to rogues, vagabonds, sturdy beggars, and vagrants, into one act of Parliament; and for the more effectual punishing such rogues, vagabonds, sturdy beggars, and vagrants, and sending them whither they ought to be sent, as relates to common players of interludes. (10 Geo. II, c. 28).

Plays (1736), CTS *p. 103.*

The Licensing Act of 21 June, 1737.

173 THE E—— OF C——F——D'S SPEECH in the H——se of L——ds, against the Bill for licensing all dramatic performances. To which are prefixed, some loose thoughts, that were found in the closet of a gentleman lately deceased.

pp. [1–3] 4–16 L

Dublin 1749

Lord Chesterfield's speech.

¶ An Act to prevent the counterfeiting of gold and silver lace; and for settling and adjusting the proportions of fine silver and silk; and for the better making of gold and silver thread. (15 Geo. II, c. 20)

Gold and silver thread (1741), CTS *p. 106.*

See note to 9 Will. III, c. 39 (1697), p. 22 above.

¶ An Act to amend and make more effectual the laws relating to rogues, vagabonds, and other idle and disorderly persons, and to houses of correction. (17 Geo. II, c. 5).

Justices Commitment (1743), CTS *p. 107.*

✠ Fitz-Crambo, Patrick, *pseud.* Tyranny triumphant! . . . or . . . remarks on the famous cartel lately agreed on by the masters of the two theatres. 1743. *See no. 1340.*

Attacks the theatrical monopoly.

✠ The theatrical contest. 1743. *See no. 1335.*

On Garrick's attempt to obtain a licence to open a new playhouse.

¶ An Act for the better preventing thefts and robberies, and for regulating places of publick entertainment, and punishing persons keeping disorderly houses. (25 Geo. II, c. 36).

Disorderly Houses (1751), CTS *p. 116.*

¶ An Act for making perpetual an act passed in the twenty fifth year of the reign of His present Majesty, for the better preventing thefts and robberies, and for regulating places of publick entertainment, and punishing persons keeping disorderly houses . . . (28 Geo. II, c. 19).

Thefts, Robberies, etc. (1755), CTS *p. 119.*

The above two Acts provided for the licensing by Justices of the Peace of establishments such as Sadler's Wells for 'music, dancing and public entertainments', as distinguished from plays.

✠ Cibber, Theophilus. Dissertations on theatrical subjects . . . With an appendix . . . in which the laws, relative to the theatres are considered. 1756. *See no. 2615.*

174 [HILL, JOHN?] OBSERVATIONS on the importance and use of theatres; their present regulation, and possible improvements.

pp. [3–7] 8–40 MH

M. Cooper. And J. Jackson 1759

Reviewed in Gentleman's Magazine, May 1759. Against government control of the theatre. Probably inspired by the failure of his play The Rout.

¶ An Act for the better securing a fund, belonging to certain persons of the Theatre Royal in Drury-lane, applicable to charitable uses; and for other purposes therein mentioned. (16 Geo. III, c. 13).

Drury Lane Theatre (1776), CTS *p. 149. See also below nos. 1348–1355.*

¶ An Act for securing a fund belonging to certain persons of the Theatre Royal, Covent-Garden, applicable to charitable uses; and for other purposes. (16 Geo. III, c. 31).

Theatre Royal, Covent Garden (1776), CTS *p. 149. See also below nos. 1159–1162.*

✠ Theatrical monopoly; being an address to the public on the present alarming coalition of the managers of the winter theatres. 1779. *See no. 1358.*

✠ Candid remarks upon the stage-bill . . . Dublin. 1785. *See no. 1800.*

Legalization of the theatre out of London

See also p. 28 below at the year 1803 (Glasgow, Establishment of Theatre); at the year 1807 (Birmingham, Establishment of Theatre); and p. 31 below at the year 1826 (Ramsgate, Theatre)

¶ An Act for extending the royalty of the city of Edinburgh over certain adjoining lands; and for giving powers to the magistrates of Edinburgh for the benefit of the said city; and to enable His Majesty to grant letters patent for establishing a theatre in the city of Edinburgh, or suburbs thereof. (7 Geo. III, c. 27).

Edinburgh: improvements (1766), CTS *p. 134.*

175 AN ACT for extending the royalty of the city of Edinburgh, over certain adjoining lands; and for giving powers to the magistrates of Edinburgh, for the benefit of the said city; and to enable His Majesty to grant letters patent for establishing a theatre in the city of Edinburgh, or suburbs thereof.

pp. [1] 2–15 [16]; head-title   EP
[Edinburgh: printed by Alexander Kincaid, His Majesty's Printer]   [1768]

⚔ [Bonar, John, *solicitor of excise*] considerations on the proposed application to His Majesty and to Parliament, for the establishment of a licensed theatre in Edinburgh. [Edinburgh]. 1767. *See no. 1916.*

¶ An Act to enable His Majesty to licence a playhouse in the city of Bath. (8 Geo. III, c. 10).

Theatre, Bath (1768), CTS *p. 136.*

¶ An Act for licensing a playhouse within the city of Norwich. (8 Geo. III, c. 28).

Theatre, Norwich (1768), CTS *p. 136.*

¶ An Act for enabling His Majesty to licence a playhouse in the city of York; and in the town and county of the town of Kingston upon Hull. (9 Geo. III, c. 17).

Theatres, York and Hull (1769), CTS *p. 137.*

¶ An Act to enable His Majesty to licence a playhouse in the town of Liverpoole, in the County Palatine of Lancaster. (11 Geo. III, c. 16).

Liverpool Theatre (1771), CTS *p. 140.*

¶ An Act to enable His Majesty to licence a theatre in the city of Chester. (17 Geo. III, c. 14).

Chester Theatre (1776), CTS *p. 150.*

⚔ A full and authentic account of what passed in the House of Commons on the second reading of the Birmingham Playhouse Bill. [Birmingham. 1777]. *See no. 1569. See also nos. 1570–1572.*

¶ An Act to enable His Majesty to licence a theatre in the city of Bristol. (18 Geo. III, c. 8).

Bristol Theatre (1778), CTS *p. 152.*

¶ An Act to enable His Majesty to licence a playhouse within the town and port of Margate, in the Isle of Thanet, in the County of Kent, under certain restrictions therein limited. (26 Geo. III, c. 29).

Margate Theatre, (1786), CTS *p. 168.*

¶ An Act to enable His Majesty to licence a playhouse in the town and county of the town of Newcastle upon Tyne. (27 Geo. III, c. 50).

Newcastle Theatre (1787), CTS *p. 171.*

The Closing of the Royalty Theatre

John Palmer, the actor, conceived the scheme of building a theatre at the East End, independent of the authority of the Lord Chamberlain, thinking that a licence from the local magistrates would be sufficient. The theatre was opened 20th June 1787 with "As You Like It"; but the performances were immediately suspended. On 3rd July the theatre again opened, this time for pantomimes and irregular pieces. In April 1826 it was burnt down and on its site was erected the Brunswick Theatre—Lowe.

176 ★GRAY'S ELEGY, as delivered by Mr. Palmer at the Royalty.
                                                           [1787]
Lowe.

177 ★A LETTER to the author of the burletta called Hero and Leander, in refutation of what he has advanced in his dedication to Philips Glover, on the statutes for the regulation of theatres, the conduct of Mr. Palmer, of Mr. Justice Staples, and the other justices; and also of his observations on the consequences that must arise from the establishment of a theatre in Wellclose Square.

pp. (1) 48   MB
G. Kearsley   1787

Written to refute the statements made in the Letter to Phillips Glover *(no. 181 below).*

178 PINDAR, PETER, JUN., *pseud.* The plotting managers, a poetical satyrical interlude: to which is prefixed a letter to Lord S–dn–y, on his recommending the suppression of the Royalty-Theatre; by Peter Pindar, jun.

pp. [iii–v] vi–xii [13] 14–22   L
Printed and sold by J. James; Scatchard and Whitaker; W. Randall; and J. Debrett   [1787?]

179 POLYDORE, AUGUSTUS, *pseud.* The trial of Mr. John Palmer, comedian, and manager of the Royalty Theatre, in Wells Street, near Wellclose-Square, for opening the said Theatre in defiance of an Act made in the 10th year of George II. Tried in the Olympian shades, before the Right Honourable Lord Chief-Justice Shakespear, and the following august special jury: John Milton, Joseph Addison, Thomas Otway, Nicholas Rowe, Thomas Gray, John Dryden, Edward

Young, Sir John Vanbrugh, Richard Savage, John Sheffield, D. of B. William Congreve, and David Mallet. Taken in short-hand, by Augustus Polydore.

pp. [1–3] 4–20   DFo

J. Ridgeway   1787

180 A REVIEW of the present contest between the managers of the winter theatres, the Little Theatre in the Hay-Market, and the Royalty Theatre in Well-Close Square. To which are added, several authentic papers.

pp. [4] [1] 2–79 [80 (bl.)]   MH

Charles Stalker   1787

181 [JACKMAN, ISAAC.] ROYAL AND ROYAL-TY THEATRES. Letter to Phillips Glover, Esq. of Wispington, in Lincolnshire; in a dedication to the burletta of *Hero and Leander*, now performing, with the most distinguished applause, at the Royalty Theatre, in Goodman's Fields.

pp. [i–iv] v–vii [viii], [1] 2–84   L

J. Murray   1787

See also no. 177 above.

182 [COLMAN, GEORGE.] A VERY PLAIN STATE OF THE CASE, or the Royalty Theatre versus the Theatres Royal, respectfully inscribed to the Right Honourable the Earl of Salisbury, Lord Chamberlain of England.

pp. [i–v] vi–vii [viii], [1] 2–54 [55 (errata), 56 (bl.)]   MH

Printed for the author, and sold by J. Murray. . . .1787

Published 9th July. See Page, *pp. 291–294. Page claims that this pamphlet, "in Colman's best style", "brought to an end" John Palmer's venture.*

¶ A Bill, intituled, An act to enable justices of the peace to license theatrical representations occasionally, under the Restrictions therein contained. 1788. (Public Bills *1788, 18, 565*).

¶ An Act to enable justices of the peace to licence theatrical representations occasionally under the restrictions therein contained (28 Geo. III, c. 30).

Theatrical Representations (1788), CTS *p. 172.*

Enabled justices to license performances for a period of sixty days beyond a twenty-mile limit from London.

183 THE CASE of Messrs. Wroughton and Arnold, the lessees and proprietors of Sadler's Wells, and reasons humbly offered and submitted by them to the consideration of the public in general, and more especially, and with the utmost respect and duty, most humbly laid before the Right Honourable and Honourable the Members of both Houses of Parliament.

pp. [1] 2–3 [4]   L

[London]   [1788]

The case against the inclusion of the Royal Grove, Royal Circus and Royalty Theatre in the clause freeing Sadler's Wells from some of the provisions of the Bill of Restriction in Regard to Places of Public Amusement, then before Parliament.

184 CASE of the renters of the Royalty Theatre. Addressed to the intended purchaser of the said theatre.

fold. doc., pp. [1] 2–10 [11 (bl.) 12 (filing-title)]   MH

[London]   [1788]

185 OBSERVATIONS on the petition to the House of Commons for a bill to enable His Majesty to grant a patent for Sadler's Wells.

pp. [1] 2–3 [4]   L

[London]   [1788]

186 [PALMER, JOHN?] *CASE of the theatre in Well Street.

                                                  [1790]

Lowe.

187 ANSWERS to all the objections which have been raised against the petition to Parliament for the Royalty Theatre.

pp. [1–3] 4–8   LGk

[London]   [1794?]

188 CONSIDERATIONS upon how far the present winter and summer theatres can be affected by the application to Parliament for an act to enable his majesty to license, as a playhouse for the summer season, the Royalty Theatre in Well-Street, in the liberty of the Tower Hamlets.

pp. [1–3] 4–15 [16 (bl.)]   L

[London]   [1794]

Letters from the Royalty Theatre proprietor D. Steel, dated March 1794.

189 A PAPER having been distributed, called "Reasons why the Bill for licensing the Royalty Theatre should not pass into a law," the following analysis of and answer to it, is most respectfully addressed to the Honorable the House of Commons.

pp. [1] 2–3 [4 (bl)]; head-title   LGk

[London]   [1794?]

¶ An Act to amend and render more effectual an act, made in the fifteenth year of His late Majesty King George the Second, intituled, An act to prevent the counterfeiting of gold and silver lace, and for settling and adjusting the proportions of fine silver and silk, and for the better making of gold and silver thread (28 Geo. III, c. 7).

Gold and Silver Thread (1788), CTS *p. 172.*

See note to 9 Will. III, c. 39 (1697) p. 22 above

¶ An Act to explain and amend an act, made in the seventeenth year of the reign of His late Majesty King George the Second, intituled, An act to amend and make more effectual the laws relating to rogues, vagabonds, and other idle and disorderly persons, and to houses of correction (32 Geo. III, c. 45).

Rogues and Vagabonds (1792), CTS *p. 180.*

✖ To the most noble the Marquis of Salisbury, Lord High Chamberlain. The memorial of John Johnstone . . . and other performers of the Theatre-Royal, Covent-Garden. [1800]. *See no. 1185.*

Complaint by the actors over new restrictions.

190 CUTSPEAR, W. Dramatic rights: or, private theatricals, and pic-nic suppers, justified by fair argument. With a few whip-syllabubs for the editors of newspapers. By W. Cutspear.

pp. [i–iii] iv [v–vi], ²[i] ii [3] 4–60 [61 ("Explanation") 62 (bl.)]   MH
Printed by T. Burton . . . sold (for the author) by J. Badcock   1802

Copy at MB has a printed slip, inserted after the title-page, "Address to the Public on Pic-Nic", offering an etymology for the word "pic-nic". The "Explanation" on the last leaf concerns the price, and some copies have the price 2s. (printed on the verso of the title-page) altered in MS to 1s.; the "Prefatory Advertisement" (pp. [iii]–iv) concerns a method of preventing piracy by fixing a two-penny stamp to the title-page, and the notice "To the Public" (pp. ²[i]–ii) concerns the at least temporary failure of this scheme. Dedicated to "the nobility and gentry of both sexes, who have patronized the plan of a private theatre, in Tottenham-Court Road". The plan was Colonel Greville's Pic Nic Society, formed to present opera. See also below no. 4096.

191 ——†[another issue]

pp. [2] [v–vi], ²[i] ii [3] 4–60 [61 ("Explanation") 62 (bl.)]   MH
"Sold, by the Author[,] at 23 Maiden-Lane Cov[ent Garden]"   1802

The imprint is printed on a slip of paper (torn in the copy seen) cancelling the original imprint. The printed slip about the etymology of "picnic" follows the title page.

¶ An Act to enable His Majesty to grant letters patent for establishing a theatre under certain restrictions in the city of Glasgow. (43 Geo. III, c. 142 — Local and Personal).

Glasgow, Establishment of Theatre (1803), ILPA *p. 446.*

192 THE NUMBER of little theatres already opened within the City and Liberty of Westminster, by the Lord Chamberlain's license, having greatly injured the Theatres Royal . . .

pp. [1–2] 3–9 [10]   L
C. Lowndes, printer   [*ca.* 1807]

¶ An Act to enable His Majesty, His Heirs and Successors, to grant letters patent for establishing a theatre or playhouse, under certain restrictions, in the town of Birmingham, in the County of Warwick (47 Geo. III, c. 44 — Local and Personal).

Birmingham, Establishment of Theatre (1807), ILPA *p. 400.*

The "Third Theatre" 1810–1813
The project of a third theatre was much discussed. A bill was introduced into Parliament, but, owing to the exertions of Mr. Whitbread, did not pass — Lowe.

193 SUBSCRIPTION THEATRE. Proposals for raising by subscription a sum not exceeding £200,000, in shares of £100 each, for the purpose of building and maintaining a theatre in the Metropolis for dramatic entertainments.

pp. [1] 2–3 [4]; head-title
Printed by S. Gosnell   [1809 or 1810]

JFA.

194 ACCOUNT of the proceedings before His Majesty's Most Hon. Privy Council, upon a petition for a third theatre in the metropolis; with the arguments of Counsel, and copies of all the petitions and documents.

pp. [2] [1] 2–117 [118], ²[1] 2–48   L
W. H. Wyatt, Secretary to the Committee of Sub-scribers   1810

195 JACKSON, RANDLE. ★Third theatre. The argument of Randle Jackson, Esq., before the Lords of the Privy Council, on behalf of the trustees, and other parties interested in the late Theatre Royal, Drury Lane. With copies of the petition for a charter to erect a third theatre in the metropolis.

pp. 48   MB
Deans   1810

196 ROYAL CIRCUS. Mr. Elliston's statement, on his application to Parliament. 1st March, 1810.

fold. doc., ff. [2]; filing-title.   LGk
Hartnell Albion Press   1810

197 CASE of Thomas Harris, Esq.—John Philip Kemble, Esq. — George White, Esq.—Richard Jackson, Esq., a trustee for Mrs. Ann Martindale; and Henry Harris, Esq.; the proprietors of the New Theatre-Royal Covent Garden; against the "Bill for erecting and maintaining a new theatre, for dramatic entertainments, within the cities of London and Westminster, or liberties thereof." The second reading of this bill is fixed for Monday the 18th of March 1811.

fold. doc., pp. [1] 2–3 [4]; filing-title, headed "(In Parliament.)" MH

Farrer, Steadman, & Uhthoff [1811]

✠ Heads of plan for a private theatre. [1811]. *See no. 1083.*

198 THIRD THEATRE. We trust that there can be but one opinion amongst the Honourable Members of this House as to the importance of a Bill, that has for its object the amelioration of the National Drama . . .

bs. MH

Printed by S. Gosnell [1811]

Circulated at first or second (March 1811) reading of the Third Theatre Bill. In support of the Bill.

198.1 A BILL for erecting and maintaining a new theatre for dramatic entertainments within the cities of London and Westminster, or liberties thereof.

fold. doc., pp. [1] 2–18; filing-title L

The "Third Theatre" Bill.

1812

199 *PROPRIETORS of the Theatres Royal. To the Honourable the Lords Spiritual and Temporal of the United Kingdom of Great Britain and Ireland, in Parliament assembled. The humble petition of the proprietors of the Theatres Royal, Drury Lane and Covent Garden; sheweth. . . .

pp. 3

1812

STR.

✠ Wyatt, George. A compendious description of a design for a theatre . . . for carrying into effect the project of erecting a third theatre. 1812. *See no. 795.*

200 LAWRENCE, JAMES. Dramatic emancipation, or strictures on the state of the theatres, and the consequent degeneration of the drama; on the partiality and injustice of the London managers; on many theatrical regulations; and on the regulations on the Continent for the security of literary and dramatic property. Particularly deserving the attention of the subscribers for a third theatre. By James Lawrence, Knight of Malta. Original. 1813.

In The pamphleteer: respectfully dedicated to both Houses of Parliament. No. IV. December, 1813 (1813), pp. 369–395 L

Against the monopoly of the Patent Houses — Lowe.

¶ An Act for rebuilding the late Theatre-Royal Drury-Lane upon the conditions and under the regulations therein mentioned (50 Geo. III, c. 214 — Local and Personal).

London, Drury Lane Theatre, Rebuilding (1810), ILPA *p. 501.*

¶ An Act for altering and enlarging the powers of an act of His present Majesty, for rebuilding the late Theatre Royal Drury Lane (52 Geo. III, c. 19 — Local and Personal).

London, Drury Lane Theatre, Rebuilding (1812), ILPA *p. 501.*

¶ An Act for altering and enlarging the powers of two acts of the fiftieth and fifty-second years of the reign of His late Majesty, for rebuilding the Theatre Royal Drury Lane (1 Geo. IV, c. 60 — Local and Personal).

London, Drury Lane Theatre, Rebuilding (1820), ILPA *p. 501.*

Major v. Minor Theatres 1816–1835

¶ An Act to enable Temple West Esquire, sole proprietor of The Royal Circus or Surrey Theatre, situate in the Parish of Saint George, in the County of Surrey, to continue the same open, for public amusement, for a limited time (56 Geo. III, c. 13 — Local and Personal).

London, Surrey Theatre or Royal Circus (1816), ILPA *p. 502.*

✠ Dramaticus, *pseud.* An impartial view of the stage . . . shewing the necessity of a reform in the system. 1816. *See no. 905.*

201 COPY of a memorial presented to the Lord Chamberlain, by the committee of management of the Theatre-Royal Drury-Lane, and by the proprietors of the Theatre-Royal Covent-Garden, against the Olympic and Sans Pareil theatres; with copies of two letters, in reply to the contents of such memorial, addressed to the Lord Chamberlain, by Robert William Elliston, comedian.

pp. [4] [i] ii–viii, [1] 2–140 [*2*] 141 [*1*] 142 [143] [=146] L

John Miller 1818

Elliston opened the Olympic Pavilion, formerly managed by Philip Astley, on 19th April 1813, under the name of Little Drury Lane Theatre, but the Chamberlain made him close it. In the next year he reopened it. His 1818 season was specially successful — Lowe.

202 [REYNOLDS, FREDERICK?] IMPARTIAL OBSERVATIONS on the proceedings instituted by the proprietors of the Theatres Royal, Drury Lane and Covent Garden, against the minor establishments.

pp. [*2*] [1–3] 4–33 [34 (bl.)] L

Thomas Boys 1820

203 THE WINTER THEATRES.

bs.   MH

Lowndes, printer   [1820]

> Begins, "*Since the patentees of the winter theatres . . .*"
> *Against the lengthened seasons at Drury Lane.*
> *Reprinted in George Raymond,* Memoirs of Robert William Elliston (*Concluding Series, 1845*), *pp.269–270.*

204 A LETTER to a Member of Parliament, on the impropriety of classing players with rogues and vagabonds in the Vagrant Act. By the author of "The Vagrant Act in relation to the liberty of the subject".

pp. [1–3] 4–22 [23–24 (bl.)]   E

John Murray   1824

> *Dated at the end April 29, 1824.*

205 CHAPMAN, J[ohn] K[emble]. To the public. Charles Kemble's mercies or the "999" increasing.

bs.   MH

[London]   [1826?]

> *Objecting to Charles Kemble's attempts to suppress Chapman's City Theatre.*

206 DIGEST of the statutes regarding theatres and places of public entertainment.

pp. [1] 2–3 [4]; head-title   MH

[Edinburgh: printed by John Stark]   [ca. 1827?]

207 [JACKSON, RANDLE.] LETTER to the Right Hon. Robert Peel, respecting the proposed introduction of a bill, to repeal so much of the act of 10th Geo. II. cap. 28, as requires notice to be sent to the Lord Chamberlain, previously to the representation of any new play or entertainment of the stage, or any addition to an old play; and showing that the consequence of such an act would be, to confirm the monopoly claimed by the proprietors of Drury Lane and Covent Garden, and to enable them to annihilate the minor theatres.

pp. [1–3] 4–12   L

Printed for the author   1829

> *Signed: A friend to "Fair play and a free stage".*

208 ——[another edition]

pp. [1–3] 4–11 [12]   LUC

J. Ridgway   1829

209 REPORT of the Lord Chancellor and the other judges to his Majesty, on the investigation of the subject of the different theatrical petitions, was as follows:

pp. 1–2   L

[London]   1831

In favour of extending the season of the English Opera House to include May and October, months formerly reserved for the Major Theatres.

210 MACARTHY, EUGENE. A letter to the King, on the question now at issue between the "major", and "minor" theatres. By Eugene Macarthy.

pp. [1–3] 4–16   L

Effingham Wilson   1832

> *Dated 23 February 1832.*

211 ——*second edition

pp. 16   MB

             1832

212 ONE OF THE PUBLIC, *pseud.* of Frederick Guest Tomlins. Major and minor theatres. A concise view of the question, as regards the public, the patentees, and the profession. With remarks on the decline of the drama, and the means of its restoration. To which is added the petition now lying for signature. By one of the public.

pp. [1–3] 4–24   L

W. Strange; F. Tomlins; Purkess; Berger   1832

> *Attributed by* Lowe *to Tomlins.*

¶ Report from the Select Committee on Dramatic Literature; with the minutes of evidence 1832.

Dramatic Literature *in* (Reports, Committees *1831–32 (679), VII, 1*).

> *Reprinted in* British parliamentary papers. Stage and theatre 1 (*Shannon: Irish U.P., 1968*).

¶ 1. A Return, specifying the number and name of each theatre which has been licensed annually by the Lord Chamberlain from the year 1820 to the present time; — Also, 2. A return of the number and title of each dramatic piece or song licensed by the examiner of plays during the years 1829, 1830, and 1831, to the present time. 1832. (Theatres and Dramatic Pieces, *in* Accounts and Papers *1831–32 (543), XXXV, 409.*)

213 THACKERAY, THOMAS JAMES. On theatrical emancipation, and the rights of dramatic authors. By Thomas James Thackeray, Esq. Member of the University of Cambridge . . .

pp. [1–3] 4–47 [48 (advt.)]   GU

C. Chapple   1832

> *Against the restrictions on the erection of new theatres, and the lack of protection of authors' mss.*

¶ A Bill intituled An act for licensing theatres, and for the regulation of dramatic performances. 1833. (Dramatic Performances, House of Lords Sessional Papers *1833 (143)*.)

¶ A Bill for licensing theatres, and for the regulation of dramatic performances in the Cities of London and Westminster, and within a certain distance thereof. 1833. (Public Bills 1833 (74), II, 121.)

¶ A Bill (as amended by the Committee) for licensing theatres, and for the regulation of dramatic performances in the Cities of London and Westminster, and within a certain distance thereof. 1833. (Public Bills 1833 (513), II. 141.)

214 CAUSE of the drama.

bs.   MB

[London]   [1833]

> Begins: "*At a most numerous and highly respectable Meeting of the Friends of the National Drama, holden, pursuant to public advertisement, at the Crown and Anchor, Strand, on Wednesday, the 13th August, 1833*".

215 COPY of a petition which was presented by the proprietors of the Theatres Royal Drury Lane and Covent Garden, to the Hon. the Lords Spiritual and Temporal of the United Kingdom of Great Britain and Ireland, in Parliament assembled.

fold. doc., pp. [1] 2–3 [4]; filing-title   L

[London]: [Alfred Robins, printer]   [1833?]

216 *THE NATIONAL DRAMA, or the histrionic war of majors and minors.

                                                                        1833

With folding caricature frontispiece — Lowe.

¶ A Bill intituled An act for licensing theatres, and for the regulation of dramatic performances, in the Cities of London and Westminster and within twenty miles thereof. 1834. (Dramatic Performances, *in* House of Lords, Sessional Papers 1834 (97.))

217 PLACE, FRANCIS. A brief examination of the dramatic patents. By Francis Place. Extracted from "The monthly magazine" for March, 1834.

pp. [1–2] 3–12   L

Printed by Baylis and Leighton   1834

An attack upon the monopoly of the patent theatres — Lowe.

¶ A Bill intituled An act to repeal so much of two acts of the twenty-fifth and twenty-eighth years of King George the Second as restrains the amusements of public music, dancing, or other public entertainment of the like kind in the Cities of London and Westminster or within Twenty Miles thereof. 1835. (Public Amusements, House of Lords Bills 1835 (152).)

¶ A Bill to repeal so much of an act of the twenty-fifth year of King George the Second, as restrains the amusements of music and dancing. 1835. (Public Bills 1835 (349), III, 503.)

---

218 THE MODERN STAGE. A letter to the Hon. George Lamb, M.P. on the decay and degradation of English dramatic literature: with a proposal for the encouragement of composition for the stage, by the legislative protection of new pieces; so that they might be produced in the provincial theatres, or otherwise published, with an adequate reward, independent of the caprice of arbitrary judges.

pp. [1–5] 6–28   L

London: Edwards and Knibb; Windsor: Knight and Son   1819

219 PLUMPTRE, *Rev.* JAMES. *A letter to the Most Noble the Marquis of Hertford, Lord Chamberlain of His Majesty's Household, and Master of the Revels, on the subject of a dramatic institution. By James Plumptre, B.D.

pp. 13   MB

Cambridge: Hodson   1820

¶ Papers relating to a riot at Dublin Theatre; on the 14th December 1822. 1823. (Ireland, *in* Reports, Committees 1823 (165), VI, 533.)

¶ Copies of the addresses of the Corporation of the City of Dublin, and of the freemen, freeholders, and inhabitants of the City of Dublin, to His Excellency the Lord Lieutenant of Ireland; respecting the riot at the Theatre Royal in Dublin, on the 14th December last; — and His Excellency's answers thereto. 1823. (Riot at Dublin Theatre, *in* Reports, Committees 1823 (381), VI, 817.)

¶ Minutes of evidence, taken before the Committee of the whole House appointed to inquire into the conduct of the Sheriff of the City of Dublin. 1823. (Reports, Committees 1823 (308), VI, 545.)

The Monopoly in Edinburgh 1825

For the disputes over the monopoly of the theatre in Edinburgh see nos. 1970–1971

¶ An Act to enable His Majesty to license a playhouse within the town and port of Ramsgate in the Isle of Thanet in the County of Kent (7 Geo. IV, c. 32 — Local and Personal).

Ramsgate, Theatre (1826), ILPA *p. 534.*

¶ A Bill intituled An act to amend the laws relating to dramatic literary property. 1833 (Dramatic Authors, House of Lords Sessional Papers 1833 (49.)

¶ An Act to amend the laws relating to dramatic literary property. (3 & 4 Will. IV, c. 15).

Dramatic Copyright (1833), CTS *p. 293.*

⌘ Rodwell, George Herbert Buonoparte. A letter to the musicians of Great Britain; containing a prospectus of proposed plans . . . for the erection and management of a grand opera in London. 1833. *See no. 2079.*

⌘ Gray, George. A lecture on the mischievous effects of theatrical monopolies, twice delivered before the citizens of Glasgow. Glasgow: Edinburgh: London. 1835. *See no. 2011.*

220 OTWAY. An attempt to deduce from facts, the causes of the present disgraceful state of our national theatres. By Mr. Otway, a gentleman whose case forms some illustration of the danger arising to the professors of the drama from a monopoly, and the difficulty of even received merit obtaining the least support without either a rivalry on the part of Covent Garden and Drury-Lane, or a superintendance of a more liberal policy, unconnected with other theatres, and having for its object the support of our native talent alone.

pp. [1–3] 4–15 [16] L
C. Harris 1835

¶ A Bill, intituled, An act for the regulation of theatres. 1837. (Theatres Regulation, Public Bills *1837 (514), IV, 473.*)

¶ An Act for further improving the police in and near the metropolis (2 & 3 Vict., c. 47).

Metropolitan Police (1839), CTS *p. 319.*

¶ An Act for regulating the police in the City of London (2 & 3 Vict., c. 94 — Local and Personal).

London, Police (1839), ILPA *p. 499.*

⌘ Tomlins, F. G. A brief view of the English drama . . . with suggestions for elevating the present condition of the art, and its professors. 1840. *See no. 924*

Treats of the monopoly.

The 1843 Act

¶ Copies of any communications which have been addressed to the Secretary of State for the Home Department, in the course of the present year, complaining of the state of the laws in reference to dramatic entertainments. 1842. (Dramatic Entertainments, *in* Accounts and Papers *1842 (429), XXXIII, 565.*)

¶ A Bill to repeal part of an act of the tenth year of King George the Second, to explain and amend so much of an act made in the twelfth year of the Reign of Queen Anne, intituled, An act for reducing the Laws relating to rogues, vagabonds, sturdy beggars and vagrants, into one act of Parliament, and for the more effectual punishing such rogues, vagabonds, sturdy beggars and vagrants, and sending them whither they ought to be sent, as relates to common players of interludes, and to make other provisions in lieu thereof. 1843. (Players of Interludes, Public Bills *1843 (131), III, 497.*)

¶ A Bill for regulating theatres. 1843. (Theatres Regulation, Public Bills *1843 (487), IV, 479.*)

¶ Amendments made by the Lords to the Bill for regulating theatres 1843. (Theatres Regulation Bill, Public Bills *1843 (582), IV, 487.*)

¶ A Bill intituled An act for regulating theatres. 1843.

Clause to be proposed on third reading by Earl of Glengall. 1843. (Theatres Regulation, *in* House of Lords Sessional Papers *1843*), (*228*), (*228a*).

¶ An Act for regulating theatres (6 & 7 Vict., c. 68).

Theatres (1843), CTS *p. 336.*

221 [A BRIEF HISTORY of the theatrical question, with reference to Mr. Duncombe's late motion.]

pp. [1] 2–16 LGk
[William Stevens, printer] [1843]

In the copy seen, the title page is missing; the running-title is here transcribed.

¶ Copies of any memorial or petition from the inhabitants of Liverpool to the Queen, praying Her Majesty to grant a second licence for theatrical representations in that Town; with correspondence relating thereto, &c. &c. 1843. (Liverpool Theatre 1843, *in* Accounts and Papers *1843 (56), XLIV, 161.*)

⌘ Old Playgoer, An, *pseud. of* S. Parlby? Desultory thoughts on the national drama. 1850. *See no. 930.*

Discusses Government regulation of the theatre.

¶ Report from the Select Committee on Public Houses, &c; together with the proceedings of the Committee, minutes of evidence, appendix, and index. 1853. (Public Houses, *in* Reports, Committees *1852–53 (855) XXXVII, 1.*)

⌘ Mathews, Charles. Lettre de M. Charles Mathews aux auteurs dramatiques de la France. 1852. *See nos. 3312–3313.*

On the International Copyright controversy.

¶ Report from the Select Committee on Public Houses; together with the proceedings of the committee, minutes of evidence, appendix and index. 1854. (Public Houses, *in* Papers of the House of Commons *1854 (231), 14.*)

¶ An Act to confer powers on the commissioners of Her Majesty's Works and Public Buildings to acquire the Theatre Royal, Edinburgh, and adjacent property, for the erection of a new General Post Office; and for other purposes (21 & 22 Vict., c. 40).

New General Post Office, Edinburgh (1858), CTS *p. 411. See also no. 1994 below*

¶ Return of the number of the Metropolitan Police Force employed on special duty and not in the ordinary duties of the police; the number to whom the issue of the usual police uniform has been discontinued, and who are allowed a sum of money in lieu thereof; and the number employed at the several docks, dockyards, public buildings, museums, institutions, and theatres; &c. 1858. (Metropolitan Police, *in* Accounts and Papers *1857-58 (384), XLVII, 653.*)

¶ A Bill to amend the acts concerning theatres and public houses. 1860. (Theatres and Public Houses, Public Bills *1860 (266), VI, 521.*)

¶ An Act for granting to Her Majesty certain duties on wine licences and refreshment houses, and for regulating the licensing of refreshment houses and the granting of wine licences (23 Vict., c. 27).

Refreshment Houses (1860), CTS *p. 420.*

222 READE, CHARLES. The eighth commandment. Charles Reade.

pp. [4] [1] 2–88, ²[1–2] 3–6 95–161 [162–172] 181–380 = [370]   LVA

Trübner & Co.   1860

²[1–2] 3–6: *title-page and preface of* Poverty and pride. A drama in five acts. *1856.*

223 ——*[abridged edition] Extracts.

ff 19.   MB

[London?]   [1860]

——[American edition] Boston: Ticknor and Fields. 1860.

¶ Copies of a Letter relating to precautions against fire addressed by the Lord Chamberlain to the managers of theatres, dated 7th February 1864; and, of a memorandum by the Lord Chamberlain, dated 5th February 1864, and transmitted by him to managers of theatres; together with a copy of regulations for better protection against accidents by fire. 1864 (Theatres (Precautions against Fire) *in* Accounts and Papers *1864 (64), L, 489.*)

224 A HANDY-BOOK on the law of the drama and music: being an exposition of the law of dramatic copyright, copyright in musical compositions, dramatic copyright in music, and international copyright in the drama and music; the law for regulating theatres; the law affecting theatres; and the law relating to music, dancing, and professional engagements; with the statutes, forms, &c., referring thereto.

pp. [i–vii] viii, [1] 2–79 [80]   E

T. H. Lacy   1864

225 BELL, ROBERT. Dramatic literature and the laws affecting its production and representation. By Robert Bell, F.S.A. (Reprinted, by permission, from the "Shilling Magazine.")

pp. [1–3] 4–15 [16 (bl.)]; title headed: "In support of Theatres, &c, Bill. In Parliament, 1865."   LGk

Printed by Woodfall and Kinder   1865

¶ A Bill to amend the law relating to theatres and other places of public amusement. 1865. (Theatres, &c., Public Bills *1865 (64), IV, 521.*)

226 REASONS for the repeal or amendment of the laws affecting theatres and other places of public amusement.

pp. [1–3] 4–11 [12 (colophon)]; title headed "In Parliament, Session 1865"   LGk

Printed by Woodfall and Kinder   1865

¶ Report from the Select Committee on Theatrical Licenses and Regulations; together with the proceedings of the committee, minutes of evidence, and appendix. 1866. (Theatrical Licenses and Regulations, *in* Reports, Committees *1866 (373), XVI, 1.*)

Copy at MH.

227 EVANS'S, Covent Garden. Minutes of evidence taken before the select committee on theatrical licenses and regulations. Mr John Green called in and examined.

pp. [8]   L
[William Barth, printer]   [1866]

228 vacant.

229 CORYTON, JOHN. Stageright A compendium of the law relating to dramatic authors, musical composers, and lecturers as regards the public representation of their works. With an appendix containing notes on various matters connected with the stage, statutes (including the Lord Chamberlain's Act). etc. By John Coryton, Esq. of Lincoln's Inn, barrister-at-law late recorder of Moulmein, British Burmah.

pp. [i–iii] iv–viii, [1] 2–100, ²i–lii (appendix)   E

D. Nutt   1873

¶ A Bill intituled An act to amend the law relating to musical and other entertainments in the metropolis and neighbourhood. 1875. (Musical Entertainments, House of Lords Sessional Papers *1875 (49)*.)

¶ A Bill intituled An act for amending the law relating to houses of public dancing, music, or other public entertainment of the like kind, in the Cities of London and Westminster. 1875. (Public Entertainments (H.L.) Public Bills *1875 (178)*, *V, 59*.)

¶ A Bill intituled An act for amending the law relating to houses of public dancing, music or other public entertainment of the like kind, in the Cities of London and Westminster. 1875.
Amendments to be moved in Committee by the Lord Steward 1875. (Public Entertainments (Hour of Opening) (H.L.), House of Lords Sessional Papers *1875. (51) (51a)*.)

¶ A Bill (as amended in Committee) intituled An act for amending the law relating to houses of public dancing, music, or other public entertainment of the like kind, in the Cities of London and Westminster. 1875.
Amendment to be proposed on the Third Reading by the Lord Steward 1875. (Public Entertainments (Hour of Opening) (H.L.) House of Lords Sessional Papers *1875 (77) (77a)*.)

¶ An Act for amending the law relating to houses of public dancing, music, or other public entertainment of the like kind, in the Cities of London and Westminster. (38 & 39 Vict., c. 21).
Public Entertainments (1875), CTS *p. 508.*

230 HOLLINGSHEAD, JOHN. Theatrical licenses. Reprinted from "The Daily Telegraph" and "Times" by John Hollingshead.

pp. [1–3] 4–24   L
Chatto and Windus   1875

✖ [Chevalier, W. A.] Outlines of a scheme for reforming the stage, and elevating the actor's calling to the status of a liberal and legitimate profession. [1877?] *See no. 951.*

¶ Copies of any papers relating to the burning down of the Brooklyn Theatre. 1877. (Brooklyn Theatre, *in* Accounts and Papers *1877 (93)*, *LXVIII, 379*.)

¶ An Act to amend the Metropolis Management Act, 1855, the Metropolitan Building Act, 1855, and the Acts amending the same respectively. (41 & 42 Vict., c. 32).
Metropolis Management and Building Acts Amendment (1878), CTS *p. 529.*

¶ An Act to regulate the employment of children in places of public amusement in certain cases. (42 & 43 Vict., c. 34).
Children's Dangerous Performances (1879), CTS *p. 535.*

¶ Return (pursuant to an Order of the House of Lords, dated 5th April 1881,) showing the various modes of exit for theatres licensed by the Lord Chamberlain. 1881. (Theatres, *in* House of Lords Sessional Papers *1881 (80)*.)

¶ An Act to amend the law of copyright relating to musical compositions. (45 & 46 Vict., c. 40).
Copyright (Musical Compositions) (1882), CTS *p. 545.*

¶ A Bill for the better regulation of theatres and other places of public entertainment. 1883. (Theatres Regulation, Public Bills *1883 (81)*, *X, 1*.)

¶ A Bill intituled An act to amend the law for regulating theatres. 1883. (Stage Plays in aid of Charities (HL.), House of Lords Bills *1883 (32)*.)

✖ The regulation of music halls. A summary of the attempts made by music hall proprietors to obtain an improvement in the law. [1883]. *See no. 2121.*

¶ Report of Hugh Shield, Esquire, Q.C., M.P. upon the disaster at Sunderland on the 16th of June 1883. 1883. (Accounts and Papers *1883 (C–3721)*, *LIV, 555*.)

¶ A Bill for the better regulation of theatres and music halls within the Metropolitan area. 1884. (Theatres, &c. Regulation (Metropolis), Public Bills *1884 (61)*, *VII, 257*.)

¶ A Bill to amend the law relating to the licensing and performance of stage plays in the City of Oxford and Town of Cambridge (Not Printed). 1884. (Stage Plays (Oxford and Cambridge) Public Bills *1884 (84)*, *VII, 107*.)

Note: only title is printed in volume.

231 AMATEURS' GUIDE to the law of musical & dramatic performances.

pp. [1–3] 4–12   E
Manchester: Abel Heywood & Son; London: F. Pitman
                              [1885]

232 GEARY, [*Sir*] W[ILLIAM] N[EVILL] M[ONTGOMERIE]. The law of theatres and music-halls including contracts and precedents of contracts. By W. N. M. Geary, of Christ Church, Oxford, and of the Inner Temple, Barrister-at-law, J.P. for the county of Kent.

With Historical introduction by James Williams, B.C.L., M.A., of Lincoln College, Oxford, and of Lincoln's Inn, Barrister-at-Law.

pp. [2] [i–v] vi–xii, [1] 2–230   L
Stevens and Sons   1885

With an appendix of statutes and London and provincial acts and regulations.

¶ A Bill for the better regulation of theatres and music halls in the Metropolis. 1886. (Theatres, &c. (Metropolis), Public Bills *1886* (*69 sess. 1*), *VI, 35*.)

¶ A Bill for the better regulation of theatres and music halls in the Metropolitan area. 1887. (Theatres (Metropolis) Public Bills *1887* (*15*), *VI, 327*.)

¶ A Bill for the better regulation of theatres and music halls in the Metropolis. 1888. (Theatres (Metropolis), Public Bills *1888* (*37*), *VII, 415*.)

¶ A Bill to confer further powers upon the Metropolitan Board of Works for inspecting theatres and music halls and granting certificates. 1886. (Metropolitan Board of Works (Theatres, &c.) Public Bills *1886* (*44 sess. 1*), *IV, 119*.)

¶ A Bill to confer further powers upon the Metropolitan Board of Works for inspecting theatres and music halls and granting certificates. 1887. (Metropolitan Board of Works (Theatres, &c), Public Bills *1887* (*117*), *IV, 227*.)

¶ An Act to amend the laws relating to local government in England and Wales, and for other purposes connected therewith. (51 & 52 Vict., c. 41).

Local Government (1888), CTS *p. 577*.

¶ An Act to amend the law relating to the recovery of penalties for the unauthorised performance of copyright musical compositions. (51 & 52 Vict., c. 17).

Copyright (Musical Compositions) (1888), CTS *p. 575*.

¶ Report by Captain Eyre M. Shaw, C.B., to the Right Hon. the Secretary of State for the Home Department concerning the fire which occurred at the Theatre Royal, Exeter, on the 5th of September 1887. 1888. (Accounts and Papers *1888* (*C–5306*), *LXXX, 451*.) *See also below no. 1595*

¶ An Act to amend the Public Health Acts. (53 & 54 Vict., c. 59).

Public Health Acts Amendment (1890), CTS *p. 593*.

¶ A Bill to make better provision for the regulation of theatres in London (not printed). 1890. (Theatres (London), Public Bills *1890* (*133*), *IX, 93*.)

¶ A Bill to amend and extend the law relating to theatres, music halls, and places of public entertainment or resort in the Administrative County of London (Not Printed). 1890. (Theatres (London), No. 2, Public Bills *1890* (*159*), *IX, 95*.)

¶ A Bill to provide for the control and regulation of theatres, music halls, and places of public entertainment in the Administrative County of London; and for other purposes. 1891.
(Theatres, &c. (London), Public Bills *1890–91* (*106*), *X 329*.)

233 CUTLER, EDWARD, THOMAS EUSTACE SMITH and FREDERIC E. WEATHERLY. The law of musical and dramatic copyright. By Edward Cutler, one of her majesty's counsel, Thomas Eustace Smith and Frederic E. Weatherly, Esquires, Barristers-at-law.

pp. [i–iii] iv, [1–2] 3–163 [164]   E
Cassell & Company, Limited   1890

234 ——Revised edition.
pp [i–iii] iv, [1] 2–172   L
Cassell and Co. Ltd.   1892

235 ——*[another edition]
pp. ix, 155
The Era   1898
    STR.

236 ——*Second edition
pp. xii, 184
The Era   1901
    STR.

237 ——*Third edition
pp. xii, 243
The Era   1910
    STR.

238 LONDON COUNTY COUNCIL theatres bill. Preliminary observations . . . Fladgates, Craig's Court, S.W.
fold. doc., pp. [1] 2–3 [4]; filing-title   LGk
[London]   [1891?]

239 HAMLYN, CLARENCE. A manual of theatrical law containing chapters on theatrical licensing, music and dancing generally, and dramatic copyright, with an appendix of all the Lord Chamberlain's forms and those of the County Council for licensing. By Clarence Hamlyn, of the Middle Temple and the Northern Circuit, Barrister-at-Law.
pp. [i–v] vi–xii, [1] 2–216   L
Waterlow & Sons Limited   1891

¶ An Act for regulating the police and sanitary administration of towns and populous places, and for facilitating the union of police and municipal administration in burghs in Scotland. (55 & 56 Vict., c. 55).

Burgh Police (Scotland) (1892), CTS *p. 606.*

¶ Report from the Select Committee on Theatres and Places of Entertainment; together with the proceedings of the Committee, minutes of evidence, appendix and index. 1892. (Theatres and Places of Entertainment, *in* Reports, Committees 1892 *(240), XVIII, 1.*)

¶ An Act to regulate and restrict the wearing of naval and military uniforms. (57 & 58 Vict. c. 45).

Uniforms (1894), CTS *p. 620.*

The wearing of uniform in plays is exempted.

✂ Cooke, Peter Joseph. A handbook of the drama. Its philosophy and teaching. With a chapter on the law of copyright. [1895]. *See no. 977.*

¶ An Act to extend the age under which the employment of young persons in dangerous performances is prohibited. (60 & 61 Vict., c. 52).

Dangerous Performances (1897), CTS *p. 641.*

240 STRONG, A[LBERT] A[MBROSE]. Dramatic and musical law being a digest of the law relating to theatres and music halls and containing chapters on theatrical contracts, theatrical, music and dancing and excise licences dramatic and musical copyright, &c. with an appendix containing the acts of Parliament relating thereto and the regulations of the London County Council and the Lord Chamberlain by A. A. Strong, LL.B. (London) solicitor.

pp. [i–vii] viii–ix [x–xii], [1] 2–155 [156]; inset (addendum leaf, opp. p. 30)   L
'The Era' Publishing Office   1898

Dedicated to Edward Ledger.

241 ———by Albert Strong, LL.B. (London) solicitor second edition.

pp. [i–vii] viii–ix [x–xii], [1] 2–184   L
'The Era' Publishing Office   1901

Strong also published The Law of Copyright for Actor and Composer *(1901).*

242 ———★Third edition

pp. xii, 184
The Era   1910

STR.

243 NORTHBROOKE, JOHN. †*Spiritus est vicarius Christi in [terra].* A treatise wherein dicing, daūcing, vaine playes or enterluds with other idle pastimes &c. commonly vsed on the Sabboth day, are reproved by the authoritie of the word of God and auntient writers. Made dialoguewise by Iohn Northbrooke minister and preacher of the word of God.

pp. [*14*] 1–148   L

George Byshop   [1577?]

Lacks A4. Perfect copy at MH. STC *18670.*

244 ——[another edition] *Spiritus est vicarius Christi in terra.* A treatise wherein dicing, daūcing, uaine plaies or enterludes with other idle pastimes, &c. commonly used on the Sabboth day, are reprooved, by the authoritie of the worde of God and auncient vvriters. Made dialoguewise by Iohn Northbrooke minister, and preacher of the worde of God.

ff. [*8*] 1–72, *misnumbering 22 as "26", 24 as "28".*   L

George Bishoppe   1579

STC *18671.*

245 ——[another edition] A treatise against dicing, dancing, plays, and interludes. With other idle pastimes. By John Northbrooke, minister. From the earliest edition, about A.D. 1577. With an introduction and notes. [Edited by J. P. Collier].

pp. [i–v] vi–xx, [1–3] 4–188   L

The Shakespeare Society   1843

Reissued in Early Treatises on the Stage; *viz.* Northbrooke's Treatise against Dicing,... (*The Shakespeare Society, 1853*).

246 GOSSON, STEPHAN. *†The shoole of abuse, conteining a pleasaunt invective against poets, pipers, plaiers, iesters, and such like caterpillers of a cōmonwelth; setting vp the flagge of defiance to their mischieuous exercise, & ouerthrowing their bulwarkes, by prophane writers, naturall reason, and common experience: a discourse as pleasaunt for gentlemen that fauour learning, as profitable for all that wyll follow vertue. By Stephan Gosson. Stud. Oxon.

8⁰ ★2–★7 A–E⁸ F⁵; ff. [*6*] 1–37 [38–45]   CSmH

Printed by Thomas Woodcocke   1579

An edition of perhaps 3000 copies. The work may have been commissioned by the city fathers. See Ringler, pp. 26–28, 140–141. STC *12097. See also nos. 251, 256.*

247 ——[another edition] †The schoole of abuse ...

8⁰ → 2 –→ 7 A–E⁸ F³; ff. [*6*] [1] 2–36 [37–43]   L

Thomas VVoodcocke   1579

Ringler, *pp. 143–144.*

248 ——†[another edition]

8⁰ A1–A3 A6 B–F⁸; ff. [*46*]   L

Thomas Woodcocke   1587

Ringler *143–144.* STC *12098. Perfect copy at CSmH.*

249 ——[another edition] The school of abuse, containing a pleasant invective against poets, pipers, players, jesters, &c. By Stephen Gosson. With an introduction regarding the author and his works.

pp. [i–v] vi–xviii, [1–3] 4–51 [52]   NbU

The Shakespeare Society   1841

Reissued in Early Treatises on the Stage; *viz ...* Gosson's School of Abuse ... (*The Shakespeare Society, 1853*).

250 ——[another edition] Stephen Gosson Stud. Oxon. The schoole of abuse. [August?] 1579. And A short apologie of The schoole of abuse. [November?] 1579. Edited by Edward Arber, F.S.A. Fellow of King's College, London ...

pp. [1–3] 4–80; *t.p. headed "English Reprints"; on t.p., "No. 3."; t.p. in red and black*   NbU

Birmingham: 35 Wheeleys Road   2 March 1868

250.1 ——★[large paper issue of no. 250]

pp. 80   MB

                  1868

250.2 ——★[another edition of no. 250]

             MB

             1869

Reprinted in A Collection of Scarce and Valuable Tracts. *Second edition, vol. 3, 1810.*

251 GOSSON, STEP[HEN]. †The *Ephemerides* of Phialo, deuided into three bookes. The first, A method which he ought to follow that desireth to rebuke his freend, when he seeth him swarue: without kindling his choler, or hurting himselfe. The second, A canuazado to courtiers in foure pointes. The third, The defence of a curtezan ouerthrowen. And A short apologie of The schoole of abuse, against poets, pipers, players, & their excusers. By Step. Gosson, Stud. Oxon.

8⁰ →2–→7 A–G⁸ H¹–H² H5–H8 I–L⁸ M⁴ (*missigning M2 as "M3"*); ff. [*7*] [1] 2–92. many misnumbered, including 92 misprinted as "29"   L

Imprinted at London by Thomas Dawson   1579

Wants first leaf (blank) and H3 and 4. Perfect copy at CSmH. Ringler, *pp. 144–145.* STC *12093.*

252 ——[another edition]

8⁰ –→8 A–L⁸ M⁴; ff. [*8*] [1] 2–92, *misnumbering 92 as "65"*   L

Imprinted by Thomas Dawson   1586

Two copies in L, one lacking the first leaf, and the other signatures L and M. Ringler, p. 145. STC 12094.
A short apologie of *The schoole of abuse* is reprinted in Arber's ed. *of* The school of abuse *(1868), no. 250 above.*

253 [LODGE, THOMAS. *†A REPLY to Stephen Gosson's *Schoole of Abuse* in defence of poetry musick and stage plays].

pp. [1] 2–9 14 15 12 13 10 11 16 1 [for 17?] 8 [for 18?] 19–48 [=48]; lacking t.p.   CSmH

[1579–1580]

According to Lodge himself, this pamphlet was suppressed before publication. STC 16663. Univ. microfilms 12357.

254 ——[another edition] A defence of poetry, music and stage-plays, by Thomas Lodge, of Lincoln's Inn. To which are added, by the same author, *An alarum against usurers;* and the delectable history of *Forbonius and Priscaria.* With introduction and notes. [Ed. David Laing].

pp. [i–v] vi–lxxvii [lxxviii], [1–3] 4–129 [130]   L
The Shakespeare Society   1853

Reprinted in The Complete Works of Thomas Lodge *(The Hunterian Club, 1883), in G. G. Smith,* Elizabethan Critical Essays *(Oxford 1904), I, 61–86, and in G.E.B. Saintsbury,* Elizabethan and Jacobean Pamphlets *(1892), pp. 1–42.*
On Lodge's source, see W. Ringler, RES, XV, 1939.

255 ANGLO-PHILE EUTHEO, *pseud. of* Anthony Munday. A second and third blast of retrait from plaies and theaters: the one whereof was sounded by a reuerend byshop dead long since; the other by a worshipful and zealous gentleman now aliue: one showing the filthines of plaies in times past; the other the abhomination of theaters in the time present: both expresly prouing that that common-weale is nigh vnto the cursse of God, wherein either plaiers be made of, or theaters maintained. Set forth by Anglo-phile Eutheo.

pp. [12] 1–128 [129 (colophon) 130 (bl.)]   L
[Henry Denham]   1580
STC 21677.
Reprinted in Hazlitt, pp. [97] 98–154.

256 GOSSON, STEPH[EN]. Playes confuted in fiue actions, prouing that they are not to be suffred in a Christian common weale, by the waye both the cauils of Thomas Lodge, and the "Play of playes", written in their defence, and other obiections of players frendes, are truely set downe and directlye aunsweared. By Steph. Gosson, Stud. Oxon.

8⁰ π⁵ A–G⁸; unnumbered   L
Thomas Gosson   [1582]
A cancellans slip on B4ᵛ in CSmH copy. Ringler, pp. 145–146. STC 12095.
Reprinted in Hazlitt, pp. [157]–218.

257 STUBBES, PHILLIP. *The anatomie of abuses.

O

1st May 1583

STC 23376.

258 ——[another edition] The anatomie of abuses: containing, a discouerie, or briefe summarie of such notable vices and imperfections, as now raigne in many countreyes of the world: but (especiallye) in a famous ilande called Ailgna: together, with most fearefull examples of Gods Iudgements, executed uppon the wicked for the same, aswel in Ailgna of late, as in other places, elsewhere. Very godly, to be reade of all true Christians: but most needefull to be regarded in Englande. Made dialogue-wise by Phillip Stubbes. Seene and allowed, according to order.

ff. [7] 1–5 7–125 [126]   L
Richard Iones   16. August 1583

STC 23377.

259 ——The anatomie of abuses: containing a discouerie, or briefe summarie of such notable vices and corruptions, as nowe raigne in many Christian countreyes of the worlde: but (especially) in the countrey of Ailgna: together, with most fearefull examples of Gods Iudgementes, executed vpon the wicked for the same, aswell in Ailgna of late, as in other places, elsewhere. Very godly, to be read of all true Christians, every where: but most chiefly, to be regarded in England. Made dialogue-wise by Phillip Stubs. And now newly reuised recognized, and augmented the third time by the same author.

8⁰ A⁴ B–Q⁸ R⁴; ff. [7] [1] 2–124 [125] [=128], many misnumbered   L
Richard Iones   1585

STC 23378.

260 ——The anatomie of abuses. Containing a description of such notable vices and enormities, as raigne in many countries of the world, but especiallie in this realme of England: together with most fearefull examples of Gods heauie Iudgements inflicted vpon the wicked for the same as well in England of late, as in other places else where. Verie godly to be read of all true Christians every where, but most chiefly, to bee regarded in England. Made dialogue-wise by Philip Stubs, Gent. Now, the fourth time, newly corrected and inlarged by the same author.

4⁰ A–T⁴; pp. [8] 1–144, some misnumbered   L
Richard Johnes   1595

STC 23379.

261 ——Reprinted from the third edition of MDLXXXV, under the superintendence of William B.D.D. Turnbull, Esq. Advocate, F.S.A. Scot.

pp. [i–v] vi–xi [xii], ²[i–ii] iii–xix [xx], [1] 2–229 [230 (text) 231–232 (bl.)]   E

London: W. Pickering; Edinburgh: W. & D. Laing
1836

One hundred copies printed.

262 ———[another edition] (Miscellaneous Tracts. Temp. Eliz. & Jac. I.)

pp. [2] [i] ii–xviii [19] 20–194; printed wrappers   L
[1870]

Edited by J. P. Collier.

263 ———[another edition] Phillip Stubbes's Anatomy of the abuses in England in Shakspere's youth, A.D. 1583. Part I. (Collated with other editions in 1583, 1585 and 1595.) With extracts from Stubbes's "Life of his wife", 1591, and his "Perfect pathway to felicitie", 1592 (1610), and Bp. Babington on the "Ten commandments", 1588; also the fourth book of Thomas Kirchmaier's (or Naogeorgus's) "Regnum papismi, or Popish Kingdome", (Englisht by Barnabe Googe, 1570,) on popular and popish superstitions in 1553. Edited by Frederick J. Furnivall. (New Shakspere Society. Series VI. Nos. 4 and 6.)

pp. [4] [1★–2★] 3★–10★ ff. 11★–15★ pp. 17★–20★ ff. 21★–33★ [=ff. 18] pp. 35★–98★ [99★–102★] [=pp. 82], [i–iii] iv–xx ²[21] 22–376; illus.; pl. [1] = 2 leaves   L

For The New Shakespere Society by N. Trübner & Co.
1877 and 1879

An extract ("Stage-plaies and Enterludes, with their wickednesse".) from the 1584 edition reprinted in Hazlitt, pp. 218–225.
For "The second part of the anatomie of abuses", which is of no theatrical interest, see Appendix.

264 RANKINS, WIL[LIAM]. A mirrour of monsters: wherein is plainely described the manifold vices, & spotted enormities, that are caused by the infectious sight of playes, with the description of the subtile slights of Sathan, making them his instruments. Compiled by Wil. Rankins. Seene and allowed.

ff. [1] [1] 2–24   L

T[homas] H[acket]   1587

STC *20699.*

265 RAINOLDES [JOHN], GAGER, [WILLIAM], and GENTILES [*i.e.* Gentili, Alberico.] Th'over-throw of stage-playes, by the way of controversie betwixt D. Gager and D. Rainoldes, wherein all the reasons that can be made for them are notably refuted; th'objections aunswered, and the case so cleared and resolved, as that the iudgement of any man, that is not froward and perverse, may easelie be satisfied. Wherein is manifestly proved, that it is not onely unlawfull to bee

an actor, but a beholder of those vanities. Whereunto are added also and annexed in th'end certeine latine letters betwixt the sayed Maister Rainoldes, and D. Gentiles, reader of the civill law in Oxford, concerning the same matter.

pp. [8] 1–163 [1] 164–190 [191 (bl.)], misprinting 100 as "200", 164 as "264"   L

[Middelburg: Richard Schilders].   1599

STC *20616.*

266 ———[another issue]

pp. [8] 1–163 [1] 164–190 [191], misnumbering 74 as "73", 156 as "158", 178 as "168"; misprinting 100 as "200", 164 as "264"   L

Middleburgh, imprinted by Richard Schilders   1600

STC *20617.*

267 ———the second edition

pp. [8] 1–164 164–190 [191 (bl.)], misprinting 191 as "190" [=192]   L

Oxford: E. Forrest, and W. Webbe   1629

The title-page has the following variant spellings: 'The overthrow'; 'answered'; 'bee satisfied'; 'be an actor'; 'the end'; 'certaine'; 'the said'. With some mispagination. STC *20618.*

For an account of this controversy see F. S. Boas, University Drama in the Tudor Age (1914), in which Gager's reply to Rainold's first letter is summarised. Th'overthrow contains two letters to Gager, dated 10 July 1592 and 30 May 1593, and two letters to Gager's friend Gentiles, with two shorter replies from him.

268 HEYWOOD, THOMAS. An apology for actors. Containing three briefe treatises. 1 Their antiquity. 2 Their ancient dignity. 3 The true use of their quality. Written by Thomas Heywood.

4° A⁴ a⁴ B–G⁴   L

Printed by Nicholas Okes   1612

Arthur M. Clark, in "A Bibliography of Thomas Heywood", Oxford Bibliographical Society Proceedings & Papers (Oxford, 1927), I, 99–153, describes this book from two Bodley copies and this copy, and gives more information; Perkinson, in the 1941 edition (below no. 271) draws attention to 21 copies and three different states of sig. B. STC 13309.

269 ———[another edition] The actors vindication, containing, three brief treatises, *viz.* I. Their antiquity. II. Their ancient dignity, III. The true use of their quality.

pp. [16] 1–46 [47–48 (bl.)]   L

W[illiam] C[artwright]   [1658]

Omits the letter to Okes. Dedication to Lord Dorchester. Wing H *1777.*

270 ———[another edition] An apology for actors. In three books. By Thomas Heywood. From the edition of 1612, compared with that of W. Cartwright. With an introduction and notes. [Ed. John Payne Collier].

pp. [4] [i] ii–xvi, [1–5] 6–66 L

The Shakespeare Society 1841

Reissued in Early Treatises on the Stage; *viz. . . .* Heywood's Defence of Stage Plays (*The Shakespeare Society, 1853*).

271 ———[another edition] An apology for actors (1612) by Thomas Heywood A refutation of 'The apology for actors' (1615) by I.G. With introductions and bibliographical notes by Richard H. Perkinson.

pp. [2] [i–vi] vii–xvii [xviii], sigs. A^4 a^4 B–G^4 (facsim. reprint of no. 268), pp. [2] [i–ii] iii–ix [x], [2] [1] 2–62 55 58–59 62 [=66] (facsim. reprint of no. 272) [4] L

New York: Scholars' Facsimiles & Reprints 1941

Reprinted in A Second Collection of Scarce and Valuable Tracts *vol. 1 (1750), pp. 172–203, without the letter to Okes; in* A Collection of Scarce and Valuable Tracts *The Second Edition Volume Third (1810), pp. 574–600, without the letter to Okes, and with a brief note; in* Chambers, *Elizabethan, IV, 250–254, (condensed).*

272 G., I. A refutation of the "Apology for actors". Divided into three briefe treatises. Wherein is confuted and opposed all the chiefe groundes and arguments alleaged in defence of playes: and withall in each treatise is deciphered actors, 1. Heathenish and diabolicall institution. 2. Their ancient and moderne indignitie. 3. The wonderfull abuse of their impious qualitie. By I.G.

pp. [2] 1–62 55 58 59 62 [=66] L

Imprinted at London by W. White 1615

STC *12214.*

273 ———[another issue]

pp. [2] 1–62 55 58 59 62 [=66] L

Imprinted at London by W.W. and are to be sold by Tho. Langley and I. White 1615

STC *12215.*

The work is sometimes attributed, without good authority, to J. Green(e).

For the facsimile reprint edited by R. Perkinson (New York, 1941), see no. 271 above.

274 vacant.

✠ Field, Nathan. The remonstrance of Nathan Field . . . addressed to a preacher . . . who had been arraigning against the players at the Globe theatre . . . [Ed. by J. O. Halliwell Phillips]. 1865. *See no. 1040.*

Written in 1615.

275 A SHORTE TREATISE against stage-playes.

pp. [1–2] 3–28 L

n.p. Printed in the yeere 1625

Alexander Leighton (1568–1649) has been suggested as author and Middleburgh as the place of publication. In his Speculum Belli Sacri *(1624) Leighton refers to a treatise of his against stage plays (pp. 269, 280), as the BM cataloguer noticed. See also below no. 280.*

Reprinted in Hazlitt, *pp. [231]–352.*

STC *24232.*

Prynne's Histrio-mastix

276 PRYNNE, WILLIAM. Histrio-mastix. The players scourge, or, actors tragaedie, divided into two parts. Wherein it is largely evidenced, by divers arguments, by the concurring authorities and resolutions of sundry texts of Scripture; of the whole primitive church, both under the Law and Gospell; of 55 Synodes and Councels; of 71 Fathers and Christian writers, before the yeare of our Lord 1200; of above 150 foraigne and domestique Protestant and Popish authors, since; of 40 heathen philosophers, historians, poets; of many heathen, many Christian nations, republiques, emperors, princes, magistrates; of sundry apostolicall, canonicall, imperiall constitutions; and of our owne English statutes, magistrates, universities, writers, preachers. That popular stage-playes (the very pompes of the Divell which we renounce in baptisme, if we beleeve the Fathers) are sinfull, heathenish, lewde, ungodly spectacles, and most pernicious corruptions; condemned in all ages, as intolerable mischiefes to churches, to republickes, to the manners, mindes, and soules of men. And that the profession of play-poets, of stage players; together with the penning, acting, and frequenting of stage-playes, are unlawfull, infamous and misbeseeming Christians. All pretences to the contrary are here likewise fully answered; and the unlawfulnes of acting, of beholding academicall enterludes, briefly discussed; besides sundry other particulars concerning dancing, dicing, health-drinking, &c. of which the table will informe you. By William Prynne, an utter-barrester of Lincolnes Inne.

pp. [36] 1–512; ff. 513–568; pp. 545–832 [833–834 (bl.)], 831–1006 [40] L

Michael Sparke 1633 [1632]

Pforzheimer, *p. 833;* STC *20464a. Some copies without errata on* *** 4^v (STC *20464*).

—[Dutch translation] *Histrio-mastix, ofte schouw-spels trevr-spel, dienende tot een klaer bewijs van de onwetlijckheden der hedendaechsche comedien* (Leyden: W. Christiaens), 1639

277 MR. WILLIAM PRYNN his defence of stage-plays, or a retraction of a former book of his called "Histrio-Mastix".

pp. [1–2] 3–8 L

1649

Wing *M 2278*.

This was a forgery — Lowe. *In no. 279 below Prynne denies writing it, and attributes the authorship to 'some of the imprisoned stage-players, or agents of the army'.*

278 ——— [another edition]

pp. [1–3] 4–8 L

[London] 1822

On p. [2]: Reprinted, [not for sale,] 1822.
Reprinted in E. W. Brayley, An enquiry into the genuineness of Prynne's "Defence . . ." *(London, 1825), pp. [7]–11 (no. 1008 below), and in* Hazlitt, *pp. [266]–271.*

279 [PRYNNE, WILLIAM]. THE VINDICATION of William Prynne Esquire, from some scandalous papers and imputations, newly printed and published, to traduce and defame him in his reputation.

bs. L

[London] [1649]

Signed: From the Kings head in the Strand, Jan 10 1648, William Prynne.
Reprinted in E. W. Brayley, An enquiry into the genuineness of Prynne's "Defence . . ." *(London, 1825), p. 14 (no. 1008 below);* Hazlitt, *p. 271. They are both curtailed, being copied from the reprint in J. P. Collier,* Poetical Decameron *(1820), II, 322.* Wing *P 4129.*

✠ Baker, *Sir* Richard. Theatrum redivivum, or the theatre vindicated . . . in answer to Mr. Pryn's *Histrio-mastix*. 1662. *See no. 282.*

✠ Visits from the Shades: or, dialogues . . . II. Pryn, and "The loyal observator." 1704. *See no. 336.*

✠ Ralph, James. The taste of the town . . . and the stage-entertainment fully vindicated from the exceptions of old Pryn, The Reverend Mr. Collier, Mr. Bedford and Mr. Law. 1731. *See no. 870.*

✠ Brayley, E. W. An enquiry into the genuineness of Prynne's "Defence of stage plays", &c. together with a reprint of the said tract, and also of Prynne's "Vindication". 1825. *See no. 1008.*

✠ Gardiner, Samuel, *ed.* Documents relating to the proceedings against William Prynne. Camden Soc. 1877. *See no. 1054.*

---

280 *A SHORTE TREATISE against stage-playes pp. 36

1638

Bertram Dobell Catalogue 201 (1911) no. 860. Present location unknown. Possibly another edition of no. 275 above.

281 ROWE, JOHN. Tragi-comoedia. Being a brief relation of the strange, and wonderfull hand of God discovered at Witny, in the comedy acted there February the third, where there were some slaine, many hurt, with severall other remarkable passages. Together with what was preached in three sermons on that occasion from Rom. I. 18. Both which may serve as some check to the growing atheisme of the present age. By John Rowe of C.C.C. in Oxford, lecturer in the towne of Witny.

pp. [*20*] 1–48 51–81 [82 (bl.)]; illus. L

Oxford: Henry Cripps 1653

While some country folks were playing the comedy of "Mucedorus" at Whitney, the room in which they were playing fell in, and many people were killed or hurt. The enemies of the stage saw in this a direct interposition of Providence — Lowe. Wing *R 2067.*

282 BAKER, *Sir* RICHARD. *Theatrum redivivum*, or the theatre vindicated by Sir Richard Baker in answer to Mr. Pryn's *Histrio-mastix:* wherein his groundless assertions against stage-plays are discovered, his misstaken allegations of the Fathers manifested, as also what he calls his reasons, to be nothing but his passions.

pp. [*8*] 1–141 [142–144 (bl.)] L

Francis Eglesfield 1662

Wing *B 513.*

283 ———[reissue]. *Theatrum triumphans* or a discourse of plays. Shewing the lawfulness and excellent use of drammatique poesy, and vindicateing the stage from all those groundless calumnies and misrepresentations, wherewith it is aspersed. Wherein all scruples are removed, and the vain objections of "Histro-matrix" and others fully answered and confuted, their mistaken allegations of Scripture and Fathers discovered, and their pretended reasons manifested to be nothing but their passions. Written by the learned Sir Richard Baker, Kt.

pp. [*8*] 1–141 [142] E

Francis Eglesfield 1670

Wing *B 514.*

The Collier Controversy 1698–1707

Jeremy Collier (1650–1726) . . . *A nonjuring clergyman, whose* Short View, *is the most serious attack ever made on the stage in this country. It was replied to by Congreve and other dramatists, but Collier was completely victorious, and the best proof of his success, and of the necessity for his attack, was the marked improvement in decency which it produced* — Lowe.
For some notes on the practical side of the Collier *controversy, see A. H. Scouten, "The S.P.C.K. and the Stage",* TN *XI (1957).*
Listed first are Collier's own contributions.

284 COLLIER, JEREMY. A short view of the immorality, and profaneness of the English stage, together with the sense of antiquity upon this argument, by Jeremy Collier.

pp. [*16*] 1–288   L

S. Keble, R. Sare, and H. Hindmarsh   1698

> *The preface dated 5 March; advertised 16–21 April, 1698 (Hooker 1). Wing C 5263.*

285 ———The second edition

pp. [*16*] 1–288, misnumbering 73 as "37", 126 as "621", 165 as "195"   GU

S. Keble, R. Sare, and H. Hindmarsh   1698

> *Advertised 12–14 May 1698 (Hooker 3). Wing C 5264.*

286 ———The third edition

pp. [*16*] 1–288   L

S. Keble, R. Sare, and H. Hindmarsh   1698

> *Wing C 5265. Not in Hooker.*

287 ———The fourth edition

pp. [*16*] 1–288   L

S. Keble, and R. Sare   1699

> *Wing C 5266. Not in Hooker.*

288 ———*[fifth edition corrected.] With the several defences of the same. In answer to Mr. Congreve, Dr. Drake, &c.

pp. (*14*), 437   MB

G. Strahan   1728

289 ——— [reissue of 288?] A short view of the profaneness and immorality of the English stage, &c. The fifth edition corrected, with the several defences of the same. In answer to Mr. Congreve, Dr. Drake, &c.

pp. [*14*] 1–437 [438–440 (advts.)]; pl. [*1*]   L

G. Strahan, Richard Williamson, and T. Osborne 1730

290 ——— [reissue of 289]

pp. [*14*] 1–437 [438–440 (advts.)]   E

Samuel Birt and Thomas Trye   1738

> *"The fifth edition, corrected" on half-title.*

291 COLLIER, JEREMY. A defence of the Short view of the profaneness and immorality of the English stage, &c. Being a reply to Mr. Congreve's Amendments, &c. and to the Vindication of the author of the Relapse. By Jeremy Collier.

pp. [*4*] 1–139 [140 (advt.)]   L

S. Keble, R. Sare, and H. Hindmarsh   1699

> *Sometimes said to have been published in 1698; advertised 8–10 Nov. 1698 (Hooker 19). Wing C 5248.*

292 ———[another edition]

pp. [*4*] 1–139 [140]   LGk

S. Keble, R. Sare   1705

293 COLLIER, JEREMY. A second defence of the Short view of the prophaneness and immorality of the English stage, &c. being a reply to a book, entituled, The ancient and modern stages surveyed, &c. By Jeremy Collier.

pp. [*4*] 1–142   L

S. Keble, R. Sare, and G. Strahan   1700

> *The preface is dated 26 Nov. 1699; advertised 8–10 Feb. 1700 (Hooker 27).*

294 [COLLIER, JEREMY.] MR. COLLIER'S DIS-SUASIVE from the play-house; in a letter to a person of quality, occasioned by the late calamity of the tempest.

pp. [*1–2*] 3–15 [16 (advt.)]   L

Richard Sare   1703

> *Dated 10 Dec. 1703; initialled J.C.*

295 ———[another edition]

pp. [*1–2*] 3–16   MH

Dublin: Printed and sold by Peter Lawrence   1704

296 ———[another edition] Mr. Collier's dissuasive from the play-house; in a letter to a person of quality, occasion'd by the late calamity of the tempest. To which is added, a letter written by another hand; in answer to some queries sent by a person of quality, relating to the irregularities charged upon the stage.

pp. [*1–2*] 3–32   MH

Richard Sare   1704

297 COLLIER, JEREMY. A farther vindication of the Short view of the profaneness and immorality of the English stage, in which the objections of a late book, entituled, A defence of plays, are consider'd. By Jeremy Collier.

pp. [*1–2*] 3–46 [47–48 (advt.)]   L

R. Sare and G. Strahan   1708

298 [CONGREVE, WILLIAM.] AMENDMENTS of Mr. Collier's false and imperfect citations, &c. from the Old Batchelour, Double Dealer, Love for Love, Mourning Bride. By the author of those plays.

pp. [*4*] 1–80 71–109 [110 (bl.)] [=120]; cancellans, pp. 43–44   L

J. Tonson   1698

> *Advertised 9–12 July (Hooker 13). P. 44 cancellandum misprinting "superstition" for "supposition". Copies with the cancellans note the correction on sig A1ᵛ. Wing C 5844.*
> *Reprinted (uncancelled version) in Congreve, The dramatic works (S. Crowder, C. Ware, and T. Payne, 1773), II, [231]–285.*

299 ANIMADVERSIONS on Mr. Congreve's late answer to Mr. Collier. In a dialogue between Mr. Smith and Mr. Johnson. With the characters of the present poets; and some offers towards new-modeling the stage.

pp. [*32*] 1–88   DFo

John Nutt   1698

> *Advertised 3–8 Sept. 1698 (Hooker 15). Wing A 3195.*

300 ——The second edition

pp. [*30*] 1–88   L

J. Nutt   1698

> *Advertised 15–18 Oct. 1698 (Hooker 15).*

301 BOSSUET, JAMES [*i.e.* Jacques] BÉNIGNE. *Maxims and reflections on plays. Written in French by James Bénigne Bossuet, Bishop of Meaux, Counsellor to the French King, and formerly preceptor to the Dauphine. Translated into English.

J. Nutt   1698

> *Advertised Oct. 11–13 1698 (Hooker 17). Not seen by Hooker. Bossuet's Maximes sur la comédie, a reply to Caffaro (see no. 303 below), were published in 1694 in Paris.*

302 ——[another edition] Maxims and reflections upon plays. (In answer to a discourse of, the lawfullness and unlawfullness of plays. Printed before a late play entituled, *Beauty in distress.*) Written in French by the Bp. of Meaux. And now made English. The preface by another hand.

pp. [*16*] 1–127, ²112–118 [119–120 ("Books Printed for Richard Sare")] [=136]   MH

R. Sare   1699

> *Advertised 9–11 Feb. 1699 (Hooker 22). Wing B 3786. Another copy (also MH) perhaps representing another issue, has a variant setting of the title: instead of "by the Bp. of / Meaux" it has "by / the Bp. of, Meaux". The preface of the copy with the variant setting of the title reprinted in facsimile in The Augustan Reprint Society Series Three: Essays on the Stage No. 4 (Michigan 1948).*

303 CAFFARO, *Father* [FRANCOIS], MOTTEAUX [PETER ANTHONY]. Beauty in distress. A tragedy. As it is acted at the theatre in Little Lincolns-Inn-Fields. By His Majesty's Servants. Written by Mr. Motteaux. With a Discourse of the lawfulness & unlawfulness of plays, lately written in French by the learned Father Caffaro, Divinity-Professor at Paris. Sent in a letter to the author by a divine of the Church of England.

pp. [i–iii] iv–xxxi [xxxii], 1–58 [59–60 (advt.)]   L

Daniel Brown; and Rich. Parker   1698

> *Advertised 16–21 June 1698 (Hooker 10). Cunningham 13. Macdonald 36. François Caffaro's Lettre d'un théologien illustre pour sçavoir si la comédie peut estre permise ou doit être absolument défendue, in favour of the theatre, was published in 1694. It is also translated in Robert Mansel's Free thoughts upon Methodists. 1814, see below no. 485.*

304 [SETTLE, ELKANAH.] A DEFENCE of dramatick poetry: being a review of Mr. Collier's View of the immorality and profaneness of the stage.

pp. [*8*] 1–118 [119–120 (bl.)], misnumbering 77 as "67" and 103 as "113"   L

Eliz. Whitlock   1698

> *Sometimes wrongly ascribed to Edward Filmer. Wing F 905. Advertised 31 May–7 June 1698 (Hooker 6).*

305 ——[another edition] A defence of dramatick poetry: being a review of Mr. Collier's View of the immorality and profaneness of the stage.

pp. [*8*] 1–118 [119–120 (bl.)], misnumbering 103 as "113"   DFo

Eliz. Whitlock   1698

306 [SETTLE, ELKANAH.] A FARTHER DEFENCE of dramatick poetry: being the second part of the *Review of Mr. Collier's "View of the immorality and profaneness of the stage"*. Done by the same hand.

pp. [*8*] 1–72   L

Eliz. Whitlock   1698

> *Advertised 18–21 June 1698 (Hooker 11). Wing F 906.*

307 ——[reissue of nos. 304, 306] A defence of dramatick poetry: being a review of Mr. Collier's View of the immorality and profaneness of the stage.

pp. [*16*] 1–118, misnumbering 103 as "113", ²[*8*] 1–72   DFo

Eliz. Whitlock   1698

> *Includes a dedication of the whole work to Viscount Lisburne, signed in Folger copy "E. Settle".*

308 DENNIS, [JOHN]. The usefulness of the stage, to the happiness of mankind. To government, and to religion. Occasioned by a late book, written by Jeremy Collier, M.A. By Mr. Dennis.

pp. [*8*] 1–143 [144 (errata)]   L

Rich. Parker   1698

> *Advertised 4–7 June (Hooker 7). Some copies without the list of errata. Reprinted in Miscellaneous Tracts (1725), I, pp. 295–417, and in Hooker, I, 146–193, with notes. Wing D 1046.*

309 ——[another edition] The usefulness of the stage to religion, and to government: shewing the advantage of the drama in all nations since its first institution. With an account of the rise and progress of the play-houses that were put down, and remarks on all the dramatick pieces which have been published and played since the late Act of Parliament for licencing the stage, with the reasons that occasioned it. Also a distinction between the stage and the press, and our present written plays and the drama in its purity, with reflections on the taste of the times, as to Ballad Operas, Pantomines, [*sic*] Dumb Shew, Tumbling, Dancing, and Entertainments.

pp. [*4*] [*1*] 2–51 [52 (appendix)]; pl. [front.]   L
Thomas Harper   1738

310 ———the second edition

pp. [*4*] [*1*] 2–60; pl. [front.]   L
T. Cooper   1738

A reissue of no. 309, with some new matter replacing the appendix. "A mutilated reprint of portions of Dennis's book" (Hooker I, 468).

311 D'URFEY, [THOMAS]. The campaigners: or, the pleasant adventures at Brussels. A comedy, with a familiar preface upon a late reformer of the stage. Ending with a satyrical fable of The dog and the ottor. Written by Mr. D'urfey.

pp. [*8*] 1–32, ²1–60   L
A. Baldwin   1698

Advertised 9–12 July 1698 (Hooker 12). Wing D 2705. A facsimile reprint of the preface (pp. 1–27) was issued by the Augustan Reprint Society (1948).

312 ———[another issue, with variant t.p.] The campaigners: or, the pleasant adventures at Brussels. A comedy. As it is acted at the Theatre-Royal. With a familiar preface. . . .

pp. [*8*] 1–32, ²1–60   E
A. Baldwin   1698

313 THE IMMORALITY OF THE ENGLISH PULPIT, as justly subjected to the notice of the English stage, as the immorality of the stage is to that of the pulpit. In a letter to Mr. Collier. Occasion'd by the third chapter of his book, entitl'd, "A short view of the immorality of the English stage", &c.

pp. [*1–2*] 3–8   L
                                                 1698

A very weak production. Of the immorality of the pulpit no proofs are advanced — Lowe. Hooker 18. Wing I 57a.

314 [HOPKINS, CHARLES?] A LETTER to A.H. Esq; concerning the stage.

pp. [*2*] 1–22   L
A. Baldwin   1698

Advertised June 11–13 1698 (Hooker 9). Addressed to Anthony Hammond? or Horneck? See Hooker's Review of The Jeremy Collier Stage Controversy. 1698–1726 *by Sister Rose Anthony, S.C., MLN LIV (1939) 386–9. Wing M 2033. Attributed in Wing to Luke Milbourne. Reprinted in facsimile with an introduction by H. T. Swedenberg, Jr. by The Augustan Reprint Society (Series Three: Essays on the Stage), (1946).*

315 A LETTER to Mr. Congreve on his pretended amendments, &c. of Mr. Collier's Short view of the immorality and prophaneness of the English stage.

pp. [*1–2*] 3–42 [43–46 (advts.) 47–48 (bl.)]   DFo
Samuel Keble   1698

Advertised 30 Aug.–1 Sept. 1698 (Hooker 14). Wing L 1713 a.

316 [WILLIS, RICHARD, *Bishop of Winchester*.] THE OCCASIONAL PAPER: number IX. Containing some considerations about the danger of going to plays. In a letter to a friend.

pp. [*1–2*] 3–23 [24 (advt.)]   L
M. Wotton   1698

Advertised 19–21 May 1698 (Hooker 5). Reprinted in facsimile with an introduction by H. T. Swedenberg, Jr. by The Augustan Reprint Society (Series Three: Essays on the stage No. 1), (1946).

317 ———[another edition] Some considerations about the danger of going to plays. In a letter to a friend.

pp. [*1–2*] 3–23 [24 (advts.)]   L
M. Wotton   1704

318 [GILDON, CHARLES.] PHAETON: or, the fatal divorce. A tragedy. As it is acted at the Theatre Royal. In imitation of the antients. With some reflections on a book call'd, *A short view of the immorality and profaneness of the English stage.*

pp. [*22*] 1–33 [34 (epilogue)]   L
Abel Roper   1698

Advertised 28–30 April 1698 (Hooker 2). Wing G735.

319 [VANBRUGH, *Sir* JOHN.] A SHORT VINDICATION of the *Relapse* and the Provok'd Wife, from immorality and prophaneness by the author.

pp. [*4*] 1–79 [80]   L
H. Walwyn   1698

Vanbrugh's comedies were specially indecent, and were singled out for censure justly by Jeremy Collier — Lowe. Advertised 9–11 June 1698 (Hooker 8). Wing V 59.

320 SOME REMARKS upon Mr. Collier's *Defence of his Short view of the English stage, &c.* In vindication of Mr. Congreve, &c. In a letter to a friend.

pp. [*2*] 1–18   L
A. Baldwin   1698

Advertised 3–6 Dec. 1698 (Hooker 20). Wing S 4605.

321 [RIDPATH, GEORGE.] THE STAGE condemn'd, and the encouragement given to the immoralities and profaneness of the theatre, by the English schools, universities and pulpits, censur'd. King Charles I. Sundays mask and declaration for sports and pastimes on the Sabbath, largely related and animadverted upon. The arguments of all the authors that have writ in defence of the stage against Mr. Collier, consider'd. And the sense of the fathers, councils, antient philosophers and poets, and of the Greek and Roman states, and of the first Christian emperours concerning the drama, faithfully deliver'd. Together with the censure of the English state and of several antient and modern divines of the Church of England upon the stage. And remarks on diverse late plays, as also on those presented by the two universities to King Charles I.

pp. [8] 1–216   L
John Salusbury   1698

Advertised 13–15 Sept. 1698 (Hooker 16). Wing R 1468.

322 ———the second edition

pp. [8] 1–216   L
Printed, and sold by B. Bragg   1706

Title-page differs from that of first edition in omitting "King Charles . . . animadverted upon" and the "u" in "emperours", and in substituting "Also remarks . . ." for 'And remarks . . .'. A reissue.

323 A VINDICATION of the stage, with the usefulness and advantages of dramatick representations, in answer to Mr. Collier's late book, entituled, *A view of the prophaness and immorality, &c.* In a letter to a friend.

pp. [1–2] 3–29 [30 (bl.)]   MH
Joseph Wilde, at the Sign of the Elephant at Charing-Cross   1698

Advertised 17–19 May (Hooker 4). Krutch, p. 270, suggests that Charles Gildon may be the author. Wing V 532.

324 [DRAKE, JAMES.] THE ANTIENT AND MODERN STAGES survey'd. Or, Mr. Collier's "View of the immorality and profaness of the English stage" set in a true light. Wherein some of Mr. Collier's mistakes are rectified, and the comparative morality of the English stage is asserted upon the parallel.

pp. [32] 1–367 [368 (bl.)]   L
Abel Roper   1699

Advertised 11–14 March 1699 (Hooker 23). Wing D 2123.

325 [OLDMIXON, JOHN.] REFLECTIONS on the stage, and Mr. Collyer's Defence of the Short View. In four dialogues.

pp. [14] 1–194 (misnumbering 193 as "163")   E
R. Parker   1699

Advertised 2–4 May 1699 (Hooker 24). Wing O 262.

326 THE STAGE acquitted. Being a full answer to Mr Collier, and the other enemies of the drama. With a vindication of King Charles the Martyr, and the clergy of the Church of England, from the abuses of a scurrilous book, called, *The stage condemned.* To which is added, the character of the animadverter, and the Animadversions on Mr Congreve's answer to Mr Collier.

pp. [6] 1–185 [186], misnumbering 61 as "64", 64 as "61", 97–112 as "85–89 82–84 93–96 89–92"   L
John Barnes   1699

Advertised 7–9 Feb. 1699 (Hooker 21). Preface dated 1 Jan. and signed A.D., who says the book is written by a friend. Wing S 5160.

327 [DEFOE, DANIEL.] THE PACIFICATOR. A poem.

pp. [2] 1–14   L
[J. Nutt]   1700

Advertised 17–20 Feb. 1700 (Hooker 28). Wing D 839; Moore 23. Reprinted in A Second Volume of the Writings of the author of the True-Born Englishman (1705).

328 [BAKER, THOMAS.] AN ACT at Oxford. A comedy. By the author of the *Yeoman o' Kent.*

pp. [14] 1–11 11 12 14–60 [=60]   E
Bernard Lintott   1704

"The Epistle Dedicatory" discusses the Collier controversy.

329 PERSON OF QUALITY, THE, *pseud.* of John Dennis. The person of quality's answer to Mr. Collier's letter, being a disswasive [*sic*] from the play-house. In which are inserted the apologies of a young lady, and young gentleman, in behalf of the ladies and gentlemen who frequent the play-house.

pp. [2] 1–34   MH
Printed and are to be sold by the booksellers of London and Westminster   1704

Dated 1st January.
Reprinted, with an introduction, in Original letters, familiar moral and critical. In two volumes, *W. Mears (1721) and in Hooker, I.*

330 A REPRESENTATION of the impiety & immorality of the English stage, with reasons for putting a stop thereto: and some questions addrest to those who frequent the play-houses.

pp. [1–2] 3–24   L
Printed, and are to be sold by J. Nutt   1704

This work consists chiefly of select profane passages from plays which had appeared since Collier's Short View — *Lowe. Sometimes ascribed to Collier, for no good reason (Hooker, I, 501).*

331 ――――[another edition]

pp. [1–2] 3–24   L

Printed, and are to be sold by J. Nutt   1704

With changes in sig. B.

332 ――――*the third edition.

pp. [1–2] 3–24   MB

Printed, and are to be sold by J. Nutt   1704

With changes in sig. [B4]. A facsimile reprint was published by the Augustan Reprint Society (Series Three: Essays on the Stage No 2), (1947).

333 [COLLIER, JEREMY?] SOME THOUGHTS concerning the stage in a letter to a lady.

pp. [1–2] 3–13 [14–16 (bl.)]   MB

Printed, and are to be sold by J. Nutt   1704

Sometimes thought to be by Jos. Woodward, but ascribed by John Dennis to Collier (Hooker, I, 505); and, possibly, to some members of the S.P.C.K., by A. H. Scouten, "The S.P.C.K. and the Stage", TN 11 (1957) 60.

334 ――――[another edition]

pp. [1–2] 3–13 [14 (bl.)]   MH

London   1704

A facsimile reprint was published by the Augustan Reprint Society (Series Three: Essays on the Stage No. 2), 1947. Lacking a name in the imprint; perhaps the printing was done for the Society for the Promoting of Christian Knowledge, who ordered 200 copies to be distributed at the "principal coffee-houses". See A. H. Scouten, "The S.P.C.K. and the Stage", TN 11 (1957) 60.

335 [GILDON, CHARLES.] THE STAGE-BEAUX toss'd in a blanket: or, hypocrisie alamode; expos'd in a true picture of Jerry――a pretending scourge to the English stage. A comedy. With a prologue on occasional conformity; being a full explanation of the Poussin Doctor's book; and an epilogue on the reformers. Spoken at the Theatre-Royal in Drury-lane.

pp. [12] [1] 2–60 [61–64 (epilogue and advt.)]   DFo

Printed and sold by J. Nutt   1704

"I have Maidment's copy which is on large paper. It is a presentation copy to Rich and the dedication to him is signed by Charles Gildon who is thus proved to be the author." — Wilbur Eames, in a note in his copy of Lowe, now in the Folger Library.

336 VISITS from the shades: or, dialogues serious, comical, and political. Calculated for these times. Between I. Jo Hains's ghost, and the reforming Mr. Collier. II. Pryn, and the Loyal Observator. III. Nat. Lee the tragedian, and Colly Cibber, the plagiary. IV. Pasquil, and Heraclitus Ridens. V. Hobs, and the pious Mr. Asgill. VI. Ben Jonson, and Mr. Bak – – – r, the author of the *Oxford-Act*. VII. The famous Luxemburgh, and Mynheer Obd – – – m.

VIII. John Sobiesky, and the present king of P – – – d.
IX. Gustavus Adolphus, and the present King of S – – – n.

pp. [4] 1–70 [71–72 (comical advt.)]   L

                                                                      1704

337 ――――*second edition

                                                                   1709–10

Boyce *p. 166.*

Visits from the shades. Part II, (1705 [for 1704]) contains only one dialogue of theatrical interest, between "Heywood and Tom Durfey the songster".

338 PROLOGUE spoken at the first opening of the Queen's new theatre in the Hay-Market.

pp. [2]   L

Printed, and sold by B. Bragg   1705

On the reverse, The opening prologue paraphras'd in a familiar stile, for the better conception of the true meaning, and for the particular use of Mr. Jer. Collier.

339 FILMER, EDWARD. A defence of plays: or, the stage vindicated, from several passages in Mr. Collier's *Short view, &c.* Wherein is offer'd the most probable method of reforming our plays. With a consideration how far vicious characters may be allow'd on the stage. By Edward Filmer, Doctor of the Civil Laws.

pp. [16] 1–167 [168 (bl.)]   MH

Jacob Tonson   1707

Appears to have no connection with A defence of dramatick poetry (1698), with which it is sometimes confused. (See above no. 304).

✗ [Ralph, James.] The taste of the town . . . and the stage-entertainment fully vindicated from the exceptions of old Pryn, The Reverend Mr. Collier, Mr. Bedford and Mr. Law. 1731. *See no. 870.*

――――――――――――――

340 ANSTRUTHER, SIR WILLIAM. Essays, moral and divine; in five discourses: viz. I. Against atheism. II. Of providence. III. Of learning and religion. IV. Of triffling [sic] studies, stage-playes, and romances. V. Upon the incarnation of Jesus Christ, and redemption of mankind. By Sir William Anstruther of Anstruther, one of the Senators of the Colledge of Justice.

pp. [20] 1–238 [239–240 (bl.)]   E

Edinburgh: George Mosman   1701

341 AMES, *Dr.* WILLIAM. Stage-plays arraigned and condemned; by that eminent foreign theologist, namely William Ames, Doctor and Professor of Divinity of Francker in Friesland; in a solution by him given to this following question, Quest. What is to be thought of stage-plays?

pp. [1–2] 3–8   MH

Printed, and are to be sold by A. Baldwin   1702

342 BURRIDGE, RICHARD. *A scourge for the play-houses.

DFo

1702

343 FEILD, JOHN. An humble application to the Queen, and her great council, the Parliament of England, to suppress play-houses and bear-baitings, with all prophaness and immorality. By John Feild.

pp. [1–2] 3–15 [16 (bl.)]   L

Printed and sold by T. Sowle   1703

Dated: 10 Dec. 1702.

344 A LETTER from several members of the Society for Reformation of Manners. To the most reverend father in God Thomas by divine providence, Lord Arch-bishop of Canterbury.

pp. 1–4; head-title   L

[London]   [10 December 1704]

An attack on Vanbrugh, protesting against his being appointed manager of the new theatre in the Haymarket, on account of the notorious indecency and profanity of his plays, which are illustrated by quotations — Lowe.

345 BEDFORD, ARTHUR. Serious reflections on the scandalous abuse and effects of the stage: in a sermon preach'd at the parish-church of St. Nicolas in the city of Bristol, on Sunday the 7th day of January 170⅘. By Arthur Bedford, M.A. vicar of Temple-church in the aforesaid city.

pp. [26] 1–44 [45–46 (list of books against the stage)]   L

Bristol: printed and sold by W. Bonny   1705

See also below nos. 351, 377.

346 [BEDFORD, ARTHUR.] A SECOND ADVERTISEMENT concerning the profaneness of the play-house.

pp. [1] 2–16   L

[Bristol: printed by W. Bonny]   [1705]

347 BEDFORD, ARTHUR. The evil and danger of stage-plays: shewing their natural tendency to destroy religion, and introduce a general corruption of manners; in almost two thousand instances, taken from the plays of the last two years, against all the methods lately used for their reformation. By Arthur Bedford, M.A. chaplain to his grace Wriothesly Duke of Bedford; and vicar of Temple in the city of Bristol.

pp. [14] 1–227 [228 (bl.) 229 (errata) 230 (bl.) 231 (advt.) 232 (bl.)]; cancellans, pp. 1–2   L

Printed and sold by W. Bonny, and the Booksellers of Bristol and by Henry Mertlock, London.   1706

The head-title of the cancellandum, sig. B 1, reads: "Hell upon Earth: or, the Language of the Play-House". The

head-title of the cancellans is: "The Evil and Danger of Stage-Plays". Copies with cancellandum: L; MH. Also at MH is Lowe's own copy, with cancellans.

✠ A letter to a lady concerning the new play house. 1706. See no. 1503.

A strong attack on theatres and on the new Queen's Theatre in particular.

348 MELMOTH, WILLIAM. *New representations of the corruption of the stage.

1706

TN (1957), II, 258.

349 DE BOURBON, ARMAND. The works of the most illustrious and pious Armand de Bourbon Prince of Conti. With a short account of his life. Collected and translated from the French. To which are added some other pieces, and a discourse of Christian perfection, by the Archbishop of Cambray, never before published.

pp. [46] i–lix [lx (bl.)], [4] [1–2] 3–47 [48 (bl.)], ²[1–2] 3–74 [2], ³1–32 [2], ⁴1 [2–4], ⁵[1] 2–14 [2], ⁶1–29 [30 (bl.)] [8], ⁷1–49 [50 (bl.)] [8], ⁸1–14 [18], ⁹1–70 [2], ¹⁰1–13 [14 (bl.)] [2], ¹¹1–15 [16 (errata) 17–21 (advts.) 22 (bl.)]; t.p. in red and black   L

W. Bray   1711

With continuous signatures. Includes: "A treatise on plays and shews", "A second treatise against plays and shews", "The decrees of the councils concerning plays and publick shews", "The sentiments of the fathers, relating to plays and publick shews", "The opinion of St. Francis de Sales, concerning balls, plays, games, &c. with remarks upon it"; these items run from pp. [2] ⁶1–29 to pp. ¹⁰1–13 [14].

350 ——[reissued as] The works of Armand de Bourbon Prince of Conti, viz. I . . . V. A treatise of plays and shews, with the decrees of the councils, and the sentiments of the Fathers on that subject. With a short account of his life. Translated from the French. Also, A discourse of Christian perfection by the Archbishop of Cambray, and some other pieces, by which it may appear, how little the life of the player, and the diversion of the play-house in its present state is consistent with the profession of Christianity.

L

W.B.   1713

Cancellans title-page; pagination as no. 349.

351 BEDFORD, ARTHUR. A serious remonstrance in behalf of the Christian religion, against the horrid blasphemies and impieties which are still used in the English play-houses, to the great dishonour of Almighty God, and in contempt of the statutes of this realm. Shewing their plain tendency to overthrow all piety, and advance the interest and honour of the devil in the world; from almost seven thousand instances, taken out of the plays of the present century, and especially of the five last years, in defiance of all methods hitherto used for their reformation. By Arthur Bedford, M.A. chaplain to the most noble Wriothesly Duke of Bedford, and rector of Newton St. Loe in the county of Somerset.

pp. [i–ii] iii–xx, 1–383 [384 (advt.)]   L
Bath: Henry Hammond; Bristol: Richard Gavett; Oxford: Anth. Piesley   1719

For Bedford's other writings against the theatre see nos. 345–347; 377.

352 THE OCCASIONAL PAPER. Vol. III. Numb. IX. Of plays and masquerades. The second edition.

pp. [1–3] 4–28   MH
Em. Matthews; J. Roberts; J. Harrison; and A. Dodd
1719

The first edition formed a part of Vol. III of A collection of the occasional papers for 1716–18. There seems to be no connection between Willis's work (nos. 316–317 above) and the present item.

353 ———An essay on plays and masquerades. By the author of the Occasional Paper. The third edition.

pp. [1–3] 4–30 [31 (advts.) 32 (bl.)]   MB
Eman. Matthews   1724

With additions.

354 *STAGE PLAYS justly condemned in a letter to a friend in Scotland.

1720

An 8-page pamphlet, 8vo, with no title page. Dated "Calvinopoli, January 1720–21" — Lowe.

355 THE CONDUCT of the stage consider'd. Being a short historical account of its original, progress, various aspects, and treatment in the pagan, Jewish and Christian world. Together with the arguments urg'd against it, by learned heathens, and by Christians, both antient and modern. With short remarks upon the original and pernicious consequences of masquerades. Humbly recommended to the consideration of those who frequent the play-houses.

pp. [1–2] 3–43 [44 (advts.)]   MH
Printed Eman. Matthews   1721

Has been ascribed to Charles Owen.

356 HEIDEGGER, [JOHN JAMES]. Heydegger's letter to the Bishop of London.

pp. [1–3] 4–8   L
N. Cox   1724

A defence of masquerades, which Heidegger organised and which the Bishop had condemned in a sermon. For further references to masquerades etc. see nos. 864, 866, 869, 870 below.

357 [W., P.]? A SEASONABLE APOLOGY for Mr. H———g———r. Proving the usefulness and antiquity of masquerading from scripture, and prophane history. With observations on the several species of masks now in use: and likewise the report from the committee appointed to state and examine the advantages arising from our present masquerades.

pp. [6] 1–26   L
A. Moor   1724

Dedication signed P.W.

Law's Absolute Unlawfulness

358 LAW, WILLIAM. The absolute unlawfulness of the stage-entertainment fully demonstrated. By William Law, A.M.

pp. [2] [1] 2–50 [51–52 (advts.)]   L
W. and J. Innys   1726

359 vacant

360 ———The second edition

pp. [2] 2–50 [51–54 (advts.)]   E
W. and J. Innys   1726

✖ ———[abridged edition] A discourse shewing the danger and sinfulness of the stage. Edinburgh. 1751. *See no. 398.*

361 ———The third edition

pp. [1–3] 4–56   L
W. Innys and J. Richardson   1755

362 ———The fourth edition. Reflections on a favourite amusement.

pp. [1–3] 4–55 [56 (bl.)], ²1–3 [4 (bl.)]   L
[Dublin?]   1756

The Absolute Unlawfulness slightly abridged.

363 ———[another issue] Reflections on a favourite amusement. The fourth edition.

pp. [1–3] 4–55 [56 (bl.) 57 (post-script) 58 (bl.)]   L
n.p.   1756

The postscript is shorter than in the Dublin edition; it ends with the words "Sacrifice much more than even this Amusement to their Duty."

364 ———The absolute unlawfulness of the stage-enterainment [sic] fully demonstrated. By William Law, A.M. The fourth edition.

pp. [1–3] 4–56   MH
Londons [sic]: J. Richardson   1759

365 ———*another edition. Reflections . . .
Dublin   1764
  Lowe.

366 ———*fifth edition. The absolute unlawfulness. . . .
pp. 56   MB
M. Richardson   1765

367 ———The sixth edition
pp. [1–3] 4–56   L
G. Robinson   1773

  This copy bound up to form part of the L copy of the
  collected Works *(1775?). See note following no. 369*
  below.

368 ———A new edition
pp. [2] [1] 2–95 [96]   MH
Printed and sold by Kent and Co.; J. Denis; and by
Darton and Hervey   1798

369 AUDLEY, JOHN. *Abridgement of Law's
Unlawfulness of stage plays. By John Audley.
                                                          1802

  Mentioned by Allibone — Lowe. See also David Love
  Catalogue, no. 49.
  A collected edition of Law's works, consisting of reissued
  copies of individually published items, was published in
  about 1775, with a general title-page dated 1762.
  Different editions of The Absolute Unlawfulness *are*
  found in different copies of the collected edition. The
  collected edition was reprinted in 1892.

370 DENNIS, [JOHN]. The stage defended, from
scripture, reason, experience, and the common sense of
mankind, for two thousand years. Occasion'd by Mr.
Law's late pamphlet against stage-entertainments. In a
letter to ****** By Mr. Dennis.
pp. [i–iii] iv–xii, 1–34   L
N. Blandford   1726

  Reprinted in Hooker, II, 300–321.

371 O———, Mrs. S———. Law outlaw'd: or, A short
reply to Mr. Law's long declamation against the stage.
Wherein the wild rant, blind passion, and false reasoning
of that piping-hot Pharisee are made apparent to the
meanest capacity. Together with an humble petition
to the governours of the incurable ward of Bethlehem
to take pity on the poor distracted authors of the town,
and not suffer 'em to terrify mankind at this rate.
Written at the request of the orange-women, and for the
publick good, by the impartial pen of Mrs. S—— O———,
a lover of both houses. London, printed for the benefit
of the candle-snuffers, and sold by the booksellers of
London and Westminster.
pp. [1–3] 4–15 [16 (bl.)]   L
[A. Moore]   1726

372 PHILOMUSUS, S., *pseud.* *Mr. Law's Unlawfulness of the stage entertainment examin'd: and the
insufficiency of his arguments fully demonstrated. By
S. Philomusus, M.A.
pp. (1) 31   MB
Sold by J. Roberts   1726

373 THE ENTERTAINMENT of the stage, a cor-
rupt and sinful entertainment, contrary to the whole
nature of Christian piety, and constantly to be avoided
by all sincere Christians.
pp. [1–2] 3–44   L
Edinburgh: printed by Mr. James Davidson and
Company   1727

374 [RAMSAY, ALLAN.] SOME FEW HINTS, in
defence of dramatical entertainments.
pp. 1–24; head-title   E
[Edinburgh]   [1728]

✖ [Ralph, James.] The taste of the town . . . and the
stage-entertainment fully vindicated from the exceptions of old Pryn, the Reverend Mr. Collier, Mr. Bedford and Mr. Law. 1731. *See no. 870.*

———————————

375 [A] PRELUDE TO THE PLAYS: or, a few
serious questions proposed to the gentlemen, ladies, and
others, that frequent the play-house; which they are
desired to answer deliberately, to themselves, before
they go again to those diversions.
pp. [i–ii] iii–vi [7] 8–23 [24]   L
J. Roberts   1729

376 ———*second edition
pp. 24   MB
J. Roberts   1729

377 BEDFORD, ARTHUR. A sermon preached in
the parish-church of St. Butolph's Aldgate, in the city
of London, on Sunday the thirtieth day of November,
in the year of our Lord 1729. Occasioned by the erecting
of a play-house in the neighbourhood. Published at the
request of several of the auditors. By Arthur Bedford,
M.A. Chaplain to the worshipful the Haberdasher's
Hospital at Hoxton, and preacher of the afternoon
sermons on Sundays at St. Butolph's Aldgate, aforesaid.
pp. [2] [1–3] 4–40   L
Printed by Charles Ackers   1730

  For Bedford's other writings against the theatre see above
  nos. 345–347; 351. See also no. 870.

378 ——The second edition. The evil and mischief of stage-playing: [title continues as in 377].

pp. [1–3] 4–40   L

J. Wilford   1735

A reissue.

✠ Citizen, A, *pseud.* A letter to the right honourable Sir Richard Brocas, Lord Mayor of London. By a citizen. 1730. *See no. 158.*

Objecting to Goodman's Fields.

379 HORNECK, ANTHONY. *A testimony against stage-plays. Being an extract of a letter written to a young gentleman, by the reverend and learned Anthony Horneck, D.D. . . .

                   MH

[London]   1730

✠ Order forbidding undergraduates to attend . . . the new playhouse. Cambridge. 1730. *See no. 1587.*

380 COOKE, [THOMAS]. The triumphs of love and honour, a play, as it is acted by His Majesty's Servants, at the Theatre-Royal in Drury-Lane. To which are added, Considerations on the stage, and on the advantages which arise to a nation from the encouragement of arts. By Mr Cooke.

pp. [i–iii] iv–viii [9] 10–41 [42–46] 47–74 [75–76 (bl.)]; p. [45]: separate title of "Considerations on the stage."

                   DFo

J. Roberts   1731

The "Considerations on the stage" occupy pp. [43]–74; they were apparently not issued separately.

381 ANDERSON, REV. GEORGE. The use and abuse of diversions. A sermon on Luke xix. 13. With an appendix, shewing that the stage in particular is an unchristian diversion.

pp. [i–ii] iii–iv 5–59 [60 (bl.)]   L

Edinburgh: printed by R. Fleming and Company 1733

"If you take my preaching for the first publication, (and it is a verbal one) this is but a second edition with additions" (p. iii).

382 ——The second edition corrected

pp. [i–ii] iii–iv 5–59 [60 (bl.)]   L

Edinburgh: printed by R. Fleming and Company 1733

383 ANDERSON, REV. GEORGE. A reinforcement of the reasons proving that the stage is an unchristian diversion. Or, A vindication of the appendix to *The uuse* [sic] *and abuse of diversions, a sermon on Luke xix. 13.* In answer to the remarks of an anonymous author.

pp. [4] 1–149, 140 [for 150] [151–2 (bl.)]   L

Edinburgh: J. M.'Euen   1733

384 SOME REMARKS upon the Rev^d. Mr. Anderson's positions concerning the unlawfulness of stage-plays. In a letter to the author.

pp. [1–2] 3–27 [28 (bl.)]   L

Edinburgh: Gavin Hamilton   1733

385 PORÉE, CHARLES. An oration, in which an enquiry is made whether the stage is, or can be made a school for forming the mind to virtue; and proving the superiority of theatric instruction over those of history and moral philosophy. With reflections on operas. Spoke March 13, 1733, in the Jesuits College at Paris, in presence of the Cardinals de Polignac and de Bissy, the Pope's Nuncio, and several other persons of the highest distinction by Charles Porée of the Society of Jesus, translated into English by J. Lockman.

pp. [6] [1–3] 4–111 [112 (advt.)]   L

C. Davis   1734

Latin and English on opposite pages.

386 *A LETTER to Father Porée, and a preface prefixed to the tragedy of Oedipus.

n.d.   [1734?]

Recorded but not seen by Lowe.

387 WELL-WISHER, A, *pseud.* *The inconsistency of comedies and stage-plays with true Christianity proved by Scripture and authorities, by a well-wisher to the King and the people.

pp. 16   MB

[London]   [1735]

388 *A COMPANION TO THE THEATRE: or the usefulness of the stage to religion, government, & the conduct of life. . . .

                   1736

Chase.

389 THE FLIGHT of religious piety from Scotland, upon the account of Ramsay's lewd books, &c and the Hell-bred play-house comedians, who debauch all the faculties of the souls of our rising generation.

pp. 1–16   L

[Edinburgh]   [1736?]

In verse.

390 OF THE USE AND IMPROVEMENT OF THE STAGE. An epistle to Charles Fleetwood, Esq.

pp. [1–2] 3–16   DFo

T. Cooper   1737

391 GORDON, ——. *An essay on publick sports and diversions, to which is subjoined an epilogue, addressed to the nobility, gentry, &c. of Edinburgh, spoke by

Mr. Este, on Monday the 17th of January, 1743, at the Taylors' Hall, Cowgate.
Edinburgh 1743

Lowe.

392 WERENFELS, [SAMUEL]. The usefulness of dramatic interludes, in the education of youth: an oration spoke before the masters and scholars of the University of Basil, by Mr. Werenfels. Translated from the Latin by Mr. Duncombe.
pp. [i–iii] iv, [1] 2–27 [28]; vignette on t.p. L
R. Dodsley 1744

Translated by William Duncombe, dramatist and miscellaneous writer.

393 A SERIOUS ADDRESS to the frequenters of play-houses: or rather, serious motives to draw people to a just consideration of the folly, sin and danger of encouraging, and being present at those unlawful assemblies. Earnestly recommended to parents, matrons, guardians, mistresses of boarding schools — and all others whom it may concern.
pp. [2] [1–3] 4–21 [22] L
[London?]: printed in the ever memorable year of the Scottish Rebellion 1746

394 THE VENGEANCE OF GOD, and the impenitency of man, demonstrated, in the country's being laid waste in blood and misery; while the inhabitants, particularly in Edinburgh, are rioting in lewdness and vice, and encouraging that source of wickedness, the play-house. With an absract [*sic*], shewing the danger and sinfulness of the stage.
pp. [i–ii] iii–xv [xvi], 1–31 [32] E
Edinburgh: [printed by T. Lumisden and J. Robertson] 1747

395 HARLEQUIN METHODIST. To the tune of, *An old woman cloathed in grey.*
bs., illus. L
Sold at the Print and Pamphlet Shops [1750?]

With an engraving of Harlequin preaching. The tune is used for the first air in The Beggar's Opera.

396 BETSON, A. Miscellaneous dissertations historical, critical, and moral, on the origin and antiquity of masquerades, plays, poetry, &c. with an enquiry into the antiquity of free masonry, and several other old heathenish customs. As also, whether plays conduce more to the improvement or corruption of morals: which is most excellent, a poem in rhyme or in blank verse; and finally, what spirit introduc'd masquerades originally into the world. With several other curious enquiries. By A. Betson, O.A.M.
pp. [2] [i–iii] iv–vii [viii] [9] 10–105 [106 (bl.)] MH
Printed for T. Meighan and sold by C. Corbett, the publisher [1751]

Published February — LS.

397 ———*[another edition] Miscellaneous dissertations, historical, critical, and moral in the origin and ambiguity of masquerades, plays, poetry, &c.
DFo
n.p. [1807?]

398 A DISCOURSE shewing the danger and sinfulness of the stage. Extracted from the works of an eminent author [William Law].
pp. [2] 1–31 [32] E
Edinburgh: printed by T. Lumisden and Company 1751

399 [CAMPBELL, JOHN.] A LETTER from the Prince of the Infernal regions, to a spiritual lord on this side the great gulf, in answer to a late invective epistle levelled at his Highness, containing many material and intertaining observations, worthy to be perused not only by his many friends, (witness the late earthquakes) but likewise by his few enemies in London, Westminster, and ten miles round.
pp. [2] [1–2] 3–29 [30] E
Printed and published for the benefit of the publick 1751

399.1 AN ADDRESS to the ladies on the indecency of appearing at immodest plays.
pp. [2] [1] 2–22 L
R. Griffiths 1756

✠ Some considerations on the lawfulness and expediency of frequenting the theatre at Exeter. Exon. 1756. *See no. 1593.*

400 [LOBB, THEOPHILUS.] *AN ANSWER to that important question, whether it is lawful for the professors of the Christian religion to go to plays? With some soliloquies annexed.
pp. (1), 32 MB
J. Buckland 1757

Douglas Controversy

For the controversy aroused in Edinburgh by Home's play *see below EDINBURGH nos. 1860–1904.*

---

401 THE UNLAWFULNESS of the stage evinced; or, the immoralities and prophaneness of the theatre exposed. In a series of papers, selected from the most celebrated authors, both antient and modern. Addressed to the inhabitants of the city of Glasgow.

pp. [1] 2–40; head-title; published in five numbers   GU
Glasgow: printed by John Bryce   [1757?]

402 WITHERSPOON, JOHN. A serious enquiry into the nature and effects of the stage. Being an attempt to show, that contributing to the support of a public theatre, is inconsistent with the character of a Christian. By John Witherspoon, M.A. Minister of the Gospel in Beith.

pp. [4] 1–72   L
Glasgow: printed by J. Bryce and D. Paterson   1757

Lefèvre *128.*

403 ———*[another edition]
Glasgow   1762

Lowe.

———[American edition] New York: Whiting and Watson, 1812.

Includes also A sermon, on the burning of the theatre at Richmond &c. by Samuel Miller.

404 ———[another edition] A serious inquiry into the nature & effects of the stage [originally published in 1757]; with A letter respecting play-actors, [first published in 1793,] by the Rev. John Witherspoon, D.D., some time minister of the gospel at Paisley, and late president of Princeton College, New Jersey. With preface by the Rev. D. T. K. Drummond, B.A., Oxford, and memoir of the author, by the Rev. William Moffat, M.A., Cairnie.

pp. [i–iii] iv–xxxvi, [1] 2–100   L
Edinburgh: Lyon & Gemmell   1876

"A letter" was first published (with "A serious enquiry") in New York.
Collected editions of Witherspoon's works were published in America (2nd edition, Philadelphia: William W. Woodward, 1802); and in Edinburgh (1804–5, 1815).

405 *A DISCOURSE concerning plays and players, occasioned by a very late and very extraordinary sermon.
                                                    1759

Recorded but not seen by Lowe.

406 ROUSSEAU, JEAN JACQUES. A letter from M. Rousseau, of Geneva, to M. D'Alembert, of Paris, concerning the effects of theatrical entertainments on the manners of mankind. Translated from the French.

pp. [i–ii] iii–xii, [1] 2–190 [191–192 (advts.)]   MH
J. Nourse   1759

The French edition was published in Amsterdam, 1758. Reprinted in Kenrick's translation in The Miscellaneous Works of Mr. J. J. Rousseau, T. Becket and P. A. de Hondt, 1767, Vol. III; The Works, Edinburgh: John Donaldson, 1774, Vol. VIII.

The "Minor" Controversy 1760

For the controversy over Foote's The Minor see nos. 2776–2796.

———

407 GENTLEMAN OF THE UNIVERSITY OF OXFORD, A, *pseud. of Sir* Richard Hill. An address to persons of fashion, containing some particulars relating to balls: and a few occasional hints concerning play-houses, card-tables, &c. In which is introduced the character of Lucinda, a lady of the very best fashion, and of most extraordinary piety. By a gentleman of the University of Oxford.

pp. [i–iii] iv [5] 6–48   L
George Keith   1761

408 ———the second edition, revised, corrected, and enlarged.

pp. [i–iii] iv–vi [7] 8–58   L
George Keith   1761

409 ———the third edition, revised, corrected, and enlarged

pp. [i–iii] iv–vi [7] 8–63 [64 (bl.)]   L
George Keith   1761

410 ———*fourth edition, enlarged

pp. 86   MB
Dublin: W. Watson   1761

411 ———An address to persons of fashion, relating to balls... By the author of Pietas Oxoniensis. The sixth edition. Revised, corrected, and very much enlarged.

pp. [i–iv] v–xvi [17] 18–176   MH
Shrewsbury: printed by J. Eddowes   1771

———[American editions] Boston: printed by W. McAlpine, 1767; Baltimore: Cole and I. Bonsal, et al., 1807.

412 GEERE, JOHN. Serious considerations on plays, games, and other fashionable diversions. Shewing the sinfulness, and dangerous tendency thereof. By John Geere, of Farnham, Surry.

pp. [i–iii] iv [5] 6–47 [48]   GM
Guildford: printed for the author, by Charles Martin
                                                    1763

413 H[UME], S[OPHIA]. A short appeal to men and women of reason; distinguished by titles of worldly honour; or by riches exclusive of titles; who may be walking according to the course of this evil world, living in the pleasures thereof, and frequenting theatres, balls, &c. by S.H.

pp. [1–2] 3–35 [36]   L
Bristol: printed by E. Farley   1765

✖ Bristol Theatre: a poem. Bristol. 1766. *See no. 1582. See also no. 1581*

✖ [Bonar, John, *solicitor of excise*]. Considerations on the proposed application to His Majesty and to Parliament, for the establishment of a licensed theatre in Edinburgh. [Edinburgh. 1767]. *See no. 1916.*

✖ Hill, *Sir* Richard. A letter from Richard Hill . . . containing some remarks on a letter signed 'A Player'. Shrewsbury. 1767. *See no. 1685.*

414 THE STAGE THE HIGH ROAD TO HELL: being an essay on the pernicious nature of theatrical entertainments; shewing them to be at once inconsistent with religion, and subversive of morality. With strictures on the vicious and dissolute characters of the most eminent performers of both sexes. The whole enforced and supported by the best authorities, both antient and modern.

pp. [*12*] [1] 2–43 [44 (bl.)]   L
W. Nicoll; and J. Williams   [1767?]

415 [CHATER, JOHN]. ANOTHER HIGH ROAD TO HELL. An essay on the pernicious nature and destructive effects of the modern entertainments from the pulpit. Occasioned by a pamphlet, entitled *The stage the high road to Hell, &c.*

pp. [*12*] [1] 2–35 [36 (bl.)]   L
T. Vernor and J. Chater   1767

Preface signed "Ignotus". Said by W. Wilson, The history and antiquities of dissenting churches and meeting houses, in London, Westminster, and Southwark (1808–1814), III, 112–113, to be by John Chater, minister, bookseller, and novelist.

416 [FLITCROFT, HENRY?]. THEATRICAL ENTERTAINMENTS consistent with society, morality, and religion. In a letter to the author of *The stage the high road to Hell.* Shewing that writer's arguments to be fallacious, his principles enthusiastic, and his authorities (particularly from the ancients) misconstrued and perverted. With a counter-dedication to the Rev. Mr. Madan.

pp. [*4*] [i] ii–ix [x], [1] 2–32   L
Sold by Baker and Leigh; Dodsley; and Flexney   1768

Dedicated to Colman and Garrick.

417 LUCIFER'S LETTER to Tersa, capital of Bellicosa, concerning religion and the theatre: offering sage proposals for the improvement of both. Translated

from a curious old M.S. very scarce, and humbly presented as a New Year's gift to all the learned and pious in Britain.

pp. [1–3] 4–17 [18]   L
Edinburgh   1769

An attack on the habits of society, especially in the matter of churches and theatres — Lowe.

✖ An epistle to Henry Mossop, Esq; on . . . the drama, and the present state of the Irish stage. With some observations on Mr. Sheridan's plan of education for the young nobility . . . Dublin. [*ca* 1770]. *See no. 1793.*

418 ★THE BRITISH THEATRE, and the Church of England contrasted; or, an attempt to shew the inconsistency of stage entertainments with the profession of Christianity.

    MB
Sheffield: sold by John Smith   [177–?]

419 ——★[another edition]
Sheffield   1803

See American edition.

——[American edition] Philadelphia: Solomon W. Conrad, 1804

Imprint reads: Printed at Sheffield (G.B.) 1803 Reprinted by Solomon W. Conrad . . .

420 HAYWARD, Mr. ★Reflections on the innocence and usefulness of the stage. By Mr. Hayward.

[Edinburgh]: W. Gray   [1770]

Baine, Theatre licentious, second edition, pp. 37, 40.

The "Minor" Controversy 1770
For the controversy in Edinburgh over the production of Foote's The Minor see below, nos. 2797–2803.

———

421 THE ADVANTAGES of theatrical entertainments briefly considered.

pp. [1–2] 3–16   DFo
Glasgow   1772

An ironical defence of the stage.

✖ Griffith, *Mrs.* Elizabeth. The morality of Shakespeare's drama illustrated. 1775. *See no. 2964.*

422 HILL, ROWLAND. By command of the king of kings! And at the desire of all who love his appearing. —At the theatre of the universe; on the eve of time, will be performed the Great Assize: or, Day of Judgement.
bs. in red and black   L
Printed by George Cooke   [1800]

422.1————[another edition]

bs., headed: The following is a copy of the bill written by the late Rev. Rowland Hill, which was stuck up at Richmond. On Saturday, 4th of June, 1774. . . .

Hull: sold at Simpson's   L [1840?]

422.2————[another edition]

b.s., headed as 422.1

E. Palmer and Son   L [1848]

422.3————[another edition]

bs. with royal arms, headed: [Copy of the Rev. Rowland Hill's celebrated playbill.]

G. J. Stevenson   L [1868]

423 ORTON, [*Rev.*] J[OB]. *A serious dissuasive from frequenting the playhouse. By J. Orton.

pp. 22   MB

Shrewsbury: printed by J. Eddowes and sold by J. Buckland, and T. Longman. London   1776

Reprinted in Job Orton, Discourses on practical subjects *(John Heaton. 1814), pp. 476–492; and in* The practical works of the Rev. Job Orton, S.T.P. *(Thomas Tegg, 1842), pp. 302–312.*

424 THE SINFULNESS OF PLAYS.

pp. [1–2] 3–8   L

Canterbury: printed for the author by J. Grove [1780?]

425 THE FOLLOWING EXTRACTS from the writings of pious men, of different denominations, and at different periods of time, exposing the evil and pernicious effects of stage plays, and other vain amusements, are recommended to the serious perusal of all who profess christianity.

pp. [1–2] 3–19 [20]   L

Dublin: printed by Robert Jackson   1785

P. 17: "*The foregoing extracts were handed to the Mayor of Waterford, with the following letter, which, being printed by his permission, is now annexed thereto*"; *letter signed by Thomas Ross and John Pemberton, two American Quakers.*

426 THOUGHTS on the entertainments of the stage. Second edition.

pp. [1–2] 3–24   L

Leeds: J. Binns   1786

427 DUNCAN, *Rev.* JOHN. The lawfulness of the stage, enquired into. By the Rev. John Duncan, of Winbourn Minster, Dorset.

pp. [i–v] vi–x, [1] 2–77 [78 (bl.)]   L

Printed and sold by T. Wilkins   1787

428 SIMPSON, *Rev.* DAVID. A discourse on stage entertainments. By the Rev^d. David Simpson, M.A.

pp. [i–vii] viii [9] 10–88   L

Birmingham: printed and sold by M. Swinney   1788

Reissued in David Simpson, Discourses on several subjects, *(Birmingham, 1789).*

429 EXTRACTS from the writings of divers eminent authors, of different religious denominations; and at various periods of time. Representing the evils and pernicious effects of stage plays, and other vain amusements.

pp. [1–3] 4–22   L

Sheffield: printed by J. Gales   1789

————[American edition] Philadelphia: Joseph James, *printer*, 1789.

✠ Murray, Lindley. The sentiments of pious and eminent men . . . 1789. *See nos. 486–491 below and Addenda.*

430 HILL, ROWLAND. Aphoristic observations proposed to the consideration of the public, respecting the propriety of admitting theatrical amusements into country manufacturing towns. By Rowland Hill, A.M. late of St. John's College, Cambridge.

pp. [2] [1–2] 3–87 [88 (bl.)] [4]   GU

J. Mathews   1790

431 MANNERS, NICHOLAS. Remarks on the Memoirs of Tate Wilkinson, Esquire, manager of the Theatres-Royal, York and Hull. By Nicholas Manners.

pp. [1] 2–12; head-title   L

n.p.   [1790?]

432 KENDALL, JOHN. Remarks on the prevailing custom of attending stage entertainments: also on the present taste for reading romances and novels: and on some other customs; submitted, with a heart overflowing with good will, to the notice and consideration of the professors of the Christian name, in the different religious societies; by John Kendall.

pp. [1–5] 6–31 [32 (bl.)]   MH

Printed by James Phillips   1794

433 ————the second edition. To which is added, Remarks on subjects not noticed before.

pp. [1–3] 4–24   L

Printed by James Phillips   1796

434 ————the third edition. To which are added, Remarks on subjects not noticed in the former editions.

pp. [1–3] 4–24   L

Printed and sold by W. Phillips   1801

435 KILHAM, *Rev.* ALEXANDER. The hypocrite detected and exposed; and the true Christian vindicated and supported: in a sermon, preached from a passage in a play-bill, December 15, 1793, in the Methodist chapel in this city. With a reply, in an appendix, to a paper signed Civis, concerning dancing. And a post-script, with remarks, on Mr Lee Lewes's answer. By Alexander Kilham, Minister of the Gospel.

pp. [i–iii] iv [5] 6–48   L
Aberdeen: printed by J. Chalmers & Co.   1794

Dated 6 Jan. 1794.

436 LEWES, CHARLES LEE. The stage, and the pulpit. The player and the preacher. Or, a serio-comic answer to Mr. Kilham, preacher. By Charles Lee Lewes, comedian.

pp. [1] 2–8; head-title   GM
[Aberdeen?]   [1794]

Dated 4 Jan. 1794.

437 HILL, ROWLAND. An expostulatory letter to the Rev. W. D. Tattersall, A.M. Rector of Westbourne, Sussex, and Vicar of Wotton-Underedge, Gloucester-shire. In which the bad tendency of the admission of stage amusements, in a religious and moral point of view, is seriously considered. By Rowland Hill, A.M. late of St. John's College, Cambridge.

pp. [1–5] 6–44   L
Printed by A. Paris   1795

438 DEFENCE OF THE STAGE. A speech in verse, delivered in a public assembly, upon the following question: "Do public and private theatrical representa-tions tend to vitiate or improve the morals of mankind?"

pp. [1–3] 4–14   MH
J. S. Jordan   1798

439 THE DEMORALISING INFLUENCE of the playhouse.

pp. [1] 2–12; caption title   MB
Edinburgh: William Oliphant   [18—]

440 [PORTER, JANE?] A DEFENCE of the pro-fession of an actor.

pp. [2] [1–3] 4–42   L
W. Miller   1800

Dedicated to Sarah Siddons. The half-title reads: "A defence, &c." Said by Lowe to be by "Miss Porter", i.e. Jane Porter or her sister Anna Maria.

441 HILL, ROWLAND. A fifth village dialogue on the evil nature and effects of stage plays by the Rev. R. Hill, A.M.

pp. [1] 2–20; head-title   GU
T. Williams   [1801]

Reprinted in Village Dialogues, *by Rowland Hill, which reached 24 editions by 1824, and was published in an abridged edition by The Religious Tract Society [1858].*

442 COBBIN, I[NGRAM]. Stage playing immoral, vain, and dangerous in its tendency. A sermon, preached at South Molton, Devon, on Sunday evening, April 4, 1802. By I. Cobbin. Published by request.

pp. [i–iii] iv–vi [7] 8–31 [32]   L
London: printed by W. Nicholson . . . and sold by T. Williams . . . Cobbin, Warren Street, Tottenham Court Chapel; Woolmer, Exeter; and the author . . .
                                                   [1802]

Against strolling players in South Molton.

443 GREEN, EDWARD. Observations on the drama, with a view to its more beneficial effects on the morals and manners of society. In three parts. By Edward Green, corresponding member of the literary and philosophical society of Manchester.

pp. [i–ii] iii–iv, [1] 2–60   MH
Cadell and Davies   [1803?]

444 ——second edition

pp. [1] 2–60   L
Cadell and Davies   [1814]

✂ Thirlwall, *Rev.* Tho. Oct. 17, 1803. Royalty Theatre. A solemn protest against the revival of scenic exhibitions and interludes at the Royalty Theatre. By the Rev. Tho. Thirlwall. A member of the Society for the Suppression of Vice. 1803. *See nos. 1505–1507.*

445 OBSERVATIONS on the effect of theatrical representations, with respect to religion and morals: occasioned by the preface to the third volume of the works of Mrs. H. More.

pp. [i–iii] iv [5] 6–32   L
Bath: printed by J. Hume   1804

The Ryland/Clayton Controversy 1804–1805

446 [CLAYTON, JOHN, *the elder*]. A COUNTER AND IMPARTIAL STATEMENT of circumstances relative to a late withdrawment from a dissenting inde-pendent church.

pp. [1–3] 4–48   L
London: printed by Bye and Law; Bucklersbury: sold by Thomas Conder   1804

John Clayton was the minister of the church from which Mr and Mrs Richard Ryland withdrew in consequence of a dispute over dancing and the theatre.

447 ——*[another edition] To which are added notes and an appendix, designed as a reply to Mr. Rylands "Remarks."

pp. 63   MB
Biggs & Co.   1805

448 CHRISTIAN, OBADIAH. A letter to John Clayton, the elder, occasioned by his Counter and impartial statement, &c. By Obadiah Christian, one of the people called Quakers.

pp. [3–5] 6–16   L
R. Ogle   1805

449 FOUR LETTERS, occasioned by two pamphlets, recently published, entitled "A statement," and "A counter and impartial statement of circumstances relative to a late withdrawment from a dissenting independent church."

pp. [1–3] 4–35 [36]   L
Printed by Biggs & Co.   1805

Dated 28 December 1804 and initialled A.Z.

❌ Harvey, Daniel Whittle. Letters [o]ccasioned by a pamphlet. 1805. *See below no. 456.*

450 [CLAYTON, JOHN, *the younger*]. *LETTERS, occasioned by a recent controversy between R. R. Esq. and the Rev. J. C. Second edition enlarged.

pp. (4), 68   MB
Biggs & Co.   1805

451 vacant

452 [RYLAND, RICHARD]. *A SECOND EDITION of "The statement", "The address", and "The remarks" on the "Counter-statement", relative to a late withdrawment from a dissenting independent congregation. With a postscript by the writer of the statement.

pp. (2) 202   MB
Bye & Law   1805

Rowland Hill's Warning to Professors *1805–1810*

453 HILL, ROWLAND. A warning to professors; containing aphoristic observations on the nature and tendency of public amusements. By Rowland Hill, A.M.

pp. [i–v] vi–viii, [1] 2–76   MB
Printed by Joseph Hartnell . . . sold by M. Jones, and J. Wallis T. Conder, T. Williams and at Surry-Chapel.
                                                  1805

Preface dated February 5, 1805.

454 ——second edition, corrected

pp. [i–v] vi–viii, [1] 2–76   MB
Printed by Joseph Hartnell . . . sold by M. Jones and J. Wallis T. Conder, T. Williams, Champante and Whitrow.   1805

455 ——[another edition] with remarks on some anonymous publications, in two letters to the Rev. George Burder. By Rowland Hill, A.M.

pp. [i–iii] iv–vi [7] 8–81 [82–84 (bl.)]   L
Page and Sons   1833

456 HARVEY, DANIEL WHITTLE. *Letters [o]ccasioned by a pamphlet, recently published by Rowland Hill, entitled, "A warning to professors, containing aphoristic observations on the nature and tendency of public amusements"; with concise remarks on a late withdrawment from a dissenting independent church.

pp. 46   MB
Jordan & Maxwell   1805

The late remarks on the "withdrawment from a dissenting independent church" relate to the controversy between Richard Ryland and the Rev. John Clayton (see nos. 446–452 above).

457 INDEPENDENT, AN. *The dissenters appeal, against the attacks of the Rev. Rowland Hill, in the conclusion of a book, entitled "A warning to professors, containing aphoristic observations on the nature and tendency of public amusements." By an Independent.

pp. viii, 38.   MB
Conder   1805

458 MᶜCULLA, *Rev.* V. An address to Rowland Hill, A.M. minister of Surrey Chapel, Southwark, with some needful remarks on his pamphlet, entitled, "A warning to professors." By V. MᶜCulla, minister of the Gospel, Nethaneel Chapel, Eden Street, Tottenham Court-Road.

pp. [1–5] 6–47 [48]   L
Printed for the author   [1810?]

A furious, but not specially intelligible attack on Hill. It seems as if some sectarian spite dictated it — Lowe. Refers only briefly to Hill's views on the theatre.

Burder's Lawful Amusements *1805*

459 BURDER, GEORGE. Lawful amusements; a sermon, preached at the Thursday-evening lecture Fetter-Lane, January 10, 1805, by George Burder.

pp. [4] [1] 2–36   L
Printed by Biggs and Co.   1805

460 ——The second edition. With an appendix.

pp. [4] [1] 2–47 [48]   L
Printed by Biggs and Co.   1805

461 A LETTER to the Rev. George Burder, occasioned by his sermon on lawful amusements; preached at the Thursday evening lecture, Fetter Lane, Jan. 10, 1805.

pp. [1–3] 4–36 L
H. D. Symonds, Hatchard & R. Bickerstaffe [1805]

462 POSTSCRIPT to the letter to the Rev. G. Burder, occasioned by his appendix to his sermon on lawful amusements.
pp. [4] [1] 2–39 [40] L
H. D. Symonds, Hatchard, Conder, and Mathews 1805

---

463 STYLES, JOHN. An essay on the character, immoral, and antichristian tendency of the stage. By John Styles.
pp. [i–v] vi–xi [xii], [1] 2–132 L
Isle of Wight: printed for the Author at the Medina Press, Newport, by R. Tilling; London: sold by Williams and Smith 1806

464 ———An essay on the character and influence of the stage on morals and happiness. Second edition, with an appendix
pp. [i–v] vi–xii, [1] 2–188 GM
Messrs. Williams and Smith 1807
Appendix contains "Strictures on an article in the fifth volume of The Annual Review, *which is a critique on the preceding essay, and avowedly a defence of the stage."*

465 ———An essay on the character and influence of the stage. Third edition, newly arranged and considerably enlarged
pp. [i–v] vi–xi [xii] [13] 14–234 [235 ("By the same author.") 236 (bl.)] L
Williams and Son 1815
The half-title reads: An essay on the stage.

466 ———[another issue] Third edition, newly arranged and considerably enlarged.
pp. [i–v] vi–xii [13] 14–234 [235 ("By the same author.") 236 (bl.)] MH
Williams and Son 1816

✠ ———[abridged edition] The immoral and anti-Christian tendency of the stage exhibited . . . Selected principally from Dr Styles's "Essay on the stage". Newcastle. 1819. *See below no. 525.*

467 ———The stage: its character and influence. By John Styles, D.D. Fourth edition, revised.
pp. [i–iii] iv–vi, [1] 2–210 L
Thomas Ward and Co. 1838

468 PHILOKOSMOS, *pseud.* *The fashionable world reformed; being reflections on theatrical representations, &c. By Philokosmos.
1807
Recorded but not seen by Lowe.

The Halesworth Controversy

469 AUDI ALTERAM PARTEM, hear me first. [second issue]
pp. [1–3] 4–8 L
Halesworth: printed by T. Tippell 1808
With postscript dated 19 Sept. added after publication of no. 471. Attributed to J. G. Morgan, but possibly through reading too much into the MS note on verso of title of this item, number one in the collection, "The Halesworth Controversy" in L, which states only that Morgan formed the collection. Written just before "the season for the Players coming", to forestall John Dennant's avowed intention of preaching against them.

470 vacant

471 DENNANT, J[OHN]. An appeal to the candour and common sense of the public, respecting the present controversy on the subject of plays. By J. Dennant.
pp. [1] 2–12 L
[Halesworth: Harper, printer] [1808]
Dated Oct 8 1808. A reply to To the printer *(see below no. 480). Dennant was pastor of the Independent church at Halesworth.*

472 DENNANT, JOHN. *Five minutes intrusion on your time before you go to a play.
Halesworth: Harper 1808
Referred to in no. 475.

473 *GENTLE STRICTURES on the Halesworth Review, by the author of the "Dunciad Anatomised."
[Halesworth] [1808]
Chase.

474 [HUGMAN, JOHN, Junr.]. THE HALESWORTH DUNCIAD; satire on pedantry. Addressed to the censor of the stage.
pp. [1–3] 4–12 L
Halesworth: printed by T. Tippell 1808
So ascribed in MS note on copy in L. "The censor" is Dennant.

475 THE HALESWORTH REVIEW from 14th September to 14th October, 1808.
pp. [1–3] 4–18 L
Halesworth: printed by T. Tippell [1808]

476 [DENNANT, JOHN]. A LETTER to the writer of an anonymous pamphlet in defence of plays.
pp. [1] 2–8 L
[Halesworth: Harper, printer] [1808]
Signed J. Dennant, and dated 22 Sep. 1808.

477 [MORGAN, J. G. and JAMES JERMYN] THE PAMPHLETS.

bs.   L

Halesworth: Tippell, printer   [1808]

478 *A POEM on the combin'd defence of the stage, at H——h, or a satire on vanity, dogmatism and malice . . .

Halesworth   1808

Chase.

479 [MORGAN, J. G. ?]. STANZAS objurgatory and interrogatory.

pp. [1–3] 4–7 [8]   L

Halesworth: printed by T. Tippell   [1808]

With MS annotations.

480 [MORGAN, J. G. and JAMES JERMYN.] TO THE PRINTER.

pp. [1] 2–8   L

[Halesworth: Tippell, printer]   [1808]

Reveals that the company was led by Fisher and Scragg.

———

✄ Four letters on the theatre, written during the dispute between the public and the proprietors of the new Theatre Royal, in Covent Garden, on its opening in 1809 . . . [1809]. *See no. 1219.*

481 PLUMPTRE, JAMES. Four discourses on subjects relating to the amusement of the stage: preached at Great St. Mary's Church, Cambridge, on Sunday September 25, and Sunday October 2, 1808; with copious supplementary notes. By James Plumptre, B.D. Fellow of Clare Hall.

pp. [i–iii] iv–xv [xvi (bl.)], [1] 2–184   L

Cambridge: printed by Francis Hodson, for Messrs. F. C. and J. Rivington, St. Paul's Church-yard; and sold by J. Hatchard, No 190, Piccadilly, London; J. Deighton, and J. Nicholson, Cambridge; and Cook and Parker, Oxford.   1809

Rev. James Plumptre, (1770–1832) [was] a somewhat eccentric clerical defender of the stage. One of his eccentricities was an essay to prove that Hamlet was written as a censure on Mary Queen of Scots!—Lowe.

482 PLUMPTRE, JAMES. An inquiry into the lawfulness of the stage. Taken principally from "Four discourses on subjects relating to the amusement of the stage, preached at Great St. Mary's Church, Cambridge, on Sunday September 25, and Sunday October 2, 1808"; and from the preface to "The English drama purified": published in 1812. By James Plumptre, B.D. Fellow of Clare Hall.

pp. [1–3] 4–32   L

Cambridge: printed by F. Hodson; and sold by F. C. and J. Rivington, No 62 St Paul's . . . and J. Hatchard, No 190 Piccadilly, London; and J. Deighton, and J. Nicholson and Son, Cambridge.   1812

In answer to Law's Absolute unlawfulness.

483 [ALEXANDER, ANNE TUKE]. REMARKS on the theatre, and on the late fire at Richmond, in Virginia.

pp. [1–3] 4–32   L

York: for the author   1812

484 ———second edition

pp. [1–3] 4–24   L

York: W. Alexander   1814

485 MANSEL, ROBERT. Free thoughts upon Methodists, actors, and the influence of the stage; with an introductory letter to Mrs.——, of ——Castle, Glamorganshire, upon the origin of the drama, &c. &c. &c. By Robert Mansel, of the Theatres Royal York and Hull. Likewise, A discourse on the lawfulness and unlawfulness of plays; written by the learned Father Caffaro, divinity professor at Paris.

pp. [i–iii] iv [v–xii], [1] 2–206 [207 (errata) 208 (bl.)] L

Hull: printed for the author, and J. Craggs   1814

For an earlier edition of Caffaro's Discourse see Motteaux, Beauty in distress, 1698 (see above no. 303). For Mansel's conflict with the Rev. Thomas Best see below nos. 508–510.

———[American edition] A defence of the drama, containing Mansel's Free thoughts, extracts from the most celebrated writers, and a discourse on the lawfulness and unlawfulness of plays, by the celebrated Father Caffaro, divinity professor at Paris. New York: George Champley, 1826

486 MURRAY, LINDLEY. *Sentiments of pious and eminent persons on the pernicious tendency of dramatic entertainments and other vain amusements; with a few reflections on the same subject subjoined.

Printed by William and Samuel Graves   1815

STR. *First published ca. 1789 (see Addenda).*

487 ———*[another edition]

Dublin: Graiseberry and Campbell   1816

Smith.

488 ———a new edition

pp. [i–iii] iv [5] 6–24   MB

Printed by William and Samuel Graves   1817

"No. 18. 2nd Ed." on the title-page.

489 ——A new edition

pp. [i–iii] iv [5] 6–24   L

Printed by William and Samuel Graves, Sherborne-Lane; for the Tract Association of the Society of Friends
1823

"No. 18. 4th Ed." on the title-page.

490 ——[another edition]

pp. [1–3] 4–16   L

The Tract Association of the Society of Friends 1855

"No. 18" on the title-page.

491 ——[another edition] (Tract association of the Society of Friends, General series no. 18)

pp. [1–3] 4–16   GM

Tract Association of the Society of Friends   1864

——[American edition] Extracts from the writings of divers eminent authors, of different religious denominations; and at various periods of time, representing the evils and pernicious effects of stage plays, and other vain amusements. By Lindley Murray, with some additions. Philadelphia: Benjamin & Jacob Johnson, 1799.

Smith records further British and American editions.

492 QUISNAM?, *pseud.* *The budget, or a collection of letters which recently appeared in the public prints on theatrical amusements. To which is added The stage, a familiar epistle in mock verse. By Quisnam?

MH

Cork   1815

A reprint of correspondence which appeared in some of the Cork papers for and against the stage. The "familiar epistle" is addressed to the Cork Advertiser — Lowe.

493 THE STAGE. Veluti in speculum.

pp. [1–3] 4–13 [14]   L

Huddersfield: J. Brook, printer   1816

Pamphlets on the Death of Cummins 1817–1818

494 REMARKS ON THE THEATRE, occasioned by the awful death of Mr. Cummins, which took place at the play-house, in Leeds, on the evening of the 20th of June.

pp. [1–3] 4–16   L

Leeds: G. Walker   1817

495 *REMARKS ON THE THEATRE, occasioned by the awful death of Mr. Cummins, which took place at the playhouse in this town, the 20th of June.

pp. 3–34   MB

Leeds: Dewhirst   1817

496 ——*second edition

pp. 34   MB

Leeds: Dewhirst   1817

497 CHURCHMAN, A, *pseud. of* Thomas Greenwood. An answer to a pamphlet in defence of stage amusements, intituled "Further remarks on the theatre", by "A Churchman". Second edition, with an appendix.

pp. [1–4] 5–36   LdP.

Leeds: printed by Inchbold & Gantress; sold by T. Inchbold   [1817]

498 [HOLMES, R. B.]. FURTHER REMARKS on the theatre, occasioned by the awful death of Mr. Cummins, which took place at the play-house, in this town, on the evening of the 20th of June.

pp. [1–7] 8–35 [36]   MH

Leeds: printed by G. Wright   1817

On p. [5]: "The following trifle is addressed (not dedicated) to those whom it may concern". By R. B. Holmes, the Curate of St. Paul's Church, Leeds according to Leeds Public Library. Dated 18 July 1817.

499 CHURCHMAN, A, *pseud. of* Thomas Greenwood. *More remarks on the theatre: addressed to those who take the trouble to read them.

pp. 36   MB

Leeds: Wright   1818

Rev. Thomas Best's Sermons (1818–1865)

Best preached against the stage annually from 1817–1864.

500 BEST, *Rev.* T[HOMAS]. Two sermons on the subject of theatrical amusements, preached at Sheffield, on Sunday, Nov. 2, 1823, by the Rev. T. Best, A.M., minister of St. James's Church.

pp. [1] 2–16; head-title   L

[Sheffield: James Montgomery, printer]   [1823]

501 ——[another edition] Sermons on the amusements of the stage, preached at St. James's Church, Sheffield, by the Rev. T. Best, A.M.

pp. [i–iii] iv–x [xi–xii], [1] 2–305 [306]   L

Sheffield: George Ridge; London: Hamilton and Adams   1831

Includes revised versions of Two Sermons [1823]. Preface: "most of the following Discourses were printed in newspapers or otherwise, at the time of their delivery." Now published by a reformed theatre-goer who has already "printed and gratuitously circulated" 1000 copies of a discourse of Best's which had altered his convictions.

502 BEST, *Rev.* THOMAS. Theatrical amusements. Sermon preached at St. James's Church, Sheffield, on Sunday, the third day of November, 1833, by the Rev. Thomas Best.

pp. [1–3] 4–14 [15–16 (bl.)]   L
Wakefield: John Stanfield, printer   [1833]

503 BEST, *Rev.* THOMAS. Theatrical amusements: a sermon preached by the Rev. Thomas Best, M.A. Oxon. At St. James's Church, Sheffield, on Sunday, October 29, 1848.

pp. [1] 2–12; head-title   L
[Sheffield: G. Ridge, printer]   [1848]

504 BEST, *Rev.* THOMAS. A sermon on the amusements of the stage, preached in St. James's Church, Sheffield, on Sunday, Nov. 16, 1851. By the Rev. Thomas Best, M.A., Oxon.

pp. [1–3] 4–15 [16]   L
Sheffield: J. Pearce, Jun.   1851

505 BEST, *Rev.* THOMAS. Theatrical amusements. A sermon on theatrical amusements, preached at St. James's Church, Sheffield, on Sunday morning, November 4th, 1860, by the Rev. Thomas Best, M.A., Oxon., incumbent.

pp. [1–3] 4–14 [15 (imprint) 16 (bl.)]   L
Sheffield: George Ridge, printer   [1860]

506 BEST, *Rev.* THO[MA]S. *The sinners in Zion are afraid.* A sermon preached at St. James's Church, Sheffield, on Sunday morning, November 6th, 1864, by the Rev. Thos. Best, M.A. Oxon., incumbent.

pp. [1–3] 4–19 [20]   L
Sheffield: Pawson and Brailsford   1864

507 BEST, *Rev.* THOMAS and *Rev.* R. E. ROBERTS, *ed.* Sermons on theatrical amusements: delivered in St James's Church, Sheffield. By the late Rev. Thomas Best, M.A., Oxon. Edited by the Rev. R. E. Roberts, M.A., Rector of Richmond, Yorkshire, and Rural Dean.

pp. [i–iii] iv–ix [x], [1] 2–293 [294]   L
London: Seeley, Jackson, and Halliday; Sheffield: Pawson & Brailsford   1865

Contains sermons for 1832–37, 39–42, 46, 47, 49–51.

508 [MANSEL, ROBERT.] A SHORT STRUGGLE for stage or no stage; originating in a sermon, preached by the Reverend Thomas Best, in St. James's Church, Sheffield.

pp. [1–4] 5–16   L
Sheffield: W. Todd, printer   [1818]

A republication, by Robert Mansel, of letters which appeared in the Sheffield Mercury *and other papers. On the title page is the motto, "Facts, but not comments, if you please." — Lowe. A compilation, privately printed by Mansel, manager of the Sheffield Theatre, containing his letters to the press replying to a sermon of Best's, and further correspondence on both sides by various hands, not however, by Best. For an earlier defence of the stage by Mansel see no. 485.*

509 LAYMAN, A, *pseud.* "Facts, but not comments;" being strictures on the stage: in a letter to Robert Mansel, Esq. on his attempt to represent the Saviour of the world as an approver of theatrical exhibitions. By a layman.

pp. [1–5] 6–24   L
Sheffield: printed for the author   1819

510 STAGE-PLAYS considered, and contrasted with the Bible.

pp. [1–2] 3–14 [15 (text) 16 (bl.)]   L
Sheffield: printed for the author   1819

511 CALVERT, F[REDERICK] B[ALTIMORE]. A defence of the acted drama, in a letter addressed to the Rev. Thomas Best, M.A. of Sheffield, by F. B. Calvert, formerly of St. Edmund's College, now of the Theatres Royal York and Hull.

pp. [1–3] 4–29 [30 (bl.)]   L
Hull: printed by Thomas Topping   1822

An answer to a sermon preached by Mr. Best, as reported in the Sheffield Mercury — Lowe.

512 [B., F.] THEATRE versus conventicle; or, the drama attacked and defended: containing Mr. Calvert's letters in defence of the stage, to the Rev. T. Best, of Sheffield; with the subsequent controversy, in the Leeds Independent of 1824.

pp. [i–iii] iv, [1–3] 4–112   SP
Hull: printed and sold by I. Wilson; London: sold by Baldwin, Cradock and Joy.   1826

513 LACY, T[HOMAS] H[AILES]. The theatre defended chiefly in reference to the last annual sermon of the Rev. Thomas Best against theatrical amusements. By T. H. Lacy, manager of the Sheffield Theatre.

pp. [2] [i] ii, [5] 6–23 [24]   SP
Sheffield: Whitaker & Co.   1840

Three letters to the Sheffield Iris.

514 LACY, T[HOMAS] H[AILES]. Three letters by T. H. Lacy, manager of the Sheffield Theatre in reference to the last annual sermon of the Rev. Thomas Best, preached on Sunday, October 30, in St. James's Church, against theatrical amusements.

pp. [1] 2 [3] 4–12   SP
[Sheffield]: Whitaker and Co., Printers   [1841]

The letters are to the Sheffield Iris.

---

515 THOMSON, *Rev.* ANDREW. The sin and danger of being "lovers of pleasure more than lovers of God" stated and illustrated in two discourses on 2 Timothy iii. 4. By the Rev. Andrew Thomson, A.M. Minister of St. George's, Edinburgh.

pp. [1–5] 6–148   L
Edinburgh: William Blackwood; London: T. Cadell
and W. Davies   1818

516 ———[another edition] Lovers of pleasures more
than lovers of God two discourses by the late Andrew
Thomson, D.D. Minister of St. George's Church,
Edinburgh republished with an introductory essay by
Robert S. Candlish, D.D. Principal of the New College,
Edinburgh, and Minister of Free St. George's Church.

pp. [4] [1] 2–64   L
Edinburgh and London: William Blackwood and Sons
     1867

*Price ninepence, but on back printed paper cover: "A
considerable reduction in the price of this book will be given
when purchased in quantities for distribution."*

"Mr. Clement and Mr. Mortimer" 1819–1834

517 THE STAGE. Three dialogues between Mr.
Clement and Mr. Mortimer.

pp. [1] 2–36; head-title   L
The Religious Tract Society   [1819?]

*By the head-title, "No. 112". Theophilus Clement and
Albert Mortimer are fictional characters.*

518 ———[second edition]

pp. [1] 2–36; head-title   MH
Printed by P. White and sold by F. Collins; and J. Nisbet
     [1819?]

*By the head-title, "No. 112" [of the Religious Tract
Society's tracts]; on p. 2, "2nd Ed 10,000".*

519 ———[another edition]

pp. [1] 2–36; head-title   MH
[Liverpool: printed and sold by R. Tilling]   [ca. 1830?]

By the head-title, "No. 198."

520 ———[another edition]

pp. [1] 2–36; cover-title   MH
The Religious Tract Society. No. 112.   [1834]

521 THEATRICAL AMUSEMENTS; or, a dialogue
between Mr. Clement and Mr. Mortimer in which the
present state of the stage is fully considered: with
interesting anecdotes.

pp. [1–2] 3–8; cover-title; illus.   MH
The Religious Tract Society   [ca. 1820]

522 ———[another edition] (The Second Series
Tracts of the Religious Tract Society No. 542)

pp. [1–2] 3–8; illus.   L
The Religious Tract Society   [1830?]

This is a version of Dialogue Three of The Stage. Three
dialogues between Mr. Clement and Mr. Mortimer
(no. 517 above.)

523 PLUMPTRE, JAMES. A letter to the author of
a tract entitled "The stage: three dialogues between
Mr. Clement and Mr. Mortimer." Published by the
Religious Tract Society. By James Plumptre, B.D.
Vicar of Great Gransden, Huntingdonshire; and
formerly Fellow of Clare Hall, Cambridge.

pp. [1–3] 4–21 [22 23–24 (advts.)]   L
Cambridge: printed by James Hodson. And sold by
Deightons and Nicholsons, Cambridge; F. C. and J.
Rivington, St. Paul's Church-Yard; J. Hatchard,
Piccadilly, London; and T. Lovell, Huntingdon   1819

524 CLERGYMAN, A, *pseud.* Testimonies of pagans,
of infidels, of Christian Fathers, of councils, of states and
sovereigns, and of members of the Church of England,
on the nature and tendency of theatrical amusements. By
a clergyman. Second edition, enlarged.

pp. [1–3] 4–16   L
Sheffield: printed by James Montgomery   1819

525 †THE IMMORAL AND ANTI-CHRISTIAN
TENDENCY of the stage exhibited, in a variety of
extracts from Sir M. Hale, Sir John Hawkins, Wm.
Wilberforce, Esq. Archbishop Tillotson, Dr. Wither-
spoon, Rousseau, and others. Selected principally from
Dr Styles's "Essay on the stage." (No. 5. N.R.T.S.)

pp. [1–3] 4 9 [10] 11–12   NwP
Newcastle: printed by Edward Walker   1819

526 ———*third edition
Newcastle   1823
   STR.

527 ———[another edition] exhibited in extracts
from various authors. (Religious Tract Society No. 32)

pp. [1] 2–8; head-title   L
The Religious Tract Society   [ca. 1830?]

528 MORRIS, WILLIAM, Motives of ministerial
animadversion, on theatrical exhibitions, being the
substance of two lectures, delivered by William Morris,
at Zion Chapel, St. Helier.

pp. [2] [1–3] 4–24   MB
Jersey: printed by W. Marston   1829 [for 1819]

Occasioned by Bickerstaff's The Hypocrite. *See also
nos. 536 and 540.*

✖ Layman, A, *pseud.* Remarks, occasioned by the
perusal of a pamphlet, entitled Motives of ministerial
animadversions on theatrical exhibitions. By a layman.
Second edition. Jersey. 1823. *See below no. 536.*

⌘ Pack, James. Some account of the life and experience of James Pack . . . late celebrated actor, . . . but now, by the grace of God, a disciple and follower of the Lord Jesus Christ. 1819. *See no. 3392.*

529 TESTIMONIES on the nature and tendency of theatrical amusements.

pp. [1] 2–16; head-title MB

[Dublin: printed by M. Goodwin] [*after* 1816. 1819?]

530 ———[another edition?] *Testimonies on the nature and tendency of theatrical amusements

pp. 12

n.p. n.d.

Thomas Thorp Catalogue 610, item 1462.

531 *WARD, VALENTINE. The stage: a dangerous and irreconcilable enemy to Christianity.

pp. 45 AP

Aberdeen: Chalmers 1819

532 ———The stage, a dangerous and irreconcilable enemy to Christianity, asserted and proved, in a letter addressed to a comedian. By Valentine Ward, minister, Aberdeen. Second edition.

pp. [1–5] 6–45 [46 (postscript) 47 (advts.) 48 (bl.)] L

Aberdeen: printed by D. Chalmers 1819

533 ———*[another edition]

Dublin 1824

STR.

⌘ [Macarthy, Eugene] A brief defence of the stage, against the attacks of the Methodists and other sectarians . . . intended chiefly as a reply to . . . Mr. Valentine Ward. Dublin. 1824. *See no. 541.*

534 SUTOR, ALEXANDER. An essay on the stage: in which the arguments in its behalf, and those against it, are considered; and its morality, character, and effects illustrated. By Alexander Sutor, surgeon.

pp. [*10*] [i–iii] iv–ix [x] [11] 12–166 MB

Aberdeen: printed by D. Chalmers & Co. 1820

Cf. no. 542 below.

535 *THE THEATRE. Its injurious influence on the morals of the community; and the consequent obligations of those who make a serious profession of the Gospel, stated and illustrated.

Edinburgh 1820

Lowe.

⌘ [Mangin, *Rev.* Edward?] The Bath stage: a dialogue. Bath. 1822. *See no. 1553.*

⌘ Calvert, F. B. A defence of the acted drama, in a letter addressed to the Rev. Thomas Best of Sheffield. Hull. 1822. *See no. 511.*

536 LAYMAN, A, *pseud.* Remarks, occasioned by the perusal of a pamphlet, entitled Motives of ministerial animadversions on the theatrical exhibitions, purporting to be the substance of two lectures, delivered at Zion Chapel, by William Morris. By a layman. Second edition.

pp. [1–3] 4 [2] [5] 6–31 [32] MH

Jersey: printed by P. Payn 1823

Preface dated 2nd January 1823; text dated 15th April 1819. Ascribed to one "M.T." in an old hand in the copy seen (MH). See also above no. 528.

537 M'NICOLL, DAVID. A rational enquiry concerning the operation of the stage on the morals of society. By David M'Nicoll.

pp. [1–5] 6–88 L

Newcastle upon Tyne: printed by Edward Walker and sold by Messrs. Charnley, Finlay, Horn, &c. &c. 1823

Enlarged from contributions to The Newcastle Courant. *See also no. 543.*

⌘ A melancholy event improved. [Newcastle. 1823]. *See no. 1656.*

538 TELL-TRUTH, TIM, *pseud.* *Tim Tell-Truth on the state and influence of the acting drama. 1823

Recorded but not seen by Lowe.

539 *TWENTY REASONS for not attending the theatre nor contributing towards its support.

pp. 12 SP

Sheffield: printed and sold by J. Blackwell; Newcastle-upon-Tyne: sold by T. Horn. 1823

540 ACTOR, AN, *pseud.* Shakespeare, and honest King George, versus Parson Irving and the puritans; or, taste and common sense, refuting cant and hypocrisy. By an actor. Embellished with a coloured plate, by Cruikshank.

pp. [1–3] 4–19 [20]; pl. [front.] by Robert Cruikshank L

C. Harris 1824

Refers to the King's commanding a performance of The Hypocrite *in answer to Irving's preaching. See also above no. 528.*

541 [MACARTHY, EUGENE.] *A BRIEF DEFENCE of the stage, against the attacks of the Methodists and other sectarians; in a letter to a friend, intended chiefly as a reply to a pamphlet, written by

Mr. Valentine Ward, entitled "The stage; a dangerous and irreconcilable enemy to Christianity."

pp. (3) 36   MB
Dublin: Underwood   1824

Signed E.M.

542 DWIGHT, TIMOTHY. An essay on the stage: in which the arguments in its behalf, and those against it, are considered; and its morality, character, and effects illustrated. By Timothy Dwight, S.T.D. L.L.D. Late president of Yale College.

pp. [10] [i–iii] iv–ix [x] [11] 12–166   L
Middletown, Connecticut: printed; London: reprinted for Sharp, Jones & Co.   1824

Cf. no. 534 above.

543 Mc'NICOLL, DAVID. Pro & con: or, the claims of the stage briefly and candidly examined. By David Mc'Nicoll.

pp. [1–3] 4–15 [16 (bl.)]   L
Stockton: printed by T. Jennett   1824

See also no. 537.

544 [EAST, TIMOTHY.] ON THEATRICAL AMUSEMENTS.

4 parts. pp. [1–2] 3–12 + [1–2] 3–12 + [1–2] 3–12 + [1–2] 3–12   L
Francis Westley   1824

The four parts are nos. 87, 90, 91, and 93 of The Evangelical Rambler (nos. 1–108, 1824–1825). There were new editions of The Evangelical Rambler in 1836 and 1857.

545 *A SERIOUS ADDRESS to the frequenters of theatres.
                                                   1824

In the corner of the title-page is "No. 160," I presume the number of a Tract — Lowe.

546 TO THE THEATRICAL PUBLIC.

bs., illus.   MH
C. Harris   1824

Begins, "When we perceive fanatics endeavouring, by pious cant and specious hypocrisy, to undermine every laudable institution. . . ." Includes a version of the eight questions in The Play! The Fair! The Races! (No. 568), with replies. Signed 'Jaspero.'

Bunn and Angell James

John Angell James, a leading Birmingham pastor, attacked the theatre in A Christian father's present to his children, and Youth warned (1824). The Controversy continued until September or later, with the publication of Anti-Cant, an answer to Bunn's [?] Cant.

547 vacant

548 BUNN, ALFRED. A letter to the Rev. J. A. James, of Carr's lane meeting house. With notes, critical, religious, and moral. By A. Bunn, Manager of the Theatre Royal, Birmingham.

pp. [4] [1] 2–34   L
Birmingham: printed for the author   1824

The letter is dated 26 July 1824.

549 ——third edition
pp. [4] [1] 2–34   L
Birmingham: printed for the author   1824

550 ——*seventh edition
                                                   MB
Birmingham: for the author   1824

551 ——eighth edition
pp. [4] [1] 2–34   MH
Birmingham: printed for the author   1824

552 [BUNN, ALFRED?]* CANT. A satirical poem by a late member of Carr's Lane Meeting House.
                                                   BP
Birmingham   1824

553 CHURCHMAN, A, *pseud.* of Alfred Bunn. The reprover admonished. Being the substance of a sermon, which may be preached any where. By a churchman.

pp. [1–5] 6–35 [36]   MH
Birmingham: J. Drake   1824

Attributed to Bunn by Urwin. A reply to J. A. James's The scoffer admonished (August, 1824).

553.1 HUDIBRAS THE YOUNGER, *pseud.* *Anti-Cant: an extra-satirical burlesque; with notes that may be useful. By Hudibras the younger.

pp. 24   BP
Birmingham   1824

In reply to nos, 548, 552.

554 JAMES, JOHN ANGELL. *The scoffer admonished. Second edition.

pp. 53   BP
Birmingham   1824

555 MEMBER OF THE CHURCH OF ENGLAND, A, *pseud.* A letter to Mr. Alfred Bunn, manager of the Theatre Royal, Birmingham; being a review of his epistle to the Rev. J. A. James. By a member of the Church of England.

pp. [1–5] 6–22 [23–24 (bl.)]   L
Birmingham: B. Hudson   1824

Dated 23 August 1824 and signed "Mercator".

556 [PARKES, JOSEPH.] THE PLAGIARY "warned". A vindication of the drama, the stage, and public morals, from the plagiarisms and compilations of the Revd. John Angell James, Minister of Carr's Lane Chapel, Birmingham: in a letter to the author.

pp. [i–iii] iv–vii [viii], [1] 2–113 [114] L

Birmingham: J. Drake; London: Baldwin, Cradock, and Joy 1824

Dated at end Oct. 30. 1824.

557 ———second edition, with alterations

pp. [1–2] 3–59 [60]; alternative vol. pp. [217–218] 219–275 [276] L

Birmingham and London 1824

Pamphlet no. 49 in Vol. 25 of The Pamphleteer *(1825), issued separately. Initialled I.P.*

558 [BUNN, ALFRED.] *THE REFORMER admonished.

BP

Birmingham [1824?]

---

559 BOWDEN, GEORGE. The life and conversion of George Bowden, formerly a player; wherein is set forth the glory of God's distinguishing grace, through the revelation of Jesus Christ, to him when in bondage of soul. Written by himself, for the glory of God and the comfort of His tried people.

pp. [i–iii] iv–vii [viii] [9] 10–95 [96] L

Printed for the author, by Gold and Walton 1825

560 ———second edition

pp. [i–iii] iv–vii [viii] [9] 10–95 [96] GU

Palmer and Higham 1826

561 *A DISSUASIVE from frequenting the theatre. By the author of "An essay on early rising."

pp. 33 MB

Wellington, Salop: Houlston 1825

562 MORISON, JOHN. *Fashionable amusements the bane of youth: a sermon, preached Dec. 9, 1824, before the churches associated in the Pimlico, Chelsea, and Brompton monthly lecture. Third edition.

pp. 58 MB

Westley 1825

✠ [Mangin, Edward]. A letter to Thomas Moore, Esq. on the subject of Sheridan's *School for Scandal*. Bath. 1826. *See no. 3504.*

✠ [B.,F.] Theatre versus conventicle containing Mr. Calvert's letters . . . to the Rev. T. Best of Sheffield, with the subsequent controversy. Hull. 1826. *See no. 512.*

563 HURN, WILLIAM. *A glance at the stage, by the light of truth, and for the benefit of the public.

pp. 36

Ipswich 1827

STR.

564 WAIT, WILLIAM PIGUENIT. An answer to certain letters addressed to the Rev. W. P. Wait, Rector of Norton Malreward, and Chewstoke, in the County of Somerset, on the subject of the Chew-Magna theatricals.

pp. [i–iii] iv–ix [10–11] 12–59 [60 (bl.)] L

Bristol: printed and published for the author by J. Chilcott 1827

Wait stuck up the tract Why do you not go to the play? *(no. 568?) on the turnpike gate at Chew-Magna, and received letters of disagreement; tract and letters here reprinted. On title-page: "The profits arising out of the sale of this pamphlet, if any, will be given to the Society for the Suppression of Vice and Immorality."*

565 THE SIN and danger of frequenting the theatre. A discourse, preached in the parish church of Sunderland, on Sunday, the 16th of March, 1828.

pp. [1–3] 4–18 L

Sunderland: printed by Reed and Son 1828

A sermon on Exodus xxiii, 2.

✠ Smith, *Rev.* George Charles. Dreadful catastrophe. Destruction of the Brunswick Theatre. 1828. *See nos. 1127–1130. See also no. 1125.*

✠ Morris, William. Motives of ministerial animadversion. 1829 [for 1819]. *See no. 528.*

566 [GREVILLE, ROBERT KAYE]. THE DRAMA brought to the test of Scripture, and found wanting.

pp. [1–3] 4–131 [132] L

Edinburgh: William Oliphant 1830

Preface signed "R.K.G."

567 GREVILLE, ROBERT KAYE. An appeal to Christians on the subject of dramatic entertainments. By Robert Kaye Greville, LL.D.

pp. [1] 2–12; ptd. wrappers E

Edinburgh: William Oliphant 1830

568 THE PLAY! The Fair! The Races!

bs. MH

Ipswich: Piper, printer [*ca.* 1830?]

Eight reasons for not going to plays, fairs, or races. In prose, within a black border, with an introductory poem:
Why don't you go to the Play? *or the* Fair?
Because I'm afraid there's no good *doing there. . . .*
See also nos. 546, 564.

✖ Best, *Rev.* Thomas, Sermons on the amusement of the stage. Sheffield. 1831. *See no. 501.*

569 KEMPTHORNE, *Rev.* JOHN. A warning against attendance at the theatre, the fair, and the race-course, being the substance of a sermon preached last year in the parish church of St. Michael, in the city of Gloucester, previous to the annual recurrence of revelry in or near that city; and now published in an enlarged form, by Rev. John Kempthorne, B.D., rector of St. Michael's.

pp. [i–iii] iv [5] 6–35 [36 (colophon)]   L
Gloucester: printed and sold by W. Verrinder   1831

570 NORTON, THEODORE. *Verbum sap. Or, time passed in coffee houses, hells, theatres, etc. A poem.
F. C. Westley   [1832]
STR.

✖ Best, *Rev.* Thomas. Theatrical amusements. Sermon preached at . . . Sheffield. Wakefield. [1833]. *See no. 502.*

✖ Hill, Rowland. A warning to professors . . . with some remarks on some anonymous publications, in two letters to the Rev. George Burder. 1833. *See no. 455.*

571 [C., W. C.,] *AN ESSAY on the evil tendency of the theatre. Read before one of the Young Men's Societies in Edinburgh, August 21, 1834.

Edinburgh   1834

Preface initialled "W. C. C." — Lowe.

572 MAN OF THE WORLD, *pseud.* A parody and answer to W. C. C.'s Essay on the evil tendency of the theatre. Dedicated to Sir Andrew Aguecheek, M.P. Issued for the diffusion of useful knowledge, and for the confusion of useless essayists. By a "Man of the World;" but not a "Macsycophant."

pp. [2] [1–3] 4–37 [38]; paper covers   MH
Edinburgh: printed for the author   1834

573 DENMAN, JOHN [DOE]. The drama vindicated; with copious notes. By John Denman, Esq. S.C.L. of St. John's College, Cambridge.

pp. [4] [1–3] 4–120   GU
Cambridge: W. H. Smith   1835

574 NANTZ, F[REDERIC] C[OLEMAN]. An actor's vindication, of his profession; by F. C. Nantz, comedian, (member of the Norwich Company.) In reply to a sermon, preached by the Reverend John McCrea, on Sunday evening, March 19th. 1837, at Saint Margaret's Church, King's Lynn.

pp. [1–5] 6–18   MH
Lynn: printed and sold by W. Whittingham   [1837]

Printed on green paper, and dated 21 March 1837.

575 BENNETT, *Rev.* JOHN B. The evil of theatrical amusements, stated and illustrated in a sermon, preached in the Wesleyan-Methodist Chapel, Lower Abbey-St., on Sunday, November 4, 1838; with an appendix. By Dr. John B. Bennett. Published by request.

pp. [i–iii] iv [5] 6–48   L
Dublin: John Fannin and Co.   1838

576 ——*second edition
pp. 48   DN
London: John Mason; Dublin: John Fannin   1839

Reprinted in Exeter Hall lectures. *Vol. II (Lectures delivered before the Young Men's Christian Association 1846–47), pp. [211]–236, (James Nisbet & Co., 1875). See also no. 580 below.*

577 BINNEY, *Rev.* THOMAS. Objections to theatrical amusements. A discourse, delivered on Wednesday evening, April 4, 1838, by the Rev. Thomas Binney, at Wells Street Chapel, Oxford Street. (Corrected by the author of Animadversions on the stage, quoted by the reverend lecturer.)

pp. [119] 120–134   L
James Paul   1838

In: A course of lectures on important practical subjects, addressed especially to young men, delivered at Wells Street Chapel, Oxford Street, in the year 1838. By ministers in connexion with the Christian Instruction Society.

578 WILKS, THOMAS EGERTON. Letter to the Rev. T. Binney, in defence of the drama; showing the futility of the objections made by him against theatrical amusements, in his lecture recently delivered in Wells Street Chapel. By Thomas Egerton Wilks, author of several popular dramas.

pp. [1–3] 4–16   L
William Sams   1838

579 ——second edition. Revised and altered
pp. [1–3] 4–16   L
William Sams   1838

580 CALCRAFT, JOHN WILLIAM, *pseud.* of John William Cole. A defence of the stage, or an inquiry into the real qualities of theatrical entertainments, their scope and tendency. Being a reply to a sermon entitled "The evil of theatrical amusements stated and illustrated," lately published in Dublin, and preached in the Wesleyan methodist chapel in lower Abbey-Street, on Sunday, November 4th, 1838, by the Rev. Dr. John B. Bennett. Including an examination of the authorities on which that sermon is founded. By John William Calcraft, lessee and manager of the Theatre Royal, Dublin.

pp. [i–iii] iv–vii [viii], [1] 2–175 [176 (errata)]; cancellans, pp. 163–164   MH
Dublin: Milliken and Son   1839

See also no. 575 above.

581 HALFORD, J. *A reply to a sermon on the theatre, preached in Richmond church, on Sunday, August 25, 1839, by the Rev. Edward Hoare, A.M. With brief observations on the drama, dedicated to the inhabitants of Richmond and its vicinity. By J. Halford, (comedian).

pp. 15   MB

Pattie   1839

✠ Lacy, Thomas Hailes. The theatre defended chiefly in reference to the last annual sermon of the Rev. Thomas Best. Sheffield. 1840. *See nos. 513, 514.*

✠ A.B.C., *pseud.* The drama, the press, and Mr. Macready. [1842]. *See nos. 3278, 3279.*

Praises Macready's attempts to make the theatre respectable

582 *THE OPERA TICKET; a dialogue.

pp. 52   MB

Nisbet & Co.   1843

Censures the theatre, particularly opera and ballet.

Rev. John East of Bath

583 EAST, *Rev.* JOHN. The pulpit justified, and the theatre condemned: in a letter to some members of the Association for Increasing the Attractions and Promoting the Improvement of Bath. By the Rev. John East, M.A., Rector of St. Michael's, Bath.

pp. [1–3] 4–47 [48]   L

Hamilton, Adams, & Co.   1844

Written after the second edition of The theatre *(no. 585).*

584 EAST, *Rev.* JOHN. The theatre: a discourse on theatrical amusements and dramatic literature, delivered in St. Michael's Church, Bath, on Sunday evening, January VII., MDCCCXLIV. By the Rev. John East, M.A., Rector of the Parish. Delivered by request.

pp. [1–3] 4–28   TnSA

Hamilton, Adams, & Co.   1844

585 ———second edition

pp. [1–3] 4–28   L

Hamilton, Adams & Co.   1844

"Delivered by request" is omitted from title-page.

586 CHURCHMAN, A, *pseud. of.* P. R. Saumarez? A temperate answer to the sermon of the Rev. John East M.A., Rector of St. Michael's Bath, delivered on the day of 7th January 1844. By a churchman.

pp. [1–3] 4–11 [12]   BhP

Bath: printed by John and James Keene.   1844

587 OBSERVER, AN, *pseud.* *The theatre, as it is: or, remarks upon a pamphlet, entitled "The Bath theatre vindicated." By an observer.

pp. 20   MB

Hamilton, Adams & Co.   1844

588 RESIDENT, A, *pseud.* The Bath Theatre vindicated from the aspersions of the Rev. John East, M.A., Rector of St. Michael's, Bath. By a resident.

pp. [1–3] 4–16   L

Bath: printed by John and James Keene   1844

Three editions came out in the same year — Loewenberg.

589 VISITOR, A, *pseud.* The theatre. Observations on a recent pamphlet, entitled *The pulpit justified, and the theatre condemned,* by the Rev. John East, M.A., Rector of St. Michael's Bath: in a letter, addressed and dedicated, by permission, to Thomas Noon Talfourd, Esq., Serjeant at Law, by a visitor.

pp. [1–7] 8–24   L

London: Longman, Orme, and Co.; Bath: Collings   1844

Letter dated from Bath 29 March 1844.

---

590 SMITH, EDWARD. The theatre: its history and moral tendency. A paper read at the Islington Literary and Scientific Institution, February 2, 1844. By Edward Smith.

pp. [i–v] vi–vii [viii] [9] 10–42   L

Printed for private circulation.   [1844]

591 THOUGHTS ON THE THEATRE: a letter addressed to the Honourable Her Majesty's Justices of the Peace for the County of Renfrew; and suggested by the late discussions in the Court of Petty Sessions, on an application by Mr. G. F. Adams, of Greenock, for license to erect a theatre in Paisley.

pp. [1–3] 4–8   MH

Paisley: Caldwell and Son   1844

592 [WEBSTER, *Rev.* GEORGE EDIS.] THE THEATRE and the church; or, Gospel truth to be realized.

pp. [4] [1] 2–15 [16]   L

Woodbridge: printed and sold by J. Loder   1845

593 VILLIERS, *Rev.* H[ENRY] MONTAGU. Balls and theatres; or, the duty of reproving the works of darkness. A sermon, by the Hon. and Rev. H. Montagu Villiers, M.A. preached at the Church of St. George, Bloomsbury, on Sunday morning, March 15, 1846.

pp. [1–5] 6–20   L

James Nisbet and Co.   1846

"Price 2d., or 14s. per 100".

594 ——*seventh edition

1853

Lowe.

595 A PLEA FOR THE DRAMA.

pp. [1–5] 6–15 [16]   MH

Printed and published for the author by J. W. Thomas
1847

Printed on grey paper. Preface dated November.

☒ Best, *Rev.* Thomas. Theatrical amusements: a
sermon preached . . . at . . . Sheffield. [Sheffield. 1848.]
See no. 503.

☒ Drummond, *Rev.* David Thomas Kerr. Memoir
of Montague Stanley. Edinburgh and London. 1848.
See no. 3560. See also no. 3562.

596 ON THE THEATRE. No. 228.

pp. [1] 2–8; title on wrapper   MH
[J. and W. Rider, printers]   [ca. 1850?]

The Rev. Francis Close's Attacks

597 CLOSE, *Rev.* FRANCIS. *The stage, ancient and
modern; tendencies on morals and religion.

Hatchard   1850

*IKF. A lecture attacking the stage delivered on 24 October
1850 at Cheltenham, when Close was rector there.*

598 ——[another edition] The stage, ancient and
modern; its tendencies on morals and religion. A lecture by Francis Close, D.D., Dean of Carlisle.

pp. [i–iii] iv–v [vi], [1] 2–67 [68–70 (bl.)]   L
London: Hatchard; Carlisle: C. Thurnam & Sons 1877

*A lecture, attacking the stage, which its author re-published
on account of some remarks by the Bishop of Manchester
on the other side of the stage controversy — Lowe.*

599 *AN APOLOGY for secular recreations: a letter
to the Rev. Francis Close.

pp. 32   MB
London: Rivingtons   1855

——————

☒ Best, *Rev.* Thomas. A sermon on the amusements
of the stage preached in . . . Sheffield. Sheffield. 1851.
See no. 504.

600 MACDONALD, *Rev.* JOHN. What is the
theatre? By the late Rev. John Macdonald, A.M.
Missionary minister, Calcutta.

pp. [1–3] 4–30 [2]   GM
Edinburgh: John Greig & Son; London: James Nisbet
& Co.   1851

*A strongly worded attack on the theatre, elicited by some
remarks made at a theatrical dinner in Calcutta on 7th
January 1842 — Lowe. The dinner was in honour of
"Mrs Leach and the Sans Souci". A further tract by
Macdonald is no. 606 below.*

——[Calcutta edition] What is the theatre?
An inquiry suggested by some recent circumstances.
[From the Calcutta Christian Observer.] [Calcutta:
American Mission Press, 1842.] *Signed 'J.M.D.'; No. 4
in Pastoral Tracts by ministers of different denomina-
tions, 1851.*

——[Tasmanian edition] Launceston, Tasmania:
J. S. Waddell, printer, 1856.

601 KEDDIE, WILLIAM. The theatre: its pernicious
tendency. Addressed to young men. By William
Keddie

pp. [i–iii] iv, [1] 2–123 [124]   GM
Glasgow: Glass and Duncan   1853

602 YATE, W. *A letter to the congregation of
St. John's Mariners' Chapel, Dover, upon theatrical
amusements.

Dover   1853
STR.

603 CLERICUS, M.A., *pseud. of Rev.* Richard Hibbs.
Remarks on the Italian opera in Edinburgh; with
reference to Dr. Guthrie's proposed "placard," and some
observations thereon in a recent letter to the *Scotsman*.
By Clericus, M.A. The profits arising from the sale of
this tract will be given to the Apprentice School
Association.

pp. [1–3] 4–32   L
Edinburgh: W. P. Kennedy; Glasgow: D. Bryce;
London: Hamilton, Adams, & Co.   1854

*The placard was to be placed on the building belonging to
the Association, announcing that the institution was closed
because the people of Edinburgh preferred spending their
money on hearing an Italian sing or seeing a Frenchman
dance.*

604 CLERICUS, M. A., *pseud. of Rev.* Richard Hibbs.
A few more words on the introduction of the Italian
opera into Edinburgh: or, "Robert the Devil," *versus*
Lazarus. By Clericus, M.A.

pp. [1–3] 4–29 [30 (imprint) 31–32 (advts.)]   L
Edinburgh: Moodie & Lothian; Glasgow: David Bryce
1855

☒ An apology for secular recreations: a letter to the
Rev. Francis Close. 1855. *See no. 599.*

605 LADY, A, *pseud.* An appeal to the women of
England to discourage the stage. By a lady.

pp. [1–3] 4–15 [16]   L

Joseph Masters   1855

606 MACDONALD, *Rev.* J[OHN]. The theatre: fourteen reasons why we should not go to it. By the late Rev. J. Macdonald, formerly of London and latterly of Calcutta. With an introduction by Rev. W. Clarkson, Ipswich. Reprinted, with modifications, from the Calcutta edition.

pp. [1–3] 4–31 [32]   E

Simpkin, Marshall, and Co.   1856

See also no. 599.

607 REMARKS on the morality of dramatic compositions: with particular reference to "La Traviata", etc.

pp. [1–2] 3–8   E

John Chapman   1856

Socialist plea for realism in literature.

608 THE THEATRE.

bs.   L

Stirling: Peter Drummond   October, 1856

609 BELLOWS, *Rev. Dr.* [HENRY WHITNEY]. *Published by request — An address upon the claims of the drama, delivered before the president and members of the American Dramatic Fund Society, 1857. By the Rev. Dr. Bellows, of All Soul's Church, New York. (Verbatim from the "New York Herald".) With an introduction by J. B. Buckstone, Esq.

pp. (1) 29   MB

Anson   [1857?]

One of the few clerical defences of the stage — Lowe.

———[American edition] The relation of public amusements to public morality, especially of the theatre to the highest interests of humanity. An address, delivered at the Academy of Music, New York, before "The American Dramatic Fund Society," for the benefit of the Fund. New York: C. S. Francis & Co., 1857.

———[Australian edition] With an introduction to the dramatic profession of England, by J. B. Buckstone, Esq., and to the Australian Colonies, by the Hon. George Coppin, M.L.C., comedian. Presented gratuitously to the visitors of the theatres, by the Hon. George Coppin, M.L.C., during his performances for the benefit of the charitable institutions of the Colonies. Melbourne: Charlwood & Son, printers, 1859.

610 BLAND, HARCOURT, *stage name of* Harcourt Beatty. The exposure dissected, and the foul calumnies of Aitken & Co. fully established: or the theatrical profession thoroughly vindicated. By Harcourt Bland, comedian.

pp. [1–5] 6–31 [32]   GU

Glasgow: Richard Stobbs, William Love; Edinburgh: Peter Pollock   1857

611 BLAND, HARCOURT, *stage name of* Harcourt Beatty. Two letters from Harcourt Bland, comedian, to Mr. J. H. Aitken, the anti-theatrical lecturer.

pp. [1–3] 4–11 [12]; title headed: "Moral and spiritual necessity for a total abolition of the drama"   GU

Glasgow: Richard Stobbs   1857

Aitken delivered his lectures in March 1857. They were reported in the Daily News.

✖ Best, *Rev.* Thomas. Theatrical amusements. A sermon . . . preached at . . . Sheffield. Sheffield. [1860]. *See no. 505.*

612 BINCKES, THOMAS A. Preaching in theatres. An essay, delivered at the east branch of the Young Men's Christian Association, by Thomas A. Binckes.

pp. [1–3] 4–15 [16]   L

Ward and Co.; J. Elliott   1860

613 THE STAGE considered as a moral institution.

pp. [1] 2–11 [12]   E

n.p.   [ca. 1860]

✖ Best, *Rev.* Thomas. "The sinners in Zion are afraid." A sermon preached at . . . Sheffield. Sheffield. 1864. *See no. 506.*

614 BAXTER, *Rev.* A[NDREW] J[OSEPH]. The theatre "a religious institution." By the Rev. A. J. Baxter, Nottingham.

pp. [1–3] 4–8   L

G. J. Stevenson   [1865]

On the opening of the new Theatre Royal, Nottingham, on 25th September 1865, the manager made a statement to the effect that attending theatres was not inconsistent with a religious life. This caused a bitter newspaper controversy, and produced the above tract—Lowe.

✖ Best, *Rev.* Thomas. Sermons on theatrical amusements delivered in Sheffield. By the late Rev. Thomas Best. Edited by the Rev. R. E. Roberts. London & Sheffield. 1865. *See no. 507.*

615 FRECKELTON, THOMAS WESLEY. *The church and the drama. A sermon preached at Bradford, January 29th, 1865.

pp. 27   MB

Maxwell & Co.   1865

In favour of the theatre—Brown.

616 GHOST OF WALTER S. LANDOR, THE, *pseud.* An imaginary conversation between Mr. Phelps, and Dr. Cumming. By the ghost of Walter S. Landor. Price one penny.

pp. [1–3] 4–8 MH
n.p. [*ca.* 1865]

617 KERR, R[OBERT]. The play-house: its hurtful influence on society and morals. Specially addressed to those who attend both church and play-house. By R. Kerr.

pp. [1–3] 4–40 GU
Paisley: printed by J. & J. Cook 1865

Kerr was opposed to "granting a licence to the Exchange Rooms for dramatic purposes".

618 LADY AMATEUR ACTRESS OF MANCHESTER, A, *pseud.* of Louisa Nosworthy. *The stage and Christianity reconciled. The simple story of the real troubles of an inquirer after truth. By a lady amateur actress of Manchester.

pp. 16 MB
Manchester: The Guardian Steam-Printing Offices 1866

With an A.L.S. from the authoress.

✠ Duncan, George. Origin and history of the British drama: containing a review of the stage — its aims and purpose. Glasgow. 1867. *See no. 859.*

619 CALLENDER, E. ROMAINE. *Dr. Thomson on the stage. A reply.

pp. 16 MB
Manchester: Heywood [187?]

Defends the stage against charges of immorality made in a sermon preached at Manchester by Dr. Thomson, probably the then Archbishop of York, William Thomson, D.D.

✠ [Hambleton, John.] The converted actor. Glasgow, London, New York, Sydney, Melbourne, Brisbane. [*ca.* 1870?]. *See no. 3003.*

620 MILNE, JOHN. *The stage vindicated: a defence of the actor. By John Milne, acting member of the Aberdeen Medical Students' Dramatic Club.

pp. 19 AP
Aberdeen: printed by W. Bennett 1870

✠ Taylor, Tom. The theatre in England. Some of its shortcomings and possibilities. 1871. *See no. 2025.1.*

621 KINGSLEY, CHARLES. Plays and Puritans, and other historical essays. By Charles Kingsley.

pp. [*6*] [1–3] 4–271 [272 (colophon)]; pl. [front.] L
Macmillan and Co. 1873

With 58 pages of advertisements bound in as issued.

622 ——[new edition]

pp. [*6*] [1–3] 4–282 [*6* (advts.)]
Macmillan and Co. 1889

JFA.

——[American edition] New York: Macmillan & Co., 1873

A defence of the Puritan attitude to Elizabethan drama. The title essay first published in The North British Review, *vol. xxv (1856).*

✠ Knowles, James Sheridan. Lectures on oratory gesture and poetry to which is added A correspondence with four clergymen in defence of the stage. 1873. *See no. 737.*

623 STEVENS, SAMUEL J. The Sunday history of the English stage. . . . By Samuel J. Stevens, (of the council of the League.) [Being a paper read at the monthly meeting of the members of the National Sunday League, February, 1873.]

pp. [*2*] [1] 2–8; t.p. headed: National Sunday League L
Printed by T. Taylor 1873

624 DRUMMOND, ROBERT B. The theatre: its bearings on morals and religion. A lecture delivered in St. Mark's Chapel, Edinburgh, on April 18, 1875. Published by request.

pp. [1–3] 4–15 [16 (bl.)] MH
Edinburgh [1875]

A moderate and sensible defence of the theatre, by a Unitarian clergyman — Lowe.

625 TALMAGE, J [for T?] de WITT. The average theatre by the Rev. J. de Witt Talmage Brooklyn, New York with introductory note by the Rev. William Arnot, Edinburgh.

pp. [i–iii] iv [5] 6–32 GM
Edinburgh: Andrew Elliot [1875]

Originally two sermons delivered in America.

626 FOSTER, JOHN. The theatre. By John Foster. Not included in his collected works. With a prefatory note by the Rev. John Donaldson, senior minister of the Free Church, Ceres.

pp. [1–3] 4–8 GM
Edinburgh: Maclaren & Macniven; Glasgow: D. Bryce & Son; Aberdeen: A. R. Milne; London: J. Nisbet & Co. [*ca.* 1876]

Originally printed in "The Visitor" *February, 1845. Donaldson suggests that it was originally written about 1813 because of references to the O.P. riots in that year.*

627 AMATEUR LECTURER, AN, *pseud.* Views of an amateur lecturer in regard to professional & amateur play-acting: and also as to public and private balls and dancing: with a few words of advice to the young; hints to unmarried folk — sportsmen — tenant-farmers as statesmen, and farmers as politicians — the Game Laws; and a shot at the heroes of the 1875 East Aberdeenshire election! &c.

pp. [1–3] 4–26   GM

Aberdeen: printed by Davidson & Smith   1876

    Satire, in prose and rhyme, on the theatre.

✂ Close, Francis. The stage, ancient and modern. 1877. *See no. 598.*

628 HEADLAM, STEWART D[UCKWORTH] Theatres & music halls: a lecture given at the Commonwealth Club, Bethnal Green on Sunday, October 7, 1877 by The Rev. Stewart D. Headlam, Curate of St. Matthew's, Bethnal Green, with A letter to the Bishop of London and other correspondence. Second edition.

pp. [i–iii] iv [v] vi–xi [xii], [1] 2–11 [12 (advt.)]

Westminster: printed by the Women's Printing Society   [1877?]

    IKF. *Copy in MB. The lecture, first published in* The Era, *led to the termination of Headlam's curacy.*

629 MANCHESTER LAYMAN, A, *pseud.* The theatre: its character and tendency; being a lecture delivered in the Free Library, Regent Road, Salford, February 22nd, 1877 . . . in reference to the recent utterances of the Bishop of Manchester on theatrical performances.

pp. [1–3] 4–16   MH

Manchester: John Heywood; Salford: Thomas Walker; London: Elliot Stock   [1877]

✂ [Chevalier, W. A.] A tribute to the Shakespeare Memorial . . . Outlines of a scheme for reforming the stage, and elevating the actor's calling to the status of a liberal and legitimate profession. [1877?]. *See no. 951.*

630 HAM, *Rev.* J[AMES] PANTON. The pulpit and the stage. Four lectures, by the Rev. J. Panton Ham with illustrative notes, by Fred. Whymper.

pp. [i–ii] iii–xv [xvi] [17] 18–184; pl. [front. (photo.)]
                                                                                                        L

Charles Henry Clarke   [1878]

    Defence of the stage. See Nicoll *V, 15. See also no. 645.*

631 HAWEIS, *Rev.* H[UGH] R[EGINALD]. Shakspere and the stage: a tribute to the Shakspere memorial at Stratford-on-Avon. A sermon, preached at St. James's, Westmoreland Street, Marylebone, April 28, 1878. By the Rev. H. R. Haweis, M.A. incumbent of St. James's, Westmoreland Street, Marylebone.

pp. [1–3] 4–48   L

C. Kegan Paul and Co.   1878

    The sermon printed in part in the Era *and* New York Tribune. *Sold for the benefit of the Shakspere Memorial Fund.*

✂ Journal of Dramatic Reform. Boston. 1878. *See no. 4394.*

632 LITTLEWOOD, WILLIAM EDENSOR. *Theatrical amusements and Christian duty.

Bath   1878

    Bibliotheca Somersetensis.

633 STARR, FRANK. *Stage theology: or colloquy of clowns. Written upon reading the brave speech made by the Bishop of Manchester, on the stage of the Theatre Royal in that city, before Wm. Sidney and his company.

pp. 39 (1)   MB

Southwell   1878

634 WALKER, *Rev.* V. *The theatre.

                                                                                                        BP

[Birmingham?]   1878

    A reply to Irving's lecture on "The stage" (see below no. 3065).

635 WRIGHT, *Rev.* J[OHN]. The theatre; the ally, not the enemy of morality and religion. Second edition. A lecture delivered at Trim-Street Chapel on Sunday evening, January 20th, 1878, by the Rev. J. Wright, B.A. Reported for "The Bath Herald" and published by permission of the lecturer.

pp. [1–3] 4–14 [15–16]   BhP

Bath: William Lewis "The Herald" Office   1878

636 DAVIS, J. The attitude of society to the stage, past and present. A paper read by J. Davis before the monthly meeting of the Church and Stage Guild, Tuesday, Oct. 7, 1879.

pp. [1–3] 4–16   L

J. Masters and Co.   1879

637 DRAMATIC REFORM ASSOCIATION. First report of committee; with proceedings at the general meeting, Nov. 3, 1879; and a list of members.

pp. [1–5] 6–23 [24]   MH

Manchester: A. Ireland & Co.   1879

    See also PERIODICALS no. 4394

638 DRAMATIC REFORM ASSOCIATION. Objects.

pp. [4]   MH

[Manchester]   [*ca.* 1879]

639 FLUCK, ARTHUR W. A paper on theatrical reform. By Arthur W. Fluck. Any profits arising from the sale of this publication will go towards the formation of a London Theatrical Reform Association. Persons interested in the movement will please communicate with the author of this pamphlet.

pp. [4] [1] 2–27 [28 (bl.)]   L

William Ridgeway   1879

640 [DIXON, JAMES MATTHIAS.] THE PULPIT and the stage.

pp. [1] 2–8; head-title   L

[E. W. Allen, printer]   [1879?]

    Signed J. M. Dixon, Minister of Bowlalley Lane Chapel, Hull.

641 BULLOCK, CHARLES. *Popular recreation. (A church congress paper.) The theatre as it is; and the Ober-Ammergau play.

pp. 80   MB

"Hand and Heart" Publishing Office   [1880]

642 CROUCH, *Rev.* WILLIAM. *The objects of the Church and Stage Guild.

Womens Printing Society Ltd.   [*ca.* 1880?]

    STR.

643 CROUCH, *Rev.* WILLIAM. *What we go to the theatre for.

Womens Printing Society.   [*ca.* 1880?]

    STR.

644 FELL, BEATRICE. *Mistakes about the theatre.

[Church and Stage Guild]   [*ca.* 1880?]

    STR.

645 HAM, J[AMES] PANTON. The stage and the drama in their relation to society. A lecture delivered before the Sunday Lecture Society, on Sunday afternoon, April 11th, 1880.

pp. [1–3] 4–20   L

Sunday Lecture Society   1880

    Reissued in A selection of lectures delivered before the Sunday Lecture Society. *Fourth Selection.* (*London: published by the Society, 1886*). *See also no. 630.*

646 HEADLAM, *Mrs.* STEWART [BEATRICE R.] The ballet: a paper read before the Church and Stage Guild, December 2, 1879. By Mrs. Stewart Headlam.

pp. [1–3] 4–16   L

William Poole   [1880]

    See also below no. 2125.

647 HEADLAM, STEWART DUCKWORTH. *A preliminary paper (read to Church & Stage Guild).

Printing Society, Ltd.   [*ante* 1881]

    STR.

648 BAKER, *Rev.* WILLIAM. Church and stage. A sermon preached before the Church and Stage Guild, in the Crypt Chapel of St. Paul's Cathedral, Sept. 24, 1880, by the Rev. William Baker, D.D., Prebendary of St. Paul's, and Head Master of Merchant Taylors' School.

pp. [1–5] 6–14 [15 (text) 16 (advt.)]   L

William Poole   [1881]

649 LYNE, *Rev.* AUGUSTUS A[DOLPHUS]. Theatres, their uses and abuses; bringing forward a remedy. By the Rev. Augustus A. Lyne, late an officer Royal Navy.

pp. [1–5] 6–23 [24 (bl.)]   L

Cheltenham: Marshall, Norman, and Co.   [1881]

    A lecture delivered in December, 1881, and published soon afterwards. Price 6d., or 5/– a dozen.

650 MERION, CHARLES. *The music hall stage and its relation to the dramatic stage and the church.

?   [*ca.* 1881]

    STR.

651 SPICER, HENRY. Church and stage. By Henry Spicer.

pp. [1–3] 4–32   L

Tinsley Brothers   1881

652 STEPHENSON, C. H. *The stage and the daughter of the Church.

Church and Stage Guild   1881

    STR.

653 ADAMSON, *Rev.* WILLIAM. The theatre: its influence on actors and audience. A lecture, by the Rev. William Adamson, D.D., Edinburgh. Published by request.

pp. [1] 2–32   E

Edinburgh: Andrew Elliot; D. Macara   1883

654 LILLINGTON, *Rev.* FREDERICK ARTHUR CECIL. *Shall I go to the theatre?

pp. 15

Marshall Bros.   [1883]

    BMC., *but L copy destroyed.*

655 MURSELL, ARTHUR. *The stage, the pulpit and the people.

      BP

[Birmingham?]   1883

656 PORTEOUS, J[AMES] MOIR. Theatres and Christians: the revived question viewed in the most brilliant lights, by J. Moir Porteous, D.D.

pp. [1] 2–24   LE

Edinburgh, Glasgow, Stirling, Belfast, London   1883

657 BLAU, HENRY. Some notes on the stage, and its influence on the education of the masses, players, and playgoers. By Henry Blau, F.S.Sc. Read at a meeting of the members of the Society of Science, Letters, and Art, of London. Sir Henry Valentine Goold, Bart., presiding.

pp. [1] 2–16   GM

The Society of Science, Letters, and Art, of London
                                                              1884

See also below no. 663.

658 KENDAL, *Mrs.* [MADGE]. The drama: a paper read by Mrs. Kendal at the Congress of the National Association for the Promotion of Social Science, Birmingham, September, 1884.

pp. [1–3] 4–16   MH

Birmingham: printed at the Herald Press   [1884]

This lecture raised a terrific storm in the theatrical world: some of Mrs. Kendal's remarks being vehemently resented alike by critics and actors. It is impossible to characterise it as a judicious production — Lowe. See also no. 3213.

659 ——[another edition] The drama By Mrs. Kendal A paper read at the Congress of the National Association for the Promotion of Social Science, Birmingham, September 1884.

pp. [4] [1] 2–24; pl. [front.]; t.p. in red and black   MH

David Bogue   [1884]

First Bogue edition. With two leaves of advertisements bound in, as issued.

660 ——[second edition]

pp. [4] [1] 2–24; pl. [front.]; t.p. in red and black   MH

David Bogue   [1884]

On the back of the half-title is a facsimile A. N. S, "I desire that all profits arising from the sale of my Paper on "The Drama" shall be devoted to the Chelsea Hospital for Women Madge Kendall". With two leaves of advertisements bound in, as issued. The words "Second Edition" on verso of title-page.

661 ——[third edition]

pp. [8] [1] 2–24 [25–28 (advts.) 29–32 (bl.)]; illus. (facsims.); pl. [front., port.]; vignette on t.p.; t.p. in red and black   GM

David Bogue   [1884]

"Third Edition" on verso of title-page.

662 ——[fourth edition]

pp. [4] [1] 2–24; pl. [front.]; t.p. in red and black   L

David Bogue   [1884 or 1885]

With two leaves of advertisements bound in, as issued. "Fourth Edition" on verso of title-page.

663 BLAU, HENRY. *Some more notes on the stage, and its influence on the education of the masses, players, and playgoers. Read at a meeting of the members of the Society of Science, Letters, and Art.

pp. 32   MB

Trübner & Co.   [1885]

See also above no. 657.

664 CHARRINGTON, FRED[ERIC]K N[ICHOLAS]. The battle of the music halls by Fredk. N. Charrington.

pp. [1–3] 4–16; illus.   MH

Book Saloon   [1885?]

See Guy Thorne, The Great Acceptance, (London, 1912), pp. 104–134.

665 CORIN, *pseud. of* Lind. The truth about the stage. By Corin.

pp. [2 (advt.)] [i–iii] iv–vi, [1] 2–180 [181–184 (advt.)]
                                                               L

Wyman & Sons   1885

Motto: ' "Something is rotten in the state of Denmark." Shakespeare.'

666 ——second edition

pp. [i–iii] iv–vi, [1] 2–180   MH

Wyman & Sons   1885

667 ——third edition

pp. [i–iii] iv–vi, [1] 2–180   MH

Wyman & Sons   1885

The author was said to be an old actor named Lind, who occupied a position of trust in the household of the late Charles Reade. His experiences seem to have been very unfortunate, and he appears to consider them as the usual experiences of young actors — Lowe.

✖ Dechmann, George. Histrions and the histrionic art. [ca. 1885]. See no. 753.

668 FOWLER, J[OHN] H[ENRY]. The influence of the theatre on life & character, the Chancellor's essay, 1886, by J. H. Fowler, B.A., late scholar of Trinity Coll.

pp. [1–5] 6–28   L

Oxford: B. H. Blackwell; London: Simpkin, Marshall & Co.   1886

669 HUDSON, WILLIAM HENRY. The church and the stage by William Henry Hudson.

pp. [1–3] 4–71 [72 (bl.)]   L
Trübner & Co.   1886

A history of the church-stage controversy.

670 GEIER, JOHN. Thespis on tryal, or the moralitie of playes considered. Translated out of the Latin of John Geier, by A. C. Gent. 1685. (Bibliotheca Curiosa.)

pp. [1–7] 8–36   L
Edinburgh: privately printed   1887

671 ———[large paper issue.]

pp. [1–7] 8–32   MH
Edinburgh: privately printed   1887

The title and licence pages here reprinted allege that it was published by John Leadbeater at "Honestapolis" in "Play House Lane", indicating that Edmund Goldsmid's(?) phrase "translated out of the Latin of John Geier by A. C. Gent 1685" is facetious. Includes also much of Historia Histrionica (1699) and an essay by Edmond Malone from the Drama (1822). "Limited to 275 small-paper and 75 large-paper copies."

672 HERONDO, F., *pseud.* of Frank A. Swallow. The world's argument: or, justice and the stage. A dramatic debate. By F. Herondo.

pp. [4] [1–5] 6–149 [150 (imprint) 151–152 (bl.)]   L
Sedwyn Publishing Company   1887

In verse and prose, printed within a red framework.

✠ Adderley, *Hon.* James Granville. The fight for the drama at Oxford. Oxford. 1888. *See no. 1672.*

673 HEADLAM, STEWART D[UCKWORTH]. The function of the stage. A lecture by Stewart D. Headlam.

pp. [1–4] 5–29 [30 (bl.)] 31–37 [38–40 (bl.)]; illus.   E
Frederick Verinder   1889

Pp. 31–37: "Some opinions of the press on The theory of theatrical dancing with a chapter on pantomime edited by [sic] Carlo Blasis' code of Terpischore [sic], with the original plates by Stewart D. Headlam."

674 KENSIT, JOHN. *The theatre: shall we go?

      1889
STR.

675 LEEDS, JOSIAH W[OODWARD]. The theatre: an essay upon the non-accordancy of stage-plays with the Christian profession. By Josiah W. Leeds, of Philadelphia.

pp. [8] [1] 2–77 [78]   GM
Newport, Mon: John E. Southall; London: E. Hicks, Jr.
      1890

Originally an American Quaker tract published in Philadelphia in 1884. This British edition edited by John E. Southall was instigated by "a newspaper discussion which followed the presentation of the so-called Welsh National Opera in Cardiff, by an amateur company, largely drawn from professing Christian Churches . . . I would therefore especially commend this book to the intelligent public of South Wales"—Editor's preface.

———[American editions] Philadelphia: The Author, 1884, 1886.

676 FORREST, *Rev.* A[NDREW] F. *The theatre and theatre going. By Rev. A. F. Forrest, Glasgow.
      1892
STR.

677 ———[another edition]

pp. [1] 2–23 [24]; title on wrappers   GM
Edinburgh: R. W. Hunter; Glasgow: S.A.C. Todd
      [ca. 1930?]

Rev. A. F. Forrest was minister of the Renfield Street U.P. Church.

✠ Lund, T. W. M. "The Second Mrs. Tanqueray;" what? And why? Liverpool. 1894. *See no. 4006.*

678 BLATHWAYT, RAYMOND. Does the theatre make for good? An interview with Mr. Clement Scott by Raymond Blathwayt. (Reprinted from *Great Thoughts.*) Replies from leading actors, press comments, &c.

pp. [1–3] 4–23 [24]; illus. incl. facsims.   L
A. W. Hall   [1898]

679 LIGHTFOOT, J[OSEPH] B[ARBER]. The drama. A sermon by the late J. B. Lightfoot, D.D., Bishop of Durham. Published under the direction of the Tract Committee.

pp. [1–4] 5–16   L
Society for Promoting Christian Knowledge   1898

Previously published in "The use and abuse of the world." Six sermons preached on the Sundays after Easter, 1873, in the Church of St. James's, Piccadilly, ed. J. E. Kempe (S.P.C.K., 1873), with other sermons on the World, Music, the Adornments of Life, Society, and Popular Literature.

THE ARTS OF THE THEATRE
THE ART OF ACTING

For sections on acting contained in more general works see GENERAL HISTORY *nos. 829, 830, 880, 882, 885, 906, 954, 961, 985;* THEATRE OUT OF LONDON *no. 1658;* IRELAND *no. 1817, 1818 (Dublin);* BIOGRAPHY: COLLECTIVE *nos. 2244, 2363;* BIOGRAPHY: INDIVIDUAL *nos. 2939, 2941, 3028, 3080, 3086, 3637;* THEORY AND CRITICISM *nos. 3701, 3716. For amateur handbooks on acting, make-up etc. see* THE AMATEUR THEATRE *especially nos. 2162–2165, 2168–2169, 2172.1, 2176–2179, 2182, 2190–2194. See also* PERIODICALS *nos. 4238, 4242, 4289. For minstrel shows see* IRREGULAR FORMS *nos. 2128, 2129.*

680 AN ESSAY on the theatres: or, the art of acting. In imitation of Horace's *Art of Poetry*. MS. Never before printed.

Vol. V, pp. 543–549 of The Harleian miscellany *(T. Osborne, 1745) Reprinted in subsequent editions of* The Harleian miscellany: *(1810), V, 580–585; (1811), XII, 146–157. Originally composed ca. 1735.*

681 [HILL, AARON.] THE ART OF ACTING. Part I. Deriving rules from a new principle, for touching the passions in a natural manner. An essay of general use, to those, who hear, or speak in public, and to the practisers of many of the elegant arts; as painters, sculptors, and designers: but adapted, in particular, to the stage: with view to quicken the delight of audiences, and form a judgment of the actors, in their good, or bad, performances.

pp. [i–iii] iv–viii, [5] 6–22   L

J. Osborn   1746

Heroic couplets; an expansion of a short poem originally published in The Prompter *(no. 4075 below). No Part II, apparently. Reprinted without the dedication in* The works of the late Aaron Hill, Esq. *(1753), III, 387–408; 2nd ed. (1754), III, 387–408. Hill's prose* Essay on the art of acting, *based on numbers of* The Prompter, *is printed in* The works of the late Aaron Hill, Esq. ... with An essay on the art of acting *(1753), IV, [353]–414; 2nd ed. (1754), IV, [337]–396.* The actor *(1821), see below no. 721, is based on this. For the relationship of these and Hill's other writings on acting, see Leo Hughes "The actor's epitome", RES, xx, 306–7.*

682 WEEKS, JAMES EYRE. *A rhapsody on the stage, or, the art of playing. In imitation of Horace's Art of Poetry. Humbly addressed to His Excellency Philip, Earl of Chesterfield, Lord Lieutenant General, and General Governor of Ireland. By James Eyre Weeks.

DFo

Dublin: printed for the author   1746

683 [HILL, *Sir* JOHN.] THE ACTOR: a treatise on the art of playing. Interspersed with theatrical anecdotes, critical remarks on plays, and occasional observations on audiences.

pp. 1–326   L

R. Griffiths   1750

Advertised 28 April 1750 — LS, p. 195. Sometimes wrongly attributed to Aaron Hill. Translated (with additions) from P. R. de Sainte-Albine's Le comédien *(1747). A French adaptation (1769) prompted Diderot's* Paradoxe sur le comédien *(1770).*

684 ———*[another edition]
R. Griffiths   1752

Advertised 30 November 1752.

685 ———*[another edition] The actor. A treatise on the art of playing, interspersed with observations on the performances of Garrick, Quin, Barry, Berry, Macklin, Ryan, Havard, Woodward, Foote, &c; Mrs Cibber, Mrs Pritchard, Mrs Woffington, Mrs Ward, Mrs Elmy, Mrs Green, Mrs Clive, Miss Bellamy, &c. Also some anecdotes of Betterton, Booth and Wilkes and other celebrated performers; together with occasional remarks upon managers and audiences, and upon the principal tragedies, comedies, masques and farces.

R. Griffiths   1753

Advertised 30 October 1753—LS, pt. 4, p. 387.

686 ———[another edition] The actor: or, a treatise on the art of playing. A new work, written by the author of the former, and adapted to the present state of the theatres. Containing impartial observations on the performance, manner, perfections, and defects of Mr. Garrick, Mr. Barry, Mr. Woodward, Mr. Foot, Mr. Havard, Mr. Palmer, Mr. Ryan, Mr. Berry, &c. Mrs. Cibber, Mrs. Pritchard, Miss. Nossiter, Mrs. Gregory, Mrs. Woffington, Mrs. Clive, Mrs. Green, Miss. Bellamy, &c. in their several capital parts.

pp. [2] [1] 2–284 [285–303 (index) 304 (bl.) 305–308 (advts.)]   L
R. Griffiths   1755

A re-written and shortened version of the first edition. Published 12 March 1755—LS, pt. 4, p. 473.

687 AN ESSAY on the stage; or, the art of acting. A poem.

pp. [4] [1] 2–17 [18]   E

Edinburgh: printed and sold by John Yair   1754

Said, in the preface, to be written by a young gentleman, without whose knowledge it is printed by a friend, who signs himself "A Comedian" —Lowe.

688 [PICKERING, ROGER.] REFLECTIONS upon theatrical expression in tragedy. With a proper introduction, and appendix.

pp. [2] [1] 2–81 [82]   L
W. Johnston   1755

Published 13 March 1755 — LS.

689 [LLOYD, ROBERT.] THE ACTOR. A poetical epistle. To Bonnell Thornton, Esq.

pp. [4] 1–20   L
R. and J. Dodsley   1760

690 ———The actor. A poetical epistle to Bonnell Thornton, Esq.; by the Rev. Mr. Loyd, [*sic*] one of the masters of Westminster school. The third edition.

pp. [1–2] 3–20   MH
London: R. and J. Dodsley; Dublin: re-printed for W. Whitestone   1760

691 ———The actor. Addressed to Bonnell Thornton, Esq. By R. Lloyd, A.M. The fourth edition.

pp. [4] [1] 2–16   L
G. Kearsly   1764

692 ———[another edition] The actor, a poem. By Robert Lloyd. With some critical alterations, by the author of *The prompter.*

pp. [1–5] 6–18   L
Dublin: printed for, and presented to, W. Husband, Esq. by his obliged friend, Smollet Holden   1811

See also no. 717 below.

693 ———[another edition] The actor a poem by Robert Lloyd to which is prefix'd an essay by Edmund Blunden the whole embellish'd with theatrical figures by Randolph Schwabe.

pp. [2] [i–iv] v–xix [xx] [21–22] 23–42 [43–46]; illus.; t.p. in two colours   L
C. W. Beaumont   1926

60 copies on "Japanese vellum", and 210 on "hand-made paper". Pp. vii–xix: "On familiar poetry and Robert Lloyd" by Edmund Blunden. Reprinted in Lloyd's Poems (1762); and The Poetical Works of Robert Lloyd, ed. by W. Kenrick (1774), vol. I, which contains a memoir of Lloyd by Kenrick, and also other poems of theatrical interest.

694 THE SENTIMENTAL SPOUTER: or, young actor's companion. Containing: I. A treatise on oratory in general, and theatrical acquirements in particular: in which rules are laid down, and if properly observed, cannot fail to possess the dramatic genius with taste to discern, and judgement to enforce the meaning and conception of his author, with propriety and applause. II. A collection of the most celebrated scenes, speeches and soliloquies, selected from the most admired tragedies and comedies, represented on the English stage. The whole comprising the essence of theatrical delivery. And the beauties of dramatic poetry.

pp. [4] [i] ii–xvi, [1] 2–124   L
J. Wheble; and T. Axtell   1774

Lowe records a frontispiece.

695 [STEELE, JOSHUA]. AN ESSAY towards establishing the measure and melody of speech to be expressed and perpetuated by certain symbols.

pp. [i–iv] v–xvii [xviii], [1] 2–193 [194–198].   L
J. Almon   1775

696 ———Prosodia rationalis; or, an essay towards establishing the melody and measure of speech, to be expressed and perpetuated by certain symbols. The second edition amended and enlarged.

pp. [i–iv] v–xvii [xviii], [1] 2–243 [244]   L
Printed by J. Nichols   1779

Dedication signed: Joshua Steele.

697 CAREY, GEORGE SAVILLE. A lecture on mimicry, as it was delivered with great applause, at the theatres in Covent-Garden and the Hay-Market, and the great room in Panton-Street. In the course of which were introduced a great variety of theatrical imitations. To which is added Jerry Sneak's return from the Regatta; and A lecture on lectures. By George Saville Carey.

pp. [2] [i] ii–iii [iv] [5] 6–57 [58]; pl. [front.]   DFo
J. Bew   1776

698 *RUSTED, ROBERT, *ed.* The new spouter's companion.

pp. 20; [front.]
        [1781?]
PH. and KB.

699 PALMER, [JOHN] *ed.* The new spouter's companion; or, a choice collection of prologues and epilogues being a complete theatrical remembrancer, and universal key to theatrical knowledge . . . to which is prefixed an introduction including rules to be observed in theatrical representation and public speaking. A new edition, carefully revised and corrected by Mr. Palmer.

pp. [1–5] 6–112; pl. [front.]   L
Alex Hogg   [ca 1790]

700 *THE NEW THESPIAN ORACLE; containing original strictures on oratory and acting. And a select collection of all the modern prologues, and epilogues, spoken at the Royal and private theatres.

        1791

With a frontispiece—Lowe.

701 *THE THESPIAN ORACLE; or, a new key to theatrical amusements. Containing the new prologues and epilogues, and an introduction on oratory and acting.

pp. iii   MB

Printed and sold by J. Barker   1791

702 *THE SCHOOL of Roscius, or theatrical orator. Containing a select collection of all the modern prologues & epilogues, spoken at the Theatre's Royal, &c., with a preface on oratory & acting.

pp. (1) 94   MB

J. Roach   1792

    Lowe *records a frontispiece.*

703 STONE, W. The beauties of the stage: or, dramatic companion. Being a collection of the most favourite and admired scenes, soliloquies, speeches, passages, &c. Selected from the most celebrated and approved tragedies, comedies, farces, and other entertainments of the stage. Interspersed with a number of parodies, burlesques, addresses, &c. Together with several originals, and an essay on the art of acting. The whole calculated for the use and amusement of the lovers of the drama, particularly candidates for either sock or buskin. By W. Stone.

pp. [i–iii] iv–xi [xii], [5] 6–241 [242 (bl.)] 243–244 (advts.)]; pl. [front.]   L

A. Hamilton   [1792]

    "The art of acting: or, instructions for candidates for sock or buskin" in heroic couplets, pp. [iii]–xi.

704 HENDERSON, WILLIAM. *The spouter's new guide, containing all the modern prologues and epilogues; including the celebrated address spoken by Mr. Lewis. To which are added the most approved rules for oratory and acting; addrest to the candidates for theatrical fame of both sexes, by William Henderson, Esq.

                                    1796

    Lowe.

705 *THE READER, or reciter: by the assistance of which any person may teach himself to read or recite English prose with the utmost elegance and effect. To which are added, instructions for reading plays. On a plan never before attempted.

pp. iv, 186   MB

T. Cadell jun. and W. Davies   1799

706 ST. MAINE. St. Maine's book of useful information, or stage guide.

pp. [1–4] 5–47 [48], incl. ptd. wrappers   GU

n.p.   [18–?]

    Brochure advertising St. Maine's course of private instruction, with brief information on each subject.

707 WANTED, FOR ACTIVE SERVICE in the North of Ireland, during the ensuing theatrical campaign, half a dozen aspiring young heroes, and as many heroines, under the banners of Mr. Boreas Buskin . . . Apply to the Manager at O.P. and P.S. Tavern, Russell-Court, Drury-Lane. . . .

bs.   DFo

[London]: printed by Harrison   [1800?]

708 AUSTIN, *Rev.* GILBERT. Chironomia; or a treatise on rhetorical delivery: comprehending many precepts, both ancient and modern, for the proper regulation of the voice, the countenance, and gesture. Together with an investigation of the elements of gesture, and a new method for the notation thereof: illustrated by many figures. By the Reverend Gilbert Austin, A.M.

pp. [4] [i–iii] iv–xiii [xiv–xvi], [1] 2–583 [584 (bl.)] 585–599 (indexes) 600 (errata)]; illus.; pls. 1–12 (incl. 1 fold.)   E

T. Cadell and W. Davies   1806

709 TEGG, THO[MAS]. †The new myrtle and vine; or, complete vocal library. . . . To which is added, An essay on the science of singing, and The art of acting. By Tho. Tegg.

Vol. I nos. [I–II] III–IV pp. [i–ii] iii–iv 5–231 [232–240 (index)] added t.p., engr.; pls. [3]   GU

Thomas Tegg   1806

    Issued in parts. Lacking An essay.

709.1 *EXTRACT from a poem entitled The art of acting.

                                  MH

Dublin   1807

710 SIDDONS, HENRY. Practical illustrations of rhetorical gesture and action, adapted to the English drama. From a work on the same subject by M. Engel, Member of the Royal Academy of Berlin. By Henry Siddons. Embellished with numerous engravings, expressive of the various passions, and representing the modern costume of the London theatres.

pp. [i–iii] iv, [1] 2–352 ²351–352(cancellans) 353–387 [388–407 (index) 408 (errata) 409–410 (list of pls.) 411–412 (advts.)]; pls. [69] = 66 leaves   L

Richard Phillips   1807

    The son of Mrs. Siddons. He was manager of the Edinburgh Theatre Royal from 1809–1815 — Lowe. This work is taken from J. J. Engel's Ideen zu einer Mimik (Berlin 1785–1786). An appendix, pp. 359–387, consists of "some account of the dresses now worn on the London theatres".

711 ——second edition, improved

pp. [i–v] vi–viii, [1] 2–393 [394–408 (index)]; pls. 1–69 [= 66 leaves]; illus.   MH

Sherwood, Neely, and Jones   1822

The plates are numbered, some very faintly, or, in some copies, not at all. The order of the first three plates varies; the intended order is apparently 'Suspicion', 'Contempt', and 'Pride' (numbered 1). The half-title reads: Illustrations of gesture and action.

712 THE THEATRICAL SPEAKER; or an elucidation of the whole science of acting: containing comprehensive rules for accurately exhibiting the dramatic passions, with numerous examples for representation.

pp. [4] [1] 2–233 [234]; pl. fold. [front.]   L

Printed for the author, and published by J. Smeeton
    1807

713 ——second edition

pp. [4] [1] 2–233 [234]; pl. fold. [front.]   L

J. Smeeton; and H. D. Symonds   1807

A reissue of the first edition.

714 [LYDDAL, DAVID?] THE PROMPTER, or cursory hints to young actors. A didactic poem. To which are prefixed strictures on theatrical education.

pp. [1–5] 6–60   L

Dublin: printed for and presented to W. Husband Esquire, by the Hibernia Press-Company   1810

Dedicated to "the author of some Familiar Epistles. . . ." [J. W. Croker].

715 ——*[another edition] The prompter; or, elementary maxims for the art of acting. A didactic poem.

pp. [4] 125   O

Dublin: twelve copies, printed for the author, by A. O'Neil, at the Minerva Press   1827–8

Pencilled attribution: assumed name of Willcocks Hubard.

716 ——*[another edition] The prompter: or, elementary maxims for the art of acting. A didactic poem. To which are prefixed strictures on theatrical education, and a prologue.

pp. [4], 125

Dublin: ten copies, printed for the author, by William Holden   1831

    STR.

717 THE THESPIAN PRECEPTOR; or, a full display of the scenic art: including ample and easy instructions for treading the stage, using proper action, modulating the voice, and expressing the several dramatic passions: illustrated by examples from our most approved ancient and modern dramatists; and calculated not only for the improvement of all lovers of the stage, actors and actresses, but likewise of public orators, readers, and visitors of the Theatres Royal.

pp. [1–3] 4 [13] 14–156 [=148]   L

J. Roach, at the Theatrical Library   1811

718 ——*[second edition] The Thespian preceptor, or a full display of the scenic art: including ample and easy instructions for treading the stage.

pp. [2] i–ii, [13] 14–176 [=164]; pls; fold. [front]

J. Roach, at the Britannia office.   [1818]

    Cohn *792*

    ——[American edition] Boston: Bliss, 1810.

719 BROWN, JOHN. The stage: a poem. By John Brown.

pp. [2] [1] 2–50   DFo

John Souter   1819

Addressed to William Farren.

720 *AN ESSAY on the art of acting; in three epistles. Epistle 1.
    1819

Recorded but not seen by Lowe.

721 [HILL, AARON.] THE ACTOR; or, guide to the stage; exemplifying the whole art of acting: in which the dramatic passions are defined, analyzed, and made easy of acquirement. The whole interspersed with select and striking examples from the most popular modern pieces.

pp. [6] [1] 2–29 [30]; pl. [front.]   MB

John Lowndes   1821

An arrangement of Aaron Hill's essay originally published in The Prompter *(see note to no. 681 above). The editor promises a forthcoming book,* System of study for the stage.

    ——[American editions] Philadelphia: Turner & Son; and C. Neal, [1830]; New York: Circulating Library and Dramatic Repository, 1823.

722 [CROOK, EDWARD] THE RISING CHARACTER of the theatrical profession, especially as relating to provincial actors, has for some time required a corresponding respectability in the method of communication between managers and performers . . . some reputable and avowed centre of theatrical information has long been a desideratum. . . . With these views, Mr. Edward Crook of the Theatre Royal, Drury Lane, has opened an office for the settling of engagements. . . .

bs.   DFo

[London]   [1823]

A circular.

723 REDE, LEMAN THOMAS [TERTIUS]. The road to the stage; or, the performer's preceptor.

Containing clear and ample instructions for obtaining theatrical engagements; with a list of all the provincial theatres, the names of the managers, and all particulars as to their circuits, salaries, &c. With a description of the things necessary on an outset in the profession, where to obtain them, and a complete explanation of all the technicalities of the histrionic art! By Leman Thomas Rede, author of *The modern speaker*, &c.

pp. [*2*] [i] ii–iv [*5*] 6–106; pl. [front.]   L
Joseph Smith   1827

724 ———The road to the stage, contains clear and ample instructions for obtaining theatrical engagements; with a list of the provincial theatres, names of the managers, and particulars as to salaries, rules, fines, &c.; an account of things necessary on an outset in the profession, how and where obtained; and a clear elucidation of all the technicalities of the histrionic art. To which is added, a list of the London theatres; copies of their rules and articles of engagement; an account of the Dramatic Authors' Society; the members; scale of prices; and a copy of the Dramatic Copyright Act. By the late Leman Thomas Rede. A new edition, revised and improved.

pp. [i–iii] iv–viii, [1] 2–100; pl. [front.]   LVA
J. Onwhyn   1835

Edited by William Leman Rede, the dramatist and brother of the author.

725 ———*[another edition]
pp. viii, 100   DLC
J. Onwhyn   1836

726 ———[another edition] The guide to the stage: or, how to enter the theatrical profession, obtain an engagement and become an actor. Founded on, and partly taken from Leman Rede's book; with modern list of theatres, &c. Corrected to August, 1868.

pp. [1–3] 4–43 [44]
T. H. Lacy   [1868]
    JFA.

727 ———*[another edition] The guide to the stage: or, how to enter the theatrical profession, obtain an engagement, and become an actor. Founded on, and partly taken from Leman Rede's book; with modern list of theatres, &c. Corrected to August, 1871.

pp. 43   MB
Lacy   [1871]

———[American editions] New York: Samuel French, 1863, 1864, and 1872.

728 VETERAN STAGER, A, *pseud. of G. Grant. An essay on the science of acting. By a veteran stager.

pp. [i–iii] iv–xii, [1] 2–201 [202 (bl.) 203–204 (advts.)]; pl. [front.]   MH
Cowie and Strange   1828

Said by H. B. Wheatley to be by Grant.

729 BELL, ALEXANDER. The tongue, a poem, in two parts, by Alexander Bell, professor of elocution.

pp. [*6*] [I] 2–72 [73 (advt.) 74 (bl.)]   L
W. J. Cleaver   1846

730 OLD STAGER, AN, *pseud.* of James Shirley Hodson. A complete guide to the stage, and manual for amateurs and actors; containing a list of the principal London and provincial theatres: with the names of their managers, etc., also instructions in the various requisites for the stage, together with such useful information and advice, as render it of the highest value to the young artist. By an old stager.

pp. [1–5] 6–36; ptd. covers.   MH
Henry Beal   [1851]

The author acknowledges his debt to Leman Rede's The road to the stage. Preface dated 1 Jan. 1851.

731 [BERTRAM, JAMES GLASS.] THE WAY TO THE STAGE; or, how to become an actor and get an engagement.

pp. [1–3] 4–22 [23–24 (advts.)]   EP
Edinburgh: James G. Bertram & Co.   [1852]

Motto on title — "Advice to persons about to go upon the stage — DON'T!" — Lowe. Bertram, under the pseudonym Peter Paterson, wrote: The confessions of a strolling player. 1852. See below no. 2446–2449.

732 [SMITH, CHARLES WILLIAM?] THE ART OF ACTING.

pp. [i–iii] iv [5] 6–28   E
Thomas Hailes Lacy   [ca. 1855]

Probably reissued at various dates until 1863. With blue printed paper covers. A different work from Smith's The actor's art (no. 735 below).

733 ———[another edition] The art of acting, or, guide to the stage: in which the dramatic passions are defined, analyzed, and made easy of acquirement.

pp. [i–iii] iv [5] 6–24; on cover: No. ccxxvii. French's minor drama.   MH
New York: Samuel French; London: Samuel French, Ltd.   [ca. 1860]

———[American editions] New York: Samuel French, [1855?]; O. A. Roorbach, Jr., 1855; Boston: W. V. Spencer, [1856?].

734 [REYNOLDS, ARTHUR.] ON ACTING and kindred subjects, considered in relation to genius and talent. Also, on theories of chemistry.

pp. [1–5] 6–32   L
J. & F. C. Mathieson   [1865]

The preface consists of the following sentences: "Various circumstances have induced me to have this printed. It has been written and printed very hurriedly. I throw myself on the indulgence of the reader. A.R." I am not sure that I have ever seen a more eccentric preface — Lowe.

735 SMITH, CHARLES WILLIAM. The actor's art: its requisites, and how to obtain them; its defects, and how to remove them. By Charles William Smith, sometime professor of elocution in the University of Oxford, by permission of the Reverend, the Vice-Chancellor.

pp. [i–iii] iv [5] 6–48   L

Thomas Hailes Lacy   [1867?]

736 ——*[another edition]

pp. 48   MB

London: Samuel French; New York: Samuel French [187–?]

On cover "French's Acting Edition (Late Lacy's)".

——[American edition] New York: O. A. Roorbach, [ca. 1870?].

737 KNOWLES, JAMES SHERIDAN. Lectures on oratory gesture and poetry to which is added A correspondence with four clergymen in defence of the stage. By James Sheridan Knowles.

pp. [8] [1] 2–134ª–134⁰[134ᵖ] [135] 136–249 [250 (bl.)]; pl. [autograph facsim.]; insets [2 (type facsims.)]   L

Privately printed for James McHenry   1873

Only twenty-five copies printed. Revised and edited by Francis Harvey. Uniform with Knowles's Lectures on dramatic literature, 1873 (see no. 3745 below) and R. B. Knowles's Life of James Sheridan Knowles, 1872. (See no. 3215 below).

738 "HARESFOOT AND ROUGE", *pseud.* How to "make-up." A practical guide to the art of "making-up", for amateurs, &c. Shewing, by a series of novel illustrations, the manner in which the face may be "made-up" to represent the different stages of life, viz: youth, manhood, maturity, old age, etc. By "Haresfoot and Rouge".

pp. [2] [9] 10–48 [49–50 (advt.)]; col. pls 1–6   L

London: Samuel French; New York: Samuel French & Son   1877

739 [WAGNER, LEOPOLD.] THE STAGE, with the curtain raised: by an actor.

pp. [1–3] 4–15 [16]   L

Leopold Wagner   [1881?]

740 ——*third edition, revised and enlarged.

Advertised in The pantomimes, 1881. (no. 2120 below). Probably to be identified with no. 741.

741 ——New, revised and enlarged edition. By Leopold Wagner.

pp. [1–3] 4–32; cover-title   L

London and Manchester: John Heywood   [1881?]

742 GARCIA, GUSTAVE. The actors' art: a practical treatise on stage declamation, public speaking and deportment, for the use of artists, students and amateurs, by Gustave Garcia, Professor of Singing and Declamation at the Royal Academy of Music, and the London Academy of Music; Professor of Singing at the Guildhall School of Music, etc., etc. Illustrated by A. Forestier.

pp. [4] [i–iii] iv–viii [9] 10–201 [202–204 (bl.)]; pl., Fig. 52, fold.; errata slip; illus.   NbU

T. Pettitt & Co.   1882

Dedicated to Irving.

743 ——including a sketch on the history of the theatre, from the Greeks to the present time, by Gustave Garcia. . . . Professor of Singing at the Royal College of Music. . . . Second edition.

pp. [i–ix] x–xv [xvi], [1] 2–286 [287–8 (bl.)]; illus. LGk

Simpkin, Marshall, & Co.   1888

744 BARLOW, GEORGE. An actor's reminiscences and other poems.

pp. [i] ii–xiv [xv–xvi], 1–332   MB

Remington and Co.   1883

745 CHARLES H. FOX, theatrical, mechanical, & private wig maker. Wholesale, retail, and for exportation. [The fourth edition.]

pp. [64]; illus.   MH

[London: C. H. Fox]   1887–8

Running-title: C. H. Fox's Illustrated Catalogue. Quotes press notices of first edition (1883).

746 ——*[another edition] . . . wig maker, costumier, &c.

illus.   L

C. H. Fox   1888–9

Issued with Dramatic & Musical Directory (no. 4258).

747 FOX, CHARLES H. The art of making-up for public and private theatricals advice to amateurs, etc., by C. H. Fox.

pp. [1–5] 6–218; illus.   MH

C. H. Fox   [1888?]

748 ——[another edition]

pp. [1–5] 6–240; illus.   MH

C. H. Fox   [1890]

749 ——[another edition]

pp. [1–5] 6–106; illus.   L

C. H. Fox   [1892]

750 *C. H. FOX'S THEATRICAL CATALOGUE.
illus.   L

C. H. Fox   1891?

Issued with Dramatic and Musical Directory (*no.
4258*) *in 1891 and 1892. See also no. 745 above.*

751 POLLOCK, WALTER HERRIES. The paradox
of acting. Translated with annotations from Diderot's
'Paradoxe sur le comédien'. By Walter Herries Pollock.
With a preface by Henry Irving.

pp. [i–ix] x–xx, [1] 2–108   GU

Chatto & Windus   1883

————[American edition] with Masks or faces?
By William Archer. Introd. Lee Strasberg. New York:
Hill and Wang, 1957. (Dramabooks.)

752 TALMA [FRANÇOIS JOSEPH.] Talma on the
actor's art, with preface by Henry Irving. Any proceeds
of the sale of this essay will be given to the Actors'
Benevolent Fund.

pp. [1–3] 4–26 [27 (colophon) 28 (bl.)]; cover-title   L

Bickers and Son   [1883]

A translation of Réflexions sur Lekain et l'art théâtral
(*1825 and 1856*) *originally published, at Irving's suggestion, in the* Theatre (*1877*) (*see below no. 4240*).

————[American edition] with a review by H. C.
Fleeming Jenkin, and notes by Brander Matthews
(Publications of the Dramatic Museum of Columbia
University, Second Series, no. IV), New York, 1915.

753 DECHMANN, GEORGE. Histrions and the
histrionic art. By George Dechmann.

pp. [1–3] 4–87 [88 (advts.)]   DFo

City of London Publishing Company   [ca. 1885]

754 DREW, EDWIN. How to recite: being studies
of poems, with fresh readings, recitations, anecdotes,
sketches, and articles connected with elocution. By
Edwin Drew.

pp. [4] [1] 2–138 [139–142 (advts.)]; illus.   E

Dean & Son   [1886]

755 ARCHER, WILLIAM. Questions on the art of
acting formulated on behalf of the editor of *Longmans'
Magazine* by William Archer When answered, kindly
return to W. Archer, Esq. c/o Messrs Longmans, Green,
& Co. 39 Paternoster Row, London, E.C.

pp. [1] 2, [i] ii 3–35 [36]   MH

[Printed by Spottiswoode & Co.]   [1887]

*Seventeen questions, with space for the answers. A parody
appeared in the* St. James's Gazette, *16 Nov. 1887.*

756 ARCHER, WILLIAM. Masks or faces? A study
in the psychology of acting by William Archer.

pp. [8] [1] 2–232   L

Longmans, Green, and Co.   1888

"Considerable portions" of this work first appeared in
Longmans' Magazine, *January, February, and March
1888, under the title of "The anatomy of acting."*

————[American edition] with The paradox of
acting by Denis Diderot. Introd. Lee Strasberg. New
York: Hill and Wang, 1957. (Dramabooks.)

757 ILLUSTRATED CATALOGUE of theatrical
and private wigs. W. Clarkson.

pp. [1–5] 6–95 [96 97–104 (advts.)]; inserted leaves of
coloured paper [3] (advts. for Clarkson's Lillie Powder);
illus.   MH

[London: Clarkson]   [1889]

758 FITZGERALD, PERCY [HETHERINGTON].
The art of acting in connection with the study of char-
acter, the spirit of comedy and stage illusion by Percy
Fitzgerald, M.A., F.S.A. (The Dilettante Library, no. 10).

pp. [i–vii] viii–xii, [1] 2–194 [195 (advts.) 196 (bl.)];
pl. [front.]   L

London: Swan Sonnenschein & Co.; New York:
Macmillan & Co.   1892

*"The substance of the following little Treatise was
delivered in the form of Lectures at the Royal Institution,
the Society of Arts, and the Royal Institute, Hull".*

759 MACLAUGHLIN, EMILY. *A handy book
upon elocution and dramatic art.

pp. lvi, 179

Iliffe & Son   1892

BMC., *but L copy destroyed.*

760 [LYNN, NEVILLE.] LYNN'S PRACTICAL
HINTS on making-up. For plays, charades, tableaux-
vivants, private purposes, teetotal entertainments, etc.
Alphabetically arranged. With an appendix on making-
up by electric light; and a classified list of the best-known
typical stage characters; naming the wig, etc., profes-
sionally allotted to each.

pp. [1–7] 8–20; illus.; ptd. wrappers, illus.   E

London: Capper and Newton; Dublin: McWillis &
Co.   [1894–5]

761 ————new and entirely revised edition.

pp. [1–7] 8–20; illus.   L

Capper & Newton   [1897]

762 BUCHANAN, R. C. †Steps to the stage, or how to become an actor.

A. Malcolm & Co.   L
                                                          [1895]

Copy imperfect, lacks all after p. 12.

763 CAMPBELL, HUGH., R. F. BREWER and HENRY G. NEVILLE. Voice, speech and gesture: a practical handbook to the elocutionary art by Hugh Campbell, M.D., R. F. Brewer, B.A. and Henry Neville including essays on reciting and recitative by Clifford Harrison, and on recitation with musical accompaniment by Frederick Corder, R.A.M., with upwards of a hundred illustrations by Dargavel and Ramsey comprising also selections in prose also selections in prose and verse adapted for recitation, reading, and dramatic recital edited, with an introduction, by Robt. D. Blackman.

pp. [i–ix] x–xvi, [1–3] 4–888; illus., incl. music   E
Charles William Deacon & Co.   1895

764 ——new and enlarged edition

pp. [i–ix] x–xviii, [1–3] 4–1132; illus., incl. music   E
Charles William Deacon & Co.   1897

765 ——new and enlarged edition

pp. [iii–ix] x–xix, [1–3] 4–1196; illus., incl. music   E
Charles William Deacon & Co.   1904

Lacks half-title.

——[American edition] New York: Putnam's Sons, 1895

766 "PAINTER, A", *pseud.* Turner's complete guide to theatrical make-up giving detailed instructions as to painting, lining, wigs, &c., &c., by "A painter."

pp. [1–3] 4–47 [48 (advts.)]; illus.; ptd. wrappers   L
John Alvey Turner   [1896?]

767 CORLETTE, CHA[RLE]S M[AYNE]. The universal theatrical stage guide by Chas. M. Corlette, theatrical agent, etc. 2, Snowden Street, Gaylor Street, Manchester. First edition.

pp. [1–2] 3–8   L
[Manchester]   [1896]

768 ——The universal theatrical stage tutor and guide. Second edition. By Chas. M. Corlette.

pp. [1–3] 4–14 [15 (illus.) 16 (bl.)]; illus.; ptd. wrappers
                                                      L
Manchester: T. Cusack, Junr.   [1897]

769 BUCHANAN, R. C. How to become an actor. By R. C. Buchanan, F.R.S.L.

pp. [1–11] 12–104; incl. ptd. front wrapper   E
Samuel French, Limited   [1897]

Articles on make-up, stage slang, etc. as first published in the Glasgow Weekly Herald *with additional chapters.*

770 HAMMERTON, Sir J[OHN] A[LEXANDER], *ed.* The actor's art Theatrical reminiscences methods of study and advice to aspirants specially contributed by leading actors of the day Edited by J. A. Hammerton Prefatory note by Sir Henry Irving.

pp. [i–iv] v–vi [vii–viii], [1] 2–267 [268 (imprint)]; illus. (facsim. autographs)   E
George Redway   1897

771 ——second edition

pp. [i–iv] v–vi [vii–viii], [1] 2–267 [268 (imprint)]; illus. (facsim. autographs on cover)   NbU
George Redway   1897

The leading actors include Ellen Terry, George Alexander and J. L. Toole.

772 WAGNER, LEOPOLD. How to get on the stage and how to succeed there by Leopold Wagner.

pp. [i–vii] viii–ix [x], [1] 2–181 [182]   L
Chatto & Windus   1899

773 HUBERT, PHILIP G[ENGEMBRE]. The stage as a career A sketch of the actor's life; its requirements, hardships, and rewards The qualifications and training essential to success — expert opinions from famous actors, including Sir Henry Irving, Lawrence Barrett, Dion Boucicault, Joseph Jefferson, Helen Modjeska, Mary Anderson, and Maggie Mitchell — disappointments and pitfalls — the actor and society — how to begin — dramatic schools and teachers — contracts and salaries. By Philip G. Hubert, Jr.

pp. [i–ii] iii–vii [viii (bl.)], 1–192   L
New York and London: G. P. Putnam's Sons   1900

With one leaf of advertisements bound in as issued.

774 RYDER, MAXWELL. Elocution and stage training. By Maxwell Ryder.

pp. [4] [1–5] 6–232 [233–236 (advts.)]; errata slip   L
Thomas Burleigh   1900

"Part II. Stage Training. Notes of Lectures" pp. [45]–232.

COSTUME

See also GENERAL HISTORY no. 959; ACTING nos. 710, 757; THE AMATEUR THEATRE passim especially nos. 2178–2179, 2181, 2185, 2187–2189, 2197, 2198; BIOGRAPHY 3122–3123 (Charles Kean), 3418–3426 (Planché); THEORY AND CRITICISM no. 3924; GOVERNMENT REGULATIONS for the year 1697 etc. (pp. 22, 25, 27 above), 1894 (p. 36 above). See also SALE CATALOGUES, nos. 53–137, passim.

775 [JEFFERYS, THOMAS.] A COLLECTION of the dresses of different nations, antient & modern. Particularly old English dresses. After the designs of Holbein, Vandyke, Hollar and others. With an account of the authorities, from which the figures are taken; and some short historical remarks on the subject. To which are added the habits of the principal characters on the English stage. (Recueil des habillements de différentes nations etc.)

4 vols. in 2. pp. [i–vii] viii–xiii [14–15] 16–47 [48 (bl.)]; pls. 1–119 + pp. [49–55] 56–83 [84 (errata)]; pls. 120–240 + pp. [1–7] 8–35 [36 (bl.)]; pls. 1–120 + pp. [1–7] 8–39 [40 (bl.)]; pls. 121–240   L

Thomas Jefferys   1757–72

In English and French.

776 ——★large paper issue

vols. I and II only; col. pls.   L

777 LACY, THOMAS HAILES, *comp.* ★Female costumes, historical, national and dramatic.

pls. 200   MB

Lacy   1865

Running title: Lacy's Dramatic Costumes.

778 LACY, THOMAS HAILES, *comp.* ★Male costumes, historical, national & dramatic.

pls. 200   MB

Lacy   1868

Running title: Lacy's Dramatic Costumes.

779 vacant.

780 BOWEN, CYRIL. Practical hints on stage costume, including instructions and patterns for making hats, boot tops, sword belts, lace ornaments, ballet shirts, and other necessary articles of costume generally supplied by the actor himself. By Cyril Bowen, of the Globe, Duke's, Aquarium, Park and Alexandra Palace Theatres, London: Newcastle, Bradford, and principal provincial theatres of England.

pp. [1–3] 4–36; illus.   GU

London and New York: Samuel French   [ca. 1881]

SCENERY AND MACHINES

See also THE LONDON THEATRE nos. 1095–1096, 1307, 1498; THE THEATRE OUTSIDE LONDON no. 1624; AMATEUR THEATRE no. 2191; BIOGRAPHY no. 3109 (Inigo Jones); THEATRICAL CRITICISM nos. 3877, 3924. For Sale Catalogues of individual theatres see nos. 53–67, 69, 126.

781 STEPHENSON, R. M. ★Stephenson's patent theatre machinery.

folio: pls. 10

                                                    [1845?]

STR.

782 DIRCKS, HENRY. The ghost! As produced in the spectre drama, popularly illustrating the marvellous optical illusions obtained by the apparatus called the Dircksian phantasmagoria: being a full account of its history, construction, and various adaptations. By Henry Dircks, civil engineer, life member of the British Association (1837), &c. &c. the inventor.

— Come, let me clutch thee: —
I have thee not, and yet I see thee still.
Art thou not, fatal vision, sensible
To feeling as to sight?

                                                Macbeth

pp. [4] [1] 2–102; inset [blue slip: "All communications . . ."]; illus.   L

E. and F. N. Spon   1863

See also below no. 785.1.

783 LLOYDS, F. Practical guide to scene painting and painting in distemper. By F. Lloyds. With illustrations drawn by the author.

pp. [i–v] vi, [1] 2–97 [98 (bl.)]; pls. [17 (five col.) (12 leaves in all)]; col. patches [37 (stuck to pages 29, 43, 44)]; illus.   MH

George Rowney & Co.   [1875]

784 CLARE, WALTER F. ★Theatrical decoration.

                                                    1879?

Advt. in Dramatic and Musical Circular. (no. 4243 below)

785 ★ART OF SCENE-PAINTING by practical scenic artists.

[French?]   [ca. 1881]

Advt. in Fox (1890), p. 127 (see above no. 748).

785.1 PEPPER, [JOHN HENRY], *Professor.* The true history of the ghost; and all about metempsychosis. By Professor Pepper.

pp. [*6*] [1] 2–46; illus.; pl., fold. [front.]; ptd. covers

L

Cassell & Company   1890

Title on cover reads: The True History of Pepper's Ghost. *Describes the stage illusion first shown at the Polytechnic in 1862, and refutes Dircks's claim (see no. 782) to be the sole inventor.*

786 HOPKINS, ALBERT A[LLIS]. Magic stage illusions and scientific diversions including trick photography Compiled and edited by Albert A. Hopkins. With an introduction by Henry Ridgely Evans. With four hundred illustrations.

pp. [i–v] vi–xii, [1] 2–556 [557–560 (advts.)]; illus., incl. [front.]

L

Sampson Low, Marston and Company Limited   1897

First published by Munn & Co., New York, 1897, parts having previously appeared in Scientific American. *Book Four, pp. 251–366: "Science in the Theatre."*

ARCHITECTURE, FIRE PRECAUTIONS etc.

See also GOVERNMENT REGULATION OF THE THEATRE for the years 1881, 1883, 1884, 1886, 1887, 1888 (see above pp. 33–35); THE LONDON THEATRE nos. 1098, 1100, 1113, 1125, 1178, 1179, 1195–1199, 1296, 1312.1, 1366–1379, 1451, 1458, 1472, 1489, 1500; THE THEATRE OUT OF LONDON nos. 1573, 1607, 1653, 1937.

787 SAUNDERS, GEORGE. A treatise on theatres.

pp. [i–vii] viii–x [xi–xiv], [1] 2–94; pls. I–XIII, incl. 4 fold.

L

Printed for the author, and sold by I. and J. Taylor 1790

788 ———[another edition] A treatise on theatres and on the plays performed therein.

pp. [i–vii] viii–x [xi–xiv], [1] 2–94; pls. I–XIII, incl. 4 fold.

O

Oxford: J. Lichfield   1790

———[American edition] New York: Benjamin Blom, Inc., 1968.

789 [HOWARD, FREDERICK, *Earl of Carlisle.*] THOUGHTS upon the present condition of the stage, and upon the construction of a new theatre.

pp. [1–3] 4–43 [44 (advt.)]

L

W. Clarke   1808

790 ———A new edition, with additions.

pp. [*4*] [1] 2–59 [60 (advt.)]

L

W. Clarke   1809

791 *LIBERTY ABOVE ALL THINGS; or, important and original observations on the liberty of the press, &c. To which will be added, timely hints to prevent theatres, manufactures, and other public buildings of magnitude, and also large private houses from demolition by fire. . . .

Printed by J. Dean   [1809?]

Advertised in Authentic account *(no. 1366 below).*

792 [WARE, SAMUEL.] REMARKS on theatres; and on the propriety of vaulting them with brick and stone: with observations on the construction of

domes, and the vaults of the Free and Accepted Masons. By the author of A treatise of the properties of arches and their abutment piers.

pp. [i–iii] iv–viii, [1] 2–75 [76 (bl.)]; pls. [3] incl. 1 fold.

L

T. Bensley   1809

Follows the author's letters to The Times *on the fire at Drury Lane, and includes a scheme for the rebuilding.*

793 ———*[another edition]

pp. viii, 75; pls. [3]

J. Taylor   1809

STR.

794 ———*[another edition]

1812

STR.

795 WYATT, GEORGE. A compendious description of a design for a theatre; made in pursuance of an order (and now published under permission) from the committee of subscribers for carrying into effect the project of erecting a third theatre in the metropolis. By George Wyatt, F.S.A. architect.

pp. [1–3] 4–22 [23–24 (bl.)]; pls. [front.] 1–4 (fold.)   L

J. Taylor   1812

796 KITCHINER, WILLIAM, *Dr.* The economy of the eyes: precepts for the improvement and preservation of the sight. Plain rules which will enable all to judge exactly when, and what spectacles are best calculated for their eyes observations on opera glasses and theatres, and an account of the pancratic magnifier, for double stars, and day telescopes. By William Kitchiner, M.D.

pp. [i–iii] iv–viii, [1–2] 3–246; illus. (music); pls. [front. (fold.), 1]

L

Hurst, Robinson, & Co.   1824

797 ——*second edition. Part I.

pp. viii, 242   MB

Whittaker   1826

——[American edition] Boston: Wells & Lilly, 1824.

798 SHAW, EYRE M[ASSEY]. Fires in theatres. By Eyre M. Shaw, London Fire Brigade.

pp. [1–3] 4–48   LGk

London and New York: E. and F. N. Spon   1876

799 ——second edition

pp. [i–iii] iv–xx, [1] 2–86   L

London and New York: E. & F. N. Spon   1889

800 *THE STATE of the London theatres and music halls.

                                                   MH

                                                   1887

On the title-page is also a note: "These articles are reprinted from the Saturday Review *exactly as they appeared, without addition or omission, except some clerical alterations." They have reference to the provision made for the safety of the public, in case of fire, in the different places of amusement in London. The first article is dated June 11; the last, September 10, 1887. Just as the articles were coming to an end, the terrible catastrophe at Exeter emphasised the lesson they were teaching — Lowe. On the fire at Exeter see below no. 1595.*

801 BUCKLE, J[AMES] G[EORGE]. Theatre construction and maintenance: a compendium of useful hints and suggestions on the subjects of planning [,] construction, lighting, fire prevention, and the general structural arrangements of a model theatre; including the regulations prepared by the Metropolitan Board of Works and the Lord Chamberlain; together with a model set of rules, based upon the metropolitan, provincial, American, and continental theatre regulations. By J. G. Buckle, A.R.I.B.A.

pp. [1–5] 6–157 [158–160 (bl.)]; pl. [front., fold.]   L

"The Stage" Office   1888

Dedicated to Wilson Barrett. Includes tables of the principal dimensions of a large number of theatres.

802 ROTH, WALTER E[DMUND]. Theatre hygiene: a scheme for the study of a somewhat neglected department of the public health. By Walter E. Roth, B.A., late demy of Magdalen Coll., Oxon, author of *The elements of school hygiene*, etc.

pp. [i–vii] viii [9] 10–53 [54]; illus.   L

Baillière, Tindall and Cox   [1888]

803 GERHARD, WILLIAM PAUL. Theatre fires and panics: their causes and prevention. First edition.

pp. [2] [i–ii] iii [iv] v–vii [viii], [1] 2–175 [176]   GM

New York: John Wiley & Sons; London: Chapman & Hall   1896

804 SACHS, EDWIN O[THO]. and ERNEST A. E. WODROW. Modern opera houses and theatres. Examples selected from playhouses recently erected in Europe, with descriptive text, a treatise on theatre planning and construction, and supplements on stage machinery, theatre fires, and protective legislation; by Edwin O. Sachs architect and Ernest A. E. Wodrow, A.R.I.B.A.

3 vols. pp. [16] [1] 2–60 [61–62]; illus.; pls. [85] [=99 leaves] + pp. [18] [1] 2–54 [2] 55–56; illus.; pls. [91] [=101 leaves] + pp. [16] [1] 2–122 [10] ²[1] 2–170 [2] [i] ii–viii; illus. pls. [front., 18]; t.pp. in red and black.
                                                   GM

B. T. Batsford   1896 (vol. I), 1897 (vol. II), 1898

                                                   (vol. III).

Volumes II and III by Sachs alone.

——[American edition] New York: Benjamin Blom, Inc., 1968.

805 ——Stage construction. Examples of modern stages selected from playhouses recently erected in Europe with descriptive and critical text, being a supplement to "Modern Opera Houses and Theatres." By Edwin O. Sachs, architect.

pp. [12] [1] 2–86 [87–88 (bl.)]; illus.; pls. [front., 5]; running title: Modern Opera Houses and Theatres
                                                   LGk

B. T. Batsford   1898

806 YOUNG, ARCH[IBAL]D. Theatre panics and their cure. By Archᵈ. Young, Edinburgh. With plans for a safe theatre prepared by Thomas T. Paterson, architect, Edinburgh.

pp. [1–4] 5–20; illus.   GU

Edinburgh: Andrew Elliot; London: B. T. Batsford
                                                   1896

807 DARBYSHIRE, ALFRED. Theatre exits. A paper by Alfred Darbyshire, architect . . . With a description and plan of Sir Henry Irving's "safety theatre". (Publications of the British Fire Prevention Committee, No. 4, ed. by Edwin O. Sachs.) (Bound in Publications of the British Fire Prevention Committee, vol. 1, 1898.)

pp. [2] [1–5] 6–13 [14]; illus. [front., plan]   GM

Issued at the offices of the British Fire Prevention Committee; Charles & Edwin Layton, publishers 1898

808 GERHARD, W[ILLIA]M PAUL. The safety of theatre audiences and the stage personnel against danger from fire and panic. A paper by Wm. Paul Gerhard, consulting engineer. (Publications of the British Fire Prevention Committee. No. 41, ed. by Edwin O. Sachs.)

pp. [1–5] 6–43 [44]   GM

The British Fire Prevention Committee   1899

MANAGEMENT, INCLUDING STAGE MANAGEMENT

For rules and regulations of particular companies see THE LONDON THEATRE nos. 1181, 1298, 1403, 1407, 1480; THE THEATRE OUT OF LONDON: ENGLAND nos. 1536, 1541, 1686, SCOTLAND no. 1976; THE AMATEUR THEATRE no. 2153.
See also GOVERNMENT REGULATION OF THE THEATRE no. 152; ARTS OF THE THEATRE no. 722; GENERAL HISTORY no. 985; MEDIEVAL AND RENAISSANCE STUDIES no. 1033; PERIODICALS nos. 4258, 4266, 4395.

809 BROWNSMITH, J[OHN]. The dramatic time-piece: or perpetual monitor. Being a calculation of the length of time every act takes in the performing, in all the acting plays at the Theatres-Royal of Drury-Lane, Covent-Garden, and Hay-Market, as minuted from repeated observations, during the course of many years practice. As also the time of night when half-price will be taken, and the certain period when any play will be over. By J. Brownsmith, prompter to the Theatre-Royal in the Hay-Market.

pp. [4] [1] 2–75 [76 (bl.) 77–80 (index)]   L
J. Almon; T. Davies; J. Hingeston   1767

810 BROWNSMITH, JOHN. The theatrical alphabet. Containing a catalogue of several hundred parts (both mens and womens) in different plays and farces; with the number of lengths noted that each part contains, carefully disposed in alphabetical order, and accurately distinguished by initial letters, denoting whether they are in a tragedy, comedy, opera, farce, &c. The number of lengths are justly calculated, as they are performed at the Theatres Royal; with a vacancy reserved to insert many more, as they may occur in new pieces, or otherwise. By John Brownsmith.

pp. [40]; thumb-indexed by hand in red and black ink   L
Printed for the author, and sold by Mr. Rowland, at the Black-Lion, in Russel-Street, Covent-Garden. Price 1s. plain, or 1s. 4d. cut and lettered.   1767

811 SOME GENERAL ADVICE to theatrical managers. The third edition.

pp. [i–v] vi–xi [xii] [13] 14–34   DFo
C. Stalker   1789

Satirises the dishonest practices of stage managers.

812 R., N. ✶"No salary required"; or, theatricals at Winklegate, by N.R. Being a satirical expose of some of the adveriements which appear in several of our leading papers.

pp. 20; illus.   MB
Wright & Co.   [18–?]

813 [HOGG, WENTWORTH, *comp.*] GUIDE to selecting plays; or, managers' companion. Giving a complete description of 1500 pieces, showing the number of characters — acts and scenes — the class of play — the costumes — time in representation — an account of the dramatis personae — the plot or advice connected with each. Arranged according to the requirements of any company.

pp. [1–3] 4–78 [79–80 (list of music for hire)]   L
London: Samuel French; New York: Samuel French & Son   [1882?]

PLAYWRITING

See also GENERAL HISTORY no. 925; PERIODICALS no. 4324. For the problem of copyright see GOVERNMENT REGULATION OF THE THEATRE for the years 1832, 1833, 1882, 1888 (see above pp. 30–31, 34–35); also nos. 200, 213, 218, 222–225, 229, 233, 239, 240–241 note; GENERAL HISTORY no. 977; BIOGRAPHY no. 3312 (Mathews). For the Dramatic Author's Society see nos. 2134–2137.

814 MAYHEW, EDWARD. Stage effect: or, the principles which command dramatic success in the theatre. By Edward Mayhew

pp. [1–11] 12–103 [104 (imprint) 105–107 (advts.) 108 (bl.)]   L
C. Mitchell   1840

815 DRAMATIST, A, *pseud.* †Playwriting: a handbook for would-be dramatic authors. By a dramatist.

pp. [i–v] vi–viii, [1] 2–111 [112], ²[i] ii–vii [viii]; illus.   L
The Stage Office   1888

This copy lacks pp. 103–106. Contains an appendix of stage plans and sketches. Possibly by Jerome K. Jerome — Motley 1.

816 CALMOUR, ALFRED C[ECIL]. Practical playwriting and the cost of production. By Alfred C.

Calmour. With an introduction by Wm. Davenport Adams.

pp. [i–vii] viii–xii, [1] 2–62 [63–66 (advts.)]   L
Bristol: J. W. Arrowsmith; London: Simpkin, Marshall, Hamilton, Kent & Co. Limited   [1891]

A paper delivered "at the Playgoers' Club, and at Professor Herkomer's School of Art, Bushey" in 1891. Dedicated to Irving.

817 ARCHER, FRANK *pseud. of* Frank Bishop Arnold. How to write a good play. By Frank Archer.

pp. [i–vii] viii–xi [xii], [1] 2–224; illus. (diagrams)   E
Sampson Low, Marston & Company Limited   1892

818 ———[another edition]

pp. [i–vii] viii–xi [xii], [1] 2–224; illus. (diagrams).   E
London: Samuel French, Ltd.; New York: Samuel French   [1920]

819 WAGNER, LEOPOLD. How to publish a book or article and how to produce a play Advice to young authors by Leopold Wagner.

pp. [i–iv] v–ix [x] [11] 12–210, [1] 2–6 (advts.); half-title: How to publish   L
George Redway   1896

HISTORIES

For histories of the theatre contained in playlists, dictionaries etc. see LISTS AND DICTIONARIES nos. 30–33, 35–40, 42, 44.

820 FLECKNOE, RICHARD. Love's kingdom. A pastoral trage-comedy. Not as it was acted at the Theatre near Lincolns-Inn, but as it was written, and since corrected by Richard Flecknoe. With a short treatise of the English stage, &c.

pp. [8] 1–81 [82–96]   L

Printed by R. Wood for the author   1664

This play was acted three times without much success. Genest remarks that, judging from the play and the short treatise, Flecknoe cannot have been so dull a writer as Dryden represented him to be — Lowe. Wing F 1229. The "short treatise" reprinted in Hazlitt, pp. 275–281 and Spingarn, II, 91–96.

821 ———[another issue]

pp. [8] 1–81 [82–96]   L

Simon Neale   1674

Wing F 1230.

822 [WRIGHT, JAMES.] HISTORIA HISTRI-ONICA: an historical account of the English-stage, shewing the ancient use, improvement, and perfection, of dramatick representations, in this nation. In a dialogue, of plays and players.

pp. [6] 1–32   L

William Haws   1699

Advertised in the Post Boy, *4–6 July 1699 — Hooker. Wing W 3695.*

823 ———[another edition] "Historia histrionica:" from the rare original printed at London in 1699. (Mr. Ashbee's Occasional Fac-Simile Reprints.)

pp. [6] 1–32; cover-title   L

Printed for subscribers only   1872

100 copies printed.

Reprinted in Dodsley's A select collection of old plays, 11, i-xxvii (1774 and later editions); in An apology for the life of Colley Cibber, comedian, 3rd ed., (R. Dodsley, 1750), pp. 489–520, new ed. (1889), I, xix-li; The old English drama (1830), I, i-xvii. Reprinted in part in Social England illustrated, a collection of XVIIth century tracts with an introduction by Andrew Lang (Constable, 1903), pp. 421–432; In Bentley, II, 691–696.

824 [DOWNES, JOHN.] ROSCIUS ANGLI-CANUS, or an historical review of the stage: after it had been suppres'd by means of the late unhappy civil war, begun in 1641, till the time of King Charles the IIs. restoration in May 1660. Giving an account of its rise again; of the time and places the governours of both the companies first erected their theatres. The names of the principal actors and actresses, who perform'd in the chiefest plays in each house. With the names of the most taking plays; and modern poets. For the space of 46 years, and during the reign of three kings, and part of our present Sovereign Lady Queen Anne, from 1660, to 1706.

pp. [4] 1–52   L

Printed and sold by H. Playford, at his house   1708

Summers, in his edition (p. x), claims that "there were various issues, & in certain of these the author corrected some few of the more patent errors due to the printer's carelessness . . ." Stratman, Play Lists 16.

825 ———with additions, by the late Mr. Thomas Davies [edited by F. G. Waldron].

pp. [i–iii] iv [5] 6–70 [71–72]   L

Printed for the editor   1789

826 ———[reissue of no. 825 with appendix] (The Literary Museum)

pp. [iv] [5] 6–70 [71–72], ²1–27 [28]   L

Printed for the editor   1792

Signed F.G.W[aldron] (p. ²27); "Appendix to Downes's Roscius Anglicanus. Edition 1789" (pp. ²1–27).

827 ———A fac-simile reprint of the rare original of 1708. With an historical preface by Joseph Knight.

pp. [i–v] vi–xxxv [xxxvi (bl.)], [4] 1–52 [8]   L

J. W. Jarvis   1886

Limited to 125 copies. Reprints also A Declaration of the Lords and Commons, 1642 (see above no. 143).

828 ———edited by the Rev. Montague Summers.

pp. [i–vi] vii–xiii [xiv–xviii], 1–286   L

The Fortune Press   [1928]

"Fifty copies on Alton Mill hand-made paper, numbered 1–50; and six hundred copies on Arnold unbleached hand-made paper, numbered 51–650."

————[American edition (the Summers edition)] New York: Benjamin Blom, Inc., 1968.

John Downes was prompter at the theatre in Lincoln's Inn Fields from 1661 to 1706. To him we are indebted for most of our information regarding the Restoration stage and actors — Lowe.

829 BETTERTON, THOMAS. The history of the English stage, from the Restauration to the present time. Including the lives, characters and amours, of the most eminent actors and actresses. With instructions for public speaking; wherein the action and utterance of the Bar, stage, and pulpit are distinctly considered. By Mr. Thomas Betterton.

pp. [8] [1] 2–167 [168] [2], 2[1] 2–86; illus.   L
E. Curll   1741

Advertised 13 June 1741 — Straus. By Curll and William Oldys from notes and information from Betterton and John Bowman, according to CBEL. Pp. 2[1] 2–86: an abridged version of Egerton's Faithful memoirs of . . . Mrs. Anne Oldfield, 1730 (see below no. 3384).

————[American edition] Boston: printed by William S. & Henry Spear, 1814.

830 RICCOBONI, LEWIS. An historical and critical account of the theatres in Europe. Viz, the Italian, Spanish, French, English, Dutch, Flemish, and German theatres. In which is contain'd a review of the manner, persons and character of the actors; intermix'd with many curious dissertations upon the drama. Together with two celebrated essays: viz. an essay on action, or, the art of speaking in public: and, a comparison of the ancient and modern drama. By the famous Lewis Riccoboni of the Italian Theatre at Paris. The whole illustrated with notes by the author and translator.

pp. [16] [1] 2–333 [334 (bl.) 335–336 (catalogue of German plays) 337–352 (The Table)]   L
T. Waller; and R. Dodsley   1741

Dedicated by the translator to Charles Fleetwood. Luigi Riccoboni's Réflexions historiques et critiques sur les differents théâtres de l'Europe. Avec les pensées sur la déclamation was published in Paris (Jacques Guéron) in 1738.

831 ————[another edition?] *Reflections upon declamation; or, the art of speaking in publick. With an historical and critical account of the theatres in Europe . . . By the famous Lewis Riccoboni, of the Italian theatre in Paris.

[Cooper]   1741

Recorded but not seen by Lowe.

832 ————*An historical account of all the theatres in Europe. With a review of the manner, persons, and character, of the actors. With two essays; viz. on action, or the art of speaking in public; and a comparison of the

antient and modern drama. By Lewis Riccoboni, of the Italian Theatre of Paris. The second edition.

pp. [16] [1] 2–333 [334 (bl.) 335–336 (Catalogue . . . German Theatre)] [18 (Table)]   NNUQ
T. Waller   1747

833 ————A general history of the stage, from its origin. In which the several theatres of Europe, those particularly of Italy, Spain, France, England, Holland, Flanders, and Germany, with regard to their excellencies and defects, are critically compared with each other; the various management of them described; and the characters, manners, and persons of the principal performers considered. Together with two essays; on the art of speaking in public, and a comparison between the antient and modern drama. Translated from the eminent Lewis Riccoboni. The second edition. To which is prefixed, An introductory discourse concerning the present state of the English stage and players.

pp. [4] [i] ii–xx, [1] 2–333 [334 (bl.) 335–336 (catalogue of German plays) 337–352 (The Table)]   L
W. Owen; and Lockyer Davis   1754

A reissue of Riccoboni's An historical and critical account (1741) with new preliminary matter. Dedicated by the translator to David Garrick.

834 ————[another edition] Declamation; or, an essay on the art of speaking in public; with an historical and critical account of the theatres in Europe. Viz. Italian, Spanish, French, English, Dutch, Flemish, and German theatres. With a review of the manner, person, and character of actors. With curious dissertations on the drama; and a comparison of the dramas of ancient and modern [sic]. By Lewis Riccoboni of the Italian Theatre at Paris. Illustrated with notes by the author and the translator.

pp. [2] [1] 2–333 [334 (bl.) 335–336 (catalogue of German plays) 337–352 (The Table)]   L
R. Dodsley   1790

A reissue, without the preliminaries, of Riccoboni's An historical and critical account (1741).

835 CHETWOOD, W[ILLIAM] R[UFUS]. A general history of the stage, from its origin in Greece down to the present time. With the memoirs of most of the principal performers that have appeared on the English and Irish stage for these last fifty years. With notes, antient, modern, foreign, domestic, serious, comic, moral, merry, historical, and geographical, containing many theatrical anecdotes; also several pieces of poetry, never before published. Collected and digested by W. R. Chetwood, twenty years prompter to His Majesty's company of comedians at the Theatre-Royal in Drury-Lane, London.

pp. [8] 1–256   L
W. Owen   1749

This work has been abused in unmeasured terms, but it contains much valuable information—Lowe.

836 ———[another edition] A general history of the stage; (more particularly the Irish theatre) from its origin in Greece down to the present time. With the memoirs of most of the principal performers, that have appeared on the Dublin stage, for the last fifty years. With notes, antient, modern, foreign, domestic, serious, comic, moral, merry, historical, and geographical, containing many theatrical anecdotes; also several pieces of poetry, never before published. Collected and digested by W. R. Chetwood, twenty years prompter to His Majesty's company of comedians of the Theatre Royal in Drury-Lane, London.

pp. [*16*] 1–259 [260]; pls. [front., 1]   L
Dublin: printed by E. Rider for the author   1749

837 [CHETWOOD, WILLIAM RUFUS?] THE BRITISH THEATRE. Containing the lives of the English dramatic poets; with an account of all their plays. Together with the lives of most of the principal actors, as well as poets. To which is prefixed, a short view of the rise and progress of the English stage.

pp. [*2*] [i] ii–xvi, [*6*] [1] 2–200 [201–227 (index) 228 (errata)]   L
Dublin: Peter Wilson   1750

   Stratman, *Play Lists 23.*

838 ———[reissue]
pp. [*2*] [i] ii–xv [xvi], [*6*] [1] 2–200 [201–227 (index) 228 (errata)]   L
R. Baldwin, jun.   1752

839 VICTOR, [BENJAMIN]. The history of the theatres of London and Dublin, from the year 1730 to the present time. To which is added, An annual register of all the plays, &c. performed at the Theatres-Royal in London, from the year 1712. With occasional notes and anecdotes, by Mr. Victor, late one of the managers of the Theatre-Royal in Dublin.

2 vols. pp. [i–v] vi–viii, [1] 2–272 + [*4*] [1] 2–218   L
T. Davies; R. Griffiths, T. Becket, and P. A. De Hondt; G. Woodfall; J. Coote; and G. Kearsley   1761
   Stratman, *Play Lists 28.*

840 ———*[another edition]
2 vols.
Dublin: G. Faulkner & J. Exshaw   1761
   IKF.

841 VICTOR, [BENJAMIN]. The history of the theatres of London, from the year 1760 to the present time. Being a continuation of the annual register of all the new tragedies, comedies, farces, pantomimes, &c. that have been performed within that period. With occasional notes and anecdotes. By Mr. Victor, author of the two former volumes.

pp. [i–iii] iv–xi [xii], [1] 2–232   L
T. Becket   1771

   Stratman, *Play Lists 30. See also below no. 843.*

842 CENSOR DRAMATICUS, *pseud.* A complete history of the drama, from the earliest periods to the present time. By Censor Dramaticus.

pp. [1–3] 4–140   L
Printed and Sold by T. Wilkins   1793

   Stops abruptly at Chapter XII, (the quarrel between Wilks and Powell).

843 [OULTON, WALLEY CHAMBERLAIN.] THE HISTORY of the theatres of London: containing an annual register of all the new and revived tragedies, comedies, operas, farces, pantomimes, &c. that have been performed at the Theatres Royal, in London, from the year 1771 to 1795. With occasional notes and anecdotes.

2 vols. pp. [i–v] vi, [1] 2–196 + [i–v] vi, [1] 2–217 [218 219–220 (advt.)] [misprinting 217 as "117"]   GU
Martin and Bain   1796

   A continuation of Benjamin Victor's History, 1761, 1771 (see above nos. 839–841). Stratman, *Play Lists 37.*

844 ———*A history of the theatres of London, containing an annual register of new pieces, revivals, pantomimes, &c. With occasional notes and anecdotes. Being a continuation of Victor's and Oulton's histories, from the year 1795 to 1817 inclusive. By W. C. Oulton.
3 vols.   MB
Chapple   1817–1818

   Vol. 1, Drury Lane; vol 2, Covent Garden; vol 3, Haymarket and English opera. Stratman, *Play Lists 46.*

845 ROACH, JOHN. Roach's new and complete history of the stage, from its origin to its present state, including, all the entertaining anecdotes, of London, Dublin, and Edinburgh, &c. Recorded by our most eminent historians. Viz. Strutt, Stow, Cibber, Langborow, Gildon, Chetwood, Carew, Dodsley, Baker, Malone, Stevens, Victor, Oulton, &c. Intended as a companion to Roach's *Authentic memoirs of the green room.*

pp. [1] 2–144; engr. t.p.; pl. [front.]   L
J. Roach   1796

   For Roach's Authentic Memoirs see below no. 2214.

846 DIBDIN, [CHARLES]. A complete history of the English stage. Introduced by a comparative and comprehensive review of the Asiatic, the Grecian, the Roman, the Spanish, the Italian, the Portugese [*sic*], the

German, the French, and other theatres, and involving biographical tracts and anecdotes, instructive and amusing, concerning a prodigious number of authors, composers, painters, actors, singers, and patrons of dramatic productions in all countries. The whole written, with the assistance of interesting documents collected, in the course of five and thirty years, by Mr. Dibdin.

5 vols. pp. [4] [i] ii, [1] 2–386 + [1–5] 6–400 + [1–5] 6–392 + [1–5] 6–329 340–458 [=448] + [4] [i] ii–iii [iv (bl.)], ²[i] ii–v [vi (bl.)] [5] 6–96 99–387 [388 (bl.)], ³[i] ii–viii; misprinting 387 as "487" [=386]   L

Printed for the Author, and sold by him at his Warehouse   [1797–1800]

> *Originally published in monthly parts, beginning May 1797 — Dibdin. The title of vols. II–V is: "A complete history of the stage", and the half-title of each volume is: "Dibdin's history of the stage". Vol. V [i] ii–iii: "To the most noble the Marquis of Salisbury"; this dedication is dated 25 March, 1800, and is meant to be bound up with vol. I. Vol. V ²[i] ii–v: Preface. Vol. V ³[i] ii–viii: Contents. Dibdin, pp. 93, 101–102.*

847 A COMPENDIOUS HISTORY of the English stage, from the earliest period to the present time. Containing a candid analysis of all dramatic writings, a liberal and impartial criticism on the merits of theatrical performers, and a sketch of the lives of such as have been eminent in their profession. By Waldron, Dibdin, &c.

pp. [4] [1] 2–174 [175–176 (advt.)]; added engr. t.p., dated 1797, which reads "The curtain; or an impartial history of the English stage; digested from the most undoubted authorities."; pl. [front.]   L

J. S. Jordan   1800

> *A compilation — Lowe.*

848 WALDRON, F[RANCIS] G[ODOLPHIN]. *The origin of the English stage; with memoirs of celebrated performers, accompanied by their portraits; of many of whom there are no other prints extant. By F. G. Waldron.

1802

> *Recorded but not seen by Lowe.*

849 [GENEST, *Rev.* JOHN.] SOME ACCOUNT of the English stage, from the Restoration in 1660 to 1830.

10 vols. pp. [4] [i] ii–cxl, [1] 2–499 [500 (imprint)] + [4] [1] 2–660 + [4] [1] 2–655 [656 (imprint)] + [4] [1] 2–664 + [4] [1] 2–632 + [4] [1] 2–607 [608 (bl.)] + [4] [1] 2–719 [720 (bl.)] + [4] [1] 2–704 + [4] [1] 2–600 + [4] [1] 2–550 [2] [i] ii–vii [viii (corrections)]   L

Bath: printed by H. E. Carrington   1832

> *This, the only complete history of the stage since the Restoration, was the work of a Bath clergyman, who must have devoted his life to it. No words can do adequate justice*

to the honest and thorough nature of the work; and its value cannot be over-estimated. Yet it fell dead from the press. (Lowndes says it was published at £5, 5s., but reduced to £1, 10s.) It was for years a drug in the market but is now becoming one of the most valued of theatrical books. — Lowe. Stratman, *Play Lists 47.*

850 HARVEY, FRANCIS. List of portraits, views, etc. contained in this illustrated copy of Genest's History of the English stage 1600–1830.

pp. [4] [1] 2–122 [123 (imprint) 124 [(bl.)]   L

[Chiswick Press, printed by Whittingham and Wilkins]
1876

851 CHAPMAN, J[OHN] K[EMBLE], *ed.* A complete history of theatrical entertainments, dramas, masques, and triumphs, at the English Court, from the time of King Henry the Eighth to the present day, including the series of plays performed before Her Majesty, at Windsor Castle, Christmas, 1848-9. Containing many curious particulars of our early dramatic literature and art. Embellished with beautiful engravings on steel, by Finden, from designs by Grieve, Telbin, and Absolon. Edited by J. K. Chapman.

pp. [4] [1] 2–86; engr. tp., engr. ded.; pls. [front., 5]; insets in blue and gold [5]   L

John Mitchell   [1849?]

852 ——[another issue] The court theatre, and royal dramatic record; being a complete history of theatrical entertainments at the English court, from the time of King Henry the Eighth down to the termination of the series of entertainments before Her Most Gracious Majesty Queen Victoria, His Royal Highness Prince Albert, and the Court at Windsor Castle, Christmas 1848-9. With illustrations on steel, by Finden, from designs by Messrs. T. Grieve, Telbin, and John Absolon.

pp. [4] [1] 2–86; engr. t.p., engr. ded.; pls. [front., 5]; insets in blue and gold [5]   LGk

J. Mitchell   [1849?]

853 ——*[another edition]

1852

> *Recorded, but not seen by Lowe. For the Windsor Castle performances, see also below no. 929.*

854 DORAN, *Dr.* [JOHN]. "Their majesties' servants." Annals of the English stage, from Thomas Betterton to Edmund Kean. Actors-authors-audiences. By Dr. Doran, F.S.A.

2 vols. pp. [8] [1] 2–591 [592]; illus., incl. [front.] + pp. [4] [1] 2–586; illus., incl. [front.]   GM

Wm. H. Allen & Co.   1864

855 ——second edition. (Revised, corrected, and enlarged.)

pp. [i-vii] viii, [1] 2-459 [460 (bl.) 461-464 (advts.)]; pl. [front.]   E

Wm. H. Allen   1865

A "People's Edition" — Dedication.

856 ——[another edition] edited and revised by Robert W. Lowe.

3 vols. pp. [i-v] vi-vii [viii-ix] x [xi-xiv], [1] 2-436; illus.; pls. [front., 15] + pp. [i-v] vi [vii-x], [1] 2-414; illus.; pls. [front., 15] + pp. [i-v] vi [vii-x], [1] 2-428; illus.; pls. [front., 17]   L

John C. Nimmo   1888

The illustrations include wood engravings on Japanese paper mounted on pages of text. Stratman, Play Lists 51 A.

857 ——[large paper issue *of no. 856*]

JFA.

Edition limited to 300 numbered copies; plates in duplicate.

858 ——People's edition with portrait and eighty wood engravings.

pp. [i-vii] viii [ix-x], [1] 2-459 [460 (bl.)]; pls. [front., 28]; illus.   L

John C. Nimmo   1897

A reprint of the 1865 edition (no. 855 above).

——[American editions] New York: W. J. Widdleton, 1865; New York: Armstrong, 1880, with a memoir of Dr. Doran and an introduction and conclusion by R. H. Stoddard; Philadelphia: D. McKay, 1890.

859 DUNCAN, GEORGE. Origin and history of the British drama: containing a review of the stage — its aims and purpose; the lives of all the celebrated dramatists, with specimens of their writings; and anecdotes of Garrick, Foote, Elliston, Palmer, Macready, Edmund Kean, the Kembles, Young, Phelps, Mrs. Jordan, Mrs. Siddons, Miss O'Neill, Mr. and Mrs. Charles Kean, G. V. Brooke, Fechter, and other celebrated actors. By George Duncan. To be issued in monthly parts.

Parts 1-4. pp. [1-3] 4-64   GM

Glasgow: George Duncan   1867

Breaks off at Marlowe.

860 DORAN, *Dr.* [JOHN]. In and about Drury Lane and other papers reprinted from the pages of the *Temple Bar* magazine. By Dr. Doran.

2 vols. pp. [8] [1] 2-316 [317-320 (advt.)] + [8] [1] 2-349 [350 (imprint) 351-352 (advt.)]

Richard Bentley & Son   1881

JFA.

——[American editions] Boston: F. A. Niccolls & Co., [19—?].

861 HERFORD, C[HARLES] H[AROLD]. †A sketch of the history of the English drama in its social aspects being the essay which obtained the Le Bas Prize, 1880 by C. H. Herford, B.A. Trinity College.

pp. 96   L

Cambridge: E. Johnson   1881

862 FITZGERALD, PERCY [HETHERINGTON]. A new history of the English stage from the Restoration to the liberty of the theatres, in connection with the patent houses, from original papers in the Lord Chamberlain's Office, the State Paper Office, and other sources. By Percy Fitzgerald.

2 vols. pp. [i-vii] viii-xii, [1-3] 4-437 [438 (bl.) 439-440 (advts.)] + [i-v] vi-viii, [2] [1] 2-463 [464]   GU

Tinsley Brothers   1882

862.1 MOLLOY, J[OSEPH] FITZGERALD. Famous plays with a discourse by way of prologue on the play-houses of the Restoration. By J. Fitzgerald Molloy.

pp. [i-vii] viii-xvi, [1-3] 4-313 [314 (bl.) 315-328 (advts.)]

Ward & Downey   1886

JFA.

862.2 ——*third edition

Advertised in Molloy's Kean.

862.3 ——*new edition. Famous plays: their histories and their authors.

pp. xvi, 313   MB

Ward & Downey   1888

863 HAMILTON, WALTER. A sketch of the drama in England during the last three centuries. By Walter Hamilton, F.R.G.S., F.R.H.S. Parodist to ye Sette of Odd Volumes. Read at a Meeting of "The Sette", held at Limmer's Hotel, on Wednesday, January 8th, 1890. (Privately printed opuscula issued to the members of The Sette of Odd Volumes. No. XXI.)

pp. [1-7] 8-79 [80]; illus.; pl. [front.], fold.   E

Imprynted at the Chiswick Press   1890

Edition limited to 201 copies.

CONTEMPORARY SURVEYS, MISCELLANIES 1700–1900

864 R., C. The danger of masquerades and raree-shows, or the complaints of the stage, against masquerades, opera's, assemblies, balls, puppet-shows, bear-gardens, cock-fights, wrestling, posture-masters, cudgel-playing, foot-ball, rope-dancing, merry-makings, and several other irrational entertainments, as being the ground and occasion of the late decay of wit in the island of Great-Britain. By C.R. of C.C.C. Oxford. Inscribed to Mrs. Oldfield.

pp. [1–8] 9–37 [38]   L
W. Boreham   1718

865 *THE DANCING DEVILS: or, the Roaring Dragon. A dumb farce. As it was lately acted at both houses, but particularly at one, with unaccountable success.

pp. 70
Bettesworth   1724

Against pantomimes and raree shows. Very scarce — Lowe.

866 A LETTER TO MY LORD ******* on the present diversions of the town. With the true reason of the decay of our dramatic entertainments.

pp. [1–4] 5–30   MH
J. Roberts   1725

Blames the decay on opera and masquerades and the "three Men, who call themselves the Managers of our Stage."

867 D'URFEY, THOMAS, *pseud.* The English stage Italianiz'd, in a new dramatic entertainment, called Dido and Æneas: or, Harlequin, a butler, a pimp, a minister of state, generalissimo, and Lord High Admiral, dead and alive again, and at last crown'd King of Carthage, by Dido. A tragi-comedy, after the Italian manner; by way of essay, or first step towards the farther improvement of the English stage Written by Thomas D'Urfey, Poet Laureat *de Jure.*

pp. [i–ii] iii–vi [vii–viii] [9] 10–24   L
A. Moore   1727

See Nicoll, II, 256–257. "B. Moore" signs an affidavit concerning the pretended authenticity of the work. Didone abbandonata da Enea was produced at the King's Theatre 17 Dec. 1726.

868 D'ANVERS, CALEB, *pseud.* of Nicholas Amhurst. The Twickenham hotch-potch, for the use of the Rev. Dr. Swift, Alexander Pope, Esq; and company. Being a sequel to *The Beggars Opera*, &c. Containing, I. The state of poetry . . . V. The rival actresses, *viz.* Mrs. O——d, Mrs. P——r, Mrs. B——h,

Miss Y——ger, and Miss Polly Peachum. VI. A poetical catalogue of Polly Peachum's gallants. VII. An epistle from Signora F——na to a lady. VIII. A true copy of Polly Peachum's opera. Also, her panegyrick. Written by Caleb D'Anvers.

pp. [2] [i] ii–vii [viii (bl.)], [1] 2–54   L
J. Roberts   1728

Published 13 May — Schultz. Includes some reprinted pieces. On page 54: "This work will be continued", but no other parts are recorded.

869 [RALPH, JAMES.] THE TOUCH-STONE: or, historical, critical, political, philosophical, and theological essays on the reigning diversions of the town. Design'd for the improvement of all authors, spectators, and actors of operas, plays, and masquerades. In which every thing antique, or modern, relating to musick, poetry, dancing, pantomimes, chorusses, cat-calls, audiences, judges, criticks, balls, ridottos, assemblies, new oratory, circus, bear-garden, gladiators, prizefighters, Italian strolers [*sic*], mountebank stages, cock-pits, puppet-shews, fairs, and publick auctions, is occasionally handled. By a person of some taste and some quality. With a preface, giving an account of the author and the work.

pp. [2] [i–ii] iii–xxviii, 1–237 [238]   L
Printed and Sold by the Booksellers   1728

Dedication signed: "A. Primcock".

870——— [reissue] The taste of the town: or, a guide to all publick diversions. Viz. I. Of musick, operas and plays. Their original, progress, and improvement, and the stage-entertainment fully vindicated from the exceptions of old Pryn, the Reverend Mr. Collier, Mr. Bedford and Mr. Law. II. Of poetry, sacred and profane. A project for introducing scripture-stories upon our stage, and acting them on Sundays and Holy-Days after divine service, as is customary in most polite parts of Europe. III. Of dancing, religious and dramatical. Reflections on this exercise, public and private, with the learned Bishop Potter's sentiments thereon. IV. Of the mimes, pantomimes and choruses of the antients; and of the imitation of them in our modern entertainments after plays. V. Of audiences, at our theatrical representations, their due behaviour, and of cat-calls and other indecent practices, concluding with remarks on our pretenders to criticism. VI. Of masquerades; ecclesiastical, political, civil and military: their antiquity, use and abuse. Also of ridottos, assemblies and Henley's oratory. VII. Of the athletic sports of the antients: their circus compared with our bear-garden, and their gladiators with our prize-fighters. Of cock-fighting, puppet-shews, mountebanks and auctions.

pp. [i–ii] iii–xxviii, 1–237 [238]; t.p. in red and black L
Printed and Sold by the Booksellers   1731

871 THE DRAMATIC POETASTER a vision. Humbly inscrib'd to the most illustrious the Viscount Nessuno.

pp. [2] 1–30   L

T. Cox; T. Astley; S. Harding   1732

A satire on pantomimes, "Hurlothrumboicks," ballad-operas, and the debasement of the drama.

872 B———, *Right Honourable the Lord, pseud.* ⋆See and seem blind: or, a critical dissertation on the publick diversions, &c., of persons and things, and things and persons, and what not. In a letter to A—— H——, Esq.

pp. 30   MB

H. Whitridge   [1733]

873 THE PLAYERS: a satire.

pp. [46]   L

W. Mears   1733

Heroic couplets, with a preface. Sometimes attributed to Edward Phillips.

874 ⋆THE SESSION of the critics; or, the contention for the nettle. A poem. To which is added, a dialogue between a player and a poet.

pp. [1–2] 3–16   TxU

T. Cooper   [1737]

Foxon.

875 SCRIBLERIUS TERTIUS, *Esq., pseud.* The hard-us'd poet's complaint: inscrib'd to the theatric-managers, and bibliopolians, of the great, little world. By Scriblerius Tertius, Esq. of neither university, and indeed barely of gramatical erudition.

pp. [4] [i] ii, [5] 6–8; pl. [front.]   L

Printed for the author, publish'd by G. Woodfull [*ca.* 1750]

Variously ascribed to Paul Whitehead (probably erroneously) and to Thomas Cooke; both used the pseudonym "Scriblerius Tertius".

876 ⋆A GUIDE to the stage: or, select instructions and precedents from the best authorities towards forming a polite audience; with some account of the players, &c.

                                                    1751

Published 10 Dec 1750 (LS., pt. 4, p. 225). An Addisonian essay on how to behave at the playhouse.

877 ———the second edition, with additions.

pp. [1–3] 4–30   L

D. Job; and R. Baldwin   1751

Advertised as "newly publish'd this day" 12 Dec 1750 (LS., pt. 4, p. 226).

878 THE PRESENT STATE OF THE STAGE in Great-Britain and Ireland. And the theatrical characters of the principal performers, in both kingdoms, impartially considered.

pp. [1–2] 3–55 [56 (bl.)]   L

Paul Vaillant; and M. Cooper   1753

A very valuable work. Its criticisms on the actors of the day are excellent — Lowe. Published in March. See LS., pt. 4, p. 364.

879 †[THE] UPPER GALLERY. A poem.

pp. [1–3] 4–12   L

W. Owen   1753

A descriptive poem, without any special interest or motive — Lowe.

880 THE THEATRICAL EXAMINER: an enquiry into the merits and demerits of the present English performers in general; the substance of theatric character; public taste; conduct of the managers; advice to young actors; some slight remarks on late productions; with a short consideration on *Douglas.*

pp. [2] 1–98   L

J. Doughty   1757

A very trenchant criticism upon Garrick, Barry, Mossop, and the other actors of the time — Lowe.

881 [WOTY, WILLIAM?] THE SPOUTING CLUB: a mock heroic, comico, farcico, tragico, burlesque poem. By the author of The Robin Hood society: a satire.

pp. [4] 1–16   MH

R. Withy   1758

"Published clandestinely" — DNB. Sometimes ascribed to Richard Lewis.

882 WILKES, [THOMAS]. A general view of the stage. By Mr. Wilkes.

pp. [2] [i–iii] iv–viii, [1] 2–335 [336]; vignette on t.p.   L

London: J. Coote; Dublin: W. Whetstone   1759

Advertised as "this day publish'd" on 28 March 1759 — LS., pt. 4, p. 718. Contains a section on the art of acting.

883 AN ESSAY upon the present state of the theatre in France, England and Italy. With reflections upon dramatic poetry in general, and the characters of the principal authors and performers of those nations. A work absolutely necessary to be read by every lover of theatrical exhibitions.

pp. [8] [1] 2–220   L

Printed for I. Pottinger, at the Dunciad   1760

Published in January — LS.

883.1 A THEATRICAL LOVE EPISTLE from Honest Ranger, to Miss Polly Honeycombe. Compos'd from the titles of plays, farces, &c.

bs.   MH
Printed at No. 41, (take notice pray,)
Leadenhall-Street, the little a
(London is needless without doubt,
Only it makes the metre out)   [*ca.* 1760]

In prose, within borders. Polly Honeycomb by George Colman, the elder was first produced at D.L. 5 December 1760. See also below no. 967 for a similar item based on play titles.

884 F——B——L——, *pseud.* The rational Rosciad. On a more extensive plan than any thing of the kind hitherto published. In two parts. *viz.* I. On the stage in general and particular, and the merits of the most celebrated dramatic writers. II. On the merits of the principal performers of both theatres. By F——B——L——.

pp. [*4*] [1] 2–35 [36 (bl.)]   MH
C. Parker; and J. Wilkie   1767

Published 11 Feb. 1767 — LS., pt. 4, p. 1220.

885 HIFFERNAN, PAUL. Dramatic genius. In five books. By Paul Hiffernan, M.D.

pp. [i–iv] v–viii, [1–2] 3–125 [126 (advts.)]   L
Printed for the Author   1770

Dedicated to David Garrick. Book 1, Plan of a temple to the memory of Shakespeare; 2, The progress of the human mind in inventing the drama; 3, A philosophical analysis of the pre-requisites to succeed in the art of acting; 4, Composition and acting; 5, Architecture, painting and other arts as far as they are necessary to theatrical representation.

886 ——second edition

pp. [1–4] 5–220 [221–222 (advts.) 223–224 (bl.)]   L
T. Becket and P. de Hondt   1772

887 [PILON, FREDERICK.] THE DRAMA, a poem.

pp. [2] [i–iii] iv, [1] 2–25 [26]   L
J. Williams   1775

Some copies have imprint: printed by J. Chapman and sold by J. Williams. The attribution to Hugh Downman is mistaken.

888 [GENTLEMAN, FRANCIS.] THE MODISH WIFE, a comedy, performed with uninfluenced applause at the Theatre-Royal, Haymarket. To which is prefixed A summary view of the stage, as it has been, is, and ought to be. With biographical anecdotes of Messrs. Mossop, Dexter, Derrick, and the author, school-fellows, and public cotemporaries.

pp. [*4*] [1] 2–30 [31–32], ²[1] 2–80   L
Sold by T. Evans; and J. Bell   [1775]

Gentleman's The Modish Wife was produced at the Haymarket 18th September 1773. "A summary view of the English, Scots, and Irish Stages", pp. 1–30.

889 WOTY, W[ILLIAM]. The stage; a poetical epistle, to a friend. By W. Woty.

pp. [1–3] 4–12   L
Derby: printed for the Author by J. Drewry [*ca.* 1780?]

Rouze! Britons, rouze! and banish from the Scene, Dumb shows, and noise, the frivolous, and mean.

890 DAVIES, THOMAS. Dramatic micellanies [*sic*]: consisting of critical observations on several plays of Shakespeare: with a review of his principal characters, and those of various eminent writers, as represented by Mr. Garrick, and other celebrated comedians. With anecdotes of dramatic poets, actors &c. By Thomas Davies.

3 vols. pp. [i–iii] iv–xxiv, [1] 2–451 [452]; pl. [front.] + pp. [1–5] 6–410 [2] 411–425 [426] + [*4*] [1] 2–508
                                                      GM
Printed for the author   1784 (Vol. I), 1783 (Vol. II), 1784 (Vol. III)

891 ——[another edition] ["Miscellanies" correctly spelled]

3 vols. [bound in one] pp. [i–iii] iv–v [vi–vii] viii–xii, [1] 2–263 [264] + [1–3] 4–286 + [2] [1] 2–310   L
Dublin: S. Price, H. Whitestone, W. Wilson, R. Moncrieffe, L. White, R. Marchbank, T. Walker, P. Byrne, R. Burton, J. Cash, W. Sleater   1784

892 ——a new edition

3 vols. pp. [i–v] vi–xi [xii (bl.)], [1] 2–451 [452 (bl.)]; pl. [front.] + pp. [1–5] 6–427 [428 (bl.)] + pp. [2] [1] 2–605 [606 (bl.)]   L
Printed for the author   1785

The half-title (to vols. I and II) reads: "Dramatic Miscellanies". The words "A new edition" do not occur on the title-page of vol. III.

893 ★THE CLOVEN FOOT; or a peep into Hell: being a most impartial critique on the Devil, and a few of his liege subjects. A fragment.

pp. [3] 4–18   DFo
Printed for E. Macklew   1786

A satire on contemporary literature and the theatre.

894 THE EASTERN THEATRE erected. An heroi-comic poem. In three cantos.

pp. [*4*] [i] ii [iii–iv], [1] 2–35 [36]   DFo
William Brown   1788

895 *THE MODERN STAGE EXEMPLIFIED, in an epistle to a young actor. Part I.

pp. viii, 32   DFo

W. Flexney   [1788]

Apparently only Part I was published.

896 DISBANDED SON OF THESPIS, A, *pseud.* *A serio-comic poem, entitled, The budget, or, truth's candle lighted: intended as a theatrical scourge for naughty boys and girls, by a disbanded son of Thespis.

1791

Recorded but not seen by Lowe.

897 BELLAMY, THOMAS. Miscellanies: in prose and verse; written by Thomas Bellamy.

2 vols. pp. [8] [1] 2–248; pl. [front.] + pp. [1–5] 6–130 [131 (note) 132 (bl.)], ²[1] 2–4, ³[1–3] 4–76, ⁴[1–7] 8–33 [34 (bl.) 35 ("Advertisement") 36 (bl.)]; pls. [front., 1] L

Printed for the author   1794–1795 [*for* 1796]

Vol. 2 contains "The life of William Parsons, comedian. Written by Thomas Bellamy. To which are added his dramatic character, by John Litchfield, Esq. and a letter of intelligence, from Charles Dibdin, Esq." (pp. ³[1–3] 4–76), and "The London theatres; a poem. Interspersed with sentiments of pity on the fair unfortunate: and free reflections on the lobby lounger, the orange woman, the place keeper, and other nuisances which degrade a London theatre. By Thomas Bellamy." (pp. ⁴[1–7] 8–33); each of these has a full title-page and separate signatures and pagination (and so may be found separately), but on p. ⁴[35]: "It was the original intention of Mr. Bellamy to sell "The life of Parsons", and "The London theatres" by themselves, as well as with the Miscellanies: and for that purpose they were titled, priz'd, and separately paged. As he has renounced that intention, it is necessary respectfully to inform the public, that, the present edition of the Miscellanies, the life, and the poem, cannot be had any other way than together".

898 OXONIENSIS, *pseud. of* Thomas Munro. Philoctetes in Lemnos. A drama, in three acts. To which is prefixed, a green room scene, exhibiting a sketch of the present theatrical taste: inscribed, with due deference, to the managers of Covent-Garden and Drury-Lane theatres, by their humble servant Oxoniensis.

pp. [i–iv] v–xi [xii], [1–5] 6–100   GU

William Bingley   1795

The "green room scene" is satirical on the use of animals on the stage, and other follies of public and managerial taste—Lowe.

899 *A REVIEW of the present state of the British theatre, on [sic] useful hints to Mr. Pitt, on taxation.

pp. 12   MB

Printed for the author   [1795?]

900 [TAYLOR, JOHN.] VERSES on various occasions.

pp. [6] [1] 2–140   L

Printed by B. Millan; Sold by J. Debrett   1795

Includes a long poem "The Stage", and many other theatrical pieces. Dedicated to Mary Robinson. For Taylor's autobiography Records of my life, *1832 see below no. 920.*

901 ——[another edition.] Poems on several occasions: consisting of sonnets, miscellaneous pieces, prologues and epilogues, — tales, imitations, &c.

pp. [i–v] vi [vii–x], [1–3] 4–246   L

Edinburgh: Archibald Constable and Co.; London: John Murray   1811

902 ——[Another edition.] Poems on various subjects, by John Taylor, Esq.

2 vols. pp. [i–v] vi–xxxii, [1–5] 6–316 + [i–v] vi–xv [xvi], [1–3] 4–308   L

Payne and Foss; Longman, Rees, Orme, and Co.; J. Richardson; and J. Murray   1827

902.1 [PENN, JOHN.] LETTERS on the drama.

pp. [1–5] 6–80   L

Elmsly; Faulder; Sewell; and Owen and White. 1796

By John Penn of Stoke Park, author of a tragedy called "The Battle of Eddington" — Lowe. See below no. 4000.

903 THE STROLLING PLAYER; or, life and adventures of William Templeton.

3 vols. pp. [4] [1] 2–293 [294] + [4] [1] 2–262 + [4] [1] 2–294   L

Printed by B. McMillan   1802

Apparently fictional.

904 GILLILAND, THOMAS. A dramatic synopsis, containing an essay on the political and moral use of a theatre; involving remarks on the dramatic writers of the present day, and strictures on the performers of the two theatres. By Thomas Gilliland.

pp. [i–iii] iv, [1] 2–146   L

Lackington, Allen, and Co; Symonds; Jordan and Maxwell; S. Highley; Roach; Williams; Bell; and Ginger   1804

905 DRAMATICUS, *pseud.* An impartial view of the stage, from the days of Garrick and Rich to the present period; of the causes of its degenerated and declining state, and shewing the necessity of a reform in the system, as the only means of giving stability to the present property of the two winter theatres. By Dramaticus.

pp. [2] [i] ii–vii [viii (bl.)], [1] 2–26   L

C. Chapple   1816

  Dated 21st November 1815.

906 [M., G. and W., C.?] AN ESSAY on the profession of a player, &c. &c. To which is added A description of the first theatre that ever was built, called the theatre of Bacchus, at Athens. N.B. The profits arising from the sale of this essay, will be given in aid of the Theatrical Fund.

pp. [1–3] 4–18

York: printed by C. Peacock   1816

  IKF. *Another copy at MB.*

907 MONNEY, WILLIAM. Caractacus, a new tragedy, in five acts: with previous Remarks on English dramatic tragedy; including a blank verse gamut, and strictures on theatrical committees, managers, and players. By William Monney, Gent.

pp. [2] [i–iii] iv–v [vi] [7–9] 10–117 [118]   L

Printed for the Author   1816

  Stratman, *Tragedy, 4502.*

908 ———*With an appendix, including an answer to, and critique on, some unique criticism contained in a publication entitled "The Critical Review." Second edition. By William Monney, Gent.

pp. 141   MH

For the author   1817

  Stratman, Tragedy, *4503.*
  A work so dreadfully bad, that it is difficult to conceive that even Mr. Monney believed in it. Its publication fully justified the manager who refused to produce it. The first edition received some well-deserved criticism, and the appendix to the second edition is devoted to abusing the reviewers—Lowe.

909 THE DRAMATIC SCORPION. A satire, in three cantos, with explanatory notes.

pp. [2] [i] ii–ix [x–xii], [5–9] 10–29 [30] [4] [31] 32–71 [72 (bl.)] 73–74 ("An alphabetical list of the persons mentioned in this satire")] [=88]   MH

R. S. Kirby; J. Barker; Rodwell and Martin   1818

  Dedicated to J. P. Kemble. Formerly ascribed to Hazlitt, but not so by Keynes.

910 DIDDLER, JEREMY, *pseud.* Theatrical poems: comic, satirical, and descriptive; containing "The strolling manager", "The scene painter's blunder", "Studies from nature", "Kean, and his imitators", &c. &c. &c.

pp. [i–v] vi–vii [viii] [9] 10–43 [44]   MH

H. Price   1822

Poems refer also to the West of England and Ch——Kl—— manager of the summer theatre "not 10 miles west of London". Jeremy Diddler is a character in Kenney's "Raising the wind".

911 LEE, HENRY. The manager. A melo-dramatic tale. By Henry Lee.

pp. [4] [9] 10–68   TnSA

Sherwood, Neeley, and Jones   1822

  Dedicated to Edmund Kean. In verse. A tale for recital about a fictitious manager named Burr.

912 SAMS, W. *Studies from the stage, or the vicissitudes of life.

W. Sams   [1823]

  Tooley *442.*

913 *THE LONDON GALLIMAUFRY, or theatrical scrapbook.
                                                        1824
STR.

914 IMPORTANT THEATRICAL FACTS.

pp. [1] 2–4; head-title   MH

[Printed by J. Warwick]   [ca. 1825?]

  A facetious brochure.

915 [RYAN, RICHARD.] DRAMATIC TABLE TALK or scenes situations & adventures, serious & comic, in theatrical history & biography.

3 vols. pp. [i–ii] [xi] xii–xiii [xiv] [vii] viii–li [lii] [iii] iv–x [=60], [1] 2–288; engr. t.p.; pls. [front., 5] incl. 3 fold. + pp. [i–iii] iv–x, [1] 2–288; eng. t.p.; pls. [front., 7] incl. 3 fold. + pp. [i–iii] iv–ix [x] [misprinting iv as "vi"], [1] 2–317 [318 (list of engravings) 319–320 (advts.)]; eng. t.p.; pls. [front., 6] incl. 2 fold.   L

John Knight & Henry Lacey   1825 (Vols. I, II);
                                       1830 (Vol III)

  The engraved title-page to Volume I is found in two states.

  ———[American edition] (Stage Lovers series)
Boston: Page, 1903.

916 GRAVES, HENRY MERCER. An essay on the genius of Shakespeare, with critical remarks on the characters of Romeo, Hamlet, Juliet, and Ophelia; together with some observations on the writings of Sir Walter Scott. To which is annexed, A letter to Lord ——, containing a critique on taste, judgment, and rhetorical expression, and remarks on the leading actors of the day. By Henry Mercer Graves.

pp. [i–vii] viii, [1] 2–206   L

James Biggs   1826

  Jaggard *p. 120.*

917 GRIN, GEOFFREY, GENT. *pseud.* Rhyming reminiscences in comical couplets. By Geoffrey Grin, Gent.

pp. [i–ix] x–xii, [1] 2–168; illus. (allegorical front.) MH
C. S. Arnold   1826

The half-title reads: "Rhyming reminiscences in comical couplets; being a versification of the good things supposed to have been uttered by all the witty wags since the Deluge; interspersed with many novelties, quips, quiddities, and quotations". A number of these poems are on theatrical matters, and the author was apparently an actor ("the public, before whom he has had the honour of appearing frequently, though not in the capacity of an author").

918 HERBERT, THOMAS. A nostrum for theatrical insipidity; or the legitimate drama, versus horror and hobgoblinism: a satiric poem, (in length 944 lines,) with explanatory notes. By Thomas Herbert.

pp. [1–5] 6–33 [34 (bl.)]   L
T. Herbert   [1826]

919 OXBERRY, [WILLIAM]. Oxberry's anecdotes of the stage, &c. &c.

pp. [2] [1] 2–96; pl. [front.]   E
G. Virtue   1827

920 TAYLOR, JOHN. Records of my life; by the late John Taylor, Esquire, author of "Monsieur Tonson".

2 vols. pp. [i–v] vi–viii, [1] 2–432; pl. [front.] + pp. [i–v] vi–viii, [1] 2–412 [413–416 (advts.)]   L
Edward Bull   1832

The Records are full of theatrical information, for Taylor was on intimate terms with actors, authors, and managers for nearly two generations — Lowe.

————[American edition] New York: Harper & Brothers, 1833.

The "anecdotal substance" reprinted in Personal reminiscences of O'Keeffe, Kelly, and Taylor, ed. by R. H. Stoddard (Bric-a-Brac Series, New York, 1875). For Taylor's Verses on various occasions 1795, 1811, 1827, see above nos. 900–902.

921 [TOMLINS, FREDERICK GUEST.] *THE PAST AND PRESENT STATE of dramatic art and literature; addressed to authors, actors, managers, and the admirers of the old English drama.

pp. 32   MB
C. Mitchell   1839

922 ————The past and present state of dramatic art and literature; addressed to authors, actors, managers, and the admirers of the old English drama. Second edition.

pp. [1–3] 4–32   MH
C. Mitchell   1839

923 COOKE, JAMES. The stage. Its present state, and prospects for the future. By James Cooke.

pp. [1–5] 6–16   L
J. Pattie   [1840]

924 TOMLINS, F[REDERICK] G[UEST]. A brief view of the English drama, from the earliest period to the present time: with suggestions for elevating the present condition of the art, and of its professors. By F. G. Tomlins.

pp. [i–iii] iv–viii, [1] 2–152   GM
C. Mitchell   1840

Proposes a Royal Academy for Dramatic Art. Originally published in part in the Sunday Times.

925 HERAUD, JOHN A. *The present position of the dramatic poet in England. By John A. Heraud.

                                                                             MH
                                                                             1841

926 TOMLINS, F[REDERICK] G[UEST]. The nature and state of the English drama. A lecture delivered at a meeting of the Syncretic Association, at the Gallery of British Artists, Suffolk Street, on Thursday, January 28th, 1841. By F. G. Tomlins.

pp. [1–5] 6–24   L
C. Mitchell   1841

927 À BECKETT, GILBERT ABBOTT. The quizziology of the British drama. Comprising I.—stage passions. II.—stage characters. III.—stage plays.

pp. [i–iii] iv, [1] 2–87 [88]; illus.; pl. [front.] by Leech L
Punch office   1846

928 SHAKESPERE'S HOUSE.

bs.   MH
E. M. Hodges, printer, (from Pitt's)   [1847]

In verse (with another poem "Thou art gone from my gaze"), on the impending auction of Shakespeare's birthplace, and P. T. Barnum's bid for it; and on the popularity of ballet and opera at the expense of Shakespeare's plays. A street ballad. See also Shakespere Newspaper [1847] (no. 4192 below).

929 WEBSTER, BENJAMIN, *ed.* The series of dramatic entertainments performed by Royal Command, before Her Majesty the Queen, His Royal Highness Prince Albert, the royal family, and the court, at Windsor Castle. 1848-9. Comprising Merchant of Venice. (Shakspere.) Used up. (Dion Bourcicault.) The stranger. (Thompson.) The housekeeper. (D. Jerrold.) Hamlet. (Shakspere.) Box and Cox. (J. M. Morton.)

Twice killed. (John Oxenford.) Sweethearts & wives. (J. Kenny.) Printed verbatim from the authorised versions. With fac-similes of the bills of performance, and a corrected list of the royal personages and the nobility and gentry present on each occasion. Edited by Benjamin Webster, lessee of the Theatres Royal, Haymarket and Adelphi. The greater number of the above dramas are copyright.

pp. [6] [1] 2–372; col. pls. [front., 9 (incl. half-title)]; insets [5 (laced paper programmes)]   L

Mitchell, Royal Library; McLean's; National Acting Drama Office   [1849]

See also nos. 851–2.

930 OLD PLAYGOER, AN, *pseud. of Major-general Samuel Parlby?* *Desultory thoughts on the national drama, past and present. By an old playgoer.

pp.(5), 62   MB
Onwhyn   1850

931 ———second edition
pp. [4] [1–2] 3–70   LGk
Onwhyn   1850

Dedicated to W. C. Macready. A preliminary note is dated 28 June 1850.

932 ANECDOTES of the stage, or dramatic table-talk in theatrical history & biography.

pp. [1] 2–36; cover-title   MH
Edinburgh: James G. Bertram & Co.; London: W. Winn; Manchester: Abel Heywood; Glasgow: W. Love; Dunfermline: J. Henderson   1851

933 TOMLINS, FREDERICK GUEST. *Remarks on the present state of the English drama.

pp. 15   MB
Lacy   1851

934 RICHARDSON, JOHN. *Recollections political, literary, dramatic and miscellaneous of the last half century.

2 vols.

C. Mitchell   1856

    DLC Cat.

935 DONNE, WILLIAM BODHAM. Essays on the drama. By William Bodham Donne.

pp. [i–v] vi [vii–viii], [1] 2–256   L
John W. Parker and Son   1858

Essays reprinted from the Quarterly *and* Westminster Reviews, *and* Fraser's Magazine.

936 ———*Essays on the drama, and on popular amusements. By William Bodham Donne, Examiner of stage plays, Lord Chamberlain's Office. Reprinted from the Quarterly Review, the Westminster Review, and Fraser's Magazine. Second edition.

pp. (5), 256   MB
Tinsley   1863

936.1 WATKINS, BEN WILLIAM ("B.W.W.") Outlines of the life of William Bestow, Esq., editor and proprietor of the "Theatrical Journal." With occasional reference to contemporary theatrical events and personages. Traced by Ben William Watkins, Esq. ["B.W.W."]

pp. [2] [i] ii, [1] 2–110 [111–112 (advts.)]   MH
Published for the proprietor by Thomas Hailes Lacy   1864

First published in The Theatrical Journal *June 18, 1862–June 17, 1863 in fifty chapters; reprinted in forty-nine chapters.*

937 TUCKERMAN, HENRY T[HEODORE]. The collector Essays on books, newspapers, pictures, inns, authors, doctors, holidays, actors, preachers. By Henry T. Tuckerman. With an introduction by Dr. Doran.

pp. [4] [1] 2–353 [354], ²[1] 2–10 (advts.); inset t.p. with vignette.   L
John Camden Hotten   [1868]

On actors pp. 221–245.

938 HODDER, GEORGE. Memories of my time, including personal reminiscences of eminent men.

[i–vii] viii–xx, [1] 2–420   L
Tinsley Bros.   1870

Stories of Jerrold, Van Amburgh, Albert Smith, John Poole, Miss Kelly, J. S. Knowles, Macready, amateur performance, theatrical fund dinner, Charles Kean.

——[American edition] Personal reminiscences by Barham, Harness and Hodder, *ed.* R. H. Stoddard, (Bric-à-brac Series), New York: Scribner, Armstrong, and Company, 1875.

Selections.

939–940 vacant

941 SIMPSON, J. BELL. Literary and dramatic sketches. By J. Bell Simpson, Glasgow.

pp. [6] [1] 2–150   GM
Glasgow: David Bryce & son   1872

942 SNOW, WM. R. The drama on crutches. A satire of the day. By Wm. R. Snow, author of *Britannia's box of soldiers*.

pp. [1–9] 10–32   MH
(For the Author) J. C. Hotten   1872

Heroic couplets, on the present degraded state of the theatre, shown in its "sensation", "nude Burlesque", "Ballet", and "mediocrity":
Show to the Pit, with realistic pride
Some choice selections from their world outside!
Drive a real Hansom on the scene, and there
Pay him a real bad sixpence for his fare . . .

943 FITZGERALD, PERCY [HETHERINGTON]. The book of theatrical anecdotes. Selected and edited by Percy Fitzgerald, M.A.

pp. [1–5] 6–128   L
George Routledge and Sons   [1874]

944 FITZGERALD, PERCY [HETHERINGTON]. The romance of the English stage. By Percy Fitzgerald.

2 vols. pp. [i–vii] viii–ix [x–xii], [1] 2–334 [335–336 (advt.)] + [8] [1] 2–328   E
Richard Bentley & Son   1874

945 PAUL, G[EORGE] H[ENRY] HOWARD, J. TIMBS and P[ERCY HETHERINGTON] FITZGERALD. Book of modern anecdotes. Humour, wit, and wisdom. American — legal — theatrical. Edited by Howard Paul, J. Timbs, and P. Fitzgerald.

pp. [1–5] 6–448   L
Routledge & Sons   [1874]

946 NEVILLE, HENRY. The stage: its past and present in relation to fine art. By Henry Neville. Being the subject of a lecture delivered by the author at the Fine Art Gallery, Conduit Street, for the Society for the Encouragement of the Fine Arts on the 13th July, 1871. Revised and enlarged.

pp. [i–vii] viii–x [xi–xiii] xiv–xvi, [1–3] 4–96; errata slip; copyright slip   NbU
Richard Bentley and Son   1875

947 COOK, [EDWARD] DUTTON. A book of the play: studies and illustrations of histrionic story, life, and character. By Dutton Cook.

2 vols. pp. [i–vii] viii–xii, [1] 2–322 [323–324 (advts.)] + [i–v] vi–vii [viii], [1] 2–328   L
Sampson Low, Marston, Searle, & Rivington   1876

948 ——second edition

2 vols. pp. [i–vii] viii–xii, [1] 2–322 + [i–v] vi–vii [viii], [1] 2–328   LVA
Sampson Low, Marston, Searle, & Rivington   1876

949 ——third and revised edition

pp. [i–v] vi–viii, [1] 2–391 [392]   GU
Sampson Low, Marston, Searle, & Rivington   1881

950 ——*fourth edition

                                                                                    1882
STR.

951 [CHEVALIER, W. A.] OUTLINES of a scheme for reforming the stage, and elevating the actor's calling to the status of a liberal and legitimate profession.

pp. [2] [1–3] 4–22; title headed: A tribute to the Shakespeare Memorial at Stratford-on-Avon.   L
R. J. Bush   [1877?]

Motto: "O! reform it all together." Dedicated to W. E. Gladstone.

952 DIPROSE, JOHN. Diprose's book of the stage and the players. By John Diprose.

pp. [1–5] 6–111 [112] [8] [113] 114–288; illus.; pl. [front.]   L
Diprose & Bateman   [1877]

✖ Irving, Henry. The stage. 1878. *See no. 3065.*

953 *STAGE GOSSIP or theatrical tit-bits, ancient and modern.

pp. 96   MB
Jennings   [1880?]

954 [DIETZ, ELLA.] *A FEW WORDS on the work of an actor, and the duties of art criticis and audiences. A paper read before the Church and Stage Guild on April 6th, 1880.

                                                                                    MH
Women's Printing Society Ltd.   [1880]

955 HOLLINGSHEAD, JOHN. Plain English by John Hollingshead.

pp. [i–v] vi [vii–viii], [1] 2–191 [192 (bl.)]   L
Chatto and Windus   1880

A collection of papers on theatrical subjects, by the manager who made the Gaiety Theatre famous — Lowe.

956 FITZGERALD, PERCY [HETHERINGTON]. The world behind the scenes. By Percy Fitzgerald. (The Wanderer's Library.)

pp. [8] [1] 2–320, misprinting 61 as "63"   L
Chatto and Windus   1881

957 vacant.

✖ Irving, Henry. The stage as it is. [1881]. *See no. 3067.*

958 LENNOX, *Lord* WILLIAM PITT. Plays, players and playhouses at home and abroad with anecdotes of the drama and the stage by Lord William Pitt Lennox.

2 vols. pp. [i–v] vi–viii, [1] 2–303 [304] + [i–v] vi–viii, [1] 2–271 [272 (bl.)], ²1–16 (advts.)   GU

Hurst and Blackett   1881

Lord William Pitt Lennox's two series of Celebrities I have known *(Hurst & Blackett: 1876, 1877) contains some theatrical information.*

959 ROSS, CHARLES H[ENRY]. "Stage whispers," and "shouts without." A book about plays and playgoers, actors and actresses. With coloured costumes by Archibald Chasemore, heads by Alfred Bryan, comic scenes by Judy's artists, and chatter at the wing by Charles H. Ross.

pp. [3–8 (advts.) 13–14 (prelims)] 15–100 [101–102 (text) 103–110 (advts.)]; illus.; col. pls. [8, incl. front.]   E

"Judy" Office   [1881]

960 LARWOOD, JACOB, *pseud. of* Herman Diederik Johan Van Schevichaven. Theatrical anecdotes or fun and curiosities of the play, the playhouse, and the players, by Jacob Larwood (The Mayfair Library.)

pp. [8] [1] 2–328   MH

Chatto and Windus   1882

Sometimes ascribed to L. R. Sadler.

961 COOK, [EDWARD] DUTTON. On the stage. Studies of theatrical history and the actor's art. By Dutton Cook.

2 vols. pp. [i–iii] iv–viii, [1] 2–287 [288 (imprint)]; pl. [front.] + pp. [i–iii] iv, [1] 2–332; illus.   NbU

Sampson Low, Marston, Searle, and Rivington   1883

962 OLD PLAYGOER, AN, *pseud. of* Peter Hanley. Random recollections of the stage. By an old playgoer.

pp. [1–5] 6–70   E

Printed for the author for private circulation   [1883]

963 ——— [second edition]

pp. [1–5] 6–86   L

Printed by Diprose and Bateman for the Author for private circulation   [1884]

"Carefully revised" with "additional matter", according to "Preface to second edition". "Second edition" also on cover.

964 ——— [third edition] A jubilee of playgoing. By Peter Hanley.

pp. [1–5] 6–113 [114]   E

Tinkler and Hillhouse   1887

First public edition.

965 DAY, W. C. Behind the footlights; or, the stage as I knew it. By W. C. Day. Illustrated by G. B. Le Fanu.

pp. [6] [i] ii [iii–iv], [1] 2–191 [192]; illus., incl. [front.]   NbU

London and New York: Frederick Warne and Co. 1885

A collection of sketches — Lowe.

966 SCOTT, CLEMENT [WILLIAM]. *The stage and the age. A lecture delivered at the Playgoers' Club, on March 17, 1885. By Clement Scott.

[1885]

Lowe.

967 *HALL, HENRY THOMAS. Dramatic letters, a titular novelty.

pp. 20   MB

Cambridge: Wallis   1886

The incidents of these letters are told almost entirely by piecing together the titles of English plays—Brown. For a similar jeu d'esprit see no. 883.1.

968 NEWTON, H[ENRY] CHANCE. The penny showman and other poems. By H. Chance Newton. [Reprinted by permission from the *Referee, Fun, Weekly Times, &c., &c.*]

pp. [2] [1–2] 3–64   L

London: Samuel French; New York: Samuel French & Son   [1886]

969 BROADLEY, A. M. The craft, the drama, and Drury Lane, by A. M. Broadley, Barrister-at-law, P.M. 1717 and 1835, P.D.D.G.M. of Malta, and P.D.G.M.M. of the Mediterranean, secretary of the Drury Lane lodge, no. 2127.

pp. [2] [1–5] 6–15 [16] [17–18 (bl.)]; illus.

[1887]

Reprinted from the Christmas number of The freemason. IKF.

970 LYNN, [RICHARD A.] NEVILLE. The Thespian papers, being a series of humorous essays on subjects of professional and amateur interest. By Neville Lynn, F.S.L.A.

pp. [1–13] 14–134   GU

Walter Scott   1887

Short articles, some reprinted from journals.

971 JEROME, JEROME K[LAPKA]. Stage-land: curious habits and customs of its inhabitants. Described by Jerome K. Jerome. Drawn by J. Bernard Partridge.

pp. [4] [1] 2–80; pls. [front., 13]; illus.   L

Chatto & Windus   1889

972 ——*[another edition] Sixteenth thousand.
pp. [4], 80; illus.   MB
Chatto & Windus   1890

973 ——*[another edition]
pp. 84; illus.
Chatto & Windus   1892

Motley 1.

——[American editions] New York: Henry
Holt & Co., 1890; 1891; George Munro, 1890.

974 ADAMS, WILLIAM DAVENPORT. With
poet and player. Essays on literature and the stage. By
William Davenport Adams.
pp. [i–vii] viii, [1] 2–228   GU
Elliot Stock   1891

——[American edition] New York: A. C.
Armstrong & Son, 1891.

975 MOORE, GEORGE. Impressions and opinions
by George Moore.
pp. [8] [1] 2–346   GM
David Nutt   1891

*Contains papers upon An actress of the 18th century
[Mlle. Clairon]; mummer-worship; our dramatists and
their literature; note on "Ghosts"; Théâtre Libre; on the
necessity of an English Théâtre Libre.*
*"Since their first appearance in the Reviews these papers
have all been revised, and in some cases entirely
rewritten."—prefatory note.*

——[American edition]. New York: Scribner,
1891.

976 DOROTHY WALLIS. An autobiography with
an introduction by Walter Besant.
pp. [i–v] vi–xi [xii], [1–3] 4–319 [320]   L
London and New York: Longmans, Green and Co.
                                                            1892

Evidently a fictitious autobiography.

977 COOKE, P[ETER] J[OSEPH]. A handbook of
the drama. Its philosophy and teaching, by P. J. Cooke
With a chapter on the law of copyright in its relation
to dramatic works by Edmond Browne.
pp. [8] [1] 2–160; pl. [front.]   GU
The Roxburghe Press   [1895]

978 SALA, GEORGE AUGUSTUS. The life and
adventures of George Augustus Sala written by himself.

2 vols. pp. [i–v] vi–xvi, [1] 2–442; pl. [front.] + pp.
[i–iii] iv–viii, [1] 2–457 [458 (bl.)]; pl. [front.]
                                                            GM
London, Paris & Melbourne: Cassell and Company,
Limited   1895

979 ——second edition
2 vols. pp. [i–v] vi–xvi, [1] 2–442; pl. [front.] + pp.
[i–iii] iv–viii, [1] 2–457 [458 (bl.) 459–460 (advts.)];
pl. [front.]   L
London, Paris & Melbourne: Cassell and Company,
Limited   1895

980 ——third edition
2 vols. pp. [i–v] vi–x, [1] 2–4, [xi] xii–xv, 2[1] 2–442;
pl. [front.] + pp. [i–iii] iv–viii, [1] 2–457 [458 (bl.)
459–460 (advts.)]; pl. [front.]   L
London, Paris & Melbourne: Cassell and Company,
Limited   1895

Pp. [1]–4: "Preface to the third edition".

——[American edition] New York: Charles
Scribner's sons, 1895.

*Mr. Sala is one of the most distinguished of English
journalists, the founder of* Temple Bar *magazine, the war
correspondent of the* Daily Telegraph, *and one of the best
known and most popular men in London — Lowe.*

981 À BECKETT, ARTHUR W[ILLIA]M. Green-
room recollections by Arthur Wm. A'Beckett (Arrowsmith's 3/6 Series. Vol. XXV.)
pp. [i–v] vi–ix [x–xiv] 15–296   L
Bristol: J. W. Arrowsmith; London: Simpkin, Marshall,
Hamilton, Kent and Company Limited   [1896]

982 COWDEN-CLARKE, MARY. My long life
An autobiographic sketch by Mary Cowden-Clarke
pp. [8] [1] 2–264; pls. [front., 7]   L
T. Fisher Unwin   1896

Wife of the author and dramatic critic.

——[American edition] New York: Dodd,
Mead, & Co., 1896.

983 FILON, AUGUSTIN. The English stage being
an account of the Victorian drama by Augustin Filon
translated from the French by Frederic Whyte with an
introduction by Henry Arthur Jones
pp. [1–4] 5–319 [320]   NbU
London: John Milne; New York: Dodd, Mead &
Company   1897

First appeared in Le Revue des Deux Mondes.

984 GANTHONY, ROBERT. Random recollections, by Robert Ganthony.

pp. [1–7] 8–244 245–6 (advts.); illus.; pls. [front., 7]   L

Henry J. Drane   [1898]

985 JONES, STANLEY. The actor and his art Some considerations of the present condition of the stage by Stanley Jones.

pp. [8] 1–215 [216]   L

Downey & Co. Limited   1899

Motto, from John Stuart Mill: "The diseases of Society can, no more than corporeal maladies, be prevented or cured, without being spoken about in plain language".

986 SCOTT, CLEMENT [WILLIAM]. The drama of yesterday & to-day by Clement Scott in two volumes.

2 vols. pp. [i–vii] viii–xviii [xix–xx], [1] 2–607 [608 (bl.)]; illus.; pls. [front., 65 = 23 leaves] + pp. [i–v] vi–x [xi–xii], [1] 2–581 [582 (bl.) 583–584 (advts.)]; illus.; pls. [front., 80] = 24 leaves   L

London: Macmillan and Co., Limited; New York: the Macmillan Company   1899

Stratman, *Play Lists 57.*

MEDIEVAL AND RENAISSANCE STUDIES

Some of the works in this section are literary, rather than theatrical, and have been included because they are in Lowe. For 19th century reprints of Elizabethan and Jacobean tracts against the stage see also MORALITY OF THE THEATRE nos. 245, 249–250, 254, 261–263, 270, 278.

987 STROLING PLAYER, A, *pseud.* of John Roberts. An answer to Mr. Pope's preface to Shakespear. In a letter to a friend. Being a vindication of the old actors who were the publishers and performers of that author's plays. Whereby the errors of their edition are further accounted for, and some memoirs of Shakespear and stage-history of his time are inserted, which were never before collected and publish'd. By a stroling player.

pp. [1–3] 4–48   L

1729

Letter signed Anti-Scriblerus Histrionicus.

988 [UPTON, JOHN.] REMARKS on three plays of Benjamin Jonson. Viz. Volpone, or The Fox: Epicoene, or The Silent Woman: and The Alchimist.

pp. [8] [1] 2–124 [125–128 (index)]   L

G. Hawkins   1749

989 CHETWOOD, W[ILLIAM] R[UFUS]. Memoirs of the life and writings of Ben. Jonson, Esq; poet laureat to King James the first, and King Charles the first. With an abstract of the lives of their favourites, Somerset and Buckingham. Collected from the writings of the most eminent historians, and interspersed with the pasquils of those times. To which are added, two comedies, (wrote by Ben. Jonson, &c. and not printed in his works) called *The Widow*, and *Eastward Hoe*. By W. R. Chetwood.

pp. [16] [i] ii–x [11] 12–72, 2[1–3] 4–126 [127–128 (advts.)]   L

Dublin: W. R. Chetwood   1756

990 COLMAN, GEORGE, *the elder.* The dramatic works of Philip Massinger, compleat in four volumes. Revised, corrected, and all the various editions collated, by Thomas Coxeter. With notes critical and explanatory of various authors. To which are prefixed, critical reflections on the old English dramatick writers; intended as a preface to the works of Massinger. Addressed to David Garrick, Esq,

Vol. I. pp. [4] [1] 2–27 [28], [v] vi–xxii, 2[1–3] 4–347 [348].   L

T. Davies   1761

Critical reflections (*pp. [1]–[28]*).

Reprinted in The dramatick works of Philip Massinger, ed. *John Monck Mason (1779)*, I, [xiii]–xlvi; *George Colman*, Prose on several occasions *(1787)*, II, *105–148. See E. R. Page*, George Colman, *(1935) p. 51.*

✂ [Warner, Richard.] A letter to David Garrick Esq. concerning a glossary to the plays of Shakespeare. 1768. *See no. 2884.*

991 HAWKINS, THOMAS. The origin of the English drama, illustrated in its various species, viz. mystery, morality, tragedy, and comedy, by specimens from our earliest writers; with explanatory notes by Thomas Hawkins, M.A. of Magdalene College, Oxford.

3 vols. pp. [8] i–xvii [xviii ('Advertisement')], [1–5] 6–251 254–317 [318 (bl.) 319 ('Epilogue') 320–322 (bl.)]; illus. + pp. [4] [1–5] 6–352; cancels, pp. 43–44, 59–60 + pp. [4] [1–7] 8–377 [378 (bl.)]   MH

Oxford: printed at the Clarendon Press, for S. Leacroft, Charing-Cross, London   1773

The second leaf of vol. 3 contains "Additional Notes"; this leaf is found variously bound: in the place here

described, following the preface of vol. 1, or concluding vol. 3. One of the copies at MH. has the cancellandum leaf for pp. 59–60; there are changes on both pages.

☒ Old Comedian, An, *pseud.* The life and death of David Garrick.... And Messrs. Alleyn, Mohun, Hart ... compared with Mr. Garrick. To which is added, The life of Edward Alleyn. 1779. *See no. 2920.*

992 [DAVIES, THOMAS.] SOME ACCOUNT of the life and writings of Philip Massinger.

pp. [2] [1] 2–44 [45 (ded.) 46 (advt.)]   L
                                          1789

Dedication to Dr Johnson signed.
First published as "A short essay on the life and writings of Massinger" in The dramatick works of Philip Massinger, ed. John Monck Mason (1779), I, [xlvii–xlix] l–xcii [xciii (ded.)–xciv (advt.)].

993 MALONE, EDMOND. An historical account of the rise and progress of the English stage, and of the economy and usages of the ancient theatres. By Edmond Malone, Esq.

pp. [4] [1] 2–331 [332]; illus.; pls. [4] incl. 1 fold.   BP
Henry Baldwin   1790

"Only a few copies, for presents, were struck off."—Field.

994 ——*[another edition.] Edited by James Boswell.

Rivington   1821

Offprinted from "The variorum Shakespeare." Jaggard.

——[Swiss edition] Historical account of the rise and progress of the English stage, and of the economy and usages of the ancient theatres in England; by Edmund Malone, Esqr. Basil: J. J. Tourneisen, 1800.

Reprinted in, among others, the following editions of Shakespeare's works: Rivington & Sons, 1790, with additions by G. Steevens; Dublin: John Exshaw, 1794; Rivington, 1805; and Rivington, 1821 (much enlarged). Jaggard.

995 [PERCY, THOMAS, *Bishop of Dromore.*] AN ESSAY on the origin of the English stage, particularly on the historical plays of Shakespeare.

pp. [1–3] 4–28   L
n.p.   1793

First printed in Volume I of Percy's Reliques of Ancient English Poetry, 1765 and in subsequent editions of the Reliques; here reprinted with alterations.

996 [WALDRON, FRANCIS GODOLPHIN.]*THE ANCIENT AND MODERN MISCELLANY; or, Shakesperean museum: containing a re-publication of scarce and valuable tracts; biographical anecdotes of theatrical performers, with scarce and original poetry.

Pagination irregular   MB
E. and S. Harding   1794

997 ——[another edition] The Shakspearean miscellany: containing a collection of scarce and valuable tracts; biographical anecdotes of theatrical performers; with portraits of ancient and modern actors: (of many of whom there are no prints extant) scarce and original poetry; and curious remains of antiquity ... A concise history of the early English stage, with anecdotes and portraits of the following authors and performers. Perkins, Bond, Cartwright, Harris, Penkethman, Farquhar, Miss Norsa, Theo. Cibber, Redman, and T. Davies. Printed chiefly from manuscripts, in the possession of, and with occasional notes by, F. G. Waldron.

pp. [4] [1] 2–50, ²[1] 2–45 [46], ³[1] 2–3 [4], ⁴[1] 2–84; pls. [front., 11]   L
Printed by Knight and Compton, and sold by Lackington, Allen, and Co.   1802

998 ——[reissue]

pp. [4] [1] 2–45 [46], ²[1] 2–3 [4], ³[1] 2–84, ⁴[1] 2–50; pls. [front., 11]   L
John Manson   1804

Differences in title include "And two plates of antiquities." Plates and text bound in different order.

999 GILCHRIST, OCTAVIUS. An examination of the charges maintained by Messrs. Malone, Chalmers, and others, of Ben Jonson's emnity, &c. towards Shakspeare. By Octavius Gilchrist.

pp. [4] [1] 2–62; errata slip   E
Taylor and Hessey   1808

1000 GILCHRIST, OCTAVIUS. A letter to William Gifford, Esq. on the late edition of Ford's plays; chiefly as relating to Ben Jonson. By Octavius Gilchrist, Esq.

pp. [1–5] 6–45 [46 (bl.) 47 (advts.) 48 (bl.)]   L
John Murray   1811

1001 [WHITTINGTON, G. D.?] A LETTER to J. P. Kemble, Esq. involving strictures on a recent edition of John Ford's dramatic works.

pp. [2] [1–3] 4–29 [30 (bl.)]   L
Cambridge: printed by F. Hodson   1811

1002 [MITFORD, *Rev.* JOHN.] A LETTER to Richard Heber, Esq. containing some observations on the merits of Mr. Weber's late edition of Ford's dramatic works.

pp. [1–7] 8–30 [31–32 (advts.)]   L
Sold by White, Cochrane, and Co.   1812

1003 HONE, WILLIAM. Ancient mysteries described, especially the English miracle plays, founded on apocryphal New Testament story, extant among the unpublished manuscripts in the British Museum; including notices of ecclesiastical shows, the festivals of fools and asses—the English boy bishop—the descent into Hell—the Lord Mayor's Show—the Guildhall giants—Christmas carols, &c. By William Hone. With engravings on copper and wood.

pp. [2] [i] ii–x [xi–xii] [13] 14–298, [1] 2 (advt.); illus.; [pls. front., 3 (incl. one fold. and two by Cruikshank, one of which was issued col. and plain)]; t.p. in red and black L

William Hone 1823

Cohn *401.*

1004 ———[another edition] By William Hone. With engravings on copper and wood.

pp. [4] [i] ii–x [11–12] 13–264 [2] 265–268 [2] 269–299 [300]; illus. (incl. front.); pl., fold. [1]; ptd. cover L

[Reeves and Turner; Richard Griffin] [*ca.* 1860?]

A reprint of no. 1003 above, preserving original imprint; yellow cloth cover.

1005 ———[another edition] With glossary and index. By William Hone. With engravings by G. Cruikshank and others.

pp. [2] [i] ii–x [xi–xii] [2] 13–264 [2] 265–268 [2] 269–300; illus.; pls. [front., 1 (fold.)]; t.p. in red and black NbU

William Reeves [*ca.* 1860?]

A reprint of the first edition; probably another issue of the Reeves and Turner reprint, with variants. Black cloth, white end-papers.

1006 ———[another edition]

pp. [6] [i] ii–x, 13–264 [2] 265–268 [2] 269–300; illus. (incl. front.); pl. fold.

[William Reeves?] [*ca.* 1860?]

JWR.

This is another issue, with variants, of no. 1005. Black cloth cover, yellow end-papers.

✠ Planché, James Robinson. Costume of Shakespeare's historical tragedy of King John. 1823. *See no. 3418. See also nos. 3419–3423.*

1007 SKOTTOWE, AUGUSTINE. The life of Shakspeare; enquiries into the originality of his dramatic plots and characters; and essays on the ancient theatres and theatrical usages. By Augustine Skottowe.

2 vols. pp. [i–v] vi–viii, [1] 2–360 + [4] [1] 2–328 NbU

Longman, Hurst, Rees, Orme, Brown, and Green 1824

1008 BRAYLEY, E[DWARD] W[EDLAKE]. An enquiry into the genuineness of Prynne's "Defence of stage plays", &c. together with a reprint of the said tract, and also of Prynne's "Vindication". By E. W. Brayley, F.A.S., and F.R.S.L.

pp. [1–7] 8–16 L

1825

Only fifty copies printed "for gratuitous circulation".

1009 SHARP, THOMAS. A dissertation on the pageants or dramatic mysteries anciently performed at Coventry, by the trading companies of that city; chiefly with reference to the vehicle, characters, and dresses of the actors. Compiled, in a great degree, from sources hitherto unexplored. To which are added, the Pageant of the Shearmen & Taylors' Company, and other municipal entertainments of a public nature. By Thomas Sharp.

pp. [6] [1] 2–114, 115–118 (music, verso unnumbered) [119] 120–226 [227–230 (index)] [=234]; illus; pls. [front.] II–X, incl. pl. V col. L

Coventry: Merridew and Son 1825

1010 COLLIER, J[OHN] PAYNE. The history of English dramatic poetry to the time of Shakespeare: and annals of the stage to the Restoration. By J. Payne Collier, Esq., F.S.A.

3 vols. pp. [i–v] vi–xxxvi, [1] 2–454 [455 (imprint) 456 (bl.)]; vignette on t.p.; illus. (facsim. signatures) + [2] [i–iii] iv–vi, [1] 2–488; vignette on t.p.; illus. (facsim. signatures) + [2] [i–iii] iv–vi, [1] 2–508; cancel (pp. 269–270); vignette on t.p.; illus. (facsim. signatures) L

John Murray 1831

1011 ———a new edition

3 vols. pp. [i–iii] iv–xvi, ²[i] ii–ix [x] [11] 12–489 [490]; illus.; vignette on t.p. + pp. [2] [1] 2–544; illus.; vignette on t.p. + pp. [2] [1] 2–506; illus.; vignette on t.p. L

George Bell & Sons 1879

The illustrations are facsimile autographs.

✠ London pageants. I. Accounts of fifty-five royal processions and entertainments. 1831. *See no. 1088.*

✠ Catalogue of early English poetry and other miscellaneous works illustrating the British drama, collected by Edmond Malone and now preserved in the Bodleian Library. Oxford. 1836. *See no. 111.*

1012 MARRIOTT, WILLIAM. A collection of English miracle-plays or mysteries; containing ten dramas from the Chester, Coventry, and Towneley series, with two of latter date. To which is prefixed, an historical view of this description of plays. By William Marriott, Ph.Dr.

pp. [i–iii] iv–lxiii [lxiv], [1–3] 4–271 [272] GU

Basel: Schweighauser & Co; Paris: Brockhaus & Avenarius 1838

1013 OLIVER, *Rev.* GEORGE. *An account of the Corpus pageants, miracle plays, religious mysteries, &c. which were practised at Sleaford.

1838

Loewenberg.

✖ Kemp, William. Kemps nine daies wonder. 1840. *See no. 3210.*

Contains a life of Kemp.

1014 HALLIWELL, JAMES ORCHARD, *later* Halliwell-Phillipps, *ed.* Ludus Coventriae. A collection of mysteries, formerly represented at Coventry on the Feast of Corpus Christi. Edited by James Orchard Halliwell, Esq. F.R.S. Hon. M.R.I.A., F.S.A., F.R.A.S., &c.

pp. [i–v] vi–xvi, [1] 2–434   L
The Shakespeare Society   1841

Reissued in A Supplement to Dodsley's Old Plays, (*The Shakespeare Society, 1853*). *Vol. II.*

1015 CUNNINGHAM, PETER, *ed.* Extracts from the accounts of the revels at court, in the reigns of Queen Elizabeth and King James I., from the original office books of the masters and yeomen. With an introduction and notes by Peter Cunningham.

pp. [i–vii] viii–li [lii], [1] 2–228   L
Shakespeare Society   1842

On the authenticity of this work see Chambers, Elizabethan, IV, 136–141 and Shakespeare, II, 330–331.

1016 DANIEL, GEORGE. Merrie England in the olden time. By George Daniel.

2 vols. pp. [i–v] vi [vii–viii], [1] 2–292; pls. [front., 3]; illus; vignette on t.p. + pp. [4] [1] 2–296; pl. [front.]; illus.; vignette on t.p.   L
Richard Bentley   1842

Revised from Bentley's Miscellany. Engravings by John Leech, Robert Cruikshank, and Thomas Gilks.

1017 ——*a new edition
pp. viii, 422   MB
Warne & Co.   1873

1018 HALLIWELL, JAMES ORCHARD, *later* Halliwell-Phillipps. Tarlton's jests, and News out of purgatory: with notes, and some account of the life of Tarlton, by James Orchard Halliwell, Esq.

pp. [i–vii] viii–xlvii [xlviii], [1–5] 6–135 [136]; illus. L
The Shakespeare Society   1844

See also below no. 1042.

1019 COLLIER, J[OHN] PAYNE, *ed.* The diary of Philip Henslowe, from 1591 to 1609. Printed from the original manuscript preserved at Dulwich College. Edited by J. Payne Collier, Esq., F.S.A.

pp. [i–vii] viii–xxiv, [1] 2–290   L
The Shakespeare Society   1845

Portions of the diary were first printed by Malone in his "Historical Account of the Rise and Progress of the English Stage" (no. 993. above), 1790.

Reissued in Henslowe and Alleyn: being the Diary of of Philip Henslowe and the Life of Edward Alleyn to which is added the Alleyn Papers (*The Shakespear Society, 1853*).

1020 vacant

1021 ——[another edition] Henslow's diary edited by Walter W. Greg, M.A.
2 vols. pp. [i–viii] ix–li [lii], [1] 2–240; spine label; illus.; + pp. [i–vi] vii–xvi, 1–400; pls. [5]   L
A. H. Bullen   1904–1908

Henslowe Papers being Documents Supplementary to Henslowe's Diary, *edited by W. W. Greg, was published by Bullen in 1907 uniform with the two volumes of the Diary.*

1022 ——[another edition] Henslow's diary edited with supplementary material introduction and notes by R. A. Foakes and R. T. Rickert.
pp. [i–vi] vii–lix [lx], [1–2] 3–368; pls. I–IV   L
Cambridge: at the University Press   1961

1023 COLLIER, J[OHN] PAYNE. Memoirs of the principal actors in the plays of Shakespeare. By J. Payne Collier, Esq., F.S.A. (Shakespeare Society Publications, no. 32.)
pp. [2] [i–vii] viii–xxxviii, [2] [1] 2–296, ²[1] 2–12 (Annual report)   GU
The Shakespeare Society   1846

1024 ——[reissue] Lives of the original actors in Shakespeare's plays. By J. Payne Collier.
pp. [2] [i–vii] viii–xxxviii, [2] [1] 2–296   NbU
The Shakespeare Society   1853

1025 RIMBAULT, EDWARD F[RANCIS]. Who was "Jack Wilson," the singer of Shakespeare's stage? An attempt to prove the identity of this person with John Wilson, Doctor of Musick, in the University of Oxford, A.D. 1644. By Edward F. Rimbault, L.L.D., F.S.A., member of the Royal Academy of Music in Stockholm, etc. etc. etc.
pp. [1–3] 4–16   GU
John Russell Smith   1846

Of Collier's note on "Jack Wilson" as a composer for Shakespeare's company. Rimbault says "Mr. Collier has adopted a favourite hypothesis of mine that Wilson was the composer of much of the music to Shakespeare's plays." He disagrees with Collier, however, about the songs which he claims for Wilson; and his attempted identification of Wilson with the Doctor of Music is new. He also refers to Robert Johnson.

✠ Chapman, John Kemble, *ed.* A complete history of theatrical entertainments, dramas, masques, and triumphs, at the English Court. [1849?]. *See no. 851.*

1026 COLERIDGE, S[AMUEL] T[AYLOR]. Notes and lectures upon Shakespeare and some of the old poets and dramatists. With other literary remains of S. T. Coleridge. Edited by Mrs. H. N. Coleridge.

2 vols. pp. [i–v] vi–xv [xvi], [1] 2–372; vignette on t.p. + pp. [i–iii] iv–v [vi], [1] 2–371 [372]; vignette on t.p.   E
William Pickering   1849

Literary rather than theatrical.

1027 [CROKER, THOMAS CROFTON.] REMARKS on an article inserted in the papers of the Shakespeare society.

pp. [1–4] 5–15 [16 (bl.)]   L
[priv. ptd.]   [1849]

The article related to Massinger's 'Beleeve as you list' — Lowe. Not theatrical.

1028 MITFORD, JOHN. Cursory notes on various passages in the text of Beaumont and Fletcher, as edited by the Rev. Alexander Dyce; and on his "Few notes on Shakespeare." The author John Mitford.

pp. [1–3] 4–56   L
John Russell Smith   1856 [*for* 1855]

1029 EDLIN, P. H. *A lecture on the old English dramatists, delivered at the St. Philip's Athenæum, Bristol, on Monday, February 8th, 1857, by P. H. Edlin, Esq.

Bristol   1857

   Lowe.

1030 SMITH, WILLIAM HENRY. Bacon and Shakespeare. A[n] inquiry touching players, playhouses, and play-writers in the days of Elizabeth. By William Henry Smith, Esq. To which is appended an abstract of a ms. respecting Tobie Matthew.

pp. [i–v] vi–viii, [1–3] 4–162   L
John Russell Smith   1857

1031 HALLIWELL, JAMES O[RCHARD] *later* Halliwell-Phillipps. A dictionary of old English plays,

existing either in print or in manuscript, from the earliest times to the close of the seventeenth century; including also notices of Latin plays written by English authors during the same period. By James O. Halliwell, Esq., F.R.S.

pp. [i–v] vi–viii, [1] 2–296   L
John Russell Smith   1860

   Stratman, Play Lists *48.*

1032 ———[a thick paper impression]
pp. [i–v] vi–viii, [1] 2–296   MB
John Russell Smith   1860

"Thick paper copy 25 printed No. 1 J. R. Smith" MS note on half-title.

1033 HALLIWELL, JAMES O[RCHARD], *later* Halliwell-Phillipps, *ed.* The theatre plats of three old English dramas: namely, of The battle of Alcazar, Frederick and Basilea, and of The dead man's fortune, from the originals, which were suspended near the prompter's station, in the Fortune Theatre, in the latter part of the sixteenth century. Edited by James O. Halliwell, Esq., F.R.S. The fac-similes by Messrs. Ashbee & Dangerfield.

pp. [4]; pls. 1–4   L
For private circulation   1860

1034 [CARTWRIGHT, ROBERT.] THE FOOT-STEPS of Shakespere; or a ramble with the early dramatists, containing much new and interesting information respecting Shakespere, Lyly, Marlowe, Greene, and others.

pp. [i–iii] iv [v–vi], [1] 2–186   L
John Russell Smith   1862 [*for* 1861]

1035 LIFE AND TIMES OF SHAKESPEARE: actor and dramatist.

pp. [1–3] 4–16; illus. (port.)   L
H. Vickers   [1864]

A leaflet, a copy of which is at MB, was put out by Vickers in 1864 advertising this work as "now ready".

1036 [CARTWRIGHT, ROBERT.] SHAKSPERE and Jonson. Dramatic, versus Wit-Combats. Auxiliary forces:—Beaumont and Fletcher, Marston, Decker, Chapman, and Webster.

pp. [2] [1] 2–122   L
John Russell Smith   "Twelfth Night," 1864

1037 VYSE, BERTIE, *pseud.* of Arthur William à Beckett. *William Shakespeare behind the scenes of the Globe Theatre. From a rare MS. edited by Bertie Vyse.

pp. 8   MB
Nichols   1864

1038 COHN, ALBERT. Shakespeare in Germany in the sixteenth and seventeenth centuries: an account of English actors in Germany and the Netherlands and of the plays performed by them during the same period. By Albert Cohn.

pp. [2] [I] II–III [IV–VIII], 2[I] II–CXXXVII [CXXXVIII], [1–4]; columns [5–6] 7–422; p. [423]; pls. I–II [=3 leaves]   GU

London & Berlin: Asher & Co.   1865

1039 ———[large paper issue]
pp. [2] [I] II–III [IV–VIII], 2[I] II–CXXXVII [CXXXVIII], [1–4]; columns [5–6] 7–422; p. [423]; pls. I–II [=3 leaves]   L

London and Berlin: Asher & Co.   1865

✕ [Halliwell, James Orchard, *ed.*] A copy of a letter . . . to Sir Dudley Carleton . . . in May, 1619, containing a curious account of the performance of the drama of "Pericles" at the English court. 1865. *See no. 4028.*

1040 FIELD, NATHAN. The remonstrance of Nathan Field, one of Shakespeare's company of actors, addressed to a preacher in Southwark, who had been arraigning against the players at the Globe theatre in the year 1616. Now first edited from the original manuscript. [Edited by J. O. Halliwell.]

pp. [1–5] 6–15 [16]   L

[London: printed by Whittingham and Wilkins] 1865

This tract "the unwearying labours of Mr. Halliwell have given us" — Lowe. Only 25 copies printed, and of these only 10 preserved (15 destroyed by the editor).

1041 JORDAN, JOHN, [JAMES ORCHARD HALLIWELL, *ed.*] Original memoirs and historical accounts of the families of Shakespeare and Hart, deduced from an early period, and continued down to this present year 1790. By John Jordan, of Stratford-upon-Avon. With drawings of their dwelling houses, and coats of arms. Now first printed, A.D. 1865.

pp. [i–v] vi–vii [viii], [1] 2–84   L
Printed by Thomas Richards   1865

Only ten copies printed.

✕ Kelly, William, *ed.* Notices illustrative of the drama . . . chiefly in the sixteenth and seventeenth centuries . . . extracted from the Chamberlain's accounts . . . of the borough of Leicester. 1865 [*for* 1864]. *See no. 1599.*

✕ Green, John [*or* Townsend, George Henry.] Evans's music and supper rooms, Covent Garden. . . . the ancient drama [*etc*] [1866?]. *See no. 1423.*

1042 HALLIWELL, J[AMES] O[RCHARD], *later* Halliwell-Phillipps, *ed.* Papers respecting disputes which arose from incidents at the death-bed of Richard Tarlton,

the actor, in the year 1588. Now first printed from the original manuscripts. Edited by J. O. Halliwell, Esq., F.R.S.

pp. [1–5] 6–31 [32]   L
Printed for the editor   July, 1866

Only ten copies printed. See also no. 1018 above.

1043 HALLIWELL, J[AMES] O[RCHARD], *later* Halliwell-Phillipps. Notices of players acting at Ludlow, selected from the original manuscripts belonging to the corporation of that town. By J. O. Halliwell, F.R.S.

pp. [1–5] 6–12.   L
Priv. ptd.   1867

Only ten copies printed.

1044 INGLEBY, C[LEMENT] M[ANSFIELD]. Was Thomas Lodge an actor? An exposition touching the social status of the playwright in the time of Queen Elizabeth. By C. M. Ingleby, LL.D.

pp. [1–3] 4–16; pl. [fold.]   L
Printed for the author, by Richard Barrett and Sons 1868

Dated 29 October 1867.

1045 [HAZLITT, WILLIAM CAREW, *ed.*] THE ENGLISH DRAMA and stage under the Tudor and Stuart princes 1543–1664 illustrated by a series of documents, treatises and poems. With a preface and index.

pp. [i–v] vi–xvi, [1–3] 4–289 [290]; illus.   E
The Roxburghe Library   1869

1046 ———[large paper issue]
pp. [i–v] vi–xvi, [1–3] 4–289 [290]; illus.   L
The Roxburghe Library   1869

———[American edition] New York: Burt Franklin, 1964.

1047 [HALLIWELL, JAMES ORCHARD, *later* Halliwell-Phillipps, *ed.*] A collection of ancient documents respecting the office of Master of the Revels, and other papers relating to the early English theatre, from the original manuscripts formerly in the Haslewood collection.

pp. [4] [1–2] 2–100   L
Printed by T. Richards   1870

Only eleven copies printed.

✕ Roffe, Alfred. A musical triad from Shakespeare. . . . To which is added old English singers, and Mr. Bowman — actor, singer, and ringer! 1872. *See no. 2243.*

✕ Kingsley, Charles. Plays and puritans. 1873. *See no. 621.*

1048 PAGET, A[LFRED] H[ENRY]. Shakespeare's plays: a chapter of stage history. An essay on the Shakesperian drama. By A. H. Paget.

pp. [1–7] 8–47 [48 (bl.)]   L

John Wilson   1875

A paper read before the Leicester Literary and Philosophical Society, 1875.

1049 WARD, ADOLPHUS WILLIAM. A history of English dramatic literature to the death of Queen Anne by Adolphus William Ward, M.A.

2 vols. pp. [i–vii] viii–xlvii [xlviii], [1] 2–604 + [6] [1] 2–643 [644]   L

Macmillan and Co.   1875

1050 ———new and revised edition

3 vols. pp. [i–v] vi–xiii [xiv], [1] 2–575 [576] + [i–v] vi–xii, [1] 2–766 [767 (errata) 768 (imprint)] + [i–v] vi–xiv, [1] 2–599 [600]   L

London: Macmillan and Co., Limited; New York: The Macmillan Company   1899

1051 HALLIWELL-PHILLIPPS, J[AMES] O[RCHARD]. A brief hand-list of the selected parcels in the Shakespearian and dramatic collections of J. O. Halliwell-Phillipps at No. 11, Tregunter Road, London.

pp. [1–7] 8–32   E

Privately printed by J. E. Adlard   1876

1052 JEREMIAH, JOHN. Notes on Shakespeare, and memorials of the Urban Club. Comprising a succinct account of the life and times of the great dramatist; also a history of the Urban Club, and an account of the Boar's Head Feast and ceremonies formerly observed at St. John's Gate. By John Jeremiah. Subscriber's copy.

pp. [1–5] 6–112 115–129 [130 (erratum)] [=128]; illus. incl. music; pls. [front., 2]; inset (on blue paper)   L

Clayton & Co.   1876

Originally privately published in April 1876 without the section on Elizabethan playhouses. With an appendix: "Memorials of the Urban Club, St. John's Gate, Clerkenwell; being a complete collection of the programmes and circulars since the first issued on April 24th, 1875, to July 7th, 1876" and supplement: "The National Theatre Project".

1053 ———[large paper issue.]

pp. [2] [1–7] 8–169 [170]; illus., incl. music; pls. [front., 2]; inset (on blue paper).   LVA

H. Sotheran & Co.   1877

Fifty copies only printed.

✖ Blanch, William Harnett. Dulwich College and Edward Alleyn. 1877. *See no. 2382.*

1054 GARDINER, SAMUEL RAWSON, *ed.* Documents relating to the proceedings against William Prynne, in 1634 and 1637. With a biographical fragment by the late John Bruce. Edited by Samuel Rawson Gardiner. (The Camden Society New Series XVIII.)

pp. [4] [i] ii–xxxviii, [2] [1] 2–121 [122]   L

The Camden Society   1877

1055 HALLIWELL-PHILLIPPS, J[AMES] O[RCHARD]. A budget of notes and memoranda on the life and works of Shakespeare, and on the history of the early English stage. By J. O. Halliwell-Phillipps, F.R.S.

pp. [1–5] 6–48   L

Printed by James Evan Adlard   1880

Only twenty-five copies printed.

1056 FLEAY, FREDERICK GARD. ★On the actor lists, 1578–1642.

pp. 39, [1]; cover-title, tables   PP

Printed for private circulation   1881

Reprinted in Transactions of the Royal Historical Society (1881), IX, 44–81.

✖ Warner, George Frederic. Catalogue of the manuscripts . . . of Alleyn's College. 1881. *See no. 56.*

1057 FLEAY, FREDERICK GARD. ★On the history of the theatres of London. From their first opening in 1576 to their closing in 1642.

pp. 20

Priv. ptd.   1882

STR.

Reprinted in Transactions of the Royal Historical Society, vol. X, pp. 114–133, 1882.

1058 B[OWER], G[EORGE] S[PENCER]. A study of the prologue and epilogue in English literature from Shakespeare to Dryden By G.S.B.

pp. [i–ix] x–xi [xii (bl.)], [1] 2–187 [188 (bl.)]   L

Kegan Paul, Trench & Co.   1884

1059 [HALLIWELL-PHILLIPPS, JAMES ORCHARD, *ed.*] TWO OLD THEATRES. Views of the Globe and the Bear Garden, the former being the theatre belonging to Shakespeare's company of actors, which was erected on the site of the original building that was destroyed by fire in the year 1613, a wood engraving, taken from an unique view of London, published by Visscher in the early part of the reign of Charles the First.

pp. [8]; illus.   L

Brighton: for private circulation only   1884

Only thirty copies printed.

1060 GREENSTREET, JAMES [HARRIS]. Documents relating to the players at the Red Bull, Clerkenwell, and the Cockpit in Drury Lane, in the time of James I (Read at the 106th meeting of the N. Sh. Society, on April 10, 1885). By James Greenstreet, esq.

pp. [489] 490–508; head-title; headed: "A second copy will be issued in the Transactions." L

[priv. ptd.] [1885]

1061 IRESON, *Brother* FRANK. A sketch of the pre-Shakspearian drama by Bro. Frank Ireson, B.A. Lond. Artificer to the sette, delivered at the Freemasons' Tavern, on Friday, January 9, 1884. (O.V. Miscellanies. No. 7.)

pp. [1–5] 6–33 [34 (bl.)]; cover-title L

Imprynted by Bro^r C. W. H. Wyman 1885

"1884" altered by hand to "1885". Limited to 133 copies, "for private circulation only."

1062 FLEAY, FREDERICK GARD. A chronicle history of the life and work of William Shakespeare player, poet, and playmaker. By Frederick Gard Fleay.

pp. [i–vii] viii, [1] 2–364; pls. [front., 1] GU

John C. Nimmo 1886

1063–1065 vacant

1066 HALLIWELL-PHILLIPPS, J[AMES] O[RCHARD], *ed.* A hand-list of sixty folio volumes, containing collections made by J. O. Halliwell-Phillipps, from 1854 to 1887, on the life of Shakespeare, and the history of the English stage.

pp. [1–5] 6–7 [8] L

Brighton: printed by John George Bishop 1887

1067 HALLIWELL-PHILLIPPS, J[AMES] O[RCHARD], *ed.* The visits of Shakespeare's company of actors to the provincial cities and towns of England, illustrated by extracts gathered from corporate records by J. O. Halliwell-Phillipps, F.R.S.

pp. [1–5] 6–47 [48] L

Brighton: for Private Circulation and for Presents only 1887

Half-title: Shakespeare's Tours.

1068 WHEATLEY, HENRY BENJAMIN. ★On a contemporary drawing of the interior of the Swan Theatre, 1596.

MB

1888?

Reissued in New Shakespeare Society Transactions. *No. 12, 1887–1892. Pt. II. The De Witt drawing.*

1069 FLEAY, FREDERICK GARD. A chronicle history of the London stage 1559–1642 by Frederick Gard Fleay, M.A.

pp. [i–vii] viii–x, [1] 2–424 L

Reeves and Turner 1890

"Four hundred and sixty copies of the Edition have been printed, and the type distributed".

1070 FLEAY, FREDERICK GARD. A biographical chronicle of the English drama 1559–1642, by Frederick Gard Fleay, M.A.

2 vols. pp. [8] [1] 2–387 [388] + [8] [1] 2–405 [406 (imprint) 407–408 (bl.)] GU

Reeves & Turner 1891

1071 PAGET, ALFRED HENRY. ★The Elizabethan play-houses.

14 pp. PU

Leicester: G. Gibbon & Co., printers 1891

Reprinted from the Transactions of the Leicester Literary and Philosophical Society, *II, vi.*

1072 HAZLITT, W. CAREW, *ed.* A manual for the collector and amateur of old English plays. Edited from the material formed by Kirkman, Langbaine, Downes, Oldys, and Halliwell-Phillipps, with extensive additions and corrections by W. Carew Hazlitt.

pp. [2] [i–v] vi–viii, [1] 2–62 ★61[★62] 63–284, ²1–4 (advts.); t.p. in red and black E

Pickering and Chatto 1892

Only two hundred and fifty copies printed. Stratman, Play Lists 54.

———[American edition]. New York: Burt Franklin, 1965. (Burt Franklin: Bibliography and Reference Series no. 109.)

1073 CALMOUR, ALFRED C[ECIL]. Fact and fiction about Shakespeare with some account of the playhouses, players, and playwrights of his period by Alfred C. Calmour with notes and illustrations.

pp. [8] [1] 2–61 [2 (illus.)] 62–105 [2 (illus.)] 106–112; pls. [front., 7]; insets [2 (double)]; errata slip; illus.; t.p. headed "Stratford-on-Avon Edition"; t.p. in red and black L

Stratford-on-Avon: George Boyden; London: Henry Williams [1894]

✂ Ordish, Thomas Fairman. Early London theatres. 1894. *See no. 1109.*

1074 vacant

1075 GODFREY, JOHN T[HOMAS]. Notes on the drama in Nottingham in the 16th and 17th centuries (1569–1624): by John T. Godfrey. Reprinted from *The Newark Advertiser*.

pp. [1–3] 4–10 [11–12 (bl.)]   E
[Nottingham?]   1896

1076 WALKER, [CHARLES] CLEMENT. John Heminge and Henry Condell friends and fellow-actors of Shakespeare and what the world owes them by Clement Walker.

pp. [2] [1–3] 4–26 [27–30 (bl.)]; pl. [front.]; title headed: "Presented to. . . . by Charles Clement Walker"   L
n.p.   1896

Brown cloth cover. Published on the occasion of the erection of their monument, which still stands at St. Mary's Aldermanbury, although the ruined church has been dismantled and re-erected in Fulton, Missouri.

1077 ———[another issue]
pp. [1–3] 4–26 [27–28 (bl.)]; pl. [front.]   L
n.p.   1896

Stiff paper cover.

1078 ———[another edition]
pp. [6] [1–3] 4–26 [27–30 (bl.)]; pls. [front., 7]   L
n.p.   1896

Apparently an invitation to attend the ceremony of the unveiling of the monument. Red cloth cover.

1079 CLARKE, SIDNEY WRANGEL. The miracle play in England. An account of the early religious drama, by Sidney W. Clarke.

pp. [10] [1] 2–94 [14 (advts.)]; pls. [front., 3]; t.p. in red and black.
William Andrews & Co.   [1897]
JWR.

1080 FLEAY, F[REDERICK] G[ARD]. Queen Elizabeth, Croydon, and the drama. By F. G. Fleay, M.A. A paper read before the Balham Antiquarian and Natural History Society, January 24, 1898.

pp. [1–3] 4–16   GM
Balham and District Antiquarian and Natural History Society; [A. Bonner, printer]   [1898]

✠ Poel, William. An account of the Elizabethan Stage Society. 1898. *See no. 2138.*

THE LONDON THEATRE

GENERAL

See also GOVERNMENT REGULATION OF THE THEATRE passim; ARTS OF THE THEATRE nos. 730, 800, 805; GENERAL HISTORY especially nos. 839, 843, 860, 897; MEDIEVAL AND RENAISSANCE STUDIES nos. 1057, 1069, 1071; OPERA no. 2079; THEORY AND CRITICISM especially nos. 3762, 3782, 3784–3786, 3792, 3798, 3802–3803, 3808–3810; PERIODICALS nos. 4068–4326.

1081 *THE THEATRICAL REGISTER: or, complete list of every performance at the different theatres, for the year 1769. Illustrated with critical observations.

pp. 3–74   MB
[London]   [1770]

1082 A PLAN for the improvement of theatrical and other public entertainments.

pp. [1] 2–3 [4]; title on p. [4]   DFo
[London]   [22 March 1784]

Proposals by Thomas Harris (in partnership with Henry Holland) to build by subscription a Prince of Wales's Theatre behind Grosvenor Place 'being possessed of two antient Freehold Patents for the Exhibition of all kind of Theatrical Performances, (under the Authority of one of which such Entertainments were formerly exhibited at the Theatre in Lincoln's-Inn Fields, and under the other the Theatre in Covent Garden was built and opened)'.

1083 HEADS of plan for a private theatre.

pp. [4]   L
W. Bulmer, printer   [1811]
Dated 1 March 1811.

1084 WILKINSON, R[OBERT] [and WILLIAM HERBERT]. Theatrum illustratum. Graphic and historic memorials of ancient playhouses, modern theatres, and places of public amusement, in London and Westminster. By R. Wilkinson.

25 leaves PP¹ N⁴ X³ Y² Z⁴ XX² UU² MM¹ SS¹ QQ² 3A¹ 3G²; pls. [34]   E
                                                            1825

Separate issue of part of Londina Illustrata (2 vols. 1819, 1825, originally issued in 36 numbers 1808–1826). Wilkinson was assisted in the work by William Herbert.

1085 DIBDIN, CHARLES. History and illustrations of the London theatres: comprising an account of the origin and progress of the drama in England; with historical and descriptive accounts of the Theatres Royal, Covent Garden, Drury Lane, Haymarket, English Opera House, and Royal Amphitheatre. By Charles Dibdin, Jun. Illustrated with engravings.

pp. [2] [1] 2–94; pls. 16 (variously numbered, in roman and arabic)   L

The Proprietors of the "Illustrations of London Buildings"   1826
"Only twenty-five copies worked".

1086 BRAYLEY, EDWARD WEDLAKE. Historical and descriptive accounts of the theatres of London: by Edward Wedlake Brayley, F.A.S. &c. &c. Secretary to the Russell Institution. Illustrated with a view of each theatre, elegantly coloured, drawn and engraved by the late Daniel Havell.

pp. [i–iv], [1] 2, [v] vi [vii–viii], ²[1] 2–92, ³[1] 2–4 (addenda); col. pls. I–XVI   L
J. Taylor   1826 [for 1827]
Also issued with uncoloured plates (MH). Dedication to Charles Mathews dated 9 June 1827.

1087 [CLARKE, WILLIAM.] *EVERY NIGHT book; or, life after dark. By the author of "The Cigar."

pp. 192   MB
Richardson   1827

1088 LONDON PAGEANTS. I. Accounts of fifty-five royal processions and entertainments in the city of London; chiefly extracted from contemporary writers. II. A bibliographical list of Lord Mayors' pageants.

pp. [1–3] 4–121 [122 (imprint)], ²[1] 2 (advts.)
J. B. Nichols and son   1831
    JFA.

1089 THE THEATRICAL ALPHABET.

bs.   DFo
Birmingham: printed by T. King, and sold by G. Green
                                                        [ca. 1845]

1090 LEECH, AUGUSTUS E. *Theatres as they are, physically, quizzically, and critically discussed.

pp. iv, 68   MB
The Theatrical Times Office   1848

1091 MARX, W. P. The box book keeper's guide or London theatrical and amusement directory by W. P. Marx.

pp. [36]; pls. 1–23 (some fold.); ptd. covers   L
Jullien & Co.   [1848?]
The twenty-three plates are plans of the boxes.

1092 ———The box book-keeper's guide: and London theatrical amusement directory. Second edition.

pp. [*24*]; pls. 1–23 (some fold.); ptd. covers.   L
Jullien & Co.   1849

The title omits the name W. P. Marx, which is, however, on the cover. With descriptions of theatres by H. G. Brooks.

1093 ★THE PRESS PRIVILEGE at the theatres.

pp. 3   MB
[London]   [1853]

1094 SMITH, ALBERT, *ed.* ★"Press orders": being the opinions of the leading journals on the abolition of newspaper privileges. Edited by Albert Smith.

pp. 91   MH
W. Kent and Co.   [1853]

Reprints published articles and letters with Smith's commentary on the controversy concerning the moves during December 1852 and January 1853 by Smith, Charles Mathews and Benjamin Webster to discontinue the system of free passes for newspapers.

1095 [ERLE, THOMAS WILLIAM.] LETTERS from a theatrical scene-painter.

pp. [*6*] [1] 2–107 [108]   L
Printed by desire   1859

1096 ———Letters from a theatrical scene-painter. (Second series.)

pp. [*6*] [1] 2–95 [96]   L
n.p.   1862

1097 ———[another edition] Letters from a theatrical scene-painter; being sketches of the minor theatres of London as they were twenty years ago.

pp. [*116*]   L
Marcus Ward & Co.   1880

"Printed for private circulation only". On the green cloth cover: "by T. W. Erle." Reprints the 1859 and 1862 series, with the omission of three letters, and a new preface.

1098 ★METROPOLITAN BOARD OF WORKS. Rules and regulations for theatres.

              1878
STR.

1099 METROPOLITAN BOARD OF WORKS. Prevention of fire in theatres. Report by the Chief Officer of the fire brigade on the condition of various theatres in London.

pp. [1–5] 6–93 [94 (bl.)]   LGk
Confidential.—Printed for the consideration of members of the board only. Judd & Co., Phœnix Printing Works.   1882

Signed at the end by the Chief Officer, Eyre M. Shaw, and dated at the beginning 21 March 1882. Reports on Adelphi, Covent Garden, Drury Lane, Gaiety, Lyceum, Opera Comique, Strand, and Vaudeville Theatres. Printed on the title-page: No. 1035

1100 METROPOLITAN BOARD OF WORKS. Prevention of fire in theatres. Report by the Chief Officer of the fire brigade on the condition of various theatres in London.

pp. [i–v] vi, [1] 2–370; errata slip   LGk
Confidential. — Printed for the consideration of members of the board only. Judd and Co., Printers to the Metropolitan Board of Works   [1882]

Signed by the Chief Officer, Eyre M. Shaw, and dated 17th July 1882. Reports on thirty-four theatres. Printed on the title page: No. 1035

1101 SALA, GEORGE AUGUSTUS. Living London: being "Echoes" re-echoed by George Augustus Sala.

pp. [i] ii–xxi [xxii–xxiv], [1] 2–568; pls. [front., 11 (incl. engr. t.p. and dedication)]; illus.   L
Remington & Co.   1883

A "selected republication" of the "Echoes of the Week" and "The Playhouses" which appeared in the Illustrated London News, *1882.*

———[American edition] New York: Scribner & Welford, 1893

1102 WILLIAMS, MICHAEL. Some London theatres past and present. By Michael Williams.

pp. [*8*] [1] 2–215 [216]; errata slip   L
Sampson Low, Marston, Searle, & Rivington   1883

1103 ———★[another edition]
              1898
Chase.

1104 HAXELL, EDWARD NELSON. A scramble through London and Brighton. With anecdotes of the stage, past and present. By Edward Nelson Haxell. Second edition.

pp. [i–v] vi–viii, [1] 2–186; pls. [front., 16]   LGU
Isaac Pitman   1888

1105 BAKER, H[ENRY] BARTON. The London stage: its history and traditions from 1576 to 1888. By H. Barton Baker.

2 vols. pp. [i–v] vi–xiv [xv–xvi], [1] 2–296; pl. [front.]
+ pp. [6] [1] 2–323 [324]; pl. [front.]   L
W. H. Allen & Co.   1889

1106 ——[second edition] History of the London
stage and its famous players (1576–1903) by H. Barton
Baker.
pp. [i–vii] viii–xiv [xv–xvi], [1–3] 4–557 [558 (colophon)
559–560 (bl.)]; pls. I–X, incl. front.   E
London: George Routledge and Sons, Limited; New
York: E. P. Dutton and Co.   1904

*"Thoroughly revised" from the 1889 edition. Dedicated to
Sir Charles Wyndham "as the doyen manager of the
London stage."*

1107 HOLLINGSHEAD, JOHN. The story of
Leicester Square by John Hollingshead, with numerous
illustrations by M. Faustin, Howell Russell, Phil May,
and others, and facsimile reproductions of rare engravings, original water-colour drawings, etc. in the British
Museum, and various private collections. Art editor —
Mons. Charles Alias.
pp. [1–9] 10–75 [76]; illus. (incl. front.)   L
Simpkin, Marshall, Hamilton, Kent & Co., Limited
                                                         1892

1108 PLAYBILLS a collection and some comments.

pp. [4] [1] 2–37 [38]   L
Francis Edwards   1893

*Describes a collection of playbills, with comments on the
Tottenham Street House, Marylebone Theatre, Soho
Theatre, Pavilion Theatre, Garrick Theatre, Effingham
Theatre and Covent Garden 1828–9.*

1109 ORDISH, T[HOMAS] FAIRMAN. Early London theatres. [In the Fields.] By T. Fairman Ordish,
F.S.A. (The Camden Library.)
pp. [i–vii] viii–xvi, [1] 2–298 [299–300]; illus.; pls., fold.
[3]   GU
Elliot Stock   1894

*The companion volume, London theatres in the town,
announced on p. [299], was not published.*

1110 ——[large paper issue]
pp. [i–vii] viii–xvi, [1] 2–298 [299–300]; illus.; pls., fold.
[3]   L
Elliot Stock   1894

1111 ——[another edition]
pp. [i–vii] viii–xvi, [1] 2–298 [299–300]; illus.; pls., fold.
[3]   L
Elliot Stock   1899

INDIVIDUAL THEATRES

*Theatres are listed in alphabetical order under the name of the theatre, ignoring the prefixes Royal, New, Theatre Royal
etc (e.g. for Theatre Royal Covent Garden see Covent Garden).*

Alhambra Palace

*Also known as the Royal Alhambra Palace. Opened 1858
as a music hall, converted into a theatre in 1871. Destroyed
by fire December 12 1882. Rebuilt and reopened December 3
1883. In 1884 it reverted to music hall, see also no. 2125.*

1112 [WHITE, W.] THE ILLUSTRATED HAND-
BOOK of the Royal Alhambra Palace Leicester
Square. By the author of *The illustrated handbook of the
Royal Panopticon.*
pp. [1] 2–31 [32]; cover-title; pl. [front. (fold.)]; illus. L
Printed by Nicholls Brothers   [1869]

1113 THE ALHAMBRA alterations and decorations.
bs.   L
                                                  Sept. 1892

Argyle Theatre

*Also known as the Argyle Rooms. Opened July 1807 (as the
New Private Saloon Theatre).*

1114 GREVILLE, [HENRY   FRANCIS].   Mr.
Greville's statement of Mr. Naldi's case.

pp. [2] [1–3] 4–20   L
C. Chapple   1811

*Greville was proprietor of the Argyle Theatre. He engaged
Naldi, and the "case" between them was regarding breach
of contract — Lowe.*

1115 NALDI, GUISEPPI. The alien; or, an answer to
Mr. Greville's statement with respect to Mr. Naldi's
action for arrears of salary: including, also, a short
history of the Argyle Theatre. By Guiseppi Naldi.
pp. [2] [i–iii] iv–vi [7] 8–81 [82]   L
J. Blacklock   1811

1116 *ARGYLE ROOMS. Under the immediate
patronage of the haut ton . . .
bs.[?]; illus. (by G. Cruikshank)
Jas. Bullock   1827
  Cohn 32.

Astley's Royal Amphitheatre

*Also known as Astley's Amphitheatre and The Royal
Amphitheatre. Built in 1780. Astley relinquished it in 1817.
See no. 192.*

Bear Garden

See no. 1059.

Blackfriars

See no. 151.

Bridges-Street, Theatre Royal

The first theatre on the Drury Lane site. Opened 7 May 1663. Destroyed by fire 25 January 1672.

1117 ON THE UNHAPPY CONFLAGRATION OF THE THEATRE ROYAL. Jan the 25th. $167\frac{1}{2}$.

bs.   L

Daniel Brown   1672

In verse. Wing O 328.

Brunswick Theatre

The Royal Brunswick Theatre, which took the place of the Royalty Theatre, burned in April 1826, was opened on February 25, 1828, under the management of Percy Farren, with the Mermaiden's Well, *and a farce* An uncle too many. *These pieces were repeated the following night; there was no performance on the 27th; and on the 28th, while the performers were in the theatre at a rehearsal, the building fell, burying nearly all in the theatre under its ruins. The number killed was fifteen — Lowe.*

1118 CARRUTHERS, RICHARD and DAVID SAMSON MAURICE. To the worshipful the Magistrates of the County of Middlesex, in general session assembled. The humble petition of Richard Carruthers, citizen and goldsmith, of Gracechurch Street, and of David Samson Maurice, citizen and stationer, of Fenchurch Street, both in the City of London.

fold. doc., pp. [1] 2 [2 (bl.)]; caption-title   L

                               [1827]

Dated 18 October; seeking renewal of licence for Brunswick Theatre when rebuilt after the fire of 1826.

1119 AWFUL DESTRUCTION OF THE NEW BRUNSWICK THEATRE, attended by the loss of nearly 100 lives!!

bs.   MH

Printed by T. Birt   [1828]

In verse and prose.

1120 THE CHARGE of Maurice Thomas, Esq. deputy steward and coroner of His Majesty's Tower of London, its liberties, and precincts, delivered in the Court-House, Wellclose Square, on Thursday the 10th day of April, 1828, to the jury there impanelled and sworn, to enquire, on behalf of the King, when, where, and in what manner eleven of the sufferers, by the fall of "The Royal Brunswick Theatre" came to their deaths.

pp. [1–3] 4–31 [32 (bl.)]   LGU

W. Banning; W. Mason; H. Steel   1828

1121 DREADFUL ACCIDENT AT THE BRUNSWICK THEATRE, nearly 100 persons killed. This morning at about twelve o'clock. . . .

bs.   MH

Printed by T. Birt   [1828]

1122 FALLING OF THE BRUNSWICK THEATRE. The Rev. Mr. Smith's statement concerning the falling of the new Brunswick Theatre, Wellclose Square, Feb. 28, 1828, minutely detailing the awful situation in which the unfortunate sufferers were found in the midst of the ruins. And the means used to extricate them that were alive from their perilous situation. To which is added important particulars to the present time. List of killed, wounded, &c. &c. Second edition, with additions.

pp. [1–3] 4–14 [15–16 (advts.)]   MB

John Fairburn, (senior)   [1828]

L copy has pp. [1–2] 3–14, and only one "&c." on the title page.

1123 THE FALLING OF THE NEW BRUNSWICK THEATRE.

bs.; pl. by Robert Cruikshank   L

J. Didsbury   [1828]

1124 A FULL AND ACCURATE ACCOUNT of the destruction of the Brunswick Theatre, with the statements of Rev. G. C. Smith, & Messrs. Wm. & Percy Farren; letters of the architect; reports of public meetings; and every particular connected with the melancholy event: together with a history of the Theatre, from its origin: and of the introduction of theatres in the eastern part of the metropolis.

pp. [1–3] 4–36   L

J. Robins   1828

Copy at MB has plate.

1125 *THE GROUND OF THE THEATRE. An interesting review of circumstances connected with the ground upon which the late "Royalty", and the more recent "New Brunswick Theatre" stood. This site of ground having formerly been occupied as a place of worship, where the Gospel of salvation was preached for many years, with proposals for restoring the ground back to its original appropriation, by erecting a building that shall be devoted to purposes of benevolence and religion, where the sounds of prayer & praise shall again be heard glorifying God.

pp. 34   MB

W. K. Wakefield   [1828]

1126 ROYAL BRUNSWICK THEATRE, Goodman's Fields. Licensed pursuant to Act of Parliament, 25th Geo. II. The public are respectfully informed, that the above new, elegant, and commodious theatre will open, for the winter season, on Thursday, January 31, 1828.

bs.   MH
Maurice, printer   [1828]

1127 SMITH, *Rev.* GEORGE CHARLES *Dreadful catastrophe. Destruction of the Brunswick Theatre, Wellclose Square. First part.

pp. 12   MB
Wakefield   [1828]

1128 ———Dreadful catastrophe. Destruction of the Brunswick Theatre, Wellclose Square. By the Rev. G. C. Smith. Third edition.

pp. [1–2] 3–12; illus. t.p.   L
W. K. Wakefield   [1828]

This tract was divided in six parts. The above is the title of the first; the second bore the following title: — Lowe.

1129 ———Brunswick Theatre; or the second [–sixth] part of observations on the destruction of the new Brunswick Theatre, Wells Street, Wellclose Square. By the Rev. G. C. Smith, Minister of the London Mariner's Church.

pp. [1–2] 3–12 + [1–2] 3–12 + [1–2] 3–12 + [1–2] 3–12 + [1–2] 3–12   L
W. K. Wakefield   [1828]

The four succeeding parts differ very slightly in the punctuation of the title-page, and of course in the number of the parts, from the title of the second part — Lowe.

1130 ———A narrative of the falling of the Brunswick Theatre, Wells Street, Wellclose Square. By the Rev. G. C. Smith, Minister of the Mariners' Church, and formerly an officer in the Navy.

pp. [4] [1–2] 3–12, ²[1–2] 3–12, ³[1–2] 3–12, ⁴[1–2] 3–12, ⁵[1–2] 3–12, ⁶[1–2] 3–12; illus., incl. [front.]   LGk
W. K. Wakefield   1828

A reissue in one volume of the first(?) edition of parts 2–6 and of the fifth edition of part 1.

1131 THOMSON, JAMES, *ed.* A brief narrative of the opening, and sudden destruction of the Royal Brunswick Theatre, in a letter from Percy Farren, stage-manager of the late establishment. To which is subjoined, the new musical farce of An uncle too many; by James Thomson. Never performed but on the only two evenings the Brunswick Theatre was open, Monday 25th, and Tuesday 26th of February, 1828. Published in aid of the subscription for the sufferers by the late awful calamity.

pp. [1–5] 6–56   L
Effingham Wilson; and Smith, Elder, and Co.   1828

1132 TOTAL DESTRUCTION OF THE BRUNS-WICK THEATRE; with the loss of nearly 100 lives!

bs.; illus.   MH
Printed and sold by J. Catnach   [1828]

In verse and prose, with a large woodcut.
Last Thursday morn, oh, fatal day,
Near Well-close-square, alas,
The New Brunswick Theatre,
Fell with a dreadful crash.

1133 [THOMSON, CHARLES.] THE BRUNS-WICK: a poem.

pp. [4] [1] 2–64 [67] 68–103, 106–108 [=108]   L
William Marsh   1829

Motto: "Fallen, fallen, fallen" — Dryden.

1134 ———second edition

pp. [4] [1] 2–108   L
William Marsh   1829

Circus, Royal

Opened 1782. Later renamed the Surrey (see below nos. 1521–1523) See also GOVERNMENT REGULATION OF THE THEATRE for the year 1816 (p. 29); and nos. 193 seq.

1135 [DIBDIN, CHARLES.] ROYAL CIRCUS epitomized.

pp. [i–iii] iv–vi [vii–viii] ix–xx, [1] 2–79 [80 (bl.)]   L
Printed for the Author   1784

The dedication to William Davis, Esq. [one of the proprietors of the Royal Circus] is a most vicious attack on him, and accuses him of the grossest bad faith to Dibdin. In "Decastro's Memoirs" [no. 2672] some particulars regarding Davis are given — Lowe. Dibdin, p. 51.

1136 *THE CASE OF CHARLES HUGHES of the Royal Circus.

                                                                      1790
PH and KB.

1137 READ, T. *The history of the Royal Circus, introductory to the case of Mr. Read, late stage manager of that theatre; in a letter, to a friend.

pp. (4), 138   MB
London   1791

1138 vacant

Coburg, Theatre Royal

Opened 11 May 1818. Became the Royal Victoria Theatre on 1 July 1833, then the New Victoria Palace (music hall) in 1871 and the Royal Victoria Hall and Coffee Tavern (temperance music hall) in 1880. (See below nos. 1525–1533). Now the Old Vic Theatre.

1139 PROPOSALS FOR THE ROYAL COBURG THEATRE.

bs.   L

Goyder, printer   [1816?]

1140 ROYAL COBURG THEATRE. In order to form a just opinion as to the advantages . . .

pp. [2]   L

Goyder, printer   [ca. 1816]

1141 ROYAL COBURG THEATRE. Mr. Jones, late proprietor of the Royal Circus, is now engaged. . . .

bs.   L

[London]   [1816?]

1142   vacant

Cockpit

In Drury Lane. Converted into a theatre in 1616. Burned down by apprentices in 1617. It was rebuilt and renamed the Phoenix. See nos. 151, 1060.

Covent Garden, Theatre Royal

The first Covent Garden Theatre was built by Rich, and opened 7th December 1732. From Rich's death, in December 1761, until 1767, his son-in-law, Beard, was manager. Then Colman, Powell, Harris and Rutherford became proprietors, and their quarrels produced many pamphlets. Harris was the next manager, and he improved the theatre in 1792. But his improvements and the raising of the prices caused a riot. In 1803 John Kemble became part-proprietor. In 1808 the theatre was burnt, and at the reopening in 1809 the famous O.P. Riots occurred. The theatre was again burned down on 5th March 1856. — Lowe. The present theatre opened 15th May 1858.

See also SALE CATALOGUES nos. 53, 54; GOVERN-MENT REGULATION OF THE THEATRE especially nos. 166–172, 180–9, 192, 193–217, 220; ARTS OF THE THEATRE nos. 809–810; GENERAL HISTORY especially nos. 844, 904, 905; THE LONDON THEATRE nos. 1356, 1358 (Drury Lane), 1423 (Evans'); OPERA passim especially nos. 2078, 2092; BIOGRAPHY: COLLECTIVE especially nos. 2203, 2206, 2209–2223, 2314, 2321, 2325, 2344, 2350; THEORY AND CRITICISM nos. 3755–3758, 3762, 3764, 3972; PERIODICALS especially nos. 4081, 4109, 4110, 4113.

1143 RICH, JOHN. *Proposals. Whereas Mr. Rich has obtained from his Grace the Duke of Bedford a lease of a peice [sic] or parcel of ground contiguous to Bow Street and Covent Garden . . . upon which ground there is now building a new theatre . . .

[1730/1731]

TN XII, 1, 17.

1144 *TOM K——G's: or, the Paphian Grove. With the various humours of Covent Garden, the theatre, the gaming-table, &c. A mock-heroic-poem. The second edition.

pp. (4) 64; pls.   MB

John Torbuck   1738

1145 RICH [JOHN]. Mr. Rich's answer to the many falsities and calumnies advanced by Mr. John Hill, apothecary, and contained in the preface to Orpheus, an English opera, as he calls it, publish'd on Wednesday the 26th of December last.

pp. [2] 1–27 [28]   L

J. Roberts   1739

1146 HILL, JOHN. Orpheus: an English opera. By Mr. John Hill. With a preface, appealing to the publick for justice, and laying before them a fair and impartial account of the quarrel between the author and Mr. Rich, who intends in a few weeks to perform such an entertainment without his concurrence.

pp. [1–3] 4–7 [8], ²1–16 [17 (postscript) 18 (advt.)]   L

John Clarke   1740

In the preface Hill accuses Rich, manager of Covent Garden, of having stolen his pantomime of Orpheus and Eurydice from this work, which had been submitted to him and rejected. Rich effectually rebutted the accusation — Lowe. Rich's Orpheus and Eurydice, with the Metamorphoses of Harlequin was produced at Covent Garden 12 February 1740.

1147 HILL, JOHN An answer to the many plain and notorious lyes advanc'd by Mr. John Rich, Harlequin; and contain'd in a pamphlet, which he vainly and foolishly calls, An Answer to Mr. Hill's preface to Orpheus. By Mr. John Hill.

pp. [1–3] 4–24 [25 (postscript) 26 (bl.)]   L

J. Clarke   1740

Hill says that the title-page of Rich's answer is by Theo. Cibber; the head, tail, and certain dark passages in the middle, Mr. Theobald's; the impertinence, Captain Egan's; and the folly, Mr. Rich's own — Lowe.

Disputes of 1743

See DRURY LANE nos. 1336–1346

1148 A LETTER to a certain patentee: in which the conduct of managers is impartially considered; and a few periods bestowed on those darlings of the publick, Mr. G——k, Mr. F——e, Mrs. P——d, &c.

pp. [1–3] 4–28   L

H. Mumford   [1747]

A vicious criticism of Rich's management. The performers alluded to in the title are, of course, Garrick, Foote and Mrs Pritchard—Lowe.

The *"Bottle Conjurors"*

For this controversy at Covent Garden in 1749 see below Haymarket nos. 1425–1433

1149 [COOKE, THOMAS.] A PROLOGUE on comic poetry, and an epilogue on the comic characters of women, as spoke at the Theatre Royal in Covent-Garden, with a pastoral dialogue as performed at the same theatre: to which is prefixed an ode to John Rich, Esq;

pp. [1–3] 4–12   L
Printed, and sold, by J. Purser   1753

1150 MR. LEE'S CASE. November 13th, 1758.

old. doc., pp. [1] 2–4; filing-title   L
                                       1758

Head-title: "Case. Deliver'd Gratis at such Places as are advertiz'd in the Gazetteers of the 14th and 15th of November, 1758".

1151 [MADDISON, ROBERT.] AN EXAMINA-TION of the oratorios which have been performed this season at Covent-Garden Theatre.

pp. [i–iii] iv, [1] 2–63 [64]   L
G. Kearsly; R. Davis; and J. Walter   1763

     LS, pt. 4, 979.

1152 vacant

Riots of 1763

See also BIOGRAPHY: GARRICK nos. 2874–2882 for the Drury Lane riots.

1153 [BEARD, JOHN.] THE CASE CONCERN-ING THE LATE DISTURBANCE at Covent-Garden Theatre, fairly stated, and submitted to the sense of the public in general.

fold. doc., pp. [1] 2–3 [4]; head-title   L
[London]   [1763]

Head-title the same as the filing-title.

1154 *FITZ-GIGGO, a new English uproar, as it was performed at the Theatre-Royal in Covent-Garden, on Thursday last, by Mr. Beard, Miss Brent, Signior Tenducci, pit, boxes, galleries, &c. &c. The words adapted, (al burlesquo,) to the favourite airs in the opera of Artaxerxes.

bs.; illus. (engr. by L. Boitard)   L
Sold by E. Sumpter   [Feb. 1763]

The "uproar" was produced during the performance of Arne's Artaxerxes at Covent Garden on 24th February 1763. Stephens (1883) no. 4004.

1155 ——The second edition, price six-pence. Nothing under the full price can be taken.

bs.; illus.   MH
Sold by E. Sumpter   [1763]

1156 ——Fitz-giggo, a new English uproar; with The way to make him; or, a new overture upon the old score; as it was performed at the Theatre Royal in Covent-Garden, by Mr. Beard, Miss Brent, Sig. Tenducci, Mr. Smith, Mr. Woodward, pit, boxes, galleries, &c. &c. The words adapted (al burlesquo) to the favourite airs in the opera of *Artaxerxes.* The third edition. Price six-pence. Nothing under the full price can be taken.

bs.; illus.   MH
Sold by E. Sumpter   [1763]

Advertised 10th March 1763. Stephens (1883) no. 4004.

1157 THE SECOND AND LAST ACT of *Fitzgiggo, or All's well that ends well,* a new English uproar, as it was performed on Thursday the 3d of March 1763, at the Theatre Royal in Covent-Garden, by Messieurs Beard, Smith, Woodward, Pit, Boxes, Galleries, &c. &c. The words adapted to the favourite airs in the opera of Artaxerxes.

bs.; illus.   MH
J. Williams   [1763]

Farquar's The Inconstant was performed at Covent Garden on 3rd March 1763. Advertised in The Public Advertiser 10th March 1763.

1158 [BEARD, JOHN and JOHN SHEBBEARE.] LETTERS which have passed between John Beard, Esq; manager of Covent-Garden Theatre, and John Shebbeare, M.D.

pp. [2] 5–50   L
G. Kearsley   1767

Dr. Shebbeare wrote a comedy, and sent it to Beard, who politely declined it; being, however, injudicious enough to give his reasons for doing so in detail. Dr. Shebbeare thereupon poured out reams of argument and rudeness on the unfortunate manager, and published the letters —Lowe. Beard, however, is said to have kept the play for two years without replying.

Covent Garden Theatrical Fund

For Parliamentary Acts see GOVERNMENT REGULA-TIONS for the year 1776 (p. 26). Bs. announcements of the anniversary dinners of the Covent Garden Theatrical Fund, with other relevant material, from the 10th anniversary dinner (1825) to the 27th (?) (1844) are in L.

1159 THEATRICAL FUND, instituted at the Theatre Royal, Covent Garden, December 22, 1765. . . .

pp. [1] 2–4; head-title   MH
[London]   [1767]

A report.

1160 ———instituted at the Theatre Royal, in Covent-Garden, December 22, 1765, and confirmed by Act of Parliament, 1776.

pp. [2] [1–4] 5–20   L
Printed by E. Macleish   1811

1161 ———*instituted at the Theatre Royal in Covent Garden, 1765, and confirmed by Act of Parliament, 1776, 1794.

                                                  1819

STR.

1162 *COVENT GARDEN THEATRICAL FUND. Rules and regulations.

                                                  1872

IKF.

————————————————

The Proprietors' Dispute 1768

These disputes arose really from the attempt made by Harris to force his mistress, Mrs. Lessingham, into parts she could not play. Legal proceedings were taken, and harmony was not restored until Harris quarrelled with Mrs. Lessingham —Lowe. See Page, pp. 150–185, and 306–307; LS, pt. 4, vol. 3, pp. 1268 seq.

1163 ANIMADVERSIONS on Mr. Colman's True state, &c., with some remarks on his little serious piece called The Oxonian in town.

pp. [4] [1] 2–20   L
Walter; Dodsley; Fletcher and Company; Richardson and Urquhart; and Robson   1768

> *Unfriendly to Colman — Lowe. Reviewed in the* Critical Review *for March 1768. The Oxonian in town was produced at Covent Garden 7th November 1767.*

1164 COLMAN G[EORGE]. T. Harris dissected. By G. Colman.

pp. [2] [1] 2–36   L
T. Becket   1768

> *Dated 16 August 1768.*

1164.1 COLMAN, GEORGE. A true state of the differences subsisting between the proprietors of Covent-Garden Theatre; in answer to a false, scandalous, and malicious manuscript libel, exhibited on Saturday, Jan. 23, and the two following days; and to a printed narrative, signed by T. Harris and J. Rutherford. By George Colman.

pp. [1–3] 4, ²1–63 [64]   L
T. Becket; R. Baldwin; and R. Davis   1768

> *Advertised 10 February — Page. On p. [2]: "Although the following state of our case has been drawn up by Mr. Colman, I desire to be considered as equally responsible for its contents. William Powell."*

1164.2 ———the second edition

pp. [1–3] 4, ²1–63 [64]   L
T. Becket; R. Baldwin; and R. Davis   1768

1165 THE CONDUCT of the four managers of Covent-Garden Theatre freely and impartially examined, both with regard to their present disputes, and their past management. In an address to them, by a frequenter of that theatre.

pp. [4] 1–25 [26 (bl.)]   L
J. Wilkie; J. Williams; J. Almon   1768

> *Advertised 18 February 1768 — Page.*

1166 HARRIS, T[HOMAS]. A letter from T. Harris, to G. Colman, on the affairs of Covent-Garden Theatre. To which is prefixed, an address to the public.

pp. [2] [i] ii–vii [viii], [1] 2–56   LGk
J. Fletcher and Co.   1768

1167 KENRICK, W[ILLIAM]. An epistle to G. Colman.

pp. [4] [1] 2–15 [16]   L
J. Fletcher   1768

> *Advertised 22 February 1768 — Page.*

1168 ———the second edition

pp. [4] [1] 2–15 [16]   L
J. Fletcher and W. Anderson   1768

1169 THE MANAGERS: a comedy: as it is acted in Covent-Garden.

pp. [1–5] 6–13 [14 (bl.)] 15–16 (Epilogue)]   L
J. Nokes   1768

> *Advertised 27 February 1768 — Page.*

1170 *THE MANAGERS MANAGED: or, the characters of the four kings of Brentford.

                                                  1768

> *A rhymed attack upon all the contending parties, describing each of them in the most uncomplimentary manner. Prefixed is a short Address to Kenrick — Lowe.*

1171 [HARRIS, THOMAS and JOHN RUTHERFORD.] A NARRATIVE of the rise and progress of the disputes subsisting between the patentees of Covent-Garden Theatre.

pp. [2] ii [iii], 1–38   L
J. Fletcher   1768

> *Published in January.*

1172 *THE RING, an epistle addressed to Mrs. Lessingham.

                                                  [1768]

> LS. *pt. 4, vol. 3, p. 1269.*

1173-1174   vacant

The Macklin Riots 1773
See BIOGRAPHY nos. 3258-3265 (Macklin)

1175 RESIGNATION; or, majesty in the dumps; an ode. Addressed to George Colman, Esq. late manager of the Theatre Royal in Covent-Garden.

pp. [*2*] [1] 2–16   L
J. Bew   1774

Occasioned by Colman's retirement from management.

1176 *A LETTER to the patentees of Covent Garden Theatre on the conduct of Mr. Harris, the acting manager, who calls it *his* theatre.

                                            1780
Lowe.

1177 MR. HARRIS, proprietor of the Theatre-Royal in Covent-Garden, being desirous of discharging the incumbrances of seven-twelfths of that theatre, proposes to raise a sum of £25,000 for that purpose, on the following plan.

pp. [1] 2–3 [4]   DFo
[London]   29 Sept., 1784

1178 *POOR COVENT GARDEN! or, a scene rehearsed; an occasional prelude, intended for the opening of the new Theatre Royal, Covent-Garden, this season.

pp. 16   MB
Printed by T. Wilkins   1792

A satirical piece decrying the changes made in the theatre, which had been almost rebuilt during 1792, and the shilling gallery abolished.—IKF.

1179 [FOOT, JESSE?] A VINDICATION of a right in the public to a one shilling gallery either at the new Theatre Royal in Covent-Garden, or somewhere else.

pp. [1–3] 4–40   L
J. Owen; and H. D. Symonds   1792

When Harris altered the theatre, he abolished the upper gallery, and made 2s. the lowest admission. He had, however, to build a shilling gallery — Lowe. Signed "Pythagoras", and dated 15 September 1792. On the title-page of the copy at LGk an old hand attributes this work to Jesse Foot.

1180 *TRUTH and treason! Or a narrative of the Royal procession to the House of Peers, October the 29th, 1795. To which is added, an account of the

martial procession to Covent-Garden Theatre, on the evening of the 30th.

[London]   1795
Lowe.

1181 A TABLE of forfeits to be incurred by the performers of the Theatre Royal, Covent-Garden . . .
bs.   DFo
E. Macleish, printer   4 June, 1798

Forfeits for absence from rehearsal or performance, and for refusing parts.

1182 [HOLMAN, JOSEPH GEORGE?] A STATEMENT of the differences subsisting between the proprietors and performers of the Theatre-Royal, Covent-Garden. Given in the correspondence which has passed between them. By John Johnstone, Joseph George Holman, Alexander Pope, Charles Incledon, Jos. S. Munden, John Fawcett, Thomas Knight, Henry Erskine Johnston.

pp. [i–v] vi–vii [viii], [1] 2–69 [70], ²[1] 2–3 [4]   MH
W. Miller   1800

This dispute arose from the dislike of the actors to new restrictions on their power of giving orders for admission, to a change in the charge for benefits, &c. They submitted a case to the Marquis of Salisbury, then Lord Chamberlain, who practically decided against them — Lowe. "Generally supposed" to have been written by Holman — Genest. The final two leaves contain a Supplement.

1183 ———second edition

pp. [i–v] vi–vii [viii], [1] 2–69 [70] ²[1] 2–3 [4]   L
W. Miller   1800

Pp. ²1–3: Supplement.

1184 ———*third edition
                                            MH
                                            1800

Copy at MH interleaved with manuscript annotations, and a manuscript title-page in a fair hand: "Observations on the Statement of the Differences . . . Respectfully Submitted to the Most Noble the Marquis of Salisbury His Majesty's Lord Chamberlain. By the Proprietors. . . ." The copy of the second edition at L is similarly interleaved and entitled. According to Genest, VII, 483, the proprietors "sent to the Lord Chamberlain a copy of the Statement, interleaved with their own observations in manuscript — it was understood that this book was to be shown to the King — the King did read it, and the book was returned to Harris."

1185 TO THE MOST NOBLE THE MARQUIS OF SALISBURY, Lord High Chamberlain. The memorial of John Johnstone, Joseph George Holman, Alexander Pope, Charles Incledon, Joseph Samuel Munden, John Fawcett, Thomas Knight, and Henry

Erskine Johnston, on behalf of themselves, and other performers of the Theatre-Royal, Covent-Garden.

pp. [1] 2–3 [4]; p. 3: Marquis of Salisbury's award . . . with Mr. Estcourt's letter   DFo

Printed by E. Macleish   [1800]

1186 GILLILAND, THOMAS. Elbow room, a pamphlet; containing remarks on the shameful increase of the private boxes of Covent Garden, with a variety of original observations relating to the management of that theatre. Also A comparative view of the two houses, shewing the puerility of a great man's prophecy, who was to have turned Drury Lane Theatre into a "splendid desert", &c. &c.

pp. [i–iii] iv [5] 6–30 [31 (errata) 32 (bl.)]   L

Printed for the author and sold by Chapple   1804

1187 KEMBLIANA: being a collection of the jeu d'esprits, &c. that have appeared respecting *King John;* including the preternatural appearances of the ghost of Covent Garden.

pp. [1–5] 6–20   L

F. Sims, and V. Griffiths   1804

A shabby little tract — Lowe. First published "in the Newspapers" and here "rescued from oblivion". A note on p. 20: "Kembliana, Part II. is in the Press, and will be published in a few days", but no further parts are known.

1188 MR. G. WHITE'S LETTER, to Mr. Harris, June 5, 1804. With Mr. Harris's answer, June 17, 1804.

fold doc., pp. [1] 2–3 [4]; filing-title   L

[E. Macleish, printer]   [1804]

1189 MAJOR, JOHN. The Yorkshireman in London: or Humphrey Hobnail's return from the play. Sung by Mr. Emery, with unbounded applause, at the Theatre Royal Covent Garden. (Written by Mr. John Major.)

bs.; illus., (engr.)   MH

Laurie and Whittle   8 Nov. 1806

Five stanzas — Humphrey's impressions of the theatre; he saw Bold Stroke for a Wife *and the farce of* The Devil to Pay.

The Fire of 1808

It is probable that the wad of a gun fired in "Pizarro" was the cause of the fire which destroyed the theatre, 20th September 1808—Lowe.

1190 *ACCOUNT of the burning of Covent Garden Theatre.

1808

Recorded, but not seen by Lowe.

1191 AN ACCOUNT of the dreadful fire, which broke out on Tuesday morning, Sept. 20th, 1808, at Covent Garden Theatre, and totally destroyed that and a great number of other houses, and occasioned the death of upwards of twenty persons, besides greatly hurting many others.

pp. [1–2] 3–8; illus.   DFo

Printed and sold by Howard & Evans   [1808]

Cut and mounted.

✄ Liberty above all things . . . To which will be added, timely hints to prevent theatres . . . from demolition by fire. [1809?]. *See no. 791.*

1192 SMEETON, [GEORGE.] Smeeton's authentic statement of the dreadful conflagration of Covent Garden Theatre, and adjacent buildings, on Tuesday morning, September 20th, 1808. Also, An account of the melancholy accident that ensued, whereby near fifty persons were killed and dangerously burnt. With the proceedings of the coroner's inquest, and the names and other particulars of the unhappy sufferers. accompanied by An exact representation of the ruins of the theatre, &c. as they appeared on Tuesday morning, September 20, 1808 — 7 o'clock.

pp. [1–3] 4–16; col. pl. fold.   L

G. Smeeton   [1808]

1193 *A DETAILED STATEMENT of the losses of the several performers of Covent Garden Theatre in the late Fire. To which is added, the examination before the Magistrates relative to its origin; with the charge of the Coroner to the Jury.

1809

Recorded but not seen by Lowe.

The New Theatre 1808–1809

The rebuilding of the theatre was inaugurated by a great Masonic demonstration on 30th December 1808, and the Prince of Wales laid the foundation stone — Lowe.

1194 A NEW THEATRE will be erected with all possible expedition, by Robert Smirke, Junior, Esquire, Architect, on the scite of the late Theatre Royal in Covent Garden . . .

bs.   MH

[London]   [1808]

Offer of shares.

✄ [Howard, Frederick, *Earl of Carlisle*] Thoughts upon the present condition of the stage, and upon the construction of a new theatre. 1808. *See no. 789.*

1195 EXPLANATION of the sculpture, in basso relievo, in the grand front of Covent Garden Theatre, and a particular description of its interior.

bs.   MH

Printed and sold by J. Jennings   [1809]

1196 ——[another edition] Explanation of the sculpture, in basso relievo, in the grand front of Covent-Garden Theatre.

bs. MH
Sold, Wholesale, by N. Hewitt; Grant, printer [1809]

1197 ——[another edition]

pp. [2] MH
Swan and Son, printers [1809]

1198 ——[another edition] Description of Covent Garden Theatre.

bs.; illus. MH
Sold by N. Hewitt. Higley, printer [1809]

See also below no. 1245: A new song, on Covent Garden.

1199 PADDY O'FOGGERTY'S DESCRIPTION of the exterior of the new Covent Garden Theatre.

bs.; col. illus. DFo
[London]: sold at Mr. Abrahams, and by the Author;
Higly, printer [1809]

1200 [DONNE, JOHN WILLIAM]. WHEREAS, A FEW EVIL DISPOSED PERSONS have falsely and maliciously. . . .

bs. MH
A. Newman, printer 15 May 1809

1201 [DONNE, JOHN WILLIAM]. LAW and justice, against oppression! or, struggling through difficulty!!! Price three-pence.

pp. [1] 2–4; headed "sixth edition" MH
A. Newman, printer [1809]

Signed and dated 22 May. Donne (an actor) owned premises in Bow Street, which the Covent Garden proprietors were trying to obtain.

The O.P. Riots 1809

The opening night was 18th September 1809, when the increase in the price of admission and in the number of private boxes led to the disgraceful "O.P." or "Old Price" Riots, which lasted for sixty-seven nights. The advanced prices were 7s. for the boxes, and 4s. for the pit. Previously they had been 6s. and 3s. 6d. respectively. In the end the proprietors were forced to give way; the private boxes were reduced in number, and the prices were fixed at 7s. and 3s. 6d. The riots were renewed at the beginning of the next season, because the private boxes were not sufficiently reduced in number; and the rioters again carried their point — Lowe.

1202 THE AFFECTING FAREWELL of Othello, Moor of Covent Garden; a "finished" actor. (Exit in a rage.)

bs.; illus. (by George Cruikshank) MH
For the proprietor by J. Johnston Nov. 1809

A fourteen-line parody. Issued both coloured and uncoloured. Cohn 871.

1203 AT THE THEATRE NAPOLEON, Covent Garden, will be repeated the popular comedy of The truth will out; or, knaves detected.

bs., headed "This, and every evening, till further notice." DFo
[London] [1809]

1204 ATTALUS, *pseud.* Justice and generosity against malice, ignorance, and poverty: or, an attempt to shew the equity of the new prices at the Theatre Royal, Covent Garden. By Attalus.

pp. [2] [1–4] 5–16 [17–18 (advt.)] L
Sherwood, Neely, and Jones 1809

1205 AUTHOR OF NOTHING ELSE THE, *pseud.* *The "Old Price-iad;"* or Thespian bear garden: an epic poem, in two parts. By the author of nothing else. [Part I.]

pp. (1) 36 (1). MB
Ryan [1809]

1206 A BOW STREET CASE. A young man was last night taken out of the pit, and charged by two of the officers . . .

bs. DFo
T. Romney, printer November 23d. 1809

1207 BRITONS BE FIRM!

bs. MH
[London] [1809]

A handbill, reprinted in Baker, p. 308.

1208 BULL, JOHN, *pseud.* Covent Garden Theatre!! Remarks on the cause of the dispute between the public and managers of the Theatre Royal, Covent Garden, and on their right to raise the prices of admission; with A circumstantial account of the week's performances, from the opening of the Theatre on Monday Sept. 18, until the closing of the same, on Saturday Sept. 23, 1809. By John Bull. Illustrated with a large caricature frontispiece of The House that Jack Built.

pp. [2] [1–3] 4–45 [46 (advt.)]; pl. fold. [front., by George and Isaac Cruikshank] L
John Fairburn [1809]

Cohn 168. The plate was issued both plain and coloured.

1209 BY PARTICULAR REQUEST, the new prices will be continued a night or two longer. New Theatre, Covent-Garden. This evening will be presented, a medley of entertainments, called *The Jugglers, or, half the truth.* . . . After which *A peep behind the curtain.* . . . To conclude with the new national drama, John Bull victorious. . . . To-morrow evening (by general desire) Empty benches, with A house to be sold.

bs. MH

Printed by W. Glindon [1809]

A mock play-bill.

1210 CANDIDUS, *pseud.* The statement of a few facts, and an impartial appeal on the subject at issue between the public and the proprietors of the Theatre-Royal, Covent-Garden. By Candidus.

pp. [1–3] 4–16 L

Richards and Co. [1809]

Dated 23 September.

1211 CAUTION. Lord Mansfield, on the trial of the rioters in the case of Mr. Macklin . . .

bs. DFo

Printed by E. Macleish [1809]

1212 CESSATION OF HOSTILITIES. Basis of a speedy, lasting, and honorable peace!!

bs. DFo

Printed by A. Macpherson [1809]

In defence of Brandon.

1213 CLIFFORD FOR EVER! O. P. AND NO P. B. The trial between H. Clifford, plaintiff, and J. Brandon, defendant, for an assault and false imprisonment, as the plaintiff was quitting Covent Garden Theatre, October 31, 1809. With the speeches of counsel and the charge to the jury. Which was tried before Sir James Mansfield, and a special jury, in the Court of Common Pleas, Westminster, Dec. 5, 1809.

pp. [1–3] 4–27 [28 (advt.)] L

John Fairburn [1809]

Clifford was a barrister, and the ringleader of the rioters. He won this action: damages £5 — Lowe.

1214 CONSIDERATIONS on the past and present state of the stage; with reference to the late contests at Covent Garden; to which is added, A plan for a new theatre for the purpose of hearing plays.

pp. [4] [1] 2–58 L

C. Chapple 1809

Unfriendly to the managers of Covent Garden. Its real purpose is to advocate a small theatre, in which it would be possible to hear what is said on the stage — Lowe.

1215 COUNSELLOR O. P., — defender of our theatric liberties.

bs.; illus. (col. by J. Gillray) MH

H. Humphrey 5 Dec. 1809

Six lines of verse. A caricature of Henry Clifford. George *(1947) 11430*

1216 THE COVENT-GARDEN A.B.C.

bs. MH

[London] [1809]

Begins *A was an actor, well shaven and shorn,*
B was a Bull. . . .

1217 COVENT GARDEN THEATRE. It having been stated in some of the publick prints, that the profits of the late theatre were more than sufficient, the proprietors think it their duty to state, that the average profits of the last ten years have not been six per cent.

bs. DFo

[London]: printed by E. Macleish [1809]

1218 COVENT GARDEN THEATRE. Public Office, Bow Street. Mr. M. Thomas, a gentleman of respectability. . . .

bs. MH

Printed by W. Glindon [1809]

Dated 14 October 1809. M. Thomas, who had "hissed and hooted . . . from a principle of unbiassed judgment", was discharged by the magistrate.

1219 *FOUR LETTERS ON THE THEATRE; written during the dispute between the public and the proprietors of the new Theatre Royal, in Covent Garden, on its opening in 1809: wherein are discussed, the merits of players, and the morality of the stage; originally published in "The Times", and now collected, with additional notes and observations.

pp. xi, 96 MB

Wilson [1809]

⌘ Friend of the People, A, *pseud.* A private peep into the treasury of the Theatre-Royal, Covent Garden . . . By a friend of the people. 1809. *See no. 1278.*

A reissue of Theatricus: Theatrical taxation *(see below no. 1277).*

1220 THE GHOST OF O.P.

bs. DFo

[London] [1809]

Begins *November's drizzling dark fogs lowered.*

1221 GIBBS, *Sir* VICARY. Covent Garden Theatre. The speech of Sir Vicary Gibbs, Knt. His Majesty's attorney-general, in the Court of King's Bench at Westminster, on Monday the 20th November, 1809, on moving for a rule to shew cause why a criminal information should not be filed against Henry Clifford, Esq. and others. Accurately and impartially taken in short hand, by Mr. Farquharson.

pp. [1–5] 6–24   L

J. Ridgway   1809

The above rule was made absolute on 28th November, and the trial was to come on in the next session — Lowe.

1222 GRAND THEATRICAL MEDAL. Obverse. An allegorical head, illustrative of folly and avarice . . . Sold at Hathway's Newspaper Office, Royal Exchange.

bs.   DFo

[London]   [1809]

1223 HEIGH HO! SAYS KEMBLE. With an accopaniment [*sic*] for the piano forte.

pp. [1] 2–3 [4]; illus., music; head-title   DFo

[London]   [1809]

Begins Jack Kemble would as an actor go.

1224 THE HOUSE that Jack built.

bs.; illus.   L

[London]   [1809]

Begins This is the house that Jack built.
These are the boxes let to the great, that visit the house . . .
Signed: Bow-Wow.

1225 £100 REWARD! Absconded from the duties of his employment, a man who has the audacity to call himself an actor.

bs.   DFo

[London]   [1809]

1226 IS THIS A RATTLE which I see before me?

bs.; illus. (col. caricature of Kemble by I. Cruikshank) L

S. W. Fores   30 Oct. 1809

Kemble as Macbeth, with twelve lines of parody. George (1947) 11422.

1227 JOHN BULL to the galleries. Worthy brethren of the galleries.

bs.   DFo

[Pri]nted by E. Macleish   [1809]

1228 JOHNNY leave the pit alone, let 'em sing O.P.

bs.   L

[London]   [1809]

Begins Air —"Molly put the kettle on." Four stanzas, with a chorus.

1229 *A JOURNAL OF THE WAR, carried on in the New Theatre Royal, Covent Garden, from the 18th of September to the 18th of November 1809.

                                                         1809

Recorded but not seen by Lowe. The rebellion; or, all in the wrong, no. 1270 below, (pp. 1–80 and 124–128) contains a Journal of the war carried on in the new Theatre-Royal, Covent Garden.

1230 vacant

1231 KING JOHN and John Bull.

bs.; illus. by Cruikshank   DFo

J. Johnston   November 1809

Begins KING JOHN. What means this thund'ring clamour here? Cohn 1290.
Different from the caricature of the same title, issued by Fairburn in October 1809 — George (1947) 11419, Cohn 1289.

1232 *KING JOHN IN A COCK'D HAT, or heighho says Kemble.

bs.

T. Tegg   Nov. 14, 1809

Cohn 1291.

1233 KING JOHN WAS A MANAGER. Air — "My master's a conjuror."

bs.   MH

T. Gibson   [1809]

Six stanzas, beginning:
    King John was a manager mighty and high —
    Hey populorum jig.
    He built private boxes, the devil knows why —
    Hey populorum jig. . . .

See also no. 1258 below.

1234 LIBERTY OF THE SUBJECT. BRITISH FORUM, Trader's Hall, Skinner's Street, Snowhill. Thursday next, the 26th October, 1809.

bs.   DFo

[London]   [1809]

Announcement of a public meeting.

1235 THE LIFE OF JOHN PHILIP KEMBLE, Esquire, a proprietor, and stage manager of Covent Garden Theatre, interspersed with family and theatrical anecdotes.
        O, my "aitches!!!"
                Tempest, (new reading.)

pp. [4] [1] 2–52; pl. fold. [front.]   L
J. Johnston   [1809]

> *The frontispiece O.P. caricature by I. and G. Cruikshank issued both plain (at L.) and coloured (at L.). Cohn 459 (but with a half-title).*

1236 ———*to which is added strictures on Mrs. Galindo's curious letter to Mrs. Siddons. Second edition.
pp. [4] [1] 2–64   MH
                                                   [1809]

> *'O, my "aitches"!!!' on plate, not title-page. Cohn 459.*

1237 LONGBOW, *Signor, pseud.* This is the house that Jack built. Composed by Signor Longbow of Grand Caero.
pp. 1–3 [4]; engr. words, music; with vignette   DFo
Printed and sold at Bland & Weller's   [1809?]

1238 THE MANAGER turned an O.P.
bs.   DFo
[London]   [1809]

1239 THE MANAGER with his opera hat; or, heigho! says Kemble.
bs.   DFo
Printed and sold by J. Jennings   [1809]

1240 MENDOZA & Kemble. It is a notorious fact, that the managers of Covent Garden Theatre . . .
bs.   DFo
James Whiting, printer   [1809]

1241 MR. MUNDEN WILL NEXT, as he has previously declared an ungrateful people little deserving of, come forward, and edify the public.
bs.   DFo
[London]   [1809]

1242 NATIONAL AIR. Humbly submitted to the placarding committee.
bs.   L
Glindon, printer   [1809]

> *Begins "God save Great JOHNNY BULL"*

1243 THE NEW GRAND O P DANCE, with characteristic figure, by that eminent composer, O.P: M.D. now performing with universal applause at the Theatre-Royal Covent Garden.
bs., engr.; illus. (music); headed: "A new edition with embellishments"   DFo
For the author by J. Girtin   November 23 1809

1244 A NEW SONG. New Covent Garden. Tune Ally Croker. A house there was of great renown.
bs.   DFo
[London]   [1809]

1245 A NEW SONG ON COVENT GARDEN THEATRE. Come all you lads and you lasses, fond of sport, And listen to my ditty, and hear, but my report . . .
bs; illus.   DFo
Printed and sold by J. Pitts   [1809]

1246 ———[another edition] A new song on Covent Garden Theatre. Come all you lads and you lasses, fond of sport, And listen to my ditty, and hear but my report . . .
bs.   DFo
J. Pitts   [1809]

> *Same as no.1245 with printer's device instead of illustration.*

1247 A NEW SONG, on Covent Garden Theatre. *Tune* — Madam Fig's Gala.
[2]   L
Higly, printer   [1809]

> *On the reverse, Description of Covent Garden Theatre. Perhaps another edition of no. 1198.*

1248 NEW THEATRE, Covent-Garden, this evening will be presented for the last time, an operatic farce, in one act, called Imposition.
bs.; headed: Last night of performance at the New Prices   DFo
Printed by Glindon   [1809]

1249 NEW THEATRE ROYAL, Covent-Garden, this present Wednesday, October 4, 1809, will be acted a comick opera called The Beggar's Opera.
bs.   DFo
[London]   [1809]

> *Includes statement of accounts of the theatre.*

1250 NEW THEATRE ROYAL, Covent Garden. This present Wednesday, Oct. 11, 1809, will be presented. . . . Hockley in the hole. . . . To conclude with a grand chorus of hired ruffians, fighting Israelites, and Bow-Street officers . . .
bs.   MH
W. Glindon, printer   1809

1251 NEW THEATRE ROYAL, Covent-Garden, this present Friday, Oct. 6, 1809, will be acted a comedy called John Bull; or, an Englishman's fire-side.
bs.   DFo
[London]   [1809]

> *Includes statement of accounts of the theatre for the previous six years.*

1252 OLD PRICES: comprising an answer to the pamphlets in favour of the imposition, entitled *Theatrical taxation*, and *The statement of a few facts, and an impartial appeal on the subject at issue between the public and Covent Garden Theatre.*

pp. [1–3] 4–19 [20 (bl.)]   L
Gale and Curtis   1809

1253 OLD PRICES FOR EVER HUZZA! An appeal to the public by order of the committee appointed to conduct the patriotic opposition, now in a state of great activity, against the scandalous impositions on the public, attempted by the rapacious proprietors of the new Theatre Royal Covent-Garden . . . (Signed) Robert Row. Tommy Trumpet. Ralph Rattle. Humphrey Horner. Kit Catcall. Gregory Groaner, Secretary, Peter Placard.

bs.   DFo
Printed by W. Glindon   [1809?]

1254 ONE WHO DARES TO THINK FOR HIMSELF, *pseud.* *Reason versus passion; or, an impartial review of the dispute between the public and the proprietors of Covent Garden Theatre: with strictures on the Times and Morning Chronicle newspapers: comprising a defence of the committee. By one who dares to think for himself.

pp. iv, 60   MB
Wilson   [1809]

1255 O.P., AN, *pseud.* *"What do you want?" A poetical epistle from an O.P.

[1809]

One night, while the riot raged, Kemble, instead of asking "what the pleasure of the audience was?" asked "What is it that you want?" This was seized upon as want of respect—Lowe. Not seen by Lowe.

1256 *O.P. The interesting trial at large of Henry Clifford, Esq.

MH
1809

1257 O.P. JACK! It is only one step you know.
bs.; illus.   DFo
W. Evans   [1809]

1258 †O P KING JOHN WAS A MANAGER a new ballad.
bs.   DFo
[London]   [1809]

Begins Air — 'My Master's a Conjuror.' King John was a Manager mighty and high. This is another edition or version of no. 1233.

1259 †THE O P MAGIC DANCE in the new-built playhouse, O!
bs.   DFo
Printed by J. Bailey for T. Gibson   [1809]

Begins Tune. "The Bay of Biscay, O!" Loud roar'd the watchman's rattle. Also includes The OP's victory.

1260 OP THE KING OF THE JEWS in a cocked hat, or Jemmy deceived.
bs.   L
W. Evans   [1809]

Begins AIR — "Bull in a China Shop". I'll sing you a song mayhap. "Jemmy" was the box-keeper, Brandon.

1261 *O.P.'s manual.
1809
Recorded but not seen by Lowe.

1262 A PARODY OF MACBETH'S SOLILOQUY at Covent Garden Theatre. Boxes 7/-.
bs.; illus.   DFo
Walker   October 1809

Begins Is this a "seven shilling piece" I see before me? George 11423 (col. impression.)

1263 *A PEEP into the treasury of Covent Garden theatre.
[1809]
Recorded but not seen by Lowe.

1264 PINDARIC, PETER, *pseud.* This day is published, Broad hints at retirement, a rebellious ode to a tragedy king, being a rhyming, chiming, pertinent and satirical epistle to J. P. Kemble, Esq. author of the Row and principal Manager of the Revels at Covent Garden. By Peter Pindaric.
bs.   DFo
John Bailey   [1809]

See also no. 1276.

1265 PITY POOR KEMBLE, gentlefolks, pray.
bs.; illus.   L
Printed and sold by J. Pitts   [1809]

1266 A POETICAL EPISTLE to Henry Clifford, Esq. on the late disturbances in Covent Garden Theatre.
pp. [1–3] 4–8   L
Edinburgh: printed by John Moir   1810

Published at 2 shillings!! A most extravagant eulogy of Clifford — Lowe.

1267 THE PRESENT ANNUAL EXPENSES of Covent-Garden Theatre.

bs.   DFo

[London]: printed by E. Macleish   [1809]

1268 PROPOSALS submitted to Mr. Kemble at the Crown and Anchor Tavern, Strand, last night.

bs.   DFo

Printed by W. Glindon   Dec. 15, 1809

Six demands of the O.P. rioters.

1269 PUBLIC OFFICE, BOW-STREET. Whereas great riot and disturbances have taken place at Covent Garden Theatre . . . By order of the Magistrates, John Stafford, Chief Clerk.

bs.   DFo

Printed by E. Macleish   10 October, 1809

1270 THE REBELLION; or, all in the wrong. A serio-comic hurly-burly, in scenes, as it was performed for two months at the new Theatre Royal, Covent-Garden, by his Majesty's servants, the players, and his liege subjects, the public. To which is added, A poetical divertisement, concluding with A panoramic view of the new theatre, in prose.

pp. [i–iii] iv–viii, [1] 2–128; pl. [front.]; t.p. in red and black   L

Vernor, Hood, and Sharpe; Taylor and Hessey; Sharpe and Hailes; and J. Booker   1809

1271 ——*second edition

pp. viii, 128; port.   MB

Vernor, Hood & Sharpe   1809

1272 *A SHORT ADDRESS to the public on the raising the prices at Covent Garden Theatre.

                                                               MH
                                                             1809
    Lowe.

1273 SPLITTING THE DIFFERENCE; or the ready reckoner.

bs.   DFo
                                                             [1809]

Begins *To H——s, quoth K——e, "I question much whether".*

1274 *STRICTURES on the engagement of Madame Catalani.

                                                             1809

The engagement of Catalani was one of the grievances of the rioters—Lowe. Not seen by Lowe.

1275 *THE THEATRIC COUNT, a tragic comedy, in five acts. From the Orgoglio Cupitoso, conte teatrino, of Gonzago Bicchieri. Adapted for representation on the English stage.

pp. 56   DLC

Sherwood, Nealy and Jones   1809

1276 THEATRICAL REBEL, A., *pseud.* Broad hints at retirement, an ode to a tragedy king, addressed to J. P. Kemble, Esq. author of The row, and principal Manager of the Revels at Covent-Garden. By a theatrical rebel.

pp. [i–iii] iv [5] 6–15 [16]   L

John Bailey   [1809 or 1810]

The tone of this pamphlet may be gathered from the motto on the title-page:
    "This fact know, John, the public can dispense,
    Both with thine acting and impertinence!" — Lowe.
See also no. 1264.

1277 THEATRICUS, *pseud.* Theatrical taxation; which embraces reflections on the state of property in the Theatre-Royal, Covent-Garden, and the engagement of Madame Catalani: also, an analysis of the grounds upon which the proprietors have been induced to raise the prices of admission to the pit and boxes of that theatre. By Theatricus.

pp. [2] [1] 2–22   MH

G. Hughes   [1809]

A defence of the new prices. The author attributes much of the opposition to Taylor, the lessee of the Opera House, who was annoyed at the engagement of Catalani at Covent Garden — Lowe.

1278 ——[reissue] FRIEND OF THE PEOPLE, A, *pseud.* A private peep into the treasury of the Theatre-Royal, Covent-Garden, and the exposition of the engagement of Madame Catalani. By a friend of the people.

pp. [2] 2–22   MH

G. Shade   [1809]

1279 ——EXTRACTS FROM A PAMPHLET, entitled Theatrical Taxation.

pp. [1] 2–16   DFo

[London]: Hughes   [1809]

1280 TO THE PUBLIC. A private school was opened in Bow-Street, on the 18th of September, 1809, where all the unlettered O.P.'s and N.P.B's are taught to read by a certain knightly parson.

bs.   DFo

[London]   [1809]

1281 *TRIAL of James Brandon for assault and false imprisonment committed on the person of H. Clifford.

[1809]

Chase.

1282 THE UPROAR! or John Bull and the manager. A melo drame, performed six nights, with unbounded applause, at the Theatre Royal, Covent-Garden; with the chorusses, and accompaniments for the horn and other wind instruments. To which is added, a new comic song, called John Bull's concert; or, Mr. Rooney O'Rogherty's visit to Covent Garden Theatre.

pp. [3–7] 8–37 [38]; col. pl., fold. [front.]   L

John Fairburn   [1809]

Plate by Isaac and George Cruikshank (Cohn 821).

1283 UPROAR AT COVENT GARDEN THEATRE.

bs.; illus.   L

Printed and sold by J. Pitts   [1809]

1284 VERUS AMICUS, *pseud.* *A letter to John Kemble, Esq. upon the present disturbances at the Theatre Royal, Covent Garden; with some hints for the better accommodation of the public. By Verus Amicus.

1809

Lowe.

1285 WESTMINSTER SESSIONS. Thursday, 26th October, 1809. The riot act read.

pp. [1] 2–3 [4]   MH

[Printed by E. Macleish]   [1809]

The stern voice of authority, doubtless reprinted by the Covent Garden proprietors.

1286 WHO IS BRANDON? Is Brandon not in the employ of the theatre? . . .

bs.   MH

Printed by A. Macpherson   [1809]

1287 THE WHOLE PROCEEDINGS on trial of an action brought by Henry Clifford, Esquire, against Mr. James Brandon, for an assault and false imprisonment. Before Sir James Mansfield, Knight, and a special jury, in the court of common pleas, on Tuesday the 5th day of December, 1809. Taken in short hand by Messrs. Blanchard and Ramsey.

pp. [i–v] vi–xxii, [1] 2–118   L

Printed by E. Blackader   1809

1288 [STOCKDALE, JOHN JOSEPH, *ed.*] THE COVENT GARDEN JOURNAL.

2 vols. pp. [1–5] 6–368; pls. [front., 2] + pp. [4] 369–816; pl. [front.]   L

J. J. Stockdale   1810

The "directions to the binder" (p. [16]) allow for binding in either one volume or two; a head-title ("The Covent Garden Journal. vol. II") and a title-page for the second volume are provided. Originally issued in weekly numbers with printed wrappers; the last number issued 28 April 1810. Volume II reprints some of the OP literature (unillustrated).

1288.1 ——[large paper issue].

pp. and pls. as no. 1288   LU

J. J. Stockdale   1810

1289 A GENUINE COLLECTION of O.P. songs, whimsical and satirical, among which are many originals, never before printed . . . To which is added the toasts and sentiments, given by the O.P.'s, at the Crown & Anchor Tavern, before and after the reconciliation, also the terms of peace.

pp. [1–3] 4–23 [24]   DFo

B. Mace   [1810]

1290 MAD BULL, A, *pseud.* The O-Poeiad, a satire. By a mad bull.

pp. [1–3] 4–16   L

Printed for the Author, and Sold by James Cawthorn

1810

1291 MAD TOM, *pseud.* of Sowerby. A series of letters on the late theatric festival, interspersed with remarks on some serio-comic pantomimes fresh in the memory. By Mad Tom, "a daring, obstinate enthusiast."

pp. [i–v] vi–xii [xiii–xiv], [1] 2–64   L

Sherwood, Neeley, & Jones   1810

Attribution to one Sowerby reported by Lowe.

1292 THE O.P. SONGSTER for 1810; containing all the O.P. songs that have made their appearance on this occasion; together with the most popular songs now singing at the different places of amusement: to which are added, A new comic song, of the exciseman outwitted; and Mr. Mathew's celebrated song of Bartholomew Fair, never before published.

pp. [1–3] 4–28; col. pl., fold. [front.]   L

W. Evans   [1810]

The plate is signed 'Cruikshank'. Not in Cohn.

1293 †TEGG, THOMAS. The rise, progress, and termination of the O.P. war, in poetic epistles, or hudibrastic letters, from Ap Simpkins in town, to his friend Ap Davies in Wales; including all the best songs, placards, toasts, &c. &c. which were written, exhibited, or given on the occasion; with illustrative notes, by Thomas Tegg.

pp. [i–vii] viii–xi [xii], [1] 2–179 [180]   L

Thomas Tegg   1810

> *Half-title reads "The O.P. War." Dedicated to Henry Clifford with "deference and respect". Cohn 786, with a note on a frontispiece, which varies in different copies, and was issued both plain and coloured.*

1293.1 *THE VICTORY of the O.P.'s; an account of the O.P. dinner.

          MH
          1810

> *At a dinner held on 14th December at the Crown and Anchor Tavern, Clifford in the chair, Kemble attended, and peace was made — Lowe.*

✠   Theatrical Fund instituted at the Theatre Royal, in Covent Garden. 1811. *See no. 1160.*

1294 *DRURY'S RESURRECTION, or the drama versus the menagerie.

          MH
          1812

> *I have not seen this pamphlet, but, no doubt, it refers to the degradation of the stage by Harris at Covent Garden, where horses were introduced in plays — Lowe.*

1295 SAPPHO, *pseud.* Elephantasmagoria; or, the Covent Garden elephant's entrance into Elysium: being a letter from the shade of Garrick to John Philip Kemble, Esq. by Sappho.

pp. [i–v] vi–xv [xvi], [1] 2–47 [48]; pl. [front.]   MH

Cradock and Joy; Collins; and Hookham   1812

> *Dedicated to "Romeo Coates, Esq." In octosyllabics, with the caption title: "Elephantasmagoria Solomonharrisoria." A live elephant was introduced by Harris on the stage at Covent Garden, 26th December 1811. The plate may not belong to the book.*

1296 CHABANNES, JEAN BAPTISTE MARIE FREDERIC, *Marquis de.* *On conducting air by forced ventilation and regulating the temperature in dwellings. With a description of the application of the principles as established in Covent Garden Theatre and Lloyd's Subscription Rooms.

          LRO

London   1818

✠   Theatrical Fund instituted at the Theatre Royal in Covent Garden. 1819. *See no. 1161.*

1297 THE THEATRICAL HOUSE that Jack built. With thirteen cuts.

pp. [1–10] 11–27 [28]; illus.   L

Joseph Grove   1819

> *An attack on the management of Covent Garden; Fawcett, the actor, and Brandon, the box-keeper, are specially abused — Lowe. On Brandon Lowe adds: Boxkeeper at Covent Garden during the O. P. Riots. He made himself specially obnoxious to the Rioters, who insisted on his dismissal. He was, however, reinstated.*

1298 INSTRUCTIONS for the admission of orders into Covent Garden Theatre.

bs.   MH

Printed by E. Macleish   [1820?]

> *Signed T. Harris.*

1299 TO THE PUBLIC. A number of foreigners are engaged at Covent Garden Theatre. . . .

bs.   MH

          Sept. 27th, 1820

> *Signed "Fairplay".*

1300 FITZGEORGE, GEORGE. *A letter addressed to the Lord Chamberlain, on the present state of the drama. By George Fitzgeorge, of Lincoln's-Inn, Esq.

          [1821?]

> *A furious attack upon Mr. Harris, the proprietor of Covent Garden Theatre — Lowe.*

1301 O.P. AMATEUR, AN, *pseud.* *A plain statement of facts; containing the whole of the particulars relative to the various circumstances which have hitherto transpired connected with the existing differences between the present management of Covent Garden Theatre and Mr. James Brandon: interspersed with remarks on the impolicy of again risking another theatrical war, *alias* an O.P. row! By an O.P. amateur.

          1823

> *Charles Kemble and the other managers alleged misconduct against Brandon, and tried to eject him, but he declined to go. How the matter ended I cannot trace — Lowe. Brandon was the treasurer. According to Saxe Wyndham (Annals of Covent Garden, 1906, I, 348) he left Covent Garden with an annuity of £200 p.a. and went to Drury Lane. He died in 1825.*

1302 THEATRE ROYAL, Covent-Garden. Saturday, November 29, 1828.

bs.

Printed by W. Reynolds   1828

> *Copy in the Nag's Head Tavern, Covent Garden. No play on Monday, pending report from persons employed to remove gasometers.*

1303 COVENT-GARDEN Theatre. Closed for one week. Address.

bs.

Printed by W. Reynolds 1828

Copy in the Nag's Head Tavern, Covent Garden. Closed while gasometers removed after an explosion of gas on 27 November which killed two persons.

1304 RE-OPENING of Covent-Garden Theatre. Thursday, December 4, 1828. The public attention is respectfully solicited to the following important documents . . .

bs.

Printed by W. Reynolds 1828

Copy in the Nag's Head Tavern, Covent Garden.

1305 HARRIS, HENRY. A letter from Mr. Henry Harris, the principal proprietor and lessor of Covent Garden Theatre, to Mr. White, one of the real creditors of the Theatre, in reply to remarks and assertions made by Messrs. Kemble, Willett, & Forbes, the lessees of the Theatre, and their solicitor, at the recent meetings; with the judgments of Sir John Leach, Knt. Master of the Rolls; and Lord Lyndhurst, Chancellor.

fold. doc., pp. [1–3] 4–15 [16]; filing-title L

[1829]

1306 CHANCELLOR, E. BERESFORD. The annals of Covent Garden and its neighbourhood by E. Beresford Chancellor M.A., F.S.A. With 16 illustrations.

pp. [1–8] 9–288; pls. [front., 15] L

Hutchinson & Co. [1830]

1307 S[CHARF], G[EORGE], *Sir.* Recollections of the scenic effects of Covent Garden Theatre during the season 1838–9. Dedicated (by permission) to W. C. Macready Esqr. by G. S.

pp. [4] mounted on 2 leaves; engr. t.p.; pls. [43] LVA

Pattie [1839]

"Dedication. To W. C. Macready, Esq. This humble and imperfect attempt to convey an idea of the many and great improvements introduced by him during his management of Covent Garden Theatre, especially in the restoration of the text of Shakspere, is dedicated, with every sentiment of respect and admiration . . ."

1308 HALLIWELL, JAMES ORCHARD, *later* Halliwell-Phillipps. The management of Covent Garden Theatre vindicated from the attack of an anonymous critic, in a letter to the editor of the "Cambridge Advertiser." By James Orchard Halliwell, Esq.

pp. [1–5] 6–12 E

(Not printed for sale) 1841

In answer to an attack on his critical opinions. The attack was entitled "Madam Vestris and the National Theatre," and attacked Madame Vestris — Lowe. *Reprinted, with changes, from the* Cambridge Advertiser.

1309 SMITH, ALBERT. Theatrical ashes. By Albert Smith.

pp. [1–7] 8–35 [36] LGk

For private circulation 1856

Reprinted from Household Words. *On the burning of Covent Garden, 5 March 1856. Bound in wood from Covent Garden after the fire of 1856.*

1310 *ROYAL ITALIAN OPERA, Covent Garden. Season 1864.

pp. 20 MB

[Miles & Co.] 1864

Prospectus.

1311 *IN CHANCERY. Between Brownlow William Knox, plaintiff, and Frederick Gye, defendant. The answer of Frederick Gye the above named defendant to the bill of complaint of the above named plaintiff.

pp. [1]–64

Tamplin & Tayler 1865

IKF.

1312 GRUNEISEN, C[HARLES] L[EWIS]. The opera and the press, by C. L. Gruneisen, F.R.G.S.

pp. [1–3] 4–70 [71 (bl.) 72 (imprint)] L

Robert Hardwicke 1869

On the managements of Lumley and Gye.

⌘ Covent Garden Theatrical Fund. Rules and regulations. 1872. *See no. 1162.*

Crown Theatre

Opened October 31 1898

1312.1 SACHS, EDWIN O[THO]. The Crown Theatre, Peckham, Ernest Runtz, architect. Some illustrations and notes with comments by Edwin O. Sachs, architect, author of "Modern Opera Houses and Theatres," "Stage Construction," &c., &c.

pp. [4] 1–12, ff. 13–16 [17–18] 19–22, pp. 23–36 [37–38 (bl.)]; illus.; pls. MH

Gilbert Wood 1898

Folios 13–22 are the plates, from photographs.

Daly's Theatre

Opened 1893 and closed in 1937.

1313 SCOTT, CLEMENT. Song of dedication! On the occasion of laying the foundation stone of "Daly's

Theatre", London, 30th October, 1891. Spoken by Miss Ada Rehan.

bs.　　　　　　　　　　　　　　　　　　DFo

[London]　　　　　　　　　28th October, 1891

1314 DALY'S THEATRE Leicester Square.

pp. [*12*]; illus; cover-title　　　　　　　MH

[Winchell Press, New York]　　　　　　1893

Dorset Garden Theatre

Originally the Duke's Theatre. Demolished June 1709.

1315 THE PATENTEE: or, some reflections in verse on Mr. R——'s forgetting the design of His Majesty's Bear-Garden at Hockly in the Hole, and letting out the Theatre in Dorset-Garden to the same use, on the day when Mr. Dryden's obsequies were perform'd; and both play-houses forbore acting in honour to his memory.

pp. [*2*]　　　　　　　　　　　　　　L

[London]　　　　　　　　　　　　1700

　　Macdonald *299.*

1316 [ADDISON, JOSEPH?] *DESCRIPTION of the playhouse in Dorset Garden.

bs.　　　　　　　　　　　　　　　ICN

[London]: sold by B. Bragg　　　　　1706

　　Edited by Emmett L. Avery, "A Poem on Dorset Garden Theatre", TN 18 (1964) 121–124. Different versions reprinted in The Poetical Works of . . . Sir Charles Sedley (1707) pp. 202–207 (as "The Play-House. By J. Addison, Esq") and in C. N. Greenough, 'Did Joseph Addison write "The Play-House"?', Harvard Studies and Notes in Philology and Literature, XVII (1935) 55–65.

Drury Lane, Theatre Royal

Was built near the site of the old Cockpit; opened on 7th May 1663; burned down 1672; rebuilt; reopened 1674; interior considerably altered 1775; closed 1791; and pulled down; new theatre opened 12th March 1794; burned 24th February 1809; rebuilt; reopened 10th October 1812 — Lowe. The last is the present theatre, with a new interior.

Note that all items on Drury Lane printed during the period of Garrick's management until his death (1747–1779) are listed under BIOGRAPHY: GARRICK.
See also GOVERNMENT REGULATION OF THE THEATRE, especially nos. 153, 154–6, 166–172, 180–9, 192, 193–217, 220; ARTS OF THE THEATRE nos. 792, 809–810, GENERAL HISTORY especially nos. 844, 904, 905; LONDON THEATRES no. 1186; THEATRE OUT OF LONDON no. 1701; BIO-GRAPHY COLLECTIVE especially nos. 2203, 2206, 2209–2223, 2316–2320, 2322–2325, 2344, 2348, 2350, 2356; THEORY AND CRITICISM especially nos.

3749, 3755–3757, 3762, 3764, 3777; PERIODICALS especially nos. 4109, 4111, 4113.

✠ On the unhappy conflagration of the Theatre Royal. 1672. See no. 1117.

　　The destruction by fire of the Theatre Royal, Bridges Street, the first theatre on the Drury Lane site.

1317 *A JUSTIFICATION of the letter to Sir J——n St——ley, relating to his management of the playhouse in Drury-Lane.

pp. 2

n.p.　　　　　　　　　　　　　　　n.d.

　　This is said to be an answer to a printed letter. It contains references to the principal players and a violent attack upon Mrs. Oldfield — Thorn-Drury.

1318 vacant.

1319 [BAGGS, ZACHARY.] ADVERTISEMENT CONCERNING THE POOR ACTORS, who under pretence of hard usage from the patentees, are about to desert their service.

pp. 1–4; head-title　　　　　　　　　L

[London]　　　　　　　　　　　　1709

　　Signed Zachary Baggs, Treasurer at the Theatre Royal in Drury Lane, 8 July 1709. Gives actors' incomes.

1320 THE PLAY-HOUSE SCUFFLE, or, passive obedience kickt off the stage. Being a true relation of a new tragi-comedy, as it was acted last week at the Play-house in Drury Lane; by several notorious actors, frequently call'd Her Majesties Servants, but of late turn'd their own masters. In two canto's.

pp. [1–2] 3–16　　　　　　　　　　L

J. Bethel　　　　　　　　　　　1710

　　Dated 1 July by Luttrell.

1321 *THE HUMBLE REMONSTRANCE of Robert Wilks and Colley Cibber of the Theatre Royal. January 16th, 1713/14.

　　　　　　　　　　　　　　　　1713/14

STR.

1322 RT. HON. BARON BUNGEY, *pseud. To diabebouloumenon: or, the proceedings at the Theatre-Royal in Drury-Lane. Occasion'd by the much lamented death of the late celebrated Sir Harry Wildair; with an apotheosis, spoken on that occasion, and a tragi-comi-farsi-cal scene call'd, Love and friendship: or, the rival passions. As it was acted before the three mock kings, Phyz, Trunk, and Ush. Faithfully collected from the original mss. and journals of the house, at their*

Majesty's command. By the Rt. Hon. Baron Bungey, Secretary of State to their Majesties.

pp. [1–4] 5–40   L
T. Payne   1723

> *This curiously titled pamphlet seems to refer to Wilks' retirement from the character of Sir Harry Wildair, in which he excelled. On 18th April 1723, the date mentioned in the pamphlet as that of Sir Harry's death, Wilks played the part for the last time. Of the three mock kings, Phyz is certainly Colley Cibber; Trunk, from his indolence, must be Booth; and Ush must be Wilks himself. Cibber is scurvily treated throughout—Lowe. Daily Journal, 16 April 1723: "On Thursday next Mr Wilks acts the part of Sir Harry Wildair . . . and it will be the last time he will perform that part". (See LS. pt. 719) Despite this advertisement Wilks continued to act the part for many more seasons.*

1323 RENNEL, GABRIEL. Reflections, of a moral and political tendency, occasioned by the present state of the two rival-theatres in Drury-Lane and Lincolns-Inn-Fields. By Gabriel Rennel, Esq.

pp. [1–5] 6–30 [31–32 (bl.)]   L
A. Moore   [1725?]

> *Strong against raree-shows, pantomimes, and all irregular forms of dramatic production — Lowe.*

Dispute of 1733

The dispute of 1733 arose from the secession of the leading actors of Drury Lane from the manager, John Highmore, who had recently purchased Cibber's share of the patent. The seceders played at the Haymarket. Highmore tried to force them to return, and even prosecuted Harper as a rogue and vagabond, but unsuccessfully. He, after a few months, gave up the struggle; and Fleetwood became manager — Lowe.

1324 *THE CASE OF THE COMEDIANS.
folio
London   1733

> *Recorded but not seen by Lowe. Perhaps same as The case of the comedians, &c. belonging to the theatre in Goodman's Fields (no. 167 above).*

1325 CIBBER, THEOPHILUS. A letter from Theophilus Cibber, comedian, to John Highmore, Esq;

pp. [1] 2–4; head-title   L
                                                               [1733]

> *An attempted defence of Cibber's conduct in stirring up the actors of Drury Lane to revolt against Highmore, who had recently purchased a large share in the Patent.—Lowe*

1326 GENTLEMAN, A, LATE OF TRINITY-COLLEGE, CAMBRIDGE, *pseud.* of Edward Phillips. The stage-mutineers: or, a play-house to be lett. A tragi-comi-farcical-ballad opera, as it is acted

at the Theatre-Royal in Covent-Garden. By a gentleman late of Trinity-College, Cambridge.

pp. [8] 1–40   L
Richard Wellington   1733

> *Produced at Covent Garden 27th August 1733.*

1327 ——the second edition
pp. [8] 1–40; cancellans t.p.   L
H. Slater; F. Noble; T. Wright; J. Duncan   [1733]

> *"Let" for "lett" on t.p.*

1328 AN IMPARTIAL STATE of the present dispute between the patent and players.
fold. doc., pp. [1] 2–6; filing-title   L
[London]   [1733]

1329 *THE LAMENTATION OF MR. H——during his confinement in Bridewell.
                                                               1733

> *Mr. H—— is Harper the actor, who was proceeded against by Highmore, manager of Drury Lane, as a "rogue and vagabond." He was committed to Bridewell, November 12, 1733, but on trial was discharged upon his own recognisances—Lowe. Not seen by Lowe.*

1330 *THE THEATRE turned upside down; or, the mutineers. A dialogue, occasioned by a pamphlet, called, The theatric squabble. . . .
pp. 8   DLC
Printed, and sold by A. Dodd   1733

> *Eulogises Mr Clive R——r (Raftor) who remained loyal to Highmore.*

1331 THE THEATRIC SQUABBLE: or, the p——ntees. A satire . . .
pp. [2] [4] 5–8   DFo
E. Nutt; and A. Dodd   1733

> *A satire on the secession of the leading actors of Drury Lane during the management of John Highmore.*

——————

1332 CAREY, HENRY. Of stage tyrants. An epistle to the Right Honourable Philip Earl of Chesterfield. Occasion'd by *The Honest Yorkshire-man* being rejected at Drury-Lane play-house, and since acted at other theatres with universal applause. By Mr. Carey.

pp. [2] 1–8 [9 ("Proposals for printing by subscription one hundred English ballads. Set to music by Mr. Carey. . . .") 10 (bl.)]   L
London: J. Shuckburgh, and L. Gilliver; J. Jackson; Bath: J. Leake   1735

> *An attack on Fleetwood, in heroic couplets. For the background to this epistle see LS. pt. 3, pp. cxliv–cxlv. Carey's The Honest Yorkshireman was produced at the Haymarket 15th July 1735. Reprinted in The Poems of Henry Carey, ed. F. T. Woods (1930), pp. 104–108.*

1333 CHARKE, CHARLOTTE. The art of management; or, tragedy expell'd. By Mrs. Charlotte Charke.

pp. [1–10] 11–47 [48 (bl.)]   L

Printed by W. Rayner   1735

> *A satire on Charles Fleetwood, manager of the Theatre Royal, Drury Lane, who is in it called Squire Brainless. The farce was performed at York Buildings on 24th September 1735, and on 1st October it was advertised that on "Friday next, printed books of the farce will be sold at the Great Room". Fleetwood, according to Genest (IV, 568–569) endeavoured to buy up the whole impression.*

1334 A SEASONABLE REBUKE to the playhouse rioters, contained in two new prologues. Proper, at this turbulent juncture, to be exhibited in the British theatre. To which is prefixed, a petitionary dedication to the fair members of the Shakespear-Club.

pp. [1–9] 10–16   L

C. Corbett   1740

> *A prefatory note explains that the piece was finished shortly after the tumult at Drury Lane [on 23 January 1740], but that it is still topical though publication was delayed (till 9 March, according to MS note) "as scarce a night has since passed without some disturbance in the theatre."*

1335 *THE THEATRICAL CONTEST.
                                        DFo

G. Foster   Octob^r, 24th, 1743

> *On Garrick's attempt to obtain a licence to open a new playhouse.*

Dispute of 1743

Fleetwood's misconduct led to the serious dispute of 1743. The actors, headed by Garrick and Macklin, seceded; but, failing to get a licence to play elsewhere, were forced to return to Drury Lane. They had agreed to stand or fall together, and Fleetwood's refusal to receive Macklin again, to whom he ascribed the revolt, led to a violent dispute between Garrick and Macklin, particulars of which will be found under GARRICK [see below nos. 2829–2833]. Numerous pamphlets appeared for and against Fleetwood during the original dispute: his champion being Paul Whitehead, and William Guthrie writing on the actors' side — Lowe.

1336 THE CASE BETWEEN THE MANAGERS of the two theatres, and their principal actors, fairly stated, and submitted to the town.

pp. [1–2] 3–23 [24 (bl.)]   L

J. Roberts   1713 [*for* 1743]

> *Against Fleetwood and Rich.*

1337 THE CASE OF OUR PRESENT THEATRICAL DISPUTES, fairly stated. In which is contained, a succinct account of the rise, progress and declension of the ancient stage; a comprehensive view of the management of the Italian, Spanish, French and Dutch theatres, with some free remarks upon our own. Calculated entirely for the use of the public, and wherein, the only method is suggested, that can prevent all future debate.

pp. [2] 1–64   L

Jacob Robinson   1743

> *Sometimes attributed to James Ralph.*

1338 COMEDIAN, A, *pseud.* A full answer to Queries upon queries. In which the conduct of the players is vindicated, and the misrepresentations of the querist expos'd. By a comedian.

pp. [1–2] 3–22 [23 (advt.) 24 (bl.)]   L

J. Roberts   1743

> *For Queries upon queries see below, no. 1342.*

1339 [CHETWOOD, WILLIAM RUFUS]. THE DRAMATIC CONGRESS. A short state of the stage under the present management. Concluding with a dialogue as it lately passed between the illustrious bashas of Dr—ry Lane and Co—nt Garden, and the chiefs of the revolted players. In a letter to Messieurs B—th and W—ks, in the Shades, from W.R. C—d, *nuper* Monitor *Theat. Reg.* Londin. & *nunc* Elanensis.

pp. [1–2] 3–27 [28 (bl.)]   L

M. Cooper   1743

> *On the side of the actors — Lowe. Chetwood was prompter at Drury Lane.*

1340 FITZ-CRAMBO, PATRICK, *pseud.* Tyranny triumphant! and liberty lost; the muses run mad; Apollo struck dumb; and all Covent-Garden confounded. Or, historical, critical, and prophetical remarks on the famous cartel lately agreed on by the masters of the two theatres. In a letter to a friend in the country. To which is added, An essay towards a farce on the same subject. By Patrick Fitz-Crambo, Esq; secretary to the minor poets.

pp. [2] [1] 2–29 [30 (bl.)]   L

G. Lyon   1743

1341 QUERIES TO BE ANSWER'D by the manager of Drury-Lane Theatre, for the satisfaction of the publick, in regard to the present dispute between him and his actors.

pp. [1–4] 5–19 [20 (bl.)]   L

J. Roberts   1743

1342 QUERIES UPON QUERIES, to be answer'd by the male-content players. For the satisfaction of the publick, in regard to the present dispute between them and the manager.

pp. [1–2] 3–19 [20 (bl.)]   L

W. Bickerton   [1743]

> *Answered in A full answer to Queries upon queries, by a Comedian (no. 1338 above).*

1343 THEATRICAL CORRESPONDENCE in death. An epistle from Mrs. Oldfield, in the shades, to Mrs. Br—ceg—dle, upon earth: containing, a dialogue between the most eminent players in the shades, upon the late stage desertion.

pp. [4] [1] 2–24   L
Jacob Robinson   1743

1344 THE DISPUTES between the managers of the theatres, and their actors adjusted: with an impartial examination of the players right to appeal to the publick. In a letter to a friend.

pp. [2] 5–25 [26]; misnumbering 13 as "5", 16 as "8", 17 as "9", 20 as "12"   L
Jacob Robinson   1744

1345 THE DISPUTES between the Director of D—y, and the pit potentates: being a letter to a friend, concerning the behaviour of the melancholly manager of the suff'ring theatre; and some considerations on the late disturbances and the causes thereof: with a few hints on the heroes and heroines, G—rr—k, C—bb—r, Q—in, M—ls, M—ck—n; C—bb—r, R—b—ts, H—rt—n, and M—ls; not forgetting 'Squire Poor, 'Squire Swift-Timber, Mr. Knotty-Nob, the orator; and Hard-Head the constable. The whole relating to some remarkable occurrences in the year 1744.

pp. [1–4] 5–27 [28 (bl.)]   L
M. Cooper   1744

> *Serious riots occurred on 17th and 19th November 1744, owing to Fleetwood's ['Squire Swift-Timber] charging advanced prices to old entertainments — Lowe. Signed: B.Y. Tom's Coffee-House, Covent-Garden, Nov. 20, 1744.*

1346 MR. NEITHER-SIDE, *pseud.* An impartial examen of the present contests between the town and the manager of the theatre. With some proposals for accomodating the present misunderstandings between the town and the manager, offer'd to the consideration of both parties. By Mr. Neither-side.

pp. [1–5] 6–24   L
M. Cooper   1744

1347 A NEW MUSTER of Bays's troops.
bs.; with pl.   DFo
[London]: sold at the print and pamphlet-shops   1745

> *An engraving showing the Drury Lane company mustering, in suitable theatrical costumes, to engage the Pretender's forces; the Laureate and Rich also appear; with a key and eight stanzas describing their military preparations.*

Garrick's management

For the history of Drury Lane from 1747 until Garrick's death in 1779 see BIOGRAPHY (Garrick), especially nos. 2835, 2840, 2851, 2855, 2857, 2862, 2867, 2870, 2874–2882.

Drury Lane Theatrical Fund

See also GOVERNMENT REGULATION OF THE THEATRE for the year 1776 (p. 26). Bs. announcements of the anniversary festivals of the Drury Lane Theatrical Fund (4th anniversary, 1821, and 30th anniversary, 1847) are at MH, together with a collection of clippings, concerning the festivals 1829–1851, formed by George Daniel, who wrote the speeches delivered on these occasions by John Pritt Harley: after 1851, a note — "This speech closes these yearly festivals. There has been no Dinner since. . . ."

1348 BE IT REMEMBER'D, that at the Theatre-Royal, in Drury-Lane, in the year of Our Lord, 1766, a contribution was set on foot, and encouraged by the patentees and members of said theatre, in order to institute and establish a fund, for the support of such performers, whose age or infirmities should oblige them to retire from the stage.

pp. [1] 2–13 [14]; head-title, headed: London, April 24, 1775   LGk
[London]   [1775]

> *Probably lacks title "Rules and orders" etc.*

1349 ——[another edition] Rules and Orders to be observed by the society established for the relief of indigent persons, belonging to His Majesty's Company of Comedians of the Theatre-Royal in Drury-Lane.

pp. [2] [1] 2–26 [27 (text) 28 (bl.)]   LGk
                                                         1777

1350 ——†[another edition] Rules and orders, to be observed by the society established for the relief of indigent persons, belonging to his Majesty's Company of Comedians of the Theatre-Royal in Drury-Lane; who from age or infirmity may be obliged to retire from the stage.

pp. [2] [1] 2–19 [20]   LGk
                                                         1781

1351 ——[another edition] The fund, for the relief of indigent persons belonging to His Majesty's Company of Comedians of the Theatre Royal, Drury Lane. Established, endowed, and incorporated, by that great master of his art, David Garrick, Esq. 1777.

pp. [2] [1–5] 6–28   LGk
Printed by C. Lowndes   1806

1352 ——[another edition]
pp. [1–5] 6–30   L
Printed by Lowndes and Hobbs   1813

1353 ——[another edition]
pp. [2] [1] 2–30   LVA
Printed by C. Lowndes   1814

1354 ———[another edition]

pp. [1–5] 6–42   MH

Printed by C. Lowndes   1819

Contains the proceedings of the first dinner in aid of the Drury Lane Theatrical Fund, 11th March, 1818, and a list of 'donators', etc.

1355 FUND. Theatre-Royal, Drury-Lane, April 6th, 1778.

bs.   LGk

[London]   [1778]

Announcing that the Committee of the Fund have expunged the Ninth Article of the Rules and Orders.

———

1356 COALITION, a farce; founded on facts, and lately performed, with the approbation, and under the joint inspection of the managers, of the Theatres-Royal.

pp. [i–iii] iv–viii, [1] 2–31 [32]   L

D. Browne   1779

In 1778 a coalition between the patentees of Drury Lane and Covent Garden took place, and actors were lent by the one to the other in the strangest way — Lowe. The preface is signed "A poor player".

1357 ———the second edition. Dramatis personae. Brainsley, Senior. Brainsley, Junior, Harras. Tickler. Lyric, a pragmatic poet. Servants, bailiffs, &c. Mrs. Brainsley. Scene lies in London.

pp. [i–iii] iv–viii, [1] 2–31 [32]   L

J. Barker, at the Pit-Door in Russell-Court, Drury-Lane

                                               1779

Instead of "the Theatres-Royal" the title-page reads "both theatres". Brainsley = Sheridan, Harras = Harris, Tickler = Richard Tickell.

1358 THEATRICAL MONOPOLY; being an address to the public on the present alarming coalition of the managers of the winter theatres.

pp. [4] [i] ii–vi [vii–viii], [1] 2–32   L

Fielding and Walker   1779

Dedicated to George Colman.

1359 [REED, JOSEPH]. THE RETORT courteous; or a candid appeal to the public on the conduct of Thomas Linley, Esq, manager of Drury-Lane Theatre, to the author of Dido. Containing original letters and just remarks on the manager's arbitrary and indefensible rejection of that tragedy.

pp. [1–3] 4–48   L

Printed for the Author   1787

Contains an account of the circumstances surrounding Reed's MS narrative "Theatrical Duplicity", now in the Harvard Theatre Collection.

1360 FENTON, W. The itinerant Thespians, or the theatre dissected. By W. Fenton.

pp. [i–iii] iv–v [6] 7–30, misprinting 30 as "29"   L

[London?] Printed for the Author   1792

A satire by a disgruntled actor, apparently on the Drury Lane management and company.

1361 THE PARTICULARS of a new renter's share in the Theatre Royal, Drury Lane . . . which will be sold by auction, by Messrs. Skinner and Dyke, on Thursday the 23rd of October, 1794, at twelve o'clock, at Garraway's Coffee-House . . .

pp. [1–2] 3–4   L

[London]   [1794]

The new renter's share is Lot 1. It is "For One Hundred Years, Paying to the Holder Two Shillings and Six-pence for each Night that Theatrical or Musical Entertainments shall be exhibited, and Free Admission into any Part of the House, behind the Scenes excepted." The price paid for this was £470. The other lots are non-theatrical.

1362 A STATEMENT of facts.

pp. [1] 2–16; head-title   MB

                                              [1797]

"Copy of a deposition made at the Sessions-House, Clerkenwell, Feb. 17, 1797", concerning J. E. Burghall, Mrs. Booth, and Miss Granger, of the Theatre Royal Drury Lane. Signed J. E. Burghall, Feb. 1797.

1363 THE TRIAL of James Hadfield, at the Court of King's Bench, before Lord Kenyon, on the 26th of June, 1800, for high treason, in attempting the life of the King, at Drury-Lane Theatre, on the fifteenth of May last, with the whole of the evidence.

pp. [1–3] 4–42 [43–44 (bl.)]   MH

Newcastle Upon Tyne: printed and sold by Matthew Brown   [1800]

1364 HOULTON R[OBERT]. A review of the musical drama of the Theatre Royal, Drury Lane, for the years 1797–98–99– & 1800. Which will tend to develope a system of private influence injurious to musical emulation, and public entertainment — and to elucidate several interesting points of matter in Mrs Plowden's late distinguished publication. Addressed to the proprietors of the theatre. By R. Houlton, M.B.

pp. [1–5] 6–79 [80 (postscript)]   L

R. H. Westley; W. Stewart; H. D. Symonds   1801

Mrs. Plowden's publication was, I suppose, her comic opera Virginia, which was damned the first night — Drury Lane, 30th October 1800 — Lowe.

1365 WEST, JOSHUA. *A poetical epitome of the proceedings of the chancery-court at Lincoln's-Inn-Hall, on the 23d day of December, 1801, relative to the celebrated Drury-Lane-Theatre cause heard before the Right Hon. John Lord Eldon, now Lord High Chancellor of Great-Britain, written in allusion to an antique history of the last revel held in the Inner-Temple, on the 2d of February, 1733; in the presence of the Right Hon. Charles Lord Talbot, then Lord High Chancellor. By Joshua West.

pp. 20   MH

Printed for the author, by J. and E. Hodson; and sold by T. Bright   1802

✗ The Fund for the relief of indigent persons belonging to His Majesty's Company of Comedians of the Theatre Royal, Royal Drury Lane. 1806. *See no. 1351.*

Fire of 1809 and rebuilding of Drury Lane

The theatre was burnt down on 24th February, 1809, through the carelessness of some workmen. The performances were carried on at the Lyceum. Drury Lane was not rebuilt till 1812. It was, through Sheridan's mismanagement, almost bankrupt when the fire occurred, and it was only by the exertions of Mr. Whitbread that the necessary funds to rebuild it were raised — Lowe.

For Government publications on the rebuilding see GOVERNMENT REGULATION OF THE THEATRE *for the years 1810, 1812, 1820 (p. 29).*

1366 AUTHENTIC ACCOUNT of the fire which reduced that extensive building of the Theatre-Royal, Drury-Lane, to a pile of ruins, on the evening of the 24th of February, 1809; to which is added, a chronological list of all the places of public amusement, destroyed by fire, in England.

pp. [1–3] 4–12 5 16–24 37 [38 (advt.)] (=24); col. pl., fold. [front.]   L

T. Broom; J. Herbert; W. Wilson; W. Evans   [1809]

✗ [Ware, Samuel]. Remarks on theatres and on the propriety of vaulting them with brick and stone. 1809. *See no. 792.*

Includes a scheme for rebuilding Drury Lane.

1367 [WYATT, BENJAMIN.] *DESIGNS for the building of Drury Lane Theatre.

pls.

              [1811]

Recorded but not seen by Lowe. See also below nos. 1377, 1378, 1390.

1368 PROPOSALS for rebuilding Drury Lane Theatre.

fold. doc., pp. [4]; filing title   L

Printed by Lowndes and Hobbs   [1811]

1369 REBUILDING DRURY-LANE THEATRE. Wednesday, July 3, 1811. The Committee under the Act of Parliament met, Samuel Whitbread, Esq. in the chair.

ff. [1] 2–5   LGk

Lowndes and Hobbs, printers   [1811]

Minutes of the meeting, signed by Whitbread.

1370 REPORT of the committee for rebuilding Drury Lane Theatre, by shares of £100 each, erected into a joint stock company, by Act of Parliament. Samuel Whitbread, Esq. chairman.

fold. doc., pp. [1] 2–4; filing-title. Headed 3d July 1811   MH

Lowndes and Hobbs, printers   [1811

1371 REPORTS of the committee under the act for rebuilding Drury-Lane, Theatre, &c. &c. &c.

pp. [2] [1–3] 4–20 [21–22 (bl.)]   L

Lowndes & Hobbs, printers   [1811]

1372 REPORTS presented to the first and second general assemblies of subscribers to the re-building of the Theatre-Royal, Drury Lane, from the committee appointed under the act passed in the 50th year of His Majesty's reign, entitled "An act for re-building the late Theatre-Royal, Drury-Lane, upon the conditions, and under the regulations therein mentioned."

pp. [1–3] 4–46 [47–48 (bl.)]   DFo

Printed by J. McCreery; and sold by J. Ridgeway 1811

1373 ———Report presented to the third general assembly of Subscribers to the re-building of the Theatre-Royal, Drury Lane, from the committee appointed under the acts passed in the 50th and 52nd years of His Majesty's reign, entitled, "An act for re-building the late Theatre-Royal, Drury-Lane, upon the conditions, and under the regulations therein mentioned;" and "An act for altering and enlarging the powers of" the said act. April 11, 1812.

pp. [1–5] 6–23 [24]   DFo

Printed by J. McCreery; and sold by J. Ridgeway 1812

1374 ———Fourth Report presented to the general assembly of subscribers to the rebuilding of the Theatre-Royal, Drury Lane, (including the report of the sub-committee of management,) from the committee appointed under the act passed in the 50th year of his majesty's reign, entitled. "An act for re-building the late Theatre-Royal, Drury-Lane, upon the conditions, and under the regulations therein mentioned;" and "An act for altering and enlarging the powers" of the said act.

pp. [1–3] 4–15 [16 (bl.)]   DFo

Printed by J. McCreery; and sold by J. Ridgeway   1813

1375 ———Fifth Report presented to the general assembly of subscribers to the re-building of the Theatre-Royal, Drury Lane, September 2, 1814, (including the report of the sub-committee of management,) from the committee appointed under the act passed in the 50th year of His Majesty's reign, entitled "An act for re-building the late Theatre-Royal, Drury-Lane, upon the conditions, and under the regulations therein mentioned;" and "An act for altering and enlarging the powers" of the said act.

pp. [1–5] 6–17 [18–20 (bl.)]   DFo
Printed by J. McCreery; and sold by J. Ridgeway 1814

1376 ★THE SHADE of Drury, a vision; inscribed to one of the patentees of the Theatre Royal, Drury Lane.
MH
1811

1377 WYATT, BENJAMIN. Observations on the principles of the design for the theatre, now building in Drury Lane, by Benjamin Wyatt, No. 22, Foley Place.

pp. [2] [1–3] 4–46; pls. 1 (with pasted ptd. slip) [2 (col.)] 3 (col., fold.)   MH
Printed by Lowndes and Hobbs   1811

1378 ———[another edition] Observations on the principles of a design for a theatre, by Benjamin Wyatt, No. 22, Foley Place.

pp. [1–3] 4–58; pls. 1 (with flap ptd. in red) [2 (col.)] 3   L
Printed by Lowndes and Hobbs   1811

See also nos. 1367, 1390.

1379 [PLACE, FRANCIS?] "A NEW WAY to pay old debts;" or observations on the reports made to the subscribers to the rebuilding of the Theatre Royal, Drury-Lane.

pp. [1–3] 4–32   L
Sherwood, Neely, and Jones   1812

Ascribed to Place in BMC.

1380 ★DRURY, a poem. To which is prefixed an address to the critics.
Miller   1812
IKF.

The "Rejected Addresses" 1812

For the opening night the committee advertised for a poetical address, but none sent in was thought good enough, and Lord Byron wrote an address which was spoken by Elliston. The happy idea of a series of parodies of well-known poets, in supposed competition for the prize offered, led to the immortal "Rejected Addresses" of Horace and James Smith; and the success of the burlesque suggested the idea of publishing a collection of the actual addresses sent in and rejected — Lowe.

1381 FRANCIS, SAMUEL LOCK. ★Address: written to have been spoken at the opening of Drury-Lane-Theatre. By Samuel Lock Francis.
DFo
1812

A genuine rejected address — Lowe. Dedicated to Lord Byron.

1382 THE GENUINE REJECTED ADDRESSES, presented to the committee of management for Drury-Lane Theatre; preceded by that written by Lord Byron, and adopted by the committee.

pp. [i–iii] iv–ix [x], [1] 2–130   L
Printed and sold by B. McMillan   1812

The little book is now very scarce — Lowe.

1383 ———[another edition]
pp. [i–iii] iv–ix [x], [1] 2–134   L
Printed and sold by B. McMillan   1812

A reissue.

1384 LORD———. A critique, on the address written by Lord Byron, which was spoken at the opening of the new Theatre Royal, Drury Lane, October 10, 1812. By Lord———

pp. [2] [1–3] 4–18   L
Printed by T. Bayley   [1812]

The half-title reads, "A critique on Lord Byron's address".

1385 ———★second edition
O
[1812]

1386 NEW RENTER, A, *pseud.* An heroic address to old Drury, from a new renter.

pp. [2] [1] 2–9 [10]   L
Becket and Porter   1812

In verse.

1387 STANLEY, WILLIAM. The rejected addresses; or, the triumph of the Ale-King: a farce. By William Stanley, Esq.

pp. [i–v] vi [vii–viii], [1] 2–68   L
John Cawthorn   [1812]

The Fire-King routed by the Ale-King — that is, Whitbread, the chairman of the Drury Lane Committee, who was a brewer — Lowe.

THE LONDON THEATRE   – 1398

1388 WIZARD, PHILOMATH, *pseud.* Anticipation: or, the prize address; which will be delivered on the opening of the new Drury-Lane Theatre, by the manager, in the character of Peter Puncheon, a landlord. Now first published, for the sake of gratifying the impatient curiosity of every rank of society. By Philomath Wizard, astrologer.

pp. [1–5] 6–15 [16 (bl.)]   L
John Walker   1812

1389 ACCEPTED ADDRESSES; or proemium poetarum. To which are added, *Macbeth travestie,* in three acts, and miscellanies, by different hands. Fourth edition.

pp. [8] [1] 2–195 [196]   L
Thomas Tegg   1813

1390 WYATT, BENJAMIN. Observations on the design for the Theatre Royal, Drury Lane, as executed in the year 1812: accompanied by plans, elevation, & sections, of the same. Engraved on eighteen plates. By Benjamin Wyatt, F.S.A. Architect.

pp. [iii–vii] viii–xii, [1] 2–77 [78]; pls. 1–18, incl. 11 fold, 1 col., 1 with attached slip   LVA

J. Taylor   1813

This copy lacks pl. 8. Also printed in Architectural Curiosities, 1812 *(TN XVII, 43). In his Preface Wyatt rejects the insinuation that his plan (that actually executed) was indebted to George Wyatt's* Compendious description, *advancing reasons for the indebtedness being the other way. See also above nos. 1367, 1377, 1378.*

✗ The Fund for the relief of indigent persons belonging to His Majesty's Company of Comedians of the Theatre Royal Drury Lane. 1813, 1814. *See nos. 1352–1353.*

The Amateur Committee

The management of the amateur committee resulted in the failure and confusion which were bound to come. Recriminatory pamphlets were written, and much ill-feeling was caused. The Committee ended their mismanagement in 1818–1819. Elliston, the "Great Lessee", had the theatre the next season — Lowe.

1391 MOORE, [PETER]. Copy. Letter from Mr. Moore to Mr. Raymond. Dated October 14, 1817.

pp. [1] 2–8   LGk
[London]   [1817]

1392 MOORE, P[ETER]. Observations submitted to the consideration of the Committee of Management of Drury Lane Theatre, by Mr. P. Moore.

pp. [3] 4–11 [12 (bl.)]   LGk
[London]   [1817?]

1393 ARNOLD, SAMUEL JAMES. A letter to all the proprietors of Drury-Lane Theatre, (excepting Peter Moore, Esq. and others who are, or have been concerned in the management thereof); being a commentary on certain parts of an anonymous pamphlet, called *A brief review of the season 1817–18, at the Theatre Royal, Drury-Lane, &c. &c. &c.* and a conclusive detection of the author, by Samuel James Arnold, Esq. a proprietor. Also, a letter, relative to the subject, from the late Samuel Whitbread, Esq. M.P. &c. &c.

pp. [2] [1] 2–86   L
William Fearman   1818

1394 *AN AUTHENTIC STATEMENT of facts connected with the interior management of Drury-Lane Theatre, for the last three seasons; together with an appendix of documents.

                                                                       MH
                                                                      1818
Lowe.

1395 [RAYMOND, JAMES GRANT, *ed.*] DRURY-LANE THEATRE. To the editor of [blank].

pp. [2] [1] 2–10; head-title   MH
[Printed by B. McMillan]   [1818]

Copy of a letter from P. Moore to J. G. Raymond, manager of Drury Lane, and of the reply, with a covering letter from Raymond's son, James Grant Raymond.

1396 [MOORE, PETER?] FACTS are stubborn things! Being a brief review of the season 1817–18, at the Theatre Royal, Drury-Lane: also, an inquiry into the conduct of the sub and special committees; with explanatory notes; and an appendix, containing the celebrated letter from Peter Moore, Esq. M.P. to the late J. G. Raymond; also his *Observations,* addressed to the sub-committee. The report of the sub to the general committee. The report of the general committee to the proprietors, &c. &c.

pp. [4] [1] 2–63 [64]   L
Sherwood, Neely, and Jones   1818

Attributed to Moore by Samuel Arnold. Half-title reads, "A brief review, &c. &c. &c."

1397 *THE NEW WAY TO ACT OLD PLAYS. A familiar epistle to the management of Drury Lane Theatre, on the present state of their stage.

pp. 36   MB
Stodart   1818

This pamphlet attacks the Drury Lane Company. Kean was playing fast and loose, and was, to use Bucke's expression, "saving the theatre with his right hand and ruining it with his left." — Lowe.

1398 REPORT OF THE GENERAL COMMITTEE to the proprietors of the Theatre Royal, Drury Lane.

pp. [1] 2–7 [8 (bl.)]   MH
Rodwell, printer, Theatre Royal, Drury Lane   [1818]

Signed by the Secretary, 29 August 1818.

1399 PRYNNE, PEREGRINE, *pseud.* of J. Cahuac?
Histriomastrix or, the untrussing of the Drury Lane
squad. By Peregrine Prynne.

pp. [1–5] 6–24   MH
J. Cahuac   1819

*In verse and prose. Includes "Churchill Redivivus; or
the Drury-Lane Rosciad".*

1400 ——second edition, with additions

pp. [1–5] 6–24   L
J. Cahuac   1819

1401 WAG, WALTER, *Esq., pseud.* The fudge committee, or creditors wanting more: a hudibrastic poem,
in three cantos, with occasional notes; dedicated to the
amateur manager of the Theatre Royal, Drury Lane.
By Walter Wag, Esq.

pp. [4] [1] 2–102 [103 (advt.) 104 (bl.)]   L
W. Lewis   1819

✗ The Fund, for the relief of indigent persons,
belonging to His Majesty's Company of Comedians,
of the Theatre Royal, Drury Lane. 1819. *See no. 1354.*

*Contains the proceedings of the first dinner in aid of the
Drury Lane Theatrical Fund.*

1402 TO R. W. ELLISTON, Esq. on his becoming
lessee and manager of Drury Lane Theatre.

bs.   MH
[London]   [1819]

Heroic couplets, signed H. R[.] H.P.D.

1403 *REGULATIONS instituted of good order in
the Theatre Royal, Drury Lane. Oct. 28, 1820.

STR.

1404 PHILO-DRAMATICUS, *pseud.* *A letter to C.
Kemble and R. W. Elliston, on the present state of the
stage.

pp. (2) 17   MB
Marsh   1825

1405 DRURY LANE THEATRE. Outline of the
conditions.

fold. doc., pp. [1] 2–3 [4]   LGk
[London]   [1826]

Conditions for leasing the theatre.

1406 HUM, HUMPHREY, *Esq., pseud.* *Manage-
ment, a dramatic satire by Humphrey Hum, Esq.
Illustrated with notes, &c., by Paulus Purgantius
Pedasculus. With an original essay on the science of
humbugging, from the unpublished M.S. of the late
George Alexander Stevens.

pp. 20; col. pl.   MB
Holt   [1826]

A satire on Elliston.

1407 THE TABLE OF REGULATIONS and forfeits
to be observed and paid by the band of the Theatre
Royal, Drury Lane.

bs.   MB
[London]   [1828?]

1408 THE MODERN TANTALUS or, the demon
of Drury Lane Theatre.

bs.   LGk
                                                  [1830?]

Extract from Monthly Magazine, Nov. 1830. *Account
of an interview with the box-office keeper at Drury Lane,
"the late eccentric Mr. Massingham."*

1409 [WILSON, F. A.] EPISTOLARY REMON-
STRANCE to Thomas Morton, Esq., dramatic writer
and professed critic and reader to Captain Polhill, and
His Majesty's servants of Drury Lane Theatre.

pp. [1–3] 4–40; errata slip   LGk
Effingham Wilson   1832

Signed F. A. Wilson.

Riots of 1848

*Riots broke out on the night of 12 June 1848 when Bunn
brought over the French company of Le Théâtre Historique
to Drury Lane. The Palais Royale Troupe was at St.
James's in the same month.*

1410 BRITONS STAND BY THE BRITISH
DRAMA! And help to restore it to its pristine health
and vigour.

bs.   MH
W. Turner, printer   [1848]

1411 ENGLISHMAN, AN, *pseud.* The late riots at
Drury Lane: a defence of the British drama in reply to
Albert Smith's pamphlet and advocacy of the French
stage. By an Englishman.

pp. [1–3] 4–16   LGk
Printed and published for the author, by W. Strange,
and W. Barth   1848

1412 MACREADY, WILLIAM CHARLES. *A letter from Mr. Macreadyto the director of the Theatre Historique.

bs.

1848

STR. *On the same sheet is an inflamed criticism of his letter, signed "A Jolly Brick". In the letter Macready expresses regret at the Drury Lane riots against the French actors.*

1413 SMITH, ALBERT. Why our theatres are not supported, with a few words about the late riots at Drury Lane. By Albert Smith.

pp. [1–3] 4–40   LGk
Published for the author; by Kent and Richards, Barth, Schulze and Co.   1848

1414 vacant

1415 SPILLAN, HARRY GERALD. *The stage and the press: or, revelations theatrical and journalistic.

no. 1 May 1852, pp. 16   MB
The Author   1852

1416 SHAKESPEARE AT DRURY LANE.

bs.   MB
J. W. Last, printer   [1864]

Begins *That the national poet is becomingly commemorated and worthily represented at the national theatre, has been unanimously testified by all the Press critics, as will be seen by the following extracts from their published opinions.*

1417 *FALCONER v CHATTERTON. Complaint and answer.

          MH
[London]   [1866]

Copies of legal documents and letters regarding the partnership between Edmund Falconer (otherwise O'Rourke) and Frederick Balsir Chatterton, in the management of Drury Lane Theatre. No title-page — Lowe.

1418 KENNEY, CHARLES LAMB. Poets and profits at Drury Lane Theatre. A theatrical narrative. Suggested by F. B. Chatterton, and written by Charles Lamb Kenney.

pp. [i–v] vi–ix [x] [11] 12–58   L
Aubert's steam printing works   1875

A defence of Mr. Chatterton's much criticised statement that, in his experience as a manager, "Shakespeare spelt ruin and Byron bankruptcy," which was made by him in the course of a controversy regarding his production of Boucicault's Formosa, on 5th August 1869. Mr. Kenney

gives figures to prove that in each of the nine seasons during which Mr. Chatterton had then managed Drury Lane, poetic drama had invariably resulted in monetary loss. When this pamphlet was published, another of Boucicault's plays, The Shaughraun, which proved an enormous success, was being prepared for production. Mr. Chatterton in 1879 failed disastrously, and the theatre remained shut for some time, when Mr. Augustus Harris, the present lessee, stepped into the breach, and has gone on from success to success—Lowe.

1419 OLD PLAYGOER, AN, *pseud.* Renters and lessees. A review of the judgment in the suit of Dauney *v.* Chatterton. By an old playgoer.

pp. [1–3] 4–16   LGk
Printed by J. W. Last   1875

A review of a case regarding the rights of "new renters" at Drury Lane Theatre — Lowe.

1420 KENNEY, CHARLES LAMB. The coming season at Drury Lane Theatre, being the thirteenth under the management of F. B. Chatterton. An introductory address by Charles Lamb Kenney. September 28, 1878.

pp. [1–3] 4–23 [24 (bl.)]   LGk
W. S. Johnson, Nassau Steam Press   [1878]

1421 FIVE YEARS at Old Drury Lane, 1879–1884, being a record of the productions at the national theatre during the past five years of the management of Augustus Harris. Drury Lane Theatre, 1884.

pp. [1–4] 5–32   LVA
[Alfred Gibbons]   1884

East London Theatre
See Royalty Theatre (nos. 1505–1508) and Brunswick Theatre (nos. 1118–1134).

Eastern Theatre
See Royalty Theatre (nos. 1505–1508).

Empire Theatre
Opened as music hall on 17 April 1884. Now a cinema. See no. 2125.

Empress Theatre
Also known as the Empress Palace. Opened 1898.

1422 AN ACCOUNT of the "Empress" Theatre of Varieties, Brixton. With original illustrations.

pp. [1–9] 10–15 [16]; illus.   MH
[Wilkes & Co., printers]   December 26th 1898

English Opera House
See Lyceum (nos. 1488–1492).

English Opera House, Royal

See Palace Theatre (nos. 1496–1497).

Evans's Music and Supper Rooms

Also known as Evans's Song-and-Supper Rooms. See also no. 227.

1423 GREEN, JOHN [or TOWNSEND, GEORGE HENRY.] Evans's music and supper rooms, Covent Garden. Odds and ends about Covent Garden and its vicinity, the ancient drama, the early English divinity and controversial plays, &c.; compiled from various sources by Mr. John Green. Also, A selection of madrigals, glees, songs, choruses, &c., sung every evening in the above rooms.

pp. [*2*] [1–3] 4–60 [61–62 (bl.)]; illus.   L
[Privately printed for John Green]   [1866?]

> *Cover title: Odds and ends about Covent Garden, the Ancient Drama, &c. "Although the title-page attributes this work to John Green, it was actually written by George Henry Townsend" — Brown.*

Fortune Theatre

In the parish of St. Giles's without Cripplegate, in the street called Playhouse Yard, the Fortune was built of wood for Henslowe and Alleyn, and opened in 1600. In 1621 it was burnt down, and rebuilt of brick. In 1649 it was dismantled, and "no acting seems to have taken place at the Fortune after 1649" — Chambers, Elizabethan. See no. 1033.

Gaiety Theatre

Opened 21 December 1868. Formerly the Strand Music Hall. For the French Plays at the Gaiety Theatre (1879–1880) see nos. 3789–3790.

1424 HOLLINGSHEAD, JOHN. Gaiety chronicles by John Hollingshead.

pp. [i–viii] ix–xvi, 1–493 [494 (bl.)] 495–497 (advt.) 498 (bl.) [=404]; facsims.; pls. [front., 47]   LGk
Westminster: Archibald Constable & Co.   1898

> *Title-page in red and black. The plates are unnumbered, but are each, except the frontispiece, counted as two pages in the pagination.*

Globe Theatre

The Globe was situated on the Bankside, and was the summer house of Shakespeare's company. It was built in 1599; rebuilt, after a fire, in 1613; pulled down in 1644. See nos. 1037, 1059.

Goodman's Fields Theatre

First opened by Thomas Odell on 31 October 1729. A new building erected and opened 2 October 1732. Closed under the Licensing Act of 1737 but continued to give performances until finally closed on 27 April 1742. See GOVERNMENT REGULATION OF THE THEATRE nos.

158–172; MORALITY OF THE THEATRE nos. 377, 378.

Haymarket, Theatre Royal

The present theatre, opened 1821, is the successor of another building erected in 1720 by a builder named Potter, next to the site on which the present theatre stands. The history of the Haymarket, though not so important as that of the Winter Theatres, is yet of great interest; the managers having been such men as Fielding, Foote, the elder and younger Colman, Webster, Buckstone, and Bancroft. Mr. Beerbohm Tree, a very notable artist, is the present lessee — Lowe. Known first as the New or Little Theatre in the Hay-Market. The present name of Theatre Royal, Haymarket goes back to 1767, when Foote was given permission to use it.

See also ARTS OF THE THEATRE nos. 809–810; GENERAL HISTORY no. 844; LONDON no. 1312; BIOGRAPHY: COLLECTIVE nos. 2206, 2209–2223, 2344; BIOGRAPHY especially nos. 2793, 2804 (Foote).

The "Bottle Conjurors"

1425 ANGLICANUS, M.D., *pseud.* ★The bottle heroes, or, madness & folly à-la-mode. Humbly inscribed to Mr. H—g—h, and Mr. G—k. With a humorous copper-plate head-piece. By Anglicanus, M.D.

1749

> *Reported in R. S. Kirby's* The Wonderful and scientific museum.

1426 THE BOTTLE CONJURER, from head to foot, without equivocation.

bs, with pl.   L
Sold in Mays Building, Covent Garden   1749

> *Dated Jan. 24th. Stephens 3026.*

1427 A COMPANION to the bottle; or Don Jumpedo in the character of Harlequin jumping down his own throat.

bs; pl.   L
B. Dickinson   1748/9

> *The plate, dated March 20, "is an exact Representation of Harlequin's Escape, introduc'd in the Pantomime Entertainment of the Royal Chace, or Merlin's Cave, now acting at the Theatre Royal, in Covent Garden . . ." Stephens 3024. Stephens records (3023) a second print depicting this feat of Lun's.*

1428 ★ENGLISH CREDULITY; or, Ye're all bottled. A humorous print . . . to which is annexed a poem. headed: Jan. 30. This day is published (6d. plain 1s. coloured)

Jan. 30 1749

> *Reported in R. S. Kirby's* Wonderful and scientific museum. *He also mentions a print alone: FEB 25 THIS DAY is published (6d plain 1s coloured) a comical print of the bottle conjuror's reflecting mirror.*

1429 ———[another edition?] The Magician, or bottle cungerer. English credulity; or ye're all bottled.

bs; pl.   L

B. Dickinson   1748/9

Plate dated "5th of March" Stephens 3022.

1430 AN EPISTLE from the bottle conjurors unto the Gothamites; containing the eighth chapter of the Acts of the seducers, sharpers and conjurors in three parts. Part the first, wherein the conjuror proposes to . . . jump into a quart bottle. Part the second. A full and true account of the tragi-comical farce, as it was acted at the Theatre in the Hay-market, on Monday the 16th of January, 1748-9. Part the third. Harlequin's . . . escape by virtue of a funnel from a quart bottle, as it is acted at the Theatre in Covent-garden . . . Printed from the manuscript of Signore Dolocio Ufrontorio, son to the wonder working chymist, lately deceas'd in Alsatia.

pp. [1–2] 3–30 [31 (errata) 32 (bl.)]   L

R. Freeman, and B. Habrin   [1749]

1431 A LETTER TO THE TOWN, concerning the man and the bottle.

pp. [1–5] 6–20   L

Printed and sold by W. Reeve; and A. Dodd   1749

1432 A MODEST APOLOGY FOR THE MAN IN THE BOTTLE. By himself. Being a full answer to all that ever was, or ever will be said upon that important occasion.

pp. [1–3] 4–25 [26]   L

J. Freeman   [1749]

1433 NICK-ALL, J.,* *pseud.* An apology to the town, for himself and the bottle, by J.* Nick-All.

bs.; pl.   L

B. Dickinson   1749

The print dated 8 February consists of "an exact representation of Harlequin's escape into the bottle; introduc'd in the pantomime entertainment of Apollo and Daphne *. . . acted at the Theatre Royal in Covent Garden" (on 26 January and 2 March, see LS. pt. 4, i, p. 93). Stephens 3025.*

The "French Strollers"

1434 SOME CONSIDERATIONS on the establishment of the French strolers; the behaviour of their bully-champions, and other seasonable matters, at this critical juncture. Humbly addressed to the publick in general; but, particularly, to the inhabitants of Westminster.

pp. [2] [1] 2–25 [26 (bl.)]   L

R. Freeman   [1749]

Published November 1749 — Gentleman's Magazine. This refers to Jean Louis Monet's company at the Haymarket, of whom Colley Cibber wrote to Victor on 21st November 1749. He says that there was a monstrous tumult the first night but that the young men of quality overpowered the dissentients, and turned them out of the house — Lowe.

✄ The Covent-Garden journal. 1749. *See no. 4076.*

On the French Strollers.

1435 GENTLEMAN IN TOWN, A, *pseud.* An impartial state of the case of the French comedians, actors, players, or strollers, who lately opened a theatre at the Hay-Market. In which some notice is taken of another set, now occupying that theatre. In a letter from a gentleman in town, to his friend in the country.

pp. [2] [1–2] 3–25 [26 (bl.)]   L

M. Shepey; R. Sparvan; W. Myer; G. Woodfall   1750

Woodward v. Hill 1752

For the fracas which ensued when Woodward was insulted and attacked in the theatre see below BIOGRAPHY nos. 3671–3679 (Woodward).

1436 THE ORANGE-GIRL AT FOOTE'S to Sally Harris: or, the town to the country pomona. An heroic epistle.

pp. [4] 1–11 [12]   L

S. Bladon   1773

1437 ———*a new edition

pp. [3] 11   MB

S. Bladon   1773

1438 SHERLOCK, THOMAS. To George Colman, Esq. Proprietor of the Theatre-Royal in the Haymarket.

bs.   L

[London]   June 9, 1779

An open letter from Sherlock, then a prisoner in the Fleet, calling upon Colman to inform the public why he should not pay a debt which Sherlock alleges to be due to him for printing.

1439 THEATRE, HAYMARKET, Feb. 17, 1794. When the late dreadful accident happened at this theatre . . .

bs.   L

[London?]   1794

A Republican leaflet, complaining of the lack of mourning by their Majesties for the fifteen people trampled to death at the Command Performance on 3 February 1794.

1440 BRERETON, AUSTIN. Haymarket Theatre
A short history of "She stoops to conquer" "The
rivals" and "The school for scandal".

pp. [1–3] 4–21 [22–24 (bl.)]; illus.; cover title   L
The Nassau Press (H. Virtue & Co., Ltd.)   1900

1441 ———new and revised edition

pp. [1–3] 4–23 [24 (bl.)]; illus.; title headed: Haymarket
Theatre   L

The Nassau Press (H. Virtue & Co., Ltd.)   1900

> She Stoops to Conquer *was revived at the Theatre
> Royal, Haymarket 9 Jan. 1900.*

Her Majesty's Theatre

*Vanbrugh's new theatre in the Haymarket was opened 9th
April 1705. It was burnt down 17th June 1789; rebuilt 1791;
again burnt in 1867. During its existence it has been known
as the Queen's Theatre [see below nos. 1503–1504], the
Opera House, the King's Theatre [see below nos. 1452–1487],
and Her Majesty's Theatre. It is now practically non-existent
as a theatre — Lowe. Rebuilt 1868–1869; demolished 1891.
The present theatre opened 1897. See also SALE
CATALOGUES nos. 57, 58, 59; COVENT GARDEN
no. 1312; BIOGRAPHY no. 3237; PERIODICALS
no. 4197.*

1442 AMATEUR, AN, *pseud.* ★Her Majesty's Theatre,
&c. By an amateur.

                               1838

> *A criticism on the operatic performance of the previous
> season — Lowe.*

1443 HER MAJESTY'S THEATRE. A list of the
subscribers for the season 1839. P. F. Laporte, Esq.
manager.

pp. [1–9] 10–64; pl. = 2 leaves; ptd. on pink paper; in
slip-case

Messrs Andrews, Ebers, Hookham, and Mitchell;
Mr. W. Seguin; and Mr. Sams   1839

   JFA.

1444 HER MAJESTY'S THEATRE. A list of subscribers for the season 1845.

pp. [1–7] 8–53 [43]; pl., fold. [1]   L
C. Nugent, at the box office; J. Mitchell   [1845]

1445 MARVEL, SEDGLEY, *pseud.* The opera:
views before and peeps behind the curtain. By Sedgley
Marvel, (Old) Bachelor of Arts, S.A.H.M.T., etc.

pp. [1–3] 4–34   L
C. Mitchell   1847

1446 HER MAJESTY'S THEATRE. A list of the
subscribers for the season 1856.

pp. [1–7] 8–39 [40]; pls., fold. [2]   L
Ryan and Co.   [1856]

1447 HER MAJESTY'S THEATRE. Season 1857.

pp. [8]; head-title; ptd. covers, illus. (vignette with
royal arms)
[London]   [1857]

   JFA.

1448 IN THE HOUSE OF LORDS, in error from
the Exchequer Chamber upon a judgment in eject-
ment brought after a special case stated. Between
Faithful Croft . . . and Benjamin Lumley [and others].

fold. doc., pp. [1–2] 3–6 [6] ²[1] 2–74
[J. Wodderspon]   [1857]

> IKF. *Croft sought to recover possession of the theatre on
> the grounds that the lease had expired, but judgment was
> given on 17 April 1858 in favour of Lumley.*

1449 IN CHANCERY. — WYATT v. HASLE-
WOOD. Particulars and conditions of sale of the Box
no. 124, in Her Majesty's Theatre, in the Haymarket:
which will be sold by auction, by Messrs. Chinnock &
Galsworthy, . . . the commodious family box . . .

pp. [4]

                               [1860]
   IKF.

1450 LUMLEY, BENJAMIN The Earl of Dudley,
Mr. Lumley, and Her Majesty's Theatre. A narrative
of facts addressed to the patrons of the opera, his friends,
and the public generally, by their faithful servant,
B. Lumley. Second edition.

pp. [1–3] 4–32   E
Bosworth and Harrison   1863

> *Lumley took the management of the opera about 1842,
> Mapleson in 1863—Lowe. See also below nos. 3244,
> 3301.*

1451 HER MAJESTY'S THEATRE Haymarket
Description.

pp. [2] [1] 2–3 [4–6 (bl.)]; pl. (phot.); cover-title
[London]   [1897]

> IKF.
> *The old theatre was demolished in 1892. A new building
> was erected by Beerbohm Tree and opened on 28 April
> 1897.*

King's Theatre, Haymarket

*Also known as the Opera House, and the Italian Opera
House. From 1705–1714 had been known as the Queen's
Theatre (see nos. 1503–1504). Renamed Her Majesty's
Theatre in 1837 (see nos. 1440–1451). See also SALE
CATALOGUES no. 60: OPERA passim, especially nos.
2031–2051, 2057–2058, 2073.*

1452 TRUTH on all sides. A new masquerade ballad, as it is intended to be sung, at the K——g's Theatre in the H——ym——t to the tune of Tantararara, masters all, masters all.

pp. [1–2] 3–8   MH

H. Carpenter   1750

Foxon.

1453 LOCKMAN, [JOHN]. A faithful narrative of the late pretended gun-powder plot: in a letter to the Right Honourable Stephen Theodore Janssen, Esq; Lord Mayor of London. By Mr. Lockman, secretary to the Society of the Free British Fishery.

pp. [4] 1–27 [28 (bl.)]   L

Printed for the Author, and Sold by G. Woodfall   1755

A "squib" regarding the King's Theatre in the Haymarket, and Benjamin May, the manager — Lowe.

1454 A DEFENCE OF F. GIARDINI, from the calumnies, falshoods, and misrepresentations, of Cacophron, in a pamphlet, published by him in the name of Gabriel Leone. To which is subjoined, a short account of the cause of Cacophron's resentment against Giardini.

pp. [2] i–iv, 1–15 [16]   MH

R. Davis   1765

Dedication signed R.P.

1455 THE MASQUERADE; a poem. Inscribed to the King of Denmark.

pp. [4] 1–24   L

T. Evans   1768

1456 *A MOB in the pit; or, lines addressed to the D——ch——ss of A——ll.

S. Bladon   1773

Lowe.

1457 ——A mob in the pit; or, lines addressed to the D——ch——ss of A——ll. The second edition.

pp. [4] [1] 2–7 [8]   L

S. Bladon   1773

A satirical poem on the behaviour of the Duchess of Argyll on a night when Anne Heinel was dancing.

1458 LADY OF FASHION, A, *pseud.* A descriptive plan of the new opera house, with the names of the subscribers to each box taken from the theatre itself by a lady of fashion.

32 engr. leaves, incl. t.p. and plan of the boxes   L

T. Becket   [1782?]

Usually dated 1791 by cataloguers, when a similar, more elaborate list was produced for the King's Theatre, Pantheon; William Van Lennep dated the MH copy 1782.

1459 THE OPERA RUMPUS; or, the ladies in the wrong box! A serio-comic-operatic burlesque poem! With explanatory notes, by the ablest commentators.

pp. [i–v] vi–viii, [1] 2–20   L

R. Baldwin   1783

A poem on the subject of some quarrel about a box at the Opera. The box was the property of some Mr. B——d——d, and Lady Jersey seems to have been the lady turned out of it — Lowe.

1460 THE CASE of the Opera-House disputes, fairly stated.

pp. [4] [1] 2–41 [42 (bl.)]   L

Printed and sold by H. Reynell   1784

"We mutually pledge ourselves to be responsible for the contents. W. Allen, T. Luppino, H. Reynell" — [A2^v].

1461 TAYLOR, WILLIAM. *The testament or will of Mr. William Taylor, proprietor of the King's Theatre in the Haymarket.

    1785

STR.

1462 A LIST OF THE SUBSCRIBERS to the boxes, at the King's-Theatre, 1788.

pp. [6]   MH

[London]   [1788]

1463 LE TEXIER, [A. A.] Ideas on the Opera, offered to the subscribers, creditors, and amateurs of that theatre. By Mr. Le Texier. Translated from the French.

pp. [4] [1] 2–66 [67–68 (bl.)]   L

J. Bell   1790

Removal to Pantheon Theatre 1789–1791

After the fire of 1789 the opera company moved to the Pantheon Theatre, see nos. 1498–1500.

1464 O'REILLY, ROBERT BRAY. †An authentic narrative of the principal circumstances relating to the Opera-House in the Hay-Market; from its origin to the present period; but more particularly including the transactions from the year 1778. With an appendix, containing copies or extracts from all the original papers referred to. By Robert Bray O'Reilly, Esq.

pp. [2] [1] 2–71 [72]   L

J. and J. Taylor; and J. Southern   1791

This copy has no appendix.

1465 TAYLOR [WILLIAM]. A concise statement of transactions and circumstances respecting the King's Theatre, in the Haymarket. By Mr. Taylor, the proprietor. Together with the official correspondence upon the same subject, between the Rt. Hon. the Lord Chamberlain, and Earl Cholmondeley, &c.

pp. [4] [1] 2–46 [47–48 (bl.)]   MH

J. Debrett; T. Beckett; and J. Murray   1791

The half-title reads: 'Opera Statement, &c.'

1466 ———the second edition

pp. [4] [1] 2–48   MH

J. Debrett; T. Beckett; and J. Murray   1791

With new matter on the last three pages.

1467 BY PERMISSION OF THE MANAGER. The plan of the boxes at the King's Theatre, Haymarket. With an alphabetical list of the subscribers are most respectfully submitted to the nobility & gentry by their most humble, dutiful & obed.^t serv.^t William Lee. N°. 51, G^t Marybone Street, Portland Place.

pp. 1–93 [94–96 (bl.)]; pls. [6, incl. engr. t.p.]   LVA

[William Lee]   1794

1468 THE PLAN OF THE BOXES at the King's Theatre, Haymarket, with an alphabetical list of the subscribers, for the season 1804, are most respectfully submitted to the nobility and gentry, by their most humble, dutiful, and obedient servant, William Lee, no. 8, Walnut-tree Walk, Lambeth.

pp. [4] 1–15 [16–18 (bl.)] 19–33 [34–36 (bl.)] 37–51 [52–54 (bl.)] 55–69 [70–72 (bl.)] 73–82 [83–84 (bl.) 85–86] 87–119 [120 (advt.)]; pls. [6, incl. engr. t.p.]; title headed "By permission of the manager."   L

Printed by D. N. Shury   [1804]

With a second, printed, title-page.

1469 ———. . . for the season 1805 . . . No. 18, . . .

pp. and pls. as for 1804.   L

Printed by D. N. Shury   [1805]

1470 ———. . . for the season 1807 . . . No. 18, . . .

pp. and pls. as for 1804, except the concluding leaves: –117 [118–119 (advts.) 120 (bl.)]   L

Shury, printer   [1807]

1471 MEMORANDUM, August, 1799. King's Theatre.

pp. [1] 2–6   L

Printed by W. Glindon   1799

Taylor's dispute with Signor Namiani, an Italian singer.

1472 [MATHIAS, THOMAS JAMES.] PANDOLPHO attonito! Or, Lord Galloway's poetical lamentation on the removal of the arm-chairs from the pit at the Opera House! (Printed originally in the *Morning Herald*

of May 1, 1800.) With a preface and some remarks by the editor.

pp. [iii–v] vi–xviii, [1–5] 6–13 [14]   L

T. Becket   1800

1473 PHILOFIDDLE, *pseud.* A letter from Philofiddle to the public, on the management of the Opera.

pp. [2] [5] 6–30   LGk

Printed by C. Stower for J. Ginger   1805

1474 WATERS, EDMUND, *ed.* Kings Theatre, Hay Market, January 11, 1808. To the nobility, gentry, subscribers to the opera, and the public.

pp. [4]; head-title   L

[London]   [1808]

1475 WATERS, E[DMUND]. The opera glass; exhibiting all the curious proceedings of the King's Theatre; together with the original letters and papers, which have passed between the present proprietors, since the decease of Francis Goold, Esq. joint proprietor with Mr. Taylor in the above property. The whole forms an address to the public. By E. Waters, Esq. sole executor of Mr. Francis Goold, and principal mortgagee of Mr. Taylor's share in the King's Theatre.

pp. [2] [1] 2–148   L

C. Chapple   1808

Taylor, who had been a clerk in a bank, lent Sheridan, who was at the time connected with the King's Theatre, one thousand pounds, and in some mysterious way contrived to insinuate himself into the ownership of the property. Lord Thurlow declared that "no magnifying power could render his right visible," yet he sold the property — Lowe.

1476 KING'S THEATRE, HAY-MARKET. Harrison's plan of the boxes: with an alphabetical list of the subscribers. For the season 1809.

pp. [4] [1] 2–67 [68]   LVA

Printed by Brettall and Co.   1809

1477 GREVILLE, H[ENRY] F[RANCIS]. A letter to the subscribers to the opera. By H. F. Greville, Esq.

pp. [2] [1–3] 4–15 [16 (bl.) 17–18 (advts.)]   L

C. Chapple   1811

An attack on Taylor.

1478 R., W. Prosecution of Alex. Read, Esq. on false charges of perjury, by W. Taylor, Esq. of the Opera House, before Lord Ellenborough, and a special jury, at Westminster Hall, Saturday, Feb. 22, 1812. On which charges the defendant was honourably acquitted by the tergiversation of the prosecutor. Taken in short hand, by W. R. The second edition.

pp. [1–3] 4–40   L

C. Chapple   1812

1479 THEATRICAL INTELLIGENCE. The public are respectfully informed that the King's Theatre will be opened with an entire new company . . .

bs.   MH

Printed by Dobson & Co.   [*ca.* 1815]

1480 *KING'S THEATRE: Regulations to be hence-forth observed by the performers at this Theatre.

1st. Jan. 1816

In English, French and Italian — Lowe.

1481 VERITAS, *pseud.* Opera house. A review of this theatre, from the period described by the Enterprizer, . . . A recital of the litigations, loans, embarrassments, partnerships, the annuity, concert room, debenture, and Leominster issue of silver tickets, their objects and consequences, the original forty one, the final Pantheon arrangement, and the roman letter encroachment of property boxes. A review of the management of Gallini, Taylor, Goold and Waters, demonstrating the cause, why? as the subscriptions have gradated 126 *l.* 157 *l.* 10s. 189 *l.* 252 *l.* and 315 *l.* the performances from splendour have degraded nearly to the exhibitions of the minor theatres, deducing the question, whether it would not benefit the community, as in capitals where the receipts of the theatres are not commensurate to the expenditure, for their absolute government to be vested in the Lord Chamberlain, or a similar authority, rather than in a metropolis, where the annual receipt drawn from the public purse to the dramatic expenditure is greater than the disproportion of 60,000 *l.* to 15,000 *l.* the legitimate drama should be distressed and degraded by equivocal patents or licences, in the administration of presumptuous adventurers, who, have exercised them as unconscionable pretexts for levying contributions upon the community. By Veritas.

pp. [6] [3] 4–80   GU

Printed for the author   [1818?]

1482 WATERS, E[DMUND]. A statement of matters, relative to the King's Theatre. By E. Waters, Esq. Second edition.

pp. [4] [1] 2–27 [28]   L

J. Ebers; Hookham and Sons; E. Lloyd; and J. Fentum

1818

Dated 16 June 1818.

1483 IN CHANCERY, 13 Dec. 1823. Winchester, v. Chambers. Judgment of the Lord Chancellor on a motion for appointing a receiver at the King's Theatre, or the Opera House, from the notes of the short-hand writer.

fold. doc., pp. [1] 2–3 [4]; filing-title   L

Derbery and Haslewood   [1823]

1484 EBERS, JOHN. Seven years of the King's Theatre. By John Ebers, late manager of the King's Theatre in the Haymarket.

pp. [i–v] vi–xxviii, [1] 2–395 [396]; pls. [front., 5]

MH

William Harrison Ainsworth   1828

On opera at the King's Theatre.

————[American edition] Philadelphia: Carey, Lea & Carey, 1828.

1485 AN EXPLANATION OF THE DIFFER-ENCES existing between the manager of the Italian Opera and the non-conforming members of the late orchestra. Written among themselves.

pp. [i–iii] iv–viii [9] 10–50 [51–52 (bl.)]   GU

Published for the authors by Hunt and Clarke   1829

1486 IN CHANCERY. The King's Theatre, or Opera House. Copy of the short-hand writer's notes, taken at the hearing of the cause before the Vice-Chancellor; in which Abraham Henry Chambers, formerly a banker in New Bond Street, and his assignees, under a commission of bankrupt issued against him in the year 1826, were the plaintiffs, and Edmund Waters, claiming to be the owner and proprietor of the King's Theatre; and the executors of the late William Taylor, formerly a proprietor of the said theatre, were the defendants. Together with the judgment pronounced by the Vice-Chancellor in the said cause: and against which judgment the said Edmund Waters has determined, under the advice of his counsel, to appeal to the Lord High Chancellor, with as little delay as the forms of the Court of Chancery will admit of. London, June 1st. 1829.

pp. [1–5] 6–333 [334 (colophon)]   L

[Printed by T. Brettell]   [1829]

1487 MASON, THOMAS MONCK. Prospectus of the plan intended to be pursued in the direction of the Italian Opera House, by Thomas Monck Mason, Esq.

pp. [1–5] 6–16   MH

James Cochrane and Co.   1831

Lamb's Conduit Private Theatre

See THE AMATEUR THEATRE no. 2153.

Lincoln's Inn Fields Theatre

Converted into a theatre ca. 28 June 1661. On 7 December 1732 the company transferred to the new Covent Garden theatre. Fell into virtual disuse as a theatre after 1743. Pulled down 1848. See nos. 1323, 1671, 2047, 3749.

Little Theatre in the Haymarket

See Haymarket Theatre (nos. 1425–1439).

Lyceum (English Opera House)

Also called the Large Theatre, Lyceum, and the Royal Lyceum. Became Theatre Royal, Lyceum in 1809 (with summer licence). After 1816 also known as the English Opera House. Originally erected 1765. Converted into a theatre in 1794. Finally closed as a theatre in 1939. See also BIOGRAPHY: IRVING, nos. 3068 passim.; also GOVERNMENT REGULATION OF THE THEATRE nos. 203, 209; OPERA especially nos. 2085, 2097; THEORY AND CRITICISM no. 3807.

1488 GENERAL OUTLINE of a project for purchasing the Opera House.

pp. [1] 2–3 [4 (bl.)]; head-title   MH

[Printed by J. Brettell]   [1815?]

1489 A DESCRIPTION OF THE ENGLISH OPERA-HOUSE, in the Strand: erected A.D. 1816. Opened for the encouragement of native talent, and as a school for English music, on the 15th of June in the same year, under the express sanction of His Majesty. Together with a short account of the first establishment of the English opera.

pp. [1–3] 4–20   MH

[Lowndes, printer]   [1816?]

Imprint and date torn off in the copy seen.

1490 *ROYAL ITALIAN OPERA, Lyceum Theatre. Season 1857.

pp. 8

                                               1857

IKF. Two pages contain notes on season and list of company.

1491 LINES ON THE LYCEUM Provident and Benevolent Fund.

pp. [4]; head-title   MH

Redford & Son, printers   [1879?]

Eight stanzas within a coloured border. The copy seen (MH) has a pencil note, "By Hal Louther", in unknown hand. The Fund was founded by Irving when he became manager.

1492 HOLLINGSHEAD, JOHN. A Lyceum historiette by John Hollingshead inscribed to an old friend, Sir Henry Irving, 1859–1899.

pp. [1–3] 4–14 [15 (advts.) 16 (bl.)], incl. ptd. paper covers

The Nassau Press   1899

JFA.

Marylebone, The Royal

Originally opened in 1831 as the Royal Sussex (later the Royal Pavilion and the Portman Theatres). The Marylebone Theatre opened on 13 November 1837 and became the Royal

Marylebone (Theatre Royal, Marylebone) in 1842. From 1866 until 1870 was renamed the Royal Albert. Became the West London Theatre in 1893. Was a cinema from 1932 until 1941 before finally closing down.

1493 [LOVERIDGE, G. A.]. Royal Marylebone Theatre. 1842 1892. Jubilee souvenir. 12th December, 1892

folder, pp. [12]   L

                                               [1892]

Metropolitan Theatre of Varieties

Opened in 1862 as Turnham's Grand Concert Hall. Renamed the Metropolitan Music Hall in 1864 (The "Met"). Functioned as a music hall or for touring revues until 1960.

1494 SOME ACCOUNT of the New Metropolitan Theatre of Varieties and early history of its site and associations. With original illustrations. First edition.

pp. [1–7] 8–18 [19 (list of sub-contractors) 20 (bl.)]; pls. [5 (3 glued in, and one double leaf sewn in)]; illus.   MH

267, Edgware Road   January 1898

The half-title reads: "The Metropolitan Old and New"; on the upper cloth cover: "Ye Met."

New

All theatres using the prefix New are listed under the name of the theatre (e.g. New Brunswick Theatre see Brunswick Theatre).

Olympic Theatre

Originally opened in 1806 as the Olympic Pavilion (also called the Olympic Saloon, Astley's New Olympic Pavilion, Astley's Pavilion, The Pavilion, Little Drury Lane). In 1816 became the Olympic Theatre. Its most famous manager was Madame Vestris. Finally closed in 1899. See SALE CATALOGUES no. 61; GOVERNMENT REGULATION OF THE THEATRE no. 201.

Opera House, The

See King's Theatre (nos. 1452–1487).

Oxford Music Hall

Opened 26 March 1861. Finally demolished 1926.

1495 THE OXFORD. Inaugurated 1861. Rebuilt 1893. Architects: Messrs. Wylson & Long . . . Contractor: Mr. Frank Kirk . . . Annals of old and new.

pp. [2] [1–5] 6 [2] 7–8 [2] 9–10 [2] 11–12 [2] 13–14 [2] 15 [16 (imprint)] = 28 pp.; illus. (incl. [front.]); cover title: The Oxford 1893

Proprietors, "The Oxford, Limited"   1893

Copy in Members' Library, Greater London Council. A souvenir of the re-opening.

Palace Theatre

Opened on 31 January 1891 as the Royal English Opera House. Also called the Palace Theatre of Varieties. Still in use.

1496 MONOGRAPH of the Royal English Opera House. R. D'Oyly Carte proprietor & manager.

pp. [1] 2–16; pls. [8]

[London]   [1891]

IKF. *Another copy in L.*

1497 SOUVENIR the opening of the Palace Theatre Dec. 10th 1892. Sir Augustus Harris, Managing Director.

pp. [4] [1] 2 [2] 3–4; illus.; pl.; cover title

[London]   [1892]

IKF.

Pantheon

Also called the King's Theatre, Pantheon. Reconstructed as a theatre in 1790 to rehouse the King's Theatre opera company after the fire of 1789. Virtually closed as a theatre in 1814 after losing its licence.

1498 DESCRIPTION OF THE ALLEGORY, painted for the curtain of the King's Theatre, Pantheon.

pp. [1–3] 4–8; pl. [front.]   L

Printed by T. Bensley   1791

1499 THE PLAN & section of the boxes at the King's Theatre, Pantheon with An alphabetical list of the subscribers are most respectfully submitted to the nobility & gentry by their most humble, dutiful & obed.^t serv.^t William Lee. N⁰. 51, G^t Marybone Street, Portland Place.

pp. [2] [1] 2–31 [32]; pls. [3 (engr. t.p. and folding plans)]   L

[W. Lee]   1791

The alphabetical list has the title-page: By permission of R. B. O'Reilly, Esquire. An alphabetical list of the subscribers to the King's Theatre, Pantheon: with references to their different boxes.

1500 HARTLEY, DAVID. Proposals for the security of spectators in any public theatre against fire. By David Hartley, Esq.

pp. [1–3] 4–16   L

Stockdale, Ridgeway, Debrett, Dilly, Newbery, and Sewell   [1792]

Dated 27 Jan. 1792. On the misapplication of safety devices in the Pantheon, burnt 14th January 1792.

Prince's Theatre, The

See St James's Theatre (no. 1517).

Princess's Theatre

The Princess's was opened in 1840 with promenade concerts, but it was not till December 1842 that dramatic performances were given in it, J. M. Maddox being lessee, 1843. In 1850 Charles Kean and Keeley took the theatre. Keeley retired in 1851, and Charles Kean's tenancy ended in 1859 — Lowe. See also BIOGRAPHY nos. 3121–3127 (Charles Kean).

1501 PARTICULARS AND CONDITIONS OF SALE of the lease of the Queen's Bazaar, on the north side of Oxford Street. For sale, at Garraway's Coffee House, 'Change Alley, Cornhill, on Monday, the 14th of March, 1836, at twelve o'clock. E. Foster & Son, 14, Greek Street, Soho Square and 54, Pall Mall.

fold. doc., pp. [1–2] 3 [4]; pl., fold. [ground plan]; filing-title   MH

[London]   [1836]

1502 THE PRINCESS'S THEATRE, grand concert room, and premises, in Oxford Street. For sale by auction. . . . on Thursday, 9th September, 1841 . . . E. Foster and Son . . .

fold. doc., pp. [1–3] 4–5 [6]; filing-title   MH

[London]   [1841]

Queen's Bazaar

See Princess's Theatre (nos. 1501–1502).

Queen's Theatre, Haymarket

Opened 9 April 1705. From 1714–1837 known as the King's Theatre (nos. 1452–1487). From 1837 renamed Her Majesty's Theatre (nos. 1442–1451). See also THEATRE AND MORALITY no. 338.

1503 A LETTER TO A LADY concerning the new play house.

pp. [1–2] 3–16   L

Printed and sold by Joseph Downing   1706

A strong attack on theatres, and on the new house in the Haymarket specially — Lowe. Dated 29 September 1705. Variously and without authority attributed to Collier and Josiah Woodward. One of the tracts distributed in bulk by the S.P.C.K.

1504 ADVERTISEMENT. Friday the 17th 17$\frac{9}{10}$. It has been publish'd . . .

bs.   L

n.p.   [1710]

A dispute between the management and Cavalier Nicolini, one of the singers.

Red Bull

See no. 1060.

Royal

All theatres using the prefix Royal are listed under the name of the theatre (e.g. Royal Coburg see Coburg).

Royalty Theatre

Opened on 20 June 1787 but denied a licence (see no. 894). In 1810 renamed the East London Theatre. Burnt down in April 1826. Rebuilt as the Brunswick Theatre (see above nos. 1118–1134). For John Palmer's attempts to break the monopoly of the Patent Theatres see above GOVERNMENT REGULATION OF THE THEATRE nos. 176–189.

1505 THIRLWALL, *Rev.* THOMAS. Oct. 17, 1803. Royalty Theatre. A solemn protest against the revival of scenic exhibitions and interludes, at the Royalty Theatre. By the Rev. Tho. Thirlwall, M.A. a member of the Society for the Suppression of Vice.

pp. [1–3] 4–14   MH
Printed by T. Plummer and sold by Barnfield; Ratcliff; Taylor; Moxon; New; Watkinson   1803

1506 ——Oct. 17, 1803. Royalty Theatre. A solemn protest against the revival of scenic exhibitions and interludes, at the Royalty Theatre; containing remarks on Pizarro, The stranger, and John Bull; with a post-script. By the Rev. Tho. Thirlwall, M.A. a member of the Society for the Suppression of Vice.

pp. [1–3] 4–14 [15 (postscript) 16 (advt.)]; headed "A second edition, price sixpence."   L
Printed by T. Plummer and sold by Rivingtons; Richardson; Spragg; Barnfield; Taylor; Moxon; Harris; Watkinson.   [1803]

1507 ——*third edition, enlarged. Prefixed, a review of the conduct of the stage in general, and the expediency and lawfulness of dramatic entertainments.

pp. 29 (1)   MB
             1805

1508 PERCIVAL, JOHN. Society for the Suppression of Vice. A few observations in defence of the scenic exhibitions at the Royalty Theatre, and on the intolerant censure of the drama in general; contained in the "Solemn protest" of the Rev. Tho. Thirlwall, M.A. in the name of the Society for the Suppression of Vice by John Percival, Esq.

pp. [4] [i] ii [3] 4–42   MB
Printed for V. Griffiths, German Bookseller to Her Royal Highness the Dutchess of York, Pall Mall; and Egerton, Military Library, Whitehall   1804

The half-title reads, "A defence of the drama, against the Society for the Suppression of Vice, &c. &c." Dated 26 March.

Sadler's Wells

Originally opened as Sadler's Musick House on 3 June 1683 (later becoming Miles' Musick House), then Sadler's Wells Theatre. In 1804 also called the Aquatic Theatre. See also GOVERNMENT REGULATION OF THE THEATRE nos. 183, 185.

1509 [WARD, EDWARD.] A WALK to Islington: with a description of New Tunbridge-Wells, and Sadler's Musick-House.

pp. [1–2] 3–16   L
             1699

Wing W 765.

1510 ——the second edition
pp. [1–2] 3–12   L
             1701

1511 LONSDALE, MARK. The names, &c. of the gentlemen whose likenesses are exhibited in the picture, placed within the bar of the Sir Hugh Myddleton's Head Tavern, near Sadler's Wells, compiled by the late Mr. Mark Lonsdale, formerly manager of that summer theatre.

bs.   L
D. Deans, printer   [*ca.* 1801?]

MS note to picture "by Francis Hayman". It depicts Rosoman, a builder who took over Sadler's Wells in 1746, his friends and others associated with him in the conduct of the theatre.

1512 DREADFUL CATASTROPHE. Fairburn's authentic account of the accident at Sadler's Wells, with the whole of the examination, at Hatton Garden, of the persons charged with causing a false alarm of fire in the theatre, and occasioning the death of eighteen persons, October 15, 1807. With the investigation of the coroner's inquest, and the names of the persons killed. Including an address to the frequenters of theatres, on the late calamity. To which is added, An account of a fire that happened in a barn, in Cambridgeshire, wherein a number of persons were assembled to witness an exhibition, and of whom no less than eighty persons were trampled to death, in endeavouring too eagerly to escape from the furious element.

pp. [1–3] 4–32   L
John Fairburn   [1807]

The account of the Cambridgeshire fire, 8 September 1727, is reprinted from Thomas Gibbons, An account of a most terrible fire (1769). (See below no. 1586).

1513 SADLER'S WELLS THEATRE, contiguous to the New River Head and Islington. The particulars of valuable shares or interests in a most desirable property, Sadler's Wells Theatre, one of the oldest and most popular in the Metropolis, and which, possessing exclusive local advantages, both for dramatic and aquatic representations, has long been a decided favourite of a liberal public, to be sold by auction, by Mr. G. Scott, at Garraway's Coffee House, 'Change Alley, Cornhill, on Friday, 21st of July, 1820, at 12 o'clock, in three lots, without any reservation.

pp. [1–2] 3 [4]   L
             [1820]

1514 NEW SADLER'S WELLS.

pp. [*2*]; illus.   L

J. Catn[a]ch   [*ca.* 1822?]

A song in praise of the establishment.

1515 SADLER'S WELLS THEATRE. Particulars and conditions of sale, of nineteen-fortieth shares, or nearly one undivided moiety, in the valuable lease of the Sadler's Wells Theatre, together with its appropriate and well-arranged stage machinery, scenes, &c. which will be sold by auction, by Mr. Leifchild, at Garraway's, Cornhill, London, on Wednesday, April, 20th 1842, at 12 for 1 o'clock precisely, by order of the assignees of Richard Hughes, a bankrupt, and with the concurrence of the mortgagee.

pp. [*4*]   L

R. Clay, printer   [1842]

1516 MRS. WARNER and Mr. Phelps, of the Theatres Royal, Drury Lane, Covent Garden, and Haymarket, present their respectful compliments, and request attention to the following outlines of a plan which they trust will not be without interest for the respectable inhabitants of this neighbourhood.

pp. [*2*]   LVA

[London]   [1844]

St James's Theatre

Opened 14 December 1835. Known as the Prince's Theatre from 1838–1842. Demolished 1957. See also nos. 1410, 2111.

1517 *A CHRONICLE of the St James's theatre from its origin in 1835.

pp. 87; pls., incl. front.; cover-title: A souvenir of the St James's theatre. 1835–1900.

     NN

Produced by the Guild of Woman Binders   1900

Sans Pareil

Opened on 27 November 1806. Became the Adelphi in October 1819 (later the Royal Adelphi and the Century Theatre). Still in use as the Adelphi Theatre. See GOVERNMENT REGULATION OF THE THEATRE no. 201.

Savoy Theatre

Opened 10 October 1881. Still in use. See OPERA no. 2098.

Strand, The Royal

Opened as a theatre in 1831 as Rayner's New (Strand) Subscription Theatre. Became the New or Royal Strand. Demolished in 1905.

1518 PRESENTATION of testimonial to Miss Swanborough, lessee and directress of the Royal Strand Theatre, on Friday, September 23rd, 1859.

pp. [1–3] 4–11 [12]   MH

Nassau Steam Press — W. S. Johnson   [1859]

1519 THE STRAND MUSICK HALL. Historie of ye building. Programme of inauguration.

pp. [1–5] 6–16; printed wrappers   LGU

[Strand Music Hall]   [1871]

Souvenir programme.

1520 BRERETON, AUSTIN. A short history of the Strand Theatre by Austin Brereton.

pp. [1] 2–16; cover serves as t.p.   MH

With the compliments of Broadhurst Brothers, Lessees and managers   [1899]

Surrey Theatre

Formerly Royal Circus (see above nos. 1135–1137). Renamed "Surrey" in 1810. Reverted to original name 1814–1819. Burned down 1869, but reopened the same year. Became cinema 1920. Demolished 1934. See also GOVERNMENT REGULATION OF THE THEATRE under the year 1816 (p. 29).

1521 SURREY THEATRE. Thursday, October 8th, 1829. To the public. Mr. Elliston, in the forenoon of Wednesday, received from the solicitors of Messrs. Yates, Mathews and [Cu]mberland, an order, intimating that an injunction had been granted against the performance of *The Flying [Du]tchman* at the Surrey Theatre. . . .

bs.   MH

S. G. Fairbrother, printer   1829

1522 SURREY THEATRE. Under the direction of Mr. Elliston. Friday, October 16th, 1829. Injunction refused!!! By the Master of the Rolls.

bs.   MH

S. G. Fairbrother, printer   [1829]

1523 [M., H. D. *i.e.* HENRY DOWNES MILES] THE TWO "CIRCUSES," and the two "Surrey Theatres." Topographical, historical, dramatic and descriptive.

pp. [1–3] 4–16; ptd. wrappers

Thomas Hailes Lacy   1866

     IKF. *Another copy at MH.*

Swan Theatre

See no. 1068.

Theatre Royal

For theatres granted the title Theatre Royal (e.g. Theatre Royal, Lyceum; Theatre Royal, Covent Garden) see under name of theatre e.g. Lyceum, Covent Garden etc.

Vauxhall Gardens, Royal

Originally opened as a place of entertainment called Spring Gardens in 1660. Closed after riots and disorders in 1859. See also SALE CATALOGUES no. 66; PERIODICALS no. 4136.

1524 [PARTINGTON, C. F.] A BRIEF HISTORICAL AND DESCRIPTIVE ACCOUNT of the Royal Gardens, Vauxhall.

pp. [1–3] 4–43 [44 (bl.)]   L
Royal Gardens, Vauxhall; published by the Proprietors.
                                                            1822

Victoria Hall and Coffee Tavern, Royal

Also called the Royal Victoria Coffee Hall. Formerly the Coburg Theatre, (see above nos. 1139–1141) the Royal Victoria Theatre, and the New Victoria Palace. Opened as a temperance music hall on 27 December 1880. Is now the Old Vic Theatre, temporary home of the National Theatre.

1525 THE ROYAL VICTORIA COFFEE HALL.

pp. [1] 2–4; head-title   L
[London]: For private circulation only   [1881]

Report.

1526 ROYAL VICTORIA COFFEE HALL.

pp. [1] 2–4; head-title   L
[London]   1882

Report.

1527 ROYAL VICTORIA COFFEE HALL.

pp. [1–3] 4–9 [10–12 (accounts)]   L
[London: House-Boy Brigade, printers]   [1883]

Report.

1528 ROYAL VICTORIA COFFEE HALL

pp. [1–3] 4–9 [10–12 (accounts)]   L
[London: printed by G. Pulman]   [1883, December]

Report.

1529 ROYAL VICTORIA HALL, and Coffee Tavern.

pp. [1–3] 4–15 [16]   L
[London]   [1884?]

Report of a meeting in support of the Hall.

1530 THE ROYAL VICTORIA HALL, and Coffee Tavern . . . List of subscribers and donors, and balance sheet, 1884–85.

pp. [1–2] 3–5 [6–7 (balance sheet) 8 (bl.)]   L
[London]   [1885]

1531 ROYAL VICTORIA HALL, and Coffee Tavern.

pp. [1–3] 4–6 [7 (subscription form) 8 (bl.)]   L
[London: Bowers Brothers, steam printers]   [1885]

Report.

1532 ROYAL VICTORIA HALL, and Coffee Tavern.

pp. [2] [1] 2–10 [11 (form) 12 (press report)]   L
[London: Bowers Brothers, steam printers]   [1886]

Report.

1533 *The HISTORY of the Royal Victoria Hall and Morley Memorial College, Waterloo Road. Reprinted from the Morley College Magazine.

pp. 35
[Morley College]   [1894]

STR.

Victoria Theatre, Royal

See the Coburg Theatre (nos. 1139–1141) and the Royal Victoria Hall and Coffee Tavern (nos. 1525–1533).

Wyndham's Theatre

Opened 16 November 1899. Still in use as a theatre.

1534 WYNDHAM'S THEATRE Charing Cross Road. Corner of Cranbourne Street. Opened, Nov: 16th, 1899.

pp. [16 (including paper covers)]; title on cover; illus.
                                                            MH
[London]   [1899]

THE THEATRE OUT OF LONDON

GENERAL

See also SALE CATALOGUES nos. 126 (Richardson), 135 (Winston); ARTS OF THE THEATRE nos. 723, 730; GENERAL HISTORY no. 903; MEDIEVAL AND RENAISSANCE STUDIES no. 1067; BIOGRAPHY nos. 2446-9 (Peter Paterson), 2693 (R. Dyer), 2709 (Alma Ellerslie), 2960 (Wm. Gomersal), 3172 (Ch. Keith), 3221 (R. Legge), 3315 (John Mathews), 3346 (Mozeen), 3398 (Geo. Parker), 3471 (Ryley), 3636 (Wild); PERIODICALS no. 4231.

1535 QUEARMOODE, HUMPHREY, *pseud.* ★An essay on the summer entertainments in the neighbourhood of London. By Humphrey Quearmoode, Esq.

pp. 3-21   MB

D. Job   1750

1536 ARTICLES to be observed by the members of Messrs. Austin and Whitlock's company of comedians.

pp. [2]   L

n.p.   [ca. 1780]

See Cecil Price, "An Eighteenth Century Theatrical Agreement", TN, II, (1948) 31–34.

1537 MOORE, MARK. The memoirs and adventures of Mark Moore, late an officer in the British navy. Interspersed with a variety of original anecdotes, selected from his journals, when in the Tuscan, Portuguese, Swedish, Imperial, American, and British service, in each of which he bore a commission. Written by himself. As the author has been at intervals the manager of a respectable company of comedians, in several of the principal towns of England, France, and Flanders, he has also added some original sketches of several theatrical characters, who now rank high in the Thespian corps — With descriptions of the various scenes in which he has been lately involved, through the machinations of petty-fogging attornies, in which the arts of those terriers of the law are fully exposed, for the benefit of society.

pp. [iii–v] vi–xi [xii], misprinting xi as "ix", [1] 2–267 [268]   L

Printed for the author by J. W. Myers   1795

Gathering R has four leaves only.

1538 THEATRICAL AMATEUR, A, *pseud. of* James Winston. Under the patronage of Her Serene Highness the Margravine of Anspach, by whose permission, an engraving of her elegant theatre, will be given as a frontispiece to the publication. Prospectus of a work (never before presented to the public.) entitled The theatre tourist; being a genuine collection of correct views, with brief and authentic historical accounts of all the principal provincial theatres in the United Kingdom. By a theatrical amateur.

bs.   L

[London]   [1803]

1539 THEATRIC AMATEUR, A, *pseud. of* James Winston. The theatric tourist; being a genuine collection of correct views, with brief and authentic historical accounts of all the principal provincial theatres in the United Kingdom. Replete with useful and necessary information to theatrical professors, whereby they may learn how to chuse and regulate their country engagements; and with numerous anecdotes to amuse the reader. By a theatric amateur.

pp. [2] [1] 2–72; col. pls. [24]

Printed by T. Woodfall   1805

Accounts, descriptions and exterior views of the theatres at Bath, Andover, Margate, Tunbridge Wells, Reading, Brighton, Richmond (Surrey), Newbury, Portsmouth, Grantham, Lewes, Exeter, Newcastle, Edmonton, Maidstone, Liverpool, Windsor, Chichester, Birmingham, Manchester, Southampton, Plymouth, Winchester and Norwich — Loewenberg. Also issued with plain plates (LGk). 12 copies with coloured plates mounted on cardboard are recorded by Lowndes. Originally published in 8 parts, 1804–1805. A prospectus (no. 1538) was issued about the end of 1803 (in Burney scrap-book of private theatres at L). A copy containing the 24 original drawings, and additional drawings for 66 other provincial theatres was sold at Sotheby's June 1898 (Catalogue of William Wright Collection, p. 88). Winston's work was continued by William Douglas in a MS note-book "Account of the Provincial Theatres", now at NN. See "The Manuscript of Winston's Theatric Tourist" by C. B. Hogan and others, TN, I (1947) 86–95; J. E. Cunningham, "The Origin of The Theatric Tourist" TN IV (1950) 38–40; Philip H. Highfill, Jr. "Folger Manuscripts Relating to The Theatric Tourist", TN, XX (1966), 121–124; Alfred L. Nelson, "The Periodicity of The Theatric Tourist", TN, XXI (1966/7), 59–62. Dr. Alfred L. Nelson's dissertation, unpublished, is entitled "James Winston's Theatric Tourist, A Critical Edition, with a Biography and a Census of Winston Material" (1968); copies at George Washington University Library, Washington, D.C., and at LSTR. Tooley 512; Loewenberg.

1540 MILLER, JOHN. ★An alphabetical list of theatres in the United Kingdom, with the names of the managers, &c., &c. Compiled and published by John Miller, Henrietta Street, Covent Garden, London. (Agent to the Dramatic Authors' Society.)

pp. (30)

          Dec. 1833

Loewenberg.

1541 *RULES to be observed by the members of Mrs. Latimer's Mammoth Theatre.

[ca. 1850]

A printed handbill, concerning the management of a "theatrical booth travelling the Midlands in the middle of the nineteenth century". Edited by Cecil Price, TN, IV (1949), 8–9.

1542 [TOMKINS, SIMON, *pseud.*] SUSARION, *pseud., ed.* The adventures of a strolling player. An autobiography. Edited by Susarion.

pp. [i–iii] iv–viii, [1] 2–311 [312]   L

Charles Griffin & Co.   [1868]

Satirical fiction.

ENGLAND

INDIVIDUAL TOWNS

See also PERIODICALS: ENGLISH PROVINCES (nos. 4327–4418). Consult also the INDEX OF PLACES OF PUBLICATION for towns not listed below.

Bath

See also INDEX OF PLACES OF PUBLICATION; also GOVERNMENT REGULATION OF THE THEATRE for the year 1768 (p. 26 above); THE MORALITY OF THE THEATRE nos. 583–589; THE THEATRE OUT OF LONDON no. 1584 (Bristol), BIOGRAPHY no. 3022 (Henderson).

1543 [L., J. M. ie John Lee?] THE BATH COMEDIANS. A poem: in two cantos. Written in imitation of *Hudibras.*

pp. [1–3] 4–24   L

Printed for the Author   1753

Dated from Bath 21 April 1753 and initialled J.M.L. Includes also "A poem on friendship".

1544 ——*[another edition]

1755

Dated at end Pontefract 16 June 1755 and signed J.L. = John Lee? — Loewenberg.

1545 PASSERINI, JOSEPH. *An appeal to the public by Signor Passerini, being an answer to Mr. Brown's advertisement in the Bath Journal of last Monday.

pp. 8

Bath   1756

Loewenberg.

1546 BROWN, H. A letter to the public.

pp. [1–2] 3–8   BhP

Bath: printed by S. Martin   [1757]

On the management of the Orchard Street Theatre, complaining of "unmerited strokes of malice" which Brown had suffered since he arrived in Bath six years before; and explaining why he had had to raise the price of boxes.

1547 HULL, THOMAS. *Mr. Hull's case, adress'd to the consideration of the public.

MH

Bath: printed by Stephen Martin, and given gratis at Mr. Hull's, and nowhere else.   [1759]

Hull is best known as the founder of the Theatrical Fund. —Lowe. This pamphlet is Hull's account of his dispute with John Palmer over the fulfilling of Hull's contract as actor and manager of the Theatre in Orchard Street. He published twelve letters which passed between them. In 1759 he left Bath and went to Covent Garden.

1548 BROWNSMITH, JOHN. The danger of a Lee shore: or, an impartial view of the Bath T*****e, in the year 1759. To which is prefix'd, (by way of introduction) an allegorical letter, from a sailor on board, to his friend on shore, with a key to it. And a wonderful prophecy, for the year 1760. By J. Brownsmith, late prompter to the said T*****e.

pp. [3] 4–46   DFo

Bath   [1760]

1549 [LEE, JOHN] *AN ADDRESS TO THE JUDGES and the public, on a decision lately made in one of our courts of judicature.

pp. 21   MB

Printed for the author   1772

This is a letter from John Lee to Mr. Justice Nary on a decision given in a cause between Lee and Davy respecting a contract for building a theatre in Bath.

1550 *THEATRICAL FUND instituted at the Theatre Royal, Bath, March 22, 1800.

Bath: printed by William Meyler in the Grove   1800

Typescript in BhP.

1551 MEYLER, WILLIAM. Poetical amusement on the journey of life; consisting of various pieces in verse: serious, theatric, epigrammatic and miscellaneous. By William Meyler.

pp. [i–v] vi–xvi, [1] 2–207 [208 (bl.)], ²207–210 [=212]; ptd. boards   TnSA

Bath: printed by W. Meyler   1806

Contains numerous addresses, prologues &c. spoken at Bath and Bristol, with explanatory notes, also An Address spoken ... on opening the new theatre at Stourbridge, 1793 — Loewenberg.

1552 LIST OF SUBSCRIBERS to the Tontine annuity of £600 per annum, issuing out of the New Theatre Royal, Bath.

pp. [1] 2–3 [4] BhP
Bath: Anne Keene, printer 1807

1553 [MANGIN, *Rev.* EDWARD?] THE BATH STAGE: a dialogue.

pp. [i–v] vi–xv [xvi], [1] 2–25 [26 (bl.)] BhP
Bath: printed and sold by Henry Gye 1822

In verse; preface signed X. Y. Z., 49 Milsom Street — Loewenberg. See also below no. 1561.

1554 *TO THE EDITOR of the Bath Theatrical Review.

pp. 4
Bath Dec. [1822]

Loewenberg.

1555 *TO THE EDITOR of the Bath Theatrical Review.

pp. 4
Bath Jan. [1823]

Loewenberg.

1556 SIGMOND, GEORGE. *The Royal Dramatic Fête, Wednesday, January 26th, 1825.

Bath: printed for private circulation only 1825

Loewenberg.

1557 BARRY, FREDERICK. *An address written for the Bath Dramatic Fête, and spoken by Mr. Grainger.

[Bath] [1831]

Loewenberg.

1558 PRY, PAUL, *pseud. of* Frederick Barry. The Bath Dramatic Fete, 1836. By Paul Pry.

pp. [1–3] 4–16 BhP
Bath: printed by Benj. Higman 1836

In verse.

1559 M., A. *A letter to James Woulds, manager of the Theatre Royal, Bath.

pp. 4 MH
?: printed by W. H. Millard [1837]

1560 ONE THAT WHISTLES IN THE WOOD, *pseud.* A brief account of the Drum-atic Fete holden at that rum-antic seat the Aqueduct Inn on that ever to be remembered day, Tuesday, Sept. 12th., and in the present remarkable year 1843. By One that whistles in the wood.

pp. [1] 2–4 BhP
Bath: printed by J. Fryer 1843

1561 MANGIN, EDWARD. Miscellaneous essays. By the Rev. Edward Mangin, M.A.

pp. [i–vii] viii–xi [xii], [1] 2–382 [383–384 (bl.)] L
Hope and Co. 1851

See also above no. 1553.

1562 *"OUR BOYS" at the Bath Theatre Royal, Wednesday, 5th Febr., 1879. Being an account of the performance and some subsequent proceedings on its having been played for 1000 times in the provinces by Mr. Duck's company. Reprinted from the Bath Herald, for private circulation.

Bath 1879

Loewenberg.

1563 IDLER, AN, *pseud.* The past and present of the Bath theatre. By an idler.

pp. [2] [1–3] 4–12 [13–14 (bl.)] BhP
Bath 1886

Reprinted from the Bath Herald, *11 Sept. 1886. Wrapper title reads: The Bath theatre past and present.*

1564 BATH Theatre Royal Season 1888–9.

pp. [1–2 (advts.) 3–11] 12–21 [22–24 (advts.)] BhP
Bath 1888

1565 BATH THEATRE ROYAL. AUTUMN SEASON, 1890. Acting manager . . . Mr. Walter D. Hartree. Musical conductor . . [.] Mr. W. F. C. Schottler.

pp. [2] [1–11] 12–22 [23–26 (advts.)]; illus. (front.) MH
Bath: The Herald Office [1890]

1566 PENLEY, BELVILLE S. The Bath stage: a history of dramatic representations in Bath. By Belville S. Penley.

pp. [i–vii] viii–xv [xvi], [1] 2–180 (text) 181–196 (advts.); illus. incl. [front.] TnSA
London and Bath: William Lewis & Son 1892

MS indexes, by R. W. Boodle and by B. Cooke, are in the Bath Municipal Libraries—Loewenberg. Originally published in the Bath Herald.

1567 [LEWIS, WILLIAM.] A SHORT HISTORY of the Bath stage, abridged from Mr. B. S. Penley's popular work, with a list of engagements at the Theatre Royal, Bath 1894–5.

pp. [1–5] 6–34 BhP
Bath: printed at the Herald Office [1895]

Birmingham

See also INDEX OF PLACES OF PUBLICATION; also GOVERNMENT REGULATION OF THE THEATRE for the years 1777 and 1807 (pp. 26, 28 above); THE AMATEUR THEATRE nos. 2171, 2175, 2180, 2184, 2186; BIOGRAPHY no. 3273 (Macready).

1568 SMOKE'EM, SIMON, TIMOTHY TOUCH-'EM, CHRISTOPHER CATCHPENNY, pseuds. The Campaign; or the Birmingham theatrical war: with a review of the conduct of the rival generals and the officers under their command on that expedition. By Simon Smoke'em, Timothy Touch'em, Christopher Catchpenny.

pp. [2] [1–3] 4–43 [44 (bl.)] L
R. Baldwin 1775

The "rival generals" were R. Yates and Joseph Younger.

1569 A FULL AND AUTHENTIC ACCOUNT of what passed in the House of Commons, on the second reading of the Birmingham Playhouse Bill. Tuesday, April 29, 1777.

pp. [1–2] 3–16 BP
[Birmingham] [1777]

1570 TO THE GENTLEMEN, clergy and inhabitants in general of the town of Birmingham.

bs. BP
[Birmingham] [1777]

Petition dated 17 February 1777. Begins A petition having been lately presented to the Honourable House of Commons for leave to present a bill to licence a theatre lately erected on New-Street, in the said . . .

1571 THE PROPRIETORS of the Birmingham Theatre, having by one of their resolutions at a special general meeting, held this day, determined upon opening the new house for dramatic performances . . .

bs. L
Birmingham 1794

Dated 26 Nov 1794.

1572 MEETING at the Shakspeare Tavern the 21st day of February, 1820, for the purpose of forming a new proprietory or company for the purchase of the property belonging to the proprietors of the theatre, for re-building the theatre. . . .

pp. [1] 2–3 [4] DFo
[Birmingham: Thomas Knott, printer] 1820

Birmingham Theatre Royal, destroyed by fire 6 Jan. 1820.

1573 BOROUGH OF BIRMINGHAM. Report of the Committee of Justices appointed on the subject of the protection of the public from fire in theatres and music halls within the borough.

pp. 1–19 [20] BP
Birmingham: Geo. Jones and Son [1888]

Report dated 28th December 1887 and was approved by the Justices on 4th January 1888.

1574 MANTON, H. *Letters on theatres.

 BP
[Birmingham?] 1888

1575 PEMBERTON, T[HOMAS] EDGAR. The Birmingham theatres: a local retrospect. By T. Edgar Pemberton.

pp. [6] [1] 2–216 L
Birmingham: Cornish Bros.; London: Simpkin, Marshall, Hamilton, Kent & Co., Limited [1890]

Reprinted from the Birmingham Daily Mail. The London imprint is stamped on the title-page, cancelling the imprint: "London: Simpkin, Marshall & Co."

Boston

1576 *AN IMPARTIAL CRITIQUE, or, a peep into the Boston theatre, during the season of 1813; being a comprehensive view of the corps dramatique, who are "ever anxious to please."

 MH
Boston [1813]

1577 ——*second edition

 MH
Boston [1813]

1578 *AN IMPARTIAL CRITIQUE, or, a peep into the Boston Theatre, during the season of 1814; being a review of the corps dramatique, with remarks on the wonderful exhibitions, and theatrical novelties.

Boston [1814]

Lowe.

Brandenburgh House

See THE AMATEUR THEATRE no. 2152.

Brighton

See also INDEX OF PLACES OF PUBLICATION; also THE LONDON THEATRE no. 1104; BIO-GRAPHY no. 3035.

1579 PORTER, HENRY C. The history of the theatres of Brighton, from 1774 to 1885, by Henry C. Porter, (twenty-four years dramatic critic at Brighton.) Dedicated to Miss Amy Sedgwick (the celebrated actress.) Mrs. H. N. Chart (proprietress T.R.B.), by the author, with every sentiment of admiration, esteem and respect.

pp. i–viii (advts.), [1–3] 4–42 47–206 [=202] incl. engr. t.p., I–XIV [XV–XVI (advts.)] title headed: "The only standard work of the Brighton stage"; ptd. wrpprs.   GU

Brighton: printed by King and Thorne   1886

1580 PLAY-GOER, A, *pseud.* of Charles Fleet. Reminiscences of the Brighton Theatre. (By a Playgoer).

pp. [1] 2–31 [32]; head-title   BiP

Brighton   1891

> *Colophon: Reprinted from the Brighton Gazette, Thursday June 11th, 18th, 25th and July 2nd 1891.*

Bristol

See also INDEX OF PLACES OF PUBLICATION; also GOVERNMENT REGULATION OF THE THEATRE for the year 1778 (p. 26 above). THE THEATRE OUT OF LONDON no. 1551 note.

1581 [?CHAMPION, ——]. *THE CONSE-QUENCES of a new theatre to the city of Bristol considered, with some interesting thoughts on plays in general: humbly submitted to the consideration of the wiser and more serious part of the inhabitants of the said city.

pp. [1–3] 4–51 [52]   BrP
Bristol: T. Cadell   1765

1582 *BRISTOL THEATRE: a poem.

Bristol   1766

> *A bitter and silly attack on the stage, curious as being in rhyme. The author apologises for this peculiarity thus — "The author would rather have chosen to publish his sentiments on this important subject in plain prose; but for this single reason, that many sooner peruse sentiments conveyed in poetry, and longer retain them." The author's poetry is certainly remarkable — e.g.*
>   *"So Nile's amphibious Crocodiles decoy,*
>   *And, softly soothing, Sycophants destroy." — Lowe.*

1583 [COURTNEY, ——]. *THE ASSOCIA-TION of theatrical opposers, or Bristol in commotion against the Muses.

    MH

Bristol   1773

1584 *AN ADDRESS to the actors of the Bristol and Bath theatres.

6 leaves

    1798

    STR.

1585 JENKINS, RICHARD. Memoirs of the Bristol stage, from the period of the theatre at Jacob's Well, down to the present time; with notices, biographical and critical, of some of the most celebrated comedians who have appeared on its boards. By Richard Jenkins.

pp. [i–v] vi–xii, [1] 2–103 [104]   L
Bristol: printed for the Author by W. H. Somerton   1826

Burwell

1586 GIBBONS, THOMAS. An account of a most terrible fire that happened on Friday the eighth of September, 1727, at a barn at Burwell in Cambridgeshire, in which by computation about one hundred and forty persons were assembled at a puppet-show, of which number no less than eighty persons perished, or received such injury by the flames as to expire soon after. Taken in part from the parish-register of baptisms and burials belonging to the said town, and more largely from the relation of Mr Thomas Howe, who, being at that time about sixteen years of age, was present in the barn, and an eye-witness of the dreadful calamity. To which account are subjoined some serious and impor-tant inquiries relating to the melancholy event, and some observations designed as a practical improvement of the awful catastrophe. By Thomas Gibbons, D.D.

pp. [i–iii] iv–vii [viii], [1] 2–55 [56 (bl.) 57 (advts.) 58 (bl.)]   L

James Buckland   1769

> *Excerpts from this pamphlet are reprinted in Fairburn's account of the Sadler's Wells accident, 1807. (See no. 1512).*

Cambridge

See also INDEX OF PLACES OF PUBLICATION; also GOVERNMENT REGULATION OF THE THEATRE for the years 1736, 1884 (pp. 24, 34 above) THE AMATEUR THEATRE no. 2166.

1587 *[ORDER forbidding undergraduates to attend either the new playhouse near the paper mills or Sturbridge Fair.]

bs.

Cambridge   1730

> *Dated Aug. 29, 1730, and signed by R. Lambert, vice-chancellor of the University.—Loewenberg.*

1588 THE ALBUM of the Cambridge Garrick Club: containing original and select papers on the drama, and the proceedings of that society. With illustrations. Edited by a member of the club.

pp. [i–vii] viii–xvi [xvii–xxii], [1] 2–287 [288]; pls. [front., 7]; lithographed facsims. [2]   L
Cambridge: W. H. Smith, for the society   1836

1589 [HALL, HENRY THOMAS.] *A MEMORIAL of the Tercentenary of Shakespeare, in Cambridge.

pp. 16   CP
Cambridge   [1864]

    Loewenberg

1590 [HALL, HENRY THOMAS.] *CAMBRIDGE DRAMATIC ALBUM.

pp. 131   MB
Cambridge: Wallis   1868

Cardiff

See no. 675.

Cheltenham

See also INDEX OF PLACES OF PUBLICATION.

1591 THE CHELTENHAM ASSEMBLY ROOMS and Theatre Company Ltd. Prospectus.

pp. [4]   GrP
Cheltenham   1890

An account of the company and the theatre, with the Memorandum of Association and application forms for preference and ordinary shares, and debentures.

Chester

See INDEX OF PLACES OF PUBLICATION; also GOVERNMENT REGULATION OF THE THEATRE for the year 1776 (p. 26 above); MEDIEVAL AND RENAISSANCE STUDIES no. 1012; THEATRE OUT OF LONDON nos. 1608, 1686.

Chew-Magna

See THE MORALITY OF THE THEATRE no. 564.

Cornwall

See also BIOGRAPHY no. 2666.

1592 SANDYS, W. *On the Cornish drama.

STR.   1865

Coventry

See MEDIEVAL AND RENAISSANCE STUDIES nos. 1009, 1012, 1014.

Croydon

See no. 1080.

Edgbaston

See THE AMATEUR THEATRE nos. 2171–2173, 2180, 2184, 2186.

Exeter

The Exeter stage is chiefly notable for Edmund Kean's connection with it. Unfortunately it has gained new interest from an appalling catastrophe which occurred on 5th September 1887, when the theatre was burned down and about 150 persons were killed by burning or suffocation — Lowe.
For the Government report of the fire see GOVERNMENT REGULATION OF THE THEATRE for the year 1888 (p. 35 above).

1593 *SOME CONSIDERATIONS on the lawfulness and expediency of frequenting the theatre, as it is at present circumstanced at Exeter. Addressed to the citizens of that city.

Exon   1756

   Loewenberg.

1594 COTTON, WILLIAM. The story of the drama in Exeter, during its best period, 1787 to 1823. With reminiscences of Edmund Kean. By William Cotton, F.S.A.

pp. [4] [1] 2–66; pls. [front., 5]; errata slip   L
London: Hamilton, Adams & Co; Exeter: William Pollard and Co.   1887

1595 NARRATIVE of the disastrous fire and loss of life at the Theatre Royal, Exeter, Monday, 5th September, 1887. With illustration.

pp. [1–3] 4–16; pl. [1]   L
[Exeter: H. Besley & Son, printers]   [1887]

Bound with this copy is a report of the Exeter Theatre Disaster Fund Finance Sub-Committee, 24th April, 1888.

1596 vacant

Gravesend

See WORTHING no. 1702.

Halesworth

See THE MORALITY OF THE THEATRE nos. 469–480.

Hull

See also INDEX OF PLACES OF PUBLICATION; also GOVERNMENT REGULATION OF THE THEATRE for the year 1769 (p. 26 above); BIOGRAPHY no. 3637.

1597 THE TRIUMPH of public opinion over injustice and oppression! In accordance with advertisements (and upon the suggestion of several gentlemen of Hull), the public meeting (composed of at least 2,000 persons) took place at the Mechanics' Institute, Hull, Yorkshire, on Monday evening, Feb. 21st, 1848. to hear the statement and reply of George Jones, Esq, to the Lessee of the Theatre Royal, Hull, and the Editor of the *Hull Advertiser*, and to decide upon the following proposition, viz.:—"To take into consideration the passing of resolutions condemnatory of the conduct of the Lessee of the Theatre Royal, Hull (Mr. J. L. Pritchard), in reference to 'The Shakespeare Memorial Nights' at Hull and Leeds."

bs.   DFo
Kingston-upon-Hull   21st Feb. 1848

Signed "John Peck, Chairman of the above Public Meeting."

Hythe

See WORTHING no. 1702.

Ipswich

See also INDEX OF PLACES OF PUBLICATION.

1598 BELLAMY, B. P. A letter to the dramatic censor of the *Suffolk Chronicle;* by B. P. Bellamy, of the Theatre Royal, Norwich.

pp. [2] [1] 2–38   L

Ipswich: printed by C. Battely   [1814]

Lancashire

See no. 3636.

Leicester

See also INDEX OF PLACES OF PUBLICATION.

1599 KELLY, WILLIAM, *ed.* Notices illustrative of the drama, and other popular amusements, chiefly in the sixteenth and seventeenth centuries, incidentally illustrating Shakespeare and his cotemporaries; extracted from the Chamberlain's accounts and other manuscripts of the borough of Leicester. With an introduction and notes by William Kelly.

pp. [i–v] vi–viii, [1] 2–310 [311–312 (advts.)]; illus.; pls. fold. [front. 1]   NbU

John Russell Smith   1865 [*for* 1864]

> *Partly previously published in Trans. Leicester Lit. and Phil. Soc.*

1600 ———[large paper issue]
    L

John Russell Smith   1865

Lincoln

See also INDEX OF PLACES OF PUBLICATION.

1601 FRIEND TO JUSTICE, A, *pseud.* *A letter addressed to the authors of the Lincoln Dramatic Censor, containing strictures and observations upon their conduct towards the manager of the Lincoln Theatre. By a friend to justice.

pp. 8   MB

Lincoln: Brooke   1809

1602 ROBERTSON, THOMAS. *An appeal to the city of Lincoln in refutation of the charges brought against the theatres. By Thomas Robertson.

    MH

Lincoln   1809

> Loewenberg.

Liverpool

See also INDEX OF PLACES OF PUBLICATION; also GOVERNMENT REGULATION OF THE THEATRE for the years 1771, 1843 (pp. 26, 32 above); THE THEATRE OUT OF LONDON no. 1608.

1603 LETTERS ON THE SUBJECT OF HALF PRICE ADMISSION to the theatre. The small charge of 3d. for this pamphlet will be excused, when it is considered, that were it given gratis, the friends of managers might find means to suppress the whole, by so cheaply getting them into their own possession — should they attempt the same by purchase, they will defeat their own object, as whatever is received from the sale of these will be expended on more impressions. Vox populi vincit.

pp. [1–3] 4–16   MH

Liverpool: printed by J. Gore   1810

1604 REPORT OF THE PROCEEDINGS upon a criminal information against Abraham Lemon, Thomas Turner, Barton Wilson, John Webster, John Robinson Mulleneux, and Charles Rowlinson, for a conspiracy and riot at the Theatre-Royal, Liverpool, in the month of May last, tried at the summer assizes for the County of Lancaster, on Friday the 14th September 1810, before Sir Robert Graham, Knt. one of the barons of His Majesty's Court of Exchequer, and a special jury. Taken in short hand by Mr. Farquharson

pp. [4] [1] 2–104   L

Liverpool: printed by Thos. Kaye   1810

1605 *TRIAL of Lemon, Turner and others for riot at the Theatre [Royal] Liverpool in May 1810.

Liverpool   1810

> *Recorded but not seen by Lowe. May be the same item as no. 1604.*

1606 RAMBLER, REUBEN. *Remarkable adventures of Reuben Rambler, Gent. during a sixty minute excursion near the Theatre Royal, Liverpool.

pp. 8

Liverpool: R. Stebbing   1829

> Loewenberg. *Copy at LvP destroyed.*

1607 *THEATRES and places of public resort. Reports of the Town Clerk, the Head Constable and the City Engineer.

Liverpool Council Proceedings   1881–82

> Loewenberg.

Ludlow

See no. 1043.

Manchester

See also INDEX OF PLACES OF PUBLICATION; also THE MORALITY OF THE THEATRE no. 633.

1608 CENSOR, C., *pseud.* †The Thespian mirror, or poetical strictures; on the professional characters of Mr. Cooke, Mr. Ward, Mrs. Powell, Mr. Bates, Mrs. Taylor, Miss Cornely's, Mr. Banks, Mr. Harding, Mrs. Banks, Mr. Grist, Mr. Richardson, Miss Daniels, Mr. Tyrrel, Mr. Davis, Mrs. Cornely's Mr. Barrett, Mr. Francis, Mr. Clegg, and Mr. Ryley. Of the Theatres Royal, Manchester, Liverpool, and Chester. By C. Censor.

pp. [1–3] 4–40; wanting pp. 9–32   L
[Manchester?]: printed for the author   1793

> *Besides the actors mentioned in the title, several more are apostrophized in the actual text, as for instance, Mr. Congdon and Miss Valois — Loewenberg.*

1608.1 CANDID, *pseud.* A letter to Mr. Ward, one of the managers of the Theatre-Royal, Manchester. Occasioned by his intemperate change of "malignity and falsehood" against the writer of *Impartial reflections,* &c. By Candid.

pp. [1–3] 4–11 [12]   L
Manchester: printed and sold by W. Shelmerdine and Co.   [1800]

1609 CROSS, WILLIAM. An expostulatory address, to the public. By William Cross, of the Theatre-Royal, Manchester

pp. [1–3] 4–14 [15 (colophon) 16 (bl.)]   L
Manchester: printed and sold by W. Cowdroy; also sold by B. Hopper   1800

1610 IMPARTIAL REFLECTIONS, on the conduct of the managers, and merits of some of the performers of the Theatre-Royal, Manchester. With observations on a late publication, entitled *A peep into the theatre,* &c.

pp. [1–3] 4–11 [12 (bl.)]   L
Manchester: printed and sold by W. Shelmerdine and Co.   [1800]

> *Signed "Candid". Defends some of the actors, and fiercely attacks Ward, one of the managers — Lowe.*

1611 A PEEP INTO THE THEATRE-ROYAL, Manchester; with some remarks on the merits and demerits of the performers.

pp. [1–7] 8–30 [31 (colophon) 32 (bl.)]   L
Manchester: printed and sold by G. Bancks   1800

> *Signed "Philipi". The Manchester correspondent of the* Monthly Mirror *says, in March 1800, that this was written "by an ignorant barber, who is tolerated by these very managers in playing once annually for a benefit."*

It abuses the managers and actors in unmeasured terms — Lowe. *William Cross's* An expostulatory address (*1800*) *is a reply by one of the actors.*

1612 ——— *second edition
pp. 36   MH
Manchester: E. Bancks   1800

1613 LAVISH, CHARLES. *Letter to the proprietors of the Theatre Royal, Manchester.
bs.
Manchester   1800

> PH *and* KB.

1614 vacant.

1615 TOWNSMAN, A, *pseud.* of James Watson? An address to the inhabitants of Manchester, on theatricals by a townsman.

pp. [i–iii] iv [5] 6–8   L
Manchester: G. Bancks, printer   [1803]

> *Preface dated 1 December 1803. James Watson edited the periodical* The Townsman: *see no. 4385.*

1616 *ARGUS'S ANSWER TO THE HISTRIONIAN MR. HUDDART; addressed to the inhabitants of Manchester.

pp. 10   MH
Manchester: R. & W. Dean   1804

> *Huddart, who was attacked in the first number of Argus, inserted an answer in the Manchester newspapers, to which this is a reply — Lowe.*

1617 A LITTLE AMUSEMENT for the gentlemen of Monmouth-street, Rosemary-Lane, and the neighbourhood; vulgarly called Cannon-st. and McDonald's-lane. With observations on clerical, military, mercantile, & theatrical characters.

pp. [1–3] 4–29 [30 (announcement about "our next theatrical campaign")]   L
Manchester: printed and sold by R. & W. Dean & Co.
                                                          1804

1618 THE THEATRICAL INQUISITOR; or, an enquiry into what two worthy managers have promised, and what performed.
    Words are but air, and air but wind,
    Too feeble instruments to bind.   Pope.
Dedicated to the said managers; with a sincere wish to remove the axiom which appears so deeply grafted.
    ———Populus me sibilat; at mihi plaudo
    Ipse domo, simul ac nummos contemplor in arca.
                                                          Hor.

The fame of their last season's performers, is so indelibly stampt upon the public mind, that it is requested they may not be again offered, as there is a probability that they will not be accepted.

pp. [1–3] 4–28   L

Manchester: printed and sold by R. & W. Dean & Co. 1804

The managers in question were Ward and Thomas Ludford Bellamy — Loewenberg.

1619 BENWELL, J. M. An essay on the danger of unjust criticism. By J. M. Benwell, of the Theatre-Royal, Manchester. Occasioned by a publication entitled *The Thespian review.*

pp. [1] 2–8; head-title   L

[Manchester:] Wardle, printer   [1806]

Dated 8 March 1806. The Thespian Review, see no. 4388.

1620 A LETTER FROM MR. B. to Miss F.

pp. [1–3] 4–12   MB

Manchester: printed by J. Leigh   1814

Bound in a volume labelled Manchester Theatre Tracts; correspondents not identified.

1621 [EASBY, JOHN?] RANDOM SCENES from the life of a Manchester green-coated schoolboy; his trials on the stage, the press, the platform, and the pulpit. Written, from memory, by himself.

pp. [1–3] 4–16

Manchester: Abel Heywood   1851

IKF. *This copy has MS attribution to John Easby.*

1622 PROCTER, RICHARD WRIGHT. Our turf, our stage, and our ring. By Richard Wright Procter. With illustrations by William Morton.

pp. [i–v] vi [vii–ix] 10–100; illus., incl. [front.]

Manchester: Dinham & Co.; London: Simpkin, Marshall, & Co.   1862

JFA.

1623 PROCTER, RICHARD WRIGHT. Manchester in holiday dress. By Richard Wright Procter.

pp. [i–v] vi–viii, [1] 2–179 [180 (bl.) 181–184 (advts.)] L

London: Simpkin, Marshall & Co.; Manchester: Abel Heywood & Son   1866

1624 DARBYSHIRE, ALFRED. *Address delivered at the Arts Club, Manchester, April 22nd, 1893, by Alfred Darbyshire, F.S.A.

pp. 39; Running title: Stage representation of Shakespeare   DLC

Manchester: Guardian Printing Works. "Printed for private circulation"   1894

Deals with Charles Calvert's Shakespearean revivals at the Prince's Theatre, Manchester.

1625 THE MANCHESTER STAGE 1880–1900 Criticisms reprinted from "The Manchester Guardian."

pp. [1–4] 5–241 [242 (bl.) 243–244 (advts.)] GU

Archibald Constable & Co.   [1900]

Contributors: William Thomas Arnold, Oliver Elton, Allan Noble Monkhouse, Charles Edward Montague.

Margate

See also INDEX OF PLACES OF PUBLICATION; also GOVERNMENT REGULATION OF THE THEATRE for the year 1786 (p. 26 above).

1626 *MARGATE THEATRE ROYAL, in which the great Edward Kean, Mrs. Siddons, and Mr. Booth have played in their earliest days. Its history, ancient and modern, with a full description of the present elegant structure and critiques by the leading daily and local journals, also a reprint of some of the play bills of 60 years ago.

pp. 16   MgP

Margate: Keble's Gazette Office   [1874]

Newcastle

See also INDEX OF PUBLICATION; also GOVERNMENT REGULATION OF THE THEATRE for the year 1787 (p. 26, above); SCOTLAND no. 1912.

1627 HEATTON, MICHAEL and JOSEPH AUSTIN. To the Right Worshipful John Baker, Esq.

bs.   L

Newcastle   1 April 1769

Application for the lease of the Newcastle Theatre to the Mayor. Edited by Cecil Price in "Joseph Austin and his Associates 1766–1789", TN, IV (1949) 89–94.

1628 LIST of subscribers to the Theatre Royal, Newcastle.

fold. doc., pp. [4]; filing-title   NwP

[Newcastle-upon-Tyne]   [1789]

1629 THOUGHTS ON THE LATE DISTURBANCE at the Theatre-Royal, Newcastle.

pp. [1–5] 6–19 [20]   NwP

Newcastle: printed by M. Brown   1789

The disturbance was caused by the conduct of Mrs. Whitlock, sister to Mrs. Siddons, and wife of the Newcastle manager, who was asked by Cooke to play Marcia to his Cato, on the occasion of his benefit. This she refused to do — Lowe.

Kemble–Edwin Dispute 1793

1630 EDWIN, J[OHN]. To the public.

pp. [1] 2–4; head-title   L

[Newcastle]   [4 June 1793]

> *Stephen Kemble, then manager of the Newcastle Theatre, is accused of cruel injustice in the matter of salary towards Mr. and Mrs. Edwin — Lowe. Signed and dated from Newcastle 4 June 1793.*

1631 EDWIN, J[OHN]. To the public.

pp. [1] 2–7 [8 (bl.)]; head-title   L

[Newcastle]   [12 June 1793]

1632 [KEMBLE, STEPHEN.] TO THE PUBLIC.

pp. [1] 2–6; head-title   L

[Newcastle]   [10 June 1793]

> *As Edwin and Kemble confine themselves to flat contradiction of each other, the truth cannot now be arrived at — Lowe.*

1633 THE NEWCASTLE JESTER; being a choice collection of entertaining jests, humourous tales, droll stories, lively puns, &c. To which are added, the following comic pieces . . .

pp. [1–3] 4–60   NwP

Newcastle: printed and sold by David Bass   1804

> *Includes a prologue spoken by Liston at the opening of the Theatre Royal, Newcastle.*

Mara v. Mitchell Controversy

1634 MARA, S[AMUEL] D[ELAVAL]. (No. I.) of the Mitchelliad; or Tyne Mercury analyz'd. By S. D. Mara, of the Theatre-Royal, Newcastle.

pp. [1–3] 4–8   NwU

Newcastle: printed and sold by David Bass   1804

1635 ——(No. two,) of the Mitchelliad; *continues as in no. 1634.*

pp. [1–2] 3–8   NwU

Newcastle: printed and sold by David Bass   1804

1636 ——(No. II.) of the Mitchelliad; *continues as in no. 1634.*

pp. [1–2] 3–8   NwU

Newcastle: printed for the author   1804

> *A counterfeit number as appears from the contents and different imprint; signed S. D. Mara and dated Feb. 28, 1804, but in fact a counter-attack, by or on behalf of Mitchell, alleging that Mara's real name was "Thomas Hoggers" — Loewenberg.*

1637 ——(No. three,) of the Mitchelliad; *continues as in no. 1634.*

pp. [1–2] 3–8   NwU

Newcastle: printed and sold by David Bass   1804

1638 ——(No. Four.) of the Mitchelliad; *continues as in no. 1634.*

pp. [1–2] 3–8   L

Newcastle: printed and sold by David Bass   1804

1639 ——*[no. ix] of the Mitchelliad

[Newcastle?]   [1804?]

> *Catalogue of Newcastle Literary and Philosophical Society.*

1640 MARA, S[AMUEL] D[ELAVAL]. The barber's pig; or, a tickler for Typo. By S. D. Mara of the Theatre-Royal, Newcastle.

pp. [1] 2–4   NwP

[Newcastle: printed by D. Bass]   [1804]

1641 MARA, S[AMUEL] D[ELAVAL]. The Dean-street Dunciad; or, a peep into pandaemonium. A poem, in four cantos. By S. D. Mara, of the Theatre-Royal, Newcastle. Dedicated without permission to Mr. John Mitchell, proprietor, editor, compositor, conductor, paragraph-monger, and printer of the Tyne Mercury. With a preface, and notes, analytical and explanatory.

pp. [1–8] 9–24   NwP

Newcastle: printed and sold by David Bass   1804

> *Preface dated July 18, 1804.*

1642 [MARA, SAMUEL DELAVAL.] AN EASTER GIFT; or, *The house where Jack lives.*

bs., illus.   L

Newcastle: printed and sold by D. Bass   [1804]

> *Dedication signed: S. D. Mara.*

1643 MARA, S[AMUEL] D[ELAVAL] The trial of Typo; or, news from Parnassus: a vision. Communicated by Peter Parable to S. D. Mara, of the Theatre-Royal, Newcastle.

pp. [1] 2–8; head-title   L

[Newcastle: printed by D. Bass]   [1804]

1644 ——Second part of the trial of Typo; or, news from Parnassus: a vision. Communicated by Peter Parable, to S. D. Mara, of the Theatre-Royal, Newcastle.

pp. [1] 2–8; head-title   L

[Newcastle: printed by D. Bass]   [1804]

1645 MARA, S[AMUEL] D[ELAVAL]. Typo's travels; or, a flight from Carlisle. (Tune— *The Rogue's March*.) By S. D. Mara.

bs.   L

Newcastle: D. Bass, printer   [1804]

1646 TYPO'S LAST SHIFT.

pp. [1] 2–4; head-title   L

[Newcastle: printed by D. Bass]   [1804]

Letter to Bass from J. Mitchell, and a reply to Mitchell from Mara, dated 2 April, 1804.

1647 ★VINDICATION of the Tyne Mercury. The editor of the Tyne Mercury received the following communication, in vindication of his character and conduct, at a late hour last night. It was intended for publication in the Mercury of this day; but the Editor being unwilling to deprive his friends of other information of importance, has determined to deliver copies of it (gratis) to his subscribers, in a detached form. Tyne Mercury Office, March 6, 1804.

pp. 8

Newcastle upon Tyne   [1804]

Loewenberg.
Another contribution to the controversy is the manuscript in L of "The dream. A doggerel poem, humbly dedicated to the readers of a Tuesday's newspaper, by Timothy Touchall, Gentn. In which is included a celebrated poem entituled

A queer epistle to my brother Jack,
Upon the vile stage players base attack.

Newcastle: Printed for all the Booksellers 1804." It is either a copy of a publication otherwise unknown, or a work never printed.

✠ Grim Typo, the Tyne demon; or, the resurrection of *The barber's pig*. A satirical miscellany ... of the demon, both before and since his defeat by Mara, in 1804, to the present period. Newcastle Upon Tyne. [1818.] *See no. 4401.*

J. P. Edwin v. Macready, the elder, 1807

1648 EDWIN, JOHN PROSSER. An appeal to the public, relative to the conduct of William McCready, Esq. in the case of the author, John Prosser Edwin, comedian, of the Theatre-Royal, Newcastle.

pp. [1–3] 4–35 [36 (bl.)]; misprinting 4 as "3"   L

Newcastle upon Tyne: printed for the author by S. Hodgson   1807

The dedication, to the Mayor of Newcastle, is dated 4 April 1807.

1649 M'CREADY, WILLIAM. ★Fact versus Fallacy; or the true state of the case between (the man who calls himself) John Prosser Edwin, comedian, late of the Theatre-Royal, Newcastle, and William M'Cready.

pp. 40   MB

Newcastle on Tyne: Mitchell   1807

1650 EDWIN, JOHN PROSSER. Candour versus calumny; being an ample refutation of the malignant falsehoods and despicable misrepresentations lately published by the man-ager, William McCready. Written by the man calling himself John Prosser Edwin, comedian.

pp. [1–3] 4–28   NwP

Newcastle upon Tyne: printed for the author by S. Hodgson   1807

These three pamphlets relate to a dispute of the usual nature between manager and actor; the latter alleging cruelty and injustice on the part of the manager who replies by charges of misconduct. Of Edwin I known nothing, except that he was in the army before he became an actor — Lowe.

1651 CAUSTIC, *pseud.* The Newcastle critic, or a poetic epistle to the dramatic Draco of the Tyne Mercury, the self-created standard of theatric taste. By Caustic.

pp. [1–2] 3–8   NwP

Newcastle: printed for the author by K. Anderson 1814

1652 Y., G. Newcastle Theatre in an uproar, with the bear, the horses, and the dogs as principal performers. A new song. — By G.Y.

bs.   NwP

Newcastle: J. Marshall, printer   [1819]

1653 DE CAMP, *Mr.* Theatre-Royal, Newcastle upon Tyne, Friday, Feb. 21, 1823. Mr De Camp, labouring under sincere grief for the melancholy event which took place here on Wednesday night last, begs to inform the public ...

bs.   L

Newcastle: W. A. Mitchell, printer   1823

Announcing new arrangements after the panic (following upon an alarm of fire) of 19 February 1823, which led to the death of seven persons.

1654 DREADFUL ACCIDENT.

pp. [4]   NwP

[Newcastle-upon-Tyne]   [1823]

1655 MELANCHOLY ACCIDENT.

bs.   NwP

Gateshead: W. Stephenson, printer   [1823]

1656 A MELANCHOLY EVENT improved.

pp. [1] 2–8   NwP

[Newcastle: G. Angus, printer]   [1823]

1657 TEN GUINEAS REWARD.

bs.   MB

Newcastle: Mitchell, printer   1827

> Begins *Whereas, during the last Winter Season, a gong was borrowed from a gentleman of the town for the use of the Theatre . . . Dated 16th March, 1827.*

Norfolk

1658 [HARRAL, THOMAS?] *†THE NORFOLK THESPIAD: a poem, in three parts; with notes, biographical, critical, and illustrative: to which are prefixed, strictures on the requisites of an actor.

pp. 64; pls.   MH

Ipswich: printed by John King   1814

> Published in 4 monthly parts of 16 pages each from Jan. 1814. According to Loewenberg up to 14 parts were projected. MH copy complete only through stanza XIV of Part I. —

Norwich

See also INDEX OF PLACES OF PUBLICATION; also GOVERNMENT REGULATION OF THE THEATRE for the year 1768 (p. 26 above).

1659 [PINN, D.] ROSCIUS: or, a critical examination. Into the merits of all the principal performers. Belonging to Norwich theatre. For the last season.

pp. [4] 1–26   L

Norwich: printed by S. White   1767

1660 ———*the second edition, with additions and corrections. By D. Pinn.

pp. [iv] 20

Norwich   1767

> Loewenberg.

1661 STRICTURES, in verse, on the performances at the Theatre-Royal, Norwich towards the close of the season of 1799.

pp. [2] [1–5] 6–29 [30]; vignette on t.p.   L

Norwich: printed by Bacon; London: J. Wright, Robert Baldwin; Cambridge: Hodson; Bury: Rackham; Lynn: Marshall; Yarmouth: Downes and Boulter; Ipswich: Jermyn; Colchester: Keymer   [1799?]

The Dispute between Philo Thespis and the Norwich Theatrical Observer 1827

1662 *CANTERBURY EPISTLE.

[Norwich]   [1827]

> Alluded to in no. 1664 below.

1663 THE EDITOR of "The Norwich theatrical observer", to the friends, subscribers, & readers of that publication.

pp. [1] 2–4   MH

[Norwich: Cranefield, printer]   1827

> Dated 18 July 1827.

1664 PHILO THESPIS, *pseud.* A quid pro quo; or, the doctor and his conclave. A satirical poem. By Philo Thespis.

pp. [i–iii] iv–viii [9] 10–24   MH

Norwich: printed by C. Berry   1827

> A defence against the Canterbury epistle (*see above no. 1662*).

1665 PHILO THESPIS, *pseud.* A slap at slip-slop; or, the doctor physicked, a satirical poem by Philo Thespis.

pp. [1–3] 4–8   MH

Norwich: printed by Stewardson & son   [1827]

> Signed at end "*Ching Chilly*".

1666 PHILO THESPIS, *pseud.* To Rivers. By Philo Thespis.

bs.   MH

[Norwich]   [1827]

> Contains an open letter and poem "*Tasso & the pastry-cook. A sketch.*"

1667 PHILO THESPIS, *pseud.* To the editor of the "Observer". By Philo Thespis.

pp. [1] 2–4   MH

Norwich: printed by Christopher Berry   1827

> Dated 23 July 1827.

1668 THEPSIS, *pseud. of* John Smith. The following acrostic has been refused admission, by the impartial editor of The Observer.

bs.   MH

Norwich: C. Berry, printer   [1827]

> Also contains "Ode" signed "Philo-Thespis".

1669 TO PHILO-THESPIS. Acrostick.

bs.   MH

[Norwich: G. Kitton, printer]   [1827]

> The acrostic spells SMITH. Also contains a bogus announcement "By permission, to be seen alive, near the Theatre Royal, Norwich, that astonishing natural curiosity the moon-calf, alias, Jack Ching-Chilly . . .", signed "Rivers".

1670 THEATRE ROYAL NORWICH. Opinions of the press of Mr. G. H. Chaplin's gorgeous Christmas pantomime for 1875–6.

bs. DFo

Norwich: "Herald Office". W. H. Stewardson, printer [1876]

Nottingham

See INDEX OF PLACES OF PUBLICATION; also THE MORALITY OF THE THEATRE no. 614.

Oxford

See also INDEX OF PLACES OF PUBLICATION; also GOVERNMENT REGULATION OF THE THEATRE for the years 1736, 1884 (pp. 24, 34, above).

1671 THE PLAYERS TURN'D ACADEMICKS: or, a description (in merry metre) of their translation from the Theatre in Little Lincolns-Inn-Fields, to the Tennis-Court in Oxford. With a preface relating to the proceedings of the University the last act: as also the Wadhamite prologue that was spoken there, with a prologue and epilogue, by way of answer to it, at the Theatre Royal.

pp. [4] 1–12 L

1703

Banter of a visit of Betterton and his companions to Oxford. The prologue quoted was spoken by Betterton on 5th July 1703, and the answer was spoken by Mills at Drury Lane on the 16th and 23rd July — Lowe. "The Wadhamite prologue" was written by Joseph Trapp. See also Wiley Rare Prologues, p. 124. "The Wadhamite prologue", by Joseph Trapp, was published anonymously as A prologue to the University of Oxford. Spoke by Mr. Betterton [n.p., n.d.], and reprinted in The life and times of that excellent and renowned actor Thomas Betterton (Reader, 1888) pp. 153–154. The 'answer' was published as A prefatory prologue, by way of introduction, to one spoken by Mr. Betterton at Oxford, on Monday the 5th of July. Spoken by Mr. Mills at the Theatre-Royal in Drury-Lane, on Friday the 16th of July, 1703. (n.p., n.d.).

1672 ADDERLEY, Hon. JAMES GRANVILLE. The fight for the drama at Oxford Some plain facts narrated by the Hon. and Rev. J. G. Adderley with a preface by W. L. Courtney, M.A.

pp. [i–ix] x–xiv, [1] 2–35 [36] L

Oxford: B. H. Blackwell; London: Simpkin, Marshall, and Co. 1888

Dedicated to the O.U.D.S. Originally an address delivered before members of the Church and Stage Guild.

Portsmouth

See INDEX OF PLACES OF PUBLICATION; also BIOGRAPHY no. 3624.

Ramsgate

See GOVERNMENT REGULATION OF THE THEATRE for the year 1826 (p. 31 above).

Richmond (Surrey)

See also INDEX OF PLACES OF PUBLICATION; also THE MORALITY OF THE THEATRE no. 422.

1673 DON BUSKINSOCKO, pseud. The squabble of the Richmond players: a pleasant, melancholy, occasional, egotic, poetic doggrel narrative. Including some choice hints, and curious theatrical remarks. With a criticism, on a remarkable Twickenham play-bill. Inscrib'd to the gentry of Richmond and Twickenham, &c.

pp. [i–ii] iii–vii [viii] 9–38 [39–40 (advt.)] MB

Printed for the author, Don Buskinsocko, member of the company [17–?]

1674 [WALDRON, FRANCIS GODOLPHIN.] TO THE NOBILITY, gentry, and others, inhabitants of Richmond, and the adjacent villas and villages.

pp. [1–2] 3–8 MB

[Richmond] [September 2, 1776]

Signed Francis Waldron. An appeal for subscriptions to help him purchase the Richmond Theatre.

1675 BINGHAM, FREDERICK. A celebrated old playhouse. The history of Richmond Theatre (in Surrey), from 1765 to 1884. By Frederick Bingham.

pp. [1–9] 10–42; illus., incl. [front.]

London: Henry Vickers; Richmond-on-Thames: R. W. Simpson and Storey, printers 1886

GS.

1676 ★THE THEATRES of Richmond, 1719–1899.

pp. 21; illus.; headed: Theatre Royal and Opera House, Richmond Souvenir. Monday, September 18th, 1899.

RdP

Richmond [1899]

Rochdale

1677 MEMORANDUM AND ARTICLES OF ASSOCIATION of the Rochdale Theatre Company, Limited, incorporated under the Act 1862. Table A.

pp. [1–5] 6–26 ReP

Rochdale [1866]

Salisbury

See also INDEX OF PLACES OF PUBLICATIONS.

1678 *AN EPISTLE to the author of Candour. By the author of The Prospect of Liberty, The Country Spy. etc.

[London]: T. Davies and Salisbury: E. Easton   1768

STR. *In verse.*

1679 PERSON OF FORTUNE, A, *pseud.* *Occasional remarks on the Salisbury comedians.

Salisbury   [*ca.* 1768]

STR. *Headed: Remarks on Mr. Johnson's company.*

1680 PERSON OF NO QUALITY, A, *pseud.* *An enquiry into the real merits of the Salisbury company of comedians.

pp. viii, 41   DFo
Salisbury   [*ca.* 1768]

1681 BROWNSMITH, J. The contrast; or, new mode of management. Being a peep behind the curtain of the Salisbury theatre, in 1776: wherein the requisites to form a brace of managers — their plain dealing, artless innocence, and public gratitude — are all nicely weigh'd, duly consider'd, and justly display'd. To which are added, (by way of supplement) a few spontaneous fragments, pick'd up at the foot of Parnassus. By J. Brownsmith, late nominal prompter to the said theatre.

pp. [2] [1] 2–33 [34]   MH
Salisbury: printed by J. Hodson   1776

1682 *THE RIVALS: or Green room controversy.

Salisbury   1776
STR.

Sheffield

See also INDEX OF PLACES OF PUBLICATION; also THE THEATRE OUT OF LONDON no. 1686.

1683 MEMBER OF THE CLUB, A, *pseud.* Proceedings of the Sheffield Shakespeare Club from its commencement, in 1819, to January, 1829. By a member of the Club.

pp. [2] [i–v] vi–xii, [1] 2–163 [164 (bl.)]; pl. [front., engr.]
     L
Sheffield: printed for the Editor by H. and G. Crookes
     1829

250 copies only.

Shrewsbury

See also INDEX OF PLACES OF PUBLICATION; also BIOGRAPHY no. 3531 (Mrs. Siddons).

1684 *A LETTER FROM A PLAYER to Sir Richard Hill.

     1766

See no. 1685.

1685 HILL, *Sir* RICHARD. A letter from Richard Hill, Esq; to his friend near Shrewsbury, containing some remarks on a letter signed "A Player". Which letter is also prefixed.

pp. [1–3] 4–30   L
Shrewsbury: printed by J. Eddowes and sold for the benefit of the prisoners in Shrewsbury goal [*sic*]   1767

> *The letter by a Player accuses Hill, who was a magistrate, of grievously oppressing some poor strolling actors. Hill's reply is pretty much the usual cant — Lowe. The player's letter, dated Newport, 3 December 1766, was "handed about the county", and appeared in "one of the evening papers".*

1686 RULES AND REGULATIONS to be observed by the members of the theatres Shrewsbury, Chester and Sheffield.

bs.   MH
Printed by J. France, Shrewsbury   [1830?]

Sleaford

See no. 1013.

South Molton

See no. 442.

Southampton

See INDEX OF PLACES OF PUBLICATION; also BIOGRAPHY no. 3274.

Southend

See below WORTHING no. 1702.

Southport

1687 THE SOUTHPORT Opera House and Winter Gardens, Ltd. Prospectus. Registered Office:– 41 Corporation Street, Manchester.

fold. doc.   SptP
"Guardian" Printing Works, Manchester   [1898]

Dated May 28, 1898.

Staffordshire

1688 PARODY ON THE UNFORTUNATE MISS BAILEY. An excellent comedian, in Staffordshire had played the part of Risk, in *Love laughs at the Locksmiths*, with much applause, but, a, [*sic*] week before his benefit, was arrested for a small sum, which the manager immediately defrayed, and set the Thespian at liberty. On his night, to a very crowded house, he sung the following curious parody on Miss Bailey, "which was loudly encored. — Vide Monthly Mirror for Feby. 1804, Page 133." [Song follows].

bs.; illus.   MH
Laurie & Whittle   1804

Stockton

See also INDEX OF PLACES OF PUBLICATION.

1689 [RITSON, JOSEPH.] *ST–CKT–N JUBILEE. Shakespeare in all his glory.

Newcastle 1781

PH and KB. See also below no. 1699.

Stourbridge

See above BATH no. 1551 note.

Stratford-upon-Avon

See also INDEX OF PLACES OF PUBLICATION; also SALE CATALOGUES no. 65; BIOGRAPHY nos. 2885–2896 (Garrick and the Shakespeare Jubilee), nos. 3412–3413 (Phelps).

1690 AT A GENERAL MEETING of the inhabitants of the town and neighbourhood of Stratford-upon-Avon, held at the Town Hall, this 19th day of December, 1820, agreeably to the suggestion of Mr. Mathews the preceding evening, to consider the best mode of erecting, in the form of a theatre, a national monument to the immortal memory of Shakspeare: Captain Sanders in the Chair. . . .

pp. [1] 2–3 [4] MB
Ward, printer, Stratford [1820]

1691 A DESCRIPTIVE ACCOUNT of the late Gala festival, at Stratford-upon-Avon, in commemoration of the natal day of Shakespeare; the King's adopted birth-day, and the Festival of St. George, on the 23rd, 24th, & 25th days of April, 1827. Transcribed from the notes of a gentleman connected with the Newspaper press.

pp. [1–5] 6–59 [60 (bl.)] L
Stratford-on-Avon: R. Lapworth 1827

1692 AN ACCOUNT of the second Commemoration of Shakspeare, celebrated at Stratford-upon-Avon, on Friday, the 23d of April, 1830, and three subsequent days: including full particulars of the various festivities given on that occasion, in honor of the anniversary of the natal day of the poet, and the adopted birth-day of the august patron of the Club — His Majesty George the Fourth. Dedicated to the members of the Royal Shakspearean Club.

pp. [1–3] 4–62; illus. DFo
Leamington: printed at the Courier office, by J. Sharp; and sold by James Ward, Stratford-on-Avon [1830]

1693 [FLOWER, CHARLES EDWARD.] *A HISTORY of the Shakespeare Memorial, Stratford-on-Avon.

pp. 80; illus.

[1878]

Loewenberg.

1694 ——*second edition, abridged and revised.

pp. 40; illus.

1882

Loewenberg.

1695 MARSTON, Dr. [JOHN] WESTLAND. Address by Dr. Westland Marston on the inauguration of the Shakespeare memorial theatre at Stratford-upon-Avon, April 23rd, 1879. Delivered by Miss Kate Field.

pp. [1] 2–8; title on cover. DFo
Bradbury, Agnew and Co, printers [1879]

Heroic couplets.

1696 [HUTCHINGS, WILLIAM.] THE SHAKESPEARE MEMORIAL BUILDINGS, Stratford-Upon-Avon. A complete record of the festival connected with the inauguration of the theatre portion of the Shakespeare memorial buildings, from April 23rd to May 3rd, 1879. Reprinted from the "Stratford-Upon-Avon Herald."

pp. [1] 2–39 [40 (bl.)]; title on cover DFo
Stratford-Upon-Avon: Herald Office [1879]

1697 SHAKESPEARE MEMORIAL THEATRE, library, & picture gallery. Fourth ordinary meeting of governors, to be held at the Town Hall, Stratford-on-Avon, on Wednesday, the 23rd day of April, 1879, at eleven o'clock in the morning.

pp. [2] DFo
[Stratford-upon-Avon] [1879]

1698 HUTCHINGS W[ILLIAM]. Past dramatic performances in Stratford-upon-Avon. A paper read before the members of the Shakspere Club at Stratford-upon-Avon, by W. Hutchings, on Thursday, December 6th, 1894.

pp. [1–3] 4–24 L
Stratford-upon-Avon: George Boyden 1895

Strawberry Hill

See THE AMATEUR THEATRE nos. 2154–2155.

Sunderland

See also INDEX OF PLACES OF PUBLICATION; also GOVERNMENT REGULATION OF THE THEATRE for the year 1883 (p. 34 above).

1699 CAWDELL, J[AMES]. The miscellaneous poems of J. Cawdell, comedian: consisting of a variety of serious and comic prologues, epilogues, pastorals, songs, descriptions, and epigrams. Together with several sentimental pieces. To which is annexed An answer to a late libellous compilation, called The Stockton jubilee.

pp. [1–5] 6–194; pl., fold. [front.]   L

Sunderland: printed for the author, by James Graham
1785

According to Loewenberg, *the actor shown in the frontispiece is Cawdell, and the stage is that of the Sunderland theatre. For the Stockton Jubilee see no. 1689.*

Twickenham

See above RICHMOND no. 1673.

Wakefield

See also INDEX OF PLACES OF PUBLICATION.

1700 SENIOR, WILLIAM. The old Wakefield theatre by William Senior.

pp. [8] 1–151 [152]; pl. [front.]   L

Wakefield: printed at the Radcliffe Press by W. H. Milnes   1894

Wargrave

See BIOGRAPHY nos. 2420–2424 (Earl of Barrymore).

Warwick

1701 FOUR THEATRICAL ADDRESSES: upon the providential preservation of His Majesty's life, at Drury-Lane Theatre. Upon the preliminaries of peace. Upon the opening of the new theatre at Warwick. And a farewell epilogue.

pp. [2] [1–5] 6–31 [32]   L

Dwyer   [1803?]

Windsor

See GENERAL HISTORY nos. 851–853, 929.

Witney

See THE MORALITY OF THE THEATRE no. 281.

Wooton-under-Edge

See THE MORALITY OF THE THEATRE no. 437.

Worthing

1702 PARTICULARS of the Worthing, Southend, Hythe, and Gravesend theatres; which will be sold by auction, by Messrs. Robins at their rooms, on Monday, the 1st of May, 1826. . . .

fold. doc., pp. [1–2] 3 [4]; filing-title   MH

[Printed by W. Smith and Co.]   [1826]

York

See also INDEX OF PLACES OF PUBLICATION; also GOVERNMENT REGULATION OF THE THEATRE for the year 1769 (p. 26 above).

1703 CROFT, JOHN. Memoirs of Harry Rowe: constructed from materials found in an old box, after his decease.

pp. [1–5] 6–144; pl. [front.]

York: Wilson and Spence   [1800?]

GS. *See also below no. 1708. Rowe was a puppet showman.*

1704 BURTON, W[ILLIAM]. A pasquinade, on the performances of the York company. By W. Burton, comedian.

pp. [1–5] 6–24   L

Leeds: printed by Edward Baines for the author   1801

1705 WILSON, GEORGE. The retort courteous; with the addition of a few rhapsodical miscellanies. By George Wilson.

pp. [1–3] 4–24   L

Leeds: printed by J. H. Leach for the Author   1801

A reply to Burton's A pasquinade (1801) *"in which I am lugg'd in by the ears".*

1706 THEATRICAL FUND, instituted at the Theatre-Royal, in York, July the 22nd, 1815.

pp. [1–3] 4–13 [14 (bl.) 15 ("Names of subscribers.") 16 (bl.)]

Hull: Myrton Hamilton   [1815]

SR.

1707 BENSON, GEORGE. *York Theatre. A brief biographical sketch of the drama in York, the Theatre Royal, its history and associations.

pp. 24   YP

York: W. Pickwell   1885

1708 CAMIDGE, WILLIAM. *The life and character of Harry Rowe: trumpet major and High Sheriff's trumpeter for the county of York.

pp. 19   YP

York   1894

See also above no. 1703. Printed in Burdekin's Old Moore's Almanac.

Yorkshire

See no. 3636.

IRELAND

GENERAL

See also GENERAL HISTORY nos. 835–6.

1709 HITCHCOCK, ROBERT. An historical view of the Irish stage; from the earliest period down to the close of the season 1788 interspersed with theatrical anecdotes, and an occasional review of the Irish dramatic authors and actors. In two volumes. By Robert Hitchcock, prompter of the Theatre-Royal, Dublin.

2 vols. pp. [*32*] [1] 2–315 [316] + [*16*] [1] 2–263 [264]; t.p. omits "prompter" L

Dublin: printed by R. Marchbank (vol. I) and William Folds (vol. II) 1788 (vol. I) 1794 (vol. II)

In the preface to the second volume the author explains that he has decided to end his history at 1774.

1710 WALKER, JOSEPH C[OOPER]. An historical essay on the Irish stage. By Joseph C. Walker, Esq. Member of the Royal Irish Academy; Fellow of the Literary and Antiquarian Society of Perth; and Honorary Member of the Etruscan Academy of Cortona.

pp. [1–3] 4–18; vignette on p. 18 DFo

Dublin: George Bonham 1789

First printed in the Transactions of the Royal Irish Academy, *vol. ii, 1788. Stops at 1690.*

⌘ An answer to the Memoirs of Mrs. Billington. With the life and adventures of Richard Daly, Esq. and an account of the present state of the Irish theatre. 1792. *See no. 2497.*

1711 *†AN ESSAY on the welfare of the Irish Stage. Dublin, 30 June 1792.

DN

[Dublin: W. Slater] 1792

This copy lacks title-page.

⌘ [Moore, Thomas?]. The private theatre of Kilkenny, with introductory observations on other private theatres in Ireland, before it was opened. 1825. *See no. 2160.*

⌘ O'Keeffe, John. Recollections of the life of John O'Keeffe. 1826. *See no. 3373.*

1712 HERBERT, J. D., *pseud. of* James Dowling. Irish varieties, for the last fifty years: written from recollections, by J. D. Herbert. Consisting of sketches of character, customs, manners, occurrences, events, professions, establishments, the stage, the bar, the pulpit; and a plan for relieving the Irish peasantry. The first series.

pp. [i–vii] viii–xii, [1] 2–310 L

William Joy 1836

Dedicated to James Sheridan Knowles.

1713 McGEE, T. B. *Irish writers and actors.

[Dublin?]: Duffey 1848

STR.

⌘ The life of Mrs. Abington (formerly Miss Barton) . . . including also interesting notes upon the history of the Irish stage. 1888. *See no. 2369.*

1714 MOLLOY, J[OSEPH] FITZGERALD. The romance of the Irish stage with pictures of the Irish capital in the eighteenth century. By J. Fitzgerald Molloy.

2 vols. pp. [i–iv] v–xi [xii], 1–250 [251–252]; pl. [front.] + pp. [i–iv] v–vii [viii], 1–255 [256]; pl. [front.] L

Downey & Co. Ltd. 1897

1714.1 ——second edition

2 vols. pp. [i–iv] v–xi [xii], 1–250 [251 (text) 252 (imprint)]; pl. [front.] + pp. [i–iv] v–vii [viii], 1–255 [256]; pl. [front.] LGk

Downey & Co. 1897

——[American edition] New York: Dodd, Mead & Co., 1897.

1715 WOLFE, FRANCIS R. *Theatres in Ireland.

pp. 23

Dublin: Amateur Dramatic Defence Association 1898

Loewenberg.

1716 ——*second edition

pp. 37 DN

Dublin: Amateur Dramatic Defence Association 1898

INDIVIDUAL TOWNS

See also PERIODICALS: IRELAND nos. 4419–4440. Consult also the INDEX OF PLACES OF PUBLICATION for towns not listed below.

Cork

See also INDEX OF PLACES OF PUBLICATION.

1717 NORMAN, *Mr.* To the public. Theatre-Royal, Cork. 2nd, April, 1829, Mr Norman (late of the Theatres-Royal Covent-Garden and Dublin,) begs leave . . .

bs.   L

Cork: J. Connor, printer   1829

> *Soliciting support for a subscription ball, Norman being stranded in Cork after a disagreement with Alfred Bunn.*

1718 FLYNN, J. W. The random recollections of an old playgoer. A sketch of some old Cork theatres.

pp. [1–5] 6–55 [56]   DN

Cork: Guy & Co., Ltd.   1890

Dublin

See also INDEX OF PLACES OF PUBLICATION; also GENERAL HISTORY especially nos. 839–840.

1719 POOR POET, A, *pseud.* ★The humble petition of a poor poet to the players of Dublin.

bs.

[Dublin]   [1726–27]

> *Refers to Charles Shadwell, who had died on 12 Aug. 1726; the author proposes to succeed him as poet to the Dublin theatre — Loewenberg.*

1720 PERSON OF HONOUR, A, *pseud.* An excellent new ballad inscrib'd to the Irish Polly Peachum, on her benefit of *The Beggar's Opera:* given, at the general desire of the nobility and gentry of Dublin, April, XI. MD, CC, XXVIII. By a person of honour. Tune. Pretty Polly say, &c.

bs.   L

Dublin: printed by Rich. Dickson   1728

> *Schultz (p. 41) suggests this refers to Mrs Barbier.*

1721 ★AN EPISTLE to Mr. Thomas Elrington, occasioned by the murder of the tragedy of *Cato* last Monday night.

ff. [4]

[Dublin]   1730

> *Thorn-Drury. Thomas Elrington managed Smock Alley from 1720 until 1732.*

1722 ★THE UPPER GALLERY, a poem, inscribed to the Revd. Dr. Swift, D.S.P.D.

pp. 8

Dublin   1733

> Loewenberg.

Sheridan and Cibber Dispute 1743

A quarrel between T. Sheridan and Theo. Cibber, who were acting together in Dublin. The former wanted a particular robe for Cato, and as he could not get it, would not play. Cibber then read Cato, and acted his own part, Syphax. A vehement paper war ensued — Lowe. See also Sheldon, pp. 40–47, and bibliography.

1723 ★ANCIENT PISTOL. A letter from Ancient Pistol, to Young Pistol, who acted that part on Monday the 15th of August, 1747, at the Theatre in S——k-A——y, being an epistle from the dead to the living.

pp. 8

Dublin   1743

> *Thorn-Drury. Cibber and Sheridan (no. 1725 below) reprints a work of this title, pp. 52–55.*

1724 AN ANSWER to the young lady; or, a letter from Mrs. Slammekin to Miss Tabitha Tammy, the suppos'd authoress of A letter from a young lady to Mr. Cibber.

pp. [1–3] 4–16   DFo

Dublin   1743

1725 CIBBER AND SHERIDAN: or, the Dublin miscellany. Containing all the advertisements, letters, addresses, replys, apologys, verses, &c, &c, &c. lately publish'd, on account of the theatric squabble. To which are added, several prologues and epilogues, spoke at the theatre in Smock-Alley, this summer, by Mr. Cibber, some of which were never before printed. Also, two songs by Mr. Worsdale, one call'd "An act of grace, the poet's release", the other, on the routing of the French forces at Dettingen, &c.

pp. [1–3] 4–79 [80 (bl.)]   L

Dublin: Peter Wilson   1743

1726 ——[another edition] The buskin and sock; being controversial letters between Mr. Thomas Sheridan, tragedian, and Mr. Theophilus Cibber, comedian; just published in Dublin.

pp. [2] 1–40 ²33–56 [=64]   L

Dublin printed; London reprinted for Jacob Robinson
                                                            1743

> *Copy at E has: pp. [2] 1–40 ²33–40 49–64 [=64]. Reprints less of the literature of the dispute than does the Dublin edition, no. 1725.*

1727 CIBBER, THEOPHILUS. An epistle from Mr. Theophilus Cibber, comedian, to Mr. Thomas Sheridan, tragedian.

pp. [1-3] 4-14 [15-16 (bl.)]   DFo
Dublin   [1743]

> Dated 19 July 1743. Signed T.C. Reprinted in Cibber and Sheridan (see above no. 1725) pp. 11-17, and The buskin and sock (above no. 1726) pp. 9-23. Cibber and Sheridan also contains, pp. 17-19 "a postscript added to a new edition of the foregoing epistle".

1728 *A PROPER REPLY to a late scurrillous libel entitled, Mr. Sheridan's address to the town.

Dublin   1743

> Loewenberg. Dated July 27 1743. Reprinted in The buskin and sock pp. 40-56 (see above no. 1726) and Cibber and Sheridan, pp. 36-51, where it is signed "T.C.", (above, no. 1725).

1729 SHERIDAN [THOMAS]. *Mr. Sheridan the tragedian's answer to Mr. Cibber the comedian's epistle.

pp. 8
Dublin   1743

> Thorn-Drury.

1730 SHERIDAN, [THOMAS]. *Mr. Sheridan's address to the town.

pp. 16
Dublin: printed by Martineau and Kinneir   1743

> Loewenberg. Reprinted in Cibber and Sheridan (see above no. 1725) pp. 26-35.

1731 YOUNG LADY, A, pseud. *A letter from a young lady to Mr. Cibber.

pp. 16
Dublin: printed by Martineau and Kinneir   1743

> "It is suggested in a MS note in the volume of tracts containing the copy of this that I examined that it is by Mrs. Chamberlaine whom Sheridan married in 1748" — Thorn-Drury. Cibber and Sheridan (no. 1725 above) reprints a work of this title, pp. 56-61.

1732 *A POEM on Mr. Sheridan and Mr. Barry.
                                                    DA
Dublin   1746

> Loewenberg.

1733 SCH——R, A. *An apology for Mr. Sheridan. By a Sch——r.
Dublin   1746-47

> Loewenberg.

Kelly's Riot 1747

On 19th January 1747, when "Æsop" was being played, a fellow named Kelly, a gentleman, went into the pit of the Smock Alley Theatre, drunk. He climbed on the stage, and going into the green room, grossly insulted Mrs. Dyer, an actress. Sheridan had him turned out; and Kelly, going back to the pit threw oranges at Sheridan, with one of which he struck him on the face. After the play, Kelly found his way on the stage, and abused Sheridan, who gave him a well-deserved thrashing, which Kelly took like a lamb. Kelly and his friends caused several riots in the theatre on subsequent evenings, in one of which they insulted a Trinity College student. The students, who were great supporters of their former comrade, Sheridan, effectually resented this insult to their body. They captured the leading rioters, carried them to the college, and forced them to kneel and abjectly apologise. Kelly was tried before the Lord Chief Justice, sentenced to three months' imprisonment, and fined £500. After being confined for a week, he begged Sheridan's mercy, and, by the latter's intercession, the fine was remitted and Kelly released. From this time no one was allowed behind the scenes of the theatre. — Lowe. See also Sheldon, pp. 76-107, and bibliography.

1734 *DUBLIN in an uproar; or, the ladies robb'd of their pleasure. Being a full and impartial relation of the remarkable tumult that lately happen'd at the Dublin Theatre. With the genuine letters that pass'd on both sides.

pp. (iv), 22
Dublin   [1747]

> Loewenberg. Dated 16 February.

1735 ——[another edition]
pp. [2] [1] 2-21 [22]   L
Dublin, printed; London: reprinted; and sold by Charles Corbett   [1747]

1736 [SHERIDAN, THOMAS.] A FAITHFUL NARRATIVE of what happen'd at the theatre on Monday the 19th instant, which gave rise to the following disturbance there, with some observations upon it, humbly submitted to the consideration of the publick.

pp. [1-2] 3-14   MH
[Dublin]: printed and sold by Ebenezer Rider   1747

1737 FREEMAN, A pseud. of Charles Lucas? A letter to the free-citizens of Dublin. By a freeman, barber and citizen.

pp. [1] 2-4; head-title   L
[Dublin]   [1747]

> Signed A. [sic] Freeman, barber. See also no. 1744 below.

1738 ——*The fourth edition, with alterations and amendments.
pp. 8; head-title   DN
[Dublin]   [12 Feb 1746/7]

1739 [SHERIDAN, THOMAS.] A FULL VINDICA-
TION of the conduct of the manager of the Theatre-
Royal. Written by himself.

pp. [1–3] 4–19 [20]   L
Dublin: printed by S. Powell   1747

> *Dated March 4, 1746–7.*

1740 *THE GENTLEMEN. An heroic poem.

pp. 23   DP
Dublin   1747

> Loewenberg.

1741 *THE GENTLEMEN'S APOLOGY to the
ladies for their being disappointed at the playhouse on
Wednesday, the 11th of February, 1746–7.

Dublin   1747

> Loewenberg.

1742 PLEBEIAN, A, *pseud.* *An humble address to
the ladies of the city of Dublin by a plebeian.

pp. 20   DA
Dublin   1747

> *Signed "Plebeius".*

1743 *REFLECTIONS of a gentleman in the country
on the present theatrical disturbances, in a letter to the
printer of the "Dublin Courant".

single sheet.

[Dublin]   [1747]

> Loewenberg. Sheldon: *"incomplete".*

1744 A. F. BARBER AND CITIZEN, *pseud.* of
Charles Lucas? *A second letter to the free-citizens of
Dublin. By A. F. barber and citizen.

pp. 20   DA
[Dublin]   [1747]

> Sheldon. *See also no. 1737.*

1745 [BROWN, JOHN?] *A SERIOUS ENQUIRY
into the causes of the present disorders in the city,
humbly offered to the consideration of the inhabitants.
No. 1.

pp. 16   DA
Dublin   1747

> *See* Sheldon, *pp. 99–100.* Loewenberg.

1746 SHERIDAN, [THOMAS]. *A state of Mr.
Sheridan's case, humbly submitted to the consideration
of the public.

single sheet.

Dublin   1747

Sheldon: *copy in Marsh's Library, Dublin. Loewenberg's* A statement of Mr. Sheridan's case (1747) *is
probably an incorrect description of the same work.*

1747 PUNCH'S PETITION to Mr. S——n, to be
admitted into the Theatre Royal.

bs.   L
Dublin: printed for the author   [1747 or 1748]

> *Signed "Punchinello".*

1748 A LETTER to the admirers of Mr. S——n.

pp. [2]; head-title   L
[Dublin]   [1748]

1749 [WILSON, JOHN.] THE CASE of a master
clothier in the Liberty. Relative to what happened at
the theatre in Smock-Alley, last Monday sevennight.

bs.   L
[Dublin]   [5 Jan. 1750?]

1750 FITZ-HENERY, *The Rev., pseud.* A full and true
account of the woefull and wonderfull apparition of
Hurloe Harrington, late prompter to the Theatre-Royal
in Dublin: who, by the instigation of some evil spirits,
threw himself down a considerable precipice, by which
great violent and sudden fall, he first destroyed his
intellectuals, and soon after departed this mortal life,
to the great grief of His Majesty's company of com-
medians of Ireland, as well, male as female. In a letter
from the reverend parson Fitz-Henery to His G——e
the A. B. of C——y.

pp. [1–3] 4–32   L
R. Watkins   1750

Dispute between Mosse and Sheridan 1750

1751 [SHERIDAN, THOMAS.] A STATE of the case
in regard to the point in dispute between Mr. Mosse and
Mr. Sheridan.

pp. [1–2] 3–26, [1] ii–xix [xx]   L
Dublin   1750

> *One Mr. Mosse managed entertainments at the New
> Garden in Great Britain Street, Dublin. He engaged
> the orchestra of the theatre to perform at these, but owing
> to some misunderstanding they failed to appear. A very
> abusive series of advertisements and manifestos followed.
> The above gives a full account of the transaction from
> Sheridan's point of view, while the following pamphlet
> [no. 1753 below] abuses the manager violently—Lowe.*

1752 ——the second edition

pp. [1–2] 3–26, [i] ii–xix [xx (bl.)]   L
Dublin   1750

> *A reissue of the first edition.*

1753 THE MAN of honour; but not of his word. Inscribed to Mr. Sheridan.

pp. [1–2] 3–16   L

Dublin   1750

L copy cut down; full title given by Thorn-Drury.

1754 B——N, B——T. *The stage, or Coronation of King Tom, a satyr by B——t B——n.

pp. 16   DP

Dublin: printed for the Author   1753

Loewenberg.

1755 ——*[another edition] Tom's Stage, a satyr.

pp. 16   DP

Dublin   1758

Loewenberg.

The "Mahomet" Affair 1754

Sheridan was unpopular with a certain party because of his "Castle" proclivities; and a revolutionary speech in "Mahomet" having been forbidden by him to be spoken twice, when demanded by the Anti-Court party, disturbances ensued, which drove him from Ireland — Lowe. See Genest X 381–391, and Sheldon, pp. 195–214, and bibliography.

1756 *A GRAND DEBATE betwen [*sic*] court and country. At the Theatre-Royal in Smock Alley. Lately in a letter to the C——t party, with Mr Sh——n's Apology to the C——ry party.

pp. 8   DN

[Dublin]   [1754]

1757 L——H——N, THOMAS. *A friendly letter from Thomas L——H——N, gent. to Thomas S——d——n.

pp. 16

Dublin   1754

Thorn-Drury.

1758 MR. SH——N'S APOLOGY to the town; with the reasons which unfortunately induced him to his late misconduct. Written by himself. And publish'd by his very good friend H——y S——r.

pp. [1–2] 3–8   L

Dublin   2754 [i.e. 1754]

1759 *THE PLAYHOUSE prorogued, or, a vindication of the conduct of the manager addressed to the town.

           D

Dublin   1754

1760 REMARKS on two letters signed "Theatricus" and "Hibernicus", and published in the Dublin Journal of the 12th and 23rd of February, 1754.

pp. [1–3] 4–15 [16 (bl.)]   L

Dublin   1754

The letters were in support of Sheridan in the disturbance over Mahomet — Lowe. *The Remarks are signed "Libertas"; he reprints the two letters and says they were attributed to Sheridan himself.*

1761 *RULES OF ACCOMMODATION as drawn up by a select committee of gentlemen, appointed for that purpose, in order to establish a right understanding between the town and the manager of Smock-Alley Theatre. Humbly submitted to the consideration of the public. To which is annex'd a number of new toasts, to be drank by the reconcilers at their next meeting at the Phoenix Tavern.

pp. 8   D

Dublin   1754

Thorn-Drury; Sheldon.

1762 *THE SIGHS and groans of Mr. Sh——n, with a full and comical farce that was acted last Saturday night at the Theatre in Smock Alley, and the occasion thereof. Also, an account of the manager's rude behaviour to the audience at the play of Mahomet.

           C

Dublin   1754

1763 [SHERIDAN, THOMAS.] A VINDICATION of the conduct of the late manager of the Theatre-Royal humbly address'd to the publick.

pp. [1–3] 4–23 [24 (bl.)]   L

Dublin   1754

Reprinted in Sheridan's An humble appeal, 1758 (no. 1778 below).

1764 ——The third edition.

pp. [1–3] 4–23 [24 (bl.)]   MH

Dublin   1754

1765 A LETTER to Messieurs Victor and Sowdon, managers of the Theatre-Royal.

pp. [1–3] 4–15 [16 (bl.)]   L

Dublin   1755

A general criticism. It specially alludes, however, to the production of Mahomet, *which caused so much party feeling—Lowe.*

Sheridan's dispute with Lee

See also Sheldon, pp. 215–254, and bibliography.

1766 [LEE, JOHN.] A LETTER from Mr. Lee to Mr. Sheridan.

pp. [4] [1] 2–18 [19–20 (bl.)]   MH
Dublin   1757

1767 ———[another edition]

pp. [1–2] 3–18   MH
Dublin   1757

The title-page of this edition continues with "A public acknowledgement . . .", matter which appears on a separate leaf following the title-page in no. 1766.
A series of letters, dated 12 Aug. 1756 to 4 June 1757. Complaint of ill-treatment, by Lee, who was engaged by Sheridan as a "star" at a salary of £400 for the season 1756–57. Lee declares that Sheridan treated him badly both pecuniarily and artistically — Lowe.

1768 *A LETTER from Tom the First, King of Ireland, to John the Second, King of Scotland. With the King of Scotland's answer thereto.

     DA
Dublin   1757

1769 *REMARKS on Mr. Lee's letter to Mr. Sheridan.
pp. 8   DA
[Dublin]   1757

Sheridan's dispute with Spranger Barry

See also Sheldon, pp. 215–254, and bibliography.

1770 AN ANSWER, in behalf of Spranger Barry, the proprietor of the new theatre in Crow-Street, to the "Case" and "Petition" of Thomas Sheridan, manager and lessee of the united theatres of Aungier-Street and Smock-Alley, and also to the "Petition" of two of the proprietors of said united theatres; humbly submitted to the consideration of the honourable the knights, citizens and burgesses in Parliament assembled.

pp. [1] 2–4   L
[Dublin]   [1758]

1771 *The CASE of the stage in Ireland; containing the reasons for and against a Bill for limiting the number of theatres in the City of Dublin; wherein the qualifications, duty, and importance of a Manager are carefully considered and explained, and the conduct and abilities of Mr. Sheridan, the present manager of the Theatre in Smock-Alley, are particularly reviewed and examined. The whole occasionally interspersed with critical observations on Mr. Sheridan's oration. And a summary of the principal advantages that must necessarily accrue to the Kingdom of Ireland from an academy, connected with the theatre.

pp. 51   NNC(?)
Dublin   [1757 or 1758]

Loewenberg. Lowe *gives a title with some differences ("this kingdom" instead of "the Kingdom of Ireland," etc.), and gives also an imprint date, 1758, and is probably describing a different Dublin edition.*

1772 ———[another edition]

pp. [1–3] 4–48   L
Dublin: printed; London: reprinted, for J. Coote [1758]

In support of Sheridan against Barry — Lowe.

1773 *THE CURTAIN LECTURE: or, the manager run mad. A dialogue between a stage-director and his wife.

pp. 8   DFo
J. Howel   1758

In verse.

1774 A FULL VINDICATION of Thomas Sheridan, Esq. Being an answer to a scurrilous pamphlet, intitled The case of the stage.

pp. [1–3] 4–23 [24]   DN
Dublin   1758

Signed P. Shea.

1775 PUNCH, THOMAS, *pseud.* To the honourable k*****s, c******s and b*******s in P*********t assembled. The humble petition of Thomas Punch, Esq; principal performer and sole manager of the still-life-Theatre in Caple-Street.

pp. [1] 2   L
[Dublin]: [printed at the Caple-Street Theatre printing office]   [1758]

A satire on Sheridan's petition — Loewenberg.

1776 PUTLAND, JOHN. To the honourable the knights, citizens and burgesses, in Parliament assembled: the humble petition of John Putland, Esquire, and Captain Theophilus Desbrisay, in behalf of themselves and the other proprietors of the united theatres of Aungier-Street and Smock-Alley, in the city of Dublin.

pp. [1] 2   L
[Dublin]   [1758]

Incomplete copy? Page 2 has catchword.

1777 SHERIDAN, THOMAS. The case of Thomas Sheridan, lessee and manager of the united theatres of Aungier-Street and Smock-Ally.

pp. [2]   L
[Dublin]   [1757 or 1758]

Contains also "A proposal for saving the stage in Dublin", which is reprinted in Sheridan's An humble appeal . . . (1758), pp. 86–92 (see below no. 1778).

1778 SHERIDAN, THOMAS. An humble appeal to the publick, together with some considerations on the present critical and dangerous state of the stage in Ireland. By Thomas Sheridan, deputy Master of the Revels, and manager of the Theatre-Royal.

pp. [1–3] 4–91 [92 (bl.)], ²[1] 2–46 misnumbering 91 as "92"   L

Dublin: G. Faulkner   1758

An appeal against the threatened opposition by Barry, who was engaged in getting up a new theatre in Crow Street. In this pamphlet Sheridan gives an account of what he had done for the Dublin stage—Lowe. Thorn-Drury describes a copy with a final blank leaf, missing in this copy.

1779 ———*[another edition]   MB

Re-printed for W. Faden   1758

1780 ———*[another edition] An appeal to the public: containing an account of the rise, progress, and establishment of the first regular theatre in Dublin: with the causes of it's [sic] decline and ruin. By Thomas Sheridan, formerly manager of the Theatre-Royal. First published in the year 1758.
                                NN

Dublin   1771
Sheldon.

1780.1 ———*the sixth edition   NN
Dublin: printed by J. Hoey   1771
Sheldon.

1781 SHERIDAN, THOMAS. An humble address to the publick, from Mr. Sheridan, in consequence of his *Appeal.*

pp. [1] 2–3 [4 (bl.)]; head-title   L
[Dublin]   [1758]
Dated 6 May, 1758.

1782 [SHERIDAN, THOMAS.] TO THE HONOURABLE THE KNIGHTS, citizens, and burgesses, in Parliament assembled: the humble petition of Thomas Sheridan, manager and lessee of the united theatres of Aungier-Street and Smock-Alley; sheweth . . .

bs.   L
[Dublin]   [1758]

✖ Beauclerk, Mrs. D. J. Mrs. Beauclerk's letters to Mr. Sheridan and Mr. Victor. Dublin. 1758. *See no. 2429.*

A novice who accuses Sheridan of treating her badly.

1783 AN ESTIMATE of the theatrical merits of the two tragedians of Crow-Street. In a letter from a gentleman in Dublin, to his friend in London.

pp. [1–3] 4–23 [24 (bl.)]   L
Dublin   1760
A comparison of Barry and Mossop, strongly favouring the former — Lowe.

1784 [JAUNICE, CLAUDE.] *A GENUINE LETTER from a French officer, late prisoner of war in Ireland, to his friend at Plymouth. Describing the customs and manners of the inhabitants of Dublin, the theatres and performers there; the routs, drums, assemblies, and many other curious particularities, as were in season in the months of November and December, 1759.

pp. 44   DN
Dublin: Peter Wilson   1760
Author's name written on t.p. of this copy.

✖ Mr. Stayley's reference to the publick. Dublin. 1760. *See no. 3563.*

1785 [LEWIS, RICHARD?] *THE BATTLE of the players, exhibiting the characters of all the actors and actresses of the Irish stage.

Dublin   1762
Loewenberg.

1786 THE CASE of Mr. Anthony Minelli.
pp. [1] 2   L
[Dublin]   [1762]
On Minelli's losses due to the demands of Amicis. See also no. 1787.

1787 THE CASE of Mr. Dominick De Amicis.
bs.   L
[Dublin]   [1762]
See also no. 1786.

1788 GENTLEMAN OF TRINITY COLLEGE, A, *pseud.* *Crow Street in an uproar, or the battle of the buskin and sock, in imitation of Mr. Lewis's battle of the players. By a Gentleman of Trinity College.

pp. 20
Dublin   1762
Loewenberg.

1789 McLOUGHLIN, CHARLES [*i.e.* Charles Macklin?]. *Zanga's triumph; or, Harlequin and Othello at war. Being a full and impartial account of a certain theatrical partnership lately dissolved; with all its attendant circumstances. To which are added, five original advertisements, now collected together, for the use of those, who may chuse to keep them by them, or remit them as presents into the country. With a postscript, or the combatants reconciled. In a letter to a friend. By Charles McLoughlin, Esq.

pp. 16
Dublin   1762

Relates to the Dublin contest between Mossop (Zanga), Woodward (Harlequin), and Barry (Othello). In 1762 Woodward dissolved his partnership with Barry at Crow Street, and went to law with him. To this disagreement this pamphlet no doubt refers—Lowe. McLoughlin was Macklin's real name, but no other ground for ascription.

1790 ——*another edition

Dublin   1762

Loewenberg.

1791 SCRIVEN, PATRICK, *pseud.?* *A familiar dialogue between Mr. Crowe and Mr. Alley, two theatrical taylors. By Patrick Scriven, public notary, and teacher of shorthand in the Isle of Man.

pp. 16   MB

Dublin: printed by James Hunter   [1762]

Mr. "Crowe" and Mr. "Alley" are of course Crow Street and Smock Alley Theatres — Lowe.

1792 K***, S**** *The Hibernian Rosciad. By S**** K***.

pp. 16

Dublin   1765

Loewenberg.

1793 AN EPISTLE to Henry Mossop, Esq; on the institution and end of the drama, and the present state of the Irish stage. With some observations on Mr Sheridan's plan of education for the young nobility and gentry. The second edition.

pp. [34]   DFo

Dublin: J. Milliken   [ca. 1770]

Signed "S.W."

1794 *A FAMILIAR LETTER to Sam Foote.

Dublin: J. Milliken   [ca. 1770]

From a reference in no. 1793.

1795 AN APPEAL to the public, against Mr. Sheridan's intended scheme for a monopoly of the stage.

pp. [1–3] 4–27 [28]   DFo

Dublin: R. Moncrieffe   1772

1796 SHERIDAN, [THOMAS]. *Mr. Sheridan's speech addressed to a number of gentlemen, assembled with a view of considering the best means to establish one good theatre in this city.

pp. 24   NNC

Dublin: George Faulkner   1772

1797 [ARNE, MICHAEL.] MR. ARNE'S ADDRESS to the public.

pp. [1–3] 4–14

[Dublin]   [1776 or 1777]

*This pamphlet sets out the financial details of the Crow Street Theatre, Dublin, in answer to criticisms of mismanagement which had been made against Arne. It is probably to be dated late in 1776 or early in 1777, after Arne's arrival from England and before he was thrown into a Dublin sponging-house in the summer of 1777.
As his leading lady, Ann Catley, was paid £47/10/- a week, it is not surprising that he went bankrupt—IKF.*

1798 LEFANU, PETER. *Smock Alley secrets; or the manager worried. A prelude.

[Dublin]   [1780]

A ms. of this prelude which was produced at the Smock Alley Theatre, Dublin, on 1 Nov. 1780 is in the Houdini Collection, New York — Loewenberg.

✖ Lady of Distinction, A, *pseud.* *Observation of Mrs. Siddons. Dublin. 1784. See no. 3525.

Reissued as The beauties of Mrs. Siddons 1786 (see no. 3526). Describes her performances "when she last appeared in Ireland".

1799 THE AESOPIAD; a poem. Being a critique on the merits of the following performers, at the Theatre-Royal, Smock Alley. Viz: Mr. D—gg—s. Mr. W—ld—r. Mr. D—ly. Mr. F—tt—r—l. M. O'R—ly. Mr. Cl—ch. Mr. M—tch—l. Mr. G. D—ws—n. Mr. Gr—h—m. Mr. C—rn—lys. Mr. J—hn—n. Mr. K—m—ble. Mr. K—ne, and Mr. R—d—r.

pp. [1–2] 3–47 [48]   DFo

Dublin   1784–5

1800 CANDID REMARKS upon the stage-bill, now depending. Humbly addressed to the Rt. Hon. the Lord Mayor, sheriffs, commons, and citizens of Dublin.

pp. [1–5] 6–31 [32 (bl.)]   L

Dublin: printed and sold by R. Marchbank   1785

In favour of a city theatre, proposed by the Lord Mayor.

1801 THE MIRROR; a panegyrical, satirical, and Thespian epistle in rhyme. From the Theatre in Crow-Street, to the Theatre in Smock-Alley.

pp. [i–iii] iv, 1–31 [32]   DA

Dublin: printed by B. Dornin   1790

1802 THE TRIAL of John Magee, for printing and publishing a slanderous and defamatory libel, against Richard Daly, Esq. held before the Right Honourable Lord Viscount Clonmel, by a special jury of the city of Dublin. At the sittings by *nisi prius* of the Court of King's Bench. After Trinity term, viz. on Monday, June 28, 1790.

pp. [1] 2–68   DA

Dublin: printed and sold by P. Byrne   1790

1803 WHYTE, SAMUEL. The theatre: a didactic essay. Including an idea of the character of Jane Shore, as performed by a young lady in a private play, &c. &c. By Samuel Whyte.

pp. [iii–v] vi–xiv [xv–xvi], [1] 2–30 [31–36 (prologue, address, and verses)]   L

Dublin: John Jones   1790

Contains, besides the poem, casts and prologues of various plays performed at private theatres in Dublin, 1773–90; the young lady mentioned in the title is R. B. Sheridan's sister Alicia, later Mrs. Lefanu; some dated prologues, with casts and notes, were contained already in Whyte's earlier collection, The Shamrock, or Hibernian Cresses, *Dublin 1772 (pp. 53–5, 443–5, &c.) — Loewenberg.*

1804 ———A collection of poems, on various subjects, including The theatre, a didactic essay; in the course of which are pointed out, the rocks and shoals to which deluded adventurers are inevitably exposed. Ornamented with cuts, and illustrated with notes, original letters and curious incidental anecdotes. By Samuel Whyte. The second edition, carefully revised and conducted through the press, by Edward Athenry Whyte, F.C.T.C.D.

pp. [i–iii] iv–vii [viii], ²[i] ii–vii [viii (directions to the binder)], ³[iii] iv–x (list of subscribers), ⁴[ix] x–lvi [lvii–lviii], [1] 2–260 [261–262], ²[255–256] 257–343 [344] [=352]; pls. [front., 4 (incl. engr. t.p. for "The theatre", dated 1793, and a pl. opp. p. [255] not incl. in the binder's directions]; vignettes   L

Dublin: printed by Robert Marchbank   1792 [*for 1794*]

The "second edition" on the title-page refers to The theatre *(1790) (see above no. 1803). Contains also a large number of prologues, addresses, and other material relating to the Irish public and private theatres.*

1805 ———*the third edition, carefully revised. Poems on various subjects . . .

pp. viii, viii, iii–x, ix–xl, 365, xli–lxxx, [2]

Dublin   1795

Loewenberg.
Samuel Whyte's Miscellanea Nova, *New Edition (Dublin 1800) contains much material relevant to the stage in Dublin.*

1806 MACHUMBUG, LEONARD, *pseud. of* Leonard McNally? *Thespis to Apollo. An heroic epistle proving the declining state of the Irish stage, and the necessity of improving it. With critical notes and explanatory. By the ingenious Leonard MacHumbug, Esq.

pp. 16   MB

Dublin: printed by H. Colbert   1792

Loewenberg.

1807 *A SHORT VINDICATION of the Right Hon. and Hon. the Subscription Company of Comedians.

Dublin   1792

Loewenberg.

1808 A LETTER to the manager of the Theatre-Royal, Dublin.

pp. [1–3] 4–13 [14]   DA

Dublin   1794

Croker's "Familiar Epistles" 1804–1806

These celebrated Epistles . . . raised a tremendous storm in Dublin theatrical society, and were the cause of many pamphlets—Lowe.

1809 [CROKER, JOHN WILSON.] FAMILIAR EPISTLES TO FREDERICK J——S, Esq. on the present state of the Irish stage.

pp. [i–v] vi–xix [xx (bl.)], [1] 2–78 [79 (errata) 80 (bl.)] L

Dublin: John Barlow   1804

The dedication to Lord Hardwicke is initialled T.C.D., and the preface is dated January 10, 1804.

1810 ———second edition, with considerable additions.

pp. [i–v] vi–xxiii [xxiv] [25] 26–122   L

Dublin: John Barlow   1804

A last-minute paragraph is dated March 24, 1804.

1811 ———third edition, with considerable additions.

pp. [i–v] vi–xxiii [xxiv] [25] 26–122   L

Dublin: printed by M. N. Mahon, and sold in London by Messrs. Vernor and Hood   1805

A reissue of the second edition, with cancellans title-leaf.

1812 ———fourth edition, with considerable additions.

pp. [i–vii] viii–xxx [31] 32–84 97–178 [179 (errata) 180 (bl.)] [=168]   MH

Dublin: printed by Graisberry & Campbell   1805

The "Advertisement to the fourth edition" is initialled T.C.D., and dated Dec. 26 1804.

1813 ———fifth edition

pp. [i–v] vi–xxii [23] 24–110   L

Dublin: printed by Graisberry and Campbell   1806

1814 ———[another edition] The familiar epistles. Written by Wilson Croker, Esq. (Of Trinity College, and afterwards Secretary of the Admiralty.) These epistles were written in 1804, and addressed to Frederick Jones, Esq., patentee of the Dublin Theatre, on the inefficiency of the actors; and now, in these modern days, a contemporary, Walter Donaldson, Esq., presents them to the public, with remarks from personal knowledge.

pp. [1–4] 5–59 [60]   GM
London: Livermore & Robinson; Southampton: Gutch & Co; Portsmouth: Charpentier   [1875]

1815 AN ANSWER to *Familiar epistles to Frederick J——s, Esq. on the present state of the Irish stage.*

pp. [1–5] 6–24   L
Dublin: J. Parry   1804

Octosyllabics. Dedicated to Lady Hardwicke, and, at the end, signed "Frederick E. J——s", and dated March 17, 1804.

1816 ——second edition

pp. [1–5] 6–24   L
Dublin: J. Parry   1804

A reissue of the first edition.

1817 *CURSORY HINTS to young actors.

pp. 22
Dublin: M. M. Mahon   1804
  STR.

1818 ——CURSORY HINTS to young actors. Second edition.

pp. [1–7] 8–30 [31–32 (bl.)]   L
Dublin: printed by H. Fitzpatrick   1805

Heroic couplets, dedicated to Croker and laudatory of him. His opponents declared that he wrote it himself as a "puff" — Lowe.

1819 [OWENSON, SYDNEY, *afterwards Lady* Morgan.] A FEW REFLECTIONS occasioned by the perusal of a work, entitled, *Familiar epistles, to Frederick J——s Esq. on the present state of the Irish stage.*

pp. [i–iii] iv–vi [7] 8–77   L
Dublin: printed by J. Parry   1804

The dedication to Frederick Jones is initialled S.O., and the last page is dated March, 1804.

1820 JONES, FREDERICK EDWARD. *Thoughts on Familiar Epistles.

Dublin   1804
  Loewenberg.

1821 STUDENT OF T.C.D., A, *pseud.* Tea Table Conversation, an epistle to the author of *Familiar epistles.* By a student of T.C.D.

pp. [i–iii] iv [v–vi] [7] 8–51 [52 (bl.)]   LGk
Dublin: J. Parry   1804

The preface is dated June 25.

1822 [OWENSON, ROBERT NUGENT.] THEATRICAL TEARS, a poem, occasioned by *Familiar epistles to Frederick J——s, Esq.*

pp. [1–9] 10–47 [48 (bl.)]   L
Dublin: J. Parry   1804

Prefatory note signed R.N.O.

1823 *THE THESPIAD: a poem in answer to the author of six familiar epistles addressed to F. Jones, Esq., patentee of the Irish Theatre Royal, Dublin &c., on the present state of the Irish stage; in which the comparative merits of the London and Dublin players are depicted.

pp. [2?] 1–32   DA
Lacy   1804

Loewenberg. DA copy wants title-page.

1824 JACK IN A PASSION, or the critic criticised.

pp. [i–iii] iv–viii [9] 10–59 [60 (bl.)]   L
Dublin: printed by C. Lewis   1805

The dedication to "Jonathan Prattle", is signed "Dunce". A reply, in dramatic form, to Familiar epistles.

1825 *The AMAZONIAD; or, figure and fashion: a scuffle in high life. With notes critical and historical, interspersed with choice anecdotes of *bon ton.*

                                                      DN
Dublin   1806

Attributed to J. W. Croker.

1826 ——second edition, with additions.

pp. [i–iii] iv–viii [9] 10–73 [74 (bl.)]   L
Dublin: printed by John King   1806

1827 A MODEST REPLY from F. J. Esq. to the author of *Familiar epistles* to the manager.

pp. [i–iii] iv–xii, [1] 2–43 [44 (errata) 45–46 (bl.)] LGk
Dublin: printed by John Parry   1806
Octosyllabics. The preface is signed Scriblerus.

1828 HISTRIONIC EPISTLES.

pp. [i–iii] iv–xxiv [25] 26–82 [83 (errata) 84 (bl.)]
                                                       L
Dublin: John Barlow   1807

Heroic couplets. On p. 82, "End of Epistle I"; no others are known. Sometimes attributed to John Wilson Croker, for no known reason.

✄ Macauley, Elizabeth Wright. A pamphlet on the difficulties and dangers of theatrical life. Dublin. 1810. *See nos. 3245–3246.*

1829 *THE O.P.; or, theatric dog.
Dublin   1815
  Loewenberg.

1830 [JONES, FREDERICK EDWARD.] PUBLIC JUSTICE, and private right: or, a vindication of the patentee of the Theatre-Royal, including general observations on the professions of the stage together with a full refutation of the allegations contained in the report of the committee of the friends of the drama proving that two theatres cannot be successfully opposed to each other in the city of Dublin.

pp. [1–3] 4–37 [38]   DN
Dublin: printed by J. J. Nolan   1818

1831 CROWQUILL, CALEB. *Familiar epistles addressed to H—— H—— Esq., of the United Theatres of Great Britain and Ireland. By Caleb Crowquill.

nos. 1–6 14 March 1821 to 1822

Dublin   1821–1822
  Loewenberg.

1832 CROWQUILL, CALEB. The new patent or, theatrical secrets worth knowing, in a series of familiar epistles addressed to H—— H—— Esq. [Henry Harris].

pp. [i–ii] [iii (advt.)] iv (advt.) [v] vi–xxiii [xxiv–xxvi], [75] 76–95 [96]   DA
Dublin: printed by J. J. Nolan   1822
  Advertisement and sixth epistle only.

The Riot of 1823

See also GOVERNMENT REGULATION OF THE THEATRE for the year 1823 (p. 31 above).

1833 [RAFFLE, MOLL.] *ADDRESS to the bottle.
bs.
[Dublin]   [1823]
  Signed Moll Raffle; concerning the assault on the Lord Lieutenant at the Theatre-Royal, Dublin, on 14 Dec. 1822 — Loewenberg.

1834 EMINENT REPORTER, AN, *pseud.* *The only accurate and impartial report. The trial of James Forbes, Henry Handwich, William Graham, Matthew Handwich, George Graham, and William Brownlow, in the Court of King's Bench, Monday, February 3, 1823, and following days for a conspiracy, riot, and an attempt to assault the most noble Marquis Wellesley, Lord Lieutenant of Ireland, &c. &c. on his visit to the theatre, 14th December, 1822, on an ex-officio information, filed by the Right Hon. W. C. Plunkett, His Majesty's Attorney General. By an eminent reporter. Embellished with a correct likeness of the noble Marquis.

pp. [2] 98; headed: Second edition   DN
Dublin: printed by Richard Grace   1823

1835 GREENE, RICHARD WILSON. A report of the trial of James Forbes, William Graham, George Graham, Mathew Handwich, Henry Handwich, and William Brownlow, for a conspiracy to create a riot, and to insult and assault his excellency the Lord Lieutenant, in the Theatre Royal, and also for a riot. By Richard Wilson Greene, Esq.

pp. [2] [1] 2–371 [372]   E
Dublin: Richard Milliken   1823

1836 LEES, *Rev. Sir* HARCOURT, *Bart.* An address to the Orangemen of Ireland, relative to the late riot at the Theatre Royal, Hawkins's-St.

pp. [1–3] 4–24   DN
Dublin   1823
  Reprinted from The Antidote *and* The Irish Protestant.

1837 *LETTERS of "an old juror", on the late ex-officio proceedings, in the Court of King's Bench. Re-published from the Warder newspaper.

pp. 38   DN
Dublin: printed by W. Underwood   [1823]

1838 *A REPORT of the speech of the Attorney General, upon the trial of James Forbes and others, in the Court of King's Bench, Dublin, for a conspiracy.

pp. [4] 36   DA
Dublin: Richard Milliken   1823

1839 *X.O. FISH. O.!!! A patched, vamp'd, future, old, revived, bran new poem, descriptive of some recent important transactions.

pp. 34   DN
Dublin   1823
  A satirical poem on events before and after the attempted assault.

———————————

1840 *A REVIEW of the performances at the Theatre Royal, Dublin, during the season 1827–8. Commencing with the opening of the theatre, in November, 1827, under the auspices of Mr. Bunn.

Dublin   1829
  Loewenberg.

✄ Opinions of the press on the performances of Miss Catherine Hayes in London, and . . . Ireland. 1851. *See no. 3014.*

1841 FAREWELL ADDRESS spoken by Mr. Barry, of the Queen's Royal Theatre, Dublin, on Wednesday, 15th December, 1858, who, in consequence of declining health, is compelled to resign his professional duties; and, acting upon the advice of some kind friends, anxious to promote his interest, made a final appeal to the public, on the above evening, under the patronage of the Right Honourable the Lord Mayor; and was also liberally responded to by his brethren of the Independent Order of Oddfellows, of the Dublin district.

pp. [1–3] 4–8   MH
Dublin: printed by S. G. Downes   1858

1842 THE HISTORY OF THE THEATRE ROYAL, Dublin, from its foundation in 1821 to the present time. Reprinted, with additions, from *Saunders' News-letter*.

pp. [1–5] 6–204 [205 (corrigenda) 206 (bl.)]   L
Dublin: Edward Ponsonby   1870

1843 LEVEY, R[ICHARD] M[ICHAEL] and J. O'RORKE. Annals of the Theatre Royal, Dublin, from its opening in 1821 to its destruction by fire, February,

1880; with occasional notes and observations. By R. M. Levey and J. O'Rorke.

pp. [2] [i–iii] iv–vi [7] 8–71 [72 (bl.) 73–75], ²74–271 [272 (bl.)] [=274]   L
Dublin: Joseph Dollard, printer   1880

1844 [HALL, JOHN B.] *SOUVENIR of the twenty-fifth anniversary of the opening of the Gaiety Theatre, [Dublin], 27th. November 1896.

pp. 40   MH
Dublin: Dollard Pr. House   [1896]

Kilkenny

See *THE AMATEUR THEATRE nos. 2156–2157; BIOGRAPHY no. 3390 (Eliza O'Neill).*

SCOTLAND

BIBLIOGRAPHY

See also CATALOGUES no. 110.

1845 CAMERON, JAMES. A bibliography of Scottish theatrical literature. By James Cameron. (The Edinburgh Bibliographical Society. Session 1891–92. Printed Paper No. IV.)

pp. [1] 2–8   GU
Edinburgh   1892

1846 ———Supplement to a bibliography of Scottish theatrical literature. By James Cameron. (The Edinburgh

Bibliographical Society. Session 1894–95. Printed Paper No. II.)

pp. [1] 2   GU
Edinburgh   1896

Both items also issued in Papers of the Edinburgh Bibliographical Society 1890–95 *(half-title:* Publications of the Edinburgh Bibliographical Society Volume I.) *(Edinburgh: printed for the Society, 1896).*

GENERAL

See also GOVERNMENT REGULATION OF THE THEATRE at the year 1892 (p. 36).

1847 JACKSON, JOHN. The history of the Scottish stage, from its first establishment to the present time; with a distinct narrative of some recent theatrical transactions. The whole necessarily interspersed with memoirs of his own life, by John Jackson, ten years manager of the Theatre Royal of Edinburgh.

pp. [i–vii] viii–xvi (misprinted "16") [xvii (errata) xviii (bl.)], [1] 2–424, ²[1–2] 3–41 [42]   E
Edinburgh: Peter Hill; London: G. G. J. and J. Robinson
                                           1793

✄ Ryley, Samuel William. The itinerant, or memoirs of an actor. 1808–1827. *See no. 3471.*

Vols 7–9 were entitled The itinerant in Scotland.

1848 INGLIS, RALSTON. The dramatic writers of Scotland. By Ralston Inglis.

pp. [2] [1–5] 6–155 [156 (errata)]   L
Glasgow: G. D. Mackellar   1868

A curious little book—Lowe. Stratman, Play Lists 50.

1849 CLARK, WILLIAM [and WILLIAM HUGH LOGAN, *ed.*] Marciano; or, the discovery. A tragicomedy, by William Clark, advocate.

pp. [i–iii] iv–xvi, [1–2] 3–8, ²1–71 [72]   GU
Edinburgh: reprinted for private circulation 1871

Edition limited to 75 copies. A reprint of Marciano *as first published in 1663, with the addition of Clark's name on the title page and of an introduction by W. H. Logan on the early history of the drama in Scotland.*

INDIVIDUAL TOWNS

See also PERIODICALS: SCOTLAND nos. 4441–4506. Consult also the INDEX OF PLACES OF PUBLICATION for towns not listed below.

Aberdeen

See also INDEX OF PLACES OF PUBLICATION.

1850 ANGUS, J. KEITH. A Scotch play-house; being the historical records of the old Theatre Royal, Marischal Street, Aberdeen. By J. Keith Angus.

pp. [1–9] 10–69 [70 (ornament) 71–72 (advt.)]   E
Aberdeen: D. Wyllie & Son; Edinburgh: John Menzies
& Co.; London: Simpkin, Marshall & Co.   1878

1851 ——second edition

pp. [1–9] 10–69 [70–72 (advts.)]   MH
Aberdeen: D. Wyllie & Son; Edinburgh: John Menzies
& Co.; London: Simpkin, Marshall & Co.   1878

Ayr

1852 MORRIS, JAMES. Recollections of Ayr theatricals from 1809. By James Morris. Printed for private circulation.

pp. [1–5] 6–40   E
Ayr: printed at the Ayr Advertiser Office   1872

Dundee

1853 BOYD, FRANK. Records of the Dundee stage from the earliest times to the present day.

pp. [4] [i] ii [iii–vi], [1] 2–96 [97–98 99–100 (bl.)]; pls.
[front., 4]   E
Dundee: W. & D. C. Thomson   1886

Edinburgh

See also INDEX OF PLACES OF PUBLICATION; and GOVERNMENT REGULATION OF THE THEATRE for the years 1766, 1858 (pp. 25, 33 above).

Tony Aston and Allan Ramsay

1854 UNTO THE RIGHT HONOURABLE, THE LORDS OF COUNCIL AND SESSION, the petition of the Magistrates of the City of Edinburgh . . .

pp. 1–7 [8]; filing-title: Petition for the Magistrates of the City of Edinburgh. Against Anthony Aston, &c. 1727.   EP
[Edinburgh]   26 Dec. 1727

Signed 'Ch. Areskine'. Against the interlocutor of the Court of Session of 15 December, suspending the Magistrates' prohibition of Aston and his company from performing.

1855 ANSWERS FOR CHARLES EARL OF LAWDERDALE, James, Lord Somervell, John Lord Belhaven, and Anthony Aston their Servant, to the Petition of the Magistrates of Edinburgh.

pp. [1] 2–6   EP
[Edinburgh]   17 Jan. 1728

Signed "Geo. Ogilvie".

1856 A MERRY DIALOGUE, in the Tolbuith of Edinburgh; betwixt Tonny Ashton, and John Curry.

bs.   E
[Edinburgh]   [1728]

1857 A PIL to Tonny Ashton or the play-house puld down.

bs.   E
[Edinburgh]   [1728]

1858 *PRINTED DOCUMENTS issued in connection with the prosecution of Anthony Aston, comedian, by the magistrates of Edinburgh . . . January 17, 1728.

pp. 6
[Edinburgh]   [1728]

Loewenberg.

1859 RAMSAY, ALLAN. To the Honourable, Duncan Forbes of Culloden, and all our other good judges, who are careful of the honour of the government, and the property of the subject; the address of Allan Ramsay . . .

pp. [1] 2–4   EP
[Edinburgh]   [1737]

Begins

> *To you, my Lords, whase elevation*
> *Makes you the wardens of the nation . . .*

Protesting against the closing of his theatre under the Act; dated 25 July. Martin 120.

The Douglas Controversy

Douglas, which caused the fiercest storm in Scotch religious circles that ever raged over the theatre . . . was produced first in Edinburgh, 14th December 1756, then at Covent Garden, 14th March 1757. It was conspicuously successful, and still remains a popular play. Home was persecuted by the Church, and resigned his charge; but this ill-treatment commended him to the Earl of Bute — Lowe.

1860 THE MANAGER OF THE THEATRE [i.e. John Dudley West Digges]. *Address to the public by the manager of the theatre relative to the tragedy of Douglas.

bs.
Edinburgh   December 1756

Loewenberg.

1861 A PROLOGUE to the long expected tragedy of Douglas, as it is to be acted this evening at the theatre in the head of the Canongate, Edinburgh.

bs.   DFo

[Edinburgh]   14 December 1756

Lefèvre *145.*

1862 THEATRE.

bs.   MH

[Edinburgh]   [1756]

Begins *As the manager has been informed, That a Report prevails, that no Persons will be admitted into the Theatre on Tuesday the 14th instant, but CLERGYMEN, at which Rumour many other Persons are offended; He thinks it his Duty to acquaint the Public, That the PIT ALONE IS PARTICULARLY kept BY ORDER FOR THE FRATERNITY* . . . Lefèvre *147.*

1863 AN ADDRESS to the Synod of Lothian and Tweedale, concerning Mr. Home's tragedy and Hume's Moral Essays.

pp. [1] 2–8   E

[Edinburgh]   [1757]

Lefèvre *103.*

1864 [BANNATYNE, G.] THE ADMONITION. An execrable new ballad, to the tune of *the Times.*

pp. [1] 2–4; head-title   E

[Edinburgh]   [January 1757]

Begins
The clergy in dugeon! poor laymen are hector'd!
Lefèvre *104.*

1865 ADMONITION and exhortation by the Reverend Presbytery of Edinburgh to all within their bounds.

pp. [1] 2   DFo

Edinburgh   5 Jan., 1757

"*Extracted from the records of Presbytery, by James Craig, Presb. Clerk.*" Lefèvre *138.*

1866 ADVERTISEMENT. On S——y next, being the 30th, will be acted in all the —— of this city, a new farce, called, Old Mother P——y run mad; or, much ado about nothing. Written by Dr. Alexander Bonum Magnum [Alexander Webster] and Dr. Patrick Turnstile [Patrick Cumming] . . .

bs.   E

[Edinburgh]   [1757]

The ascription is, of course, facetious. Lefèvre *139.*

1867 ADVERTISEMENT. That there is lately come to town, a new set of curious puppets, commissioned by the R—— ——d P—— ——y of Edinburgh, in order to afford a proper innocent entertainment for the remaining part of the winter-season . . .

pp. [1] 2–4   E

[Edinburgh]   [1757]

The Advertisement is followed by a Prologue, beginning "In a dark dismal corner long had stood/Poor Punchinello in a pensive mood . . ." Lefèvre *105.*

1868 ADVERTISEMENT. This is to acquaint the public, that a certain person, of eminent and jovial sanctity, has conceived a mortal aversion to tragedy . . .

bs.   E

[Edinburgh]   [1757]

Against the Rev. Alexander Webster. Lefèvre *140.*

1869 ADVERTISEMENT. Whereas some malicious persons have represented the R——d Mr. H——h B——r, as the author of the execrable ballad called The admonition . . .

bs.   E

[Edinburgh]   [1757]

Lefèvre *141.*

1870 ADVICE to the writers in defence of Douglas.

pp. [1] 2–4   EU

[Edinburgh]   [1757]

Begins
      I who's weak numbers struggled to display
      The hidden beauties of our Scottish play,
Lefèvre *106.*

1871 [MACLAURIN, JOHN, *Lord* DREGHORN.] APOLOGY for the writers against the tragedy of Douglas. With some remarks on that play.

pp. [1–3] 4–15 [16]   E

Edinburgh   1757

Lefèvre *107.*

1872 THE APOSTLE to the theatre his garland. An excellent new song, to the tune of, *De'il stick the minister.*

pp. [1] 2–4; head-title   E

[Edinburgh]   [1757]

Begins
Ye wolves in sheep's clothing I pray you draw near . . .
Lefèvre *108.*

1873 THE SECOND PART of The apostle to the theatre his garland. Containing the lamentation of a beautiful young damsel in Athelstaneford. All which you have for the small and easy charge of a penny. To the tune of, *Had awa frae me, Donald.*

pp. [1] 2–4; head-title   E

[Edinburgh]   [1757]

Begins
Had awa, had awa . . . Lefèvre *109.*

1874 [CARLYLE, ALEXANDER.] AN ARGU-MENT to prove that the tragedy of Douglas ought to be publickly burnt by the hands of the hangman.

pp. [1–2] 3–24   E
Edinburgh   1757
   Lefèvre *110.*

1875 BY PARTICULAR DESIRE of the Reverend Members of the G——l As——m——y. On Sunday next, being the 5th of June, will be performed a concert of music, consisting of several favourite overtures. After which will be presented (gratis) a tragedy, called, The sufferings of Job. [By W——M W——E A——te.] ...

bs.   E
[Edinburgh]   [1757]
   Lefèvre *142. This copy expands name as George Wallace, Advocate.*

1876 [MACLAURIN, JOHN, *Lord* DREGHORN.] THE DEPOSITION, or fatal miscarriage: a tragedy.

pp. [1–5] 6–14 [15 (epilogue) 16 (bl.)]   E
[Edinburgh]   [1757]
   Lefèvre *111.*

1877 DOUGLASIANA.

pp. [1] 2–8; head-title   EU
[Edinburgh]   [1757]

Contents

I.   *The battle of the ministers. To be sung over a bowl of punch, to the tune of,* Down the burn Davie.
      Begins
            To me repair, ye martial sons
            Of the church militant.

II.   *The revolution. To the tune of,* A cobler there was.
      Begins
            Learned men whilom were under no fetters,
            But made what was call'd the republic of letters;

III. *An epistle, from the manager of the theatre, to the Rev. member of the synod of Lothian and Tweeddale, who maintained, in open court, that the profession of a player is lawful and honourable; and that the stage, without any reformation, is the great support of religion and virtue.*
      Begins
            Some call you, from their want of taste,
            The pattern of the true bombast.

IV.   *The confession. Humbly inscribed to the Rev. gentleman who has owned, "That he has been some-times at Mr. Digges's house, along with the author, and had some conversation about the tragedy; but that he had never ate or drunk with Mrs. Ward, or con-versed with her, further than in agreeing or disagreeing to what was about the play." Scots Mag. for March, p. 160. To the tune of,* Gill Morris.
      Begins
            About your dialogues with Ward,
            What you say may be true:

V.   *An epistle, to Mr Genius, a——st in Edinburgh.*
      Begins *My dear sir,*
            It would most certainly have been odd,
            Had J——n been censur'd by the synod;

Lefèvre *113*. The battle of the ministers *is advertised in* The history of Agis.

✖ English Critic, An. A letter to Mr. David Hume, on the tragedy of Douglas. 1757. *See no. 3929.*
   Lefèvre *121.*

1878 AN EPILOGUE to the tragedy of Douglas, spoke by the author.

bs.   E
[Edinburgh]   [1757]
   Begins
      Shrouded in glory, and with praise full blown,
      Permit your bard his gratitude to own. Lefèvre *143.*

1879 THE FINISHING STROKE; or, nothing. A ballad.

pp. [1] 2–4; head-title   E
[Edinburgh]   [1757]
   Lefèvre *114.*

1880 THE FIRST NIGHT'S AUDIENCE: an excellent new ballad. To the tune of, *A cobler there was, &c.* Humbly inscribed to the author of Douglas, a tragedy.

pp. [1] 2–4; head-title   E
[Edinburgh]   [1757]
   Begins
      Your success, dear Jacky, was great as my wish,
   Lefèvre *115.*

1881 [CARLYLE, ALEXANDER.] A FULL AND TRUE HISTORY of the bloody tragedy of Douglas, as it is now to be seen acting at the Theatre in the Canongate.

bs.   E
[Edinburgh]   [1757 or ? 1756]
   Lefèvre *144.*

1882 GENTLEMAN, A, *pseud.* Douglas, a tragedy, weighed in the balances, and found wanting. Being an answer to two important questions respecting that per-formance. In a letter from a gentleman to his friend.

pp. [2] [1] 2–38   EU
Edinburgh: W. Gray and W. Peter   1757
   Signed "A.B." 21 April 1757. A reply to The morality of stage plays seriously considered *(no. 1892)* Lefèvre *112.*

1883 GENTLEMAN, A, *pseud.* Remarks upon the play of Douglas, in a letter by a gentleman to his friend in the country.

pp. [1] 2   E
[Edinburgh]   [1757]
   Lefèvre *146.*

1884 [CRAIG, JAMES.]
THE GOOD EXHORTATION of the sons of Korah,
    To all that reside in this wicked Gomorrah.
A new song, to its own tune,
    The presbyt'ry taking in consideration . . .
pp. [1] 2–4; head-title   E
[Edinburgh]   [1757]
> 'Extracted from church rolls by scriv'ner James Craig.'
> Lefèvre 116.

1885 I SMILE, my easy friend at you . . .
bs.; without title   EU
[Edinburgh]   [1757]
> An epigram by one of Home's admirers on Home and Rev.
> Robert Walker of the New Kirk (of St. Giles). Lefèvre
> 149.

1886 THE IMMORALITY of stage-plays in general, and of the tragedy called Douglas, in particular, briefly illustrated; in a letter from Athelstaneford to the Moderator of the Presbytery of Haddingtoun.
pp. [1–3] 4–26   E
Edinburgh   1757
> Lefèvre 117.

1887 THE INFERNAL COUNCIL. An excellent new ballad. To the tune of, The devils were brawling, &c.
pp. [1] 2–4; head-title   EU
[Edinburgh]   [1757]
> Begins
> Grim Belzebub's council assembled of late,
> Where matters important were weigh'd in debate:
> Lefèvre 118.

1888 [M'DEBIT, JOHN], pseud. THE IRISH PARSON'S ADVICE concerning the play-house, or the reverend revenge, a poem.
pp. [1] 2–4; head-title   EU
[Edinburgh]   [1757]
> Signed 'John McDebit'.
> Begins
> The reverend D——s, my brethren hear,
> Revenge I'll whisper in your ear.
> Lefèvre 119.

1889 A LETTER to the reverend the moderator, and members of the Presbytery of Haddingtoun.
pp. [1–3] 4–8   E
Edinburgh   1757
> Lefèvre 122.

1890 MAGNUM, ALEXANDER BONUM, pseud. The petition of poor Alexander Bonum Magnum, humbly sheweth, that your petitioner hath, tho' during a very cold season, been laid under the disagreeable necessity of abstaining from the use of his favourite catholicon . . .
bs.; headed: "14th February, 1757. Unto the Right Aetherial the Siplers."   E
[Edinburgh]   [1757]
> The attribution to Alexander Bonum Magnum [Rev.
> Alexander Webster] is of course facetious. Lefèvre 148.

1891 THE MODERATOR. Number II.
pp. [1] 2–12   DFo
[Edinburgh]   [1757]
> Lefèvre 123.

1892 [FERGUSON, ADAM.] THE MORALITY of stage-plays seriously considered.
pp. [2] [1] 2–29 [30]   E
Edinburgh   1757
> A defence of "Douglas". By Adam Ferguson—Lowe. See
> nos. 1882, 1895. Lefèvre 124.

1893 O'QUEER, SIMON, pseud. Letter from Simon O'Queer, to Mrs. Grissel Gray at Edinburgh.
pp. [1] 2–4; head-title   E
[Edinburgh]   [1757]
> Begins
> Dear honey, as logic I hate all delay . . . Lefèvre 120.

1894 [MACLAURIN, JOHN, Lord DREGHORN.] THE PHILOSOPHER'S OPERA.
pp. [i–iii] iv, [1] 2–23 [24]   E
[Edinburgh]   [1757]
> An attack on Douglas and on Home's supporters, including
> David Hume. Lefèvre 125.

1895 [HALDANE, JOHN.] THE PLAYERS SCOURGE: or a detection of the ranting prophanity and regnant impiety of stage plays, and their wicked encouragers and frequenters; and especially against the nine prophane pagan priests, falsely called ministers of the gospel, who countenanced the thrice cursed tragedy called Douglas.
pp. [1] 2–8   E
[Edinburgh]   [1757]
> Signed "H.I." A reply to The morality of stage-plays
> seriously considered (no. 1892). Lefèvre 126.
> A most scurrilous attack upon Home and his supporters,
> who are accused in it of profanity, impiety, swearing,
> Sabbath-breaking, conniving at adultery, drinking, calling
> for profane songs, such as "De'il Stick the Minister,"
> &c. — Lowe.

1896 H[ALDA]NE, J[OH]N. The second part of the players scourge exhibited to the world. Wherein is contained the true character of playhouses, play-actors,

& play-haunters. With an humble advice to the occupant upon the throne. By J——n H——ne.

pp. [1–3] 4–16   E
[Edinburgh]   1768
   Lefèvre *127*.

1897 THE SEVEN CHAMPIONS of the stage. In imitation of Gill Morice. An excellent new old fashioned song. All to the melancholy tune of Gill Morice, except the 17th, 18th, and 19th stanzas, which ought to be sung to the merry tune of the C——s are coming, O ho!

pp. [2] ¹[1] 2–8, ²[3] 4–11 [12] [=20]   DFo
[Edinburgh? Glasgow?]   [1757]
   Lefèvre *129*.

1898 [HARPER, *Rev.*? THOMAS.] SOME SERIOUS REMARKS on a late pamphlet, entituled, The morality of stage-plays seriously considered. In a letter to a lady.

pp. [2] [1] 2–32   E
Edinburgh   1757
   Lefèvre *130*.

1899 [WEDDERBURN, ALEXANDER.] A SONG: or, a sermon. A new ballad.

pp. [1] 2–4; head-title   EU
[Edinburgh]   29th January 1757
   Begins
          Since the Presbyt'ry sage,
          Attacking the stage,
   Lefèvre *131*.

1900 THE STAGE or the pulpit: a sermon. Sung by the Reverend author of *Douglas* the first night he went to see his own play represented. To the tune of Gill Morice.

pp. [1] 2–4   DFo
[Edinburgh]   [1757]
   Lefèvre *132*.

1901 THE STAGE or the pulpit, part II. Sung by the Reverend author after the play was over, but before the curtain fell.

pp. [1] 2–4   DFo
[Edinburgh]   [1757]
   Though this is separately paginated, it may not have been issued independently of part I. The MH copy has a MS ascription in an old hand to John Maclaurin, Lord Dreghorn. Lefèvre *133*.

1902 THE STAGE or the pulpit. Part III.

pp. [1] 2–4; head-title   EU
[Edinburgh]   1757
   Begins with note
   It was advertised in the news-papers, that the tragedy of Douglas was to be published this day, being the 29th of March 1757.

Then poem
        Prepare ye Scottish connoisseur,
         To criticise the play:
Lefèvre *134*.

✖ The theatrical examiner . . . with a short consideration on *Douglas*. 1757. *See no. 880.*

✖ The tragedy of Douglas analysed. 1757.
   See no. 3930.1

1903 THE USEFULNESS of the Edinburgh theatre seriously considered. With a proposal for rendering it more beneficial.

pp. [2] [1] 2–12   E
Edinburgh   1757
   An ironical seconding of Morality of the stage seriously considered, *quoted on title page. The proposal is that Edinburgh should not rely on England for actors, but cast plays from the ample resources of Edinburgh society. The attack ranges beyond* Douglas *to the position of the theatre in Edinburgh.* Lefèvre *136*.

1904 VOTES of the P——y of E——h.

pp. [1] 2–4; head-title   E
[Edinburgh]   [1757]
   Lefèvre *137*.

✖ Brickface, Lack-Limb, *pseud.* A fragment: found in the ruins of Aquileia. [Edinburgh. 1760?]. *See no. 3931.*

"Gentlemen Musicians" Controversy 1758

Six leaflets occasioned by West Digges' attempts to escape payment of arrears of salary to the orchestra (described by themselves in the first pamphlet as 'gentlemen musicians'). See Dibdin pp. 97 seq.

1905 TO THE PUBLIC.
bs.   MH
[Edinburgh]   [March–April 1758]
   The first in the series. Begins That a certain number of gentlemen musicians in this city, having agreed with West Digges, manager of the concert hall in the Canongate . . .

1906 ANSWERS to Mr. Digges's paper, intitled A short detection, &c.
bs.   MH
[Edinburgh]   [1758]
   The fifth in the series.

1907 FROM THE PUBLIC.
bs.   MH
[Edinburgh]   [1758]
   The sixth in the series. Begins Whereas some low and scurrilous papers have lately been imposed upon us, by that respectable society, who are pleased to term themselves, the gentlemen musicians of this city. . . .

1908 OBSERVATIONS on a printed paper, addrest to the public by Mr. Digges, comedian, dated at the Theatre of Edinburgh, April 5th, in answer to an address to the public, by the band of music in this city, for their vindication against the scandalous aspersions of that man.

pp. [1] 2–3 [4 (bl.)]; head-title   MH

Edinburgh   7 April 1758

The third in the series.

1909 A SHORT DETECTION of an infamous libel, called Observations, &. on Mr. Digges's appeal to the public.

bs.   MH

[Edinburgh]   [8 April 1758]

The fourth in the series. In vindication of Digges.

1910 THEATRE OF EDINBURGH, April 5. To the public.

pp. [1] 2   MH

[Edinburgh]   5 April [1758]

The second in the series. Signed 'West Digges'.
These six broadsides are reprinted in Fragmenta Scoto-Dramatica *(1835) pp. 29–48. (no. 1983).*

1911 CONTRACT betwixt the proprietors of the Concert-Hall, Canongate, and Mess. Beatt and Dowson.

pp. [1] 2–7 [8]; head-title   EP

[Edinburgh]   [1759?]

1912 DIGGES, [JOHN DUDLEY WEST]. Mr. Digges's case, in regard to his present dismission from the theatres of Newcastle and Edinburgh.

pp. [1] 2–8; head-title   EP

[Edinburgh]   24 November 1759

1913 SOCIETY OF GENTLEMEN, A, *pseud.* A view of the Edinburgh theatre during summer season, 1759. Containing, an exact list of the several pieces represented, and impartial observations on each performance. By a society of gentlemen.

pp. [2] i–ii, ²i–iv, 9–50   L

A. Morley   1760

Several of these pieces first appeared in the Edinburgh Chronicle. *Dedicated to West Digges.*

1914 CITY OF EDINBURGH, THE, *pseud.* A letter from the city of Edinburgh to the town of Glasgow.

pp. [1–2] 3–12   EP

[Edinburgh]   [1766]

Signed "Edina". Includes an ironical eulogy of the Edinburgh management and company.

1915 GENTLEMAN, A, *pseud.* A letter from a gentleman in Edinburgh, to his friend in the country: occasioned by the late theatrical disturbances.

pp. [1–2] 3–16   E

Edinburgh   1766

Attributed, without the least probability, to Allan Ramsay the younger.

1916 [BONAR, JOHN, *solicitor of excise.*] CONSIDERATIONS on the proposed application to His Majesty and to Parliament, for the establishment of a licensed theatre in Edinburgh.

pp. [2] [1] 2–18   EP

[Edinburgh]   1767

An attack on the proposed application, and on the stage generally — Lowe.

1917 THE CONTEST; a comic uproar. Al-burlesquo. As performed at the Theatre, Edinbro.

pp. [1–3] 4–8   EP

[Edinburgh]   [1767]

On the rioting in the theatre when the proprietors refused to re-engage George Stayley. See Dibdin, pp. 138 seq.

1918 [TRUTH, *pseud.*] TO THE PUBLIC.

pp. [1] 2   EP

[Edinburgh]   [1767]

A defence of Stayley. Signed "Truth".

The Patent dispute between Lee and Ross

Ross was an actor who might have been great if he had not been neglectful and indolent. — Lowe. See also Dibdin, pp. 144 seq.

1919 AN ADDRESS to the public.

pp. [1–3] 4–24   EP

Edinburgh   1767

1920 AS IT IS NOW CERTAIN that the gentlemen who took upon them this day se'nnight to form a resolution with regard to the disposal of the patent for a theatre in this place, . . .

bs., headed "Friday, November 27th"   EP

[Edinburgh]   27 November [1767]

1921 AT A VERY NUMEROUS MEETING of the gentlemen of this place and neighbourhood, held this day at Fortune's, to consider of the present situation of the Theatre . . .

bs., headed "Edinburgh, 28th November 1767"   EP

Edinburgh   28 November 1767

1922 AT THE THEATRE ROYAL in Gray's Close, on Saturday, December 12th, will be presented a comedy, (altered from Congreve, in four acts) called The Double Dealers.

bs.   EP
[Edinburgh]   [1767]

1923 CONSIDERATIONS upon the intended disposal of the patent.

pp. [1] 2–21 [22]   EP
[Edinburgh]   [1767]

1924 A FEW BRIEF CONSIDERATIONS upon the means of establishing a regular theatre in Edinburgh.

pp. [1] 2–8; head-title   EP
[Edinburgh]   [1767]

1925 ———[another edition] Considerations upon the means of establishing a licensed theatre in Edinburgh.

pp. [1] 2–24; head-title   EP
[Edinburgh]   [1767]

1926 A FEW PLAIN TRUTHS, addressed to Mr. Ross.

bs.   EP
Edinburgh   4 December 1767

1927 LEE, [JOHN]. Mr. Lee's address to the public.

pp. [1] 2–4; head-title   EP
[Edinburgh]   [4 December 1767]

1928 NEXT WEEK will be published, a full history of the proceedings in the case of sister Peg's puppetshow.

bs.   EP
[Edinburgh]   [1767]

1929 *NIL MORTALIBUS ARDUUM;* or, a vindication of the disposal of the puppet-shew house.

pp. [1–3] 4–18   EP
Edinburgh   1767

1930 *PUNCH'S ADDRESS to the public.

pp. 8; head-title
[Edinburgh]   [1767]
    Loewenberg.

1931 QUERIES addressed to the town.

bs.   EP
[Edinburgh]   [1767]

1932 ROSS, [DAVID]. Mr. Ross's address to the public.

pp. [1] 2–3 [4]; head-title   EP
[Edinburgh]   [30 November 1767]

1933 *A SERIOUS AND EARNEST ADDRESS to the inhabitants of this city, upon a subject in which they are all most nearly concerned.

pp. 11   MB
[Edinburgh]   [1767]

1934 A SHORT VINDICATION of the proprietors of the theatre; with a word to the querist.

bs.   EP
[Edinburgh]   [1767]

1935 STAYLEY, GEORGE. The theatrical hurricane or, all's well which ends well. A poetical description. To which are added, proposals for the teaching of reading; with a poem applicable to the occasion. By George Stayley, comedian.

pp. [1–3] 4–7 [8–11] 12–16   E
Edinburgh: printed by J. Robertson   1767
    Reprinted in Dibdin, pp. 141–142.

1936 TO THE FRIENDS of virtue and liberty.

bs.   EP
[Edinburgh]   [1767]

�封 An Act for extending the royalty of the City of Edinburgh . . . and to enable His Majesty to grant letters patent for establishing a theatre [1768]. *See no. 175.*

1937 PROPOSALS for building a new Theatre-Royal in the new streets of Edinburgh. The ground being feued by Mr. Ross, behind the Orphan Hospital, to the east side of the new bridge.

bs.; illus. (engr.)   EP
Edinburgh   1 March 1768

The "Minor" Controversy

For the controversy over the production of Foote's The Minor see BIOGRAPHY nos. 2797–2803 (Foote).

———

1938 A LETTER to the author of a panegyric on Mrs B——r, entitled, A new Rosciad.

pp. [2] [1] 2–5 [6]   E
[Edinburgh]   1770
    Signed 'Candidus'.

1939 A NEW ROSCIAD.

pp. [1–3] 4–13 [14]   L
[Edinburgh]   1770
    Half-title is "A new Rosciad for the year MDCCLXX".

1940 ACCOUNT of the entertainment of the Jubilee, intended to be performed at the Theatre-Royal, Edinburgh.

pp. [1] 2–8   EP
[Edinburgh]   [1771]

1941 THE DEPUTY-MANAGER of the Theatre-Royal detected. To which is prefixed, an address to the people of Edinburgh; by the editor.

pp. [1–3] 4–21 [22]   EP
Edinburgh   1772

1942 A NARRATIVE of a remarkable breach of trust committed by a nobleman, five judges, and several advocates of the Court of Session in Scotland.

pp. [4] 1–36   E
Printed for the Author; and sold by G. Kearsly   1772

Signed John Lee. Refers to Lee's experiences while manager of the Theatre Royal, Edinburgh.

1943 *THE EDINBURGH THEATRE ROYAL displayed.
Edinburgh   1773

Loewenberg.

1944 THE EDINBURGH ROSCIAD, for 1775.

pp. [2] [5] 6–16   E
Edinburgh: sold by C. Elliot   [1775]

1945 vacant

1946 MR. DIGGES'S PROPOSALS to his creditors.
bs.   E
Edinburgh   16 July 1777

1947 IN THE PROCESS at the instance of John Howe, some time carpenter of the Theatre-Royal of Edinburgh, against John Bland residing in Edinburgh, June 24, 1782.

pp. [1] 2–4   MH
[Edinburgh]   [1782]

Prints the contract between West Digges and John Bland regarding their interests in the Theatre-Royal, Edinburgh.

1948 [JACKSON, JOHN.] CASE OF JOHN JACKSON, Patentee of the Edinburgh Theatre-Royal.

pp. [1] 2–16; head-title   L
[Edinburgh]   [1786]

In support of Jackson's application for a new patent, the original being due to expire on 29 September 1788; rival applicants were the other shareholders in the Edinburgh Theatre.

1949 FENNELL, JAMES. A statement of facts occasional of and relative to the late disturbances at the Theatre-Royal Edinburgh, by James Fennell.

pp. [1–3] 4–54   L
Edinburgh: John and James Ainslies   [1788]

Dated: Walker's Hotel July 24, 1788.

1950 ——second edition

pp. [1–3] 4–54   E
Edinburgh: John and James Ainslies   [1788]

1951 ——third edition

pp. [1–3] 4–56   L
John Bell   1788

1952 DEEDS RELATIVE TO THE EDINBURGH CIRCUS.

pp. [1–3] 4, ²[1] 2–6, ³[1] 2–3[4], ⁴[1] 2–6, ⁵[1] 2–7 [8], ⁶[1] 2–5 [6]   EP
[Edinburgh]   [1790]

1953 TO THE KING'S most excellent majesty, the humble petition of the subscribers, inhabitants of Your Majesty's City of Edinburgh, and of the neighbourhood . . .

pp. [1] 2–3 [4 (bl.)]; head-title   L
[Edinburgh]   [1790?]

A petition for new, more efficient, patentees.

The Jackson–Kemble dispute 1792–1793

1954 JACKSON, J[OHN]. A statement of facts, explanatory of the dispute between John Jackson and Stephen Kemble, relative to the Theatre Royal of Edinburgh. By J. Jackson.

pp. [4] [1] 2–114 [115 (advt.) 116 (bl.)]   L
Edinburgh: Peter Hill   1792

Reprinted, with minor variations, in Jackson's History of the Scottish Stage (no. 1847 above.) — "a portion of that work published in advance, to give an early statement of Jackson's arguments in the quarrel between Stephen Kemble and himself" — Lowe. The half-title reads: A statement of facts, concerning the Edinburgh Theatre.

1955 *ANSWERS for Robert Playfair . . . to petition of Stephen Kemble.

       1793
PH and KB.

1956 A COMPARATIVE VIEW of the rights and merits of Mrs. Harriet Pye Esten, &c. and Mr. Stephen Kemble.

pp. [1–5] 6–31 [32]   E
Edinburgh   1793

1957 KEMBLE, STEPHEN. *Petition of Stephen Kemble, manager of the New Theatre of Edinburgh, against Lord Swinton's *Interlocutor*, Feb. 7, 1793.

[Edinburgh]   1793

     STR.

1958 *MEMORIAL for R. Playfair . . . trustee for the creditors of J. Jackson, late manager of the Theatre Royal, Edinburgh, and for Mrs. H. P. Esten, lessee of the said theatre, *etc.*

Headed: January 29, 1793.

[Edinburgh]   [1793]

     BMC., *but copy at L destroyed.*

1959 CRITO'S LETTER to the Manager of the Edinburgh Theatre, with additions, alterations, and the letter of Philo-Crito, never before published.

pp. [1–3] 4–16   E

Edinburgh: printed by T. Maccleish and Co.   1800

     Attacks Stephen Kemble. See Dibdin pp. 237–238.

1960 *DISCOVERY and description of Timothy Plain.

     1800

     PH and KB. *A poem.*

1961 PLAIN, TIMOTHY, *pseud.* of Moncrieff Threepland. Letters respecting the performances at the Theatre Royal, Edinburgh, originally addressed to the editor of the Scots Chronicle, under the signature of Timothy Plain, and published in that paper during the years 1797, 1798, 1799, and 1800.

pp. [i–iii] iv–v [vi] [7] 8–284   L

Edinburgh: G. Gray   1800

     A reprint of letters said to have been written by Stewart Thriepland, [i.e. Moncrieff Threepland] advocate, sharply criticising the company [at] the Edinburgh Theatre under the management of Stephen Kemble — Lowe.

1962 EDINBURGH THEATRICAL REPORTS for November and December, 1800. (To be continued occasionally.) Containing the criticisms of Crito and Timothy Plain; and the letters of Verus and Cassandra. (The second part to be published at the end of the winter season, and will contain farther strictures upon the Edinburgh theatre, anecdotes of the principal performers, with various letters concerning the Scottish stage.)

pp. [4] [1] 2–39 [40]   DFo

Edinburgh: printed by C. Stewart & Co.   1801

1963 CANDIDUS, *pseud.* The theatre; or the letters of Candidus, &c. on the performances of the Edinburgh stage, in 1802. With considerable additions by the author.

pp. [i–iii] iv–xxxii, [1] 2–98 [99 (errata) 100 (bl.)]   L

Edinburgh: J. Buchanan   1802

Reprinted in part from the Edinburgh Herald and Chronicle. *Introduction dated May.*

1964 CANDIDUS, *pseud.* *Supplement to The theatre. By Candidus.

pp. 101–148

Edinburgh   1802

     The letters had originally appeared in the Edinburgh Herald and Chronicle — Loewenberg.

1965 FRIENDLY HINTS, addressed to the manager of the Theatre Royal, Edinburgh.

pp. [1–3] 4–35 [36 (bl.)]; errata slip   L

Edinburgh: printed for the author   1807

     A criticism of the performers of the time — Lowe. In octosyllabics.

1966 †REMARKS ON THE THESPIAN CRITIQUE.

pp. [1–3] 4–8   EP

[Edinburgh]   [1816]

     On caption title: "Inscribed (without permission) to Patrick Pitt, Esq." Pp. 7–8 replaced by typescript.

1967 ALEXANDER, [JOHN HENRY]. A plain statement of facts, by Mr. Alexander, late of the Theatre-Royal, Edinburgh.

pp. [1] 2–10; head-title   E

[Edinburgh]: W. Aitchison, printer   [1821]

1968 ——second edition

pp. [1] 2–10; head-title   E

[Edinburgh]: W. Aitchison, printer   [1821]

1969 CALCRAFT, JOHN WILLIAM, *stage name* of John William Cole. An address to the public, containing observations on some late criticisms connected with the Edinburgh Theatre. By John William Calcraft, of the Theatre-Royal, Edinburgh.

pp. [1–3] 4–15 [16]   L

Edinburgh: John Anderson, Jun.   1822

     A reply to attacks made on the management and company in the Edinburgh Dramatic Review. *A broadside (copy at MB) advertising this pamphlet ("This day is published . . .") was distributed by Anderson.*

1970 [JAMESON, R.] ANSWERS for Mr. Corbet Ryder: to the reasons of suspension and interdict for Mrs. Harriet Murray or Siddons, of the Theatre-Royal, Edinburgh.

pp. [1] 2–5 [6]   E

[Edinburgh?]   [1825?]

     Mrs Siddons' attempts to maintain her monopoly at the Theatre Royal against Ryder who was at the Caledonian Theatre.

1971 REPORT of the trial of the proceedings in the action of suspension and interdict at the instance of Mrs. H. Siddons, of the Theatre Royal, against Mr Corbet Ryder, of the Caledonian theatre, containing bill of suspension and answers; the patent of the Theatre-Royal; assignation thereof, and lease of the patent; with the *viva voce* pleadings of the counsel, and opinions of the counsel, and opinions of the judges. Taken in short-hand.

pp. [1–3] 4–78   L

Edinburgh: Edward West and company; Glasgow: R. Griffin & Co.; London: Sherwood, Jones, & Co. 1825

1972 vacant

1973 OBSERVATIONS on the present state of the stage, with particular reference to that of Edinburgh.

pp. [4] [1] 2–20   EP

Edinburgh: John Hunter & Co. . . . and George Hamilton   1826

An attack on the management of W. H. Murray, who is accused of following the lax moral example of the contemporary London stage.

1974 AN ACCOUNT of the first Edinburgh Theatrical Fund Dinner, held at Edinburgh, on Friday 23rd February 1827; containing a correct and authentic report of the speeches; which include, among other interesting matter, the first public avowal, by Sir Walter Scott, of being the author of the Waverley Novels.

pp. [1–3] 4–24   E

Edinburgh: John Anderson, Jun.   1827

1975 RULES AND REGULATIONS of the Edinburgh Theatrical Society, instituted April 2, 1819.

pp. [1–5] 6–13 [14]   E

Edinburgh: printed by John Stark   1827

1976 REGULATIONS to be observed by the company of the Theatre-Royal, Edinburgh.

pp. [1–3] 4–15 [16]   GU

[Edinburgh]   [1828?]

Watermark: 1828.

1977 I[NNES], F[REDERICK] M[AITLAND]. On the causes of the decline of the drama, and the means by which its reputation may be vindicated. With a letter addressed to the manager of the Theatre-Royal, Edinburgh. By F.M.I.

pp. [i–v] vi–x [11–13] 14–24   MH

Edinburgh: George Abercromby Douglas   1834

Preface dated 5 May 1834, and a letter to William Murray, manager of the Theatre Royal, Edinburgh signed 'F——d——k M——t——d I——n——s'.

Nugae Histrionicae

1978 [LOGAN, WILLIAM HUGH.] A CAP AND BELLS for those whom it may fit.

pp. [1] 2–14; head-title   E

[Edinburgh]   [1834]

[No. 4] of Nugae Histrionicae (no. 1982).

1979 [LOGAN, WILLIAM HUGH]. *THE EDINBURGH ROSCIAD; for the summer season, 1834.

pp. 8   E

Imprinted at Modern Athens   1834

[No. 3] of Nugae Histrionicae. (no. 1982).

1980 GENTLEMAN IN TOWN, A, *pseud. of* William Hugh Logan. *Letter from a gentleman in town to his friend in the country, regarding Keeley, the theatre, and other matters connected with the drama in Edinburgh.

pp. [8]

[Edinburgh]   1834

Signed H.M. and dated 7 June 1834 — Loewenberg. [No. 1] of Nugae Histrionicae (no. 1982).

1981 [SPITFIRE, PEREGRINE, *pseud. of* William Hugh Logan]. PLAYS AND PLAYERS at the Edinburgh Adelphi Theatre. July, 1834.

pp. [1] 2–8; title headed: Fourth edition   E

[Edinburgh]   [1834]

[No. 2] of Nugae Histrionicae (no. 1982).

1982 ——[reissue of nos. 1978–1981] NUGAE HISTRIONICAE. Emanations from the pen of Peregrine Spitfire, Gent.

pp. [2] [1–3] 4–8, ²[1–3] 4–8, ³[1] 2–8, ⁴[1] 2–14, ⁵[1] 2
                                                   EP

Edinburgh: Buchanan and Co.   1834

1983 [LOGAN, WILLIAM HUGH and JAMES MAIDMENT, *eds.*] FRAGMENTA SCOTO-DRAMATICA. 1715–1758.

pp. [1–3] 4–48

Edinburgh   1835

IKF. *Another copy at L. 'A very few copies have been printed at the private expense of the editor.' Edited by W. H. Logan, as he claimed (H and L), or by James Maidment, according to Stevenson, p. 10; probably edited jointly.*

The Disputes of William Black

A very litigious shareholder of the Edinburgh Adelphi Theatre. He was a merchant in Leith, but gave up his business, and became lessee of the Queen's Theatre, Edinburgh, which he opened in 1855. He had a good company, Tom

Mead being his leading man, and he did everything well; but he failed in about 18 months, and, it is said, had to take a clerk's situation in the business he had once owned — Lowe.

1984 CORRESPONDENCE anent the Adelphi Theatre, Edinburgh, betwixt W. H. Murray, Esquire, the lessee; James Spence, Esquire, W.S., the secretary for the trustees; and Mr William Black, merchant, Leith, a shareholder of said theatre.

pp. [1–3] 4–24, misnumbering 18 as "81"   E

Edinburgh: printed by James Brydone   1850

The correspondence was published by Black, who complained that Murray by performing at the Theatre Royal in preference to the Adelphi, was not fulfilling his contract with the shareholders of the latter theatre, of which he was also lessee; and that Spence was not faithfully representing their interests.

1985 BLACK, WILLIAM. Letter, Mr. William Black, merchant, Leith, to the trustees of the Edinburgh Circus, now Adelphi Theatre.

pp. [1] 2–3 [4]; head-title   E

[Edinburgh]: James Brydone, printer   1851

1986 BLACK, WILLIAM. Letters, &c. anent the Adelphi Theatre, Edinburgh, to James Maidment, Esq., advocate, John Reid, Esq., Dollar, and James Spence, Esq., writer to the signet, the secretary for the trustees, by William Black, Merchant, Leith, a shareholder of said theatre.

pp. [1–3] 4–7 [8]   MH

Edinburgh: printed by James Brydone   1851

1987 BLACK, WILLIAM. Additional correspondence anent the Adelphi Theatre, Edinburgh, betwixt James Spence, Esquire, W.S., the secretary for the trustees, and Mr William Black, merchant, Leith, a shareholder of said theatre.

pp. [1–3] 4–15 [16]   E

Edinburgh: printed by James Brydone   1852

Supporting Black's complaint that his trustees and their secretary were withholding the accounts from the shareholders.

1988 BLACK, WILLIAM. Case for William Black, merchant in Leith, a shareholder, and one of the trustees for the shareholders, of the Edinburgh Circus, thereafter called the Adelphi Theatre, and now named the Queen's Theatre and Opera House, against John Spence, Esq., surgeon-dentist, 50 Great King Street, Edinburgh.

pp. [1–3] 4–16   EP

Edinburgh: printed by James Brydone   1854

Objecting to Spence's continuing as a trustee, on the ground that he was not a bona fide *shareholder. Black states (p. 9) that twenty copies of the 'Case' (dated 9 Nov) were already printed before further action by Spence led him to add the 'Appendix': it is not known if these copies were published.*

1989 ———Addition to "Case" for William Black, merchant in Leith, against John Spence, 50 Great King Street, Edinburgh.

pp. [1] 2–4; head-title   EP

[Edinburgh]   1854

1990 ———[another edition of no. 1988, with Addition to "Case"].

pp. [1–3] 4–20   E

Edinburgh: printed by James Brydone   1854

1991 BLACK, WILLIAM. Case for William Black, merchant in Leith, a shareholder, and one of the trustees for the shareholders, of the Edinburgh Circus, thereafter called the Adelphi Theatre, and now named the Queen's Theatre and Opera House, against unclaimed shares.

pp. [1–3] 4–14 [15–16 (bl.)]   E

Edinburgh: printed by James Brydone   1854

Alleging that there have been irregularities in the re-sale of long dormant shares.

1992 BLACK, WILLIAM. Objections for William Black, merchant in Leith, a shareholder, and one of the trustees for the shareholders, of the Edinburgh Circus, thereafter called the Adelphi Theatre, and now named the Queen's Theatre and Opera House, to the report by James Maidment, advocate, David Smith, W.S., and Thomas Scott, accountant, Edinburgh, the committee of the trustees of the Adelphi Theatre appointed to revise the list of shareholders.

pp. [1–3] 4–8   EP

Edinburgh: printed by James Brydone   1855

✂ Clericus, M.A., *pseud. of the Rev.* Richard Hibbs. Remarks on the Italian opera in Edinburgh; with reference to Dr. Guthrie's proposed "placard" . . . Edinburgh, Glasgow and London. 1854. *See no. 603.*

1993 REPORT by the trustees of the Queen's Theatre and Opera-House to a general meeting of the shareholders, held on the 25th May 1857. Approved, and ordered to be printed and circulated.

pp. [1–3] 4–12   E

Edinburgh: printed by Murray and Gibb   1857

✂ An Act to confer powers on the commissioners of Her Majesty's Works and Public Buildings to acquire the Theatre Royal, Edinburgh. [1858.]

See GOVERNMENT REGULATION OF THE THEATRE for the year 1858 (p. 33 above).

1994 EVIDENCE IN ARBITRATION. The owners of the Theatre-Royal of Edinburgh, Claimants; The Commissioners of Her Majesty's works and public buildings, Respondents. George Moir, Esq., Oversman. David Rhind, Esq., and James Horne, Esq., Arbiters. George Patton, Esq., and Patrick Fraser, Esq., Counsel for the Claimants. The Lord Advocate, Edward S. Gordon, Esq., and A. T. Boyle, Esq., Counsel for the Respondents. Grant & Wallace, W.S., Agents for Claimants. Donald Horne, W.S., Agent for Respondents. Hugh James Rollo, W.S., Clerk to the Arbitration. J. Irvine Smith, Short-Hand Writer.

pp. [i–iii] iv, [1] 2–169 [170]; pl., fold. [1] hand coloured   E

[Edinburgh]: W. Burness, Printer to Her Majesty
September 1859

Details of the sale of the Theatre Royal to the Government, who had aquired the whole site to erect the new G.P.O. buildings. For the price finally agreed upon see Dibdin, *pp. 468–469.*

1995 [CHAMBERS, ROBERT.] SKETCH of the history of the Edinburgh Theatre-Royal prepared for this evening of its final closing, May 25, 1859. With a poetical address delivered on the occasion.

pp. [2] [1–3] 4–24 [25 (imprint) 26 (bl.)]   EP
Edinburgh: Wood and Co.   1859

The address was by Wyndham (reprinted Dibdin, *pp. 466 seq.).*

1996 THE EDINBURGH STAGE from 1816 to 1821. (From 'Reminiscences of a writer's clerk,' in the 'Montrose Standard'.)

pp. [1–3] 4–8   EP
Edinburgh: printed by James Turner & Co.   1877

✖ Wilson, Frank. Miss Alma Murray as Juliet. 1887. *See no. 3359.*

Alma Murray in Edinburgh 1884.

1997 DIBDIN, JAMES C. The annals of the Edinburgh stage with an account of the rise and progress of dramatic writing in Scotland, by James C. Dibdin.

pp. [i–v] vi–viii, [1–3] 4–511 [512]; pls. [front., 6]; facsim. playbills [2]; errata slip   NbU
Edinburgh: Richard Cameron   1888

1998 HARRIS, DAVID FRASER. St. Cecilia's Hall in the Niddry Wynd   A chapter in the history of the music of the past in Edinburgh By David Fraser Harris M.D., C.M., B.Sc. (Lond.), F.R.S.E., F.S.A. Scot. Lecturer on Physiology in the University of St. Andrews.

pp. [i–vi] vii–xv [xvi], [1] 2–303 [304 (bl.)]; illus., incl. facsims.   GU
Edinburgh and London: Oliphant Anderson and Ferrier
1899

1999 ———second edition . . . by David Fraser Harris . . . formerly Fellow of the Society of Antiquaries, Scotland, Lecturer, on Physiology in the University of Birmingham.

pp. [6] iii–iv ix–xv [xvi] [=16], [1] 2–303 [304 (bl.)]; illus., incl. facsims.   GU

Edinburgh and London: Oliphant Anderson and Ferrier   1911

Glasgow

See also GOVERNMENT REGULATION OF THE THEATRE *for the year 1803 (p. 28 above);* INDEX OF PLACES OF PUBLICATION.

2000 THE QUEEN STREET GHOST; or theatrical spectre!!

pp. [1–3] 4–16   GM
Glasgow: printed by Duncan Mackenzie   1806

Signed "A Spectre". An estimate of the stage qualities of the company.

2001 FOOT, J[OHN] F[ORRESTER]. A general review of the management of Thomas Beaumont, ★★★ alias, Capt. —— ††† lessee of the Theatre Royal, Glasgow, from the commencement of the present season, to the appointment of the new acting-manager. To which is added, A faithful account of the mode adopted by the manager's friends in suppressing "A reply to all facts"; with remarks on the alleged interposition of the committee of proprietors. By J. F. Foot, Esq. late of the Theatre Royal.

pp. [4] [1] 2–47 [48 (bl.)]   L
Glasgow: printed by D. McKenzie   [1809]

2002 HILL, *Mr.* A plain statement of facts, addressed to the inhabitants of Glasgow, by Mr. Hill, from the Theatre Royal, Covent Garden.

pp. [1–3] 4–11 [12]   E
Glasgow: printed by James Hedderwick and Co.   1809

✖ Bell, John Montgomerie. Answers for William Johnson of the Tontine Theatre . . . Paisley, to the reasons of suspension and interdict. . . And for the late concern of [those] designing themselves proprietors and patentees of the Theatre Royal, Glasgow; and Francis Seymour, designing himself tenant. 1826. *See no. 2022.*

2003 M., E. A brief reply to a pamphlet, entitled. "The state of public amusements, in Glasgow, &c. &c." By E.M.

pp. [1–2] 3–8   GU
Paisley: printed by G. Caldwell   1829

A defence of Seymour of the Theatre Royal. The pamphlet originally appeared as an article in the Edinburgh Evening Post.

The Management of J. H. Alexander

Familiarly known as "Alec", Mr. Alexander was one of the most amusing of characters. He was the manager of the Carlisle and Dumfries theatres; became manager of minor theatres in Glasgow and Edinburgh; and in 1829 purchased the Glasgow patent, which he made a paying speculation. Numberless anecdotes of his oddities are told — Lowe.

2004 ALEXANDER, JOHN HENRY. *Persecution and oppression. No. 1. Account of the proceedings and prosecution against John Henry Alexander, manager of the Caledonian Theatres of Glasgow and Edinburgh, instituted by Francis Seymour, designating himself manager of the Theatre Royal, Glasgow, as a common informer on an old act passed in the reign of Queen Anne, and amended by the 10th Geo. II. so far as relates to "Common players of interludes, rogues, vagabonds, and sturdy beggars," &c.

Glasgow   1828

An appeal by Alexander against the legal proceedings against him by the then patentee of the Theatre Royal. He is very impressive in his denunciations of tyranny, &c., but, when he himself became patentee, he was a most vigorous assertor of his rights — Lowe.

2005 HARDY, ROBERT BURNS. *To the public.

pp. 4

[Glasgow]   [1830]

A four page sheet, 12 mo, in reply to J. H. Alexander's Appeal to the Public regarding his throwing into prison a poor Showman for infringing his patent — Lowe.

2006 HARDY, R[OBERT] B[URNS]. *Reply to Alexander's second appeal to the public; in which he insults the citizens of Glasgow in his usual style, and basely insinuates, that the meeting held in the Bazaar was not a public meeting; with a brief notice of a visit to the theatre, &c. &c. By R. B. Hardy.

pp. 8; head-title

[Glasgow]   [ca. 1830]

Loewenberg.

2007 HARDY, R[OBERT] B[URNS]. *Lectures on the drama: First Series — Shakespeare.

pp. [i–v] vi [vii–viii], 1–134 [135–136 (bl.)]   BP
Glasgow: Reid; Edinburgh: Oliver & Boyd; London: Whittaker *et al.*   1834

The author states in his Preface: "The following Essays were written in prison . . . where I was thrown at the instance of the manager of the Glasgow theatre, for publishing an alleged libel on his character". Dedicated to James Sheridan Knowles. The second, third and fourth series announced at the end never appeared, it seems.

2008 ALEXANDER, JOHN HENRY. Letter to the Lord Provost, Magistrates, Town Council, and citizens of Glasgow, on the subject of a pamphlet addressed to them *On the present state of the Theatre-Royal, and the duties incumbent upon them regarding its patent*, by an individual styling himself "Walter Dennistoun, Esq."

pp. [1–3] 4–23 [24]   E
Glasgow: Muir, Gowans, & Co.   1835

2009 DENNISTOUN, WALTER. *Letter to the Lord Provost, Magistrates, and Town Council of Glasgow, on the present state of the Theatre Royal, and the duties incumbent upon them regarding its patent. By Walter Dennistoun, Esq.

Glasgow   1835

An attack upon Alexander — Lowe.

2010 DENNISTOUN, WALTER. Walter Dennistoun's second letter to the Lord Provost & Magistrates of Glasgow, in reply to John Henry Alexander's pamphlet, in which he attempts to defend his position as a theatrical monopolist.

pp. [1–2] 3–12   GM
Glasgow: James Duncan   1835

2011 GRAY, GEORGE. A lecture on the mischievous effects of theatrical monopolies, twice delivered before the citizens of Glasgow: containing a concise history of the stage, and an exposition of all the laws affecting the drama and its professors. By George Gray, of the London and Dublin theatres, and member of the London Dramatic Committee.

pp. [1–5] 6–21, [i] ii [iii] (Appendix)   GU
Glasgow: John Reid & Co; Edinburgh: Oliver & Boyd; London: Whittaker & Co.   1835

2012 RECORD in suspension and interdict John Henry Alexander, against John Henry Anderson.

pp. [2] [1] 2–19 [20]   GM
Edinburgh Printing Company   1842

Dated June 30.

2013 ADDITIONAL APPENDIX in suspension and interdict, John Henry Alexander against John Henry Anderson.

pp. [1] 2–4   GM
Edinburgh Printing Company   1842

Dated July 4.

2014 REVISED CASE John Henry Alexander against John Henry Anderson.

pp. [2] [1] 2–59 [60]   GM
Printed by Edinburgh Printing Company   1842

Dated 30 May.

2015 REVISED CASE for John Henry Anderson, of the Minor Theatre in Glasgow; in the process of suspension and interdict against him at the instance of John Henry Alexander, of the Theatre Royal, Glasgow.

pp. [1] 2–28   GM

Edinburgh: printed by W. Burness   1842

     Dated June 3.

2016 REVIEW OF THE LATE CORRESPONDENCE between Mr John Henry Alexander, manager and proprietor of the Glasgow Theatre, and Mr Lloyd, of the Theatre-Royal, Edinburgh.

pp. [1] 2–16; head-title   E

[Glasgow: William Gilchrist, printer]   [1843]

     Against Alexander: calls for the erection of an additional theatre in Glasgow. Of Lloyd, Lowe writes "A popular and accomplished comedian, whose name has been a household word in Scotland for two generations. He made his first appearance, I believe, at Edinburgh on December 30, 1829, at the Caledonian Theatre, then under the management of Bass."

2017 [FULTON, JAMES.] THE ELDER'S FIRST AND LAST VISIT to the play-house. Price one penny. The poet and the public are much indebted to Mr. James Fulton of Greenock, for this most amusing story.

bs.   MH

Copies can only be had in the Poet's Box, 6 St Andrew's Lane, Gallowgate, Glasgow   5 September 1857

2018 BERNARD, CHARLES. Letters from Charles Bernard, of the Gaiety Theatre, Glasgow, to the Justices of the Peace.

pp. [1–3] 4–31 [32]   GM

[Glasgow: priv. ptd.]   [1877]

     On the subject of a licence to sell exciseable liquors in the Theatre.

2019 BAYNHAM, WALTER. The Glasgow stage. By Walter Baynham.

pp. [8] 2–221 [222], [i] ii–viii; pl. [front.]   L

Glasgow: Robert Forrester   1892

     "Only 400 copies printed."

2020 ———[large paper issue]

pp. [8] 2–221 [222], [i] ii–viii; pl. [front.]

Glasgow: Robert Forrester   1892

     JFA. *"Only 100 copies printed."*

Hawick

2021 TYNTE, CHARLES K. and AUSTIN BURNS. *Noctes Hawickianae; or, ye drama on ye Borders, being ye feates and adventures of a dramaticke companie. What they did and how they did it . . . Illustrated in upwards of one hundred humorous sketches. . . .

     MH

Edinburgh   [*ca.* 1850]

Paisley

See also INDEX OF PLACES OF PUBLICATIONS: SCOTLAND.

2022 BELL, J[OHN] M[ONTGOMERIE]. Answers for William Johnson of the Tontine Theatre, Bank Street, Paisley, to the reasons of suspension and interdict for John Hamilton, Henry Monteith, and Colin Campbell, merchants in Glasgow, John Maxwell of Dargavel, Hugh Bogle of Calderbank, Kirkman Findlay, merchant in Glasgow, Laurence Hill, writer in Glasgow, and as taking burden on him for the late concern of James and Laurence Hill, writers in Glasgow, Andrew Mather, merchant in Glasgow, James Denniston of Golf-hill, banker in Glasgow, and Robert Ferrie, wright and builder in Glasgow, designing themselves proprietors and patentees of the Theatre Royal, Glasgow; and Francis Seymour, designing himself tenant of the said theatre.

fold. doc., pp. [1] 2–7 [8]; headed: "Outer-House, February 11, 1826"   MH

     1826

     The proprietors of the Theatre Royal sought to stop Johnson from presenting theatrical performances in Paisley on the grounds that he was infringing their patent rights in Glasgow and also their rights under a licence from the sheriff depute of Renfrewshire.

A NATIONAL THEATRE

See also nos. 975, 1052, 4306 (1897).

2023 DRAMATICUS, *pseud*. The stage as it is: by Dramaticus.

pp. [4] [1] 2–24   L
F. Newton   1847

A plea for a national theatre.

2024 WILSON, WILLIAM. A house for Shakspere. A proposition for the consideration of the nation. By William Wilson. Reprinted from "Hoods Magazine" for September.

pp. [1–3] 4–8   LGk
H. Hurst   1848

Advocates a national theatre for the representation of Shakespeare's plays, as being more important than the Stratford-on-Avon birthplace, which had just been purchased.

2025 WILSON, WILLIAM. The second and concluding paper, containing a review of the reception of the first, and a few digressions. By William Wilson.

pp. [1–3] 4–16   LGk
C. Mitchell   [1848?]

Bound in this copy are two leaves of press comment on Wilson's two pamphlets.

2025.1 TAYLOR, TOM. The theatre in England Some of its shortcomings and possibilities By Tom Taylor. Reprinted from "The Dark Blue" for August.

pp. [1–3] 4–11 [12]   MH
The British and Colonial Publishing Company, Limited   1871

A judicious lament over the shortcomings of the theatre — Lowe. Reprinted with the addition of two paragraphs. Proposes permanent employment for actors at a British Comédie Française, privately financed.

2026 [BATE, SAMUEL STRINGER?] SCHEME for the establishment of a national theatre (somewhat similar to the "Comédie Française") by the formation of a national dramatic institute from amongst real and influential patrons of dramatic art and literature, and eminent artistes earning their livelihood thereby.

pp. [1] 2–15 [16 (bl.)]; head-title   LGk
                                            [ca. 1875]

Copy inscribed: "To Joseph Knight Esq with the author's complts Walter S Raleigh". "Walter S. Raleigh" was a pseudonym used by S. Stringer Bate, dramatic writer, according to BMC, which does not, however, include this item.

2027 GODWIN, GEORGE. On the desirability of obtaining a national theatre not wholly controlled by the prevailing popular taste. A paper read at the Cheltenham Congress of the Social Science Association (Art Department), October, 1878. By George Godwin, F.R.S., F.S.A.

pp. [1–3] 4–32   L
Wyman & Sons   1878

Supported by Planché in his Suggestions for establishing an English Art Theatre *(no. 3426).*

See also SALE CATALOGUES nos. 54, 112; LONDON: KING'S THEATRE passim, especially nos. 1454, 1471, 1479, 1484, 1485; HER MAJESTY'S passim, especially nos. 1445, 1447, LYCEUM (ENGLISH OPERA HOUSE) passim, especially no. 1490; QUEEN'S THEATRE no. 1504; BIOGRAPHY nos. 2392 (Arditi), 2400 (Balfe), 2427 (Beale), 2519 (Braham), 2538 (Catalani), 2539 (Catley), 2694 (Sutherland Edwards), 2746 (Fenton, i.e. "Polly Peachum"), 2976 (Grossmith), 3014 (Hayes), 3033 (Aaron Hill), 3173 (Frances Kelly), 3174 (Michael Kelly), 3176 (Kemble), 3232 (Lind), 3244 (Lumley), 3292 (Malibran), 3301 (Mapleson), 3340 (Mingotti), 3403 (Pasta), 3404 (Paton), 3416 (Phillips), 3443 (Sims Reeves), 3478 (Santley), 3547 (Soldene), 3552 (Sontag), 3575 (Sullivan), 3579 (Templeton), 3580 (Tenducci); PERIODICALS nos. 4068, 4144, 4189, 4197, 4203, 4243.

2028 DENNIS, [JOHN]. An essay on the opera's after the Italian manner, which are about to be establish'd on the English stage: with some reflections on the damage which they may bring to the publick. By Mr. Dennis.

pp. [8] 1–15 [16 (postscript)]   L
John Nutt   1706

Reprinted in Dennis's Select Works (1718) and in Hooker, I, 382–393, with notes.

2029 A COMPARISON between the French and Italian musick and opera's. Translated from the French; with some remarks. To which is added A critical discourse upon opera's in England, and a means proposed for their improvement.

pp. [6] 1–86   L
William Lewis   1709

In part from F. Raguenet's Parallèle des Italiens et des François, &c.

✄ Baldassarii, Benedetto. A letter from Sig. Benedetto Baldassarii. 1720. See no. 3572.

2030 [SETTLE, ELKANAH?] AN EPISTLE to Mr. Handel, upon his operas of *Flavius* and *Julius Caesar*.

pp. [2] [1] 2–3 [4]   MH
J. Roberts   1724

Heroic couplets. Flavius was produced at King's 14th May 1723, and Julius Caesar 20th February 1724. Advertised as published "this day" in the Post Boy 7th March 1724. Reprinted in Otto E. Deutsch, Handel: a Documentary Biography (London, 1955), pp. 158–160. Doubtfully ascribed to Elkanah Settle (F. C. Brown, Elkanah Settle, Chicago, 1910, p. 132).

Pasquinades on the Opera Singers 1724–1736

Involving producers, composers and opera singers, including Heidegger, Handel, Faustina, Senesino, Anastasia Robinson, Carestini, and Farinelli.

2031 AN EPISTLE from S——o, to A——a R——n
pp. [2] [1] 2–3 [4]   MH
M. Smith   1724

Advertised 27th February 1724. For the scandal of 1724 concerning Mrs. Robinson and Senesino, see DNB, "Anastasia Robinson".

2032 ——[another edition]
pp. [2] [1] 2–3 [4]   MH
London   1724

2033 HILL, AARON. *Answer to a scurrilous, obscene poem, entitled *An epistle from Mrs. Robinson to Senesino*. 1724.

    1724

From DNB, "Anastasia Robinson". Not in Brewster. In Hill's The Plaindealer, no. 7, 13th April 1724 there is "An Answer from Mrs. Robinson to Senesino" in verse.

2034 IT CANNOT RAIN BUT IT POURS: or, the first part of London strow'd with rarities. Being a full and true account of a fierce and wild Indian deer that beat the breath out of Mr. U****k's body. As also how Madam Faustina the rare singing woman has been taken hoarse. Together with a lamentable story of their being blooded. And likewise a true relation of the arrival of the two marvellous black Arabian ambassadors, who are of the same country with the wonderful horse lately shewn in King-Street. N.B. The second part of this book by mistake of the printer was published first.

pp. [1–2] 3–11 [12 (bl.)]   L
J. Roberts   1726

Sometimes attributed to Swift. The "second part" perhaps by Arbuthnot. The "second part" which was "published first" is apparently It cannot rain but it pours: or, London strow'd with rarities. Being an account of the arrival of a white bear . . . (Roberts, 1726) This mentions Faustina, but in the title only.

2035 [CAREY, HENRY.] MOCKING IS CATCHING, or, a pastoral lamentation for the loss of a man and no man. In the simple stile. By the author of "Namby pamby".

pp. [2]   L
[N. Blandford]   [1726]

2036 ——[another edition]
pp. [2]   L
[Dublin: reprinted by George Faulkner]   [1726]

Reprinted, with a different title, in The Poems of Henry Carey, ed. by Frederick T. Wood (1930), pp. 108–109.

2037 ★AN ANSWER from F——

pp. [1-4] 5-8   PPL

J. Roberts   1727

Foxon.

2038 ★THE CONTRE TEMPS: or, rival queans: a small farce. As it was lately acted, with great applause, at H——d——r's private Th——re near the H——y M——t.

A. Moore   1727

Groves. *A pungent satire in verse on squabbles among opera singers, composers and producers, including Faustina, Heidegger, Handel and Senesino.*

2039 THE DEVIL TO PAY AT ST. JAMES'S: or, a full and true account of a most horrid and bloody battle between Madam Faustina and Madam Cuzzoni. Also of a hot skirmish between Signor Boschi and Signor Palmecini. Moreover, how Senesino has taken snuff, is going to leave the Opera, and sing psalms at Henley's Oratory. Also about the Flying Man, and how the Doctor of St. Martin's has very unkindly taken down the scaffold, and disappointed a world of good company. As also how a certain great lady is gone mad for love of William Gibson, the Quaker. And how the Wild Boy is come to life again, and has got a dairy maid with child. Also about the great mourning, and the fashions, and the alterations, and what not. With other material occurrences, too many to insert.

pp. [1-2] 3-15 [16 (bl.)]   L

A. Moore   1727

Reprinted in The Miscellaneous Works of the Late Dr. Arbuthnot *(1751 and 1770), but not by Arbuthnot.*

2040 AN EPISTLE FROM S——R S——O to S——a F——A

pp. [1-5] 6-8; vignette on t.p. (two singers in costume on the stage)   MH

J. Roberts   1727

Heroic couplets. The lament of the castrato Senesino.

2041 ★AN EPISTLE from Signora F——a to a lady

pp. [1] 2-4   DFo

Venice [for London]   1727

Reprinted in Caleb D'Anvers, The Twickenham hotch-potch *(1728) (no. 868 above).*

2042 vacant

2043 [CAREY, HENRY.] FAUSTINA: or the Roman songstress, a satyr, on the luxury and effeminacy of the age.

pp. [1-3] 4-11 [12 (bl.)]   L

J. Roberts   [1727]

Another version is printed in The Poems of Henry Carey, *ed. F. T. Wood, 1930, pp. 97-101.*

2044 F——NA'S ANSWER to S——no's epistle.

pp. [1-3] 4-8   L

A. Moore   1727

Heroic couplets. Published 18 March.

2045 ——★second edition corrected

A. Moore   1727

STR.

✠ Arnoux, Claude. New and familiar phrases and dialogues — to which is added a French ode, intituled *The Triumphs of Signora Faustina and of the English Theatre. 1743. See no. 2054.*

2046 AN EPISTLE FROM THE PLATONICK MADAM B——IER, to the celebrated Signor Car——ino.

pp. [1-4] 5-11 [12 (bl.)]   MH

R. Smith   1734

2047 JOHNSON, HURLOTHRUMBO, *pseud.* ★Harmony in an uproar; a letter to F——d——k H——d——l; m——r of the O——a H——e in the Hay-market, from Hurlothrumbo Johnson, Esq. In which the rights and merits of both O——S are properly considered.

pp. 23   MB

R. Smith   1734

A defence of Handel, in the form of an ironical attack, occasioned by the rivalry between Handel at the King's Theatre and the "Opera of the Nobility" at Lincoln's Inn Field, 1733-1734. Dated 12 February 1733 (i.e. Old Style). Hurlothrumbo, by Samuel Johnson of Cheshire, was produced at the Haymarket 29 March 1729. Harmony in an uproar is reprinted in The Miscellaneous Works of the Late Dr. Arbuthnot *(1751 and 1770), but is not by Arbuthnot. Reprinted in part, with notes, in Otto E. Deutsch,* Handel: a documentary biography *(London, 1955) pp. 344-358.*

2048 THE FATE of Courtezans and their enamerato's. A new ballad. Inscrib'd to Mrs. C—— P—— and the angelick Signior F——lli.

pp. [1] 2-4   L

F. Cook   1735

To the tune of "To you, fair ladies, now at land."
Mrs. C. P. has been identified as Constantia Phillips.

2049 THE HAPPY COURTEZAN: or, the prude demolish'd. An epistle from the celebrated Mrs. C—— P——, to the angelick signior Far——n——li.

pp. [2] [1] 2-16   L

J. Roberts   1735

2050 ★THE SECRETS of a woman's heart. An epistle from a friend to Signor F——lli. Occasioned by the epistle of Mrs C—— P—— to the angelick F——li.

pp. [1–2] 3–15 [16 (bl.)]; engr. t.p.

E. Cook   1735

Foxon.

2051 *AN EPISTLE to John James H——dd——g ——r, Esq; on the report of Signor F——r——n——lli's being with child.

pp. [1–2] 3–8

1736

Foxon.

✖ A letter to my Lord *******. With the true reasons of the decay of our dramatic entertainments. 1725. *See no. 866.*

✖ D'Urfey, Thomas, *pseud.* The English stage Italianiz'd. 1727. *See no. 867.*

✖ [Ralph, James.] The touch-stone. 1728. *See no. 869.*

Gay's Beggar's Opera *1728*

For pamphlets on the Beggar's Opera *see THEORY AND CRITICISM nos. 3904–3908; BIOGRAPHY nos. 2746–2752 (Fenton).*

✖ Porée, Charles. An oration . . . With reflections on operas . . . Translated into English by J. Lockman. 1734. *See no. 385.*

See also below no. 2052.

2052 LOCKMAN, [JOHN]. Rosalinda, a musical drama. As it is performed at Hickford's Great Room, in Brewer's Street. By Mr. Lockman. Set to music by Mr. John Christopher Smith. To which is prefixed, An enquiry into the rise and progress of operas and oratorios, with some reflections on lyric poetry and music.

pp. [6] [i] ii–xxiv, [7–8] 9–19 [20]   L

Printed by W. Strahan for the Author   1740

Lockman also contributed "A Discourse on Operas", differing from the present essay, to F. Vanneschi's Fetonte *(London: Woodfall, 1747). See also no. 385.*

2053 ——*[another edition]

pp. xxiv, 7–12

Printed by W. Strahan for the author   1740

STR.

2054 ARNOUX, CLAUDE. *New and familiar phrases and dialogues in French and English . . . to which is added a French ode, intituled, *The Triumphs of Signora Faustina, and of the English Theatre,* preceded by a copy of verses in English by Dr. Merrick on the subject of the Ode, etc.

J. Nourse   1743

STR.

2055 ——*second edition

J. Nourse   1761

STR.

2056 ORPHEUS and Hecate. An ode. Inscribed to the patroness of the Italian opera.

pp. [1–5] 6–7 [8 (bl.)]   L

W. Webb   1746

✖ Faddle found out: or, the draining of Hal W——dw——d's coffee-pot. [ca. 1748]. *See no. 3669.*

Woodward's scheme to bring over Italian opera.

2057 *A SCHEME for having an Italian Opera in London, of a new taste.

pp. 22   MB

W. Owen   1753

A proposal to employ parodies to increase the popularity of the operas to be given at the King's Theatre, Haymarket. The text is in English and French on opposite pages. The last page of the English text has no corresponding page in French — Brown.

2058 *THE VOICE of discord, or the battle of the fiddles. A history of a seditious and unnatural attempt upon the lives and properties of fifty singers and fiddlers. (With French translation).

?   1753

Lowe. *An answer to no. 2057.*

✖ Passerini, Joseph. An appeal to the public by Signor Passerini. Bath 1756. *See no. 1545.*

✖ An examination of the oratorios performed this season at Covent Garden Theatre. 1763. *See no. 1151.*

2059 A FAIR ENQUIRY into the state of operas in England.

pp. [1–3] 4–16   L

M. Cooper   [1763?]

On the unpopularity of opera in England.

✖ An elegy on the death of *The guardian outwitted,* an opera; written and composed by Thomas Augustine Arne. 1765. *See no. 3825.*

2060 ALGAROTTI, Count [FRANCESCO]. An essay on the opera written by Count Algarotti F.R.S. F.S.A. etc.

pp. [i–v] vi [vii–viii], [1] 2–192   L

L. Davis and C. Reymers   1767

A translation of Algarotti's Saggio sopra L'Opera in Musica *(1755).*

2061 ———[another edition] Written in Italian by Count Algarotti F.R.S. F.S.A. etc.

pp. [2] [i–iii] iv, [2] 5–124 [2] 125–182 E

Glasgow: R. Urie 1768

2062 ———[another edition] Francesco Algarotti A reprint of his Essay on Opera and a sketch of his life by Richard Northcott.

pp. [1–2] 3–48; illus. L

The Press Printers Ltd. 1917

A "revised reprint" of the Essay on the Opera *(1767). Cover title: "A tribute to Algarotti".*

2063 THE OPERA: a poem. By the author of The coach drivers. Book I.

pp. [4] [1] 2–19 [20] L

Printed for the Author; and sold by W. Flexney; C. Bathurst; G. Kearsly; and M. Hingeston 1767

Apparently no more books published.

2064 THE LYRIC MUSE revived in Europe or a critical display of the opera in all its revolutions.

pp. [2] [i] ii–vi, [1] 2–128, ^{2}127–147 [148] [=150] L

L. Davis and C. Reymers 1768

2065 THE REMARKABLE TRIAL of the Queen of Quavers, and her associates, for sorcery, witchcraft, and enchantment, at the assizes held in the moon, for the County of Gelding, before the Rt. Hon. Sir Francis Lash, Lord Chief Baron of the Lunar Exchequer. Taken in short hand by Joseph Democritus, and William Diogenes.

pp. [1–3] 4–148 L

J. Bew [1777 or 1778]

A satire on the popularity of Italian opera. The "Queen of Quavers" is Polly Farmer, according to BMC.

2066 [BURGOYNE, JOHN.] THE LORD OF THE MANOR, a comic opera, as it is performed at the Theatre Royal Drury-Lane, with a preface by the author.

pp. [2] v–xxvi, [1] 2–96 L

T. Evans 1781

The preface is a dissertation on opera, especially English comic opera. The Lord of the Manor was produced at Drury Lane 27 December 1780.

2067 ———*another edition

Dublin 1781

CBEL.

Reprinted, with the preface, in The Dramatic and Poetical Works of the late Lieut. Gen. J. Burgoyne; to which is prefixed, Memoirs of the Author *(London), 1808, vol. I.*

2068 BROWN, JOHN. Letters upon the poetry and music of the Italian opera; addressed to a friend. By the late Mr. John Brown, painter.

pp. [2] [i–iii] iv–xx, [1] 2–141 [142]; illus. L

Edinburgh: Bell and Bradfute; London: Elliott and Kay 1789

The letters were addressed to Lord Monboddo, who introduces the volume.

2069 ———Letters on the Italian opera: addressed to the Hon. Lord Monboddo. By the late Mr. John Brown. Second edition.

pp. [i–iii] iv–xviii, [1] 2–141 [142 (bl.) 143 (errata) 144–146 (bl.)]; illus. (diagram) E

Sold by T. Cadell 1791

✠ Houlton, R. A review of the musical drama of the Theatre Royal, Drury Lane for the years 1797 . . . 1800. Which will tend to develop a system of private influence injurious to musical emulation . . . and to elucidate . . . Mrs. Plowden's late distinguished publication. 1801. *See no. 1364.*

2070 BRANDON, I[SAAC]. Kais: or, love in the deserts. An opera. In four acts: as performed at the Theatre Royal, Drury-Lane. With a few words by way of preface. By I. Brandon, Esq.

pp. [iii–vii] viii–xv [xvi], [1] 2–68; cancellans, pp. 19–20 L

London: sold by J. Murray; J. Harding; Edinburgh: A. Constable & Co. 1808

Kais was produced at Drury Lane on 11 February 1803.

2071 ———second edition

pp. [i–vii] viii–xv [xvi], [1] 2–68 L

London: sold by J. Murray; J. Harding; Edinburgh: A. Constable and Co. 1808

2072 ———*third edition

DLC

J. Murray 1808

✠ Strictures on the engagement of Madame Catalani. 1809. *See no. 1274.*

✠ Greville, [Henry Francis]. Mr. Greville's statement of Mr. Naldi's case. 1811. *See no. 1114. See also no. 1115.*

2073 [EDGCUMBE, RICHARD, *Second Earl of Mount Edgcumbe.*] MUSICAL REMINISCENCES of an old amateur, for fifty years, from 1773 to 1823.

pp. [i–v] vi–xii [13] 14–148 L

W. Clarke 1824

2074 ——Musical reminiscences of an old amateur chiefly respecting the Italian opera in England for fifty years, from 1773 to 1823, the second edition, continued to the present time.

pp. [i–v] vi–xii [13] 14–183 [184]   L
W. Clarke   1827

This edition concludes with a charitable appeal on behalf of the singer Miss Cecilia Davies.

2075 ——Musical reminiscences chiefly respecting the Italian Opera in England from the year 1773 to the present time. By the Earl of Mount Edgcumbe. The Third Edition.

1828

Lowe.

2076 ——Musical reminiscences, containing an account of the Italian opera in England. From 1773. The fourth edition, continued to the present time, and including the Festival in Westminster Abbey. By the Earl of Mount Edgcumbe.

pp. [i–v] vi–xvi, [1] 2–193 [194–197] 198–224   GU
London: John Andrews; Richmond: F. H. Wall   1834

✖ Ebers, John. Seven years of the King's Theatre. 1828. *See no. 1484.*

2077 VOCAL AND DRAMATIC INSTITUTION. February 1829.

fold. doc., pp. [1] 2–3 [4]; filing-title   L
Mallett, printer   1829

A prospectus of the Institution; Secretary at 286, Regent Street. Head-title: "Vocal and dramatic institution for instruction in singing, combining all dramatic requisites to qualify for the orchestra and theatre, with an exclusive department to accomplish for the ballet."

2078 PARKE, W[ILLIAM] T[HOMAS]. Musical memoirs; comprising an account of the general state of music in England, from the first commemoration of Handel, in 1784, to the year 1830. Interspersed with numerous anecdotes, musical, histrionic, &c. By W. T. Parke, forty years principal oboist to the Theatre Royal Covent Garden.

2 vols. pp. [i–v] vi–vii [viii], [1] 2–350 + [4] [1] 2–333 [334 (advts.)]   L
Henry Colburn and Richard Bentley   1830

2079 RODWELL, G[EORGE] HERBERT [BUONOPARTE]. A letter to the musicians of Great Britain; containing a prospectus of proposed plans for the better encouragement of native musical talent, and for the erection and management of a grand national opera in London by G. Herbert Rodwell.

pp. [1–3] 4–32   GU
James Fraser   1833

Prospectus for a new opera house. Criticism of Covent Garden, the Opera House and Drury Lane for the operas they have performed.

2080 ——*[another edition]

pp. 16   DLC
Printed by W. Clowes   1834

2081 CHALON, A. E. *Recollections of the Italian Opera 1835.

pls. 7
J. Mitchell   1836
IKF.

2082 HOGARTH, GEORGE. Memoirs of the musical drama. By George Hogarth.

2 vols. pp. [i–v] vi–xii [xiii (list of ports.) xiv (bl.)], [1] 2–465 [466]; pls., [front., 1] + pp. [i–v] vi–viii, [1] 2–464; pls. [front., 5]   L
Richard Bentley   1838

2083 ——A new edition. Memoirs of the opera in Italy, France, Germany, and England. By George Hogarth.

2 vols. pp. [i–iii] iv–viii, [1] 2–376; pl. [front.] + pp. [i–iii] iv–v [vi (bl.)], [1] 2–379 [380]; pl. [front.]   L
Richard Bentley   1851

Printed end-papers. Cheap edition, with omissions and additions.

2084 EGESTORFF, GEORGE. A lecture on music, with especial reference to the German opera, as introduced into this country; by George Egestorff, formerly a member of King George the Fourth's private band.

pp. [1–5] 6–30 [31–32 (advts.)]   E
Published by the author   1840

2085 ENGLISH OPERA HOUSE. Statement and correspondence between Mr. Balfe, and Mr. H. Phillips, relative to the affairs of the above theatre. Price one shilling.

pp. [2] [1–3] 4–24 [25–26 (bl.)]; half-title: English Opera House. Correspondence, &c. between Mr. Balfe and Mr. H. Phillips   MH
W. S. Johnson   1841

A narrative of the quarrel caused by the sudden withdrawal of Phillips, the singer, from his engagement with Balfe, published by the latter — Lowe.

✖ The opera ticket. 1843. *See no. 582.*
An attack on the theatre, especially opera and ballet.

2086 BEAUTIES of the opera and ballet. Illustrated with ten highly-finished portraits, engraved on steel, and numerous engravings on wood, under the superintendence of Mr. Charles Heath.

pp. [i–ix] x–xiv [xv–xvi], [1] 2–160; illus. (ptd. in various colours); pls. [10] L

David Bogue [1844]

Plates by A. E. Chalon and others; text from Les Beautés de l'Opéra, *by Gautier and others.*

2087 LUNN, HENRY C. Musings of a musician: a series of popular sketches, illustrative of musical matters and musical people. By Henry C. Lunn, Associate of the Royal Academy of Music.

pp. [iii–v] vi [vii–viii], [1] 2–205 [206] GU

Simpkin, Marshall, and Co. 1846

2088 ———a new edition

pp. [i–iii] iv [v–vii] viii, [1] 2–204 [205–207 (advts.) 208 (bl.)] GU

Robert Cocks and Co., Simpkin, Marshall, and Co. 1854

2089 *LYRIC RECOLLECTIONS of the Marchioness of C—— after beholding her on various occasions at the Italian opera, and other places of public entertainment, during the years 1845–6.

Printed for private circulation 1847

STR.

✠ A review of the performances of Mademoiselle Jenny Lind, at Her Majesty's Theatre, and their influence and effect upon our national drama. 1847. *See no. 3236.*

✠ Clericus, M. A., *pseud. of the Rev.* Richard Hibbs. Remarks on the Italian opera in Edinburgh; with reference to Dr. Guthrie's proposed "placard". Edinburgh, Glasgow and London. 1854. *See no. 603.*

✠ Remarks on the morality of dramatic compositions: with particular reference to "La Traviata", etc. 1856. *See no. 607.*

2090 EDWARDS, [HENRY] SUTHERLAND. History of the opera, from its origin in Italy to the present time. With anecdotes of the most celebrated composers and vocalists of Europe. By Sutherland Edwards.

2 vols. pp. [i–iii] iv, [1] 2–303 [304 (advt.)] + [i–iii] iv, [1] 2–324 L

Wm. H. Allen & Co. 1862

2091 ———*second edition

2 vols. in 1 MB

1862

✠ Clayton, Ellen Creathorne. Queens of song . . . To which is added a chronological list of all the operas that have been performed in Europe. 1863. *See no. 2241.*

2092 THE ENGLISH OPERA ASSOCIATION (LIMITED). Prospectus.

pp. [*4*]; filing-title L

Printed by J. Miles & Co. [1864?]

✠ Royal Italian Opera, Covent Garden. Season 1864. *See no. 1310.*

2093 [COX, JOHN EDMUND.] MUSICAL RECOLLECTIONS of the last half-century.

2 vols. pp. [i–v] vi–xv [xvi], [1–3] 4–345 [346 (bl.) 347–348 (advts.)] + [*2* (advts.)] [i–iii] iv–vi, [1] 2–370 [371–372 (advts.)] L

Tinsley Brothers 1872

Issued in blue cloth, with an additional 14 pages and 16 pages of advertisements in vols. 1 and 2, and also in green cloth without the additional advertisements.

2094 EDWARDS, H[ENRY] SUTHERLAND. The lyrical drama. Essays on subjects, composers, & executants of modern opera. By H. Sutherland Edwards.

2 vols. pp. [1–2], [i–iii] iv, [3] 4–316 + [i–iii] iv, [1] 2–312 L

W. H. Allen & Co. 1881

2095 ROOSEVELT, BLANCHE, *pseud. of* Blanche Roosevelt Tucker Macchetta. Stage-struck; or, she would be an opera-singer. By Blanche Roosevelt.

2 vols. pp. [*4*] [i–iii] iv [5] 6–278 [279–280 (bl.)] + [*4*] [1] 2–271 [272] L

Sampson Low, Marston, Searle & Rivington 1884

A "narration of truth in the form of fiction" written to "persuade American girls who come over to Europe to study music, that they might be wiser to stay at home".

———[American edition] New York: Fords, Howard & Hulbert, 1884.

2096 EDWARDS, H[ENRY] SUTHERLAND. The prima donna Her history and surroundings from the seventeenth to the nineteenth century by H. Sutherland Edwards.

2 vols. pp. [*8*] [1] 2–320 + [*4*] [1] 2–302 [303–304 (bl.)] L

Remington and Co. 1888

✠ Leeds, Josiah Woodward. The theatre: an essay upon the non-accordancy of stage-plays with the Christian profession. Newport, Mon.: London. 1890. *See no. 675.*

A British edition of an American Quaker tract, instigated by the presentation of the Welsh National Opera in Cardiff.

2097 MAUREL, VICTOR. Lyceum Theatre, December 8th, 1890. Address on the modern development of the lyric art, supplemented by practical demonstrations.

pp. [1] 2–14 [15] 16

[London] [1890]

IKF.

2098 FITZGERALD, PERCY [HETHERINGTON].
The Savoy Opera and the Savoyards by Percy Fitzgerald, M.A., F.S.A.

pp. [i–vii] viii [ix] x–xii [xiii] xiv–xv [xvi], [1] 2–248;
pls. [front., 1]; illus. L

Chatto & Windus 1894

This copy wants plate facing page 240.

2099 ——*new edition
illus.

1899

Clunes

2100 STREATFEILD, R[ICHARD] A[LEXANDER].
The opera A sketch of the development of opera.
With full descriptions of every work in the modern repertory by R. A. Streatfeild with an introduction by J. A. Fuller-Maitland.

pp. [i–iv] v–xx, [1] 2–336; t.p. in red and black L
London: John C. Nimmo; Philadelphia: J. B.
Lippincott Company 1897

An edition of 1,500 copies according to a publisher's note in the 1902 edition.

2101 ——new edition, revised and enlarged.

pp. [i–iv] v–xx, [1] 2–351 [352]; t.p. in red and black L
London: John C. Nimmo; Philadelphia: J. B.
Lippincott Company 1902

Title-page differs from that of first edition in having "all works" instead of "every work"

2102 ——third edition, revised and enlarged.

pp. [i–iv] v–xix [xx], [1] 2–363 [364]; t.p. in red and black L

George Routledge & Sons, Limited 1907

2103 ——fifth edition, revised, enlarged and brought down to date by Edward J. Dent.

pp. [4] [i–ii] iii–xx, [1] 2–402 [403–404 (bl.)] L
London: George Routledge & Sons, Ltd.; J. Curwen & Sons, Ltd.; New York: E. P. Dutton & Co. 1925

A cheaper version of the fifth edition was published in 1931, and the fifth edition was reprinted in 1934. Fuller-Maitland's introduction is revised in each edition.

For London music halls see THE LONDON THEATRE: INDIVIDUAL THEATRES especially nos. 1112, 1422–1424, 1494–1497, 1524–1533.

See also SALE CATALOGUES no. 126 (Richardson); GOVERNMENT REGULATION OF THE THEATRE passim; MORALITY OF THE THEATRE nos. 309, 355–357, 628, 650, 664, 673; GENERAL HISTORY nos. 864–871, 889, 918, 968; MEDIEVAL AND RENAISSANCE STUDIES no. 1016, THE LONDON THEATRE no. 1323 (Drury Lane & Lincoln's Inn Fields); THEATRE OUT OF LONDON nos. 1586 (Burwell), 1670 (Norwich), 1703, 1708 (York); BIOGRAPHY: GARRICK 2851 (Drury Lane); THEORY & CRITICISM no. 3730; INDIVIDUAL PLAYS no. 4066 (Queen Mab). See also BIOGRAPHY nos. 2450 (Betterton), 2498 (Blanchard), 2546 (Cave), 2554 (Chevalier), 2649 (Sam Cowell), 2729 (Nellie Farren), 2963 (Corney Grain), 2966 (Grimaldi), 3048 (Holtum), 3050 (Houston), 3172 (Keith), 3225–6 (Lewes), 3271 (Mackney), 3315 (Mathews), 3335 (Prince Miller), 3392 (Pack), 3430 (Purvis), 3440 (German Reeds), 3450 (Roberts), 3614 (Wallet); PERIODICALS nos. 4136, 4186, 4196, 4210, 4213, 4214, 4222, 4224, 4229, 4233, 4243, 4254, 4260, 4273, 4276, 4277, 4286, 4288, 4297, 4298, 4300, 4311, 4316, 4317, 4318, 4321, 4326, 4350, 4351, 4352, 4353, 4383, 4384, 4503–4.

2104 THE BRITISH STAGE; or, the exploits of Harlequin: a farce. As it is performed by a company of wonderful comedians at both theatres, with universal applause; with all its original songs, scenes, and machines. Design'd as an after-entertainment for the audiences of *Harlequin Doctor Faustus*, and *The necromancer.*

pp. [i–iv] v–vii [viii], 1–24   L

T. Warner   1724

Not a genuine play, but a satire on the taste for pantomime. John Thurmond's Harlequin Doctor Faustus *was produced at Drury Lane 26th November 1723 and* The necromancer *at Lincoln's Inn Fields 20th December 1723. See also below no. 3921.*

2105 WEAVER, JOHN. The history of the mimes and pantomimes, with an historical account of several performers in dancing, living in the time of the Roman emperors. To which will be added, a list of the modern entertainments that have been exhibited on the English stage, either in imitation of the ancient pantomimes, or after the manner of the modern Italians; when and were first performed, and by whom composed. By John Weaver, dancing-master.

pp. [4] 1–56   L

J. Roberts and A. Dod   1728

John Weaver's An essay towards an history of dancing (1712) *contains a short section on "stage-dancing".*

2106 [MILLER, JAMES.] HARLEQUIN-HORACE: or, the art of modern poetry.

pp. [10] [1] 2–59 [60 (advts.)]; pl. [front.]; t.p. in red and black   L

Lawton Gilliver   1731

With a dedication to John Rich, and a frontispiece depicting a performance with the legend "Serpentes avibus geminentur; Tigribus agni", (Ars Poetica, l. 13). On this poem and its frontispiece see Stephens 1834.

2107 ——the third edition, corrected. With several additional lines and explanatory notes.

pp. [10] 2–61 [62 (advts.)]; pl. [front.]; t.p. in red and black   L

Lawton Gilliver   1735

With a dedication to John Rich, and a frontispiece caricature with the legend
Shakespear, Rowe, Johnson, now are quite undone
These are thy Tryumphs, thy Exploits O Lun!
This frontispiece was originally published separately (Stephens 1838) and may in fact not be integral to this edition of Harlequin-Horace, of which only one copy has been seen.

2108 ——[*another edition].

1735

CBEL.

Reprinted (from the first edition) in A collection of scarce, curious and valuable pieces in verse and prose *[ed. W. Ruddiman] (Edinburgh, 1773), pp. 231–268.*

2109 MÖSER, JUSTUS. Harlequin: or, a defence of grotesque comic performances. By Mr. Justus Möser, Councellor of the High Court of Justice at Osnabruck, etc. Translated from the German by Joach. Andr. Fred. Warnecke, LL.C.

pp. [i–v] vi–xv [xvi], [1] 2–104; pl. [front.]   L

Printed and sold by W. Nicoll, P. A. de Hondt, Drybutter   1766

Dedicated by the translator to Garrick.

2109.1 [COLLIER, JOHN PAYNE.] PUNCH AND JUDY, with illustrations designed and engraved by George Cruikshank. Accompanied by the dialogue of the puppet-show, an account of its origin, and of puppet-plays in England.

pp. [2] [1] 2–111 [112]; illus.; pls. [front.] 1–23   GU

S. Prowett   1828

Issued with plates both plain and coloured. Cohn 150. On this work see Speaight, pp. 185–188 and notes, and P. McPharlin "The Collier-Cruikshank Punch and Judy", The Colophon, N.S. I, 3 (1936), 371–387. Collier was paid £50, and produced his work at short notice. According to Cruikshank, the puppet showman

Piccini put on a special performance for Prowett, Collier, and himself.

2109.2 ——second edition [with additional text]
pp. [2] [1] 2–141 [142]; illus.; pls. [front.] 1–23

S. Prowett   1828

> GS. *Title reads "drawn and engraved".*

2109.3 ——third edition [reissue of 2109.2 with press criticisms].
pp. [8] [1] 2–141 [142]; illus.; pls. [front.] 1–23
W. H. Reid   1832

> GS. *Title reads "designed and engraved".*

2109.4 ——[reissue of 2109.2] Punch's real history. With twenty-eight illustrations, drawn and engraved by George Cruikshank. Accompanied by the tragical comedy or comical tragedy of Punch and Judy; the explanation of the puppet-show, and account of its origin. The third edition.

Thomas Tegg   1844

> GS.

2109.5 ——fourth edition
pp. [1–2] 3–94; illus.; pls. [front.] 1–23
Thomas Hailes Lacy   [1859]

> GS. *Copy at L.*

2109.6 ——fifth edition.
pp. [2] [1–5] 6–94; illus.; pls. [front.] 1–23
Bell & Daldy   1870

> GS. *Copy at L. With additional extract from the Catalogue of the Cruikshank exhibition.*

2109.7 ——sixth edition [reissue of 2109.5]
Bell & Daldy   1873

> GS. *Copy at L.*

2109.8 ——sixth edition (Bohn's Illustrated Library) [reissue of 2109.6 omitting hair-line borders]
George Bell & Sons   1881

> GS.

2109.9 ——*seventh edition (Bohn's Illustrated Library)
George Bell & Sons   1890

> DLC Cat.

——[American editions] New York: S. King, [1828]; New York: Happy Hours Company, 1879; New York: Rimington & Hooper, 1929.

2110 EGAN, PIERCE. The show folks! By Pierce Egan. Embellished with nine characteristic designs on wood, by the late Mr. Theodore Lane, and engraved by Mr. John Thompson. To which is added, A biographical sketch of the life of Mr. Theodore Lane. Dedicated to the President of the Royal Academy, Sir Martin Archer Shee, Knt.

pp. [3–5] 6–59 [60 (directions to binder) 61–64 (advts.)]; pls. [front., 8]   L
M. Arnold; and Simpkin and Marshall   1831

> *In verse. Copy with half-title-page recorded by Stott.* Stott *253.*

2111 THE ETHIOPIAN SERENADERS, G. W. Pell, G. W. White, G. A. Harrington, M. G. Stanwood, F. G. Germon, in their celebrated performances . . . as given at the St. James's Theatre, London, during the years, 1846–7.

pp. [8 (two title-pages and two blank leaves)]; pls. [10]
                                                  MH
John Mitchell   1847

> *Lithographs by J. H. Maguire. Second t.p. reads* Portraits of the Ethiopian Serenaders, G. W. Pell . . .

2112 SMITH, ALBERT [RICHARD]. The natural history of the ballet-girl by Albert Smith. Illustrated by A. Henning.

pp. [1–5] 6–103 [104]; illus.; on ptd. wrapper: Fourth edition   L
D. Bogue   1847

2113 ——*another edition
                                                  1851
STR.

2114 HALLIDAY, ANDREW, *pseud. of* Andrew Halliday Duff. *Comical fellows: or, the history and mystery of the pantomime: with some curiosities and droll anecdotes concerning Clown and Pantaloon, Harlequin and Columbine.

pp. 96   MB
Thomson   1863

2115 *WAR among the blacks. A full report of the celebrated chancery suit, Montague & Wilson versus Moore, Crocker, Ritter, and Hamilton, proprietors and managers of the Christy Minstrels, February 8th, 1865.

pp. (4) 80   MB
Liverpool: Holme & Copley   1865

> *See also below no. 2118.*

2116 WOOD, *Mrs.* HENRY, STIRLING COYNE, ANDREW HALLIDAY, *pseud. of* Andrew Halliday Duff, and others. Mixed sweets from Routledge's Annual.

pp. [4] [1] 2–143 [144]; pls. [front., 3]; illus. L
George Routledge and Sons   [1867]

> *Includes "Private theatricals" by C. H. Ross and "About pantomimes" by Andrew Halliday Duff.*

2117 A GUIDE TO THE PANTOMIMES OF 1869. The history of pantomime, and a full account of all the pantomimes.

pp. [1–3] 4–16   L

H. Vickers   [1870]

2118 CHRISTY MINSTRELS. Full report of the trial for libel, Matthews brothers versus Moore, Crocker, and Burgess, before Mr. Justice Lush and a special jury, at Westminster Hall. On the 11th of February, 1869.

pp. [1] 2–24; cover-title

1874

> IKF. *"Transcript of the short-hand notes of Messrs. Cherer and Bennett, 38 Lincolns Inn Fields." See also above no. 2115.*

2118.1 PUNCH and puppets (No. 38 British Standard Hand Book).

pp. 1–32; illus.; ptd. wrappers; title on wrapper

J. & R. Maxwell   [188?]

GS.

2119 SPECTATOR, A, *pseud.* *The music hall, as it is, as it might be. By a spectator.

pp. (1), 93   MB

Smart & Allen   1880

2120 WAGNER, LEOPOLD. The pantomimes and all about them: their origin, history, preparation and exponents.

pp. [1–7] 8–60 [61–64 (advts.)]

London and Manchester: John Heywood   [1881]

> IKF. *A copy at MB.*

2121 THE REGULATION of music halls A summary of the attempts made by music hall proprietors to obtain an improvement of the law regulating places of public entertainment; with some opinions of the press on the subject.

pp. [1–3] 4–34   LE

Printed by F. Chiffenel and Co.   [1883]

> *Brought out by the Music Hall Proprietors' Protection Association.*

2122 FITZGERALD, PERCY [HETHERINGTON]. Music-hall land. An account of the natives, male and female, pastimes, songs, antics, and general oddities of that strange country. By Percy Fitzgerald. With eight illustrations by Alfred Bryan.

pp. [i–v] vi, [1] 2–90; illus.   L

Ward and Downey   [1890]

2123 ADAMS, WILLIAM DAVENPORT. A book of burlesque. Sketches of English stage travestie and parody, by William Davenport Adams. With portraits of F. C. Burnand, W. S. Gilbert, and G. R. Sims, (The Whitefriars Library of wit and humour, vol. vi. ed. by W. H. Davenport Adams.)

pp. [i–v] vi [vii–viii], [1] 2–220 [4 (advts.)]; pls. [3]   GM

Henry and Co.   1891

2124 *"POUF-LA". A string of wheezes by thirty-nine music-hall artistes.

pp. 122; illus.

Gilbert Dalziel, "Judy" Office.   1892

> Motley.

2125 HEADLAM, STEWART D[UCKWORTH]. The ballet by Stewart D. Headlam.

pp. [1] 2–16; cover-title   L

Frederick Verinder   1894

> *A paper read to The Playgoers' Club, 3rd February 1894. See also above no. 646.*

2126 BAILEY, FRED. Sally in the ballet! The famous parody on "Sally in our alley".

bs.   L

[F. J. Croger]   [1895?]

2127 STUART, CHARLES DOUGLAS and A. J. PARK. The variety stage A history of the music halls from the earliest period to the present time by Charles Douglas Stuart and A. J. Park.

pp. [i–vii] viii–xii, [1] 2–255 [256]   L

T. Fisher Unwin   [1895]

✠   Variety stars. [1895]. *See no. 2198.*

2128 WALLACE, JOHN. How to form and conduct a nigger minstrel troupe, with practical and valuable advice to committee of management, manager, musical director, secretary and treasurer, and interlocutor. Directions as to vocalists, "piccaninnies," corner men. Instructions as to rehearsals, arrangement of platform. How to procure and perform jokes, first part finales, stump speeches and farces. By John Wallace, Jun., author of "The nigger corner man — his book"; "Nigger knockers," etc., etc. (Abel Heywood & Son's Winter Amusements.)

pp. [1–5] 6–39 [40]   L

Manchester: Abel Heywood & Son; London: F. Pitman
                                                                      [1896]

2129 WALLACE, JOHN. The minstrel troupe instructor Practical and valuable advice to manager, musical director, interlocutor, secretary and treasurer, singers and corner-men. Hints on management, platform decoration, rehearsals, seating of troupe, etc. Directions on how to plot out a programme, and how to get-up jokes, stump speeches, &c. By John Wallace, Jun., author of "Modern minstrel boys", "Good business", etc.

pp. [1–4] 5–46 [47–48 (advts.)]; illus.   L

John Alvey Turner   [1897]

2130 CLARK, G[EORGE] F[REDERICK] SCOT-SON-, *artist.* The "halls". Pictured by G. F. Scotson-Clark.

pp. [1–8] 9–47 [48–134]; col. pls. [5]; illus. (incl. 19 full-page col. ports.)   L

T. Fisher Unwin   [1899]
With two leaves of advertisements and printed end-paper, as issued. "Chiefly concerning the music halls" by George Gamble, pp. 9–[48].

SOCIETIES

GENERAL

2131 *OBSERVATIONS on raising subscriptions for the families of deceased actors.

1822

Recorded but not seen by Lowe.

INDIVIDUAL SOCIETIES

Actors' Benevolent Fund

2132 REPORT OF THE PROCEEDINGS at the first dinner of the actors' benevolent fund, held at the Hôtel Métropole, on Wednesday, 24th June, 1891. Henry Irving, Esq., in the chair.

pp. [1–5] 6–22 [23–24 (bl.)]   DFo

[Nassau Steam Press]   [1891]

Partly reprinted from The Era, *27th June 1891. With a note inserted, "With the Secretary's Compliments"; the Secretary of the Fund was C. I. Colston, 8 Adam Street, Adelphi, London W.C.*

Amateur Dramatic Defence Society

See above IRELAND *no. 1715.*

Artists' General Benevolent Fund

2133 *A POETICAL ADDRESS . . . on behalf of the artists' general benevolent fund.

1818

STR.

Bath Theatrical Fund

See above no. 1550.

Church and Stage Guild

See above no. 642.

Covent Garden Theatrical Fund

See above nos. 1159–1162.

Dramatic Authors' Society

✠ Rede, Leman Thomas Tertius. The road to the stage . . . To which is added . . . an account of the Dramatic Authors' Society. 1835. *See no. 724.*

2134 CATALOGUE OF DRAMATIC PIECES, the property of the members of The Dramatic Authors' Society, or their representatives; brought down to September, 1865.

pp. [1–3] 4–40 [41 (text) 42 (bl.)]   L

Published for The Dramatic Authors' Society, by Thomas Hailes Lacy   [1865 or 1866]

2135 ———[reissue] Catalogue of dramatic pieces, the property of the members of The Dramatic Authors' Society, or their representatives; brought down to September, 1865.

pp. [1–3] 4–40 [41 (text) 42 (bl.) 43 (additions to Sept 1866) 44 (bl.)]   E

Published for The Dramatic Authors' Society, by Thomas Hailes Lacy   [1886]

2136 [DRAMATIC AUTHORS' SOCIETY.] †ALPHABETICAL LIST &c &c &c.

pp. [3] 4–14 [15 16 (bl.)]; lithographed throughout   MH

[Dramatic Authors' Society?]   [1866]

2137 DRAMATIC AUTHORS' SOCIETY'S TARIFF. Provincial & London. Seventh issue — in force to the 30th June, 1882.

pp. [1–6] 7–96   MH

[The Dramatic Authors' Society]   [1881?]

Lists fee for performance. Classifies London and provincial theatres into four classes. Lists authors and proprietors.

Drury Lane Fund

See above nos. 1348–1355.

Edinburgh Theatrical Fund

See above nos. 1974–1975.

Elizabethan Stage Society

2138 POEL, WILLIAM. *An account of the Elizabethan Stage Society.

pp. 12

Printed for the Society   1898

R. Speaight, William Poel and the Elizabethan revival *(1954).*

General Dramatic Authors' Benevolent Fund

2139 THE GENERAL DRAMATIC AUTHORS' BENEVOLENT FUND, established 1861, for the relief of distressed and necessitous dramatic authors. (Registered pursuant to Section XI of 18 & 19 Vict., cap. 63.) President. The Right Hon. Sir Edward Bulwer Lytton, Bart., M.P. Trustees. Charles Dickens, Esq. Jonas Levy, Esq. Honorary Secretary. J. Stirling Coyne, Esq. Bankers. The London and Westminster Bank, Temple Bar Branch. Offices. 28, King Street, Covent Garden.

pp. [1–5] 6–12   MH

Printed by W. S. Johnson & Co.   1862

Rules and a list of members.

General, Dramatic, Equestrian and Musical Agency and Sick Fund Association

See PERIODICALS nos. 4210, 4272.

General Theatrical Fund, Royal

Anniversary festivals of the General Theatrical Fund were held from 1846 to at least 1887, under the chairmanship of Lytton, Thackeray, C. J. Mathews, Tom Taylor, Alfred Wigan, Dickens, Shirley Brooks, Boucicault, J. L. Toole, the Dukes of Edinburgh and Beaufort, and others. Accounts of the proceedings of all or most of these festivals were published. Lowe records the Proceedings at the fourth anniversary festival of the General Theatrical Fund, held at the London Tavern, Bishopgate Street, on Monday, May 21, 1849. Charles Kean, Esq. in the chair, 1849; and copies of the proceedings of the 18th, 19th, and 21st anniversary festivals (1863, 1864, 1866) are at L.

2140 PATRONESS, HER MAJESTY, THE QUEEN. Rules and regulations of the General Theatrical Fund Association, finally adopted and agreed to at an open meeting of the committee, held at the English Opera House, on the 22nd of January, 1839. Altered and amended, June the 13th, 1843; and further amended, November the 10th, 1847. Enrolled with the magistrates, according to the acts of Parliament.

pp. [i–v] vi–x [11] 12–43 [44]   L
S. G. Fairbrother, Garrick Press   1848

2141 *[ROYAL] GENERAL THEATRICAL FUND. Rules and regulations adopted and agreed to at an open meeting of the Committee held at the English Opera House on 22nd January 1839. (Altered and amended to 1856.)

pp. 43
T. H. Lacy   [1856]
  IKF.

2142 ——[another edition] Amended to 20th November 1868.
pp. 36
T. H. Lacy   [1869]
  STR.

London Theatrical Reform Association

✗ Fluck, Arthur W. A paper on theatrical reform. Any profits arising from the sale of this publication will go towards the formation of a London Theatrical Reform Association. 1879. *See no. 639.*

Lyceum Provident & Benevolent Fund

See above no. 1491.

Music Hall Proprietors' Protection Association

See above no. 2121.

Royal Dramatic College

A home for actors in retirement.

2143 DODD, HENRY. Royal dramatic college. Correspondence respecting proposed gift of land at Langley, Bucks, by Mr. Henry Dodd.
pp. [i–iii] iv [5] 6–42   MH
Waterlow and Sons, printers   1859

2144 ——second edition, with additions
pp. [i–iii] iv [v] vi–viii [ix], [1–5] 6–85 [86 (bl.)]   L
Waterlow and Sons, printers   1859

2145 THE ROYAL DRAMATIC COLLEGE NEWS ... and programme of the fêtes.
no. 5,001 July 1863   L
[Printed at the Nassau Steam Press]   [1863]
  The number "5,001" is evidently facetious.

2146 CLINTON, JOHN WADE. *Mabury: or musings around the Royal Dramatic College.
pp. (ii) 9
Cheltenham: T. Harper   1875
  IKF.

✗ Catalogue of the valuable and interesting collection of pictures, water-colour drawings and prints, books, manuscript plays, and a variety of items connected with the drama. The property of the trustees of the Royal Dramatic College, and others. 1881. *See no. 63.*

Royal General Theatrical Fund

See under, General Theatrical Fund nos. 2140–2142 above.

Stage Society

2147 THE STAGE SOCIETY first annual report 1899–1900.
pp. [1–2] 3–15 [16]; title on cover   L
[London]   [1900]
  Annual reports issued until the Twenty-first Annual Report 1919–1920 are at L.

Theatrical Mission Institute & Orphanage

2148 [THE THEATRICAL MISSION.] "FOOTLIGHT FLASHES" of light and love, record of work in the Theatrical Mission, with list of contributors and balance sheet, from November 1st, 1889, to October 31st, 1890.
pp. [1–9] 10–56 [57–60]; illus.   MH
Theatrical Mission Institute   [1890]

2149 [THE THEATRICAL MISSION.] "STARS," a year's work in the Theatrical Mission, with lists of contributors, and balance sheet, November, 1891–1892.
pp. [4] [7] 8–72 [73–82]; illus.; insets [2]   MH
Theatrical Mission Institute and Orphanage   [1892]

THE AMATEUR THEATRE

See also THEATRE ARTS *nos. 745–749;* IRREGULAR FORMS *no. 2116;* BIOGRAPHY *2420–2425 (Earl of Barrymore), 3012, 3034, 3223, 3429;* PERIODICALS *nos. 4149, 4256, 4261, 4309, 4316, 4339, 4348, 4349, 4399, 4415, 4498, 4502.*

2150 *PROLOGUE and epilogue to The Orphan . . . at a private school at Isleworth April 25 1728.

Manchester: L. Gulliver 1728

Foxon.

2151 A SATIRICAL DIALOGUE between a sea captain and his friend in town: humbly address'd to the gentlemen who deform'd the play of Othello, on Th——rs——y, M—— the 7th, 1750, at the Th——tre R——y——l, in Dr——y L——ne: to which is added, a prologue and epilogue, much more suitable to the occasion than their own.

pp. [1–3] 4–8 L

J. River [1751]

This tract is very abusive, but the performance was really wonderfully good—Lowe.
Refers to the private performance, by Sir Francis Delaval, family and friends, of Othello *at Drury Lane 7th March 1751. It has been conjectured that William Kenrick is the author.*

⌘ A Catalogue of all the valuable materials of the theatre and several erections . . . late the property of the Right Hon. Earl Barrymore. [1792]. *See no. 69.*

2152 *PROLOGUE written for the opening of the Hall at Brandenburgh House, after it was embellished and enlarged in 1795.

pp. 13 [ca. 1795]

STR.

2153 †RULES AND REGULATIONS for the Lambs Conduit private theatre.

pp. [1–2] 5 6 3 4 7 8; second and third leaves reversed. MH

Printed by J. Hammond 1799

A society of amateurs; each member to act once every three months.

2154 BAILLIE, JOHANNA. Epilogue to the theatrical representation at Strawberry-Hill. Written by Johanna Baillie and spoken by the Hon. Anne S. Damer, Nov., 1800.

pp. [1–2 (text) 3–4 (bl.)]

n.p. [1804]

JFA. *Watermark 1804.*
Reprinted in Fugitive Verses. By Joanna Baillie *(1840), pp. 128–130; and in* The Dramatic and Poetical Works of Joanna Baillie *(1851; second edition, 1853), p. 794.*

2155 [EDGCUMBE, RICHARD] MOUNT EDGCUMBE, *Earl of.* Prologue written by the Earl of Mount Edgcumbe, and spoken by him at the opening of the theatre, Strawberry Hill, Nov. 1800.

pp. [1 text (2–4) (bl.)]

n.p. [1804]

JFA. *Watermark 1804.*

2156 KILKENNY THEATRICAL SOCIETY. 1818.

bs. L

[Kilkenny] [1818]

A list of members.

2157 *ACCOUNTS of the Kilkenny Theatre.

pp. 20

1819

Dawsons of Pall Mall, Catalogue 344 (1962).

2158 BURTON, J. G. *The Critic's Budget, or, a peep into the amateur green room. Pourtraying a view of the most popular and well-known private actors!!! of the present day. Subjoined, a list of the several amateur theatres, reading and concert rooms. Also the original members, &c. composing the late Black Tye Committee.

pp. 5–51 MB

Onwhyn [1819]

2159 ARTICLES for the regulation of the Society of Thalians, Berwick-Street, Soho.

bs. MB

[London] Egan, printer [*ca.* 1820]

2160 [MOORE, THOMAS?] THE PRIVATE THEATRE of Kilkenny, with introductory observations on other private theatres in Ireland, before it was opened.

pp. [4] [1] 2–11 [12], [i] ii–iv [5] 6–134; pls. [front., 10] DFo

n.p. 1825

Sometimes ascribed to Richard Power, but he died 18th December 1824, before the introduction was written. Miss Stockwell, cited by Loewenberg, refers to Thomas Moore's Journal *VIII, 130, 217, 242.*

2161 vacant

2162 SORRELL, WILLIAM J. The amateur's handbook and guide to home or drawing room theatricals. How to get them up and how to act in them. By W. J. Sorrell. To which is added How to "get up" theatricals in a country house. By Captain Sock Buskin. And a supplement containing a list of suitable plays, with the number of male and female characters. Complete lists of the modern plays. The law for amateurs. The free drama. Addresses of theatrical tradesmen. And many particulars of great utility and interest. By Thomas Hailes Lacy, theatrical publisher, London.

pp. [1–5] 6–93 [94–98] 99–120; illus.   E
[London: Thomas Hailes Lacy]   [1856]

2163 ———[another edition] The amateur's handbook and guide to home or drawing room theatricals. How to get them up and how to act in them. By W. J. Sorrell. To which is added How to "get up" theatricals in a country house. By Captain Sock Buskin.

pp. [2] [1–5] 6–120; on cover: Amateur Series. The Amateur's Guide   L
Thomas Hailes Lacy   [1866]

With a supplement by T. H. Lacy.

2164 ———[seventh edition] And a supplement containing a list of suitable plays, with the number of male and female characters. Complete lists of the modern plays. The law for amateurs. The free drama. Addresses of theatrical tradesmen. And many particulars of great utility and interest. By Thomas Hailes Lacy, theatrical publisher, London.

pp. [1–5] 6–94 [101] 102–123 [124–126 (advts)]; on cover: Seventh thousand. Corrected to November, 1870.   L
[Thomas Hailes Lacy]   [1870 or 1871]

Advertised as "Seventh Edition". No authors' names or pseudonyms on the title-page. A large number of further editions were published.

———[American edition] New York: S. French, 1866.

✖ Views of an amateur lecturer in regard to professional & amateur play-acting. Aberdeen, 1876. *See no. 627.*

2165 FREDERICKS, L. The stage and histrionic education. A few words to amateurs. By L. Fredericks, (of the principal London theatres.)

pp. [1–3] 4–8   L
Published by the author   [1878]

Mr. Fredericks is, or was, a teacher of elocution, &c. — Lowe.

2166 BURNAND, *Sir* F[RANCIS] C[OWLEY]. The "A.D.C." Being personal reminiscences of the Univer-

sity Amateur Dramatic Club, Cambridge. Written by F. C. Burnand, B.A., Trin. Coll. Camb.

pp. [2] [i–v] vi–xix [xx (bl.)], [1] 2–267 [268]; illus.; half-title: Personal reminiscences of the "A.D.C." Camb.   L
Chapman and Hall   1880 [*for* 1879]

2167 ———*second edition   MH
1880 (?)

2168 POLLOCK, WALTER HERRIES and *Lady* [JULIET] POLLOCK. Amateur theatricals. (Art at home series). By Walter Herries Pollock and Lady Pollock.

pp. [i–vii] viii, [4] [1] 2–71 [72]; illus., incl. front. [some by Kate Greenaway]   GM
Macmillan and Co.   1879

2169 ANGUS, J. KEITH. Amateur acting by J. Keith Angus.

pp. [1–5] 6–171 [172 (bl.) 173–6 (advt.)]; illus.; col. pls., [4], incl. t.p.   E
George Routledge and Sons   [1880]

2170 NORTHUMBERLAND AMATEUR DRAMATIC CLUB, 1880.

pp. [4]   NwP
[Newcastle-upon-Tyne]: printed by Septimus A Cail   1880

Rules and list of office-bearers.

2171 "OLD BOY", AN, *pseud.* of Edward Bellasis. *"The Pincerna" at the Oratory School, 1880. By an "old boy".

pp. 17   BP
          [1880]
Loewenberg.

See also nos. 2175, 2180, 2184, 2186.

2172 ———second issue
pp. [3] 4–17 [18]; cover-title   L
Printed by C. Bowles   [1880]

2173 CALLOW, FRANCES [ELIZABETH] and ALICE [MARY]. Home theatricals made easy, or, busy, happy, and merry. By Frances and Alice Callow.

pp. [1–9] 10–14 [2] 15–20 [2] 21–84; illus.   L
T. H. Roberts and Co.   1881

"Charade" texts, with a chapter "Remarks on general management."

2174 ———[another edition] Containing: three easy charades, a burlesque tragedy, a fairy-tale drama, and a comedy farce. With directions for general management of drawing room performances.

pp. [1–9] 10–84 [85–96 (advts.)]   L

London, New York, and Melbourne: Ward, Lock and Co.   [1890]

2175 "OLD BOY", AN, *pseud.* of Edward Bellasis. "The Phormio" at the Oratory School, 1881. By an "old boy". Second issue.

pp. [1–3] 4–20   L

Printed by Nichols and Sons   [1881]

See also nos. 2171, 2180, 2184, 2186.

2176 OLD STAGER, AN, *pseud.* of James Shirley Hodson. Private theatricals: being a practical guide for the home stage. By an old stager. With pictorial suggestions for scenes, after designs by Shirley Hodson.

pp. [i–iii] iv–viii, [1] 2–118 [119–120 (advts.)]; col. pls. [front., 1] both = two leaves; inset, fold. [1]   L

W. H. Allen   1881

Preface signed J.S.H.

2177 DAKIN, HENRY J. The stage in the drawing-room; or, the theatre at home Practical hints on amateur acting for amateur actors by Henry J. Dakin.

pp. [6] [1] 2–98 [99–102 (advts.)]; illus. (incl. front.); ptd. paste-downs   L

Griffith & Farran successors to Newbery and Harris   [1882]

On the cover: Griffith & Farran's Household Hand-Books.

2178 HARRISON, CHARLES. Theatricals and tableaux vivants for amateurs. Giving full directions as to stage arrangements, "making up," costumes, and acting. With ninety-two illustrations. By Charles Harrison.

pp. [2] [i–iii] iv–vi, [1] 2–126 [127 (advt.) 128 (bl.)]; illus.   L

L. Upcott Gill, "The Bazaar" Office   1882

2179 PRITCHARD, J. V. *Tableaux vivants. Arranged for private representation. By J. V. Pritchard. Containing 80 selected tableaux, with instructions how to get them up, cast of characters, costumes required, and full description of each picture. Also information respecting the use of tableaux lights, and other effects, and describing the music required for each representation.

[1881–2?]

Advt. in Descriptive catalogue of plays and dramatic works (*Samuel French, 1881–2*).

2180 ANCIENT ACTOR, AN, *pseud.* of Edward Bellasis. The Latin play at a Catholic school. (Edgbaston, 1883.) By an "ancient actor."

pp. [1–3] 4–20   L

St. Nicholas Cole Abbey   [1883]

The Eunuchus. See also nos. 2171, 2175, 2184, 2186.

2181 [FARREN, ROBERT, *illustrator.*] PENCIL JOTTINGS from the Ajax as presented at Cambridge Nov. 29th, 30th Dec. 1st, 2nd, 1882.

f. [1] engr., with vignette; pls. [7]; wrappers, engr., with vignette; title on wrappers   E

Cambridge: Macmillan and Bowes   1883

See also nos. 2185, 2187–2189, 2197.

2182 OLD STAGER, THE, *pseud.* The actor's hand-book, and guide to the stage for amateurs. By the old stager.

pp. [1–5] 6–28 [29–32 (advts.)]   E

Dicks   [1884?]

2183 ———*another edition

[London]   [*ca.* 1890]
  STR.

2184 BELLASIS, EDWARD. The Money Jar of Plautus at the Oratory School: an account of the recent representation by Edward Bellasis.

pp. [6] [9] 10–48; illus.   L

Kegan Paul, Trench, and Co.   1884

See also nos. 2171, 2175, 2180, 2186.

2185 FARREN, ROBERT, *illustrator.* The Birds of Aristophanes as performed by members of the University at the Theatre Royal Cambridge November 1883 drawn & etched by Robert Farren.

pls. [12], incl. illus. t.p.; ptd. wrappers   L

[Cambridge: Macmillan and Bowes]   [1884]

Cover title: The Birds of Aristophanes a series of etchings to illustrate the "Birds" of Aristophanes, as represented at Cambridge by members of the university, Nov. 27 to Dec. 1, 1883 by Robert Farren. See also nos. 2181, 2187–2189, 2197.

✗ Amateurs' Guide to the law of musical & dramatic performances. Manchester, and London. [1885]. *See no. 231.*

2186 BELLASIS, EDWARD. The new Terence at Edgbaston: being notices of the performances in 1880 and 1881. By Edward Bellasis. Third issue.

pp. [1–7] 8–54 [55–56 (advts.)]   L

Kegan Paul, Trench, and Co.   1885

A revised edition of "The Phormio" at the Oratory School (see above no. 2175) and "The Pincerna" at the Oratory School (no. 2171), published uniformly with The Money Jar of Plautus at the Oratory School (no. 2184).

2187 FARREN, ROBERT, *illustrator*. The *Eumenides* of Aeschylus as performed by members of the university at the Theatre Royal Cambridge December 1885 drawn & etched by Robert Farren.

pls. [1 (engr. t.p.) 3–8] [=7]; pp. [2]   L

Cambridge: Macmillan and Bowes   1886

Cover-title: The Eumenides *of Aeschylus a series of etchings to illustrate the* Eumenides *of Aeschylus, as represented at the Theatre Royal, Cambridge, by members of the university, December 1st to 5th, 1885. Proof sets also issued. See also nos. 2181, 2185, 2188, 2189, 2197.*

2188 FARREN, ROBERT, *illustrator*. The *Oedipus Tyrannus* of Sophocles as performed at Cambridge Nov. 22–26 1887 with a portrait of C. Villiers Stanford M.A. drawn & etched by Robert Farren.

pls. [1 (engr. t.p.) 2–7]; pp. [2]   L

Cambridge: Macmillan & Bowes   1887

Cover-title: "The Oedipus Tyrannus *of Sophocles a series of etchings to illustrate the* Oedipus Tyrannus *of Sophocles, as represented at Cambridge by members of the university, Nov. 22 to 26, 1887 together with a portrait of Professor C. Villiers Stanford, M.A. by Robert Farren" dated 1888. Proof sets also issued. See also nos. 2181, 2185, 2187, 2189, 2197.*

✖ Lynn, [Richard A.] Neville: The Thespian papers, being a series of humorous essays on subjects of professional and amateur interest. 1887. *See no. 970.*

2189 SPEED, L. and F. R. PRYOR. *The Oedipus Tyrannus. A record by L. Speed and F. R. Pryor of the performance at Cambridge in November 1887.

pp. 63; illus.   MB

Cambridge: Macmillan & Bowes   [1888]

See also no. 2188.

2190 TOWNSEND, STEPHEN. *A short account of the Amateur Dramatic Club of St. Bartholomew's Hospital. With a few hints to amateurs on the art of acting and stage management.

pp. vi, 72

W. Speaight   1888

STR.

2191 BAKER, SIDNEY. *A guide to theatrical scene painting in distemper, for the use of amateurs, . . .

pp. 31

Brodie & Middleton   [1889]

BMC (*L copy destroyed*).

2192 MILMAN, CONSTANCE [ANGELENA], *afterwards Lady* Arbuthnot. "Evenings out" or the amateur entertainer A truthful record of facts and hints for popular entertainments by Constance Milman.

pp. [1–7] 8–126 [127–8 (bl.)]; illus.; printed covers   E

Griffith Farran Okeden & Welsh   [1891]

2193 [MOSCROP, HUGH, *ed.*] THE AMATEUR ACTOR'S DRAMATIC HANDBOOK and guide. Containing the names of the principal dramatic clubs and their addresses, with a few hints to amateur actors.

pp. [1–7] 8–39 [40–43 (advts.) 44 (bl.)]   L

Bury: printed by T. Crompton and Co.   1892

2194 GANTHONY, ROBERT. Amateur entertainments for charitable or other objects; how to organise and work them with profit and success. By Robert Ganthony.

pp. [i–vii] viii, [1] 2–66 [67–70 (advts.)]; illus.   L

L. Upcott Gill   1893

2195 SMITH, LITA, *comp.* and [RICHARD A.] NEVILLE LYNN, *ed.* Lynn's theatrical handbook for 1894–95. Compiled by Lita Smith, and edited, with a preface, by Neville Lynn; F.S.L.A. Including a full, detailed, and illustrated guide to the selected plays, duologues, readings, and recitations in "Lynn's acting edition;" list, seating-accommodation, and fees of the principal London and suburban halls; the best theatrical clubs and newspapers; laws on copyright and procedure of licensing; music-hall and Christy minstrel play, triple bills, musical and pastoral plays; special plays for the provinces, pier, and town hall entertainments, political, service, and volunteer clubs, etc., etc.

pp. [1–3] 4–16 48–63 [33] 34–40 [1] 41–47, ²48–63 illus.; ptd. illus. wrappers   L

Capper and Newton   [1894]

2196 ———[third edition]

pp. [1–8] 9–40 [1] 41–61 [62–63] [=64]; illus.; ptd. wrappers illus.; title headed "enlarged and revised edition"   E

Capper and Newton   [1895]

2197 FARREN, ROBERT, *illustrator*. Iphigenia in Tauris of Euripides performed by members of the university at the Theatre Royal Cambridge November & December 1894 drawn & etched by Robert Farren.

pls. [engr. t.p., 1–7]; pp. [2]   L

Cambridge: Macmillan and Bowes   [1895]

Cover-title: "The Iphigenia in Tauris *of Euripides a series of etchings to illustrate the* Iphigenia in Tauris *of Euripides, as represented at Cambridge by members of the university, Nov. 30, Dec. 1–5, 1894." Proof sets also issued. See also nos. 2181, 2185, 2187–2189.*

2198 VARIETY STARS

pp. [1–4] 5–40 [41–48 (advts.)]   L

The Variety Publishing Company   [1895]

Preface signed: A. J. Park, Chas. Douglas Stuart. Contributions from Marie Lloyd, Dan Leno, Gus Elen, Harry Payne and other variety stars methods of work.

2199 PARKE, WALTER. The Tantalus tour A theatrical venture chronicled by Walter Parke joint-author of *Les manteaux noirs,* and other comic operas with illustrations by J. Harrison.

pp. [i–iv] v–viii [9–10] 11–183 [184]; illus.   MH
Bellairs & Co.   1896

"*The following fanciful (but not utterly unreliable) record of a theatrical tour, under amateur management, first appeared as a Serial in* Funny Folks . . . *many of the incidents, although extravagant, have a certain foundation in fact. . . .* " (*page v*).

2200 DOUGLASS, ALBERT. The amateurs' hand-book and entertainers' directory, 1897. Compiled by Albert Douglass. Late of the Globe, Opera Comique, Crystal Palace and Standard Theatres.

pp. [1–3] 4–5'[6], ²5–6 7–8 [9] 10 [3] 15–85 [86] [=90] L
Potter Bros; A. Douglass   [1897]

2201 ELLIOT, W. G., *ed.* Amateur clubs & actors edited by W. G. Elliot with illustrations by C. M. Newton and from photographs.

pp. [i–vi] vii–xv [xvi], [1] 2–320; pls. [front., 19] LGk
Edward Arnold   1898

✠ Wolfe, Francis F. Theatres in Ireland. Dublin, The Amateur Dramatic Defence Society, 1898. *See no. 1715.*

2202 ★PIONEER PLAYERS.
pp. 4
                                                                  [*ca.* 1900]
STR. *Describes objects of the society.*

BIOGRAPHY
COLLECTIVE

Divided into three sections: Collections of biographical notices; Collections of anecdotes; Rosciads and other appraisals of groups of actors and actresses.

COLLECTIONS OF BIOGRAPHICAL NOTICES

See also PLAYLISTS AND DICTIONARIES nos. 30, 42, 44; GENERAL HISTORY especially nos. 835–837, 847, 848, 854, 859, 878, 880, 883; MEDIEVAL AND RENAISSANCE STUDIES nos. 996–997, 1023, 1056; IRELAND nos. 1713, 1785, 1792, 1799; OPERA nos. 2086, 2096; IRREGULAR FORMS no. 2124; BIOGRAPHY no. 2570; THEORY AND CRITICISM especially nos. 3755, 3762, 3764, 3768; PERIODICALS nos. 4139, 4298, 4305. For collected biographies of dramatists see PLAYLISTS AND DICTIONARIES, espeicially nos. 10, 19, 28, 30, 42–44; IRELAND no. 1713; SCOTLAND no. 1848; THEORY AND CRITICISM especially nos. 3737–3742, 3744, 3762, 3767.

2203 *GENTLEMAN, A, *pseud.* Both theatres opened. A history of the lives of the most noted actors and actresses. . . . By a gentleman conversant with them in five reigns.

[1727–1730?]

PH and KB.

2204 DRAMATIC CHARACTERS, or different portraits of the English stage.

pp. [1] 2; pls. 1–24 [25–38]; engr. t.pp. [2]   MH

Robt. Sayer, and Jnº. Smith   1770 [*for* 1772 *or* 3]

With two engraved title-pages (one in French, one in English) and a letter-press table of contents. Though the imprint is that of the first edition, this is an issue of the second edition (in which the number of plates was increased from twenty-four to thirty-eight). Some plates dated 1772.

2205 ——[another issue] Dramatic characters or different portraits of the English stage. In the days of Garrick &c.

pls. [1 (engr. t.p.)] 2–24 [25–38]   L

Robt. Sayer & Co.   [1773]

This copy mounted and extra-illustrated, with engraved list of contents. IKF (Catalogue 203) also records an edition with twenty-seven plates.

2206 THEATRICAL BIOGRAPHY: or, memoirs of the principal performers of the three Theatres Royal.

DRURY-LANE.

Mr. Garrick,	Mr. King,	Mr. Vernon,
Mr. Barry,	Mr. Moody,	Mr. Parsons,
Mr. Reddish,	Mr. Dodd,	Mr. Baddely.
Mr. Aickin,	Mr. Love,	
Mrs. Barry,	Miss Hayward,	Mrs. Egerton,
Mrs. Abington,	Mrs. Baddely,	Mrs. W. Barry,
Miss Younge,	Miss Pope,	Mrs. Jefferies.

COVENT-GARDEN.

Mr. Ross,	Mr. Yates,	Mr. Bensley,
Mr. Smith,	Mr. Shuter,	Mr. Mattocks,
Mr. Savigny,	Mr. Dyer,	Mr. Clark.
Mr. Woodward,		
Mrs. Yates,	Miss Macklin	Mrs. Green,
Mrs. Mattocks,	Mrs. Bulkley,	Mrs. Thompson.

HAY-MARKET.

Mr. Foote,	Mr. J. Aickin,	Mr. Davies.
Mr. Weston,	Mr. Didier,	
Mrs. Gardner,	Mrs. Jewell,	Mrs. Didier.

Together with critical and impartial remarks on their respective professional merits.

2 vols. pp. [4] [i] ii–vii, [1] 2–156 + [4] [1] 2–147 [148 (bl.) 149–152 (index)]   L

S. Bladon   1772

2207 ——[another edition]

2 vols. pp. [i–v] vi–viii [ix–xii (contents)], [1] 2–106 + [1–3] 4–122   L

Dublin: H. Saunders, E. Lynch, W. Slater, D. Chamberlaine, J. Potts, J. Williams, W. Wilson, R. Moncrieffe, T. Walker, L. Flin and C. Jenkins.   1772

Title differs from that of first edition in spelling Bensley "Bensly", Jewell "Jewel" and in punctuation. There are additions to the text, consisting of a "Postscript" by Shuter and an extract from The Smithfield Rosciad.

2208 GENUINE REFLECTION, A, *pseud.* The green-room mirror. Clearly delineating our present theatrical performers, by a genuine reflection.

pp. [i–ix] x–xv [xvi], [1] 2–63 [64 (bl.)]   L

Printed for the author, and sold by E. Macklew; and T. W. Swift   1786

2209 THE SECRET HISTORY of the green rooms; containing authentic and entertaining memoirs of the actors and actresses in the Theatres Royal. Vol. 1. — Drury-Lane. Vol. 2. — Covent-Garden and Haymarket.

pp. [*2*] [i] ii–x, [1] 2–291 [292] [misnumbering pp. 158–167] + [*2*] [i] ii–iii [iv–vi], [1] 2–309 [310–312] L

J. Ridgway; J. Forbes; and H. D. Symmonds 1790

2210 ———The secret history of the green room: [continues as in 2209 but inserts 'three' before "Theatres Royal"]. The second edition.

pp. [i–iii] iv–xii, [1] 2–336 [337–339 (index) 340 (bl.)] + pp. [*2*] [1] 2–335 [336], [i] ii–xix [xx–xxiv] L

H. D. Symonds 1792

None of the three copies seen has the appendix mentioned in the index.

2211 ———the third edition

pp. [i–iii] iv–xii, [1] 2–331 [332], ²[i] ii–vi [vii] [ix (index) x (bl.)] + [*2*] [1] 2–335 [336], [i] ii–xix [xx (bl.) xxi–xxiv (index)] L

H. D. Symmonds 1793

Although vol. I has been entirely reset, the index provided, in the copies seen, is suitable only for the second edition.

2212 ———[another edition] A new edition, with improvements. To which is prefixed A sketch of the history of the English stage, &c.

pp. [*2*] [i–iii] iv [v] vi–ix [x–xi] xiv–liii [liv–lv] lvi [lvii] lviii–lx [=lviii], [1] 2–216 209–357 [=365] [358–359] 360–361 [362] + *4* [1] 2–387 [388 (bl.) 389 (index)] 390–391 (index) [392 (bl.)] L

J. Owen 1795

Sometimes implausibly attributed to Joseph Haslewood.

2213 [CROSBY, B., *ed.*?] CROSBY'S POCKET COMPANION to the playhouses. Being the lives of all the principal London performers. To be re-printed at the commencement of each winter season, with the addition of those new performers, who may hereafter be engaged in the theatres of Drury-Lane, Covent-Garden, and the Haymarket. To which are subjoined, particulars of the life of Mr. Dibdin. Dedicated to Richard Brinsley Sheridan, Esq.

pp. [i–v] vi [vii–ix] x–xi [xii], [1] 2–34 33*–38* 35–105 [106 (bl.) 107–108 (advts.)]; pl. [front.] L

B. Crosby 1796

The Monthly Mirror, *January 1796 says that "the editor of this little volume has been particularly attentive to the accuracy of his materials." The particulars of the life of Dibdin are a rather amusing attack on him, for forbidding Crosby to publish anything about him. The portrait of Sheridan is frequently wanting* — Lowe. *Issued on both ordinary and fine paper, according to the half-title page.*

2214 ROACH'S AUTHENTIC MEMOIRS of the green room, containing the lives of all the performers of the Theatres Royal, Drury Lane Covent Garden and the Haymarket, with poetic criticisms to each and characters of the patentees, the whole being entirely new.

pp. [1] 2–130; pls. [front., engr. t.p.] L

J. Roach 1796

Imprint dated 10 February 1796.

⌘ Roach's new and complete history of the stage . . . Intended as a companion to Roach's *Authentic memoirs of the green room. 1796. See no. 845.*

2215 [OULTON, WALLEY CHAMBERLAIN] *AUTHENTIC MEMOIRS OF THE GREEN-ROOM, (for 1799.) Containing the lives of all the performers of the Theatres-Royal, Drury-Lane, Covent-Garden and the Hay-Market.

J. Roach [1799]

The Monthly Mirror *for March 1799 says: "These* authentic *memoirs want but one thing to entitle them to that epithet, and that is, to use the words of Father Philip, in the Castle Spectre;* 'they are not true.' *They are manufactured by a needy and malignant scribbler, of the name of Oulton"* — Lowe.

2216 *AUTHENTIC MEMOIRS OF THE GREEN ROOM (for 1800.) containing particulars of all the Theatres Royal, Drury Lane, Covent Garden, and the Hay market. To which are now first added, absentees and provincial performers.

2 vols.

J. Roach 1800

Lowe.

2217 AUTHENTIC MEMOIRS OF THE GREEN-ROOM, (for 1801.) involving sketches, biographical, critical and characteristic, of the performers of the Theatres-Royal, Drury-Lane, Covent-Garden and the Hay-Market.

pp. [1–3] 4–119 [120] LLib

J. Roach 1801

2218 *AUTHENTIC MEMOIRS OF THE GREEN-ROOM (for 1802).

MB

J. Roach 1802

2219 AUTHENTIC MEMOIRS OF THE GREEN-ROOM, (for 1803.) involving sketches, biographical, critical and characteristic of the performers of the Theatres-Royal, Drury-Lane, Covent-Garden, and the Hay-Market.

pp. [1–3] 4–107 [108] LLib

J. Roach 1803

2220 ———(for 1804.) . . .

pp [1–3] 4–95 [96]; pl. [front.] LLib

J. Roach 1804

2221 AUTHENTIC MEMOIRS OF THE GREEN-ROOM; involving sketches, biographical, critical, & characteristic, of the performers of the Theatres Royal, Drury-Lane, Covent-Garden, and the Hay-Market. In two volumes. Embellished with seven portraits of eminent performers.

2 vols. pp. [2 (index)] [1–3] 4–212; pls. [front., 3] + pp. [2 (index)] [1–3] 4–95 [96 (advt.)], ²[1–3] 4–100; pls. [front., 2]   L

J. Roach   [1806]

> *Originally published in four parts, 1801 to 1804. The present item is an edition of parts 2, 3, and 4, with a new part (dated 1806) substituting for the original part 1. The title-page of the second, but not the first, volume says "Second Edition".*

2222 AUTHENTIC MEMOIRS OF THE GREEN-ROOM; including sketches, biographical, critical, & characteristic, of the performers of the Theatres Royal, Drury-Lane, Covent-Garden, and Haymarket; containing original lives and anecdotes, never before published.

pp. [i–v] vi–xii [13] 14–260   L

J. Roach   [ca. 1814]

> Lowe *records a copy with a portrait.*

2223 ———[another edition]

pp. [i–v] vi–ix [x–xii] [13] 14–269 [270] ²257–260   L

J. Roach   [1815]

2224 BREWER, J[AMES] NORRIS. Histrionic topography: or, the birth-places, residences, and funeral monuments of the most distinguished actors. Illustrated by engravings, executed by Messrs. J. & H. Storer, and by historical and descriptive notices, written by Mr. J. Norris Brewer.

pp. [i–iii] iv, [1] 2–37 [38]; pls. [front., 13 (incl. added engr. t.p.]   L

J. Cole   1818

2225 *MEMOIRS and intrigues of the green room.

pp. 142; col. pl.; head title

[Duncombe]   [ca. 1820]

> *A copy of this occurred in Maidment's sale catalogue, wanting title. This is the only copy I have heard of —* Lowe. *Memoirs include Mrs. Waylett, Benjamin Webster, Miss Craddon, Charles Sinclair, Mrs. Faucitt, Mrs. Tayleure, Benjamin Wrench, George Colman, Mr. and Mrs. Gibbs, Mary Paton, Robert Keeley, Esq.*

2226 COOKE, [CHARLES] *ed.* Cooke's illustrations to the British theatre.

engr. t.p.; pls. [55]   LGk

C. Cooke   1821

2227 THE BIOGRAPHY OF THE BRITISH STAGE; being correct narratives of the lives of all the principal actors & actresses, at Drury-Lane, Covent-Garden, The Haymarket, The Lyceum, The Surrey, The Coburg, and The Adelphi theatres. Interspersed with original anecdotes and choice and illustrative poetry. To which is added, a comic poem, entitled "The actress."

pp. [i–v] vi–xii, [1] 2–295 [296–300 (advts.)]; illus.; pl. [1]   GM

Sherwood, Jones, & Co.   1824

———[American edition] New York: Collins and Hannay, 1824

2228 TERRY, D[ANIEL]. *British theatrical gallery, a collection of whole length portraits, with biographical notices, by D. Terry Esq.

pp. [76]; col. pls. [front., 19]   LGk

H. Berthoud   1825

> *Terry, Daniel (1789–1829). Actor. The friend of Sir Walter Scott, many of whose novels he adapted for the stage. First appearance in London, Haymarket, 20th May 1812. In 1825 Yates and he bought the Adelphi, but after two seasons Terry had to give up the partnership, owing to private embarrassments —* Lowe.

2229 OXBERRY, WILLIAM. *Oxberry's dramatic mirror; containing the biography of eminent performers.

pp. (1) 476; ports.   MB

Virtue & Co.   1827

> *Projected by William Oxberry and edited after his death by his widow. The running title is, Dramatic Biography* —Brown.

2230 ———*[another edition] Oxberry's dramatic mirror; containing the biography, and an excellent likeness on steel, of the following eminent performers: Bland, Booth, Carew, Elliston, Emery, Fawcett, Foote, Harley, Jordan, Kean, Kelly, Kemble, C. Kemble, J. Knight, Liston, Mardyn, Munden, O'Neill, Orger, Oxberry, Sherwin, Siddons, Stephens, West.

LLib
1828

Lowe.

2231 *ANNALS OF THE GREEN ROOM, and biography of the stage, comprising the lives of the most eminent London performers . . . Part I Memoirs of Mrs. Honey; Part II Brief account of Mrs. Waylett, Louisa Turner, Miss Vincent, and Mrs. Humby.

2 parts in one vol.; illus.

1830

STR.
Part I reprinted, pp. 24, 1842 (copy at MB).

2232 *CUMBERLAND'S THEATRICAL ILLUSTRATIONS; consisting of portraits of eminent actors, engraved on steel from original paintings by Buss and Wageman . . .

pls. [204]   MB
                                                                [1831]

2233 GALT, JOHN. The lives of the players. By John Galt, Esq.

2 vols. pp. [iii–v] vi [vii] viii, [1] 2–315 [316] + [6] [1] 2–308   GU

Henry Colburn and Richard Bentley   1831

2234 ——[another edition]

pp. [i–v] vi–xii [13] 14–338 [2], ²[1] 2–8 (advts.)   GM

London: Hamilton, Adams & Co.; Glasgow: Thomas D. Morison   1886

A "boil-down" of memoirs of actors and actresses, of little real value — Lowe.

——[American edition] Boston: Hill, 1831.

2235 LANE, R[ICHARD] J[AMES]. Theatrical sketches, drawn from life, by R. J. Lane, Lithographer in ordinary to Her Majesty, and to His Royal Highness the Prince Albert, A.R.A.

pls. [49]   LGk
John Mitchell   [1840]

2236 THE DAUGHTERS OF THESPIS: or, a peep behind the curtain! Comprising biographical sketches, brilliant repartees, witty sallies, extraordinary adventures, and amusing anecdotes, never before presented to the public, of the dramatic beauties, Mrs. Honey, Madame Vestris, Mrs. Nisbett, Miss Murray, Mrs. Humby, Mrs. Stirling, Countess of Harrington, late Miss Foote, Mrs. Chatterley, Miss Chester, Mrs. West, Mrs. Waylett, Mrs. Orger, and Miss Vincent.

pp. [1–3] 4–206 [207 (misnumbered 305) 208 (misnumbered 206) 209–210 (advts.)] col. pls. [front., 5]   MH
Jackson & Co.   1841

2237 ——[reissue] †SCENES BEHIND THE SCENES[;] or the secrets of the green room, disclosed in the extraordinary adventures of Madam Vestris, Mrs. [Ho]ney, Mrs. Nisbett, Miss Murray, Mrs. Humby, and other celebrated dramatic beauties, their amours with favorite actors noble lords, dukes, and royalty, with curious anecdotes, never before presented to the public, from a prompter's private note book. Fine coloured plates.

pp. [1–3] 4–206 [207 (misnumbered 305) 208 (misnumbered 206)]; col. pls. [5]   MH

W. Edwards   [1841?]

A reissue of The daughters of Thespis (1841).

2238 MATHEWS, *Mrs.* [ANNE]. Anecdotes of actors: with other desultory recollections, etc. etc. etc. By Mrs. Mathews, author of the "Memoirs of Charles Mathews, comedian;" to which this is a supplementary volume.

pp. [i–v] vi–vii [viii (bl.)], [1] 2–430   L
T. C. Newby   1844

2239 MARSHALL, THOMAS. Lives of the most celebrated actors and actresses. By Thomas Marshall, Esq. Dedicated to the General Theatrical Fund Association.

pp. [2] [1–2] 3–18 [6] 19–36 [6] [37] 38–56 [4] [57] 58–72 [8] [73] 74–89 [90] [6] [91] 92–110 [4] [111] 112–131 [132] [2] [127] 128–167 [168] [6] [167] 168–185 [186] [4] [187] 188–232; illus.   NbU

E. Appleyard   [1847]

A valuable little work — Lowe. Published in eleven or twelve parts, dated 25 January to 29 September 1847. Binding in of the unpaginated leaves varies. The running-title is: National Dramatic Biography. The editor or author promises further volumes. Another copy at L.

2240 OXBERRY, WILLIAM HENRY. Oxberry's dramatic chronology containing the names, dates of births, first appearances and deaths, of most of the principal London actors and actresses, up to 1849.

pp. [1–3] 4–43 [44 (addenda)]   MH
Published for the Collector, by H. Harris, Bow-street, Covent-Garden Mr. Duncombe, Holborn   [1850?]

On title page "This work will be continued annually".

2241 CLAYTON ELLEN CREATHORNE *afterwards* Needham, Ella Creathorne. Queens of song; being memoirs of some of the most celebrated female vocalists who have appeared on the lyric stage, from the earliest days of opera to the present time. To which is added a chronological list of all the operas that have been performed in Europe.

2 vols. pp. [i–vii] viii–xvi, [1] 2–381 [382]; pl. [front.] + pp. [4] [1] 2–452; pls. [front., 4]   L
Smith, Elder & Co.   1863

——[American edition] New York: Harper, 1865.

2242 MAYALL'S CELEBRITIES of the London stage, a series of photographic portraits in character.

nos. 1–18; photographs [18] by Mayall, J[ohn] E[dwin]; title on wrappers   L
A. Marion, Son & Co.   [1865–66]

Published in monthly parts.

2243 ROFFE, ALFRED. A musical triad from Shakespeare The clown in Twelfth Night; Autolycus;

— the Lord of Amiens. Also Shakespeare upon art and nature. To which is added Old English singers, and Mr. Bowman — actor, singer, and ringer! Written by Alfred Roffe. (Engraver)

pp. [4] [1] 2–92 [93–95 (colophon) 96 (bl.)]   L

Somers Town, London: [Edwin Roffe] Ye Rochester Press   1872

Twenty copies printed.

2244 RUSSELL, W[ILLIAM] CLARK. Representative actors. A collection of criticisms, anecdotes, personal descriptions, etc. etc. Referring to many celebrated British actors from the sixteenth to the present century; with notes, memoirs, and a short account of English acting. By W. Clark Russell. (The Chandos Library.)

pp. [i–vii] viii–xv [xvi], [1] 2–496; pl. [front.]   L

Frederick Warne and Co.   [1872]

2245 ——[another edition] (The "Chandos Classics")

pp. [i–vii] viii–xv [xvi], [1] 2–496; pl. [front.]   PU

London: Frederick Warne and Co; New York: Scribner, Welford and Co.   [1875]

2246 ——[another edition]

pp. [i–vii] viii–xv [xvi], [1] 2–496

Frederick Warne and Co.   [1883]

JFA.

2247 ——[another edition] (The "Chandos Classics")

pp. [i–vii] viii–xv [xvi], [1] 2–496   GU

London & New York: Frederick Warne and Co.   1888

——[American edition] New York: Scribner, Welford and Co., 1872

A book whose value to the worker can scarcely be overstated. It is most comprehensive, and wonderfully accurate — Lowe.

2248 ★THE ARTISTS of the London stage. Musical and dramatic portrait gallery.

                                                        1876

A reissue of portraits and memoirs which had appeared in a publication entitled The Saturday Programme, *issued by the proprietor of the* London Figaro—*Lowe. First number, 1876.*

2249 BRYAN, ALFRED, *illustrator.* Footlight favorites from original sketches by Alfd. Bryan.

vol. 1 nos. 1–3; pp. [4]; pls. 1–4; cover-title + pp. [4]; pls. 5–8; cover-title + pp. [4]; pls. 9–2; cover-title   MH

Tinsley Bros   [*ca.* 1876]

"To be published in 12 monthly numbers, each containing four character portraits". The first three parts were published on 10 March, 3 May and 8 July respectively. The fourth part is promised in No. 3 but no further numbers are known. Each plate lithographed and tinted, with tissue shields (Maclure & Macdonald, Litho.).

2250 BAKER, HENRY BARTON. Our old actors. By Henry Barton Baker.

2 vols. pp. [i–iii] iv–xii, [1–3] 4–402; photos. [front., 1]; errata slip + pp. [i–iii] iv–x, [1–3] 4–379 [380 (bl.)]; photos. [front., 2]   L

Richard Bentley and son   1878

2251 ——popular edition

pp. [i–vii] viii, [1] 2–460 [461–464 (advts.)]; pl. [front.]
                                                        GU

Richard Bentley and son   1881

——[American edition] English actors from Shakespeare to Macready. New York: Holt & Co, 1879.

2252 PASCOE, CHARLES EYRE. The dramatic list: a record of the principal performances of living actors and actresses of the British stage. With criticisms from contemporary journals. Compiled and edited by Charles Eyre Pascoe.

pp. [2] [i–iii] iv–v [vi], [1] 2–358, 359–360 (advts.); t.p. in red and black; vignette on t.p.   GU

London: Hardwicke and Bogue; Boston, U.S.: Roberts Brothers   1879

2252.1 ——The dramatic list: a record of the performances of living actors and actresses of the British stage. Second edition, revised and enlarged. Edited by Charles E. Pascoe.

pp. [2] [i–iii] iv, [1] 2–432; t.p. headed: Our actors and actresses.   GU

David Bogue   1880

2253 COOK, [EDWARD] DUTTON. Hours with the players.

2 vols. pp. [i–iii] iv–vi [vii–viii], [1] 2–277 [278 (bl.) 279 (emblem) 280 (bl.)]; vignette on t.p. + pp. [4] [1] 2–263 [264]; vignette on t.p.   NbU

Chatto and Windus   1881

Reprinted journalism. Another copy in L.

2254 ——new edition

pp. [i–vii] viii–x [xi–xii], [1] 2–359 [360]; pl. [front.]   GU

Chatto & Windus   1883

2255 MARSTON, [JOHN] WESTLAND. Our recent actors: being recollections critical, and, in many cases, personal, of late distinguished performers of both sexes. With some incidental notices of living actors.

2 vols. pp. [i–iii] iv–xviii, [1] 2–288 + pp. [i–v] vi–xix [xx], [1] 2–310   L

Sampson Low, Marston, Searle & Rivington, Ltd. 1888

2256 ———[another edition]
pp. [i–iii] iv–viii, [1] 2–392   GU
Sampson Low, Marston, Searle & Rivington, Limited
1890

———[American edition] Boston: Roberts Brothers, 1888

2257 REID, ERSKINE, and HERBERT COMPTON. The dramatic peerage, 1891. Personal notes and professional sketches of the actors and actresses of the London stage. Compiled by Erskine Reid, and Herbert Compton.

pp. [1–3] 4–266; t.p. headed: The 'Peerage' Series   L
The General Publishing Co., Ltd.; Dodd, Eyton & Co.
[1890]

2258 ———[revised edition] The dramatic peerage. 1892. Personal notes and professional sketches of the actors and actresses of the London stage. Compiled by Erskine Reid and Herbert Compton. (The Peerage series).

pp. [1–3] 4–243 [244]; headed: Revised and corrected by the profession.   GU
Raithby, Lawrence   [1892 or 1893]

2259 GODDARD, ARTHUR. Players of the period. A series of anecdotal, biographical, and critical monographs of the leading English actors of the day. By Arthur Goddard, with numerous illustrations by "Alma," Fred. Barnard, Alfred Bryan, Phil May, J. Bernard Partridge, Georges Pilotelle, F. H. Townsend, etc., photographs of the subjects and autograph quotations. First Series.

pp. [i–v] vi–xii [13] 14–368; illus., incl. [front] and facsims.; errata slip.   GU
Dean & Son   1891

2260 ———With numerous illustrations by and after "Alma", Fred. Barnard, Alfred Bryan, Phil May, J. Bernard Partridge, Georges Pilotelle, F. H. Townsend, etc. photographs of the subjects and autograph quotations. Second series.

pp. [i–v] vi–ix [x–xi] xii [13] 14–316 [317–320 (advts.)]; illus. incl. [front.] and facsims.   GU
Dean & Son   1891

2261 vacant

2262 ———[a reissue of nos. 2259 and 2260]
pp. [i–v] vi [vii] viii–x [xi] xii [13] 14–368, ²[i–v] vi–ix [x–xi] xii [13] 14–316 [317–320 (advts.)]; errata slip; illus.; facsims.   L
Dean & Son   1891
In one volume.

2263 DIRCKS, RUDOLPH. Players of to-day. By Rudolph Dircks. With sixty-six illustrations.

pp. [4 (advts.)] [i–v] vi–xxi [xxii (ornament)], [1–2] 3–150 [151–152 (advts.) 153–154 (bl.)]; illus.   L
London: Simpkin, Marshall, Hamilton, Kent, & Co., Ltd.; Newcastle-upon-Tyne: Andrew Reid, Sons & Co.
[1892]

The illustrations are portraits from photographs.

2264 vacant.

2265 THE LEADING ENGLISH ACTRESSES with their autographs.

col. pls. [10]; cover-title   L
F. Harris & Wells   [1892?]

2266 "CALL BOY, THE", *pseud.* "On and off." Thirty-five actresses interviewed by "the call boy." With five illustrations by William Parkinson, and thirty-five portraits.

pp. [1–16] 17–87 [88] [89–96 (advts.)], incl. ptd. wrappers; illus., incl. [front.]; head-title: Judy's annual for 1894   GM
Gilbert Dalziel, "Judy" office   [1894]

2267 BLACK, HELEN C. Pen, pencil, baton and mask   Biographical sketches by Helen C. Black.

pp. [i–ix] x [xi–xii], [1] 2–370, ²[1] 2–4 [5–6]; pls. [front., 5]   L
Spottiswoode & Co.   1896

The half-title reads "Biographical Sketches." Most of these sketches appeared originally in periodicals. The last three leaves contain advertisements.

2268 WHYTE, FREDERIC. Actors of the century A play-lover's gleanings from theatrical annals by Frederic Whyte translator of "The English stage" by M. Augustin Filon.

pp. [i–v] vi–xii, [1] 2–204; collotype pls. [front., 7]; other pls. [84]; errata slip; t.p. in red and black   NbU
George Bell and Sons   1898

With Appendix by the photographer Adolphe Beau

2269 LAWRENCE, BOYLE, *ed.* Celebrities of the stage. Edited by Boyle Lawrence.

pp. [4] [1–10] 11–106, incl. 49 col. pls.   L
George Newnes, Ltd.   [1899–1900]

Issued in parts, weekly, then fortnightly, bound in printed wrappers.
A continuation of Celebrities of the stage, players of the day, *in twelve parts, each part with four coloured plates, was published by George Newnes Limited 1902–1903. Volume title-page and "cloth binding case" were provided.*

2270 ROBINS, EDWARD. Twelve great actors.

pp. [4] [i–iv] v–xiv, 1–474 [475–6 (advts.)]; pls. [front., 22]; ptd. guard pls. [12]   GM

New York and London: G. P. Putnam's Sons. The Knickerbocker press   1900

2271 ROBINS, EDWARD. Twelve great actresses by Edward Robins.

pp. [4] [i–ii] iii–x, 1–446; pls. [front., 19 (incl. 11 with ptd. tissues)]   L

New York and London: G. P. Putnam's Sons   1900

Title-page in red and black. Printed within borders.

COLLECTIONS OF ANECDOTES

See also BIOGRAPHY: INDIVIDUAL nos. 2587 (Cibber); 2700 (Edwin); 2813 (Foote); 2938 (Garrick); 3339 (Miller).

2272 *THE COMEDIAN'S TALES; or jests, songs, and pleasant adventures of several famous players.

pp. (4) 92   MB

T. Warner & W. Pepper   1729

"Excessively rare. I never saw another copy. This curious volume is full of low humour, and contains some odd anecdotes of the old actors, Spiller, Joe Haynes, A. Leigh, and others, nowhere else to be found" — MS note in Daniel's copy, which sold for 58s. — Lowe.

2273 THE THEATRICAL JESTER: or green-room witticisms. Being a collection of entertaining and original anecdotes, bon mots, repartees, &c. relating to the stage.

pp. [1–3] 4–32; pl. [front.]   L

Printed by J. Hammond   [1795?]

2274 GABBLE, GRIDIRON, *pseud.* of Joseph Haslewood. Green room gossip; or, gravity gallinipt: a gallimaufry, consisting of theatrical anecdotes — bon-mots — chit-chat — drollery entertainment — fun — gibes — humour — jokes — kickshaws — lampoons — mirth — nonsense — oratory — puns — quizzing — repartee — stories — tattle — vocality — wit — yawning — zest. Got up to guile gymnastical and gyne-cocratic governments. With an appendix of grave subjects. Gathered and garnished by Gridiron Gabble, gent. godson to Mother Goose.

pp. [1–3] 4–184   L

Given in Gimmal, under guidance of J. Barker, Dramatic Repository   1809

Copy prepared for an intended second edition was included in the 1833 Haslewood sale.

2275 OXBERRY, WILLIAM. The theatrical banquet; or, the actor's budget: consisting of monologues, prologues, addresses, tales, &c. &c. serious and comic; together with Collins's "Evening brush", and a rare and genuine collection of theatrical anecdotes, comic songs, &c. &c. By W. Oxberry, of the theatres of Aberdeen and Glasgow, and late of Covent Garden.

2 vols. pp. [4] [i] ii–viii, [1] 2–263 [264 (bl.) 265 (errata) 266 (bl.)] + [2] [i] ii, [1–3] 4–320 [321 (errata) 322 (bl.)]   L

Appleyards   1809

2276 ———[another edition] The actor's budget; consisting of monologues, prologues, epilogues, and tales, serious and comic: together with a rare and genuine collection of theatrical anecdotes and comic songs. By W. Oxberry, of the Theatre Royal, Drury Lane.

pp. [4] [i] ii–iv [v–viii], [1]2–346 [347–348]   L

W. Simpkin and R. Marshall   1820

———[Calcutta edition] With additions. Calcutta: Columbian Press, 1824

2277 THE THEATRICAL BANQUET, or, actors chum; a superior collection of droll stories, comic tales, laughable occurrences, queer jokes, good things, anecdotes, recitations, terrific legends, &c. including many originals.

pp. [2] [1–3] 4–142; col. pls. [8]   MH

Duncombe   [1810?]

An almost completely different collection from Oxberry's.

2278 FLECK, DUDLEY and WILLIAM ARTIS. Tales from the note-book of an ex-actor, by Dudley Fleck & William Artis.

pp. [1–5] 6–56 [57 (advt.) 58 (bl.) 59 (advt.) 60 (bl.)]   L

Isle of Wight: printed by S. C. Joyce, West Cowes   1865

Dudley Fleck's Thrown upon the world (1865), *a novel about a ballet girl, is advertised.*

2279 HUGHES, FREDERICK. *The hare's foot papers; or, peeps behind the scenes; containing upwards of 300 anecdotes of actors and actresses.

Lacy   [1869]

IKF.

2280 HERMAN, HENRY. Between the whiffs. Being short stories, anecdotes, odd sayings, principally about celebrities literary, theatrical, etc., and about Savage clubmen.

pp. [4] [1] 2–188   L

Bristol: J. W. Arrowsmith; London: Simpkin, Marshall, Hamilton, Kent and Co. Limited   [1890]

2281 *BEHIND THE SCENES: being thirty-two stories by actors and actresses. Illustrated by Judy's artists.

pp. 96; illus.; vignette; autograph facsims.   MB

[London]; Dalziel   [1891]

ROSCIADS AND OTHER APPRAISALS OF GROUPS OF ACTORS AND ACTRESSES

See also THE LONDON THEATRE no. 1399 (Drury Lane); THEATRE OUT OF LONDON no. 1543; IRELAND nos. 1792, 1799; SCOTLAND nos. 1939, 1944 (Edinburgh); BIOGRAPHY no. 2910 (Garrick); THEORY AND CRITICISM no. 3738.

2282 BROADBOTTOM, J. *J. Broadbottom on the performers.

I have seen this title mentioned; but know nothing whatever about the work. I suppose it to be theatrical. — Lowe.

2283 THE ROSCIAD. A poem.

pp. [2] [1] 2–24   L

J. Robinson   1750

Principally a critical estimate of Quin, Garrick, and Barry. Quin and Garrick are praised tolerably equally: Barry not as favourably — Lowe.

The Rosciad Controversy 1761

2284 [CHURCHILL, CHARLES.] THE ROSCIAD. By the author.

pp. [4] [1] 2–28   L

Printed for the author, and sold by W. Flexney   1761

Churchill, Charles (1731–1764). The famous author of the Rosciad: *a dissipated clergyman. . . . This well-known satire on the actors was published anonymously in March 1761. Its keen and merciless criticisms caused an awful sensation among the criticised. It praised Garrick, and most unfairly depreciated Barry, Quin, and Mossop. In the "Apology" Smollett, Murphy, and others are viciously handled. These two publications caused a crop of pamphlets — Lowe. Williams, p. 191.*

2285 ——The Rosciad. By C. Churchill. The second edition, revised and corrected, with additions.

pp. [4] [1] 2–34 [35–36 (bl.)]   L

Printed for the author, and sold by W. Flexney   1761

2286 ——the third edition, revised and corrected.

pp. [4] [1] 2–34   NbU

Printed for the author, and sold by W. Flexney   1761

2287 ——*[fourth edition]

                                                       DFo

                                          1741 [for 1761]

2288 ——the fifth edition, revised and corrected, with large additions.

pp. [4] 2–39 [40]; cancellans slip (pasted to p. 16)   L

Printed for the author, and sold by W. Flexney   1761

2289 ——*[sixth edition]

                                                       DFo

                                                       1762

2290 ——the seventh edition. With large additions.

pp. [4] [1] 2–49 [50]   L

Printed for the author, and sold by W. Flexney   1763

2291 ——the eighth edition, with large additions.

pp. [2] [1] 2–51 [52]   E

Printed for the author, and sold by W. Flexney   1763

2292 ——the ninth edition. With large additions.

pp. [4] [1] 2–52   L

Printed for the author, and sold by W. Flexney   1765

In the 9th edit. the names were printed at full length for the first time — Lowe.

2293 ——*[another edition]

Dublin   1765

  CBEL.

2294 ——another edition

pp. [1–3] 4–34   L

[London]   1772

2295 ——and The apology. By Charles Churchill. Edited by Robert W. Lowe. With eight illustrations.

pp. [i–vii] viii–xviii [xix–xx], [1] 2–78 [79 (printer's imprint) 80 (bl.)]; pls. [I (front.)–VIII]; t.p. in red and black   L

Lawrence and Bullen   1891

Limited to forty-five copies on japon, four hundred on laid paper.

Reprinted from the eighth edition, in Churchill, Poems, (For the Author, 1763), pp. [1]–52 and subsequent editions (see CBEL, II 339–40); in The British Satirist (Glasgow, 1826), pp. [255]–288, with notes and introduction (pp. xiv–xvi); with notes, in The Poetical Works of Charles Churchill, ed. Douglas Grant (Oxford, 1956).

2296 CHURCHILL, C[HARLES]. The apology. Addressed to the critical reviewers. By C. Churchill.

pp. [4] [1] 2–20   L

Printed for the author and sold by W. Flexney   1761

Smollett, Murphy, and others are viciously handled here — Lowe. Published in May. Williams, p. 192.

2297 ——the fourth edition, revised and corrected.

pp. [2] [1] 2–20   MH

Printed for the author, and sold by W. Flexney   1761

2298 ——the fifth edition, revised and corrected.

pp. [4] [1] 2–20   MH

Printed for the author, and sold by W. Flexney   1761

2299 ——the sixth edition, revised and corrected.

pp. [4] [1] 2–24   MH

G. Kearsly; W. Flexney; and J. Coote   1763

Reprinted in Churchill's Poems (1763), and in other collections of Churchill's poems (see CBEL II 339–40), the most recent of which is that edited by Douglas Grant (Oxford, 1956). Reprinted also in R. W. Lowe, The Rosciad and The Apology by Charles Churchill (1891), with the review from The Critical Review which provoked Churchill's reply (no. 2295).

2300 [MORELL, THOMAS.] THE ANTI-ROSCIAD. By the author.

pp. [2] [1] 2–10   L

Printed for the author, and sold by G. Kearsly   1761

In Field's copy was a note: — "This was written by Dr. Thomas Morell, as he inform'd Mr. Stevens" — Lowe.

2301 THE CHURCHILIAD: or, a few modest questions proposed to the reverend author of 'The Rosciad'.

pp. [i–iii] iv–viii, [1] 2–48   L

J. Williams; and T. Lewis   1761

The author enthusiastically defends Quin, among others — Lowe.

2302 AN EPISTLE to the author of The Rosciad and The apology.

pp. [1–3] 4–15 [16]   PU

Thomas Hope   1761

Urges Churchill to be more tolerant.

2303 HAYES, D[ANIEL]. An epistle to C. Churchill, author of The Rosciad, &c. By D. Hayes, Esq;

pp. [2] [1] 2–22   L

W. Bristow   1761

Critical of Churchill's opinions, but not abusive. The author defends, among others, Barry and Mossop, whom Churchill specially attacked — Lowe.

2304 LLOYD, R[OBERT]. An epistle to C. Churchill, author of The Rosciad. By R. Lloyd, M.A.

pp. [i–ii] iii–iv, 1–14   L

William Flexney   1761

Reprinted in The Poetical Works of Robert Lloyd, ed. W. Kenrick (1774), vol. I.

2305 MURPHY, ARTHUR. The examiner. A satire. By Arthur Murphy, Esq;

pp. [1–4] 5–32   L

J. Coote   1761

A reply to the "Rosciads, Apologies, Murphyads, Meretriciads, &c. &c. &c." The poem was originally entitled "The Expostulation", but Murphy's opponents advertised a poem of that name, and so Murphy provided his with a new title — "and now the Sons of Darkness are welcome to avail themselves of their Design". The head-title reads: "The Expostulation". See also Murphy's attack on Churchill's Apology in his Ode to the Naiads (no. 2306).

2306 MURPHY, ARTHUR. An ode to the naiads of Fleet-ditch. By Arthur Murphy, Esq;

pp. [2] i–iv 5–16   L

M. Cooper   1761

A furious attack on Churchill in answer to his mention of Murphy in the Apology — Lowe.

2307 VAUGHAN, THOMAS. *The retort.

1761

I have not seen this, but understand it to refer to the Rosciad. Vaughan is said to have been the original of Dangle in "The Critic" — Lowe.

2308 *VERITAS, pseud. The triumvirate, a poetical portrait . . . by Veritas, an unknown hand.

1761

I have not seen this; but I believe it to be an attack on Churchill, Colman and Robert Lloyd—Lowe. See Page, p. 70. The triumvirate is mentioned in the Critical Review XII, 318, Oct 1761.

2309 WHACKUM SMACKUM, pseud. *The scrubs of Parnassus, or all in the wrong. A comi-tragical heroic poem in Hudibrastic verse addressed to the authors of the Rosciad, the Fribbleriad, the Churchiliad, the Naiads of Fleet Ditch, and the gentlemen of the Bath theatres. By Whackum Smackum, Esq.

1761

Loewenberg.

2310 WOTY, WILLIAM. ★The Muses' advice, addressed to the poets of the age. By W. Woty.

1761

Has reference, I believe, to Churchill's "Rosciad" — Lowe. Not seen by Lowe.

2311 THE BATTLE OF THE PLAYERS. In imitation of Dean Swift's *Battle of the books.* In which are introduced, the characters of all the actors and actresses on the English stage. With an impartial estimate of their respective merits. By the author.

pp. [1–2] 3–52   L
W. Flexney   1762

2312 ——★second edition.

1762

Lowe.

2313 ——the third edition
pp. [2] [1–2] 3–52   MB
R. Richards   1762

2314 [PYE, HENRY JAMES.] ★THE ROSCIAD of C——v——nt G——rd——n. By the author.

Printed by the author   1762

PH and KB.
The Preface expresses admiration for Churchill's Rosciad *and announces the author's intention of dealing with those characters omitted in this work.*

2315 SHAW, CUTHBERT. ★The four farthing candles, a satire. By Cuthbert Shaw.

1762

A satire on Churchill, Lloyd, Colman and Shirley (DNB). Cuthbert Shaw's The Race (1765) included by Lowe, who had not seen it, is literary, not theatrical, being a satire on booksellers, poets and reviewers. Shaw was an actor.

2316 THE SMITHFIELD ROSCIAD. By the author.
pp. [4] 1–28   DFo
Printed for the author: and sold by W. Flexney; G. Kearsly; and J. Coote   1763

The author, who seems to wish the reader to believe that he is Garrick, reviews the leading actors and actresses of the day in the first part of the poem; the second part is a Dunciad in which the chief butt is Thaddeus Fitzpatrick.

2317 ★A CRITICAL BALANCE of the performers at Drury Lane Theatre for 1765.

[1765]

LS, pt. 4, vol. I, p. ccxxiv. A huge broadside chart, awarding points to each actor for figure, grace, spirit, etc.

The Thespis Controversy 1766–1767

2318 [KELLY, HUGH.] THESPIS: or, a critical examination into the merits of all the principal performers belonging to Drury-Lane Theatre.

pp. [4] [1] 2–42 [43–44 (bl.)] with errata slip pasted to [43]   DFo
G. Kearsly   1766

2319 ——the second edition, with corrections and additions.
pp. [4] [1] 2–47 [48]   DFo
G. Kearsly   1766

2320 ——[another edition]
pp. [1–5] 6–46 [47–48 (bl.)]   DFo
Dublin: J. Exshaw   1767

Reprinted from the first edition.

2321 KELLY, HUGH. Thespis: or, a critical examination into the merits of all the principal performers belonging to Covent-Garden Theatre. Book the second. By Hugh Kelly, author of the first.

pp. [1–4] 5 2 [7] 8–28 25–32 37–53 [54], misprinting 17 as "71" [=54]; errata slip pasted to [4]   DFo
G. Kearsly   1767

A continuation of his work on Drury Lane (no. 2318). Reprinted in The works of Hugh Kelly. To which is prefixed The life of the author (printed for the author's widow, and sold by T. Cadell et al., 1778) pp. 345–403.

2322 ANTI-THESPIS: or, a vindication of the principal performers at Drury-Lane Theatre from the false criticisms, illiberal abuse, and gross misrepresentations of the author of a poem lately published, entitled, Thespis.

pp. [4] [1] 2–19 [20]   DFo
H. Gardner; J. Walter; and S. Bladon   1767

2323 BROWNSMITH, JOHN. ★The rescue: or, Thespian scourge. Being a critical enquiry into the merit of a poem, intituled, Thespis. With some candid remarks on the modesty, good-nature, and impartiality of that piece. Written in Hudibrastic verse.

pp. (3) 28   MB
J. Williams   1767

2324 STAMMA, LOUIS. The Kellyad: or a critical examination into the merits of Thespis. By Louis Stamma.

pp. [4] [1] 2–36   MH
J. Williams   1767

An attack on [Hugh] Kelly. The last lines advise him to return to Ireland, and—
> *"There pass in quiet thy remaining days,
> In writing elegies, or mending stays."*
Kelly was originally apprenticed to a staymaker — Lowe.

––––––––––––––

2325 NIPCLOSE, *Sir* NICHOLAS, *pseud. of* Francis Gentleman. The theatres. A poetical dissection.

pp. [i–vii] viii, [5] 6–80 [=84]; illus.; vignette on t.p. of Garrick   L

London: John Bell; York: C. Etherington   1772

With vignette, on title, of Garrick treading on writings of Shakespeare, &c., with motto—
> *"Behold the Muses Roscius sue in vain,
> Taylors & Carpenters usurp their reign."*
On page 63, the criticism of Covent Garden begins, and is headed by a caricature of Colman, with the lines —
> *"View Colman in the lap of Mother Shipton
> A better subject Satire never whipt on." — Lowe.*
A critique of the two theatres, opposed to Garrick and in favour of Mrs Abington, Mossop and Foote. Reviewed in the Gentleman's Magazine *Jan 1772 "blasting its contentions". (LS, pt. 4, pp. 1592, 1597).*

2326 ––––––the second edition
pp. [i–v] vi–viii, [5] 6–80 [=84]; illus.   L
London: John Bell; York: C. Etherington   1772

2327 [MACARONI, A, *pseud. of* — Taylor?]. THEATRICAL PORTRAITS, epigramatically delineated; wherein the merit and demerit of most of our stage heroes and heroines are excellently painted by some of the best masters. Inscribed to the performers of both theatres.

pp. [i–iii] iv vii–ix [x], [1] 2–14   L
J. Bew   [1774]

The "epigrams" are not specially brilliant, e.g.:—
BADDELEY.
*'Play Frenchmen, Baddely, for that's your plan —
You make a devil of an Englishman.'*

On the two Mr. LEWIS'S.
> *"In different paths these actors tread,
> To make the audience feel,
> One does it from his heart and head,
> The other from his heel." — Lowe.*

Preface signed A Macaroni. Published in June. Attributed to one Taylor by Tee Bee in Notes and Queries *(14 December 1861), pp. 473–474.*

2328 A PARODY on *The Rosciad* of Churchill. To which, amongst other pieces, are added several occasional essays, addressed to Mr. Lee Lewes, upon his exhibition of Mr. Alexander Steven's 'Lecture on heads'.

pp. [i–iii] iv–vi [7] 8–55 [56]   L
Printed for the author and sold by J. Macgowan   1780

Criticises the actors and actresses of the period — Lowe. Preface dated 22 Sept 1780, and signed Grubstreticus.

2329 THEATRICAL PORTRAITS.
pp. [1–5] 6–40   MH
[London]   [*ca.* 1780]

Twenty-nine poems on actors and actresses of the day, "originally conveyed through the medium of a public print to the Town".

2330 THE NEW ROSCIAD, in the manner of Churchill: containing a judicious, humourous and critical description of our present dramatic characters. Dedicated to George Colman, Esq.

pp. [i–vi] vii–x, [1] 2–42; errata slip (pasted on p. 42)   MH
E. Macklew   1785

Not Leigh's poem of the same name (no. 2336 below).

2331 THE STROLLIAD: an hudibrastic mirror.
pp. [1–3] 4–26   L
Printed for the Author, and Sold by J. Ridgeway, and W. Richardson   1785

2332 [PASQUIN, ANTHONY], *pseud. of* John Williams. The children of Thespis. A poem. Part first.

pp. [i–v] vi–vii [viii] [9] 10–67 [68]; with vignette on t.p.   GU
[London]: printed by Denew and Grant and sold by J. Bew, T. Hookham, R. Jameson   1786

2333 ––––––The children of Thespis. A poem. Part first. The second edition.
pp. [i–v] vi–vii [viii] [9] 10–67 [68]; vignette on t.p.   L
[London]: printed by Denew and Grant and sold by J. Bew, T. Hookham, R. Jameson   1786

2334 ––––––The children of Thespis. A poem. By Anthony Pasquin Esq. Part the third.
pp. [i–v] vi [7] 8–63 [64]; vignette on t.p.   L
J. Strahan   1788

2335 ––––––The children of Thespis, a poem, by Anthony Pasquin, Esq. The thirteenth edition, with additional characters and emendations.
pp. [i–vi] vii–xxii [xxiii–xxiv] [25] 26–95 [96] [xcvii–xcix] c–cv [cvi] [107] 108–164 [clxv–clxvii] clxviii [169] 170–251 [252]   GU
Kirby and Co.   1792

See also nos. 2346, 2347 below.

2336 [LEIGH, HENRY JAMES.] THE NEW ROSCIAD: a poem.
pp. [2] [1] 2–28   DFo
G. and T. Wilkie   1786

2337 ———[another edition]

pp. [2] [1] 2–28   L

Thomas Hookham   1787

Reprinted in Poems on several occasions (*T. Hookham, 1790*), *pp. 1–37.*

2338 GENTLEMAN, A, *pseud.* The Garriciad, a poem, being a companion to the Rosciad of Churchill. By a gentleman.

pp. [2] [1] 2–32   DFo

Printed for the author: sold by H. D. Symonds [1787]

2339 *THE THEATRICAL REVIEW: being remarks on favourite performers.

                                                            1787

Recorded, but not seen by Lowe.

2340 McDONALD, A[NDREW]. The miscellaneous works of A. McDonald; including the tragedy of Vimonda, and those productions which have appeared under the signature of Matthew Bramble, Esq. With various other compositions, by the same author.

pp. [i–iv] v [vi] vii–viii, [1] 2–358 [4], ²[1] 2–82 [83–84 (Epilogue)]   MH

J. Murray   1791

pp. [1] 2–60: Odes to actors.

2341 LADY, A, *pseud. of* Mary Julia Young. Genius and fancy; or, dramatic sketches. By a lady.

pp. [1–5] 6–16   L

H. D. Symonds; and J. Gray   [1792]

Heroic couplets. "Some hundred copies printed, and many presentation ones circulated" — from note to 1795 edition.

2342 ———[another edition] with other poems on various subjects. By Mary Julia Young.

pp. [1–5] 6–48   L

Sold by H. D. Symonds; W. Lee; and J. Gray   1795

With a note on the title page about the publication of "Genius and fancy."

2343 [FOX, J.] *A PEEP INTO PARIS, being a series of amusing and incidental French anecdotes, with a description of the Parisian theatres, and a comparative view of the French and English actors. By the author of Tancred &c.

pp. xxviii, 186

Printed for the author   1794

STR.
Introduction signed by Fox. There is a list of subscribers, mostly actors.

2344 CANDID AND IMPARTIAL STRICTURES on the performers belonging to Drury-Lane, Covent-Garden, and the Haymarket theatres. Dedicated to that great admirer and patron of the stage, His Grace the Duke of Leeds.

pp. [i–v] vi [vii–viii], [1] 2–71 [72]   L

Martin and Bain   1795

2345 ———second edition

pp. [i–v] vi [vii–viii], [1] 2–71 [72]; "Second edition" on half title page   MB

Martin and Bain   1795

2346 PASQUIN, A., ANTHONY, *pseud.* The pin basket. To the children of Thespis. A satire. By Anthony Pasquin, A. With notes biographical, critical, and explanatory. Involving [a list of ninety-seven players and others]. Dedicated to the Countess of Jersey.

pp. [1–5] 6 [vii] viii [9] 10–64   L

Printed for the author and sold by J. S. Jordan   1796

Certainly not by John Williams. Apparently an attempt to trade upon the reputation of his Children of Thespis *(nos. 2332–2335) and to anticipate his continuation of that poem (no. 2347). It is probably by the author of* The Cap, *who borrowed the signature of Dr. Wolcot (Peter Pindar) for that production*—Lowe.

2347 WILLIAMS, JOHN [PASQUIN, ANTHONY, *pseud.*] The pin-basket to *The children of Thespis.* With notes historical, critical, and biographical. By John Williams, whose public appellation is Anthony Pasquin.

pp. [1–5] 6–232; vignette on t.p.   GU

H. D. Symonds and T. Bellamy   1797

A forgery of this was issued in 1796 — Lowe. *(no. 2346). For* The children of Thespis *see nos. 2332–2335.*

2348 THE DRURIAD: or strictures on the principal performers of Drury-Lane Theatre: a satirical poem: with notes critical and explanatory.

pp. [i–iii] iv, [1] 2–28   LGk

W. J. & J. Richardson   1798

2349 THE FASHIONABLE CYPRIAD: in a series of elegant and interesting letters, with correlative anecdotes of the most distinguished characters in Great Britain and Ireland. Second edition.

2 parts pp. [2] [1] 2–248 + [2] [1] 2–153 [154 (bl.)]   L

Part I   Printed for the author   1798
Part II M. Bull   1799

A scurrilous work which includes accounts of Mrs. Gibbs, Mrs. Jordan and Mrs. Eston.

2350 MYRTLE, MARMADUKE, *pseud. of* Thomas Dermody. The histrionade: or, theatric tribunal; a poem, descriptive of the principal performers at both houses. In two parts. By Marmaduke Myrtle, Esq.

pp. [4] [9] 10–56   L

R. S. Kirby; C. Chapple; J. Ginger   1802

2351 [BUTLER, GEORGE.] THE ROSCIAD, a poem: dedicated to Mr. Kemble. 1802.

pp. [4] [1] 2–61 [62 (bl.)]   L

Robert Butler   [1802]

Dedication signed Geo. Butler. The poem is highly favourable to J. P. Kemble.

2352 THE THESPIAD.

pp. [i–iii] iv–viii [9] 10–50   L

Stockdale, Junior   1809

Poetical criticisms on Mrs Siddons, Kemble, Cooke, Pope &c. &c. — Lowe.

2353 K.L.M.N.O.P.Q., *pseud.* The Rosciad; a heroi-serio-comical poem. In two cantos. By K.L.M.N.O.P.Q.

2 parts. pp. [1–3] 4–15 [16] + [1–3] 4–16   L

Bath: printed by Wood and Cunningham for the author   1812

On p. 15: "The Second Canto will be published on Saturday next the 22d inst."

2354 THE TRIAL OF K.L.M.N.O.P.Q. author of the "Rosciad." Intended as an X.Y.Z. to the subject.

pp. [1–3] 4–8   L

Bath: printed by Wood and Cunningham   1812

2355 [BARRETT, EATON STANNARD.] *THE THESPIAD. By the author of All the Talents.

                                                            1816

STR.

2356 UNDER GRADUATE, AN, *pseud.* *Actors and editors, a poem; by an under graduate.

pp. 44   MB

Sherwood, Neely, and Jones   1817

2357 VAN DYK, HARRY STOE. Theatrical portraits; with other poems: by Harry Stoe Van Dyk.

pp. [2] [i–v] vi [ix] x [xi–xii] [=x], [1] 2–151 [152]   L

John Miller; Simpkin and Marshall; and Chappell and Son   1822

Poems on twenty-three contemporary actors and actresses.

2358 R., G. F. The actress of the day. A poem.

pp. [1–3] 4–12   MB

Printed and published for the author by W. Dugdale
                                                            [183?]

Criticisms of Misses Jarman, Phillips, Kemble, Tree, whom the author thinks surpassed by "Surrey's fair heroine", who is "the Actress of the day."

2359 FINLAY, JOHN. Miscellanies. The foreign relations of the British Empire: the internal resources of Ireland: sketches of character: dramatic criticism: etc. etc. etc. By John Finlay, LL.D., Barrister at Law.

pp. [i–vii] viii, [1] 2–282   L

Dublin: John Cumming; London: Whittaker, Treacher, and Co.   1835

The half-title reads "Miscellanies". Pp. 206–282: "Dramatic Criticism".

2360 BARON WILSON, C. Our actresses; or, glances at stage favourites, past and present. By Mrs. C. Baron Wilson.

2 vols. pp. [4] [1] 2–312; pls. [front., 4] + pp. [4] [1] 2–315 [316]; pls. [front., 4]   L

Smith, Elder and Co.   1844

2361 VALENTINE, HENRY. Behind the curtain. By Henry Valentine, Esq.

pp. [i–iii] iv–vi, [1] 2–102; illus.   L

G. F. Frost   [1848?]

Dedication, to W. C. Macready, is dated January 1848. Monologues of twenty-seven contemporary players, and of David Garrick, at rehearsal.

2362 MUNDUS DRAMATICUS (THE NEW ROSCIAD). A satire.

pp. [i–v] vi [7–9] 10–44 [45 (bl.) 46 (printer's imprint)]
                                                            MH

Hailes Lacy   1852

" . . . part of this Satire appeared in a magazine, wherein it was so favourably received, that the publisher suggested this reprint. It has since been revised, completed, and partly re-written" — Advertisement.

2363 LEWES, GEORGE HENRY. On actors and the art of acting by George Henry Lewes.

pp. [2] [i–v] vi–xiv, [1] 2–278 [279–280 (bl.)]   NbU

Smith, Elder, & Co.   1875

A "collection of articles from various periodicals" — Preface.

2364 ——second edition

pp. [2] [i–v] vi–xiv, [1] 2–278 [279–280 (bl.)]

Smith, Elder, & Co.   1875

JFA.

————[American editions] New York: Holt & Co., 1878; Grove Press, [1957].

2365 BRERETON, AUSTIN. Some famous Hamlets from Burbage to Fechter By Austin Brereton With an appendix giving extracts from the criticisms on Hamlet by Goethe, Coleridge, Schlegel, Hazlitt, Ulrici, etc.

pp. [i–v] vi–viii [ix–xii], [1] 2–74 [75–76 (bl.)]   E

David Bogue   1884

2366 BRERETON, AUSTIN. Shakespearean scenes and characters: with descriptive notes on the plays, and the principal Shakespearean players, from Betterton to Irving. By Austin Brereton. Illustrated by thirty steel plates and ten wood engravings.

pp. [1–11] 12–96; pls. [front., 39]; t.p. in red and black   L

London, Paris, New York & Melbourne: Cassell & Company, Limited   1886

2367 SCOTT, CLEMENT [WILLIAM]. Some notable Hamlets of the present time (Sarah Bernhardt, Henry Irving Wilson Barrett, Beerbohm Tree and Forbes Robertson). By Clement Scott. Illustrated by W. G. Mein.

pp. [1–2 (advts.) 3–13] 14–193 [194 (imprint) 195–196 (advts.)]; pls. [6]   L

Greening & Co. Ltd.   1900

Cancellans title-leaf.

2368 ————new and cheaper edition with a new chapter on Mr. H. B. Irving by W. L. Courtney.

l. [1], pp. [1–9] 10–183 [184], l. [1]; leaves in wrappers; pls. [6]   L

Greening & Co., Ltd.   1905

INDIVIDUAL

For further information consult also the AUTHOR INDEX for works written by theatrical personalities; SALE CATALOGUES (see above nos. 68–137, listed alphabetically under the name of the owner); THEORY AND CRITICISM: INDIVIDUAL PLAYS (nos. 3811–4067 below, listed alphabetically under the name of the playwright).

Abington, Frances (1737–1815)

Actress.

2369 THE LIFE OF MRS. ABINGTON (formerly Miss Barton) celebrated comic actress, with full accounts of her various performances in the theatres of London and Dublin. Including also interesting notes upon the history of the Irish stage and copious notices, anecdotes, and criticisms of her theatrical contemporaries. Embellished with a portrait in steel after Cosway. By the editor of the "Life of Quin".

pp. [2] [1–5] 6–124 [125–126 (bl.)]; pl. [front.]; t.p. in red and black   L

Reader   1888

Bound in eights.

2370 ————[large paper issue]

pp. [2] [1–5] 6–124 [125–126 (bl.)]; pl. [front.]; t.p. in red and black   NbU

Reader   1888

Bound in fours.

Actor, An

2371 *THE ADVENTURES of an actor, in the characters of a merry-Andrew, a Methodist-preacher, and a fortune-teller. Founded on facts.

pp. (1) 334   MB

For the author   [17–?]

2372 EGAN, PIERCE, *the elder.* The life of an actor. By Pierce Egan. Dedicated to Edmund Kean, Esq. The poetical descriptions by T. Greenwood. Embellished with twenty-seven characteristic scenes, etched by Theodore Lane; enriched also with several original designs on wood, executed by Mr. Thompson.

pp. [i–iii] iv–xvi, [1] 2–272; illus.; col. pls. [front., 26]   L

C. S. Arnold   1825

2373 ————[another edition] (Dicks' English novels).

pp. [1–7] 8–96; illus., incl. [front.]; printed wrapper, illus.   GU

John Dicks   [1891]

2374 ————[another edition] The life of an actor. By Pierce Egan author of "Life in London", "Tom and Jerry," &c. The poetical descriptions by T. Greenwood. Embellished with twenty-seven characteristic scenes, etched by Theodore Lane.

pp. [2] [i–iii] iv–xvi, [1] 2–257 [258 (bl.)]; illus.; col. pls. [front., 26]; t.p. in red and black   L

Pickering and Chatto   1892

ECB Dec. 1891.

2375 ————a new edition. (The Illustrated Pocket Library of Plain and Coloured Books.)

pp. [i–iv] v–xix [xx], [1] 2–263 [264 (imprint)]; illus.; col. pls. [front., 26]   L

Methuen & co.   1904

Alberg, Albert (1838–)

Swedish actor appearing in England.

2376 ANSON, W. S. W., *pseud. of* William Swan Sonnenschein, *afterwards* Stallybrass. Life of Albert Alberg (actor–author).

pp. [1–3] 4–37 [38 (bl.)]   L
n.p.   [1882?]

Aldridge, Ira (1807–1867)

Ira Aldridge was a genuine negro, who was educated in America for the Church, but took to the stage. He probably made his first major appearance in this country in October 1825, at the Royal Coburg, playing Oroonoko, Gambia, &c., with great success. He was very successful in the Provinces, and in 1833 appeared at Covent Garden as Othello. He died at Lodez, in Poland, 7th August 1867 aged 63 — Lowe. See Herbert Marshall and Mildred Stock, Ira Aldridge, *1958.*

2377 [COLE, JOHN.] A CRITIQUE on the performance of Othello by F. W. Keene Aldridge, the African Roscius. By the author of *The talents of Edmund Kean delineated . . .*

pp. [1–3] 4   L
Scarborough: printed (only 30 copies) for John Cole
      1831

Ira Aldridge, using the forename Keene, performed at Scarborough in August, 1831.

2378 [ALDRIDGE, IRA.] WILLIAM TELL, the Swiss patriot! Written by the African Roscius, and to be delivered gratuitously to each person on entering the theatre, on his benefit, April 2nd, 1832, at the Royal Clarence Theatre, Hull.

bs.   DFo
Hull: Peck and Smith, printers   1832

2379 MEMOIR and theatrical career of Ira Aldridge, the African Roscius.

pp. [1–5] 6–28; pl. [front.]   MH
Published by Onwhyn   [1848?]

Dedicated to Sir Edward Lytton Bulwer Lytton "distinguished philanthropist, author, and friend to the drama".

Alexander, John Henry (1796–1851)

See SCOTLAND no. 1967 (Edinburgh); nos. 2004–2016 (Glasgow).

Alleyn, Edward (1566–1626)

This contemporary of Shakespeare is one of the most famous actors in English stage history: his reputation as a player being of the highest order. He is no less famous as the Founder of Dulwich College — Lowe. See William A. Armstrong, "Shakespeare and the Acting of Edward Alleyn", Shakespeare Survey, 7, 1954, *and G. L. Hoskin,* The Life and Times of Edward Alleyn, 1954. *See also SALE CATALOGUES no. 56; BIOGRAPHY no. 2923 (Garrick).*

2380 COLLIER, J[OHN] PAYNE. Memoirs of Edward Alleyn, founder of Dulwich College: including some new particulars respecting Shakespeare, Ben Jonson, Massinger, Marston, Dekker, &c. By J. Payne Collier, Esq., F.S.A.

pp. [i–v] vi, [1] 2–219 [220 (bl.)], ²[1] 2–4; cancellans, pp. 3–4   E
The Shakespeare Society   1841

Reissued with a second title-page, in Henslowe and Alleyn: Being the Diary of Philip Henslowe . . . and the Life of Edward Alleyn . . . 2 vols. ([London] The Shakespeare Society, 1853). Copy with both cancellans and cancelland at NbU.

2381 COLLIER, JOHN PAYNE. The Alleyn papers. A collection of original documents illustrative of the life and times of Edward Alleyn, and of the early English stage and drama. With an introduction by J. Payne Collier, Esq., F.S.A. (Shakespeare Society).

pp. [i–v] vi–xxxi[xxxii], [1] 2–110   GU
Shakespeare Society   1843

Reissued in volume two of Henslowe and Alleyn . . . to which is added the Alleyn Papers. 2 vols. ([London] The Shakespeare Society, 1853).

2382 BLANCH, WILLIAM HARNETT. Dulwich College and Edward Alleyn. A short history of the foundation of God's gift College at Dulwich. Together with a memoir of the founder. By William Harnett Blanch.

pp. [i–iii] iv–viii, [1] 2–136; vignette on t.p.; pls. [front., 3]; ptd. wrappers   L
E. W. Allen   1877

Memoir of Alleyn: pp. [53] 54–75.

Anderson, John Henry (1815–1874)

Conjuror and actor.

2383 KIRKALDY, A. Poetic address to "The Wizard of the North."

bs.   L
      1857

Deals with Anderson as conjuror.

Anderson, Joshua

Actor and singer, brother-in-law of Madame Vestris. See below no. 3602.

Anderson, Mary (*Madame de Navarro*) (1859–1940)

American actress.

2384 FARRAR, J. M[AURICE]. Mary Anderson The story of her life and professional career by J. M. Farrar, M.A. With a portrait on steel from an original drawing by Henry van der Weyde.

pp. [*10*] [1] 2–86; pl. [front.]; t.p. in red and black   L
David Bogue   1884

2385 vacant

2386 [WILLIAMS, HENRY LLEWELLYN.] THE STAGE LIFE of Miss Mary Anderson. With tragic and comic recitations, from the répertoire of this favourite actress "The bright particular star" of the stage.

pp. [1–2] 3–16; illus. on t.p.   E
George Vickers   [1884]

2387 ANDERSON, MARY. Girlhood of an actress, by Mary Anderson (Mme de Navarro).

pp. [2] 1–105 [106]   L
Osgood, McIlvaine & Co.   1895

Running title "A few memories." The work has the appearance of having been first published in parts.

2388 ANDERSON, MARY. A few memories by Mary Anderson (Mme. de Navarro). With portraits.

pp. [*8*] 1–266 [267 (index cont.) 268 (bl.)]; illus.; pls. [front., 5]   L
Osgood, McIlvaine & Co.   1896

The earlier chapters reprint Girlhood of an actress.

————[American edition] New York: Harper, 1896.

Precedes English edition.

Angelo, Henry (1760–1839)
Fencing master.

2389 ANGELO, HENRY [CHARLES WILLIAM]. Reminiscences of Henry Angelo, with memoirs of his late father and friends, including numerous original anecdotes and curious traits of the most celebrated characters that have flourished during the last eighty years.

2 vols. pp. [i–v] vi–viii, [1] 2–510; pl. [front.] + pp. [4] [1] 2–558   E
Henry Colburn (vol. I); Henry Colburn and Richard Bentley (vol. II)   1828, 1830

*Angelo's picnic (*John Ebers, 1834; second edition, G. Willis, 1840*) also contains information of theatrical interest.*

Anson, J. W. (1817–1881)
Actor, manager and worker for charities. See also PERI-ODICALS no. 4210.

2390 [ANSON, F. W.?] MEMOIR of the late Mr. J. W. Anson.

pp. [1–3] 4–16; illus.   MH
                                           [1881?]

This copy contains a printed slip "With the compliments of F. W. ["F.W." in MS] Anson". J. W. Anson died 6th February 1881.

Anspach, *Margravine of* (1750–1825)
This lady was the daughter of the Earl of Berkeley. She was married to Lord Craven, and, on his death, to the Margrave of Anspach. She was a tolerably voluminous dramatic writer — Lowe. See also THE AMATEUR THEATRE no. 2152.

2391 ANSPACH, ELIZABETH, *Margravine of.* Memoirs of the Margravine of Anspach. Written by herself.

2 vols. pp. [i–iii] iv–viii, [1] 2–430; pl. [front.] + pp. [i–iii] iv–vii [viii], [1] 2–406 [407–408 (advts.)]; pl. [front.]   E
Henry Colburn   1826

Arditi, Luigi (1822–1903)
Conductor and composer.

2392 ARDITI, LUIGI. My reminiscences. By Luigi Arditi With numerous illustrations, facsimiles, etc. Edited and compiled with introduction and notes by the Baroness von Zedlitz.

pp. [2] [i–v] vi–xxv [xxvi], [1] 2–352 [353 (advt.) 354–356 (bl.)], illus. incl. facsims.; pls., [front., 10]   E
Skeffington and Son   1896

2393 ————second edition

pp. [2] [i–v] vi–xxv [xxvi], [1] 2–352 [353 (advt). 354–356 (bl.)], illus., incl. facsims.; pls., [front., 10]   E
Skeffington and Son   1896

————[American edition] New York: Dodd, Mead & Co., 1896.

Arnold, Samuel James (1774–1852)
Manager of the Lyceum Theatre, opened by him in 1809 with English opera. In 1812 he became manager at Drury Lane, but resigned in 1815. In 1816 he re-opened the Lyceum.—Lowe. See AUTHOR INDEX.

Astley, Philip (1742–1814)
The most famous of circus proprietors. He was, when a young man, a private in a cavalry regiment, where he conceived the idea of becoming a trainer of horses—Lowe. See R. Toole Stott, Circus and Allied Arts, I (1958), 137–144. See no. 2672.

Aston, Anthony (fl. 1712–1735)

A noted strolling player, of whom Chetwood, in his "History of the Stage" gives a curious account. Of the facts of his life little is known. He was announced to play for the first time at Lincoln's-Inn-Fields Theatre, January 13, 1722. Chetwood in 1749 believed that he was then travelling in the country —Lowe. See Watson Nicholson, Anthony Aston, Stroller and Adventurer, South Haven, Michigan, 1920. See also SCOTLAND nos. 1854–1858 (Edinburgh); BIOGRAPHY no. 2570.

2394 MEDLEY, MAT., *pseud.* of Anthony Aston. The fool's opera; or, the taste of the age. Written by Mat. Medley. And performed by his company in Oxford. To which is prefix'd, A sketch of the author's life, written by himself.

pp. [6] [1] 2–22 [23–24 (advts.)]; pl. [front.]   L

T. Payne   [1731?]

> *Pp. 12–14: A ballad, call'd, A dissertation on the Beggar's Opera; pp. 15–22: A sketch of the life, &c. of Mr. Anthony Aston.*

2395 †TONY ASTON'S PETITION and speech (with his deportment) before the Honble H——se of C——ns in behalf of himself and the actors in town and country. To which is prefix'd, His visionary introduction, &c.

pp. [1–4] 9–12   L

For the Author   1735

> *Lacks pp. 5–8. On p. 12, Aston states that his memoirs of the stage will be published "next year".*

Austin, Joseph

Actor under Garrick and theatrical manager. See no. 1536.

Baddeley, Sophia (1745–1786)

A very beautiful woman with a very bad character. She married the well-known actor, Baddeley, and was by him introduced to the theatre, where she became very popular. Her amours are, however, more interesting than her acting. She died, a prey to drink, disease, and want, in Edinburgh — Lowe.

2396 STEELE, *Mrs.* ELIZABETH. The memoirs of Mrs. Sophia Baddeley, late of Drury Lane Theatre. By Mrs. Elizabeth Steele.

6 vols. pp. [4] [1] 2–199 [200] + [1–5] 6–223 [224] + [4] [1] 2–215 [216] + [1–5] 6–240 + [1–5] 6–228 + [1–5] 6–199 [200 (errata) 201–204 (advts.)]   L

Printed for the author at the Literary Press   1787

> *Neither well done nor improving in tone — Lowe. Sometimes attributed to Alexander Bicknell, author of An Apology for the Life of George Anne Bellamy (1785).*

2397 ——[another edition]

3 vols. pp. [4] [1] 2–252 + [4] [1] 2–263 [264] + [4] [1] 2–250 [251 (errata) 252 (bl.)]   L

Dublin: Colles, Moncrieffe, Gilbert, Exshaw, Wogan, Walker, White, Byrne, Parker, Sleater, H. Whitestone, W. Porter, Moore and Dornin.   1787

2398 ——*[another edition] Abridgement in one volume.

                                                      MH
                                                      1787

2399 ——*[another edition]

For the author   1788

   STR.

Balfe, Michael William (1808–1870)

Musical composer. See also OPERA no. 2085.

2400 KENNEY, CHARLES LAMB. A memoir of Michael William Balfe. By Charles Lamb Kenney. With portrait.

pp. [i–v] vi–x, [1] 2–309 [310 (colophon)]; pls. [front., 1 (fold.)]; illus.   L

Tinsley Brothers   1875

——[American edition] New York: Geo. Routledge & Sons, 1875

2401 BARRETT, W[ILLIA]M ALEXANDER. Balfe: his life and work. By Wm. Alexander Barrett.

pp. [12] [1] 2–313 [314–316 (bl.)]; pls. [front., 5]   E

Remington and Co.   1882

2402 ——second edition

pp. [8] [1] 2–313 [314] [315–316 (bl.)]   LVA

Remington and Co.   1883

2403 ——[another edition]

pp. [4] [1] 2–312   L

William Reeves   [1890?]

Bancroft, *Sir* Squire (1841–1926) and *Lady* Marie Effie (1839–1921)

Actor managers.

2404 [BANCROFT, *Sir* SQUIRE and *Lady* MARIE] MR. & MRS. BANCROFT on and off the stage. Written by themselves. With portraits.

2 vols. pp. [i–v] vi–xi [xii], [1–3] 4–443 [444]; illus. (facsim.); pl. [front.]; inset, fold., [1 (facsim.)] + pp. [i–iii] iv–x, [1–3] 4–457 [458]; illus. (facsim.); pl. [front.]; inset, fold., [1 (facsim.)]   L

Richard Bentley and Son   1888

2405 ———Second edition.

2 vols. pp. [i–vii] viii–xiii [xiv], [1–3] 4–433 [434] +
[i–v] vi–xii, [1–3] 4–457 [458]   LVA

Richard Bentley and Son   1888

2406 ———*third edition

2 vols.
                                                      1888

Clunes.

2407 ———*fourth edition
                                                      MB
                                                      1888

2408 ———fifth edition

2 vols. pp. [i–vii] viii–xiii [xiv], [1–3] 4–443 [444];
illus. (facsim.); pl. [front.]; inset, fold., [1 (facsim.)] +
pp. [i–iii] iv–x, [1–3] 4–457 [458]; illus. (facsim.); pl.
[front.]; inset, fold., [1 (facsim.)]

Richard Bentley and Son   1888
JFA.

2409 ———A new edition, being the sixth.

pp. [6] [1] 2–410; illus. (facsims.)   L

Richard Bentley and Son   1889

2410 ———*seventh edition

pp. vi, 410

R. Bentley   1889
    STR.

2411 ———A new edition, being the eighth.

pp. [4] [1] 2–410; illus. (facsims.)   L

Richard Bentley and Son   1891

2412 BANCROFT, *Mrs.* [MARIE]. Gleanings from
"On and off the stage" by Mrs. Bancroft

pp. [1–7] 8–320   L

George Routledge & Sons, Limited   1892

2413 ———[another issue]

pp. [1–7] 8–320; cancellans t.p.   L

George Routledge and Sons, Limited   [1897?]

Bannister, John (1760–1836)

*Son of Charles Bannister, the noted singer and actor. He was
a pupil of Garrick and gave promise of being a successful
tragic actor, but ultimately made his reputation as a comedian.
His early training, however, stood him in good stead in parts
combining tragedy and comedy, and his most famous part
might be said to be one of that description, Walter in
Children in the Wood. He was a man of high character,
and was universally esteemed—Lowe.*

2414 ADOLPHUS, JOHN. Memoirs of John
Bannister, comedian. By John Adolphus, Esq.

2 vols. pp. [i–vii] viii–xix [xx], [1] 2–399 [400]; pl.
[front.] + pp. [i–iii] iv–xi [xii], [1] 2–199 *182–*199
200–368 [=386]; pl. [front.]   L

Richard Bentley   1839

*Chapter XXVII on pp. *182–*199; chapter XXVII*
begins on p. 200. Dedicated to the members of the
Garrick Club.*

2415 ———[another edition]

pp. [iii–vii] viii–xix [xx], ²[iii] iv–xi [xii], [1] 2–399
[400], ²[1] 2–199 *182–199* 200–368 [=386]; pls.
[front., 1]   L

Richard Bentley   [1839?]

An issue in one volume.

Barbier, *Mrs.*

Singer. See IRELAND no. 1720 (Dublin).

Barker, *Mrs.* (–1876)

*Née McPhain, married first George Barker, second —
Malison, third Henry Willoughby Gratton Plunkett.
Actress.*

2416 [BARKER, GEORGE.] IMPUNITY OF MILI-
TARY INSOLENCE and licentiousness, exhibited in a
correspondence between George Barker, of the Theatre
Royal, Drury Lane, and Captain Sutton, of the 7th
Hussars, and the Commander in Chief, His Grace the
Duke of Wellington.

pp. [4] [1] 2–23 [24 (bl.)]   L

James Ridgway   1845

*This correspondence relates to a very gross speech of
Captain Sutton's regarding Mrs. Barker, which he neither
endeavoured to substantiate nor withdrew. Mr. Barker
appealed for some redress to Sutton's colonel, and to the
Duke of Wellington, but without result — Lowe.*

Barrett, Wilson (1847–1904),

*Stage name of William Henry Barrett. Actor manager.
See also nos. 3826–3827.*

2417 *VERBATIM REPORT of the reception of
Lawrence Barrett, by Wilson Barrett. Langham Hotel,
London, England, April 2nd, 1884.

                                                      MB

[London]   [1884]

Lawrence Barrett (1838–1891), American actor.

2418 [COBBE, JOHN.] WILSON BARRETT
MEMORANDA for Press use only

ff. [1–3] 4–18   MH

[Walter Smith, printer]   [1886?]

2419 BATH THEATRE ROYAL. Luncheon and presentation to Wilson Barrett, Esq. October 14th, 1887.

pp. [1–3] 4–7 [8 (bl.)]   BhP
Bath   1887

Barry, *Mrs.* Anne Spranger

See below CRAWFORD, Mrs. ANNE, nos. 2652–2655.

Barry, Spranger (1719–1777)

This 'silver-toned' actor was the most serious rival that Garrick ever had. He was the Romeo at Covent Garden in the famous contest between the two houses — Lowe. See IRELAND nos. 1732, 1770–1783; (Dublin); BIO-GRAPHY; COLLECTIVE nos. 2284 et seq; 2303; BIOGRAPHY; INDIVIDUAL nos. 2770–2773 (Foote); 2914 (Garrick); THEORY AND CRITICISM no. 4042.

Barrymore, *Earl of* (1769–1793)

Amateur actor.

✖ A catalogue of all the valuable materials of the theatre . . . at Wargrave . . . late the property of the Right Hon. Earl of Barrymore. 1792. *See no. 69.*

2420 PASQUIN, ANTHONY, *pseud.* of John Williams. The life of the late Earl of Barrymore. Including A history of the Wargrave theatricals, and original anecdotes of eminent persons. By Anthony Pasquin, Esq.

pp. [1–5] 6–79 [80 (advt.)]; pl. [front.]   L
H. D. Symonds   1793

2421 ——a new edition, corrected and much enlarged.

pp. [3–5] 6–119 [120 (advt.)]; pl. [front.]   L
H. D. Symonds   1793

"*The public are requested to be particular in sending for 'Pasquin's Life of Lord Barrymore', as there are some catchpenny accounts of him in circulation!*"

2422 ——third edition, corrected and much enlarged.

pp. [1–5] 6–119 [120 (advt.)]; pl. [front.]   L
H. D. Symonds   1793

2423 ——fifth edition

pp. [1–3] 4–24   L
Dublin: C. Jackson   [1794?]

The title-page has a list of the "eminent personages", and also names other works written by Pasquin. The head-title on the second leaf is "Convivials. Number I", as though a series were intended. This copy is complete but mutilated—imprint date not visible. Severely abridged.

2424 PERSONAL OBSERVER, A, *pseud.* Truth opposed to fiction. Or, an authentic and impartial review of the life of the late right honourable the Earl of Barrymore. Being a recital of every transaction calculated to exite the attention of the public. Compre-hending . . . a faithful delineation of his destructive theatrical connections and dramatic representations . . . By a personal observer, (the author of several popular publications.) With a striking likeness of his lordship, from an original painting.

pp. [i–iii] iv–vii [viii], [1] 2–121 [122]   L
C. and G. Kearsley   1793

Preface dated 20 April 1793. No plates or illustrations in this copy.

2425 ROBINSON, JOHN ROBERT. The last Earls of Barrymore 1769–1824 By John Robert Robinson.

pp. [i–v] vi–xiv [xv–xvi], [1] 2–272; pls. [front., 4]   L
Sampson Low, Marston & Co.   1894

Barton, Frances (1737–1815)

Actress. See above ABINGTON, FRANCES no. 2369.

Bateman, Kate (1843–1917)

Actress.

2426 KENNEY, CHARLES LAMB. *The new actress and the new play at the Adelphi Theatre.

pp. 19   MB
Johnson & Co.   1863

An account of Miss Kate Bateman in Augustin Daly's Leah. (Adelphi 1 Oct. 1863).

Beale, Thomas Willert (1828–1894)

Writer and opera manager.

2427 MAYNARD, WALTER, *pseud. of* Thomas Willert Beale. The enterprising impresario. By Walter Maynard.

pp. [4] [1] 2–407 [408 (bl.)]   L
Bradbury, Evans, & Co.   1867

2428 BEALE, [THOMAS] WILLERT. The light of other days seen through the wrong end of an opera glass. By Willert Beale (Walter Maynard).

2 vols. pp. [6] [1] 2–368; pl. [front.] + pp. [6] [1] 2–364
                                                             L
Richard Bentley & Son   1890

Beard, John (1716–1791)

Singer and actor. He married a daughter of John Rich, and from Rich's death, in 1761, until 1767, he managed Covent Garden—Lowe. See no. 1158.

Beauclerk, *Mrs.*

2429 [BEAUCLERK, *Mrs.* D. J.] MRS. BEAU-CLERK'S LETTERS to Mr. Sheridan and Mr. Victor, with their answers. To which is prefixed, An occasional prologue, spoken by Mr. King the first night of her appearing on the stage.

pp. [i–ii] iii–iv 5–32   L
Dublin   1758

> *Mrs. Beauclerk was a novice, who wished to be introduced to the public in Dublin. She made her first appearance, 11th November 1757, as Andromache. She was full of grievances against Sheridan, whom she accused of treating her very badly — Lowe.*

Bedford, Paul John (ca. 1792–1871)

A well-known comedian, who made his first appearance at Drury Lane as long ago as November 1824 — Lowe.

2430 BEDFORD, PAUL [JOHN]. Recollections and wanderings of Paul Bedford. Facts, not fancies.

pp. [8] [1] 2–160; pl. [front.]   L
Routledge, Warne, & Routledge   1864

2431 ——*[another edition]
Routledge, Warne etc.   1867

Lowe.

Bellamy, George Anne (1727–1788)

A noted actress, whose private history is of rather a sensational order — Lowe. See C. H. Hartman, Enchanting Bellamy, 1956.

2432 BELLAMY, GEORGE ANNE. An apology for the life of George Anne Bellamy. Late of Covent Garden Theatre. Written by herself. To which is annexed her original letter to John Calcraft, Esq. advertised to be published in October 1767, but which was then violently suppressed. In five volumes.
5 vols. pp. [3–4] 5–12, ²[1] 2–215 [216 (bl.)] + [2] [1] 2–226 + [2] [1] 2–216 + [2] [1] 2–215 [216 (advt.)] + [2] [1] 2–144 [145–164 (index)]   LGk
Printed for the author, by the Literary Society, at the Logographic press and sold by J. Bell   1785

> *Edited by Alexander Bicknell.*

2433 ——the second edition. In two volumes.
2 vols. pp. [10] [1] 2–330 + [1] 2–299 [300 (bl.) 301–318 (index)], misprinting 71 as "51", 292 as "92"   L

Dublin: Moncrieffe, Burnet, Jenkin, Wilson, Exshaw, Burton, White, Byrne and H. Whitestone   1785

2434 ——the second edition. In five volumes.
5 vols. pp. [iii–v] vi–xii, [1] 2–200 + [1] 2–215 [216 (bl.)] + [1] 2–199 [200 (advt.)] + [4] [1] 2–212 + [1] 2–195 [196 (errata) 197–215 (index) 216 (bl.)]   L
For the author and sold by J. Bell   1785

2435 ——the third edition. In five volumes.
5 vols. pp. [i–v] vi–xii, [1] 2–200, ²[1] 2–4 (advts.) + [4] [1] 2–215 [216] + [4] [1] 2–199 [200] + [4] [1] 2–212, ²[1–2] 3–4 (advts.) + [4] [1] 2–195 [196–216]   L
Printed for the author, and sold by J. Bell   1785

2436 ——An apology for the life of George Anne Bellamy, late of Covent-Garden theatre. Written by herself. To the fifth volume of which is annexed, Her original letter to John Calcraft, Esq. advertised to be published in October 1767, but which was then violently suppressed. In six volumes. Vol. VI.
pp. [i–v] vi–ix [x] [11] 12–162 [163–169 (index) 170 (bl.) 171–181 (critical notices) 182 (bl.) 183–190 (advts.)]   L
Printed for the author, and sold by J. Bell   1785

> *This supplementary volume was published in May 1785. "Those who are possessed of either of the former editions," runs the Advertisement (p. viii) "may add this to it".*

2437 ——the fourth edition. In five volumes.
5 vols. pp. [i–v] vi–xii, [1] 2–232, ²[1] 2–6 (advt.), misprinting 219 as "119"; pls. [front., 1] + pp. [4] [1] 2–226; pl. [front.] + pp. [4] [1] 2–207 [208 (bl.)]; pl. [front.] + pp. [4] [1] 2–224; pl. [front.] + pp. [4] [1] 2–242, misprinting 229 as "189"; pl. [front.]   L
For the author   1786

> *Incorporates part of supplementary vol. VI.*

2438 ——[abridged edition] *Memoirs of a celebrated actress; containing a true account of her various amours, adventures, and vicissitudes; and interspersed with curious anecdotes of several distinguished persons.
pp. 60; front.
Champantre & Whitrow   [1785]

> *A condensation of the "Apology" — Lowe.*

——[French editions] Mémoires de Miss Bellamy, célèbre actrice de Londres; traduits de l'anglais. 2 vols. Paris: à la librairie, Rue André-des-Arcs, an vii [1799]; Mémoires de Mistriss Bellamy, actrice du Théâtre de Covent-Garden, [translated by P. V. Benoist and P. B. Lamare.] Avec une notice sur sa vie, par M. Thiers. (Collection des mémoires sur l'art dramatique.) 2 vols. Paris: Ponthieu, 1822.

2439 GENTLEMAN OF COVENT-GARDEN THEATRE, A, *pseud.* Memoirs of George Anne Bellamy, including all her intrigues; with genuine anecdotes of all her public and private connections.

pp. [*4*] [1–2] 3–204

J. Walker and J. Debrett   1785

     IKF. *Another copy at MB.*

2440 ——[another edition]

pp. [*2*] [1] 2–198 201–204 [=202]   L

J. Walker   1785

2441 ——*[another edition]

Debrett   1785

     STR.

2442 WILLETT, EDWARD. Letters addressed to Mrs. Bellamy, occasioned by her Apology. By Edward Willett.

pp. [1–5] 6–75 [*76*]   L

Printed by J. Rozea   [1785]

     Willett was the attorney of Woodward, the comedian, whose friend Mrs. Bellamy was. She accused Willett, in her Apology, of misconduct regarding a legacy left her by Woodward. He replied in this tract — Lowe.

Belton, Fred (1815–1889)

2443 BELTON, FRED. Random recollections of an old actor. By Fred. Belton.

pp. [*8*] [1] 2–248   L

Tinsley Brothers   1880

Bennett, Charles Frederick (1775?–).

Actor.

2444 BENNETT, CHARLES FREDERICK. His memoirs and poetry, by Charles Frederick Bennett, second son of the late Rev. Thomas Bennett, D.D. formerly of Trinity-College, Cambridge, and one of His Majesty's justices of the peace for the County of Middlesex.

pp. [*2*] [i–iii] iv–xiv, [1] 2–144   L

Holt: printed for the author by J. Shalders   1817

     The half-title reads: Bennett's Memoirs and Poetry.

Berkeley, Elizabeth

See above ANSPACH, Margravine of (no. 2391).

Berkeley, Colonel W. Fitzhardinge

An illegitimate son of Earl Berkeley, who seduced Maria Foote. He was an amateur actor and a colonel of militia — Lowe. See nos. 2758, 2761–2764.

Bernard, John (1756–1828)

A successful actor and manager, both in America and this country. His Retrospections (edited by his son) make an interesting and valuable book — Lowe.

2445 BERNARD, JOHN. Retrospections of the stage. By the late John Bernard, manager of the American theatres, and formerly secretary to the Beef-steak Club.

2 vols. pp. [i–iii] iv–xii, [1] 2–381 [*382*] + pp. [i–iii] iv–viii, [1] 2–337 [*338*]; pl. [front.]   GU

Colburn and Bentley   1830

     Edited by his son W. Baile (afterwards Bayle) Bernard.

     ——[American edition] Boston: Sarter & Hendee, 1832.

Bertram, James Glass (1824–1892)

Editor of the North Briton, *a somewhat notorious Edinburgh newspaper — Lowe. A "Memoir" is prefaced to his* Some memories of books, authors, and events *(Westminster: Archibald Constable and Company, 1893). See also ARTS OF THE THEATRE no. 731.*

2446 PATERSON, PETER, *pseud.* of James Glass Bertram. *The confessions of a strolling player; or three years' experience in theatres rural.

pp. 42   MB

Bertram & Co.   1852

2447 PATERSON, PETER, *pseud.* of James Glass Bertram. Behind the scenes: being the confessions of a strolling player. By Peter Paterson, late comedian of the theatres royal and rural.

pp. [iii–vii] viii [9] 10–166; illus. cover   EP

Edinburgh: D. Mathers; Glasgow: W. Love   1858

2448 ——[second edition] Fourth thousand.

pp. [i–vii] viii [9] 10–166   L

Edinburgh: D. Mathers; London: Henry Lea; Glasgow: Thomas Murray & Son   1859

     Called 'second edition' in the preface.

2449 ——[another edition, enlarged] Glimpses of real life as seen in the theatrical world and in Bohemia: being the confessions of Peter Paterson, a strolling comedian.

pp. [i–vii] viii–xii, [1] 2–352; illus.   E

Edinburgh: William P. Nimmo   1864

Betterton, Charles

Actor and showman.

2450 BETTERTON, CHARLES. The life of Mr. Charles Betterton, written by himself. In two numbers. Number one.

pp. [1–3] 4–12   MH

Portsea: printed by George Moxon   1829

2451 ──── The life of Mr. Charles Betterton, (written by himself.) No. 2.

pp. [1–3] 4–12   MH

Portsmouth: printed by W. Harrison   1829

Betterton, Thomas (1635–1710)

One of the greatest, if not indeed the greatest, of English actors. Colley Cibber says of him — "Betterton was an actor, as Shakespear was an author, both without competitors, formed for the mutual assistance and illustration of each other's genius." He was not more admirable for his great genius, than for the worth and probity of his private life — Lowe.

2452 [ROWE, NICHOLAS.] EPILOGUE spoken by Mrs. Barry, April the 7th, 1709. At a representation of Love for Love: for the benefit of Mr. Betterton at his leaving the stage.

pp. [1–3] 4–6 [7–8]   L

[Sanger & Curll]   1709

2453 [GILDON, CHARLES.] THE LIFE of Mr. Thomas Betterton, the late eminent tragedian. Wherein the action and utterance of the stage, bar, and pulpit, are distinctly consider'd. With the judgment of the late ingenious Monsieur de St. Evremond, upon the Italian and French music and opera's; in a letter to the Duke of Buckingham. To which is added, "The amorous widow, or the wanton wife". A comedy. Written by Mr. Betterton. Now first printed from the original copy.

pp. [i–ii] iii–xiv, 1–176, ²[1–2] 3–87 [88 (bl.)]; pl. [front.]
                                                  L

Robert Gosling   1710

In some copies (also at L) the Epistle Dedicatory concludes with the printed name of the author.

2454 vacant.

2455 AN ACCOUNT of the life of that celebrated tragedian Mr. Thomas Betterton. Containing a distinct relation of his excellencies in his profession, and character in private life. And interspersed with an account of the English theatre during his time.

pp. [i–ii] iii–iv [5] 6–36   L

J. Robinson   1749

2456 THE LIFE and times of that excellent and renowned actor Thomas Betterton, of the Duke's and United Companies, at the theatres in Portugal Street, Dorset Gardens, Drury Lane, &c., during the latter half of the seventeenth century. With such notices of the stage and English history, before and after the Restoration, as serve generally to illustrate the subject. By the author and editor of the Lives of "Mrs. Abingdon," "James Quin," etc., etc.

pp. [4] [1] 2–144 149–160 [=156]; pl. [front.]   NbU

Reader   1888

Bound in eights.

2457 ──── large paper edition.

pp. [4] [1] 2–144 149–160 [=156]; pl. [front.]   L

Reader   1888

Bound in fours.

2458 LOWE, ROBERT W[ILLIAM]. Thomas Betterton by Robert W. Lowe.

pp. [i–v] vi [vii–viii], [1] 2–196   GU

Kegan Paul, Trench, Trübner, & Co., Ltd.   1891

Reissued in one volume with Archer's Macready and Parry's Macklin with title on spine: "Eminent Actors. Macready, Betterton, Macklin". See below no. 3291.

Betty, Henry (1819–1897)

The son of the famous W.H.W. Betty—a highly respected gentleman, whose wealth is liberally used by him for the aid of unfortunate members of his old profession—Lowe. See no. 2486.

Betty, William Henry West (1791–1874)

The celebrated Young Roscius, over whom all England went mad. He appeared in London on 1st December 1804, and was a great attraction, drawing immense sums of money. He left the stage and went to Cambridge; but returned to it when a man. His success, however, was not great — Lowe. See Giles Playfair, The Prodigy, 1967. See also below Mrs. SIDDONS, no. 3532.

2459 [BEST, WILLIAM.] ANIMADVERSIONS on Mr. J. Jackson's Dramatic strictures upon the merits of Young Roscius. By the editor of "The Glasgow Theatrical Register."

pp. [2] [1] 2–70   E

Glasgow: Cameron & Co.; Edinburgh: John Buchanan; London: Vernor & Hood   1804

2460 vacant

2461 AUTHENTIC MEMOIRS of that wonderful phenomenon, the Infant Roscius; in which is interspersed a variety of theatrical anecdotes, and a criticism on his performance.

pp. [8] [11] 12–34; pls. [4]   MH
W. Hodgson   [1804]

2462 BISSET, J[AMES]. Critical essays on the dramatic excellencies of the Young Roscius, by gentlemen of distinguished literary talents and theatrical amateurs, opposed to the hypercriticisms of anonymous writers, who assume the signatures of Justus, Ennius, & Crito. Interspersed with authentic and interesting anecdotes of this wonderful phenomenon, who so brightly illumines the theatric hemisphere; containing also an account of his Irish, Scotch, and English provincial and metropolitan engagements, &c. &c. Faithfully compiled by J. Bisset, Museum, Birmingham, author of 'The patriotic clarion', &c. &c.

pp. [i–v] vi–xii, [1] 2–91 [92 (bl.)]   L
Birmingham: printed for the author by Knott and Lloyd, published in London by J. Johnson; Cadell and Davies   [1804 or 1805]

Copies at MB and Shrewsbury Public Library have a frontispiece.

2463 *CRITIQUE on the first performance of Young Roscius at Covent Garden Theatre, Dec. 1, as it appeared in the British Press (newspaper), Dec. 3. 1804.

pp. 34   MB
[London]: Kirby   1804

2464 DEMOCRITUS, JUNIOR, *pseud.* *The Young Roscius dissected; or, an account of the parentage, birth and education of William Henry West Betty; strictures on his acting; reasons for the decline of his popularity; and an appendix dedicated to parents and guardians, containing hints, which may enable them to instruct children in the art of acquiring a fortune, by Junior Democritus.

pl. [front.]
Liverpool   [ca. 1804]

IKF. *Copy at MH.*

2465 HARLEY, GEORGE DAVIES, *pseud.* of George Davies. An authentic biographical sketch of the life, education, and personal character, of William Henry West Betty, the celebrated Young Roscius. By George Davies Harley, of the theatres of Birmingham and Sheffield, late of the Theatre Royal Covent-Garden.

pp. [1–5] 6–76; pl. [front.]   L
Richard Phillips   1804

Preface dated Sheffield 28 November 1804.

2466 ——*second edition
pp. 3–76   MB
Phillips   1804

2467 ——third edition
pp. [3–5] 6–7 [8–9] 10–76   NbU
Richard Phillips   1804
Copy at MB with pl.

2467.1 ——*[another edition] An authentic sketch of the life of William Henry West Betty, the celebrated Young Roscius: with a critique of his performances at Covent Garden Theatre.

pp. 5–40; port.   MB
Hughes   1804

2468 ——*[another edition]
Richard Phillips   1805
Thorn-Drury.

2469 HARRAL, T[HOMAS]. *The Infant Roscius; or, an inquiry into the requisites of an actor: comprising a critical analysis of young Betty's acting, on the London boards; a complete sketch of his life; an investigation of the merits of the four pamphlets which have been published respecting him, by Mess. Jackson, Bissett, Merritt, and Harley; strictures on the present state of the Covent Garden company, &c. By T. Harral, Esq.

pp. (1), 50   MB
Allen   [1804]

2470 IMPARTIAL OBSERVER, AN, *pseud.* The wonderful theatrical progress of W. Hen. West Betty, the Infant Roscius, in Ireland, Scotland, and various parts of England, also, at the Theatres Royal Covent Garden & Drury Lane; with An accurate sketch of his life. By an impartial observer.

pp. [1–3] 4–70 [71–72 (advt.)]; pl. [front.]   L
Manchester: Dean and Co. and M. Swindells; Nottingham: E. B. Robinson; Birmingham: Wilkes and Co., Belsher and Peart; Liverpool: Milner, Newett, and Jones; Sheffield: Todd; Leeds: Binns; London: Crosby and Co.   [1804]

On the cover: Memoirs of Master Betty, the Infant Roscius. See no. 2482 below.

2471 ——*[second edition]
Barnard & Sultzer   MB
On the cover: Memoirs of Master Betty, the Infant Roscius.

2472 JACKSON, J[OHN]. *Strictures upon the merits of Young Roscius. By J. Jackson.
Glasgow   1804
Lowe.

2473 ———second edition

pp. [1–5] 6–77 [78 (bl.)]; pl. [front.]   L

Glasgow: printed by W. Lang   1804

With an addendum.

2474 ———third edition

pp. [4] [1] 2–82; pl. [front.]   E

Longman, Hurst, Rees and Orme, and J. Hatchard 1804

2475 THE LIFE OF WM. HENRY WEST BETTY, the celebrated and wonderful Young Roscius: containing the particulars of his theatrical career, his education, character, & abilities; together with An impartial account of his astonishing performances on the London theatres. Illustrated with a striking likeness of this brilliant theatrical star.

pp. [1–3] 4–36; pl. [front.]; "Advertisement" slip (inserted between [A1] and A2)   MH

John Fairburn   [1804]

The slip announces that the work will be continued, and the second part published "early next week"; it is dated 6th December 1804.

2476 *MEMOIRS and interesting anecdotes of the Young Roscius, with critical remarks on the wonderful phenomenon.

pp. 33
                                                    1804
STR.

2477 MERRITT, JOHN. *Memoirs of the life of Wm. Henry West Betty, known by the name of the Young Roscius, with a general estimate of his talents, and a critique on his principal characters.

pp. 140   MB
Liverpool: Wright   1804

2478 ———Memoirs of the life of Wm. Henry West Betty, known by the name of the Young Roscius, with a general estimate of his talents, and a critique on his principal characters. Second edition.

pp. [1–9] 10–140   L
Liverpool: printed by J. Wright; London: sold by Longman, Hurst, Rees, and Orme   1804

2479 THE NESTOR ROSCIUS, aged ninety five!!! The public is most respectfully informed that this most astonishing phenominon of *second childhood* is engaged to perform the principal parts in. . . . He will make his debut on the London boards in Young Norval. The part of Lady Randolph by his great grand daughter.

bs.   DFo
[London?]   [1804–5]

The title is headed with the motto
Flos est senectutis virtus,
et
Virtus in actione consistit . . .

2479.1 R., W. P. *i.e.* W. P. Russell? *The prose-Rosciad; or an easy cure for popular phrenzy in theatrical concerns, having reference to the indecent plaudits, and exhorbitant recompence, bestowed by the English, Scotch, and Irish on that puerile performer, called the Young Roscius: thereby tending to disparage the merits of the adult performers; and to manifest the ingratitude of the British people. By W.P.R.

                                                    1804
STR.

2480 *A MEDLEY, and a letter respecting the Theatrical Game Chicken.

                                                    1805
Recorded but not seen by Lowe.

2481 PANGLOSS, PETER, *pseud.* The Young Rosciad, an admonitory poem, well-seasoned with Attic salt, *cum notis variorum.* By Peter Pangloss, Esq. L.L.D. & A.S.S.

pp. [i–iii] iv–viii [9] 10–35 [36 (advt.)]   L
W. Gordon   1805

Against Betty — Lowe.

2482 ROSCIUS IN LONDON. Biographical memoirs of William Hen. West Betty, from the earliest period of his infancy. Including the history of his Irish, Scotch, and English engagements. With analytical strictures on his acting at the London theatres. Dedicated to Richard Brinsley Sheridan, Esq. M.P.

pp. [4] [1] 2–59 [60 (advt.)]; pl. [port.]   L
B. Crosby and Co.   1805

Enlarged from The Wonderful Theatrical Progress of W. Hen. West Betty *(1804) (no. 2470, above).*

2483 ———second edition, with a postscript respecting his late indisposition.

pp. [4] [1] 2–62 [63–64 (advts.)]; pl. [front.]   LGk
B. Crosby and Co.   1805

———[American edition] The Young Roscius. Biographical memoirs, etc. New York: Robert M'Dermut, 1806.

2484 WOODWARD, G[EORGE] M[OUTARD]. The Bettyad, a poem: descriptive of the progress of the Young Roscius in London. By G. M. Woodward.

pp. [1–5] 6–17 [18]; pl., fold. [front.]   L
M. Allen   1805

Plate is "*Striking likenesses of John Bull and the Young Roscius*", published *10 January 1805. An engraving by I. Cruikshank of "Young Roscius and his Pappa in Company with John Bull" was published by Fores 4 January 1805 (George 10458).*

2485 *A TRIBUTE to the genius of the Young Roscius.

Wisbech   1808

STR.

2486 MEMOIRS OF MR. W. H. W. BETTY, the English Roscius. To which is affixed A sketch of the theatrical career of his son, Mr. Henry Betty.

pp. [2] [1] 2–22   L

B. D. Cousins   [1847?]

Printed in columns.

Beverley, *Mrs.*

Mrs. Beverley was an actress who, failing to get an engagement, engaged in business, and failed. She issued these publications to make a little money — Lowe.

2487 BEVERLEY, *Mrs.* R. *i.e.* Elizabeth Beverley. The actress's ways and means, to industriously raise the wind! Containing the moral and entertaining poetical effusions of Mrs. R. Beverley, comedian; professor of elocution; and author of the popular *Coronation sermon, Modern times,* &c. &c.

pp. [1–3] 4–31 [32 ("To the public")]   L

Printed for the author, by Macdonald and Son [*ca.* 1820]

2488 ———fourth edition

pp. [1–3] 4–32   L

Printed for the author by W. Glendinning   1822

2489 ———tenth edition

pp. [1–3] 4–29 [30 (bl.) 31 (advts.) 32 (bl.)]   L

Printed for the author by T. Dolby, Britannia Press [1825?]

2490 BEVERLEY, *Mrs.* ELIZABETH. The book of variety; containing laughable anecdotes, entertaining poetry, and various other pieces of interest and amusement, by Mrs. Elizabeth Beverley, comedian . . .

pp. [1–3] 4–22 [23] [24 (advts.)]   L

Printed for the author by T. Traveller   1823

2491 ———*third edition

                                                   MB

Printed for the authoress   1824

2492 ———fifth edition

pp. [1–3] 4–23 [24 (advts.)]   L

Printed for the authoress by T. H. Coe   1824

2493 B[EVERLEY], *Mrs.* E[LIZABETH]. *Reflections by Mrs. E.B., comedian.

                                                   MH
                                                   1829

2494 BEVERLEY, *Mrs.* ELIZABETH. The indefatigable, bound on a voyage to the island of Liberality, fitted out and stored (with what it is respectfully hoped will please her numerous friends,) by the sole owner, Mrs. Elizabeth Beverley, comedian.

pp. [1–5] 6–36   L

Printed for the authoress   1830

Includes an essay "on the management of theatres", and notices of Mrs. Beverley's entertainments. The essay had appeared earlier in Mrs. Beverley's Veluti in speculum (For the Authoress 1827, "second edition" 1827).

2495 ———[another issue]

pp. [1–5] 6–36   L

Printed for the authoress   1831

Billington, *Mrs.* Elizabeth (*ca.* 1768–1818)

Singer. A most beautiful woman, whose career was marked by many scandals — Lowe.

2496 MEMOIRS OF MRS. BILLINGTON, from her birth: containing a variety of matter, ludicrous, theatrical, musical, and — With copies of several original letters, now in the possession of the publisher, written by Mrs. Billington, to her mother, the late Mrs. Weichsel: a dedication; and a prefatory address.

pp. [8] [i] ii–xv [xvi], [1] 2–78 [79–80 (bl.)]; pl. [front.]
                                                   MH

James Ridgway   1792

An attack of the most virulent nature. According to The secret history of the green room, 1793, II, 116, an action was brought against the publisher, which was, however, compromised, and the pamphlet was withdrawn. This is not a scarce book, but, being very coarse, it is much sought after — Lowe.

2497 AN ANSWER to the *Memoirs of Mrs. Billington.* With the life and adventures of Richard Daly, Esq. and An account of the present state of the Irish theatre. Written by a gentleman, well acquainted with several curious anecdotes of all parties.

pp. [8] [1] 2–71 [72 (bl.)]   L

Printed for the author   1792

Half-title has pasted slip: "Sold by L. Whitaker. . . . 1792". On the spine of one of the L copies: "Fox's Memoirs of Mrs. Billington."

Blanchard, Edward Leman (1820–1889)

Writer and producer of pantomimes.

✄ Catalogue of the . . . library of the late Frank A. Marshall . . . To which is added the library of the late E. L. Blanchard . . . [1890]. *See no. 113.*

2498 SCOTT, CLEMENT [WILLIAM] and CECIL HOWARD. The life and reminiscences of E. L. Blanchard, with notes from the diary of Wm. Blanchard. By Clement Scott and Cecil Howard.

2 vols. pp. [i–v] vi–xv [xvi], [1] 2–351 [352]; illus.; pls. [front., 3]; errata slip; misnumbering 246 as "244" + pp. [4] [353] 354–736; pls. [front., 4]; errata slip   GU
Hutchinson & Co.   1891

Bland, *Miss* Dorothy

See below JORDAN, *Mrs Dorothy nos. 3110–3120.*

Booth, Barton (1681–1733)

A very great actor, the legitimate successor of Betterton. He was one of Cibber's partners in management, and was the original Cato — Lowe. An account of Booth's death and autopsy is given in Daniel Turner's The Ancient Physicians Legacy *(1733).*

2499 *LIFE OF THAT EXCELLENT TRAGEDIAN, Barton Booth, by the author of *A Pastoral Elegy on the death of Calista.*

1733

Chase.

2500 *LIFE OF THAT EXCELLENT TRAGEDIAN Barton Booth. Late one of the managers at the Theatre in D-L. To which is added, a poem to his memory.

J. Cooper   1733
STR.

2501 [VICTOR, BENJAMIN.] MEMOIRS of the life of Barton Booth, Esq; with his character. To which are added several poetical pieces, written by himself, *viz.* Translations from Horace, Songs, Odes, &c. To which is likewise annex'd, The case of Mr. Booth's last illness, and what was observ'd (particularly with regard to the quick-silver found in his intestines) upon opening of his body, in the presence of Sir. Hans Sloan, by Mr. Alexander Small, surgeon. Publish'd by an intimate acquaintance of Mr. Booth, by consent of his widow.

pp. [1–3] 4–58; pl. [front.]   MH
John Watts   1733

2502 ———*[another edition]
John Watts   1733
STR. *Excluding the poetical pieces.*

2503 CIBBER, THEOPHILUS. The lives and characters of the most eminent actors and actresses of Great Britain and Ireland, from Shakespear to the present time. Interspersed with a general history of the stage. By Mr. Theophilus Cibber. Part I. To which is prefixed, A familiar epistle from Mr. Theophilus Cibber to Mr. William Warburton.

pp. [i–vii] viii–xcix [c], ²[i–iii] iv [v] vi–xiv, [1] 2–89 [90]
                                                     L
R. Griffiths   1753

Part I consists mainly of "The life and character of that excellent actor Barton Booth, Esq.; sometime one of the patentees and directors of His Majesty's company of comedians". No other parts known.

2504 ———[another edition] In three parts. Part I . . .
pp. [i–vii] viii–xli [xlii–xlv] xlvi–lii [53] 54–100.   L
Dublin: Abraham Bradley and John Bradley   1753

On p. [4]: "Purchasers are desired to be careful of this number, as the second and third are in the press, and will speedily be published."

Booth, Junius Brutus (1796–1852)

An actor who bore a strong resemblance to Edmund Kean, and who tried unsuccessfully to rival him. He was unfairly treated by Kean, and injudiciously advised by his own friends. He engaged both at Covent Garden and Drury Lane, and his changing from one theatre to the other caused great disturbances. He became very popular in America. Edwin Booth is his son — Lowe. A flow of pamphlets followed his failure to take the stage with Kean at Drury Lane on 22 February 1817, having previously appeared (unsuccessfully, and while still under contract to Covent Garden) two days before.

2505 LOVER OF TRUTH, A, *pseud.* To Mr. Junius Brutus Booth.

bs.   DFo
[London]   28 Feb. 1817

2506 vacant

2507 MEMOIRS OF JUNIUS BRUTUS BOOTH, from his birth to the present time; with an appendix, containing original letters, from persons of rank and celebrity; and copious extracts from the journal kept by Mr. Booth, during his theatrical tour on the continent.

pp. [i–v] vi, [9] 10–32 37–44 49–86 [87 (errata) 88 (bl.)]
[=80]; pl. [front.]   L
Chapple, Miller, Rowden, and E. Wilson   1817

Dedication dated 22 March 1817.

2508 MIDDLESEX⎱
     to wit. ⎰ James Salter, of No. 2, Norton
Falgate, in the County of Middlesex, Gentleman,
Attorney at Law, maketh oath. . . .

bs.   MH

E. Macleish, printer   [1817]

Affidavit sworn 25th February 1817 in Booth's defence.

2509 MR. BOOTH. Covent Garden Theatre. Monday, Feb. 24. (Circular.)

bs.   DFo

Printed by E. Macleish   [1817]

Justifying the proprietors of Covent Garden, in a dispute about the employ of Booth, with Drury Lane.

2510 MR. BOOTH. The sub-committee of Drury-Lane Theatre, consisting of five gentlemen . . .

bs.   MH

E. Macleish, printer   [1817]

With a copy of a letter from Thomas Harris to the Hon. Douglas Kinnaird, a member of the sub-committee, 27th February 1817.

2511 MR. BOOTH. Theatre Royal, Drury-Lane.

bs.   DFo

Lowndes, printer   1817

Dated Tuesday, February 25, 1817.

2512 MR. BOOTH'S APPEAL to the public.

bs.   DFo

Printed by E. Macleish   26 February 1817

2512.1 OLD ACTOR, AN, *pseud.* *Memoirs of the
life of Mr. Booth, containing a true statement of all
the circumstances attending his engagements at the
rival theatres, with a few remarks upon his conduct;
by an old actor.

pp. 27   MB

Keys   [1817]

2513 ORIGINAL MEMOIR and portrait of
Mr. Booth. Presented, gratis, to the purchasers of
Bell's Original Weekly Dispatch.

bs.; illus.   MH

[London]: printed by Hay and Turner   March 9, 1817

2514 THEATRICAL SQUABBLES, or a Booth in
Covent Garden.

bs; illus.   MH

Printed and sold by Jⁿº Green   [1817]

A street ballad.

2515 THEATRE ROYAL, COVENT-GARDEN.
Mr. Booth.

bs.   DFo

Printed by E. Macleish   [1817]

Justification of Covent Garden proprietors.

2516 CLARKE, ASIA BOOTH. The elder and the
younger Booth by Asia Booth Clarke (American
Actor Series).

pp. [8] [1–3] 4–194 [195–196 (bl.)]; pls. [front., 6 (incl.
1 fold.)]   L

David Bogue   [1882]

The American Actor Series edited by Laurence Hutton.

———[American edition] Boston: Osgood and
Co., 1882.

Bowman, *Mr.* (1651–1739)

Actor and singer. See above no. 2243.

Bracegirdle, Anne (1673 or 1674?–1748)

*A brilliant actress, whose chastity seems to have surprised
her contemporaries, and exercised the minds of more recent
historians. Good Genest quaintly remarks that she was
"perhaps a woman of cold constitution." Congreve was one
of her admirers, and some of the indecent poetry of the period
asserted that he married her — Lowe. See Lucyle Hook,
"Anne Bracegirdle's First Appearance", TN, XIII, 133–136,
and "Portraits of Elizabeth Barry and Anne Bracegirdle,"
TN, XV, 129–137. See also THE LONDON THEATRE
no. 1343; also below MOUNTFORD, WILLIAM no.
3344.*

2517 THE TRYAL OF CHARLES LORD MOHUN,
before the House of Peers in parliament, for the murder
of William Mountford; which began the 31 of January
1692. And continued by several adjournments till the
fourth of February following; the most honourable the
lord marquiss of Carmarthen, lord president of their
majesties council, being lord high steward *pro hac vice.*
Together with the questions in points of law, put by
their lordships to the judges; with the arguments of
my Lord Mohun's counsel, and the opinions of the
judges upon the said questions. Published by command
of the House of Peers.

pp. [4] 1–4 9–28 33–36 ²33–60 [=60]   MH

Edward Jones; and Randal Taylor   1693

*A privilege leaf, dated 4 March 1693, precedes the title-
page. Pagination in different copies varies from: pp. [1–4]
5–28 33–64 [=60] to pp. [4] 1–4 9–28 33–36 ²33–40
45–48 ²45–56 61 58–59 64 [=60]. Wing T 2181.
The players' tragedy. Or fatal love. A new novel
(1693) is about Anne Bracegirdle and the Lord Mohun
scandal.*

2518 B——LE, *Mrs.* The ladies answer, in vindication of the hoop'd pettycoat. Written by the famous actress Mrs. B——le.

bs.; illus.   MH
Printed for the author   [*ca.* 1710]

Not, of course, by Mrs. Bracegirdle. Cp. The fifteen plagues of a maiden-head. Written by Mrs. B——le (1707). According to C. W. Cunnington, the hoop-petticoat was worn from "c. 1710" (A Dictionary of English Costume, 1960).

Braham, John (1777–1856)

One of the greatest of English singers — Lowe. See also below KEMBLE, J. P. no. 3197.

2519 CRIM. CON. Damages one thousand pounds!! The trial between Mr. Henry Wright, (purser of an Indiaman), and Mr. Braham, (of musical celebrity), for criminal conversation with the plaintiff's wife, at the Court of Common-Pleas, Guildhall, before Sir Vicary Gibbs, and a special jury, on Tuesday, July 23, 1816. Taken in short-hand.

pp. [1–3] 4–16   L
John Fairburn   [1816]

2520 *REPORT OF THE TRIAL for Criminal Conversation, Wright versus Braham, of the King's Theatre . . . July 23, 1816 . . . with memoirs of Mr Braham

pp. 40   MH
                                                          1816

2521 *TRIAL OF MR. BRAHAM for Crim. Con. To which is added, the life of Mr. Braham.

                                                          1816

Recorded but not seen by Lowe. Same as no. 2520?

Brandon, James (?–1825)

In service of Covent Garden from 1768 to 1823; boxkeeper during O.P. Riots, and later treasurer. See THE LONDON THEATRE nos. 1297, 1301 (Covent Garden).

Brent, John Frederick

2522 OCTOGENARIAN ACTOR, AN, *pseud.* of John Frederick Brent. Memories of a mistaken life. An autobiography. By an octogenarian actor.

pp. [i–iii] iv [5] 6–48   L
Elliot Stock   1897

Mainly about his wife, an actress.

Brindal

2523 REPORT OF THE IMPORTANT THEATRICAL TRIAL, Martin v. Brindal. April 4th, 1844. Printed by order of the court.

pp. [1–3] 4–8   MH
W. S. Johnson, Nassau Steam Press   [1844]

A jeu d'esprit. Brindal was an actor, and Martin a dresser. There is a short notice of Brindal in W. Davenport Adams, A Dictionary of the Drama (1904).

Brooke, Gustavus Vaughan (1818–1866)

A popular tragedian; drowned in the London while on a voyage to Melbourne — Lowe.

2524 *G. V. BROOKE, the eminent tragedian: opinions of the London Press.

Belfast   [*ca.* 1848]
    STR.

2525 HERAUD, JOHN A[BRAHAM]. The wreck of the London: a lyrical ballad, by John A. Heraud. Published in aid of the fund for building a life-boat, to be called *The G. V. Brooke.*

pp. [1–3] 4–16   L
J. W. Anson (Honorary Secretary to the Fund), W. Walker & Co., and C. W. Stevens   1866

2526 TOMLIN, EDWIN. The wreck of the London. In memory of G. V. Brooke, a poem by Edwin Tomlin.

bs.; illus.
                                                          1866
    IKF.

2527 LAWRENCE, W[ILLIAM] J[OHN]. The life of Gustavus Vaughan Brooke, tragedian. By W. J. Lawrence.

pp. [2] [i–v] vi–x, [1] 2–44 [45] 46–283 [284]; pl. [front.]
                                                          GU
Belfast: W. & G. Baird   1892

Edition limited to five hundred copies, each signed by the author.

Brownsmith, John

A prompter who seems to have been a very quarrelsome person—Lowe. See AUTHOR INDEX.

Buckstone, John Baldwin (1802–1879)

A popular actor, author, and manager. He managed the Haymarket Theatre from 1853 to 1878, when he virtually retired from the stage—Lowe. See AUTHOR INDEX.

Bunn, Alfred (1798–1860)

The "Poet Bunn" of Punch. He was manager at Birmingham; stage-manager at Drury Lane under Elliston; became lessee both of Drury Lane and Covent Garden; was bankrupt; after an interval became lessee of Drury Lane for a second time; but again failed, and died in poverty at Boulogne — Lowe. See G. G. Urwin, "Alfred Bunn 1796–1860: A Revaluation", TN, XI, 96–102, and on the critical and moral controversies of Bunn's Birmingham management, see Urwin, *pp. 33–45. Bunn also edited* The Vauxhall Papers *(1841), a thrice weekly (?) periodical, 10 July 1841 to 23 August 1841, concerning the Gardens. For Bunn's part in various controversies etc. see AUTHOR INDEX; see also* THE THEATRE OUT OF LONDON *(Dublin) no. 1840.*

2528 STARGAZER, A, *pseud.* ★Alfred the Little; or, management! A play. As rejected at the Theatre Royal, Drury Lane, October, 1833. By a *Stargazer.*

pp. 16

1833

A severe satire on Bunn — Lowe.

2529 BAILEY, WILLIAM. A brief continuation of Father Isla's history of that renowned personage, Don Gerundio di Campazaz, otherwise Zotes, who is now, and hath been for the last twenty years, manager general of the Theatres Royal Drury Lane & Covent Garden: and where Dr. Millman, poetry professor at Oxford, is charged with pirating Fazio from the MS. of Grimaldi. By William Bailey.

pp. [1–3] 4–87 [88 (errata)]   LGk
B. Steill   1835

2530 BUNN, ALFRED. The stage: both before and behind the curtain, from "observations taken on the spot." By Alfred Bunn, late lessee of the Theatres Royal Drury Lane and Covent Garden.

3 vols. pp. [2] [i–iii] iv–xxvii [xxviii (publisher's disclaimer)], [1] 2–295 [296 (bl.) 297 (errata) 298 (bl.)]; illus. + pp. [i–iii] iv–vii [viii (bl.)], [1] 2–308; errata slip; cancels (pp. 157–158, 191–192, 227–228, 251–254) + pp. [2] [i–iii] iv–vi, [1] 2–304; errata slip; cancels (pp. 7–8, 165–166)   L
Richard Bentley   1840

———[American edition] Philadelphia: Lea & Blanchard, 1840.

2531 ADAM, J. R. ★"A word" with Bunn, after Burns's "Address to the Deil." By J. R. Adam, the Cremorne Poet.

pp. 12   MB
W. Brittain   [1847]

2532 BUNN, ALFRED. A word with *Punch* by Alfred Bunn.

pp. [1] 2–12; illus.   L
W. S. Johnson, printer   [1847]

This pamphlet is got up in imitation of Punch, *with an illustrated cover, &c. In the upper corner is "No. 1, –(to be continued, if necessary.)" It is a reply to the chaff and criticism showered upon "the poet Bunn" by* Punch, *and is distinguished by its strength of language, at least. Albert [Richard] Smith is said to have aided in writing it —*

Lowe. *According to a note by F. W. Fairholt in the L copy the pamphlet "was too true to be pleasant, and has been industriously bought up, and destroyed . . ."*

2533 BUNN, ALFRED. The case of Bunn versus Lind, tried at the Court of Queen's Bench, Guildhall, City, before Mr. Justice Erle and a special jury, on Tuesday, February 22nd, 1848, given in full, from shorthand notes taken at the time, with a series of letters from plaintiff and defendant, produced thereat, with others from both, now for the first time published. To which are added, notes explanatory and critical. By Alfred Bunn.

pp. [1–3] 4–73 [74 (bl.)]   L
W. S. Johnson, Nassau Steam Press   1848

Breach of contract by Lind. Bunn got £2500 damages — Lowe. *See also no. 3232 below.*

2534 BUNN, ALFRED. Old England and New England, in a series of views taken on the spot. By Alfred Bunn.

2 vols. pp. [i–v] vi–xxi [xxii], [1] 2–313 [314]; inset, fold [1]; col. pl. [front.] + pp. [i–iii] iv–viii, [1] 2–328 L
Richard Bentley   1853

———[American edition] Philadelphia: Hart, 1853.

Butler, *Mrs.* Frances
See below KEMBLE, FRANCES ANNE *nos. 3178–3184.*

Calvert, Charles Alexander (1828–1879)
Actor.

2535 MEMORIALS OF CHARLES CALVERT'S PRODUCTIONS of Shakspere and the poetic drama collected, edited, and prefaced by Thomas W. Charles.

pp. [1–3] 4–8, ²[1] 2–10   MH
William Aubert   1875

Productions include Byron's Sardanapalus.

2536 ———[another edition]
pp. [1–3] 4–8, ²[1] 2–20   MH
William Aubert   1875

Cane, Andrew (fl. 1622–1652)
A famous comedian belonging to the Fortune Theatre.— Lowe. *See no. 141.*

Cantelo, *Mr.*
A Bath musician.

2537 ★PARTICULARS of the performance for Mr. Cantelo's annual night. Wed. April 26, 1786.
Bath   1786
STR.

Catalani, Angelica (1780–1849)

A famous Italian vocalist, whose engagement at Covent Garden was one of the causes of the O.P. Riots — Lowe. See also THE LONDON THEATRE no. 1274 (Covent Garden).

2538 SIMPSON, ARTHUR. Secret memoirs of Madame Catalani. By Arthur Simpson, Esq.

pp. [i–v] vi–vii [viii], [1] 2–46   L
Bath: printed for the author by M. Gye   1811

A most gushing production, relating high-flown adventures of Catalani and her husband, M. de Valle Bregue [Valabrèque] — Lowe.

Catley, Ann (1745–1789)

An actress and singer, of very eccentric manners. She was said to be married to General F. Lascelles, in whose house she lived — Lowe.

2539 SHANDY, TRISTRAM, *pseud.* Miss C——y's cabinet of curiosities; or, the green-room broke open. By Tristram Shandy, Gent.

pp. [1–2] 3–48   L
Utopia: printed for William Whirligig, at the Maiden's Head, in Wind-mill-street.   1765

Among the curiosities are Genuine and authentic memoirs of Miss C—y. By a gentleman of quality. Sterne's Tristram Shandy was published 1759–1767; Vols. VII and VIII were published in 1765.

2540 ★MEMOIRS of the celebrated Miss Ann C——y
2 vols.; port.

                                                         1773

Recorded but not seen by Lowe.

2541 A BRIEF NARRATIVE of the life of the celebrated Miss C★tl★y, containing the adventures of that lady, in her public character of a singer, and private one of a courtezan, in England, Ireland, &c. Also, some of the most remarkable occurences [sic] in the high court of gallantry, on the stage, in the public gardens, and in the polite world, or court-end of the town; with many curious anecdotes, never before published.

pp. [1–2] 3–56   MH
Printed by W. Bailey   [ca. 1780]

Copy at DLC with a frontispiece.

2542 ———[another edition]
pp. [1–2] 3–56   L
[London]   [ca. 1780]

With a long list of contents on the title-page, and an advertisement on the verso. Punctuation of title also differs slightly from that of the first edition.

2543 AMBROSS, *Miss.* The life and memoirs of the late Miss Ann Catley, the celebrated actress: with biographical sketches of Sir Francis Blake Delaval, and the hon. Isabella Pawlet, daughter to the earl of Thanet. By Miss Ambross.

pp. [1–3] 4–56; pl. [front.]   L
J. Bird   [1789 or 1790]

2544 THE LIFE OF MISS ANNE CATLEY celebrated singing performer of the last century including an account of her introduction to public life her professional engagements in London and Dublin and her various adventures and intrigues with well-known men of quality and wealth. Carefully compiled and edited from the best and most authentic records extant.

pp. [1–3] 4–78 [79–80 (bl.)]; pl. [front.]   L
                                                         1888

2545 ———★[large paper issue]
                                                        MH
                                                        1888

Cave, Joseph Arnold

Actor, singer and manager.

2546 CAVE, JOSEPH A[RNOLD], and ROBERT SOUTAR, *ed.* A jubilee of dramatic life and incident of Joseph A. Cave author, manager, actor, and vocalist Edited by Robert Soutar With portrait of the author and of above twenty past and present celebrities.

pp. [8] [1] 2–218 [219 (advts.) 220 (colophon)]; pls. [front., 22]; illus.   L
Thomas Vernon at the office of the Weekly Dispatch
                                                      [1892]

"The following chapters first appeared in that witty hebdomadal, The Man of the World" — Preface. Dedicated to Edward Terry.

Charke, *Mrs.* Charlotte (1713–1760?)

The youngest daughter of Colley Cibber. She had considerable ability as an actress, but the chief interest in her life centres in her wildly eccentric private career — Lowe. See George Speaight, "Charlotte Charke: An Unpublished Letter", TN, XII, 33–34. See also no. 1333.

2547 [CHARKE, *Mrs.* CHARLOTTE]. A NARRATIVE of the life of Mrs. Charlotte Charke, (youngest daughter of Colley Cibber, Esq;) containing, I. An account of her birth, education, and mad pranks committed in her youth. II. Her coming on the stage; success there; and sundry theatrical anecdotes. III. Her marriage to Mr. Charke, and its consequences. IV. Her adventures in mens cloaths, and being belov'd by a lady of great fortune, who intended to marry her. V. Her being gentleman to a certain peer. VI. Her commencing strolling-player; with various and surprizing vicissitudes of fortune, during nine years peregrination. VII. Her turning pastry cook, &c. in Wales. With several extremely humourous and interesting occurrences. Written by herself.

pp. [2] [i–iii] iv–x [11] 12–277 [278]; pl. [front.]

W. Reeve; A. Dodd; and E. Cook   1755

> GS. *Another copy at L. First published in eight weekly parts, April–May.*

2548 ———the second edition. Title adds after "in mens cloaths" "going by the name of Mr. Brown, and being belov'd . . ."

pp. [2] [i–iii] iv–x [11] 12–277 [278]; pl. [front.]   MH

W. Reeve; A. Dodd; and E. Cook   1755

2549 ———[another edition] A narrative of the life of Mrs. Charlotte Charke, youngest daughter of Colley Cibber, Esq. Written by herself.

pp. ²[i–v] vi–viii [9] 10–167 [168]   L

Hunt and Clarke   1827

> *In* Autobiography. A collection of the most instructive and amusing lives ever published, written by the parties themselves. With brief introductions, and compendious sequels carrying on the narrative to the death of each writer. Volume VII. Mary Robinson — Charlotte Charke (*Whittaker, Treacher, & Arnot, 1829*).

2550 ———[another edition] A narrative of the life of Mrs. Charlotte Charke daughter of Colley Cibber. (Constable's Miscellany of Original & Selected Publications in Literature No. 29)

pp. [1–4] 5–223 [224 (bl.)]

Constable and Co. Limited   1929

> GS. *Another copy at L. "No. 29" on jacket.*

2551 CHARKE, CHARLOTTE. ★The history of Henry Dumont, Esq; and Miss Charlotte Evelyn. Consisting of variety of entertaining characters, and very interesting subjects; with some critical remarks on comick actors. By Mrs. Charke. The second edition.

H. Slater   1756

> IKF.

2552 ———The history of Henry Dumont, Esq; and Miss Charlotte Evelyn. Consisting of variety of entertaining characters, and very interesting subjects; with some critical remarks on comick actors. By Mrs. Charke. The third edition.

pp. [i–iii] iv–v [vi–xii], [1] 2–257, ²1–7 (advts.) (=264)   L

Printed for H. Slater; and H. Slater, jun. and S. Whyte   1756

> *Fiction: with occasional remarks of theatrical interest.*

Chatterton, Frederick Balsir (1835–1886)

Manager of Drury Lane from 1863 to 1879, when he failed, with liabilities of about £40,000. He was the author of the notorious saying:—"That Shakespeare spelt ruin, and Byron bankruptcy."—Lowe. See no. 1417.

Chester, Eliza (1799–   )

A lady who owed her position on the stage chiefly to her remarkable beauty. She first appeared 3rd July 1820, at Drury Lane, as Portia. Her readings of Shakespeare to George IV caused some merriment and scandal. When she died I have been unable to discover — Lowe.

2553 ★THE PUBLIC AND PRIVATE LIFE of Miss Chester, Private Reader, &c. to our late beloved King, George IV.; formerly chere-amie to Mr. Calcraft, M.P. Introducing numerous amatory anecdotes of His Majesty, at the festive board and private boudoir.

pp. 16

[1830]

> Lowe. *With portrait of Miss Chester as the Widow of Cornhill.*

Chetwood, William Rufus (–1766)

Originally a bookseller, he became prompter at Drury Lane, where he continued for twenty years. In 1741–2 he went to Smock Alley Theatre, Dublin, in which city he seems to have remained until his death. He was considered a good tutor, and is said to have instructed Barry in the rudiments of theatrical education—Lowe. See AUTHOR INDEX.

Chevalier, Albert (1861–1923)

Actor and dramatic author.

2554 CHEVALIER, ALBERT, and BRIAN DALY. Albert Chevalier A record by himself Biographical and other chapters by Brian Daly.

pp. [2] [i–iv] v–xii [xiii–xiv], [1] 2–295 [296 (bl.)]; cancellans t.p.; illus.   L

John Macqueen   1895

Cibber, Colley (1671–1757)

Colley Cibber is, to those unacquainted with his real character, simply the prince of dullards, whom Pope elevated to the throne of Dulness in the second edition of The Dunciad. *But this is a misconception, for dulness is the last crime of which Cibber could be accused, and indeed it is for levity rather than dulness that he is noted. He was a good comedian, a clever dramatist, a successful manager, and a keen and accomplished critic —* Lowe. *See R. H. Barker* Mr. Cibber of Drury Lane *(New York, 1939). For Cibber's dispute with Pope, see C. D. Peavy, "The Pope-Cibber Controversy: A Bibliography",* Restoration and 18th Century Theatre Research III *(2) (1964) 51–55. See also MORALITY OF THE THEATRE no. 336; THEORY AND CRITICISM nos. 3851–3861 (The Non-juror); AUTHOR INDEX.*

2555 CIBBER, COLLEY. An apology for the life of Mr. Colley Cibber, comedian, and late patentee of the Theatre-Royal. With an historical view of the stage during his own time. Written by himself.

pp. [16] [1] 2–346; pl. [front.] L

Printed by John Watts for the author 1740

One of the most famous and valuable of theatrical books — Lowe. *Dedication dated 6 November 1739; published 7 April 1740 — a handsome quarto, price one guinea.* Barker, pp. 194–203.

2556 ———the second edition

pp. [24] [1] 2–488; pl.; t.p. in red and black L

Printed by John Watts for the author 1740

Published 14 May. A more modest edition than the first, which cost a guinea; this cost five shillings. The text, however, was revised. See Lowe's edition of the book, I, ix, and Barker, p. 194.

2557 ———the fourth edition. [i.e. another edition]

pp. [12] [1] 2–346 [347–348 (advts.)] L

Dublin: reprinted by and for George Faulkner 1740

2558 ———the third edition. To which is now added, A short account of the rise and progress of the English stage: also, A dialogue on old plays and old players.

pp. [24] [1] 2–555 [556 (bl.)]; pl. [front.] MH

R. Dodsley 1750

The 'Short account' is from the preface of Dodsley's Old Plays, and 'A dialogue' is Wright's Historia Histrionica. On 24 March 1750, Cibber assigned the copyright of his book to Robert Dodsley, for fifty-two pounds ten shillings — N & Q (1911), I, 266.

2559 ———the fourth edition. With An account of the rise and progress of the English stage: A dialogue on old plays, and old players: and A list of dramatic authors and their works.

2 vols. pp. [14] [1] 2–324; pl. + pp. [4] [1] 2–303 [304 (bl.) 305–334 (index to authors and plays) 335–336 (bl.)] L

R. and J. Dodsley 1756

2560 ———[another edition] An apology for the life of Mr. Colley Cibber, comedian and patentee of the Theatre Royal. Written by himself; and interspersed with characters and anecdotes of his theatrical cotemporaries; the whole forming a complete history of the stage for the space of forty years. A new edition, with many critical and explanatory notices, by Edmund Bellchambers.

pp. [i–iv] v–xxiii [xxiv], [1] 2–514, ²[i] ii–vii (index) [viii (bl.)], misprinting 453 as "455"; pl. L

W. Simpkin and R. Marshall 1822

Without Dodsley's additions.
Notices in fact by J. H. Burn? of whom Lowe writes: Although this gentleman's name does not appear on any title-page which I have catalogued, I must draw attention to the fact that it is claimed for him that he really wrote the notes to Bellchamber's edition of Colley Cibber's Apology, and to Whitehead's edition of Dickens's Grimaldi. Regarding the latter Mr. Burnett says: "They have the peculiarity of contradicting the editor (Dickens) point-blank on almost every page; and are said to be as correct as the original biography is vague and inaccurate." On the subject of the Cibber notes I cannot do better than quote an extract from a catalogue of that excellent bookseller, Mr. Salkeld, of 314 Clapham Road. In cataloguing a copy of Bellchambers's Cibber he says: "On the back of title is the following — 'In 1821, while residing at No. 28 Maiden Lane, Covent Garden, the elder Oxberry, who frequently called in as he passed, found me one day adding notes in MS to Cibber's Apology. Taking it up, he said he should like to reprint it; he wanted something to employ the spare time of his hands, and preferred to buy my copy, thus annotated. I think it was two pounds I said he should have it for; this sum he instantly paid, and the notes throughout are mine, not Bellchambers's, who having seen it through the press or corrected the proofs whilst printing, added his name as the editor' — J. H. Burn". See also no. 2968.

2561 ———[another edition] An apology for the life of Mr. Colley Cibber, comedian. Written by himself. (Autobiography. A Collection Of The Most Instructive And Amusing Lives Ever Published, Written By The Parties Themselves. With Brief Introductions And Compendious Sequels . . . Volume 1 — Colley Cibber)

pp. [6] [i] ii [iii–vi], [1] 2–340; pl. [front.] L

Hunt and Clarke 1826

Without Dodsley's additions.

2562 ———[a reissue of no. 2561]

pp. [14] [i] ii, [1] 2–340; pl. LSTR

Whittaker, Treacher, and Arnot 1829

2563 ———[a reissue of no. 2561]

pp. [6] [i] ii, [1] 2–340 [341–344 ("Contents")] MH

Whittaker, Treacher, and Arnot 1830

2564 ———[another edition] An apology for the life of Mr. Colley Cibber written by himself A new edition with notes and supplement by Robert W. Lowe with twenty-six original mezzotint portraits by R. B. Parkes, and eighteen etchings by Adolphe Lalauze.

2 vols. pp. [i–v] vi–lxxi [lxxii (bl.)], [1] 2–337 [338]; pls. [I (front.) II–XIII]; etched chapter-headings, pasted to the page [I–IX] + pp. [i–v] vi [vii–viii], [1] 2–416 [417] [418 (bl.)]; pls. [I (front.) II–XIII]; etched chapter headings, pasted to the page [I–IX]; t.p. in red and black L

John C. Nimmo 1889 [*for* 1888]

Only 350 copies printed. The leaves with the etchings are inserted. Each plate is reproduced twice, once on Japanese paper, and once in 'Indian proof'. Reprints Wright's Historia Histrionica, Aston's Brief Supplement.

2565 ——[another edition] Colley Cibber written by himself (Beaux & Belles of England).

2 vols. pp. [i–iv] v–vii [viii (bl.)] [2], ²vii–xiv [1–2] 3–399 [400 (bl)]; pls. [front. (col.), 5]; ptd. tissue guards [6]; t.p. in red and black + pp. [i–iv] v–vii [viii (bl.) ix (list of illustrations) x] 1–400; pls. [front. (col.), 5]; ptd. tissue guards [6]; t.p. in red and black   NbU

Printed by the Grolier Society   [190–?]

"Imperial edition limited to one thousand copies for England and America." Another edition of Lowe's edition (no. 2564), with his notes and supplementary material.

——[American edition] Beaux and Belles of England. New York: Athenaeum Press, n.d. [1907?].

2566 ——*[another edition] (Days of the Dandies).

2 vols. col. front, col. pls., col. ports.   CLaU

The Grolier Society   [190–?]

Edition de luxe, limited to one thousand copies for England and America.

2567 ——[another edition] An apology for his life by Colley Cibber. (Everyman's Library.)

pp. [i–vi] vii–xv [xvi], [1] 2–302 [303–304 (bl.)]   E

London: J. M. Dent & Sons Ltd.; New York: E. P. Dutton & Co.   [1914]

With an appreciation by William Hazlitt. Without Dodsley's additions.

2568 ——[another edition] An apology for the life of Colley Cibber, comedian, and late patentee of the Theatre-Royal. Written by himself.

2 vols. pp. [i–viii] ix–xii, 1–160 + [8] 1–163 [164 (bl.) 165 (publisher's notice) 166 (bl.)]; t.p. in turquoise and black   L

The Golden Cockerel Press   1925

Only 450 copies printed.
An abridged version of The apology appeared in The history of the stage, 1742. (See below no. 2569).

2569 THE HISTORY OF THE STAGE. In which is included, the theatrical characters of the most celebrated actors who have adorn'd the theatre. Among many others are the following, *viz.*

Mr. Betterton,   Mrs. Barry,
Mr. Montfort,   Mrs. Montfort,
Mr. Dogget,   Mrs. Gwin,
Mr. Booth,   Mrs. Bracegirdle,
Mr. Wilks,   Mrs. Porter,
Mr. Nokes,   Mrs. Oldfield
Together with, The theatrical life of Mr. Colley Cibber.

pp. [4] 1–144 147–230 [=228]   L

J. Miller   1742

A "boil-down" of Cibber's Apology — Lowe.

2570 ASTON, ANTHONY. A brief supplement to Colley Cibber, Esq; his lives of the late famous actors and actresses. By Anthony, *vulgò* Tony Aston.

pp. [1–3] 4–24   L

Printed for the author   [1747]

Reprinted in Bell's Cabinet (1808); Watson Nicholson, Anthony Aston (Michigan, 1920); in Lowe's ed. of Cibber's Apology (1889) (no. 2564).

2571 THE LAUREAT: or, the right side of Colley Cibber, Esq; containing, explanations, amendments and observations, on a book intituled An apology for the life, and writings of Mr. Colley Cibber. Not written by himself. With some anecdotes of the laureat, which he (thro' an excess of modesty) omitted. To which is added, The history of the life, manners and writings of Æsopus the tragedian, from a fragment of a Greek manuscript found in the library of the Vatican; interspers'd with observations of the translator.

pp. [1] 2–126   L

J. Roberts   1740

A furious attack on Cibber. The life of Æsopus is a burlesque life of Cibber — Lowe. Published in November.

2572 THE TRYAL OF COLLEY CIBBER, comedian, &c. for writing a book intitled "An apology for his life", &c. Being a thorough examination thereof; wherein he is proved guilty of high crimes and misdemeanors against the English language, and in characterising many persons of distinction. Together with An indictment exhibited against Alexander Pope of Twickenham, Esq; for not exerting his talents at this juncture: and The arraignment of George Cheyne, physician at Bath, for the philosophical, physical, and theological heresies, uttered in his last book on regimen.

pp. [i–iii] iv–viii, [1] 2–40, misnumbering viii as "vii", vii as "viii"   L

Printed for the author   1740

With motto — "Lo! He hath written a Book!" The Dedication is signed "T. Johnson." A most odd production. It seems to be only a pretended attack on Cibber — Lowe. A reprint, with introduction and comment, of papers in Henry Fielding's The Champion, April to May, 1740. The intention is to belittle Fielding's criticism, not Cibber.

2573 CIBBER, COLLEY. A letter from Mr. Cibber, to Mr. Pope, inquiring into the motives that might induce him in his satyrical works, to be so frequently fond of Mr. Cibber's name.

pp. [1–5] 6–66   L

Printed and sold by W. Lewis   1742

Published 27th July. For an account of Pope's facial expressions as he read this work, see Barker, p. 214.

2574 ——the second edition
pp. [1–5] 6–66 [67–68 (bl.)]   L
Printed and sold by W. Lewis   1742

2575 ——the third edition
pp. [4] [1] 2–72; pl. [front]   L
Glasgow: W. Macpharson   [1742?]

2576 ——[another edition]
pp. [4] [1] 2–40   L
     1777

In 1777 the collected plays of Cibber were published.

2577 CIBBER, COLLEY. †A second letter from Mr. Cibber to Mr. Pope. In reply to some additional verses in his *Dunciad*, which he has not yet published.
pp. [3–5] 6 (bl.)   L
[London]   [1743]

    Published 15th February 1743. Barker, p. 265. This copy lacks t.p.

2578 CIBBER, COLLEY. Another occasional letter from Mr. Cibber to Mr. Pope. Wherein the new hero's preferment to his throne, in the *Dunciad*, seems not to be accepted. And the author of that poem his more rightful claim to it, is asserted. With An expostulatory address to the Reverend Mr. W. W——n, author of the new preface, and adviser in the curious improvements of that satire. By Mr. Colley Cibber.
pp. [1–5] 6–56   MH
Printed and sold by W. Lewis   1744

    Dated 9 Jan. and published in that month.

2579 ——[another edition]
pp. [1–5] 6–56   L
Glasgow: W. Macpharson   [1744?]

2580 A BLAST upon Bays; or, a new lick at the laureat. Containing, remarks upon a late tatling performance, entitled, *A letter from Mr. Cibber to Mr. Pope &c.*
pp. [2] [1] 2–26   L
T. Robbins   1742

    Dated 29th July. Published August. Motto: ' "And lo there appeared an Old Woman!" Vide the Letter throughout.'

2581 ——the second edition
pp. [2] [1] 2–26   MH
T. Robbins   1742

    On the title-page: "Tattling" instead of "Tatling" of the first edition.

2582 [HERVEY, *Lord* JOHN.] THE DIFFERENCE between verbal and practical virtue. With a prefatory epistle from Mr. C——b——r to Mr. P.
pp. [4] [1] 2–7 [8]   L
J. Roberts   1742

2583 [HERVEY, *Lord* JOHN] A LETTER to Mr. C——b——r, on his letter to Mr. P——.
pp. [4] 1–26   L
J. Roberts   1742

    Abusive of Pope — laudatory towards Cibber — Lowe.

2584 SAWNEY AND COLLEY, a poetical dialogue: occasioned by a late letter from the Laureat of St. James's, to the Homer of Twickenham. Something in the manner of Dr. Swift.
pp. [2] [1] 2–21 [22 (bl.)]   L
J.H.   [1742]

    A coarse and ferocious attack on Pope in rhyme — Lowe. Published August 1742. Reprinted in facsimile by The Augustan Reprint Society (No. 83) (Los Angeles, 1960).

2585 [CIBBER, COLLEY.] THE EGOTIST: or, Colley upon Cibber, being his own picture retouch'd, to so *plain* a likeness, that no one, *now*, would have the face to own it, but himself.
pp. [1–5] 6–78 [79–80]   L
Printed and sold by W. Lewis   1743

2586 [DODD, WILLIAM.] A NEW BOOK of The Dunciad: occasion'd by Mr Warburton's new edition of *The Dunciad* complete. By a gentleman of one of the Inns of Court. With several of Mr Warburton's own notes, and likewise notes variorum.
pp. [i–v] vi–viii, [1] 2–27 [28 (bl.)]   L
J. Payne and J. Bouquet   1750

    Cibber dethroned by Warburton — Lowe. Warburton's Pope's Dunciad *(1749) was published January, 1750: Griffith 638.*

2587 COLLEY CIBBER'S JESTS; or, the diverting witty companion. Being a choice collection of the most ingenious jests, diverting stories, pleasing jokes, and satyrical epigrams now extant, &c. &c.
pp. [2] [1–3] 4–98   L
Newcastle: W. Charnley   1761

2588 COLLEY CIBBER'S TRENCHER-MAKERS. (As related by him at Drury Lane Theatre.)
bs.   L
Nursey, printer, 4, Long Acre   [1780?]

2589 ——[another edition] Colley Cibber's whimsical wager.
bs.   L
Salisbury: Fowler, printer   [1785?]

Cibber, Susanna Maria (1714-1766)

A very eminent actress: the second wife of Theo. Cibber, who treated her in blackguardly fashion. She was the sister of Dr. Arne — Lowe. See also below CIBBER, THEOPHILUS nos. 2595-2608.

2590 LUN, *junior.* *The beggar's pantomime, or, the contending columbines. By Lun, junior.

1736

This is a skit on the contest between Mrs. Cibber and Mrs. Clive for the part of Polly in the Beggar's Opera. *It is probably by Woodward, who, however, was only nineteen at the time—Lowe. Not seen by Lowe.*

2591 *A DIALOGUE IN THE SHADES between the celebrated Mrs. Cibber, and the no less celebrated Mrs. Woffington, both of amorous memory.

1766

Genest describes this as a catch-penny production. It contains no information of value, but it is curious and is very rare—Lowe. Not seen by Lowe.

2592 [KEATE, GEORGE.] A POEM to the memory of the celebrated Mrs. Cibber.

pp. [*4*] [1] 2–7 [8 (bl.)]   MH

J. Dodsley   1766

Reprinted in: The poetical works of George Keate, Esq., (*J. Dodsley, 1781*), II, [*97*]–*105.*

2593 AN ACCOUNT of the life of that celebrated actress, Mrs. Susannah Maria Cibber with interesting and amusing anecdotes. Also the two remarkable and romantic trials between Theophilus Cibber and William Sloper.

pp. [1–3] 4–56; ptd. in red; pl. [front.]   L

Reader   1887

Reprints The Tryals of Two Causes (*1740*). *See below no. 2599. Bound in eights.*

2594 ——[large paper issue]

pp. [1–3] 4–56; ptd. in red; pl. [front.]   L

Reader   1887

Bound in fours.

Cibber, Theophilus (1703-1758)

This disreputable son of Colley Cibber was an actor of undoubted merit in certain parts in comedy, but dissipated habits and extravagance prevented his making a good position for himself. He was drowned in crossing to Ireland to fulfil an engagement in Dublin — Lowe. See also THE LONDON THEATRE no. 1325 (Drury Lane); IRELAND nos. 1723-1731 (Dublin); also above BOOTH, BARTON no. 2503.

Lawsuit between Cibber and Sloper

The details given in these reports of the trial are very gross, and the pamphlets are naturally much sought after — Lowe.

2595 THE TRYAL of a cause for criminal conversation, between Theophilus Cibber, Gent. plaintiff, and William Sloper, Esq; defendant.

pp. [1–2] 3–32   L

T. Trott   1739

Cibber, it is said, sold his wife to Sloper, and then brought an action for £5000 against him. The jury showed their opinion of his conduct by a verdict for £10. Mrs. Cibber continued to live with Sloper, and Theo. brought a second action against him for detaining his wife. In this he got £500 damages—Lowe. Price on title-page. Reissued in no. 2599 below.

2596 ——[another issue] The tryal of a cause or [*sic*] criminal . . .

pp. [1–2] 3–32   MH

T. Trott   1739

No price on title-page.

2597 ——[another edition] A collection of remarkable trials, *viz.* I. The trial between Theophilus Cibber, Gent. plaintiff, and William Sloper, Esq; defendant, for criminal conversation with the plaintiff's wife. With a frontispiece representing a principal scene. II. Four original letters, *viz.* two from a husband to a gentleman; and two from a husband to a wife. . . .

pp. [1–3] 4–35 [36 (bl.)], [xxxvii–xxxix] xl–xliii [xliv (bl.)], [45] 46–130; pl. [front.]   L

Glasgow: printed for Tom Tickle, and sold by Mr. Tuz at the sign of the River Midway   [1739?]

The Four original letters *reprinted from no. 2604 below.*

2598 *TRYAL of William Sloper Esq. for criminal conversation with Mrs. Cibber

1739

Recorded but not seen by Lowe.

2599 THE TRYALS of two causes, between Theophilus Cibber, Gent. plaintiff, and William Sloper, Esq; defendant. The first for criminal conversation. The second, for detaining the plaintiff's wife.

pp. [2] 1–8 11–12 [=10], ²3–32   L

T. Trott   1740

Pp. 1–8, 11–12, "A short account of a tryal, &c" concerns Cibber's suit against Sloper for trespass and assault (4 December 1739). Pp. ²3–32 are a reissue of The tryal of a cause (*no. 2595*).

2600 ——[another edition]

pp. [1–2] 3–32   L

T. Trott   1740

Reprinted in An account of the life of that celebrated actress, Mrs Susannah Maria Cibber, *Reader, 1887, pp. 23–56: see above no. 2593.*

2601 vacant

2602 [TRUELOVE, FRANCIS, *pseud.?*] THE COMFORTS OF MATRIMONY; exemplified in the memorable case and trial, lately had upon an action brought by Theo——s C——r against ——S——, Esq; for criminal conversation with the plantiff's wife. Wherein a true and impartial account is given of the occasion which first began the acquaintance between Mr. C—bb—r's wife and the defendant; how they proceeded in their amour; Mr. C—bb—r's taking his wife from him in the country; his bringing her to town; her escape from him; and, lastly, the trial in the Court of King's Bench, with the evidence that was given on both sides.

pp. [2] [1–2] 3–37 [38]   DFo
Sam. Baker   1739

2603 ——the sixth edition
pp. [1–4] 5–13 12–37 [38 (bl.)] [=40]   L
Sam. Baker   1739

Epistle Dedicatory, "To all the unmarried Esquires in Great Britain," signed "Francis Truelove" — Lowe.

2604 FOUR ORIGINAL LETTERS, viz. two from a husband to a gentleman: and two from a husband to a wife.

pp. [2] [i] ii–iv, [1] 2–38   DFo
T. Read   1739

Ostensibly written by Cibber to his wife and to Sloper. Reprinted in A collection of remarkable trials. *(Glasgow: Tom Tickle, [1739?]). See above no. 2597.*

2605 ——the second edition
pp. [i–iii] iv–vi, [1] 2–38   L
T. Read   1739

2606 ——the third edition
pp. [i–iii] iv–vi, [1] 2–38   MH
T. Read   1739

"These letters had been offer'd to the Publick much sooner, had not some Booksellers, and Printers, been intimidated from publishing 'em; one in particular, by some Means, was alarm'd even to the breaking of the Press, when the whole was compleatly compos'd and ready to be work'd off" — p. 38.

2607 ——*fourth edition, with some additions.

[1739]
STR.

2608 HORNER, *Reverend Mr., pseud.* Cuckoldom's glory; or, the horns of the righteous exalted: in a sermon preached at Salters-Hall, on Sunday the 29th of October, 1738. By the Reverend Mr. Horner, minister of the Gospel.

pp. [1–4] 5–36; pl. [front.]   DFo
J. Wilford   [1739]

Lowe, who continued to annotate books after the publication of his Bibliographical Account, *described this in 1894 as "abominable" in his copy, now at MH.*

2609 AN APOLOGY FOR THE LIFE OF MR. T......... C....., COMEDIAN. Being a proper sequel to the *Apology for the life of Mr. Colley Cibber, comedian.* With an historical view of the stage to the present year. Supposed to be written by himself. In the stile and manner of the Poet Laureat.

pp. [i–iii] iv–viii, [1] 2–144   L
J. Mechell   1740

For Henry Fielding's possible share in this, see Barker, p. 202. Published early in July. Another copy in L has sig. C reset and variations in pagination.

2610 ——[another edition]
pp. [i–iii] iv–xi [xii (advt.)], [1] 2–178 [179–180 (advt.)]
L
Dublin: George Faulkner   1741

Title-page has "The' Cibber" for the omission marks of first edition and also "style" for "stile".

2611 CIBBER, THEOPHILUS. A serio-comic apology for part of the life of Mr. Theophilus Cibber, comedian. Written by himself. In which is contain'd, a prologue, an epilogue, and a poem, wrote on the play of Romeo and Juliet being first revived in 1744; also some addresses to the publick, on different occasions; likewise, original letters that passed between the late Sir Thomas de Veil, and Mr. Theo. Cibber, (relating to the Stage Act) on a stop being put to the playing at the Hay-Market. Interspersed with memoirs and anecdotes concerning the stage-management and theatrical revolutions, in the years 1744, 1745, and 1746, &c. And cursory observations on some principal performers; particularly Mr. Quin, Mr. Ryan, Mr. Delane, Mrs. Woffington, Mr. Sherridan [*sic*], Mrs. Ward, and Miss Bellamy; Mr. Garrick, Mr. Barry, Mr. Macklin, Mrs. Cibber, Mrs. Clive, Mrs. Pritchard, and others. Concluding with a copy of verses, call'd The contrite comedian's confession.

pp. [1–3] 4–48   DFo
Dublin: printed by A. Long   1748

2612 ——[another edition] Romeo and Juliet, a tragedy, revis'd, and alter'd from Shakespear, by Mr. Theophilus Cibber. First reviv'd (in September, 1744,) at the Theatre in the Hay-Market: now acted at the Theatre-Royal, in Drury-Lane. To which is added, A serio-comic apology, for part of the life of

Mr. Theophilus Cibber, comedian. Written by himself. Interspersed with memoirs and anecdotes, relating to stage-management, theatrical revolutions, &c. Also, cursory observations on some principal players. Concluding with a copy of verses, call'd, The contrite comedian's confession.

pp. [4] [1] 2–108   L

C. Corbett, and G. Woodfall   [1750]

Advertised 1st October 1750 — LS. Dedication dated 25 Nov. 1748. The title of the "Serio-comic apology", which begins on p. 69 is: "A serio-comic apology for part of the life of Mr. Theophilus Cibber, comedian. Written by himself. In which is contained, a prologue, an epilogue, and a poem, wrote on the play of Romeo and Juliet being first revived in 1744; also some addresses to the publick, on different occasions; likewise original letters that passed between the late Sir Thomas De Veil, and Mr. Theo. Cibber, (relating to the stage-act) on a stop being put to the playing at the Hay-Market. Interspersed with memoirs and anecdotes concerning the stage-management and theatrical revolutions, in the years 1744, 1745, and 1746, &c. And cursory observations on some principal performers; particularly Mr. Quin, Mr. Ryan, Mr. Delane, Mrs. Woffington, Mrs. Ward, and Miss Bellamy; Mr. Garrick, Mr. Barry, Mrs. Cibber, Mrs. Clive, Mrs. Pritchard, and others. Concluding with a copy of verses, called, The contrite comedian's confession." This "apology" perhaps also issued separately (such a copy at MB).

2613 CIBBER, THEOPHILUS. A lick at a liar: or, calumny detected. Being an occasional letter to a friend from Theophilus Cibber, comedian.

pp. [i–ii] iii–iv 5–23 [24 (advt. by Cibber)]   L

R. Griffites [*sic*]   [1752]

The "liar" is some actor who had reported that Theo. had run away from Ireland in debt, and had left his bail to pay a debt for him in Liverpool — Lowe. Dated 20 Oct.

2614 CIBBER, THEOPHILUS. An epistle from Mr Theophilus Cibber to David Garrick, Esq; to which are prefixed, some occasional verses, petitions, &c.

pp. [4] [1] 2–27 [28 (bl.)]   L

R. Griffiths   1755

Reprinted in Cibber's Dissertation on theatrical subjects 1756 etc. See below no. 2615.

2615 CIBBER, [THEOPHILUS]. Dissertations on theatrical subjects, as they have several times been delivered to the public, (with general approbation) by Mr. Cibber. With an appendix, which contains several matters, relative to the stage, not yet made public; and in which the laws, relative to the theatres, are considered.

pp. [4] [1] 2–76 [77–78], ²[1] 2–47 [48], ³[1–5] 6–32, ⁴17–113 [114 (errata)]   L

Printed for the author, and are to be had of Mr Griffiths (the publisher)   1756

P. 113 contains a notice of "Cibber, and Company, Snuff-Merchants"; pp. [77–78], "Contents of Second Dissertation", follow p. [114] in the reissue (i.e. no. 2616). The appendix reprints An Epistle from Mr. Theophilus Cibber, to David Garrick, Esq. [1755] (see no. 2614); To the Public (1 January, 1755) (see no. 2618); petitions, addresses, speeches, etc. concerning theatrical monopolies.

2616 ———[another edition] Cibber's two dissertations on the theatres. With an appendix, in three parts. The whole containing a general view of the stage, from the earliest times, to the present: with many curious anecdotes relative to the English theatres, never before published; and remarks on the laws concerning the theatres.

pp. [8] [1] 2–76 [2], ²[1] 2–47 [48], ³[1–5] 6–32, ⁴17–113 [114 (errata) 115 (Contents of Second Dissertation) 116 (bl.)]   DFo

Printed for the author, and are to be had of Mr. Griffiths [*ca.* 1757]

A reissue of the 1756 edition, with a new title-page, and dedication (to the friends of liberty). In all copies seen the 1756 title-page is also present: possibly, therefore, the present item is the only genuine issue. Pp. 113 [114–116] are also found bound together preceding p. ²[1] (L and DFo).

2617 ———[a reissue] Theophilus Cibber, to David Garrick, Esq; with dissertations on theatrical subjects . . . Adorn'd with a frontispiece, and curious copper-plates.

pp. [2] [1] 2–76 [4], ²[1] 2–47 [48], ³[1–5] 6–32, ⁴17–112 [=128]; pls. [front.], "Frontispiece Vol 1ˢᵗ", "Frontispiece. Vol 2ᵈ", [2, incl. 1 fold.] [=5]   L

W. Reeves, and J. Phipps   1759

2618 CIBBER, THE[OPHILUS]. To the public.

pp. [1] 2–4   DFo

[London]   [1756]

Announcing a benefit "concert" at the theatre in the Hay-Market on 14 January 1756, and challenging the actors of either company to perform alternately with Cibber in a round of parts. Challenge appears also in An Epistle from Mr. Theophilus Cibber, to David Garrick, Esq. (1755). See above nos. 2614, 2615 note.

Clarke, John Sleeper (1834–1899)

Actor and manager.

2619 SKETCH OF THE LIFE OF MR. JOHN S. CLARKE, comedian.

pp. [1] 2–8; head-title   L

[J. W. Last & Co., printers]   [1872]

The printed cover has a portrait on the front.

2620 ★VIS COMICA: an essay from "Belgravia, a London magazine, conducted by M. E. Braddon."

pp. 31

London: J. W. Last, printer [n.d.]

Chase.
In praise of humour, with an account of John S. Clarke, whose portrait is mounted on the cover.

Clive, *Mrs.* Catherine (1711–1785)

One of the greatest of comic actresses—Lowe. See also nos. 2590, 3666 note.

2621 [CLIVE, CATHERINE.] THE CASE OF MRS. CLIVE submitted to the publick.

pp. [1–5] 6–22 L

B. Dod 1744

When Fleetwood re-engaged Garrick after the secession, he did not re-engage Mrs. Clive. In this tract she complains of both managers — Rich and Fleetwood — Lowe.

2622 FITZGERALD, PERCY [HETHERINGTON]. The life of Mrs. Catherine Clive with an account of her adventures on and off the stage a round of her characters together with her correspondence By Percy Fitzgerald, M.A., F.S.A.

pp. [i–v] vi–viii, [1] 2–112; pl. [front.] E

A. Reader 1888

Bound in eights.

2623 ———[large paper issue]

pp. [i–v] vi–viii, [1] 2–112; pl. [front.] L

A. Reader 1888

Bound in fours.

Clun, Walter (–1664)

Actor. According to Historia Histrionica, *a boy actor with the King's Men before the closing of the theatres.*

2624 AN EGLEY UPON THE MOST EXECRABLE MURTHER OF MR. CLUN on of the comedeans of the Theator Royal, who was rob'd and most inhumanely kill'd on Tuseday-night, being the 2ᵈ, of August, 1664. near Tatnam-Court, as as [sic] he was riding to his country-house at Kentishtown.

bs. MH

Printed by Edward Crowch [1664]

Within a plain black border, beginning,
  Mourn Royal Stage, your Poets *pens implore,*
  To cease to write, since Clun *can be no more;*
  Turn all your Sceans *to black, and let them be,*
  The Emblimes *of our cares;* Cluns *Tragedy:*
  Go hide your Tapestry, *and Clothes of green,*
  Act now on black, Clun *will no more be seen.*
Wing E 481.

2625 ———[another edition] An elegy upon the most execrable murther of Mr. Clun, one of the comedians of the Theator Royal, who was rob'd and most inhumanely kill'd on Tuesday night, being the 2d of August, 1664, near Tatnam Court, as he was riding to his country house. at Kentish Town.

bs. MH

Printed by Edward Crouch [18–?]

This is either a reduced facsimile of another 1664 edition, or an inaccurate reprint of the "Egley" edition. Reprinted in facsimile in J. W. Draper, A Century of Broadside Elegies (1928), p. [101].

Coates, Robert (1772–1848)

The notorious "Amateur of Fashion." He had a passion for exhibiting himself and his diamonds on the stage, and made a fool of himself on every possible opportunity. Charles Mathews, in 1813, burlesqued him on the stage — Lowe.

2626 SWIFTSURE, JONATHAN, *pseud.* ★Report of the extraordinary trial, of Charles Momus, comedian, of Covent-Garden Theatre, for stealing privately from the person of Romeo Lothario Doodledoo, Esq. certain articles his property. Taken in shorthand, by Jonathan Swiftsure.

MH

1814

Refers to the imitation by Mathews of the Amateur of Fashion, Robert Coates — Lowe.

2627 ROBINSON, JOHN R[OBERT], and HUNTER H. ROBINSON. The life of Robert Coates better known as "Romeo" and "Diamond" Coates the celebrated "amateur of fashion" by John R. and Hunter H. Robinson.

pp. [i–iii] iv–viii, [1] 2–255 [256]; pls. [front., 1] GU

Sampson Low, Marston & company 1891

Cole, John William (–1870)

Under the stage name of John William Calcraft, actor in Edinburgh and from 1824 to 1851 manager in Dublin. Biographer of Charles Kean. See AUTHOR INDEX.

Coleman, John (1831–1904)

A well-known actor and manager—Lowe.

2628 COLEMAN, JOHN. Players and playwrights I have known. By John Coleman.

2. vols. pp. [4] 1–329 [330 (bl.)] + [4] 4–397 [398–400]
L

Chatto & Windus 1888

Later copies dated 1889.

———[American edition] "Second edition". Philadelphia: Gebbie & Co., 1890.

Colman, George, *the elder* (1732–1794)

A noted dramatist and manager. He was a partner in the management of Covent Garden from 1767 to 1774, where his quarrels with his partners occasioned some lively pamphlets. In 1776 he took the Haymarket from Foote, and was the means of introducing many famous performers to the stage. He became imbecile before his death — Lowe. *See Eugene R. Page,* George Colman the elder, Essayist, Dramatist and Theatrical Manager 1732–1794 (*New York, 1935*). See also nos. *1163* et seq.; *1438 and* AUTHOR INDEX.

2629 COLMAN, GEORGE, *the elder.* Some particulars of the life of the late George Colman, Esq. Written by himself, and delivered by him to Richard Jackson, Esq. (one of his executors,) for publication after his decease.

pp. [4] [1] 2–33 [34]; pl. [front.] L

T. Cadell, jun. and W. Davies 1795

Particulars relating to Colman's private affairs, the interest of which to the public is difficult to see — Lowe.

2630 POSTHUMOUS LETTERS, from various celebrated men; addressed to Francis Colman, and George Colman, the elder: with annotations, and occasional remarks, by George Colman, the younger. Exclusive of the letters, are, An explanation of the motives of William Pulteney (afterwards Earl of Bath) for his acceptance of a peerage; and Papers tending to elucidate the question relative to the proportional shares of authorship to be attributed to the elder Colman and Garrick, in the comedy of "The clandestine marriage."

pp. [i–v] vi–ix [x–xi] xii–xvi, [1] 2–347 [348] L

London: T. Cadell and W. Davies; Edinburgh: W. Blackwood 1820

"Letters on theatrical subjects to George Colman, the Elder," pp. 137–229; "Letters from David Garrick to George Colman, the Elder," pp. 231–325.

✠ Peake, Richard Brinsley Memoirs of the Colman family. 1841 *See below no. 2635.*

Colman, George, *the younger* (1762–1836)

Son of the preceding. Succeeded him in the management of the Haymarket. He was a very successful dramatist; his Heir at Law, Poor Gentleman, &c. *still holding the stage. He was made Examiner of Plays, in which foolish office he behaved with great arrogance* — Lowe.

2631 THINKS-I-TO-MYSELF-WHO? *pseud.* The preface to *The Iron chest.* A satirical poem. Written by Thinks-I-to-myself-who?

pp. [1–3] 4–12 L

J. Roach [1796]

Principally an attack on Colman, but Kemble also is treated with very scant courtesy — Lowe. *Preface signed "Sylvester Daggerwood," who is supposed to have found the poem.*

2632 LEE, HENRY. Caleb Quotem and his wife! Or, Paint, poetry, and putty! An opera, in three acts. To which is added a postscript, including the scene always play'd in *The review, or wags of Windsor,* but omitted in the edition lately published by G. Colman, Esq. With prefatory remarks, &c. . . . By Henry Lee, manager of the theatres, Taunton, Barnstaple, Wells, Dorchester, Bridgwater, &c.

pp. [4] [1] 2–6 [7–9] 10–66 [67–68 (bl.)]; pl. [front.] TnP

J. Roach [1809]

In his preface Lee accuses Colman of stealing the character of Caleb Quotem in his farce of "The Review" from him, and makes a very strong case. The pamphlet bears the rather amusing motto—"See where he steals! !"—Shakespear—Lowe.

2633 COLMAN, GEORGE, *the younger.* Random records; by George Colman, the younger.

2 vols. pp. [i–v] vi–xii, [1] 2–323 [324]; pl. [front.] + pp. [i–iii] iv–vi, [1] 2–305 [306] GU

Henry Colburn & Richard Bentley 1830

Genest says of this work that Colman's "theatrical information is of no great importance — his morality (see what he says of Terence) is disgusting — Valverde moralising!" — Lowe.

2634 vacant

2635 PEAKE, RICHARD BRINSLEY. Memoirs of the Colman family, including their correspondence with the most distinguished personages of their time. By Richard Brinsley Peake.

2 vols. pp. [i–vii] viii–xi [xii], [1] 2–432; pl. [front.] + pp. [i–iii] iv–viii, [1] 2–454 [455–6]; pl. [front.] GU

Richard Bentley 1841

2636 ———*[another edition]

2 vols. in one MB

Richard Bentley [1841]

2637 BUCKSTONE, GEORGE B., *ed.* Broad grins My nightgown & slippers and other humorous works prose and poetical of George Colman the younger. Now first collected. With life and anecdotes of the author edited by George B. Buckstone.

pp. [i–iii] iv–vii [viii (bl.)], [1–3] 4–492; pl. [front.] L

John Camden Hotten [1872]

The earlier editions do not include the life and anecdotes.

Compton, Henry (1805–1877)

A very great actor; one of the few whom we can fancy in such company as Garrick and his associates. In all he did he was a thorough artist, and may fairly be considered the greatest comedian this century has produced. He was a good man and a gentleman. His real name was Charles Mackenzie.

2638 COMPTON, CHARLES and EDWARD, *eds.* Memoir of Henry Compton. Edited by Charles and Edward Compton. With anecdotes and personal recollections of the eminent comedian by Mrs. W. H. Kendal (Miss Madge Robertson), Messrs. E. L. Blanchard, F. C. Burnard, Henry J. Byron, R. Brudenell Carter, W. Chippendale, Henry Howe, Henry Irving, Charles Mathews, J. R. Planché, Tom Taylor, J. L. Toole, and Hermann Vezin.

pp. [i–vii] viii, [I] 2–348; pl. [front.] NbU

Tinsley Brothers 1879

 Lowe *noted that Edward Compton was Henry Compton's son and "himself a most promising and talented actor".*

Congreve, William (1670–1729)

Dramatist. See also MORALITY OF THE THEATRE nos. 298–300.

2639 MR. CONGREVE'S LAST WILL AND TESTAMENT, with characters of his writings. By Mr. Dryden, Sir Richard Blackmore, Mr. Addison and Major Pack. To which are added, two pieces, viz. I. Of rightly improving the present time. An epistle from Mr. Congreve to the Right Honourable Richard Lord Viscount Cobham. II. The game of quadrille. An allegory.

pp. [2] 1–34 [35–38 (advts.)] L

E. Curll 1729

2639.1 —— With characters of his writings. By Mr. Dryden, Sir Richard Blackmore, Mr. Addison, Major Pack, and Mr. Pope. To which are added, two pieces, *viz.* I. of rightly improving the present time. An epistle, from Mr. Congreve, to the Right Honourable Richard Lord Viscount Cobham. II. The game of quadrille. An allegorical court-satire. The second edition.

pp. [1–2] 3–24 L

E. Curll 1730

2640 [MALLET, WILLIAM.] A POEM to the memory of Mr. Congreve, inscribed to her Grace, Henrietta, Dutchess of Marlborough.

pp. [1–6] 7–20 [21–23 (advt.) 24 (bl.)] MH

J. Millan 1729

 Often attributed to Thomson. For correct attribution, see Alan D. McKillop, MLN, LIV (1939), p. 599.

2641 ——[another edition] A poem to the memory of William Congreve, by James Thomson. With a preface and notes, by Peter Cunningham, Esq. (Early English poetry, ballads and popular literature of the Middle Ages. Edited from original manuscripts and scarce publications. Vol. IX).

pp. [i–v] vi–xvii [xviii] [19–21] 22–32 GU

Reprinted for the Percy Society by T. Richards 1843

 Ascribed to Thomson by Peter Cunningham. Reprint of 1729 edition. Preface mainly on Thomson as the author.

2642 WILSON, CHARLES, *pseud.* of John Old-mixon? Memoirs of the life, writings, and amours of William Congreve Esq; interspersed with miscellaneous essays, letters, and characters, written by him. Also some very curious memoirs of Mr. Dryden and his family, with a character of him and his writings, by Mr. Congreve. Compiled from their respective originals, by Charles Wilson Esq;

pp. [i–iii] iv–xvi, [I] 2–112, ²1–156 [157–160 (index)], ³1–38; pl. [front.] L

[Edmund Curll] 1730

 Published 12 August 1729 — Straus. By Oldmixon, according to Straus. Pp. ³1–38 include Congreve's will, various "characters" and verse, and Curll advertisements; these pages are included in the index. Also bound in, in two copies at L is Mr. Congreve's Last Will and Testament . . . Second Edition (Curll: 1730), pp. 24. Macdonald 332. See above no. 2639.1.

Conway, William Augustus (1789–1828)

An unfortunate actor, who drowned himself off Charleston. He was of gigantic height, and very handsome, but a bad actor. The gibes of the press at his expense are said to have crazed him — Lowe.

2643 PIOZZI, *Mrs.* HESTER LYNCH. Love letters of Mrs. Piozzi, written when she was eighty, to William Augustus Conway.

pp. [1–5] 6–39 [40 (bl.)] L

John Russell Smith 1843

 Preface is dated 10th January 1843. On this "diabolical fabrication" see James L. Clifford, Hester Lynch Piozzi (Oxford, 1952), pp. 451–453, 470–471.

Cook, Dutton (1829–1883)

A learned critic and dramatic historian, whose Nights at the Play *is a contribution of the utmost value to the history of the contemporary stage—Lowe. See AUTHOR INDEX.*

Cooke, George Frederick (1756–1812)

An actor of real genius, who for some time was the rival of John Kemble; but his dissipated habits ruined his reputation, and ultimately killed him. He was great in the same class of parts as Macklin — Lowe. See also NEWCASTLE no. 1629; also below KEMBLE, J.P. no. 3193.

2644 ★THE LIFE OF GEORGE FREDERIC COOKE, Esq.

pp. 1–8

G. Smeeton   [1812]

Cohn *163. Reprinted in Smeeton's* Universal Pamphleteer, *no. 7 (1829)?*

2645 DUNLAP, WILLIAM. Memoirs of George Fred. Cooke, Esq. late of the Theatre Royal, Covent Garden. By William Dunlap, Esq. Composed principally from the personal knowledge of the author, and from the manuscript journals left by Mr. Cooke. Comprising original anecdotes of his theatrical contemporaries, his opinions on various dramatic writings, &c.

2 vols. pp. [i–iii] iv–xiv, [1] 2–344; pl. [1] + pp. [i–iii] iv–vi, [1] 2–362 [363–364 advts.]   L
Henry Colburn   1813

2646 ——The life of George Fred. Cooke, (late of the Theatre Royal, Covent Garden.) Composed principally from journals and other authentic documents left by Mr. Cooke, and the personal knowledge of the author. Comprising original anecdotes of his theatrical contemporaries, his opinions on various dramatic writings, &c. By William Dunlap. Second edition, revised and improved.

2 vols. pp. [i–iii] iv–xiii [xiv], [1] 2–441 [442 (imprint)]; pl. [front.] + pp. [i–iii] iv–vi, [1] 2–410   L
Henry Colburn   1815

——[American edition] Memoirs of the life of George Frederick Cooke. New York: D. Longworth, 1813.

2647 ★THE LIFE OF GEORGE FREDERIC COOKE, Esq. (the legitimate successor to Garrick, Macklin, and Henderson) late of the Theatre-Royal, Covent-Garden; and of New York, Philadelphia, &c. Containing an account of the whole of his theatrical career from his first treading the boards, down to his final dramatic exit, at Rhode Island, in America: the various characters he performed: with critical remarks upon his genius, taste, judgement, and talents as an actor: reviewing his beauties defects eccentricities infirmities wit sarcasms urbanity, and benevolence: interspersed with a variety of original, interesting, witty, humourous, and pathetic anecdotes, among whom are the most prominent, [*here follows a list of anecdotes*]. With an account of the mortality of the stage, enumerating the loss it has sustained within the last forty years, independent of secession, &c. including some observations on its present degeneracy; the whole forming a most interesting piece of theatrical biography, of that extraordinary man! Embellished with a highly coloured humorous print, engraved by Mr. G. Cruikshank, representing The whiskey-shop in an uproar; or, the grand climacteric of a tragedian!

pp. 34; col. pl. [front]   MB
Egan   1813

Lowe. Cohn *162.*

Coppinger, Matt (–1695)
Actor.

2648 ★AN ACCOUNT of the life, conversation, birth, education, pranks, projects, and exploits, and merry conceits, of the famously notorious Mat. Coppinger, once a player in Bartholomew Fair, and since turned bully of the town, who receiving sentence of death at the Old Baily on the 23rd of February, was executed at Tyburn on the 27th 1695. Also an account of his behaviour in Newgate after condemnation and his dying words at the place of execution, &c.

T. Mobs   1695

Thorn-Drury.

Cowell, Joseph Leathley (1792–1863)
Known as Joe Cowell; stage name of Hawkins Witchett. See APPENDIX (p. 434 below).

Cowell, Samuel Houghton (1820–1864)
Known as Sam Cowell. Actor and star of early music halls. Son of Joe Cowell, he began his career in America and appeared first in this country in Edinburgh.

2649 COWELL, SAM. ★Collection of comic songs.

DFo
Edinburgh   1853

With sketch of his life.

Cowper, John Curtis
Real name Curtis. Actor.

2650 [COWPER, JOHN CURTIS.] ★BIOGRAPHICAL SKETCH of J. C. Cowper, tragedian. (from the Liverpool Era).

Liverpool   1864

Chase.

Cradock, Joseph (1742–1826)
Patron of the theatre.

2651 CRADOCK, J[OSEPH]. Literary and miscellaneous memoirs; by J. Cradock, Esq. M.A. F.S.A.

4 vols. pp. [i–v] vi–xlviii xlvii–xlviii xlix–lx [=62], [1] 2–294; pl. [front.] + pp. [2] [1] 2–376; pls. [front., 2 (fold.)] + pp. [4] 1–333 [334] 164 [1] [335–336] 337–410 [=412]; pl. [1 (facsim.)] + pp. i–iv, 1–416   GU
J. B. Nichols   1828

Edited by J. B. Nichols. Joseph Cradock was an intimate associate of Garrick, Foote etc.

Craven, Elizabeth, *Baroness* Craven
See above ANSPACH, Elizabeth, Margavine of, no. 2391.

Crawford, Ann (1734–1801)

A famous actress alike in tragedy and comedy. She married, first, Dancer, an actor; next, Spranger Barry; and last, one Crawford, an Irish barrister [and occasional actor], who treated her badly — Lowe. Née Street.

2652 ROSALIND: or, an apology for the history of a theatrical lady.

pp. [i–iv] v–xx 21–112   L

Dublin: printed, and sold by the Booksellers   1759

A biography of Mrs. Dancer and her husband, having special reference to a scandal caused by her supposed elopement with Poicteur, a dancer. One of the epigrams on the subject began with the line—
"When Rosalind chose from Champansi to fly" —
Lowe. The half-title reads: Rosalind: or, the theatrical lady.

2653 O'BLUNDER, *Mrs.* SHARP-SET, *pseud. of* Mrs. Elizabeth Franchett. Granny's prediction revealed to the widow Brady, of Drury-Lane theatre. By her relashion Mrs. Sharp-set O'Blunder.

pp. [i–ii] iii–iv, 1–53 [54 (bl.)]; cancellans, pp. 5–6   L

Printed for the authoress: and sold by M. Folingsby
                                                              1773

An attack on Mrs. Crawford (then Mrs. Barry) by her relative, Mrs. Franchett. . . . Mrs. Barry was the original Widow Brady in The Irish Widow *— Lowe. Garrick's* The Irish Widow *was produced 23 October 1772 at Drury-Lane.*

2654 *A REVIEW OF MRS. CRAWFORD, and Mrs. Siddons, in the character of Belvidera: in a letter to a gentleman at Bath.

                                                              MH
                                                              1782

Exceedingly rare. Written in the interests of Mrs. Craw-ford. Subjoined is a poem on "Genius and Fame," addressed to Mrs. Crawford, by Mr. W. of Edinburgh —Lowe.

2655 FUNEREAL STANZAS, inscribed to the revered memory of Mrs. Anne Crawford. With a comparative dissertation between her theatrical merits and those of Mrs. Siddons.

pp. [i–iii] iv–viii, ²[vii] viii–xii [=xiv]   L
Dublin: R. Milliken   1803

Creswick, William (1813–1888)

Actor.

2656 CRESWICK, WILLIAM. *An autobiography: a record of fifty years of the professional life of the late William Creswick.

pp. 128 (incl. front.)

James Henderson   [1889?]

IKF. *This copy with a presentation inscription from Mrs. Creswick, dated April 1889. Another copy at MH.*

Crouch, *Mrs.* Anna Maria (1763–1805)

A very beautiful woman; an excellent singer and actress —Lowe

2657 YOUNG, M[ARIA] J[ULIA]. Memoirs of Mrs. Crouch. Including a retrospect of the stage, during the years she performed. By M. J. Young.

2 vols. pp. [6] [1] 2–284; pl. [front.] + pp. [2] [1] 2–328
                                                              GU

James Asperne   1806

Cumberland, Richard (1732–1811)

A noted dramatist. The original of Sir Fretful Plagiary —Lowe.

2658 CUMBERLAND, RICHARD. Memoirs of Richard Cumberland. Written by himself. Containing an account of his life and writings, interspersed with anecdotes and characters of several of the most distinguished persons of his time, with whom he has had intercourse and connexion.

pp. [2] [1] 2–533 [534]; pls. [front., 3]   L
Lackington, Allen & Co.   1806

2659 ——[second edition]
2 vols. pp. [4] [1] 2–432; pls. [front., 2] + pp. [4] [1] 2–500 (text) [501] 502–504 (advts.); pl. [1]   L
Lackington, Allen, & Co.   1807

Includes Supplement.

2660 CUMBERLAND, RICHARD. Supplement to the Memoirs of Richard Cumberland. Written by himself. With an index.

pp. [2] [1] 2–72 [42 (index)]   GU
Lackington, Allen & Co.   1807

——[American editions] New York: Brisban & Brannan, 1806 (without the Supplement); Boston: West, 1806 (without the Supplement); Philadelphia: Parry & McMillan, 1856 (with illustrative notes by Henry Flanders).

2661 MUDFORD, WILLIAM. *The life of Richard Cumberland, Esq. embracing a critical examination of his various writings. With an occasional literary inquiry into the age in which he lived, and the contemporaries with whom he flourished. By William Mudford.

                                                              1812

Lowe.

2662 ———A critical examination of the writings of Richard Cumberland, Esq. with an occasional literary inquiry into the age in which he lived, and the contemporaries with whom he flourished. Also, memoirs of his life. And an appendix, containing twenty-six of his original letters, relating to a transaction not mentioned in his own memoirs. By William Mudford. A new and improved edition.

2 vols. pp. [i–ix] x–xxxi [xxxii], [1] 2–168 *168–*168 169–244 *244–*244 245–300 [=304]; pl. [front.] + pp. [4] 301–348 *348–*348 349–601 [602] [=604], ²[1] 2–68 [603] 604–621 [622]   L

Sherwood, Neely, and Jones; and J. Asperne   1812

> *The publishers of Cumberland's own* Memoirs *(1807) and other works (Lackington, Allen & Co.) obtained an injunction restraining the sale of the first edition of this hostile work. The new edition is much altered by cancellation.*

Cummins, *Mr.*

For the series of anti-theatrical pamphlets which followed the death of Cummins in the Leeds playhouse, see above MORALITY OF THE STAGE nos. 494–499.

Curling, Henry

2663 CURLING, HENRY. Recollections of the messtable and the stage. By Henry Curling.

pp. [i–vii] viii, [1] 2–248   GU

T. Bosworth   1855

> *Short anecdotes.*

Daggerwood, Sylvester

Fictional character.

2664 DAGGERWOOD, SYLVESTER, *ed.* PANGLOS, PETER, *pseud.* Memoirs of Sylvester Daggerwood, comedian, &c. deceased: including many years of provincial vicissitudes, interspersed with genuine anecdotes of many eminent persons, and several deceased and living actors and managers. To which is added, his last will and testament containing "Secrets Worth Knowing." With an epistle dedicatory from the author to G. Colman, Esq. The whole collected from the deceased author's M.S. with notes, critical and explanatory, by Peter Panglos [*sic*], Esq. LLD. and A.S.S.

2 vols. pp. [i–v] vi–xxii 23–186 + [i–iii] iv–x [11] 12–192   MH

M. Allen   1807

> *From the "Advertisement": "These Memoirs, in all probability, would never have appeared, but from the liberty Mr. G. Colman, the younger, had taken with the name of Daggerwood. The real Actor, of that name, was a provincial performer of some respectability ... The Anecdotes, we can venture to affirm, are all genuine, and within the memory of several living Provincial and London Actors, though never yet made public."*

2665 ———the second edition

2 vols. pp. [i–v] vi–xxii 23–186 + [i–iii] iv–x [11] 12–192   L

M. Allen   [1807?]

Daly, Richard (–1813)

Daly was manager of Smock Alley Theatre, Dublin, for seventeen years. He retired in 1797. He was a man of indifferent character — Lowe. See IRELAND no. 1802 (Dublin); BIOGRAPHY no. 2497.

Dancer, *Mrs.* Ann

See above CRAWFORD, Mrs ANN no. 2652–2655.

Darbyshire, Alfred (1839–1908)

Architect. See also AUTHOR INDEX.

2666 DARBYSHIRE, ALFRED. An architect's experiences: professional, artistic, and theatrical. By Alfred Darbyshire, F.S.A., F.I.B.A.

pp. [i–ix] x–xv [xvi], [1] 2–351 [352]; pls. [6]; errata slip   L

Manchester: J. E. Cornish   1897

> *Partly reprinted from the Manchester City News.*

Davies, Thomas (ca. 1712–1785)

Twice an actor and twice a bookseller. It is said that he gave up the stage finally on account of the satire of Churchill. He was an excellent and amiable character, but died in poverty. His widow, I believe, died in the workhouse—Lowe. See AUTHOR INDEX.

Dawson, James

Provincial actor and manager, especially in Cornwall.

2667 DAWSON, JAMES. The autobiography of Mr. James Dawson.

pp. [i–v] vi–viii, [1] 2–171 [172 (bl.)]   L

Truro: J. R. Netherton   1865

> *With list of subscribers.*

Dawson, Nancy (*ca. 1730–1767*)

A lady with no character worth mentioning. She made her appearance as a dancer at Sadler's Wells, and was afterwards engaged at Covent Garden. She was Shuter's mistress — Lowe. See also below SHUTER, EDWARD no. 3519.

2668 AUTHENTIC MEMOIRS of the celebrated Miss Nancy D★ws★n.

pp. [1–2] 3–30   L

Printed for Tom Dawson, in Drury-Lane   [1760?]

> *Probably the same work as Lowe's Genuine memoirs of the celebrated Miss Nancy D———n (1760), which he had not seen.*

2669 NANCY DAWSON'S JESTS: to which is added The merry hornpipe; being a collection of songs written for the delight and amusement of all her admirers.

When first with Nancy Dawson
The Hornpipe came in fashion,
We ev'ry one to dance begun,
And jigg'd throughout the nation,
And a jigging we will go.

Embellished with a beautiful print of Miss Dawson in the famous hornpipe.

pp. [4] 1–44; pl. [front.]   L
J. Seymour   1761

2670 *THE JOVIAL LIFE, amorous exploits, and singular adventures, of the celebrated Miss Nancy Dawson, a Cyprian singer and dancer, in the first circles of Old Drury and the Garden; containing a variety of anecdotes, theatrical, musical, eccentrical, and unaccountable, of the most noted performers of her time, with her death and character. The whole forming a camera obscura; or, magic lanthorn of wit and humour.

n.d.

Lowe.

Deans, *Mrs.* Charlotte (1768–   )

Actress, née Lowes.

2671 DEANS, CHARLOTTE. Memoirs of the life of Mrs. Charlotte Deans, from her earliest infancy, comprising the periods when she was Miss Charlotte Lowes, Mrs. Johnston, and Mrs. Deans; being a journal of a seventy years pilgrimage, with anecdotes of many with whom it has been her good and bad fortune to associate. Arranged by herself.

pp. [1–3] 4–111 [112]   MH
Wigton: printed by H. Hoodless, Market-Place   1837

Decastro, Jacob (1758–1824)

An actor.

2672 DECASTRO, J[ACOB]. The memoirs of J. Decastro, comedian. In the course of them will be given anecdotes of various eminently distinguished characters, with whom he has been intimate in his peregrinations. Amongst others are Dr. Johnson, Garrick, Foote, Wilson, Charles Bannister, J. Palmer, C. Dibdin, Sen., the late Earl of Barrymore, R. B. Sheridan, Esq., G. F. Cooke, J. P. Kemble, Esq., &c. Never before in print; accompanied by an analysis of the life of the late Philip Astley, Esq., founder of the Royal Amphitheatre, Westminster-Bridge; with many of his managerial peculiarities. Also an accompanying history of the Royal Circus, now the Surrey Theatre; and an historical sketch of Sadler's Wells. Likewise, scarce theatrical advertisements, from Garrick's first attempt in Goodman's-Fields; his last moments. Old Grimaldi's dream, &c. To which will be added the origin of poetry; a chapter on *Bent's*, &c. &c. &c. Edited by R. Humphreys.

pp. [i–iii] iv–xx, [1] 2–279 [280]; pls. [front., 1 (fold.)]   L
Sherwood, Jones, & Co.   1824

Lowe records another plate, "certificate of birth", "often wanting". There is no apparent connection between Decastro and a four volume novel, The History of Mr. John Decastro and his Brother Bat, commonly called Old Crab. The Merry Matter written by John Mathews; the Grave by a Solid Gentleman (London, 1815; Boston, 1815; Pittsburg, 1902), sometimes attributed to George Colman.

Delaval, *Sir* Francis Blake (1727–1771)

A performance of Othello was given by Sir F. Delaval and his friends at Drury Lane on 7th March 1751. It was a capital performance for amateurs, but it is bitterly attacked. —Lowe. See above nos. 2151, 2543.

Dennis, John (1657–1733)

The renowned critic; the sworn enemy of Pope; the bitter opponent of Steele. He was an acute, though abusive, critic; and was constantly at war with somebody. Nevertheless most modern writers have a liking for "stout John Dennis" — Lowe. For Dennis's part in various controversies see also AUTHOR INDEX.

2673 DENNIS, JOHN and CHARLES GILDON. *A new project for regulating the stage. By John Dennis and Charles Gildon.

1720

I have not seen this, but believe that it is satirical on Dennis and Gildon — Lowe. Loftis (p. 78) suggests it may have never been published.

2674 DENNIS, [JOHN]. Original letters, familiar, moral and critical. By Mr. Dennis.

2 vols. bound in 1. pp. [16] [1] 2–224 + [2] 225–486   L
W. Mears   1721

2675 THE LIFE OF MR. JOHN DENNIS, the renowned critick. In which are likewise some observations on most of the poets and criticks, his contemporaries. Not written by Mr. Curll.

pp. [2] [1–2] 3–59 [60 (bl.)]; pl. [front.]   L
Printed for J. Roberts   1734

Derby, *Countess of*

See below FARREN, ELIZABETH nos. 2718–2728.

Dibdin, Charles (1745–1814)

Our great sea-song writer. In addition to his musical gifts he possessed considerable powers as a comedian, and was also a successful dramatic writer—Lowe. See also above no. 2213 and AUTHOR INDEX.

2676 DIBDIN, CHARLES. The musical tour of Mr. Dibdin; in which — previous to his embarkation for India — he finished his career as a public character.

pp. [*8*] [i] ii–iv, [1] 2–308 307–338 335–443 [444 (directions to the binder)] [=450]; pls. [20 (=15 leaves)]; vignette on dedication leaf   L

Sheffield: printed for the Author by J. Gales   1788

Printed for subscribers. 600 copies printed, according to the preface. A second, London, edition is announced in the preface, but is not known. E. R. Dibdin, pp. 60–65.

2677 DIBDIN, CHARLES. The professional life of Mr. Dibdin, written by himself. Together with the words of six hundred songs selected from his works, and sixty small prints taken from the subjects of the songs. And invented, etched, and prepared for the aqua tinta by Miss Dibdin. Embellished also with an elegant engraving by Mr. Smith, from a portrait of Mr. Dibdin, a striking likeness, and an admirable picture painted by Mr. Devis. In four volumes.

4 vols. pp. [i–v] vi–xxv [xxvi], [1] 2–229 [230 (bl.) 231–35 (index) 236 (bl.)]; additional engr. t.p. with port. + pp. [*4*] [1] 2–303 [304 (bl.) 305–11 (index) 312 (bl.)] + pp. [*4*] [1] 2–387 [388 (bl.) 389–95 (index) 396 (bl.)] + pp. [*4*] [1] 2–328 [329–36 (index)]   L

Published by the author, J. Cundee, printer   1803

Without plates, as issued. Copies with plates have eight in the first volume, sixteen in the second, fifteen in the third, and twenty-one in the fourth.

2678 ——[another issue] The professional life of Mr. Dibdin, written by himself. Together with the words of six hundred songs selected from his works. Interspersed with many humorous and entertaining anecdotes incidental to his public character. In four volumes.

4 vols. pp. [i–v] vi–vii [viii], [1] 2–229 [230 (bl.)] + pp. [*2*] [1] 2–303 [304 (bl.) 305–11 (index) 312 (bl.)] + pp. [*4*] [1] 2–387 [388 (bl.) 389–95 (index) 396 (bl.)] + pp. [*4*] [1] 2–328 [329–336 (index)]   L

Published by the author   1803

2679 ——[another issue] †Second edition. The professional life of Mr. Dibdin, containing a narrative of such circumstances as relate to the pursuits of the author, during forty-four years, in his character of writer, composer, and performer; with the addition of six hundred songs, and sixty plates, from their subjects. Second edition. In this edition new particulars are introduced concerning Mr. Dibdin's late tour to Ireland, and the whole of Britons strike home, the war songs, and such others as have been brought forward at Sans Souci, up to the present time, are superadded.

4 vols. pp. [*2*] vi–xxv [xxvi], [1] 2–229 [230 231–235 (index) 236 (bl.)]; pls. [8]; additional engr. t.p. + pp. [*2*] [1] 2–303 [304 (bl.) 305–311 (index) 312 (bl.)]; pls. [16] + pp. [*2*] [1] 2–387 [388 (bl.) 389–395 (index) 396 (bl.)]; pls. [14] + pp. [*2*] [1] 2–328 [329–336 (index and directions to binder)]; pls. [21]   MH

Printed by James Cundee. Published by the author 1804

Vol. III lacking 1 plate and vol. IV lacking the supplement.

2680 ——[another edition] †The professional life of Mr. Dibdin, written by himself; together with the words of eight hundred songs, two hundred and twenty of which will have their appropriate music. Selected from his works, and embellished with an elegant engraving by Mr. Smith, from a portrait of Mr. Dibdin, a striking likeness, and an admirable picture painted by Mr. Devis. In six volumes.

2 vols. pp. [i–v] vi–vii [viii], [1] 2–94 [*2*] 95–251 [252]; additional engr. t.p. with port.; engr. music, songs [1–2] 3–28 [=59 leaves] + pp. [*4*] [1] 2–220; engr. music, songs 29–36 38–56 [=83 leaves]   L

Published by the author, Cantwell, printer   1809

Lacking songs 56–61. Only two volumes appeared. Originally issued in parts.

2681 ——Plates from Dibdin (title on cover).

engr. t.p., with port., of the 1809 edition of *Professional life of Mr. Dibdin;* pls. [60] of the 1803 edition   L

Published by the author   [1809?]

2682 ——*[reissue]

1 vol.; paper-covered boards

Black, Kingsbury, Parbury, & Allen   [*ca.* 1818]

The complicated bibliographical history of The professional life *is discussed in E. R. Dibdin, A Charles Dibdin bibliography (Liverpool, 1937) pp. 106–7, 109–110, 129–130.*

2683 DIBDIN, [CHARLES]. *The public undeceived, written by Mr. Dibdin; and containing a statement of all the material facts relative to his pension.

[1807]

Dibdin had a pension of £200 a year, which was stopped on a change of administration — Lowe.

2684 KITCHENER, *Dr.* WILLIAM. A brief memoir of Charles Dibdin, by the late Dr. William Kitchener, with some letters and documents never before published, supplied by his grand-daughter, Mrs. Lovat Ashe.

pp. [1–4] 5–24   L
M. Walbrook   [1884?]

2685 THORN, HENRY G[EORGE]. Charles Dibdin, one of Southampton's sons; what he did for the nation, and what the nation has done for him. Written and compiled by Henry G. Thorn. Dedicated to those who would do honour to themselves by helping to perpetuate the memory of a remarkable man, one of our greatest national lyrists, and a fellow-townsman.

pp. [1–7] 8–32; on ptd. paper cover: Fourth thousand   L

Southampton: Geo. Buxey, "Observer" Office; London: Geo. Vickers   [1888]

Dibdin, Thomas John (1771–1841)

Author of 800 dramas. He was son of Charles Dibdin, and was an actor of some merit. His Reminiscences *is a most amusing and interesting book — Lowe.*

2686 DIBDIN, THOMAS. The reminiscences of Thomas Dibdin, of the Theatres Royal, Covent-Garden, Drury-Lane, Haymarket, &c. and author of the Cabinet, &c.

2 vols. pp. [i–v] vi–xii, [1] 2–446; pl. [front.] + pp. [i–v] vi–xi [xii], [1] 2–431 [432]; illus., incl. facsim.

Henry Colburn   GU 1827

2687 ——[reissue]

2 vols. pp. [4] 1–446; illus.; + pp. [2] 1–431 [432]   L

Henry Colburn   1837

——[American edition.] 2 vols. in 1. New York: Collin & Hannay, 1828.

Dibdin also published T. Dibdin's Penny Trumpet *in four penny numbers in October–November 1832. This is non-theatrical, concerned only with the Reform Bill. See DNB.*

Dickens, Charles (1812–1870)

The novelist. See also AUTHOR INDEX.

2688 PEMBERTON, T[HOMAS] EDGAR. Charles Dickens and the stage. A record of his connection with the drama as playwright actor and critic. By T. Edgar Pemberton. With new portraits in character of Miss Jennie Lee, Mr. Irving, and Mr. Toole.

pp. [8] [1] 2–260, [1] 2–4 (advts.); illus. (facsims.); pls. [front., 2] by F. G. Kitton   GU

George Redway   1888

Digges, West (1720–1786)

West Digges was an actor of some note, and was for some time manager at Edinburgh. — Lowe. Full name was John Dudley West Digges. See also above EDINBURGH nos. 1905 et seq.

2689 [MAIDMENT, JAMES, and WILLIAM HUGH LOGAN, *eds.*] LETTERS which passed between Mr. West Digges, comedian, and Mrs. Sarah Ward, 1752–1759.

pp. [1] 2–4 (advts.), [i–iii] iv–xi [xii (bl.)], ²[1] 2–160 NbU

Edinburgh: Thomas Stevenson   1833

60 copies printed (p. [ii]). Stevenson, p. 9. Mrs. Sarah Ward, the actress, was Digges' mistress for many years.

Dodd, James William (1774–1796)

Actor. See above SALE CATALOGUES no. 73.

Donaldson, Walter Alexander (1793–1877)

Actor.

2690 DONALDSON, W[ALTER] A[LEXANDER]. Fifty years of an actor's life; or, Thespian gleanings. By W. A. Donaldson, Sen., professor of elocution.

pp. [1–3] 4–56   L

Lacy   1858

"Part I" on the printed cover.

2691 DONALDSON, WALTER [ALEXANDER]. Recollections of an actor by Walter Donaldson comedian Never before printed.

pp. [i–iii] iv [4] [v] vi–viii, [1] 2–360; pl. [front.]   L

John Maxwell and Company   1865

Pp. [4] are 2 leaves of subscribers' names printed on recto only.

2692 ——[another edition] Fifty years of green-room gossip; or, recollections of an actor.

pp. [i–iii] iv–viii, [1] 2–360   GU

John and Robert Maxwell   [1881]

Doran, *Dr.* John (1807–1878)

Dr. Doran's first literary effort was a play produced at the Surrey when he was seventeen years old. He was engaged on the Literary Chronicle *till it was purchased by Sterling, and was also editor of* Notes and Queries. *At various times he was acting editor of the* Athenaeum. *("Men of the Time.") —Lowe. See AUTHOR INDEX.*

Downes, John (*fl.* 1662–1710)

See nos. 824–828.

Dryden, John (1631–1700)

See THE LONDON THEATRE no. 1315 (Dorset Gardens); also above CONGREVE, WILLIAM no. 2642; AUTHOR INDEX.

Dyer, Robert

Provincial actor.

2693 DYER, ROBERT. Nine years of an actor's life. Robert Dyer, late of the Theatres-Royal Plymouth, Worcester, Derby, Nottingham, Taunton, Barnstable, &c. &c.

pp. [16] [1] 2–219 [220] [1] 221–241 [242 (imprint) 243 (bl.)]   L

London: Longman, Rees, Orme, Brown & Co.; Symons; Kenneth; and Plymouth: Edward Nettleton   1833

Edwards, Henry Sutherland (1828–1906)

Author and journalist.

2694 EDWARDS, H[ENRY] SUTHERLAND. Personal recollections by H. Sutherland Edwards.

pp. [i–v] vi–viii, [1] 2–280   L

Cassell and Company   1900

Edwards, John (d. 1706)

Actor in Pinkethman's company.

2695 *PINKEMAN'S COMPANY in mourning; or, an elegy on the much unlamented death of John Edwards, the horse-doctor and merry-andrew.

bs.

T. Goodall   1706

Foxon.

Edwin, John, *the elder* (1749–1790)

A celebrated comedian, who was noted for his extravagant humour and reckless "gagging". He died of drink — Lowe.

2696 *EDWIN'S PILLS to purge melancholy: containing all the songs sung by Mr. Edwin, of Covent-Garden Theatre, since his first appearance in London; and many duets that Mr. Edwin has a part in. With an humourous account of Mrs. Siddons's first reception in Dublin; and a portrait of Mr. Edwin finely executed.

Dublin   1783

Loewenberg.

2697 ——Edwin's pills to purge melancholy: containing all the songs sung by Mr. Edwin, of Covent-Garden Theatre, since his first appearance in London; and many duets that Mr. Edwin has a part in. With An humourous account of Mrs. Siddons's first reception in Dublin; and a portrait of Mr. Edwin finely executed. The second edition, with considerable additions.

pp. [2] [v] vi–viii, [7] 8–56 59–104 [=102] [105–106 (advts.)]; pl. [front.]   L

William Holland   1788

2698 ——the third edition, with considerable additions.

pp. [i–iii] iv vii–viii, [7] 8–56 59–66 65 68–69 68–69 72–104 [=102], [1] 2 (advt.); pl. [front.]   L

William Holland   [1789?]

"A second part of this work will be speedily published" with a print of Mr. Edwin and Mrs. Wells — p. 104. This "second part" is not known. The print mentioned is bound in with the L copy of the present book, and is dated 8 March 1789.

2699 *EDWIN'S LAST LEGACY. Containing a collection of his oddities, songs, and various efforts of humour, as given at the Theatres Royal, &c. To which is prefixed, authentic memoirs of his public and private

life. With an account of his death and the order of his funeral. Printed from original copies, and embellished with his portrait, most beautifully executed.

[ca. 1790]

Pp. 80 (really 84 pages, for Nos. 9 to 12 occur twice; the Memoirs ending on page 12, while the Oddities, which follow, have their first page numbered 9.) Portrait— Lowe.

2700 EDWIN'S JESTS, humours, frolicks and bonmots: containing all the good things, he has said and done in his whole life: being the richest and best mental feast, ever offered to the public; interspersed with many occasional traits of several eminent persons in England and Ireland.

pp. [1–3] 4–60; pl. [front.]

J. Roach   1791

IKF. Roach's address is given as "Russel-Court, near the Pit-Door of Drury-Lane Play House."

2701 vacant

2702 OLD CRONEY, AN, *pseud.* The life and adventures of John Edwin, comedian. By an old croney. To which are added the whole collection of his songs, oddities, &c. &c.

pp. [4] [1] 2–36, ²[9] 10–80; pl. (port.)   MH

J. Aitkin   1791

The second leaf contains "Edwin's Tomb" by "Anthony Pasquin".

2703 PASQUIN, ANTHONY, *pseud.* of John Williams. The eccentricities of John Edwin, comedian. Collected from his manuscripts, and enriched with several hundred original anecdotes. Arranged and digested by Anthony Pasquin, Esq.

2 vols. pp. [8] [1] 2–326 [327–328 (bl.)]; vignette on t.p. + pp. [4] [1] 2–349 [350 (bl.) 351 (advt.) 352 (bl.)]; illus.; vignette on t.p.   L

J. Strahan   [1791]

Dedication dated February 20, 1791. At the end of the second volume is "A calm enquiry into the present state of our theatres" — Lowe.

2704 ——a new edition

2 vols. pp. [6] [1] 2–326 + [2] [1] 2–349 [350 (bl.) 351 (advt.) 352 (bl.)]; illus.   L

J. Strahan   [1791]

Without title page vignettes.

2705 ——a new edition

2 vols. pp. [2] [1] 2–326; vignette on t.p. + pp. [2] [1] 2–349 [350 (bl.)]; illus.; vignette on t.p.   L

J. Strahan   [1791]

2706 ——[another edition]

2 vols. pp. [4] [1] 2–336 + [2] [1] 2–312   L

Dublin: P. Byrne, J. Moore, J. Jones, A. Grueber, W. Jones, and R. White   1791

2707 ——a new edition

2 vols. pp. [8] [1] 2–326 [327–328 (bl.)]; vignette on t.p. + pp. [4] [1] 2–349 [350 (bl.) 351 (advt.) 352 (bl.)]; illus.; vignette on t.p.   E

J. Strahan   [1791]

2708 ELEGY WRITTEN IN A LONDON CHURCH-YARD.

pp. [1–3] 4–10 [11 ("Epitaph") 12 (bl.)]   L

J. Bell   1792

On Edwin's tomb.

Edwin, John, *the younger* (1768–1805)

Died, like his father, of drink. His wife was an actress of considerable ability, and was very popular — Lowe. For his quarrel with Stephen Kemble see above NEWCASTLE nos. 1630–1632.

Edwin, John Prosser

Of Edwin I know nothing, except that he was in the army before he became an actor — Lowe. For his dispute with William Macready senior, see above nos. 1648–1650.

Ellerslie, Alma

Provincial actress.

2709 [ELLERSLIE, ALMA.] THE DIARY of an actress or realities of stage life. Edited by H[enry] C[ary] Shuttleworth, M.A., Rector of St Nicholas Cole-Abbey; sometime minor canon of St Paul's.

pp. [1–7] 8–160   L

Griffith, Farran, Okeden & Welsh   1885

Anonymous; but, as the young lady gives dates and characters at an easily recognised provincial theatre, I, by consulting my Edinburgh bills, identified her at once. The "Diary" is a pleasing relation of her experiences as a young actress in country theatres —Lowe.

Elliston, Robert William (1774–1831)

The "Great Lessee," of whom Charles Lamb writes so delightfully. He was a most successful actor and an enterprising manager; while, as an advertiser, he stood alone. He was manager of the Surrey Theatre, of the Olympic, and of several provincial theatres. In 1819 he took Drury Lane, which he leased and managed till 1826, in the winter of which year he was bankrupt. In 1827 he again leased the Surrey, the last years of his management being brightened by the production of Black Eye'd Susan — Lowe. See also GOVERNMENT REGULATION OF THE THEATRE no. 196; THE LONDON THEATRE

nos. 1402 et seq. (Drury Lane), 1521–1522 (The Surrey); THEORY AND CRITICISM no. 4009; SALE CATALOGUES no. 74.

2710 RAYMOND, GEORGE. Memoirs of Robert William Elliston comedian. 1774 to 1810. By George Raymond, Esq. With illustrations by George Cruikshank.

pp. [i–iii] iv–xxxvi, [1] 2–438; pls. [front., 3]; illus.   L

John Mortimer   1844

Cohn 686. L copy lacks last two pp. of advts. recorded by Cohn.

2711 RAYMOND, GEORGE. Memoirs of Robert William Elliston comedian. By George Raymond Esq. With illustrations by "Phiz". Concluding series.

pp. [2] [i–iii] iv–ix [x], [1] 2–554; pls. [2]; illus.   L

John Mortimer   1845

Cohn 686.

2712 ——*[reissue of 2710 and 2711]

2 vols.

John Mortimer   1845

Cohn 686.

2713 ——*second edition

2 vols. pls. [front., 5]   1846

Lowe.

2714 ——[another edition] The life and enterprises of Robert William Elliston, comedian. By George Raymond. Illustrated by George Cruikshank and "Phiz".

pp. [i–iii] iv–xiv [xv–xvi], [1] 2–416; pls. [front., 5]   L

London and New York: G. Routledge & Co.   1857

Abridged.

Elrington, Thomas (1688–1732)

Irish actor and manager. See above DUBLIN no. 1721.

Estcourt, Richard (1668–1712)

An actor familiar to all readers of the Spectator. Steele's partiality for him may have affected his judgment, for Cibber does not praise him. He was an incorrigible "gagger" — Lowe.

2715 ESTCOURT, [RICHARD]. *A letter from Dick Estcourt, the comedian, to the Spectator.   1713

CBEL.

2716 ESTCOURT, [RICHARD]. The infernal congress: or, news from below. Being a letter from Dick Estcourt, the late famous comedian, to the Spectator. The second edition corrected.

pp. [1–6] 7–32 E
J. Baker 1713

Signed Richard Estcourt.

Esten, *Mrs* Harriet Pye

Actress. She obtained the lease, in opposition to Stephen Kemble, of the Theatre Royal Edinburgh in 1792, but gave it up the following year. See EDINBURGH no. 1956.

Everard, Edward Cape (1755–)

A poor strolling actor, whose tale is most pitiable. I do not know when or where the poor fellow died—Lowe.

2717 EVERARD, EDWARD CAPE. Memoirs of an unfortunate son of Thespis; being a sketch of the life of Edward Cape Everard, comedian, twenty-three years of the Theatre-Royal, Drury-Lane, London, and pupil of the late David Garrick, Esq. With reflections, remarks, and anecdotes, written by himself.

pp. [i–iii] iv–viii, [1] 2–274 L
Edinburgh: printed by James Ballantyne and Co. 1818

Falconer, Edmund (1814–1879)

A well-known Irish actor and dramatic author. He was said to have made £13,000 at the Lyceum, which he embarked in Drury Lane, and lost every penny—Lowe. See no. 1417.

Farinelli (1705–1782)

Stage name of Carlo Broschi, singer. See above OPERA nos. 2048–2051.

Farren, Elizabeth (1759–1829)

A noted actress, especially of fine ladies, who married the Earl of Derby, to whom she was engaged for some years before his first wife's death — Lowe.

2718 *ARBITER, PETRONIUS, Esq. *pseud.* Memoirs of the present Countess of Derby, (late Miss Farren); including anecdotes of several distinguished persons, particularly the Right Hon. C.J.F.——, R.B.S——n, Esq., the Earl of D——y, Lord St——nl——y, the late General Burgoyne, Lord M——t——wn, the late Mr. Parsons, the Duke of R——m——d, Mr. King, the actor, Mr. Farren, her Ladyship's father, Mrs. Farren, her Ladyship's mother, Mrs. Knight, her Ladyship's sister, George Colman, the Elder, the late Earl of Chesterfield, Mr. J. Palmer, the actor, the late Mr. Younger, &c. &c. By Petronius Arbiter, Esq.

pp. 27 MB
Symonds [1797]

This is a very sneering account of Miss Farren's history, seasoned with a few gratuitous nastinesses, which do much to increase its value, for it is now extremely scarce, and much sought after. At the time of publication it went through at least seven editions. The replies written to this Memoir are however, less accurate than itself — Lowe.

2719 ——[the second edition]
pp. [4] [i] ii, [5] 6–27 [28] L
H. D. Symonds [1797?]

"The Second Edition" on half-title.

2720 ——[the third edition]
pp. [4] [i] ii, [5] 6–27 [28] L
H. D. Symonds [1797?]

"The Third Edition" on half-title.

2721 ——[the fifth edition] With a postscript extraordinary!
pp. [i–v] vi [7] 8–31 [32] L
H. D. Symonds [1797?]

"The fifth edition, with considerable additions" on half-title. Title-page also varies from preceding editions in the insertion of the names of Capt. Farren, her ladyship's uncle, of Mr. Dignum, and of The Shoreditch prophet.

2722 ——[seventh edition]
pp. [i–v] vi [7] 8–31 [32] L
H. D. Symonds [1797?]

"The Seventh Edition, with considerable additions" on half-title. Title-page as for fifth edition.

2723 SCRIPTOR VERITATIS, *pseud.* *The memoirs of the present Countess of Derby, rescued by truth from the assassinating pen of Petronius Arbiter; and proving the stage, from the patronage of the most exalted personages, to have been always considered as a school for morality. By Scriptor Veritatis.

1797

On the title-page is a long list of "exalted personages" who had been patrons of the stage—Lowe.

2724 ——*another edition
Manchester 1797
STR.

2725 THE TESTIMONY OF TRUTH to exalted merit: or, a biographical sketch of the Right Honourable the Countess of Derby; in refutation of a false and scandalous libel.

pp. [2] [1–3] 4–37 [38]; pl. [front.] L
George Cawthorn 1797

"We know this biographical sketch to be authentic, for it is stolen . . . from the brief account of Lady Derby (then Miss Farren) given in No. 13 of this work. . . . But lest this mark of friendly attention to the Monthly Mirror should not be recognised by the proprietors, the publisher of the pamphlet has rendered himself liable to prosecution by pirating the plate . . ." — The Monthly Mirror (October, 1797). The "libel" is Petronius Arbiter's Memoirs of the present Countess of Derby (no. 2718 above). The half-title reads: A biographical sketch of the Right Honourable the Countess of Derby.

2726 ———third edition

pp. [1–3] 4–37 [38]   L

George Cawthorn   1797

A reissue of the first edition. No plate in this copy.

2727 ———*[another edition]

pp. 35   MB

For the booksellers   1797

2728 THALIA TO ELIZA: a poetical epistle from the comic muse to the Countess of D——. In which various eminent dramatic and political characters are displayed.

pp. [1–3] 4–32   L

W. J. and J. Richardson; Hookham and Carpenter; J. Wright; and R. H. Wesley   1798

The Monthly Mirror *says of this: "A jumble of malignity and falsehood" — Lowe.*

Farren, Ellen ("Nellie") 1848–1904

Burlesque actress at the Gaiety from 1868–1891. Married Robert Souter.

2729 THE NELLIE FARREN TESTIMONIAL FUND benefit performance, Thursday, March 17th, 1898. Theatre Royal, Drury Lane.

pp. [1–4]

Waterlow and Sons, Limited   [1898]

Pp. [2–3]: "Lines to be spoken by Edward Terry, Esq.," by Henry Hamilton. IKF.

Farren, Percival (17 –1843)

Elder brother of the greater William Farren. He is best known as the early tutor of Helen Faucit in her theatrical studies. She writes of him with affectionate appreciation and gratitude. He was stage-manager of the Brunswick Theatre —Lowe. See nos. 1125 and 1133.

Farren, William (1786–1871)

One of the greatest of English comedians. He was a perfect representative of such characters as Lord Ogleby, Sir Peter Teazle, &c. His vanity was proportionate to his talent, and he was known in the profession as the "Cock Salmon." — Lowe. See nos. 719 and 1125.

Faucit, Helena Saville (ca. 1817–1898)

The most notable actress of modern times. She made her first appearance, at Covent Garden, on 5th January 1836; the last occasion on which she has played was for the benefit of Charles Calvert's widow in October 1879. She was for a long period associated with Macready in his worthy efforts to support the dignity of the stage. In 1851 she married Sir Theodore Martin, K.C.B. — Lowe. See also Addenda.

2730 FAUCIT, HELENA [*Lady* Martin]. On Desdemona. By Helena Faucit Martin.

pp. [4] [51] 52–96 [97 (imprint)–98 (bl.)]

For strictly private circulation. [Printed by William Blackwood and Sons]   [1881]

JFA. Postscript dated 12th February 1881.

2731 FAUCIT, HELENA, [*Lady* Martin]. On Juliet. By Helena Faucit Martin.

pp. [2] [1] 2–88

For strictly private circulation   [1881]

JFA. Dated 5th January, 1881.

2732 FAUCIT, HELENA, [*Lady* Martin]. On Imogen By Helena Faucit Martin.

pp. [4] [1] 2–86 [87–88 (blank)]

For strictly private circulation. [Printed by William Blackwood and Sons]   [1882]

JFA. Dated Oct. 1822.

2733 FAUCIT, HELENA, [*Lady* Martin]. On Beatrice By Helena Faucit Martin.

pp. [4] [1] 2–60

For strictly private circulation. [Printed by William Blackwood and Sons]   [1885]

JFA. Dated 6th January, 1885.

2734 FAUCIT, HELENA, [*Lady* Martin]. On some of Shakespeare's female characters Ophelia Portia Desdemona Juliet Imogen Rosalind Beatrice. By Helena Faucit, Lady Martin.

pp. [i–vii] viii–ix [x–xii], [1–3] 4–422 423–443 (appendix) [444 (bl.)]; pls. [front., 2]; t.p. in red and black; vignette on t.p.   GM

Edinburgh: William Blackwood and Sons   1885

2735 ———new edition

pp. [i–vii] viii–ix [x–xii], [1–3] 4–354; pl. [front.]   E

Edinburgh and London: William Blackwood and Sons   1887

2736 ———third edition

pp. [i–vii] viii [ix–x], [1–3] 4–364; pl. [front.]   L

Edinburgh and London: William Blackwood and Sons   1888

2737 ———new and enlarged edition

pp. [2] [i–vii] viii [ix–x], [1–3] 4–410 [411–412 (bl.)]; pl. [front.]   L

Edinburgh and London: William Blackwood and Sons   1891

Adds Hermione to list of characters in title.

2738 ———fifth edition

pp. [i–vii] viii [ix–x], [1–3] 4–410; pl. [front.]

Edinburgh and London: William Blackwood and Sons
1893

JFA.

2739 ———sixth edition

pp. [i–vii] viii–xii [xiii–xiv], [1–3] 4–410; pl. [front.]
LGk

Edinburgh & London: William Blackwood and Sons
1899

———[German translation] Leipzig, 1890

2740 MARTIN, *Sir* THEODORE. Helena Faucit
(Lady Martin) by Sir Theodore Martin K.C.B.,
K.C.V.O.

pp. [i–vii] viii–x [xi–xii], [1] 2–416; pls. [front., 3]   L
Edinburgh and London: William Blackwood and Sons
1900

This copy lacks a plate.

2741 ———second edition

pp. [i–vii] viii–x [xi–xii], [1] 2–416; pls. [front., 4]   L
Edinburgh and London: William Blackwood and Sons
1900

Faustina [Bordoni] (1700–1781)

*Opera singer, married to J. H. Hasse, the composer. Appeared
in London from 1726 for two seasons only. Her quarrel with
Francesca Cuzzoni at the King's Theatre was satirized in
Gay's Beggar's Opera (1728). For the series of pamphlets
on Faustina, Senesino, etc. see above OPERA nos. 2034–
2045, 2054.*

Fawcett, John (1769–1837)

*An admirable comedian, who was stage-manager of Covent
Garden for a considerable period. His Caleb Quotem
[in H. Lee's Throw Physic to the Dogs! (Haymarket,
6 July 1798)] is one of the traditions of the stage—Lowe.
See no. 1182.*

Fechter, Charles Albert (1824–1879)

*A French actor, whose performance of Hamlet (in English)
aroused a storm of controversy. He was the first, in recent
times, to try to throw a little naturalness into the part. He
played it first at the Princess's Theatre on 20th March 1861,
and it ran for 115 nights. His Othello was as bad as his
Hamlet was good — Lowe. See Mary Katherine Kemble
Field, Charles Albert Fechter (American Actors Series)
(Boston, 1882), which includes (pp. 143–193) a review of
British criticism of Fechter.*

2742 OTTLEY, HENRY. Fechter's version of
Othello, critically analysed. By Henry Ottley, with
prefatory observations on the stage, the audience, and
the critics.

pp. [1–3] 4–32   E
T. H. Lacy   1861

*A severe criticism on Fechter, reprinted, with additions,
from the Morning Chronicle of October 24 and 26 —
Lowe.*

2743 WILMOT. *A retrospective glance at
Mr. Fechter's Iago, and acting edition of Othello.
By Wilmot.

pp. 31   MB
Lacy   1862

2744 vacant

2745 HAMLEY, *Sir* EDWARD. Shakespeare's funeral
and other papers by Sir Edward Hamley.

pp. [6] 1–311 [312 (bl.)]   GU
Edinburgh and London: William Blackwood and Sons
1889

Includes a criticism of Fechter's acting in "Othello".

Fennell, James (1766–1816)

*Was a very promising actor. He made his first appearance
at Edinburgh in 1787. During the next season a quarrel
occurred regarding the cast of Venice Preserved, and
Fennell was brutally treated by a section of the public, and
driven from the Edinburgh stage. He ultimately went to
America.... His real name was Cambray — Lowe. See
AUTHOR-INDEX.*

Fenton, Lavinia (1708–1760)

*The original Polly in the Beggar's Opera (1728), by which
part she at one bound became famous. [See below nos.
3904–3908]. At the end of 1727–1728 she quitted the stage,
and became the mistress of the Duke of Bolton, a married
man. On his wife's death in 1751, he, oddly enough, married
Miss Fenton — Lowe.*

2746 AN ANSWER TO POLLY PEACHUM'S
BALLAD. The following lines being sent to the author
as an answer to the foregoing ballad, he to shew what he
publish'd was not done out of malice to Polly Peachum,
has annex'd them to this edition, having so much value
for the female sex as to give them fair play to a fair
woman.

bs.   L
Printed by A. Moore   [1728]

*Apparently published with another edition of A new
ballad (see below no. 2750). Reprinted in the Twickenham Hotch-Potch, 1728 (see above no. 868).*

2747 *LETTERS IN PROSE AND VERSE to the
celebrated Polly Peachum from the most eminent of
her admirers and rivals.

A. Miller   1728
STR.

2748 ——Letters in prose and verse, to the celebrated Polly Peachum: from the most eminent of her admirers and rivals. The second edition.

pp. [1–4] 5–24   L
A. Millar   1728

Advertised in July — Schultz.

2749 THE LIFE OF LAVINIA BESWICK, alias Fenton, alias Polly Peachum: containing, her birth and education. Her intrigues at a boarding school. Her first acquaintance with a certain Portugueze nobleman. The time when, and the person to whom she bestow'd her first favours. A particular account of her conversation with a mercer, now living near the Royal Exchange. Of the Portugueze nobleman being confin'd in the Fleet, and the honourable method she took to gain him his liberty. A copy of verses which she composed on a Fop, which conduced to her acquaintance with Mr. Huddy, for whose benefit, at the New Theatre in the Haymarket, she first appear'd on the stage. A particular account of a benefit she shar'd with one Mr. Gilbert, a few weeks after Mr. Huddy's, at the same theatre. Her first admittance into the Theatre-Royal in Lincoln's-Inn-Fields: her weekly salary, both now and then; and the time when, and the cause why, it was raised. Of her wit gaining her more lovers than her beauty. The horse-courser dismounted, yet saves his distance. A poet strutting under the protection of the nine Muses. Another poet, who would attack Ulysses and Penelope in a barbarous manner, is severely handled by Polly in a satyrical stanza. Her judgment in poetry, and history painting. And the reasonable reason why so many great men have been her humble servants. The whole interspers'd with convincing proofs of her ingenuity, wit, and smart repartees. And concluding with some remarkable instances of her humanity to the distressed.

pp. [2] [1] 2–48   L
A. Moore   1728

Advertised 24 May 1728 — Schultz.

2750 A NEW BALLAD INSCRIPE'D [sic] TO POLLY PEACHUM To the tune of Pretty parrot say, by the author of Leheup's ballad.

pp. [1] 2; head-title   L
[London]   1728

Reprinted in the Twickenham Hotch-Potch, *1728. (no. 868).*

2751 *POLLY PEACHUM on fire.

pp. [2] 1–29 [30 (bl.)]   MH
     1728

Foxon.

2752 POLLY PEACHUM'S JESTS. In which are comprised most of the witty apothegms, diverting tales, and smart repartees that have been used for many

years last past, either at St. James's or St. Giles's: suited aliked [sic] to the capacities of the peer, and the porter.

pp. [4] 1–44   L
J. Roberts   1728

Advertised in April — Schultz.

Field, Nathan (1587–1619 or 20)

One of the old actors, who was the controversial champion of his profession—Lowe. *See Roberta F. Brinkley,* Nathan Field *(Yale Studies in English, 77) (New Haven, 1928); E. Verhassalt, A Biography of Field, Dramatist and Actor (Revue Belge, xxv) (Bruxelles, 1947); W. Perry, ed.* The Plays of Nathan Field *(Austin, 1950). See no. 1040.*

Fisher, Clara (1811–1898)

An infant phenomenon who made her appearance at Drury Lane in 1817, when only six years old. She retained her talent after she grew up, and was for many years a popular actress in America, where she married a musician, Mr. James G. Maeder — Lowe.

2753 *A SKETCH of the life of Miss Clara Fisher, the lilliputian actress, of the Theatres-Royal, Drury-Lane, and Covent Garden.

     MH
     1818

2754 ——*second edition, with additions.
     1819
Lowe.

2755 ——third edition
pp. [2] [1–3] 4–24; illus. [front.]   GU
Glasgow: printed by William Tait   1820

Fitzball, Edward (1792–1873)

A voluminous dramatic writer, who, in his later years, fell on evil days — Lowe. *Known also as Edward Ball.*

2756 FITZBALL, EDWARD. Thirty-five years of a dramatic author's life. By Edward Fitzball, Esq.

2 vols. pp. [2] [i] ii–x, [1] 2–308; pl. [front.] + pp. [4] [1] 2–414   E
T. C. Newby   1859

Fitzgerald, Percy Hetherington (1834–1925)

One of the most industrious and best informed of living theatrical historians—Lowe. *This is rather exaggerated praise: Thorn-Drury comments,* 'Lowe was a most amiable man and a member of the Garrick where he was constantly meeting Fitzgerald and others whom he compliments in his notes, and it was difficult if not impossible for him to tell the truth about them". *See Fitzgerald's* An output. A list of writings ... 1853–1912 *(London, [1912]). See AUTHOR INDEX.*

Fleetwood, Charles (– *ca.* 1745)

A man of fortune and fashion, who purchased the greater part of the Drury Lane patent in 1733–34, and retained it till 1745. He was a reckless, shiftless, and unprincipled man, very unjust to his actors — Lowe. For Fleetwood at Drury Lane see above nos. 1332 et seq.

Foot, John Forrester

Actor, of whom I know little, except that he played at Bath in 1818, and that his name appears in the Haymarket and Drury Lane bills subsequently. His line, in 1818, seems to have been "old men."—Lowe. See no. 2001.

Foote, Maria (1797?–1867)

A beautiful actress, whose amatory and matrimonial affairs were somewhat sensational. She was seduced, under promise of marriage, by Colonel Berkeley (a militia colonel), who did not marry her. Joseph Hayne, Esq. — generally known as "Pea-green Hayne," from the colour of coat he affected — proposed to her, with full knowledge, I believe, of her amour with Berkeley; but declined to fulfil his engagement, and she got £3000 damages out of him. In 1831 she married the Earl of Harrington — Lowe.

2757 DAMAGES THREE THOUSAND POUNDS!! Fairburn's edition of the trial between Maria Foote, the celebrated actress, plaintiff, and Joseph Hayne, Esq. defendant, for a breach of promise of marriage; including the evidence at full length, speeches of counsel, &c. and the whole of the love letters. Tried in the Court of King's Bench, Westminster, before the Lord Chief Justice Abbott, and a special jury, Dec. 21, 1824. Taken in short hand.

> "May God strike me dead if ever I consent to separate myself from you."
>
> Hayne

pp. [1–3] 4–76 [77–78 (advts.)]   L
John Fairburn   [?1824]

Some copies have one of the several coloured caricature engravings of this affair issued by Fairburn, bound in as frontispieces, and may have been so published.

2758 FULL REPORT of the trial between Miss Foote and J. Hayne, Esq. for a breach of promise of marriage: detailing the opening speech of the Attorney General, at full length, narrating a most interesting history: the first introduction of the parties and consequent intimacy; unfolding the whole of this hitherto mysterious affair: the evidence; with copies of the numerous and highly interesting love letters that passed on each side. Mr. Scarlett's skilful and amusing speech for the defence, reply of the Attorney General, and the summing up of the evidence by the Lord Chief Justice, with Col. Berkeley's letters in explanation of his conduct.

pp. [4] [6] 7–17 19–28 [=26]; illus.; title headed: "Damages £3000. Duncombe's edition"   E
Duncombe   [1824]

2759 ——seventh edition!!! With the whole of the letters.

pp. [3–4] 5–26; col. pl. [front.]   MH
Duncombe   [1825?]

2760 *THE RAPE OF JOSEPH: a mock heroic poem. The characters and subect taken from the present day. Principal characters, Miss F***e and Mr. H***e.

       MH
       [1824]

✂ [Foote, Maria?] *An appeal to the justice and common sense of the friends of the true drama; wherein is compared the treatment experienced by Miss Foote . . . with that experienced by Mr. Kean . . . [1825]. *See no. 3138.*

2761 BLACKMANTLE, BERNARD *pseud. o,* Charles Malloy Westmacott? Fitzalleyne of Berkeley. A romance of the present times. By Bernard Blackmantle.

2 vols. pp. [i–v] vi–xx, [1] 2–219 [220 (bl.)]; engr. on t.p. + pp. [i–v] vi–x, [1] 2–201 [202 (bl.)]; engr. on t.p.
       L

Sherwood and Co.   1825

2762 THE COLONEL AND THE EDITOR; a new song to an old tune, on a recent affair at Cheltenham. (From the *Telescope*, Sunday Newspaper, April 3, 1825.)

bs., illus. (col.)   MH
T. Holt   [1825]

Eight stanzas, and a coloured wood-cut. George (1952) no. 14869.

2763 FACTS ILLUSTRATIVE OF THE EVIDENCE of the late trial of Foote v. Hayne: with a brief review of the speech of the Attorney-General.

pp. [1] 2–29 [30]   L
John Miller   1825

A strong attack upon Miss Foote's father and mother, and a defence (partially) of Colonel Berkeley — Lowe.

2764 ——second edition

pp. [1] 2–29 [30]   L
John Miller   1825

2765 REAPPEARANCE OF MISS FOOTE, who was kindly received on Saturday evening at Covent Garden Theatre.

bs.; illus.   L
J. Pitts, printer   [1825]

2766 S., H.T. *An account of Miss Foote's reappearance at the Theatre-Royal, Covent-Garden, on the fifth of February, 1825; and of her reception and performances, during a tour of eight months, at the Theatres-Royal of Dublin, Edinburgh, and Bath &c.

pp. v, 85   MB

[Edinburgh?]   [1825]

2767 ——[another edition] *AN ACCOUNT of Miss Foote's reappearance at the Theatre-Royal, Covent Garden, on the fifth of February 1825; and of her first appearance at the Theatres-Royal, Dublin, Liverpool, Edinburgh, Glasgow, Dumfries, &c.

[Edinburgh]   [1825]

Lowe. *Preface initialled "H.T.S."*

2768 SECOND-SIGHT; or, the consequences of the reception given to Miss Foote, on Saturday, the 5th February, 1825. Dedicated (without permission) to the husbands, fathers, and brothers of the British metropolis.

pp. [1–3] 4–24   L

Sherwood, Jones, and Co.   1825

Signed: Archibald McMoral. Edinburgh, 10 Feb. 1825. Brown lists a copy with portrait.

❌ The theatrical mince pie . . . Containing a correct account of the several appearances of Mr. Kean and Miss Foote, since their late actions in the Court of King's Bench . . . 1825. *See no. 4141.*

2769 *AN ACCOUNT of the third and fourth theatrical tour made by Miss Foote, in 1826 and 1827, to Liverpool, Bath, Edinburgh, &c.

pp. 92   MB

Smith   1827

Foote, Samuel (1720–1777)

"The English Aristophanes," as he has been called. As a mimic and broad comedian he holds a very high place, while as an author he was facile and clever. His abuse of private persons, by producing them on the stage, was objectionable in the last degree, and was terribly punished; the accusation which precipitated his death being made in revenge for a threatened attack on a private individual. An account of this is given below [see nos. 2805–2807] — Lowe. See M. M. Belden, The Dramatic Work of Samuel Foote (New Haven, 1929). Foote took over the Haymarket Theatre in 1747 and sold it to Colman in 1777.

Treatise on the Passions

2770 [FOOTE, SAMUEL.] A TREATISE on the passions, so far as they regard the stage; with a critical enquiry into the theatrical merit of Mr. G——k, Mr. Q——n, and Mr. B——y. The first considered in the part of Lear, and the two last opposed in Othello.

pp. [1–2] 3–44   L

C. Corbet   [1747]

2771 AN EXAMEN of the new comedy, call'd "The suspicious husband". With some observations upon our dramatick poetry and authors; to which is added, A word of advice to Mr. G——rr——ck; and a piece of secret history.

pp. [1–4] 5–56   L

J. Roberts   1747

Dr. Hoadley's "Suspicious Husband [Covent Garden 12 February 1747] is one of the best comedies ever written. The "Word of Advice" to Garrick is a criticism of Foote's "Treatise on the Passions"; and the "Piece of Secret History" is a "sell" — Lowe.

2772 FOOTE, S[AMUEL]. The Roman and English comedy consider'd and compar'd. With Remarks on *The suspicious husband*. And An examen into the merit of the present comic actors. By S. Foote.

pp. [1–2] 3–45 [46]   L

T. Waller   1747

2773 A LETTER OF COMPLIMENT to the ingenious author of A treatise on the passions, so far as they regard the stage; with a critical enquiry into the theatrical merit of Mr. G——k, Mr. Q——n, and Mr. B——y, &c. With some further remarks on Mr. M——n. And a few hints on our modern actresses, particularly Mrs. C——r and Mrs. P——d.

pp. [1–4] 5–47 [48]   L

C. Corbertt   [1747]

An ironical defence of Foote — Lowe. Signed J.T.

2774 [SKEWBALL, PETER, *pseud.*] A CATALOGUE of curiosities, chiefly theatrical, which are to be sold by auction; being part of the effects of a virtuoso, lately deceas'd.

pp. [i–v] vi–vii [viii] [9] 10–22   MB

M. Cooper   1748

Satirical. The peculiarities and weaknesses of certain actors are sharply alluded to — Lowe. Particularly those of Foote.

2775 WHIPPING RODS, for trifling, scurrhill, scriblers; as Mr. F——t on taste, Spectorhill his late pamphlets and papers: his Theophrastus on stones or gems, with other of his principal performances.

pp. [i–ii] iii–ix xii–xv [xvi (bl.)] [=xiv], [1] 2–34   L

M. Cooper   1752

F—t is Samuel Foote . . . Spectorhill is Dr. John Hill, author of The Inspector. Both are roundly abused — Lowe. Foote's comedy Taste was produced at Drury Lane 11 and 24 January 1752 to a noisy audience — LS. Dedication signed K——y.

The Minor 1760

The Minor was first produced in Dublin without success in January 1760. Foote extended it, and on its production at the Haymarket in the summer (28 June 1760), it was very successful. It is a bitter attack on the Methodists — Lowe. For its reception in Edinburgh in 1770 see below, nos. 2797–2803.

2776 MINISTER OF THE CHURCH OF CHRIST, A, *pseud. of* Martin Madan? Christian and critical remarks on a droll, or interlude, called *The Minor.* Now acting by a company of stage players in the Hay-market; and said to be acted by authority. In which the blasphemy, falshood, and scurrility of that piece is properly considered, answered, and exposed. By a minister of the church of Christ.

pp. [2] [1] 2–41 [42]   MH
Mr. Keith; Mrs. Lewis; Mr. Andrews; Mr. Rolls; Mr. Burd and Mr. Taylor   1760

This pamphlet, published in August, is "supposed by some to be by Whitefield, but [is] probably by Martin Madan" (Belden, p. 86).

2777 ——the second edition corrected.

pp. [2] [1] 2–41 [42], misprinting 32 as "42"   L
Mr. Keith; Mrs. Lewis; Mr. Andrew; Mr. Rolls; Mr. Burd; Mr. Taylor   1760

2778 FOOTE, [SAMUEL]. A letter from Mr. Foote, to the Reverend author of the Remarks, critical and Christian, on The Minor.

pp. [4] 1–40   L
T. Davies; T. Becket; and J. Coote   1760

Reprinted in William Cooke, Memoirs of Samuel Foote (1805), III, 160–201, (see below no. 2816) and in The Works of Samuel Foote, ed. Jon Bee [John Badcock], 3 volumes (1830), I, xciii ff.

2779 vacant

2780 [MADAN, *Rev.* MARTIN?] A LETTER TO DAVID GARRICK, Esq; occasioned by the intended representation of "The Minor" at the Theatre-Royal in Drury-Lane.

pp. [4] [1–3] 4–48   L
Sold by Mr. Field; Mr. Flexney; Mr. Hurd   1760

Signed "Anti-Profanus"; the Postscript signed "A.P." Sometimes attributed, probably erroneously, to Abraham Portal; Belden, and L. Tyerman, Life of the Rev. George Whitefield (1878) II, 434, attribute it to Madan. In Baine's The Theatre Licentious (1770) it is said to be by a "very worthy English clergyman".

2781 ——the third edition

pp. [1–3] 4–24   MH
Edinburgh: [W. Gray]   1770

Advertised as "published by W. Gray" in the second edition of Baine's Theatre Licentious (1770).

2782 A LETTER TO MR. FOOTE, occasioned by his *Letter to the reverend author of The christian and critical remarks on The Minor,* containing a refutation of Mr.

Foote's pamphlet, and a full defence of the principles and practices of the Methodists. By the author of the *Christian and critical remarks.*

pp. [2] [1] 2–28   L
P. Wicks   1760

"Clearly not" by the author of Christian and Critical Remarks *(Belden, p. 90).*

2783 A LETTER TO MR. F——TE. Occasioned by the *Christian and critical remarks* on his interlude, called *The Minor.* To which is added, An appendix, relative to a serious address to the Methodists themselves.

pp. [4] [1] 2–28   L
T. Pote   1760

"A poor piece of work and may well have given Foote the impetus to write a reply of his own" (Belden, p. 87).

2783.1 MINISTER OF THE CHURCH OF CHRIST, A, *pseud.* *An exhortatory address to the Brethren in the faith of Christ, occasioned by a remarkable letter from Mr. Foote to the reverend author of Christian and critical remarks on the Minor. With a serious word or two on the present melancholy occasion. By a minister of the Church of Christ.

                                                                    1760

Belden, p. 198.

2784 *AN OLD WOMAN'S ANSWER to the Minor.

                                                                    1760

Belden, p. 199.

2784.1 ——*A word to the public, in answer to The Minor.

                                                                    1760?

This is the preface, separately published, to An old woman's answer (no. 2784) (Belden, pp. 90–91).

2785 *SATIRICAL DIALOGUE between the celebrated Mr. F——te and Dr. Squintum; as it happened near the Great Lumber-House in Tottenham-Court Road.

Ranger   1760
   STR.

2786 AN ADDITIONAL SCENE to the comedy of *The Minor.*

pp. [1–9] 10–19 [20 (bl.)]   L
J. Williams   1761

A vicious attack on Foote for his taking off people who had befriended him — Lowe. Dedicated to Garrick.

2787 GENIUS, A, *pseud. of* James Boswell *the elder.* Observations, good or bad, stupid or clever, serious or jocular, on Squire Foote's dramatic entertainment, intitled, "The Minor." By a Genius.

pp. [1–5] 6–15 [16 (bl.)]   L
J. Wilkie   1761

2788 [SQUINTUM, GEORGE, *pseud.*] A LETTER OF EXPOSTULATION from the manager of the Theatre in Tottenham-Court, to the manager of the Theatre in the Hay-Market. Relative to a new comedy, called "The Minor".
pp. [1–2] 3–12 L
R. Stevens [1761?]

Signed "George Squintum."

2789 [POTTINGER, ISRAEL?] THE METHODIST, a comedy; being a continuation and completion of the plan of *The Minor*, written by Mr. Foote, as it was intended to have been acted at the Theatre Royal in Covent-Garden, but for obvious reasons suppressed. With the original prologue and epilogue.
pp. [4] [1] 2–60 L
I. Pottinger [1761]

2790 ———the third edition
pp. [4] [1] 2–60 [61–63 (songs) 64 (bl.)] L
I. Pottinger [1761]

2791 *THE MIMIC: a poem. By the author.
pp. viii, 9–20 MB
Printed for the author and sold by J. Scott 1761

Dedicated and addressed to Samuel Foote — Brown.

2792 PARAGRAPH, PETER, *pseud.* The methodist and mimick. A tale, in hudibrastick verse. By Peter Paragraph. Inscribed to Samuel Foot, Esq.
pp. [1–4] 5–21 [22 (bl.) 23 (advt.) 24 (bl.)] MH
C. Moran 1766

Belden *and* Lowe *appear to know of copies dated 1767.*

⌘ Wilkinson, Tate. The wandering patentee; or, a history of the Yorkshire theatres . . . To which are added . . . Foote's trial for a libel on Peter Paragraph. Written by the late Samuel Foot, Esq. York, 1795. *See no. 3640.*

2793 [CAREY, GEORGE SAVILLE.] MOMUS, a poem; or a critical examination into the merits of the performers, and comic pieces, at the Theatre Royal in the Hay-Market.
pp. [1–5] 6–22 [23–24 (bl.)] L
[1769–70?]

An attack on Foote and his company — Lowe. *So dated by* Belden. *Copy at MH lacks the final blank leaf, but has a half-title leaf, missing in this copy. Reprinted in George Saville Carey's* Analects in Verse and Prose *(1770), I, 93–107.*

2794 PHILO-TECHNICUS MISO-MIMIDES, *pseud. of* Paul Hiffernan? Foote's prologue detected; with a miniature-prose epilogue of his manner in speaking it. By Philo-technicus Miso-mimides.
pp. [1–4] 5–35 [36 (bl.)] L
Printed for the author and sold by J. Williams [1770]

A bitter attack on Foote, whose prologue on opening his theatre alluded to the Jubilee of Shakespeare in an uncomplimentary manner. The description of Foote's personal appearance and manner of delivery is a piece of the plainest speaking. I do not doubt that Dr. Paul Hiffernan was the author of this and the following tract [*no. 2795*]. *Both are extremely rare*—Lowe.

2795 PHILO-TECHNICUS MISO-MIMIDES, *pseud. of* Paul Hiffernan? An appendix to "Foote's prologue detected"; containing with other curious articles a new occasional epilogue, for the close of his theatre, on Saturday September 15, 1770. By Philo-technicus Miso-mimides.
pp. [1–4] 5–39 [40 (advt.)] L
Printed for the author and sold by J. Williams 1770

2796 PHILO-TECHNICUS MISO-MIMIDES, *pseud. of* Paul Hiffernan? *Thoughts on the cause of discontent in Foote's prologue.
[1770]

Belden, *p. 32.*

The Minor *in Edinburgh 1770*

2797 BAINE, *Rev.* JAMES. The theatre licentious and perverted. Or, a sermon for reformation of manners. Preached on the Lord's Day, Dec 2. 1770. Partly occasioned by the acting of a comedy, entitled, *The Minor*, in the licensed theatre of Edinburgh, on Saturday the 24th of November preceding. By James Baine, A.M. Minister of the Gospel at Edinburgh. Inscribed to Samuel Foote, Esq;
pp. [i–iii] iv–ix [x] [11] 12–40, misprinting 31 as "32" E
Edinburgh: printed by J. Reid 1770

2798 ———the second edition
pp. [i–iii] iv–ix [x] [11] 12–40 L
Edinburgh: printed by J. Reid 1770

2799 ———the third edition
pp. [i–iii] iv–ix [x (bl.)] [11] 12–40 L
Edinburgh: printed by J. Reid 1771

2800 FOOTE, SAMUEL. Apology for the Minor, in a letter to the Rev. Mr. Bain. By Samuel Foote, Esq.
pp. [1–3] 4–33 [34 (bl.)] PU
Edinburgh 1771

2801 ———[another edition] Apology for the Minor. In a letter to the Rev. Mr. Baine. To which is added, the original epilogue. By Samuel Foote, Esq.
pp. [1–3] 4–24 L
Edinburgh: J. Wood 1771

2802 BELINDA'S ACCOUNT of a comedy, called *The Minor*, introduced upon the stage, at Edinburgh, Saturday, November 24 1770.

pp. [1] 2–4; head-title   L

[Edinburgh]   [1770]

A furious attack on The Minor — Lowe.

2803 [SIMPLEX], *pseud. of* —— Young. A letter to Mr. James Baine, minister in Edinburgh; occasioned by his sermon, intitled *The theatre licentious and perverted: or, strictures upon the doctrine, lately insisted on against Samuel Foote, Esq; &c. on account of a late representation of the comedy, called The Minor, at the Theatre Royal, Edinburgh.*

pp. [2] [1] 2–47 [48]   E

Edinburgh: W. Coke   1771

Signed Simplex and dated January.

✖ An epistle to Henry Mossop, Esq; on ... the drama, and the present state of the Irish stage. Dublin, [*ca.* 1770]. *See no. 1793.*

The Mossop affair in Ireland. See also no. 1794.

2804 THE STAGE OF ARISTOPHANES.

pp. [2] [1] 2–21 [22]   E

H. Setchell   1774

A poetical review of Foote and the members of his company.

2805 THE CASE OF THE DUCHESS OF KINGSTON.

pp. [4] [i] ii [3] 4–30 [31–32 (bl.)]   L

J. Wheble   1775

Into a piece called "The Trip to Calais" Foote introduced a character, Lady Kitty Crocodile, which was an obvious attack upon the notorious Duchess of Kingston, afterwards convicted of bigamy. Whether he did this as a means of blackmailing the Duchess or not cannot be decided. She, at any rate, heard of his intention, and had influence enough to have the piece prohibited by the Licenser, in spite of Foote's protests. (See "Letter to the Licenser," below.) Foote then altered the piece to one called "The Capuchin", in which, in the character of Dr. Viper, he attacked Dr. Jackson, the confidential friend and adviser of the Duchess. This fellow, who afterwards committed suicide to escape hanging for treason, was editor of a newspaper, in which, from the time of Foote's reported intentions regarding the Duchess, obscure hints and innuendoes charging him with a most infamous crime had appeared (see "Sodom and Onan") and these accusations finally took formal shape in July 1776, when a bill of indictment was preferred against Foote for a criminal assault on a coachman whom he had recently dismissed for drunkenness. On trial, Foote was most clearly acquitted without the jury's leaving the box, and it was shown that the prosecution was got up by Jackson; but the horror of the accusation broke Foote's health, and he died little more than a year after — Lowe. See Belden, pp. 36–49.

2806 [FOOTE, SAMUEL.] ★A LETTER TO THE LICENSER [regarding the prohibition of the *Trip to Calais.* By Samuel Foote.]

                           1775

I have never seen this even catalogued, but I believe that such a pamphlet was published—Lowe. Ghost? *Perhaps the letter in* Morning Chronicle *of 3 August*

2807 [NETTLE, HUMPHREY] *pseud. of* William Jackson? SODOM and Onan. A satire. Inscrib'd to [portrait of Foote and a drawing of a human foot] Esq ͬ alias the Devil upon two sticks.

pp. [i] ii, [1] 2–29 [30 (bl.)]; engr. t.p.   L

n.p.   [1776]

The dedication to Foote begins "Most infernal sir" and is signed Humphrey Nettle.

✖ Particulars of the trial of Foote. 1830. *See no. 2818.*

2808 HOLCROFT, THOMAS. Elegies. I. On the death of Samuel Foote, Esq. II. On age. By Thomas Holcroft, of the Theatre Royal, Drury-Lane.

pp. [i–iii] iv [5–7] 8–24   L

J. Bew   1777

2809 MEMOIRS OF THE LIFE AND WRITINGS OF SAMUEL FOOTE, Esq; the English Aristophanes: to which are added the bon mots, repartees, and good things said by that great wit and excentrical genius.

pp. [2] 5–42 41–88 [=88]   L

J. Bew   [1777?]

2810 WIT FOR THE TON! The convivial jester; or, Sam Foote's last budget opened. Containing original and authentic anecdotes, bon mots, jocose remarks, poignant repartees, whimsical occurrences, queer hums, inimitable witticisms, &c. of that immortal child of humour the English Aristophanes; with authentic memoirs of his life and writings, and a particular recital of the many laughable incidents which befel him in the former, and the various whimsical occurrences that gave rise to the latter.

pp. [i–ii] iii [iv] 5–47 [48]; pl. [front.]   L

W. Adlard   [1777?]

2811 ——the second edition, with additions.

pp. [i–ii] iii [iv] 5–47 [48]; pl. [front.]   L

W. Adlard   1779

2812 BOSCHERECCIO, *pseud.* An elegy on the death of Samuel Foote, Esq. By Boschereccio.

pp. [1–3] 4–11 [12 (bl.)]; vignette on t.p.   L

G. Kearsley   1778

2813 GENTLEMAN, A, *pseud.*, *ed.* Aristophanes, being a classic collection of true Attic wit, containing the jests, gibes, bon-mots, witticisms, and most extraordinary anecdotes of Samuel Foote, Esq., the Lords Chesterfield, Tyrawley, Messrs. Churchill, Thornton, Cox, Lloyd, and their cotemporaries; being a high-seasoned olio, of more variety than was ever offered to the public before. Wherein is given the lively jeux-d'esprit of the first ladies of the age, whether celebrated at court or in the theatre: with some singular anecdotes of their fames and fortunes. Collected, during the course of twenty years, by a gentleman, who was a constant companion to the wits of his time. With an engraved head of Samuel Foote, Esq.

pp. [4] [i] ii–lv [lvi], [1] 2–148 [misnumbering xxxii as "xxxi"]; pl. [front.]   DFo

Robert Baldwin   1778

2814 THE NEW THEATRE OF FUN; or, the modern Aristophanes in high glee. Being a genuine collection of the jests, gibes, witticisms, bonmots, puns, repartees, anecdotes, remarks, and singular jokes, of Samuel Foote, Esq.

pp. [1–3] 9–96; pl. [front.]   L

Sold by R. Durfey, and J. Curdell   1778

2815 †THE LIFE OF SAMUEL FOOTE, ESQ.

pp. [1] 2–23 [24 (bl.)]; head-title   L

[London]   [1788]

2816 COOKE, WILLIAM. Memoirs of Samuel Foote, Esq. with a collection of his genuine bon-mots, anecdotes, opinions, &c. mostly original. And three of his dramatic pieces, not published in his works. By William Cooke, Esq.

3 vols. pp. [i–iii] iv–xii, [1] 2–240; pl. [front.] + pp. [2] [1] 2–224 + [2] [1] 2–220

Richard Phillips   1805

     IKF; *another copy at L.*

2817 ——[another edition] The table-talk and bon-mots of Samuel Foote. With an introductory memoir. Edited by the late William Cooke. Illustrated.

pp. [i–v] vi–viii, [1] 2–268; pls. [14]   L

Myers & Rogers   1902

     Only 120 copies printed. An edition, chiefly of Vol. 2, of Cooke's Memoirs of Samuel Foote *(1805).*

2818 *PARTICULARS of the trial of Foote the dramatist, before Lord Mansfield and a special jury, 1776, for a certain crime.

     1830

     Recorded but not seen by Lowe. See above nos. 2805–2807. Badcock's edition of Foote's works was published in 1830.

2819 JERROLD, WALTER, *ed.* Bon-mots of Samuel Foote and Theodore Hook. Edited by Walter Jerrold. With grotesques by Aubrey Beardsley.

pp. [1–5] 6–13 [14 (bl.)] 15 16 (bl.) 17] 18–115 [116 (bl.) 117 118 (bl.) 119] 120–192; pls. [2]; illus.; t.p. in red and black   E

J. M. Dent   1894

2820 ——[large paper issue]

pp. [2] [1–5] 6–192; illus.; pls. [2]; t.p. in two colours   L

J. M. Dent and Company   1894

     Only 100 copies printed.

2821 ——*second edition

     1898

     "Second edition, October 1898" — no. 2822.

2822 ——[third edition]

pp. [2] [1–5] 6–192; illus.; t.p. in two colours   L

J. M. Dent and Company   1904

     Published in June.

Forbes-Robertson, Sir Johnston (1853–1937)

A popular young actor, who is an excellent painter as well as player. He made his first appearance in 1874—Lowe. See no. 3415.

Fortescue, *Miss* Finney (1862–1950)

Actress.

2823 ONE WHO KNOWS ALL ABOUT IT, *pseud.* *The peer and the actress, or incidents in the lives of Miss Fortescue and Viscount Garmoyle. By one who knows all about it.

     [*ca.* 1882]

STR.

Frere, Benjamin

Dramatist.

2824 [FRERE, BENJAMIN.] THE ADVENTURES of a dramatist on a journey to the London managers. In two volumes.

2 vols. pp. [i–v] vi [vii–viii (bl.)], [1] 2–204 + [2] [1–3] 4–204   L

Lackington, Allen and Co.   [1812]

     The dedication, to Samuel Whitbread, is signed B. Frere, and dated 1st November 1812 from Handsworth, Staffs.

2825 ——*second edition

2 vols. in one   MB

Lackington, Allen and Co.   1813

2826 vacant

2827 ——[another edition] The adventures of a dramatist.

2 vols. pp. [6] [i–iii] iv–v [vi] [7] 8–257 [258 (bl.)] + [2] [1–3] 4–46 [1] 47–224 [225 (bl.)] [=224]   L

Simpkin and Marshall   1832

Signed Benjamin Ererf.

Galindo, *Mrs.*

An actress, who accused Mrs. Siddons of improper intimacy with Mr. Galindo — Lowe. See nos. 1236; 3533.

Garrick, David (1717–1779)

The most famous of English actors. He made his first public appearance in London at Goodman's Fields Theatre on 19th October 1741, as Richard III; became joint-patentee (with Lacy) of Drury Lane in 1747; managed Drury Lane till 1776, when he retired, his last appearance being made on 10th June 1776; died 20th January 1779. An account of almost every notable occurrence in his career will be found below; for pamphlets in showers were written about everything he did. He married Eva Maria Violetti, a noted dancer who made him an excellent wife.—Lowe. See also Carola Oman, David Garrick (1958), Kalman Burnim, David Garrick, Director (Pittsburgh, 1961) and David M. Little and George M. Kahrl, Letters of David Garrick, 3 vols. (1963).

2828 A CLEAR STAGE, and no favour: or, tragedy and comedy at war. Occasion'd by the emulation of the two theatric heroes, David and Goliah. Left to the impartial decision of the town.

pp. [1–2] 3–12   MH

J. Huggonson   [1742]

David and Goliah are Garrick and Quin, the representatives of the new and the old school — Lowe. Published in December. Heroic couplets.

✖ Lamentation from the Drury-Lane Play-house. [1743?]. See no. 3650.

A satire on Peg Woffington, Garrick and (?) Lord Darnley.

The Dispute between Garrick and Macklin, 1743

In 1743 the actors of Drury Lane, headed by Garrick and Macklin, revolted against Fleetwood, the manager, but were obliged to return to their duty. Fleetwood received all but Macklin, whom he regarded as doubly ungrateful. As the revolters had agreed to stand by one another, Macklin considered Garrick's return as a breach of faith, and a bitter contest ensued — Lowe. On the 1743 riots see above nos. 1336–1346.

2829 [MACKLIN, CHARLES.] THE CASE of Charles Macklin, comedian.

fold. doc., pp. [2]; filing-title   L

                                                         1743

Dated 5 December 1743. Reprinted in Mr. Macklin's Reply to Mr. Garrick's Answer (1743) (see below no. 2831); Arthur Murphy, Life of David Garrick (1801) (see below no. 2942.)

2830 [GUTHRIE, WILLIAM.] *MR. GARRICK'S ANSWER to Mr. Macklin's case.

                                                        DFo

                                                        1743

In answer to The Case of Charles Macklin. Reprinted in Mr. Macklin's Reply (no. 2831 below).

2831 [MACKLIN, CHARLES.] Mr. MACKLIN'S REPLY to Mr. Garrick's answer. To which are prefix'd, all the papers, which have publickly appeared, in regard to this important dispute.

pp. [1–2] 3–36   L

J. Roberts; and A. Dodd   1743

2832 ———*[another edition]

pp. 32

Dublin: Jeremiah Pepyrt   1743

   Thorn-Drury.

2833 GARRICK, DAVID. To the publick. Whereas an appeal to town has this day been dispers'd by Mr. Macklin . . . I humbly hope the publick will suspend their judgments . . . David Garrick

bs.   DFo

[London]   [1743]

———

2834 AN ESSAY ON ACTING: in which will be consider'd the mimical behaviour of a certain fashionable faulty actor, and the laudableness of such unmannerly, as well as inhumane proceedings. To which will be added, A short criticism of his acting Macbeth.

pp. [4] [1] 2–27 [28 (bl.)]   L

W. Bickerton   1744

Garrick first acted Macbeth at D.L. Jan. 7, 1744. Ascribed to Garrick himself by Davies (I, 163–4) and Lowe. "With his usual terror of criticism, he wrote this humorous attack on himself to blunt the censures which he anticipated for his Macbeth." — Lowe.

2835 A LETTER TO MR. GARRICK, on his having purchased a patent for Drury-Lane Play-house.

pp. [2] 1–29 [30]   L

J. Freeman   [1747]

Published June 1747.

2836 [F., E.] *MR. GARRICK'S CONDUCT, as manager of the Theatre-Royal in Drury-Lane, considered. In a letter addressed to him.

pp. 1, 9–27   MB

C. Corbett   [1747]

An unfriendly criticism, signed "E.F." — Lowe.

2837 ———the second edition
pp. [4] 9–27 [28] L
C. Corbett [1747]
Letter dated 18 Oct. 1747, and initialled E.F.

2838 [PHILAUTUS], *pseud. of* Nathaniel Lancaster. The pretty gentleman: or, softness of manners vindicated from the false ridicule exhibited under the character of William Fribble, Esq;
pp. [i–iii] iv [5] 6–36 L
M. Cooper 1747
The introductory address, signed "Philautus," is a mock attack on Garrick; and the whole production is in ridicule of the "Fribbles," a class of effeminate beaux, whom Garrick had shown up in his successful farce of Miss in her Teens—Lowe. *Reprinted in* Fugitive pieces *(1761, etc.). I, 195–221.*

2839 ———another edition, edited by Edmund Goldsmid, F.R.H.S. (Bibliotheca Curiosa.)
pp. [1–9] 10–32 L
Edinburgh: priv. ptd. 1885
"The edition is limited to seventy-five Large Paper Copies, and two hundred and seventy-five Small Paper Copies, issued only to Subscribers."

2840 [JOHNSON, SAMUEL and DAVID GARRICK.] PROLOGUE AND EPILOGUE, spoken at the opening of the Theatre in Drury-Lane 1747.
pp. [1–3] 4–12 L
Printed by E. Cave 1747
Delivered 15th September 1747 on the opening of Drury Lane under Garrick's management. Knapp *349.*

2841 ———*[another edition]
pp. [1] 2–4
Printed by W. Webb [1747?]
Knapp *349. Pirated.*

2842 ———[another edition] The Drury-Lane prologue by Samuel Johnson and the epilogue by David Garrick 1747. Reproduced in type-facsimile from the edition printed by W. Webb.
pp. [i–iv] v [vi], [1] 2–4, [xi–xii] xiii [xiv] L
Oxford University Press; London: Humphrey Milford 1924

———[American edition, of no. 2840, incl. 30 copies on fine paper] New York: Dodd, Mead and Company, 1902.

Johnson's prologue reprinted in Gentleman's Magazine, *Oct. 1747; in Dodsley* Collection of poems *(1748), III, 150; second edition (1748), I, 206, and subsequent editions; Boswell,* Life of Samuel Johnson, *ed. Morley, IV, 389–90;* Poems of Johnson, *ed. D. N. Smith and E. L. McAdam (1941), pp. 51–53;* Works, *vol. VI, ed. E. L. McAdam and G. Milne (1964), pp. 87–90.*

⌘ [Foote, Samuel.] A treatise on the passions ... with a critical enquiry into the theatrical merit of Mr. G——k ... [1747]. *See no. 2770.*

⌘ An examen of the new comedy, call'd "The suspicious husband".... to which is added, A word of advice to Mr. G——rr——ck. 1747. *See no. 2771.*
The "word of advice" is a criticism of Foote's Treatise on the passions.

2843 D——RY-L——NE P——YH——SE BROKE OPEN. In a letter to Mr. G——.
pp. [4] [1] 2–24 L
M. Cooper 1748
On Garrick's relations with the public.

2844 A LETTER TO MR G——K, relative to his treble capacity of manager, actor, and author; with some remarks on *Lethe*.
pp. [1–5] 6–19 [20] MH
Printed and sold by W. Reeve and A. Dodd 1749
Garrick's Lethe *was produced on 2nd January, 1749 at Drury Lane.*

2845 *ODE to Mr. G——r——k.
pp. [1–2] 3–8 DFo
J. Bromage 1749
On his marriage with Eva Maria Violette.

2846 [RAMBLER, HARRY, *pseud.*] *BAYS IN COUNCIL: or, a picture of a green-room. A dramatic poem. Containing the speeches of Mr. G——rr——k, Mr. H——v——d, Mr. S——wd——n, Mr. W——d——d, Mrs. C——e, and Mrs. P——tc——d, a few days before Drury Lane was open'd. To which is added, a poem on Mrs. Bland.
pp. 22 MB
Dublin: printed for the author 1751

2847 [DERRICK, SAMUEL?] FORTUNE, a rhapsody. Inscribed to Mr. Garrick.
pp. [3–4] 5–24 L
R. Manby, and H. S. Cox 1751

2848 THE THEATRICAL MANAGER: a dramatic satire.
pp. [i–iv] v–vi [vii–viii], [1] 2–64 MH
T. Lownds 1751
Advertised in January—LS.

2849 ———[another edition]
pp. [i–ii] iii–iv 5–71 [72] L
Dublin 1751

2850 A POETICAL EPISTLE FROM SHAKESPEAR in Elysium, to Mr. Garrick, at Drury-Lane Theatre. To which is added, A view from Hermon-Hill, near Shrewsbury. A solitudinarian ode.

pp. [1–2] 3–12 [15–16] 17–29 [30 (bl.)] [=28]   L

J. Newbery   1752

Very laudatory of Garrick — Lowe.

✠ Cibber, Theophilus. An epistle from Mr. Theophilus Cibber to David Garrick. 1755. *See no. 2614.*

Cibber complains that he had to close the Haymarket when Drury Lane re-opened for the season.

2851 THE VISITATION; or, an interview between the Ghost of Shakespear and D——v——d G——rr——k, Esq.

pp. [1–3] 4–14   L

Printed for the author   1755

Against the production of dances and pantomimes — Lowe.

2852 ——*[another edition]

1757

STR.

The Chinese Festival 1755

This entertainment was produced 8th November 1755, but, as it was principally performed by foreigners, a patriotic public damned it because we were at war with France. Foote alludes to this in the "Minor", where he speaks of the patriot gingerbread baker in the Borough, who would not suffer three dancers from Switzerland, because he hated the French. Garrick persevered with the piece for six nights, on each of which there was a riot—Lowe.

2853 ANTIGALLICAN, AN, *pseud.* An ode to a player. Written extempore by an Antigallican.

pp. [3] 4–8   DFo

A. More   1755

2854 THE DANCERS DAMN'D; or, the Devil to pay at the old house.

pp. [1–3] 4–20   E

[London]: R. Griffiths   1755

An attack upon the rioters.

2855 SPECTATOR, A, *pseud.* †The nowiad: an heroic poem. Humbly inscrib'd to the most renown'd Tom Thumb the Great, patentee and grand manager of the Old–New–English–French Theatre. In which due honour will be paid to his most noble allies, our truly British spirited sons of Mars. With notes historical and critical. By a spectator.

pp. [1–3] 4–16; lacking pp. 13–16   L

[1755]

Imprint cut off. Another copy at TxU.

2856 HOWARD, HENRY. Visionary interview at the shrine of Shakespear. Inscribed to Mr. Garrick. By Henry Howard.

pp. [1–2] 3–12   DFo

R. Withy and J. Ryall   1756

At this the Bard, with diffidence withdrew,
"Farewell," he cries, "my substitute farewell".

✠ English Critic, An, *pseud.* A letter to Mr. David Hume, on the tragedy of Douglas . . . and the charge against Mr. Garrick. 1757. *See no. 3929.*

2857 [COLMAN, GEORGE.] A LETTER OF ABUSE, to D——d G——k, Esq.

pp. [1–3] 4–26   L

J. Scott   1757

Published in May—Page. Initialled A.B.

2858 [SHIRLEY, WILLIAM.] *BRIEF REMARKS on the original and present state of the drama: to which is added Hecate's prophecy, being a characteristic dialogue betwixt future managers, and their dependents.

1758

A violent attack upon Garrick . . . Davies gives a long account of it — Lowe.

2859 CANDID OBSERVER, A, *pseud.* *A bone for the chroniclers to pick; or a take-off scene from behind the curtain. A poem. By a candid observer of men and things.

1758

A coarsely written and venomous attack on Garrick by one who states, in an advertisement, that he was "taken off" by him. I think it was probably written by Shirley — Lowe.

2860 [RALPH, JAMES.] THE CASE OF AUTHORS by profession or trade, stated. With regard to booksellers, the stage, and the public. No matter by whom.

pp. [4] [1] 2–72 ²65–68 [=76]   L

R. Griffiths   1758

2861 ——[reissue] The case of authors by profession or trade, stated; with regard to booksellers, the stage, and the public. By James Ralph, Esq;

pp. [4] [1] 2–72 65–68 [=76]   L

R. Griffiths   1762

Of James Ralph, Lowe writes: This great party-writer was a disappointed dramatic author; his comedy, The Astrologer, *played at Drury Lane in 1744, having been a failure. For some reason, he conceived a dislike to Garrick, and, in his* Case of Authors by Profession, *made an acrimonious attack on him and the stage, for which the great actor never forgave him. In Davies'* Life of Garrick, *chapter xxi., a full account of Ralph's connection with Garrick will be found.*

2862 A LETTER TO MR. GARRICK on the opening of the Theatre, with observations on the conduct of managers, to actors, authors, and audiences: and particularly to new-performers.

pp. [1–3] 4–19 [20]   L

J. Coote   1758

*The advice is not of the general abusive nature, but is friendly in tone — Lowe. Signed * * * * **

2863 PITTARD, JOSEPH. Observations on Mr. Garrick's acting; in a letter to the Right Hon. the Earl of Chesterfield. By Joseph Pittard.

pp. [1–4] 5–24   L

J. Cooke and J. Coote   1758

An enthusiastic laudation of Garrick in King Lear *— Lowe.*

2864 DRAMATIC AUTHOR, A, *pseud.* A defence of Mr. Garrick, in answer to the letter-writer. With remarks upon plays and players, and the present state of the stage. By a dramatic author.

pp. [2] [1] 2–37 [38]   L

R. Stevens   [1759]

An answer to no. 2865. Published 1 November—LS.

2865 [W., H.] *pseud. of* Edward Purdon. A LETTER to David Garrick, Esq; on opening the Theatre. In which, with great freedom, he is told how he ought to behave.

pp. [2] [1] 2–33 [34]   L

I. Pottinger   1769 [*for* 1759]

Published 13 October 1759—LS. A scurrilous attack, principally on Mossop, who was then leading actor with Garrick. Purdon was, however, compelled to make a public apology for his falsehood and malice. This apology, which is a most abject production, was dated 12 Oct. 1759—Lowe. (The apology appeared in the London Chronicle, VI, 437, p. 362.) *Signed H.W. on p. 33.*

2866 REASONS why David Garrick, Esq; should not appear on the stage, in a letter to John Rich, Esq;

pp. [4] 9–42 [43–44 (bl.)]   L

J. Cooke   1759

A specimen of the "puff oblique." Very laudatory of Garrick, the principal reason given why he should not appear being that, when on the stage, he compelled the entire attention of the audience, to the neglect of the other actors – Lowe. Published October 1759 – LS. Sometimes attributed, without authority, to Garrick himself. Initialled Y.Z.

2867 *REMARKS upon the present conduct and management of the theatre, with strictures on The Rout, Antony and Cleopatra, and The Guardian.

1759

Recorded but not seen by Lowe.

2868 [HILL, *Sir* JOHN, M.D.] TO DAVID GARRICK, Esq; the petition of I. In behalf of herself and her sisters.

pp. [1–3] 4–16   L

M. Cooper and J. Jackson   1759

By Dr. John Hill, complaining that Garrick, in such words as "virtue", &c, pronounced I as if it were U. Garrick replied in a very happy epigram:—
  If it's true, as you say, I have injur'd a letter,
  I'll change my note soon, and I hope for the better.
  May the just rights of letters as well as of men
  Hereafter be fix'd by the tongue and the pen;
  Most devoutly I wish, they may both have their due,
  And that I may be never mistaken for YOU — Lowe.

✠ [Madan, *The Rev.* Martin?] A letter to David Garrick, Esq; occasioned by the intended representation of "The Minor" at the Theatre-Royal in Drury-Lane. *1760. See no. 2780.*

2869 [LLOYD, ROBERT.] †SHAKESPEARE: an epistle to Mr. Garrick; with an ode to genius.

pp. [2] 1–8   L

n.p.   [1760]

Ode missing.

2870 [GILBERT, T.] *SOME REFLECTIONS on the management of a theatre.

pp. [2] 25   MH

J. Cooke   [1760]

On Garrick's management of Drury Lane.

The Fribbleriad

2871 [FITZPATRICK, THADDEUS.] AN ENQUIRY into the real merit of a certain popular performer. In a series of letters, first published in the *Craftsman or Gray's-Inn journal;* with an introduction to D——d G——k, esq.

pp. [2] [i–ii] iii–viii, [1] 2–41 [42]   L

M. Thrush   1760

2872 [GARRICK, DAVID.] THE FRIBBLERIAD.

pp. [i–iii] iv–viii, [1] 2–20; pl. [front.]   L

J. Coote   1761

The principal person in this poem, Fizgig, is a caricature of Fitzpatrick, and is a most ludicrous picture of an effeminate character. Churchill also furiously attacked Fitzpatrick in the "Rosciad," describing him as "A motley figure, of the Fribble tribe", and representing him as a most despicable and contemptible creature — "one of the very worms of the creation", to quote Cooke. — Lowe. Knapp 61. Reprinted in Poetical Works of David Garrick, 1785 (see below no. 2937), I, [11]–34, and in The repository (1777), II, [27]–49; third edition (1790), II, [1]–23. On Fitzpatrick, Garrick, and Churchill, see Grant, p. 460.

2873 *THE MUSES address to D. Garrick Esq; with Harlequin's remonstrance. In answer to the said address.

pp. 23

W. Nicholls   1761
STR.

Churchill's Rosciad 1761

See above nos. 2284–2310.

Riots of 1763

Fitzpatrick must have bitterly regretted his attacks on Garrick. In 1763 he gratified his malevolence by heading a very serious riot, directed against Garrick. The object of the riot was to compel the managers to accept half-price at the end of the third act of every play, new or old, except a new pantomime. After two nights' violence the rioters carried their point. For very shame they had to extort a similar concession from Covent Garden — Lowe. See LS pt. 4, pp. 974–975, 980–982. See also above COVENT GARDEN nos. 1153–1157.

2874 AN APPEAL TO THE PUBLIC in behalf of the manager.

pp. [2] 1–41 [42]   L
Wilson and Fell   1763

2875 A DIALOGUE IN THE GREEN-ROOM upon a disturbance in the pit.

pp. [2] i–viii, [1] 2–32   L
George Burnett   1763

Published 10 February 1763 — LS.

2876 ENEMY TO IMPOSITION, AN, *pseud.* To the frequenters of the theatres.

bs.   DFo
[London]   [1763]

Reprinted in An appeal to the public (*see above no. 2874*).

2877 FIZGIG, or the modern Quixote, a tale: relative to the late disturbances, at Drury-Lane and Covent-Garden Theatres.

pp. [2] 5–13 [14 (bl.)]   L
Printed for the author, and sold by J. Williams 1763

A vigorous attack upon Fitzpatrick — Lowe. Octo-syllabics.

2878 AN HISTORICAL AND SUCCINCT ACCOUNT of the late riots at the theatres of Drury-Lane and Covent-Garden. Interspersed with the principal letters and advertisements that have been published on each side the question.

pp. [2] [5] 6–39 [40 (bl.)]   L
W. Morgan   1763

Published in March.

2879 LADY, A, *pseud.* Theatrical disquisitions: or a review of the late riot at Drury-Lane Theatre, on the 25th and 26th of January, with an impartial examen of the profession and professors of the drama; some few hints on the prerogatives of an audience, and, a short appendix, relative to the more flagrant disturbance committed at Covent-Garden Theatre, on Thursday the 24th of February. By a lady.

pp. [i–ii] iii–iv, 1–36   L
G. Burnet   1763

Against the rioters — Lowe.

2880 O' BLANEY, MURDOCH, *pseud.* Fizgig's triumph. A new song. To the tune of; Stand around my brave boys. Written by Murdoch O' Blaney.

bs.; illus.   MH
Printed for Tristram Shandy, Fleetstreet   1763

*Then since Fiz has the Day, let the Town loud huzza,
    Half price there shall be at both Houses;
Fizgig and his friends, have now got their ends,
    And may treat both themselves and their Spouses.*

2881 OLD MAN OF THE TOWN, AN, *pseud.* Three original letters to a friend in the country, on the cause and manner of the late riot at the Theatre-Royal in Drury-Lane. Letter the first. The introduction — with a theatrical anecdote, the cause of the riot as set forth in the printed paper. Letter the second. The complaint impartially examined; and their proceedings at the Theatre faithfully related, with proper remarks. Letter the third. A review of the condition and usuage [sic] of that Theatre forty years ago: the first rise of latter accounts: the entertainments then given to the public: the salaries, &c. compared with the present: the rights of an audience considered. Remarks on the whole. By an old man of the Town.

pp. [2] [1] 2–39 [40 (bl.)]   L
T. Becket   1763

Dated Jan. 5, 1763.

2882 [GARRICK, DAVID?] THE SICK MONKEY, a fable. "Thursday Afternoon, David Garrick, Esq; arrived at his House in Southampton-Street, Covent-Garden". Public Advertiser, April 27, 1765.

pp. [2] [1] 2–23 [24]; pl. [front.]   L
J. Fletcher, and Co.   1765

Shortly after the troubles referred to in the previous pamphlets Garrick took a tour on the Continent. On his return he published this pamphlet for the purpose of anticipating the censure and ridicule he expected, though with what reason it is difficult to see, to greet him on his return. It is a stupid production; the moral of it being that Garrick was not to disturb himself about the pamphlets in criticism and abuse of him which were published. The last two lines of the poem advise him to

"Keep the poison from your HEAD,
    And clap it to your TAIL"—

a sufficiently broad point!—Lowe. Reprinted in The

Poetical Works of David Garrick (*1785*), *I, 35 (see below no. 2937*). Knapp *145*.

❌ [Latter, Mary] The siege of Jerusalem . . . To which is prefixed, by way of introduction, An essay on the mystery and mischiefs of stage-craft. 1763. *See no. 3972.*

Occasioned by the rejection of her play by the managers.

2883 THE INTERVIEW; or Jack Falstaff's ghost. A poem. Inscribed to David Garrick, Esq.

pp. [1–5] 6–23 [24]   L

Printed for the author, and sold by S. Bladon; and
F. Blyth   1766

Visit of the ghost of Quin to Garrick — Lowe.

2884 [WARNER, RICHARD.] A LETTER TO DAVID GARRICK, Esq. concerning a glossary to the plays of Shakespeare, on a more extensive plan than has hitherto appeared. To which is annexed, a specimen.

pp. [1–2] 3–110 [111 (errata) 112 (bl.)]   L

Printed for the author: and sold by T. Davies;
T. Beckett and P. A. De Hondt   1768

The letter dated 1 January 1768 and signed Richard Warner.

❌ The Masquerade; a poem. 1768. *See no. 1455.*

Refers to Garrick being present at a ball given by the King of Denmark and his playing of Lusignan in Zara the following night.

Shakespeare Jubilee 1769

In honour of Shakespeare, Garrick got up his famous Jubilee celebration at Stratford, which gave rise to numerous satirical productions. It seems to have been really rather a silly business — Lowe. *For a contemporary account, see* J[ames] S[olas] Dodd, *Essays and poems (1770), pp. 245–278. Recent accounts are Christian Deelman, The Great Shakespeare Jubilee (1964); and Johanne M. Stochholm, Garrick's Folly (1964).*

2885 G[ARRICK], D[AVID]. An ode upon dedicating a building, and erecting a statue, to Shakespeare, at Stratford upon Avon. By D.G.

pp. [4] [1] 2–34   L

T. Becket, and P. A. De Hondt   1769

Subjoined to the ode are "Testimonies to the genius and merits of Shakespeare."—Lowe. Knapp *105.*

2886 AN ODE upon dedicating a building to Shakespeare which was erected by the subscription of the noblemen & gentlemen in the neighbourhood of Stratford upon Avon. The music composed by Dr. Arne.

pp. [2] [1] 2–4 [5 (bl.)] 6–12 [13 (bl.)] 14–27 [28];
(bl.) engr.   L

John Johnston   [1769]

2887 ———*[another edition]

pp. 27; engr.   StdC

Lukey and Johnston   [1769]

2888 ———[another edition] Ode upon dedicating the Town Hall, and erecting a statue to Shakspeare, during the Jubilee at Stratford-upon-Avon, 1769.

pp. [i–iii] iv [5] 6–16   L

Stratford-upon-Avon: John Bacon   1827

Knapp *105.*
Reprinted separately as an appendix to the Gloucester Journal (*1769*), *and in many other periodicals September 1769 (Knapp 105); also in* The repository (*1777*), *I, 69–99; the third edition (1790), I, [63] 64–99 with a parody, "Ode on dedicating a building and erecting a statue to Le Stue".*

2889 ANTI-MIDAS: a Jubilee preservative from unclassical, ignorant, false, and invidious criticism.

pp. [1–2] 3–35 [36]   L

n.p.   1769

A defence of Garrick's Ode — Lowe. *The four articles in* The Public Ledger *by "Longinus" [Thomas Sheridan], against which the defence is chiefly directed, are reprinted [pp. 23–33].*

2890 CAREY, GEORGE SAVILLE. Shakespeare's jubilee, a masque. By George Saville Carey.

pp. [1–6] 7–23 [24 (advt.)]   L

T. Becket and P. A. De Hondt   1769

Reprinted in Carey's Analects in Verse and Prose (*1770*), *II, 129–149.*

2891 GARRICK'S VAGARY: or, England run mad. With particulars of the Stratford Jubilee.

pp. [iii–v] vi–viii, [1] 2–55 [56]   L

S. Bladon   1769

2892 *LIST of the horses enter'd at the Jubilee Race.

J. Keating   1769

PH *and* KB.

2893 [GENTLEMAN, FRANCIS.] THE STRATFORD JUBILEE. A new comedy of two acts, as it has been lately exhibited at Stratford upon Avon, with great applause. To which is prefixed Scrub's trip to the Jubilee.

pp. [8] [1] 2–40   L

T. Lowndes, and J. Bell   1769

Reviewed in the London Chronicle *19–21, September 1769.*

2894 [THOMPSON, EDWARD.] TRINCULO'S TRIP to the Jubilee.

pp. [4] i–iv 5–47 [48 (advt.)]   MH

C. Moran; W. Flexney; R. Riddley   1769

  Reviewed in the London Chronicle *7–9 Nov. 1769.*

2895 JARVIS, J. Correct detail of the ceremonies attending the Shakspearean gala, celebrated at Stratford-upon-Avon, on Monday, Tuesday, and Wednesday, April 23, 24, and 25, 1827; together with some account of "Garrick's jubilee," in 1769; by J. Jarvis, reporter to the London journals.

pp. [1–5] 6–30 [31 (advt.) 32 (bl.)]; pl. [1]   L

Stratford-upon-Avon: J. Bacon; London: J. Onwhyn
[1827]

2896 A CONCISE ACCOUNT OF GARRICK'S JUBILEE, held at Stratford-upon-Avon, in honour of Shakspeare, in 1769. And of the commemorative festivals in 1827 and 1830.

pp. [1–5] 6–24   L

Stratford-upon-Avon: J. Ward   1830

2897 [WILLIAMS, DAVID.] A LETTER TO DAVID GARRICK, Esq. on his conduct as principal manager and actor at Drury-Lane.

pp. [6] [1] 2–39 [40]   L

S. Bladon   1772

2898 ——second edition. With a preface and notes, by the editor.

pp. [10] [1] 2–30   L

J. Williams; and G. Corrall   [1776?]

  This pamphlet was written by the Rev. David Williams, a friend of Mossop's, and is written in that actor's interest; but how Williams expected to benefit his friend by abusing Garrick, is a mystery. Of this Williams a very unfavourable impression is conveyed in the "Garrick Correspondence" — Lowe. Reprinted in Thomas Morris, General view of the life and writings of the Rev. David Williams (J. Ridgway, 1792), pp. 25–68.

2899 [COMBE, WILLIAM.] SANITAS, daughter of Æsculapius. To David Garrick, Esq. A poem.

pp. [4] [1] 2–32; errata slip; vignette on t.p.   L

G. Kearsley, H. Parker, W. Shropshire   1772

  To Garrick, during an illness, wishing him recovery — Lowe.

Kenrick's Dispute with Garrick 1772

"Love in the suds" *is a most vile attack on Garrick by that contemptible hound, Dr. Kenrick. "Nyky" is Isaac Bickerstaffe, who had to quit this country to escape trial for an unnatural crime. Kenrick, in this poem, insinuates that Garrick was a participator in the crime — Lowe.*

2900 KENRICK, WILLIAM. A letter to David Garrick, Esq. From William Kenrick, LL.D.

pp. [2] [i] ii [iii–iv], [1] 2–25 [26]   L

J. Wheble   1772

  Pp. [i]–ii: letter; p. [iii]: "Love in the suds; a town eclogue. Being the lamentation of Roscius for the loss of his Nyky. With annotations by the editor. J. Wheble. 1772"; pp. [1]–25: eclogue.

2901 ——the second edition

pp. [1] [i–ii] iii [iv–v], [1] 2–31 [32]   L

J. Wheble   1772

  p. [iv]: "Love in the suds; a town eclogue. Being the lamentation of Roscius for the loss of his Nyky. With annotations by the editor; and an appendix, containing queries and answers relative to the personal satisfaction, pretended to have been required of the author of the above eclogue, by the lamentable Roscius."

2902 ——the third edition

pp. [1] [i–ii] iii [iv–v], [1] 2–31 [32–34]   L

J. Wheble   1772

  L has two 'third editions.' The one described above is the genuine third edition: the other contains the title page only, bound in with a later edition of Love in the Suds. *The latter copy would seem to be that described by Lowe as 'third edition'.*

2903 ——Love in the Suds; a town eclogue. Being the lamentation of Roscius for the loss of his Nyky. With annotations and an appendix. The fourth edition.

pp. [i–iii], [1] 2–31 [32]   E

J. Wheble   1772

2904 ——Love in the suds; a town eclogue. Being the lamentation of Roscius for the loss of his Nyky. With annotations and an appendix. The fifth edition.

pp. [i–iii] iv, [1] 2–44   MH

J. Wheble   1772

  To this edition are added verses which appeared in the Morning Chronicle *on this subject. Those in defence of Garrick were signed "Benedick", and were written by Joseph Reed — Lowe.*

2905 KENRICK, [WILLIAM]. A letter to David Garrick, Esq. occasioned by his having moved the Court of King's Bench against the publisher of *Love in the suds, or the lamentation of Roscius for the loss of his Nyky.* By Dr. Kenrick.

pp. [2] 1–34   E

J. Wheble   1772

  Kenrick made a public apology in the Publick Advertiser, *23rd November 1772, and promised to withdraw and suppress the sale of the pamphlet — Lowe.*

⌘ Kenrick, *Dr* William. A letter to David Garrick, Esq., on the non-performance of "Falstaff's wedding". 1772. *See no. 3970.*

2906 THE KENRICKAD: a poem.
pp. [4] [1] 2–16 L
W. Griffin 1772

A strong attack on Kenrick — Lowe. *Signed "Ariel" on p. 16.*

2907 THE RECANTATION and confession of Doctor Kenrick, L.L.D.
pp. [2] [1] 2–12 L
Allen 1772

A mock recantation, prefaced by a rather coarse dialogue between Kenrick and his publisher, John Wheble — Lowe. *The genuine recantation appeared in the* Publick Advertiser, *23 Nov. 1772. Attributed by Kenrick to "that filthy yahoo, Paul Hiffernan".*

2908 LLOYD, E[VAN]. An epistle to David Garrick, Esq. By E. Lloyd, M.A.
pp. [1–4] 5–24; pl., fold. [front.] L
Printed for the author: and sold by Messrs. Richardson and Urquhart 1773

Inter alia, *refers with unmeasured condemnation to Kenrick's* Love in the Suds — Lowe. *In verse. See also below no. 2909.*

2909 SCRIBLERIUS FLAGELLARIUS, *pseud. of* William Kenrick. A whipping for the Welch parson. Being a comment on the Rev. Mr. Evan Lloyd's "Epistle to David Garrick, Esq". By Scriblerius Flagellarius. To which is superadded the parson's text.
pp. [4] [1] 2–23 [24] L
T. Evans 1773

⌘ Miles, William Augustus. A letter to Sir John Fielding . . . occasioned by his extraordinary request to Mr. Garrick for the suppression of *The Beggars Opera* 1773. *See no. 3907.*

⌘ [R., T.] An appeal to the publick, from the judgment of a certain manager. 1774. *See no. 4008.*

2910 THE POETICAL REVIEW, a poem. Being a satirical display of the literal characters of Mr. G*rr*ck, Mr. C*lm*n, Mr. Sh*r***n, Genl. B**rg***e, Mr. M*ckl*n, Dr. K*nr**k. The Canonical Duellist, &c. &c. &c. With a word to the Critical, London, and Monthly Reviewers. The third edition, with additions.
pp. [i–iii] iv, [1] 2–28 L
For the author [*ca.* 1775]

Favourable to Garrick: abusive of Kenrick — Lowe.

2911 [PRATT, SAMUEL JACKSON.] GARRICK'S LOOKING-GLASS: or, the art of rising on the stage. A poem. In three cantos. Decorated with dramatic characters. By the author of *****.
pp. [4] [1] 2–72 L
London: T. Evans; Dublin: W. Wilson; Edinburgh: W. Creech 1776

2912 ———[another edition]
pp. [1–3] 4–40 L
Dublin: the United Company of Booksellers 1776

2913 [MORE, HANNAH.] ODE TO DRAGON, Mr. Garrick's house-dog, at Hampton.
pp. [1–5] 6–14 [15–16 (bl.)] MH
T. Cadell 1777

A panegyric of Garrick — Lowe.

2914 PURSUIT AFTER HAPPINESS: a poem. To which is added, An ode to Mr. Garrick, on his quitting the stage. Also An elegy on the death of Mr. Barry.
pp. [i–iii] iv, [1] 2–43 [44] L
G. Kearsly 1777

The first sketch of the "Ode to Mr. Garrick" has appeared before, but is now enlarged and corrected" — Preface.

⌘ [McNally, Leonard?] The apotheosis of Punch . . . with a monody on the death of the late Master Punch. 1779. *See no. 2929.*

An attempt to ridicule Sheridan's Monody.

2915 BATH, — a simile. Bath, — a conversation-piece. Bath, — a medley. Preceded by A prologue to the critics; succeeded by A rhapsody, on the death of Mr. Garrick.
pp. [1–3] 4–61 [62] L
T. Whieldon and Co., and R. Faulder 1779

2916 [TASKER, WILLIAM.] AN ELEGY on the death of David Garrick, Esq.
pp. [*12*] L
For the author, printed at Laidler's Office 1779

2917 ———the second edition, with additions.
pp. [*12*] L
For the author, printed at Laidler's Office 1779

2918 *A FUNERAL EULOGIUM to the memory of David Garrick.
1779

Recorded but not seen by Lowe.

2919 GARRICK IN THE SHADES; or, a peep into Elysium; a farce: never offered to the managers of the Theatres-Royal.

pp. [4] [1] 2–44   L

J. Southern   1779

An attack on Garrick, conspicuous for its bad taste, it being published shortly after his death. The "Biographia Dramatica" says: "This seems to be the production of some disappointed author, whose resentment extended beyond the grave." — Lowe.

2920 MELMOTH, COURTNEY, *pseud.* of Samuel Jackson Pratt. The shadows of Shakespeare: a monody, occasioned by the death of Mr. Garrick. Being a prize poem, written for the vase at Bath-Easton.

pp. [3–4] 5–24   L
Bath: printed by R. Cruttwell   [1779?]

2921 ———the second edition

pp. [3–4] 5–24   MH
Bath: printed by R. Cruttwell   [1780?]

2922 MEYLER, WILLIAM. *A monody on the death of David Garrick.

Bath   1779
  CBEL.

2923 OLD COMEDIAN, AN, *pseud.* The life and death of David Garrick, Esq. the celebrated English Roscius. Giving an account of his figure, face, voice, and education. His great powers both in tragedy and comedy are considered, and Messrs. Alleyn, Mohun, Hart, Nokes, Leigh, Betterton, Wilks, Cibber, and Barry, compared with Mr. Garrick. Also Mr. Garrick's celebrated speech on his retiring from the stage in 1776, the procession and ceremony at his funeral, substance of his will, account of the Jubilee at Stratford upon Avon, with part of the ode and songs on that occasion; his best prologues, epilogues, bon mots, repartees, &c. To which is added, The life of Edward Alleyn, the celebrated comedian in the reigns of Queen Elizabeth and James the first, founder of Dulwich College, and who was called the Roscius of his time. Also a curious anecdote of Alleyn, Shakespeare, and Ben Jonson. By an old comedian.

pp. [4] 1–64   L
Sold by J. Pridden; S. Bladon; J. Mathews   1779

A very catchpenny production — Lowe.

2924 ———The life and death of David Garrick, Esq. the celebrated English Roscius. In which his great powers both in tragedy and comedy are considered, and Messrs Alleyn, Mohun, Hart, Nokes, Leigh, Betterton, Wilks, Cibber, and Barry, compared with Mr. Garrick. Also Churchill's beautiful character of Mr. Garrick. Lines from Sheridan's Monody on the

death of Mr. Garrick, as spoken by Mrs. Yates, at Drury-Lane Theatre. Prize Monody on the death of Mr. Garrick, for the vase at Bath Easton, by Miss Seward. Extract from "Thespis; or a critical examination into the merits of the performers at Drury-Lane Theatre." Mr. Garrick's *celebrated* speech on retiring from the stage, in 1776. The procession and ceremony at his funeral. Substance of his will. His best prologues and epilogues. Part of the ode and songs written by Mr. Garrick for the Jubilee at Stratford upon Avon. Epitaph written by Mr. Garrick at his friend Mr. Henry Hoare's, of Stourhead, Wilts. Anecdote of Mrs. Garrick and Lady Burlington. Also anecdotes, bon mots, &c. of Garrick, Quin, Foote, Mrs. Woffington, and many other theatrical performers. . . . Second edition. With considerable additions.

pp. [8] 1–72   L
Sold by J. Pridden; S. Bladon; J. Mathews   1779

2925 [SHERIDAN, RICHARD BRINSLEY.] VERSES to the memory of Garrick. Spoken as a monody, at the Theatre Royal in Drury-Lane.

pp. [1–6] 7–15 [16]; pl. [front.]   L
T. Evans; J. Wilkie; E. and C. Dilly; A. Portal; and
J. Almon   1779

A "second issue" is recorded by Rhodes, with the single correction of "difference" to "deference" in the preface. Rhodes, III, 218, no. 3.

2926 ———the second edition

pp. [1–6] 7–15 [16 (bl.)]; pl. [front.]   L
T. Evans; J. Wilkie; E. and C. Dilly; A. Portal; and
J. Almon   1779

2927 ———[another edition] The airs and chorusses, in *The monody, on the death of Mr. Garrick.* Set to music by Mr. Linley.

pp. [1] 2–3 [4]   L
[London]   [1779]

Probably sold at the theatre — Rhodes.

2928 ———[another edition] The tears of genius. A monody. On the death of Mr. Garrick. As written by Richard Brinsley Sheridan, Esq.

pp. [1–5] 6–8 [7] 8–14 [=16]   L
Dublin: C. Jackson   1780

Slightly abridged.
Reprinted in Poems selected and printed by a small party of English, who made this amusement a substitute for society, which the disturbed situation of the country prevented their enjoying (Strasburg: [priv. ptd.], February 1792), pp. [46]–50; in Rhodes, III, 213–216. See also below no. 2929.

2929 [McNALLY, LEONARD?] THE APOTHEO-SIS OF PUNCH; a satirical masque: with a monody on the death of the late master Punch. As now performing at the Patagonian Theatre, Exeter 'Change, with universal applause.

pp. [6] 9–40   L

J. Wenman; F. Newbery; and W. Thompson   1779

An attempt to ridicule Sheridan's Monody on Garrick. The "Biographia Dramatica" . . . describes it as malignant without merit. — Lowe. Dedication to R. B. Sheridan is signed "Plunder".

2930 DAVIES, THOMAS. Memoirs of the life of David Garrick, Esq. interspersed with characters and anecdotes of his theatrical contemporaries. The whole forming a history of the stage, which includes a period of thirty-six years. By Thomas Davies.

2 vols. pp. [20] [1] 2–304 *305–*312 305–336; pl. [front.]; + pp. [14] [1] 2–202 *203–*206 203–416   L

Printed for the author   1780

2931 ——[another edition]

2 vols. pp. [16] [1] 2–274; pl. [front.] + pp. [12] [1] 2–311 [312 (errata)]   L

Dublin: J. Williams, W. Hallhead, E. Cross, C. Jenkin, L. Flin, W. Gilbert, T. Walker, W. Wilson, L. White, J. Beatty, and R. Burton   1780

From the first edition.

2932 ——a new edition.

2 vols. pp. [8] [i] ii–viii, [1] 2–344; pl. [front.] + pp. [16] [1] 2–429 [430 (bl.) 431 (advt.) 432 (bl.)]   L

Printed for the author   1780

With corrections and a new appendix.

2933 ——third edition

2 vols. pp. [16] [1] 2–352; pl. [front.]; + pp. [16] [1] 2–434 [435–436 (advts.)]   E

Printed for the author   1781

With corrections.

2934 ——fourth edition: to which is added an accurate index.

2 vols. pp. [16] [1] 2–368; pl. [front.] + pp. [16] [1] 2–471 [472]   L

Printed for the author   1784

2935 ——a new edition, with ample additions and illustrations, in the form of notes [by Stephen Jones].

2 vols. pp. [i–v] vi–vii [viii–ix] x [xi] xii [xiii] xiv–xxi [xxii (errata)], [1] 2–381 [382]; pl. [front.] + pp. [i–v] vi–xii, [1] 2–502   L

Longman, Hurst, Rees, and Orme   1808

——[American edition] Boston: Wells & Lilly, 1818.

2936 [BUTT, GEORGE.] A DIALOGUE between the Earl of C——d and Mr. Garrick, in the Elysian shades.

pp. [2] [1–2] 3–30   L

Printed by J. Nichols   1785

Very laudatory of Garrick and Dr. Johnson — Lowe. Composed "as a votive offering" for Johnson's grave. Reprinted in Butt's Poems (Kidderminster, 1793), with omissions.

2937 GARRICK, DAVID. The poetical works of David Garrick, Esq. Now first collected into two volumes. With explanatory notes.

2 vols. pp. [4] [i–iii] iv–lxvii [lxviii], misnumbering lxvi as "lvi" and lxvii as "lvii", [1–2] 3–224 + [4] [225] 226–540 [541–543 (advts.) 544 (bl.)]   L

George Kearsley   1785

2938 GARRICK'S JESTS; or, genius in high glee. Containing all the jokes of the wits of the present age, *viz.* Mr. Garrick, Ld. Lyttleton, Mr. Fox, Ld. Mansf——, Mr. Burke, Mr. Foote, Mr. Selwyn, Dutchess of K. Lady H——, Lady T——, &c. Being humorous, lively, comical, queer, satirical droll, smart repartees; facetious, merry bon mots, &c. To which are added, A new selection of epigrams, poems conundrums, toasts, sentiments, hob-nobs, &c. now in fashion, and the favourite new songs sung last season at Vauxhall.

pp. [1–2] 3–11 [12], ²[1] 2–148 [=160]; pl. [front.]   L

Charles Steele, and A. Milne   [1790?]

2939 ANDERSON, J. W. The manner pointed out in which the Common Prayer was read in private by the late Mr. Garrick, for the instruction of a young clergyman: from whose manuscript notes this pamphlet is composed. By J. W. Anderson, A.M.

pp. [1–5] 6–78 [79–80 (bl.)]   DFo

F. and C. Rivington   1797

2940 ——the second edition

pp. [3–5] 6–78   L

F. and C. Rivington; R. Faulder   1797

2941 ——Garrick's mode of reading the liturgy of the Church of England. A new edition, with notes, and a preliminary discourse on public reading, by Richard Cull, tutor in elocution.

pp. [i–v] vi–xiv [xv–xvi], [1] 2–143 [144]   L

London: John W. Parker; Cambridge: J. and J. J. Deighton   1840

2942 MURPHY, ARTHUR. The life of David Garrick, Esq. By Arthur Murphy, Esq.

2 vols. pp. [4] [i] ii–xxv [xxvi], [1] 2–389 [390]; pl. [front.] + pp. [4] [i] ii–xvi, [1] 2–387 [388]   E
J. Wright   1801

2943 ———[another edition]
pp. [4] [i] ii–xxxi [xxxii], [1] 2–507 [508 (bl.)]   L
Dublin: Messrs. Wogan, Burnet, Porter, Moore, Colbert, Fitzpatrick, Jones, Dornin, Stockdale, Mercier and Codd   1801

———[French edition] Vie de David Garrick suivie de deux lettres de M. Noverre à Voltaire sur ce célèbre acteur, et de l'histoire du théâtre anglais depuis son origine jusqu'à la fin du 17e siècle, par A. Murphy et traduit p. Marigney, Paris, 1798.

———[French edition] Mémoires sur Garrick et sur Macklin, traduits de l'anglais par le traducteur des oeuvres de Walter Scott; précédés d'une histoire abrégée du théâtre anglais, par M. Després (Collection des mémoires sur l'art dramatique, publiés ou traduits par Mon. Andrieux [F.G.J.S.] et al.). Paris, 1822.

The memoir of Macklin is translated from Kirkman's Memoirs.

———[French edition] Mémoires de Mlle Clairon, de Lekain, de Préville, de Dazincourt, de Molé, de Garrick, de Goldoni, ed. F. S. Barrière. Paris, 1846.

Severely abridged.

✖ Wilkinson, Tate. Original anecdotes . . . with remarks on Mr. Murphy's "Life of Garrick." [ca. 1805]. See no. 3641.

2944 [REYNOLDS, Sir JOSHUA.] JOHNSON AND GARRICK.
pp. [1–3] 4–15 [16]   L
[Not published.] Printed by Nichols, Son and Bentley   1816

The prefatory note says: "The following jeu d'esprit was written by Sir Joshua Reynolds to illustrate a remark which he had made, 'that Dr. Johnson considered Garrick as his property, and would never suffer anyone to praise or abuse him but himself.'" In the first of these supposed dialogues, Sir Joshua himself, by high encomiums upon Garrick, is represented as drawing down upon him Johnson's censure; in the second, Mr. Gibbon, by taking the opposite side, calls forth his praise — Lowe. Written ca. 1790. The MS copy for the printer is at Yale University Library. Published in 1816 for Mary Palmer, Lady Thomond, Reynolds' niece. Reprinted in the London New Monthly Magazine (1816), in various biographies, and, with annotations, in Johnsonian Miscellanies (1897). See F. W. Hilles, The Literary Career of Sir Joshua Reynolds (1936), pp. 146–150.

2945 ———[another edition] Two dialogues with an introduction by R. Brimley Johnson (Cayme Press Pamphlet No. 9).

pp. [1–4] 5–31 [32]   L
The Cayme Press   1927

✖ Posthumous letters, from various celebrated men. London & Edinburgh. 1820. See no. 2630.

Letters from Garrick, pp. 231–325.

Garrick Sale Catalogues 1823–1825

For the sale of Garrick's house and villa at the death of his wife see SALE CATALOGUES nos. 77–87. For catalogues of Garrickiana see especially nos. 76, 120, 129–130.

———

2946 GARRICK'S CUP, carved from Shakespeare's mulberry tree. This celebrated Shakespearian relic . . .
bs.; illus.   MH
[London]   [1825?]
Offered for sale at two hundred guineas by J. Johnson.

✖ Jarvis, J. Correct detail of the ceremonies attending the Shakspearean gala . . . 1827 . . . Together with some account of "Garrick's Jubilee" in 1769. Stratford-upon-Avon. [1827]. See no. 2895.

2947 DANIEL, GEORGE. Garrick in the green room! A biographical and critical analysis of a picture, painted by William Hogarth, and engraved by William Ward. By George Daniel.
pp. [1–3] 4–33 [34 (bl.)]; pl., fold. [front.]   L
James Webb Southgate   1829
The picture represents Garrick sitting speaking with great animation, surrounded by Hogarth and some members of his company — Lowe.

✖ A concise account of Garrick's Jubilee . . . in 1769. And of the commemorative festivals in 1827 and 1830. Stratford-upon-Avon. 1830. See no. 2896.

2948 [BOADEN, JAMES, ed?] THE PRIVATE CORRESPONDENCE of David Garrick with the most celebrated persons of his time; now first published from the originals, and illustrated with notes, and a new biographical memoir of Garrick.
2 vols. pp. [12] [i] ii–lxiv, [1] 2–660; pl. [front.] + pp. [i–v] vi–xii, [1] 2–636   L
Henry Colburn and Richard Bentley   1831–1832

2949 ———*second edition
2 vols; port.
    1835
CBEL.

2950 [BUNN, ALFRED?] ODE TO DAVID GARRICK, by one of his descendants, and dedicated by him to the Garrick Club.

pp. [1–3] 4–7 [8 (bl.)]   L
                                            1847

The DFo copy is bound in a volume with an early label, "Facetiae Bunn".

2951 FITZGERALD, PERCY [HETHERINGTON]. The life of David Garrick; from original family papers, and numerous published and unpublished sources. By Percy Fitzgerald, M.A., F.S.A.

2 vols. pp. [i–vii] viii–ix [x–xi] xii–xvii [xviii], [1] 2–450; pls. [front., 1]; inset, fold. [1] + pp. [i–v] vi–vii [viii], [1] 2–492; pls. [front., 1 (facsim.)]   L

Tinsley Brothers   1868

2952 ———new and revised edition, containing additional important matter.

pp. [i–vii] viii–ix [x–xi] xii–xvi, [1] 2–480; pl. [front.]; inset, fold. [1]   L

Simpkin, Marshall, Hamilton, Kent, & Co., Ltd.   1899

2953 SMYTH, JAMES. David Garrick. By James Smyth.

pp. [1–5] 6–80   L
William Reeves   [1887]

2954 KNIGHT, JOSEPH. David Garrick by Joseph Knight, F.S.A. With etched portrait by W. Boucher from a painting by Gainsborough in the possession of Mrs. Kay.

pp. [i–v] vi [vii (errata) viii (bl.)], [1] 2–346 [347 (advts.) 348 (bl.)]; pl. [front.]   NbU

Kegan Paul, Trench, Trübner & Co., Ltd.   1894

"Originally intended to form one of a series of lives of actors" — Preface.

2955 ———[large paper issue]
pp. [2] [i–v] vi [vii (errata) viii (bl.)], [1] 2–346 [347 (advt.) 348 (bl.)]; pl. [front.]

Kegan Paul, Trench, Trübner & Co., Ltd.   1894

JFA. *"This large paper edition consists of one hundred copies, all of which are numbered."*

2956 RUSSELL, *Sir* EDWARD [*Baron* Russell of Liverpool]. *Garrick, a lecture.

Liverpool   [1895?]
  Chase.

Gay, John (1685–1732)

Most famous, theatrically, as the author of The Beggar's Opera, *which was produced at Lincoln's Inn Fields on 29th January, 1728, and was acted at least sixty-two times in its first season — Lowe. See also* THEORY AND CRITICISM *nos. 3904–3908 (Beggar's Opera); also above* FENTON, LAVINIA *nos. 2746–2752.*

2957 [CURLL, EDMUND.] THE LIFE OF MR. JOHN GAY, author of *The Beggar's Opera*, &c.

pp. [8] [1] 2–72; vignette on t.p.   L
E. Curll   1733

Advertised 1st February — Straus. Dedication signed E.C. The half-title reads: The life of Mr. Gay. With the epitaph, intended for his monument, written by himself.

Gentleman, Francis (1728–1784)

Actor, dramatic author, and editor of Bell's Edition of Shakespeare. *He was Mossop's schoolfellow, and the particulars given of this unfortunate actor in the preface to* The Modish Wife *are very valuable. The Dramatic Censor is also valuable for its criticisms of the actors— Lowe. See* AUTHOR INDEX.

German Reeds, The

See below REED, THOMAS GERMAN *no. 3440.*

Giardini, Felice

See above THE LONDON THEATRE *no. 1454 (King's Theatre).*

Giffard, Henry

Proprietor of Goodman's Fields. For the opening of Goodman's Fields under Giffard and the controversy over the Licensing Bill of 1735 see above nos. 158–172.

Gilbert, *Sir* William Schwenk (1836–1911)

One of the most notable personages in the theatrical world. His series of comic operas, written in conjunction with Sir Arthur Sullivan, have had a sustained popularity which is as phenomenal as it is well deserved — Lowe. He is particularly associated with D'Oyly Carte at the Savoy Theatre. His manner and short temper led him into many disagreements with his colleagues. See below HODSON, HENRIETTA *nos. 3037, 3038.*

Glyn, Isabella (*Mrs.* E. S. Dallas) (1823–1889)

Actress. Her real name was Gearns.

2958 OPINIONS of the press on Miss Glyn's readings.

pp. [1–3] 4–23 [24 (bl.)]
[London?]   [1866–7]
  IKF.

2959 OPINIONS of the press on Miss Glyn's reading of "Hamlet".

pp. [1–3] 4–12   [1867]
  IKF.
  These readings were given at St. James's Hall.

Gomersal, William

Actor and lessee.

2960 GOMERSAL, W[ILLIA]M. *No chestnuts! Being anecdotes of the stage, by Wm. Gomersal. Lessee of the Theatre Royal, Worcester; formerly lessee of the Theatre Royal, Hull; the Theatre Royal, Sheffield; and Her Majesty's Opera House, Aberdeen.

pp. 1–58, front.   AP

Worcester: Worcestershire Newspapers and General Printing Company   [1891]

> *In part reprinted from The Worcestershire Chronicle. An account of Mr. Gomersal's career as actor and lessee, with humorous anecdotes.*

Goodall, *Mrs.* Charlotte (formerly *Miss* Stanton) (1765–1830)

An actress at Drury Lane.

2961 CRIM. CON. Trial between Thomas Goodall, Esq. Plaintiff, and William Fletcher, attorney at law, (of 13, Took's Court, Chancery Lane,) Defendant. For criminal conversation with the plaintiff's wife. Before Lord Ellenborough, and a special jury, in the Court of King's Bench, on Monday, July 19, 1813. Damages, £5000. Taken in short hand, by an eminent reporter.

pp. [4] [1] 2–52   L

C. J. Barrington   1813

2962 CRIM. CON. or the love-sick lawyer!! The trial between Mr. Goodall, (admiral of Hayti,) plaintiff, and Mr. Fletcher, (Attorney-at-law,) defendant, for criminal conversation with the plaintiff's wife, containing the curious love-letters at full length. Tried at the Court of King's Bench, Westminster, before Lord Ellenborough and a special jury, on Monday, July 19, 1813, when a verdict was given for the plaintiff, damages — £5,000. The third edition.

pp. [1–3] 4–22   L

John Fairburn   [1813]

Gosson, Stephen (1554–1624)

Mr. Arber describes Gosson as "Poet, Actor, Dramatist, Satirist, and Preacher." He acted and wrote plays when a young man, but saw the error of his ways, and became one of the most earnest enemies of the evils of the playhouse— Lowe. See AUTHOR INDEX.

Grain, [Richard] Corney (1844–1895)

Entertainer and barrister. See also below REED, THOMAS GERMAN no. 3440.

2963 GRAIN, [RICHARD] CORNEY. Corney Grain. By himself.

pp. [i–iii] iv [5] 6–130   L

John Murray   1888

> *Based on four articles in Murray's Magazine, vol. III (1888).*

Griffin, Benjamin (1680–1740)

An actor of great merit; author of several plays—Lowe. See no. 3914.

Griffith, *Mrs.* Elizabeth (1720?–1793)

Dramatist and actress.

2964 GRIFFITH, *Mrs.* [ELIZABETH]. The morality of Shakespeare's drama illustrated. By Mrs. Griffith.

pp. [i–iii] iv [v] vi–xiii [xiv–xvi], [1] 2–528; pl. [front.]   L

T. Cadell   1775

2965 ——[another edition]

2 vols. pp. [i–ii] iii–xiv, [2] 1–298 + [4] [1–3] 4–307 [308]   L

Dublin: J. Beatty   1777

Grimaldi, Joseph (1778–1837)

The most famous of clowns — Lowe.

2966 GRIMALDI.

pp. [1 (ptd. and embossed) 2–4 (bl.)]   MH

n.p.   [1811?]

> *A poem in eleven stanzas, in praise of Grimaldi, beginning,*
>
> > *Who is it, tell me generous few,*
> > *That strives our spirits to renew,*
> > *When sad'ning care does us pursue?*
> > *GRIMALDI.*

2967 BOZ, *ed., pseud.* of Charles Dickens. Memoirs of Joseph Grimaldi. Edited by "Boz". With illustrations by George Cruikshank.

2 vols. pp. [i–v] vi–xix [xx (bl.) xxi (list of "embellishments") xxii (bl.)], [1] 2–288; pls. [front., 6] + pp. [i–v] vi–ix [x (bl.)], [1] 2–263 [264 (colophon)]; pls. [front., 5]   L

Richard Bentley   1838

> Cohn 237 (twelve etchings by Cruikshank). Eckel (*1932*) *pp. 140–141. With 36 pages of advertisements bound in at the end of volume 2, as issued. The frontispiece to volume 1 is from a portrait by S. Raven; it appears in all the editions. According to Cohn and Eckel, the first issue of this first edition was bound in pink; the later issue or issues were bound in brown or black, and a border (subsequently removed) added to the final plate ("The Last Song"). For Dickens' agreement with Bentley, see The Dickensian 31 (1935), p. 250, and for a letter from Dickens justifying his work, see The Dickensian 34 (1938), pp. 65–66. For the binding of the first issue, see Sadleir, Evolution, p. 47. Grimaldi's MS. autobiography was first edited by T. E. Wilks, and then by Dickens: see Findlater, pp. 227–229.*

——[American edition] New York: W. H. Colyer, 1838.

2968 ——a new edition, with notes and additions, revised by Charles Whitehead.

2 vols. pp. [i–v] vi–xviii, [1] 2–230; pls. [front. (col.), 6] + pp. [1] 2–211 [212 (bl.)]; pls. [front., 6]   L

Richard Bentley   1846

Cohn 238 (twelve etchings by Cruikshank). The frontispiece to volume 1 is by De Wilde, "an excellent likeness" (Lowe), and appears in this edition only. According to Lowe and to Findlater, Whitehead worked "with the aid of new material collected by J. H. Burn." For Burn see also no. 2560.

2969 ——[another edition]

pp. [i–v] vi–xvi, [1] 2–358, ²[1] 2–4 [5–10]; final five leaves contain advts.; pls. [front., 10]   L

G. Routledge & Co.   1853

With ten of the Cruikshank etchings.

2970 ——[another edition]

pp. [i–v] vi–xvi, [1] 2–256; pls. [front., 10]   L

George Routledge and Sons   1866

With ten of the Cruikshank etchings.

2971 ——[another edition] Memoirs of Joseph Grimaldi. Edited by Charles Dickens. With thirteen illustrations by George Cruikshank.

pp. [i–v] vi–vii [viii] [9] 10–98; illus.   L

John Dicks   [1883]

Printed in columns. The illustrations are the twelve Cruikshank etchings, and the S. Raven portrait. Without the Whitehead–Burn notes.

2972 ——[another edition] Grimaldi, the clown Edited by Charles Dickens Author's edition With the twelve original illustrations by George Cruikshank.

pp. [1–7] 8–10 [11] 12–184, ²3–10; the last four leaves being advts.; illus.   L

George Routledge and Sons   1884

From the revised edition.

2973 ——[another edition] (The Caxton Series).

pp. [1–7] 8–10 [11] 12–184 [185–192 (advts.)]; illus.   L

George Routledge & Sons   [1893]

2974 ——[another edition] Memoirs of Joseph Grimaldi edited by "Boz" (Charles Dickens) with Cruikshank's illustrations and Charles Whitehead's notes New edition with introduction and notes by Percy Fitzgerald, M.A., F.S.A. (Half-forgotten books, No. 7. Ed. E. A. Baker).

pp. [i–v] vi–xxiv, [1] 2–271 [272 (bl.)]; pls. [front., 10] L

London: George Routledge & Sons Ltd.; New York: E. P. Dutton & Co.   1903

2974.1 ——[another edition] Memoirs of Joseph Grimaldi by Charles Dickens with illustrations by George Cruikshank. Edited by Richard Findlater, with new notes and an introduction. (The Fitzroy Edition).

pp. [1–8] 9–311 [312]; pls. [front. (col.), 5]   L

Macgibbon and Kee   [1968]

2975 MILES, HENRY DOWNES. The life of Joseph Grimaldi; with anecdotes of his contemporaries. By Henry Downes Miles.

pp. [1–3] 4–16 [2] 17–30 [2] 31–44 [2] 45–58 [2] 59–72 [2] 73–86 [2] 87–116 [2] 117–194; pls. [front., 1]; illus. (on the uncounted pp.)   L

Christopher Harris   1838

✄ Catalogue of a collection of theatrical portraits . . . Also the following genuine property of the late inimitable Joe Grimaldi. [1848.] *See no. 90.*

Grossmith, George, *the elder* (1847–1912)

Singer in light opera.

2976 GROSSMITH, GEORGE. A society clown. Reminiscences by George Grossmith (Arrowsmith's Bristol Library, vol. XXXI).

pp. [4] [1] 2–192; incl. music   E

Bristol: J. W. Arrowsmith; London: Simpkin, Marshall & Co.   1888

Grossmith, William Robert (1818–   )

I know nothing of this "phenomenon" — Lowe.

2977 B., E. C. ★The life of the celebrated infant Roscius, Master Grossmith of Reading, Berks, only seven years and a quarter old, by E.C.B., his preceptor.

pp. 30; on cover: "Pecks of troubles. . . . June, 1825. Melo-drama"   MH

Reading: Cowslade   1825

2978 THE LIFE and theatrical excursions of William Robert Grossmith, the juvenile actor, not yet nine years of age. Second edition.

pp. [1–3] 4–24; pl. [front.]; ptd. covers, illus.   L

Reading: M. Cowslade and Co.   1827

"Price, with portrait, one shilling; without portrait, sixpence; to be had of all the booksellers; and of the Young Roscius himself." The cover depicts Grossmith in his round of parts in Shakespeare and Pecks of Troubles.

2979 ——★fourth edition

pp. 22; pl., fold.   MH

Reading   1829

Gwyn, Eleanor (1650–1687)

This noted mistress of Charles II was a fairly good actress in a limited line of parts. The chief interest of her career does not, however, lie in her theatrical history — Lowe.

2980 AN ELOGY upon that never to be forgotten matron, old Maddam Gwinn, who was unfortunately drown'd in her own fishpond, on the 29th of July 1679.

pp. [2]   L

[1679]

Wing E 459. *Reprinted in facsimile in John W. Draper, A Century of Broadside Elegies (1928), p. [133].*

2981 A TRUE ACCOUNT of the late most doleful, and lamentable tragedy of old Maddam Gwinn, mother to Maddam Elenor Gwinn; who was unfortunately drowned, in a fish-pond, at her own mansion-house, near the neat-houses.

pp. [1–4]; head-title   L

[London]   [1679]

Wing T 2384.

2982 A PLEASANT BATTLE between two lap dogs of the Utopian Court. Or, a dialogue between sleep and awake, jest and earnest, reality and fancy: being fought upon the new erected dog-pit, lately contrived purposely upon this occasion as aforesaid in the anti-chamber of the said court, where it was fought with great applause, satisfaction and content of the company there present: but by reason of the authors drowzy disposition, being late at night, and he inclin'd to sleep: he would crave your favorable censures of this his pains; and judg of them as you find occasion.

pp. [1] 2–4   MH

[Printed for R.B.]   [1681]

Wing P 2537. *In prose, with a preface in verse. "Tutty" — Nell Gwyn, "Snap-short" — Louise, Duchess of Portsmouth.*

2983 A DIALOGUE, between the Dutchess of Portsmouth, and Madam Gwin, at parting.

pp. [2]   MH

[Printed for J.S.]   1682

In verse. Wing D 1329.

2984 A LETTER FROM THE DUTCH. OF PORTSMOUTH to Madam Gwyn, on her landing in France.

pp. [2]   MH

[Printed for J.S.]   [1682]

In prose. Wing L 1518.

2985 MADAM GWINS ANSWER to the Dutchess of Portsmouths letter.

pp. [1] 2   MH

[J. Johnson]   [1682]

In prose, with three lines of verse. Wing M 243.

2986 THE DUTCHESS OF PORTSMOUTHS FAREWEL:
> The Dutchess holds a dialogue, and talks with Madam Gwin;
> Yea, doth relate the wretched state, that now she liveth in.

To the tune of, Tan tarra rara tan tivee.

bs., illus.   L

[London:] I. Clarke, W. Thackeray, and T. Passinger
[1685?]

The Luttrell copy, dated 20 (or 29) Feb. 1685. The King died 6 February. A black letter ballad similar in theme to A pleasant dialogue betwixt two wanton ladies *[1685?] no. 2987.*

2987 A PLEASANT DIALOGUE betwixt two wanton ladies of pleasure; or, the Dutchess of Portsmouths [sic] woful farwel to her former felicity.
> One lady she couragiously stands in her own defence;
> Assuredly none can deny, the words she speaks is sence:
> The other now doth seem to bow, her colours are display'd,
> She is content, her mind is bent, still to maintain her trade.

Tune of, Tan tarra rara, tan tivee.

bs.; illus.   L

[London:] I. Deacon   [1685?]

The Luttrell copy, dated 17 February 1685. The King died 6 February. A black-letter ballad.

2988 PORTSMOUTHS LAMENTATION. Or, a dialogue between two amorous ladies, E.G. and D.P.
> Dame Portsmouth was design'd for France,
>   But therein was prevented;
> Who mourns at this unhappy chance,
>   and sadly doth lament it.

To the tune of, Tom the Taylor, or, Titus Oats.

bs.; illus.   L

C. Dennisson   [1685?]

Wing P 3008. *A black-letter ballad similar in theme to* A pleasant dialogue betwixt two wanton ladies *[1685?] no. 2987.*

2989 *A SERMON preached by D.T. at the funeral of M. E. Gywnn.

[1687?]

A forgery. Dr Tenison's real sermon was never published. See Cunningham, The story of Nell Gwyn, *ed. Goodwin, pp. 154, 165 (no. 2998).*

2990 MEMOIRS OF THE LIFE OF ELEANOR GWINN, a celebrated courtezan, in the reign of King Charles II. and mistress to that monarch.

pp. [4] 1–60   L

F. Stamper   1752

Attributed by Lowndes to "John Seymour, Comedian".

2991 ——†[another edition]

pp. 3–14   L

Title-page missing. Perhaps the same item as no. 2292.

2992 ——*[another edition]

Dublin   1754

Lowe.

2993 FAIRBURN'S EDITION of the life, amours and exploits of Nell Gwinn, the fortunate orange girl, who, from the above low sphere of life became the bosom friend and mistress of King Charles the Second (of merry memory,) and who, for the comfort of old soldiers, was the cause of erecting Chelsea Hospital; with an account of the many charities she left and good deeds she performed in her retirement from public life and the stage (as Lady Simcock.)

pp. [1–3] 4–26; col. pl. [front.]   L

J. Fairburn   [1820?]

2994 CUNNINGHAM, PETER. The story of Nell Gwyn: and the sayings of Charles the Second. Related and collected by Peter Cunningham, F.S.A.

pp. [i–ix] x–xi [xii], [1] 2–212; illus., incl. [front.] GU

Bradbury & Evans   1852

2995 ——[another edition] With the author's latest corrections. Edited with an introduction, additional notes and a life of the author, by Henry B. Wheatley F.S.A.

pp. [i–iv] v–lxii [lxiii–lxiv], [1] 2–224; illus.; pls. [front., 8]

W. W. Gibbings   Fifteenth of November 1892

JFA. *Edition limited to 250 copies.*

2996 ——[another edition] The story of Nell Gwyn by Peter Cunningham edited by Gordon Goodwin with illustrations.

pp. [i–viii] ix–xii, [1] 2–236; illus. (facsims.); pls. [front., 13]; t.p. in red and black   E

A. H. Bullen   1903

2997 ——[another edition] Nell Gwyn Written by Peter Cunningham Together with Mrs. Jameson's lives of the Duchesses of Portsmouth and Cleveland (Beaux & Belles of England).

pp. [i–iv] v–lxxv [lxxvi–lxxviii], 1–305 [306]; pls. [front. (col.), 5]; ptd. tissue guards [6]; illus.; t.p. in red and black   NbU

Printed by the Grolier Society   [190–?]

"Imperial edition limited to one thousand copies for England and America." Another edition of Wheatley's edition, with his "Notes on the life of the author", introduction, and notes.

2998 ——[another edition] Edited by Gordon Goodwin.

pp. [i–viii] ix–xii, [1] 2–236; illus. (facsims.); pls. [front., 13]; t.p. in red and black

Edinburgh: John Grant   1908

JFA.

2999 ——[another edition]

pp. [1–5] 6–179 [180 (bl.)]; inset t.p. (double leaf, in black and brown)   L

Sisley's, Ltd. makers of beautiful books   [1908]

3000 ——[another edition] The story of Nell Gwyn and the sayings of Charles II related and collected by Peter Cunningham, F.S.A. with the author's latest corrections edited, with introduction, additional notes and a life of the author, by Henry B. Wheatley, F.S.A. (Hutchinson's Library of Standard Lives).

pp. [1–4] 5–283 [284 285–288 (bl.)]; pl. [double pl. of front. and t.p.]   L

Hutchinson & Co.   [1926]

3001 ——The story of Nell Gwyn and the sayings of Charles the Second related and collected by Peter Cunningham, F.S.A. New edition, with an introduction by John Drinkwater with a folding reproduction of Hollar's View of London, thirty-eight portraits and views from rare contemporary prints.

pp. [i–iv] v–xvi, 17–194 [195–196 (bl.)]; pls. [front., 38 (incl. 1 fold.)]   L

Privately printed for the Navarre Society Limited   1927

——[American editions] New York: Wiley, 1883, 1891; New York: Athenaeum Press (Beaux and Belles of England) [1907?]

Originally published in Gentleman's Magazine *for 1851, now corrected and enlarged. The preface says: "It must be read as a serious truth, not as a fiction — as a biography, not as a romance." This book, which sold at Daniel's sale in 1864 for 1s. 6d., is now one of the scarcest of theatrical biographies, and fetched 37s. at Mr. Herman's sale, while in a recent catalogue it was priced at 45s. This rise in value is to me inexplicable, and is certainly not attributable either to the beauty or value of the book — Lowe.*

3002 HART, WILLIAM HENRY, *ed.* A memorial of Nell Gwynne, the actress, and Thomas Otway, the dramatist. By William Henry Hart, F.S.A.

pp. [6]; illus. [autograph facsims.]   L

John Russell Smith   1868

Reprint of a power of attorney by Nell Gwynne to Mr. James Fraizer to receive her pension. One of the witnesses is Otway — Lowe.

Haines, Joseph

See below HAYNES, JOSEPH nos. 3016–3018.

Halliwell, *afterwards* Halliwell-Phillipps, James Orchard (1820–1889)

A very distinguished and learned Shakespearean scholar and antiquary, to whose labours we are indebted for much valuable information regarding Shakespeare and his times— Lowe. See Justin Winsor, ed. Halliwelliana: A Bibliography (Library of Harvard University. Bibliographical Contributions. Edited by Justin Winsor, No. 10) (Cambridge, Mass., 1881); George R. Wright, A Brief Memoir of the Late J. O. Halliwell-Phillipps (1889); A. N. L. Munby, The Family Affairs of Sir Thomas Phillipps (Phillipps Studies No. 2) (Cambridge, 1952). Halliwell assumed the name Phillipps in 1872. Of his many productions only those that were recorded by Lowe or that relate directly to the stage are recorded here. See AUTHOR INDEX.

Hambleton, John (fl. 1870)

An actor who became a Bible distributor.

3003 [HAMBLETON, JOHN.] THE CONVERTED ACTOR or, buds, blossoms, and fruits of the revival, being the remarkable life-story of John Hambleton actor, gold-miner, explorer, evangelist, and pioneer in the gospel. 5th edition—revised and completed. (Penny Library No. 12).

pp. [1–3] 4–32; illus.; ptd. covers   MH

Glasgow: Pickering & Inglis; London: Alfred Holness; New York: D. T. Bass; Sydney: G. Lawler; Melbourne: Gordon & Gotch; Brisbane: W. R. Smith & Co.   [ca. 1870?]

The illustrations include one of John Hambleton burning his theatrical properties.

Hare, *Sir* John (1844–1921)

Actor-manager at the Prince of Wales, the Court Theatre, St James's and the Garrick. Knighted in 1907 and retired in 1911.

3004 PEMBERTON, T[HOMAS] EDGAR. John Hare comedian 1865–1895 A biography by T. Edgar Pemberton.

pp. [2] [i–iii] iv–vi [7] 8–202; pls. [front., 4]   L
George Routledge and Sons Limited   1895

Harley, George Davies (–1811?)

Stage name of George Davies. Actor, known as the Norwich Roscius. See also AUTHOR INDEX.

3005 H[ARLEY], G. D. *Poems by G.D.H. of the Theatre Royal, Covent Garden.
?   1796
Chase.

Harley, John Pritt (1790?–1858)

Singer and actor, especially of low comedian parts. Excelled in Shakespearean clowns.

✖ A catalogue of the excellent furniture . . . of the late J. P. Harley, the celebrated comedian . . . [1858]. See no. 89.

Harper, John (–1742)

The actor who was proceeded against by Highmore, manager of Drury Lane [in the 1733 disputes] as a "rogue and a vagabond". He was committed to Bridewell, November 12 1733, but on trial was discharged — Lowe. See above no. 1329.

Harris, *Sir* Augustus Henry Glossop (1851–1896)

The present lessee and manager of Drury Lane, the only one who has made a success in the management since, it might almost be said, David Garrick. The secret of this success lies principally in the thoroughness with which Mr. Harris does everything. Lessee of Drury Lane from 1879 — Lowe. Famous for his elaborate pantomimes. See Gerald Forsyth, "Notes on Pantomime", TN, II, 22–30. Knighted in 1891 as Sheriff of the City of London. For Harris at Drury Lane see above no. 1421.

Harris, Henry (–1839)

Son of Thomas Harris. Assisted his father as manager and proprietor of Covent Garden, eventually succeeding him in 1809. See above under COVENT GARDEN nos. 1294 et seq.

Harris, Thomas (1743–1820)

Harris became part patentee in 1767, and for half a century he and his son, Henry Harris [q.v.] were managers of Covent Garden — Lowe. See above nos. 1082, 1163 et seq., 1176–7.

✖ A catalogue of a collection of theatrical portraits of a gentlemen deceased, formerly part of the gallery of the late Thomas Harris . . . 1848. See no. 90.

Hart, Charles (d. 1683)

Actor. The common assertion that Hart was Shakespeare's grand-nephew is rejected by Bentley.

3006 AN ELEGY on that worthy and famous actor, Mr. Charles Hart, who departed this life Thursday August the 18th. 1683.

pp. [2]   L
Printed by Nath. Thompson   1683

Wing E 368. Reprinted in facsimile in John W. Draper, A century of broadside elegies (1928), p. [163].

✖ Jordan, John. Original memoirs and historical accounts of the families of Shakespeare and Hart. 1865. See no. 1041.

Hartley, *Mrs.* Elizabeth (1751–1824)

A noted actress, of extraordinary personal beauty. Her portraits by Sir Joshua Reynolds are familiar to all — Lowe.

3007 [BATE, *Rev.* HENRY, *later Rev. Sir* Henry Bate Dudley, *ed.?*] THE VAUXHALL AFFRAY; or, the Macaronies defeated: being a compilation of all the letters, squibs, &c. on both sides of that dispute. With an introductory dedication to the Hon. Tho. Lyttleton, Esq;

pp. [i–ii] iii–iv [5] 6–87 [88]   MB
Sold by J. Williams   1773

3008 ——the second edition

pp. [i–ii] iii–iv [5] 6–87 [88]   L
Sold by J. Williams   1773

3009 ——the third edition

pp. [i–ii] iii–iv [5] 6–87 [88 (bl.) 89] 90–120; pl. [1]   L
Sold by J. Williams   1773

3010 ——[another issue of 3009]

pp. [i–ii] iii–iv [5] 6–120; pl. [1]   MH
Sold by J. Williams   1773

> *See the advertisement cited under no. 3011 below: "The whole pamphlet, with the appendix and caricature, may be then had complete, price 2s." MH copy is extra-illustrated with a second plate, a contemporary cartoon on the incident.*

3011 [BATE, *Rev.* HENRY, *later Rev. Sir* Henry Bate Dudley *ed.?*] AN APPENDIX to the Vauxhall affray; or, Macaronies defeated: to which is prefixed an elegant caricature, called the Macaroni sacrifice.

pp. [2] [89] 90–120; wanting pl.   MB
J. Williams   1773

> *"This morning . . . will be published. Price 1s. An Appendix to* The Vauxhall Affray . . . *To which is prefixed, an elegant caricature, designed and executed by a gentleman, entitled,* The Macaroni Sacrifice. *The whole pamphlet, with the appendix and caricature, may be then had complete, price 2s." —* The Morning Post. *Mrs. Hartley, the actress, being at Vauxhall one evening, accompanied by, among others, the well-known Rev. Mr. Bate, conceived herself insulted by the stares of a party of Macaronies. The reverend gentleman seems to have been the most courageous of her champions, and a challenge passed between him and one of the offending beaux. On the latter's discovering that his opponent was a clergyman, he withdrew from the proposed encounter; but, by some means, a fistic encounter was arranged between Mr. Bate and a supposed fellow-Captain of his*

opponent's, which was claimed as a victory by both sides. Ultimately it appeared that the supposed Captain was only a servant, which was a terrible insult to the clerical "bruiser." The correspondence, here reprinted, was of the most vigorous description. There are other pamphlets on the subject, but I do not know anything of them — Lowe. The original incident occurred on 26 July 1773.

Harvest, *Rev.* George (–1789)

Amateur actor, playgoer, and eccentric.

3012 HARVEST, GEORGE. The absent man; or, the life and singular eccentricities of George Harvest, parson and comedian. To which are added, The siege of Alicant, and *The husband's stratagem.*

pp. [1–2] 3–24   L
Penrith: printed by Anthony Soulby   [1805?]

3013 ——[another edition] The eccentric character of George Harvest of Thames Ditton.

pp. [2] [7] 8–32; engr. t.p.; pl. [front.]   L
Printed by T. Crabb   1814

Hayes, Catherine (afterwards *Mrs.* Bushnell) (1825–1861)

Singer.

3014 *OPINIONS OF THE PRESS on the performances of Miss Catherine Hayes in London, and in the chief cities and towns in Ireland.

pp. (1) v, 45 (1)   MB
Mellett   1851

3015 CONTRIBUTOR, A, *pseud.* *Memoir of Miss Catherine Hayes, "the Swan of Erin", by a contributor to the Dublin University magazine.

pp. (3), 40, (1), 9; port.   MB
Cramer & Co.   [1852?]

Haynes, Joseph (–1701)

A noted low comedian and practical joker. He was specially good at speaking prologues and epilogues. He was on the stage from 1672 to 1700 — Lowe. He eventually joined Killigrew's company at the Theatre Royal and as one of the first Harlequins. His name is also spelt Haines.

3016 [BROWN, THOMAS.] THE REASONS of Mr. Joseph Hains the player's conversion & re-conversion. Being the third and last part to the dialogue of Mr. Bays.

pp. [4] 1–32   L
Richard Baldwin   1690

> Wing B 5071.

3017 ———[another edition]

pp. [*4*] [1] 2–28 L

T. Bennet, and A. Roper 1691

Wing B 5072. This was one of his practical jokes.

3018 [THOMAS, TOBYAS, *pseud.?*] THE LIFE of the late famous comedian, Jo. Hayns. Containing, his comical exploits and adventures, both at home and abroad.

pp. [*8*] 1–63 [64] L

J. Nutt 1701

Dedication signed "Tobyas Thomas". Sometimes erroneously attributed to Thomas Brown, who, in fact, derides this work, attributing it to a "fellow actor". There is no actor of this name in LS *at this date.*

Hazlitt, William (1778–1830)

A great English critic and essayist, whose works on the theatre are most valuable—Lowe. *See* AUTHOR INDEX.

Hazlitt, W. Carew (1834–1913)

A grandson of William Hazlitt, and himself a distinguished bibliographer, critic, and authority on dramatic subjects. His edition of Dodsley's plays is one of the most valuable collections of classical plays—Lowe. *See* AUTHOR INDEX.

Heath, Caroline (1835–1887)

Actress. Wife of Wilson Barrett.

3019 DRAMATICUS, *pseud.* *Miss Heath. A biographical sketch. By Dramaticus.

pp. [1] 2–12

Leicester: E. Lamb 1879

IKF.
Reprinted with additions, from Scarborough Daily Post, Bradford Daily Chronicle, Halifax Courier, *and* Birmingham Daily Gazette. *This was issued for Caroline Heath's appearance at the Surrey Theatre, in "Jane Shore", from 12 April, 1879.*

Heminge, John (1556–1630)

Actor in Burbage's company and with the King's Men. Shareholder in the Globe and Blackfriars theatres. Editor, with Condell, of the first folio edition of Shakespeare. See above no. 1076.

Henderson, John (1747–1785)

An actor of remarkable powers, both tragic and comic, who, with no personal advantages, yet promised to be a rival to Garrick. His Hamlet and his Falstaff were equally famous, and his reading of John Gilpin *was, says Rogers, "marvellous"* — Lowe.

3020 [PILON, FREDERICK.] AN ESSAY on the character of Hamlet. As performed by Mr. Henderson, at the Theatre Royal in the Hay-Market.

pp. [*4*] [1] 2–8 11–25 [26 (bl.)] [=24] L

W. Flexney [1777]

Dedicated to George Colman, the new manager of the Haymarket, where Henderson appeared as Hamlet on 27th June 1777.

3021 ———second edition

pp. [*6*] [1] 2–8 11–25 [26 (bl.)] [=24] L

W. Flexney [1777]

3022 [DAVIES, THOMAS.] A GENUINE NARRATIVE of the life and theatrical transactions of Mr. John Henderson, commonly called the Bath Roscius.

pp. [*4*] [i] ii–vii [viii], [1] 2–60 L

T. Evans 1777

3023 ———the second edition

pp. [i] ii–vii [viii], [1] 2–60 L

J. Ireland 1778

3024 ———the third edition

pp. [*4*] [i] ii–vii [viii], [1] 2–60 LGk

J. Ireland 1778

⌘ A catalogue of the library of John Henderson . . . [1786]. *See no. 92.*

3025 IRELAND, JOHN, *ed.* Letters and poems, by the late Mr. John Henderson. With anecdotes of his life, by John Ireland.

pp. [i–v] vi–xii, [1] 2–333 [334 (bl.) 335 (errata) 336 (bl.)]; cancelled pp. [1] 2, 11–12 also present L

J. Johnson 1786

The cancelled pages omit Latin mottoes.

3026 ———[another edition]

pp. [i–v] vi–xii, [1] 2–264

Dublin: Byrne, Lewis, Jones, and Moore 1786

JFA.
John Ireland was a watchmaker. He was an intimate friend of Henderson, the actor, and is said to have persuaded the latter to invest £600 in his business. Ireland, however, who was an enthusiastic dabbler in literature, neglected his business, and the money was lost. Henderson naturally resented this misconduct, and the two never became friendly again. After the actor's death, Ireland, probably repentant, published a memoir of his former friend — Lowe.

3027 HARLEY, GEORGE DAVIES, *stage name o*, George Davies. A monody on the death of Mr. John Henderson, late of Covent-Garden, Theatre. By George Davies Harley, of the Theatre-Royal, Norwich.

pp. [*2*] [i] ii–iii [iv], [1] 2–31 [32] L

Norwich: Booth and Son 1787

3028 SHERIDAN'S AND HENDERSON'S PRAC-
TICAL METHOD of reading and reciting English
poetry. Elucidated by a variety of examples taken from
some of our most popular poets, and the manner pointed
out in which they were read or recited by the above
gentlemen: intended for the improvement of youth, and
as a necessary introduction to Dr. Enfield's Speaker.
Dedicated to Morris Robinson, Esquire.

pp. [i–iii] iv–xii, [1] 2–264   L

E. Newbery; and J. Scatchard   1796

> Sheridan and Henderson gave public readings, which were
> very successful. Henderson's reading of John Gilpin was
> a great attraction — Lowe. William Enfield's The
> Speaker (1774) was published in many editions during
> the 18th and 19th centuries.

Henslowe, Philip (d. 1616)

*Henslowe was originally a pawnbroker, who, it is supposed,
by lending money to the players, became interested in
theatrical speculations and was ultimately a theatre proprietor. — Lowe. Owner of the Rose, Fortune and Hope
playhouses. His Diary records his accounts and memoranda. See
Chambers Elizabethan, I 356–368, and above nos. 1019–
1022.*

Herbert, *Master* Henry

An Infant Roscius — Lowe.

3029 [COLE, JOHN.] A BIOGRAPHICAL
ACCOUNT of Master Herbert, the Infant Roscius!
With a brief delineation of his talents, and critiques on
his performances. By the author of *The talents of
Edmund Kean delineated.*

pp. [2] [1–3] 4–18   L

Scarborough: published, for the Infant Roscius, by
J. Cole, Newborough; J. Ainsworth, Scarborough; and
N. Walker, Wisbech   1830

> Dedicated to Charles Lamb. Reprints A critique on the
> performance of Master Herbert, the youthful Roscius
> (1830) (see below no. 3030).

3030 [COLE, JOHN.] A CRITIQUE on the performance of Master Herbert, the youthful Roscius.

pp. [1–3] 4   L

Scarborough: printed for John Cole   [1830]

> "Only sixty copies, and not for sale". On pink paper.
> Master Herbert performed at Scarborough in June 1830.

Herbert, *Miss*

3031 *COLLECTED REVIEW of Lady Audley's
Secret, a drama in two acts, as first performed at the
St. James's Theatre, February the 28th 1863, being the
criticisms on Miss Herbert's impersonation of Lady
Audley.

                                                    1863

STR.

Heywood, Thomas (1574?–1641)

*An actor, and a most voluminous dramatic author, who boasts
that he had been concerned in the production of two hundred
and twenty plays—Lowe. See AUTHOR INDEX.*

Hiffernan, Paul (1719–1777)

*A rather rascally hack-writer, who hung about the stage and
actors, writing plays, blackmailing, begging, and borrowing
— Lowe. His The Wishes of a Free People; a Dramatic
Poem (1761) contains a short account of its rejection by Rich
and Garrick. See also AUTHOR INDEX.*

3032 D——CK——N, R——D, *Mr.* †Narrative of
the barbarous and bloody murder of P——l
H——ff——n, M.D. Committed by himself, on
Monday the 17th day of October inst. Being a letter
from Mr. R——d D——ck——n of S——l——r
C——t Castle-Street, Dublin, to J——n B——ne Esq;
at the Hague.

pp. [1–2] 3–8   L
[Dublin]   [1748]

> Imprint cropped off.

Highmore, John

*Patentee of Drury Lane. He purchased half of Booth's share
in the patent, and the whole of Cibber's in 1732–33. At the
beginning of the next season the actors, headed by Theo.
Cibber, revolted, and before the end of it, Highmore sold his
share to Fleetwood. Theo. Cibber's conduct was, as usual,
that of a scoundrel—Lowe. See no. 1325.*

Hill, Aaron (1685–1750)

*A dramatic author of high character and attainments. He was
a most benevolent and amiable character, and stands out in
strong relief to the average dramatist of his time. His dispute
with Pope, regarding the latter's mention of him in The
Dunciad, is well known — Lowe. See also AUTHOR
INDEX.*

3033 *THE ANTI-ORPHEUS; or an epistle to
Mr. A——n H——ll.

                                         December 1726

Foxon.

Hill, Benson Earle (1796?–1845)

Amateur actor.

3034 HILL, BENSON EARLE. Playing about; or
theatrical anecdotes and adventures, with scenes of
general nature, from the life; in England, Scotland,
and Ireland, by Benson Earle Hill.

2 vols. pp. [i–v] vi–xvi, [1] 2–308 + [i–v] vi–viii, [1]
2–320   L

Printed for the author, and sold by W. Sams   1840

Hill was an artillery officer, smitten with theatrical mania. A very unfavourable idea of his manners is conveyed in the Memoirs of Charles Mathews (*1839*) *vol. iii, ch. 6, if, as is generally stated, he is the amateur referred to* — Lowe.

Hill, John (*ca.* 1716–1775)

This notorious character was a quack doctor, who dabbled in all sorts of literature. Davies says of him: "*He spared no character of friend or foe, when either his malice was to be gratified or his purse to be made heavier.*" *He was a noted slanderer and scandal-monger, and was always engaged in paper feuds. Garrick's happy epigram on his abilities as physician and dramatist is well known:*

"*For physic and farces, his equal there scarce is; His farces are physic, his physic a farce is.*"—Lowe.
See AUTHOR INDEX.

Hill, *Mrs.* P.

Actress.

3035 HILL, *Mrs.* [P.] Mrs. Hill's apology for having been induced, by particular desire, and the most specious allurements that could tempt female weakness, to appear in the character of Scrub, *Beaux Stratagem,* for one night only, at Brighthelmstone, last year, 1786, when the theatre was applied for by the Honourable George Hanger, and engaged for that purpose; with an address to Mrs. Fitzherbert. Also, some of Mrs. Hill's letters to His Royal Highness the Prince of Wales, Mrs. Fitzherbert, and others. The dénoûment, with events and remarks, that may not be deemed uninteresting to this nation at large. By Mrs. Hill.

pp. [1–3] 4–51 [52 (bl.)]   L
Printed for the authoress, and sold by G. Kearsley, and E. Harlow   [1787]

Mrs. Hill promises a second pamphlet "*to conclude my apology*".

Hilton, *Miss*

Miss Hilton was a member of the Liverpool company — Lowe.

3036 [COLE, JOHN.] A CRITIQUE on the performance of Juliana, in "The honey moon," by Miss Hilton. By the author of "The talents of Edmund Kean delineated;" "Biographical account of Master Herbert, the infant Roscius," &c. &c.

pp. [1–3] 4   MH
Scarborough: printed (only 30 copies) for John Cole
1831

The honeymoon was written by John Tobin. "*Miss Hilton, from Liverpool*" *performed at Scarborough in September 1831.*

Hitchcock, Robert (–1809)

*Actor. He was prompter at the Haymarket in the elder Colman's time, and afterwards prompter at Dublin—*Lowe.
See AUTHOR INDEX.

Hodson, *Miss* Henrietta (1841–1910)

Actress. In 1868 she married, as her second husband, Henry Labouchère, proprietor of the Queen's Theatre. She also took over the management of the Royalty Theatre. She produced some of Gilbert's plays and came into direct conflict with him due to his dictatorial manner.

3037 HODSON, HENRIETTA. A letter from Miss Henrietta Hodson, an actress, to the members of the dramatic profession, being a relation of the persecutions which she has suffered from Mr. William Schwenck Gilbert, a dramatic author.

pp. [1–3] 4–22 [23–24 (bl.)]   L
[London]   [1877]

Dated April 1877, from the Haymarket Theatre. In his answer, Gilbert says that Miss Hodson distributed 750 copies to the profession.

3038 GILBERT, WILLIAM SCHWENCK. A letter addressed to the members of the dramatic profession in reply to Miss Henrietta Hodson's pamphlet. By W. S. Gilbert.

pp. [1–5] 6–18   L
[priv. ptd.]   [1877]

Miss Hodson replied to this pamphlet by a long letter in the Era — Lowe. Searle 58.

Holbrook, Ann Catherine

3039 HOLBROOK, ANN CATHERINE. Memoirs of an actress, comprising a faithful narrative of her theatrical career from 1798 to the present period, giving a lively picture of the stage in general, and interspersed with a variety of anecdotes, humourous and pathetic. By Ann Catherine Holbrook, late of the new Theatre-Royal, Manchester.

pp. [i–iii] iv [5] 6–32 32–35 [=36]   L
Manchester: printed by J. Harrop at the Mercury Office
1807

Published by subscription.

3040 HOLBROOK, ANN CATHERINE. The dramatist; or, memoirs of the stage. With the life of the authoress, prefixed, and interspersed with, a variety of anecdotes, humourous and pathetic. By Ann Catherine Holbrook, late of the new Theatre-Royal, Manchester.

pp. [i–iii] iv [5] 6–68 [69–72 (subscription list and errata)]   L
Birmingham: printed by Martin and Hunter   1809

An enlarged edition of Holbrook's Memoirs of an Actress (*no. 3039). Published by subscription.*

Holcroft, Thomas (1744–1809)

A noted dramatist, whose Road to Ruin *still holds the stage. Holcroft was an advanced Liberal in politics, and was one of the persons accused of high treason in 1794 — Lowe.*

3041 [HAZLITT, WILLIAM, *ed.*] MEMOIRS of the late Thomas Holcroft, written by himself, and continued to the time of his death, from his diary, notes, and other papers.

3 vols. pp. [i–v] vi–viii, [1] 2–300; pl. [front.] + pp. [4] [1] 2–283 [284] + pp. [4] [1] 2–320   L

Longman, Hurst, Rees, Orme, and Brown   1816

> *Published in April — Colby. Preface dated January, 1810. P. P. Howe, in his Life of William Hazlitt (1922), rejects W. C. Hazlitt's statement that the work is unfinished.*

3042 ——[another edition] (The Traveller's Library Nos. 16 and 17).

2 parts pp. [2] [1–5] 6–156 + [2] 157–315 [316]   L

Longman, Brown, Green, and Longmans   1852

> *Slightly abridged. Reissued in 1856 as part of volume 17 of The Traveller's Library.*

3043 ——[another edition] The life of Thomas Holcroft written by himself continued to the time of his death from his diary notes & other papers by William Hazlitt and now newly edited with introduction and notes by Elbridge Colby.

2 vols. pp. [4] [i–ii] iii–lxii, [2] [1] 2–319 [320]; illus. (facsims.); pls. [front., 3, incl. 1 (music) = 2 leaves] + pp. [2] [i–iv] v–x, [1] 2–346 [347–348]; pls. [front., 3, incl. 2 (facsims.) each = 2 leaves]   E

Constable & Company Ltd.   1925

> *With an index and a few notes.*
> *Reprinted and annotated in Volume 2 of Hazlitt's Collected Works, ed. A. R. Waller and A. Glover (1902–1904), and in Volume 3 of Hazlitt's Complete Works, ed. P. P. Howe (1930–1934).*

3044 ——[another edition] Memoirs of Thomas Holcroft written by himself and continued by William Hazlitt (The World's Classics CCCII).

pp. [2] [i–vi] vii–xiii [xiv (bl.)], 1–390 [391–392 (bl.)]   L

Humphrey Milford Oxford University Press   [1926]

> *With an index and a few notes.*

——[American edition] New York: Benjamin Blom, Inc., 1968.

> *A reprint of the Colby edition.*

Holland, Mr.

Actor.

3045 *THE EXPOSITION; or, theatrical secrets divulged, being the interesting and extraordinary memoirs of Mr. Holland, comedian. Late of the New York Theatre and for one night a member of the Theatre Royal, Crow Street, Dublin. Interspersed with several anecdotes, amusing, and instructive, of several great personages.

DN

Dublin   1815

Hollingshead, John (1827–1904)

Theatre manager and journalist. Opened the Gaiety Theatre on 21 December 1868 and remained there until 1886 when he retired.

3046 HOLLINGSHEAD, JOHN. My lifetime by John Hollingshead author of various books (chiefly reprints from magazines) and creator of the Gaiety Theatre with photogravure portrait.

2 vols. pp. [i–ix] x–xv [xvi], [1] 2–255 [256]; pl. [front.] + pp. [i–iii] iv–viii, [1] 2–250 [251 (printer's imprint) 252 (bl.)]   MH

Sampson Low, Marston & Company   1895

> *Dedicated "To my best friends the British public". Some copies (one at L) omit the phrase "creator of" from the title.*

3047 ——My lifetime by John Hollingshead creator of the Gaiety Theatre. Second edition.

2 vols. pp. [i–ix] x–xv [xvi], [1] 2–255 [256]; pl. [front.] + pp. [i–iii] iv–viii, [1] 2–250 [251 (imprint) 252]   E

Sampson Low, Marston & Company Limited   1895

Holtum, J.

✖ Stage. no. 17. 24 April 1880. Sheffield. 1880. *See no. 4416.*

> *Contains a single sheet supplement: Herr Holtum (King of the Cannon).*

3048 HOLTUM, J. *The chief incidents of the non-professional and professional careers of Holtum the Dane, surnamed the Cannon King, related by himself.

pp. 36

Liverpool   1885

STR.

Honey, Laura (1816?–1843)

Actress. See also below no. 3606.

✖ Annals of the green room . . . Part I Memoirs of Mrs. Honey. 1830. *See no. 2231.*

> *Part I was reprinted separately in 1842.*

Hook, Theodore Edward (1788–1841)

Hook wrote many dramatic pieces, but his most noted production was Killing no murder *— Lowe. See nos. 2819, 3174; 3933–6.*

Hopson, Frederick (1855–1892)
See below LESLIE, FRED no. 3224.

Hough, Peter

3049 HOUGH, PETER. *The confession of Peter Hough, of Sadler's Wells, to the muse. An Ode. [Milford?]   1750

Foxon.

Houston, James
Scottish actor.

3050 HOUSTON, JAMES. Autobiography of Mr. James Houston, Scotch comedian. Illustrated by J. M. Hamilton.

pp. [i–v] vi–viii, [5] 6–196 [=200]; pl. [front.]; illus. E
Glasgow and Edinburgh: John Menzies & Co., and Wm. Love   1889

Howe, J. B. (1829–1908)
Actor. Real name Thomas Burdette.

3051 HOWE, J. B. A cosmopolitan actor. His adventures all over the world.

pp. [1–3] 4–242
Bedford Publishing Company   [1888]

IKF; *another copy at MH.*

Huddart, ——
Huddart was, I believe, the "gentleman" who appeared at Covent Garden as Othello on 15th October 1798. What became of him I do not know. He seems to have been at Manchester in 1804—Lowe. See no. 1616.

Hull, Thomas (1728–1808)
Actor and dramatist. He left Bath for Covent Garden and was one of the founders of the Covent Garden Theatrical Fund. Thomas Hull's Moral tales in verse, founded on real events (1797) contains a few dedicatory poems of theatrical Fund. See SALE CATALOGUES no. 94; BATH no. 1547.

Inchbald, *Mrs.* Elizabeth (1753–1821)
A well-known dramatist and novelist, who was also an actress. She edited two collections of English plays and one of farces—Lowe. See also below no. 3185.

3052 DUTTON, THOMAS. The wise man of the East; or, the apparition of Zoroaster, the son of Oromases, to the theatrical midwife of Leicester-Fields. A satirical poem, in four parts. By Thomas Dutton.

pp. [i–v] vi–vii [viii] [9] 10–74 [75 (advt.) 76 (bl.)]   L
H. D. Symonds   1800

This is a satire on Mrs. Inchbald, who had adapted Kotzebüe's play of The Writing-Desk; or, Youth in Danger, and called it The Wise Man of the East — Lowe. The Wise Man of the East was produced at Covent Garden 30 Nov. 1799.

3053 ——the second edition
pp. [i–iii] iv [v] vi–viii, [9] 10–72 57 58 [=74]   LGk
Printed by J. Fricker   1800

Chiefly a reissue of the first edition, with parts reprinted; the last leaf reprinted by J. Roach.

3054 COLMAN, GEORGE. The heir at law; a comedy: in five acts. Written by George Colman, the younger; and first performed at the Theatre-Royal, Hay-Market, on Saturday, July 15, 1797.

pp. [i–v] vi–ix [x–xii], [1] 2–86 [87–88 (epilogue)]   L
Longman, Hurst, Rees, and Orme   1808

With a letter to Mrs. Inchbald.

3055 BOADEN, JAMES, *ed.* Memoirs of Mrs. Inchbald: including her familiar correspondence with the most distinguished persons of her time. To which are added The massacre, and A case of conscience; now first published from her autograph copies. Edited by James Boaden, Esq.

2 vols. pp. [i–v] vi–xi [xii], [1] 2–380; pl. [front.]; cancels, (pp. 259–260) + pp. [i–iii] iv–vii [viii], [1] 2–375 [376 (bl.)]; cancels, (pp. 71–74, 85–86, 119–120, 217–218)   L
Richard Bentley   1833

"The following biography has been prepared from Mrs. Inchbald's autograph journals ... and from at least two hundred of her own letters ..." (p. [iii]).

Incledon, Charles (1763–1826)
One of the greatest of English singers—"the English Ballad Singer," as he described himself. He was originally a common sailor—Lowe. See no. 1182.

Irving, Henry (1838–1905)
John Henry Brodribb Irving, certainly the most remarkable actor of this generation, and the legitimate successor of Betterton, Garrick, Kemble, and Edmund Kean, learned his art in the laborious days of stock companies, now, alas! things of the past. He made his first appearance on the stage at Sunderland, on 29th September 1856, and his first London appearance at the Princess's on 24th September 1859. Not being satisfied with the opportunities afforded him, he went into the country again, and it was not till 6th October 1866 that he played in London as a leading actor. This was at the St. James's Theatre, and his part was Doricourt in The Belle's Stratagem. At the Vaudeville on 4th June 1870 he appeared as Digby Grant in The Two Roses; and at the Lyceum, on 25th November 1871, he took his place as the leading actor on the English stage by his playing of Mathias in The Bells. Charles I, Eugene Aram, Richelieu, Philip (in

Philip) *followed; then on 31st October 1874, came his crowning triumph, Hamlet, which he played for 200 consecutive performances. Macbeth, Othello, Richard III, Benedick, Malvolio, Shylock, Romeo, Louis XI, Lesurques and Dubosc in the Lyons Mail, the Vicar of Wakefield, and Mephistopheles are among his most famous parts. In September 1878 he became lessee and manager of the Lyceum, which he has made the only home of Shakespeare and the higher drama in London* — Lowe. *See Laurence Irving, Henry Irving the Actor and his World (New York, 1952). For prefaces written by Irving see AUTHOR INDEX.*

3056 CRITIQUE ON MR. HENRY IRVING'S "HAMLET". Lyceum Theatre, London, 1874. [Reprinted from the "Town Crier", Liverpool].

pp. [4]   MH
Liverpool: Albert Wainwright   [1874]

3057 RUSSELL, EDWARD R[ICHARD], *Baron Russell of Liverpool*. Irving as Hamlet. By Edward R. Russell.

pp. [4] [1] 2–54 [55–56 (bl.)]   MH
Henry S. King & Co.   1875

3058 ——second edition

pp. [4] [1] 2–54   L
Henry S. King & Co.   1875

An affectionately appreciative criticism — Lowe.

3059 TWO AMATEURS, *pseud*. Macbeth at the Lyceum. Mr. Irving and his critics. By two amateurs.

pp. [1–3] 4–34   GU
Bickers & Son   1875

A defence of Mr. Irving's view of Macbeth — Lowe.

3060 SHERIDAN KNOWLES' CONCEPTION and Mr. Irving's performance of Macbeth.

pp. [1–3] 4–19 [20]   L
Effingham Wilson   1876

Unfavourable to Mr. Irving — Lowe. *For Sheridan Knowles' Essay on Macbeth see below no. 3746.*

3061 CAINE, T[HOMAS] H[ENRY] HALL. Richard III and Macbeth: the spirit of romantic play in relationship to the principles of Greek and of Gothic art, and to the picturesque interpretations of Mr. Henry Irving: a dramatic study, by T. H. Hall Caine.

pp. [1–5] 6–46 [47–48 (bl.)]   L
London: Simpkin, Marshall & Co.; Liverpool: Edward Howell   1877

3062 [ARCHER, WILLIAM, and ROBERT WILLIAM LOWE.] THE FASHIONABLE TRAGEDIAN: a criticism. With ten illustrations [by G. R. Halkett].

pp. [1–3] 4–24; illus.   L
Edinburgh and Glasgow: Thomas Gray and Company   1877

"Undoubtedly Lowe was the moving spirit" — Laurence Irving.

3063 ——second edition

pp. [1–3] 4–28; illus.   L
George Taylor   1877

On the cover: Second edition, with postscript. According to Laurence Irving, Lowe was also the moving spirit behind the publication of the second edition, in which some of the strictures are qualified. There were rumours of legal action, and Lowe "withdrew such copies as had been issued to the trade".

3064 [IRVING, HENRY?] A LETTER concerning Mr. Henry Irving addressed to E.R.H.

pp. [1–3] 4–18 [19–20 (bl.)]   L
Edinburgh: The Edinburgh Publishing Company; London: Simpkin, Marshall, & Co.; Glasgow: J. Menzies & Co.   1877

A reply to The Fashionable Tragedian (1877), signed "Yorick", and at least partly written by Irving himself — *see Laurence Irving, pp. 291–293.*

✖ E., A. Notes on Louis XI. *1878. See no. 3829.*

Includes a note on Irving as Louis.

3065 IRVING, HENRY. The stage. Address delivered by Mr. Henry Irving at the Perry Barr Institute, near Birmingham, on March 6th, 1878. Any profit derived from the sale of this pamphlet will be appropriated to the building fund of the Perry Barr Institute.

pp. [2] [1] 2–32   L
William Ridgeway   1878

✖ Walker, *Rev.* V. The theatre. [Birmingham?] 1878. *See no. 634.*

A reply to Irving's lecture on "The stage" (1878).

3066 PORTRAIT and memoir of Henry Irving.

†pp. [2] [1] 2–21 [22]   MH
                                                       1878

Caption title: Memoir of Henry Irving. From a friendly pen. Lacks portrait. According to a printed note on the cover, the portrait is from The Theatre, (no. 4240 below).

3067 IRVING, HENRY. The stage as it is. A lecture by Henry Irving, delivered at the sessional opening of the Edinburgh Philosophical Institution, 8th November, 1881.

pp. [1–3] 4–24   LGk
[Henry Vickers]   1881

Reprinted in The Drama *(1893) (see below no. 3090).*

3068 ARCHER, WILLIAM. Henry Irving actor and manager A critical study by William Archer (The vellum-parchment shilling series of miscellaneous literature, no. III.)

pp. [1–11] 12–108 [109–112 (advts.)]; illus. [front.]   E
Field & Tuer, Ye Leadenhalle Presse; Simpkin Marshall & Co.; Hamilton, Adams & Co.   [1883]

With first leaf of printed vellum wrapper bound in.

3069 ———second edition (The vellum-parchment shilling series of miscellaneous literature No. III).

pp. [1–11] 12–108 [109–112 (advts.)]; illus. [front.]; t.p. headed: Second edition   E
Field & Tuer, Ye Leadenhalle Presse; Simpkin, Marshall & Co.; Hamilton, Adams & Co.   [1883]

With first leaf of printed vellum wrapper bound in.

3070 ———[another edition]

pp. [i–iv], [11] 12–108 [109–112 (advts.)]   E
Field & Tuer, The Leadenhall Press; Simpkin, Marshall & Co.; Hamilton, Adams & Co.   [1885]

Date written on t.p.

3071 vacant

3072 BRERETON, AUSTIN. Henry Irving. A biographical sketch by Austin Brereton illustrated with seventeen full-page portraits from drawings by Edwin Long, R.A., J. A. M'Neil Whistler, Fred. Barnard, Val. Bromley, Alf. P. Tilt, J. Fulleylove, and Mrs. Allingham.

pp. [i–v] vi [vii] viii–ix [x–xii], [1] 2–79 [80–1] 82–136 [137–140]; pls. [front., 16]; inset, fold. [1]   LVA
David Bogue   1883

3073 ———[large paper issue]

pp. [i–v] vi–ix [x–xii], [1] 2–136 [137–140 (list of subscribers)]; pls. [front., 16]; inset, fold. [1]; t.p. in red and black   L
David Bogue   1884

Brereton published a number of different works about Irving, including Henry Irving *(1905) and* The Life of Henry Irving *(1908).*

3074 IRVINGITE, AN, *pseud.* of Frank Albert Marshall. Henry Irving actor and manager A criticism of a critic's criticism. By an Irvingite.

pp. [i–v] vi–viii [9] 10–80; apology slip (on p. 13)   LGk

London and New York: George Routledge and Sons   1883

In answer to William Archer's Henry Irving *(1883). A note on this copy: Joseph Knight from F. A. Marshall the author.*

3075 STIRLING, VIOLA, *ed.* The Henry Irving birthday book composed of quotations from some of the characters which Mr. Irving has acted, etc. Compiled by Viola Stirling.

pp. [6] [1] 2–266; pls. [6]   L
London and New York: George Routledge and Sons   1883

Printed with red borders.

3076 DALY, FREDERIC, *pseud.* of Frederic Louis Austin. Henry Irving in England and America 1838–84 by Frederic Daly with vignette portrait etched by Ad Lalauze.

pp. [i–v] vi–viii, [1] 2–300 [301–302 (advts.) 303–304 (bl.)]; pl. [front.]   NbU
T. Fisher Unwin   1884

3077 HATTON, JOSEPH. Henry Irving's impressions of America, narrated in a series of sketches, chronicles, and conversations. By Joseph Hatton.

2 vols. pp. [i–v] vi [vii] viii [ix] x–xii, [1] 2–297 [298 (imprint) 299–300 (advt.)] + pp. [i–v] vi–viii, [1] 2–272 [273–280 (advt.)]   E
Sampson Low, Marston, Searle, & Rivington   1884

3078 ———new and cheaper edition

pp. [i–v] vi–xii, [1] 2–375 [376]   GU
Sampson Low, Marston, Searle, and Rivington   1884

———[American edition] Boston: J. R. Osgood and Company, 1884. 1 vol.

3078.1 IRVING, HENRY. *The art of acting. Address to the students of Harvard University March 30 1885.

Chiswick Press   1885

IKF. *Reprinted in* The Drama, *(1893) (see below no. 3090).*

———[American edition] Authorised edition. Chicago: The Dramatic Publishing Co., [1887]

3079 HATTON, JOSEPH. The Lyceum "Faust". By Joseph Hatton. With illustrations from drawings by W. Telbin Hawes Graven W. H. Margetson J. Bernard Partridge and Helen H. Hatton.

pp. [1 (advt.) 1 (bl.)] [1–4] 5–32; illus., incl. [front.]; ptd. cover, illus.   E
J. S. Virtue & Co., Limited   [1886]

Reprinted from The Art Journal *(January – February 1886). William Wills'* Faust *was performed at the Lyceum on 19 December 1885.*

———[American edition] Boston: H. J. Brooks, [1886].

3080 IRVING, HENRY. English actors. Their characteristics and their methods. A discourse by Henry Irving delivered in the University Schools at Oxford, on Saturday June 26, 1886.

pp. [*4*] [1] 2–60 [61–64 (advts.)] L

Oxford: at the Clarendon Press 1886

Reprinted with revisions as Four Great Actors *in* The drama *(1893) (see below no. 3090).*

3081 VEDDER, PAUL. *Henry Irving, actor, manager.

Maxwell [1887]

Advertisement in Vedder's Playgoer's Pocket Book.

3082 NIBLETT, F. DRUMMOND. The Henry Irving *Dream of Eugene Aram* By F. Drummond Niblett Dedicated to J. L. Toole.

pp. [*24* (incl. covers)]; ptd. slip L

The Leadenhall Press [1888]

Caricatures of Irving, with the text of Thomas Hood's poem, in red and black. Irving often recited the poem, and had first done so when on tour with J. L. Toole.

3083 DREW, EDWIN. Henry Irving on and off the stage His Macbeth, Faust, etc. etc. including a chapter on Irving in evening dress By Edwin Drew editor of *The elocutionist*, etc. etc.

pp. [1–3] 4–80 L

Henry J. Drane [1889]

On the front red paper cover, verso, Edwin Drew is said to be "our most prolific writer on the Art of Elocution".

3084 THE REAL MACBETH by the real Macduff from the text of the late William Shakspeare.

pp. [*20*]; cover-title; illus. L

Swan Sonnenschein & Co. [1889]

Satire on Irving, who revived Macbeth *at the Lyceum 29th December 1888. Text (MS facsimile) and illustrations printed by lithography.*

3085 WILLAN, J[AMES] N[ATHANIEL]. First-night impressions of Mr. Irving's "Macbeth." By J. N. Willan, M.A. Reprinted, for private circulation, from the "Bath Chronicle," January 10, 1889.

pp. [1–3] 4–14 L

Bath: printed at the "Chronicle" Office [1889]

⌘ Maurel, Victor. Lyceum Theatre, December 8th, 1890. Address on the modern development of the lyric art [1890]. *See no. 2097.*

3086 IRVING, HENRY. *The art of acting.

Edinburgh 1891

Opening address of the session at the Philosophical Institution, Edinburgh, November 9, 1891. Reprinted in The drama *(1893) (see below no. 3090);* Laurence Irving *pp. 675–684.*

3087 FITZGERALD, PERCY. Henry Irving A record of twenty years at the Lyceum. By Percy Fitzgerald, M.A., F.S.A.

pp. [i–v] vi–viii [ix] x–xvi, [1] 2–320; pl. [front.] L

Chapman and Hall, Ld. 1893

3088 ———a new edition, revised with an additional chapter.

pp. [i–iii] iv–v [vi–vii] viii, [1] 2–149 [150–152]; pl. [front.] L

Chatto & Windus 1895

3089 ———[another edition] Sir Henry Irving A biography by Percy Fitzgerald.

pp. [i–vi] vii–xvi, 1–319 [320] NbU

Fisher Unwin 1906

"A new and revised account" of the actor—Preface.

———[American edition] new and revised edition. Philadelphia: Jacobs & Co., 1906.

3090 IRVING, *Sir* HENRY. The drama. Addresses by Henry Irving.

pp. [*8*] 1–163 [164]; pl. [front.] L

William Heinemann 1893 [1892]

Contains: The Stage As It Is *(1881) (no. 3067);* The Art of Acting *(1885) (no. 3078.1);* Four Great Actors (= English actors *(Oxford 1886) (no. 3080),* The Art of Acting *(Edinburgh 1891) (no. 3086).*

3091 ———second edition

pp. [*8*] 1–163 [164] LGk

William Heinemann 1893

———[American editions] New York: Tait, Sons & Company, Copyright 1892; Boston: Joseph Knight Company, Copyright 1892.

These American editions are not reissues of the English, though they are very similar to it; and possibly preceded it.

3092 KING LEAR AT THE LYCEUM. Produced November 10, 1892. Some extracts from the press on the performance of Mr. Henry Irving and Miss Ellen Terry.

pp. [1–5] 6–118 [119 (colophon) 120 (bl.)]   MH
Printed at the Chiswick Press   1893

3093 CALVERT, WALTER. Souvenir of Sir Henry Irving.
pp. [1–5] 6–48; illus.; pl. [1]   L
Henry J. Drane, Chant & Co.   [1895]

3094 ———Sir Henry Irving and Miss Ellen Terry. A record of over twenty years at the Lyceum Theatre. Seventy-six illustrations.
pp. [8] [1–5] 6–48, ²[1–3] 4–48; illus.; pl. [1]   L
London: Henry J. Drane; New York: Smith & Streit
                                                  1897
A reissue in one volume of nos. 3093, 3582.

3095 RUSSELL, PERCY. Sir Henry Irving (published by permission) (Men and Women of The Century No. 1).
pp. [1–2] 3–63 [64 (advt.)]   NbU
S. Champness & Co.   [1895]

3096 THEATRE ROYAL, Gloucester: Centenary Irving Banquet.
bs.   GrP
[Cheltenham]   [1896]
Advertising a banquet for Sir Henry Irving and his company who gave a free performance at the theatre to mark its centenary.

3097 SIR HENRY IRVING at the Clef Club, October 1st, 1897.
pp. [2] 1–8 [9 (bl.) 10 (colophon)]   MH
Birmingham: printed by the Birmingham Guild of Handicraft Limited   [1897]

✄ A catalogue of a portion of the dramatic library of a gentleman. [1899.] *See no. 95.*
Irving's library.

3098 HIATT, CHARLES. Henry Irving. A record and review by Charles Hiatt.
pp. [i–iv] v–xiv, [1] 2–282, misprinting 274 as "472"; illus.; t.p. in red and black; pls. [front., 54]   E
George Bell and Sons   1899
Cover designed by Gordon Craig.

3099 IRVING, HENRY. *A speech delivered at Sunderland, when he was presented with a casket by the Shakespeare Society.
pp. 11
Printed by the Chiswick Press   [ca. 1900]
  IKF.

Jackson, John (1730–1806)
Actor. Manager of the Edinburgh Theatre from 1781. See above nos. 1948–1958.

Jackson, *Mrs.* Hester
Genest says, "Mrs. Jackson was a disagreeable actress" — Lowe.

3100 DODD, J[AMES] S[OLAS]. Gallic gratitude; or, The Frenchman in India: a comedy in two acts, as it is performed at the Theatre Royal in Covent-Garden. By J. S. Dodd.
pp. [1–9] 10–45 [46]; [pl. front.]   L
E. Johnson   1779
At the end are "Critical remarks on Mrs. Jackson's performance of Lady Randolph in the tragedy of Douglas . . . April 30, 1779," on which date "Gallic Gratitude" was produced for her benefit, "Douglas" being the first piece. She played Britannia *in the Prologue [to* Gallic gratitude] — Lowe.*

Jackson, *Mrs. R. Actress*
3101 THE RELUCTANT APPEAL OF MRS. R. JACKSON to the Newcastle audience.
bs.   MB
Newcastle: Blagburn, printer   [1826?]

3102 vacant

Jefferson, Joseph 1829–1905
American actor. He visited Britain and played in London and the provinces.

3103 JEFFERSON, JOSEPH. The autobiography of Joseph Jefferson.
pp. [iii–viii] ix–xv [xvi (bl.)], [1] 2–501 [502 (bl.)]; pls. [front., 76]   L
London: T. Fisher Unwin; New York: The Century Co.   [1890]
First published in the Century Illustrated Monthly Magazine—Brown. *Copy examined has 3 plates (opposite pp. 13, 386, 410) not included in the list of illustrations, giving a total of 79.*

3104 ———[another edition] "Rip Van Winkle": the autobiography of Joseph Jefferson.
pp. [i–iv] v–xxxii, 1–375 [376]; pls. [front., 15]   L
Reinhardt & Evans, Ltd.   1949

———[American editions] New York: The Century Co. 1890, 1897; New York: Appleton-Century-Crofts, 1950 (entitled *Rip Van Winkle*, foreword by E. Farjeon); Cambridge, Mass.: Harvard University Press, 1964 (edited with notes by Alan S. Downer.)

Jerome, Jerome Klapka (1859–1927)
Playwright and novelist. He also acted for a short period. See also AUTHOR INDEX.

3105 JEROME, JEROME K[LAPKA]. On the stage — and off: the brief career of a would-be actor by Jerome K. Jerome.

pp. [i–v] vi–viii, [1] 2–160   L

Field & Tuer; Simpkin, Marshall & Co.; Hamilton, Adams & Co.   1885

Mr. Jerome is well known in connection with the Play-goers' Club. His book is decidedly interesting — Lowe.

3106 ———*new edition

Field and Tuer   1890

ECB.

3107 ———[another edition] With one hundred illustrations by Kenneth M. Skeaping.

pp. [i–v] vi–viii, [1] 2–219 [220 (bl.)]; illus.   L

London: The Leadenhall Press, Simpkin, Marshall, Hamilton Kent & Co., Ltd.; New York: Charles Scribner's Sons   [1891]

With 8 leaves of advertisements bound in as issued. On the cloth cover: Illustrated edition.

3108 ———*[fifteenth edition]

Simpkin, Marshall & others   nd.

STR.

———[American edition] New York: Henry Holt and Co., 1891.

Johnston, Henry Erskine (1777–1845)

An actor who was known as the "Scotch Roscius." His first appearance in London was at Covent Garden in 1797–98 — Lowe.

Johnstone, John (1749–1828)

The famous Irish comedian. He made his first appearance in London at Covent Garden on 2nd October 1783, and was at first principally employed as a singer; but his reputation rests upon his Irish parts, he being able to play Irishmen of all classes. He retired from the stage in 1820—Lowe. See no. 1182.

Jones, Frederick Edward (1759–1834)

Originally an amateur actor and manager, Jones became lessee of the Dublin Theatre in 1796 — Lowe. For the controversy over Croker's Familiar Epistles, 1804, see nos. 1809–1828.

Jones, Inigo (1573–1652)

Architect and designer.

3109 CUNNINGHAM, PETER, JAMES ROBINSON PLANCHÉ and JOHN PAYNE COLLIER. Inigo Jones. A life of the architect; by Peter Cunningham, Esq. Remarks on some of his sketches for masques and dramas; by J. R. Planché, Esq. And five court masques; edited from the original mss. of Ben Jonson, John Marston, etc. by J. Payne Collier, Esq. Accompanied by facsimiles of drawings by Inigo Jones; and by a portrait from a painting by Vandyck.

pp. [i–v] vi–xxi [xxii–xxiv], [1] 2–148; pls. [front., 15 (incl. 2 fold.)]   L

The Shakespeare Society   1848 [*for* 1849]

Jordan, Dorothy (1761–1816)

Genest, who wrote her epitaph, says that Mrs. Jordan never had a superior in her proper line, which was that of the broader comedy, romps, and "breeches" parts. She was indeed a true comedian. Her private life was somewhat sensational: her connection with the Duke of Clarence, afterwards William IV, giving rise to much gossip and scandal — Lowe. Before her marriage she was billed as Miss Francis, after her mother's name, but also had the name Bland after her father.

3110 AN ESSAY ON THE PRE-EMINENCE OF COMIC GENIUS: with observations on the several characters Mrs. Jordan has appeared in.

pp. [4] [1] 2–27 [28 (bl.)]   L
T. Becket   1786

3111 ———*[another edition] . . . in the Theatre Royal, London: being the work of a celebrated clergyman in that city.

    1786

Eames.

3112 *LINES addressed to Mrs. Jordan.

pp. 14   MB
T. Becket   1787

3113 JORDAN'S ELIXIR OF LIFE, and cure for the spleen; or, a collection of all the songs sung by Mrs. Jordan, since her first appearance in London. With many other favourite songs, sung by her in the theatres of Dublin, York, Edinburgh, and Cheltenham, and a number of duetts, trios, glees, &c. that she has a part in. To which is prefixed, Authentic memoirs of Mrs. Jordan, now first published. Embellished with a superb engraving of Mrs. Jordan, in "Sir Harry Wildair".

pp. [1–3] 4–68 [68 *for* 69], ²[1] 2–6 (the last six pages are a "Catalogue of books, pamphlets, and prints, to be had at W. Holland's Museum of Genius . . .") 7 (bl.); pl. [front.]   L

William Holland   1789

3114 M———, *Capt. R. N.* *Dedicated to the British Nation. Memoirs and amorous adventures by sea and land, of King William IV. Interspersed with upwards of one hundred curious anecdotes. Including his intrigues with Madame Schwellenberg — the Plymouth bumboat woman — Mrs. Fisherman — Yankee Bet — the naval cock-and-hen club — battle Royal — Demarara Dolly — the Boatswain's wife's black broth — and a copious account of his intercourse with, and causes of separation from, Mrs. Jordan, and particulars of the Fitz-Clarence family. By Capt. M——, R.N. who has had the honour of being a shipmate with his Majesty.

pp. 32; front.

Lowe.   [1830]

3115 BOADEN, JAMES. The life of Mrs. Jordan; including original private correspondence, and numerous anecdotes of her contemporaries. By James Boaden, Esq. author of *The life of Kemble*, &c.

2 vols. pp. [4] [i] ii–xv [xvi (bl.)], [1] 2–368; pl. [front.] + pp. [4] [i] ii–xiv, [1] 2–364 [365–8 (advts.)]; pl., fold. [front.]   MH

Edward Bull   1831

3116 ——second edition

2 vols. pp. [2] [i] ii–xv [xvi], [1] 2–368; pl. [front.] + pp. [2] [1] 2–364 [365–368 (advts.)]; pl., fold. [front.]   GU

Edward Bull   1831

3117 ——*third edition

2 vols. in 1   MB

Edward Bull   1831

3118 ——[another edition] (Beaux & Belles of England)

2 vols. pp. [4] vii–xix [xx–xxi (list of illustrations) xxii], 1–334; pls. [front (col.), 5]; ptd. tissue guards [6]; t.p. in red and black + pp. [i–vi] vii–xv [xvi xvii (list of illustrations) xviii], 1–332 [333–334 (bl.)]; pls. [front (col.), 5]; ptd. tissue guards [6]; t.p. in red and black   NbU

Printed by the Grolier Society   [190–?]

Imperial edition limited to one thousand copies for England and America.

——[American edition] Beaux and Belles of England. New York: Athenaeum Press, [1907?].

3119 CONFIDENTIAL FRIEND, A, *pseud.* Public and private life of that celebrated actress Miss Bland, otherwise Mrs. Ford, or, Mrs. Jordan; late mistress of H.R.H. the D. of Clarence; now King William IV. Founder of the Fitzclarence family; being mother of the Earl of Munster — Col. Lord Frederic Fitzclarence — Lord Augustus Fitzclarence — Lord Adolphus Fitz-clarence, R.N. Lady Sophia Sydney — Lady Mary Fox — Countess of Errol — Lady Kennedy Erskine, and Lady Falkland. Delineating the vicissitudes attendant on

her early life; the splendor of her noon-tide blaze, as mistress of the Royal Duke; and her untimely dissolution at St. Cloud, near Paris, — resulting from a broken heart. Accompanied by numerous remarks and anecdotes of illustrious and fashionable characters. By a confidential friend of the departed. Embellished by portraits of the Fitzclarence family.

pp. [2] [5] 6–266; pls. [front., 10]; t.p. headed "The great illegitimates!!"   L

J. Duncombe   [1831?]

3120 ——[another edition]

pp. [1–3] 4–117 [118–120 (bl.)]   L

J. Duncombe   [1886?]

Omits from the title-page the heading and the sections "being mother . . . Falkland", and "Embellished . . . family". The punctuation of the title-page also differs. A reprint, with omissions, not in fact published by Duncombe.

Kean, Charles John (1811–1868)

Compared with his father, he was only a moderate actor. In 1850 he took the Princess's Theatre, at which his Shake-spearian productions were noted for their gorgeousness. His wife was Miss Ellen Tree, a very notable artist — Lowe. Kean gave up the Princess's in 1859.

3121 [KEAN, CHARLES JOHN and JERROLD, DOUGLAS.] MR. DOUGLAS JERROLD and Mr. Charles Kean.

pp. [1–4]; head-title
                                              [1854]

IKF. *An answer to Jerrold's criticism of Kean's management of the Princess Theatre.*

3122 COSTUMES in Shakspeare's historical play of *King Henry the Eighth* Published by the kind permission of Charles Kean Esqr.

pls. 18, each with imprint "Vienna: M. Trentsensky; London: A. & S. Joseph, Myers & Co."; title on cover

Joseph, Myers & Co.   [1855]

IKF. *Charles Kean's production of* King Henry the Eighth *opened at the Princess's on 16 May 1855.*

3123 COSTUMES in Shakspeare's play of *The Winter's Tale* as represented at the Princess's Theatre In four parts Published by the kind permission of Charles Kean Esqr.

col. pls. 24, each with imprint "Vienna: M. Trentsensky Theatr. Cost."; title on cover

A. & S. Joseph, Myers & Co.   [1856]

IKF. *Charles Kean's production of* The Winter's Tale *opened on 28 April 1856.*

3124 COLE, JOHN WILLIAM. The life and theatrical times of Charles Kean, F.S.A. Including a summary of the English stage for the last fifty years, and a detailed account of the management of the Princess's Theatre, from 1850 to 1859. By John William Cole.

2 vols. pp. [i–iii] iv–xii, [1] 2–368 + [i–iii] iv–viii, [1] 2–398 GU

Richard Bentley 1859

3125 ———The life and theatrical times of Charles Kean, F.S.A. Including a summary of the English stage for the last fifty years. By John William Cole. Second edition.

2 vols. pp. [i–iv] v–xii, misnumbering xi as "x", [1] 2–368; pl. [front.] + pp. [i–iii] iv–viii, [1] 2–391 [392] GU

Richard Bentley 1859

Some copies dated 1860; also issued as two volumes in one.

3126 ST. JAMES'S HALL. The Kean banquet, Wednesday, July 20, 1859. His Grace the Duke of Newcastle in the chair. T. H. Taunton, Esq., Hon. Sec.

pp. [1–3] 4–32 MH

Printed by Walter Brettell [1859]

3127 ST. JAMES'S HALL. The Kean banquet, Wednesday, July 20th. 1859, his Grace the Duke of Newcastle in the chair; and the Kean testimonial presentation, Saturday, March 22nd, 1862, Right Hon. W. E. Gladstone, M.P., Chancellor of the Exchequer, in the chair. T. H. Taunton, Esq., honorary secretary.

pp. [1–3] 4–48 MH

[Walter Brettell, printer] [1862?]

Partly reprinted from newspapers.

⌘ Catalogue of presentation silver plate. . . . &c. formerly the property of . . . Mr. & Mrs. Charles J. Kean. [1898]. *See no. 96.*

⌘ Catalogue of the library of the late Charles Kean. [1898]. *See no. 97.*

Kean, Edmund (1789?–1833)

One of the great names of the English stage. He made his first appearance at Drury Lane, on 26th January 1814, as Shylock. Hazlitt described this as "the first gleam of genius breaking athwart the gloom of the stage;" and the proprietors of Drury Lane acknowledged that he saved the theatre from bankruptcy. Artistically and financially he was a phenomenon, and it is sad to remember how dissipation ruined the actor and killed him. He died 15th May 1833 — Lowe. *See H. M. Hillebrand,* Edmund Kean *(New York, 1933) and Giles Playfair,* Kean *(1939).*

3128 *COOKE SLEEPS!—Kean lives! The life and interesting anecdotes of Mr. Kean: with remarks on his performances.

pp. 23 MB

Smeeton [*ca.* 1814]

3129 CRITICAL REMARKS on the astonishing performance of Mr. Kean, at Drury-Lane Theatre, in the characters of Shylock, Richard, and Hamlet. Embellished with a striking likeness of Mr. Kean in each character.

pp. [*16*]; col. pl., fold. [front.] DFo

John Fairburn [1814]

3130 PHIPPEN, FRANCIS. Authentic memoirs of Edmund Kean, of the Theatre Royal, Drury Lane; containing a specimen of his talent at composition. By Francis Phippen.

pp. [*2*] [7] 8–111 [112] [=108] L

J. Roach 1814

The specimen of his composition is an account of an unfortunate companion — Lowe.

3131 [COLE, JOHN.] THE TALENTS of Edmund Kean delineated.

pp. [1–3] 4–19 [20 (bl.)] L

J. Johnston 1817

Motto on the title page: "Thou Nature art my Goddess".

3132 ———*Illus. edition

Scarborough 1829

STR.

Bucke's "The Italians" 1819

For Kean's quarrel with Bucke see THEORY AND CRITICISM *nos. 3835–3844.*

3133 A CRITICAL EXAMINATION of the respective performances of Mr. Kean & Mr. Macready, in Cibber's alteration of Shakespeare's historical play of *King Richard the Third.*

pp. [*4*] [1] 2–40 MH

Sold by Simpkin and Marshall; Charles Reader; and Chappell and Son 1819

⌘ Macauley, Elizabeth Wright. Theatric revolution. 1819. *See no. 3247.*

Regarding Kean and his influence on the theatre — Lowe. *Unfavourable to Kean.*

3134 TO EDMUND KEAN, Esq.

engr. pl. with verses DFo

John Lowndes 1822

The verses, in quotation marks, begin "Thou art the sun's bright child . . ."

Cox v. Kean 1825

In this wretched case, which was Kean's ruin, the woman seems to have been chiefly to blame, and the husband seems to have acted like a fool. Kean was treated with extraordinary severity by the public, and was practically driven off the stage. He went to America for two seasons, but, on his return, was the wreck of his former self. Some of the pamphlets are extraordinarily nasty, and are very scarce. "Little Breeches" was a nickname of Kean's for Mrs. Cox — Lowe.

3135 CRIM. CON. COX v. KEAN. For criminal conversation with plaintiff's wife, damages £800. Full particulars of this interesting trial, with the letters, &c. &c. &c.

pp. [1–3] 4–8; t.p. headed "Chubb's cheap edition" MH
Chubb [1825]

3136 *CRIM. CON. third edition

pp. 20
Edward Duncombe [1825?]

> BMC, *but copy destroyed.*

3137 *CRIM. CON. Damages £800!!! Duncombe Jun.'s edition. A full report of the trial, on Monday January 17th, 1825, Albion Cox, Esq. versus Edmund Kean, Esq. of the Theatre Royal, Drury Lane, for criminal conversation with the plaintiff's wife: an accurate detail of all the circumstances connected with the case; speeches of Counsel at full length; with copies of the whole of the love letters that passed between the parties. Taken in short hand, by an eminent reporter, expressly. Embellished with a full length portrait of Mr. Kean, engraved by Kennerly.

[1825]

With portrait of Kean as Richard III — Lowe.

3138 [FOOTE, MARIA?] *AN APPEAL to the justice and common sense of the friends of the true drama; wherein is compared the treatment experienced by Miss Foote, of Covent Garden, with that experienced by Mr. Kean, of Drury Lane, on certain late occasions.

pp. 22 MH
[1825]

3139 COCKS AND CUCKOLDOM!! Original songs, on Keen, Cocks, and Little Breeches.

pp. [1] 2–16; head-title MH
[London: printed and published by John Fairburn]
[1825]

3140 COMPLETE DEFENCE OF KEAN against the unmanly attacks of "The Times."

pp. [1] 2–4; illus. DFo
[London: W. Mason, printer] [1825]

3141 CRIM CON. Little Breeches, or, the cock of Drury Lane.

bs., illus. DFo
Pitts, printer [1824 or 1825]

> *With a coloured woodcut of Kean as Richard III waving his sword, apparently signed "Byn" or "Byor". Reprinted in Kean vindicated (see below no. 3151).*

3142 ——[another edition]

bs.; illus. MH
Pitts, printer [1824 or 1825]

> *With a coloured woodcut of Kean as Richard III kneeling by Mrs. Cox in bed, labelled "A scene in the bedchamber".*

3143 ——[another edition] Little Breeches, and the cock of Drury-Lane.

bs.; illus. MH
Catnach, printer [1824 or 1825]

> *With three small wood-cuts, uncoloured.*

3144 CRIM. CON. The trial between Alderman Cox and Edmund Kean, for criminal conversation with the plaintiff's wife, including the letters, &c. Tried in the Court of King's Bench, Guildhall, January the 17th, 1825, before the Lord Chief Justice.

pp. [1–3] 4–25 [26] DFo
Printed by B. Clarke [1825]

3145 FAIRBURN's edition of the trial between Robert Albion Cox, Esq. plaintiff, and Edmund Kean, defendant, for criminal conversation with the plaintiff's wife, including the evidence, speeches of counsel, and all the curious love letters, &c. &c. Tried in the Court of King's Bench, Guildhall, January the 17th, 1825, before the Lord Chief Justice Abbott, and a special jury. To which is added, a memoir, containing eccentric anecdotes of the defendant in this cause, and also of Little Breeches.

pp. [1–3] 4–76 [77–78 (advts.)], misnumbering 64 as "63"; col. pl., fold. [front.]; t.p. headed: Cox versus Kean LGk
[London]: John Fairburn [1825]

> *Title bears as motto an inexact quotation from one of Kean's letters to Mrs. Cox: "I will hold my little darling to my heart, and sleep in spite of thunder!"*

3146 A GRAND SECRET, all the love letters: Cox versus Kean.

pp. [1–3] 4; title headed: Reed's cheap edition MH
[Reed] [1825]

3147 *KEAN versus O.P.

pp. 32 MH
[London] 1825

3148 LITTLE, THOMAS, *pseud. of* Thomas Moore? The actor and the alderman's wife; or, Kean and his little breeches! A farce in three acts. Written by Thomas Little, Esq.

pp. [1–3] 4–29 [30]   DFo
T. Holt   [1825]

By Moore, according to Hillebrand, *p. 249.*

3149 MR. KEAN'S RECEPTION.

pp. [4]; headed: second edition   MH
[C. S. Bingham]   [1825]

Signed J.P.

3150 ——[another edition]

pp. [1–3] 4   MH
C. S. Bingham, printer   [1825]

Contains also the "third edition" of Mr. Kean's second appearance. (See below no. 3152). Signed J.P.

3151 ——Kean vindicated, or the truth discovered; with is [sic] flattering reception on Monday evening.

pp. [1–2] 3 [4]; title headed: Reed's cheap edition   MH
T. Reed   [1825]

Contains "Third edition. Mr. Kean's reception", and "The Drury Lane Hero. A new song" (the same as that called "Little Breeches, or the cock of Drury Lane". See above no. 3141).

3152 ★MR. KEAN'S second appearance.
                                                              [1825]

Lowe. *A third edition is included in Mr. Kean's reception [another edition] 1825. (See above no. 3150).*

3153 THE POETIC EPISTLES OF EDMUND: with notes, illustrations, and reflections.

pp. [i–v] vi [vii–viii] [9] 10–47 [48]   L
Printed for the editor: published and sold by Effingham Wilson   1825

Dedicated "to the British people, as the guardians of virtue, both public and private. . . ."

3154 THE REAL FRIENDS OF KEAN and the drama, are earnestly requested, to remain seated, and to restrain their expressions of applause; . . .

bs.   MH
[London]   [7 Feb 1825]

Distributed at Drury Lane.

3155 ★THE ROSE OF COVENT GARDEN.
bs.; illus.
J. Catnach   [1825]

STR. *With a woodcut of Mrs. Cox.*

3156 SECRETS WORTH KNOWING. Suppressed letters. Cox versus Kean.

pp. [1] 2–4; illus.   MH
[Chubb, printer]   [1825]

A very nasty production — Lowe.

✠ The Theatrical Mince Pie . . . Containing a correct account of the several appearances of Mr. Kean and Miss Foote, since their late actions in the Court of King's Bench . . . 1825. *See no. 4141.*

3157 THE WIND-UP; or, candour versus times.

pp. [1] 2–8; title headed: Second edition   MH
C. S. Bingham, printer   [1825]

Signed: J.P.

———————————————————

3158 SMYTHSON, *Mrs.* Impromptu congratulatory address to Edmund Kean, Esq. on hearing of his return from America, and re-appearance at Drury Lane Theatre, on Monday, the 8th of January, 1827. Written by Mrs. Smythson, and published at the suggestion of several eminent professionals, who deemed this effort of the fair author's muse, a happy medium to submit to the public a well-penned memento worthy the renown of the first tragedian of the age.

bs.   MH
Printed and published by J. Poole   1827

Thirty-two lines of verse.

3159 [DANIEL, GEORGE.] OPHELIA KEEN!! A dramatic legendary tale.

pp. [1–5] 6–24   DFo
John Cumberland   1829

This is said to relate an actual occurrence in Kean's house at Mornington Place, Hampstead Road, where a Miss Benjamin, with whom Kean lived, broke up a supper party in the most admired confusion. There is a regular pot-house air about the whole business — Lowe.

3160 ✝KEMBLE, CHARLES and Mr. BARTLEY. Theatre Royal, Covent-Garden. Copy of a communication from Mr. C. Kemble to the public journals. Copies of three letters written to Mr. Kean by Mr. Bartley, stage manager of Covent Garden Theatre.

pp. [2]; containing only the three letters by Bartley   MH
Printed by W. Reynolds   [1829]

Concerning an agreement Kean is alleged to have broken with Covent Garden management.

Kean Sale Catalogues 1833–1834

See *SALE CATALOGUES nos. 98–100, 120.*

———————————————————

3161 EDMUND KEAN. (The popular portrait gallery of illustrious and eminent persons. Nos. viii–ix.)

pp. [*4*]; illus.; pls. [2] MH

London: W. Strange. G. Cowie. J. Thomas. G. Berger. G. Purkiss. J. Onwhyn; Edinburgh: J. Ebsworth; Dublin: G. Young [1833?]

3162 KNOWLES, [JAMES] SH[ERIDAN]. *The life of Edmund Kean, Esq. tragedian; with critical remarks on his theatrical performance. By Sh. Knowles, Esq.

1833

Recorded but not seen by Lowe.

3163 TO THE THEATRICAL WORLD and the curious generally. The bedstead on which Edmund Kean, the tragedian, breathed his last. This relic, as once the property of the greatest genius that ever graced the British stage, will be raffled for by 40 members, at 5s. each, at Mr. Phillips', Swan Tavern & Lord Dover Hotel, Hungerford Market, on Tuesday evening next, the 16th inst . . .

bs. DFo

[London] [1833]

Reprinted in The Era Almanack *(1875), p. 28.*

3164 MONUMENT TO THE MEMORY OF THE LATE EDMUND KEAN.

bs. MH

S. G. Fairbrother, printer [1834 or 5]

A list of subscriptions received, with an appeal for additional subscribers. The Chairman and Treasurer was Stephen Price.

3165 [PROCTER, BRYAN WALLER.] THE LIFE OF EDMUND KEAN.

2 vols. pp. [i–v] vi–xlvii [xlviii], [1] 2–216; pl. [front.] + pp. [i–v] vi–vii [viii], [1] 2–280 NbU

Edward Moxon 1835

For Procter, this work "was a mistake. He should not have been pressed to write it" — Procter: An Autobiographical Fragment, *ed. Coventry Patmore (1877), p. 105.*

3166 NORTON, THEODORE. Kean, a poem. By Theodore Norton.

pp. [1–9] 10–37 [38 (imprint) 39–40 (bl)]; lacking pl. [front.] GU

W. Kenneth 1835

An elegy, with an appendix of biographical anecdotes.

3167 HAWKINS, F[REDERICK] W. The life of Edmund Kean. From published and original sources. By F. W. Hawkins.

2 vols. pp. [i–ix] x–xxiii [xxiv (bl.)], [1] 2–420 + [i–v] vi–xiii [xiv (bl.)], [1] 2–430 L

Tinsley Brothers 1869

✖ Cotton, William. The story of the drama in Exeter. . . . With reminiscences of Edmund Kean. London & Exeter, 1887. *See no. 1594.*

3168 MOLLOY, J[OSEPH] FITZGERALD. The life and adventures of Edmund Kean tragedian 1787–1833.

2 vols. pp. [i–v] vi–x [xi–xii], [1] 2–298, ²i–vi (advts.) + pp. [i–v] vi–viii, [1] 2–286, ²i–vi (advts.) L

Ward and Downey 1888

3169 ———[another edition]

pp. [i–iii] iv–vii [viii (bl.)], [1] 2–430–[431–432 (bl.)]; pl. [front.] NbU

Downey & Co. Limited 1897

Keeley, Robert, (1793–1869) *and* Mary Ann (1806–1899)

Robert was one of the most admirable of low comedians. He married Miss Goward, a clever actress, both in serious and comic characters, and they together were extremely popular. From 1844 until 1847 they managed the Lyceum with great success. — Lowe. *See also above no. 1980.*

3170 GOODMAN, WALTER. The Keeleys on the stage and at home by Walter Goodman author of 'The pearl of the Antilles', 'People I have painted', etc. With two photo-engravings from pictures by the author, and other illustrations.

pp. [i–vii] viii–xiv, [1] 2–357 [358 (bl.)]; pls. [front., 17]; illus; t.p. in red and black NbU

Richard Bentley and Son 1895

Keene, Theophilus (–1718)

We know little of Keene, except what is told by Chetwood, and the particulars given by him are of little interest — Lowe.

3171 [CHETWOOD, WILLIAM, *ed.*] MEMOIRS of the life of Mr. Theophilus Keene, the late eminent tragedian. To which is added, elegies, pastorals, odes, and poems: by several hands.

pp. [2] [i] ii–v [vi], [1] 2–21 [22 (advts.) 23 (advts. & errata) 24 (bl.)] L

W. Chetwood 1718

Verse said to be by Richard Savage, Thomas Walker, A.R., Gent., William Wilks, Tolson, Chetwood, and C.W. "A Poem on the Memory of Mr. Keene. Written by Mr. Savage, Son of the late Earl of Rivers" is not reprinted in Savage's Works *(1775).*

Keith, Charlie

Clown in circus and pantomime.

3172 KEITH, CHARLIE. Circus life & amusements (equestrian, dramatic, & musical), in all nations. Written by Charlie Keith, the roving English clown, embracing his life, travels, and experiences of professional and non-professional men.

pp. [i–iii] iv [5] 6–155 [156] E
Derby: printed by Bewley & Roe 1879

Kelly, Francis Maria (1790–1882)

Actress and singer with the Italian opera; niece of Michael Kelly. She acted mainly at Drury Lane playing Ophelia to Kean's Hamlet and on her retirement she built a theatre (later to become the Royalty) for teaching actresses, which proved a financial failure. See Basil Francis, Fanny Kelly of Drury Lane *(1950).*

3173 [TAYLOR, JOHN.] TO MISS KELLY, on her return to the Theatre Royal, Drury Lane.

bs. MH
[London] [1819?]

A poem, in four stanzas, beginning,
"Three months, dear Fanny! oh! how short
Thy merits to display" . . .
Signed 'T'. *On Fanny Kelly's return from a season with Arnold at the English Opera House. Reprinted in Taylor's* Poems *(1827) (see above no. 902.)*

Kelly, Hugh (1739–1777)

The suporter of sentimental comedy. His Thespis *was disfigured by extreme coarseness and abuse of the actors, and produced several pamphlets in reply*—Lowe. *See AUTHOR INDEX.*

Kelly, Michael (1762–1826)

A noted singer, who was also a fairly good composer, but a very bad actor. — Lowe.

3174 [HOOK, THEODORE, *ed.*] REMINISCENCES of Michael Kelly, of the King's Theatre, and Theatre Royal Drury Lane, including a period of nearly half a century; with original anecdotes of many distinguished persons, political, literary, and musical.

2 vols. pp. [i–vii] viii–xxiii [xxiv], [1] 2–354 [355–356 (advts.)]; pl. [front.]; inset [2 leaves of music] + pp. [4] [1] 2–404, ²[1] 2–4 (the last 2 leaves cont. advts.) L
Henry Colburn 1826

3175 ——second edition

2 vols. pp. [i–v] vi–xvi, [1] 2–349 [350 (bl.) 351–352 (advts.)]; pls. [front., 1 (double)] + pp. [i–iii] iv–xii, [1] 2–367 [368] L
Henry Colburn 1826

Vol. 2 has bound in one leaf (pp. [1]–2) of Colburn advertisements.

——[American edition] New York: Collins & Hannay, 1826.

——[French translation] Paris: C. J. Trouve, 1827.

A delightful book — Lowe. *The "anecdotal substance" of Kelly's* Reminiscences *is reprinted in* Personal Reminiscences of O'Keefe, Kelly, and Taylor *ed. R. H. Stoddard, (Bric-a-Brac Series) (New York, 1875).*

Kemble, Adelaide (1814?–1879)

Afterwards Mrs. Sartoris; daughter of Charles Kemble. Singer.

3176 HAYTER, JOHN. *[Drawing executed for the Marquess of Titchfield, representing Miss Adelaide Kemble.]

1841

Text by Mrs. A. B. Jameson, reprinted in her Memoirs and Essays *(1846).*

Kemble, Charles (1775–1854)

Actor and manager. See also GOVERNMENT REGULATION OF THE THEATRE no. 205.

⌘ A catalogue of [a] most splendid theatrical wardrobe of an eminent actor . . . [1837]. *See no. 101.*

3177 LANE, RICHARD JAMES. *Sixteen portraits of Charles Kemble Esq.

pp. (1), 4, (2) MB
[London] 1840

Kemble, Frances Anne (1809–1893)

Fanny Kemble, daughter of Charles Kemble, made her first appearance on the stage, at Covent Garden, as Juliet on 5th October 1829, when her success was so great that, to quote Genest, "she enabled the proprietors to pay off a debt of £13,000." In 1832 she went to America, where her success was triumphant. In 1834 she married Mr. Pierce Butler. Her last appearance was in 1848 with Macready. She has written poems, plays, and very interesting records of her experiences — Lowe. *Frances Anne Kemble's* Notes upon some of Shakespeare's Plays *(1882) contains an introductory chapter "On the Stage", first published in the* Cornhill Magazine *(December 1863) and separately published as* On the Stage *(New York, 1926). Frances Anne Kemble's* Journal of a residence on a Georgian plantation in 1838–1839, *ed. by John A. Scott (1961) contains "Bibliographical Notes" (pp. 406–415).*

3178 BUTLER, FRANCES ANNE. Journal by Frances Anne Butler.

2 vols. pp. [i–v] vi–viii, [1] 2–313 [314 (colophon)] + [4] [1] 2–287 [288 (colophon)] L
John Murray 1835

————[American edition] Journal of a residence in America. Philadelphia: Carey, Lea, and Blanchard, 1835.

————[Belgian edition] Journal of a residence in America. Brussels: Ad. Wahlen, 1835.

3179 KEMBLE, FRANCES ANN. Record of a girlhood. By Frances Ann Kemble.

3 vols. pp. [8] [1] 2–299 [300] + [4] [1] 2–336 + [4] [1] 2–321 [322]   GU

Richard Bentley and Son   1878

First appeared in a shorter version in the Atlantic Monthly.

3180 ————[second edition]

3 vols. pp. [4] [1] 2–299 [300] + [2] [1] 2–336 + [2] [1] 2–321 [322]   GU

Richard Bentley and Son   1878

————[American edition] New York: Henry Holt & Co., 1879.

3181 KEMBLE, FRANCES ANNE. Records of later life. By Frances Anne Kemble.

3 vols. pp. [4] [1] 2–288 + pp. [4] [1] 2–295 [296] + pp. [4] [1] 2–422 [423–424 (bl.)]   NbU

Richard Bentley and Son   1882

————[American edition] New York: Henry Holt & Co., 1882.

3182 KEMBLE, FRANCES ANNE. Further records. 1848–1883. A series of letters by Frances Anne Kemble, forming a sequel to "Record of a girlhood" and "Records of later life". With two portraits engraved by J. G. Stodart.

2 vols. pp. [2] [i–v] vi–ix [x], [1] 2–323 [324]; pl. [front.] + pp. [i–v] vi–viii, [1] 2–280; pl. [front.]   NbU

Richard Bentley and Son   1890 [*for* 1891]

————[American edition] New York: Henry Holt & Co., 1891.

3183 L., S. D. *Memoir of the dramatic life of Miss Fanny Kemble.

pp. 15   MB

n.p.   [18—?]

3184 FITZGERALD, EDWARD. Letters of Edward Fitzgerald to Fanny Kemble 1871–1883. Edited by William Aldis Wright.

pp. [8] [1] 2–269 [270–272 (bl.)]; pls. [front., 1]   E

Richard Bentley & Son   1895

————[American editions] New York: Macmillan and Co., 1895 (twice).

Kemble, John Philip (1757–1823)

The greatest of English actors of classical parts. He made his first appearance in London at Drury Lane on 30th September 1783, in the part of Hamlet. He was manager of Drury Lane from 1788 to 1796 and 1800 to 1802. In 1803 he purchased a share in Covent Garden, which theatre he managed till his retirement from the stage in 1817. It was during his management that the O.P. riots occurred — Lowe. See Herschel Baker, John Philip Kemble *(Cambridge, Mass, 1942). For Kemble at Covent Garden see nos. 1187 et seq.*

3185 KEMBLE, J[OHN] P[HILIP]. Fugitive pieces. Written by J. P. Kemble.

pp. [iii–v] vi–vii [viii (bl.)], [1] 2–44   L

York: Printed by W. Blanchard and Co. for the Author
                                                               1780

Limited to 200 copies. It has been suggested that Mrs. Inchbald is the lady addressed in these poems. Kemble soon destroyed all the copies he could find. See Baker, pp. 58–61.

3186 [KEMBLE, JOHN PHILIP.] MACBETH RECONSIDERED; an essay: intended as an answer to part of the *Remarks on some of the characters of Shakspeare.*

pp. [4] [1–2] 3–36   L

T. and J. Egerton   1786

Dedicated to Edmond Malone. An answer to Thomas Whatley's Remarks *(1785). "Kemble's essay stood as proof that an actor could be a scholar and a gentleman" — Baker.*

3187 ————[another edition] Macbeth, and King Richard the Third: an essay, in answer to *Remarks on some of the characters of Shakespeare.* By J. P. Kemble.

pp. [4] [vii] viii–ix [x], [2] [1] 2–171 [172]   L

John Murray   1817

3188 A SHORT CRITICISM on the performance of Hamlet by Mr. Kemble.

pp. [i–iv] v–ix [x], [1] 2–21 [22]   L

T. Hookham   1789

Very favourable to Kemble — Lowe.

3189 COLMAN, GEORGE. The iron chest: a play; in three acts. Written by George Colman, the younger. With a preface. First represented at the Theatre-Royal, in Drury-Lane, on Saturday, 12th March, 1796.

"The principal characters"
"By Mr. Kemble." &c.
          Drury-Lane play-bill.
"I had as lieve the town-crier had spoke my lines."
                                          —Shakespeare.

pp. [*4*] [i] ii–xxiii [xxiv], [1] 2–127 [128 (bl.)]   L
Cadell and Davies   1796

This play is made famous by its preface, in which Kemble is grossly attacked for having killed the play by his bad acting. Colman produced it at his own theatre, the Haymarket, 29 August 1796, with Elliston in Kemble's place, when it was successful — Lowe. See also Baker, pp. 201–202: Kemble is said to have bought up and destroyed every copy of this edition he could lay his hands on.

3190 ——— [another edition]
pp. [i–iii] iv–xxvii [xxviii], [1] 2–96   L
Dublin: P. Wogan, J. Rice, and G. Folingsby   1796

3191 ———*second edition with a preface and a postscript.

                                                        1796
Lowe.
The motto, preface, advertisement, and postscript were all withdrawn for the third edition (1798) and fourth edition (1808).

3192 GENTLEMAN OF THE MIDDLE TEMPLE, A, *pseud.* of John Litchfield (?). Remarks on Mr. Colman's preface: also A summary comparison of the play of *The iron chest* with the novel of *Caleb Williams.* Originally written for, and inserted in, *The monthly mirror;* and now re-published (by permission of the proprietors) with alterations and additions. By a gentleman of the Middle Temple.

pp. [i–iii] iv [5] 6–31 [32 (bl.)]   L
Sold by Miller; Cawthorne; Symonds; Crosby; Martin and Bain; Vernor and Hood   [1796]

3193 *REMARKS on the character of Richard the Third; as played by Cooke and Kemble.

pp. 55   MB
Parsons   1801

3194 ——— the second edition — revised and corrected
pp. [1–3] 4–53 [54 (bl.)] 55–56   MH
Parsons and Son   [1801]

In favour of Cooke — Lowe. The matter on the final leaf is dated Oct. 1801.

3195 KEMBLE & Cooke: or, a critical review of a pamphlet published under the title of Remarks on the character of Richard the Third, as played by Cooke & Kemble. With other critical remarks on the performances of these two gentlemen. Second edition.

pp. [1–5] 6–52 [53–55 (bl.) 56 ("Advertisement")] DFo
Printed for the author, by J. Bonsor   [1801]

The author promises further instalments.

3196 [MARTIN, H.] REMARKS on Mr. John Kemble's performance of Hamlet and Richard the Third. By the author of *Helen of Glenross.*

pp. [2] [1] 2–39 [40]   L
G. and J. Robinson   1802

3197 GILLILAND, THOMAS. Jack in office; containing remarks on Mr. Braham's address to the public; with a full and impartial consideration of Mr. Kemble's conduct with respect to the above gentleman.

pp. [4] [1] 2–40   MB
C. Chapple; and T. Ostell   [1805]

Reprints Braham's address to the public, "as published in the various daily prints".

3198 [GRANVILLE, AUGUSTUS BOZZI?] CRITICAL OBSERVATIONS on Mr. Kemble's performances at the Theatre Royal, Liverpool.

pp. [2] [1–3] 4–40   L
Liverpool: E. Willan   1811

*The dedication to Kemble is signed A.B.G.********, M.D.*

✄ [Whittington, G. D.?] A letter to J. P. Kemble involving strictures on a recent edition of John Ford's dramatic works. Cambridge, 1811. *See no. 1001.*

3199 AN AUTHENTIC NARRATIVE of Mr. Kemble's retirement from the stage; including farewell address, criticisms, poems, &c. selected from various periodical publications; with an account of the dinner given at the Freemason's Tavern, June 27, 1817; an alphabetical list of the company present; speeches of Lord Holland, Mr Kemble; Mr. Campbell's ode, &c. &c. To which is prefixed, an essay, biographical and critical.

pp. [i–v] vi–xxvii [xxviii], [1] 2–71 [72] 71 [72] 73–78 [=80] incl. cancellandum K4 and cancellans L1; pls. [4] incl. 2 fold.   MH
John Miller   1817

3200 OBSERVATIONS ON MR. KEMBLE in the characters of Cato, Wolsey, and Coriolanus: to which are added his farewell address at Covent Garden Theatre, and an account of the dinner given at Freemason's Tavern; with every particular connected with his retirement from the stage.

pp. [2] [1–3] 4–33 [34]   L
Printed by D. N. Shury   1817
Reprinted with additions from the European Magazine.

3201 TO JOHN PHILIP KEMBLE, Esq. of the Theatre Royal, Covent Garden.
bs.   DFo
[London]   26 June, 1817
An appeal to Kemble not to retire finally, but to continue to play a few nights each season.

3202 WILLIAMS, JOHN AMBROSE. Memoirs of John Philip Kemble, Esq. With an original critique on his performance. By John Ambrose Williams.

pp. [4] [1–3] 4–80 [81–82 (Kemble's works) 83 (erratum) 84 (imprint)]; pls. [front., 1]; extra engr. t.p.   L

John Bowley Wood   1817

3203 ———[another edition] Memoirs of the late John Philip Kemble, Esq. With an original critique on his performance. By John Ambrose Williams.

pp. [2] [1–3] 4–82 [83–84 (Kemble's works) 85 (erratum) 86 (imprint)]; pl. [front.]   L

I. J. Burn   [1823]

A reissue of the 1817 edition, with one leaf added, and the preface omitted.

✖ Catalogue of the excellent household furniture . . . the property of J. P. Kemble. [1820]. *See no. 102.*

✖ A catalogue of the valuable and extensive miscellaneous library . . . of John Philip Kemble . . . 1821. *See no. 103.*

3204 *MONODY on the death of J.P.K.

[Manchester?]   [1823]

STR.

3205 ———Monody on the death of John Philip Kemble   The second edition.

pp. [1–3] 4–6 [7 (Notes to the Monody) 8 (colophon: "With the Types of John Leigh April MDCCCXXIII")]   MH

Manchester: John Leigh   1823

3206 BOADEN, JAMES. Memoirs of the life of John Philip Kemble, Esq. Including a history of the stage, from the time of Garrick to the present period. By James Boaden, Esq.

2 vols. pp. [i–iii] iv–x, [1] 2–477 [478 (imprint)]; pl. [front.] + pp. [2] [1] 2–595 [596], misprinting 532 as "432"   E

Longman, Hurst, Rees, Orme, Brown and Green   1825

———[American edition] Philadelphia: Robert H. Small; New York: Wilder and Campbell, 1825.

3207 *ILLUSTRATIONS OF THE LATE JOHN PHILIP KEMBLE. Drawn on stone by Richard J. Lane, from pictures painted in his lifetime by John Boaden, exhibiting that great actor in the characters of *Coriolanus, Hamlet, Hotspur, Macbeth, King John, Cato, The Stranger, Penruddock.*

pls. 8

Dickinson   October 1st 1826

IKF.

3208 FITZGERALD, PERCY [HETHERINGTON]. The Kembles An account of the Kemble family, including the lives of Mrs. Siddons, and her brother John Philip Kemble. By Percy Fitzgerald, M.A., F.S.A.

2 vols. pp. [i–vii] viii–xix [xx–xxi] xxii [xxiii–xxiv], [1] 2–353 [354]; pls. [front., 7, incl. 1 facsim.] + pp. [i–v] vi, [1] 2–414; pls. [front., 6]   L

Tinsley Brothers   [1871]

Kemble, Stephen (1758–1822)

Brother of John. His chief distinction was his ability to play Falstaff without stuffing — Lowe. Manager in Ireland, Newcastle, etc., and at the Theatre Royal, Edinburgh from 1791–1800. For his management in Edinburgh see above nos. 1954–1959 and for his dispute with John Edwin at Newcastle (1793) see above nos. 1630–1632.

Kempe, William (fl. 1585–1603)

Actor.

3209 KEMP WILLIAM. *Kemp's nine daies wonder, performed in a daunce from London to Norwich.

O

N. Ling   1600

STC *14923.*

3210 ———[another edition] Kemps nine daies wonder: performed in a daunce from London to Norwich. With an introduction and notes by the Rev. Alexander Dyce

pp. [2] [i–v] vi–xxvi, [1] 2–35 [36]; illus.   L

The Camden Society   1840

With a life of Kemp.

3211 ———"Kemp's nine daies wonder:" London, 1600. Facsimile reproduction: superintended by Edmund W. Ashbee, F.S.A.

pp. [36 (incl. 32 facsim.]   L

n.p.   [1876?]

Limited to 100 copies.

3212 ———[another edition] Kempes nine daies wonder, performed in a journey from London to Norwich. Wherein every dayes iourney is pleasantly set down, to satisfie his friends the truth against all lying ballad-makers; what hee did, how he was welcome, and by whome entertained. Edited from the original ms. by Edmund Goldsmid, F.R.H.S.

pp. [i–v] vi–vii [viii (ornament)], [1–3] 4–42; illus.; t.p. headed "Collectanea adamentaea–II."; t.p. in red and black   L

Edinburgh: privately printed   1884

Reprinted in Edward Arber's An English garner, vol. VII (1883), pp. 15–38; in Social England illustrated

(*a revised edition of* An English garner) *vol. VII* (*1903*), *pp. 138–162; in* Henrie Chettle Kind-Hartes Dreame *1592,* William Kemp Nine Daies Wonder *1600 ed. G. B. Harrison* (*Bodley Head Quartos IV, 1923*).

Kendal, *Mrs.* Madge (1849–1935)

Miss Madge Robertson, who married Mr. W. H. Kendal, is a sister of the dramatist. In a wide range of modern parts she has no superior on the stage — Lowe. For her famous paper on The drama *see above* THE MORALITY OF THE THEATRE *no. 658.*

3213 KENDAL, *Mrs.* [MADGE.] Dramatic opinions. By Mrs. Kendal.

pp. [i–iii] iv–viii, [1] 2–116

John Murray   1890

JFA.

3214 PEMBERTON, T[HOMAS] EDGAR. The Kendals. A biography by T. Edgar Pemberton.

pp. [i–iv] v–x, 1–340; pls. [front., 9]   L

C. Arthur Pearson Limited   1900

——[American edition] New York: Dodd, Mead & Co., 1900.

Knight, Thomas (–1820)

Generally known as "Little Knight"—a very popular comedian. He made his first appearance in London at Covent Garden on 25th September 1795 and retired in 1804 in consequence of having had a fortune left to him.—Lowe. See no. 1182.

Knowles, James Sheridan (1784–1862)

Dramatist. He also tried his fortune as an actor, without much success. In his old age he became serious — Lowe. For his other writings see AUTHOR INDEX.

3215 KNOWLES, RICHARD BRINSLEY. The life of James Sheridan Knowles by his son Richard Brinsley Knowles.

pp. [i–iii] iv–xi [xii (bl.)], [1] 2–177 [178 (bl.)]; pls. [2 (photos)]   L

Privately printed for James McHenry   1872

Only twenty-five copies printed. Revised and edited by Francis Harvey. Uniform with J. S. Knowles's Lectures on oratory (*1873*) *and* Lectures on dramatic litera-ture (*1873*). *See also below no. 3508.*

Lacy, Willoughby

3216 LACY, WILLOUGHBY. A memorial, humbly addressed to the public, by Willoughby Lacy, formerly one of the patentees of the Theatre Royal, Drury Lane.

pp. [1–5] 6–15 [16]   LVA

To be had at Mr. Eber's circulating library; Mr Earle's circulating library; and Mr. Asperne, Bookseller; [J. Brettell, printer]   1813

An account of Lacy's financial difficulties, with an appeal for help.

Langtry, *Mrs.* Lillie (1852–1929)

A "society beauty," who is rapidly assuming a good position as an actress — Lowe. Née Emilie Charlotte le Breton (daughter of the Dean of Jersey), married, first, Edward Langtry, second Sir (then Mr.) Hugo de Bathe.

3217 THE LIFE OF MRS. LANGTRY the Jersey Lily and queen of the stage.

pp. [1–3] 4–8   L

Leeds: Pinder & Howes   [1882]

3218 ——†[another edition] With an account of her successful tour through the provinces.

pp. [1–3] 4–8; illus.; cover-title   L

[Leeds: Pinder & Howes]   [1883]

Latimer, *Mrs.*

See no. 1541.

Leathes, Edmund (1847–1891)

Made his first appearance on 1st March 1873 at the Princess's — Lowe. True name Edmund John Donaldson.

3219 LEATHES, EDMUND, *pseud.* of Edmund John Donaldson. An actor abroad or gossip dramatic, narrative and descriptive from the recollections of an actor in Australia, New Zealand, the Sandwich Islands, California, Nevada, Central America, and New York. By Edmund Leathes.

pp. [i–vii] viii–x, [1] 2–317 [318 (bl.)]   L

Hurst and Blackett   1880

With 16 pages of advertisements, as issued. Donaldson also wrote a novel The Actor's Wife (*1880*).

Lee, Charles

Lee was Master of the Revels at the time of the secession of 1733 — Lowe. See no. 157.

Lee, Henry

See also nos. 911; 2632.

3220 LEE, HENRY. Memoirs of a manager; or, life's stage with new scenery; briefly sketched by Henry Lee.

pp. [i–v] vi [vii–viii, [1] 2–183 [184] + [4] [1] 2–178 [179–180 (bl.)]   TnP

Taunton: printed by W. Bragg, sold by him; by Simpkin and Marshall London; and may be obtained through any bookseller in the Kingdom   1830

Lee, John (d. 1781)

An actor of considerable ability, whose overweening vanity drove him from theatre after theatre. He was one of the competitors for the patent in Edinburgh when Ross got it — Lowe. *See AUTHOR INDEX.*

Legge, Robert George

3221 LEGGE, ROBERT GEORGE. Songs of a strolling player. By Robert George Legge.

pp. [i–ii] 12–59 [60 (colophon) 61–64 (advts.)]   L

A. D. Innes & Co.   1893

3222 LEGGE, ROBERT GEORGE. Player poems. By Robert George Legge.

pp. [i–ii] 12–74 [75 (poem) 76 (bl.) 77–80 (advts.)]

A. D. Innes & Co.   1895

    IKF.; *another copy in* L.

Lemon, Mark (1809–1870)

Noted humorist and editor of Punch. *He was a dramatic author, and was also famous for his playing of the part of Falstaff, which he gave on the platform with wonderful richness of humour and vividness —* Lowe. *See Arthur A. Adrian,* Mark Lemon. First editor of Punch *(1966).*

3223 HATTON, JOSEPH. With a show in the north. Reminiscences of Mark Lemon. By Joseph Hatton. Reprinted from the *Gentleman's Magazine.* Together with Mark Lemon's revised text of Falstaff.

pp. [4] [i] 2–284 [285–288 (advts.)]; pl. [front.]; illus. (music)   L

Wm. H. Allen & Co.   1871

   "The story of Falstaff, selected from King Henry IV., for drawing-room representation. By Mark Lemon", pp. 197–284.

3223.1 ———*popular edition

Grant   1871

   ECB. Lowe *records "popular edition", 1872.*

Lennox, *Lady* William

See below PATON, ANNE, nos. 3404–3407.

Lennox, *Lord* William Pitt (1799–1881)

See nos. 957, 958; 3404–3407

Leslie, Fred (1855–1892)

Stage name of Frederick Hopson, actor and singer.

3224 VINCENT, W[ILLIAM] T[HOMAS]. Recollections of Fred Leslie by W. T. Vincent with introduction by Clement Scott.

2 vols. pp. [i–xi] xii–xviii, [i] 2–259 [260]; illus. (incl. front.) + [8] [i] 2–272; illus. (incl. front.)   L

Kegan Paul, Trench, Trübner & Co., Ltd.   1894

Lessingham, Jane (1739–1783)

She was the cause of much of the disagreement between the four managers of Covent Garden in 1768, and was the mistress of Harris. She was a woman of very bad character, who had been taught the rudiments of acting by Samuel Derrick, with whom she had lived, and whom she deserted. She apparently had a son to Harris, as her benefit bill — Covent Garden 27th April 1773 *— announces that "Tickets delivered by Master Harris will be taken." —* Lowe. *See above COVENT GARDEN nos. 1163–1171.*

Lewes, Charles Lee (1740–1803)

A capital comedian and harlequin — Lowe. *See MORALITY OF THE THEATRE no. 436.*

3225 LEWES, CHARLES LEE. Comic sketches; or, the comedian his own manager. Written and selected for the benefit of performers in England, Ireland, Scotland and America Inscribed to the performers in general, by Charles Lee Lewes, comedian. The whole forming matter sufficient for two evenings' entertainment; originally intended for the East Indies, and as delivered by him, without an apparatus, in many parts of the three kingdoms with distinguished patronage.

pp. [i–iii] iv–xxxv [xxxvi (bl.)], [i] 2–194 [195–196 (advts.)]; pl. [front.]   L

H. D. Symonds   1804

   The volume is accompanied by a biographical account of Lee Lewes, which his son, the editor of the Memoirs, *declares "false" (no. 3226 below).*

3226 [LEWES, JOHN LEE, *ed.*] MEMOIRS of Charles Lee Lewes, containing anecdotes, historical and biographical, of the English and Scottish stages, during a period of forty years. Written by himself.

4 vols. pp. [8] [i] ii–viii [9] 10–223 [224] + [4] [i] 2–222 + [4] [i] 2–231 [232] + [4] [i] 2–276 [277–280 (advts.)]   L

Richard Phillips   1805

   The editor's preface dated June 1805.

Lewis, Matthew Gregory (1775–1818)

Dramatist and novelist, usually known as "Monk" Lewis from the title of his most famous novel. His plays were mainly sensational and melodramatic.

3227 [WILSON, Mrs. MARGARET BARON, *ed.*] THE LIFE and correspondence of M. G. Lewis author of "The monk", "Castle spectre," &c. With many pieces in prose and verse, never before published.

2 vols. pp. [i–iii] iv–viii, [i] 2–392; pl. [front.] + pp. [i–iii] iv, [i] 2–388; pl. fold. [front. (facsim.)]   NbU

Henry Colburn   1839

Lewis, Philip

Actor. Uncle of William Lewis of Covent Garden.

3228 LEWIS, P[HILIP]. Miscellaneous pieces in verse; with cursory theatrical remarks. By P. Lewis, comedian.

pp. [4] [1] 2–25 [26]   E
Printed for the author, and sold by Mr. Waller   1774

3229   vacant

3230 ———*fifth edition, carefully revised and corrected.

pp. 44   MB
Portsmouth   1782

3231 ———*[another edition]
pp. 65
                                                             1790
STR.

Lind, Jenny (1821–1887)

Stage name of Johanne Marie Lind, afterwards Madame Jenny Lind-Goldschmidt.

3232   THE FAMOUS JENNY LIND.

bs.; illus.   L
[London?]   [1847]

The copy seen is mutilated. A street ballad. See also above BUNN, ALFRED, no. 2533.

3233   THE JENNY LIND MANIA.

bs.; illus.   L
E. Hodges, from Pitts   [1847 or 1848]

A street ballad. Eight stanzas, with a chorus. Joan Bulman, Jenny Lind (1956), pp. 164–5.

3234   LINDIANA. An interesting narrative of the life of Jenny Lind. With a portrait by Linton.

pp. [2] [5] 6–52; pl. [1 (front.)]   L
Printed by Mitchell & Son, Arundel, Sussex. Sold in London by Joseph Thomas; Duff and Hodgson; J. & D. Darling; Allen   1847

3235   MEMOIR OF JENNY LIND.

†pp. [3–5] 6–20 [21–22 (advts.)]   L
John Ollivier   1847

DLC records copy with a frontispiece.

3236   *A REVIEW OF THE PERFORMANCES of Mademoiselle Jenny Lind, at Her Majesty's Theatre.
pp. 36   MB
Dickinson   1847

3236.1   *A REVIEW of the performances of Mademoiselle Jenny Lind, during her engagement at Her Majesty's Theatre, and their influence and effect upon our national drama; with a notice of her life.

Portrait
                                                             1847
Lowe. Perhaps the same as no. 3236.

3237   BAYLEY   F[REDERICK]   W[ILLIAM] N[AYLOR]. The souvenir of the season. The wake of extacy, a memory of Jenny Lind, by F. W. N. Bayley, with ideal illustrations by Kenny Meadows, lithographed by R. J. Hammerton.

pp. [1–6] 7–67 [68] [=52]; pls. [front., 7]   L
Willoughby and Co.   1848

Although unnumbered, the plates are included in the pagination. In verse. A souvenir of the summer season at Her Majesty's Theatre, 1847. Dedicated to Benjamin Lumley, the manager.

Linley, Thomas (1733–1795)

Sheridan's father-in-law. He managed Drury Lane for some time—Lowe. See no. 1359.

Liston, John (ca. 1776–1846)

One of the most celebrated low comedians the English stage has produced. He made his first appearance in London, at the Haymarket, on 15th August 1799. He took a formal farewell of the stage at the Lyceum in 1837. Paul Pry was his greatest original part — Lowe.

3238   PAUL PRY, in which are all the peculiarities, irregularities, singularities, pertinacity, loquacity, and audacity of Paul Pry, as performed by Mr. Liston, at the Theatre Royal, Haymarket. With unbounded applause. With the song of Cherry Ripe.

pp. [1–2] 3–24; col. pl. [front. (Liston as Paul Pry, "G. Cruikshanks, del.")]   L
T. Hughes   [1826]

Cohn 630. Poole's Paul Pry first produced on 13 Sep. 1825.

Litton, Marie (1847–1884)

Actress. Her real name was Lowe.

3239   *AS YOU LIKE IT. By William Shakespeare. Remarks on the performance under Miss Litton's management, illustrated by Frank Miles and Adrian Stokes.

[London]   [1880]

Miss Litton's notable production of As You Like It took place at the Imperial Theatre — first performance, 25th February 1880 — and was most successful. This pamphlet contains the play, a few introductory remarks by Miss Litton, and a criticism by Tom Taylor, reprinted from the Theatre — Lowe.

Lloyd, Horatio F. (1815–1889)

A popular and accomplished comedian, whose name has been a household word in Scotland for two generations. He made his first appearance, I believe, at Edinburgh on December 30, 1829, at the Caledonian Theatre, then under the management of Bass.—Lowe. *See above GLASGOW no. 2016.*

Lodge, Thomas

Elizabethan dramatist. See above RENAISSANCE AND MEDIEVAL STUDIES no. 1044; AUTHOR INDEX.

Love, James (1722–1774)

Actor and dramatist. His true name may have been James Dance.

3240 LOVE, JAMES. Poems on several occasions. By James Love, comedian.

pp. [i–ii] iii–xii [xiii–xvi], 1–115 [116]   L
Edinburgh: printed by R. Fleming   1754

Love, William Edward (1806–1867)

A mimic of the sounds of musical instruments and of birds, insects and animals, who toured widely, performing in Britain, France and the Americas.

3241 SMITH, GEORGE. *Memoirs and anecdotes of Mr. Love, the polyphonist; to which is added an explanation of the phenomenon of polyphony.

London   1834

Title taken from American edition of [1850].

———[American edition.] Abridged from the octavo volume published in London in 1834. [Boston, 1850].

3242 SMITH, GEORGE. *Programme of the entertainment: preceded by memoirs of Mr. Love, the dramatic polyphonist. . . . By George Smith.

London   1851

Chase.

3243 ———[another edition] Programme of the entertainment: preceded by memoirs of Mr. Love, the dramatic polyphonist; remarks on single-handed entertainments; anecdotes of eminent by-gone professors; an explanation of the phenomena of polyphony, &c. By George Smith.

pp. [1–3] 4–48   L
[London]: W. Kenneth   [1856]

Lumley, Benjamin (1811–1875)

Lessee of Her Majesty's Theatre. See also above THE LONDON THEATRE nos. 1448 et seq. (Her Majesty's).

3244 LUMLEY, BENJAMIN. Reminiscences of the opera. By Benjamin Lumley, twenty years director of Her Majesty's Theatre.

pp. [i–vii] viii–xx, [1] 2–448; pl. [front.]   L
Hurst and Blackett   1864

Macauley, Elizabeth Wright (1785?–1837)

An actress of little merit, and very eccentric — Lowe.

3245 MACAULEY E[LIZABETH] W[RIGHT]. A pamphlet on the difficulties and dangers of theatrical life. By E. W. Macauley, late of the Theatre Royal, Crow-Street.

pp. [2] [1] 2–27 [28 (poem) 29 (errata) 30 (advts.)]   L
Dublin: printed by Fortune and Blyth   1810

3246 *MISS MACAULEY'S ADDRESS to the public of Ireland.

pp. 16
Waterford: John Bull   [1810?]

Loewenberg.

3247 MACAULEY [ELIZABETH WRIGHT]. Theatric revolution, or plain truth addressed to common sense. By Miss Macauley, late of the Theatre-Royal, Drury-Lane.

pp. [1–5] 6–30 [31 (announcement) 32 (bl.)]   L
Printed for the author, and sold by her   1819

Regarding Kean and his influence on the theatre — Lowe.

3248 *MISS MACAULEY'S three questions to the public.

1820

Recorded but not seen by Lowe.

3249 FACTS AGAINST FALSEHOOD! Being a brief statement of Miss Macauley's engagements at the winter theatres; the subterfuges by which she has been driven from the regular exercise of her profession, and withheld from at least two thirds of the public of this metropolis. Also her letters of appeal to the present managers.

pp. [1–3] 4–15 [16 (advts.)]   L
Duncombe   1824

3250 AUTOBIOGRAPHICAL MEMOIRS of Miss Macauley. Published in numbers . . .

bs.; headed: A card   L
          [1834]

A prospectus.

3251 MACAULEY [ELIZABETH WRIGHT]. Autobiographical memoirs, of Miss Macauley.

pp. [1] 2–16; head-title   L

Printed for the author by Mudie   [1834]

Published in numbers, the first number only published.

3252 ——[another edition] Autobiographical memoirs of Miss Macauley, written under the title of Elizabeth, or "A plain and simple tale of truth."

pp. [1] 2–44; cover-title   L

Charles Fox   1835

Published in numbers, three numbers only published.

Mackintosh, Matthew

Stage carpenter.

3253 OLD STAGER, AN, *pseud.* of Matthew Mackintosh. Stage reminiscences: being recollections, chiefly personal, of celebrated theatrical & musical performers during the last forty years. By an old stager.

pp. [4] [1–5] 6–236   GM

Glasgow: printed by James Hedderwick & son   1866

This work is, Mr. Burnett informs me, written by Matthew Mackintosh, stage-carpenter in Glasgow. Mackintosh was with Madame Vestris during her famous Olympic management, and was also with Ducrow at Astley's. He was in America for some time, and was for a long time in Glasgow under John Henry Alexander, Edmund Glover, Seymour, &c. He died in Glasgow, December 1871. "He must have been a good stage-carpenter," says Mr. Burnett, "or he would never have been in the situations he held; but as a writer he is most inaccurate." — Lowe. GM catalogue ascribes it to John Stewart, journalist.

3254 ——*second edition

Glasgow   1870

Loewenberg.

Macklin, Charles (ca. 1700–1797)

This remarkable actor's reputation was made by his playing Shylock as a serious character at Drury Lane on 14th February 1741. Hitherto the part had been regarded as belonging to comedy. His own Love à la Mode and Man of the World furnished him with his two great parts of Sir Archy M'Sarcasm and Sir Pertinax M'Sycophant. His last appearance was at Covent Garden on 7th May 1789 — Lowe. See also W. W. Appleton, Charles Macklin (Cambridge, Mass., 1960); AUTHOR INDEX.

Macklin's Dispute with Garrick 1743

See above GARRICK nos. 2829–2833.

———————

✂ A letter of compliment to the ingenious author of *A treatise of the passions* . . . With some further remarks on Mr. M——n. 1747. *See no. 2772.*

3255 MEMBER OF THE COMPANY, A, *pseud.* An infallible recipe to make a wicked manager of a theatre. Wrote by a member of the company of players of which Mr. xxxxx was manager.

bs., engr.   L

Chester: Monsʳ Verité, [pseud?]   1750

Portrait of Thomas Hallam, the actor whose eye Macklin poked out with his stick in a dispute over a wig, thus killing him, 1735. The poem is an attack on Macklin.

✂ *The Censor: No. I with an epistolary dedication to orator Mack-n. 1755. *See no. 4078.*

3256 TULLY, *pseud.* *An epistle from Tully in the Shades, to orator Ma——n in Covent-Garden.

pp. 26   MB

M. Cooper   1755

An attack on Macklin, in ridicule of his extraordinary project, "The British Inquisition," at which he undertook to lecture on many subjects utterly beyond his knowledge. The undertaking soon became a burlesque, and was a complete failure—Lowe. Signed "M. T. Cicero". Attributed by Brown to Foote, but not so by Belden. See also no 3257.

3257 M——CKL——N'S ANSWER TO TULLY.

pp. [1–2] 3–19 [20 (bl.)]   L

S. Stonehouse   1755

Another attack on Macklin on the same subject — Lowe.

✂ A Scotsman's remarks on the farce of *Love à la mode.* 1760. *See no. 3977.*

An attack on Macklin's farce.

The Macklin Riots 1773

On October 23 and October 30, 1773, Macklin played Macbeth, and was hissed by some persons. He rashly accused Reddish and Sparks of being the culprits, and this was made the pretence of a serious riot against him. On November 18 he was driven from the stage, and the manager was forced to dismiss him from the theatre. He brought an action against six of the rioters, which he won — Lowe.

3258 AN APOLOGY FOR THE CONDUCT OF MR. CHARLES MACKLIN, COMEDIAN; which, it is hoped, will have some effect in favour of an aged player, by whom the public at large have for many years been uncommonly gratified.

pp. [2], [1] 2–30   MH

Sold by T. Axtell; J. Swan   1773

May have been published with a plate. Extracts from newspapers. Macklin disclaimed responsibility for this publication.

3259 ———[another edition]

pp. [2] [1] 2–38; pl. [front.] MB

Sold by T. Axtell; J. Swan 1773

The plate, unsigned, is Macklin as Shylock, bearing Shakespeare on his shoulders with two allegorical figures. Appleton *records a different plate, King David on the shoulders of the Muses, triumphing over the fallen Shylock. In some copies, sig. E is signed D. The additional pages (sig. F) contain an account of Macklin's trial in 1735 and an account of Macklin's "life and genius".*

3260 COVENT GARDEN ALL IN AN UPROAR: or, the town robbed of its liberty. Being a true and particular account of Macklin's defeat by a party of players.

bs., illus. DFo

[London]: printed by J. Sharpe [November 1773]

3261 [MACKLIN, CHARLES.] *[A handbill, circulated at Covent Garden on 22 November 1773, concerning Macklin's discharge by Colman.]

Reported in the Public Advertiser *22 November 1773, and in* Appleton, *p. 186, and* Page, *p. 213.*

3262 CITIZEN OF THE WORLD, A, *pseud. of* Charles Macklin? The genuine arguments of the council, with the opinion of the Court of King's Bench, on cause shewn, why an information should not be exhibited against John Stephen James, Joseph Clarke, Esqrs. Ralph Aldus, Attorney at Law, William Augustus Miles, James Sparks, and Thomas Leigh; for a riotous conspiracy, founded in private premeditated malice, to deprive Charles Macklin, one of the comedians, belonging to the Theatre Royal in Covent Garden, of his livelihood; by forcibly compelling the acting manager of the said theatre, against his will, to discharge the said Charles Macklin for ever therefrom; formally and publicly, on the stage of the said theatre.

pp. [8] [1] 2–72 L

Sold by J. Williams 1774

3263 CASE, MR. MACKLIN late of Covent-Garden Theatre, against Mess. Clarke, Aldys, Lee, James, and Miles.

pp. [1–5] 6–13 [14 (bl.)] MH

Edinburgh: John and James Ainslies [1775]

Half-title reads "Case, Mr. Macklin."

3264 HENDERSON, ANDREW. A second letter to Dr. Samuel Johnson. In which his wicked and opprobious invectives are shewn; the conspiracy against Mr. Macklin clear'd up; an anecdote submitted to David Garrick Esq; with an impartial character of Doctor Smollet; and a method laid down for adding to the British revenue 1,000000 sterling. By Andrew Henderson, author of the former Letter.

pp. [1–3] 4–24 E

J. Henderson, and J. Fox; J. Millan; J. Williams; W. Nicoll; W. Goldsmith [1775]

3265 *RIOT AND CONSPIRACY. The trial of Thos. Leigh, and others, for making and raising a riot, on the 18th of November, 1773, at Covent Garden Theatre, and conspiring to ruin in his profession as a player, Mr. Charles Macklin, and for compelling Mr. Colman, one of the proprietors of the said theatre, to discharge, against his will, the said Charles Macklin. Tried before Mr. Justice Aston, at the Court of King's Bench, on the 2nd of February, 1775.

[1775]

Lowe *and* BMC, *but copy in L destroyed.*

✠ Catalogue of the library of the late Mr. Charles Macklin. [1797]. *See no. 107.*

3266 CONGREVE, FRANCIS ASPRY. Authentic memoirs of the late Mr. Charles Macklin, comedian. In which is introduced a variety of particulars hitherto unknown to the public; together with notes illustrative and explanatory.

pp. [4] [9] 10–60 [=56]; pl. L

J. Barker 1798

This is the least pretentious, but probably the best, of Macklin's biographies — Lowe.

3267 KIRKMAN, JAMES THOMAS. Memoirs of the life of Charles Macklin, Esq. Principally compiled from his own papers and memorandums; which contain his criticisms on and characters and anecdotes of Betterton, Booth, Wilks, Cibber, Garrick, Barry, Mossop, Sheridan, Foote, Quin, and most of his contemporaries; together with his valuable observations on the drama, on the science of acting, and on various other subjects: the whole forming a comprehensive but succinct history of the stage; which includes a period of one hundred years. By James Thomas Kirkman, of the Honourable Society of Lincoln's Inn.

2 vols. pp. [i–iii] iv–xxi [xxii], [1] 2–471 [472 (bl.)], misnumbering iv as "v"; pl. [front.] + pp. [2] [i–iii] iv–xii, [1] 2–452 L

Lackington, Allen, and Co. 1799

———[French edition] Mémoires sur Garrick et sur Macklin, traduits de l'anglais par le traducteur des oeuvres de Walter Scott; précédés d'une histoire abrégée du théâtre anglais, par M. Després. (Collection des mémoires sur l'art dramatique, publiés ou traduits par Mon. Andreiux [F.G.J.S.] *et al.*). Paris, 1822.

3268 [COOKE, WILLIAM.] MEMOIRS of Charles Macklin, comedian, with the dramatic characters, manners, anecdotes, &c. of the age in which he lived: forming a history of the stage during almost the whole of the last century. And a chronological list of all the parts played by him.

pp. [8] [1] 2–444; pl. [front.] L

James Asperne 1804

3269 ———by William Cooke, Esq. The second edition.

pp. [1–3] 4–8 [9–16], ²[1] 2–444; pl. [front.] MH

James Asperne 1806

3270 PARRY, EDWARD ABBOTT. Charles Macklin by Edward Abbot Parry. (Eminent Actors Edited by William Archer.)

pp. [8] [1] 2–208 L

Kegan Paul, Trench, Trübner & Co. Ltd. 1891

Reissued in one volume with Archer's Macready *and Lowe's* Betterton *with title on spine: Eminent Actors — Macready, Betterton, Macklin (see below no. 3291).*

Mackney E. W. (1835–1909)

Music hall performer.

3271 MACKNEY, E. W. *The life and reminiscences of E. W. Mackney, Ethiopian entertainer.

illus.

1897

STR.

Maclaren, Archibald (1755–1826)

One of the few Scottish dramatists. He was a soldier, and being discharged, supported himself and his family by writing small dramatic pieces, which are marked by much ability — Lowe.

3272 MEMOIR OF ARCHIBALD MACLAREN, dramatist; with a list of his works.

pp. [1–2] 3–8 L

Edinburgh 1835

Twenty-five copies printed. Variously attributed to W. H. Logan and James Maidment.

Macready, William (1755–1829), *senior*

Father of W. C. Macready. He was a noted provincial manager and actor. His first appearance in London was in 1786. In 1795 he became manager at Birmingham, then he took Sheffield, and afterwards the Northern Circuit — Newcastle, Carlisle, and Berwick. He also tried the Royalty Theatre. In 1807 he became manager at Manchester, but in none of his ventures was he very successful — Lowe. *Manager of Queen Street Theatre Royal, Glasgow. For his disputes with John Prosser Edwin at Newcastle see above nos. 1648–1650.*

3273 THE DISSECTION of a Bir——g——m manager. By the author of The summers day, a poem.

pp. [i–iii] iv–vi, [1] 2–34 BP

Printed for the author 1796

A furious attack on Macready, the elder. The Monthly Mirror *says of it: "The whole matter is libellous, but too despicable for any legal notice."* — Lowe.

Macready, William Charles (1793–1873)

Macready made his first appearance in London at Covent Garden on 16th September 1816 as Orestes. The most notable points in his career were his managements of Drury Lane and Covent Garden, his conduct of which was marked by artistic excellence, and striving after the highest ideals, both on the stage and in the front of the house. Macready was emphatically a gentleman and an honest man. He took farewell of the stage on 26th February 1851—Lowe. *See also J. C. Trewin,* Mr. Macready *(1955) and A. S. Downer* The Eminent Tragedian *(Cambridge, Mass., 1966).*

⌘ A critical examination of the respective performances of Mr. Kean & Mr. Macready in. . . . *King Richard the Third.* 1819. *See no. 3133.*

3274 MR. MACREADY. Heroism and humanity.

bs. L

[1823?]

Reprinted from the Southampton Chronicle. *See* Trewin, *p. 71.*

3275 WALLACE, ELLEN. Twelve sketches of Macready's attitudes in Ion. By Ellen Wallace.

pp. [4]; pls. [7] [=12 sketches] DFo

[London]: W. Spooner October 15th, 1836

Ion *by Sir Thomas Noon Talford was first produced at Covent Garden on 26 May 1836 for Macready's benefit.*

3276 *A LETTER to his Royal Highness the Duke of Sussex, on the late management of Covent Garden Theatre. By one of the proprietors.

1839

A vehement attack on Macready, who had been entertained at a public dinner, at which the Duke of Sussex was chairman, on the conclusion of his Covent Garden management. For an account of the dinner see Macready's "Reminiscences", vol. ii — Lowe.

3277 R[OLLS], M[ARTHA] S[ARAH]. Dramatic recollections of the years 1838–9 drawn and etched from memory.

pls. [15]; wrappers; title on wrappers; issued in 2 parts

J. Mitchell [1839]

IKF.

✠ S., G. [*ie. Sir* George Scharf] Recollections of the scenic effects of Covent Garden . . . Dedicated (by permission) to W. C. Macready. *1839. See no. 1307.*
Praises Macready for his management of the theatre.

3278 A.B.C., *pseud.* The drama, the press, and Mr. Macready. By A.B.C. Respectfully inscribed to all admirers of the dramatic art.

pp. [1–3] 4–16   DFo
Printed by W. H. Ward   [1842]

Praises Macready's attempts to render the theatre respectable.

3279 A.B.C., *pseud.* Additional remarks on the drama, the press, and Mr. Macready. By A.B.C.

pp. [1–3] 4–16   DFo
W. W. Barth; W. Brittain   [1842]

3280 *A BRIEF MEMOIR of Mr. Macready.

pp. 11   MB
Printed for the author   1845

✠ Macready, William Charles. A letter from Mr. Macready to the director of the Théâtre Historique. *1848. See no. 1412.*
On the Drury Lane riots against the French actors.

3281 FOX, W[ILLIAM] J[OHNSON]. A biographical sketch of William C. Macready, Esq., by W. J. Fox, M.P.

pp. [1] 2–16; pl. [front.]   DFo
[London]   [1851]

Reissued in A biographical sketch of W. C. Macready . . . Also, Shakespeare's tragedy of Macbeth [*1851*]. *See below no. 3411.*

3282 LITTLETON, R. H. *The biography of William C. Macready, tragedian.

port.   MB
Vickers   [1851?]

3283 PUBLIC DINNER TO W. C. MACREADY, Esq., on his retirement from the stage, Saturday, March 1st, 1851. Sir Bulwer Lytton, Bart., in the chair. Selection of vocal music, under the direction of Mr. Land.

pp. [2] [1] 2–14; cover title   LGk
[London]   [1851]

3284 HOGARTH, JOHN. Mr. Hogarth has the honour to announce for immediate publication, an engraving of "Werner," representing W. C. Macready, Esq. in his celebrated personation of that character Engraved in the highest style of the art, by W. C. Sharpe, from the picture exhibited last year at the Royal

Academy, painted by D. Maclise, Esq., R.A. in the possession of John Forster, Esq.

pp. [1–2] 3 [4]   LGk
J. Hogarth   [1852]

Prospectus inviting subscriptions, and including reviews of the original painting by D. Maclise on which the engraving is based.

✠ Catalogue of a valuable collection of engravings . . . collected by the tragedian, William Charles Macready . . . [1868]. *See no. 108. See also no. 109.*

3285 POLLOCK, *Sir* FREDERICK, *ed.* Macready's reminiscences, and selections from his diaries and letters. Edited by Sir Frederick Pollock, Bart., one of his executors. In two volumes.

2 vols. pp. [i–v] vi–xi [xii (poem)], [1] 2–476; pl. [front.]; vignette on t.p. + pp. [i–v] vi–x, [1] 2–486; pl. [front.]; vignette on t.p.   L
Macmillan and Co.   1875

3286 ———new edition, complete in one volume
pp. [i–v] vi–xv [xvi–xviii], [1] 2–750; pls. [front., 2]; vignette   L
Macmillan and Co.   1876

3287 ———[another edition] The diaries of William Charles Macready 1833–1851 edited by William Toynbee.

2 vols. pp. [i–iv] v–xvi, 1–512; pls. [front. 26 (25 leaves)] + p.p [i–iv] v–vi, 1–543 [544]; pls. [front., 21]   GU
Chapman and Hall, Ltd.   1912

3287.1 ———[another edition] The journal of William Charles Macready 1832–1851 Abridged and edited by J. C. Trewin.

pp. [i–x] xi–xxxiii [xxxiv], [1–2] 3–304 305–315 (index) [316 (bl.)]; pls. [4]; illus. (facsims.)   L
Longmans   [1967]

3288 POLLOCK, *Lady* JULIET. Macready as I knew him. By Lady Pollock.

pp. [8] [1] 2–141 [142–144 (bl.)]   NbU
Remington and Co.   1884

3289 ———second edition
Remington & Co.   1885

IKF.
Although I do not profess to criticise the merits of books mentioned by me, I may be pardoned if I venture to point out how delightfully sympathetic this account of Macready is; how noble an idea of his character it furnishes; and how much it does to correct the impressions derived from the perusal of his own rather depressing records — Lowe.

3290 ARCHER, WILLIAM. William Charles Macready by William Archer (Eminent Actors).

pp. [2] [i–v] vi–vii [viii–x], [1] 2–224   GU

Kegan Paul, Trench, Trübner & Co., Ltd.   1890

3291 ———[reissue] (Eminent actors, edited by William Archer).

pp. [2] [i–v] vi–vii [viii–x], [1] 2–224, [4] ²[1] 2–208, ³[i–v] vi [vii–viii], [1] 2–196   GU

Kegan Paul, Trench, Trübner & Co., Ltd.   1890 [*for* 1891]

> *3 vols. in one: (1) Archer's Macready, (2) Parry's Macklin, (3) Lowe's Betterton. Title on spine: Eminent Actors — Macready, Betterton, Macklin.*

Malibran, *Madame* Felicita (1808–1836)

Opera singer. See also below no. 3579 (Templeton).

3292 AMATEUR, AN, *pseud.* Memoirs, critical and historical, of Madame Malibran de Beriot and Monsieur de Beriot. To which is appended, a brief biographical notice of Senor Garcia. By an amateur.

pp. [1–3] 4–81 [82 (bl.) 83 (advt.) 84 (bl.)]; pl. [front.]   L

Cookes and Ollivier   [1836]

3293 *MEMOIRS of the public and private life of the celebrated Madame Malibran . . .

pp. 8

J. Thompson   1836

> *BMC, but missing in L.*

3294 NATHAN I[SAAC]. Memoirs of Madame Malibran de Beriot. By I. Nathan.

pp. [4] [1] 2–72   L

Joseph Thomas; Cramer, Addison, and Beale; Simpkin and Marshall   1836

> *On p. 72: "A supplement to these pages will be published in a few days . . ."*

3295 ———third edition

pp. [4] [1] 2–72; pl. [front.]   L

Joseph Thomas; Cramer, Addison, and Beale; Simpkin and Marshall   1836

> *A reissue of the first edition.*

3296 PARKINSON, RICHARD. A sermon preached on the second day of October, 1836; being the day after the public funeral of the late Madame Malibran de Beriot in the Collegiate Church of Manchester. By the Rev. Richard Parkinson, M.A. Fellow of the Collegiate Church.

pp. [1–5] 6–23 [24]   L

Manchester: printed and sold by T. Sowler   1836

> *With an appendix: Statement of the Committee of the Manchester Musical Festival.*

3297 MERLIN, *The Countess de.* Memoirs of Madame Malibran, by the Countess De Merlin, and other intimate friends. With a selection from her correspondence, and notices of the progress of the musical drama in England.

2 vols. pp. [i–iii] iv–lxvi [lxvii–lxviii], misnumbering iv as "vi", [1] 2–279 [280]; pl. [front.] + pp. [i–iii] iv–v [vi–viii], [1] 2–294   GU

Henry Colburn   1840

3298 ———second edition

pp. [i–iii] iv–lxvi [lxvii–lxviii], [1] 2–279 [280]; misprinting 263 as "363"; pl. [front.] + pp. [i–iii] iv–v [vi–viii], [1] 2–294; misprinting iv as "vi"; 2 vols. in 1   LGk

Henry Colburn   1844

———[American edition.] Memoirs and letters of Madame Malibran. With notices of the progress of the musical drama in England. Philadelphia: Carey & Hart, 1840.

Mallet, David (1705?–1765)

His name was really Malloch, but having a dislike to be considered a Scotchman, he changed it to Mallet. It was said of him that he was the only Scot whom Scotchmen did not commend. He was a political hireling, and generally disreputable — Lowe. See nos. 3978, 3979, 3980.

Malone, Edmond (1741–1812)

The great Shakespearean critic and commentator. His acuteness was shown in his detection of the Rowley and Ireland Forgeries — Lowe. Stage historian. See also AUTHOR INDEX.

3299 [BOSWELL, JAMES, *the younger.*] A BIO-GRAPHICAL MEMOIR of the late Edmond Malone, Esq.

pp. [4] [1–3] 4–27 [28 (bl.)]   L

Printed by Nichols, Son, and Bentley   1814

> *Reprinted from the* Gentleman's Magazine *"for private distribution". Preface dated 20 Jan. 1814. Reprinted in* Catalogue of early English poetry . . . collected by Edmond Malone, Esq. and now preserved in the Bodleian Library *(Oxford, 1836) (no. 111 above.)*

✕ Catalogue of early English poetry . . . collected by Edmond Malone . . . and other miscellaneous works illustrating the British drama . . . preserved in the Bodleian library. Oxford. 1836. *See no. 111.*

3300 PRIOR, *Sir* JAMES. Life of Edmond Malone, editor of Shakspeare. With selections from his manuscript anecdotes. By Sir James Prior, M.R.I.A., F.S.A., &c. With a portrait.

pp. [i–iii] iv–xii, [1] 2–476; pl. [front.] L
Smith, Elder & Co. 1860

Mapleson, James Henry (1830–1901)

Opera manager.

3301 [MAPLESON, JAMES HENRY.] THE MAPLESON MEMOIRS 1848–1888 with portrait of the author.

2 vols. pp. [i–vii] viii–xi [xii], [1] 2–327 [328]; pl. [front.] + pp. [i–v] vi–viii, [1] 2–319 [320] L

Remington & Co. 1888

3302 ———second edition

pp. [i–vii] viii–xi [xii], [1] 2–327 [328]; pl. [front.] + pp. [i–v] vi–viii, [1] 2–319 [320] L

Remington & Co. 1888

3303 ———the third edition

2 vols. pp. [i–vii] viii–xi [xii], [1] 2–327 [328]; pl. [front.] + pp. [i–v] vi–viii, [1] 2–319 [320] GU

Remington & Co. 1888 [1889]

———[American edition] Chicago and New York: Belford, Clarke & Co., 1888.

✠ To opera and theatrical managers . . . A catalogue of an extensive and valuable operatic wardrobe, lately the property of Colonel Mapleson. [1898]. *See no. 112.*

Mathews, *Mrs.* Anne (–1869)

Actress. Née Jackson. Second wife of Charles Mathews, the elder. Author of Memoirs of Charles Mathews *(1838). (See below no. 3307).*

3303.1 MATHEWS, *Mrs.* [ANNE]. Tea-table talk, ennobled actresses, and other miscellanies. By Mrs. Mathews.

2 vols. pp. [i–v] vi, [1] 2–359 [360] + [i–iii] iv (misprinting iv as "v"), [1] 2–347 [348 (bl.) 349 (errata) 350 (bl.)] L

Thomas Cantley Newby 1857

Partly reprinted from Bentley's Miscellany.

Mathews, Charles, *the elder* (1776–1835)

The father of our own Charles Mathews, and, no doubt, the greater artist of the two. He made his first London appearance at the Haymarket on 16th May 1803. His last appearance was made at New York on 11th February 1835. He was the most remarkable of imitators, having the ability to enter into the mental as well as physical peculiarities of his subject — Lowe. Memoirs of the Youthful Days of Mr. Mathews *(Duncombe, 1825?) and Mathews' other monologues contain autobiographical information. See also* CATALOGUES *nos. 114–118.*

✠ Swiftsure, Jonathan, *pseud.* Report of the extraordinary trial, of Charles Momus. 1814. *See no. 2626.*

Refers to the imitation by Mathews of the "amateur of fashion" Robert Coates.

✠ At a general meeting of the inhabitants of . . . Stratford-upon-Avon, held . . . agreeably to the suggestion of Mr. Mathews . . . to consider the best mode of erecting, in the form of a theatre, a national monument, to . . . Shakespeare: . . . Stratford. [1820]. *See no. 1690.*

Mathews was appointed president and treasurer.

3304 HISTORY of the private and public life of Mr. C. Mathews, comedian; from his birth to his decease, including a variety of anecdotes.

pp. [2] 5–12; col. pl. [front.] MH

J. V. Quick; G. Hunt [1835?]

3305 SCANLAN, ROBERT R. Nine portraits forming a series of characters, illustrative of Mathews. In his fourteenth & last comic annual, performed in England & America, in 1833 By Robert R. Scanlan. Drawn on stone by Edward Morton.

illus. t.p.; pls. [9]; cover title: Mathews' characters LGk

[London]: printed by J. Graf [ca. 1835]

3306 DANIEL, GEORGE. View of Ivy Cottage, Kentish Town: with some account of the life and genius of the late Charles Mathews. Contributed by George Daniel, Esq. of Islington. Extracted from C. J. Smith's "*Historical and Literary Curiosities.*"

pp. [6]; pls. [2]; t.p. headed: Only 25 copies printed LGk

[1837]

At foot of first plate: William Pickering, 1837; for Smith's Historical & Literary Curiosities.

3307 MATHEWS, *Mrs.* [ANNE]. Memoirs of Charles Mathews, comedian. By Mrs. Mathews.

4 vols. pp. [i–v] vi–xi [xii (bl.) xiii–xiv (errata)], [1] 2–438; pls. [front., 2] + pp. [i–v] vi–xi [xii (bl.) xiii (errata) xiv (bl.)], [1] 2–472 [473 (list of pls.) 474 (bl.)]; pls. [front., 4] + pp. [i–v] vi–xiv, [1] 2–650; pls. [front., 7 (incl. 5 double)] + pp. [i–v] vi–xii, [1] 2–503 [504] (=502, sig. B being of seven leaves only); pls. [front.] L

Richard Bentley 1838–1839

LVA copy has variants: vol. I, list of plates in place of errata; vol. III, pls. [front., 5 (double)]; vol. IV, pls. [front., 2]: this is probably the intended order of pls.

3308 ———second edition

4 vols. pp. [i–v] vi–xi [xii], [1] 2–433 [434]; pls. [front., 2] + pp. [iii–v] vi–xi [xii], [1] 2–469 [470]; pls. [front., 4] + pp. [iii–v] vi–xiv, [1] 2–650; pls. [front., 5 (double)] + pp. [iii–v] vi–xii, [1] 2–503 [504] [=502, sig. B. being of seven leaves only]; pls. [front., 2] L

Richard Bentley 1839

Vols. I and II (with "Second Edition" on the title-page) reset and corrected. In the copy seen, vols. III and IV (without "Second Edition" on the title-page) are issues of the first edition. Together, these four volumes constitute the second edition. Vol. II has some new matter concerning S. J. Arnold.

3309 ———[another edition] The life and correspondence of Charles Mathews, the elder, comedian. By Mrs. Mathews. A new edition, abridged and condensed, by Edmund Yates.

pp. [i–iii] iv–xvi, [1] 2–480; pls. [front., 4] L

Routledge, Warne, and Routledge 1860

———[American edition] Philadelphia: Lea & Blanchard, 1839.

⌘ Mathews, *Mrs.* [Anne]. Anecdotes of actors By Mrs. Mathews, author of the "Memoirs of Charles Mathews, comedian;" to which this is a supplementary volume. 1844. *See no. 2238.*

3310 ARNOLD, S[AMUEL] J[AMES]. Forgotten facts in the Memoirs of Charles Mathews, comedian, recalled in a letter to Mrs. Mathews, his biographer by S. J. Arnold, Esq.

pp. [3–6] 7–52 L

Ridgway [1839]

Arnold engaged Mathews for a term of years to give his "Entertainments." Mrs. Mathews makes very severe comments on this arrangement in the Memoirs, *and Arnold replied in this tract* — Lowe.

3311 vacant

Mathews, Charles James (1803–1878)

Originally trained as an architect, he took to the stage, making his first appearance on 6th November 1835, at the Olympic. He continued to play the parts of young men till he died. His first wife was the famous Madame Vestris — Lowe.

3312 MATHEWS, CHARLES. Lettre de M. Charles Mathews aux auteurs dramatiques de la France.

pp. [2] [1] 2–35 [36 (bl.)] L

J. Mitchell 1852

A lively epistle regarding the International Copyright controversy. See Mathew's Life (1879), ii, 179 and 180 —Lowe.

3313 ———[another edition] Lettre de M. Charles Mathews aux auteurs dramatiques de la France. With a translation according to the terms of the international convention.

pp. [2] [1] 2–35 [36], [2] ²[1] 2–41 [42]; cover-title L

J. Mitchell 1852

A reissue, with translation.

⌘ Under the will of the late Charles Mathews, Esq. Sale . . . A catalogue of the . . . furniture . . . miscellaneous and interesting effects. [1878]. *See no. 119.*

3314 DICKENS, CHARLES, *the younger, ed.* The life of Charles James Mathews chiefly autobiographical with selections from his correspondence and speeches. Edited by Charles Dickens.

2 vols. pp. [i–v] vi–ix [x–xii], [1] 2–324; pls. [front., 1] inset t.p. + pp. [i–v] vi–vii [ix–xii], [1] 2–336; pls. [front., 2] GU

Macmillan and Co. 1879

———[American edition] New York: Harper & Brothers, 1879. (Franklin Square Library. Number 71.)

Mathews, John

Showman.

3315 MATHEWS, JOHN. *Bow! Wow!! Wow!!! Life and theatrical career of John Mathews, champion swordsman, showman, dogman and pantomimist; in which will be truthfully depicted the trying events and sensational situations of fourty five years in 60 Theatre Royals, 80 minor theatres, 20 circuses, 20 gardens, 100 music halls, 30 concert rooms, 50 booths, 40 fairs, 14 penny dukeys, 8 gaffs . . . as dogman, training 30 dogs. Career in theatrical life as proprietor, stage manager, leading actor, dog star, juvenile man, heavy man . . . pantomimist, utility, prompter, stage carpenter, property master . . . gas director, pyrotechnist, supermaster and bill inspector.

4 vols. MH

[1874–6?]

Mellon, Harriot (1777–1837)

She was in no way notable as an actress, but made two very remarkable marriages — her first husband being Thomas Coutts, the banker; her second, the Duke of St. Albans. Mr. Coutts was twice as old as she was, the duke was half her age, when the respective marriages occurred. It is difficult to realise how frankly libellous and indecent some of the pamphlets caused by these marriages were — Lowe.

3316 FINE ACTING; or a sketch of the life of the late Miss H. M——, of Drury-Lane Theatre, and of T. C——, Esq. banker.

pp. [i–iii] iv–v [vi] [7] 8–70   L
London: printed for [blank]   1815

3317 PERSON OF THE FIRST RESPECTABILITY, A, *pseud.* Authentic memoirs of the lives of Mr. and Mrs. Coutts. Communicated by a person of the first respectability.

pp. [2] [1] 2–16 [17 (advt.) 18 (bl.)]   MH
J. Fairburn   1819

3318 ——fourth edition

pp. [2] [1] 2–16 [17 (advt.) 18 (bl.)]   MH
J. Fairburn   1819

With motto, not on the title-page of the first edition:
"Burn, sooty slander, burn thy blotted scroll;
Greatness is greatness, spite of envy's soul."

3319 ——[another edition] Life of the late Thomas Coutts, Esq. banker, in the Strand, with biographical and entertaining anecdotes, of his first wife, Betty Starky, and of the present Mrs. Coutts. By a person of the first respectability. To which is added, An account of the manner in which his immense property has been bequeathed.

pp. [2] [1] 2–17 [18 (bl.) 19–20 (advt.)], ²[1]–2 (advt.) E
John Fairburn   [1822]

Mrs. Coutts is said by Wyndham (no. 3324 below) to have "hired a hungry pamphleteer" to write this.

3320 ——Biographical and historical addenda to the life of the late Thomas Coutts, Esq. Containing numerous interesting and amusing anecdotes of that gentleman and his first wife, Betty Starky; including an official copy, at full length, of Mr. Coutt's will, with the codicil, as proved and registered in the prerogative court: also, the curious and important Letter of the Earl of Dundonald on some statements in the narrative, &c. &c. Embellished with a correct likeness of Mr. Coutts.

pp. [3–5] 6–20, ²[1] 2; pl.   L
John Fairburn   [1822]

Cohn (167) and Douglas suggest plate is by George Cruikshank.

3321 ——[reissue] Life of the late Thomas Coutts, Esq. banker, of the Strand, to which is added, a biographical and historical addenda, containing some curious anecdotes, and an official copy at full length of his will and codicil, as proved in the prerogative court, &c. &c. With a correct portrait of Mr. Coutts.

pp. [6] [1] 2–17, ²[1] 2–3, ³[3–5] 6–20, ⁴[1] 2; pl. [front.] L
John Fairburn   [1822]

A reissue of nos. 3319 and 3320.

3322 [COCHRANE, ARCHIBALD, *Earl of* Dundonald]. THE EARL OF DUNDONALD'S answer to the mis-statements contained in the Life of the late T. Coutts, Esq. banker, (relative to his first lady), with curious and highly interesting anecdotes, never before published.

pp. [1–3] 4–8   L
J. Limbird   1822

Mr. Coutts's first wife had been described as a domestic in the service of the Earl of Dundonald, and some passages between her and the Earl's son were mentioned, which he (being now Earl) contradicted — Lowe.

3323 ONE OF HIS MAJESTY'S SERVANTS, *pseud.* ★The golden nuptuals, an epithalamium, on the marriage of T. C——tts, Esq. and Miss H. M——ll——n. By one of His Majesty's servants.

Advertised in Life of the late Thomas Coutts (*1822*). (*See above no. 3321*).

3324 WYNDHAM, PERCY. Mr. Percy Wyndham's strictures on an imposter, and old actress, formerly Bet the pot girl, alias, the banker's sham widow, with particulars of her appearance at at [*sic*] the bar of Bow Street, of the child manufactory at Highgate, and madam's sleeping at the Horns at Kennington. A copy of Lord Dundonald's letter, & a castigatory letter, to Sir Edmund Antropus: Sir Coutts Trotter, Edward Marjoribanks, & Co. as executors; and surviving partners of the late Thomas Coutts, Esq.

pp. [51–53] 54–125 [126] 126–144 [145] (=96); illus. L
Sold by W. B. Turner   [1822]

3325 SECRET MEMOIRS OF HARRIOTT PUMP-KIN, or the birth, parentage, and education of an actress. In which are developed a variety of interesting and amusing anecdotes; her private acquaintance for many years; the vicissitudes to which she was exposed; and her extraordinary marriage with Old Croesus!! To which is added the art of making an ostentatious shew-off under the color of charity: the whole pourtraying her never-forgiving and malicious disposition.

pp. [1–3] 4–51 [52 (bl.)]   MH
J. Cahuac   [1823?]

3326 GHOST OF OLD RALPH, THE, *pseud.* A tale of the last century. The secret memoirs of Harriott Pumpkin,★ a celebrated actress; from her infancy to her seduction of, and subsequent marriage with a banker; also, a poem by the father of our heroine. With strictures on charity without benevolence — the art of swindling a good name — fifteen shillings for publishing a donation of five! — the art of benefit-making; or, devil drive the hindmost — ripe fruit and the money-bags — a scene at the horns!!! — scenes at the cottage; procreative studies by Sally S——n; manager A——d; Miss M——n; Mr. R——d, &c.

With a variety of amatory anecdotes, and illustrative occurrences. By the ghost of old Ralph!!!

* Pumpkin, according to naturalists, a spurious kind of Melon.

pp. [2] [1–3] 4–117 [118]　　　　　　　　L
Duncombe　　　　　　　　　　　　[1825]

Most of the copies of this scurrilous pamphlet are said to have been bought up and destroyed — Lowe. An extended version of the Secret Memoirs *(see above no. 3325).*

3327 *THE PLAYTHING.

bs., engr.　　　　　　　　　　　　L
n.p.　　　　　　　　　　　　25 June 1827

Twelve lines of verse. George 15454. See also George 15453–15462.

3328 EPISTLE TO HARRIET [sic], Duchess of Saint Albans: or the first lash of nemesis.

pp. [1–3] 4–16　　　　　　　　　　L
James Ilbery　　　　　　　　　　1828

A rhymed defence of Miss Mellon, and a furious attack upon Westmacott and others who had defamed her — Lowe.

3329 MEMOIRS OF HARRIET [sic] MELLON, DUCHESS OF ST. ALBAN'S, [sic] including anecdotes of the Royal Academy. Vol. I.

pp. [2] [i] ii–vi, [7] 8–298　　　　　MH
John Joseph Stockdale, printer and publisher　1828

On an old fly leaf in pencil (MH copy), "No more printed the work is complete J. Stockdale".

3330 BARON-WILSON, *Mrs.* CORNWELL. Memoirs of Harriot, Duchess of St. Albans. By Mrs. Cornwell Baron-Wilson.

2 vols. pp. [i–iii] iv–xvi, [1] 2–362; pl. [front.] + pp. [i–iii] iv–vii [viii], [1] 2–354　　　　L
Henry Colburn　　　　　　　　　1839

3331 ——second edition

2 vols. pp. [i–iii] iv–xx, [1] 2–355 [356]; pl. [front.] + [2] [i–iii] iv–vii [viii], [1] 2–86 *87–*88 87–368 [=370]; pl. [front., 1 (fold.)]　　　　　L
Henry Colburn　　　　　　　　　1840

3332 ——third edition

2 vols. pp. [i–iii] iv–xx, [1] 2–355 [356 (bl.)]; pl. [front.] + pp. [i–iii] iv–vii [viii], [1] 2–86 *87–*88 87–368 [=370]; pl. [front.]　　　LGk
Henry Colburn　　　　　　　　　1844

3333 ——Memoirs of Miss Mellon afterwards Duchess of St. Albans　New edition.

2 vols. pp. [1–5] 6–311 [312 (bl.)] + [1–5] 6–301 [302 (bl.)]　　　　　　　　　L
Remington & Co.　　　　　　　1886

3334 ——[reissue]

2 vols. pp. [1–5] 6–311 [312 (bl)] + [1–5] 6–301 [302 (bl)]　　　　　　　　　NbU
Remington & Co.　　　　　　　1887

——[American editions] Philadelphia: Carey & Hart, 1840; New York: Scribner and Welford, 1886.

Miller, David Prince

Miller was manager of the Royal Adelphi Theatre, Glasgow, for some time; but was unfortunate in it, as he seems to have been in everything he undertook — Lowe.

3335 [MILLER, DAVID PRINCE.] THE LIFE of Miller, the showman.

pp. [i] ii [3] 4–144; head-title
[Glasgow]　　　　　　　　　[1842]

JFA.
Published in twelve weekly parts, mostly when Miller was lodged in gaol at the suit of J. H. Alexander for infringement of the patent of the Glasgow Theatre Royal.

3336 ——[another edition] The life of a showman: to which is added managerial struggles, by David Prince Miller, late of the Adelphi Theatre, Glasgow.

pp. [2] [1] 2–147 [148]　　　　　MB
London: Lacy; Leeds: C. A. Wilson and Co.　1849

3337 ——The life of a showman; and the managerial struggles of David Prince Miller: with anecdotes and letters of some of the most celebrated modern actors and actresses. The art of fortune telling. An exposé of the practices of begging imposters, mountebanks, jugglers, and various deceivers of the public; together with the secrets of conjuring, and an explanation of the most celebrated and striking tricks of wizards and conjurers. Second edition, with considerable additions.

pp. [1–3] 4–192
Thomas Hailes Lacy　　　　[1854 or 1855?]
JFA.

3338 ——*[another edition]
Lacy　　　　　　　　　　　1860
STR.

Miller, James (1684–1738)
Comedian.

3339 JENKINS, ELIJAH, *pseud.* of John Mottley. Joe Miller's jests: or, the wits vade-mecum. Being a collection of the most brilliant jests; the politest repartees; the most elegant bons mots, and most pleasant short stories in the English language. First carefully collected in the company, and many of them transcribed from the mouth of the facetious gentleman, whose name they bear; and now set forth and published by his lamentable friend and former companion, Elijah Jenkins, Esq; most humbly inscribed to those choice-spirits of the age, Captain Bodens, Mr. Alexander Pope, Mr. Professor Lacy, Mr. Orator Henley, and Job Baker, the kettle-drummer.

pp. [*2*] [I] 2–70   L
Printed and sold by T. Read   1739

> The jests did not really originate from Miller. Two more editions were published in 1739, and at least forty-one further editions have been published, including a facsimile reprint of the first edition with an introduction by Robert Hutchinson (New York: Dover Publications, Inc., 1963).

Mingotti, Regina

Singer.

3340 MINGOTTI, [REGINA]. *An appeal to the publick.
Printed for the authoress   [*ca.* 1755]

   STR.

3341 MINGOTTI, [REGINA]. A second appeal to the publick, by Signora Mingotti.

pp. [*4*] I–II [12]   L
Printed for Signora Mingotti   [1756]

> An appeal against the management of the King's Theatre.

Montgomery, Walter (1827–1871)

An unfortunate actor — Lowe.

3342 HORNE, R[ICHARD] H[ENGIST], *ed.* Was Hamlet mad? Being a series of critiques on the acting of the late Walter Montgomery: written in Melbourne in 1867, by the Hon. Archibald Michie, Q.C., (late Attorney-General); Dr. J. E. Neild (late President of the Medical Society, Victoria); R. H. Horne; James Smith, Esq. (late Parliamentary Librarian); David Blair, M.P.; and Charles Bright, Esq. Edited by R. H. Horne.

pp. [i–iii] iv [v–vi] [7] 8–48   L
Thomas Hailes Lacy, theatrical publisher   [1871 or 1872]

Moore, Mary (1862–1931)

Actress. Married to playwright James Albery and then to Sir Charles Wyndham, the actor manager. She continued to manage Wyndham's after her husband's death. See below no. 4015.

Moore, Peter (1753–1828)

An active and officious member of the Committee of Amateurs, who mismanaged Drury Lane.—Lowe. See AUTHOR INDEX.

Morgan, *Lady* Sydney Owenson (1783?–1859)

Daughter of Robert Owenson, the actor and Dublin manager.

3343 FITZPATRICK, WILLIAM JOHN. Lady Morgan; her career, literary and personal, with a glimpse of her friends, and a word to her calumniators. By William John Fitzpatrick, J.P.

pp. [i–v] vi, [I] 2–308; addendum slip   L
Charles J. Skeet   1860

> The early chapters of the biography are of theatrical interest.

Mossop, Henry (1729–1774)

An actor of great merit, but of equal vanity, who might have rivalled Garrick in many parts, but who wasted his life in struggling to be the head of the Irish theatre. His contest with Barry and Woodward in Dublin ended disastrously for all — Lowe. See IRELAND nos. 1783, 1789 (Dublin); BIOGRAPHY: COLLECTIVE: 2284 et seq; BIOGRAPHY nos. 2865, 2897 (Garrick).

Mountfort, William (1664–1692)

Actor and dramatist. Murdered at the instigation of an officer, Captain Hill, when he defended Mrs. Bracegirdle against Hill's attentions. Lord Mohun was also arrested in connection with the affair. See also no. 2517.

3344 *A TRAGICAL SONG: or, Mr. Wil. Montfort, the famous actor unfortunately kill'd. Tune of Mary live long.

bs.   CSmH
Charles Barnes   [1692 or 1693]

> Wing I 2016A. Reprinted in facsimile in Albert S. Borgman The life and death of William Mountfort (Cambridge: Mass. 1935) p. 159.

3345 MOUNTFORT, *Mr.* *Six plays, to which is prefixed some memoirs of the life of Mr. Mountfort.

                                       1720
   Chase.

Mozeen, Thomas (–1768)

3346 [MOZEEN, THOMAS.] YOUNG SCARRON.

pp. [*8*] [i] ii–viii, [17] 18–182   L
Printed and sold by T. Trye and W. Reeve   1752

> Published 17 Dec. 1751 — LS. A satirical novel of theatrical life based on Mozeen's experiences, especially as a strolling player.

Mudie, *Miss*

An "infant Roscius". She appeared at Covent Garden on November 23 1805 as Peggy in The Country Girl and was hissed off the stage. She may have helped to spark off the unrest which led eventually to the O.P. riots.

3347 *AUTHENTIC NARRATIVE of the theatrical career and dramatic talents of Miss Mudie (only seven years of age.)

1805

PH *and* KB.

Munden, Joseph Shepherd (1758–1832)

The great comedian in whom Lamb delighted, and of whom Talfourd wrote that "he was in high farce what Kemble was in high tragedy." He first appeared at Covent Garden, 2 December 1790, and retired 31 May 1824 — Lowe. See also below THEORY AND CRITICISM no. 3731.

3348 [MUNDEN, THOMAS SHEPHERD.] MEMOIRS of Joseph Shepherd Munden, comedian. By his son.

pp. [4] [1] 2–330 [331–332 (bl.)]; pl. [front.]   L
Richard Bentley   1844

3349 ——[another edition]

pp. [4] [1] 2–330; pl. [front.]   LGk
Richard Bentley   1846

Murphy, Arthur (1730–1805)

Actor and dramatist. Made his debut as an actor at Covent Garden during the season of 1754–1755. Retired from acting in 1756. Author of The life of David Garrick etc. (See above no. 2942). See also AUTHOR INDEX.

3350 MOCULLOCH, PHILIM, *pseud?* The Murphiad. A mock heroic poem. By Philim Moculloch, Esq.

pp. [4] [i] ii [3] 4–19 [20]   L
J. Williams   1761

A very nasty production — Lowe.

3351 FOOT, JESSÉ. The life of Arthur Murphy, Esq. By Jessé Foot, Esq. his executor.

pp. [i–iii] iv, [1] 2–464; pls. [front., 6]   L
J. Faulder   1811

Murray, Alma (1854–1945)

Actress. A volume of nine pamphlets about Alma Murray was presented to the British Museum in 1921 by Alfred Forman, Alma Murray's husband. He indicates the scarcity of each pamphlet, most of which are on Whatman's paper. He may well have sponsored their publication.

3352 MOSELY, B[ENJAMIN] L[EWIS]. Miss Alma Murray's Constance in Robert Browning's "In a balcony". A paper by B. L. Mosely, LL.B. Barrister-at-Law. Read to the Browning Society on the 27th of February, 1885. Reprinted from The Theatre for May, 1885.

pp. [1–3] 4–8; insert (one leaf of advts.)   L
For private distribution only   1885

3353 PRESTON, SYDNEY E, *ed.* The Cenci   Five act tragedy by Percy Bysshe Shelley   Extracts from reviews of the first performance 7th May 1886   With a preface by Sydney E. Preston.

pp. [1–5] 6–32; pl. [front.]   L
For private circulation   May 1886

Only 35 copies printed.

3354 [S., M. S.] SHELLEY'S BEATRICE CENCI and her first interpreter.

pp. [1–7] 8–15 [16 (printers' imprint & device)]   L
Printed for private circulation [by Chiswick Press]   1886

3355 THE FIRST PERFORMANCE of Shelley's tragedy The Cenci with additional notices of Miss Alma Murray's Beatrice. Chiefly from the Shelley Society's Notebook.

pp. [1–2] 3–40   L
Printed for private distribution [by Richard Clay and Sons]   1887

3356 AN INTERVIEW with Miss Alma Murray Her opinions of "The Cenci"   From the "Evening News" of 26th July, 1887.

pp. [1–3] 4–7 [8]   L
Reeves and Turner   1887

3357 MOSELY, B[ENJAMIN] L[EWIS]. Miss Alma Murray as Beatrice Cenci. A paper, by B. L. Mosely, Ll.B., Barrister-at-law, read and discussed before the Shelley Society on the 9th of March, 1887.

pp. [1–3] 4–24   L
Reeves and Turner   1887

3358 vacant

3359 WILSON, FRANK. Miss Alma Murray as Juliet. By Frank Wilson.

pp. [1–3] 4–16   L
Reeves & Turner   1887

A study of Alma Murray in Edinburgh, November 1884.

3360 ALMA MURRAY Portrait as Beatrice Cenci With critical notices containing four letters from Robert Browning.

pp. [1–3] 4–11 [12]; pl. [front.]　　　　L

Elkin Mathews　　　　1891

Issued with two leaves of Mathews' advertisements dated October 1890.

3361 ——[fine paper issue]

pp. [1–3] 4–11 [12]; pl. [front.]　　　　L

Elkin Mathews　　　　1891

Issued with two leaves (one blank) of Mathews' advertisements for December 1891.

3362 FAIRFAX, WALTER. Robert Browning and the drama with special reference to the point of view afforded by Miss Alma Murray's performances of his heroines. A note by Walter Fairfax.

pp. [1–3] 4–20 [21 (notes) 22 (bl.)]　　　　L

Reeves & Turner　　　　1891

3363 ——[fine paper issue]

pp. [2] [1–3] 4–20 [21 (notes) 22 (bl.)]　　　　L

Reeves & Turner　　　　1891

Watermark date 1898 on tipped-in advertisement (pp. [2]).

3364 ALMA MURRAY in poetic drama and dramatic recitals from Shakespeare, Shelley, Robert Browning, Victor Hugo, and Richard Wagner. A selection of criticisms with portrait by Chris Hammond and some additional matter.

pp. [24]; illus.　　　　L

[London]　　　　1896

Two copies at L, both paginated in manuscript in the same hand.

3365 vacant

Murray, William H. (1790–1852)

The famous Edinburgh manager. On the death of Henry Siddons in 1815, the management of the Edinburgh Theatre Royal devolved on Murray, for behoof of his sister, Mrs. H. Siddons. In 1830 he became patentee on his own account, and managed the theatre till 1848. He made his last appearance at the Adelphi in 1851. For some time he managed both the Adelphi and the Theatre Royal. Under his management Rob Roy *and the other Waverley dramas were produced —* Lowe. *For his dispute with the shareholder William Black see* SCOTLAND *nos. 1984–1992 (Edinburgh).*

3366 MURRAY, W[ILLIAM] H[ENRY]. The farewell and occasional addresses delivered by W. H. Murray, Esq., in the Theatre Royal and Adelphi, Edinburgh; with a biographical sketch.

pp. [4] [1] 2–160　　　　L

Edinburgh: James G. Bertram & Co.　　　　1851

pp. 1–36: "The rise and progress of the theatre in Edinburgh".

3367 ——A memoir of W. H. Murray, Esq., comedian; with a sketch of the rise and progress of the theatre, and anecdotes of the stage in Edinburgh.

pp. [1] 2–36　　　　EP

Edinburgh: James G. Bertram & Co.　　　　1851

Merely the first 36 pages of Murray's Addresses—Lowe. Running title: "The rise and progress of the theatre in Edinburgh".

Namiani, *Signor*

Opera singer. See above no. 1471.

Neilson, Lilian Adelaide (1846–1880)

Stage name of Elizabeth Ann Brown. Actress. Very popular, especially in the role of Juliet.

3368 MISS NEILSON. Haymarket Theatre. January 17th, 1876.

pp. [1] 2–8; cover-title　　　　LGk

Printed and perfumed by E. Rimmel　　　　[1875 or 1876]

3369 DE LEINE, M. A. Lilian Adelaide Neilson. A memorial sketch, personal and critical. By M. A. De Leine.

pp. [4] [1] 2–64; pl. [front. (photo.)]　　　　MH

Newman and Co.　　　　1881

3370 HOLLOWAY, LAURA C. Adelaide Neilson A souvenir By Laura C. Holloway Illustrated.

pp. [2] [1–5] 6–58 [59–60 (bl.)]; pls. [8 photos.]; illus.　　　　MH

New York and London: Funk & Wagnalls　　　　1885

Some copies issued sewn with pink or scarlet thread, and tied with a scarlet ribbon bow; stiff cardboard cover, with photograph.

Neville, Henry (1837–1910)

A very good and successful actor in drama. He was for some years manager of the Olympic Theatre — Lowe. Real name Thomas Henry Gartside Neville. Specialised in melodrama. For his writings on the theatre see AUTHOR INDEX.

Nicolini, *"Cavalier"*, (1673–1732) stage name of Nicolino Grimaldi

Opera singer. See also no. 1504.

3371 THE SIGNIOR IN FASHION: or the fair maid's conveniency. A poem on Nicolinis's [sic] musick-meeting. Humbly dedicated to the subscribers.

pp. [1] 2–4　　　　L

n.p.　　　　1711

Nossiter, Isabella

The lady was in love with Spranger Barry, to whom she left by will £3000. Her stage career was short — Lowe. *She made her debut at Covent Garden during the season 1753–1754.*

3372 [MORGAN, MacNAMARA.] A LETTER TO MISS NOSSITER. Occasioned by her first appearance on the stage: in which is contained remarks upon her manner of playing the character of Juliet; interspersed with some other theatrical observations.

pp. [2] [1] 2–56 L
W. Owen 1753

A very favourable criticism — Lowe. *Published 30 Oct. 1753 —* LS.

O'Keeffe, John (1747–1833)

One of the best of farce-writers — Lowe. *Acted in Mossop's company in Dublin for a time. He eventually went blind but continued his writing.*

3373 O'KEEFFE, JOHN. Recollections of the life of John O'Keeffe, written by himself.

2 vols. pp. [i–v] vi–xii, [1] 2–407 [408]; pl. [front.] + pp. [i–iii] iv–viii, [1] 2–428 L
Henry Colburn 1826

The "anecdotal substance" reprinted in Personal Reminiscences of O'Keeffe, Kelly, and Taylor, *ed. R. H. Stoddard (Bric-a-Brac Series) (New York, 1875).*

3374 THORN, HENRY G[EORGE]. John O'Keeffe: a few particulars relating to one of the illustrious dead, in Southampton, by Henry G. Thorn.

pp. [1–3] 4–11 [12] L
Southampton: Hampshire Independent Office [1889]

"Reprinted (with additions) from the Hampshire Independent, *of January 26, 1889."*

Oldfield, Anne (1683–1730)

One of the most celebrated actresses of the English stage, and the acknowledged successor of the great Mrs. Mountfort. She was a woman of extraordinary beauty, as well as talent, and famous both as a tragic and comic performer, though her chief excellence lay in the representation of ladies of high fashion. At her death she received unprecedented honour — her body lying in state in the Jerusalem Chamber, and being conveyed thence to Westminster Abbey. She is the Narcissa of whom Pope writes in his Moral Essays, *Epistle I:*

" 'Odious! in woollen? 'twould a saint provoke!'
Were the last words that poor Narcissa spoke." — Lowe.

✠ The memorial of Jane Rogers. [1712]. *See no. 3469.*

Mrs. Oldfield supplanted Mrs. Rogers as Andromache in The Distrest Mother *at Drury Lane.*

3375 AUTHENTICK MEMOIRS of the life of the celebrated actress Mrs. Anne Oldfield. Containing a genuine account of her transactions from her infancy to the time of her decease.

pp. [1] 2–8, misnumbering 7 as "5" L
J. Johnson [1730]

3375.1 ———*second edition

MH
1730

3376 ———Authentick memoirs of the life of that celebrated actress Mrs. Ann Oldfield. Containing a genuine account of her transactions from her infancy to the time of her decease. The third edition, with large additions and amendments.

pp. [2] i–viii 9–46, misnumbering 45, 46 as "43", "44". L

Printed, and sold by the booksellers of London and Westminster 1730

3377 ———Authentick memoirs of the life of, that justly celebrated actress, Mrs. Ann Oldfield. Collected from private records, by a certain eminent peer of Great Britain. The fourth edition. With large additions and amendments.

pp. [2] i–iii, ii, iv–v [=6], [9] 10–24, ²[1–3] 4–8 LGk
London: printed, and Dublin: re-printed, and sold by George Faulkner 1731

3378 ———Authentick memoirs of the life of that celebrated actress Mrs. Ann Oldfield. Containing a geneuine [*sic*] account of her transactions to the time of her death. To which is annex'd, a new pastoral elegy; and a poem, occasion'd by her decease. The sixth edition, with new additions never before printed.

pp. [i–ii] iii–x 11–46 [47–48], ²1–6 [7 (advt.) 8 (bl.)] MH
Printed and sold by the booksellers of London and Westminster 1730

3379 LITTLEMORE, S. A poem on the death of the celebrated Mrs. Oldfield, who dy'd October 23. 1730. Inscrib'd to the Hon. Brigadier Churchill, by S. Littlemore, Gent.

pp. [4] [1] 2–4 MH
A. Moore 1730

3380 *MAINWARIO'S WELCOME to Ophelia on his meeting her in the Shades. Inscribed to the Honourable Mr. Mainwaring.

1730

STR.

3381 *A PASTORAL ELEGY on the death of Calista. Humbly inscribed to the Honourable Col. C——rchill.
4 ll., incl. title
W. Trott 1730

Thorn-Drury.

ENGLISH THEATRICAL LITERATURE

3382 [SAVAGE, RICHARD?] *POEM to the memory of Mrs. Oldfield, inscribed to the Hon. Brigadier Churchill.

pp. [2] [1] 2–8 [9] [10 (bl.)]

J. Roberts   1730

"By a Gentleman Commoner of Oxford" (Morning Chronicle, *October 1730*). Foxon.

3383 ———*[another edition]

pp. [1–3] 4–8

Dublin   1731

Foxon.

✖ A catalogue of all the rich furniture of Mrs Oldfield. *1731. See no. 121.*

3384 EGERTON, WILLIAM, *pseud. of* Edmund Curll. Faithful memoirs of the life, amours and performances, of that justly celebrated, and most eminent actress of her time, Mrs. Anne Oldfield. Interspersed with several other dramatical memoirs. By William Egerton, Esq;

pp. [4] i–iv, ²i–v [vi], ³[i] ii–xi [xii], [1] 2–212, ²[1] 2–21 [22]; pl. [front., fold.]   LGk

London   1731

Advertised 26 February 1731 — Straus.

✖ Betterton, Thomas. The history of the English stage, from the Restauration to the present time. 1741. *See no. 829.*

Bound in is Memoirs of Mrs. Anne Oldfield. *1741 (an abridgement of Egerton's* Faithful memoirs, *no. 3384 above).*

3385 *THE LOVER'S MISCELLANY. Being a curious collection of amorous tales and poems. Together with some faithful memoirs of the life and amours of the late celebrated Mrs. Ann Oldfield.

London   1731

Thorn-Drury, *who records a copy with half-title.*

✖ A justification of the letter to Sir J——n St——ley, relating to his management of the playhouse in Drury-Lane. [n.d.]. *See no. 1317.*

Contains a violent attack upon Mrs. Oldfield.

✖ Theatrical correspondence in death. An epistle from Mrs. Oldfield, in the shades, to Mrs. Br——ceg——dle, upon earth. 1743. *See no. 1343.*

3386 ROBINS, EDWARD. The palmy days of Nance Oldfield by Edward Robins With portraits.

pp. [8] [1] 2–277 [278]; pls. [front., 10]; vignette on t.p.
                                                                               L

William Heinemann   1898

Lacks one plate.

———[American edition] Chicago: Herbert S. Stone, & Co., 1898.

O'Neill, Eliza (1791–1872)

Made her first appearance in London at Covent Garden on 6th October 1814, and was at once hailed as a successor to Mrs. Siddons. In 1819 she retired from the stage, having married Sir William Becher — Lowe.

3387 A DESCRIPTIVE PORTRAIT OF MISS O'NEILL, in a critique on her exhibition of the characters of Mrs. Haller, and Jane Shore.

pp. [4] [1] 2–108   L

E. Williams   1815

3388 JONES, CHARLES INIGO. Memoirs of Miss O'Neill; containing her public character, private life, and dramatic progress, from her entrance upon the stage; with a full criticism of her different characters, appropriate selections from them, and some account of the plays she has preferred for her representations. By Charles Inigo Jones, Esq. of the Middle Temple. Embellished with a striking and highly-finished portrait of Miss O'Neill.

pp. [i–iii] iv, [1] 2–100; col. pl. [front.]   L

D. Cox   1816

Dedicated to Thomas Harris.

3389 ———second edition

pp. [i–iii] iv, [1] 2–100; col. pl. [front.]   L

Sherwood, Neely, and Jones   1818

A reissue of the first edition. On the title-page of this edition "of the Middle Temple" omitted, and 'coloured' substituted for "striking".

3390 *MISS O'NEILL'S WELCOME to Kilkenny.

Dublin   1819

Chase.

3391 [BUNN, ALFRED?] *THE RIVAL ROSES. A poem. Addressed to Miss O'Neil and Miss Somerville, of the Theatre Royal, Covent Garden.

pp. 8   MB

Handy   1819

Attributed to Bunn by Urwin, *p. 23.*

Oxberry, William (1784–1824)

A comedian of no great note — Lowe. Father of William Henry Oxberry (1808–1852), actor and manager. See AUTHOR INDEX.

324

Pack, James

A converted actor.

3392 PACK, JAMES. Some account of the life and experience of James Pack, late celebrated actor, in the pantomime department, at the Theatre Royal, Drury Lane, and other places: but now, by the grace of God, a disciple and follower of the Lord Jesus Christ. In a series of letters written by himself, and addressed to Mr. Henry Paice, pastor of the Particular Baptist Church, meeting in Lewisham Street, Westminster.

pp. [2] [1–3] 4–45 [46]   L
Printed and sold by the author   1819

Paget, William (fl. 1731–1749)

Actor.

3393 PAGET, W[ILLIAM]. The humours of the Fleet. A poem. By W. Paget, comedian. With a preface, containing a sketch of the author's life.

pp. [i–iii] iv–viii, [1] 2–32   L
Birmingham: printed by T. Aris, for the author [1745?]

3394 ——[another edition] The humours of the Fleet: a humorous, descriptive poem. Written by a gentleman of the college. Under the following heads, viz. I. His being arrested for debt, and hurried away by those horrid merciless fellows the bailiffs to the spunging-house. II. His not liking the exorbitant demands of that Place, is by a *Habeas Corpus* brought over to the Fleet Prison. III. His being received by the turn-key, is introduc'd to a proper place, in order (as they term it) to *paint his face*, to prevent his making an escape in disguise through the *jigg*. IV. The merry scene between the prisoner, the chamberlain, the chum and the cook, and particularly describing several collegians. With a preface, containing a sketch of part of the author's life and family. Interspers'd with critical and explanatory notes.

pp. [i–iii] iv–vii [viii, misprinting viii as "vii"] 9–40; t.p. in red and black   L
B. Dickinson   1749

Cut up and mounted.

Palmer, John (1742–1798)

"Plausible Jack", the original Joseph Surface, which character he acted in private as well as on the stage. In 1787 he tried to open the Royalty Theatre, but the patent houses managed to stop him. He died on the stage at Liverpool on 2nd August 1798, while playing "The Stranger". The story that he died after saying "There is another and a better world" is entirely false — Lowe. See also GOVERNMENT REGULATION OF THE THEATRE nos. 176–189.

3395 HARRAL T[HOMAS]. A monody on the death of Mr. John Palmer, the comedian. To which is prefixed A review of his theatrical powers: with observations on the most eminent performers on the London stage. Inscribed to Mrs. Siddons. By T. Harral.

pp. [2] [1–3] 4–20   L
Printed by George Cawthorn   1798

3396 *A SKETCH of the theatrical life of the late Mr. John Palmer, containing an accurate and impartial summary of the incidents of his publick life, from his earliest entrance into the theatrical profession, to the melancholy event of his sudden death, while performing the character of the Stranger, on the Liverpool stage, on Thursday August 2, 1798.

                                                             MH
                                                             1798

Palmer, Minnie (1860–1936)

Actress and singer.

3397 BLYTH, HARRY. *My sweetheart! The life and adventures of Minnie Palmer. A tribute to grace and genius.

pp. 88, (5); ports.   MB
The Hansard Publishing Union, Ltd.   [189–?]

Her first appearance in Britain was in the part of Tina in My Sweetheart at the Princess's Theatre, Glasgow, in 1883.

Parker, George (1732–1800)

Actor, soldier and lecturer.

3398 PARKER, G[EORGE]. A view of society and manners in high and low life; being the adventures in England, Ireland, Scotland, Wales, France, &c. of Mr. G. Parker. In which is comprised a history of the stage itinerant.

2 vols. pp. [26] [i] ii–xiv [15] 16–236 + [8] [1] 2–276 [277 (errata) 278 (bl.)]   L
Printed for the author   1781

3399 PARKER, GEORGE. Life's painter of variegated characters in public and private life. By George Parker, Librarian to the Colleges of Wit, Mirth, and Humour ...

pp. [1–3] 4–90, ²[1] 2–239 [240]; pl. [front.]   L
James Ridgway   1789

pp. 15–90: List of Subscribers.

3400 ——Life's painter of variegated characters in public and private life, with political strokes on the ticklish times; containing a novel display of the styles of men of genius in the learned world. By George Parker, Librarian to the College of Wit, Mirth and

Humour; Fellow of the Society of Fun; mental anato-
mist; exhibitor of nature's mirror; citizen of the world.
. . . The second edition.

pp. [i–iii] iv–xii [xiii–xlviii], [1] 2–237 [238–239 (bl.)
240 (errata)]   L

[Dublin?]: printed for the author   [ca. 1800]

   pp. [xiii–xlviii]: List of Subscribers.

3401 ——[another edition] Life's painter of variegated characters in public and private life, by George
Parker, Librarian to the College of Wit, Mirth, and
Humour. . . . To which is added, a dictionary of modern
flash, or cant language, so much in use with the swells
of the town.

pp. [3–5] 6–176; pl. [front.]   L

Printed by R. Bassam   [ca. 1800?]

   *The previous editions also contain the "dictionary of
modern flash". Abridged.*

Parsons, Samuel (b. 1762)
Provincial actor.

3402 PARSONS, SAMUEL. Poetical trifles, being a
collection of songs, and fugitive pieces, by S. Parsons,
late of the Theatre Royal, York, with a sketch of the life
of the author.

pp. [i–iii] iv–v [vi–x], ²[i] ii–xii, [1] 2–66 [67–68 (bl.)]
                                                                                      MH

York: printed by R. Johnson   1822

Parsons, William (1736–1795)
*A great comedian, especially famous for his old men. He
made his first [London] appearance at Drury Lane 21st
September 1762, and died in harness—Lowe. The appearance was as Filch in The Beggar's Opera (LS, pt. 4, II,
951). For Bellamy's Life of William Parsons, comedian
see above no. 897.*

Pasta, *Madame* Giuditta (1798–1865)
Opera singer.

3403 [HAYTER, JOHN.] SKETCHES of Mad^me.
Pasta in the opera of Medea.

pp. [1] 2; pls. [9 (with paper shields)]   LGk
[London]   [1827]

   *Title blocked in gold on green cloth cover. The dedication
to the Countess of St. Antonio is signed by John Hayter,
the artist, and dated 25 April 1827.*

Paton, Anne (or Susannah) (1802–1864)
*A noted vocalist, whose marriage with Lord William Lennox
caused great speculation. She afterwards married Joseph
Woods, a singer — Lowe.*

3404 ★AN ACCOUNT of the very extraordinary
mysterious proceedings at Covent Garden Theatre,
between Lord and Lady W. Lennox.

pp. 8; pl., fold. [front.]

                                                                           [ca. 1825]

   A wretchedly got up pamphlet — Lowe.

3405 THE HIGHLY INTERESTING LIFE OF
LADY WM. LENNOX, formerly Miss Anne Paton.
From public and private sources. Containing an account
of her birth, parentage, and education, her amours
with persons both in high and low life, and every
particular to the present time.

pp. [1–3] 4–8; pl. [front. ("rude portrait" — Lowe)]   L
Printed by W. Lowe   [ca. 1825]

3406 ★THE PUBLIC AND PRIVATE LIFE OF
LADY WILLIAM LENNOX, alias Miss Anne Paton,
containing the whole of her amours, attachments, and
amiable faux-pas with persons in high and low life,
and an interesting detail of the causes which led to the
desertion of her husband. With a beautiful portrait.
(Amatory Biography, or Lives of the most seductive
characters, of both sexes, of the present day, No. 1).

                                                                           [ca. 1825]
   Lowe.

3407 ★MEMOIRS OF THE PRIVATE AND PUB-
LIC LIFE OF MR. AND MRS. WOOD.

                                                                                 1835

   *A vehement attack on both — Lowe. There are two
American works with titles beginning similarly ('Memoir
of Mr. and Mrs. Wood' etc.), but differing later: Philadelphia: Turner and Fisher, 1840, ("including the
marriage of Miss Paton to Lord William Lennox . . .");
and Boston, [1840] ("containing . . . a full statement
of the popular disturbances at the Park Theatre, New
York").*

Payne, John Howard (1791–1852)
A very noted American actor — Lowe.

3408 MEMOIRS OF JOHN HOWARD PAYNE,
the American Roscius: with criticisms on his acting,
in the various theatres of America, England and Ireland.
Compiled from authentic documents.

pp. [4] [1] 2–131 [132]; pl. [front.]   L
John Miller   1815

   *"The following pages present, perhaps, the only materials
which have ever been collected in England for a correct
estimate of the American stage, as to be inferred from the
encouragement of national talent, and the style of dramatic
criticism in that recent and interesting country. . . . " —
Preface.*

Peake, Richard Brinsley (1792–1847)

For many years treasurer of the Lyceum Theatre under Arnold. He was a successful farce-writer, and a quaintly humorous speaker. Planché writes in high terms regarding him—Lowe. See AUTHOR INDEX.

Pemberton, Charles Reece (1790–1840)

An actor who was introduced to the London stage through Talfourd's influence. He was not so successful as he hoped, and latterly confined himself rather to reading and lecturing — Lowe.

3409 FOWLER, JOHN, *ed.* The life and literary remains of Charles Reece Pemberton: with remarks on his character and genius, by W[illiam] J[ohnson] Fox. Edited by John Fowler, Secretary of the Sheffield Mechanics' Institution.

pp. [i–iii] iv–xxxii [33] 34–506; pl. [front.]   L
Charles Fox   1843

With list of subscribers.

Penley, William Sidney (1851–1912)
Actor.

3410 PENLEY, [WILLIAM SIDNEY]. Penley on himself The confessions of a conscientious artist (Arrowsmith's Bristol Library vol. LXVII)

pp. [1–5] 6–196; illus.   L
Bristol: J. W. Arrowsmith; London: Simpkin, Marshall, Hamilton, Kent & Company Limited   [1896]

Phelps, Samuel (1804–1878)

A great Shakespearean actor, whose managership of Sadler's Wells Theatre was one of the greatest achievements in the service of legitimate acting — Lowe.

3411 FOX, WILLIAM JOHNSON. A biographical sketch of W. C. Macready, Esq., by W. J. Fox, M.P. and full particulars of his last appearances at the Theatres Royal Haymarket and Drury-Lane; with a portrait by R. Thorburn. Also, Shakespeare's tragedy of Macbeth, being part IV. of his complete works revised from the original text; with introductory remarks and copious notes — critical, general, and explanatory. Under the immediate and personal supervision of Samuel Phelps, Esq. (of the Theatre Royal, Sadler's Wells.)

pp. [2] [1] 2–16 103–134; pls. [front., 1]; cover serves as t.p.   MB
Willoughby & Co.   [1851]

W. J. Fox's sketch originally appeared in the People's Journal. *It was reissued in this form apparently because of its relevance to Phelps. See also no. 3281 above.*

3412 KENNEY, CHARLES LAMB. Mr. Phelps and the critics of his correspondence with the Stratford Committee. By Charles Lamb Kenney, Esq.

pp. [1–3] 4–8   L
T. H. Lacy   1864

3413 TERCENTENARY CELEBRATION OF THE BIRTH OF SHAKESPEARE. Mr. Phelps and the Stratford-upon-Avon committee.

bs.   MB
J. W. Last, printer   [1864]

A poster, signed Sam[l]. Phelps, in vindication of the actor, and reprinting the correspondence between him and the committee.

3413.1 ———*[another edition]
pp. 8
                                                        1864
Loewenberg. *The poster issued as a pamphlet.*

✂ Ghost of Walter S. Landor, The, *pseud.* An imaginary conversation between Mr. Phelps and Dr. Cumming. [*ca.* 1865.] See no. 616.

✂ By order of the executors of the late Samuel Phelps. Theatrical costumes. A catalogue . . . [1879]. See no. 122.

3414 COLEMAN, JOHN and EDWARD COLEMAN. Memoirs of Samuel Phelps by John Coleman assisted by Edward Coleman.

pp. [1–7] 8–331 [332 (bl.)]; pl. [front.]   NbU
Remington & Co.   1886

3415 PHELPS, W[ILLIAM] MAY and JOHN FORBES-ROBERTSON. The life and life-work of Samuel Phelps by his nephew W. May Phelps and John Forbes-Robertson with three portraits and copies of letters from men of eminence and other original documents of interest to play-goers.

pp. [i–vii] viii–x [xi–xii], [1] 2–436; pls. [front., 2]   L
Sampson Low, Marston, Searle, & Rivington   1886

The frontispiece is from a painting by Johnston Forbes-Robertson.

Phillips, Henry (1801–1876)
Singer and actor. See also above OPERA no. 2085.

3416 PHILLIPS, HENRY. *Musical and personal recollections during half a century.

2 vols.; port.   MB
Skeet   1864

Phillips, Watts (1825–1874)

Artist and playwright.

3417 PHILLIPS, EMMA WATTS. Watts Phillips: artist and playwright. By E. Watts Phillips.

pp. [i–v] vi–x [11] 12–174; pls. [front., 28 = 31 ll.]   L
Cassell & Co.   1891

Pinkethman, William (16 –1725)

See above EDWARDS, JOHN no. 2695.

Planché, James Robinson (1796–1880)

The learned antiquary, and delightful writer of fairy tales and burlesques, who exerted a great influence for good on the theatrical world of his time. He was the adviser of Madame Vestris in many of the improvements she introduced — Lowe. See also above JONES, INIGO no. 3109.

3418 PLANCHÉ, J[AMES] R[OBINSON]. Costume of Shakespeare's historical tragedy of King John, selected and arranged from the best authorities, expressly for the proprietors of the Theatre Royal, Covent Garden; with biographical, critical, and explanatory notices, by J. R. Planché. The figures designed and executed on stone, by J. K. Meadows. (Dramatic Costume. No. 1).

pp. [1–3] 4–36; col. pls. [t.p.], 1–22   L
John Miller   1823

3419 PLANCHÉ, J[AMES] R[OBINSON]. Costume of Shakespeare's historical play of King Henry the Fourth, parts 1st and 2nd, selected and arranged from the best authorities, expressly for the proprietors of the Theatre Royal, Covent Garden; with biographical, critical, and explanatory notices, by J. R. Planché. The figures designed and executed on stone, by G. Scharf. (Dramatic Costume. No. II.)

pp. [1–3] 4–35 [36]; col. pls. [t.p.], 21   L
John Miller; and Rodwell & Martin   1824

3420 PLANCHÉ, J[AMES] R[OBINSON]. Costume of Shakespeare's comedy of As You Like It, selected and arranged from the best authorities, expressly for the proprietors of the Theatre Royal, Covent Garden; with biographical, critical, and explanatory notices, by J. R. Planché. The figures executed on stone, by G. Scharf. (Dramatic Costume. No. III.)

pp. [1–3] 4–28; col. pls. [t.p., 18]   L
John Miller; and Rodwell & Martin   1825

3421 PLANCHÉ, J[AMES] R[OBINSON]. Costume of Shakespeare's tragedy of Hamlet, selected and arranged from the best authorities, expressly for the proprietors of the Theatre Royal, Covent Garden; with biographical, critical, and explanatory notices, by

J. R. Planché. The figures executed on stone, by G. Scharf. (Dramatic Costume. No. IV.)

pp. [1–3] 4–34; col. pls. [t.p., 13]   L
London: John Miller; Rodwell & Martin; Edinburgh: W. Blackwood   1825

3422 PLANCHÉ, J[AMES] R[OBINSON]. Costume of Shakespeare's tragedy of Othello, and comedy of the Merchant of Venice; selected and arranged from the best authorities, expressly for the proprietors of the Theatre Royal Covent Garden; with biographical, critical, and explanatory notices, by J. R. Planché. The figures executed on stone, by G. Scharf. (Dramatic Costume. No. V.)

pp. [3–5] 6–46; col. pls. [t.p., 23]   L
London: John Miller; Rodwell & Martin; Edinburgh: W. Blackwood   1825

3423 PLANCHÉ, J[AMES] R[OBINSON]. Twelve designs for the costume of Shakespeare's Richard the Third, by C. F. Tomkins; after the drawings and with the descriptions of J. R. Planché, Esq. Fellow of the Society of Antiquaries.

pp. [*10*] [1] 2–20; col. pls. [13, incl. extra t.p.]   L
Colnaghi and Son   1830

The plates are dated May 1829 and February 1830.

3424 PLANCHÉ, JAMES ROBINSON. The recollections and reflections of J. R. Planché, (Somerset Herald). A professional autobiography.

2 vols. pp. [i–ix] x–xv [xvi], [1] 2–316 [317–320 (advts.)]; illus.; pls. [3] + pp. [i–v] vi–xii, [1] 2–308; illus.; pls. [4 (incl. 2 fold.)]   NbU
Tinsley   1872

Facsimiles of sketches by Thackeray, Maclise, and others. Previously published in part in the monthly London Society, April to October, 1871. Selections in Personal Reminiscences by Chorley, Planché, and Young ed. R. H. Stoddard (Bric-a-Brac Series) New York, 1876.

3425 ——new and revised edition
pp. [i–ix] x–xxiii [xxiv], [1] 2–464; illus; pl. [front] GM
Sampson Low, Marston & Company   1901

3426 PLANCHÉ, JAMES ROBINSON. Suggestions for establishing an English art theatre. By J. R. Planché, Somerset Herald.

pp. [1–3] 4–12   L
Wyman & Sons   1879

Supporting Godwin's national theatre scheme (no. 2027).

Poole, John (1786–1872)

See BIOGRAPHY no. 3238 (Liston); AUTHOR INDEX.

Pope, Alexander (1763–1835)

Actor. For several years he was leading tragedian of Covent Garden. His first appearance was on 8th January 1785. He retired in 1827—Lowe. See no. 1182.

Powell, William (1735–1769)

A young actor whom Garrick brought forward, and trained to act as his substitute during his Continental tour. In 1767 he became one of the proprietors of Covent Garden—Lowe. See nos. 1163–1174.

Power, Tyrone (1795–1841)

One of the most popular of Irish comedians. He was drowned in the President — Lowe.

3427 POWER, TYRONE. Impressions of America, during the years 1833, 1834, and 1835. By Tyrone Power, Esq.

2 vols. pp. [i–v] vi–xv [xvi], [1] 2–440; pl. [front.] + pp. [i–v] vi, [1] 2–408; pl. [front.]; slip (directions to binder)   L

Richard Bentley   1836

3428 GOUGH, H. T. A monody, appropriate to the memory of Tyrone Power, Esq. by H. T. Gough, Theatre Royal, Hay-Market.

pp. [3–5] 6–14; pl. [front.]   L

W. S. Johnson   1841

Price, Morton *i.e. Captain* Horton Rhys (1824–1876)

An amateur actor. Price became lessee of Sadler's Wells on Phelps retirement from it in 1862 — Lowe.

3429 RHYS, *Captain* [CHARLES] HORTON. A theatrical trip for a wager! Through Canada and the United States. By Captain Horton Rhys, ("Morton Price.")

pp. [2 (bl.) 6] [3] 4–18 [19] 20–59 59★–62★ 60–140, misnumbering 100 as "10"; col. pls. [2 fronts., 3]; illus. boards   GU

Published for the author by Charles Dudley   1861

An entertaining account of a trip made by the author, an amateur actor, in consequence of a bet that he could not, as an actor, earn £500 a year. He won his bet.—Lowe. Captain Morton Price is given as the author on the front cover.

Pritchard, Hannah (1711–1768)

A great actress, eminent both in comedy and tragedy. Off the stage she was a very commonplace person, but on it she seemed inspired with brilliancy and grace. She was especially excellent in her delivery of dialogue. First appearance, Haymarket, 26th September 1733; last appearance, Drury Lane, 24th April 1768—Lowe. See no. 2772.

Purvis, Billy

A very noted North Country clown and humourist, of whom old Newcastle men still speak with delight — Lowe.

3430 ROBSON J[OSEPH] P[HILIP]. The life and adventures of the far-famed Billy Purvis. By J. P. Robson.

pp. [1–3] 4–240; pl. [front.]   L

Newcastle-upon-Tyne: printed by John Clarke
1849 [*for* 1850]

Epilogue dated 26 March 1850.

3431 ——The life and adventures of Billy Purvis, continued to the time of his death, by J. P. Robson. Third edition, improved.

pp. [1–3] 4–253 [254]   NwP

Newcastle-upon-Tyne: John Christie   1854

3432 [ARTHUR, THOMAS.] THE LIFE of Billy Purvis, the extraordinary, witty, and comical showman; with many facts not before published.

pp. [1–3] 4–144; illus.   L

Newcastle-on-Tyne: T. Arthur; A. Everatt; Sunderland: T. Huntley   [1875]

Cover-title: Complete Edition, Illustrated. The Extraordinary Life of Billy Purvis, the Eccentric, Witty, and Popular Showman: his sayings and doings.

3433 ——[second edition]

pp. [2] [1–3] 4–153 [154 (bl.)]; illus.; pl. [front.]   L

Newcastle-on-Tyne: T. Arthur; A. Everatt; Sunderland: T. Huntley   [1875]

With additions. The preface refers to this as "second edition".

3434 ——★[another edition] The life of Billy Purvis.

MH

Newcastle: D. Bowman   1875

Quick, John (1748–1831)

Comic actor, the original Tony Lumpkin in She stoops to conquer. *Remained at Covent Garden for most of his career. For a brief spell was manager of King Street Theatre, Bristol.*

3435 QUICK'S WHIM; or, the merry medley: containing a choice collection of farcical operatical comical pantomimical jests and repartees, occasionally introduced by this son of Momus, and his jocund companions, at the tables of hospitality, hours of conviviality, and moments of mirth. Enriched with an engraving of that excellent comedian.

pp. [1–3] 4–72; pl. [front.]   L

W. Lane   [1795?]

Quin, James (1693–1766)

The great support of the Old School against Garrick, who, however, conquered. Quin was a great actor in many parts, and as a man was noted for his benevolence and for his wit — Lowe. *See also above nos. 2770–2773 (Foote); 2828, 2883 (Garrick).*

3436 THE LIFE OF MR. JAMES QUIN, comedian. With the history of the stage from his commencing actor to his retreat to Bath. Illustrated with many curious and interesting anecdotes of several persons of distinction, literature, and gallantry. To which is added, a genuine and authentic copy of his last will and testament. Dedicated to David Garrick, Esq;

pp. [4] [1] 2–116; pl. [front.]   LGk

S. Bladon   1766

An inaccurate and stupid compilation — Lowe.

3437 ———[another edition] To which is added a supplement of original facts and anecdotes, arranged from authentic sources. Together with his trial for the murder of Mr. Bowen.

pp. [2] [1–7] 8–48, 65–80, 49–107 [108 (bl)] [4 (bl)], gathering E bound before D; t.p. in red and black   GU

Reader   1887

A reprint of the 1766 edition, with an appendix of supplementary materials.

3438 ———*[large paper issue]

                                                        MH
                                                        1887

3439 QUIN'S JESTS; or, the facetious man's pocket-companion. Containing every species of wit, humour, and repartee, with a compleat collection of epigrams, bon-mots, &c. &c.

pp. [4] [1] 2–104   L

S. Bladon   1766

Reed, Thomas German (1817–1888)
Reed, Priscilla, *née* Horton (1818–1895)
Reed, Alfred German (1847–1895)

Thomas German Reed, musician and musical director and his actress wife, famous, with their son Alfred, as "The German Reeds" for their "Entertainment".

3440 WILLIAMSON, DAVID, ed. The German Reeds and Corney Grain: records and reminiscences. Edited by David Williamson. (The "Minster" Library — No. 1.)

pp. [i–v] vi [vii–viii], [1] 2–111 [112]; illus., incl. wrapper   E

A. D. Innes & Co.   1895

See also above no. 2963.

Reeve, John (1799–1838)

A comedian of marked ability, whose irregular conduct ruined his career — Lowe.

3441 BANISTER, DOUGLAS. Life of Mr. John Reeve, with original anecdotes, and portrait by Wageman. By Douglas Banister, Esq.

pp. [1–3] 4–16; pl. [front.]   L

Richardson and Son   [1838]

Reeve, Wybert (*ca.* 1829–1906)

Actor and manager.

3442 REEVE, WYBERT. From life by Wybert Reeve (comedian).

pp. [i–v] vi [vii–viii], [1] 2–248; pl. [front.]   L

F. V. White & Co.   1892

Part previously published in the Australasian.

Reeves [John] Sims (1818–1900)

Singer.

3443 EDWARDS, [HENRY] SUTHERLAND. The life and artistic career of Sims Reeves by Sutherland Edwards.

pp. [3–7] 8–80; pl. [front.]   L

Tinsley Bros.   [1881]

3444 REEVES, [JOHN] SIMS. Sims Reeves   His life and recollections written by himself.

pp. [2] [1–5] 6, ²[1] 2–279 [280]; pl. [front.]   L

Simpkin Marshall & Co. and the London Music Publishing Co. (Limited)   1888

Said to have run through seven editions. Eric Walter White, "An Opera-Goer's Bookshelf", Books: The Journal of the National Book League, No. 289 (Nov. 1954) pp. 240–245, detects another hand in the work.

3445 REEVES, J[OHN] SIMS. My jubilee or fifty years of artistic life by J. Sims Reeves with six plates, and a preface by Thomas Ward.

pp. [i–v] vi–viii, [1–3] 4–280; pls. [front., 5]   L

The London Music Publishing Company, Limited and Simpkin, Marshall & Co., and Hamilton, Adams & Co.
                                                     [1889]

Cover uniform with Reeves's Life and Recollections (1888).

Reynolds, Frederick (1764–1841)

A popular and prolific dramatist — Lowe.

3446 REYNOLDS, FREDERICK. The life and times of Frederick Reynolds. Written by himself.

2 vols. pp. [i–iii] iv–xxiv, [1] 2–373 [374]; pl. [front.] + pp. [i–ii], [1] 2–422   GU

Henry Colburn   1826

3447 ———second edition

2 vols. in 1. pp. [i–iii] iv–xxiv, [1] 2–373 [374] + [2] [1] 2–422 [2]; pl. [front.]   GU

Henry Colburn   1827

———[American edition.] Philadelphia: H. C. Cary and I. Lea, 1826.

3448 REYNOLDS, FREDERICK. A playwright's adventures. By Frederick Reynolds.

pp. [i–iv], [1] 2–356; illus. (wood engrs. by W. H. Brooke); title on spine: The dramatic annual 1831 GU

Longman, Rees, Orme, Brown, & Green   1831

In the form of a novel.

Rich, John (*ca.* 1692–1761)

Manager of Lincoln's Inn Fields and Covent Garden from 1714 to 1761. He was the father of pantomime, and his playing of harlequin [as "Lun"] was a marvellous piece of acting. As a manager he did great harm to the drama — Lowe. See TN, XII, 17–19 for his financing Covent Garden Theatre 1731. See above THE LONDON THEATRE nos. 1143–1150 (Covent Garden).

Ristori, *Madame* Adelaide (1822–1906)

Italian actress who toured widely in Britain and the continent.

3449 *OPINIONS of the London press on Madame Ristori.

                                                        1882

STR.

Roberts, Arthur (1852–1933)

Music hall comedian, who appeared also in pantomime, musical comedy and burlesque.

3450 ROBERTS, ARTHUR. The adventures of Arthur Roberts by rail, road and river told by himself and chronicled by Richard Morton (Arrowsmith's Bristol Library vol. LXV).

pp. [iii–v] vi–x [11] 12–198   MH

Bristol: J. W. Arrowsmith; London: Simpkin, Marshall, Hamilton, Kent & Company Limited   [1895]

Robertson, Thomas William (1829–1871)

Actor and dramatist.

3451 LEIGHTON, *Sir* BALDWYN. *The late Thomas William Robertson and the modern theatre.

pp. 16   MB

Bentley   1875

3452 PEMBERTON, T[HOMAS] EDGAR. The life and writings of T. W. Robertson by T. Edgar Pemberton.

pp. [i–v] vi [vii–x], [1] 2–320; pls. [5]   L

Richard Bentley and Son   1893

Lacks frontispiece.

Rob(b)ins, Miss

Actress. See below no. 3683.

Robinson, Anastasia (–1755), *afterwards Countess of* Pembroke

See above OPERA nos. 2031 et seq.

Robinson, Mary ("Perdita") (1758–1800)

An actress who is notorious as the mistress of George IV, then Prince of Wales. She first attracted his attention on 3rd December 1779, when acting Perdita in the Winter's Tale. *She left the stage at the end of the season, but the Prince separated from her in 1781. In his letters he called himself "Florizel" — Lowe.*

3453 LETTERS FROM PERDITA to a certain Israelite, and his answers to them.

pp. [4] [i] ii–iii [iv] [5] 6–43 [44]   L

J. Fielding; W. Kent; J. Stockdale; and J. Sewell 1781

A furious attack upon Mrs. Robinson, who, with her husband, is represented as systematically swindling. The letters are declared to be genuine letters between Mrs. R. and a Jewish admirer, with whom she had an amour. They are rather nasty productions — Lowe.

3454 POETICAL EPISTLE FROM FLORIZEL TO PERDITA: with Perdita's answer. And a preliminary discourse upon the education of princes.

pp. [1–7] 8–40; vignette on t.p.   MH

J. Stockdale   1781

The half-title reads: Florizel to Perdita: with Perdita'a [sic] answer.

3455 ———the second edition

pp. [1–7] 8–40; vignette on t.p.   L

J. Stockdale   1781

The half-title as in no. 3454.

3456 ———the third edition

pp. [1–7] 8–40; vignette on t.p.   L

J. Stockdale   1781

A reissue. Half-title as in no. 3454.

3457 THE MEMOIRS OF PERDITA; interspersed with anecdotes of the Hon. Charles F——x; Lord M——; Col. T——; P——e of W——s; Col. St. L——r; Mr. S——n, and many other well known characters.

pp. [i–iii] iv–viii, [1] 2–180   L

G. Lister   1784

According to a note on p. 180, this is the first of a series of volumes of "the annals of gallantry", and ought to have a plate.

3458 TO THE P. of W.

pp. [2]   E

n.p.   [1784?]

Written in letters and hieroglyphs.

3459 ROBINSON, [MARY]. Memoirs of the late Mrs. Robinson, written by herself. With some posthumous pieces.

4 vols. pp. [6] [1] 2–192; pl. [front.] + pp. [2] [1] 2–187 [188 (bl.) 189–192 (lists of works by Mary Robinson)] + pp. [4] [1–3] 4–184 + [4] [1–5] 6–192   L

R. Phillips   1801

Edited, with a continuation "by a friend", by Mary Robinson's daughter, Mary Elizabeth Robinson. Vols. 3 and 4 consist of poetry and prose by Mary Robinson, and "tributary lines addressed to Mrs. Robinson, by different friends".

3460 ——[another edition]

2 vols. pp. [6] [1] 2–192; pl. [front.] + pp. [2] [1] 2–258 [259–262 (lists of works by Mary Robinson)]   L

Richard Phillips   1803

Without the "posthumous works" of the 1801 edition, but with the "tributary lines".

3461 ——[another edition] Memoirs of the late Mrs. Robinson, written by herself. From the edition edited by her daughter.

pp. [3–7] 8–155 [156]; pl. [front.]   L

Hunt and Clarke   1826

In: Autobiography. A collection of the most instructive and amusing lives ever published, written by the parties themselves. With brief introductions, and compendious sequels carrying on the narrative to the death of each writer. Volume VII. Mary Robinson — Charlotte Charke.

3462 ——*[a reissue of no. 3461]

pp. 3–155   MB

Whittaker, Treacher & Arnot   1829

In: Autobiography. A collection of the most instructive and amusing lives ever published.

3463 ——[another edition] Memoirs of Mary Robinson "Perdita" from the edition edited by her daughter with introduction and notes by J. Fitzgerald Molloy.

pp. [i–iv] v–xv [xvi], [1] 2–243 [244] 245 [246 (bl.)] 247–251 [252]; pls. [front., 8]   LGk

Gibbings and Company, Ld.   1894

Edition limited to five hundred copies: three hundred and fifty for England, and one hundred and fifty for America.

3464 ——[another edition]

pp. [i–iv] v–xv [xvi], 1–251 [252]; pls. [front., 8]   L

London: Gibbings and Company, Ld.; Philadelphia: J. B. Lippincott Co.   1895

Fine paper edition, limited to "one hundred and twenty-fife [sic] copies". Dated 1894 on the spine.

3465 ——[another edition] Mrs. Mary Robinson written by herself with the lives of the Duchesses of Gordon and Devonshire by Grace and Philip Wharton (Beaux & Belles of England).

pp. [2] [i–iv] v–xvii [xviii xix (list of illustrations) xx], 1–336 [337–338 (bl.)]; pls. [front. (col.), 6]; ptd. tissue guards [7]; t.p. in red and black   NbU

London: printed by the Grolier Society   [190–?]

"Imperial edition limited to one thousand copies for England and America." With the preface by J. Fitzgerald Molloy.

3466 ——a new edition with an introduction

pp. [i–iv] v–xv [xvi], 1–197 [198–200 (bl.)]; pl. [front.]   L

Cobden-Sanderson   1930

——[American editions] Philadelphia: T. and W. Bradford, 1802; New York: T. & J. Swords, P. A. Mesier, and W. A. David, 1802; (Beaux and Belles of England) New York: Athenaeum Press, [1907?].

——[French edition] Mémoires. Paris: Ouvrier, 1802.

3467 [EGAN, PIERCE.] THE MISTRESS OF ROYALTY; or, the loves of Florizel and Perdita, portrayed in the amatory epistles, between an illustrious personage, and a distinguished female: with an interesting sketch of Florizel and Perdita, including other characters.

pp. [1–5] 6–44   L

Printed by and for P. Egan   1814

This copy has an autograph note: "With the author's best respects, to J. Richardson, Esq. If there is any merit attached to this little Book — it is from its singularity. The Author having, in the capacity of a Printer — composed the Types, and worked it off, at the Press. Pierce Egan". Note dated 25th January 1843.

Robson, Frederick (1821–1864)
stage name of Thomas Robson Brownbill

One of the most remarkable actors of the century. His wonderful combination of tragic and comic force has never been equalled — Lowe.

3468 SALA, GEORGE AUGUSTUS. Robson: a sketch. By George Augustus Sala.

pp. [1–3] 4–64   E

John Camden Hotten   1864

> *pp. [3]–28: "The late Frederick Robson," signed J[ohn] C[amden] H[otten].*

Rogers, Jane
Actress.

3469 THE MEMORIAL OF JANE ROGERS humbly submitted to the town.

pp. 1–2   MH

[London]   [1712]

> *Mrs. Oldfield supplanted Mrs. Rogers as Andromache, in Philips' The Distrest Mother, produced at Drury Lane 17th March 1712.*

Rose, *Miss*
Child actress, daughter of Mrs Franchett.

3470 [FRANCHETT, *Mrs.* E. D.] INFANT MORALITY DISPLAYED, in Miss Rose's address to the impartial admirers of theatrical merit.

pp. [2] [i] ii–iv [5] 6–26   L

Printed for the authoress   [1774]

> *Miss Rose seems to have been an infant phenomenon. She was the daughter of Mrs. E. D. Franchett, and, according to that lady, met with ill-treatment from the managers. She appeared and delivered this "Address" in a room. It is abusive of Garrick and Foote — Lowe. A "Miss Rose" and "Miss Rose's Mamma" are listed in LS as being at the Haymarket under Foote in 1770/1771. Mrs. Franchett wrote Granny's Prediction (see above no. 2653).*

Rowe, Harry (1726–   )
See THE THEATRE OUT OF LONDON nos. 1703, 1708 (York).

Ryley, Samuel William (1759–1837)
The noted "Itinerant" — Lowe.

3471 RYLEY, SAMUEL WILLIAM. The itinerant, or memoirs of an actor. By S. W. Ryley.

vol. 1 pp. [1–13] 14–326   L

Taylor and Hessey   1808

———vols. 2, 3 pp. [4] [13] 14–332 + [4] [9] 10–398   L

Sherwood, Neely, and Jones   1809

———vol. 4 pp. [6] [1] 2–155 [156], ²[1] 2–162   L

Sherwood, Neely, and Jones   1816

———vols. 5, 6 pp. [4] [1] 2–371 [372] + [4] [1] 2–446; pl. [front.]   L

Sherwood, Neely, and Jones   1817

———vols. 7, 8, 9. The itinerant, in Scotland. By S. W. Ryley.

pp. [8] [i] ii–iv, [1] 2–336 + [2] [1–3] 4–322 + [2] [1–3] 4–322   L

London: Sherwood and Co.; Edinburgh: Constable; Glasgow: Griffin   1827

> *Lowndes says vols. 7–9 were sold as waste-paper.*

3472 ———*second edition of vols 1–3.

      1817

Lowe.

3473 ———*[new abridged edition] The adventures of an actor, or, life of a strolling player.

pp. [1] 158; illus.

      [ca. 1860]

Loewenberg.

3474 ———[another edition] Reprinted from the author's edition.

pp. [1–3] 4–128   L

Oldham: Hirst and Rennie, printers, Chronicle Office   1880

> *Volumes 1–3 of original edition only.*

———[American edition] New York: Inskeep & Bradford, 1810. Vol I.

Salvini, Tommaso (1829–1916)
Italian actor.

3475 WILSON, H. SCHÜTZ. Salvini and Othello. By H. Schütz Wilson.

pp. [1–3] 4–8   LGk

[London]   [1875]

> *Dated 23rd April 1875 from the Arts Club, London. Highly critical of Salvini's performance.*

3476 SALVINI, TOMMASO. Salvini on Shakspere preceded by a biographical sketch of Tommaso Salvini from *The century* (Scribner's magazine) of November 1st, 1881.

pp. [1–3] 4–31 [32 (bl.)]

[London and Manchester: Emmott & Co.]   1884

> IKF. *The biographical sketch is by Emma Lazarus.*

3477 SALVINI, TOMMASO. Leaves from the autobiography of Tommaso Salvini.

pp. [6] 1–240; pls. [front., 7]   GU
T. Fisher Unwin   1893

————[American edition] New York: New Century Co., 1893.

Santley, *Sir* Charles (1834–1922)
Singer.

3478 SANTLEY, CHARLES. Student and singer The reminiscences of Charles Santley.

pp. [i–vii] viii–xv [xvi], [1] 2–327 [328]; pls. [front., 2]   L
Edward Arnold   1892

3479 ————new edition

pp. [i–vii] viii–xvii [xviii], [1] 2–358; pl. [front.]   L
Edward Arnold   1893

————[American edition] New York: Macmillan & Co., 1892.

Santley also wrote Reminiscences of My Life (1909).

Scott, Clement William (1841–1904)

The very well known dramatic critic of the Daily Telegraph, *Mr. Scott has exerted enormous influence on the theatre of the time. He was one of the band of young enthusiasts who before the* Prince of Wales's Theatre *became the home of Robertsonian comedy, prepared the way for the reforms which have now made the theatre once more a factor in the social and intellectual progress of the age. Though still a young man, Mr. Scott has been a critic for a quarter of a century, his appointment to the* Sunday Times *dating as far back as 1863—Lowe. See also AUTHOR INDEX. Scott also published some reminiscences as* The Wheel of Life (1897).

Blathwayt, Raymond. Does the theatre make for good? An interview with Mr. Clement Scott. [1898]. *See no. 678.*

3480 vacant

Senesino (1680–1750)
Opera singer. (Stage name of Francesco Bernardi). See above OPERA nos. 2031–2051.

Seymour, Francis
Manager of the Theatre Royal, Glasgow—Lowe. See no. 2004.

Shakespeare, William (1564–1616)
See MEDIEVAL AND RENAISSANCE STUDIES, especially nos. 995, 999, 1007, 1030, 1034–1038, 1041, 1048, 1052, 1055, 1062, 1066, 1067, 1073; THEATRE

OUT OF LONDON nos. 1690–1698 passim (Stratford upon Avon); BIOGRAPHY nos. 2885–2888; 2889–2896 (Garrick); THEORY AND CRITICISM nos. 4026–4029 (Individual plays: Shakespeare)

Sheridan, Richard Brinsley (1751–1816)
Sheridan was joint patentee of Drury Lane from 1776 to 1812. He mismanaged the theatre shamefully — Lowe. See Cecil Price, The letters of Sheridan (1966); Quentin Skinner, "Sheridan and Whitbread at Drury Lane 1809–1815", TN, XVII, 40–46, 74–79.

[McNally, Leonard?] The apotheosis of Punch. 1779. *See no. 2929.*

An attempt to ridicule Sheridan's Monody on Garrick's death 1779. (See no. 2925 above).

3481 SURFACE, JOSEPH, *pseud.* An epistle from Joseph Surface, Esq. to Richard Brinsley Sheridan, Esq. of Great Queen Street; chairman of the sub-committee for Westminster.

pp. [4] [1] 2–23 [24]   L
G. Kearsly   1780

3482 *THE BEAUTIES OF THE BRINSLEIAD: or a sketch of the opposition. A poem. Interspersed with notes.

pp. 37   1785
STR.
A satire on Sheridan in the form of verses in the manner of The Rolliad, *with elaborate commentary.*

3483 [MATHIAS, THOMAS JAMES.] THE POLITICAL DRAMATIST, in November, 1795. A poem.

pp. [3–5] 6–18   L
J. Parsons   [1795 or 1796]

3484 THE TRIAL OF THOMAS SHERIDAN, Esq. for criminal conversation with the lady of Peter Campbell, Esquire. In the Sheriff's Court, on July the 7th, 1807. Damages fifteen-hundred pounds!!! With the memoirs of the Right-Hon. Richard Brinsley Sheridan, and his son Thomas Sheridan, Esquire.

pp. [1–3] 4–16, ²[3] 4–14 [15 (advt.) 16 (bl.)]; pl. [front.]   E
J. Day   [1807]

3485 AUTHENTIC MEMOIRS of the life and death of the Right Honourable R. B. Sheridan. With an estimate of his character and talents.

pp. [1–3] 4–16   L
W. Hone   1816

According to Lowe, written by Hone (the publisher) himself; but this seems doubtful.

3486 GENT, THOMAS. Monody: to the memory of the Right Honourable Richard Brinsley Sheridan. By Thomas Gent.

pp. [1–5] 6–15 [16]   L
Longman, Hurst, Rees, Orme, and Browne; and Taylor and Hessey   1816

The half-title reads: "Monody".

3487 THE LIFE of the Right Honourable Richard Brinsley Sheridan, containing a comprehensive review of his abilities as a poet, a statesman, an orator, and a dramatist, with the remarks of Pitt, Fox, and Burke, on his most celebrated speeches, and many curious anecdotes of his parliamentary, literary, and private career, never before published: including his Monody on Garrick, verses to Miss Linley, and a collection of his fugitive poetry, &c. &c. Second edition, including an account of the funeral.

pp. [1–3] 4–42   L
John Fairburn   [1816]

3488 [MOORE, THOMAS.] LINES ON THE DEATH OF———from the *Morning Chronicle* of Monday, August 5, 1816. Ascribed to a personage of the highest poetical talent, and, to gratify the anxious curiosity of the public, re-published, without note or comment.

pp. [1–3] 4–8   L
W. Hone   1816

Reprinted in The Poetical Works of Thomas Moore *(1840–1841) and in* The Poetical Works of Thomas Moore, *ed. A. D. Godley (1910), pp. 454–455.*

3489 [BYRON, GEORGE GORDON NOEL, *Baron*]. MONODY on the death of the Right Honourable R. B. Sheridan, written at the request of a friend, to be spoken at Drury Lane Theatre.

pp. [1–5] 6–12 [13–15 (advts.) 16 (bl.)]   L
John Murray   1816

The half-title reads: "Monody". The first line on page 11 reads: "To weep the vanished beam", but some copies have the variant "To mourn the vanished beam". Delivered at Drury Lane 7 Sept. 1816, and first published in The Courier *11 Sept. 1816. Wise, pp. 115–116.*

3490 ———[another issue]

pp. [1–5] 6–11 [12 (bl.) 13–15 (advts.) 16 (bl.)]   L
John Murray   1816

Wise, p. 116.
Reprinted in The Works of Lord Byron, *ed. E. H. Coleridge, vol. 4 (1901), pp. 67–75.*

3491 PHILLIPS, CHARLES. A garland for the grave of Richard Brinsley Sheridan. By Charles Phillips, Esq. Barrister at law.

pp. [1–7] 8–15 [16]   L
N. Hailes   1816

3492 ———*second edition

                                                             1816
Lowe.

3493 A SHORT MEMOIR of the life, of the late right honourable Richard Brinsley Sheridan, being an attempt to draw a true estimate of his character as it may regard posterity. To which is added a report of his celebrated speech delivered on the following days in Westminster Hall, June 3d, 6th, 10th, & 13th, 1788, on his summing up the evidence on the Begum charge, in the trial against Warren Hastings, Esq.

pp. [2] [i] ii–xxxiv, [2] [1] 2–82   GU
Sold by J. Booth; T. Egerton; and Messrs. Hookham
                                                             1816

3494 WATKINS, JOHN. Memoirs of the public and private life of the Right Honorable Richard Brinsley Sheridan, with a particular account of his family and connexions. By John Watkins, LL.D. [Part I].

pp. [i–iii] iv–viii [ix–x], [1] 2–352; pls. [front., 1]   L
Henry Colburn   1817

P.[ix]: directions to the binder, and a notice to the reader.

3495 ———Part II. Embellished with a portrait of the present Mrs. Sheridan.

pp. [i–iii] iv–x, [1] 2–398; pl. [front.]   L
Henry Colburn   1817

Published separately from Part I.

3496 ———*second edition, embellished with portraits.

2 vols.; ports.; autograph facsim.   MB
Henry Colburn   1817

3497 ———*third edition, embellished with portraits.
2 vols.

                                                             1818
Lowe. *See also below no. 3498 note.*

3498 LEFANU, ALICIA. Memoirs of the life and writings of Mrs. Frances Sheridan, mother of the late Right Hon. Richard Brinsley Sheridan, and author of *Sidney Biddulph, Nourjahad,* and *The discovery.* With remarks upon a late life of the Right Hon. R. B. Sheridan; also criticisms and selections from the works of Mrs. Sheridan; and biographical anecdotes of her family and contemporaries. With a portrait. By her grand-daughter, Alicia Lefanu.

pp. [i–v] vi–xi [xii (bl.)], [1] 2–435 [436]; pl. [front.]   L
G. and W. B. Whittaker   1824

The "late life" is John Watkins's Memoirs *(1817) (see above no. 3494).*

3499 MOORE, THOMAS. Memoirs of the life of the Right Honourable Richard Brinsley Sheridan. By Thomas Moore.

pp. [i–vii] viii–xii, [1] 2–719 [720]; pls. [front., 1]   L

Longman, Hurst, Rees, Orme, Brown, and Green 1825

3500 ———second edition

2 vols. pp. [i–v] vi–viii, [1] 2–543 [544]; pl. [front.] + pp. [i–iii] iv, [1] 2–492; pl. [front. (facsim.)]   GU

Longman, Hurst, Rees, Orme, Brown, and Green 1825

3501 ———the third edition

2 vols. pp. [i–v] vi–viii, [1] 2–543 [544]; pl. [front.] + pp. [i–iii] iv, [1] 2–492; pl. [front., (facsim.)]   GU

Longman, Hurst, Rees, Orme, Brown, and Green 1825

3502 ———*[fourth edition]

2 vols. port.

1826

Rothwell.

3503 ———*fifth edition

2 vols. port.; facsim.   MB

Longman, Rees, Orme, Brown & Green   1827

———[American editions] Philadelphia: Carey & Lea, 1825; New York: Redfield, 1853.

3504 [MANGIN, EDWARD.] A LETTER TO THOMAS MOORE, Esq. on the subject of Sheridan's *School for Scandal*.

pp. [1–3] 4–24   L

Bath: printed by George Wood   1826

A severe attack on The School for Scandal, *for dramatic as well as moral shortcomings — Lowe. Occasioned by Moore's* Memoirs of the Life of . . . Sheridan *(1825).*

3505 SHERIDANIANA; or, anecdotes of the life of Richard Brinsley Sheridan; his table-talk, and bon mots.

pp. [i–iii] iv–xi [xii], [1] 2–334; pl. [front.]   GU

Henry Colburn   1826

3506 [SMYTH, WILLIAM.] MEMOIR OF MR. SHERIDAN.

pp. [4] [i] ii [iii–iv], [1] 2–74   L

Leeds: J. Cross   1840

Privately printed. A collection of reminiscences of Sheridan by William Smyth, of St. Peter's College, Cambridge, who was tutor to Tom, Sheridan's son. It is a most valuable biography — Lowe.

3507 OCTOGENARIAN, AN, *pseud.* Sheridan and his times. By an octogenarian, who stood by his knee in youth and sat at his table in manhood.

2 vols. pp. [i–vii] viii–x [xiii] xiv–xv [xvi] [=14], [1] 2–316; pl. [front.] + pp. [i–v] vi–vii [viii], [1] 2–326 L

J. F. Hope   1859

Sometimes ascribed to William Earle.

3508 HARVEY, FRANCIS. Genealogical table of the families of Sheridan, Lefanu and Knowles compiled by Francis Harvey.

pp. [4]; pls. [2 (incl. one double)]   L

Privately printed for James McHenry   1875

Only forty copies printed. Compiled to illustrate The Life of James Sheridan Knowles *(1872). See above no. 3215.*

3509 OLIPHANT, *Mrs.* [MARGARET]. Sheridan by Mrs. Oliphant   (English Men of Letters.)

pp. [i–v] vi [vii–viii], [1] 2–210 [211–216 (advts.)]   L

Macmillan and Co.   1883

———[American edition] New York: Harper & Bros., 1883.

3510 FITZGERALD, PERCY [HETHERINGTON]. The lives of the Sheridans. By Percy Fitzgerald.

2 vols. pp. [i–v] vi–viii [ix–xii], [1] 2–431 [432]; pls. [front., 2]; inset, fold. [1 (genealogical table)]; errata slip + pp. [8] [1] 2–480; pls. [front., 2]; inset, fold. [5 (facsim. playbills)].   GM

Richard Bentley and Son   1886

3511 ———[another edition] The Sheridans written by Percy Fitzgerald (Beaux & Belles of England).

2 vols. pp. [i–iv] v–viii [ix–xii] 1–438; pls. [front. (col.), 5]; ptd. tissue guards [6]; inset, fold. [6 (1 genealogical table and 5 facsim. playbills)]; t.p. in red and black + pp. [8] 1–481 [482–484 (bl.)]; pls. [front (col.), 5]; ptd. tissue guards [6]; t.p. in red and black   NbU

London: printed by the Grolier Society   [190–?]

"Imperial edition limited to one thousand copies for England and America."

———[American edition] (Beaux and Belles of England.) New York: Athenaeum Press, [1907?].

3512 SANDERS, LLOYD C[HARLES]. Life of Richard Brinsley Sheridan   (Great Writers. Edited by Professor Eric S. Robertson, M.A.)

pp. [1–5] 6–177 [178], [i] ii–xi [xii (bl.) xiii–xiv (advts.)]   L

London, New York and Melbourne: Walter Scott [1890]

3513 RAE, W[ILLIAM] FRASER. Sheridan A biography by W. Fraser Rae with an introduction by Sheridan's great-grandson the Marquess of Dufferin and Ava.

2 vols. pp. [i–vii] viii–xxii [xxiii–xxvi], [1] 2–422; pls. [front., 8 (incl. 1 fold.)] + pp. [i–vii] viii, [1] 2–451 [452]; pls. [front., 12 (incl. 1 fold.)]   L

Richard Bentley and Son   1896

————[American edition] New York: Henry Holt & Co., 1896.

Sheridan, Thomas (1719–1788)

The father of Richard Brinsley. He made his first appearance as an actor in Dublin on 29th January 1743. He became manager of the Dublin Theatre in 1745, and made most important reformations in its conduct. In 1754 a riot over a political question drove him from his post; but he resumed his management in 1756, finally giving it up in 1758. He then "starred" in London, and in 1778 became manager of Drury Lane under the new patentees — Lowe. See Esther K. Sheldon, Thomas Sheridan of Smock Alley, Princeton, N.J., 1967. For the many pamphlets Sheridan wrote in Dublin see AUTHOR INDEX. See also SHERIDAN, R. B. no. 3484; PERIODICALS: IRELAND nos. 4419, 4421.

3514 SHERIDAN, THOMAS. *An oration, pronounced before a numerous body of the nobility and gentry, assembled at the Musick-Hall in Fishamble-street.

Dublin   1757

Contains a few paragraphs about the theatre. For Sheridan's other writings on the English language and on education, see Sheldon, pp. 492–495.

3515 AN ENQUIRY INTO THE PLAN and pretensions of Mr. Sheridan. Grammaticus, rhetor, geometres, pictor, aliptes, augur, schoenobates, medicus, magus—Juv. Sat. 3. For the benefit of the good people of Ireland: [a poem of 22 lines].

pp. [1–4] 5–47 [48 (bl.)]   L
Dublin   1758

3516 NO-BODY, NICHOLAS, *pseud.* A critical examination of the sense, style, and grammar, of Mr. Sheridan's printed oration. Humbly submitted to all noblemen, gentlemen, and others, who sincerely wish to see a well-planned publick school and academy established in this Kingdom, under the conduct of able instructors; and whose attachment is not to the man, but to the thing. By Nicholas No-Body, Esq;

pp. [1–2] 3–23 [24]   L
Dublin: printed by Alex. McCulloh   1758

Advertised on p. 24 is: "An infallible Cure for the Bite of a mad Stage-Player".

3517 BY PETER SHEE, painter, who continues copying pictures of value on the same conditions that he formerly advertised——By Thomas Sheridan, orator, who continues to receive subscriptions of value on the same conditions that he formerly advertised . . .

bs.   L
Dublin   [ca. 1759]

Shuter, Edward (1728–1776)

A brilliant comedian. His first London appearance was at Covent Garden, 15th April 1746; his last, 23rd September 1776, at the Haymarket. Between drink and religion he was somewhat bewildered in his brain before he died. He was an enthusiastic follower of Whitfield in his later years — Lowe.

3518 SHUTER'S JESTS; or, the wit's banquet, for the year 1758. Being a collection of repartees and humorous stories, not one of which were ever printed before.

pp. [8] [1] 2–48, misprinting '48' as '58'   LGk
A. Kincaid   [1758]

A preface to Shuter apologises for calling the collection after him.

3519 [STEVENS, GEORGE ALEXANDER.] THE DRAMATIC HISTORY of Master Edward, Miss Ann, Mrs. Llwhuddwhydd, and others. The extraordinaries of these times. Collected from Zaphaniel's original papers.

pp. [2] [1] 2, ²1–192; pls. [front., 13 (incl. 1 fold.)]   L
T. Waller   1743 [for 1763]

3520 ————[reissue] The dramatic history of Master Edward, Miss Ann, and others, the extraordinaries of these times. Collected from Zaphaniel's original papers. By George Alexander Stevens. To which are prefixed, Memoirs of the life of the author. A new edition.

pp. [i–iii] iv–xi [xii], [1] 2 (cancellandum), ²1–192; illus.; pls. [front., 13 (incl. 1 fold.)]   L
J. Murray   1785

The leaf, "Zaphaniel's Exhortation to his Fellows in the Faith," with vignette, satirical upon Whitfield, Wesley, and Romaine, was cancelled — Lowe. Some copies dated 1786.

3521 AN ELEGY, on the much lamented death of Edward Shuter, the player, who departed this life on the 29th of October, 1776, in the 66th year of his age.

bs., illus. (*momento mori* emblem)   DFo
[London]   [1776]

Siddons, *Mrs.* Harriet (1783–1844)

Actress and manager, wife of Henry Siddons (see no. 710). See SCOTLAND nos. 1970–1971 (Edinburgh).

Siddons, *Mrs.* Sarah (1755–1831)

The greatest English tragic actress. Her first appearance at Drury Lane, 29th December 1775, was a failure, and she retired to the country again; but on her reappearance, 10th October 1782, she was triumphantly successful. She took her farewell of the stage, 29th June 1812, but appeared occasionally for charitable purposes. Her last appearance was at Covent Garden, 9th June 1819. She was a good and excellent woman, as well as a grand artist — Lowe.

✖ A review of Mrs Crawford, and Mrs Siddons, in the character of Belvidera. 1782. *See no. 2654.*

3522 WHALLEY, *Rev.* [THOMAS SEDGWICK]. Verses addressed to Mrs. Siddons, on her being engaged at the Theatre-Royal, Drury-Lane, in 1782. By the reverend Mr. Whalley, author of "Edwy and Edilda", "Fatal Kiss", &c. &c. &c.

pp. [4] [1] 2–19 [20 (bl.)] L

T. Cadell 1782

"Accept as a public offering, a trifle which was long since presented to you as a private tribute of friendship" — Dedication.

✖ Edwin's pills . . . With an humourous account of Mrs. Siddons's first reception in Dublin. Dublin. 1783. *See no. 2696.*

3523 THE THEATRICAL PORTRAIT, a poem, on the celebrated Mrs. Siddons, in the characters of Calista, Jane Shore, Belvidera, and Isabella.

pp. [i–vii] viii, 1–20 DFo

Printed by T. Wilkins, and sold by G. Kearsley 1783

3524 [RUSSELL, WILLIAM.] THE TRAGIC MUSE: a poem. Addressed to Mrs. Siddons.

pp. [1–5] 6–16 L

G. Kearsley 1783

Dedication dated 30 Jan. 1783 and signed W.R.

3525 LADY, A, *pseud.* *Observations on Mrs. Siddons, in the following characters: Margaret of Anjou, Belvidera, Jane Shore, Lady Randolph, Isabella and Zara. By a lady.

pp. (8), 47 MB

Dublin: printed by P. Byrne 1784

3526 ———[another edition] The beauties of Mrs. Siddons: or, a review of her performance of the characters of Belvidera, Zara, Isabella, Margaret of Anjou, Jane Shore,—and Lady Randolph; in letters from a lady of distinction, to her friend in the country.

pp. [i–v] vi–vii [viii–x], [1] 2–65 [66 (bl.)] GU

John Strahan 1786

Describes her performances when she last appeared in Dublin.

3527 [YOUNG, THOMAS.] THE SIDDONIAD: a characteristical and critical poem. Most respectfully inscribed to the Honourable Mrs. O'Neil.

pp. [i–v] vi [7] 8–26 L

Dublin: printed by R. Marchbank 1784

In heroic-couplets. Dedication signed Thomas Young. Not the same work as The Siddoniad, *1785 (no. 3529 below).*

3528 STOCKDALE, PERCIVAL. Three poems: I. Siddons:—a poem. II. A poetical epistle to Sir Ashton Lever. III. An elegy on the death of a young officer of the army. By Percival Stockdale.

pp. [i–iii] iv–vi, [3–5] 6–30 [31 (bl.) 32 (advts.)] L

W. Flexney 1784

Stockdale's Memoirs *(1809) contains some theatrical reminiscences.*

3529 THE SIDDONIAD; a poetical essay.

pp. [1–3] 4–12 L

Printed for the author by H. Reynell 1785

In blank-verse. Not the same work as Young's Siddoniad *(1784) (no. 3527 above).*

3530 CRITIQUE on the theatrical performance of Mrs. Siddons.

pp. [1–3] 4–18 DFo

Edinburgh: T. & J. Ruddiman July 1788

3531 *THE WONDERFUL SECRETS of stage trick; or, a peep behind the curtain: by the author of the Generous attachment, a novel in four volumes, Royal magnificence, or the effusion of ten days, a satirical poem in five cantos . . .

pp. v, 61 DFo

Printed for the author [1793]

An attack upon Mrs. Siddons and other players who had appeared at the theatre at Shrewsbury. Brown *records a copy with 54 pages.*

✖ Funeral stanzas . . . of Mrs. Anne Crawford. With a comparative dissertation between her theatrical merits and those of Mrs. Siddons. Dublin. 1803. *See no. 2655.*

3532 MELPOMENE IN THE DUMPS; or, child's play defended by theatrical monarchs.

bs., illus. (col., by Rowlandson) MH

Printed by D. N. Shury, for Ackerman [1804]

Portrays Sarah Siddons disgruntled at W. H. Betty's success, and at the success of The Blind Bargain, *produced at Covent Garden 24th October 1804. The illustration also portrays T. Harris and J. P. Kemble. A dialogue, in prose.* George *10318.*

3533 [GALINDO, *Mrs.* CATHERINE.] MRS. GALINDO'S LETTER to Mrs. Siddons: being a circumstantial detail of Mrs. Siddons's life for the last seven years; with several of her letters.

pp. [4] [1] 2–80 MH

Printed for the authoress: sold by M. Jones 1809

A venomous attack on Mrs. Siddons, in which, among other things, she is circumstantially charged with improper connection with Mr. Galindo, who was a fencing-master — Lowe.

3534 ——second edition

pp. [2] [1] 2–80   MH

Printed for the authoress: sold by M. Jones   1809

✖ The life of John Philip Kemble, Esquire . . . to which is added Strictures on Mrs. Galindo's curious letter to Mrs Siddons. Second edition. [1809.] *See no. 1236.*

3535 [BALLANTYNE, JAMES.] CHARACTERS by Mrs. Siddons.

pp. [2] [1–3] 4–41 [42]; head-title: "Dramatic characters of Mrs Siddons"   DFo

[Edinburgh]   [1812]

Criticisms by James Ballantine, most of which had appeared in the Edinburgh Courant, and were reprinted by the express wish of Mrs. Siddons—Lowe. The final notice, of her farewell performance, had not been previously published. Signed "James Ballantyne".

3536 BOADEN, JAMES. Memoirs of Mrs. Siddons. Interspersed with anecdotes of authors and actors. By James Boaden, Esq.

2 vols. pp. [i–v] vi–xxvii [xxviii], [1] 2–382 [383–384 (advts.)]; pl. [front.] + pp. [i–v] vi–xii, [1] 2–394 [395–400 (advts.)]   L

Henry Colburn   1827

3537 ——second edition

2 vols. pp. [i–iii] iv [ix] x–xix [xx], [1] 2–382; pl. [front.] + pp. [2] [v] vi–xii, [1] 2–412   LVA

Henry Colburn   1831

This edition has a preface and eighteen pages of "Supplement" (pp. [395]–412) relating to the death of Mrs. Siddons — Lowe.

3538 ——[another edition]

pp. [i–v] vi–xv [xvi], [1] 2–471 [472 (imprint)]; pls. [front., 3]   NbU

Gibbings and Company, Ld.   1893

150 copies on large paper. Lacks one plate.

3539 ——*[another edition]

                                                      MB

Gibbings and Co., Ltd.   1896

3540 ——[another edition] Mrs. Sarah Siddons written by James Boaden (Beaux & Belles of England).

2 vols. pp. [i–viii] ix–xviii, 1–383 [384 (bl.)]; pls. [front. (col.), 6]; ptd. tissue guards [7]; t.p. in red and black + pp. [10] 1–326 [327–328 (bl.)]; pls. [front. (col.), 4]; ptd. tissue guards [5]; t.p. in red and black   NbU

London: printed by the Grolier Society   [190–?]

"Imperial edition limited to one thousand copies for England and America."

——[American edition] Philadelphia: H. C. Carey & I. Lea, and E. Littell, 1827; New York: C. & C. Carvill, 1827; (Beaux and Belles of England). New York: Athenaeum Press, [1907?].

✖ Very excellent household furniture . . . the property of the late Mrs. Siddons. A catalogue . . . [1831]. *See no. 127.*

3541 CAMPBELL, THOMAS. Life of Mrs. Siddons. By Thomas Campbell.

2 vols. pp. [5] viii–ix [x], [1–3] 4–299 [300]; pl. [front.] + pp. [i–iii] iv–vii [viii], [1–3] 4–394   E

Effingham Wilson   1834

3542 ——[another edition]

pp. [i–vi] vii–xi [xii (bl.)], [1] 2–378 [379–380 (advts.)]; pl. [front.]   L

Edward Moxon   1839

According to a letter from Rev. Alexander Dyce to Sir Egerton Brydges, once in the possession of G. Thorn-Drury, Campbell was assisted by Dyce in the writing of this work. Dyce did not wish the fact to be publicly known.

——[American edition] New York: Harper & Brothers, 1834.

✖ Fitzgerald, Percy. The Kembles. An account of the Kemble family, including the lives of Mrs. Siddons, and her brother John Philip Kemble. [1871]. *See no. 3208.*

3543 M[AIR], E[LIZABETH] H[ARRIETT]. Recollections of the past   A series of letters by E.H.M.

pp. [i–vii] viii–xii, [1] 2–102 [103 (ornament) 104 (bl.)]   L

Edinburgh: privately printed by R. & R. Clark   1877

Mrs. Mair was the daughter of Mr. H. Siddons, who was for many years the manager of the Edinburgh theatre, and this book contains many curious recollections of the great Mrs. Siddons, whose grand-daughter she was — Lowe. Reprinted from the Ladies' Edinburgh Magazine.

3544 KENNARD, *Mrs.* A., [*i.e.* NINA H.]. Mrs. Siddons. By Mrs. A. Kennard. (Eminent Women Series, ed. John H. Ingram.)

pp. [i–v] vi [vii–viii (bl.)], [1] 2–268 [269–272 (advts.)]; errata slip   LGk

W. H. Allen & Co.   1887

Mrs. Kennard also wrote Rachel (1885) for this series.

——[American edition] Boston: Roberts Bros., 1887.

3545 CARR, J[OSEPH WILLIAM] COMYNS. *Macbeth and Lady Macbeth* An essay by J. Comyns Carr.

pp. [1–5] 6–39 [40]   L

Bickers & Son   1889 [*for* 1888]

Contains some passages about Mrs. Siddons, as a source of stage tradition.

Smith, Albert (1816–1860)

The famous "Entertainer."—Lowe. See AUTHOR INDEX.

Soane-Roby, G. Bernard

Actor and manager.

3546 SOANE-ROBY, G. B. *True stories of personal experience. Stage stories by actors & actresses. Series No. 1* by G. B. Soane-Roby. No. 1 A night of change — my first experience of Hamlet.

pp. [1–3] 4–31 [32]; illus.; cover-title; also on cover: "Short tales for railway journeys."   L

Birmingham: Moody Bros. Theatrical printers. [1895]

No other numbers published.

Soldene, Emily (1840–1912)

Singer.

3547 SOLDENE, EMILY. *My theatrical and musical recollections*, by Emily Soldene.

pp. [i–v] vi–xviii [xix–xx], [1] 2–315 [316 (imprint)]; pls. [front., 6]   GM

Downey & Co., Limited   1897

3548 ——second edition

pp. [i–v] vi–xviii [xix–xx], [1] 2–315 [316 (imprint)]; pls. [front., 6]

Downey & Co. Limited   1897

JFA.

3549 ——*new edition

pp. 320

Downey & Co.   1898

ECB.

3550 ——*new edition

pp. 318

T. S. Clarke   1906

ECB.

Somerville, Margaret Agnes (1799–1883)

Miss Somerville, who married Alfred Bunn, made her first appearance at Drury Lane, 9th May 1816. She retired rom the stage when comparatively a young woman. Her

married life was unhappy — Lowe. See also above O'NEIL Miss, no. 3391.

3551 FITZALLEN, ALLEN *pseud. of* Alfred Bunn?. *Memoirs of Miss Somerville*; comprising a notice of her private life, with a full and correct review of her dramatic career. Collected from the various public journals, and compiledfrom authorities, by Allen Fitzallen, Esq. of the Middle Temple.

pp. [4] [1] 2–58 [59–60 (bl.)]   L

J. Lowndes   1819

See Urwin, p. 23.

Sontag, Henrietta (1806–1854)

Singer.

3552 A MEMOIR OF THE COUNTESS DE ROSSI (Madame Sontag.)

pp. [1–5] 6–111 [112]   L

Published by Mr. Mitchell, Royal Library   [1850?]

A fashionable volume, evidently published on the occasion of the singer's return to the stage, under Lumley, at Her Majesty's in 1849.

Sothern, Edward Askew (1826–1881)

Actor.

3553 PEMBERTON, T[HOMAS] EDGAR. *A memoir of Edward Askew Sothern.* By T. Edgar Pemberton.

pp. [i–iii] iv [v–viii], [1] 2–314 [315 (imprint) 316 (bl.)]; pls. [front., 5 (incl. 2 fold.)]   NbU

Richard Bentley and Son   1889

3554 ——*[second edition]

pp. 314

Richard Bentley and Son   1889

STR.

3555 ——fourth edition

pp. [i–iii] iv [v–viii], [1] 2–210 [2] 211–345 [346]; inset, fold. [1]; illus. (facsims.)   LGk

Richard Bentley and Son   1890

With a photograph of Sothern as Lord Dundreary inlaid on the upper cover.

3556 ——new and cheaper edition

pp. [i–iii] iv [v–viii], [1] 2–210 [2] 211–345 [346]; pl. on cover; inset, fold. [1]; illus. (facsims.)   L

Richard Bentley and Son   1890

Spiller, James (1692–1730)

A comedian of great merit, especially famous for his "old men." — Lowe.

3556.1 AKERBY, GEORGE. The life of Mr. James Spiller, the late famous comedian. In which is interspers'd much of the poetical history of his own times. By George Akerby, painter.

pp. [2] [1] 2–44; lacks t.p.   L

J. Purser   1729

    Title-page seen by Lowe.

3556.2 ——*[reissue] Spiller's jests: or the life and pleasant adventures of the late celebrated comedian Mr. James Spiller: containing his merry jests, diverting songs, and entertaining tales.

pp. [3–4] 5–48   L

H. Cook, and S. Hester   [1729]

    *George Daniels' copy had the following MS note in it:—
"Exceedingly rare. Spiller's Jests (viz., his Life with a
new title-page) I have never seen in any other collection —
George Daniel." Lowe. Some copies issued with author's
name on title-page (BMC).*

3557 THE COMICAL ADVENTURES of Mr. Jas. Spiller, comedian, at Epsom, in England. A true humorous tale. To which is added, The pleasant story of Obadiah Mousetrap.

pp. [1–2] 3–24   L

Stirling: printed by C. Randall   [ca. 1800]

3558 ——[another edition]

pp. [1] 2–24   L

Stirling: printed and sold by C. Randall   [ca. 1800]

    *The title-page reads, differing from the other edition, "the
late Mr. J. Spiller".*

Stanley, *Miss* (1795–)
Actress.

3559 MEMOIRS OF MISS STANLEY, of the Theatre Royal, Drury Lane, with criticisms on her acting, intended to accompany the fine portrait, painted by I. P. Davis, and engraved by Bond.

pp. [1–3] 4–40   L

Printed by B. R. Howlett   1815

Stanley, Montague (1809–1844)
*He was a favourite Scotch actor. He retired from the stage,
from conscientious motives, I believe; his last appearance
being made at Edinburgh on 28th April 1838, when he played
Laertes to the Hamlet of Charles Kean. After leaving the
stage he taught elocution, fencing, painting, &c., but latterly
devoted himself entirely to painting, at which he became very
proficient — Lowe.*

3560 DRUMMOND, *Rev.* D[AVID] T[HOMAS] K[ERR]. Memoir of Montague Stanley, A.R.S.A. By the Rev. D. T. K. Drummond.

pp. [i–v] vi–viii, [1] 2–172; illus.; pl. [front.]   L

Edinburgh: W. P. Kennedy; London: Hamilton, Adams, & Co.   1848

3561 ——*second edition, revised

pp. 163; port.   MB

Edinburgh: Kennedy   [1852]

3562 MONTAGUE STANLEY, the actor.

pp. [1] 2–23 [24]   MH

The Religious Tract Society   [ca. 1848]

    On the title page: "No. 974".

Stayley, George (1727–1778?)
*Stayley was a quarrelsome, conceited actor, who was
dismissed by Mossop for giving an improper toast on the
stage. He was the cause of a riot in Edinburgh in 1767 —
Lowe. See also SCOTLAND nos. 1917–1918, 1935
(Edinburgh).*

3563 MR. STAYLEY'S REFERENCE to the public.

pp. [1] 2–8   DN

Dublin   1760

    *On Stayley's dismissal by H. Mossop, manager of
Smock-Alley Theatre, Dublin.*

3564 STAYLEY, GEORGE. †The life and opinions of an actor. A real history, in two real volumes. By Mr. George Stayley, late of Smock-Alley, comedian.

pp. [12] [1] 2–215 [216]; illus.; vol. II missing   L

Dublin: printed for the author, and sold by G. Faulkner, Dublin; J. Hinton, London   1762

    The work in part imitates the manner of Sterne's Tristram
Shandy. *It is therefore possible that the second volume
does not exist. The "history" is complete.*

3565 STAYLEY, GEORGE. The art of reading; in two lectures: the serious and the comic. With general rules, and observations: and exemplary quotations from the most eminent English authors. Published for the use of schools: and all ladies and gentlemen, public and private, who desire to be instructed in the knowledge of reading, or speaking, with taste, elegance, propriety and expression. To which is added, Bucks have at you all. By George Stayley.

pp. [1–5] 6–63 [64]   GU

Glasgow: printed for the benefit of the author's widow and children   1778

    *Full title of third part: Bucks have at you all: or, the
description of a theatrical audience. Half-title and running
title: Lectures on reading.*

Steele, *Sir* Richard (1672–1729)

Steele's connection with the stage was most intimate. He wrote excellent comedies; he took a fatherly care of the actors, in his Tatler *and* Spectator, *and he was a sharer in the Drury Lane license, which he got changed to a patent, for 1714 to 1720, when, from political reasons, it was withdrawn. Steele, however, seems to have been reinstated in 1721. He is said to have sold his share in the patent about 1724, and to have entered into a lawsuit with the managers, which was decided against him in 1726 —* Lowe. *See* John Loftis, Steele at Drury Lane *(Berkeley, 1952). See also* GOVERNMENT REGULATION OF THE THEA-TRE *nos. 154–155;* THEORY AND CRITICISM *no. 3819;* PERIODICALS *nos. 4068–4072.*

Dennis v. Steele 1720

3566 [DENNIS, JOHN.] THE CHARACTERS and conduct of Sir John Edgar, call'd by himself sole monarch of the stage in Drury-Lane; and his three deputy-governors. In two letters to Sir John Edgar.

pp. [4] 1–35 [36]   L
M. Smith   1720

> *Published early February —* Hooker. *Reprinted in* The Theatre, *ed. J. Nichols (1791) (no. 4069 below) and in* Hooker, II, 181–199.

3567 ——the second edition

pp. [4] 1–35 [36]   L
M. Smith   1720

3568 ——[another issue]

pp. [2] 1–35 [36]   L
M. Smith   1720

> *Title-page reset. Another issue of the first edition.*

3569 [DENNIS, JOHN.] THE CHARACTERS and conduct of Sir John Edgar, and his three deputy-governours. During the administration of the late separate ministry. In a third and fourth letter to the knight. With a picture of Sir John, drawn by a pen, exactly after the life.

pp. [4] [i] ii–vii [viii (bl.)], [1] 2–36   L
Printed and sold by J. Roberts   1720

> *Reprinted in* The Theatre, *ed. J. Nichols (1791) (no. 4069 below) and in* Hooker, II, 200–217.

3570 AN ANSWER TO A WHIMSICAL PAMPHLET, call'd The character of Sir John Edgar, &c. Humbly inscribed to Sir Tremendous Longinus. Written by Sir John Edgar's baker, mention'd in the 3d Theatre.

pp. [10] 1–22   DFo
J. Roberts   1720

Published 11 February — Hooker. *Sir Tremendous is John Dennis. Dedication signed Timothy Rag. Reprinted in* The Theatre, *ed. J. Nichols (1791) (no. 4069 below).*

3571 THE BATTLE of the authors lately fought in Covent-Garden, between Sir John Edgar, General-issimo on one side, and Horatius Truewit, on the other. With a list of the general officers, and some of their characters: also an account of Sir John Edgar's being taken prisoner; with his tryal and condemnation, being sentenc'd to have his eyes pick'd out with a ballad-maker's pen, &c. The whole being occasion'd by the late revolutions of the Theatre in Drury-Lane. Dedicated to Count He——cre, masquerade master general of Great Britain.

pp. [i–iii] iv–xvi, 1–44   L
J. Roberts, and A. Dod   1720

> *Published 12 March —* Hooker.

———————————————

3572 BALDASSARII, BENEDETTO. A letter from Sig. Benedetto Baldassarii, of the Hay-Market, to Sir R——d S——e, of Drury-Lane.

pp. [4] 1–14 [15–16 (bl.)]   DFo
W. Boreham   1720

3573 AITKEN, GEORGE ATHERTON. The life of Richard Steele by George A. Aitken.

2 vols. pp. [i–vii] viii–xix [xx], [1–3] 4–419 [420]; illus. (facsims.); pls. [front., 2]; inset, fold. [1] + pp. [i–v] vi [vii–viii], [1–3] 4–452; pls. [front., 2]   E
Wm. Isbister Limited   1889

Stephens, Catherine, *later Countess of* Essex (1794–1882)

Singer and actress.

✄ Catalogue of the choice collection of old French decorative furniture . . . of the late Dowager Countess of Essex . . . [1883]. *See no. 132.*

Stirling, Edward (1809–1894)

Mr. Stirling made his first appearance at the Pavilion Theatre in 1828. He was stage-manager of Drury Lane under E. T. Smith, who became lessee in 1852, and under F. B. Chatterton. His wife is the Mrs. Stirling, the famous actress—Lowe.

3574 STIRLING, EDWARD. Old Drury Lane. Fifty years' recollections of author, actor, and manager. By Edward Stirling.

2 vols. pp. [i–v] vi, [1–3] 4–363 [364] + [6] [1–3] 4–369 [370]   GM
Chatto and Windus   1881

Sullivan, *Sir* Arthur (1842–1900)
Composer.

3575 LAWRENCE, ARTHUR. Sir Arthur Sullivan: life-story, letters, and reminiscences. By Arthur Lawrence. With critique by B. W. Findon, and bibliography by Wilfrid Bendall.

pp. [i–vii] viii–xvi, [1] 2–360 [361–384 (advts.)]; illus.; pls. [front., 13 (incl. 3 fold.)]; t.p. in red and black   L

James Bowden   1899

Sullivan, Barry (1821–1891)
Actor.

3576 OPINIONS OF THE PRESS upon the famous tragic actor, Barry Sullivan throughout England, Scotland, and Ireland, the United States of America, the Canadas, Nova Scotia, and Australia.

pp. [1] 2–13 [14–16]; cover-title   MH

D. and J. Allen, printers … Belfast   [1875?]

Printed in green and purple throughout; the front cover is printed in green, purple and yellow.

3577 LAWRENCE, W[ILLIAM] J[OHN]. Barry Sullivan: a biographical sketch. By W. J. Lawrence.

pp. [1–7] 8–98; illus.   L

W. & G. Baird   1893

"It is to be hoped that the issuing of this monograph at once in a popular form will meet with due appreciation at the hands of that pit-and-gallery section of the public whose suffrages it was ever Barry Sullivan's especial delight to win" — Prefatory Note.

Sumbel, *Mrs.* Mary Leah Wells
See below WELLS, Mrs. MARY no. 3620.

Swanborough, *Miss*
Lessee of the Strand Theatre. See above no. 1518.

Tarlton, Richard (1530–1588)
A noted Clown. Sir Richard Baker says of him that he, "for the part called the Clown's part, never had his match, never will have." — Lowe. See above MEDIEVAL AND RENAISSANCE STUDIES nos. 1018, 1042.

Taylor, John (b. 1811)
Actor, preacher and lawyer.

3578 TAYLOR, JOHN. Autobiography of a Lancashire lawyer, being the life and recollections of John Taylor, attorney-at-law, and first coroner of the borough of Bolton, with notice of many persons and things met with during a life of seventy-two years lived in and about Bolton. (With engraved portrait of the author.) Edited by James Glegg.

pp. [4] [i] ii–vi [vii–viii], [1] 2–361 [362], ²[i] ii–xxx; pl. [front.]; t.p. in red and black   L

Bolton: The Daily Chronicle Office; Manchester: Tubbs, Brook, and Chrystal   1883

Green cloth? with gold lettering "Autobiography of a Lancashire lawyer with theatrical and preaching reminiscences".

Taylor, William
Generally known as "Opera" Taylor — Lowe. See Ian Donaldson, "New Papers of Henry Holland and R. B. Sheridan II", TN, XVI, 117–125. See THE LONDON THEATRE nos. 1460 et seq. (King's Theatre.)

Templeton, John (1802–1886)
Singer.

3579 H[USK?], W. H., *ed.* Templeton & Malibran. Reminiscences of these renowned singers, with original letters & anecdotes. Three authentic portraits by Mayall. Edited by W.H.H.

pp. [i–iv] v–xii, [3] 4–50 [51 (advts.) 52 (colophon)]; pls. [3 photos attached to pp. v, vii, and ix)]   L

William Reeves   [1880?]

Includes also letters from Alfred Bunn.

Templeton, William
Apparently fictional. See above no. 903.

Tenducci, Giusto Ferdinando (b. 1736)
Italian opera singer. He eloped with his pupil, Dorothy Maunsell, an Irish girl of good family.

3580 A TRUE AND GENUINE NARRATIVE OF MR. AND MRS. TENDUCCI. In a letter to a friend at Bath. Giving a full account, from their marriage in Ireland, to the present time.

pp. [1–2] 3–68   L

J. Pridden   1768

Terriss, William (1847–1897)
Stage name of William Charles James Lewin. Actor. Father of Ellaline Terris. He was assassinated outside the Adelphi Theatre by a madman in 1897.

3581 SMYTHE, ARTHUR J. The life of William Terris actor by Arthur J. Smythe with an introduction by Clement Scott.

pp. [i–iv] v–xxviii, 1–212 [= 140, pls. except front. being included in pagination], [8 (advts.)]; illus. (facsims.); pls. [front., 36]   GU

Archibald Constable & Co.   1898

Terry, Daniel (1789–1829)
Actor. See above no. 2228.

Terry, *Dame* Ellen Alice (1847–1928)

Irving's leading lady at the Lyceum. Mother of Edward Gordon Craig. See also above IRVING no. 3092.

3582 CALVERT, WALTER. Souvenir of Miss Ellen Terry.

pp. [1–3] 4–48; illus.   L

Henry J. Drane   [1897]

> *Reissued in one volume, Sir Henry Irving and Miss Ellen Terry, 1897. See above no. 3094.*

3583 HIATT, CHARLES. Ellen Terry and her impersonations An appreciation by Charles Hiatt

pp. [2] [i–iv] v–x, 1–274 [275 (imprint) 276 (bl.)]; pls. [front., 27]; t.p. in red and black.   L

George Bell and Sons   1898

> *Cover designed by Gordon Craig. Lacks four plates.*

3584 ———[another edition]

pp. [i–iv] v–x, 1–274 [275 (imprint) 276 (bl.)]; pls. [front., 31]; t.p. in red and black   GU

George Bell and Sons   1899

3585 ———*[another edition]

pp. x, 274; pls. [front., 31]

George Bell   1900

STR.

Thew, William

Actor.

3586 THEW, WILLIAM. Poems on various subjects, chiefly theatrical. By William Thew. To which is prefixed, a life of the author.

pp. [16] [1] 2–112; pl. [1]   L

Printed for the author, and published by C. Chapple; and Sherwood, Jones, and Co.   1825

> *The Life is one of the most wildly eccentric even of theatrical productions. Mr. Thew had a furious stammer, but got it cured in order that he might be the greatest actor that ever lived! His ruling passion was to play against John P. Kemble for 100 guineas. If I were to express my candid opinion, I should say that Mr. Thew was a lunatic —* Lowe.

Thorne, George (1856–1922)

Touring actor and dramatist.

3587 THORNE, GEORGE. Jots by George Thorne.

pp. [1–8] 9 x–xii 13–192; illus. (incl. front.) (Arrowsmith's Bristol Library LXXVI)   MH

Bristol: J. W. Arrowsmith; London: Simpkin, Marshall, Hamilton, Kent & Co. Limited   [1897]

Tobin, John (1770–1804)

Dramatic author. His Honeymoon still holds the stage — Lowe. *See also no. 3036 above.*

3588 BENGER, [ELIZABETH OGILVY]. Memoirs of Mr John Tobin, author of The Honey-Moon. With a selection from his unpublished writings. By Miss Benger.

pp. [i–v] vi–xiii [xiv–xvi], [1] 2–444   E

Longman, Hurst, Rees, Orme, and Brown   1820

> *Includes some of Tobin's works (but not* The Honey-Moon).

Toole, John Lawrence (1830–1906)

Actor and manager.

3589 A SHORT NOTICE of the complimentary farewell banquets given to Mr. J. L. Toole, on the occasion of his leaving England for America, July, 1874.

pp. [1] 2–11 [12 (bl.)]; title on cover   MH

Liverpool: Daily Post Printing Works   [1874]

> *Reprints newspaper reports, in prose and verse:*
> *Vale, John Lawrence! Sadly Liverpool*
> *To ocean's care commits its J. L. Toole . . .*

3590 HATTON, JOSEPH. Reminiscences of J. L. Toole related by himself, and chronicled by Joseph Hatton Illustrated by Alfred Bryan and W. H. Margetson.

2 vols. in 1. pp. [i–vii] viii–xx, [1] 2–295 [296]; illus., incl. music; pl. [front.] + pp. [iii–vii] viii–xii, [1] 2–305 [306–308 (bl.)]; illus.; pl. [front.]   GU

Hurst and Blackett, Limited   1889

3591 ———second edition

pp. [i–vii] viii–xx, [1] 2–295 [296]; illus., incl. music; pl. [front.] + pp. [i–vii] viii–xii, [1] 2–305 [306–308 (bl.)]; illus.; pl. [front.]

Hurst and Blackett, Limited   1889

JFA.

3592 ———*third edition

pp. 447   1889

STR.

3593 ———[extracts] Souvenir of Mr. J. L. Toole.

pp. [1–3] 4–34 [35–36 (advts.)]; pls. [front., 4]   MH

Charles Yates & Co.   1890

> *Contains extracts from Hatton's* Reminiscences *and an Introduction, signed G.A.S.*

3594 ———[another edition] Reminiscences . . . This edition is abbreviated from the one-volume and the two-volume editions published by Messrs. Hurst & Blackett, Limited.

pp. [i–viii] ix–xv [xvi] [17] 18–281 [282], ²[1] 2–3 (press opinions) [4–6 (advts.)]; illus., incl. music   L

George Routledge and Sons, Limited   1892

> *First serialised in the* Sunday Times *May 6 to August 19, 1888.*

Tree, *Sir* **Herbert [Draper] Beerbohm (1853–1917)**

Actor-manager. Built Her Majesty's Theatre in 1897.

3595 *MR. H. BEERBOHM TREE.
                                                                    1877

> *A paper-covered booklet containing opinions of critics on some of his performances. (H. Pearson,* Beerbohm Tree, *London, 1956, pp. 12–13).*

3596 TREE, HERBERT BEERBOHM. Some interesting fallacies of the modern stage An address delivered to the Playgoers' Club at St. James's Hall, on Sunday, 6th December 1891 by Herbert Beerbohm Tree.

pp. [1–3] 4–36   L
William Heinemann   1892

> *Reprinted in Tree's* Thoughts and After-Thoughts *(1913 and 1915), with alterations and additions.*

3597 TREE, HERBERT BEERBOHM. The imaginative faculty A lecture delivered at the Royal Institution May 26th 1893 by Herbert Beerbohm Tree With a portrait from a drawing by the Marchioness of Granby.

pp. [4] 1–48; lacking pl. [front.]   L
Elkin Mathews and John Lane   1893

> *Reprinted in Tree's* Thoughts and After-Thoughts *(1913 and 1915).*

3598 A BRIEF SKETCH of the life of Mr. Herbert Beerbohm Tree.

pp. [1–3] 4–19 [20 (bl.)]   MH
n.p.   [1894 *or* 1895]

3599 TREE, HERBERT BEERBOHM. Hamlet from an actor's prompt book The substance of a lecture delivered by Herbert Beerbohm Tree to the Wolverhampton Literary Society, October, 1895, and published in the "Fortnightly Review," December, 1895.

pp. [1–2] 3–40   L
Printed at the Nassau Press   1897

> *Reprinted with alterations and additions in Tree's* Thoughts and After-Thoughts *(1913 and 1915).*

Vandenhoff, George (1813–1885)

Actor; son of John Vandenhoff, the tragedian — Lowe.

3600 VANDENHOFF, GEORGE. Dramatic reminiscences; or, actors and actresses in England and America. By George Vandenhoff. Edited, with preface, by Henry Seymour Carleton.

pp. [i–v] vi–xvi, [1] 2–318 [319–320]   L
Thomas W. Cooper & Co.; John Camden Hotten 1860

> *First published in America under title:* Leaves from an actor's note book; with reminiscences and chitchat of the green room and the stage, in England and America. *By George Vandenhoff. (New York: D. Appleton and Company, 1860).*

3601 ———*[another edition] An actor's note-book: or, the green-room and stage.

John Camden Hotten   1865
    ECB.

———[German edition, *trans.* A. V. Winterfeld]. Blätter aus dem Tagebuche eines Schauspielers. . . . Aus dem Englischen übersetzt. Berlin: B. Behr's Buchhandlung, 1860.

Vestris, *Madame* **Eliza Lucy (1797–1856)**

Née Lucia Elizabeth Bartolozzi. Wife, first, of Armand Vestris, then of Charles James Mathews. She appeared at Drury Lane in 1820. She managed, in turn, the Olympic, Covent Garden, and the Lyceum, and during her management introduced most valuable improvements in stage-setting, &c. She was a charming actress and singer — Lowe. *See William A. Armstrong, "Madame Vestris: A Centenary Appreciation,"* TN, *XI, 11–18. See also above no. 1308.*

3602 MADAME VESTRIS, & Anderson, my Joe! Harmony in discord; or, the rival Macheaths! A chaunt between Madame Vestris and Signor Anderson, as received with unbounded applause at Drury-Lane theatre.

bs.   MH
John Fairburn   [1830]

> *On the rivalry of Joshua Anderson and Madame Vestris in April at Drury Lane.*

3603 MEMOIRS of the life of Madame Vestris, ot the Theatres Royal Drury Lane and Covent Garden. Illustrated with numerous curious anecdotes.

pp. [1–6] 7–20 19–34 33–64 67–72 [=74]   L
Privately printed   1830

3604 MEMOIRS of the public and private life, adventures and wonderful exploits of Madame Vestris, the female Giovanni, Macheath, and Don Juan of the present day. Including numrous [sic] interesting and curious anecdotes. (Amatory Biography, no. 7) pp. [1–4] 5–8; illus.; t.p. headed "Chubb's genuine edition."   L

William Chubb   [1830?]

3605 ——*[another edition] Memoirs of the public and private life, amourous [*sic*] adventures and wonderful exploits of Madame V——.

pp. 8; illus.   MH

Chubb   [1830?]

> *Extracted from* Amatory Biography No. 7, *in which "those who are desirous of procuring a lengthened life of the lady will find a perfect treat in the perusal" — p. 8.*

3606 ——[another edition] Memoirs, public & private life, adventures, and secret amours, of Mrs. C. M. late Mad. V. of the Royal Olympic Theatre, with interesting & curious anecdotes of celebrated & distinguished characters in the fashionable world; detailing an interesting variety of singular, curious, and amusing scenes, as performed before and behind the curtain, &c. to which is added, The extraordinary and secret amours of Mrs. Honey.

pp. [1–4] 5–6 [7] 8; illus.   L

J. Thompson   [*ca.* 1838]

> *The text is the same as in "Chubb's genuine edition", omitting page 8 and some of page 7 and adding an account of Mrs. Honey.*

3607 †MEMOIRS of the life, public and private adventures of Madame Vestris; formerly of the Theatre Royal San Carlos; and now of the Theatres Royal Drury Lane & Covent Garden. With interesting and curious anecdotes of celebrated and distinguished characters in the fashionable world. Detailing an interesting variety of singularly curious and amusing scenes, as performed before and behind the curtain, both in public and private life, "at home" and abroad. Dedicated to the King. Embellished with portraits, and curious coloured plates.

pp. [2] [v] vi [7] 8–168; pls., col., [5]; headed: John Duncombe's edition   L

John Duncombe   [1836]

> *An extra-illustrated copy: five of the plates seem to belong to the book as issued. Signed "Arthur Griffinhoofe." Dated 1826 by Lowe.*

3608 ——[another edition] Memoirs of the life, public and private adventures, of Madame Vestris: of the Theatres Royal Drury Lane, Covent Garden, Olympic and Haymarket, with interesting and amusing anecdotes of celebrated characters in the fashionable world, detailing an interesting variety of singularly curious and amusing scenes, as performed before and behind the curtain. To which is added, the amorous confessions of Madame Vestris, carefully selected by Charles Molloy W——m——e, Esq., from a series of

letters written by Madame to Handsome Jack, in which will be found most curious anecdotes of many eminent roues and debauchees of the day; with various others of public notoriety.

pp. [1–3] 4–61 [62–64 (bl.)]; pl. [front.]   L

Printed for the booksellers   1839 [*for* 1886?]

> *Charles Molloy Westmacott and Handsome John Phillipson were prominent in scandals concerning Madame Vestris. Said, in BMC., to be compiled chiefly from no. 3607.*

✄ Chesham Place, Belgrave Square. A catalogue of all the elegant household furniture . . . the entire property of Madame Vestris. [1837]. *See no. 134.*

3609 PUBLIC OFFICE, Bow Street Tuesday, March 5th, 1839. £100 reward. Whereas a diabolical attempt has been this day made by some person or persons to maim or destroy Mad^me. Vestris. . . .

bs.   MH

S. G. Fairbroth[e]r, "Garrick" Printing office   [1839]

> *A poster.*

Victor, Benjamin (d. 1778)

This excellent dramatic historian was sub-manager and treasurer, at the Smock Alley theatre in Dublin, and then treasurer at Drury Lane — Lowe. See also IRELAND nos. 1765 passim (Dublin); AUTHOR INDEX.

3610 VICTOR, BENJAMIN. Original letters, dramatic pieces, and poems. By Benjamin Victor.

3 vols. pp. [i–iii] iv–xvi, [1] 2–360 + [2] [i–iii] iv–vi [vii–viii], [1] 2–79 [80–83] 81, ²[83] [84–85] 86–331 [332] [=334]; [83] 81, inset leaf + [2] [i–iii] iv 5–304   L

T. Becket   1776

Vokes, Rosina, *later Mrs.* Cecil Clay (1858–1894)

Actress

3611 [CLAY, CECIL *ed.*] ROSINA VOKES.

pp. [6] [1] 2–98 [99–100 (bl.)]; illus.; pl. [front.]   L

Printed for private circulation by Rivington, Percival & Co.   1894

Wagner, Leopold

Actor. See also AUTHOR INDEX.

3612 WAGNER, LEOPOLD. Roughing it on the stage. By Leopold Wagner.

pp. [1–6] 7–13 [14] 15–200 [201 (text) 202–205 (advt.) 206–208 (bl., 208 pasted to board)]   L

Iliffe & Son   [1895]

Waldron, Francis Godolphin (1744–1818)

An actor, who at one time was a bookseller. He dabbled in literature — Lowe. Also, editor and dramatist. See AUTHOR INDEX.

Waller, *Mrs.* Emma (1816–1899)

3613 A RESUMÉ of the comprehensive talent of Mrs. Emma Waller, as an actress in tragedy, comedy, and operatic drama.

pp. [1–3] 4–24; pls. [4]   MH
T. H. Lacy   [1856?]

Wallett, William Frederick (1808–1892)

'*The Queen's Jester.*'

3614 WALLETT, WILLIAM FREDERICK. The public life of W. F. Wallett, the Queen's jester: an autobiography of forty years' professional experience and travels in the United Kingdom, the United States of America, (including California,) Canada, South America, Mexico, the West Indies, &c. Edited by John Luntley.

pp. [2] [i–v] vi–xvi, [1] 2–188 [189–192 (advts.)]; illus. [front.]   MH
London and Derby: Benrose and Sons; London: Thomas Hailes Lacey; Edinburgh: John Menzies   1870

3615 ——third edition

pp. [2] [i–v] vi–xvi, [1] 2–188 [189–192 (advts.)]; illus. [front.]   MH
London and Derby: Benrose and Sons; London: Thomas Hailes Lacey; Edinburgh: John Menzies   1870

Wallis, Dorothy

Fictional character. See above no. 976.

Ward, *Dame* Genevieve (1838–1922)

One of the few really tragic actresses on the English stage — Lowe. Full name Lucy Genevieve Teresa Ward. Known in the earlier part of her career as an opera singer under the name of Madame Guerrabella until her voice was impaired by illness. Was made a D.B.E. in 1921.

3616 GUSTAFSON, ZADEL BARNES. Genevieve Ward. A biographical sketch from original material derived from her family and friends. By Zadel Barnes Gustafson.

pp. [i–iii] iv–xv [xvi–xviii], [1–2] 3–208; illus. (music); pl. [front.]   E
David Bogue   [1881]

——[American edition] Boston: J. R. Osgood and Company, 1882.

Ward, *Mrs.* Sarah (*ca.* 1727–1771)

Mrs. Ward was the original Lady Randolph in Douglas, in Edinburgh, where it was first produced, and where she was very popular. She was a very beautiful woman. — Lowe. See TN, XIII, 119–123. See above DIGGES, WEST no. 2689.

3167 vacant.

Waylett, *Mrs. née* Harriet Cooke (1798–1851)

A noted vocalist and actress. She made her first appearance at Bath in 1816 — Lowe.

3618 INTIMATE ACQUAINTANCE, AN, *pseud.* The public and private life of Mrs. Waylett, of Drury-Lane, Hay-Market, Adelphi, and Olympic Theatres: with a beautiful full-length portrait. Written by an intimate acquaintance of the lady (Amatory biography; or, lives of the most seductive characters of both sexes of the present day. No. VI.)

pp. [1] 2–16; pl. [front.]; cover title   LGk
W. P. Chubb   [1803?]

3619 ——*[another edition] The life and amours of Mrs. Waylett, of the Haymarket, Adelphi, and Olympic theatres.

pp. 16; port. (Mrs. W. as Davie Gelletly)
                                                       [1830?]
Lowe.

Webster, Benjamin Nottingham (1797–1882)

A great "character actor," whose name is familiar to all playgoers. He was lessee and manager of the Haymarket Theatre from 1837 to 1853, and lessee of the Adelphi from 1844 to 1874. The date of his first appearance in London is somewhat difficult to ascertain, but absolutely the last appearance he made was on 15th May 1878, when he spoke part of a rhymed address at Drury Lane, on the occasion of Mrs. Alfred Mellon's benefit. He died 8th July 1882 — Lowe. See above no. 929.

Wells, *Mrs.* Mary, *later* Mrs. Mary Leah Wells Sumbel, *née* Davies (1781?–1826?)

3620 SUMBEL, *Mrs.* [MARY LEAH WELLS]. Memoirs of the life of Mrs. Sumbel, late Wells; of the Theatre-Royal, Drury-Lane, Covent-Garden, and Haymarket. Written by herself. Including her correspondence with Major Topham, Mr. Reynolds the dramatist, &c. &c. &c.

3 vols. pp. [i–vii] viii–xv [xvi (errata)], [1] 2–239 [240]; cancels, pp. 83–84, 181–182 + [4] [1] 2–241 [242 (bl.) 243–244 (advts.)]; cancels, pp. 129–130, 145–146 + [4] [1] 2–232; cancels, pp. 229–230   MH

C. Chapple   1811

3621 ———[reissue] Anecdotes and correspondence of celebrated actors and actresses. Including Mr. Reynolds, Mr. Kelly, Mr. Kemble, Mr. Colman, Mrs. Siddons, &c. &c. Also, an account of the awful death of Lord Lyttleton. In three volumes.

3 vols. pp. [iii–vii] viii–xv [xvi (errata)], [1] 2–239 [240]; cancels, pp. 83–84, 181–182 + [2] [1] 2–241 [242]; cancels, pp. 129–130, 145–146 + [2] [1] 2–232; cancels, pp. 229–230   MH

Edgerley & Co.   1828

Dedication signed Leah Wells Sumbel.

3622 ———[reissue] Anecdotes and correspondence of celebrated actors and actresses. Including Mr. Reynolds, Mr. Kelly, Mr. Kemble, Mr. Colman, Mrs. Siddons, &c. &c. Also, an account of the awful death of Lord Lyttleton. In three volumes.

3 vols. pp. [iii–vii] viii–xv [xvi], [1] 2–239 [240] + [2] [1] 2–241 [242 (bl.) 243–4 (advts.)] + [2] [1] 2–232

Edgerley & Co.   1830

IKF

Wemyss, Francis Courtney (1797–1859)

A well-known American manager, who was born and trained in England — Lowe.

3623 [WEMYSS, FRANCIS COURTNEY.] THEA-TRICAL BIOGRAPHY: or, the life of an actor and manager. Interspersed with sketches, anecdotes, and opinions of the professional merits of the most celebrated actors and actresses of our day.

pp. [1–7] 8–324   GU

Glasgow   1848

First published in America as Twenty-six years of the life of an actor and manager. *New York: Burgess, Stringer & Co., 1847.*

West, James

Actor and professor of dancing.

3624 [WEST, JAMES] THEATRE PORTSMOUTH. Mr. West's benefit postponed. Oppression struggling through difficulty.

pp. [1–3] 4–34   L

Schulze & Dean   1813

A protest against Maxfield's refusing him the use of the theatre.

3625 [WEST, JAMES.] FALLEN, never to rise again.

bs.   L

n.p.   [1817]

An appeal for subscriptions. West acted seven years with Garrick "sixty odd years back".

3626 [WEST, J.] MORE NEWS and fresh information! An appeal to friends.

bs.   L

Remmish, printer   [1817]

3627 [WEST, J.] APPEAL to the nobility, gentry, and public at large.

bs.   L

n.p.   [1823]

A handbill hawked by West from door to door. His benefit at the English Opera House had been cancelled at the last minute because he could not raise the £40 deposit.

Weston, Thomas (1737–1776)

One of the greatest of English comedians, who unfortunately killed himself by habitual drunkenness — Lowe. He alternated between the Haymarket and Drury Lane.

3628 MEMOIRS of that celebrated comedian, and very singular genius Thomas Weston.

pp. [4] [1] 2–60   MH

S. Bladon   1776

Motto: "I knew him well;
  He was a fellow of infinite humour."

Wewitzer, Ralph (1748–1825)

An actor of no great ability — Lowe. For his other writings see AUTHOR INDEX.

3629 WEWITZER, RALPH. *Green room gossip, or dramatic reminiscences.

S. Spencer   [c. 1826]

Published in parts by Duncombe in 1826. Advertised in Matthew's Invitation.

3630 WEWITZER, RALPH. *Dramatic remini-scences, anecdotes, comical sayings and doings. Collected by Ralph Wewitzer, comedian.

pp. 3–108; port.   MB

Lacy   [185?]

3631 ——[another edition] *Dramatic reminiscences, anecdotes, comical sayings and doings. Added, his dramatic chronology.

pp. 3–112, 68; ports. MB
[185–?]

Whitbread, Samuel (1758–1815)

Head of the Committee which rebuilt and managed Drury Lane after the fire of 1809. The anxieties of office drove him to suicide.

3632 AN AUTHENTIC ACCOUNT OF THE LATE MR. WHITBREAD. Consisting of facts & anecdotes relating to his latter days and death, developing the causes which led to that deplorable event. With the genuine report of the inquest, now first published — taken in short-hand by Francis Phippen, the only reporter present at the sitting of the inquest held in Mr. Whitbread's house. Including a brief memoir of his life. Illustrated by a fac-simile engraving of his handwriting and autograph, from a document in the possession of the publisher.

pp. [i–v] vi–vii [viii], [5] 6–42 [43–44 (advts.)]; pl., fold. L
William Hone 1815

> On p. vii, "The publisher is requested to state, that Mr. Phippen has supplied nothing more to the Authentic Account, than the Report of the Inquest, and is wholly unconnected with the Publication."

3633 ——the third edition
pp. [i–v] vi–vii [viii], [5] 6–42 [43–44 (advts.)]; pl., fold.
MB
William Hone 1815

White, J. F.
Actor.

3634 W[HITE] J. F. An appeal to the public at large, of the town of Manchester, but chiefly addressed to the violent opposers of J. F. White, comedian: with many particular observations on the management of theatres, and the peculiar situation of performers in general. By J.F.W.

pp. [1–3] 4–9 [10 (bl.)] L
Manchester: G. Bancks, printer 1803

> An ad misericordiam *appeal. He allows that he had not acted specially well, but says that he had had unsuitable parts — Lowe.*

Wightwick, George
Actor.

3635 WIGHTWICK, GEORGE. Theatricals, 45 years ago.
pp. [2] [1] 2–16; cover-title L
Portishead, Somersetshire 1862

Wild, James (1771–1836) *and* Sam Wild (1815–1883)
Father and son, strolling players.

3636 TRIM, *pseud.* of William Broadley Megson, *ed.* The original, complete, and only authentic story of "Old Wild's" (the Yorkshire "Richardson's," and the pioneer of the provincial theatre): a nursery of strolling players and the celebrities who appeared there. Being the reminiscences of its chief and last proprietor, "Sam" Wild. Edited by "Trim." Reprinted from the "Halifax Courier."

pp. [1–3] 4–244 L
London: G. Vickers; Bradford: J. Morgan [1888]

Wilkes, Robert
See below WILKS, ROBERT *nos. 3642–3647.*

Wilkinson, Tate (1739–1803)
The famous manager of the York circuit, to whose books we are indebted for so much of our knowledge of the actors and actresses of two generations. Wilkinson was a pupil of Foote, and was so remarkable a mimic that he could reproduce even the face of a beautiful woman. His fame as an actor was very slight otherwise — Lowe. See Sybil Rosenfeld, Strolling Players & Drama in the Provinces 1660–1765, Cambridge, 1939.

3637 WILKINSON, TATE. Memoirs of his own life, by Tate Wilkinson, patentee of the Theatres-Royal, York & Hull.

4 vols. pp. [i–v] vi–xxiv, [1] 2–240 + [2] [1–3] 4–266 + [2] [1–3] 4–266 + [2] [1–3] 4–170 173–274 [275 (errata) 276 (bl.)] [=274] L
York: Printed for the author, by Wilson, Spence, and Mawman; and sold by G. G. J. and J. Robinson, and T. and J. Egerton, London 1790

> Printed proposals were issued. Vol. IV contains "The Mirror; or, Actor's Tablet. With a Review of the Old and New Theatrical Schools" (pp. [75]–242), and some letters.

3638 ——[another edition]
3 vols. pp. [i–v] vi–xii, [1] 2–288 + [2] [1] 2–299 [300] + [2] [1] 2–299 [300] L
Dublin: P. Byrne, P. Wogan, J. Parker, J. Moore, A. Grueber, W. Jones, J. Rice, R. White, and G. Draper 1791

3639 ——*[another edition]
4 vols YP
York: printed for the author, by Wilson, Spence and Mawman 1795

——[German edition] Werkwürdigkeiten aus der Lebensgeschichte Tate Wilkinsons, privilegierten Direcktors der Königlichen Theater zu York und Hull, von ihm selbst beschrieben. Berlin & Stettin: Nicolai, 1795.

☒ Manners, Nicholas. Remarks on the Memoirs of Tate Wilkinson . . . [1790?]. *See no. 431.*

3640 WILKINSON, TATE. The wandering patentee; or, a history of the Yorkshire theatres, from 1770 to the present time: interspersed with anecdotes respecting most of the performers in the three kingdoms, from 1765 to 1795. By Tate Wilkinson. To which are added, never published, The diversions of the morning, and Foote's trial for a libel on Peter Paragraph. Written by the late Samuel Foote, Esq.

4 vols. pp. [i–v] vi–xi [xii] [13] 14–312 + [1–5] 6–268 + [1–5] 6–268 + [1–5] 6–267 [268]   L
York: printed for the author, by Wilson, Spence, and Mawman; London: sold by G. G. & J. Robinson; T. Egerton; and J. Deighton   1795

3641 WILKINSON, TATE. *Original anecdotes respecting the stage, and the actors of the Old School, with remarks on Mr. Murphy's "Life of Garrick".

[*ca.* 1805]

Reprinted from Monthly Mirror. *Mullins says: "Only 12 copies taken in this form"* — Lowe.

Wilks, Robert (1665–1732)

One of the partners of Cibber in the management of Drury Lane, and one of the greatest light comedians of the stage — Lowe. *See also above* THE LONDON THEATRE *no. 1321 (Drury Lane).*

3642 MEMOIRS of the life of Robert Wilks, Esq; containing an account of his transactions before his coming to England, the rise of his reputation on the British stage, his adventures among the ladies, particularly his amours with Mrs. Rogers, Mrs. B——, &c. an exact view of the principal parts he performed both in tragedy and comedy, the remarkable friendship between him and Mr. Farquhar, and other memorable circumstances of his life. Dedicated to Colley Cibber, Esq; poet-laureat.

pp. [6] i–xiv, 1–36; pl. [front.]   DFo
Printed by W. Rayner   1732

3643 ——the second edition
pp. [6] i–xiv, 1–36   L
                                                    1732

3644 ——the third edition   Together with a true copy of his will.
pp. [6] i–xiv, 1–36 [37–40]   L
                                                    1732

3645 O'BRYAN, DANIEL. Authentic memoirs or, the life and character of that most celebrated comedian, Mr. Robert Wilks; who died on Wednesday the 27th of September 1732, in his grand climacterical year. —

To which is added An elegy on his death. By Daniel O'Bryan Esq;

pp. [1–2] 3–30 [31–32]   L
S. Slow   1732

The elegy is by G.G. "That very silly pamphlet, said to be writ by one O'Bryan (if there be any such person)"— Curll's Life *(no. 3647 below).*

3646 ——the second edition. To which is annex'd, an exact coppy [*sic*] of his last will and testament.

pp. [1–2] 3–30 [31–32] 33–35 [36]   LGk
S. Slow   1732

Rest of title as in first edition, except for comma after "September".

3647 [CURLL, EDMUND]. THE LIFE of that eminent comedian Robert Wilks, Esq;

pp. [i–v] vi–viii, 2[i] ii–viii [ix–xii] [2 (advts.)], [1] 2–53 [54–56 (advts.)]; engr. port. on t.p.   DFo
E. Curll   1733
Straus, pp. 146–148.

Williams, John (1761–1818)

The notorious "Anthony Pasquin," one of the dirtiest and most disreputable fellows that ever disgraced the literary profession. For his character see John Taylor, Records of My Life [*no. 920*], I, 276 *and John Bernard,* Restrospections of the Stage [*no. 2445*], II, 215 — Lowe. *See* AUTHOR INDEX.

Wills, William Gorman (1828–1891)

Playwright and artist.

3648 WILLS, FREEMAN, *later* Freeman Wills Crofts. W. G. Wills dramatist and painter by Freeman Wills.

pp. [8] [1] 2–284; pl. [front.]
Longmans, Green, and Co.   1898
   JFA.

Wilson, John (1595–1674)

Lutenist. See above MEDIEVAL AND RENAISSANCE STUDIES *no. 1025.*

Winstanley, Eliza

Comedian.

3649 WINSTANLEY, ELIZA. Shifting scenes in theatrical life. By Eliza Winstanley, comedian.

pp. [2] [i–iii], [1] 2–295 [296], 2[7–8] 9–32 [33–34 (advts.)]   L
London and New York: Routledge, Warne, & Routledge   1859

A novel, founded on facts "gathered in the course of an extensive professional career".

Winston, James (1779–1843)

Manager and part proprietor of the Richmond and Plymouth theatres, and latterly of the Haymarket. He was also manager of the Garrick Club — Lowe. *LS gives his true name as James Bowes. Author of* The theatric tourist *(1805). See THE THEATRE OUT OF LONDON nos. 1538, 1539.*

Woffington, Margaret (*ca.* 1715–1760)

'Peg' Woffington "was perhaps," says Genest, "the most beautiful woman that ever appeared on the stage." Her first appearance in London, at Covent Garden on 6th November 1740; last on 3d May 1757, when she had a fit on the stage when speaking the epilogue to As You Like It — Lowe.

3650 LAMENTATION FROM THE DRURY-LANE PLAY-HOUSE. A new ballad.
pp. [2] MH
[London] [1743?]

The MH card catalogue suggests this is a satire on Peg Woffington, Garrick, and Lord Darnley.

3651 THE CONTEST DECIDED Address'd to Mrs. Woffington.
bs. L
[Dublin?] [1750?]

Reprinted in Augustin Daly, Woffington. A tribute to the actress and the woman *(Philadelphia, 1888).*

3652 A POEM on the celebrated Mrs. Woffington's performing the character of Andromache, in *The Distrest-Mother*. At the Theatre-Royal in Smock-Alley.
bs. L
Dublin: S. Cottor 1751

3653 LADY, A, *pseud.* The vision. Inscribed to Mrs. Woffington. Decus et deliciae theatri. Wrote by a lady.
pp. [1–2] 3–8 L
Dublin: printed by James Esdall 1753

3654 *MEMOIRS of the celebrated Mrs. W*ff**gt*n. Interspersed with several theatrical anecdotes; the amours of many persons of the first rank; and some interesting characters, drawn from real life.
1760

Lowe.

3655 ———Memoirs of the celebrated Mrs. Woffington, interspersed with several theatrical anecdotes; the amours of many persons of the first rank; and some interesting characters drawn from real life. The second edition, with additions.
pp. [1–3] 4–60 MH
J. Swan 1760

3656 [HOOLE, JOHN.] A MONODY: to the memory of Mrs. Margaret Woffington.
pp. [2] 1–17 [18 (bl.)] L
Printed for the author: and sold by R. Withy, book and printseller 1760

Reprinted in A collection of poems in two volumes. By several hands *(G. Pearch, 1768);* A collection of poems in four volumes. By several hands *(G. Pearch, 1770, 1775), II, 85–93;* ibid *ed. I. Reed 1783).*

3657 vacant.

3658 *A SUPPLEMENT to the memoirs of Mrs. Woffington. Being the atchievements of a pickle-herring: or, the life and adventures of Butter-milk Jack.
1760

Lowe.

3659 ———The history of a pickle-herring: or, the adventures of Butter-milk Jack. The second edition, with additions.
pp. [1–3] 4–48 51–64 MH
London printed: Dublin re-printed for the Worshipful Fraternity of News-Hawkers 1760

3660 ———*third edition, with additions
pp. [1–3] 4–64 DN
London printed, Dublin reprinted: Worshipful Fraternity of News-Hawkers 1760

A satire on Mrs. Woffington and on the Memoirs *(1760) (above, nos. 3654–5). Butter-milk Jack is John Magill, member of the Irish Parliament.*

3661 *WOFFINGTON'S GHOST. A poem. In answer to the Meretriciad.
1761

Reprinted in Augustin Daly, Woffington. A tribute to the actress and the woman *(Philadelphia, 1888).*

✠ A dialogue in the Shades between the celebrated Mrs. Cibber, and the no less celebrated Mrs. Woffington . . . 1766. *See no. 2591.*

3662 MOLLOY, J[OSEPH] FITZGERALD. The life and adventures of Peg Woffington with pictures of the period in which she lived. By J. Fitzgerald Molloy.
2 vols. pp. [i–vii] viii–xiv, [1] 2–293 [294] + [i–v] vi–viii, [1] 2–284 L
Hurst and Blackett 1884

Lowe *and* Brown *record copies with a portrait. Dedicated to Ellen Terry.*

3663 ——*second edition

                    MB

Hurst & Blackett   1885

3664 ——third edition
pp. [i–vii] viii–xv [xvi], [1] 2–352; pl. [front.]   L
Hurst and Blackett   1887

3665 ——new and revised edition
pp. [i–v] vi–viii, [1] 2–340; pl. [front.]   L
Downey & Co. Limited   1897

3666 ——[another edition] Peg Woffington Written by J. Fitzgerald Molloy (Beaux & Belles of England).
2 vols. pp. [i–vi] vii–x [xi (list of illustrations) xii] 1–312; pls. [front. (col.), 6]; ptd. tissue guards [7]; inset, fold., [1]; t.p. in red and black + pp. [4] vii–ix [x xi (list of illustrations) xii] 1–303 [304]; pls. [front. (col.), 6]; ptd. tissue guards [7]; t.p. in red and black
                        NbU
Printed by the Grolier Society   [190–?]

"Imperial edition limited to one thousand copies for England and America". Vol. 2 pp. 163–[304] is a biography of Catherine Clive.

3667 ——*[another edition] (Days of the Dandies).
2 vols. col. fronts., col. pl., col. ports., fold. facsim.   NjP
The Grolier Society   [190–?]

Edition de luxe, limited to one thousand copies for Britain and America.

——[American editions] New York: Dodd, Mead & Co., 1892; New York: Scribner's, 1899; (Beaux and Belles of England) New York: Athenaeum Press, [1907?].

Wood, *Mrs.* Ann

See above PATON, ANN nos. 3404–3407.

Woodward, Henry (1717–1777)

"An actor who for various abilities to delight an audience in comic characters had scarcely an equal," is Genest's description of Woodward, founded on Davies. Woodward was also an excellent harlequin — Lowe. In the earlier part of his career, when he was at Covent Garden, he was known as Lun Junior. In 1758 he took over the Crow Street Theatre in Dublin, along with Spranger Barry in "that deplorable management, which was so fatal to all concerned" — Lowe.

3668 THE BLOODY MURDER of Sir Harry Wildair, by Harry W——dw——d, the coffee-tosser, or Harlequin triumphant. In a letter to Mrs. Pilkington: with her answer.

pp. [1] 2; head-title   L
[Dublin]   [1748]

Letter signed: "Hibernicus."

3669 FADDLE found out: or, the draining of Hal W——dw——d's coffee-pot.
bs.   L
[Dublin]   [1748]

Woodward's scheme to bring over Italian opera.

3670 A LETTER to Mr. W——dw——rd, comedian.
bs.   L
[Dublin]   [1748]

Signed: "T.S", but not by Sheridan (Sheldon, p. 127).

Woodward's Dispute with Hill

In November 1752 Woodward was disgracefully insulted by a person in a stage-box, and, in the controversy which followed, this fellow Hill took the side of the insulter, and attacked Woodward. — Lowe.

3671 WOODWARD, HENRY. A letter from Henry Woodward, comedian, the meanest of all characters; (see Inspector, No. 524.) to Dr. John Hill, Inspector-General of Great-Britain, the greatest of all characters; (see all the Inspectors.)
pp. [1–2] 3–22   L
M. Cooper   1752

3672 ——the second edition
pp. [1–2] 3–22   L
M. Cooper   1752

A corrected reissue of the first edition.

3673 ——the third edition
pp. [1–2] 3–22   L
M. Cooper   1752

A reissue of the second edition.

3674 EDWARDS, SAMPSON, *pseud.?* A letter to Mr. Woodward, on his triumph over the Inspector. By Sampson Edwards, the merry cobler of the Hay-Market:
pp. [1–2] 3–24   L
C. Corbett   [1752]

Published in December — LS, pt. 4, p. 337.

3675 ——*second edition
                       [1752]
LS, pt. 4, p. 341.

3676 AN ESSAY ON THE RATIONALITY OF BRUTES. With a philosophical comparison between Dr. Codgill Inspector General of Town-Island. And Mango, the great monkey, Director General of the pantomime performers in the Haymarket.

pp. [2] [1–3] 4–24   MH

J. Bouquet   [1752]

A satirical reply to Dr. John Hill's "Inspector" pieces in the London Daily Advertiser 30 November 1752, and 1 December 1752. Attributed in old hand on L copy to "D. Henry."

3677 FLESTRIN, QUINBUS, *pseud. of* Charles Smart? *Dr Bobadil's monody: occasioned by an unhappy accident he met with at Ranelagh last summer, with a preface and notes variorum by Quinbus Flestrin.

Sold by W. Owen   1752

Advertised 23 December 1752 (LS, pt. 4, pp. 341–2).

3678 PARTRIDGE, SIMON, *pseud.* A letter to Henry Woodward, comedian, occasion'd by his letter to the Inspector. By Simon Partridge, the facetious cobler of Pall Mall. And son of the late Mr. Partridge, famous for his dispute with Isaac Bickerstaff.

pp. [1–2] 3–24   L

H. Jeffry   [1752 or 1753]

3679 THE THEATRICAL CONTENTION. A fable.

pp. [1–3] 4–6   L

W. Owen   [1752]

Reviewed in the Monthly Review November 1752, p. 398. References are made in this pamphlet to Captain Otter (a character in The Silent Woman). During a performance of this play on November 11 at Drury Lane, there was another fracas in the Woodward-Hill affair. (LS, pt. 4, p. 330).

✘ Whipping rods for trifling, scurrhill, scriblers; as Mr. F——t . . . Spectorhill his late pamphlets. 1752. *See no. 2775.*

Spectorhill is Dr. Hill, who is roundly abused.

3680 EARL OF ——, *pseud.* *An answer to Henry Woodward, comedian. With some occasional remarks on the Greek and Roman stage. By the Rt. Hon. the Earl of ——

pp. (1) 25   MB

M. Cooper   1753

3681 THE GEESE STRIPT OF THEIR QUILLS: or, proposals for depluming and rusticating the rival literati. With an impartial examination into some important concerns.

pp. [2] [1] 2–50   MH

M. Cooper   1753

✘ Gentleman of Trinity College, A, *pseud.* Crow Street in an uproar. Dublin 1762. *See no. 1788.*

In 1762 Woodward dissolved his partnership with Barry at Crow Street, Dublin. This pamphlet no doubt refers to this disagreement.

✘ McLoughlin, Charles. Zanga's triumph, or Harlequin and Othello at war. Being a full and impartial account of a certain theatrical partnership lately dissolved . . . Dublin. 1762. *See no. 1789.*

Same subject as item 1788.

✘ A catalogue of all the elegant household furniture . . . of Henry Woodward. [1777]. *See no. 137.*

✘ Willett, Edward. Letters addressed to Mrs. Bellamy. [1785]. *See no. 2442.*
Regarding a legacy left to Mrs. Bellamy by Woodward.

Wrighten, *Mrs.* Mary (1756–1796)

Mrs. Wrighten was the wife of James Wrighten, the prompter, from whom she eloped, and went to America — Lowe. Actress and singer.

3682 WRIGHTEN, *Mrs.* MARY *An apology for the life and conduct of Mrs. Mary Wrighten, late a favourite actress and singer.

pp. viii, viii, 77   MB

                                                                   [ca. 1775]

3683 [DAWE, M.] *MISCELLANIES, in prose and verse, on various occasions, by the author of several anonymous, well-received pieces. Added, some private memoirs of Mrs. W——n and Miss R——ns, of Drury-Lane Theatre.

                                                                    MB

Printed for the author, and sold by G. Kearsly   1776

Wycherley, William (1640?–1716)
Dramatist.

3684 [GILDON, CHARLES and] *Lord* GEORGE LANSDOWNE. Memoirs of the life of William Wycherley, Esq; with A character of his writings. By the Right Honourable George, Lord Lansdowne. To which are added, some familiar letters, written by Mr. Wycherley, and a true copy of his last will and testament.

pp. [2] 1–42   L

E. Curll   1718

Advertised 10 April — Straus. The Memoirs of the Life *is by Charles Gildon, A character of his writings by George Granville, Lord Lansdowne.*

Yates, Edmund Hodgson (1831–1894)

Is the son of the celebrated actor, Frederick Yates, who married Miss Elizabeth Brunton, a charming and clever actress. Mr. Yates was for many years in the service of the Post Office. He has had an extraordinarily varied journalistic training, and is well-known as a novelist and a dramatist. He founded the World *in 1874 — Lowe.*

3685 YATES, EDMUND. Edmund Yates: his recollections and experiences.

2 vols. pp. [i–vii] viii–xiv, [1] 2–338; pls. [front., 1] +
pp. [i–v] vi–x, [1] 2–365 [366]; pls. [front., 1]   L
Richard Bentley and Son   1884

Perhaps not strictly a theatrical book, but it is so full of valuable and interesting theatrical information that I feel bound to mention it — Lowe.

3686   vacant

3687 ——fourth edition

pp. [i–vii] viii–xx, [1] 2–485 [486]; pl. [front.]   L
Richard Bentley and Son   1885

With an additional chapter.

3688 ——*[another edition]. Fifty years of London life.

pp. (1) 310   MB
Munro   [188?]

——[American edition] Fifty years of London life. Memoirs of a man of the world . . . by Edmund Yates   (Harper's Franklin Square Library.) New York: Harper & brothers, 1885.

——[German edition] 2 vols. in 1. Leipzig: Tauchnitz, 1885.

Young, Charles Mayne (1777–1856)

An eminent actor, the rival of Kean and Macready. First appearance, Haymarket, 22nd June 1807; last, Covent Garden, 30th May 1832. — Lowe.

3689 YOUNG, JULIAN CHARLES. A memoir of Charles Mayne Young, tragedian, with extracts from his son's journal. By Julian Charles Young, A.M. Rector of Ilmington. With portraits and sketches.

2 vols. pp. [iii–v] vi–xviii [xix–xx], [1] 2–374 [375 (imprint) 376 (bl.)]; pls. [front., 1]; vignette on t.p. +
pp. [iii–v] vi–ix [x–xii], [1] 2–368; pls. [front., 2]; vignette on t.p.   L
London and New York: Macmillan and Co.   1871

3690 ——second edition

pp. [i–iii] iv–xvi, [1] 2–478; pls. [front., 5]; vignette on t.p.   L

London and New York: Macmillan and Co.   1871

With corrections and additions. Selections reprinted in Personal Reminiscences of Chorley, Planché, and Young, *ed. by R. H. Stoddard (Bric-a-Brac Series) (New York: Scribner, Armstrong and Company, 1874). Last Leaves from the Journal of Julian Charles Young (Edinburgh, 1875) contains "Extracts from the foreign journal of Charles Mayne Young" (pp. 1–36).*

Younge, *Miss* Elizabeth (1740–1797)
Actress.

3691 HORATIO, *pseud.* *For the Caledonian Mercury. Verses addressed to Miss Younge.

bs.

Edinburgh   [*ca.* 1770]

   STR.

THEORY AND CRITICISM

DRAMATIC THEORY

See also CONTEMPORARY SURVEYS nos. 864 passim; SCOTLAND no. 2007; BIOGRAPHY nos. 2770–2775 (Foote), 3597 (Tree).

3692 DRYDEN, JOHN. Of dramatick poesie, an essay. By John Dryden Esq;

pp. [8] 1–72   L

Henry Herringman   1668

> Macdonald 127 a. Reprinted in various collected editions (including Malone's collection of Dryden's prose, 1800), in a few separate editions at the end of the Nineteenth Century (ed. T. Arnold, Oxford, 1889, ed. W. H. Lowe, Clive, 1899, ed. D. Nichol Smith, Blackie, 1900) and in Ker, vol. I, Hudson, and Watson, vol. I.

3693 ———[another edition] By John Dryden, servant to His Majesty.

pp. [8] 1–51 [52 (bl.)]   L

Henry Herringman   1684

> Some copies have "Dreyden" on the title. Some copies have a cancellans imprint (pasted slip) giving two booksellers' names, Knight and Saunders. Macdonald 127 b i and 127 b ii.

3694 ———[another edition] By John Dryden, Esq;

pp. [8] 1–48   L

Henry Herringman   1693

> Macdonald 127 c.

3695 DRYDEN, JOHN. The Indian emperour, or, the conquest of Mexico by the Spaniards. Being the sequel to The Indian Queen. By John Dryden Esq; the second edition.

pp. [1–2] 3–21 [22 (bl.) 23–28], ²1–68 [69–70 (Epilogue) 71–72 (bl.)]   L

H. Herringman   1668

> Macdonald 69b. L copy lacks final blank leaf.
> The Indian emperor was produced at the Theatre Royal in Bridges Street about April 1665. With "A Defence of an Essay of Dramatique Poesy". This "Defence" does not appear in the first (1667), third (1670), or subsequent editions. It is reprinted in various collected editions, and in Ker, vol. I, Hudson, and Watson, vol. I.

3696 DRYDEN, JOHN. The conquest of Granada by the Spaniards: in two parts. Acted at the Theatre-Royall. Written by John Dryden servant to His Majesty.

pp. [24] 1–24, ²23–67 [68–72] [4] 73–175 [176]; cancellans, pp. 21–24   L

Henry Herringman   1672

> Macdonald 76 a.
> Prefixed is: "Of heroique playes. An essay," and the volume concludes with: "Defence of the epilogue. Or, an essay on the dramatique poetry of the last age." The Conquest of Granada was produced at the Theatre Royal in Bridges Street December 1670 and January 1671. "Of heroique playes" was reprinted in the second (1673), third (1678), fourth (1687), fifth (1695) and sixth (1704) editions. It is reprinted in various collected editions, and in Ker, vol. I, Hudson, and Watson, vol. I. The "Defence of the epilogue" was reprinted in the second (1673) third (1678) but not in the fourth (1687) or subsequent editions. It is reprinted in various collected editions, and by Ker, Hudson and Watson.

3697 RYMER, THOMAS. The tragedies of the last age consider'd and examin'd by the practice of the ancients, and by the common sense of all ages. In a letter to Fleetwood Shepheard, Esq; by Thomas Rymer, of Grays-Inn, Esquire.

pp. [16] 1–144   L

Richard Tonson   1678 [for 1677]

> Wing R 2430. Published Michaelmas Term, 1677 — TC. The first leaf is the licence leaf — licensed 17th July 1677.
> Reprinted in Zimansky.

3698 ——— . . . by Mr. Rymer servant to Their Majesties. Part I. The second edition.

pp. [16] 1–144   MH

Printed and are to be sold by Richard Baldwin   1692

> Wing R 2431. Sheets of the first edition (including the licence leaf), mostly, with a cancellans title-page. The Short View (no. 3705 below) is Part II, though it is not so described; and it was presumably not issued with this edition of The Tragedies, since the two works are listed separately in the TC (II 442): but the plan was to associate the old work with the new ("The Tragedies of the last Age, which being very scarce hath also been reprinted, to be bound up with the last" — Gentleman's Journal, December 1692).

3699 ———*[another edition]

    LDW

    1694

> Wing R 2432.

3700 DRYDEN, JOHN. Troilus and Cressida, or, truth found too late. A tragedy as it is acted at the Dukes Theatre. To which is prefix'd, A preface containing the grounds of criticism in tragedy. Written by John Dryden servant to His Majesty.

pp. [26] 1–69 [70 (Epilogue) 71 (advts.) 72 (bl.)]   L

Jacob Tonson; and Abel Swall   1679

> Troilus and Cressida was produced at Dorset Garden about April 1679. Macdonald 84 a i (and a ii, b, c). The

preface is reprinted in various collected editions and in Ker, vol. I, Hudson, and Watson vol. I.

3701 HEDELIN, [FRANCIS]. The whole art of the stage. Containing not only the rules of the drammatick art, but many curious observations about it. Which may be of great use to the authors, actors, and spectators of plays. Together with much critical learning about the stage and plays of the Antients. Written in French by the command of Cardinal Richelieu. By Monsieur Hedelin, Abbot of Aubignac, and now made English.

pp. [8] 1–135 [136], ²1–176   E

Printed for the author, and sold by William Cadman
1684

Wing A 4185.

———[American edition] New York: Benjamin Blom, Inc., 1968.

3702 SAINT EUREMONT, [CHARLES MARGUETEL de SAINT DENIS, *Seigneur de*]. Mixt essays upon tragedies, comedies, Italian comedies, English comedies, and opera's. Written originally in French, by the Sieur de Saint Euvremont. Licensed, August 12, 1685. Rog. L'Estrange.

pp. [8] 1–28   L

Timothy Goodwin   1685

Wing S 307.

3703 ———*[another edition]
      DFo

Timothy Goodwin   1687

Wing S 308.

3704 ———[another edition.] Miscellanea: or, various discourses upon 1. tragedy, 2. comedy, 3. the Italian & 4. the English comedy. 5. And operas, to his Grace, the D. of Buckingham. Together with Epicurus his Morals. Written originally by the Sieur de Saint Euvremont, and made English by Ferrand Spence. To which is prefixt a general dissertation, introductory to the several tracts, and dedicated to T. M. Esquire.

pp. [84] 1–180   LGk

Sam. Holford   1686

Wing S 304.

Rymer's *Short View*

3705 RYMER, [THOMAS]. A short view of tragedy; it's original, excellency, and corruption. With some reflections on Shakespear, and other practitioners for the stage. By Mr. Rymer, servant to their majesties.

pp. [16] 1–182 [183–4 (advt.)], mis-numbering p. 52 as '62' and pages of inner forme K (pp. 129–144)   L

Printed and are to be sold by Richard Baldwin   1693

Wing R 2429. Reprinted in Zimansky. See also no. 3697.

3706 DENNIS, [JOHN]. The impartial critick: or, some observations upon a late book, entituled, *A short view of tragedy*, written by Mr. Rymer, and dedicated to the Right Honourable Charles Earl of Dorset, &c. By Mr. Dennis.

pp. [16] 1–52   L

R. Taylor   1693

Advertised 27 February 1693 — Hooker. Reprinted in Spingarn, vol. III, and in Hooker, vol. I. Lowndes records editions published in 1692 and 1697; these are probably "ghosts": they are unknown to Hooker.

3707 [GILDON, CHARLES.] MISCELLANEOUS LETTERS and essays, on several subjects. Philosophical, moral, historical, critical, amorous, &c. in prose and verse. Directed to John Dryden, Esq; the honourable Geo. Granvill, Esq; Walter Moile, Esq; Mr. Dennis, Mr. Congreve, and other eminent men of th'age. By several gentlemen and ladies.

pp. [16] 1–224, ²125–131 [132 (errata)] [=232]   L

Benjamin Bragg   1694

Reissued as Letters and essays, on several subjects, 1696 and 1697. Contains "Some reflections on Mr. Rymer's Short View of Tragedy", pp. 64–118. Macdonald 275 a, b.

———

3708 LETTERS UPON SEVERAL OCCASIONS: written by and between Mr. Dryden, Mr. Wycherly, Mr. ——— Mr. Congreve, and Mr. Dennis. Published by Mr. Dennis. With a new translation of *Select letters* of Monsieur Voiture.

pp. [16] 1–128 [16] 129–190 [191 (errata) 192 (advts.)]   L

Sam. Briscoe   1696

Selections were variously reprinted in the eighteenth century. Dennis's part reprinted in Hooker, vol. II, pp. 382–386. Macdonald 285.

3709 [VOLTAIRE, FRANÇOIS-MARIE AROUET de] *AN ESSAY upon the civil wars of France. And also upon epick poetry. Fourth edition. To which is now prefixed, A discourse on tragedy, and reflections on the English and French drama.

1731

CBEL ii 803.

3710 ———[another edition?] Lucius Junius Brutus, a tragedy. As it is acted at the Theatre-Royal in Drury-Lane, by his Majesty's servants. By Mr. Duncombe. The second edition. To this edition is prefix'd, An essay on tragedy. By Mr. Voltaire.

pp. [1–13] 14–84; t.p. in red and black   LVA

J. Watts   1747

An essay on tragedy is pp. [11]–26.
William Duncombe's Lucius Junius Brutus (D.L. 25 Nov. 1734) was an adaptation of Voltaire's Brutus. It was published twice in 1735 and in 1747. Stratman, Tragedies 1712.

3711 STUDENT OF OXFORD, A, *pseud.* of John Hippisley, *Jr*? A dissertation on comedy: in which the rise and progress of that species of the drama is particularly consider'd and deduc'd from the earliest to the present age. By a student of Oxford.

pp. [3–4] 5–55 [56]   L
T. Lowndes; and J. Robinson   1750

Published in January — LS.

3712 GUTHRIE, WILLIAM. An essay upon English tragedy. With remarks upon the Abbe de Blanc's observations on the English stage. By William Guthrie, Esq;

pp. [1–3] 4–34   L
T. Waller   [1757]

The remarks are on some passages in Jean Bernard Le Blanc's Letters on the English and French Nations 2 vols (1747).

3713 GENTLEMAN OF SCOTLAND, A, *pseud.* of James Boswell. An ode to tragedy. By a gentleman of Scotland.

pp. [1–2] 3–12   L
Edinburgh: Alex. Donaldson   1661 [for 1761]

Pottle *4.*

3714 VOLTAIRE [FRANÇOIS MARIE AROUET de]. Critical essays on dramatic poetry. By Monsieur de Voltaire.

pp. [i–ii] iii–iv, 1–195 [196]   GU
Glasgow: Robert Urie   1761

3715 ——[another edition] Critical essays on dramatic poetry by Monsieur de Voltaire. With notes by the translator.

pp. [iii–ix] x–xii, [1] 2–274 [275–276 (advt.)]   L
L. Davis and C. Reymers   1761

3716 COOKE, WILLIAM. The elements of dramatic criticism. Containing an analysis of the stage under the following heads, tragedy, tragi-comedy, comedy, pantomime, and farce. With a sketch of the education of the Greek and Roman actors; concluding with some general instructions for succeeding in the art of acting. By William Cooke, Esq; of the Middle Temple.

pp. [8] [i] ii–vii [viii], [4] [1] 2–216; vignette on t.p. L
G. Kearsly and G. Robinson   1775

Dedicated to David Garrick.

——[German edition] Grundsätze der dramatischen Kritik. Lübeck: Donatius, 1777.

3717 [HODSON, WILLIAM.] ZORAIDA: A TRAGEDY. At it is acted at the Theatre-Royal in Drury-Lane. To which is added a postscript, containing observations on tragedy.

pp. [12] [1] 2–104   L
G. Kearsly   1780

The postscript is "better worth reading than the play itself — his friends at Cambridge compared him to a man with a dark lanthorn, casting a light on everybody but himself" —Genest. Postscript pp. 67–104. Zoraida was produced 13th December 1779.

3718 ——the second edition

pp. [12] [1] 2–104   L
G. Kearsly   1780

A reissue.

3719 WALWYN, B. An essay on comedy. By B. Walwyn.

pp. [iii–iv] v–xii, 1–35 [36 (bl.)]   L
M. Hookham; Miss Davis; and J. Fielding   1782

This essay first appeared in "one of the public prints", where it called forth a reply, here reprinted, from "Philo-drama" (identified as Thomas Davies).

3720 STANLEY, EDWARD. Elmira, a dramatick poem; with Thoughts on tragedy. By Edward Stanley, B.A.

pp. [1–2] 3–14 [15–16], ²[1] 2–104 [2] 105–141 [142–144 (bl.)]   L
Norwich: printed by Crouse and Stevenson   1790

3721 HAYLEY, WILLIAM. Three plays: with a preface, including dramatic observations, of the late Lieutenant-General Burgoyne, by William Hayley, Esq.

pp. [2] [i–vii] viii–xxxvi [xxxvii–xxxviii (bl.)], [1–3] 4–262 [263 (imprint) 264 (bl.)]   L
Chichester: printed by William Mason, for T. Cadell and W. Davies, Strand, London   1811

3722 AN ESSAY ON TRAGEDY.

pp. [2] [1] 2–83 [84 (bl.)]   L
Printed [by J. R. Gilmour] for the author   1824

3723 McDERMOT, M[ARTIN]. A philosophical inquiry into the source of the pleasures derived from tragic representations: from which is deduced the secret of giving dramatic interest to tragedies intended for the stage. Preceded by a critical examination of the various theories adopted on the subject by the English, French, and German philosophers. By M. McDermot.

pp. [i–iii] iv–viii, [1] 2–405 [406]   L
Sherwood, Jones, and Co.   1824

Dedicated to Francis Harriet Kelly.

3724 NASH, GEORGE. The drama, a treatise on poetry and verse, dramatic composition, dramatic authors, and the effects of dramatic amusements. To which is annexed, The poet's death, a ballad. By George Nash, author of "The outcast".

pp. [2] [1] 2–27 [28] L

Saunders and Otley 1839

⌘ Mayhew, Edward. Stage effect: or, the principles which command dramatic success in the theatre. 1840. *See no. 814.*

3725 TOMLINS, F[REDERICK] G[UEST]. The relative value of the acted and the unacted drama. A lecture delivered at a meeting of the Syncretic Association, Suffolk Street Gallery, on Thursday, March 4th, 1841, by F. G. Tomlins.

pp. [1–3] 4–14 L

C. Mitchell [1841]

Reprinted from the Monthly Magazine *(April, 1841).*

3726 PHRENOLOGY; in relation to the novel, the criticism, and the drama.

pp. [i–v] vi–vii [viii], [1] 2–69 [70 (colophon) 71–72 (advts.)] L

John Ollivier [1848]

3727 FITZGERALD, PERCY [HETHERINGTON]. Principles of comedy and dramatic effect. By Percy Fitzgerald, M.A.

pp. [1–8] [9] 10–368 E

Tinsley Brothers 1870

3728 SIMPSON, EDWIN. The dramatic unities in the present day. By Edwin Simpson.

pp. [4] [1] 2–100 L

Trübner & Co. 1874

3729 ———second edition

pp. [4] [1] 2–86 87*–94* [87] 88–101 [102 (bl.) 103–108 (reviews)]

Trübner & Co. 1875

JFA.

3730 REIVES, BLANCHE. Is burlesque art? A paper read at the monthly meeting of the Church and Stage Guild, on Thursday, October 7th, 1880. By Blanche Reives.

pp. [1–3] 4–17 [18–19 (bl.) 20 (advt.)] L

J. Jeffery [1880]

⌘ Pollock, Walter Herries. The paradox of acting. Translated . . . from Diderot's 'Paradoxe sur le comédien.' 1883. *See no. 751.*

3731 FITZGERALD, PERCY [HETHERINGTON]. The art of the stage as set out in Lamb's dramatic essays with a commentary by Percy Fitzgerald.

pp. [6] [i] ii–v [vi], [1] 2–276 [277–280]; pl. [front.] L

Remington & Co. 1885

Contains a criticism of the acting of Munden.

3732 JONES, HENRY ARTHUR. The renascence of the English drama Essays, lectures, and fragments relating to the modern English stage, written and delivered in the years 1883–94 by Henry Arthur Jones.

pp. [i–v] vi–xiv, [1] 2–343 [344] GM

Macmillan and Co. 1895

3733 ———[fine paper issue]

pp. [i–v] vi–xiv, [1] 2–343 [344] GU

Macmillan and Co. 1895

One hundred copies printed on hand-made paper March 1895.

3734 JONES, HENRY ARTHUR. *The relations of the drama to real life. A lecture delivered at Toynbee Hall on Saturday evening, November 13th, 1897.

pp. 24

Chiswick Press 1897

IKF.

COLLECTIVE CRITICISMS OF DRAMATISTS

See also no. 3767.

3735 FENTON, ELIJAH. An epistle to Mr. Southerne, from Mr. El. Fenton. From Kent, Jan. 28. 1710–11.

pp. [4] 1–19 [20 (bl.)] L

Benj. Tooke; and Bernard Lintott 1711

In heroic couplets.

3736 WEBSTER, *Mr., pseud. of Dr.* Francis Reynardson. The stage: a poem. Inscrib'd to Joseph Addison, Esq; by Mr. Webster, of Christ-Church, Oxon.

pp. [4] [1] 2–32 MH

E. Curll 1713

Published 5 April 1713. Mock-heroics. Reissued in Poems on Several Occasions *by Mr. Reynardson* (1714) *and in* A Collection of Original Poems, Translations, and Imitations (1714). *See F. W. Bateson,* "The Stage (1713)", MLN 45 (1930) 27-29.

3737 *THE DRAMATICK SESSIONS: or, the stage contest.

pp. 28   MB

A. Moore   1734

Satirical verses on British dramatists.

3738 A TRIP TO PARNASSUS; or, the judgment of Apollo on dramatic authors and performers. A poem.

pp. [2] [i-iii] iv, [1] 2-26   L

John Abraham   1788

Dedicated to Thomas Harris, manager of the Theatre Royal, Covent Garden. The "Advertisement" speaks of the "authoress", and contrasts her criticism with that of The Children of Thespis (no. 2332 above).

3739 PINDAR, PETER, *pseud. of* John Wolcot? The cap. A satiric poem. Including most of the dramatic writers of the present day. By Peter Pindar, Esq. With notes, illustrative of His Royal Highness the Duke of York, Lord Mulgrave, Doctor Moore, Mr. Cumberland, Mr. Richardson, Mr. Jephson, Mr. Greathead, Lady Wallace, Mrs. Piozzi, Miss Burney, Mrs. Gooch, Mrs. Inchbald, Mrs. Cowley, Miss Hughes, Mrs Robinson, Lord Mountmorres, Mr. Reynolds, Mr. O'Keefe, Mr. Holcroft, Mr. Boaden, Mr. Morton, Mr. Cobb, Mr. I. P. Kemble, Mr. Harris, Mr. Lewis, Mr. Dives, Mr. Colman, Mr. Brewer, Mr. Jerningham, Major Scott, Mr. Berrington, Mr. Pye, Mr. Watson, Mr. Murphy, Mr. M. P. Andrews, Mr. Hoare, Mr. Topham, Mr. Dibdin, Mr. Hurlstone, Mr. H. Bate Dudley, Mr. J. Taylor, Mr. Woodfall, Mr. Litchfield, Rev. Mr. Rose, Mr. Stewart, Mr. Oulton, Mr. Pearce, Mr. Waldron, Mr. Cross, Mr. Holman, Mr. Benson, Mr. H. Siddons, Mr. Hook, Mr. Macready, Mr. Arnold, Mr. Birch, Mr. Walter, Junr. Jew King &c. &c. Dedicated to Richard Brinsley Sheridan, Esq.

pp. [i-v] vi-viii [9] 10-41 [42]   LGk

Printed for the author   [1795]

This attack on most of the dramatists of the time caused a considerable sensation, and the authorship was much debated. It seems certain that the genuine Peter Pindar, Wolcot, was not the writer. The "Cap" is the Cap of Folly, which Boaden gains, Lady Wallace being second — Lowe. *Most authorities do not share Lowe's doubts.*

3740 ———second edition

pp. [i-v] vi-viii [9] 10-41 [42]   L

Printed for the author   [1795]

3741 [MATHIAS, THOMAS JAMES] THE GROVE. Fourth edition

pp. [i-iii] iv, [7] 8-72, misnumbering 54 as "50"   L

Printed for the author   [1798]

Closely resembles The Cap *by Peter Pindar 1795 (see above no. 3739) which it attacks.*

3742 THOMSON, ALEXANDER. *The British Parnassus, at the close of the eighteenth century; a poem, in four cantos, by Alexander Thomson, author of Whist, The paradise of taste, and The pictures of poetry.

Edinburgh   1801

A poetical criticism on the dramatic authors of the period — Lowe.

3743 MALKIN, BENJAMIN HEATH. Almahide and Hamet, a tragedy. By Benjamin Heath Malkin, Esq. M.A.

pp. [2] [1] 2-158   L

Longman and Rees   1804

pp. [1]-57: "To John Philip Kemble, Esquire" (an essay on drama). Stratman, Tragedy 3482.

3744 "Q", *pseud. of* Thomas Purnell. Dramatists of the present day by "Q" Reprinted from "The Athenaeum."

pp. [i-v] vi [vii-viii], [1] 2-140   MH

Chapman and Hall   1871

Dedicated to Swinburne.

3745 KNOWLES, JAMES SHERIDAN. Lectures on dramatic literature delivered by James Sheridan Knowles during the years 1820-1850.

pp. [8] [1] 2-228 [229 (errata) 230 (bl.)]; pl. [1 (autograph facsim.)]; insets [2 (type facsims.)]   L

Privately printed for James McHenry   1873

Only twenty-five copies printed. Revised and edited by Francis Harvey. Uniform with Knowles's Lectures on Oratory (1873) and R. B. Knowles's Life of James Sheridan Knowles (1872).

3746 KNOWLES, JAMES SHERIDAN. Lectures on dramatic literature by James Sheridan Knowles (never before published) *Macbeth.*

pp. [4] [1] 2-82 [83 (colophon) 84 (bl.)]   L

Francis Harvey   1875

First published in Knowles's Lectures on Dramatic Literature (1873) and now reprinted, in cheaper form, to coincide with the Lyceum Macbeth. See also above no. 3060.

3747 PATTERSON, R[OBERT] H[OGARTH]. Robespierre. A lyrical drama by R. H. Patterson . . . With a preface on the new phase of the modern drama.

pp. [2] [i–v] vi–lxxi [lxxii], [2] [1] 2–89 [90]   GM
Edinburgh and London: printed for the author by William Blackwood and sons   1877

Preface, pp. v–lxxi.

3748 ARCHER, WILLIAM. English dramatists of to-day. By William Archer.

pp. [4] [1] 2–387 [388]   GM
Sampson Low, Marston, Searle, & Rivington   1882

THEATRICAL CRITICISM
COLLECTIVE

3749 A COMPARISON between the two stages, with an examen of *The generous conqueror;* and some critical remarks on *The funeral, or grief alamode, The false friend, Tamerlane* and others. In dialogue.

pp. [8] 1–200   L
                          1702

A very coarse and indecent production — Lowe. Advertised 14 April 1702. Once attributed to Charles Gildon: see S. B. Wells "An Eighteenth Century Attribution", J.E.G.P., XXXVIII (1939) 233–246. 'The two stages' are Drury Lane and Lincoln's Inn Fields.

3750 ——[another edition] A comparison between the two stages A late Restoration book of the theatre edited with an introduction, and notes, by Staring B. Wells (Princeton Studies in English volume 26).

pp. [i–vii] viii–xxi [xxii], [1] 2–206; pl. [1]   L
Princeton: Princeton University Press; London: Humphrey Milford — Oxford University Press   1942

3751 [GILDON, CHARLES.] A NEW REHEARSAL, or Bays the younger. Containing an examen of *The ambitious step-mother. Tamerlane, The biter, Fair penitent, Royal convert, Ulysses,* and *Jane Shore.* All written by N. Rowe Esq; also a word or two upon Mr. Pope's *Rape of the Lock.* To which is prefix'd, A preface in vindication of criticism in general, by the late Earl of Shaftsbury.

pp. [22] 1–74 73 74 75–88 [=90]   L
J. Roberts   1714

3752 ——Remarks on Mr. Rowe's Tragedy of the Lady Jane Gray, and all his other plays. Viz. *The ambitious step-mother, Tamerlane, The biter, The fair penitent, The royal convert, Ulysses, Jane Shore.* With some observations upon, I. Mr. Smith's *Phaedra and Hyppolitus.* II. Mr. Philips's *Distress'd mother.* III. Mr. Addison's *Cato.* IV. Mr. Pope's *Rape of the Lock,* &c. To which is prefix'd, a prefatory discourse in defence of criticism in general. Collected from the works of the late Earl of Shaftsbury. The second edition.

pp. [1–4] 5–12 [20], ²1–74 73 74 75–88 [=90]   L
J. Roberts   1715

This is a reissue of A new rehearsal (1714) with additional prefatory matter. The tragedy of Lady Jane Gray was first performed at Drury Lane on 20th April 1715.

3753 CORINNA, A COUNTRY PARSON'S WIFE, *pseud.* Critical remarks on the four taking plays of this season; viz. Sir Walter Raleigh, The masquerade, Chit-chat, and Busiris King of Egypt. Dedicated to the wits at Button's Coffee-House. By Corinna, a country parson's wife.

pp. [4] [1] 2–67 [68 (bl.)]   L
James Bettenham   1719

Sir Walter Raleigh by George Sewel first performed at Lincoln's Inn Fields on 16 January 1719; The masquerade by Charles Johnson first performed Drury Lane 16 January 1719; Chit chat by Thomas Killigrew first performed Drury Lane 14 February 1719; Busiris by Edward Young first performed Drury Lane 7 March 1719.

3754 ——*second edition

[Bettenham]   1719

Lowe.

✖ [Derrick, Samuel.] The dramatic censor: being remarks upon the conduct, character, and catastrophe of our most celebrated plays. By several hands. 1752. *See no. 3999.*

3755 THE THEATRICAL REVIEW: for the year 1757, and beginning of 1758. Containing critical remarks on the principal performers of both the theatres. Together with observations on the dramatic pieces, new, or revived; that have been performed at either house within that period. To which is added, a scale of the comparative merit of the above performers.

pp. [2] i–v [vi], 1–88   L
J. Coote   1758

3756 THE THEATRICAL CAMPAIGN, for MDCCLXVI. and MDCCLXVII. Consisting of tragedy, comedy, farce, interlude, pantomime, anecdote, and secret history.

pp. [4] 1–44   L
S. Bladon   1767

A criticism on the various plays produced during the season 1766–1767 — Lowe.

3757 [GENTLEMAN, FRANCIS.] THE DRA-
MATIC CENSOR; or, critical companion.

2 vols. pp. [8] [1] 2–479 [480], misnumbering 78 as "76",
95 as "85", 216 as "612"; pl. [front.] + pp. [8] [1] 2–499
[500], misnumbering 51 as "15", 277 as "777"; pl. [front.]
                                                         NbU

London: J. Bell; York: C. Etherington   1770

Advertised in the second edition of The Theatres
*by Sir Nicholas Nipclose (1772) as obtainable "in
monthly numbers, price 1s each, or may be had complete in
two handsome octavo volumes, embellished with beautiful
frontispieces, price 12s in boards." No copy in parts is
known.*

3758 vacant

3759 *AN ESSAY on satirical entertainments. To
which is added Stevens's new Lecture on heads, now
delivering at the Theatre Royal, Hay-Market. With
critical observations.

pp. viii, 87; engr. t.p.

Printed and sold by J. Bell   1772

STR.
See also no. 2328.

3760 ——An essay on satirical entertainments. To
which is added, Stevens's new Lecture upon heads,
now delivering at the Theatre Royal, Hay-Market.
With critical observations. The second edition.

pp. [iii–iv] v–vi [vii–viii], 1–87 [88]; vignette on t.p. L
Sold by J. Bell   1772

3761 ——The third edition

pp. [iii–iv] v–vi [vii–viii], 1–87 [88]; vignette on t.p.
                                                        L
Sold by J. Bell   1772

3762 SOCIETY OF GENTLEMEN, A, *pseud. of*
John Potter. The theatrical review; or, new companion
to the play-house: containing a critical and historical
account of every tragedy, comedy, opera, farce, &c.
exhibited at the theatres during the last season; with
remarks on the actors who performed the principal
characters. The whole interspersed with occasional
reflections on dramatic poetry in general; the characters
of the best English dramatic authors; and observations
on the conduct of the managers. Calculated for the
entertainment and instruction of every lover of theatrical
amusements. By a society of gentlemen, independent of
managerial influence.

2 vols. pp. [4] [1] 2–336 + [2] [1] 2–231 [232]   L
S. Crowder; J. Wilkie and J. Walter   1772

*Reprinted with "corrections and additions" from the
Public Ledger, 21 September 1771 to 10 June 1772.*

3763 [HEARD, WILLIAM.] THE TRYAL of
dramatic genius: a poem. To which are added, a
collection of miscellaneous pieces. By the same author.

pp. [i–ii] iii–vi [vii–viii], [1] 2–96   L

Printed for the author; and sold by W. Goldsmith;
and P. Shatwell   [1773?]

*By William Heard [dramatic writer], according to James
Maidment.*

3764 HAWKINS, WILLIAM. Miscellanies in prose
and verse. Containing Candid and impartial observations on the principal performers belonging to the two
Theatres-Royal; from January 1773, to May 1775.
Likewise Strictures on two favourite tragedies, viz.
The orphan and *The fair penitent.* Being part of an
epistolary correspondence on those subjects with a
young lady. With many other agreeable and interesting
articles, such as pastoral songs, epitaphs, &c. &c. By
William Hawkins, Gent.

pp. [1–2] 3 iv–xxiii [xxiv (errata)], [1] 2–141 [142]
                                                        L
Printed for the author, and sold by T. Bell   1775

Reprinted journalism, in part. With a list of subscribers.

3765 [GARDEN, FRANCIS, *Lord* GARDEN-
STONE.] MISCELLANIES in prose and verse.

pp. [1–5] 6–7 [8], ²[1] 2–240   E
Edinburgh: printed by J. Robertson   1791

3766 ——Miscellanies in prose and verse; including
remarks on English plays, operas, and farces, and on a
variety of other modern publications. By the Honourable Lord Gardenstone. The second edition, corrected
and enlarged.

pp. [1–5] 6–335 [336 (To the Public)]   L
Edinburgh: printed by L. Robertson   1792

*The first edition of this Miscellany was not intended for
Sale — Preface. "Remarks on English Plays", pp. 117–
169.*

3767 THE CHILDREN OF APOLLO: a poem.
Containing an impartial review of all the dramatic
works of our modern authors and authoresses. Particularly Lady Wallace. Margravine of Anspach. Honourable Major North. Honourable John St. John. Sheridan.
Colman. Holcroft. Jackman. O'Keefe. Cobb. Cumberland. Morris. Bate. Miss Lee. Mrs. Cowley. — Inchbald.
Rose. Dibdin. Andrews. Morton. Stuart. Murphy.
Macklin. Jephson. M'Nally. Reynolds. Jerningham.
Hoare. Hurlstone. Topham. &c. &c. To which are
added, occasional notes. By —— —— ——, Esq. Agent
to the Sun.

pp. [1–3] 4–60   L
B. Crosby   [ca. 1794]

3768 [HUNT, JAMES HENRY LEIGH] CRITICAL ESSAYS on the performers of the London theatres, including general observations on the practise and genius of the stage. By the author of the theatrical criticisms in the weekly paper called the News.

pp. [i–v] vi–xiv [xv–xvi ("Contents")], [1] 2–229 [230 (bl.) 231 ("Appendix") 232 (bl.)], 2[1] 2–58 [2], 2[i] ii–xvii [xviii (errata)], 3[i] ii–viii [ix–x (advts.)]; engr. t.p.; cancels, pp. 23–24, 139–142, 183–184   MH

Printed by and for John Hunt   1807 [*for* 1808]

An advertisement opposite the title-page states that the author has quitted the News, *and now writes exclusively for the* Examiner, *a prospectus of which is at the end of the volume*—Lowe. Brewer, *pp. 23–24. See also below nos. 3776, 3805.*

3769 *THE STAGE: in 1816. A satirical poem, in three parts. With notes and illustrations. Part the first.

Printed and published (for the author)   1816

Recorded but not seen by Lowe.

3770 HAZLITT, WILLIAM. A view of the English stage; or, a series of dramatic criticisms. By William Hazlitt.

pp. [iii–v] vi–xix [xx], [1] 2–461 [462 (advts.)]; lacking first & last leaves   NbU

London: Robert Stodart; Anderson and Chase; Edinburgh: Bell and Bradefute   1818

"A collection of Theatrical Criticisms which have appeared with little interruption, during the last four years, in different newspapers — the Morning Chronicle, *the* Champion, *the* Examiner, *and, lastly, the* Times." *Advertised as "this day published" in* The Times *29 July, 1818. Keynes, 28.*

3771 ——[another edition]
pp. [i–v] vi–xix [xx], [1] 2–461 [462 (advts.)]   L
John Warren   1821

A reissue of the 1818 edition with cancellans half-title and title-page. The half-title reads: "Dramatic criticisms". Keynes 29.

3772 ——[another edition] Criticisms and dramatic essays of the English stage. By William Hazlitt. Second edition. Edited by his son.

pp. [i–v] vi–xix [xx], [1] 2–324   L
G. Routledge and Co.   1851

Selection from the 1818 edition. Keynes 30.

3773 ——[reissue] Criticisms and dramatic essays of the English stage. Second edition. Edited by his son. (The Works of William Hazlitt. A New and Uniform Series. Edited by his Son. Vol. 12.)

pp. [i–v] vi–xix [xx], [1] 2–324   NbU
Geo. Routledge and Co.   1854

A reissue of no. 3772. Keynes 30 note.

3774 ——[another edition] Dramatic essays William Hazlitt selected and edited, with notes and an introduction, by William Archer and Robert W. Lowe [Dramatic Essays, Second Series]

pp. [i–iii] iv–xxix [xx (bl.) xxxi xxxii (bl.)], [1] 2–231 [232 (bl.) 233–240 (advts.)]; pl. [front.]   L
Walter Scott, Limited   1895 [*for* 1894]

Keynes 31.

——[American edition.] Hazlitt on theatre. Edited by William Archer and Robert Lowe. Introduction by William Archer. New York: Hill and Wang, [1957] (Dramabooks).

3775 ——[another edition] A view of the English stage or a series of dramatic criticisms by William Hazlitt edited by W. Spencer Jackson. (Bohn's Standard Library.)

pp. [i–iv] v–xxiv, [1] 2–358 [359–360 (advts.)]   L
George Bell and Sons   1906

Keynes 32.
Reprinted in Hazlitt's Collected Works (The Roxburghe Library, 1868); in Volume 8 of Hazlitt's Collected Works, ed. A. R. Waller and A. Glover, (1902–1904), and in Volume 5 of Hazlitt's Complete Works, ed. P. P. Howe (1930–1934).

3776 [POOLE, JOHN] *TWO PAPERS: a theatrical critique, and an essay (being No. 999 of The pretender) on sonnet-writing, and sonnet-writers in general, including a sonnet on myself; attributed to the editor of The Ex——m——n——r. Preceded by proofs of their authenticity, founded upon the authority of internal evidence.

pp. xi, 24   MB
Miller   1819

A furious attack on Leigh Hunt, one of whose theatrical notices is parodied in it — Lowe. Copy at MB has manuscript note: "Poole told me that he wrote this pamphlet in wrath against Leigh Hunt because the Critic had, in one of his articles, fallen foul of an actress to whom Poole was then devoted."

3777 WOODDESON, WILLIAM FANE. *A slight sketch of the performances at the Theatre Royal Drury Lane, during the season of 1827 and 1828.

pp. 64   MB
Wooddeson   1828

3778 ROBSON, WILLIAM. The old play-goer. By William Robson.

pp. [i–v] vi–xi [xii], [1] 2–252   NbU

Joseph Masters   1846

3779 ——*[another edition]

pp. xi, 252   PP

Longman   1854

3780 ——*[another edition]

     1875

Lowe.

3781 FLETCHER, GEORGE. Studies of Shakespeare in the plays of King John, Cymbeline, Macbeth, As You Like It, Much Ado about Nothing, Romeo and Juliet: with observations on the criticism and the acting of those plays. By George Fletcher.

pp. [i–v] vi–xxiv, [1] 2–384   GU

Longman, Brown, Green, and Longmans   1847

3782 TALES OF THE DRAMA. Being historical accounts of all the popular pieces of the day, including The flowers of the forest, The wife's secret. The pearl of the ocean. The lighterman of Bankside. Naida; or, the goddess of El-Dorada. Faust; or the demon of the Drachenfels'. John Savile of Haysted. The adventures of a gentleman, &c. &c.

pp. [1] 2–8, ^{2}[1] 2–8, ^{3}[1] 2–8, ^{4}[1] 2–8, ^{5}[1] 2–8, ^{6}[1] 2–8, ^{7}[1] 2–8, ^{8}[1] 2–8, ^{9}[1] 2–8, ^{10}[1] 2–8, ^{11}[1] 2–16; illus.; cover-title   L

E. Lloyd   [1848]

First published in parts, Nos. 1–10. Nos. 11–12 form a double part. Each number undated, with a head-title giving the place of performance (London theatres).

3783 A NEW DRAMA; or, we faint!!! Decline of the drama!!! Review of the actors!!! Reprinted from "Bentley's Monthly Review."

pp. [1–3] 4–14 [15 (colophon) 16 (advt.)]   L

John Bentley and Company   1853

3784 MORLEY, HENRY. The journal of a London playgoer from 1851 to 1866. By Henry Morley Professor of English Literature in University College London.

pp. [1–5] 6–384   NbU

George Routledge & Sons   1866

An invaluable book for the student, its only defect being the absence of an index — Lowe. Dramatic criticism, in part reprinted from The Examiner. Henry Morley's Memoirs of Bartholomew Fair (1859, and subsequently) has material of theatrical interest.

3785 ——[another edition] The journal of a London playgoer from 1851 to 1866. (Books and papers by Henry Morley 1851–1866, II.)

pp. [1–5] 6–25 [26 (bl.)] 27–320   GU

George Routledge and Sons Ltd   1891

3786 HAWK'S-EYE, *pseud.* The stage of 1871: a review of plays and players. By Hawk's-eye. "Prince of Wales's Royal Theatre." "Theatre Royal, Haymarket." "Royal Princess's Theatre." "St. James's Theatre." "Olympic Theatre." "Royalty Theatre." First series.

pp. [4] [1–3] 4–61 [62], [1] 2 (advts.); two t.pp.   EU

Bickers & Son   1871

Further instalments are promised in the preface.

3787 MARTIN, *Sir* THEODORE. Essays on the drama. By Theodore Martin.

pp. [6] [1] 2–331 [332]   GM

Printed for private circulation   1874

Sir Theodore Martin is a distinguished poet and dramatist. His play of King Rene's Daughter gave Miss Faucit, whom he married, one of her best characters. Sir Theodore was the joint author, with Professor Aytoun of the famous Bon Gaultier Ballads — Lowe.

3788 ——by Sir Theodore Martin, K.C.B. Second series.

pp. [8] [1] 2–350 [351–352 (bl.)]   L

Printed for private circulation   1889

Essays, originally published in Blackwood's Magazine, Fraser's Magazine, the Quarterly Review, the Nineteenth Century, the St. James's Gazette, etc. The essays on Garrick, Rachel, and Macready are reprinted in the same author's Monographs (London: Murray; and New York: Dutton & Co. 1906).

3789 [ARCHER, WILLIAM] ENGLISH ANALYSES of the French plays represented at the Gaiety Theatre, London, June and July, 1879, by the Comédie Française. Reprinted from the *London Figaro*.

pp. [2] [1–3] 4–97 [98 (advt.)]   L

Printed and published at the Figaro Office   [1879]

With a preface. Attributed by Lowe to Archer, who began writing for the London Figaro in 1879. It was during this visit of the Comédie Française that Sarah Bernhardt made her first appearance in England.

3790 MAYER, M[ARCUS] L. Brief analyses of the repertory which will be produced at the Gaiety Theatre by the Sociétaires & Pensionnaires of the Comédie Française.

pp. [6] [1] 2–41 [42 (bl.)]

Printed by Letts, Son & Co. Limited   1879

IKF.

3791 MORRIS, MOWBRAY [WALTER]. Essays in theatrical criticism. By Mowbray Morris.

pp. [4] [1] 2–226; errata slip   L

Remington & Co.   1882

Mr. Morris was for some years the dramatic critic of the Times. *This work, which contains some extremely plain speaking, created a tremendous sensation both among actors and critics* — Lowe.

3792 THORNELL, J. HIGDEN, *ed.* The bill of the play. An illustrated record of the chief dramas, plays, operas bouffe, etc., produced or revived during the year 1881. With a short story of the plot, a critical analysis of the piece and the actors, and the full cast, and date of production. With numerous illustrations by Hal Ludlow. Edited by J. Higden Thornell.

pp. [10] 15–115 [116 117 (index) 118–128 (advts.)]; inset [advt. leaf]; illus.   MB

Pictorial World Office   [1882]

3793 COOK, [EDWARD] DUTTON. Nights at the play A view of the English stage by Dutton Cook.

2 vols. pp. [i–v] vi–xv [xvi], [1] 2–324 [325 (emblem) 326–328 (bl.)] + [i–v] vi–viii, [1] 2–350 [351 (emblem) 352 (bl.)]   NbU

Chatto and Windus   1883

3794 ———[another edition]

pp. [i–v] vi–xvi, [1] 2–480   GU

Chatto and Windus   1883

———[American edition] New York: Scribner and Welford, 1883.

A selection from criticisms contributed to the Pall Mall Gazette *and the* World, *from 1867 to 1881* — Lowe.

3795 TRISTRAM, WILLIAM OUTRAM. *The college for critics (a few facts on a new foundation). By William Outram Tristram (author of "Julian Trevor"), one of the founders.

pp. 32

[London]   [1883]

I presume Mr. Tristram is the gentleman who is author of the drama of The Red Lamp, *produced under Mr. Beerbohm Tree's management at the Comedy Theatre on 20th April 1887. The above pamphlet is apparently a satire on dramatic critics* — Lowe.

3796 ARCHER, WILLIAM. About the theatre Essays and studies by William Archer.

pp. [8], [1] 2–350 [351–352 (advts.)]   NbU

T. Fisher Unwin   1886

3797 EDWARDS, H[ENRY] SUTHERLAND. Famous first representations   By H. Sutherland Edwards.

pp. [i–v] vi–vii [viii], [1] 2–253 [254 (imprint) 255–256 (advt.)]   E

Chapman and Hall Limited   1886

3798 FULLER, EDWARD, *ed.* The dramatic year [1887–88] Brief criticisms of important theatrical events in the United States With a sketch of the season in London by William Archer   Edited by Edward Fuller.

pp. [i–iii] iv–viii, [1] 2–258 [259 (imprint) 260 (bl.)]   L

Sampson Low, Marston, Searle, & Rivington Limited   1888

3799 LAMB, CHARLES. The dramatic essays of Charles Lamb edited with an introduction and notes by Brander Matthews (My Library).

pp. [2] [i–v] vi [7] 8–265 [266]; pl. [front.]   L

Chatto & Windus   1891

See also nos. 3731, 3800.

3800 LAMB, CHARLES. Plays and dramatic essays. By Charles Lamb. With an introduction by Rudolph Dircks. (The Scott Library).

pp. [i–vii] viii–xxv [xxvi (bl.) xxvii xxviii (bl.)], [1] 2–239 [240 (bl.) 241–244 (advts.)]   L

Walter Scott   [1893]

See also nos. 3731, 3799.

———[American edition] New York: Dodd, Mead & Co., 1893.

3801 SCOTT, CLEMENT [WILLIAM]. Thirty years at the play and dramatic table talk. By Clement Scott.

pp. [8] [1] 2–246 [247–249 (advts.) 250 (stamped imprint)]   L

The Railway and General Automatic Library, Limited   [1891]

Stamped on p. 250: "Published for the Railway and General Automatic Library, Limited, by Eden, Remington & Co." Dedicated to Joseph Knight.

3802 WALKLEY, A[RTHUR] B[INGHAM]. Playhouse impressions. By A. B. Walkley.

pp. [i–v] vi–viii, [1] 2–261 [262 (imprint) 263–4 (advts.)]; illus. (music)   GM

T. Fisher Unwin   1892

Reprinted from the Speaker *and other periodicals. Includes reviews of current London plays, 1890–1892, and general and biographical articles.*

3803 KNIGHT, JOSEPH. Theatrical notes.

pp. [i–vii] viii–xvi, 1–321 [322 (imprint) 323–324 (bl.)]; pl. [front.]   NbU

Lawrence & Bullen   1893

> *Reviews of performances at London theatres 7th November 1874 to 27th December 1879, mostly reprinted from the Athenaeum.*

3804 ———[limited edition]

pp. [i–vi] [2] [vii] viii–xvi, 1–321 [322 (imprint) 323–324 (bl.)]; pls. [front., 6]   L

Lawrence & Bullen   1893

3805 HUNT, LEIGH. Dramatic essays Leigh Hunt Selected and edited, with notes and an introduction, by William Archer and Robert W. Lowe (Dramatic Essays, First Series).

pp. [i–iv] v–xlvii [xlviii (bl.)], [1] 2–241 [242 (imprint) 243–256 (advts.)]; pl. [front.]   L

Walter Scott, Ltd   1894

> *Selections from Critical Essays (1807) and from Hunt's essays in The Tatler (1830–1831). Leigh Hunt's Dramatic Criticism 1808–1831, ed. Lawrence H., and Carolyn W. Houtchens (New York, 1949) reprints and annotates "the best of Hunt's uncollected essays on the drama, primarily his theatrical reviews". See also nos. 3768, 3776 above.*

3806 FORSTER, JOHN and GEORGE HENRY LEWES. Dramatic essays John Forster George Henry Lewes Reprinted from the "Examiner" and the "Leader", with notes and an introduction by William Archer and Robert W. Lowe.

pp. [2] [i–iii] iv–v [vi–vii] viii–xliv, [2] [1] 2–284 [285–288 (advts.)]; pl. [front.]   E

Walter Scott, Limited   1896

3807 SCOTT, CLEMENT [WILLIAM]. From "The Bells" to "King Arthur". A critical record of the first-night productions at the Lyceum Theatre from 1871 to 1895 by Clement Scott. Illustrated.

pp. [i–v] vi–x, [1–2] 3–444; pls. [front. (photo.), 26]

John Macqueen   1896

> *JFA. Copy in L, lacking title-page. Copy in LGk dated 1897.*

3808 ARCHER, WILLIAM. Study & stage. A year-book of criticism. By William Archer.

pp. [i–v] vi–xi, [1] 2–250 [2 (bl)]   GU

Grant Richards   1899

3809 GREIN, J[ACOB] T[HOMAS]. Dramatic criticism by J. T. Grein.

pp. [8] [1] 2–296   NbU

John Long   1899

> *Stratman 421. Criticism of the London stage reprinted from La Revue d'Art Dramatique, The Sunday Special, and To-Morrow.*

3810 GREIN, JACOB THOMAS. Premières of the year.

pp. [1–5] 6–275 [276]   GM

John Macqueen   1900

> *Stratman 421. Covers the period from May 1899 to July 1900. Vols. III, IV, and V were published in 1902, 1904 and 1905.*

INDIVIDUAL PLAYS

Recorded here is the occasional literature associated with the performance of individual plays. For playlists and dictionaries of plays see above nos. 3–52. Souvenir programmes are not normally included.

Addison, Joseph. *Cato*

D.L., 14 April 1713. *It owed its phenomenal success at the time less to its intrinsic merits than to party feeling. Cibber gives an account of the success of the play. — Lowe. See also above IRELAND nos. 1721, 1723–1731 (Dublin).*

3811 [GILDON, CHARLES?] *CATO* EXAMIN'D: or, animadversions on the fable or plot, manners, sentiments, and diction of the new tragedy of *Cato*. With a comparison of the characters of the dramatical and historical hero. Necessary for the perusal of not only the readers of *Cato*, but of all other tragedies. Dedicated to Joseph Addison, Esq;

pp. [6] 1–21 [22 (bl.)]   L

John Pemberton   1713

Published at the end of April. See G. L. Anderson, "The Authorship of Cato Examin'd (1713)", PBSA 51 (1957), 84–90.

3812 DENNIS [JOHN]. Remarks upon *Cato*, a tragedy. By Mr. Dennis.

pp. [1–2] 3–56   L

B. Lintott   1713

> *An acute, though bitter, piece of criticism. Dr. Johnson quotes from it largely in his Life of Addison. — Lowe. For the story behind the publication of this pamphlet, see Hooker, II, 447. Reprinted in Hooker, II.*

3813 GENTLEMAN OF OXFORD, A, *pseud.* Mr. Addison turn'd Tory: or, the scene inverted: wherein it is made appear that the Whigs have misunderstood, that celebrated author in his applauded tragedy, call'd *Cato*, and that the Duke of M——'s character, in endeavouring to be a general for life bears a much greater resemblance to that of Caesar and Syphax, than the hero of his play. To which are added, Some cursory remarks upon the play it self. By a gentleman of Oxford.

pp. [1–2] 3–23 [24 (bl.)]   L

J. Baker   1713

3814 [THEOBALD, LEWIS.] THE LIFE and character of Marcus Portius Cato Uticensis: collected from Plutarch in the Greek, and from Lucan, Salust, Lucius Florus, and other authors in the Latin tongue. Design'd for the readers of Cato, a tragedy.

pp. [1–2] 3–24   E

Bernard Lintott   1713

3815 ——The life and character of Marcus Portius Cato Uticensis: collected from the best ancient Greek and Latin authors; and design'd for the readers of *Cato*, a tragedy. The second edition, with large additions.

pp. [1–4] 5–28   L

Bernard Lintott   1713

3816 [POPE, ALEXANDER.] THE NARRATIVE of Dr. Robert Norris, concerning the strange and deplorable frenzy of Mr. John Denn – – – an officer of the Custom-house: being an exact account of all that past betwixt the said patient and the doctor till this present day; and a full vindication of himself and his proceedings from the extravagant reports of the said Mr. John Denn—.

pp. [2] 5–24   L

J. Morphew   1713

This copy cut too close: imprint missing from title-page. A satire on Dennis's Remarks upon *Cato (see no. 3812). Published 28th July 1713 — Hooker. Griffith 23. Reprinted in vol. X of Elwin and Courthope's edition of Pope's works.*

3817 [SEWELL, GEORGE.] OBSERVATIONS upon *Cato*, a tragedy. By Mr. Addison. In a letter to ★★★.

pp. [1–2] 3–21 [22–24 (verses)]   L

A. Baldwin   1713

Advertised 30 April, 'to bind up with the Play' — Straus. A manuscript note on this copy: Wrote by Dr. Sewell, & of wch. I sold 20[00] EC.

3818 ——the second edition

pp. [1–2] 3–21 [22–24 (verses) 25–28 (Steele's Comparison between Cato and Caesar)].   L

E. Curll   1713

Advertised 2 May — Straus. The additional two leaves (sig ★²) are integral to this edition, which was advertised as containing Steele's Comparison. (no. 3819).

3819 STEELE, *Sir* RICHARD. ★A comparison between Cato and Caesar. By Mr. Steele.

[1713?]

A four-page sheet — Lowe. Reissued in no. 3818.

3820 THE UNFORTUNATE GENERAL: or, the history of the life and character of Cato. Together with a key, or explanation of the new-play, call'd Cato, a tragedy.

pp. [i–ii] iii–iv 5–24   L

Printed by Edw. Midwinter   [1713]

3821 DES CHAMPS [FRANCOIS MICHEL CHRÉTIEN]. Cato of Utica. A tragedy. Translated from the French of Mr. Des Champs, into blank verse. To which is added, A parallel betwixt this piece and the tragedy of *Cato* written by Mr. Addison.

pp. [*14*] [*1*] 2–56 [57–58 (bl.)]   L

Printed and sold by J. Morphew   1716

"A parallel" has its own title-page (p. [39]). Published 12th May, 1716 — Straus. Des Champs' play was produced at Lincoln's Inn Fields 16 May 1716.

3822 SEWELL, [GEORGE]. A vindication of the English stage, exemplified in the Cato of Mr. Addison. In a letter to a nobleman. By Mr. Sewell.

pp. [i–ii] iii–vii [viii], [1] 2–24   L

W. Mears   1716

—— *The Drummer*

D.L., 10 March 1715/6.

3823 [ADDISON, JOSEPH]. ★THE DRUMMER: or, The haunted-house. A comedy. As it is acted at the Theatre-Royal in Drury Lane, by His Majesty's Servants. Second edition.

1722

The second edition has a "Preface by Sir Richard Steele, occasioned by Mr. Tickell's Preface to Addison's Miscellanies." In this Steele declared that Addison was the author — Lowe.

3824 ——the third edition. With a preface by Sir Richard Steele, in an Epistle dedicatory to Mr. Congreve, occasioned by Mr. Tickell's Preface to the four volumes of Mr. Addison's works.

pp. [*24*] [1–3] 4–61 [62–63 (Epilogue) 64 (bl.)]   L

J. Darby   1722

Smithers, *pp. 345–346.*

Arne, *Dr* **Thomas.** *The Guardian Outwitted*

C.G., 12 December 1764.

3825 AN ELEGY on the death of *The guardian outwitted*, an opera; written and composed by Thomas Augustine Arne, M.D.

pp. [*2*] [*1*] 2–17 [18 (bl.)]   L
W. Nicoll   1765

> With the text of Gray's *"Elegy written in a country church-yard"*, which the present piece parodies.

Barrett, Wilson. *The Daughters of Babylon*

Lyric, 6 February 1897.

3826 SOUVENIR of the Daughters of Babylon By Wilson Barrett Illustrated by W. & D. Downey.

pp. [*24*]; illus.; cover title   L
W. & D. Downey   [1897]

——— *The Sign of the Cross*

Grand Theatre, Leeds, 26 August 1895; Lyric, 4 January 1896.

3827 SOUVENIR of the Sign of the Cross. By Mr Wilson Barrett.

pp. [*4* (advts.) *42* (text) *3* (advts.)]; illus., incl. [front.]   L
                                                  [1896]

Bentley, Richard. *The Wishes*

D.L., 27 July 1761.

3828 A LETTER to R——B—— Esq; author of the new comedy called *The Wishes*: now in rehearsal at the Theatre Royal in Drury-Lane.

pp. [1–3] 4–14   L
M. Cooper   1761

> *A puff in advance. The Wishes was a witty but eccentric drama by Richard Bentley, in which the speaking Harlequin was introduced. It was moderately well received — Lowe. On the play's reception, see LS, pt. 4, pp. 876–877.*

Bickerstaffe, Isaac. *The Hypocrite*

D.L., 17 November 1768. *See nos. 528, 540.*

Boucicault, Dion. *Louis the Eleventh*

Adapted from Louis XI *by Casimir Delavigne. First performed* Princess, *13 January 1855; revived* Lyceum, *9 March 1878.*

3829 E., A. *Notes on Louis XI. With some short extracts from Commines' "Memoirs". By A.E.

Privately printed   1878

> IKF.
> *Begins with a short note on Irving's playing of Louis — Lowe.*

Brooke, Henry. *Gustavus Vasa*

Published 1739. This was the first play forbidden by the Licenser, after the Act, limiting theatres and appointing a Licenser, was passed in 1737. It had been rehearsed several times, when it was prohibited, on account of some sentiments regarding liberty which it contained. It was printed by subscription at 5s. a copy, and, so incensed were the public at the Licenser's arbitrary action, that Brooke is said to have cleared £1000 by it. It has only been acted once in England (28th December 1805 for Betty), but it has been often played in Ireland — Lowe. See also below no. 3993.

3830 THE COUNTRY CORRESPONDENT: humbly address'd to Gustavus Vasa, Esq; and all the never-enough-to be admir'd, inimitable, and incomparable authors of that famous, excellent, and fine new patriot play, call'd, The deliverer of his country. Which lately narrowly escap'd being acted.

pp. [1–3] 4–35 [36 (bl.)]   L
Printed for R. Swan, near Charing-Cross   [1739]

3831 *THE HISTORY of the life and actions of Gustavas Vasa, deliverer of his country. Recommended to the spectators of a tragedy on that subject, now in rehearsal at the Theatre-Royal in Drury-Lane. Extracted from the best historians.

                                                     MH
[Roberts]   1739

3832 IMPARTIAL HAND, AN, *pseud.* of Samuel Johnson. A compleat vindication of the licensers of the stage, from the malicious and scandalous aspersions of Mr. Brooke, author of Gustavus Vasa. With a proposal for making the office of licenser more extensive and effectual. By an impartial hand.

pp. [3–4] 5–31 [32]; lacks half-title page   L
C. Corbett   1739

> *A sarcastic defence by Dr. Johnson — Lowe. Copy with a half-title page recorded by Courtney. Published May. Courtney, p. 10. According to R. W. Chapman (Oxford Bibliographical Society Proceedings & Papers Vol V 1936–1939, Oxford, 1940), p. 124, "there can be little doubt" that this pamphlet "was suppressed."*

Brown, *Dr* John. *Athelstan*

D.L. 27 February 1756.

3833 CRITICAL REMARKS on *The tragedy of Athelstan.* With rules necessary to be observed by all dramatic poets. By the author of *The state-farce.*

pp. [1–2] 3–36   L
Mary Cooper   1756

> *Very critical of the play and abusive of the way in which it was acted — Lowe.*

Browning, Robert. *A Blot in the 'Scutcheon*

D.L., 11 February 1843.

3834 [HUGHES, CHAS., *ed.*] A SOUVENIR of the performance of Browning's tragedy, "A Blot in the 'Scutcheon," Manchester, March 27, 1893.

pp. [*32*], illus. E

[Manchester: printed by Richard Gill for presentation]
[1893]

The performance was given before the Convocation of Victoria University by members of Calvert and Helmsley's company with the assistance of Martin Harvey. The souvenir includes the prologue, written by Walter Raleigh, and a criticism by A. W. Ward.

Bucke, Charles. *The Italians*

D.L., 3 April 1819. *The play of* The Italians *had been submitted to the Committee of Drury Lane Theatre, accepted, advertised to be produced, and put in rehearsal. Edmund Kean was cast for Manfredi, and expressed himself highly delighted with the part; but, for various reasons, the production was delayed. Before it was brought forward, Kean made a very discreditable exhibition in a play by Miss Porter entitled* Switzerland, *and Mr. Bucke withdrew his play, declining to intrust his chief character to Kean. The piece was, however, produced on April 3, 1819, with H. Kemble as Manfredi, and only played twice. Genest says it was worthy of a better fate, but that Kean's partisans were determined to damn it. A seventh edition was printed in May 1819, the personal altercation between Bucke and Kean making it sell rapidly. Genest notes that Bucke's four prefaces are well worth reading — Lowe. Hillebrand pp. 182–184.*

3835 [BUCKE, CHARLES.] THE ITALIANS; or the fatal accusation: a tragedy. With a preface; containing the correspondence of the author with the committee of Drury Lane Theatre; P. Moore, Esq. M.P.; and Mr. Kean. By the author of "The philosophy of nature."

pp. [i–v] vi–xxvi [27–29] 30–112 L

G. and W. B. Whittaker 1819

3836 ———second edition
pp. [i–v] vi–xxvi [27–29] 30–112 L
G. and W. B. Whittaker 1819

3837 ———fifth edition
pp. [i–v] vi–xxxiv, [27–29] 30–112 L
G. and W. B. Whittaker 1819

With the prefaces to the first and third editions.

3838 ———seventh edition
pp. [i–v] vi–l, [27–29] 30–112 L
G. and W. B. Whittaker 1819

With the prefaces to the first, third, sixth and seventh editions.

3839 ———The Italians; or the fatal accusation: a tragedy. With the prefaces to the first, third, sixth, seventh, and eighth editions. By Charles Bucke. A new edition.

pp. [i–v] vi–l, ²[iii] iv–viii, [27–29] 30–112 L
G. and W. B. Whittaker 1820

3840 C., *pseud.* The assailant assailed. Being a vindication of Mr. Kean, by C. Author of letters on the Portland Vase, in the *Morning Chronicle* and the Antijacobin poetry of the *New Times.*

pp. [i–iii] iv–v [vi] [7] 8–35 [36 (errata)] DFo
Fearman's Public Library 1819

Dated 2nd April 1819. A defence of Kean.

3841 ———second edition
pp. [i–iii] iv–v [vi] [7] 8–39 [40]; on t.p. "Anti-Jacobin" L
Fearman's Public Library 1819

With additions.

3842 A DEFENCE of Edmund Kean, Esq. being a reply to Mr. Buck's preface, and remarks on his tragedy of the *Italians.*

pp. [1–5] 6–42 [43–44 (bl.)] MH
John Lowndes [1819]

Preface dated 26 March 1819. See Hillebrand, p. 183.

3843 FRIEND TO JUSTICE, A, *pseud.* *A reply to the defence of Mr. Kean. By a friend to justice.
MH
1819

3844 LOVER OF HARMONY, A, *pseud.* A letter to a friend of Edmund Kean, Esq. with hints on the possibility of a reconciliation between Mr. Buck and Mr. Kean. By a lover of harmony.

pp. [2] [1] 2–42 DFo
Printed by E. Spragg for the author 1819

Buckstone, John Baldwin. *The Green Bushes*
Adelphi, 27 January 1845.

3845 ADELPHI THEATRE. A thorough hit!!! The green bushes; or, a hundred years ago, is published in 'Webster's National Acting Drama,' Suffolk St., Pall Mall East, and may be had of all booksellers. Price 1s. Opinions of the press.

bs., illus.; ptd. in black and red MH
W. S. Johnson, Nassau Steam Press [1845]

Bunn, Alfred, and Michael William Balfe.
The Bohemian Girl

D.L., 27 November 1843.

3846 HALL, C. F. C. F. Hall's Bohemian girl. The pet of Balfe and Bunn.

pp. [1–3] 4–12   L

To be had of Mr. T. H. Lacy and of the author   [1843?]

A satire on the opera.

Byron, *Lord* George Gordon. *Marino Faliero*

D.L., 25 April 1821.

3847 *A LETTER to R. W. Elliston on the injustice of his conduct in representing Lord Byron's tragedy of Marino Faliero.   MH

                            1821

This play was produced at Drury Lane, against Byron's wish, on 25th April 1821. It was not repeated till the 30th April, owing to an injunction from the Court of Chancery — Lowe.

3848 THEATRE ROYAL, DRURY-LANE. Thursday, April 26, 1821.

bs.   MB

[London]   1821

Begins Lord Byron's Tragedy of Marino Faliero, was received, last Night, with the Applause and Acclamation. . . .
Announces suspension of performances because of an injunction in chancery.

—— *Sardanapalus*

D.L., 10 April 1834. *See no. 2535 above.*

Byron, Henry James. *Our Boys*

Vaudeville, 16 January 1875. *See no. 1562 above.*

Callista

Unacted. Published 1731.

3849 [CHAMBERLE(I)N, PETER (or PAUL?)] THE PERSPECTIVE, or Calista dissected. To which are prefixed, A lock and key to the late opera of Calista.

pp. [2] i–v [vi], 1–8   L

J. Dicks   1731

Callista was published in 1731, but not performed. A contemporary manuscript note on this copy reads: "N.B. Y^e play of Calista said to be offer'd to ye New House — not offer'd at all — a puff. . . ."

Cibber, Colley. *The Careless Husband*

D.L., December 1704.

3850 EARL, THOMAS *Number IV of the Country Correspondent: or, the stage-monitor. [To be continued occasionally.] By Thomas Earl, Esq.

                           DFo

                    14 Aug 1739

The theatrical matter in this number consists chiefly of a notice of the forthcoming production of The Careless Husband *at Covent Garden — Lowe. On 21 August, 'At the particular Desire of several Persons of Quality' (LS, pt. 3, pp. 780–781).*

—— *The Non-Juror*

D.L., 6 December 1717.

Cibber's "Non-Juror" . . . was written in favour of the Hanoverian succession, and was vehemently attacked by the Jacobites and Nonjurors. Rowe wrote the prologue, which was very abusive of Nonjurors — Lowe.

3851 [POPE, ALEXANDER?] A CLUE to the comedy of *The Non-juror.* With some hints of consequence relating to that play. In a letter to N. Rowe, Esq; poet laureat to His Majesty.

pp. [1–4] 5–25 [26–28 (advts.)]   L

E. Curll   1718

Advertised 15 February — Straus. The half-title reads: "A letter to Mr. Rowe concerning The Non-Juror" *(Rowe wrote the prologue to the play). On the pro-Hanoverian politics of the play see Loftis,* Politics, *pp. 72, 85–86; on the meaning of this Clue, see Barker, pp. 205–206. The Clue is claimed by Curll to be by Alexander Pope, in an advertisement and in the second edition, and this claim is virtually allowed by G. Sherburn,* The Early Career of Alexander Pope, *Oxford, 1934, pp. 199–200. Griffith Add. 90 a.*

3852 ——The plot discover'd: or [continues as in no. 3851]. The second edition.

pp. [1–4] 5–25 [26–28 (advts.)]   L

E. Curll   1718

Advertised 25th March. The half-title reads: "A clue to The Non-Juror". *The verso of the half-title contains four lines of verse to Pope, attributing the work to him. Griffith Add. 90 b.*

3853 ——*[another issue]

pp. 25

E. Curll   1718

The title begins, "The plot discover'd." Advertised 18 February — Sherburn, Early Career, *pp. 199–200.*

3854 THE COMEDY call'd *The Non-juror.* Shewing the particular scenes wherein that hypocrite is concern'd. With remarks, and a key, explaining the characters of that excellent play.

pp. [1–4] 5–23 [24 ("The key")]   L

J.L.   1718

3855 GAY, JOSEPH, *pseud. of* John Durant Breval. A compleat key to *The Non-juror*. Explaining the characters in that play, with observations thereon. By Mr. Joseph Gay.

pp. [3–4] 5–26 [27–28 (advts.)] L
E. Curll 1718

Advertised 6 January — Straus.

3856 ——†the second edioion [*sic*]

pp. [1–4] 5–24 L
E. Curll 1718

Advertised 8 January — Straus. A reissue of the first edition.

3857 ——the third edition

pp. [8] [1–4] 5–26, lacks [27–28 (advts.)] E
E. Curll 1718

Advertised 15 February — Straus. A reissue of the first edition.

3858 A LASH for the Laureat: or an address by way of satyr; most humbly inscrib'd to the unparallel'd Mr. Rowe, on occasion of a late insolent prologue to the Non-Juror.

pp. [4] 1–8 L
J. Morphew 1718

A furious attack on Rowe on account of his prologue — Lowe.

3859 NON-JUROR, A, *pseud*. The Theatre-Royal turn'd into a mountebank's stage. In some remarks upon Mr. Cibber's quack-dramatical performance, called *The Non-Juror*. By a non-juror.

pp. [2] 1–38 MH
John Morphew 1718

3860 †SOME CURSORY REMARKS on the play call'd the Non-Juror, written by Mr. Cibber. In a letter to a friend.

pp. [2] 5–29 [30] L
William Chetwood 1718

Dated from Button's Coffee-House and signed "H.S." Very laudatory — Lowe.

3861 *A VINDICATION of a certain Middlesex Justice ... from ... the Per-Juror.

1718
STR.

—— ***Papal Tyranny in the Reign of King John***

C.G., 15 February 1744/5. *Cibber's mangling of 'King John' — Lowe.*

3862 A LETTER TO COLLEY CIBBER, Esq; on his transformation of King John.

pp. [2] 5–48 LGk
M. Cooper 1745

—— ***The Provok'd Husband***

D.L., 10 January 1728/9. *Adapted from Vanbrugh's A journey to London.*

3863 A JOURNEY TO LONDON. Being part of a comedy written by the late Sir John Vanbrugh, Knt. and printed after his own copy: which (since his decease) has been made an intire play, by Mr. Cibber, and call'd *The provok'd husband, &c.*

pp. [1–5] 6–51 [52 (bl.)] L
John Watts 1728

The Provok'd Husband, by Vanbrugh and Cibber, was produced at Drury Lane 10th January 1728; and though Cibber's Nonjuror enemies tried to condemn it, was very successful. This tract shows how much of the play was written by Vanbrugh — Lowe. Published 31st January 1728 — Barker. See Barker pp. 141–149.

3864 ——[another edition]

pp. [3–5] 6–58; pl.; t.p. in red and black L
John Watts 1735

3865 *REFLECTIONS on the principal characters in the Provoked Husband.

London 1728

Recorded but not seen by Lowe.

Collins, Wilkie. *The Woman in White*

Olympic, 9 October 1871.

3866 THE WOMAN IN WHITE, (altered from the novel for performance on the stage), by Wilkie Collins. Produced at the Olympic Theatre, Monday, October 9th, 1871. Specimens of criticism extracted from notices of "The Woman in White," in the press.

pp. [1] 2–16; head-title; ptd. cover, illus. L
[London: W. F. Johnson, printer] [1871]

On cover: Presentation copy.

3867 vacant

Colman, George, *the elder. The Jealous Wife*

D.L., 12 December 1761.

3868 GEORGE COLMAN, ESQ; analysed; being a vindication of his *Jealous wife*, against his malicious aspersions. With a dedication to the celebrated Philobiblian.

pp. [2] [1–7] 8–50 [51 (postscript), 52 (bl.)]   L
J. Scott   1761

This tract seems to be a burlesque attack on the Jealous Wife, *in banter of the critical reviewers* — Lowe. *Dedication signed:* "Witt. Criticism". *Several copies (L, E) attribute this work, in manuscript, to* "J.M."

3869 ——the second edition
pp. [4] [1–7] 8–50 [51 (postscript) 52 (bl.)]   L
J. Scott   1761

3870 ——and a key, by the author, never before printed. The second edition.
pp. [2] [1–7] 8–48 [49] [50–51 (a key) 52 (bl.)]   L
J. Scott   1761

——*The Spleen; or, Islington Spa*
D.L., 24 February 1776.

3871 [RUBRICK, JOHN, *pseud.*] ⋆THE SPLEEN: or, the offspring of folly. A lyri-comi-tragic tale. In four cantos. Cum notis variorum. Dedicated to George Colman, Esq. Author of The Spleen, a comic piece, performed with wonderful success at Drury-Lane Theatre.
    1776

Satirical frontispiece. Dedication signed John Rubrick — Lowe. *Rubrick is a character in* The Spleen.

——*The Taylors*
For Colman's adaptation, see nos. 4049–4052.

Colman, George, *the younger.* **The Iron Chest**
Haymarket, 29 Aug 1796. *See nos. 3189–3192.*

Cooke, Thomas. *The Battle of the Poets*
Haymarket, 30 November 1730.

3872 ⋆THE CANDIDATES for the bays. A poem. In which notice is taken of the Battle of the Poets as acted at the new theatre.
A. Moore   1730

Morning Chronicle, *30 December* — Foxon.

Cowley, *Mrs.* **Hannah.** *Albina, Countess Raimond*
Haymarket, 31 July 1779.

3873 COWLEY, *Mrs.* [HANNAH]. Albina, Countess Raimond; a tragedy, by Mrs. Cowley: as it is performed at the Theatre-Royal in the Hay-Market.
pp. [4] [i–ii] iii–viii [ix–xii], [1] 2–84   L
J. Dodsley; R. Faulder; L. Davis; T. Becket; W. Owen; T. Lowndes, and G. Kearsley; W. Davis; S. Crowder, and T. Evans; Messrs. Richardson and Urquhart. 1779

The preface relates a series of real or supposed injuries done by Sheridan and Harris to Mrs. Cowley. She insinuates, apparently, that the play had been shown by the managers to Miss Hannah More, who had stolen from it parts of Percy *and* The fatal falsehood. *The two ladies engaged in a war in the newspapers* — Lowe.

3874 ——the second edition
pp. [4] [i] ii–ix [x–xii], [1] 2–84   L
J. Dodsley; R. Faulder; [as for the first edition] 1779

Crisp, Samuel. *Virginia*
D.L., 25 February 1754.

3875 [CRISP, SAMUEL?] THE STORY on which the new tragedy, call'd *Virginia*, now in rehearsal at the Theatre Royal in Drury Lane, is founded.
pp. [2] [5] 6–26   DFo
Printed and sold by W. Reeve   1754

Daly, Augustin. *Leah, the Jewish maiden*
Adelphi, 1 October 1863. *See no. 2426.*

Dennis, John. *The Invader of his Country*
D.L., 11 November 1719.

3876 A SCHOOLBOY. A critick no wit: or, remarks on Mr. Dennis's late play, called The invader of his country. In a letter from a school-boy, to the author.
pp. [1–3] 4–29 [30]   L
J. Roberts   1720 [*for* 1719]

Dennis's alteration of Coriolanus, *with the above title, was a failure, deservedly* — Lowe. *This pamphlet "possibly instigated by Cibber", published 1 December 1719* — Hooker, II, 474.

Descent of Orpheus
The Cockpit, 1661.

3877 ⋆THE DESCRIPTION of the great machines, of the Descent of Orpheus into Hell, presented by the French comedians at the Cock-pit in Drury Lane. The argument taken out of the tenth and eleventh books of Ovid's Metamorphosis.
    O
[London]: Robert Crofts   [1661]

Wing O 656. A French comedy was performed at the Cockpit on Friday 30 August 1661. Rugg's Diurnal (end of August) referring to the Duchess of York's players, speaks of them as the French players (Nicoll, I 41; LS, pt. 1, p. 33).

Didone Abbandonata da Enea
King's, 17 December 1726. *See no. 867.*

Dodsley, Robert. *Cleone*

C.G., 2 December 1758.

3878 HILL, JOHN. *An account of the new tragedy of Cleone.

1758

R. Straus, Robert Dodsley (*1910*).
Garrick had rejected Cleone *and put on Hill's* The Rout. *He was later accused of sending Hill to watch* Cleone *and write against it.*

Dryden, John. *The Conquest of Granada*

Theatre Royal, Bridges Street, December 1670 (Part I), January 1670/1 (Part II). *See also nos. 3696, 4024, 4025.*

3879 [LEIGH, RICHARD?] THE CENSVRE of the rota. On Mr Driden's *Conquest of Granada.*

pp. [*2*] 1–21 [22 (bl.)]   L
Oxford: Fran. Oxlad junior   1673

Macdonald *174.*

3880 A DESCRIPTION of the Academy of the Athenian Virtuosi: with a discourse held there in vindication of Mr. Dryden's *Conquest of Granada;* against the author of the *Censure of the Rota.*

pp. [*2*] 1–35 [36 (postscript) 37 (errata) 38 (bl.)]   L
Maurice Atkins   1673

Macdonald *177.*

3881 *THE FRIENDLY VINDICATION of Mr. Dryden from *The Censure of the Rota* by his cabal of wits.

pp. [*2*] 1–17 [18 (bl.)]   O
Cambridge   1673

Macdonald *175.*

3882 [BLOUNT, CHARLES.] MR. DREYDEN VINDICATED, in a reply to *The friendly vindication of Mr. Dreyden.* With reflections on the Rota.

pp. [*2*] 1–13 [14 (bl.)]   L
T.D.   1673

Macdonald *176.*

Dryden, John and Nathaniel Lee. *The Duke of Guise*

D.L., 30 November or 1 December 1682.

3883 DRYDEN [JOHN]. The vindication: or the parallel of the French Holy-League, and the English League and Covenant, turn'd into a seditious libell against the King and His Royal Highness, by Thomas Hunt and the authors of the *Reflections upon the pretended parallel in the play called* The Duke of Guise. Written by Mr. Dryden.

pp. [*2*] 1–60; lacks first leaf (bl.)   L
Jacob Tonson   1683

Macdonald *130. The play was banned on 18 July 1682 and approved by the king on 29 October.*

3884 AN EPODE to his worthy friend Mr. John Dryden, to advise him not to answer two malicious pamphlets against his tragedy called, The Duke of Guise.

pp. [*2*]   L
Printed by J. Grantham   1683

Macdonald *224.*

3885 [SHADWELL, THOMAS.] SOME REFLEC-TIONS upon the pretended parallel in the play called The Duke of Guise, in a letter to a friend.

pp. [*2*] 1–25 [26]; lacks first and last leaves   L
Francis Smith, sen.   1683

Macdonald *222.*

3886 THE TRUE HISTORY of the Duke of Guise. Extracted out of Thuanus, Mezeray, Mr. Aubeny's Memoirs, and the Journal of the reign of Henry the Third of France. Published for the undeceiving such as may perhaps be imposed upon by Mr. Dryden's late tragedy of the Duke of Guise. Together with some remarks upon the same.

pp. [*8*] 1–30; lacks last leaf (bl.)   L
Printed and are to be sold by R. Baldwin   1683

Macdonald *223.*

D'Urfey, Thomas. *Love for Money*

D.L., January? 1691.

3887 WIT FOR MONEY: or, Poet Stutter: a dialogue between Smith, Johnson, and Poet Stutter. Containing reflections on some late plays; and particularly, on *Love for money, or, the boarding-school.*

pp. [*6*] 1–30   L
S. Burgis   1691

'Poet Stutter' is intended for Durfey — Lowe. Dedication is by "Sir Critick Catcall". Wing W 3136 A.

——— *The Marriage-Hater Match'd*

D.L., January 1692.

3888 D'URFEY, THO[MAS]. The marriage-hater match'd; a comedy. Acted at the Theatre Royal by Their Majesties Servants. Written by Tho. D'Urfey, Gent.

pp. [*12*] 1–54 [55–56 (Prologue and Song)]   L
Richard Parker; and Sam. Briscoe   1692

3889 ———*[another issue]

pp. [*12*] 1-54 [55-56 (Prologue and Song)]   MH
Richard Bentley   1692

  Wing D 2749.

3890 ———[another edition] The marriage-hater match'd: a comedy acted at the Theatre Royal by Their Majesties Servants. Written by Tho. D'Urfey, Gent.

pp. [*10*] 1-31 [*2*] 32-54 [55-56]   LVA
R. Bentley; R. Parker; Sam. Briscoe   1693

  Wing D 2750. *Prefixed is* A letter to Mr. D'Urfey, occasion'd by his play called the Marriage-Hater Match'd, *signed Charles Gildon, praising this as the best of his plays. "It is really a capital piece"— Lowe.*

The Fall of Mortimer
Haymarket, 12 May 1731. *By William Hatchett?*

3891 THE HISTORY of Mortimer, being a vindication of *The fall of Mortimer*. Occasioned by it's having been presented as a treasonable libel.

pp. [1-2] 3-27 [28 (advts.)]   L
J. Millan   1731

  Apparently by the author of the revival of the play.

3892 REMARKS on an historical play, called, The fall of Mortimer. Shewing wherein the said play may be term'd a libel against the present administration.

pp. [1-2] 3-24   L
E. Rayner   [1731]

  The Fall of Mortimer, *"alter'd from Mountfort's*[?] Edward III*", was produced at the Haymarket 12th May 1731; it is said by Lowndes to be by Hatchett (William Hatchett?). For the reception of the play and its political implications see LS, pt. 3, pp. xlix and 148, and Loftis, Politics pp. 105–106.*

3893 ———the second edition

pp. [1-2] 3-24   L
E. Rayner   [1731]

Fenton, Elijah. Mariamne
L.I.F., 22 February 1722.

3894 THE HISTORY of Herod and Mariamne; collected and compil'd from the best historians, and serving to illustrate the fable of Mr. Fenton's tragedy of that name.

pp. [1-9] 10-75 [76 (bl.)]   L
Thomas Corbet   1723

3895 ———the second edition

pp. [1-9] 10-75 [76 (bl.)]   L
Thomas Corbet   1723

  Contemporary MS note, in a copy of the second edition, reads: written by Mr. John Slide and revised by Mr. Theobald — STR.

3896 THE UNHAPPY LOVES of Herod and Mariamne, introductory to Mr. Fenton's new tragedy of that name, now acting at the Theatre Royal in Lincolns Inn Fields.

pp. [*2*] 1-19 [20]; t.p. in red and black   L
T. Payne   1723

Fielding, Henry. Miss Lucy in Town
D.L., 6 May 1742.

3897 A LETTER to a noble lord, to whom it belongs. Occasioned by a representation at the Theatre Royal in Drury-Lane, of a farce, called *Miss Lucy in town*.

pp. [*4*] 1-20   L
T. Cooper   1742

  Fielding's farce Miss Lucy in town *was produced at Drury Lane 6th May 1742, and banned by the Lord Chamberlain shortly afterwards.*

Fitzball, Edward. The Flying Dutchman
Adelphi, 1 January 1827. *See no. 1521.*

Foote, Samuel. The Knights
Haymarket, 3 April 1749.

3898 A NEW SCENE for the comedy called *The Knights*. Or, fresh tea for Mr. Foote.

pp. [1-4] 5-16   L
Printed by J. Scott   1758

  A letter to the "editor" is addressed "Dear Jack" and dated 1 March 1758. Foote's The Knight *was first performed at the Haymarket 3rd April 1749, and there were performances in January and February 1758.*

3899 ———*second edition

pp. 16   1758

STR.

———The Minor
Crow Street, Dublin, 28 January 1760; Haymarket, 28 June 1760. *See BIOGRAPHY nos. 2776–2792 (Foote); THEATRE OUT OF LONDON nos. 2797–2803 (Edinburgh).*

———A Trip to Calais
Haymarket, 19 August 1776. *See nos. 2805–2807.*

Francklin, Thomas. The Earl of Warwick
D.L., 13 December 1766.

3900 A LETTER from the rope-dancing monkey in the Hay-Market, to the acting monkey of Drury-Lane, on *The Earl of Warwick.*

pp. [1–2] 3–48   L

J. Pridden   1767

This pamphlet is sometimes ascribed to Paul Hiffernan, who apparently had two years earlier adapted a tragedy The Earl of Warwick *from La Harpe's* Comte de Warwick.

Frowde, Philip. *The Fall of Saguntum*

L.I.F., 16 January 1726/7.

3901 THE HISTORY OF SAGUNTUM, and its destruction by Hannibal: extracted from the antient historians and poets, for the illustration of a tragedy call'd *The Fall of Saguntum.* In a letter to a lady of quality.

pp. [4] [1] 2–59 [60]   L

Printed and sold by J. Roberts   1727

Letter dated 2 Jan 1726 and initialled A.B.

Garrick, David. *The Guardian*

D.L., 3 February 1759. See no. 2867.

——Lethe

D.L., 15 April 1740. See also no. 2844.

3902 *LETHE* REHEARS'D: or, a critical discussion of the beauties and blemishes of that performance, interspersed with occasional remarks upon dramatick satires in general, as well as on some that have been best received in particular. The whole in a free conversation amongst several persons of distinction.

pp. [2] [1] 2–52   L

J. Roberts   1749

Garrick's Lethe *was revived at Drury Lane 2 January 1749.* Lethe Rehearsed *was advertised 1 February 1749 —* LS.

Gay, John. *Achilles*

C.G., 10 February 1732/3.

3903 BURNET, [ALEXANDER]. Achilles dissected: being a compleat key of the political characters in that new ballad opera, written by the late Mr. Gay. An account of the plan upon which it is founded. With remarks upon the whole. By Mr. Burnet. To which is added, The first satire of the second book of Horace, imitated in a dialogue between Mr. Pope and the ordinary of Newgate.

pp. [2] [1] 2–30   L

W. Mears   1733

*The key, a parody of political interpretations of plays, is in the form of a letter to "Lady P****", dated Feb. 12, and signed "Atex* [sic] *Burnet". The dialogue is dated Feb. 26 and is signed "Guthry". On this pamphlet, see Loftis, Politics, p. 111.*

——*The Beggar's Opera*

L.I.F., 29 January 1727/8. See also BIOGRAPHY: nos. 2746–2752 (Fenton); also nos. 868, 1720, 2394, 2590, 2668, 2957, 3602.

3904 ★THE STAGE MEDLEY. Representing the polite tast [*sic*] of the town & the matchless merits of poet G——, Polly Peachum & Captn. Macheath.

bs.; illus.

                                              [1728]

Schultz.

3905 [BULLOCK, CHRISTOPHER.] WOMAN'S REVENGE: or, a match in Newgate. A comedy. As it is acted at the Royal Theatre in Lincoln's-Inn-Fields. The second edition. To which is added, A compleat key to the Beggar's Opera, by Peter Padwell of Padington, Esq;

pp. [8] [1] 2–80; pl. [front.]   L

J. Roberts   1728

An introductory letter to "Miss Polly Peachum", in which "brother Bullock's" play, first published in 1715, is said to be the source of The Beggar's Opera, *is signed "Peter Padwell". The dedication by the author of the play, Christopher Bullock, is to James Spiller, who originally played the part of Padwell, a character in the play. The "compleat key" has the head-title "A key to* The Beggar's Opera. *In a letter to Caleb Danvers, Esq." and is signed "Phil. Harmonicus"; it was also published in the* Craftsman, *February 17, 1728. "To Miss Polly Peachum, a town pastoral . . . By J.W. of Cheapside, linnen-draper", and "Newgate's garland: being a new ballad" follow the key. On the letter to D'Anvers, see Loftis, Politics pp. 95–96. See also Schultz, pp. 181–182, etc.*

3906 ★A SATYRICAL POEM: or, The Beggar's Opera dissected.

pp. [1–3] 4–8   MH

J. Welford   1729

Morning Chronicle, 1 April 1729 — Foxon.

3907 MILES, WILLIAM AUGUSTUS. A letter to Sir John Fielding, Knt. occasioned by his extraordinary request to Mr. Garrick for the suppression of the Beggars Opera. To which is added a Postscript to D. Garrick, Esq.; by William Augustus Miles.

pp. [1–5] 6–44   MH

J. Bell   1773

Dated 18 September. Sir John Fielding told the magistrates that The Beggar's Opera *"never was represented on the stage without creating an additional number of real thieves" —* Gentleman's Magazine, *September 1773. See further, Schultz, pp. 244–249.*

3908 ——*second edition. With additions.
                                                    1773
  STR.

——*The Captives*

D.L., 15 January 1723.

3909 HARRISON, ELIZABETH. A letter to Mr. John
Gay, on his tragedy, call'd, The Captives. To which is
annex'd, A copy of verses to her Royal Highness, the
Princess. By Elizabeth Harrison.

pp. [6] 1–18   L
Printed for the author   1724

  *Very favourable to the play — Lowe. Letter dated
January 21 1724.*

——*Three Hours after Marriage*

D.L., 16 January 1716/7. *Written in collaboration with
Pope and Arbuthnot*

3910 THE DRURY-LANE MONSTER. Humbly
inscrib'd to the old woman in Hand-Alley.

bs.   L
J. Roberts   [1717]

  Rothschild *931.*

3911 A LETTER TO MR. JOHN GAY, concerning
his late farce, entitled, A comedy.

pp. [4] [1–2] 3–35 [36 (bl.)]   L
Sold by J. Roberts   1717

  *The dedication to Wilks, Cibber, and Booth is signed
"Timothy Drub".*

3912 PARKER, E[DWARD]. A complete key to the
new farce, call'd *Three Hours after Marriage*. With an
account of the authors. By E. Parker, Philomath.

pp. [1–2] 3–14   MH
Printed and sold by E. Berrington   1717

  This copy of Parker's Complete key *is without a
catchword on p. 14, and was apparently issued by itself.
All the other copies seen have a catchword "A" on p. 14
linking them to copies of John Dennis'* A true character
of Mr. Pope, &c. *with which they were apparently
issued and are now bound.*

3913 ——[a reissue]

pp. [1–2] 3–14, ²3–18   L
Printed and sold by E. Berrington   1717

  With A true character of Mr. Pope, *by John Dennis,
first published May 1716.*

——*The What d'ye Call it?*

D.L., 23 February 1714/5.

3914 [GRIFFIN, BENJAMIN and LEWIS THEO-
BALD.] A COMPLETE KEY to the last new farce
The what d'ye call it. To which is prefix'd a hypercritical
preface on the nature of burlesque, and the poets design.

pp. [8] 1–32   L
James Roberts   1715

  *"The what d'ye call it," a tragi-comi-pastoral farce, by
John Gay, was a burlesque on the absurdities of some of
the tragedies then popular. It was extremely successful,
and "A complete key" is an attack on it — Lowe.*

Gentleman, Francis. *Sejanus*

Acted at Bath, 1751?.

3915 GENTLEMAN, [FRANCIS]. Sejanus, a tragedy.
As it was intended for the stage. With a preface,
wherein the manager's reasons for refusing it are set
forth. By Mr. Gentleman.

pp. [i–ii] iii–xv [xvi], 1–62   L
R. Manby and H. S. Cox   1752 [for 1751]

  *This is an alteration of Ben Jonson's tragedy. It was not
produced in London, but was, says the* Biographia
Dramatica, *acted at Bath with some degree of applause
— Lowe. Published 26 November 1751 — LS.*

Glover, Richard. *Boadicia*

D.L., 1 December 1753.

3916 FEMALE REVENGE: or, the British amazon:
exemplified in the life of Boadicia . . . The propriety of
Boadicia's character, as represented by the poet critically
examined. Calculated to instruct the readers of this
celebrated tragedy, in the true history of one of the
most memorable transactions recorded in the British
annals; and to shew wherein poetical fiction has deviated
from real facts.

pp. [1–2] 3–32   DFo
M. Cooper; W. Reeve, and C. Sympson   1753

3917 [PEMBERTON, H.] SOME FEW REFLEC-
TIONS on the tragedy of Boadicia.

pp. [4] 1–14   DFo
R. and J. Dodsley; and M. Cooper   1753

  Glover's successful play — Lowe.

3918 MILLS, CRISP, *pseud.* of Christlob Mylius.
A letter to Mr. Richard Glover on occasion of his
tragedy of Boadicia. By Crisp Mills.

pp. [2] [1] 2–51 [52]   L
A. Linde   1754

  *Praises it as a poem rather than as a play — Lowe.
The Letter, by the German visitor Mylius, was probably
translated from the German by Charles Macklin, according
to J. A. Kelly,* German Visitors to English Theatres
in the Eighteenth Century *(1936).*

3919 RIDER, W[ILLIAM]. A comment on Boadicia, with remarks on Mills's Letter. To which is added, a prologue, to be spoke at its revival. By W. Rider, A.B. late scholar of Jesus College, Oxon.

pp. [2] [1] 2–22   DFo
J. Fuller   1754

> *Very favourable — Lowe.*

3920 A SHORT HISTORY of Boadicea, the British queen. Being the story on which the new tragedy, now in rehearsal at the Theatre Royal in Drury Lane, is founded. Very proper to be bound up with the play.

pp. [1–5] 6–23 [24 (bl.)]   L
Printed and sold by W. Reeve   1754

Harlequin Doctor Faustus
D.L., 26 November 1723. *By John Thurmond.*

3921 *AN EXACT DESCRIPTION of the two grand entertainments of Harlequin Doctor Faustus, with the grand Masque of the Heathen Deities, etc., as performed in grotesque characters at both theatres.

T. Payne   [1724]
STR.

> *A comparison of the two very popular pantomimes Harlequin Doctor Faustus [by John Thurmond] first performed at Drury Lane on 26 November 1723 and The Necromancer or Harlequin Doctor Faustus [by John Rich?] first performed at Lincoln's Inn Fields on 20 December 1723.*

Harlequin Good Kynge Arthur; or, the Enchanter Merlin and the Queene of Faery Land
Sadler's Wells.

3922 OPINIONS of the press of the new grand comic Christmas pantomime, entitled *Harlequin Good Kynge Arthur; or, the enchanter Merlin and the Queene of Faery-land.* Now performing at Sadler's Wells Theatre.

bs.   L
n.p.   n.d.

Harris, Augustus and Henry Pettitt. *A Run of Luck*
D.L., 28 August 1886.

3923 CROWDY, WALLACE L. *"A Run of Luck" at Drury Lane. [A critical analysis of the play] By Wallace L. Crowdy   With illustrations . . .
illus.

[Published for Drury Lane Theatre]   [1886]

> *A Run of Luck, written by Augustus Harris and Henry Pettitt, was a tremendous success. This little book is not a copy of the play, which is not published, but an account of the plot &c. — Lowe.*

Hazlewood, Colin Henry. *Lady Audley's Secret*
Victoria, 25 May 1863? *From the novel by Mary Elizabeth Braddon. See no. 3031.*

Herman, Henry and William Gorman Wills *Claudian*
Princess's, 6 December 1883

3924 GODWIN   E[DWARD]   W[ILLIAM]. "Claudian." A few notes on the architecture and costume. A letter to Wilson Barrett, Esq., by E. W. Godwin, F.S.A.

pp. [1] 2–6 [7–8 (bl.)]; pls. [5]; cover serves as title   MH
n.p.   Nov., 1883

Hill, *Sir* John. *The Rout*
D.L., 20 December 1758. *See also no. 2867.*

3925 A LETTER to the hon. author of the new farce, called "The rout." To which is subjoined, An epistle to Mr. G——k, upon that, and other theatrical subjects. With an appendix; containing some remarks upon the new-revived play of "Antony and Cleopatra".

pp. [4] [1] 2–39 [40]   L
M. Thrush   1759

> *This pamphlet is a vigorous attack on The Rout which was a deplorable failure. Hill did not announce himself as the author, but gave out that it was written by a "Person of Honour". This produced the following epigram:*
> *Says a friend to the Doctor, "Pray give it about*
> *That this farce is not yours, or you'll miss of the pelf;*
> *What had come of your Nerves, or your P——x, or*
> *   your Gout,*
> *Had these embrios crawl'd forth as begot by yourself?*
> *Let your Muse, as your pamphlets, come forth*
> *   (I advise ye)*
> *Like a goddess of old, with a cloud cast upon her."*
> *"You're right," quoth the Doctor, "and more to*
> *   disguise me,*
> *I'll give myself out for a Person of Honour."*
> *   — Lowe.*
> *Antony and Cleopatra, revived at Drury Lane on 3 January 1759, was the first recorded performance since Shakespeare's own time. (LS, pt. 4, p. 680; see RES, January 1937).*

Hoadly, *Dr* Benjamin. *The Suspicious Husband*
C.G., 12 February 1746/7. *See nos. 2771–2772.*

Home, John. *Agis*
D.L., 21 February 1758.

3926 THE DRAMATIC EXECUTION of Agis.
pp. [1–2] 3–24   DFo
J. Cooke   1758

> *A hostile review.*

3927 THE HISTORY of Agis, King of Sparta, on which the new tragedy of *Agis* is founded.

pp. [1–3] 4–22 [23 (advt.) 24 (bl.)]   EU
Edinburgh: W. Gray and W. Peter   1758

Lefèvre *150.*

3928 *THE STORY of the tragedy of Agis. With observations on the play, the performance, and the reception.

pp. 15   MB
M. Cooper   1758

Agis . . . *was not a success* — Lowe.

———Douglas

Edinburgh 14 December 1756; C.G. March 1757. *See also* SCOTLAND *nos. 1860–1904 (Edinburgh);* BIO-GRAPHY *no. 3100 (Mrs. Jackson).*

3929 ENGLISH CRITIC, AN, *pseud.* A letter to Mr. David Hume, on the tragedy of Douglas; its analysis: and the charge against Mr. Garrick. By an English critic.

pp. [1–3] 4–19 [20]   E
J. Scott   1757

3930 ———[reissue] variant t.p.: date in roman numerals and on bottom line, price being omitted.   E

Critical of Hume's dedication, and of no. 3930.1 below.

3930.1 *THE TRAGEDY of Douglas analysed.
        O
J. Doughty   1757

Lefèvre *135. See also no. 3929 above.*

———The Siege of Aquileia

D.L., 21 February 1760. *See also below no. 3994.*

3931 BRICKFACE, LACK-LIMB, *pseud.* A fragment: found in the ruins of Aquileia. By Lack-limb Brickface, a half-pay ensign.

pp. [1–2] 3–16   E
[Edinburgh?]   [1760?]

Lefèvre *152.*

3932 †THE HISTORY of the sieges of Aquileia and Berwick. Being the story on which the new tragedy of Aquileia is founded, with some remarks on that play.

pp. [5] 6–26; t.p. pasted in   L
T. Kennersly   1760

Hook, Theodore. *Killing No Murder*

Haymarket, 21 August 1809.

3933 HOOK, THEODORE EDWARD. Killing no murder: a farce: in two acts, as performed at the Theatre Royal, Haymarket: together with a preface, and the scene suppressed by order of the Lord Chamberlain. Written by Theodore Edward Hook, Esq. The music by Mr. Hook, Sen.

pp. [i–iii] iv–ix [x], [1] 2–53 [54 (bl.)], misprinting 53 as "35"; t.p. headed "The second edition"   L
Samuel Tipper   1809

Mr. Larpent, the Reader of Plays, being a Methodist, caused this farce to be prohibited, because there was a scene in it in which Methodists were ridiculed. Hook cut out the prohibited scene, and inserted a passage in which Larpent was obviously held up to ridicule. This, having no reference either to politics or religion, the Licenser could not prohibit, and Hook had the satisfaction of holding up his oppressor to universal derision. The dispute was, of course, a magnificent advertisement for the farce — Lowe.

3934 ———*the fourth edition. Killing no murder: a farce: in two acts, as performed with great applause at the Theatre Royal, Haymarket: with the original preface, the scene suppressed by order of the Lord Chamberlain: and a new preface. Written by Theodore Edward Hook, Esq. The music by Mr. Hook, Sen.

        1809
Lowe.

3935 ———the fifth edition. With the original prefaces, and the scene suppressed by order of the Lord Chamberlain; written by Theodore Edward Hook, Esq.

pp. [i–iii] iv–xi [xii], [1] 2–51 [52 (advts.)], misprinting xi as "x"   L
C. Chapple   1811

3936 ———Killing no murder. A farce, in two acts: performed with great applause at the Theatres Royal: with the original prefaces, and the scene suppressed by order of the Lord Chamberlain; written by Theodore Edward Hook, Esq.

pp. [i–iii] iv–viii, [1] 2–44; t.p. headed "The sixth edition"   LGk
C. Chapple   1817

Hughes, John. *The Siege of Damascus*

D.L., 17 February 1719/20. *Hughes died the same night.*

3937 AN EXPLANATION [*sic*] of the several Arabick terms us'd in *The Siege of Damascus* written by Mr. Hughes. With a short account of the historical siege, and the life of Mahomet, as far as is necessary to the better understanding the play. Likewise a history of the ancient and present state of the city of Damascus.

pp. [1–2] 3–28   L
J. Brotherton and W. Meadows; J. Roberts; [T?] Tauncy, and A. Dodd; W. Lewis and W. Chetwood; and J. Graves.   [1720]

3938 *Al* WÁKIDI, ABU ABDO'LLAH MOHAM-MED EBN OMAR. The history of the siege of Damascus, by the Saracens, in the year 633. As it is related by Abu Abdo'llah Mohammed Ebn Omar Alwákidi, the Arabian historian. Very useful for the readers and spectators of the tragedy of *The siege of Damascus*, written by Mr. John Hughes.

pp. [1–2] 3–35 [36 (bl.)]   L

Printed and sold by J. Brotherton and W. Meadows; J. Roberts; A. Dodd; W. Lewis; and J. Graves   1720

Inchbald, *Mrs* Elizabeth. *The Wise Man of the East*

C.G., 30 November 1799. *See above no. 3052.*

Incle and Yarico

[By Mrs. Weddell]. See below no. 4060.

Ireland, William Henry. *Vortigern*

D.L., 2 April 1796. *The notorious* Vortigern, *produced at Drury Lane by Sheridan . . . This the audience had the good sense to condemn before hearing it all — Lowe. For a full account of the occasion, and the correction of Lowe's belief that the Ireland forgeries "were supposed to be done by the young William Henry Ireland; but there can be little doubt that his father, Samuel Ireland, was practically the culprit," see John Mair,* The Fourth Forger, *1938.*

3939 IRELAND [SAMUEL]. Mr. Ireland's vindication of his conduct, respecting the publication of the supposed Shakspeare MSS. Being a preface or introduction to a reply to the critical labors of Mr. Malone, in his *Enquiry into the authenticity of certain papers, &c. &c.*

pp. [i–ii] iii–iv, [1] 2–48   L

Faulder and Robson   1796

3940 IRELAND, WILLIAM HENRY. An authentic account of the Shaksperian manuscripts, &c. By W. H. Ireland.

pp. [2] [1] 2–43 [44 (bl.)]   L

J. Debrett   1796

3941 ———*[another edition]

Lowndes *and* Jaggard *record this edition of fifty copies reprinted, in imitation of the first edition, by Barker of London.*

3942 [IRELAND, SAMUEL *ed.*] MISCELLANEOUS PAPERS and legal instruments under the hand and seal of William Shakspeare: including the Tragedy of King Lear and a small fragment of Hamlet, from the original MSS. in the possession of Samuel Ireland, of Norfolk Street.

pp. [4] [1] 2–14 [15–16] [52], ²[1–2] 3–107 [108], ³1–7 [8]; pls., col. [3], plain [17=16 leaves], on printed sheets, [6] L

Egerton; White; Leigh and Sotheby; Robson and Faulder; and Sael   1796

3943 ———[another edition]

pp. [i–v] vi–xix [xx–xxiv], [28] [1–3] 4–152 155–6 [2], ²1–7 [8 (bl.)]; pl., fold., [1]   NbU

Egerton; White; Leigh and Sotheby; Robson and Faulder; Sael   1796

3944 IRELAND, SAMUEL. An investigation of Mr. Malone's claim to the character of scholar, or critic, being an examination of his *Inquiry into the authenticity.* of the Shakspeare manuscripts, &c. By Samuel Ireland.

pp. [i–iii] iv–vi, [1] 2–153 [154 (bl.) 155 (addenda, etc.) 156 (bl.)]; cancellans, pp. [1] 2   L

R. Faulder; T. Egerton; T. Payne; and Whites [1798?]

The cancellans leaf has head-title: "An investigation, &c." According to Lowe the cancellandum leaf head-title read "A reply to an Enquiry, &c." Attributed to the Shakespearean scholar Thomas Caldecott by the CBEL.

3945 [IRELAND, WILLIAM HENRY.] VORTI-GERN, an historical tragedy, in five acts; represented at the Theatre Royal, Drury Lane. And Henry the Second, an historical drama. Supposed to be written by the author of Vortigern.

pp. [2] [i–iii] iv–xi [xii], [1] 2–75 [76 (advts.)], [2], ²[i] ii–iii [iv], ²[1] 2–77 [78 (Epilogue)]   L

J. Barker; B. White; T. Egerton; R. Faulder   [1799]

Each of the plays has also a separate title-page ('Printed for J. Barker, 1799') and they were perhaps issued separately, as well as together in the form here described. With a preface by Samuel Ireland.

3946 ———[another edition] Vortigern; an historical play; with an original preface. By W. H. Ireland. Represented at the Theatre Royal, Drury Lane, on Saturday, April 2, 1796, as a supposed newly-discovered drama of Shakspeare.

pp. [2] [i] ii–xv [xvi], [1–3] 4–58; inset [front., fold.]   L

Joseph Thomas   1832

3947 IRELAND, WILLIAM HENRY. The confessions of William-Henry Ireland. Containing the particulars of his fabrication of the Shakspeare manuscripts; together with anecdotes and opinions (hitherto unpublished) of many distinguished persons in the literary, political, and theatrical world.

pp. [8] [1] 2–317 [318 (bl.) 319–335 (index) 336 (bl.)]; pls. [front., 1]   NbU

Thomas Goddard   1805

3948 ———*[another edition]

                                 1832

Lowe MS catalogue.

3949 ———*[another edition]

                                 BP
                               [1872?]

A large paper reprint of the 1805 edition, Jaggard p. 164.

————[American edition] With an introduction by Richard Grant White. New York: Bouton, 1874.

3950 BOADEN, JAMES. A letter to George Steevens, Esq. containing a critical examination of the papers of Shakspeare; published by Mr. Samuel Ireland to which are added, extracts from Vortigern.

pp. [4] [1] 2–72   GU
Martin & Bain   1796

3951 ————*second edition
pp. 72   DFo
Martin & Bain   1796

Pp. 57–72: "Extracts from Vortigern".

3952 [WOODWARD, GEORGE M.] FAMILIAR VERSES, from the ghost of Willy Shakspeare to Sammy Ireland. To which is added, Prince Robert: an auncient ballad.

pp. [1–5] 6–16   L
Richard White   1796

3953 [WALDRON, FRANCIS GODOLPHIN.] FREE REFLECTIONS on miscellaneous papers and legal instruments, under the hand and seal of William Shakspeare, in the possession of Samuel Ireland, of Norfolk-Street. To which are added, extracts from an unpublished MS. play, called the Virgin Queen. Written by, or in imitation of, Shakspeare.

pp. [1–5] 6–55 [56]   GU
F. G. Waldron   1796

Signed 'F. G. Waldron'.

3954 FRIEND TO CONSISTENCY, A, *pseud. of* John Wyatt? A comparative review of the opinions of Mr. James Boaden, (editor of the *Oracle*) in February, March, and April, 1795; and of James Boaden, Esq. (author of *Fontainville Forest*, and of *A letter to George Steevens, Esq.*) in February, 1796, relative to the Shakspeare MSS. By a friend to consistency.

pp. [2] [1] 2–59 [60 (bl.)]   L
G. Sael   [1796]

3955 MALONE, EDMOND. An inquiry into the authenticity of certain miscellaneous papers and legal instruments, published Dec. 24, MDCCXCV. and attributed to Shakspeare, Queen Elizabeth, and Henry, Earl of Southampton: illustrated by fac-similes of the genuine hand-writing of that nobleman, and of her majesty; a new fac-simile of the hand-writing of Shakspeare, never before exhibited; and other authentick documents: in a letter addressed to the Right Hon. James, Earl of Charlemont, by Edmond Malone, Esq.

pp. [i–v] vi–vii [viii], [1] 2–424 [425–428 (prospectus)];
pls., fold. I [II–III]   NbU
T. Cadell, Jun. and W. Davies   1796

Malone's copy, with MS notes for a second edition, is at L.

3956 [WHITE, JAMES.] ORIGINAL LETTERS, &c. of Sir John Falstaff and his friends; now first made public by a gentleman, a descendant of Dame Quickly, from genuine manuscripts which have been in the possession of the Quickly family near four hundred years.

pp. [i–v] vi–xxiv, [1] 2–123 [124]; pl. [front.]   L
Printed for the author; and published by Messrs. G. G. and J. Robinsons; J. Debrett; and Murray and Highley
                                                         1796

With a black letter dedication to "Master Samuel Irelaunde". Sometimes also attributed, with no good authority, to Charles Lamb, White's friend.

3957 ————Original letters, &c. of Sir John Falstaff selected from genuine mss. which have been in the possession of Dame Quickly and her descendants near four hundred years. The second edition. Dedicated to Master Samuel Irelaunde.

pp. [2] [v] vi–xxiv, [1] 2–123 [124]; pl. [front.]   L
Messrs. G. G. and J. Robinsons; J. Debrett; and Murray and Highley   1797

A reissue of the first edition.

————[American edition] Philadelphia: 1813.

3958 PHILALETHES, *pseud. of* F. Webb. Shakspeare's manuscripts, in the possession of Mr. Ireland, examined, respecting the internal and external evidences of their authenticity. By Philalethes.

pp. [4] [1] 2–34   L
J. Johnson   1796

3959 PRECIOUS RELICS; or the tragedy of Vortigern rehearsed. A dramatic piece. In two acts. Written in imitation of The critic. As performed at the Theatre-Royal, Drury-Lane.

pp. [1–7] 8–62 [63–64 (advts.)]   L
Debret, Hookham, and Clarke; White and Owen; Lee; Murray; Crosby; and Symonds   1796

Published 15th March 1796, according to Jaggard.

3960 VORTIGERN. A malevolent and impotent attack on the Shakspeare MSS. having appeared, on the eve of representation of the play of Vortigern. . . .

bs.   MH
[London]   [1796]

In answer to Malone's Enquiry, *requesting that Vortigern "may be heard with that candour that has ever distinguished a British audience."*

3961 [OULTON, WALLEY CHAMBERLAIN.] VORTIGERN UNDER CONSIDERATION; with general remarks on Mr. James Boaden's letter to George Steevens, Esq. relative to the manuscripts, drawings, seals, &c. ascribed to Shakespeare, and in the possession of Samuel Ireland, Esq.

pp. [1–3] 4–67 [68], misprinting 67 as "7"   L

H. Lowndes   1796

3962 [CHALMERS, GEORGE.] AN APOLOGY for the believers in the Shakspeare-papers, which were exhibited in Norfolk-Street.

pp. [i–iii] iv, [1] 2–628; pl. [facsim.]   GU

Thomas Egerton   1797

3963 CHALMERS, GEORGE. A supplemental apology for the believers in the Shakspeare-papers: being a reply to Mr. Malone's answer, which was early announced, but never published: with a dedication to George Steevens, F.R.S.S.A. and a postscript to T. J. Mathias, F.R.S.S.A. the author of *The pursuits of literature*. By George Chalmers, F.R.S.S.A.

pp. [i–iii] iv–viii, [1] 2–654 [655–656 (errata)]; ornament on t.p.   L

Thomas Egerton   1799

An appendix, concerning the Junius letters, was published in 1800.

3964 JUNIOR, *Mr.*, OWEN, *pseud.* of Thomas James Mathias *or of* George Hardinge. Chalmeriana: or a collection of papers literary and political, entitled, letters, verses, &c. occasioned by reading a late heavy *Supplemental apology for the believers in the Shakespeare papers* by George Chalmers, F.R.S.S.A. Arranged and published by Mr. Owen Junior, of Paper Buildings, Inner Temple; assisted by his friend and clerk, Mr. Jasper Hargrave. Reprinted for the *Morning Chronicle*, in which they first appeared. Collection the first.

pp. [i–iii] iv–viii, [1] 2–94 [95–96 (bl.)]   L

T. Becket   1800

3965 ——*[another issue]

Without the phrase "Collection the first" on the title-page. CBEL II 255.

3966 ——[another edition of No. IX of Chalmeriana] Antenor's letter to George Chalmers, Esq. F.R.S.S.A. author of . . . An apology for the believers in the Shakspeare papers, and of a postscript to that *Apology.* (a) Reprinted, May, 1800

pp. [1–5] 6–15 [16 (bl.)]; note (a) on t.p.: This *Letter* is taken from No. IX. of a collection of papers, literary and political, entitled, *Chalmeriana.*   L

[Printed by Jaques and Co]   1800

✖ Catalogue of the miscellaneous and dramatic library . . . of the late Charles Mathews . . . Added the unpublished writings and literary productions of the late Mr. William Henry Ireland, author of the Shaksperian forgeries. [1835]. *See no. 117.*

Johnson, Dr Samuel. *Irene*

D.L., 6 February 1748/9.

3967 *A CRITICISM on Mahomet and Irene.
                                                    1749
Recorded but not seen by Lowe.

3968 *AN ESSAY on tragedy, with a critical examen of Mahomet and Irene.

Title 1 leaf, ded. 2 leaves, pref. 1 leaf; pp. 37   MH

Griffiths   1749

Rather favourable in tone to Dr. Johnson. Irene, his solitary play, was produced by Garrick at Drury Lane — Lowe.

Jones, Henry Arthur. *The Middleman*

Shaftesbury Theatre, 27 August 1889. *See below PERIODICALS no. 4285.*

Jonson, Benjamin. *Sejanus*

See no. 3915.

Kelly, John. *The Levee*

Published 1741. *Banned by the Lord Chamberlain.*

3969 [KELLY, JOHN.] THE LEVEE. A farce. As it was offer'd to, and accepted for representation by the master of the old-house in Drury-Lane, but by the Inspector of Farces denied a licence.

pp. [4] [1] 2–42 [43–44 (advts.)]   L

The Society of Booksellers for Promoting Learning
                                                    1741
Banned because it attacked the political patron.

Kenrick, Dr William. *Falstaff's Wedding*

D.L., 12 April 1766.

3970 KENRICK, Dr WILLIAM. *A letter to David Garrick, Esq., on the non-performance of "Falstaff's wedding".

                                                    1772

DNB.
On Garrick's refusal to allow any further performances of Falstaff's Wedding at Drury Lane. It was staged again in 1774 ("by demand") as part of Kenrick's lectures on the School of Shakespeare.

3971 ———*[another edition]

1772

DNB.

Latter, Mrs. Mary. *The Siege of Jerusalem*
Published 1763. Unacted.

3972 [LATTER, MARY.] The siege of Jerusalem, by Titus Vespasian; a tragedy. To which is prefixed, by way of introduction, An essay on the mystery and mischiefs of stage-craft.

pp. [2] i–xxxvii [xxxviii (bl.)], [1–3] 4–87 [88]   L

C. Bathurst   1763

The essay (pp. i–xxxvii) has the head-title "Stage-craft, an essay". It was occasioned by the rejection of the play by the managers. The Essay may have been issued separately.

Lillo, George. *The Christian Hero*
D.L., 13 January 1735.

3973 A BRIEF ACCOUNT OF THE LIFE and character of George Castriot, King of Epirus and Albania, commonly called Scanderbeg. Inscribed to the spectators of *The Christian Hero*.

pp. [2] [1–2] 3–38   L

J. Roberts   1735

3974 [LILLO, GEORGE.] *THE LIFE OF GEORGE CASTRIOT, King of Epirus and Albania, commonly called Scanderbeg; on which is founded the tragedy of The Christian Hero. Being a most entertaining true history.

Edinburgh: [Ruddiman]   1735

Lowe.

———*The London Merchant*
D.L., 22 June 1731.

3975 DESCENDANT OF THE BARNWELL FAMILY, A, *pseud.* Memoirs of George Barnwell; the unhappy subject of Lillo's celebrated tragedy; derived from the most authentic source, and intended for the perusal and instruction of the rising generation. By a descendant of the Barnwell family.

pp. [1–3] 4–142 [143–144 (advts.)]; pl. [front.]   L

Harlow: printed by B. Flower: for M. Jones, London   1810

3976 ———[another edition]

pp. [1–3] 4–141 [142]   L

Sherwood, Neely, and Jones   1817

Not a reissue, but a genuinely new edition. A severely abridged edition, entitled The Life and History of George Barnwell; who from the highest Character and Credit, fell to the Lowest Depth of Vice . . ., *with a folding coloured plate, was published in London by Dean and Munday in 1820.*

Macklin, Charles. *Love à la Mode*
D.L., 12 December 1759.

3977 A SCOTSMAN'S REMARKS on the farce of *Love à la mode*, scene by scene. As it is acted at the Theatre Royal in Drury Lane.

pp. [2] [1] 2–38   L

J. Burd   1760

An attack by an infuriate Scot on Macklin's farce, in which latter the Scots are sharply satirised — Lowe. Published in June 1760—LS.

Mallet, David. *Elvira*
D.L., 19 January 1763.

3978 [BOSWELL, JAMES, *The Hon.* ANDREW ERSKINE, and GEORGE DEMPSTER.] CRITICAL STRICTURES on the new tragedy of Elvira, written by Mr. David Malloch.

pp. [1–6] 7–24   E

W. Flexney   1763

A very severe criticism — Lowe. Pottle 7.

———[American edition] (Augustan Reprint Society Publications, No. 35) Los Angeles, Cal.: Clark Memorial Library, 1952.

———*Eurydice*
D.L., 22 February 1730/1.

3979 REMARKS on the tragedy of Eurydice. In which it is endeavoured to prove the said tragedy is wrote in favour of the Pretender, and is a scurrilous libel against the present establishment.

pp. [1–4] 5–24   L

Printed for E. Rayner   1731

On this pamphlet, see Loftis, Politics, *p. 108.*

———*Mustapha*
D.L., 13 February 1738/39.

3980 *THE HISTORY of Solyman the magnificent, and his son Mustapha, inscribed to the spectators of Mustapha, a tragedy.

1739

Recorded but not seen by Lowe.

Martyn, Benjamin. *Timoleon*

D.L., 26 January 1729/30.

3981 REMARKS on the tragedy of Timoleon: wherein the beauties and errors are impartially consider'd.

pp. [2] 1–28 [29–30 (advts.)]   L

Printed for T. Corbett; H. Whitridge   [1730]

> *These remarks are addressed to Crites, and signed Philomusas. On this pamphlet and the politics of the play, see Loftis, Politics p. 108.*

Mason, William. *Caractacus*

Dublin, Crow Street, 30 March 1774: C.G., 6 December 1776.

3982 MASON, WILLIAM. ★Caractacus. A dramatic poem. Written on the model of the antient Greek tragedy. First published in the year 1759, and now altered for theatrical representation.

pp. (8), 76   MB

York: printed by A. Ward; and sold by R. Horsfield and J. Dodsley, in London   1777

> *Adapted for the stage by Mason. This edition contains for the first time a sonnet to Richard Hurd, and a letter to Thomas Harris, manager of Covent Garden Theatre.*

———*Elfrida*

C.G., 21 November 1772.

3983 [NEVILLE, THOMAS.] REMARKS on Mr. Mason's Elfrida, in letters to a friend.

pp. [1–3] 4–61 [62–64 (bl.)]   MH

J. and R. Tonson and S. Draper   1752

> *Mason's Elfrida, though published in 1752, was not produced till 1772.*

3984 HAWKINS, W. ★An essay on the antient and modern drama, occasioned by *Elfrida*.

Oxford   1758

> Chase. *There were editions of* Elfrida *in 1755 and 1757.*

Miller, *Rev.* James. *The Coffee House*

D.L., 26 January 1738.

3985 ADMIRER OF BAD COMPOSITION, AN, *pseud.* ★The pigeon-pye, or, a King's coronation, proper materials for forming an oratorio, opera, or play, according to the modern taste: to be represented in opposition to the Dragon of Wantley. By an admirer of bad composition, and author of — nothing.

                1738

> *A curious satire on, I believe, James Miller (1704–1744), author of* The Coffee House *— Lowe. Miller's The Coffee House was produced at Drury Lane, while Henry Carey's The Dragon of Wantley was playing at Covent Garden.*

Mitford, Mary Russell. *Rienzi*

D.L., 9 October 1828.

3986 [DANIEL, GEORGE.] REMARKS on Miss Mitford's tragedy of *Rienzi*. By the editor of Cumberland's British Theatre.

pp. [1–3] 4–12   L

John Cumberland   1828

> *A very favourable criticism — Lowe. Signed 'D——G'.*

Moore, Edward. *The Foundling*

D.L., 13 February 1748.

3987 A CRITICISM ON THE FOUNDLING. In a letter to the author.

pp. [2] [1] 2–18   L

M. Cooper   1748

> *For contemporary criticism, including the present item, see LS, pt. 4, p. 30.*

———*The Gamester*

D.L., 7 February 1753.

3988 THE GAMESTER, a true story; on which the tragedy of that name, now acting at the Theatre Royal in Drury-Lane, is founded. Translated from the Italian.

pp. [4] [7] 8–20   L

Printed and sold by W. Reeve   1753

———*Gil Blas*

D.L., 2 February 1751.

3989 THE ORIGINAL STORY; from which the new comedy of Gil Blas is taken.

pp. [2] [1] 2–26   L

W. Owen   [1751]

Moore, *Sir* Thomas. *Mangora, King of the Timbusians*

L.I.F., 14 December 1717.

3990 ★REFLECTIONS ON MANGORA.

                1718

> *Recorded but not seen by Lowe.*

3991 ★THE MUZZE muzzled, in answer to Reflections on Mangora.

            1719 (?1718)

Recorded but not seen by Lowe. *For a comment on the absurdity of Moore's play, see* LS, *pt. 2, p. 474.*

Morton, Thomas. *The School of Reform*

C.G., 15 January 1805. [*John*] *Emery's Tyke was one of the great impersonations of the stage* — Lowe.

3992 FEARON, JAMES PETER. Theatrical criticism. The present essay contains a candid critique of the new play, called *The school of reform; or, how to rule a husband.* Now acting at the Theatre Royal, Covent-Garden. Written by James Peter Fearon.

pp. [6] [i] ii–viii, [13] 14–50 [51 (notice about possibility of continuing such critical pamphlets) 52 (bl.)]   L

Printed and published (for the author) by Barker and Son, Dramatic Repository   1805

———*Zorinski*

Haymarket, 20 June 1795.

3993 MR. MORTON'S ZORINSKI and Brooke's Gustavus Vasa compared. Also a critique on Zorinski. As it appeared in the Morning Post and Fashionable World; with all such paragraphs as were inserted in the Oracle and True Briton, by Mr. Morton and his friends, in a weak and wild attempt to confute truth. With alterations and additions by Truth.

pp. [2] [5] 6–50   L

Printed for the author, and sold by Hookham and Carpenter   1795

Murphy, Arthur. *The Desert Island*

D.L., 24 January 1760.

3994 GENTLEMAN, A, *pseud.* *A letter to M. de Voltaire; with comparatory descants, on the extraordinary composition . . . The Desert Island: also remarks on the Tragedy of the Siege of Aquileia. By a gentleman.

?   1760

STR.

3995 *A LETTER TO MONS. DE VOLTAIRE on The Desert Island. By Arthur Murphy.

1760

Recorded but not seen by Lowe.

———*The Orphan of China*

D.L., 21 April 1759. *Adapted from Voltaire,* L'Orphelin de la Chine (1755)

3996 A LETTER from Mons. de Voltaire to the author of The orphan of China.

pp. [2] [1] 2–38 [39–41 (advt.) 42 (bl.)]   L
I. Pottinger   1759

The Necromancer, or Harlequin Doctor Faustus

L.I.F., 20 December 1723. By John Rich? See above no. 3921.

Paetus and Arria

Published 1809. By John Nicholson?

3997 [NICHOLSON, JOHN?] PAETUS AND ARRIA, a tragedy; in five acts. To which is prefixed A letter, addressed to Thomas Sheridan, Esq. on the present state of the English stage.

pp. [i–iii] iv–viii [ix–x], [1] 2–74 [75–76 (epilogue)]   L

Cambridge: J. Nicholson and Son; London: Lackington, Allen, and Co.   1809

The author was the son of the publisher (Notes and Queries, October, 1853). *The letter* ("of no importance" — Lowe) *is by the dramatist, and about* "that undiscerning system of rejection, so general at our Theatres." Stratman, *Tragedy, 4772.*

Nourjahad

English Opera House (Lyceum), 12 July 1834.

3998 NOURJAHAD, a grand Persian romance; on which is founded the melodramatic spectacle. Performed at the Theatre Royal, Drury Lane, with enthusiastic applause.

pp. [1–2] 3–18   E
G. Smith, and Co.   [1834]

Noverre, Jean Georges. *The Chinese Festival*

D.L., 8 November 1755. *See above* BIOGRAPHY (Garrick), *nos. 2853–2855.*

Otway, Thomas. *The Orphan*

Dorset Gardens, late February or 6 March 1679/80. *See nos. 2150, 3764.*

———*Venice Preserved*

Dorset Gardens, ? 9 February 1681/82. *Revived* C.G. 1751–2 *and* D.L. 1752–3.

3999 [DERRICK, SAMUEL.] THE DRAMATIC CENSOR; being remarks upon the conduct, characters, and catastrophe of our most celebrated plays. By several hands.

pp. [4] i–iii [iv], 1–80   DFo
Richard Manby; and H. S. Cox   1752

A2ʳ: *"Numb. I. The dramatic censor. Remarks upon the tragedy of Venice Preserv'd; with some observations on the performers. By Mr. Derrick".* Stratman 9. *The second number, on Cibber's* Richard III *"by Mr. Gentleman", is promised, but no further numbers are known.*

Penn, John. *The Battle of Eddington*

Haymarket, 10 May 1792.

4000 PENN, JOHN. *A reply to the strictures of the Monthly Reviewers, in February, 1797, on the tragedy of The Battle of Eddington. By J. Penn, Esq. Including both an abstract and supplement of his critical works on the drama.

1797

> Lowe. *Penn's defence of his tragedy, which was unfavourably received. For his 'critical works on the drama', see no. 902.1 above.*

Pettitt, Henry

Joint author of A Run of Luck. *See above no. 3923.*

Philips, Ambrose. *The Distrest Mother*

D.L., 17 March 1711/2. *See also above nos. 3469, 3652.*

4001 A MODEST SURVEY of that celebrated tragedy *The Distrest Mother*, so often and so highly applauded by the ingenious spectator. Enter'd according to order.

pp. [1–2] 3–52   L

Printed and sold by William Redmayne, and John Morphew   1712

———*Humphrey, Duke of Gloucester*

D.L., 15 February 1722/3.

4002 [SYMMONS, HENRY?] AN INTRODUCTION to the new tragedy, call'd, Humfrey Duke of Gloucester. Now in rehearsal, at the Theatre-Royal, in Drury-Lane. Faithfully collected from several of the most authentick English historians.

pp. 1–35 [36]   L

J. Roberts, and W. Pepper   [1723]

4003 MEMOIRS of Humphrey, Duke of Gloucester; (as they relate to the story of Mr. Phillips's tragedy of that name; and proper to be bound up with it.) In which the several characters, represented in that drama, are fully and faithfully drawn. With an account how far they were instrumental in the ruin and murther of that great good man.

pp. [2] 1–32   L

Thomas Corbett   [1723]

Phillips, Watts. *The Dead Heart*

Adelphi, 10 November 1859. *Walter Pollock's revision of the above to which the following item refers, was produced at the Lyceum, 28 September 1889.*

4004 COLEMAN, JOHN. *The truth about The Dead Heart, with reminiscences of the author and the actors thereof. With illustrations by Horace Petherick.

pp. (6) 119; illus.; ports.; pls.; autograph facsims.   MB

Drane   1890

Pinero, *Sir* Arthur Wing. *The Notorious Mrs. Ebbsmith*

Garrick, 13 March 1895.

4005 WILSON, H. SCHÜTZ. The Notorious Mrs. Ebbsmith.

pp. [1–3] 4–16   L

Bickers & Son   1895

———*The Second Mrs. Tanqueray*

St. James's, 27 May 1893.

4006 LUND, T[HOMAS] W[ILLIAM] M[AY]. "The Second Mrs. Tanqueray;" what? And why? By T. W. M. Lund, M.A.

pp. [1–3] 4–31 [32]; on the cover: "Published by request. Ninth edition."   L

Liverpool: Lee and Nightingale, printers   1894

> *Originally delivered as a sermon (Ezek. xxxiii, 7).*

4007 ———[tenth edition]

pp. [1–3] 4–31 [32]; on the cover: "Published by Request. Tenth edition."   L

Liverpool: Lee and Nightingale, printers   1894

Plowden, *Mrs.* Frances *Virginia*

D.L., 30 October 1800. *See above no. 1364.*

The Politician Reformed

Published March 1774. *By Thomas Ryder?*

4008 R., T. [RYDER, THOMAS?] AN APPEAL to the publick, from the judgment of a certain manager, with original letters: and the drama, of one act, which was refused representation. By T.R.

pp. [i–iii] iv–xiii [xiv], [2] [1] 2–32 35–40 [=38]   L

Printed for J. Bew   1774

> *The "Appeal" is so grotesquely conceived in tone, that I doubt whether this is not a piece of somewhat unintelligible humour. Genest, however, treats it seriously. The play is the "Politician Reformed" — Lowe. Published March 1774. LS., pt. 4 p. 1789. Favourable to Garrick.*

Poole, John. *Married and Single*

Haymarket, 16 July 1824.

4009 POOLE, JOHN. Married and single. A comedy. In three acts. First performed at the Theatre-Royal, Haymarket, on Friday, July 16th, 1824. To which is prefixed, an exposure of a recent little proceeding of the great director of the Theatre Royal, at the corner of Brydges Street. By John Poole, Esq.

pp. [i–v] vi–xv [xvi], [1] 2–67 [68]   L

John Miller   1824

The preface "gives a minute detail of an uninteresting difference between [Poole] and Elliston about this piece" — Genest. *The Theatre Royal mentioned in the title is the Theatre Royal, Drury Lane. John Poole's Sketches and Recollections (1835 and 1843) contains "My first tragedy", a fictitious account of his early dealings with London theatres.*

———*Paul Pry*

Haymarket, 13 September 1825. *See above no. 3238.*

Reade, Charles. *Dora*

Adelphi, 1 June 1867.

4010 READE, CHARLES. *Dora; or the history of a play.
London   1877
    CBEL.

Reed, Joseph. *Dido*

D.L., 28 March 1767. *Reed's MS "Theatrical Duplicity" (at MH) deals with his difficulties with the managers over the play.*

4011 WAPPINEER, A, *pseud.* Genius: a miscellaneous poetical epistle to the author of *Dido*. By a Wappineer.
pp. [2] [1–2] 3–26   PU
F. Newbery   1767
    Reed lived in Wapping.

———*Madrigal and Trulletta*

C.G., 6 July 1758.

4012 REED J[OSEPH]. Madrigal and Trulletta. A mock-tragedy. Acted (under the direction of Mr. Cibber) at the Theatre-Royal in Covent-Garden. With notes by the author, and Dr. Humbug, critick and censor-general. By J. Reed.
pp. [i–iii] iv–vii [viii], 1–64   L
W. Reeve   1758
    Produced by Theophilus Cibber at Covent Garden 6th July 1758 for one night only.

4013 HALTER-MAKER, A, *pseud.* of Joseph Reed. A sop in the pan for a physical critick: in a letter to Dr. Sm★ll★t, occasion'd by a criticism on a late mock-tragedy, call'd *Madrigal and Trulletta*. By a halter-maker.
pp. [1–3] 4–24   L
W. Reeve   1759
    A furious attack on Smollett, in whose Critical Review *an unfavourable criticism on Reed's mock-tragedy had appeared. Reed was a rope-maker by occupation, hence his assumed title of "a halter-maker"* — Lowe.

Robe, Mrs. Jane. *The Fatal Legacy*

L.I.F., 23 April 1723.

4014 ROBE, *Mrs.* JANE. ★Abstract of the lives of Etiocles and Polynices, necessary to be read by the spectators of the Fatal Legacy.
                                                   1723
    Recorded but not seen by Lowe.

Robertson, Thomas William. *David Garrick*

Prince of Wales, Birmingham, April 1864; Haymarket, 30 April 1864.

4015 CRITERION THEATRE. Lessee and manager — Mr. Charles Wyndham. Some foreign press opinions of "David Garrick."
pp. [1] 2–11 [12]; cover title   L
Printed by Farquharson Roberts & Phillips, Limited
                                                 [1888]
    Reviews of tour of Wyndham and Mary Moore to Berlin, Moscow and St. Petersburg.

4016 ———[another issue]
pp. [1] 2–11 [12]; head-title   DFo
                                                 [1888]
    On the coloured cardboard covers: Criterion Theatre. Souvenir of David Garrick. Sole lessee and manager. Mr. Charles Wyndham.

Rowe, Nicholas. *The Fair Penitent*

L.I.F., May 1703 (first recorded performance). *See above nos. 3751, 3764.*

———*Jane Shore*

D.L., 2 February 1713/4. *See also nos. 3751–2.*

4017 THE LIFE and character of Jane Shore. Collected from our best historians, chiefly from the writings of Sir Thomas More; who was her cotemporary, and personally knew her. Humbly offer'd to the readers and spectators of her tragedy written by Mr. Rowe. Inscrib'd to Mrs. Oldfield.
pp. [4] 1–20   L
Sold by J. Morphew, and A. Dodd   1714
    Mrs. Oldfield played the title role.

4018 THE LIFE and death of Jane Shore; containing the whole account of her amorous intrigues with King Edward the IVth. and the Lord Hastings: her penitence, punishment and poverty. To which are added, other amours of that king and his courtiers; with several antient love poems, written by the wits of those times. Also An heroical epistle from King Edward IV. to Jane Shore, with her answer.
pp. [4] 1–24   L
Printed and are to be sold by J. Roberts   1714
    Perhaps really published by Curll, in June — Straus.

4019 MEMOIRS of the lives of King Edward IV. and Jane Shore. Extracted from the best historians.

pp. [1–3] 4–28   L
E. Curll   1714

Published in June? — Straus.

------*Lady Jane Grey*

D.L., 20 April 1715. *See also above nos. 3751–2.*

4020 REMARKS on the tragedy of the Lady Jane Grey; in a letter to Mr. Rowe.

pp. [1–3] 4–39 [40 (bl.)]   L
J. Roberts and E. Berrington   [1715]

Unfavourable to Rowe.

------*Ulysses*

Queen's Theatre, 23 November 1705. *See also no. 3751.*

4021 CRITICAL REMARKS on Mr. Rowe's last play, call'd Ulysses. A tragedy. As it was acted at the Queen's Theatre in the Hay-Market.

pp. [1–4] 5–23 [24 (bl.) 25–27 (epilogue) 28 (bl.)]   L
Sold by Benj. Bragge   1706

Sardou, Victorien. *Robespierre*

Lyceum, 15 April 1899. *Translated by Laurence Irving.*

4022 *ROBESPIERRE. "The sea-green incorruptible" illus.; ptd. covers

Effingham Pub. Co.   [1899]

IKF.
The historical background to Robespierre, *as produced by Irving.*

Settle, Elkanah. *The Empress of Morocco*

Dorset Gardens, 3 July 1673. *Probably acted earlier at Court.*

4023 [DRYDEN, JOHN, THOMAS SHADWELL, and JOHN CROWNE.] NOTES and observations on The Empress of Morocco. Or, some few erratas to be printed instead of the sculptures with the second edition of that play.

pp. [16] 1–72; errata slip   L
                                            1674

Imprint: London, Printed in the Year, 1674.
The errata slip cancels the list of errata printed on a4ᵛ. Settle's play was published in 1673 with theatrical plates ("sculptures"). Macdonald 128.

4024 [SETTLE, ELKANAH.] NOTES and observations on *The Empress of Morocco* revised. With some

few errata's to be printed instead of the postscript, with the next edition of *The Conquest of Granada.*

pp. [4] 1–94 [95 (postscript) 96 (errata)]   L
William Cademan   1674

Macdonald *184a.*

4025 ------[reissue] *Reflections on several of Mr. Dryden's plays. Particularly, the first and second part of The conquest of Granada. By E. Settle, Gent.

William Whitwood   1687

Macdonald *184b.*

Shakespeare, William

For Charles Calvert's productions see no. 2535 above. For other notable productions of Shakespeare see nos. 2867; 3925 (Capell and Garrick's adaptation of Antony and Cleopatra); nos. 3239, 3420 (As You Like It); nos. 2365, 2367, 3020, 3056–3058, 3188, 3196, 3421, 3546, (Hamlet); no. 3122 (King Henry VIII); no. 3419 (King Henry IV); no. 3418 (King John); no. 3092 (King Lear); no. 3422 (Merchant of Venice); nos. 2151, 2377, 2742, 3422, 3475 (Othello); no. 3123 (The Winter's Tale).

------*Macbeth*

See also nos. 2834; 3059–3061, 3084–3085; 3186, 3545; 3745–6.

4026 GENTLEMAN, A, *pseud.* A key to the drama; or, memoirs, intrigues, and atchievements, of personages, who have been chosen by the most celebrated poets, as the fittest characters for theatrical representations. Calculated to gratify the public, not only with a circumstantial history of the persons, and to make the stage thereby more intelligible and interesting to those who frequent it; but that others, who from a variety of causes, have it not in their power to enjoy the representation, may nevertheless peruse the plays with a higher relish, and greater perspicuity. Vol. I. Containing the life, character, and secret history of Macbeth. By a gentleman, no professed author, but a lover of history, and of the theatre.

pp. [6] [i] ii–iii [iv (bl.)], [1] 2–237 [238 (bl.)]; t.p. in red and black   L
Printed for the author, by J. Browne   1768

No further volumes are known.

4027 RUSSELL, [*Sir*] EDWARD R[ICHARD]. *later Baron Russell of Liverpool.* The true Macbeth. A paper read before the Literary and Philosophical Society of Liverpool, November 29th, 1875. By Edward R. Russell.

pp. [2] [1] 2–52   GU
Liverpool: printed by D. Marples & Co Ltd   1875

———*Pericles*

4028 [HALLIWELL, JAMES ORCHARD, *ed.*, *later* Halliwell-Phillipps.] A COPY OF A LETTER of news written to Sir Dudley Carleton, at the Hague, in May, 1619, containing a curious account of the performance of the drama of "Pericles" at the English court.

pp. [1–5] 6–14 [15 (imprint) 16 (bl.)]   L
[London: printed for the editor by Whittingham and Wilkins]   1865

Only 25 copies printed, and of these only 10 preserved (15 destroyed by the editor).

———*Richard III*

See also nos. 3061, 3133, 3193, 3196, 3423.

4029 STUART, THOMAS. **Shakspere's tragedy of Richard III., considered dramatically and historically; and in comparison with Cibber's alteration as at present in use on the stage, in a lecture delivered to the members of the Liverpool Literary, Scientific and Commercial Institution, by Thos. Stuart, of the Theatre Royal.

[Liverpool]   [*ca.* 1850]

Recorded but not seen by Lowe. Cibber's version was first performed at Drury Lane in December 1699 or January 1700.

Shee, *Sir* Martin Archer. *Alasco*

Surrey, 5 April 1824.

4030 SHEE, [*Sir*] MARTIN ARCHER. Alasco: a tragedy, in five acts, by Martin Archer Shee, Esq. R.A. Excluded from the stage, by the authority of the Lord Chamberlain.

pp. [i–vii] viii–lvi [lvii–lx], [1] 2–169 [170]   L
Sherwood, Jones, and Co.   1824

Colman, who had recently been appointed Licenser, objected to some 85 lines in this play, and the Lord Chamberlain, whom Shee appealed to, confirmed Colman's objection. Shee indignantly withdrew the play from Covent Garden, acting, as Genest says, "with more spirit than prudence." The piece is a good one — Lowe. It was put on at the Surrey without a licence — Nicoll, IV, 400. Stratman, Tragedy 5593 (Stratman also records two American editions).

4031 [SHEE, *Sir* MARTIN ARCHER?] *REJECTED PASSAGES in the unlicensed tragedy of Alasco, with comments on the conduct of Mr. Colman.

                                   1824

Recorded but not seen by Lowe.

Shelley, Percy Bysshe. *The Cenci*

Grand Theatre, Islington, 7 May 1886. *Under the auspices of the Shelley Society. See BIOGRAPHY nos. 3353–3357, 3360 (Alma Murray).*

———*Hellas*

St. James's, 16 November 1886. *Under the auspices of the Shelley Society.*

4032 THE SHELLEY SOCIETY. First performance of "Hellas".

pp. [1] 2–3 [4]

                                   1886

IKF. Printed letter from the Hon. Sec., Jas. Stanley Little.

Sheridan, Richard Brinsley. *The Critick*

D.L., 30 October 1779.

4033 S., R.B., *pseud.* The critick anticipated; or, the humours of the green room: a farce. As rehearsed behind the curtain of the Theatre Royal, Drury-Lane. By R.B.S. Esq. &c.

pp. [i–iii] iv–xi [xii], [1] 2–30   L
S. Bladon   1779

A bitter attack — Lowe.

4034 SHERIDAN, R. B., *pseud.* *The Critick, or, a tragedy rehearsed, a literary catchpenny! by way of prelude to a dramatic after-piece, by R. B. Sheridan, Esq. With a dedication, preface, and prologue.

                                   1780

An attack upon Sheridan — Lowe.

———*Pizarro*

D.L., 24 May 1799.

4035 A CRITIQUE on the Tragedy of Pizarro, as represented at Drury Lane Theatre with such uncommon applause. To which is added, A new prologue, that has not yet been spoken.

pp. [i–iii] iv, [1] 2–27 [28 (advts.)]   L
W. Miller   1799

Pizarro is unfavourably compared with The Critic. The "new prologue" is "to be spoken by any body, in the character of a puppet-show man".

4036 ———the second edition

pp. [1–3] 4–40   L
W. Miller   1799

4037 MORE KOTZEBUE! The origin of my own Pizarro, a farce. Minor-Rosciad, or Churchillian epistle, from Dick to Jack.

pp. [6] [9] 10–32; pl. [front.]   L
Crosby and Letterman; and C. Chapple   1799

A satire on Sheridan — Lowe. The dedication to Winnifreda Whim is signed Bam-Ley Satiricon. The plate depicts a human owl under attack, crying "Who-o-o Kotzebue".

4038 [BRITTON, JOHN.] SHERIDAN and Kotzebue. The enterprising adventures of Pizarro, preceded by a brief sketch of the voyages and discoveries of Columbus and Cortez: to which are subjoined the histories of Alonzo and Cora, on which Kotzebüe [sic] founded his two celebrated plays of The virgin of the sun, and The death of Rolla. Also varieties and oppositions of criticisms on the play of Pizarro: with biographical sketches of Sheridan and Kotzebue. The whole forming a comprehensive account of those plays and the grand ballads of Cora, — and Rolla and Cora, at the Royal Circus, and Royal Amphitheatre. Dedicated to R. B. Sheridan, Esq.

pp. [i–vi] vii–viii, [1] 2–144; pl. [front.]   L
J. Fairburn   1799

Also issued: "A superior edition, on fine wove paper, hot-pressed, with proof-impressions of the plate." More than twenty editions of Pizarro were published in 1799.

4039 BARDSLEY, SAMUEL ARGENT. Critical remarks on *Pizarro*, a tragedy, taken from the German drama of Kotzebue, and adapted to the English stage by Richard Brinsley Sheridan. With incidental observations on the subject of the drama. By Samuel Argent Bardsley.

pp. [i–iii] iv–v [vi] [7] 8–48   L
T. Cadell, Junior, and W. Davies   1800

The preface is dated 14 April. Originally read to the Manchester Literary and Philosophical Society. Unfavourable to Sheridan.

4040 CARLO, The Roscius of Drury-Lane Theatre.
bs., illus.   L
Laurie & Whittle   1804

On a Newfoundland dog which performed in Pizarro.

———*The School for Scandal*
D.L., 8 May 1777. See nos. 1440; 3504.

Sheridan, Thomas. *Caractacus*
D.L., 22 April 1808.

4041 A DESCRIPTION of Caractacus. A grand ballet of action, in three parts, written by Thomas Sheridan, Esq. The action under the direction of Mr. D'Egville. As it is performed at Drury Lane Theatre, with unbounded applause. With a critique on the performers and performance.

pp. [3–7] 8–26; t.p. headed: "Scales's edition"   E
J. Scales   [1808]

Shirley, William. *Edward the Black Prince*
D.L., 6 January 1749/50.

4042 GENTLEMAN OF THE INNER-TEMPLE, A, pseud. An examen of the historical play of *Edward the Black Prince; or, The battle of Poictiers.* In which the merits and defects of that dramatick essay, are candidly

considered, and impartially pointed out. With a critical review of Mr. Barry, in the character of Ribemont. By a gentleman of the Inner-Temple.

pp. [2] 1–25 [26 (bl.)]   L
G. Jones   1750

Very laudatory of the play and of Barry's acting — Lowe.

Steele, *Sir* Richard. *The Conscious Lovers*
D.L., 7 November 1722.

4043 [DENNIS, JOHN.] A DEFENCE of Sir Fopling Flutter, a comedy written by Sir George Etheridge. In which defence is shewn, that Sir Fopling, that merry knight, was rightly compos'd by the knight his father, to answer the ends of comedy; and that he has been barbarously and scurrilously attack'd by the knight his brother, in the 65th Spectator. By which it appears, that the latter knight knows nothing of the nature of comedy.

pp. [8] 1–24   L
T. Warner   1722

Advertised 2 November 1722. An oblique attack on Steele's The Conscious Lovers. See Hooker II, 495–498. Reprinted in Hooker II, 241–250.

4044 VICTOR, B[ENJAMIN]. An epistle to Sir Richard Steele, on his play, call'd, *The Conscious Lovers.* By B. Victor.

pp. [1–2] 3–29 [30 (advt.)]   L
W. Chetwood; S. Chapman; J. Stagg; J. Brotherton; M. Smith; Tho. Edlin   1722

A furious attack on Dennis for his pamphlet A defence of Sir Fopling Flutter — Lowe. Written with Steele's encouragement, and published 29 November — Hooker.

4045 ———the second edition, corrected, with the addition of the epilogue spoken by Mrs. Oldfield, not printed with *The Conscious Lovers.*

pp. [2 (added epilogue)] 3–29 [30 (advt.)]   L
W. Chetwood; S. Chapman; J. Stagg; J. Brotherton; Tho. Edlin   1722

Dated December in a contemporary hand in this copy.

4046 *THE CENSOR CENSURED; or, The Conscious Lovers examin'd: in a dialogue between Sir Dicky Marplot and Jack Freeman. Into which Mr. Dennis is introduced by way of postscript; with some observations on his late Remarks.

     1723
Lowe.

4047 DENNIS [JOHN]. Remarks on a play, call'd, *The Conscious Lovers*, a comedy. By Mr. Dennis.

pp. [24] 1–38, 1*38–6*38, 39–42 [=48]   L
T. Warner   1723

Other copies (MH, E) have pp. [24] 1–42 (i.e. not sigs. F² ★★5, but F⁴). Published about 24th January 1723 — Hooker. Reprinted in Hooker, II, 251–274.

4048 ★SIR RICHARD STEELE, and his new comedy, called, the Conscious Lovers, vindicated from the malicious aspersions of Mr. John Dennis. Wherein Mr. Dennis's vile criticisms in defence of Sir Fopling Flutter are detected and exposed, and the author of them proved to know nothing of criticism.

1723

Published 13 December — Hooker II, 496.

Talford, *Sir* Thomas Noon. *Ion*

C.G., 26 May 1836. *See above no. 3275.*

The Taylors: A Tragedy for Warm Weather

Haymarket, 2 July 1767. *This anonymous play, sometimes attributed without authority to Foote, was abridged by George Colman, the elder, in 1778.*

4049 ★THE DEVIL AMONG THE TAILORS: the dramatic burlesque of the Tailors, with an account of the fracas at the Haymarket theatre.

1805

Recorded but not seen by Lowe.

4050 FLINT, A., *pseud.* ★The tailors' answer to the late attacks upon their profession, from the stage and press; with critical remarks on Jeremy Swell's mock-heroic poem.

pp. [i–iii] iv [5] 6–36   MH
For the author   1805

4051 SWELL, JEREMY, *pseud.* The tailors' revolt; a mock-heroic poem. In three books. By Jeremy Swell, gent.

pp. [i–iii] iv [5] 6–23 [24], misprinting iv as "v"   L
T. Hughes   1805

4052 ★THE TAILORS, or, a tragedy for warm weather; in three acts, as performed at the Theatre Royal Haymarket; to which is added, an account of the fracas at the theatre, August 15th.

1805

A serious riot took place at the Haymarket on 15th August 1805, when a mob of tailors attended to stop the performance of The Tailors, announced for Dowton's benefit — Lowe.

Thomson, James. *Edward and Eleonora*

Published 1739.

4053 THE HISTORY of the life and reign of the valiant Prince Edward, afterwards King Edward the first of England, son to King Henry the Third; and his Princess Eleonora. On which history, is founded a play, written by Mr. Thomson, call'd, Edward and Eleonora; now in rehearsal at the Theatre in Covent-Garden. Extracted from the best historians. With a geographical description of that Prince's expedition to the Holy-land, &c.

pp. [4] [1] 2–26 [27–28 (bl.)]   E
T. Cooper   1739

This tragedy was the second play prohibited under the Licensing Act. It was announced for 29 March 1739, but forbidden—Lowe. See Loftis Politics, pp. 150–151

———*Sophonisba*

D.L., 28 February 1729/30.

4054 [BIRCH, THOMAS?] A CRITICISM on the new *Sophonisba*, a tragedy. As it is acted at the Theatre-Royal in Drury-Lane.

pp. [1–2] 3–31 [32 (bl.)]   L
F. Cogan   1730

A very bitter attack on Thomson. — Lowe. Signed 'T.B.', possibly Thomas Birch, a friend of Benjamin Martyn, author of the rival tragedy of Timoleon, produced 26 January 1730. The source of the famous parody "Oh Jemmy Thomson! Jemmy Thomson Oh!"

4055 FRIEND OF THE AUTHOR'S, A, *pseud.* ★A defence of the new Sophonisba, a tragedy. In answer to a criticism on that play. By a friend of the author's.

[Cogan]   1730
Lowe.

Thurmond, John. *Harlequin Doctor Faustus*

D.L., 26 November 1723. *See above nos. 2104; 3921.*

Tobin, John. *The Honey Moon*

D.L., 31 January 1805. *See above no. 3036.*

Townley, *Rev.* James. *High Life Below Stairs*

D.L., 31 October 1759.

4056 GREY, OLIVER, *pseud.* An apology for the servants. By Oliver Grey. Occasioned by the representation of the farce called "High life below stairs", and by what has been said to their disadvantage in the public papers.

pp. [2] [1] 2–28   L
J. Newbery   1760

Appeared in parts in the Public Ledger, May 1760. Seems to be a serious defence of servants in general — Lowe.

Vanbrugh, *Sir* John. *A Journey to London*

See above nos. 3863–3865.

Villiers, George, *Duke of Buckingham. The Rehearsal*

Theatre Royal, Bridges Street, 7 December 1671.

4057 THE NEW KEY to *The Rehearsal.* Presented to his Royal Highness the Prince. Written by his Grace George, late Duke of Buckingham.

pp. [i–ii] iii–ix [x], [1] 2–14; pl. [front.]   L

S. Briscoe   1717

> *The Duke of Buckingham's play was revived at Drury Lane February 1717. A key was first provided for it in 1705.*

Wallace, *Lady* Eglantine, *née* Maxwell. *The Whim*

Published 1795.

4058 WALLACE, *Lady* [EGLANTINE], *née* Maxwell. The whim, a comedy, in three acts. By Lady Wallace. With an address to the public, upon the arbitrary and unjust aspersion of the licenser against its political sentiments. Offered to be acted for the benefit of the hospital and poor of the Isle of Thanet, but refused the Royal licence.

pp. [1–3] 4–79 [80]   GU

Margate: sold by S. and J. Read, London   1795

> *The refusal to license this comedy was one of the eccentricities of Mr. Larpent, who probably was afraid of an expression in it which plainly hinted at the connection between a certain royal personage and a lady who was commonly called "fat, fair, and forty". He meanly attributed his refusal to objectionable political passages — Lowe.*

4059 ———*second edition

                                         1795

STR.

Weddell, *Mrs. Incle and Yarico*

Unacted. Published 1742.

4060 [WEDDELL, *Mrs.*] INCLE AND YARICO: a tragedy, of three acts. As it was intended to have been performed at the Theatre-Royal, in Covent Garden. By the author of The City Farce, The Voyage up the Thames, &c.

pp. [2] [1–8] 9–69 [70]   E

Sold by T. Cooper   1742

> *This tragedy was never performed — Lowe. With "Preface: or, a general view of dramatic poetry, particularly applied to this play. By a friend."*

West, Richard. *Hecuba*

D.L., 2 February 1725/6. *Adapted from Euripides.*

4061 REFLECTIONS upon reading the tragedy of Hecuba, now in rehearsal at the Theatre-Royal in Drury Lane.

pp. [1–3] 4–12   DFo

Printed by W. Wilkins and sold by N. Blandford

                                  [1726]

4062 REFLECTIONS UPON REFLECTIONS: being some cursory remarks on the tragedy of Hecuba; in answer to the pamphlet on that play.

pp. [1–2] 3–16   L

J. Roberts   1726

> *Declares* Reflections Upon Reading the Tragedy of Hecuba, *(see above 4061) to be an author's puff.*

Whitehead, William. *The Roman Father*

D.L., 24 February 1749/50.

4063 A COMPARISON between the *Horace* of Corneille and *The Roman Father* of Mr. Whitehead.

pp. [2] [1] 2–72   L

M. Cooper   1750

> *An imaginary dialogue and correspondence between "W. Freeman" and "J. Bromley".*

4064 SPECTATOR, A, *pseud.* Remarks on the new tragedy, call'd The Roman Father. With a word to the author. By a spectator.

pp. [1–5] 6–23 [24 (bl.)]   L

Printed and sold by W. Reeve, in Fleet-Street; and A. Dodd   1750

> *Signed, on p. 23, "A.W."*

4065 *THE STORY on which the new tragedy, call'd, The Roman Father, is founded. With some account of the author, and his writings.

                                        MH

Reeve   1750

Wills, William Gorman. *Claudian*

Lyceum, 19 December 1885. *See above no. 3924.*

———*Faust*

See above no. 3079.

Woodward, Henry. *Queen Mab*

D.L., 26 December 1750. *First performed at Smock Alley, Dublin on 5 February 1748 as* Fairy friendship, or the triumph of Hibernia.

4066 THE HISTORY of Queen Mab; or, the court of fairy. Being the story upon which the Entertainment of *Queen Mab,* now exhibiting at Drury-lane, is founded. By Michael Drayton, Esq; Poet Laureat to King James I. and King Charles I.

pp. [4] [1] 2–23 [24 (advt.)]

M. Cooper   1751

Queen Mab *was a pantomime by Woodward, produced by Garrick, at Drury Lane for the purpose of fighting Rich with his own weapons. It was a great success* — Lowe. *The rivalry of the Christmas pantomimes at Drury Lane and Covent Garden is shown in the caricature* The theatrical steelyards of 1750 *(27 April 1751)* — Stephens *3090.*

Young, Edward. *The Brothers*

D.L., 3 March 1753.

4067 ★THE STORY on which the new tragedy, call'd, The Brothers, now acting at the Theatre Royal in Drury-Lane, is founded. Dedicated to the author of the play.

MH

1753

PERIODICALS

LONDON

This section contains periodicals (including annuals) outstandingly or exclusively theatrical; but, as The Dramatic Review *(No. 1, 1 Feb 1885) observes, "Every periodical of the day, including* The Nineteenth Century *and* The Fortnightly Review *— and excepting only the* Rock, *the* Record, *and the* War Cry *— is more or less a theatrical paper."*
Entries are arranged by places of publication, arranged in four sections: London, English Provinces, Ireland, Scotland (the last three subdivided into towns in alphabetical order); then by date of publication.
Carl J. Stratman, A Bibliography of British Dramatic Periodicals 1720–1960 *(New York, 1962) should also be consulted, containing as it does periodicals of a more general interest here excluded, and providing additional locations.*

Steele's The Theatre

4068 THE THEATRE. To be continu'd every Tuesday, and Saturday. By Sir John Edgar [*pseud. of* Sir Richard Steele].

In parts nos. 1–28 2 Jan 1720 to 5 April 1720; lacking nos. 16 and 28 L

W. Chetwood; J. Roberts; [Charles Lillie; J. Graves] [1720]

"The half-sheets of the original publication exist for most of the early numbers of the periodical in two or three issues, differing only slightly from one another, however, and that in accidentals"—J. Loftis, Richard Steele's The Theatre *(no. 4071, below), p. xxvii.*

4069 ———[another edition] The theatre, by Sir Richard Steele; to which are added, The anti-theatre; The character of Sir John Edgar; Steele's Case with the Lord Chamberlain The crisis of property, with the sequel, Two Pasquins, &c. &c. Illustrated with literary and historical anecdotes by John Nichols.

2 vols. pp. [i–iv] v–vii [viii], [1] 2–328; vignette on h.t. + pp. [i–ii] iii–iv, 329–615 [616 (advt.)] L

For the Editor 1791

Contains, in addition to the items mentioned on the title-page: "Cibber's statement of the conduct of the theatre under . . . Steele", Cibber's dedication to Ximenes, An answer to a whimsical pamphlet, *"A full consideration and confutation of Sir John Edgar by Sir Andrew Artlove",* The Muses Gazette, *No 8, "Three letters" from Dennis to Steele,* A Nation a Family, *by Steele, and a copy of Davenant's patent.*

4070 ———[another edition of no. 4069]

pp. [i–iv], [1] 2–580 [581–582 (advt.) 583 (printed labels) 584 (bl.)]; vignette on h.t. L

For the editor 1791

The last leaf contains printed labels for both the one volume and the two volume edition.

4071 ———[another edition] Richard Steele's *The theatre* 1720 Edited by John Loftis

pp. [i–viii] ix–xxvii [xxviii], 1–147 [148]; pl. [front.] L

Oxford at the Clarendon Press 1962

4072 *THE ANTI-THEATRE. By Sir John Falstaffe.

nos. 1–15 15 Feb to 4 Apr 1720 *twice weekly* O

[London] 1720

Reprinted in no. 4069 above. See also no. 4073.

4073 *THE THEATRE. By Sir John Falstaffe. To be continued every Tuesday and Saturday.

In parts nos. 16–26 9 April 1720 to 14 May 1720 DFo

[W. Boreham] [1720]

Nos. before 16 are those of The anti-theatre *(no. 4072), which now continues under the name of Steele's periodical,* The theatre, *which ceased publication on 5th April. The only copy known (DFo) lacks no. 19. The anonymous author announces no. 26 to be the last for the present season.*

———[American edition.] With an introduction by John Loftis (The Augustan Reprint Society. Series four: no. 1). Ann Arbor, 1948.

4074 *COTES'S WEEKLY JOURNAL; or, the English stage-player.

nos. 1–9 11 May to 6 July 1734 *weekly;* with two supplements (Shakespeare's *Julius Caesar* and Fielding's *The Miser*) O

1734

Milford.

4075 THE PROMPTER [by Aaron Hill and William Popple].

In parts nos. 1–172 12 Nov 1734 to 29 June 1736 *twice weekly* L

J. Peele [and T. Cooper] [1734–1736]

Lacks no. 173, 2 July 1736, and also nos. 138, 158. A complete run in O. See also no. 681 above.

———[American edition]. Selected and edited by William W. Appleton and Kalman A. Burnim. New York: Benjamin Blom, 1966.

✠ The country correspondent: or the stage-monitor [To be continued occasionally.] By Tho. Earl. 1739. *See no. 3850.*

4076 THE COVENT-GARDEN JOURNAL. To be publish'd once every month, during the present Westminster election. By Paul Wronghead, of the Fleet, Esq.

no. 1 5 Dec 1749 L

Printed for T. Smith, R. Welb, and S. Johnson, and sold by all the people of London and Westminster; where persons who bring advertisements or letters to the author are taken in 1749

Concerns the French actors in England (see also no. 1434 above).

4077 THE TUNER. [*ed.* Paul Hiffernan.]

In parts [no. 1] Letters 2-5, 1754-1755 ["occasionally"]; vignette on t.p. of [no. 1] MH

Printed and sold by M. Cooper [no. 1]; printed for M. Cooper [letters 2-5] 1754-1755

The title is derived from a slang use of the word "tune", explained in the preface—Lowe. At the end of Letter 5: "End of the first volume". Parts dated by Lowe 21 Jan. 1754 to 5 Nov. 1755 and by Milford 26 Jan. 1754 to [1755].

4078 *THE CENSOR: No I. with an epistolary dedication to orator Mack-n.

1755

Recorded but not seen by Lowe.

4079 THE THEATRICAL REVIEW; ⟨or, annals of the drama.⟩

vol. 1 [nos. 1-6] 1 Jan 1763 to 1 June 1763; t.p. in red and black, and with vignette., ded., introd. L

S. Williams; and Wilson and Fell 1763

4080 THE MONITOR; or, green-room laid open; with remarks thereon, which occasioned the letter to Mr. Spatter.

[no. 1 ?17 Oct 1767] L

W. Bingley 1767

I fancy that "Mr. Spatter" is meant to be Hugh Kelly —Lowe.

Then The theatrical monitor; or, stage management and green room laid open.

no. 2 24 Oct 1767 L

W. Bingley 1767

———[another edition of no. 2] 24 Oct 1767.

L

W. Bingley 1767

Then The theatrical monitor

nos. 3-18, 7 Nov 1767 to 16 April 1768 *weekly, except nos. 9, 10 and 18;* no. 10 *marked "Second edition".* L

W. Bingley (nos. 3-15); S. Bladon (nos. 16-17); S. Bladon and J. Dixwell (no. 18) 1767-68

See Page, *p. 159.*

4081 *COVENT GARDEN CHRONICLE.

no. 2 9 March 1768 O

1768

Milford. Number 3, 14 March 1768 at CtY. A rival to the Theatrical Monitor *(no. 4080).*

4082 †THE MACARONI and theatrical magazine ⟨or monthly register, of the fashions and diversions of the times conducted upon a much more elegant and liberal plan, than any other work of the kind hitherto published.⟩

Oct 1772 to March 1773 *monthly;* pls. [11 incl. fronts.]

Then The macaroni savoir vivre, and theatrical magazine

April to June 1773 *monthly;* pls. [2]

Then The macaroni, scavoir vivre, and theatrical magazine

July to Sept 1773 *monthly;* pls. [front., 6]; engr. t.p., index.

LVA

Printed for the authors 1772-1773

There should be twenty-five plates and frontispiece, according to the directions to binder.

vol. II Oct 1773 to Sept 1774 *monthly;* pls. [3]; index

L

1773-1774

Lacking title-page; head-title adds from May: "or, monthly register of taste, fashions, and amusement".

vol. III Oct 1774; t.p. L

[London]: printed by T. Bell 1774

4083 *DRAMATIC MAGAZINE; or, tragic, comic and operatical library.

nos. 1-2 [Dec] 1786 to 1787; note on No. 2: "to be continued monthly" C

1786-1787

Stratman *20.*

4084 THE PROMPTER. [*ed.* James Fennell?]

nos. 1-19 24 Oct 1789 to 10 Dec 1789 *from four times weekly to once a week* L

Printed and published (by order of the society) for Hookham; Beetham; Brett; Manson; and may be had at both the theatres [1789]

See P. A. Hummert, "The Prompter: An Intimate Mirror of the Theatre in 1789", Restoration and 18th Century Theatre Research, III, i (May 1964) 37-46.

4085 *THE LIVES AND TRAITS OF THE BON TON THEATRICALS. (To be continued weekly.) Together with the managers and performers of all the principal theatres in the three Kingdoms.

In parts nos 1-2 14 June to 21 June 1790 MH

1790

4086 †THE THEATRICAL GUARDIAN. [*ed.* James Fennell.]

nos. I–VI 5 March to 9 Apr 1791 *weekly*   L

Printed for the author   1791

Lacking nos. V–VI. For Fennell's editorship, see his autobiography (Philadelphia, 1814) p. 308. Stratman 24.

4087 vacant

4088 THE THESPIAN MAGAZINE and literary repository.

vols I–III nos [1] 2–16 [17–19] 21 [for 20] [21–27] June 1792 to April 1794, June 1794 to Sept 1794 *monthly*; pls, incl. front to each vol.; t.p., pref., index to each vol.; supplement to vols. I and II; lacking pp 69–76 of vol. III   LGk

Printed and sold by Thos. Wilkins 1793 [for 1792]–1794

4089 *DRAMATIC REVIEW; or, mirror of the stage.

                                 1795

   Stratman *26.*

4090 THE MONTHLY MIRROR: reflecting men and manners. With strictures on their epitome, the stage.

vols. 1–22 Dec 1795 to Dec 1806; pls.; t.pp., indices L

Vernor, Hood [and Sharpe]   1795–1806

new series, vols 1–9 Jan 1807 to Feb 1811; pls; t.pp., indices   L

Vernor, Hood, and Sharpe   1807–1811

A "very valuable theatrical magazine" — Lowe.

4091 HOW DO YOU DO? [*ed.* Charles Dibdin and F. G. Waldron?]

nos. 1–8 30 July 1796 to 5 Nov 1796 *fortnightly*   L

Printed for the editors by T. Woodfall   1796

Future publication, monthly, and with a greater emphasis on the stage, is promised in no. 8, but the three sets known are of 8 numbers only.

4092 *THE THESPIAN TELEGRAPH; or, dramatic mirror.

no. 1 [June?] 1796   DFo

London   1796

4093 THE DRAMATIC CENSOR; or weekly theatrical report. ⟨Comprising a complete chronicle of the British stage, and a regular series of theatrical criticism, in every department of the drama. By Thomas Dutton, A.M.⟩

vol. I–II nos. I–XIII 4 Jan to 29 March 1800 + nos. XIV–XXVI 5 Apr to 28 June 1800; each vol. with t.p., dedication, index   L

Sold by J. Roach and C. Chapple   1800

There is a four-page Supplement to no. VIII, separately paginated, and with a full title-page: "An analytical review of the German drama." No. XXVI is called the "Appendix, or Supplement" to vol. II. In no. IV, an engraved title-page is promised — apparently not published.

Then The dramatic censor; or, monthly epitome of taste, fashion, and manners. ⟨By Thomas Dutton, A.M.⟩

vols. III–IV nos. XXVII–XXXII July 1800 to Dec 1800 + nos. XXXIII–XXXVIII Jan to June 1801; t.p., dedication, index   L

J. Roach and C. Chapple   1800–1801

Then The dramatic and literary censor

vol. I nos. [3] July to Sept 1801 *monthly*, vol. V nos. XLII–L 9 Oct to 27 Nov 1801 *weekly*; nos. XLIX and L both dated 27 Nov; "End of Vol V" (no. L, p 247); pl. [front.]   LGk

Printed by J. Roach   1801

4094 *THE SPECTATOR of the stage, addressed to the King. No. 1, to be occasionally continued.

                                 1800

Recorded but not seen by Lowe.

4095 THE THEATRICAL REPERTORY. ⟨Containing criticisms on the performances which were represented at Drury-Lane and Covent-Garden theatres, during the season 1801–2. With occasional observations on other places of public entertainment.⟩

nos. 1–24 19 Sept 1801 to 1 March 1802 *weekly*; nos. 25–28 15 March 1802 to 28 June 1802 *irregularly*   L

Printed by T. Woodfall   [1802]

Suspension of publication announced. This volume reissue has four leaves of preliminaries, including a dedication to George Colman. The numbers have a head-title: "The Theatrical Repertory; or, weekly Rosciad", the last four numbers dropping the alternative title.

4096 THE PIC NIC [*ed.* William Combe].

In parts prospectus; nos. 1–14 8 Jan to 9 April 1803 *weekly*   L

R. Exton   1803

Became incorporated in The Cabinet (1803).

———— [another edition]

2 vols. t.p.; preface   L

J. F. Hughes   1803

A reprint of the parts. Preface includes a description of the theatrical society, the Pic Nic, founded by Col. Greville and Mr. Le Texier, which had to be disbanded in face of strong public opposition.

————second edition

2 vols t.p.; preface   L

Hughes   1806

A reissue of the previous item. On t.p., "Printed by D. N. Shury"; but colophon gives Exton as printer.

4097 THE MAN IN THE MOON. ⟨Consisting of essays and critiques on the politics, morals, manners, drama, &c. of the present day.⟩

nos. I–XXI 12 Nov 1803–21 Jan 1804 *twice weekly*; nos. XXII–XXIII 28 Jan 1804–4 Feb 1804 *weekly*; no. XXIV 28 Jan [*for* 11 Feb?] 1804; t.p.   E

S. Highley   1804

4098 *THE DRAMATIC ANNUAL REGISTER for 1804.

                                                     1805

Recorded but not seen by Lowe.

4099 *STAGE; or, theatrical touchstone. To be continued every fortnight. By Pertinax Probe, Esq.

[nos. 1–4] 20 July to 28 Sept 1805 *irregular*   ICN
                                                     1805

Stratman 39.

4100 THE THEATRICAL RECORDER by Thomas Holcroft.

vols. I–II nos. 1–6 Jan to June 1805 *monthly*; engr. t.p. to each no.; pls., col. [front., 6], plain [9]; index + nos. 7–12 July to Dec 1805 *monthly*; pls., col. [front., 1], plain [10]; index. Supplements, Jan 1806; pls., col. [front.], plain [1]   LU

Published for the author by H. D. Symonds 1805–1806

4101 THE THEATRICAL REVIEW.

In parts. nos. [1–3] 1 Jan 1807 to 1 March 1807 *monthly*
                                                     MB

[Printed by D. N. Shury]   [1807]

Continuous pagination. No wrappers seen. The suspension of publication is not announced, but Stratman (47) records another copy also of three numbers only. Each signature preceded by 'vol. I.' Sometimes ascribed to Thomas Holcroft, but not in E. Colby, A Bibliography of Thomas Holcroft (New York, 1922); the MB copy has in an old hand, "Said to be written by a Mr. Jackson".

4102 vacant

4103 THE DRAMATIC CENSOR: ⟨or, critical and biographical illustration of the British stage. For the year 1811. Involving a correct register of every night's performances at our metropolitan theatres, and published with a view to sustain the morality and dignity of the drama. Edited by J. M. Williams, L.L.D.⟩

vol. [I] nos. [I–III] IV–VI Jan–Dec 1811 *irregularly*; h.t., t.p., ded., index   LVA

Sold by Sherwood, Neely, and Jones; Rich and Folkard; Chapple; Ryan; and B. Wilson   [1812]

4104 THE THEATRICAL INQUISITOR; or, literary mirror. By Cerberus.

vol. I Sept 1812 to Jan 1813 *monthly*; t.p., pref., index
                                                     L

Sherwood, Neely, and Jones   1812

First number published by W. Oxberry. Each number with a plate.

Then The theatrical inquisitor, and monthly mirror.

vols. II–XIV Feb 1813 to June 1819; t.p.; pref., index
                                                     L

For the proprietors by C. Chapple   1813–1819

Each number with a plate; the number for May 1816 with two plates; plate for February 1818 missing. No index to vol. IV. Preface to vol. IV, initialled "H", to vol. V, "G.S.", to vol. VIII, "J".

Then The theatrical inquisitor

In parts. [vols. XV–XVI, new series vol. I] July 1819 to Nov 1820 *monthly*   L

For the proprietors by C. Chapple   [1819–1820]

Title-page, preface, and index for vols. XV and XVI are advertised, but for XVI at least were probably not issued. Each number of vol. XV with a plate, proof copies obtainable from Colnaghi; three plates in vol. XVI and none in New Series vol. I. A double number for October and November 1820. Numbers numbered in the signatures from September 1816 (vol. IX, No. 50) to November 1820 (NS vol. 1, No. 5); cover-titles, here missing, were probably numbered. Apparently merged with The London Magazine, and Monthly Critical and Dramatic Review (see below no. 4121) from February 1821. No numbers after November 1820 known. See also below 4121 note and 4150 note.

4105 vacant

4106 *THE DRAMATIC REVIEW and register of the fine arts.

nos. 1–3 12 Feb 1814 to 26 Feb 1814 *weekly*   ICU
                                                     1814

Stratman 55.

4107 THE MONTHLY THEATRICAL REPORTER, ⟨or, literary mirror. By T. Dutton, A.M. Embellished with superb engravings [by Robert and ? George Cruikshank]⟩

[vol I] nos I–IV [V–X] Oct 1814 to July 1815; second title and name of author as 'Thomas Dutton' added in no [V]; pls [10 fronts.]; t.p.; lacking the pls.   MH

J. Roach   1814–1815

Cohn 257. *Another copy in MH has all the frontispieces, except that to no. I.*

4108 ★THE STAGE.

vol. I nos. 1–22 17 Nov 1814 to 13 Apr 1815; vol. II nos. 1–20 20 Apr to 2 Sept 1815; new series vol. III nos. 1–47 30 Dec 1815 to 16 Nov 1816 *weekly*   O

1814–1816

Stratman 57.

4109 ★THE THEATRICAL GAZETTE.

In parts nos. [4] *daily*   MH

Printed by Plummer and Brewis, [then Swan] [1815–16]

————[vol. issue] The dramatic manual, an aid to dull apprehension, or obscure recollection; published as "Theatrical Gazettes;" being an abstract of most of the performances at Covent-Garden and Drury-Lane theatres, in the season 1815–16; comprising some of our best plays.

t.p.; index   MH
                                                                   1816

Published daily at 2d., containing the cast of the play for that night, with a synopsis of its plot. One was published for Covent Garden and one for Drury Lane. There is no date, nor hint of a date, on the numbers I have seen, but they are obviously for the season of 1815–1816 — Lowe.

4110 ★COVENT-GARDEN THEATRICAL GA-ZETTE. A complete analysis of the evening's entertainments, with the names of characters, performers, etc. Ed. by W. Leggett.

nos. 1–148 9 Sept 1816 to 9 Apr 1817; nos. 1–11 *triweekly;* nos. 12–13 *daily;* nos. 14–22 *five days a week;* nos. 23–148 *six days a week*   MH
                                                                   1816–1817

Stratman 61. L copy destroyed.

4111 ★DRURY-LANE THEATRICAL GAZETTE.

nos. 1–148 7 Sept 1816 to 9 Apr 1817   DFo

[London]   [1816–1817]

4112 THE BRITISH STAGE, AND LITERARY CABINET. By Thomas Kenrick, Esq.

vols. I–VI, nos. 1–12, Jan. to Dec. 1817; pls., col. [13 fronts.], incl. 1 dup. + nos. 13–24, Jan. to Dec. 1818; illus.; pls., col. [12 fronts.] + nos. 25–33, Jan. to Sept. 1819; illus.; pls., plain [9 fronts.] + nos. 34–48, Oct. 1819 to Dec. 1820; illus.; pls. col. [4 fronts., 1], plain [11 fronts.] + nos. 49–60, Jan. to Dec. 1821; illus.; pls. col. [11 fronts., 3], plain [1] + nos. 61–62, Jan. to Feb. 1822; illus.; pls., plain [2 fronts.]; *monthly.* Pls. by George Cruikshank, Robert Cruikshank and others. Vols. I–V each with t.p., preface, index.   L

For the Proprietor[s], by J. Chappell [and Son] 1817–1822

The numbers were issued in printed wrappers. Kenrick edited all the volumes except the fourth. From 1820 to 1822 there were issued with the numbers "reprints of scarce plays and tracts relating to the drama", separately signed and paged. Cohn 461.

4113 ★THE THEATRICAL GAZETTE; or, nightly reflector of the Theatres Royal Covent Garden and Drury Lane.

vol. I no. 1

[1818]

BMC (*but L copy destroyed*). Stratman *67 gives 7 Sept. 1818.*

4114 ★THE INSPECTOR — a weekly dramatic paper. Ed. by J. B. Collis.

nos. 1–4 2 Jan to 23 Jan *weekly*   O
                                                      1819

Stratman 70 (L copy destroyed).

4115 ★REVUE GÉNÉRALE DES THÉÂTRES de Londres et de Paris, ou journal historique, critique, et littéraire, des pièces les plus remarquables, représentées sur les différens théâtres des deux capitales. Année 1819.

nos. 1–6 *bimensuelle*   MB

Schulze & Dean   1819

4116 THE THEATRE; or, dramatic and literary mirror. Containing original theatrical essays — literary reviews — theatrical criticisms — original and selected poetry — theatrical anecdotes — provincial theatres, &c. Embellished with full length portraits, taken expressly for this work.

vols. 1–2 nos. 1–14, 1 [i.e. 15], 16–23 20 Feb 1819 to 30 Oct 1819 *weekly to no. 9, then fortnightly;* t.p. to each vol.; index to vol. 1; col. pls. [6] to nos. 4, 5, 6, 7, 18 by R. Cruikshank(?), to no. 10 by George.

MB

Duncombe   1819

Evidently wants eleven plates. Bound in are 3 other plates in the style of those integral to the magazine. Cohn records 24 parts (Cohn 790), but two sets of 23 parts only are known (MB, MH).

4117 ★THE CORNUCOPIA; or, literary and dramatic mirror, containing a variety of interesting subjects under the head of miscellanies. Embellished with coloured engravings illustrative of interesting dramatic incidents, designed and engraved by J. Findlay.

vol. I nos 1–13 Sept 1820 to Sept. 1821 *monthly;* col. pls.   BP

Sherwood & Co.   1826 [for 1820?]

A title-page and index is given to these thirteen numbers, and I suppose them to be all published. It is very curious that the title-page should be dated 1826. The coloured illustrations are scenes from plays — Lowe.

4118 *THE CRITIC; or, weekly theatrical reporter.

nos. 1–7   22 July 1820 to 2 Sept 1820 *weekly*   CtY

London   1820

Stratman 74.

4119 *THE DRAMATIC MISCELLANY and medley of literature.

no. 1   8 Apr 1820

London   1820

Stratman 75. *L copy destroyed.*

4120 KEENE'S THEATRICAL EVENING MIRROR.

In parts. vol. 1 nos. 1–25, misprinting 25 as "24" 18 June 1820 to 24 Oct 1820; *no. 2 pub. 20 Sept 1820, then from three times a week to daily*   L

J. Onwhyn   [1820]

Each number with 8 pages, including a decorative title-page. No. 7 missing from the copy seen. The suspension of publication is announced. In no. 8 there is an appeal for information concerning the "lad" who was knocked down "for vending the 'Theatrical Mirror' near the gates of Covent Garden Theatre on Thursday Evening last".

4121 THE LONDON MAGAZINE; and monthly critical and dramatic review.

vols. I–II nos. [1–12]   Jan 1820 to Dec 1820; pls. [5]; t.p., index to each vol; lacking 7 pls (for nos [1–7])   LU; L

Gold and Northhouse   1820

Vol. 1 at LU., vol. 2 at L.

Then The London magazine, and theatrical inquisitor

vol. III nos. [13] XIV–XVIII Jan 1821 to June 1821 *monthly*; pls. [5]; t.p., index; lacking 1 pl. (for no. XVII).   L

Gold and Co.   1821

Nos. 14–18 each have a title-page: Gold's London magazine, and theatrical inquisitor. The Theatrical Inquisitor (1812–1820) (no. 4104 above) ceased publication in November 1820.

Then The London magazine.

In parts vol IV no. 19   July 1821   LU

Taylor and Hessey   1821

On microfilm (from Duke University). Two copies of 19 numbers only are recorded, and probably therefore no more were published. Sometimes recorded, on no good authority, as consisting of 10 vols. 1820–1829.

4122 THE NEW DRAMATIC CENSOR; or, monthly epitome of taste, fashion and manners.

no. 1   March 1820   LGk

Roach   1820

4123 THE DRAMA; or, theatrical pocket magazine. ⟨Wholly dedicated to the stage, and containing original dramatic biography, essays, criticisms, poetry, reviews, anecdotes, bon mots, chit chat; with occasional notices of the country theatres. The whole forming a complete critical and biographical illustration of the British stage.⟩

vols. I–VI, each containing nos. 1–7; May 1821 to Sept 1824 *monthly, but 2 nos. for Jan 1822*; pl. [1] to each no.; engr. t.p., t.p., pref., index, supplement to each vol.   L

Then The drama; or, theatrical pocket magazine, ⟨forming a complete critical and biographical illustration of the British stage.⟩

vol. VII, nos. 1–7   Oct 1824 to April 1825 [not May, as stated on t.p.] *monthly*; pls. [7]; engr. t.p., t.p., pref. index   L

T. & J. Elvey   1821–1825

Then The drama; or, theatrical pocket magazine.

New series. vol. 1 nos. 1–23; pls. [22], May to Dec 1825 *fortnightly, then weekly from no. 11*; engr. t.p., pref., index   LVA

I. Gifford & Co.   1825

4124 THALIA'S TABLET, and Melpomene's memorandum-book; or, Orpheus's olio; or, the album of all sorts. Being a collective, selective medley of odd, laughable, funny, droll, tragical, comical, poetical, prosaical, elegaical, whimsical, satirical, critical, biographical, theatrical, and piratical, songs, duets, glees, chorusses, orations, recitations, lucubrations, translations, prologues, epilogues, monologues, dialogues, tales, memoirs, histories, fragments, flights of fancy, fugitive pieces, scraps, &c. &c. &c. gathered from tragedies, comedies, operas, plays, farces, burlettas, operettas, farcettas, melodrames, pantomimes, newspapers, novels, magazines & romances. Embellished with an elegant, engraved, painted portrait of a principal performer. To be continued every Saturday, as long as the public will please to patronize it.

[no. 1] [Saturday, December 8th, 1821]; col. pl. [front.]   MH

S. G. Fairbrother   [1821]

4125 ——Thalia's tablet, and Melpomene's memorandum book. Second edition. Embellished with a highly finished coloured engraving, illustrative of an interesting dramatic subject.

no. 1   Saturday, December 8, 1821; col. pl. [front.]   MH

S. G. Fairbrother, at Mr. Lowndes's   [1821]

The title page of the second edition is thus much shorter than that of the other edition here recorded. The frontispieces, both of T. P. Cooke as Mich Rattlane (or Rattlin) in The Greeks and the Turks, also differ from each other. No other copies or numbers are known.

4126 †THE THEATRICAL OBSERVER.

nos. 1–35 24 Sept to 2 Nov 1821 *daily*; lacking no 10 and final p. or pp. of no. 35   L

Printed by E. Thomas   1821

The first volume of this long-lived paper was a small shabby-looking 12mo . . . Published daily at 1d. — Lowe. Nos. 26–34 (35?) published by C. Harris.

Then ★The theatrical observer; and daily bills of the play.

nos. 1–16,950 3 Nov 1821 to 31 Aug 1876 *daily*

E. Thomas   1821–76

Lowe. *An incomplete set at MB.*

4127 ★THEATRICAL SPECTATOR.

nos. 1–11 7 Apr to 23 June 1821 *weekly*   MH
                    1821

Lacks no. 3.

4128 THE MIRROR OF THE STAGE; or, new dramatic censor; consisting of original memoirs of the principal actors; criticisms on the new pieces and performers as they appear; anecdotes, original essays, &c. &c. &c.

vols. 1–2 nos. 1–24 12 Aug 1822 to 14 July 1823 *fortnightly to no. 22, then every three weeks; t.p. to vol. 1, index to each vol.; lacking t.p. to vol. 2*   L

E. Duncombe   [1822–1823]

Vol. 1 has also an engraved coloured title-page. Each number with a coloured plate (24 plates, including 12 by I. Cruikshank). Plate for No. 24 (Mr. Hammond) is missing in this copy, which, however, has a further plate, of Mr. Yates as Grimacier. Each number in vol. 1 has an abbreviated head-title; in vol. 2, each number has a title-page. Most numbers have 16 pages. Cohn 563.

Then, The mirror of the stage; or, new dramatic censor; consisting of original memoirs of the principal actors, criticisms on the new pieces and performers; reviews of dramatic works, anecdotes, original essays, poetry, &c. &c. Embellished with accurate likenesses.

new Series vol. 3 nos. 1–12 4 Aug 1823 to 5 Jan 1824 *every three weeks to no. 2, then fortnightly to nos. 10–11, then every three weeks; t.p., index*   L

Duncombe   [1823–1824]

Each number with a title-page (except no. 12), and with a plate. The first 6 plates are coloured; the remaining 5 are stipple-engravings by Page from drawings by Meadows: of these, proofs on India paper were offered for sale. Nos. 10–11 are a single number.

Then The mirror of the stage, and new theatrical inquisitor, consisting of original memoirs of the principal actors, criticisms on the new pieces and performers; reviews of dramatic works, anecdotes, original essays, poetry, &c. &c. Embellished with accurate likenesses.

vol. 4 nos. 13–24 26 Jan 1824 to 11 Oct 1824 *every three weeks to no. 16, then approx. monthly; t.p., index*   L

Duncombe   [1824]

Each number with a title- page (except no. 24), and with a plate (11 plates, including 9 coloured). Nos. 18–19 are a single number. From no. 17, The Mirror of the Stage includes also The New Theatrical Inquisitor. Plate for no. 21 missing in this copy.

★vol. 5 nos 1–2

BMC, *but L copy destroyed. Extent of run unknown.*

4129 ★THE THEATRICAL GUIDE; or, daily chronicle of public amusements.

no. 4 4 Oct 1822
                    1822

Lowe *and* BMC, *but L copy destroyed.*

4130 THE DRAMATIC OBSERVER, and musical review.

vol. 1 no. 1 14 April 1823   MH

Published every morning at 56, Fleet Street   1823

A prospectus apparently accompanied the first number.

4131 THE DRAMATICAL & MUSICAL MAGAZINE.

In parts nos. [1–8] Jan 1823 to Aug 1823 *monthly; pls. 4, incl. 3 fold.]*   MH

Printed by R. Macdonald [no. 2] Morgan, printer [nos. 3–8]   [1823]

The publisher of the plate to no 5 is T. Holt. In no. 8, continuation is anticipated. A prospectus was apparently issued with no. 1.

4132 ★JOURNAL OF MUSIC AND THE DRAMA.

vol. 1 nos. 1–9 15 Feb 1823 to 19 Apr 1823 *weekly*   ICN

John Miller   1823

ULS. *Extent of run not known.*

4133 THE LITERARY HUMBUG; or, weekly take-in. By Jaspero, the younger, Esq.

In parts vol. 1 nos. 1–6 14 May to 18 June 1823 *weekly*   LVA

Chappell and Son   [1823]

Then, The literary exposé and fashionable Proteus, being a new series continued from no. 6, of the literary humbug; or, weekly take-in.

nos. 7–13 30 July to 10 Sept 1823 *weekly*   LVA
John Miller   [1823]

4134 ★THE LONDON THEATRICAL OBSERVER.
                    1823–1840

Lacy's catalogue has the numbers from 13th June 1823 to 6th April 1840 — Lowe.

4135 *THE THEATRICAL EXAMINER; or critical remarks on the daily performances, with the bills of the play.

vols. 1–9 21? April 1823 to 3 March 1831 *daily*

London   1823–1831

Vol. i, No. 86, Tuesday, July 29, 1823; No. 137, Friday, September 26, 1823. Vol. ii. No. 1, Wednesday, October 1, 1823. Vol. vi. No. 124, Monday, February 25, 1828. I have seen these numbers — Lowe. L copy destroyed, but a few numbers at MB, MH and LGk (printed by J. H. Cox).

4136 *THE VAUXHALL OBSERVER; or critical remarks on the amusements at the Gardens, with an account of the songs

nos. 1–51 19 May 1823–8 Nov 1823 *thrice weekly*

                                                          1823

Stratman 109. L copy destroyed.

4137 *THE PROMPTER, or theatrical review.

                                                          1824

Recorded but not seen by Lowe.

4138 *THE WEEKLY DRAMATIC CHRONICLE and entertaining miscellany.

nos. 1–10 27 Nov 1824 to 29 Jan 1825

[London]: T. Dunbar and others   [1824–1825]

BMC, but L copy destroyed.

4139 OXBERRY'S DRAMATIC BIOGRAPHY, and histrionic anecdotes. [William and Mrs Catherine Oxberry, eds.]

vols. I–V, nos. I–XVI 17–80 1 Jan 1825 to 12 Aug [?] 1826 *weekly* [?]; t.p., index, added t.p. engr. to each vol., pref. to vol. II; pl. [front.] to each no.   NbU

George Virtue   1825 (vols. I–III), 1826 (vols. IV–V)

Nos. I–XVI dated on head-titles, and originally published weekly in printed covers; nos. 17–80 dated only on plates, and published weekly as a rule. Edited by William Oxberry's widow, Mrs Catherine Oxberry, with the assistance of Leman Thomas Rede (her second husband), from materials collected by Oxberry with this work in view. Rede had probably been working on The Roscius (no. 4140); if so, there may have been a disagreement between him and the publisher, Duncombe.

Then †vol. VI, nos. [81–96]; t.p., index, added t.p., engr.; pl. [front.] to each no.; lacking nos. [93–95] + nos. [97] 98–101; pl. [front.] to each no. *weekly*

John Duncombe   1826

JFA. The run can be dated from the pieces reviewed as extending from mid-August 1826 to the end of that year. Published without the consent of Mrs Oxberry: the preface to the first volume of the new series, below, complains of an imitation published since the last number of the original series, presumably the present item.

Then Oxberry's dramatic biography, or the green room spy.

new series. vols. I–II nos. 1–16; t.p., ind., pref., added t.p., engr.; pl. [front.] to each no. + nos. 17–25; engr. t.p.; pl. [front.] to each no. *weekly*   L

G. Virtue   1827

————[another edition] Famous actors. Biographies and portraits reprinted and reproduced from [vol. I of] Oxberry's "Dramatic Biography".

pp. [8] [1–3] 4–240; illus.   E

Edinburgh: W. H. White and Co.   1894

A reprint of the biographies included in volume 1 of Dramatic Biography *without the accompanying "Histrionic anecdotes".*

4140 THE ROSCIUS, consisting of original memoirs of the principal actors and actresses; strictures on the drama, and its interests; original essays, green-room gossips, anecdotes, &c. &c. &c.

In parts. vol. 1 nos. 1–7 4 Jan 1825 to 9 Aug 1825 *the first four nos. fortnightly, then irregularly*; pls. [3 fronts.]   MB

Duncombe   [1825]

In the copy seen, no. 6 is missing, but it was apparently issued on 19th April. Each number also had a plate, according to the individual title-page, although only three plates have been seen. In no. 7 the suspension of the journal is not announced, but Stratman (124) records two other copies also of seven numbers only. In the copy seen, an old hand makes the very plausible statement, in pencil on the title-page of no. 1, that "most of the articles were written by Jerrold, Leaman Blanchard, Lemen Rede . . ."

4141 THE THEATRICAL MINCE PIE, entirely original. Containing a correct account of the several appearances of Mr. Kean and Miss Foote, since their late actions in the Court of King's Bench; together with a comical history of the drama for the last eight weeks, and divers diverting articles. By Somebody, Gent.

nos. 1–8 1 Jan to 19 Feb 1825 *weekly*   MH

[T. Holt]   1825

Imprint of nos. 2–8: "T. Holt and W. Dunbar." No. 8 is announced as the last and the fourth leaf of that number evidently provided the title-page for the volume.

4142 *THE THESPIAN SENTINEL, or theatrical vademecum.

vol. I nos. I–XLVIII [26] Sept to 19 Nov 1825; vol. II nos. I–XLVII 21 Nov 1825 to 14 Jan 1826; vol. III nos. I–LIII 16 Jan to 18 Mar 1826 *daily*   L; MB

Allman [after vol. I no. VIII, Jane Lowndes] 1825–26

Stratman 127. Vol. I at L. Vols. I–III, no. XL at MB.

4143 *THE WEEKLY DRAMATIC REGISTER. A concise history of the London stage for 1825–27. Compiled from The Theatrical Observer.

vols. I–III nos. 1–155 1 Jan 1825 to 22 Dec 1827 MB

Thomas 1825–27

✠ Cornucopia. 1826 [for 1820] *See no. 4117.*

4144 *THE OPERA GLASS, for peeping into the microcosm of the fine arts, and more especially of the drama.

Nos. 1–26 2 Oct 1826 to 24 March 1827 *weekly* O

London 1826–1827

4145 THE WASP. A literary satire. Containing an expose of some of the most notorious literary and theatrical quacks of the day. An abundance of every sort and manner of facetiae, in the shape of puns, epigrams, bon mots, epitaphs, parodies, impromptus, declarations of inefficiency, by several eminent professors, authors, actors, and others; aphorisms of notorious and celebrated characters, and every other description of witticism, perfectly original.

vol. 1 nos. 1–12 30 Sept 1826 to 16 Dec 1826 *weekly;* vol. t.p.; index L

W. Adams [W. Jeffreys] [1826]

To no. 6: "Supplement to the Wasp", headed "Second edition". The individual numbers published by W. Jeffreys. Further numbers are anticipated, but several sets of 12 numbers only are known. Stratman *133.*

4146 *SURREY DRAMATIC SPECTATOR; or critical remarks, on the daily performances, with the bills of the play.

vol. 1 nos 1–113 1827–28

London 1827–28

BMC, *but L copy destroyed; a few nos. at MH and no. 79 at MB.*

4147 THE THEATRICAL MIRROR; or, daily record of public amusements, bills of the play, and minute observations on the performances

In parts [vol. 1] nos. 1–31, misnumbering no [30] as "29" 1 Oct 1827 to 5 Nov 1827; illus.; "published every morning at 9 o'clock" MB

E. Elliot [1827]

From no. 5 on, the notation "Vol. 1" is included in the head-title.

Then The theatrical mirror; or, daily bills of the performances.

In parts vol. 1 nos. 32–36 6 Nov 1827 to [10 Nov 1827] MB

E. Elliot [1827]

The suspension of publication is not announced.

4148 THE CENSOR: an entirely original work devoted to literature poetry and the drama. Complete in one volume.

nos. 1–16 6 Sept 1828 to 4 Apr 1829 *bi-weekly* LVA

J. Clements; Cowie and Strange 1828–1829

4149 *THE DRAMATIC CORRESPONDENT and amateur's place book.

nos. 1–21 26 July 1828 to 31 Jan 1829 *weekly* MB; MH

1828–1829

ULS. Stratman *148.*

4150 THE STAGE; or theatrical inquisitor.

vol. 1 nos. 1–3 Aug to Oct 1828 *monthly*; nos. 4–7 Nov to Dec 1828 *fortnightly;* pls. [8 fronts.]; illus.; t.p., contents list MH

G. Creed 1828

vol. [2] nos. 8–11 Jan to Feb 1829 *fortnightly*; pls. [4 fronts.] MH

W. A. Wright 1829

The head-title of no. 1 continues: "Consisting of biographical memoirs of actors and actresses; strictures on the drama; reviews, essays, poetry; dramatic anecdotes, memoranda and chit chat; metropolitan, provincial, foreign and amateur theatricals. The whole forming a complete critical and biographical illustration of the British stage." Claims to be a continuation of Oxberry's Theatrical Inquisitor, *1828 (no. 4104 above).*

4151 *THE THEATRE.

vol. 1 nos. 1–13 4 Oct to 27 Dec 1828 MH

[London] [1828]

4152 *THE COLUMBINE and weekly review of literature, the sciences, fine arts, theatricals etc.

nos. 1–19 4 July 1829 to 17 Apr 1830 *irregular* MH

1829–1830

ULS.

Then, *The Columbine or, dramatic mirror.

new series. nos. 1–27 24 Apr 1830 to June 1831 *weekly* MH

1830–1831

MB has a few nos. MH has nos. 1–20, 22–23 (ULS). *Extent of run not known.*

4153 THE DRAMATIC MAGAZINE, embellished with numerous engravings of the principal performers.

In parts vols. [1]–2 nos [1–10] March 1829 to Jan 1830 + nos. [1–3] 4 [5–6] 7 [8] 8–11 Feb 1830 to Jan 1831 *monthly;* lacking Feb to April 1831 GU

Whittaker, Treacher & Co. 1829–31

4154 *THE HARLEQUIN. A journal of the drama. Conducted by the editor of the *Companion to the theatres.* [*ed.* John Timbs.]

nos. 1–9   16 May 1829 to 11 July 1829 *weekly*; illus.; pl.; facsim.; t.p.; index   MB

Sanger   1829

An editorial note states that, just as this paper was steadily making its way to popularity, the Stamp Office intimated that it was a newspaper and liable for stamp-duty. This, which was a serious matter in those days, at once stopped the publication — Lowe. L copy destroyed.

4155 THE MONTHLY THEATRICAL REVIEW.

nos. 1–4   Sept. [1829] to Dec [1829]; pls. [4]   MH

Cowie and Strange; and G. Purkess   [1829]

In the copy seen, the printed wrapper of no. 1 only is preserved; it alone carries the publishers' imprint. The suspension of publication is not announced in no. 4.

4156 †NEW EVENING THEATRICAL OBSERVER; with bills of the play.

no. 10   1 Jan 1830 *daily*   MB
                                              [1829–1830]

Extent of run not known.

4157 *CHAT OF THE WEEK and gazette of literature, fine arts, and theatricals. [*ed.* Leigh Hunt]

nos. 1–13   5 June 1830 to 28 Aug 1830 *weekly*
                                              1830

ULS; Brewer, *p. 148.*

4158 *THE DRAMATIC GAZETTE; or, weekly record of the stage, music, public exhibitions, &c.

vol. 1   nos. 1–12   9 Oct 1830 to 1 Jan 1831   MB
[London]   1830–1831

L copy destroyed.

4159 THE TATLER. A daily journal of literature and the stage. [*ed.* Leigh Hunt *and others.*]

vols. 1–4 nos 1–493   4 Sept 1830 to 31 March 1832; t.p. to each vol; sub-title: "A daily paper of literature, fine arts, music and the stage" (vols 2–4, parts 229–300); "A daily paper of literature, fine arts and public amusements" (parts from 301 on)   MP
                                              1830–1832

new series————A record of books, fine arts, music, theatricals and improvements

In parts nos. 1–59 2 April to 6 Oct 1832; sub-title dropped after no. 31; includes the *Tatler playbill for the theatres,* nos. 1–12   MP
                                              1832

————*[volume issue of the new series.]—A miscellany of literature, fine arts, music, and theatricals. Edited by R. Seton   MB

London   1833

Brewer, *p. 148.*

4160 *ACTING MANAGER; or, the minor spy. A weekly review of the public and private stage.

nos. 1–4   14 May–18 June 1831   MH

G. Hood   1831

Nos 1–2, weekly; nos 3–4, fortnightly. Stratman 179

4161 THE BRITISH STAGE; or, dramatic censor.

In parts [vol. 1, nos. 1–3] April 1831 to June 1831 *monthly;* pls. [3 fronts.]   MH

J. Duncombe   [1831]

Vol. and part no. appear only on the ptd. wrappers, which, in order, are of blue, yellow, and green paper. In no. 3 the next number is anticipated, but neither of the two MH copies consists of more than three nos.

4162 THE THEATRICAL ROD! A weekly journal of the stage, literature, and general amusement.

nos. 1–2; lacking no. 3   MH

E. Duncombe   [1831?]

MB copy includes no. 3.

4163 *THE BRITISH DRAMA, and literary humourist.

nos. 1–2
                                              1832

Only recorded copy, at L, destroyed.

4164 THE THEATRICAL ATHENÆUM.

no. 1   16 Nov 1833   L

J[ames] Holmes   [1833]

Probably a copyright sheet only, since Holmes also deposited at L a large number of single sheet periodicals, all no. 1 (the Penny Athenæum, the Critical Athenæum, etc.), on the same day. No other numbers known.

4165 THE PROMPTER; or, theatrical and concert guide.

no. 1   28 June 1834   BP

[Published every Saturday morning, by the proprietor, Isaac Bass].   1834

4166 *THE THEATRICAL CRITIC.

nos. 1–2

London   1834

BMC, *but L copy destroyed.*

4167 THE LONDON AMUSEMENT GUIDE, and theatrical reporter.

nos. 1–56   27 July 1835 to 15 Aug 1836 *weekly;* lacking no. 5   L

[William Houstoun, then Alfred Henry Bell]
[1835–1836]

Suspension of publication not announced.

4168 THE LONDON AMUSEMENT GUIDE.

nos. 1–3   18 Sept 1836 to 2 Oct 1836 *weekly*   L

[Gadsden and Percival]   [1836]

Suspension of publication not announced.

4169 *MANAGER'S NOTE-BOOK.

nos. 1–14   Nov 1837 to Dec 1838   MB

[London]   [1837–8]

A collection of biographies of the leading actors on the English Stage, extracted from the New Monthly Magazine—Brown.

4170 ACTORS BY DAYLIGHT; or ≪"and" in the parts≫ pencilings in the pit. ⟨Containing correct memoirs of upwards of forty of the most celebrated London performers; original tales, poetry and criticisms: the whole forming a faithful account of the London stage for the last twelve months.⟩

vol. 1 nos. 1–43   3 March to 22 Dec 1838 *weekly;* illus., incl. front. to no. 13; t.p., pref., index   L

Then, Actors by daylight; and miscellany of the drama, music, and literature. ⟨Containing correct memoirs of the most celebrated London performers; original tales, poetry, and criticisms.⟩

vol. 2 nos. 44–55 [27 Dec 1838] to 16 March [1839] *weekly,* illus.; t.p., pref., index; "and miscellany... literature" is dropped from the title of the parts after no. 45   L

J. Pattie, W. M. Clarke   [1838–9]

The price, to no. 43, was 1d., no. 43 is priced 2d. The publication was stopped by the illness of the editor. At no. 52 the price was reduced to 1d. — Lowe. The variation in price corresponds to the number of pages. Stratman 213.

4171 ACTORS BY GASLIGHT, or "Boz" in the boxes.

nos. 1–37   21 April 1838 to 29 Dec 1838 *weekly;* illus.   MH

[Printed for the proprietors; published by H. Hetherington and W. Strange] (from no. 25 with an imprint giving Hetherington only)   1838

From nos. 2–12, a humorous engraving was presented gratis "with each number" — apparently eleven pls. in all; seven, on thin coloured paper, have been seen (MH and MB). In no. 37 it is announced that the periodical is to be

merged with The Oddfellow. Actors by gaslight *imitates the form of* Actors by daylight. *Contains a short novel by Charles Rice,* "The Life and Adventures of Clytus Muff, Tragedian".

4172 THE CALL-BOY.

nos. 1–4   21 April 1838 12 May 1838 *weekly*   LVA

[London]   1838

4173 THE ERA.

In parts vols. 1–103 nos. 1–5,268   30 Sept 1838 to 21 Sept 1939 *weekly*   L

[London: The Era Office, then Theatrical Publications (1930) Ltd.]   [1838–1939]

The Era, *the recognised organ of the theatrical profession, was founded in 1838 (no. 1, Sunday, 30th September), as a general newspaper, with a strong sporting element. It became, next to Bell's Life, the leading sporting paper. It is under the conduct of the present editor, Mr. Ledger, that it has become exclusively a theatrical and musical paper—Lowe. Sub-title varies. Copy not collated in full.*

4174 THE THEATRICAL REGISTER, and general amusement guide.

nos. 1–5   20 Sept 1838 to 29 Oct 1838; illus. *20 Sept, 8 Oct, then weekly*   MB

[Clarke]   1838

In no. 1 (published on Thursday) it is said that a "second edition" of the "general amusement guide" occupying pp. 7–8 "will be published on Saturday afternoon". In no. 1, a "splendid steel-plate Engraving" is promised gratis monthly, to be presented with no. 4 "in order to stitch in with the monthly part"; in no. 4, there is an apology for its delay; and in no. 5, there is no mention of it. Suspension of publication is not announced in no. 5.

4175 THE THEATRICAL JOURNAL; and stranger's guide.

vol. I–III nos. 1–159   21 Dec 1839 to 31 Dec 1842 *weekly;* t.pp.   L

S. Gilbert; J. Pattie   [1839–1842]

Nos. 1–32 with head-titles: "The theatrical journal and musical intelligencer".

Then The theatrical journal

vols. IV–V nos. 160–263   7 Jan 1843 to 28 Dec 1844 *weekly;* t.pp.; index (to vol. V)   L

For the proprietor by S. Gilbert   [1843–1844]

Then The theatrical journal; a weekly review of the drama, music, & exhibitions, metropolitan, provincial, and continental.

vol. VI nos 264–315   4 Jan 1845 to 27 Dec 1845; t.p.; index   L

Samuel Gilbert   1845

Then The theatrical journal ⟨a weekly review of public amusements, metropolitan, provincial, & continental. With original articles by the editor, *etc.*⟩

vols. VII–VIII   nos. 316–420   3 Jan 1846 to 1 Jan 1848; t.pp.; indices; illus.   L

For the proprietor [by Brittain]   1846–1847

Vol. IX nos. 421–472, missing from L copy.

Then The theatrical journal ⟨a weekly review of public amusements, with original articles by gentlemen of acknowledged talent⟩.

vol. X   nos. 473–523   4 Jan 1849 to 30 Dec 1849; t.p.; index; illus.   L

For the proprietor by Collins   1849

Then The theatrical journal ⟨a weekly record of the drama, exhibitions, and amusements, with original articles by gentlemen of acknowledged talent⟩.

vols. XI–XXI   nos. 525–1098   3 Jan 1850 to 26 Dec 1860; t.pp. (except for vols. XIII–XVI, XXI); indices   L

[vols. XI–XII] For the proprietor by Collins; [vol. XIII] For the proprietor W. Bestow by Thomas Reede; [vol. XIV] . . . by G. J. Baynes; [vols. XV–XX] . . . by [Henry] Vickers; [vol. XXI] . . . by Vickers & W. J. Kelly.   1850–1860

Vol. XVII wanting. "Edited by W. Bestow" on title-page to Vols. XVIII and XX.

*vols. XXII–XXIX nos. 1099–1516 Jan 1861 to Dec 1868 weekly

Vickers for W. Bestow   1861–1868

Vols. XXIII–XXIV at CtY (Stratman).

vols. XXX–XXXII nos. 1517–1672 6 Jan 1869 to 27 Dec 1871; indices; lacking t.pp. to vols. XXXI–XXXII   L

For the proprietor, W. Bestow, by Vickers 1869–1871

Edited by W. Bestow

*vols XXXIII–XXXIV nos 1673–1747 Jan 1872 to 4 June 1873 weekly

                                                  1872–1873

Vol. XXXIV at MH (Stratman). On William Bestow, see also above no. 936.1.

4176   †THE PASTIME, theatrical and musical journal.

No. 53   Tuesday Dec 15 1840   DFo

C. Lavergne   1840

4177   †THE THEATRICAL AND CONCERT COMPANION.

no. 514   24 Aug 1840   L

[F. Coghlan]   [1840]

No. 521, 19 October 1840, is at DFo.

4178   *THE THEATRICAL CHRONICLE and dramatic review . . . *ed.* C. T. Fowler.

vols. 1–4   nos. 1–147   1840 to 11 Feb 1843

                                                  1840–1843

new series, *ed.* Frederick Fox Cooper; vol. 5 nos. 1–16 23 Sept 1848 to 3 March 1849 (?)

                                                  1848–1849

ULS. L copy destroyed; an imperfect set at MB; no complete set known.

4179   *THE ACTOR'S NOTE-BOOK *ed.* James Cooke.

nos. 1–6   26 Apr to 2 June 1841 *weekly*   MH

London   1841

Stratman 223.

4180   THE LYRE: a musical and theatrical register.

vol. 1   nos. I–XXII   31 July to 27 Dec 1841 *weekly*; pls. [fronts.] to nos. IX, XII, XXI; t.p.; index   LGk

                                                  1841

4181   *THE   DRAMATIC   AND   MUSICAL REVIEW.

vols. 1–11   nos. 1–377   2 Apr 1842 to June 1852 *vols. 1–6 weekly; vols. 7–11 alternatively monthly and semi-monthly*

                                                  BU; E

Onwhyn   1842–1852

Stratman 225; BUCOP.

4182   THE CICERONE a record of the drama music and the fine arts Edited by J. H. Stocqueler, Esq.

nos. 1–24   30 Sept 1843 to 9 March 1844 *weekly*; t.p. (engr.); index   L

William W. Barth   [1843–1844]

4183   THE CRITIC: a journal of theatricals, music, and the exhibitions.

no. 1   7 Oct 1843; illus.   MH

Gilbert   [1843]

Then The critic

nos. 2–19   14 Oct 1843 to 10 Feb 1844 *weekly*   MH

[London: Gilbert]   [1843–1844]

The publisher is given in nos. 1 and 7 only; printed wrappers, if any, may have carried fuller details. In no. 7 it is said that the periodical is delivered every Saturday and that "a country edition is also published, which will be posted every Friday evening." The suspension of publication is not announced in no. 19, but Stratman 228 records another copy also of nineteen nos. only.

4184 OXBERRY'S WEEKLY BUDGET of plays and magazine of romance, whim and interest. New and improved series.

vol. II nos. 1–52 12 June 1843–27 May 1844   LGk

[London]   [1843–1844]

Then Oxberry's weekly budget of plays and dramatic recorder: a journal of theatrical literature devoted to the interest of the manager, the author, the actor, the amateur and the playgoing public.

vol. III nos. 53–79 10 June–7 December 1844   LGk

Edw. R. Lancaster; "also published by original publishers" Vickers and Cleave.   1844

Ed. by William Henry Oxberry. Vol. I, entitled Oxberry's budget of plays, *contains texts of plays only.*

4185 THE STAGE A weekly magazine of plays and players.

nos. 1–14 19 Oct 1844 to 18 Jan 1845 *weekly*   LGk

E. Dipple; J. Allen; W. Brittain; James Gilbert; W. Jenkinson   1844–5

4186 †THE CLOWN OF LONDON. At all the theatres, sights, pleasures, and amusements with fashions for the week, with cuts, humourous numerous right and left. Droll things for the passengers on rails and boats, being a weekly collection of locomotive and other wit, from the railway chairman's down to that of the humblest stoker on the line. Out every week; sold by every-body, every-where. Price, only 4 farthings.

nos. [1–30]; illus.   L

Printed by W. S. Johnson [and H. White]   [1845]

At top of each title-page: "A friend of Punch's". Parts not dated. Nos. 1–39 at ICN (ULS).

4187 THE DRAMA. A companion to the stage and concert room.

nos. 1–2 10 Oct 1846 to 17 Oct 1846; illus.   MB

Published by A. White; R. Wynn; Cleave, Pattie and Beale; Mansell; Barth; Purkiss; Appleyard; Dyson; Norris; King; Harris   [1846]

Then The drama

nos. 3–4 24 Oct 1846 to 31 Oct 1846; illus.   MB

Published by A. White [no. 3] Printed by D. M. Aird [no. 4]   [1846]

Then The drama. A companion to the theatre and concert room.

nos. 5–7 7 Nov 1846 to 21 Nov 1846 *weekly;* illus. MB

Published by R. J. Kennett   [1846]

In no. 7, continuation is anticipated, but Stratman *(237) records another copy, also of seven nos. only.*

4188 *†THE THEATRICAL TIMES ⟨A weekly magazine of Thespian biography, original dramatic essays, provincial, continental, American, metropolitan theatricals; a complete record of public amusements, with original portraits of eminent living actors.⟩

vols. 1–4 nos. 1–34; t.p., ded., pref., index + nos. 35–86 + nos. 87–138; t.p., + nos. 139–145, misnumbering 145 as "143" 13 June 1846 to 17 March, 1849 *weekly (twice weekly from nos. 26–34 2 to 30 Dec 1846);* wanting nos. 35, 55, 71, 146–149   LGk

————no. 150 (at foot of page: no. 1 new series 13 Sept 1851).

S. Grieves, Jun.   1846–1851

ULS *adds New Series nos. 1–4 13 Sept. to 4 Oct. 1851(?)*

4189 *THE CURTAIN; or, English entr'acte, adapted to the use of the Royal Italian Operas and all the principal theatres.

nos. 1–98, 100–149 nos. 1–72 *daily, remainder every other day*   MB

[London]   [1847]

Stratman *gives dates 18 Jan 1847 to [29 Dec 1847?].*

4190 THE DRAMATIC MIRROR and review of music and the fine arts.

nos. 1–37 [14 April 1847] to [Jan 1848] *weekly;* illus.
                                            NbU

William W. Barth   1847–1848

Suspension of publication not announced, but two other copies, also of thirty-seven numbers only, are recorded (Stratman 244). Undated on title pages; last number published after 3 January. L copy destroyed.

4191 *THE DRAMATIC NEWS; a journal of theatrical progress and light reading.

vol. 1 nos. 1–6 13 Nov 1847 to 18 Dec 1847 *weekly*
                                            NjP
                                            1847
ULS. *Extent of run not known.*

4192 [THE] SHAKSPERE NEWSPAPER.

[nos. 1–2]; illus.   L

[Francis Crew]   [1847]

Published to arouse the public over the projected sale of Shakespeare's house. See above no. 928.

4193 *THEATRICAL BEAUTIES.

nos. 1–10 1 May 1847 to 3 July 1847; lacking nos. 8–9
                                            MH
                                            1847
Stratman *248; L copy destroyed.*

4194 DRAMATIC REVIEW.

nos. 1–8 15 March 1848 to 3 May 1848 *weekly*
MB

[Published by the proprietors by G. Mansell] [1848]

In no. 8 it is said that a woodcut portrait of G. V. Brooke as Lucius Junius Brutus accompanies that no.; also in no. 8 further nos., together with a series of engravings, are anticipated, but Stratman (249) records another copy also of eight nos. only.

4195 THE SCENE SHIFTER or dramatic indicator and panorama of life as it is.

In parts. vol. 1 nos. 1–3 27 Nov 1848 to 11 Dec 1848 *weekly;* illus. MB

Smith & Co. [1848]

In no. 3, the next number is promised. The title may be metaphorical, but the magazine is nevertheless of theatrical interest.

4195.1 THEATRICAL PAUL PRY.

vol. 1 no. 2 30 nov 1848 *weekly* LGk

John Collins 1848

4196 THE EUTERPEAN, a critical review of music and the drama, and a record of public entertainment

In parts nos 1–14 16 Aug to 15 Nov 1849 *weekly* BU

[Robert Palmer and Joseph Clayton] [1849]

4197 THE OPERA BOX.

†nos. [1–15] 16–24 26–63 [=62]; 15 March to 18 Aug 1849, *twice, then three times a week*

[London] [1849]

IKF. A run of 218 nos. in 3 vols. recorded in Brown at MB. "Published every day that Her Majesty's theatre is open," with sixty-one supplements giving the programme of the evening.

4198 THE STAGE: a weekly magazine of generalities, and a special guide to the sights of London. 1–14

nos. 1 [2–14] 24 March 1849 to 30 June 1849 *weekly from no.* [2] *onwards;* t.p.; pref. LGk

Andrew Vickers 1849

No more published.

4199 THE STAGE-MANAGER; a [weekly, (from no. 4)] journal of dramatic literature and criticism.

In parts vol. I nos. 1–20 17 Feb 1849 to 30 June 1849; illus. LVA

Winn [Nos 2–3: For the proprietors by H. James; nos. 4–20: For the proprietor by R. Macdonald] [1849]

new series. nos I–XIV 4 Oct 1849 to 3 Jan 1850 LVA

Printed and published by the proprietors; and Vickers [1849]

Then The literary review and stage manager. A journal of literature, music, the drama and fine arts.

new series. vol 2 nos 1–11 [12] 10 Jan to 28 March 1850 LVA

Printed and published by the proprietors and Vickers 1850

No [12], *entitled simply The Literary review, is "the last that will be published". Copy in L has plate "Presented Gratis with no. 5 New Series".*

4200 THE THEATRICAL PROGRAMME and entr'acte.

nos. 1–12 4 June 1849 to 20 Aug 1849 *weekly* L

[E. Baker, then Evans, printer] [1849]

Nos. 2–7 wanting cover-titles.

Then The theatrical mirror and playgoers' companion

nos. 13 [i.e.1] 2–6 27 Aug 1849 to 1 Oct 1849 *weekly* LGk

n.p. [1849]

Suspension of publication is not announced, but two copies of 6 numbers only are known, and therefore perhaps no more were published. Each number includes bills, and "The Stranger's Friend" (tables of cab fares, etc.).

4201 *THEATRICAL REVIEW and author's miscellany; a monthly journal of the stage.

nos. 1–5 Sept 1849 to Jan 1850; illus. MH

[London: S. J. Duffield] 1849–50

new series nos. 1–6 Feb to July 1850; illus. DLC

[London: S. J. Duffield] 1850

Sub-title varies. Stratman 258; DLC Cat.

4202 vacant

4203 *†THE STAGE MIRROR; a journal devoted to the histrionic and operatic art and literature.

nos. 1–8 31 Oct to 21 Dec 1850 *weekly* MH
1850

Nos. 1, 3, 8 in MH (ULS). Extent of run not known.

4204 TALLIS'S DRAMATIC MAGAZINE and general theatrical & musical review ⟨A new era of the stage⟩

Nov 1850 to June 1851 *monthly;* engr. t.p.; pls. [16] E
London and New York: John Tallis & Co. [1850–1851]

Then Tallis's drawing room table book of theatrical portraits, memoirs and anecdotes.

pp. [1] 2–46 [47–48]; engr. t.p.; pls. [front., 22] E
London & New York: John Tallis & Company [1851]

Issued in 6 monthly parts, July to December 1851.

Then *†Tallis's Shakspere gallery of engravings.
                                                    MB
London & New York: John Tallis & Company
                                        [1852–1853]

*Issued in 20 monthly parts, January 1852 to October
1853.*

————*[reissue] Intended as a supplementary
volume, or to illustrate all existing editions of the works
of the immortal bard of Avon: with essays on the plays,
forming a history of the sources from which he derived
his subjects, and a critical analysis of every drama.
pls.   MB
The London Printing and Publishing Co.   [185–?]

4205 †THE WORLD: a dramatic, musical, & literary
journal.
nos. 9–14 4 May 1850 to 8 June 1850 *weekly* L
[W. Thomas]   [1850]

Nos. 1–14 at MH (Stratman 266).

4206 THE MANAGER'S CIRCULAR or, general
theatrical directory. [ed. Henry Butler]
no. 1 [1] March 1851   L
[Henry Butler] subscribers only   1851

See also no. 4209 below.

4207 *THE PLAY-GOER: and literary tatler.
nos. 1–18. 25 January–24 May *weekly*   DLC
C. Harris   1851

DLC Cat.

4208 DRAMATIC REGISTER. [ed. T.F.D.C.]
[nos. 1–3] 1851 to 1853 *annually*; illus.   LGk
Thomas Hailes Lacy   1852–1854

*pp. 24, 60, and 120. The editor initials the preface to the
first number, and in this copy in a note to his "Daddy" in
the third number announces the suspension of publication.*

4209 HENRY BUTLER'S DRAMATIC ALMA-
NAC, and theatrical directory for 1853.
pp. [i–iii] iv [5] 6–31 [32]; vignette on t.p.; inset, fold.
[1]   E
[London]: Henry Butler   January 1st, 1853

See also no. 4206 above.

————Henry Butler's theatrical directory and dramatic
almanack for the year 1860, being a leap-year, [to
be continued annually.] Edited by John A. Heraud.
pp. [1–5] 6–48; insets, fold. [3 (map and facsims.)] E
Henry Butler   January 1, 1860

4210 THE GENERAL DRAMATIC EQUESTRIAN
& MUSICAL AGENCY & sick fund association for
1857 [1858, 1859] almanack by J. W. Anson secretary.
nos. [1–3] [1856 to 1858] *annually*   L
n.p.   [1856–1858]

*Each number is a large broadside, with ornamental head-
title. The first two printed in blue. A copy of the second was
presented gratis to "every Green Room throughout the
United Kingdom, America, and Australia". Presumably
published late in the old year.*

Then, Dramatic, equestrian, and musical agency, and
sick fund association almanack. Being bissextile or leap
year 1860. By J. W. Anson, secretary to the Royal
Dramatic College — treasurer of the New Theatre
Royal Adelphi — secretary to the Dramatic, Equestrian
and Musical Sick Fund Association, &c. &c.
no. [4] [1859]   L
n.p.   [1859]

*A large broadside. Presumably published late in the old
year.*

————*[another edition]
Advert. in no. [4]: "can also be had in book form"

Then Anson's (Secretary to the Royal Dramatic
College. . . .) dramatic, equestrian, musical agency,
and sick fund association almanack for 1861
no. [5] [1860]   L
Printed by William Snell   [1860]

*A large broadside, presumably published late in the old
year.*

————*[another edition]?
No. [5] in book form?

Then Anson's dramatic, equestrian, & musical sick
fund association almanack for 1862 [1863]
nos. [6–7] [1861–1862]   L
J. W. Anson   [1861–1862]

*Each number is a large broadside, presumably published late
in the old year.*

————[another edition] Dramatic, equestrian,
and musical sick fund almanack for 1862 [1863], by
J. W. Anson, secretary. . . .
[nos. 6–7] [1861–1862]   L
Printed for H. M. Arliss   [1861–1862]

*Booklets, of [80] and [84] pages respectively. No. 6 with
pink, and no. 7 with blue printed covers. Printed in blue.*

Then Dramatic, equestrian, & musical sick fund
almanack for 1864. By J. W. Anson, secretary . . .
[no. 8] [1863]   L
Printed by H. M. Arliss   [1863]

A booklet with 96 pages and blue paper cover printed in gold. No broadside edition known. Presumably published late in the old year. Printed in blue.

Then Dramatic & musical almanack for 1865. By J. W. Anson, secretary . . .

no. [9] [1864]   L

Printed by Arliss & Co.   [1864]

A booklet with 116 pages and red paper cover printed in gold. No broadside edition known. Presumably published late in the old year. Printed in blue.

Then Dramatick almanack for 1866 [1867–1872], by J. W. Anson, secretary . . .

nos. [10–16] [1865–1871] *annually*   L

Diprose [and Bateman]   [1865–1871]

Booklets. No. [10] edited by J. H. Siddons. No. [14] has three plates, no. [16] one double plate and frontispiece (portrait of Anson). Each number has a coloured paper cover (green, brown, green, green, mauve, blue, blue) printed in gold (except [13], [14] printed in black). The booklets each contain 128 pages (including a blank leaf in no. [16]), except no. [10] (124 pages) and no. [11] (112 pages, including a blank leaf). No broadside editions known. Suspension of publication is not announced in no. [16]; no other copies or numbers are known. Presumably published late in the old year. These almanacks were published in aid of the General Dramatic, Equestrian, and Musical Agency, and Sick Fund Association, founded in 1855. Printed in blue.

4211 *THE THESPIAN AND DRAMATIC RECORD, a journal especially designed to promote the interests of the British stage.

nos. 1–15   29 Apr to 5 Aug 1857 *weekly*   MB
                                                          1857

4212 †MOLIERE & SHAKESPEARE: an international review of the stage.

no. 1   29 Oct 1858; lacking pp. 5–8   BP

Alfred Cheron   1858

Bilingual.

4213 THE ENTR'ACTE: a daily programme of theatrical and other public entertainments.

nos. 1–120   16 May 1859 to 1 Oct 1859   L

[London: Thomas Barton]   [1859]

First four numbers entitled: "L'entr'acte. . . ."

Then The daily director and entr'acte: a programme of theatrical and other public entertainments.

nos. 121–432   3 Oct 1859 to 29 Sept 1860   L

[London: Thomas Barton, then George Ellis]
                                                  [1859–1860]

Sub-title varies. No more published.

4214 THE EVENING PROGRAMME and entr'acte: a programme of theatrical and other public entertainments.

no. 181, 12 Dec 1859   DFo

Thomas Barton   1859

Then The evening programme and entr'acte: a journal of the drama, music, fine arts, fashionable intelligence, &c., &c.

no. 222   30 Jan 1860   DFo

Thomas Barton   1860

4215 *THE PLAYERS. Edited [nos 5–38] by Wilfrid Wisgast, M.A. *pseud.* of George Sexton.

nos 1–8, vol 1 no 9–vol 4 no 82   2 Jan 1860 to 20 July 1861   *weekly*; illus; sub-title after no 27: a dramatic and literary journal; after no 38: a dramatic, musical and literary journal.   MH

George Abingdon, *then* H. Vickers   1860–61
   IKF (*nos. 1–18 only*); ULS.

✖   The comet [1862?] *See no.* 4442.

4216 ILLUSTRATED SPORTING NEWS and theatrical and musical review.

nos. 1–186   15 March 1862 to 30 Sept 1865 *weekly*   L

E. Harrison, then George Maddick   1862–65

Then Illustrated sporting news theatrical review

nos. 187–193   7 Oct to 18 Nov 1865 *weekly*   L

George Maddick, then J. Carter   1865

Then Illustrated sporting and theatrical news [*ed.* Henry Sampson 1869–70]

In parts vols. 4–7 nos. 194–364   25 Nov 1865 to 20 Feb 1869 *weekly*; illus.; suppl. 13 Oct 1866   L

† In parts new series vol. 1 nos. 1–44, vol. 10 nos. 2–12 27 Feb 1869 to 19 March 1870 *weekly*; illus.

[J. Carter, then others]   [1865–1870]

✖   The Royal Dramatic College news . . . [1863]. *See no.* 2145.

4217 BOOSEY'S MUSICAL & DRAMATIC REVIEW.

In parts nos. 1–9   5 March 1864 to 30 April 1864 *weekly*   MB

[Marylebone: John Boosey]   [1864]

Then The musical and dramatic review

nos. 10–14   7 May 1864 to 4 June 1864 *weekly*   MB

[Marylebone: John Boosey]   [1864]

In no. 14, "The proprietors . . . beg to announce that the publication of the paper will cease with the present number."

4218 *THE LONDON PLAYBILL.

                                                  [1864?]

STR.

4219 THE ORCHESTRA A weekly journal of music and the drama.

vols. 1–2 nos. 1–52 Oct 1863 to Sept 1864   L

Adams and Francis, and Cramer and Co.   1864

Each volume with a title-page and contents leaf.

Then The orchestra A weekly review of music and the drama.

vols. 3–10 nos. 53–260 Oct 1864 to Sept 1868   L

Adams and Francis, and Cramer and Co.   1865–1868

Each volume with a title-page and contents leaf. Vol. 5 with plates.

Then The orchestra: a weekly review: musical, dramatic, and literary.

vols. 11–22 nos. 261–561 Sept 1868 to June 1874 L

J. Swift   1869–1874

Each volume with a title-page and contents leaf. Vol. 19 with a folded inset. This copy lacks nos. 486, 487, and 538 and the title-pages and contents leaves of vols. 21 and 22.

Then The orchestra: a monthly review: musical, dramatic & literary. New series.

vols. 1–6 nos. 1–72 Aug 1874 to July 1880   L

Swift and Co., and Adams and Francis   1875–1880

Each volume with a title-page and index.

Then The orchestra and the choir. A monthly review: musical, dramatic & literary. New series.

vols. 7–8 nos. 73–98 Aug 1880 to Sept 1882   L

William Reeves   1881–1882

Volume 7, but not 8, with a title-page and index.

Then The orchestra, choir, and musical education A monthly review: musical, educational, dramatic, and literary.

In parts new series vols. 9–10 nos. 99–122 Oct 1882 to Sept 1884   L

[William Reeves]   [1882–1884]

Vol. 9 with a folded inset.

Then The orchestra musical review A weekly record of musical art, education, the drama, &c.

In parts new series [vols. 11–13] nos. 123–213 4 Oct 1884 to 26 June 1886   L

[William Reeves]   [1884–1886]

Then Orchestra musical review A record of musical art, education, the drama, &c.

In parts new series [vol. 14] nos. 214–230 Aug 1886 to Dec 1887 *monthly*   L

[William Reeves]   [1886–1887]

Discontinued. New series vols. 9 to [14], nos. 99 to 230 include vols. 5 to 8 of The Musical Review, *founded 1878.*

4220 ★THE PLAYBILL.

no. 92 2 July 1866; no. 133 20 Aug 1866

IKF.

4221 ★SOCK & BUSKIN. The drama: music: entertainments.

nos. 1–4

1867

BMC., *but L copy destroyed.*

4222 ★THE WEEKLY THEATRICAL REPORTER and music hall review.

nos. 1–14 14 Dec 1867 to 14 March 1868   MB
1867–1868

4223 THE ERA ALMANACK. Conducted by Edward Ledger.

1868–1869 *annually*   GU

Then The Era Almanack and Annual. Conducted by Edward Ledger.

1870–1905; illus.; pls., insets (facsims.)   GU

Lacking 1881–1886.

Then The Era Almanack and Annual [*ed.* Frank Desprez].

1906–1911; illus., incl. facsims.   GU

Then The Era Almanack and Annual. Edited by Frank Desprez.

1912–1913; illus., incl. facsims.   GU

Then The Era Annual. Edited by Alfred Barnard.

1914, 1915–16, 1917, 1918; illus.; col. pls.   GU

Then The Era Annual.

1919; illus.   GU

"The Era"   1868–1919

The early issues are extremely scarce and much sought after. That for 1871, which contains "How we got out of Paris", by Fred Vokes, is specially scarce — Lowe. Issued in wrappers, carrying title, until 1892: The Era Dramatic and Musical Almanack; 1893–1916: The Era Dramatic and Musical Annual; from 1917: The Era Annual.

4224 THE MUSIC HALLS' GAZETTE. A journal of intercommunication between music hall managers, their artistes at home and abroad, and the public.

In parts vol. 1 nos. 1–36 11 Apr 1868 to 12 Dec 1868 *weekly*   L

[London: Richard Allerton]   [1868]

4225 PICTORIAL SPORTING AND THEA-TRICAL GUIDE and record of music, literature and the fine arts.

In parts vol xxi nos. 1041–1044 17 Oct 1868 to 7 Nov 1868 *weekly*; illus.   L

[Alfred William Huckett]   1868

Only four numbers issued. A brief rival of the Illustrated Sporting and Theatrical News. *Sub-title changed in no. 1043 to: An authority on sport, music, art, and the drama.*

4226 *THEATRICAL AND MUSICAL REVIEW, an independent journal of criticism.

vol. 1 nos. 1–7 1 Oct to 12 Nov 1868

1868

Lowe. *L copy destroyed.*

4227 *THE DRAMATIC CHRONICLE AND OBSERVER.

nos. 1–3 4 Jan 1870 to 18 Jan 1870 *weekly* MB

1870

These three numbers were, I believe, all that were issued — Lowe.

4228 †THE LONDON ENTR'ACTE illustrated theatrical and musical critic and advertiser

nos. 27–88 8 Jan 1870 to 11 March 1871; illus. L
[London: James Welch, then others] [1870–1871]

Then London and provincial entr'acte theatrical and musical critic and advertiser.

nos. 89–137 18 March 1871 to 17 Feb 1872; illus. L
[London: H. J. Chawner] [1871–1872]

Then The entr'acte theatrical and musical critic and advertiser.

nos. 138–306 24 Feb 1872 to 8 May 1875; illus. L
[London: H. J. Chawner, then others] [1872–1875]

Then The entr'acte and limelight. Theatrical and musical critic and advertiser [sub-title varies].

nos. 307–1,974 15 May 1875 to 26 Apr 1907 *weekly;* illus. L
[London: W. H. Combes, then others] [1875–1907]

Nos. 1–26 not known. Not collated in full. Covers of the last few nos. at L.

4229 *THE MUSIC HALL CRITIC and programme of amusements.

vol. 1 nos. 1–7

1870

BMC, *but L copy destroyed.*

4230 THE VAUDEVILLE MAGAZINE A monthly journal of fact, fiction, fun, and fancy. Ed. Frederick J. Stimson and Alfred C. Skinsley.

In parts vol. 1 nos. 1–5 Sept 1871 to Jan 1872 L
F. J. Stimson and A. C. Skinsley 1871–1872

No. 4 has cover title: "Christmas Ransom A collection of amusing and entertaining stories". Each number with printed paper covers. Each number contains a theatrical section, and there are occasional theatrical articles, but "vaudeville" in the title is not used in its theatrical sense. Suspension of publication not announced, and further numbers anticipated, but no more known.

4231 THE WANDERING THESPIAN ANNUAL. *ed.* Walter Stephens.

no. [2] 1871 L

Thomas Hailes Lacy [1871]

No. [2] only (on cover: "Second Year"). Extent of run not known.

4232 vacant

4233 †THE ENTR'ACTE ALMANACK and theatrical & music hall annual for 1873[–1885].

[vols 1–13], illus; pls. L
Printed by the proprietor, H. W. Foster, and published by W. H. Combes [1872?–1884?]

Vol. 1 only at L; vols. 2, 4–13, at MH (Stratman 310), not seen.

Then The entr'acte annual. Conducted by W. H. Combes. 1886[–1906]. With illustrations by Alfred Bryan [Horace Morehen, Tom Downey]

[vols 14–34] illus; pls. L
[W. H. Combes] [1885?–1905?]

Vols. 14, 24–34 only at L; vols. 15–23, at MH (Stratman 310), not seen.

4234 †SAMUEL EYRE'S THEATRICAL PROGRAMME.

nos. 1–35 7 Oct 1872 to 2 June 1873 *weekly* L
Samuel Eyre [1872–1873]

Then The theatrical programme.

nos. 36–58 9 June 1873 to 10 Nov 1873 *weekly* L
[Samuel Eyre] 1873

Nos. 123–?, April 1875 to March 1876, are at MH, nos. 116–157 at BP. Some numbers for 1875–1876 are at NN. Last number 174? May's British & Irish Press Guide 1876 (but not 1877) records twice-weekly publication in 1876 by G. B. Huggett (from Eyre's old address).

4235 FIGARO-PROGRAMME.

In parts new series vol. [1]–2 nos. 1–49 11 July 1874 to 12 June 1875 *weekly;* each no. with pl. (photo). L
[Alfred Wilcox] [1874–1875]

Then The London programme and sketch book.

In parts vol. 2 nos. 50–51   19 June 1875 to 26 June 1875; each no. with pl. (photo.)   L

[Alfred Wilcox]   [1875]

Then The Saturday programme and sketch book.

In parts   vols. 2–6 nos. 52–181   3 July 1875 to 21 Apr 1877 *weekly;* each no. with pl. (photo.)   L

[Alfred Wilcox]   [1875–1877]

From 23 August 1876, The Wednesday Programme and Sketch Book, No. 112, was also issued, weekly, in the same numbered series as The Saturday Programme. The Wednesday Programme *also has mounted photos. After April 21st,* The Saturday Programme *was incorporated in* The London Figaro. The Wednesday Programme *continued until 20 June 1877; it then became* The Great City.

4236   THE ILLUSTRATED SPORTING & DRA-MATIC NEWS.

vols. 1–175   nos. 1–3,587   28 Feb 1874 to 25 June 1943 *weekly* then *fortnightly*   L

Thomas Fox, then others   [1874–1943]

The excellent criticism and information on theatrical matters, for which this successful weekly is noted, are supplemented by the extremely clever and humorous criticisms of the "Captious Critic," originally done by Wallis and William Mackay. The drawings are now done by Alfred Bryan, the letterpress by Montague Vizetelly — Lowe. Ceases to be theatrical, becoming Sport & Country *in the course of vol. 175, and, in October 1957,* Farm & Country. *Not collated in full.*

4237   THE LORGNETTE PROGRAMME.

In parts vol 1 nos. 1–2   23 Sept 1874 to 7 Oct 1874.   L

[John Anderson]   [1874]

Then The lorgnette programme dramatic and musical critic.

In parts vol 1   nos. 3–5   14 October 1874 to 28 Oct 1874 *weekly*   L

[John Anderson]   [1874]

The paper cost 1d., but "a special gratis edition of 4,000 copies is distributed every week". No more published.

✖ The Stage. London 1874–1875. *See The Stage, Dublin, 1874 (no. 4438 below)*

4238   THE DRAMATIC ART CIRCULAR and monthly record of the British Musical and Dramatic Institute. Edited by Mr. Charles Sleigh.

vol. I, no. 1   15 Feb. 1875; illus.   L

[Printed and published for the proprietor by F. A. Hancock]   [1875]

Discontinued, according to a note on copy at L.

4239   THE PROGRAMME, and dramatic review.

In parts. vol 1   nos. 1–2   June 1875 to July 1875   L

[Allen & Co., Dramatic Agents?]   [1875]

Discontinued, according to a note on copy at L.

4240   THE THEATRE; a weekly critical review.

*vols. 1–3   30 Jan 1877 to 23 June 1878   BP
1877–78

Then The theatre. A monthly review and magazine.

new series   vols. 1–3   Aug 1878 to Dec 1879; illus. (facsims); photos. [Woodbury types], [2] to each no.; t.p., index to each vol.   L

Wyman & Sons   1878–79

Then The theatre. A monthly review of the drama, music, and the fine arts. Edited by Clement Scott.

new series [third series] vols. I–VI   Jan 1880 to Dec 1882; illus.; pls. [2 + 5 + 20 + 8 + 3 + 3]; photos. (Woodbury types) 1 to each no. after vol I nos. 1 and 2, both with 2; t.p.; index to each vol.   L

Charles Dicken & Evans   1880–82

Then————Edited by Clement Scott [Bernard E. J. Capes (Jan to June 1890), Bernard Capes and Charles Eglington (July 1890 to June 1892), Charles Eglington (July 1892 to June 1893), Addison Bright (July 1893 to June 1894)]

new series [fourth series] vols I–XXX   Jan 1883 to Dec 1897; pls., [1 (vol II) + 2 (vol. VII) + 2 (vol VIII)] + front (vol XVII) + front. (vol XVIII) + 1 (vol XXII); photos. [1] to each no.; t.p., index to each vol. sub-title from Sept 1894: A monthly review & magazine   GM

David Bogue [Carson & Comerford (from July 1885); Strand Publishing Company (from Jan 1888); Eglington & Co. (from July 1889); Simpkin, Marshall, Hamilton, Kent & Co. Ltd. (from Jan 1894)]   1883–97

Incorporated in 1889 The Theatre Annual *(no. 4264 below).*

4241   THE CURTAIN. A weekly programme and review of the drama.

nos. 1–2   21 May 1878 to 28 May 1878   L

For the proprietors by Letts, Son & Co.   [1878]

Then The curtain. A programme and review of the drama.

nos. 3–10   4 June 1878 to 23 July 1878 [weekly]   L

For the proprietors by Letts, Son & Co.   [1878]

Nos. 1–7 on grey paper, 8–10 on white. A note from the publishers accompanying no. 10 states that further publication is postponed till September. In each no. it is claimed that "fresh editions" will be "issued daily".

4242 THE ORATOR. A monthly journal. Devoted to the interests of university men, & colleges theatres, & schools.

vol. I no. I 13 April 1877   L

[London]   [1878]

Published in the interests of "Professor Wilde" (i.e. A. H. Elworthy) "oratorical and elocutionary tutor. . . . Colleges, schools, and theatres attended." No more numbers known.

4243 THE DRAMATIC & MUSICAL CIRCULAR. An epitome of dramatic, operatic & music hall requirements issued weekly.

nos. 1–14   27 March to 28 June 1879   L

Brandon & Stevenson   1879

————nos. 15–21   5 July to 16 Aug 1879; illus.   L

Stevenson & Co.   1879

————nos. 22–27   23 Aug to 27 Sept 1879; illus.   L

[Printed by Arliss Andrews]   1879

Then The dramatic and musical circular. A theatrical and musical critic and advertiser.

nos. 28–29   4 Oct to 11 Oct 1879   L

[Printed by Arliss Andrews]   1879

Then The London mirror. In which is incorporated the dramatic and musical circular

no. 29 [*sic*: specimen no., printing THE of new title as "EHT"]–no. 31   11 Oct to 25 Oct 1879   L

[Published at 8 Bow Street, Covent Garden]   1879

4244 DRAMATIC NOTES an illustrated handbook of the London theatres 1879 by Charles Eyre Pascoe editor of 'The dramatic list' With fifty-one sketches of scenes and characters by T. Walter Wilson.

annual; illus.   L

David Bogue   1879

Then ————an illustrated year-book of the London stage edited by William H. Rideing With fifty-two sketches of scenes and characters by T. Walter Wilson 1880–1881 Second year of issue.

annual; illus.; pls. [2]   L

David Bogue   [1881]

GM copy has date on title-page.

Then————an illustrated year-book of the stage With forty-two sketches of scenes and characters by T. Walter Wilson 1881–1882 Third year of issue.

annual; illus.   GM

David Bogue   1882

————Second edition   L

David Bogue   1882

Then————By Austin Brereton With sketches of scenes and characters by T. Walter Wilson and Rudolph Blind Fourth year of issue 1882–1883

annual; illus.   GM

David Bogue   1883

————[reissue of first four annuals] a chronicle of the London stage 1879–1882

      L

David Bogue   1883

Lacking first three annuals.

Then————an illustrated year-book of the stage by Austin Brereton Fifth and sixth issues 1883–84 and 1884–85.

annual; illus; with separate half-title for 1884–85.   L

David Bogue   1885

Preface records that work did not appear in 1884.

Then————a year-book of the stage By Austin Brereton Seventh issue

annual; ptd. wrappers; pls. [13]; on wrapper: No. 7 Jan.–Dec. 1885   GM

Carson and Comerford   1886

Then————Illustrated by E. Morant Cox

annual; illus.; ptd. wrappers; on wrapper: Eighth issue   GM

Carson and Comerford   1887

Then————a year-book of the stage edited by Cecil Howard With illustrations reproduced from the "Illustrated London News".

annual; illus.; ptd. wrappers; on wrapper: Ninth issue   GM

The Strand Publishing Company   1888

Then————a year-book of the stage edited by Cecil Howard

annual; ptd. wrappers; on wrapper: Eleventh issue

      GM

Henry and Company   1890

Preface, dated May 1890, apologises for late appearance of the year book.

————[twelfth issue]

annual; ptd. wrappers; on wrapper: Twelfth issue

      GM

Hutchinson and Co.   1891

————[thirteenth issue]

annual; ptd. wrappers; on wrapper: Thirteenth issue

      GM

Hutchinson and Co.   1892

————[fourteenth issue]

annual; ptd. wrappers; on wrapper: Fourteenth issue

      GM

Gay and Bird   1893

4245 THE SATURDAY MUSICAL REVIEW A record of music and the drama. (With which is incorporated "The choir".)

In parts vol. 1 nos. 1–42 4 Jan 1879 to 18 Oct 1879 *weekly;* some nos. with separately paginated music. L

[Messrs. Metzler & Co.]   [1879]

> *Incorporates* The Choir and Musical Record (*1863 to 1878*) *and continues as* The Choir (*New Series vol. 1 Nos. 1–11, 1879–1880*).

4246 THE STAGE DOOR: stories by those who enter it edited by Clement W. Scott

pp. [1–5] 6–96; illus.; t.p. headed "Routledge's Christmas Annual" [for 1879]   L

George Routledge and Sons   [1879]

> *With 5 leaves of advertisements ("The Stage Door Advertiser") preceding the "Prologue", and 32 pages and 2 coloured leaves of advertisements following the "Epilogue".*

————The green room Stories by those who frequent it edited by Clement Scott.

pp. [1–3] 4–96; illus.; t.p. headed "Routledge's Christmas Annual" [for 1880]   L

George Routledge and Sons   [1880]

————Stories of the stage edited by Clement Scott I. The stage door II. The green room.

pp. [2] [1–5] 6–96, ²[1–3] 4–96; illus.   L

George Routledge and Sons   [1881]

> *A reissue of* The green room Stories by those who frequent it (*1880*) *and* The stage door: stories by those who enter it (*1879*).

4247 THE GREEN ROOM ⟨A weekly illustrated record of music and drama.⟩

nos. 1–2 26 June to 3 July 1880; each illus. with pl.; ptd. wrapper   L

[London]   1880

4248 THE PROMPTER a journal for amateur actors and authors.

In parts vol. 1 nos. 1–4 3 Jan 1880 to 24 Jan 1880 *weekly*   L

[George C. Bellamy & Austin Courtenay]   [1880]

> *From No. 2 sub-title is: "a journal for dramatic and musical amateurs".*

4249 THE STAGE DIRECTORY
In parts vol. 1 nos. 1–14 1 Feb 1880 to 1 March 1881 *monthly*   L
[J. A. Brook and Co., then others]   [1880–1881]

Then, The stage.
In parts nos. 1–*in progress* 25 March 1881–*in progress*
                                                             L
[Printed by J. C. Durant, then others]   [1881–   ]

> *Edited by Charles L. Carson — Lowe. Not collated in full.*

4250 THE ACTOR AND ELOCUTIONIST: a journal of elocutionary, literary, dramatic, musical, and general artistic interest, edited by Edwin Drew and Stuart St. Clair.

vol. 1 no. 1 15 Dec 1881 cover title   L
                                                             1881

4251 ★THE DRAWING ROOM, CONCERT AND STAGE.

vols. 1–3 (no. 1 of vol. 3)   O
                                                        1881–1883

> BUCOP. *L copy destroyed.*

4252 THE PLAY a chronicle of the London stage.

In parts vols. 1–3 nos. 1–119 20 Oct 1881 to 24 Jan 1884 *weekly*   L
[London: Henry Vickers]   [1881–1884]

> *From no. 9 sub-title is: "a chronicle for play-goers, a review of the drama, music, & literature"; from no. 37: "a review of the drama, music, & literature". From no. 9, each number has a "Supplement" listing the London play bills. Incorporated in no. 4255 below?*

4253 THE THEATRICAL WORLD. An international journal of the dramatic and musical profession. [*ed.* R. B. Caverly.]

In parts vol. 1 nos. 1–23, vol. 2 nos. 1–3 22 Oct 1881 to 22 Apr 1882 *weekly;* illus.   L
[R. B. Caverly]   [1881–1882]

4254 AN ACCOUNT of pantomime. The London pantomimes, 1881–1882. Fac-similes of the earliest announcements of English pantomimes, Joey Grimaldi's last speech, and verses on pantomime. By James Johnson.

annual; title on cover   L
[London]: H. Vickers   [1882]

Then †Pantomime Advertiser.

annual; running title; ptd. covers missing   L
[London]   [1883]

Then Johnson's account of pantomime (illustrated). The London pantomimes, 1883–1884. Copies of the bills of the earliest announcements of English pantomimes, with information concerning pantomime, Joey Grimaldi's last speech, and verses on pantomime. By James Johnson.

annual; ptd. covers   L

H. S. Phillips   [1884]

"Fifteenth Year of Publication", according to title-page.

4255 †THE ELOCUTIONIST. Edited by Edwin Drew.

vols. [1]–2 nos. 1–24 15 May 1882 to 1 Apr 1884; *monthly*   L

W. Nicholson & Sons "or of the editor, Mr. Edwin Drew"   [1882–1884]

Vols. 1 and 2 each with title-page and contents leaf. Nos. 1–21 each with head-title: "The elocutionist: a monthly journal of elocutionary, literary, dramatic, musical, and general artistic interest." Nos. 22–24 each with head title: "The elocutionist: with which is incorporated The play. A monthly journal of elocutionary, literary, dramatic, musical, and general artistic interests. Edited by Edwin Drew, assisted by Hinton Grove". Continuous pagination.

Then, The elocutionist: with which is incorporated *The play.* A monthly journal of elocutionary, literary, dramatic, musical, and general artistic interest. Edited by Edwin Drew. Assisted by Hinton Grove [by Charles Bradley from nos. 31 to 35 and by Ernest Douglas from Nos. 37 to 48].

In parts [vols. 3–4] nos. 25–35 37–48 1 May 1884 to March 1885 May 1885 to Apr 1886; parts issued in green and blue ptd. wrappers; separate pagination   L

[Sold by Nicholson & Sons, and privately] [1884–1886]

Willing's British & Irish Press Guide *records the cessation of publication in 1891.*

4256 THE AMATEUR THEATRICAL TIMES a journal devoted to amateur & professional news of the stage.

[no. 1 Oct 1883]   L

[Tom Whiting]   [1883]

Probably a specimen only.

4257 †THE DRAMA.

In parts vol. I – vol. II new series nos. 1–22 13 Sept 1883 to 7 Feb 1884 *weekly*; nos. 17–22 each with pl. (photo)   L

[Herbert Gray, then Messrs. Dubois and Ward] [1883–1884]

Nos. 1–30, to 3 April 1884, are recorded (Stratman 346) at NN. Published in connection with the Literary and Dramatic Agency, Savoy House, Strand.

4258 THE DRAMATIC AND MUSICAL DIRECTORY of the United Kingdom. The manager's guide, theatrical register, and handbook to the Provinces &c. The first and only complete, comprehensive, and reliable professional directory ever published.

annual.   L

The Proprietors at the offices of the Dramatic and Musical Directory   [1883–1885]

Then — incorporating Wilmot Harrison's "Manager's handbook", *ed.* C. H. Fox.

C. H. Fox [The theatrical costumier]   [1886–93]

4259 THE GENERAL THEATRICAL PROGRAMME a weekly newspaper and guide to theatres, public entertainments, &c.

In parts vols. 1–2 nos. 1–52 15 Dec 1883 to 6 Dec 1884   L

[London: for the Proprietors]   [1883–1884]

Each number with printed covers.

Then the theatrical programme. A weekly [newspaper and] guide to theatres, public entertainments, etc.

In parts vols. 2–3 nos. 53–113 13 Dec 1884 to 6 Feb 1886   L

[London: for the Proprietors, then George Edmund Shepherd]   [1884–1886]

No printed covers from no. 84. From no. 85: "newspaper and" is dropped from the sub-title.

4260 †OLD DRURY LANE CHRISTMAS ANNUAL.

[no. 1] 1882–3   L

[Alfred Gibbons]   [1883]

[No. 1] with colour printed covers, coloured plate, and words and music of "The Story of Sinbad the Sailor", 2 leaves, "presented gratis", and illustrations. 32 pages. Numbers for 1883–1884 and 1886–1887 are at MH. Extent of run unknown.

4261 THE THEATRICAL TIMES a journal devoted to amateur & professional news of the stage.

In parts vol. 1 nos. 1–22 Oct 1883 to 28 June 1884 *weekly from no. 3;* illus. (some fold.)   L

[Printed by Tom Whiting]   [1883–1884]

Further numbers are anticipated in no. 22.

4262 ★THE BOX OFFICE ENTERTAINMENT GUIDE.

vol. I–vol. XI nos. 1–271 1 Jan 1884 to 1 Apr 1895
                                              1884–1895

BMC, *but* L *copy destroyed.*

4263 THE FLY PAPER a satirical, dramatic, musical, and sporting journal.

no. 1 31 May 1884   L

[Joseph Tabrar]   [1884]

4264 *THE THEATRE ANNUAL. Edited by Clement Scott.

vols. 1–5; pls.	MH
1884–1888

Incorporated in The theatre (*see no. 4240 above*) *in* 1889.

4265 THE THEATRICAL AND MUSICAL GUIDE

nos. [1–15]	Nov [1884] to Jan 1886 *monthly*; ptd. covers	L

[For the proprietors by W. J. Goode]	[1884–1886]

Presented gratuitously to clubs, hotels, restaurants, &c.

4266 THE THEATRICAL MANAGERS' REGISTER and professional advertiser.

In parts	vol. 1	nos. 1–2	20 Feb 1884 to 27 Feb 1884
L

Foulger & Co.	[1884]

4267 *UNDER THE CLOCK. A weekly journal for playgoers.

nos. 1–64	30 Jan 1884 to 20 April 1885	MH
1884–1885

Nos. 1–52 in O.

4268 WALTER'S THEATRICAL AND SPORTING DIRECTORY.

[vols. 1–5]	1884 to 1888 *annually*	L

E. W. Kempton & Co., then others	[1884–1888]

No more published?

4269 THE WINGS. A monthly record of general, theatrical, and musical information and events. Edited by Mr. Charles Sleigh.

In parts.	vol. 1	no. 1	30 May 1884	L

[London]	[1884]

Published in connection with the Dramatic and Musical Training College founded by Charles Sleigh in 1873, Buckingham Theatre, 153, Buckingham Palace Road, S.W. No further numbers known.

4270 THE BAT. With which is incorporated The Prize Winner. [*ed. by James Davis.*]

nos. 1–153	31 March 1885 to 28 Feb 1888 *weekly*	L

Sporting Times Office	[1885–1888]

4271 THE DRAMATIC REVIEW. A journal of theatrical, musical, and general criticism.

In parts	vols. 1–17	nos. 1–313, ²1–4, 343–512	1 Feb 1885 to 26 May 1894 *weekly*; later vols. illus.	L

[London: the Proprietors]	[1885–1894]

*Edited by Edwin P. Palmer — Lowe.
Earlier volumes with signed contributions from Archer, Shaw, W. J. Lawrence, Davenport Adams, and others.*

4272 THE DRAMATIC TELEGRAM MUSIC AND THE DRAMA a journal of theatrical intelligence and universal dramatic advertiser [ornament: Dramatic, Equestrian, & Musical Sick Fund]

In parts	vol. 1	nos. 1–14	1 Nov 1865 to 6 May 1866 *fortnightly*; with a supplement to no. 5	L

[William Hawthorn Eburne at the Offices of the Dramatic, Equestrian, and Musical Sick Fund, then John Diprose for the proprietors]	[1885–1886]

No. 13 misnumbered 12, and no. 12 wanting or never published. Sub-title continues, from no. 6: "also of equestrian and musical information".

4273 INTERLUDE the organ of the variety profession.

In parts	vol. 1	nos. 1–25	14 Nov 1885 to 8 May 1886 *weekly*; illus.	L

[Henry Vickers, then Theop. Colville]	[1885–1886]

Sub-title varies.

4274 SOCK AND BUSKIN written by playgoers for playgoers.

nos. 1–2	4 Sept 1885 to 11 Sept 1885; illus.	L
[Thomas C. Hooker & Co.]	[1885]

4275 *THE CHROMATIC PROGRAMME of London amusements.

nos. 1–171	15 May 1886 to 17 Aug 1889
1886–1889

Times.

4276 M.H.A.A. GAZETTE.

nos. 1–11	30 Aug 1886 to 10 Nov 1886 *weekly*	L
[London: Music Hall Artistes' Association]	[1886]

Then, Music hall artistes' association gazette

nos. 12–42	17 Nov 1886 to 15 June 1887	L
[London: Music Hall Artistes' Association]	[1886–1887]

The Association was founded in March 1886. Secretary (and editor of the Gazette): A. Sherry Keddle.

4277 THE ARTISTE music hall gossip, theatrical and general news.

nos. 1–18	1 Jan 1887 to 2 May 1887; illus. *weekly*
L

[James Deacon]	[1887]

From No. 5 sub-title is: "Music hall gossip, theatrical, sporting and general news." With portraits of music hall artistes. No. 12 headed: "Second Edition — Music Hall Club Benefit."

4278 ENTERTAINMENT GAZETTE and guide to London.

In parts vol. 1 nos. 1–40, vol. 2 no. 41   15 Jan 1887 to 7 Jan 1888 *fortnightly until no. 12, then weekly;* illus. L

Kelly & Co.   [1887–1888]

Nos. 1–11 each with a folding plate "Supplement. What is going on". Sub-title varies. After no. 41, incorporated in Piccadilly (Nos. 1–304, 14 January 1888 to 9 November 1893)

4279 THE PLAYGOERS' POCKET BOOK. The dramatic year, 1886 [1887]. With descriptions and illustrations of all the most important new plays of the year; copies of many of the play-bills, and a record of dramatic events. Compiled by Paul Vedder. (All rights reserved.)

vols. [1–2] *annually;* illus.; pls. [4] to each vol.   MB

J. & R. Maxwell [1887]; Spencer Blackett [1888] [1887–1888]

4280 THE ELOCUTIONIST ANNUAL for 1889, consisting of original and selected readings, recitals, and elocutionary articles. Dedicated to, and with a fac-simile letter from, Mrs. Stirling. Edited by Edwin Drew, editor of *The Elocutionist* . . .

pp. [1–7] 8–136 [137–138 (text)]; illus., incl. facsim.   L

Southwood, Smith, and Co.   [1888]

No more published, apparently.

4281 MURRAY'S ENTERTAINMENT GUIDE.

[nos. 1–?] Nov 1888–? *monthly*   L

John Paul Murray   [1888–?]

Then The entertainment guide

nos. 19–? April 1890–? *monthly*   L

Andrew Reid, Sons & Co.   [1890–?]

Then Reid's London entertainment guide.

nos. 45–503 June 1892 to Feb 1931 *monthly*   L

Andrew Reid, Sons & Co [H. Grube, George Tucker, Alfred Morris, E. J. Larby and Philip Reid] [1892–1931]

The copy seen lacks nos. 2–9, 12–18, 20–44, 46–73, 77, 83–114, and a few later numbers. Extent of run not known, but discontinued by 1933. Those seen of nos. 1–80, and nos. 378–503 contain folded maps. Most numbers before 1900 also contain illustrations, and nos. 1, 10, and 11 contain coloured plates. The printed paper covers are coloured. Nos. 1–362 cost a penny each, subsequent numbers twopence. These theatrical booklets, containing details of the London (and some provincial) productions, and various short articles, have from approximately 30 to approximately 100 pages each.

4282 THE PLAYGOER a leaflet for playgoers.

In parts vols. 1–3 nos. 1–27 Nov 1888 to Oct 1890 *monthly to no. 12, then weekly to no. 18, then monthly;* illus.
                         L

[London: for the Proprietors by Harvey and Co., then others]   [1888–1890]

Sub-title varies.

4283 THE PLAYGOERS' MAGAZINE a monthly magazine for all players and playgoers. Edited by Paul Vedder.

In parts vol. 1 nos. 1–3 [Jan 1888 to March 1888]; illus.   L

Published for the Proprietors by W. Kent & Co. [1888]

4284 *COMEDY.

nos. 1–12 20 March to 24 Aug 1889   O
                            1889

Times.

4285 DRAMATIC OPINION conducted by Dr. Charles M. Clarke.

First no. [specimen] 28 Sept 1889; pl., fold. [1]; illus. L

[The Dramatic Opinion Company Ltd]   [1889]

Devoted to Henry Arthur Jones's The Middleman, produced at the Shaftesbury Theatre 27 August 1889.

4286 THE MUSIC HALL [and theatre review].

In parts vols. 1–44 nos. 1–1,229 16 Feb 1889 to 5 Sept 1912 *weekly;* illus.   L

[William McWilliam, then others]   [1889–1912]

Sub-title varies. From April 1902, incorporates The Showman (no. 4326 below). Not collated in full.

4287 †THE PROGRAMME and guide to amusements.

nos. 54–81 12 Oct 1889 to 3 May 1890 *weekly* L

[W. J. Pitt]   [1889–1890]

Wants no. 75, 22 March 1890. Nos. 65–81 with blue paper covers.

4288 THE PROMPTER AND THE FOOTLIGHTS: a music hall and theatrical review.

vol. 1 no. 1 1 March 1889; illus.   L

[Charles Douglas Stuart]   [1889]

4289 SPEECH. A monthly journal devoted to elocution, oratory, and the drama. Conducted by David J. Smithson.

In parts. vol. 1 nos. 1–8 Oct 1889 to May 1890; illus.
                         L

Henry Vickers [Hansard Publishing Union, Limited]
                      [1889–1890]

Each number with printed paper covers. No. 4 with a folded plate ("Supplement to the Christmas number of Speech") of Irving and Ellen Terry. No. 5 with an advertisement slip. No. 7 with a plate. No. 2 missing. No more published. D. J. Smithson ("formerly Lecturer on Elocution and Oratory at the University of St. Andrews, and late Director of the Scottish School of Dramatic Art, Edinburgh) was the author of Elocution and the Dramatic Art (1887, 1889, and 1897), largely an anthology.

4290 THE WEEKLY COMEDY. A review of the drama, music and literature. Edited by J. T. Grein and C. W. Jarvis.

In parts vol. 1 nos. 1–11 12 Oct 1889 to 21 Dec 1889   L

[Harvey & Co.]   [1889]

❌ The dramatic peerage, 1891. Edited by Erskine Reid and Herbert Compton. [1890]. *See nos. 2257–2258.*

Not planned by the editors as an annual or regular production.

4291 THE FOOT-LIGHTS music and the drama. A weekly journal of theatrical information.

In parts vol. 1 nos. 1–11 11 Oct 1890 to 20 Dec 1890   L

[Printed by Messrs. F. Harris and Wells]   [1890]

4292 THE ACTOR playgoer, and dramatic directory.

vol. 1 no. 1 1 Oct 1891   L

[London: for the proprietors and publishers]   [1891]

No more published.

4293 DRAMATIC OPINIONS an impartial weekly leaflet for players and playgoers. Edited by J. T. Grein & William Alison [by William Alison and Alexander Teixeira from No. 14]

In parts vol. 1 nos. 1–28 9 Dec 1891 to Aug 1892 *weekly, the last three nos. monthly;* some illus.   L

[For the proprietors by Gillingham & Henry]
                                                 [1891–1892]

4294 THE PLAYERS an independent dramatic organ.

In parts vols. [1]–2 nos. 1–47 16 Dec 1891 to 4 Nov 1892 *weekly;* illus.; ptd. covers   L

[London: "The Players" Publishing Co., Ltd., then, The Actors' Newspaper Co., Ltd.]   [1891–1892]

Sub-title from No. 21: "an illustrated paper for players and playgoers".

4295 ★THE PLAYGOERS' REVIEW: the organ of the Playgoers' Club. Edited by J. T. Grein.

vol. 1 nos. 1–5 Jan 1891 to May 1891 *monthly*   O
[London]   [1891]

BUCOP. (*L copy destroyed*).

4296 THE DRAMATIC YEAR BOOK for the year ending December 31st, 1891. An annual chronicle of the drama in Great Britain, France, United States of America and Australasia, and stage directory for the United Kingdom. Illustrated with portraits of popular actors and actresses. Dedicated with profound respect to Their Royal Highnesses the Prince and Princess of Wales. Edited by Charles S. Cheltnam.

annual; illus; pls. [24]   L
Trischler and Company   1892

A work which runs to some 740 pages. Preface dated 29 February 1892. The Dramatic Year Book 1893 edition is advertised as "now compiling" but no more were published.

4297 THE ENCORE. A music hall and theatrical review.

In parts vols. [1]–38 nos. 1–1,972 11 Nov 1892 to 9 Oct 1930 *weekly;* illus.   L

[London: The Encore Publishing Syndicate Ltd., then others]   [1892–1930]

Early numbers with plates. Sub-title varies. Not collated in full.

4298 THE PANTOMIME ANNUAL containing the portraits and biographies of the principal pantomime beauties. Edited by Henry A. Duffy.

pp. [1–2] 3–24; illus.   L
The Comet Publishing Company   1892

With printed covers, pp. [i] ii–iv. The cover title is: "The Pantomime Annual 1892–93". No other numbers known.

4299 †THE PROFESSIONAL WORLD published in the interests of the musical, dramatic, and artistic professions, and of all artistes who appear before the public. Edited by Alfred Capper and Wilson Newton

In parts vols. 1–3 nos. 1–27, new series nos. 31–34 1 March 1892 to May 1894, 1 Nov 1894 to 1 Feb 1895; illus. *monthly*   L

[For the proprietors by Alexander & Shepheard, and others]   [1892–1894]

Sub-title varies. Vol. 3 edited by Alfred Paterson. Nos. 28–30, June to September 1894 wanting.

Then The audience with which is incorporated the "Professional World" [Edited by Alfred Paterson]

In parts new series nos. 1–6 1 March 1895 to Aug 1895; illus. *monthly*   L

[For the proprietors by Francis Glass]   [1895]

4300 THE SPORTING AND DRAMATIC MIRROR.
no. 1 new series 2 May 1892; illus.   L

[Victuallers' and Brewers' Protectorate Limited] 1892

Then The sporting mirror and dramatic and music hall record.

new series nos. 2–441 9 May 1892 to 8 Oct 1900 *weekly;* illus.   L

[South Counties Press Limited, then others] [1892–1900]

Name changed after objections by the Illustrated Sporting and Dramatic News. *Incorporates* The Licensed Victuallers' Mirror (*Vol. 1 No. 1 6 February 1888 — vol. 5 no. 222 26 April 1892*), *which also contains much theatrical, especially music hall, material.*

4300.1 †THE BOHEMIAN. ⟨A monthly magazine and review of literature, drama, and art. Edited by S. L. Bensusan.⟩

vols.1–6 nos. 1–52 June 1893 to Oct 1899; illus.; t.p.p., indexes   L

The Bohemian Publishing Company   1893–1899

Lacking vols. 3 and 5; vol. 6 in parts, with pls., not illus. Later vols. ed. Charles W. Forward and H. Sidney Muller.

4301 †THEATRICALS dramatic & musical items of interest from all parts of the world.

In parts nos. 7–326 6 Oct 1893 to 9 Apr 1898 *weekly, and varies;* illus.; some nos. with pls.; some nos. with ptd. wrappers; no. for 6 October is Vol. 2 no. 1 according to cover-title, and Vol. 1 no. 7 according to head-title; Sub-title varies.   L

["Theatricals" Syndicate, then others]   [1893–1898]

Early numbers edited by "Wilford F. Field".

4302 WEST END AMUSEMENTS and souvenir of the stage.

Monday, 20 February 1893; illus.   E
                                              1893

4303 THE DRAMATIC WORLD a monthly epitome of the stage. Edited by E. and H. Gordon-Clifford.

In parts vols. 1–3 nos. 1–26 [=27] Nov 1894 to Jan 1897; illus.; each no. with pl. or pls. except nos. 21, 22, and ²13 (Sept 1896)   L

[London: The Dramatic World Syndicate] [1894–1897]

Plates to Nos. 5 and 6 wanting.

Then The dramatic illustrated world. A monthly epitome of the stage.

In parts vols. 3–9 nos 27–93 [=91] Feb 1897 to 1 Aug 1902; illus.; each no. with pl. or pls.   L

[London: The Dramatic World Syndicate] [1897–1902]

No nos. 47 or 48 issued. From no. 85 title is: The dramatic world. An illustrated journal. *Continued as* Society and the Dramatic World. Literature, Art, Music. (*Vol. 1 no. 1 New Series 1 September 1902 to May 1916*).

4304 THE GRAPHIC GUIDE to the London theatres. A succinct and descriptive digest of the plots and characters of all the plays performed at the principal theatres of the metropolis. Where to go. What to see. Edited by H. P. Priestley-Greenwood.

In parts vol. 1 nos. 1–7 June 1894 to Dec. 1894   E

Greenwood & Co.   1894

4305 PEARSON'S PHOTOGRAPHIC PORT-FOLIO of footlight favourites by eminent photographers.

In parts nos. 1–8 Dec 1894 to June 1895 *monthly*   L
C. Arthur Pearson   1894–1895

new series.

In parts nos. 1–5 Nov 1895 to March 1896 *monthly*   L
C. Arthur Pearson   1895–1896

A supplement in two parts (January and February 1895) was published: Pearson's photographic portfolio of pantomime favourites. *The first series comprises 128 portraits, the new series 80, and the supplement 32. There is no text.*

4306 THE THEATRICAL 'WORLD' for 1893. By William Archer.

pp. [i–v] vi–vii [viii–ix] x–xxxv[xxxvi], [1] 2–307 [308 (bl.) 309–332 (advts.)]   NbU

Walter Scott   [1894]

———THE THEATRICAL 'WORLD' of 1894. By William Archer. With an introduction by George Bernard Shaw, and a synopsis of playbills of the year by Henry George Hibbert.

pp. [i–v] vi–xxx [xxxi–xxxiv], [1] 2–417 [418 (bl.)], ²[1–2] 3–8 [9–10] (advt.); inset (advt. slip and spine label)   NbU

Walter Scott, Ltd.   1895

———1895 . . . With a prefatory letter by Arthur W. Pinero, and a synopsis of playbills of the year by Henry George Hibbert.

pp. [i–v] vi–xxxv [xxxvi–xl], [1] 2–445 [446 (bl.) 447–448 (advts.)], ²[1–2] 3–8 (8 pp. of advts.); inset (spine label)   NbU

Walter Scott, Ltd.   1896

———1896 . . . With an introduction "On the need for an endowed theatre" and a synopsis of play-bills of the year by Henry George Hibbert.

pp. [i–v] vi–lviii [lix–lxiv], [1] 2–423 [424 (bl.)], ²[1–2] 3–8 (8 pp. of advts.); inset (spine label)   NbU

Walter Scott, Ltd.   1897

———1897 . . . With an introduction by Sydney Grundy and a synopsis of playbills of the year by Henry George Hibbert.

pp. [i–v] vi–xxvi, [2] 1–452 [453–454 (bl.)]   L

Walter Scott   1898

Archer's dramatic criticism reprinted, mainly from the World. *The volume for 1893 has an epistle dedicatory to R.W. Lowe.*

4307 BOORMAN'S THEATRICAL DIRECTORY OF THE UNITED KINGDOM, 1895.

vol. 1 1895; cover-title   L

J. H. Boorman   [1895]

> *The head-title reads: "First edition for 1895", and in his preface Boorman promises a volume for 1896, but no others are known.*

4308 †THE DANGERFIELD GENERAL ENTERTAINMENT GUIDE. [Lockwood, E., *comp.*]

vols. [1–6] 1895–1904; *annually from vol. [4] fold. maps; wants vols. [2–3]*   L

The Dangerfield Printing Company   1895–1904

> *Extent of run not known.*

4309 THE DRAMATIC TIMES. The only organ devoted to amateur theatricals.

In parts vol. 1 nos. 1–13 2 Feb 1895 to 14 Sept 1895 *fortnightly;* illus.   L

[London: The Proprietors]   [1895]

> *Further numbers anticipated, but no more published. Sub-title varies.*

4310 THE LONDON BRIDGE THEATRE DIARY and amusement list [*ed.* Dramaticus].

nos. 2–7 June 1895 to Nov 1895 *monthly;* illus. (incl. fold. maps)   L

The London Bridge Dramatic & Musical Diary Company   [1895]

> *Booklets, each of 64 pages. Suspension of publication is not announced.*

4311 †THE VARIETY STAGE.

In parts vol. 1 nos. 1–2, new series vols. 1–2 nos. 1–50 Nov 1895 to 19 Dec 1896 *monthly,* then (*new series*) *weekly;* illus.; a few nos. with pls.   L

[W. J. Pitt, then Fred Lacey]   1895–1896

> *From no. 28, edited by C. Douglas Stuart. Nos. 51–54 (to 16 January 1897) recorded in BMC. First two numbers are specimens only.*

4312 ★ABC amusement guide and record.

nos. 1–3 7 March to 21 March 1896 *weekly*
                                          1896
Times.

4313 ★THE "ENCORE" ANNUAL.

[vols. 1–?] 1895–?
                                          [1896–?]
BMC, *but* L *copy destroyed.*

4314 †EUREKA a monthly theatre & entertainment guide and magazine.

nos. 1–2 15 Apr 1897 to 15 May 1897; illus.   L

The Favourite Publishing Co.   [1897]

> *No. 3 wanting. After no. 2 or no. 3, ceases to be especially theatrical. Sub-title changes, with no. 6[?], to "The Favourite Magazine". Continues to 1903.*

4315 THE PLAYGOER a journal of amusement.

In parts vol. 1 nos. 1–14 2 Oct 1897 to 19 Jan 1898 *weekly;* illus.   L

[London]   [1897–1898]

Then, The playgoer and playgoer's guide an illustrated journal of amusement.

In parts vols. 1–2 nos. 15–45 26 Jan 1898 to 24 Aug 1898 *weekly;* illus.   L

[London]   [1898]

4316 ★THE PLAYGOER'S MAGAZINE. A journal for theatre-goers, habitués of music halls, and amateur actors.

vol. 1 nos. 1–2

London   [1898]

> *No more published. BMC, but* L *copy destroyed.*

4317 THE PROGRAMME AND PLAYBILL, illustrated, of all the London theatres, music halls and entertainments.

In parts vol. 1 nos. 1–197 13 Oct 1898 to 7 July 1899 *daily*   L

[Frederic Winney Sabin, then George John Bell]
                                        [1898–1899]
> *Not illustrated.*

4318 THEATRICAL & MUSIC HALL LIFE.

vol. 1 no. 1 21 May 1898   L

[For the proprietors by the City Printing Co.] [1898]

4319 THEATRICAL AND PUBLIC LIFE.

nos. 1–8 Dec 1898 to June 1899 *monthly, weekly during March, no. 8 in June;* illus.   L

[Printed for the proprietors by The Castle Printing Co., then others]   [1898–1899]

4320 THE THEATRICAL PUBLIC GUIDE.

nos. 1–7 Jan 1898 to July 1898 *monthly*   L

[Printed for the proprietors by Stenlake & Simpson, then others]   [1898]

4321 VARIETY AND "VARIETY CRITIC" [*ed.* Bernard Hounsell].

In parts vol. 1 nos. 1–13 12 Feb 1898 to 7 May

1898 *weekly;* illus.; each no. with pl. ("Supplement to Variety") except the last; nos. 10–13 with ptd. covers L
[Fleet Printing Works]   [1898]

No. 1 without sub-title.

4322 THE ANGLO-FRENCH STAGE CHRONICLE international theatrical paper published every Friday.

In parts vol. 1 nos. 1–2 23 June 1899 to 14 July 1899; illus.   L
[London: For the Proprietors by Parkins and Gotto] [1899]

Bilingual.

Then, The Anglo-French chronicle political, literary and theatrical. Published in London every Saturday.

vol. 1 no. 3 29 July 1899   L
[For the proprietors by Parkins and Gotto]   [1899]

Bilingual.

4323 BELTAINE. [*ed.* William Butler Yeats,]

no. 1, May 1899; title headed: The organ of the Irish literary theatre; ptd. wrappers.   MH

London: at the Sign of the Unicorn; Dublin: at the "Daily Express" office.   [1899]

Described on wrapper as "an occasional publication".

Then Beltaine. Edited by W. B. Yeats.

In parts nos. 2–3, Feb. and April 1900; title headed: The organ of the Irish literary theatre; ptd. wrappers.
                                    MH
At the Sign of the Unicorn   [1899–1900]

————[vol. issue] The first annual volume of Beltaine. An occasional publication. Numbers one, two & three. 1899–1900. The organ of the Irish Literary Theatre. Edited by W. B. Yeats.   L
At the Sign of the Unicorn   [1900]

Note on title-page: "In response to many requests for Beltaine in a permanent form, the Publishers now re-issue the first year's Numbers in one Volume. The Numbers, in their original wrappers, have been simply encased in boards, for preservation on the bookshelf, with no addition save that of a Table of Contents to Number One." Wade 226.

4324 FOOTLIGHTS: the bulletin of the London and New York Dramatic Exchange.

no. 1 Oct 1899; illus. (facsim.)   L
[Printed by King, Sell, & Railton, Ltd. for the Proprietors]   [1899]

No more numbers recorded. A dramatists' agency.

4325 THE LONDON THEATRE, ENTERTAINMENT AND CONCERT GUIDE.

nos. [1]–16 week ending 14 July 1900 to week ending 2 March 1901 *weekly from no. 2, 17 Nov 1900.*
                                    L
R. P. Smith   [1900–1901]

Then The London theatre, concert & fine art guide.

nos. 17–623 week ending 9 March 1901 to week ending 19 Oct 1912 *weekly*   L
R. P. Smith   [1901–1912]

4326 *THE SHOWMAN; an illustrated journal for showmen and all entertainers.

vols. 1–4 nos. 1–68 Sept 1900 to 21 March 1902 *weekly*   NN
                                        [1900–1902]
ULS. *Merged in* The Music Hall (*see above no. 4286*).

THE ENGLISH PROVINCES

Bath

4327 *THE BATH THEATRICAL REVIEW: a series of criticisms on the performers and drama in general, for the season 1822–23.

vol. 1 nos. 1–25 12 Oct 1822 to 30 Apr 1823; new series vol. 1 nos. 1–3 6 Dec to 11 Dec 1823 [running title "Theatrical Review"] *weekly from no. 11* BhP
Bath   1823

See also above nos. 1554–1555.

Birmingham

4328 THE THEATRICAL LOOKER-ON ⟨at the Birmingham Theatre⟩

In parts vol. I–II nos. I–XXV 27 May to 9 Nov 1822 *weekly* + nos. I–XXV 19 May to 21 Nov 1823 *weekly*; pl. [front.] to no. XXV   MH

—[vol. issue] vol. I no. I: second edition; no. II [second edition]; t.p. to each vol.; otherwise as parts issue BP
[Birmingham: James Drake]   1822–23

Possibly edited by Alfred Bunn, or C. R. Cope. End of publication announced but see also no. 4330 below.

4329 THE BIRMINGHAM REPORTER; and theatrical review: or the opinions, doubts & perplexities of Humphrey Digbeth, manufacturer, and others.

In parts vol. I nos. 1–14 19 June 1823 to 18 Sept 1823 *weekly*   MH
[Birmingham: C. Buckton]   [1823]

In no. 14 the editor announces his departure from Birmingham, and "so it is very probable that this is the last sight that Birmingham will have of The Reporter". *R. C. Rhodes,* Theatre Royal, Birmingham *(1924), p. 22, writes that it was "suppressed because of its attacks on Mrs. Bunn."*

4330   THE BIRMINGHAM SPECTATOR, ⟨a miscellany of literature, and of dramatic criticism.⟩

[vol. 1]   nos. 1–24 29 May 1824 to 6 Nov 1824 *weekly*;
t.p., index   L

Birmingham: J. Drake   1824

Succeeds The theatrical looker-on *(see no. 4328 above). Discontinuation announced. No. 12 is labelled "Third Edition" presumably in mockery of the rapidity with which Alfred Bunn's* Letter to the Rev. J. A. James *went through a large number of "editions". Editorship attributed to William Hawkes Smith in manuscript note on copy at BP.*

4331   THE THEATRICAL JOHN BULL.

vols. 1–2 nos. 1–21 29 May to 16 Oct 1824 + nos.
1–19 28 May to 31 Sept [1825]; t.p. (covering both
vols.), index (to vol. 1 only); *weekly*   MH
[Birmingham]; W. Cooper   [1824–]1825

End of publication announced.

4332   THE THEATRICAL NOTE-BOOK.

vol. 1, no. 1. 28 June 1824   BP
Birmingham: [printed for and published by James
Drake]   1824

4333   ★THE MOUSETRAP. [*ed. Alfred Bunn?*]
Birmingham   1827

Urwin, *p. 24.* BUCOP *records* The Mouse Trap. *A very clever work without distinction, party or prejudice!! Nos. 1–2, 13–20 Sept 1824, at BP.*

4334   ★PAUL PRY.

nos. 1–8 14 June to 9 Aug 1827 *weekly*   BP
Birmingham   1827

4335   THE THEATRICAL ARGUS, and stage reporter.

no. 1 3 May 1830   BP
[Birmingham: printed and sold by W. Chidlow] 1830

4336   THE THEATRICAL TATTLER.

In parts vol. 1 nos. 2–3 24 Apr 1830 to 1 May 1830 BP
Birmingham: [printed by J. Drake]   1830

No. 1 17 April — Loewenberg.

4337   THE BIRMINGHAM musical examiner and dramatic review.

nos. 1–19 1 Sept 1845 to 3 Jan 1846 *weekly*   BP
Birmingham: Thomas Harrison   1845–6

4338   ★PRINCE OF WALES THEATRE. Play-bill and universal evening advertiser Birmingham.

nos. 1–92 1863 to 10 Nov 1865 *irregular*   BP
                                          1863–1865

4339   THE AMATEURS' GUIDE or, stage and concert hall reporter.

In parts. nos. 1–2 29 June 1867 to 13 July 1867   L
[Birmingham: printed by C. Redfern for the proprietor]
                                               [1867]

4340   THE BIRMINGHAM AND MIDLANDS MUSICAL JOURNAL and dramatic news.

nos. 1–18 29 Sept 1884 to 26 Jan 1885 *weekly*;
nos. 1–14 in ptd. wrappers, with title continuing
'containing accounts of all the concerts, theatres, musical
and dramatic entertainments, &c., with special papers,
by well-known eminent writers.'   BP
[Birmingham: James Handley]   1884

4341   THE BIRMINGHAM DRAMATIC NEWS. An illustrated record of the Midland stage.

In parts vol. 1 nos. 1–12 26 Sept 1885 to 12
Dec 1885 *weekly*; illus. by G. H. Bernasconi   E
[Birmingham: A. G. Beacon]   1885

4342   BIRMINGHAM AMUSEMENTS and souvenir of the stage.

nos. 2–65 17 July 1893 to 1 Oct 1894; illus.; col. ptd.
                                                    L
[London, Manchester, and Birmingham: Emott & Co
Ltd]   [1893–1894]

With part of No. 1 (?), published in May according to BMC.

4343   ★THE BIRMINGHAM pantomime annual 1899: a souvenir of the pantomimes. Edited by I. Waddington.

pp. 1–96; illus.   BP
[Birmingham]   [1899]

4344   ★THE CASTE: a weekly record of Birmingham plays and players.

vol. 1 nos. 1–4 5 to 26 March 1900   BP
Birmingham: Howard, Butterick & Co.   1900

Brighton

4345 *THE BRIGHTON DRAMATIC MISCEL-LANY.

nos. 1–57   26 July to 29 Sept *daily*

Brighton   1838

Stratman 215. L copy destroyed.

4346 †THE BRIGHTON MUSICAL, DRAMATIC AND LITERARY RECORD.

In parts vol. 1 nos. 1–13   Vol 2. No. 1 5 Oct 1850
to 4 Jan 1851 *weekly*   DFo

Brighton: E. Wright & Co.   1850–1851

Bristol

4347 THE THESPIAN.

In parts vol. 1 nos. 1–15   6 Jan to 14 Apr 1823 *weekly*
                                                      BrP

Bristol: W. Tyson   1823

Eaton, Cheshire

4348 THE EATON CHRONICLE; or, the salt-box.

nos. 1–20   30 Aug 1788 to [20?] Sept 1788 *daily at first
then less frequently;* t.p., ded., pref.   L

[Eaton Hall]   [1789]

*Written by and for the guests of the Earl of Grosvenor at
Eaton, Cheshire, and containing particulars of the
private theatricals there — Loewenberg.*

Leeds

4349 THE AMATEUR ACTOR. A monthly thea-trical journal. [*ed.* Fred S. Collinge]

no. 1 vol. 1   April 1886   L

[Leeds: F. S. Collinge]   1886

4350 *THE YORKSHIRE OWL PANTOMIME ANNUAL, 1893, 4.

illus.   LdP

Leeds: Barr & Co.   1893

————*1894–5. Edited by W. Lawrence.
Proprietors: N. G. Morrison and H. Burniston.
                                                      LdP

Leeds: the proprietors, at the office of the Yorkshire Owl.
                                                      1894

4351 *LEEDS PANTOMIME ANNUAL.
                                                      LdP

Leeds: [printed by W. Barrett & Co.]   [1894/5]

4352 *ROBERTS PANTOMIME ANNUAL.
1895–6. A souvenir of the pantomimes. Edited by
J. Waddington.

illus.   LdP
Leeds: Waddingtons Limited, printers   [1895]

————*Roberts' pantomime annual. Edited by
W. Lawrence.

illus.   LdP
Leeds: proprietor, B. Roberts   [1896]

————*1897–8. A souvenir of the pantomimes.
Edited by J. Waddington.

illus.   LdP
Leeds: proprietors, B. Roberts & Co.   [1898?]

4353 *THE YORKSHIRE HARLEQUIN. [Edited
by W. Lawrence.]

vols. 1–2 [nos. 1–24]   23 Dec 1896 to 9 March 1898
weekly during the pantomime season   LdP
Leeds: proprietors, B. Roberts & Co.   1896–98

4354 *LEEDS COLLEGE OF MUSIC. Quarterly
News.

vols. 1–10   Jan 1897 to Oct 1906 *quarterly*   LdP
Leeds   1897–1906

Then Leeds Triad. new series. The journal of the Leeds
College of Music, Drama and Art.

vols. 1–5 Jan 1907–July 1912   LdP
Leeds   1907–1912

Lincoln

4355 THE LINCOLN DRAMATIC CENSOR.

nos 1–4   21 Oct–13 Nov 1809   MH
Lincoln: printed by A. Stark   1809

*Occasional publication of future nos. is promised in the
first. Extent of run unknown. For A letter addressed to
the authors of The Lincoln Dramatic Censor see no.
1601 above.*

Liverpool

4356 THE LIVERPOOL DRAMATIC CENSOR,
or theatrical recorder; containing strictures on actors
and actresses, and a critical analysis of every popular
dramatic composition represented at the Theatre Royal,
in this town, during the season; with biographical
sketches of celebrated dramatists.

no. 1 [9 June] 1806; illus.   MB
Liverpool: T. Troughton   1806

*With ptd. wrappers (giving date 9 June), a t.p., and a
head-title (giving 8 June).*

Then The Liverpool dramatic censor, or theatrical
recorder.

In parts nos. 2–4   17 June 1806 to 1 July 1806 *weekly;*
illus.   MB
Liverpool: T. Troughton   1806

With ptd. wrappers, head-titles, but no title-pages. The last leaf of no. 4 is for use as the t.p. of the volume; the wording is the same as that on the t.p. of no. 1, except that it includes the words "Volume I" and gives no date. On the back cover of no. 4 the fifth no. is promised for 15 July, and further nos. fortnightly thereafter, but Stratman (42) records another copy also of four nos. only, and Lowe says only four nos. were issued.

————*second edition

pp. 286

Liverpool   1806

Loewenberg.

4357 *THE CORRECTOR: or, dramatic intelligencer. Containing original criticisms on the performances and performers of the Theatre Royal, Liverpool, for the summer season, 1816

nos. 1–8   [May to June] 1816   MH

Liverpool   1816

The numbers are not dated, but no. 2 criticises 13th May 1816 to 17th May 1816, and the last performance mentioned is that of 28th June 1816 — Lowe.

4358 *THE CENSOR, or review of public amusements in Liverpool.

nos. 1–11   Dec 1821 to Feb 1822   *monthly*

Liverpool   1821–1822

Recorded but not seen by Lowe.

4359 *THE LIVERPOOL THEATRICAL INVESTIGATOR and reviews of amusements.

2 vols. nos. 1–129   29 May 1821 to Dec 1821 *daily* + nos. 1–26   5 June 1822 to 23 Nov 1822 *weekly*; illus.

Liverpool   1821–2

Loewenberg. Copy at MB wanting some nos.

4360 *THE THESPIAN.

vol. 1 nos. 1–91   1 Aug to 1 Dec 1821 *daily, later twice a week*   DLC

[Liverpool: printed by Smith and Melling]   1821

DLC Cat.

4361 †THE DRAMATIC SPECULUM.

no. 1   21 June 1826   L

[Liverpool: printed by Worrall & Taylor]   [1826]

Nos. 1–5 at DFo (Stratman 129).

4362 THE LIVERPOOL DRAMATIC JOURNAL.

no. 1   12 Nov 1832   L

[Liverpool: S. H. Sankey, Jun.]   [1832]

No further numbers are known.

4363 *THE LOOKING GLASS, or daily theatrical mirror.

nos. 1–3   15 to 17 Aug

Liverpool   1832

Loewenberg. Nos. 2, 3 at MB.

4364 THE LIVERPOOL DRAMATIC CENSOR.

no. 1   12 July 1834   L

[Liverpool: Griffiths, printer]   [1834]

No other numbers are known.

4365 PAUL PRY IN LIVERPOOL.

vol. 1   no. 1   25 Oct 1834   L

[Liverpool: printed by J. Pannell]   1834

4366 LIVERPOOL THESPIAN REGISTER and mirror of the stage.

no. 1   15 June 1836   L

[George Thompson]   [1836]

Tri-weekly publication was promised, but no other numbers are known.

4367 THE LIVERPOOL DRAMATIC ARGUS.

nos. 1–6   20 Apr to 23 May *weekly*   LvP

Liverpool: S. A. Hurton   1846

4368 *THE CURTAIN.

14 Nov, 29 Nov, 26 Dec 1862; 17 March, 4 Dec, 15 Dec 1863, 8 Jul 1864   LvP

Liverpool: printed and published by S. Davies & Son for the Prince of Wales Theatre   1862–64

A theatrical journal issued with and incorporating the programme of the Prince of Wales' Theatre.

4369 *THE CURTAIN. Published gratuitously every morning and distributed in the Royal Amphitheatre and Theatre Royal as a free programme.

Liverpool   1863

Recorded but not seen by Lowe. Another edition of no. 4368?

4370 *THE FOOTLIGHTS.

9 June, 17 August, 14 Oct 1864; 28 Feb, 17 May 1865
                                                          LvP

Liverpool   1864–5

Issued with and incorporating the programme of the Prince of Wales' Theatre.

4371 THE PROMPTER (of Liverpool): theatrical and universal advertiser.

No. 18   4 Sept 1865   LvP

Liverpool   1865

4372 *†THE STAR: a journal devoted to the drama, literature and fine arts.

nos. 85–733   9 Sept 1865 to 25 March 1867 *daily* LvP

Liverpool: printed by W. D. Rider for the Prince of Wales Theatre   [1865–1867]

4373 *THE PLAY: a journal of literary, dramatic and musical interest.

nos 164, 176, 294, 561, 602, 638, 1337, 1346 25 April, 9 May, 25 September 1867, 28 April, 17 June, 30 July 1868, 15, 29 December 1870   LvP

Liverpool: F. C. Macdonell for the Royal Amphitheatre   [1867–1870]

4374 *†THE AMPHI.

vol. 1 no. 1 — new series vol. 1 no. 3   Christmas 1873 to Aug 1878

Liverpool   1873–1878

> Loewenberg. *Four odd numbers at LvP: 24 Dec 1873, 9 March 1874, 11 Oct 1875, 31 Aug 1878. The programme of the Amphitheatre.*

4375 *THE LIVERPOOL ENTR'ACTE. A weekly journal for theatre-goers, containing a complete programme of the entertainments at the principal places of amusement in Liverpool.

nos. 1–?   Dec 1881 to [?March 1882]

Liverpool   1881–2

> *No. 1, December 1881. Ended about March 1882 — Lowe. Not seen by Lowe.*

4376 *THE MUSICAL AND DRAMATIC WORLD.

nos. 1–89, new series nos. 1–5   22 Oct 1881 to Sept 1883 *weekly, the new series fortnightly*

Liverpool   1881–3

> Loewenberg.

4377 *THE CLARION. An illustrated theatrical and satirical journal.

nos. 1–5   24 March 1882 to 22 April 1882 *weekly* MP

Liverpool   1882

> *Only five numbers issued — Lowe.*

4378 *HAGUE'S MINSTREL and dramatic journal, edited by Henry A. Duffy.

no. 1   Sept 1882 *monthly*

Liverpool   [1882]

> *Called "New series". The editorial announcement says: "For a period of thirteen years this publication flourished under the editorship of Mr W. H. Lee, and subsequently of Mr. J. H. Stringer." There seems to have been an interval between the two series; the first was not before 1866 — Lowe.*

4379 *LLOYD'S PROGRAMME: drama, music, fine art.

nos. 1–2   14 to 21 April   *weekly*

Liverpool   1883

> Loewenberg.

4380 *THE LIVERPOOL BUSY BEE. Illustrated, comical, satirical, social, sporting, theatrical, musical.

nos. 1–10   29 Sept to 1 Dec   *weekly*

Liverpool   1886

> Loewenberg.

4381 LIVERPOOL AMUSEMENTS and souvenir of the stage.

Monday 20 Feb 1893; illus.   E
                                                       1893

> *The opening article on Nance Oldfield is the same as that appearing in* West End amusements and souvenir of the stage *of the same date (see above no. 4302).*

4382 *FOOTLIGHTS.

no. 1   Sept 1897

Liverpool   1897

> Loewenberg. *L copy destroyed.*

4383 *THE PROMPTER. Conducted by William Henderson.

nos. 1–7   [1899] to 29 Jan 1900

Liverpool   [1899]–1900

> Loewenberg.

4384 *WILL A. BRADLEY'S PANTOMIME ANNUAL. Ed. by "Dromio".

1900/1–1904

Liverpool   1900–1904

> Loewenberg.

Manchester

4385 THE TOWNSMAN, addressed to the inhabitants of Manchester, on theatricals. The profits given to the patriotic fund. [By James Watson.]

nos. 1–24 [? 8 Dec 1803 to ? 7 Dec 1805]   *weekly until no. 17, then "occasionally"*   L

Manchester: G. Bancks   1803–1805

> *Each number with a title-page, which differs slightly from the volume title-page transcribed here. No. 1 in the copy seen is "The second edition" of that number. Most numbers have 8 pages. An appendix to no. 18 was issued separately, 23rd June 1804, with 4 pages and a head-title only. The numbers are not regularly dated. Further issues are anticipated in no. 24, but another copy is*

recorded (MB) also of 24 numbers only. The Spirit of the Doctor (Manchester, 1820) contains an account of James Watson (1775–1820), amateur actor and occasional writer: "from a marvellous paucity of good Actors, at the Theatre-Royal, Manchester — occasioned by the crooked policy of a parsimonious management, — the Doctor obligingly gave to the World a weekly Stage-Review, under the title of 'The Townsman'. This pamphlet, at the time, was in the hands of half the town ..." See also above MANCHESTER no. 1615.

4386 *†ARGUS; or, the theatrical observer: containing critical, yet impartial strictures, on the merits and demerits of the principal performers, of the Theatre Royal, Manchester. To be continued every fortnight.

nos. 1–6   24 Nov 1804 to 9 Feb 1805   MB

Manchester: Dean & Co.   1804–1805

L copy (destroyed) had 7 nos., to 30 March 1805.

4387 *ARGUS CORRECTED. Containing an analytical enquiry into his qualifications as a theatrical observer; and a detection of his numerous errors.

nos. 1–2   5 Jan to 19 Jan 1805

Manchester   1805

Loewenberg. L copy destroyed.

4388 THE THESPIAN REVIEW; ⟨an examination of the merits and demerits of the performers on the Manchester stage. Pro & Con.⟩

nos. 1–7 [1 Feb 1806 to 15 March 1806] *weekly*   L

Manchester: printed and sold by J. Ashton   1806

Each number with 8 pages (pagination continuous) and a head-title only. In verse and prose. Suspension of publication is not announced. Lowe was "inclined to think that it was written by some one named Hamerton". For J. M. Benwell's remarks against some of its criticisms see his Essay on the danger of unjust criticism. Manchester, 1806. (See above no. 1619).

4389 *THE CENSOR, or theatrical review. By a candid hearer.

pp. 8 ("to be continued occasionally")   MB

Manchester: Hopper   1807

Relates to the Theatre Royal, Manchester.

4390 *THE PROMPTER; or, theatrical investigator.

nos. 1–19   Nov 1815 to March 1816 *weekly*   MB

Manchester: Wilson   [1815–1816]

————*The prompter; or, theatrical investigator. The second edition.

O

Manchester   1816

BUCOP

4391 *THE PROMPTER prompted; or, the theatrical investigator dissected. By Jeremy Collier, jun.

nos. 1–5   1816; issued not dated   NIC

Manchester   1816

4392 THE MANCHESTER THEATRICAL CENSOR.

nos. 1–6   24 May 1828 to 28 June 1828 *weekly*   MB

[Manchester: Beckett & Boyer]   1828

Then The theatrical censor.

no. [7]   [5 July 1828?]; t.p.   MB

Manchester: Beckett and Boyer   1828

The title page, apparently issued with no. [7] (which would otherwise be of one leaf only) is bound in front of no. 1 in the copy seen; on the verso an address to the public announces the suspension of the periodical.

4393 *THE MANCHESTER DRAMATIC AND MUSICAL REVIEW.

nos. 1–43 14 Nov 1846 to 4 Sept 1847 *weekly*. Supplements were issued with nos. 4, 8, 12, 16, 28. nos. 4–16 "monthly": no. 28 "occasional". Lacks nos. 3, 21–28

[Manchester]   1846–7

Loewenberg.

4394 †JOURNAL of dramatic reform [issued by the N.E. Theatre Reform Association.]

no. 1 Jan? 1878 *monthly*; title headed: Aim: — the elevation of the stage.   MH

Boston [Mass]: Geo. B. Watson, secretary   1878

nos. 2–14 lacking.

Then Journal of dramatic reform [issued by the Dramatic Reform Association].

nos. 14–17 Feb to Nov 1879 no. 19 May 1880 nos. 27 to 29 May to Nov 1882 *quarterly*; ptd. covers, with title   MH

Manchester: Abel Heyward and son, then Manchester: Scholastic Trading Institution; London: Simpkin and Marshall   1879–82

BP has nos. 1–30.

Then Journal of proceedings of the Dramatic Reform Association, in 1883; ptd. covers, with title   MH

Manchester: Scholastic Trading Company Limited; London: Simpkin Marshall, & Co.   1884

On the Dramatic Reform Association see also above nos. 637–639.

4395 THE MANAGERS' GUIDE and artistes' advertiser. A medium for the managers and members of the theatrical and music hall professions. Conducted by J. H. Cobbe.

In parts vol. 1 nos. 1–8   29 June 1878 to 17 Aug 1878 *weekly*   L

[Manchester: E. Slater and J. H. Cobbe]   [1878]

Then The managers' guide and artistes' advertiser. A medium for the managers and members of the dramatic and musical professions. Conducted by J. H. Cobbe [nos. 11–23 by W. Forrest]

In parts vol. 1 nos. 9–23 24 Aug 1878 to 3 Dec 1878 *weekly* L

[Manchester: E. Slater and J. H. Cobbe (no. 9); J. H. Cobbe (no. 10); M. Eglin (nos. 11–23)] [1878]

Distributed gratis in the United Kingdom. Suspension of publication not announced. In the copy seen, no. 17 is missing.

4396 †PROGRAMME OF MANCHESTER AMUSEMENTS.

vol. 1 no. 44 31 Aug 1891 L

Manchester 1891

Weekly? Same as no. 4398?

4397 †MANCHESTER AMUSEMENTS AND SOUVENIR OF THE STAGE.

nos. 101–347 7 Jan 1895 to 25 Sept 1899 *weekly*; illus., col. ptd. L

[London and Manchester: Emmott & Co. Limited] [1895–1899]

BMC *records nos. 3–347 20 Feb 1893 to 25 Sept. 1899.*

4398 †WHAT'S ON the pioneer programme of amusements.

nos. 343–555 11 May 1896 to 4 June 1900 *weekly*; illus; col. ptd. L

[Manchester: printed by Percy Bros., then Holbrook & Co.] [1896–1900]

In May 1896, this periodical was in its seventh year of publication.

4399 ★THE PROSCENIUM. An amateur dramatic & musical review.

vol. 1 nos. 1–4 Dec 1898 to March 1899

Manchester [1898–1899]

No more published. BMC, but L copy destroyed. Nos. 1, 3 at O.

4400 ★THE "COMEDY" GAZETTE.

O

Manchester 1899–1900
 BUCOP

Newcastle

✂ Mara, S. D. (no. 1) of the Mitchelliad [*etc.*]. Edited by S. D. Mara. Newcastle 1804. *See nos. 1634–1647.*

4401 GRIM TYPO, the Tyne demon; or, the resurrection of *The barber's pig.* A satirical miscellany; illustrated with occasional notes, anecdotes, &c. of the life, character, & behaviour of the demon, both before and since his defeat by Mara, in 1804, to the present

period; and dedicated (without permission) to the editor of the Tyne Mercury.

nos. 1–3 3 Feb to 3 Apr 1818 *monthly* L

Newcastle Upon Tyne: printed and sold by William Hall [1818]

Titles of nos. 2 and 3 differ. Each number with 8 pages. Nos. 1 and 2 preceded by prospectuses. Wholly or partly by the actor E. H. Hillington. No. 3 recorded by Loewenberg, wanting in this copy, together with the prospectuses.

4402 THE NEWCASTLE THEATRICAL OBSERVER.

nos. I–VI 24 Jan to 14 Feb 1824; *twice weekly* NwP

[Newcastle: R. T. Edgar] 1824

4403 THE THEATRICAL EXAMINER.

nos. I–V 26 Nov to 24 Dec 1827; *weekly* NwP

Newcastle: printed for the publishers by W. Boag 1827

4404 THE DRAMATIC REGISTER.

nos. I–X 27 Dec 1828 to 28 Feb 1829; *weekly*; with leaf announcing end of publication NwP

Newcastle: printed by W. Boag 1828–29

4405 THEATRICAL CRITIQUE.

†nos. [2] 7 Nov 1829 to 10 Dec 1829 MB

[Newcastle: Fordyce, Printer] [1829]

The parts are not numbered; that of 7 November was certainly not the first. The first number seems to have been published in 1827. A leaflet (copy at MB), dated 28 November 1827, and put out by Fordyce at Newcastle and Watson and Marshall at Gateshead, advertises: "Just published, no. 3 of the Theatrical Critique, Price 1d. The editor, in the present number, has retaliated upon the Theatrical Examiner, an opposition publication, brought out on Monday last, and it is probable that a paper WAR! will be the consequence. The Theatrical Critique will be published immediately after the representation of pieces of interest. . . ."

North Shields

4406 ★PAUL PRY. A weekly review of theatrical performances.

nos. 1–7 5 Nov 1827 to 9 Jan 1828 *weekly until no. 6 (10 Dec 1827)* NwP

North Shields 1827–28

Loewenberg.

4407 ★THE NORTH SHIELDS DRAMATIC CENSOR.

nos. 1–15 27 Oct 1827 to 29 Jan 1828 *weekly* NwP

North Shields 1828–29

Loewenberg. *No. 1 wanting*

Norwich

4408 THE NORWICH THEATRICAL OBSERVER, and dramatic review. *ed.* A. T. Fayerman.

vol. I nos. 1–36 10 or 13 Feb to 4 July, nos 38–42
7 Aug to 3 Oct 1827   MH
Norwich   1827

First 36 numbers issued on Wednesdays and Saturdays; Nos. 38–42 issued irregularly. Caption title beginning with no. 17 reads: Theatrical observer. Special title-page for numbers issued during Assize Week and Festival week (nos. 38–42) reads: The Norwich Theatrical Observer and Ranelagh Spectator. For the Philo-Thespis controversy see under Norwich above nos. 1662–1669.

4409 ★THEATRICAL TICKLER. By Barnaby Brother.

no. 2. 23 Jan. 1828   DFo
Norwich   1828

Stratman 159.

4410 ★THE LORGNETTE.

In parts 8 Dec 1883–3rd Jan 1891 *weekly* [unnumbered]
                                                           NoR
[Norwich: printed for the Proprietor by Burgess and Burgis]   [1883–1891]

Nottingham

4411 THE NOTTINGHAM DRAMATIC SUMMARY. Ed. John T. Godfrey.

[vols. 1–3] 1893–1895 *annually; illus.*   L
Nottingham: R. Allen & Son Ltd.   1894–1896

Each volume reprinted from Allen's Nottingham Red Book. *Suspension of publication is not announced;* Allen's Nottingham Red Book *continued publication.*

Oxford

4412 ★THE HARLEQUIN.

nos. 1–8   O
Oxford   1866

BUCOP. Copy at O wants nos. 1–2.

Plymouth

4413 THE PLYMOUTH THEATRICAL SPY; or, a pair of spectacles for the manager.

nos. 1–8 5 Jan 1828 to 23 Feb 1828 *weekly*   MH
[Plymouth: W. Haviland, printer]   [1828]

The editor calls himself Paul Pry. No. 1 is said to have been reprinted (250 copies) by demand. The suspension of the periodical is not announced.

Sheffield

4414 ★THE THEATRICAL EXAMINER for Sheffield. ⟨With a historical sketch of the beginning and progress of theatrical amusements in Sheffield.⟩

vol. I nos. 1–20 28 Oct 1824 to 24 Jan 1825 *twice weekly to no. 15 (20 Dec), then weekly*   SP
Sheffield: R. Howlden   1825

4415 ★SHEFFIELD ERA and amateur review.

24 Nov 1879 to 17 Jan 1881 [first and last number known]
                                                           1879–1881
Loewenberg

4416 THE STAGE, 1880.

no. 17 24 Apr 1880   MP
Sheffield   1880

With a single sheet supplement: Herr Holtum (King of the Cannon).

Stratford upon Avon

4417 STRATFORD THEATRICAL REVIEW, and stage reporter.

nos. 1–10 10 Dec 1827 to 8 Feb 1828 *weekly*   L
[Stratford-on-Avon: John Bacon]   [1827–1828]

In no. 10: "the title and index will form the last number... at the close of the season". Reviews the first season in the new theatre, erected 1827.

York

4418 ★THE THEATRICAL REGISTER. Containing candid and impartial strictures on the various performances at the Theatre-Royal, York, interspersed with occasional remarks by obliging correspondents.

vol. I nos. 1–18 [4 Feb to *ca.* 27 May 1788]; *weekly*   YP
York: L. Lund   1788

The work is dedicated to Tate Wilkinson, then manager of the York Theatre, and is very favourable in tone towards him and his company. It was announced to be continued annually, but I doubt if any further numbers were published. Genest founds a chapter on the work — Lowe. Last issue states "end of Vol I", and contains reviews of plays performed 23rd–26th May.

IRELAND

Dublin

4419 THE POLITICAL MANAGER: or, the invasion of the music-hall, set forth.

no. 1 2 October 1749   L

[Dublin: printed by T. Knowles]   [1749]

Presumably an ad hoc publication. On Sheridan's attempt to dissuade musical societies from performing in competition to his own theatre.

4420 THE PLAY-HOUSE JOURNAL.

no. 1 18 Jan 1750   L

[Dublin: printed by Augustus Long]   [1750]

Further numbers are anticipated, but none are known. Reprinted in Restoration and 18th Century Theatre Research *II (1) (1963).*

4421 THE NETTLE.

no. 1 24 Oct 1751   L

[Dublin: printed by T. Knowles]   [1751]

A single sheet. "To be continued occasionally", but only this one number known. Against Sheridan.

4422 THE PUBLIC ADVERTISER; or, the theatrical chronicle.

In parts vol. 1 nos. 67–68 11–14 Feb to 14–16 Feb 1774 *bi-weekly*   L

[Dublin: printed by James Parker and co.]   1774

4423 *THE EDILE or a review of the Dublin Stage.

nos. 1–5 ? to 18 Nov 1784   DA

Dublin   1784

No. 5 only at DA.

4424 *THE THEATRIC MAGAZINE; or, general repository. Comprizing uninfluenced remarks on the performances of the Dublin, provincial, and other stages, including theatric biography, characteristic traits, general dramatic criticisms, and illustrations; original poetry, on the subject of the stage, selections, etc. etc.

In parts vol. 1 nos. 1–2 Jan to Feb 1806 *monthly*
                                               DN
Dublin: R. Gibson   1806

4425 THE IRISH DRAMATIC CENSOR.

In parts nos. [1–2] 3–6 [1811 to 1812]   L

[Dublin: J. O'Callaghan]   [1811–1812]

Suspension is not announced, but Stratman (50) *records another copy also of 6 numbers only. Covers the 1811–1812 season.*

4426 *THE DRAMATIC INSPECTOR.

no. 1 20 May 1819

Dublin   1819

  Loewenberg.

4427 *THE DRAMA, a daily register of histrionic performances on the Dublin stage; and critical review of general dramatic literature. By two gentlemen of the Dublin University.

vols. I–II nos. 1–42 23 Oct 1821 to 10 Dec 1821
+ nos. 1–32 [=34], 11 Dec to 19 Jan 1822 *daily;* illus.
                                               DN
Dublin: printed by W. Underwood   1821–2

4428 *THE DRAMATIC REVIEW.

vol. i no. 1—vol. ii no. 17 19 Apr 1821 to 11 May 1821

Dublin   1821

  Loewenberg.

4429 THE STAGE. ⟨A theatrical paper. Published daily. Containing criticisms on the performances, each night, at the new Theatre-Royal, Dublin; dissertations on the British drama; dramatic portraits; satirical and other strictures on cotemporary publications; notices of incidental occurrences; and the extraordinary papers regarding the miscreants.⟩ [*ed.* Frederick W. Conway and Joseph T. Haydn.]

vol. 1 nos. 1–30, vol. 2 no. 1 9 April 1821 to 19 May 1821; t.p. to vol. 1; two leaves with notice about the editors; one leaf announcing suspension of publication

Dublin: printed by W. H. Tyrrell   1821

Nos. 1–8 were reprinted according to a notice in no. 24.

4430 †THE [ORIGINAL] THEATRICAL OBSERVER

vols. I–XII each with nos. 1–36 19 Jan 1821 to 26 July 1822 *daily;* head-title from 4 Dec 1821: The original theatrical observer; t.p., index to vols. I–IX   L

Dublin: J. J. Nolan, 3 Suffolk St. ["published at 4 Suffolk St. (from 22 Nov 1821) then J. McMullen] 1821–22

4431 *THE THEATRICAL OBSERVER [NOLAN'S THEATRICAL OBSERVER]

vols. IX nos.? –36, vols. X–XV each with 36 nos., vol. XVI nos. 1–28 ? Nov 1821 to 13 March 1823 MH

Dublin: J. J. Nolan [the original printer/publisher as proprietor]   1821–23

4432 ★THE INDEPENDENT THEATRICAL OB-
SERVER.

vol. X, no. 1–vol. XI, no. 14   17 June to 14 Aug 1822
daily   MH
Dublin   1822

*The numbering began with vol. x as this was intended to
supersede The Original Theatrical Observer (formerly
The Theatrical Observer, no. 4431 above) which however
carried on — Loewenberg.*

4433 ★THE THEATRE.

nos. 1–13 16 Nov 1822 to 30 Nov 1822 *daily*

Then The Theatre, or daily miscellany of fashion. New
series.

vols 1–2 nos. 1–25 + nos. 1–18 2 Dec 1822–21 Jan 1823
Dublin   1822–23

Lowe.

4434 †THE GENUINE THEATRICAL OBSERVER.

In parts vol. 1 nos. 2, 10, 11   Fri 31 Oct, Tues 11
Nov, and Wed Nov 12 1823   *daily*   MH
[Dublin:] T. O'Flanagan   1823

4435 ★THE DRAMATIC ARGUS.

vol. 1 no. 1–vol. 2 no. 10   18 Nov 1824 to 10 Feb 1825
daily   MB
Dublin   1824–1825
Loewenberg.

4436 ★THE NEW THEATRICAL OBSERVER.
Dublin   1833
O'Neill, *p. 86.*

4437 †TATLER, and theatrical mirror.

nos. 3 and 8   15 Nov 1834 and 22 Dec 1834; illus.   L
[Dublin: D. O'Brien, then G. Browne]   [1834]

Further numbers are anticipated in no. 8.

4438 ★THE STAGE. [Dublin edition]

vol. 1 nos. 1–14   29 Sept to 30 Dec 1874   *weekly*
                                          DN

Dublin: J. M. O'Toole and Son   1874

————[London edition]

vol 1 nos. 1–14 30 Sept to 29 Dec 1874 *weekly*; illus.
                                          BP

London [and Dublin]   1874

*BP has nos. 2–4 6 8–9 10? 11–14. No holding of
complete run recorded. The two editions may have been
merged from no. 13 onwards.*

new series. vol 1 no. 1 5 Jan 1875, illus.   BP
Dublin and London   1875

4439 †THE IRISH TURF TELEGRAPH and dramatic gazette.

nos. 1, 16   3 July 1875, 16 Oct 1875   L
[Dublin: printed for the proprietors by Pattison Jolly]
                                         [1875]

▓ Beltaine. [1899.] *See no. 4323.*

4440 THE IRISH PLAYGOER and amusement
record.

In parts vols. I–II nos. 1–30   9 Nov 1899 to 31 May
1900 *weekly*   DN
Dublin: Irish Associated Press   1899–1900

SCOTLAND

Dundee

4441 ★THE DUNDEE THEATRICAL REVIEW.
no. 1   6 Oct 1826   CtY
Dundee   1826

Stratman *130.*

4442 THE COMET: a theatrical programme and
critical journal. Established in London 1862 — Entered
at Stationers Hall.
Third series
Dundee   1879

JFA. *One no. covering performances from 17 to 20
November 1862.*

Edinburgh

4443 THE EDINBURGH THEATRICAL CENSOR.

nos. 1–12   21 March 1803 to 30 July 1803 *irregularly,
the last three nos. weekly*   MB
Edinburgh: J. Buchannan   1803

*The suspension of publication is not announced in no. 12,
but Stratman (34) records another copy also of twelve nos.
only.*

4444 ★THE THEATRE. By E. Ranger.
nos. 1–8   17 Nov 1813 to 5 Jan 1814
Edinburgh   [1813–1814]

Loewenberg. *L copy destroyed.*

4445 THE THESPIAN CRITIQUE, or theatrical censor. Inscribed (without permission) to Mr William Murray of the Theatre Royal. By Patrick Pit, Esq.

nos. I [first and] second edition II–V 8 Oct to 25 Nov 1816 *irregularly*; nos. II–V without the inscription   EP

Edinburgh: printed by W. Aitchison, for the booksellers 1816

No further nos. announced.

4446 THE THESPIAN CENSOR; or, weekly dramatic journal.

nos. I–III 19 Jan 1818 to 2 Feb 1818 *weekly*   EP
[Edinburgh: A. Brown]   1818

4447 †THE EDINBURGH DRAMATIC REVIEW.

vols. I–II nos. 1, 3–50 7 Oct to 14 Dec 1822 *daily*; t.p., dedication, index + nos. 51–100 16 Dec 1822 to 11 Feb 1823 *daily*; t.p., ded., index   GU

Edinburgh: James L. Huie   1822–1823

*vols III–IX nos 101–441 12? Feb 1823 to 6 July 1824 *daily*   MB

Edinburgh: Huie   1823–1824

————*[new series] vols. I–V nos. 1–245 15 Nov 1824–24 Dec 1825 *daily*

Edinburgh   1824–1825

   Loewenberg.

4448 THE EDINBURGH THEATRICAL OBSERVER, and musical review.

vols. I–II nos. 1–155 15 July 1823 to 30 Mar 1824 misdating no 1 "June 15" *daily during theatrical season*; t.p., ded., index, prospectus   GU

Edinburgh: W. N. Sutherland   1823–24

4449 THE LITERARY CYNOSURE.

no. 1 22 Jan 1824   E
[Edinburgh: W. Stewart]   1824

Advertised as weekly. Articles "to be continued" in next number.

4450 THE EDINBURGH DRAMATIC RECORDER. To be continued weekly.

nos. 1–12 29 Jan–5 Feb 1825 to 23 April–30 April 1825   MH

[Edinburgh: John Sutherland]   [1825]

Further nos. are anticipated in no. 12, but Stratman (122) records another copy also of twelve nos. only.

4451 THE EDINBURGH DRAMATIC AND MUSICAL MAGAZINE.

In parts vol. 1 nos. 1–3 19 Nov 1827 to 3 Dec 1827 *weekly*   MH
[Edinburgh]   [1827]

*Should perhaps have printed wrappers giving imprint. No. 2 has a leaf pp. *53–*54. In no. 3, the next no. is anticipated; according to Lowe, no more were published.*

4452 THE EDINBURGH DRAMATIC REVIEW, and Thespian inquisitor. ⟨Edited by Hannibal Hallucinate, Esq. A.M.⟩

nos. I–XLIII XLV–L [=49] 22 Oct 1827 to 31 Dec 1827, misdating 17 Nov as "16", 5 Dec as "4" *daily*; t.p. with vignette   EP
Edinburgh: D. Speare, W. Hunter and E. West 1827

No. 50 announces end of publication.

4453 THE EDINBURGH DRAMATIC JOURNAL: or, theatrical observer. (To be continued weekly)

nos. 1–11 11 Oct 1828 to 29 Nov 1828 *nos. 1–3 weekly; thereafter twice weekly*; pl. [1]   EP
[Edinburgh: T. Colquhoun]   1828

Noted by Mr. Maidment as all published — Lowe.

4454 THE EDINBURGH DRAMATIC TETE-A-TETE, or companion to the theatre.

In parts vol. 1 nos. I–XLII 20 March 1828 to 7 May 1828 *daily*   EP
Edinburgh: ["published by", then "sold by" T. Hill] 1828

4455 THE WEEKLY DRAMATIC REVIEW.

nos. 1–6 7 July 1828 to 11 Aug 1828 *weekly*   EP
[Edinburgh: M. R. Robb]   1828

4456 THE DRAMATIC CENSOR. ⟨By Proteus Porcupine, Esq. *pseud.* of C. Torrop.⟩

nos. 1–79 [=78] 23 Sept to 12 Dec 1829 *daily*; nos. 28–38 *bi-weekly*; t.p.; contents. [no. 8 omitted in numbering]   EP
Edinburgh: John Glass   1829

Cessation of publication announced at end of first volume. Maidment Catalogue (no. 110 above) identifies Porcupine as C. Torrop.

4457 †THE DRAMATIC TATLER; or, companion to the theatre.

nos. 1–17 30 March 1829 to 17 Apr 1829 *daily*   E
[Edinburgh: C. McKenzie]   1829

A daily sheet of four pages, except the last number (17) which consists of two pages—Lowe. No. 1 only at E. Copy at MH. (Stratman 163).

4458 THE THEATRE; containing a review of the performances at the Theatre Royal, &c. Edinburgh, biographical notices of principal performers; original essays, &c. on dramatic subjects; provincial intelligence, &c.

vol. I no. I 8 Oct 1831   EP

Edinburgh: Joseph Skeaf and Benjamin Strange   1831

4459 THE THEATRICAL SPECULUM and musical review.

nos. 1–9 18 June to 13 Aug 1831 *weekly*   E

Edinburgh   1831

Edited by one Greig, according to a note on the E copy of no. 4460.

4460 THE EDINBURGH THEATRICAL CASKET.

no. 1 July 1832   E

[Edinburgh: Fairgrieve and Murdoch, printers]   1832

A note on the copy states that no more numbers were published, and that this was edited by one Greig "a decayed actor who . . . performed at the Caledonian Theatre in 1824–5 during Ryder's management under the name of Gray. During the period of the publication of his dramatic criticisms he kept a book stall at the top of the Mound." See also no. 4459.

4461 THE THEATRICAL RECORD; or, review of the drama, literature, and the fine arts. Published weekly.

no. 1 1 June 1833   EP

[Edinburgh: W. Ritchie & Co.]   1833

4462 THE EDINBURGH THEATRICAL AND MUSICAL REVIEW.

In parts vols. I–II nos. 1–31 14 March to 19 Sept, misdating 11 July as "10" + nos. 32–34 (also numbered 1–3) 17 Nov to 2 Dec 1835 *weekly (5–9 twice weekly)*; wanting nos. 1–2, 4   EP

Edinburgh: at the office of the "Constitution" newspaper   1835

From the 5th No. to the end edited by W. H. Logan, aided by [Sir] Theodore Martin and other friends — Lowe. From no. 11: "under the immediate surveillance of the 'Gentleman in Black'". No. 16: Quarterly supplement to the Edinburgh theatrical and musical review.

4463 THE DRAMATIC SPECTATOR, ⟨edited by Poz, Quiz and Company⟩

nos. I–X 29 July 1837 to 30 Sept 1837 *weekly;* t.p. EP

Edinburgh: W. Glass; London: R. Crozier   1837

Nos. I–VIII edited by Poz; nos. IX and X by Quiz.

4464 THE OPERA-GLASS: a weekly musical and theatrical miscellany.

vols. I–II nos. 1–29, misnumbering no. 14 as "13", 10 Apr 1840 to 23 Oct 1840; t.p., index + nos. 1–26 30 Oct 1840 to 30 Apr 1841, misdating 6 Nov as "7" + supplements to vol. II nos. 15 and 16 *weekly* EP

Edinburgh: W. & H. Robinson   1840–1

4465 THE EDINBURGH DRAMATIC CENSOR. A weekly theatrical, musical and literary review.

nos. 1–3 12 Nov 1842 to 26 Nov 1842 *weekly*

Then, The Edinburgh dramatic censor.

nos. 4–8 3 Dec 1842 to 31 Dec 1842 *weekly*   EP

Edinburgh: published for the proprietor by J. Stampa
                                                       1842

4466 †THE PROMPTER, and Scottish dramatic review.

vols. I–II nos. I–XXIV 12 Nov [1842] to 13 May [1843] *weekly;* t.p., index + no. 1 20 May [1843]   EP

Edinburgh: W. & H. Robinson   1842–3

EP: no. IX wanting.

✂ The dramatic omnibus [Glasgow & Edinburgh] 1849–1850. *See no. 4495.*

4467 †THE STAGE, and Scottish musical & theatrical omnibus. Driven by Whip, Spur, Lash, & Co.

no. 15 11 May 1849   EP

[Edinburgh: sold by W. & H. Robinson]   1849

4468 THE PRINTER'S DEVIL. A weekly review of the stage, and a guide to the studio, &c., &c., &c.

nos. I–III 2–16 Feb 1850

Then The printer's devil, a weekly review . . .

no. IV 23 Feb 1850

Then The Edinburgh general review . . .

no. V 2 March 1850

Then The London and Edinburgh general review . . .

nos. VI–XIV 9 March 1850 to 4 May 1850 *weekly* EP

[Edinburgh: R. Reynolds]   1850

In the fifth number the title is changed, in deference to the feelings of some booksellers—Lowe. Further nos. anticipated, but Stratman (263) records another copy also of 14 nos. only.

4469 THE DRAMATIC REVIEW and weekly miscellany. ⟨A weekly journal of criticism and amusement.⟩

vol. I nos. 1–7 27 Dec 1851 to 7 Feb 1852   EP

Edinburgh: H. Robinson; Glasgow: Love   1851–52

Then The dramatic review.

vol. I nos. 8–10, vol. II nos. 1–2 14 Feb 1852 to 12 May 1852 EP

Edinburgh: H. Robinson; Glasgow: Love 1852

4470 †THE THEATRE

nos. 1–11 1 Dec 1851 to 1 May 1852 *fortnightly*; illus. E

Edinburgh: James G. Bertram & Co. 1851–2

MH also has vol. I no. 12 15 May and vol. II nos. 1–2 25 September to 2 October 1852. Stratman 270.

4471 †THE COMPANION to the theatres and other amusements of Edinburgh.

In parts vol. I nos. 1–22 4 Sept to 29 Sept 1852 *daily* EP

[Edinburgh]: J. G. Bertram & Co. 1852

Nos. 18, 20, 22 wanting.

4472 THE WEEKLY REVIEW and dramatic critic.

vols. 1–3 nos. 1–38 27 Aug 1852 to 13 May 1853; each vol. with t.p.; vols. 1–2 with contents leaf L

Edinburgh: H. Robinson; Glasgow: Love 1852–1853

†*Then* The weekly review and dramatic critic

In parts no. 39 3 June 1852, nos. 43–45 5 Aug 1853 to 2 Sept 1853 L

Edinburgh: H. Robinson [1853]

Vol. 4, no. 50, 14 October 1853, recorded by Loewenberg. Also numbered by volume (as I, 1–13, II, 1–13, III, 1–12, [IV], 1, 5–7).

4473 †THE EDINBURGH PROGRAMME. *ed.* John Wilson.

nos. 1–33 7 July 1879 to 14 Feb 1880 *weekly* EU

[Edinburgh: Edinburgh Advertising Company] 1879–80

Lacking all but no. 33, with pl. [1].

Then The weekly programme A journal of literature, art, music, and the drama

no. 1 21 Feb 1880 EU

[Edinburgh: W. Scott Wilson] 1880

Glasgow

4474 THE GLASGOW THEATRICAL REGISTER ⟨from May 18th to July 9th inclusive, containing cursory remarks on the performances at the Theatre⟩

nos. I–IX 18 May to 9 July 1803 *weekly*; wanting t.p., but title supplied on MS leaf GU

Glasgow: [W. Falconer, printer] 1803

Then The Glasgow theatrical register, from November 16 to December 8 1803, inclusive. Containing cursory remarks on the performances at the Theatre.

no. [1]; t.p. GU

Glasgow: [printed by Wm Falconer and sold by Geo. Lumsden] 1803

Criticisms on a three-weeks' season under Jackson's management — Lowe.

Then———From May 4 to July 12 1804, inclusive; containing cursory remarks on the performances at the theatre. By Timothy Tickle, Esq.

Part III nos. I–XII + 2 supplements 12 May to 14 July 1804 *weekly;* t.p., ded. GU

Glasgow: printed by W. Allan 1804

Then———From April 24 to July 26 1805, inclusive; containing cursory remarks on the performances at the Theatre Royal.

Part IV nos. I–XII 1 May to 25 July 1805 *weekly but no issue on Wed. July 10th;* t.p. GU

Glasgow: printed by Crawford and McKenzie 1805

Then———Supplement to Part IV.

nos. I–III Wed 18 Sept to Sat 5 Oct 1805 *weekly;* t.p. GU

[Glasgow: printed by Crawford and McKenzie] [1805]

4475 THE THEATRICAL OBSERVER; or, Thespian critique.

no. 1 22 July 1820 BP

[Glasgow: printed by L. Starke] 1820

4476 THE GLASGOW THEATRICAL OBSERVER. ⟨Volume first.⟩

vol. I nos. 1–6 20 Apr to 25 May 1824 *weekly;* nos. 7–12 13 July to 9 Sept 1824 *irregularly;* nos. 13–16 14 Oct to 4 Nov 1824 *weekly;* t.p., pref., index GM

Glasgow: W. R. M'Phun 1824

Weekly while the theatre was open — Lowe.

4477 ★THE CENSOR.

Glasgow 1825

From a reference in no. 4478, which is the successor to The Censor.

4478 THE GLASGOW DRAMATIC REVIEW.

In parts vol. I nos. I–XIV 9 to 27 July 1825 *daily;* (none issued on 12 and 14 July. Tues July 19th mis-dated 18th) GM

[Glasgow]: John Carmichael 1825

4479 †THE GLASGOW DRAMATIC REVIEW.

In parts vol. I nos. 1–6 9 Dec 1826 to 13 Jan 1827 *weekly* GM

Glasgow: W. R. M'Phun 1826–7
Lacking nos. 3 and 5

4480 *THE GLASGOW THEATRICAL REVIEW.

nos. 1–5 22 Sept to 3 Nov 1827 *weekly, but three weeks between nos. 3 and 4.*

[Glasgow]   [1827]

    Stratman *137.*

4481 THE OPERA GLASS; a series of criticisms on the performances of the Glasgow stage; notices of musical and rhetorical exhibitions; and in the shape of "Green room chat." A record of those occurrences of interest, which have taken place on the London and provincial boards.

vol. I nos. 1–27 and appendix Sat 19 Dec 1829 to Sat 5 June 1830; vol. II nos. 1–4 Sat 20 Nov to Sat 11 Dec 1830 *weekly*   GM/GU

Glasgow: J. Mitchell   1829–1830

    Title-page of individual issues reads: [vol. I] The opera glass. A critique on the performances of the Glasgow stage. Then [vol. II]: The opera glass containing criticisms on the theatrical and other exhibitions of Glasgow. Announced cessation of publication in vol. I, appendix (5 June 1830), but recommenced with vol. II no. 1 on 20 November 1830.

4482 THE THISTLE; or, literary, theatrical and police reporter.

vols. I–III nos. I–LII 10 Oct 1829 to 2 Oct 1830 + nos. 53–104 9 Oct 1830 to 1 Oct 1831 + nos. 105–119 8 Oct 1831 to 14 Jan 1832 *weekly;* nos. 101 to 104 drop sub-title; t.p. to vol. II; wanting t.p. to vol. I GU

Glasgow: J. Aitken & Co.   1829–1832

    End of publication announced.

4483 THE NEW OPERA GLASS; or, theatrical tribunal.

nos. 1–7, 19 Nov 1830–1 Jan 1831. *weekly*   GU

Glasgow: W. R. M'Phun   [1830–1831]

4484 THE THEATRICAL EXAMINER.

nos. 1–10 23 Nov 1833 to 25 Jan 1834

Glasgow: W. R. McPhun   1833–34

    JFA. *Another copy at MH. End of publication announced in no. 10.*

4485 THE THEATRICAL VISITOR.

nos. 1–6 16 Aug to 19 Sept [1835] *weekly*   GM

Glasgow: Francis Reid   [1835]

    Against Alexander and against monopoly.

4486 THE PEPPER-BOX; containing criticisms on theatricals and other amusements. Published weekly.

nos. 1–21 21 March to 8 Aug 1840   GM

[Glasgow: H. Alexander]   1840

    After no. 1 the title reads "theatrical" for "theatricals".

4487 THE GLASGOW DRAMATIC REVIEW ≪Published fortnightly≫ ⟨containing original essays on subjects connected with the drama and the stage. Also, critical notices of the performances at the Glasgow theatres.⟩

nos. I–LIV 13 Nov 1844 to 8 July 1846 *fortnightly, occasionally weekly;* illus.; pls. [4 incl. 3 fold.]; preface; t.p. in red and black; index   GU

Glasgow: printed for the proprietors by William Gilchrist   1844–6

4488 THE THEATRICAL CRITIC.

nos. 1–2 13 March to 27 March 1845 *fortnightly* GU

[Glasgow]: sold for the proprietors by William Love
                                                1845

    "No. III will be published on Thursday 10 April".

4489 †THE GLASGOW THEATRICAL REVIEW. Published every Wednesday morning.

In parts vols I–II nos. 1–58 25 Feb 1846 to 29 Dec 1847; lacking nos. 1–8, 10–11, 14–16, 19, 27–29, 34, 37–41, 54, 56–58   GM

[Glasgow]: J. and J. Taylor   1846–1847

4490 THE DRAMA.

nos. 1–3 2 Dec to 16 Dec 1847 *weekly*   GM

Glasgow: Jackson   1847

4491 THE DRAMATIC REVIEW. Published every Wednesday.

nos. I–II 15 to 22 Dec 1847   GM

Glasgow: published for the proprietors by William Love   1847

4492 †THE GLASGOW SATIRIST and dramatic critic.

In parts vols. [I]–2 nos. 1–12 + 13–14 26 Aug 1848 to 27 Jan 1849 *fortnightly with two "extra" (weekly) nos. 3, 6*

Then The Glasgow Punch. The satirist, and dramatic critic.

nos. 15–19 10 Feb–24 March 1849 *fortnightly (nos. 18–19 weekly)*   GM

Glasgow [Wm. F. Glassford (nos. 6–7), then others]
                                                1848–9

    Lacking no. 17.

4493 THE OPERA-GLASS, a weekly public amusement guide.

nos. 1–9 31 March 1848 to 26 May 1848 *weekly* GU

Glasgow: printed by City Printing Co.   1848

4494 THE STAGE, and literary and musical review.

[no. 1] Sept. 9 1848 *weekly*   GM

Glasgow: [Harrower & Brown, printers]   1848

4495 †THE DRAMATIC OMNIBUS.

nos. 1–36   26 May 1849 to 26 Jan 1850 *weekly*   EP

[Glasgow and Edinburgh]   [1849–50]

After no. 4, title reads Dramatic Omnibus. Licensed to carry all the theatres! EP holding ends with no. 34 which announces that Number 36 of the Omnibus will complete the first volume, the title page and index of which will be published at the usual price. Volume Two is announced and improvements promised. Nos. 1–3, 12–13 published Glasgow: W. Love; nos. 4–5 published Glasgow: J. M'Leod; nos. 6–12 published Edinburgh: J. G. Bertram; nos. 15–28, 30, 32–34 published Edinburgh: J. G. Bertram, Glasgow: W. Love; nos. 14, 29 have no imprint.

4496 THE PLAYGOER, and public amusement guide.

nos. 1–7   13 July to 24 Aug 1850 *weekly*   EP

[Glasgow: J. G. Bertram]   1850

✖ The weekly review and dramatic critic. Edinburgh and Glasgow. 1852–1853. *See no. 4472.*

4497 DRAMATIC SPECTATOR and Glasgow musical and public amusement guide.

nos. 1–7   12 Jan 1853 to 6 Apr 1853 *fortnightly*   GM

Glasgow: William Love   1853

4498 ★THE GLASGOW AMATEUR, PUBLIC AMUSEMENT RECORD and general miscellany.

nos. 1–5   1 Oct to 5 Nov 1856 *weekly*

Glasgow   1856

Stratman *274.*

4499 ★THE DRAMATIC REVIEW, a weekly journal of literature, art, music, and the drama.

vol. 1   nos. 1–7

Glasgow   1868

BMC, *but L copy destroyed.*

4500 THE DRAMATIC ALBUM of "Quiz" for 1882. By "Twym" and "Sir Oracle".

pp. [*216*], illus.; pl. [1] = 2 leaves.   GU

Glasgow: "Quiz" office   [1883]

Edition limited to 200 copies. Mainly cartoons of Glasgow theatre performances (originally published in the periodical Quiz) and drawn by Twym [A. S. Boyd], with critical commentary by Sir Oracle [William Robertson?]. Full-page cartoons.

Then Quiz album for 1883. by A. S. Boyd and Will. Robertson.

pp. [*108*]; illus.   GU

Glasgow: Quiz office   [1883]

4501 †THE AGE and dramatic journal devoted to drama, art, literature, music, and the sports. [*ed.* Paul B. Sutcliffe]

nos. 1–9   10 March to 12 May 1886   E

Glasgow: Lithgow & Son   1886

No. 1 only at E. Nos. 1–9 at O. (BUCOP).

4502 THE PROMPTER. The organ of the Scottish amateur dramatic and musical federation.

nos. 1–5 Oct 1892 to Feb 1893 [plus no. 1, preliminary, June 1892]   *monthly;* illus.   GM

[Glasgow: J. Jeffrey Hunter]   1892–3

Then, The prompter. An illustrated dramatic and musical record. Edited by J[ohn] A[lexander] Hammerton.

new series. nos. 1–21   March to 18 Nov 1893 [no issue on 28 Oct.] *monthly until July 29 then weekly;* illus.; pls., incl. music; ptd. wrappers.   GM

[Glasgow: Ye Sanct Mungo Presse]   1893

New series no. 4 "edited by 'Autolycus' ", nos. 5–13 "edited by 'Autolycus' (Andrew W. Cross)", nos. 14–18 "edited by 'Trophonius' ", nos. 19–21 "edited by 'Ariel' ". From no. 14, new series, title reads "The prompter. An illustrated weekly — drama, music, society."

4503 THE GLASGOW PANTOMIME annual and theatrical review. Written by 'Sir Oracle' of "Quiz" &c.

1894–95; illus. [incl. front.]   GM

Glasgow: J. M. Hamilton   1894–1895

Then The Glasgow theatrical annual.

1895–1901; illus. col. pls. [fronts.]   GM

Glasgow: J. M. Hamilton   1895–1901

Prefaces for 1896, 1899 signed A.S., preface for 1898 signed Alexander Stewart, preface for 1900 signed J.W. (on wrapper "written by 'Shem' ").

4504 THE GLASGOW HARLEQUIN.

nos. 1–5   17 Dec 1895 to 14 Jan 1896; illus.   L

[Glasgow: Wm. Hodge & Co.]   [1895–1896]

Head-title: "Harlequin a weekly record of Glasgow pantomimes and pantomimists".

4505 THE STAGE NEWS. The new theatrical paper.

nos. 1–2   3 March to 10 March 1897 *weekly;* illus.   GM

Glasgow: London Dramatic and Musical Agency Co.   1897

Then, The stage news and musical notes; a weekly record of art, literature and the drama.

nos. 3–8   17 March to 24 April 1897; illus.   GM

Glasgow: London Dramatic and Musical Agency Co.   1897

From No. 4, "C. W. Maxfield, editor".

Paisley

4506 PAISLEY SOCIETY AND DRAMATIC MIRROR edited by "The Bohemian".

nos. 1–3   6 Feb 1894 to 20 Feb 1894 *weekly*   L
[Paisley: Eade Montefiore]   [1894]

Then, Paisley mirror.

nos. 4–104   27 Feb 1894 to 31 Jan 1896 *weekly*   L
[Paisley: Eade Montefiore, then others]   [1894–1896]

Wants numbers for 12 February and 3 March to 23 April 1895.

ADDENDA

A429.1 [MURRAY, LINDLEY.] ★The sentiments of pious and eminent men, on the pernicious tendency of dramatic entertainments, and other vain amusements: with a few reflections on the same subject subjoined.

York: printed and sold by Wilson, Spence and Mawman;

London: sold by Darton & Harvey.   *ca.* 1789

————★[another edition]
Darton, Harvey & Darton   1811

Reprinted in Appendix of The power of religion on the mind in retirement, sickness and death, *sixth and ninth editions (York: Wilson, Spence and Mawman, 1793); eighth edition (London: printed and sold by James Phillips, 1811)*

A2729.1 FAUCIT, HELENA [*Lady* Martin]. On Ophelia and Portia. By Helena Faucit Martin.

pp. [2] [1] 2–48

For strictly private circulation [Printed by William Blackwood and Sons?]   [1880]

JFA. Ophelia *dated August 10, 1880;* Portia, *1st September 1880.*

A2732.1 FAUCIT, HELENA, [*Lady* Martin]. On Rosalind. By Helena Faucit Martin.

pp. [2] [1] 2–75 [76]

For strictly private circulation [Printed by William Blackwood and Sons.] [1884]

JFA. *Dated September 1844. Addressed to Robert Browning.*

APPENDIX OF LOWE ITEMS EXCLUDED

BUSK, HANS, *the elder.* The Vestriad, a poem: by Hans Busk, Esq. Author of *The Banquet, The Dessert,* &c.

Colburn   1819

A satire, not on Armand Vestris, as Lowe presumes, but on his father, Auguste, being a free translation of J. Berchoux, La danse ou les dieux de l'opéra *(Paris, 1806).*

COWELL, JOE. Thirty years passed among the players of England and America. By Joe Cowell. 1824.

A well-known comedian—Lowe. This item not seen by Lowe must be Cowell, Joe, i.e. Joseph Leathley Cowell, stage name of Hawkins Witchett, Thirty years passed among the players in England and America: interspersed with anecdotes and reminiscences of a variety of persons, directly or indirectly connected with the drama during the theatrical life of Joe Cowell, comedian. Written by himself. In two parts. Part I.— England. [Part II.—America.] *(New York: Harper & brothers, 1844).*

RANDALL, JACK. Rival managers; or, the elements of horse whipping. A serio-comic, operatic, gymnastic, Hudibrastic poem. By Jack Randall, P.G.A.
    [1825]

Not seen by Lowe, this is a general satire; only a small part is theatrical.

A SHORT ACCOUNT of another tryal [between Cibber and Sloper].

London   [n.d.]

I have seen only a slight allusion to this tract, and cannot tell what the correct title is — Lowe. A ghost. This is Part 2 of the Tryals of two causes *(no. 2599 above).*

STUBBES, PHILIP. The second part of the anatomie of abuses, conteining the display of corruptions, with a perfect description of such imperfections, blemishes and abuses, as now reigning in euerie degree, require reformation for feare of Gods vengeance to be powred upon the people and countrie, without speedie repentance and conuersion vnto God: made dialogwise by Phillip Stubbes.

William Wright   [1583]

This second part is of no theatrical interest.

THE THEATRICAL MUSEUM, or, fugitive repository. A collection of interludes. Added, some petitepieces, of one act each, altered from Molière. With prologues and epilogues, facetious songs, tales, droll epitaphs, epigrams, and poetical anecdotes. Prefixed, Hippesley's Drunken man.

Sold by E. Johnstone   1776

Not seen by Lowe. Plays and material for recitations only.

AUTHOR INDEX

Note: Semi-colons between item numbers denote change in subject grouping. (See note to Index of Places of Publication.) When a work goes into more than one edition, only the number of the first edition is noted.

***** 2862

——— , agent to the sun 3767

A.B. [*1727*] 3901

— [*1757*] 1882

— [*i.e. George Colman 1757*] 2857

A.B.C. 3278, 3279

A.P. 2780 *note*

A.Z. 449

À Beckett, Arthur William 981

— [*i.e. Bertie Vyse, pseud.*] 1037

À Beckett, Gilbert Abbott 927

Actor, An 540

Actors of Blackfriars, The 151

Adam, J. R. 2531

Adams, William Davenport 816 [*introd.*]; 974; 2123

Adamson, *Rev.* William 653

Adderley, *Hon.* James Granville 1672

Addison, Joseph 1316; 3823

Admirer of Bad Composition, An 3985

Adolphus, John 2414

Aitken, George Atherton 3573

Akerby, George 3556.1

Al Wakidi, Abu Abdo'llah 3938

Aldridge, Ira 2378

Alexander, Anne Tuke 483

Alexander, John Henry 1967, 2004, 2008, 2012–2014

Algarotti, Francesco 2060

Alison, William 4293 [*joint editor*]

Allen, W. 1460 [*joint author*]

Amateur, An [*1836*] 3292

— [*1838*] 1442

Amateur Lecturer, An 627

Ambross, *Miss* 2543

Ames, *Dr.* William 341

Amhurst, Nicholas [*i.e. Caleb D'Anvers, pseud.*] 868

Ancient Actor, An [*pseud. of Edward Bellasis*] 2180

Ancient Pistol 1723

Anderson, *Rev.* George 381, 383

Anderson, J. W. 2939

Anderson, John Henry 2015

Anderson, Mary (*Mme de Navarro*) 2387–2388

Angelo, Henry Charles William 2389

Anglicanus, *M.D.* 1425

Anglo-Phile Eutheo [*pseud. of Anthony Munday*] 255

Angus, J. Keith 1850; 2169

Anson, F. W. 2390

Anson, J. W. 4210 [*ed.*]

Anson, W. S. W. [*pseud. of William Swan Sonnenschein*] 2376

Anspach, Elizabeth *Margravine of* 2391

Anstruther, *Sir* William 340

Antigallican, An 2853

Anti-Profanus [*pseud. of Rev. Martin Madan?*] 2780

Anti-Scriblerus Histrionicus [*pseud. of John Roberts*] 987

Arber, Edward [*ed.*] 250

Arbiter, Petronius 2718

Arbuthnot, *Lady* Constance. *See* Milman, Constance

Arbuthnot, *Dr* John 2034 *note*, 2040 *note*, 2047 *note*

Archer, Frank [*pseud. of Frank Bishop Arnold*] 817

Archer, William 755, 756; 3062, [*joint author*], 3068, 3290; 3748, 3774 [*joint editor*], 3789 [*preface*], 3796, 3798 [*joint author*], 3805–6 [*joint editor*], 3808; 4306

Arditi, Luigi 2392

Areskine, Charles 1854

Ariel [*1772*] 2906

— [*1893*] 4502 *note* [*ed.*]

Arne, Michael 1797

Arnold, Frank Bishop [*i.e. Frank Archer, pseud.*] 817

Arnold, Samuel James 1393; 3310

Arnot, *Rev.* William 625 (*introd.*)

Arnoux, Claude 2054–2055

Arthur, Thomas 3432

Artis, William 2278 [*joint author*]

Aston, Anthony 2395, 2570

— *See also* Medley, Matthew 2394

Attalus 1204

Audley, John 369

Austin, Frederic Louis [*i.e. Frederic Daly, pseud.*] 3076

Austin, Gilbert 708

Austin, Joseph 1627 [*joint author*]

Author, The [*1761*] 2791

— [*pseud. of Charles Churchill, 1761*] 2284

— [*1762*] 2311

— [*pseud. of Henry James Pye, 1762*] 2314

— [*1763*] 2316

— of nothing else [*1809*] 1205

Autolycus [*pseud. of Andrew W. Cross*] 4502 [*ed.*]

B., *Mr.* 1620

B——. *Right honourable the Lord* 872

B——le, *Mrs.* 2518

B——n, B——t 1754

B., A. [*1727*] 3901

— [*1757*] 1882

— [*pseud. of G. Colman 1757*] 2857

B., *Mrs.* E., *comedian* [*i.e. Mrs. Elizabeth Beverley*] 2493

B., E. C. 2977

B., F. [*1826*] 512

B., G. S. [*i.e. George Spencer Bower*] 1058

B., T. [*i.e. Thomas Birch*] 4054

Baggs, Zachary 1319

Bailey, Fred 2126

Bailey, William 2529

Baillie, Johanna [Joanna] 2154

Baine, James 2797

Baker, David Erskine 30–33

Baker, Henry Barton 1105; 2250

Baker, *Sir* Richard 282

Baker, Sidney 2191

Baker, Thomas 328

Baker, *Rev.* William 648

Baldassarii, Benedetto 3572

Ballantyne, James 3535

Bancroft, *Sir* Squire 2404 [*joint author*]

Bancroft, *Mrs.* [*later Lady*] Marie 2404 [*joint author*], 2412

Bandinel, B. 111

Banister, Douglas 3441

Bannatyne, G., 1864

Bardsley, Samuel Argent 4039

Barker, George 2416

Barker, J. 37

Barlow, George 744

Barnard, Alfred. *See* 4223 [*ed.*]

Baron-Wilson, *Mrs.* Margaret Cornwall. *See* Wilson, *Mrs.* Margaret Cornwall Baron-

Barrett, Eaton Stannard 2355

Barrett, William Alexander 2401

Barron-Wilson, *Mrs.* Margaret. *See* Wilson, *Mrs.* Margaret Cornwall Barron-

Barry, *Mr.* [*fl. 1858*] 1841

Barry, Frederick 1557

— *See also* Pry, Paul 1558

Bartley, *Mr.* 3160 [*joint author*]

Bate, *Rev.* [*later Sir*] Henry Dudley 3007 [*ed.?*], 3011 [*ed.?*]

Bate, Samuel Stringer 2026

Baxter, *Rev.* Andrew Joseph 614

Bayley, Frederick William Naylor 3237

Baynham, Walter 2019

Beale, Thomas Willert 2428

— *See also* Maynard, Walter 2427

Beard, John 1153, 1158 [*joint author*]

Beatty, Harcourt. *See* Bland, Harcourt

Beauclerk, *Mrs.* D. J. 2429

Bedford, *Rev.* Arthur 345–347, 351, 377

Bedford, Paul John 2430

Bell, Alexander 729

Bell, John Montgomerie 2022

Bell, Robert 225

Bellamy, B. P. 1598

Bellamy, George Anne 2432, 2438

Bellamy, Thomas 897

Bellasis, Edward 2184, 2186
— See also Ancient Actor, An 2180
— See also Old Boy, An 2171, 2175
Bellchambers, Edmund 2560 [ed.]
Bellows, Rev. Dr. Henry Whitney 609
Belton, Fred. 2443
Benedick [i.e. Joseph Reed] 2904
Benger, Elizabeth Ogilvy 3588
Bennett, Charles Frederick 2444
Bennett, Rev. John B. 575
Benson, George 1707
Bensusan, S. L. 4300.1 [ed.]
Benwell, J. M. 1619
Bernard, Charles 2018
Bernard, John 2445
Bernard, W. Baile [afterwards Bayle]
 2445 [ed.]
Bertram, James Glass 731
— See also Paterson, Peter 2446–
 2449
Besant, Walter 976 [introd.]
Best, Rev. Thomas 500–507
Best, William 2459
Bestow, W. 4175 [ed.]
Betson, A. 396
Betterton, Charles 2450, 2451
Betterton, Thomas 829
Beverley, Mrs. Elizabeth 2487–2495
Bickley, Francis 56 note
Bicknell, Alex. 2396 note; 2432
 [ed.]
Binckes, Thomas A. 612
Bingham, Frederick 1675
Binney, Rev. Thomas 577
Birch, Thomas 4054
Bisset, James 2462
Black, Helen C. 2267
Black, William 1984–1992
Blackman, Robert D. 763 [ed.]
Blackmantle, Bernard [pseud. of
 Charles Malloy Westmacott?] 2761
Blanch, William Harnett 2382
Bland, Harcourt [stage name of
 Harcourt Beatty] 610–611
Blathwayt, Raymond 678
Blau, Henry 657, 663
Blind, Rudolf 4244 [joint illustrator]
Blount, Charles 3882
Blunden, Edmund 693 [preface]
Blyth, Harry 3397
Boaden, James 2948 [ed.?], 3055
 [ed.] 3115, 3206, 3536; 3950
Bohemian, The 4506 [ed.]
Bonar, John 1916
Boorman, J. H. 4307 [ed.]
Booth, Junius Brutus 2512
Boschereccio 2812
Bossuet, James [i.e. Jacques] Bénigne,
 Bp. of Meaux 301
Boswell, James, the elder 3978 [joint
 author]
— See also Genius, A 2787
— See also Gentleman of Scotland, A
 3713
Boswell, James, the younger 3299
Bourbon, Armand de 349

Bowden, George 559
Bowen, Cyril 780
Bower, George Spencer [i.e. B., G. S.]
 1058
Boyd, A. S. [i.e. Twym, pseud.] 4500
Boyd, Frank 1853
Boz [pseud. of Charles Dickens] 2967
 [ed.]
Bradley, Charles 4255 [ed.]
Braham 3197
Bramble, Matthew [pseud. of Andrew
 McDonald] 2340
Brandon, Isaac 2070
Brayley, Edward Wedlake 1008,
 1086
Brent, John Frederick [i.e. An Octo-
 genarian Actor, pseud.] 2522
Brereton, Austin 1440, 1520; 2365,
 2366, 3072; 4244 [ed.]
Breval, John Durant [i.e. Joseph Gay,
 pseud.] 3855
Brewer, James Norris 2224
Brewer, R. F. 763 [joint author]
Brickface, Lack-Limb 3931
Bright, Addison 4240 [ed.]
Britton, John 4038
Broadbottom, J. 2282
Broadley, A. M. 969
Bromley, J. 4063 note
Brook, H. G. 1092
Brother, Barnaby 4409 [ed.]
Brown, H. 1546
Brown, John [1747] 1745
— painter [1789] 2068, 2069
— [1819] 719
Brown, Thomas 3016–3018 note
Browne, Edmond 977 [joint author]
Brownsmith, John 809, 810; 1548,
 1681; 2323
Bryan, Alfred 2249
Buchanan, R. C. 762, 769
Bucke, Charles 3835
Buckle, James George 801
Buckstone, George B. 2637 [ed.]
Buckstone, J. B. 609 [introduction]
Bull, John 1208
Bullock, Charles 641
Bullock, Christopher 3905
Bungey, The Rt. Hon. Baron 1322
Bunn, Alfred 548, 552, 558; 2530,
 2532, 2533, 2534, 2950, 3391; 4328
 note [ed.], 4333
— See also Churchman, A 553
— See also Fitzallen, Allen 3551
Burder, George 459
Burghall, J. E. 1362
Burgoyne, General John 2066
Burnand, Sir Francis Cowley 2166
Burnet, Alexander [Atex.] 3903
Burns, Austin 2021 [joint author]
Burridge, Richard 342
Burton, J. G. 2158
Burton, William 1704
Busk, Hans the elder. See Appendix
Buskin, Captain Sock 2162, 2163
 [joint author]

Buskinsocko, Don 1673
Butler, Mrs. Frances Anne. See
 Kemble, Frances Anne
Butler, George 2351
Butler, Henry 4206 [ed.], 4209 [ed.]
Butt, George 2936
Byron, George Gordon Noel, Baron
 1382; 3489

C. 3840
C., A., Gent. 670
C., E. [i.e. Edmund Curll] 2957
C., J. [i.e. Collier, Jeremy] 294
C., T 1727 note, 1730 note
C., T. F. D. 4208 [ed.]
C., W. C. 571
C——d, W. R. [i.e. W. R. Chetwood]
 1339
C——f——d, E—— of 173
Caffaro, Father François 303
Cahuac, J. [i.e. Peregrine Prynne
 (pseud.)] 1399
Caine, Thomas Henry Hall 3061
Calcraft, John William [stage name of
 John William Cole] 580; 1969
Caldecott, Thomas 3944 note
Call Boy, The 2266
Callender, E. Romaine 619
Callow, Alice Mary 2173 [joint
 author]
Callow, Frances Elizabeth 2173
 [joint author]
Calmour, Alfred Cecil 816; 1073
Calvert, Frederick Baltimore 511
Calvert, Walter 3093, 3094, 3582
Cameron, James 1845, 1846
Camidge, William 1708
Camp, Mr. de 1653
Campbell, Hugh 763 [joint author]
Campbell, John 399
Campbell, Thomas 3541
Candid 1610, 1608.1
Candid Hearer, A 4389
Candid Observer of Men and Things,
 A 2859
Candidus [1770] 1938
— [Edinburgh 1802] 1963, 1964
— [1809] 1210
Candlish, Robert S. 516 [ed.]
Capes, Bernard 4240 [ed.]
Capper, Alfred 4299 [joint editor]
Careful Hand, A. 11 [ed.]
Carey, George Saville 697; 2793,
 2890
Carey, Henry 1332; 2035, 2037
Carleton, Henry Seymour 3600
 [ed.]
Carlyle, Alexander 1874, 1881
Carr, J. Comyns 3545
Carruthers, Richard 1118 [joint
 author]
Carson, Charles L. 4249 [ed.]
Cartwright, Robert 1034, 1036
Catcall, Sir Critick 3887
Catchpenny, Christopher 1568
Caustic 1651

Day, W. C. 965
De Camp, *Mr.* 1653
De Leine, M. A. 3369
Dean, J. 81
Deans, *Mrs.* Charlotte 2671
Decastro, Jacob 2672
Dechmann, George 753
Defoe, Daniel 327
Dempster, George 3978 [*joint author*]
Denman, John Doe 573
Dennant, John 471, 472, 476
Dennis, John 308, 370; 2028; 2673 [*joint author*], 2674, 3566, 3569; 3706, 3708, 3812, 4043, 4047
— See also Person of Quality, A 329
Dennistoun, Walter 2009, 2010
Dent, Edward J. 2103 [*ed.*]
Dermody, Thomas [*i.e. Marmaduke Myrtle, pseud.*] 2350
Derrick, Samuel 2847; 3999
Des Champ, François Michel Chrétien 3821
Desbrisay, Theophilus 1776
Descendant of the Barnwell Family, A 3975
Desprez, Frank 4223 [*ed.*]
Dibdin, Charles, *the elder* 846; 1135; 2676, 2677, 2681, 2683; 4091 [*joint editor*]
Dibdin, Charles, *the younger* 1085
Dibdin, James C. 1997
Dibdin, Thomas 2686
Dickens, Charles, *the younger* 3314 [*ed.*]
— *the elder* See Boz, 2967 [*ed.*]
Diddler, Jeremy 910
Diderot, Denis 751 [*trans.*]
Dietz, Ella 954
Digges [John Dudley] West 1860, 1910, 1912, 1946, 2689
Diprose, John 952
Dircks, Henry 782
Dircks, Rudolph 2263; 3800 [*ed.*]
Disbanded Son of Thespis, A 896
Dixon, James Matthias 640
Dodd, Henry 2143
Dodd, James Solas 3100
Dodd, William 2586
Dodsley, Robert 29 *note*
Donaldson, Edmund John [*i.e. Edmund Leathes, pseud.*] 3219
Donaldson, Walter 1814 [*ed.*]
Donaldson, Walter Alexander 2690–2692
Donne, John William 1200
Donne, William Bodham 935
Doran, *Dr.* John 854, 860, 937 [*introd.*]
Douglas, Ernest 4255 [*ed.*]
Douglass, Albert 2200 [*ed.*]
Dowling, James. See Herbert, J. D. 1712
Downes, John 824
Drake, James 324
Dramatic Author, A 2864

Dramaticus [*1816*] 905
— [*1847*] 2023
— [*Leicester 1879*] 3019
— [*1895*] 4310 [*ed.*]
Dramatist, A 815
Drew, Edwin 754; 3083; 4250 [*ed.*], 4255 [*ed.*], 4280 [*ed.*]
Dromio 4384
Drub, Timothy 3911
Drummond, *Rev.* David Thomas Kerr 3560
Drummond, Robert B. 624
Dryden, John 3692, 3695–3696, 3700, 3883, 4023 [*joint author*]
Du Plat, E. A. 62 [*ed.*]
Duff, Andrew Halliday [*i.e. Andrew Halliday*] 2114, 2116 [*joint author*]
Duffy, Henry A. 4298 [*ed.*], 4378 [*ed.*]
Duncan, George 859
Duncan, *Rev.* John 427
Dunce 1824 *note*
Duncombe, William 392 [*translator*]
Dundonald, *Earl of* [*Archibald Cochrane*] 3322
Dunlap, William 2645
D'Urfey, Thomas 311; 3888
— [*pseud. 1727*] 867
Dutton, Thomas 3052; 4093 [*ed.*], 4107 [*ed.*]
Dwight, Timothy 542
Dyer, Robert 2693

E., A. 3829
Earl of —— 3680
Earl, Thomas 3850
Earle, W. 3507 *note*
Easby, John 1621
East, *Rev.* John 583–585
East, Timothy 544
Ebers, John 1484
Edgar, *Sir* John [*pseud. of Sir Richard Steele*] 4068
Edgcumbe, Richard see Mount Edgcumbe
Edina 1914
Editor, The 1941
Edlin, P. H. 1029
Edwards, Henry Sutherland 2090, 2094, 2096; 2694, 3443; 3797
Edwards, Sampson 3674
Edwards, Sutherland. See Edwards, Henry Sutherland
Edwin, John, *the younger* 1630, 1631
Edwin, John Prosser 1648, 1650
Egan, Pierce 2110; 2372; 3467
Egerton, T. 36
Egerton, William [*pseud. of Edmund Curll*] 3384
Egestorff, George 2084
Eglington, Charles 4240 [*ed.*]
Ellerslie, Alma 2709
Elliot, W. G. 2201 [*ed.*]
Elliston, R. W. 196

Elworthy, A. H. [*i.e. Wilde, Professor*] 4242
Eminent reporter, An 1834
Enemy to Imposition, An 2876
Engel, J. J. 710 *note*
English Critic, An 3929
Englishman, An 1411
Ererf, Benjamin 2827
Erle, Thomas William 1095–1097
Erskine, *Hon.* Andrew 3978 [*joint author*]
Estcourt, Richard 2715, 2716
Eutheo, Anglo-Phile. See Anglo-Phile Eutheo
Evans, Henry 786 [*pref.*]
Everard, Edward Cape 2717
Eyre, Samuel 4234

F., A., *barber and citizen* [*pseud. of Charles Lucas?*] 1744
F., E. 2836
F—B—L— 884
Fairfax, Walter 3362
Fairplay 1299
Falstaffe, *Sir* John 4072, 4073
Farrar, J. Maurice 2384
Farren, Robert [*illustrator*] 2181, 2185, 2187–2188, 2197
Faucit, Helena [*Lady Martin*] 2730–2739; addenda
Fayerman, A. T. 4408 [*ed.*]
Feales, W. 22
Fearon, James Peter 3992
Feild, John 343
Fell, Beatrice 644
Fennell, James 1949; 4084 [*ed.?*], 4086 [*ed.*]
Fenton, Elijah 3735
Fenton, W. 1360
Ferguson, Adam 1892
Field, Nathan 1040
Field, Wilford F. 4301 [*ed.*]
Fielding, Henry 2572 *note*, 2609 *note*
Filmer, Edward 304 *note*, 339
Filon, Augustin 983
Finlay, John 2359
Fitzallen, Allen [*pseud. of Alfred Bunn?*] 3551
Fitzball, Edward [*i.e. Edward Ball*] 2756
Fitz-Crambo, Patrick 1340
Fitzgeorge, George 1300
Fitzgerald, Edward 3184
Fitzgerald, Percy Hetherington 758; 862, 943–945 [*joint author*]; 956; 2098; 2122; 2622, 2951, 2974 [*ed.*], 3087, 3208, 3510; 3727, 3731
Fitz-Henery, The *Rev.* 1750
Fitzpatrick, Thaddeus 2871
Fitzpatrick, William John 3343
Fleay, Frederick Gard 1056, 1057, 1062, 1069, 1070, 1080
Fleck, Dudley 2278 [*joint author*]
Flecknoe, Richard 820

Haldane, John 1895, 1896
Halford, J. 581
Hall, C. F. 3846
Hall, Henry Thomas 967; 1589, 1590
Hall, John B. 1844
Halliday, Andrew [*pseud. of Andrew Halliday Duff*] 2114, 2116
Halliwell, James Orchard [*later Halliwell-Phillipps*] 1014 [*ed.*], 1018 [*ed.*], 1031 [*ed.*], 1032 [*ed.*], 1040–1043 [*ed.*], 1047 [*ed.*], 1051 [*ed.*], 1055, 1059 [*ed.*], 1066–1067 [*ed.*]; 1308; 4028 [*ed.*]
Hallucinate, Hannibal 4452 [*ed.*]
Halter-Maker, A [*pseud. of Joseph Reed*] 4013
Ham, James Panton 630, 645
Hambleton, John 3003
Hamerton 4388 *note*
Hamilton, Henry 2729
Hamilton, Walter 863
Hamley, *Sir* Edward 2745
Hamlyn, Clarence 239
Hammerton, *Sir* John Alexander 770 [*ed.*]; 4502 [*ed.*]
Hanley, Peter [*i.e. An old playgoer, pseud.*] 962
Hardinge, George [*i.e. Mr. Owen junior, pseud.*] 3964
Hardy, Robert Burns 2005–2007
Haresfoot and Rouge 738
Harley, George Davies [*i.e. George Davies*] 2465, 3027
— See also H., G. D. 3005
Harper, *Rev.* Thomas 1898
Harral, Thomas 1658; 2469; 3395
Harris, David Fraser 1998
Harris, Henry 1305
Harris, Thomas 1082, 1166, 1171 [*joint author*] 1177, 1188, 1298
Harrison, Charles 2178
Harrison, Elizabeth 3909
Hart, William Henry 3002 [*ed.*]
Hartley, David 1500
Harvest, George 3012, 3013
Harvey, Daniel Whittle 456
Harvey, Francis 737 *note*; 850; 3508; 3745 *note*
Haslewood, Joseph 2212 *note*
— See also Gabble, Gridiron 2274
Hatchett, (William?) 3892 *note*
Hatton, Joseph 3077, 3079, 3223, 3590, 3593
Haweis, Hugh Reginald 631
Hawkins, Frederick W. 3167
Hawkins, Thomas 991
Hawkins, W. 3984
Hawkins, William 3764
Hawk's-Eye 3786
Haxell, Edward Nelson 1104
Haydn, Joseph T. 4429 [*joint editor*]
Hayes, Daniel 2303
Hayley, William 3721
Hayter, John 3176, 3403
Hayward, *Mr.* 420

Hazlitt, William 909 *note*; 3041 [*ed.*]; 3770
Hazlitt, William Carew 1045 [*ed.*], 1072 [*ed.*]; 3772 [*ed.*]
Headlam, Stewart Duckworth 628, 647, 673; 2125
Headlam, *Mrs.* Stewart [*i.e. Beatrice R. Headlam*] 646
Heard, William 3763
Heath, Charles 2086 [*ed.*]
Heatton, Michael 1627 [*joint author*]
Hedelin, Francis 3701
Heidegger, John James 356
Henderson, Andrew 3264
Henderson, William [*1796*] 704
Henderson, William [*1899*] 4383 [*ed.*]
Henry, D. 3676
Henslowe, Philip 1019
Heraud, John Abraham 925; 2525; 4209 [*ed.*]
Herbert, J. D. [*pseud. of James Dowling*] 1712
Herbert, Thomas 918
Herbert, William 1084 [*joint author*]
Herford, Charles Harold 861
Herman, Henry 2280
Herondo, F. [*pseud. of Frank A. Swallow*] 672
Hervey, *Lord* John 2582, 2583
Heywood, Thomas 268
Hiatt, Charles 3098, 3583
Hibbert, Henry George 4306
Hibbs, *Rev.* Richard [*i.e. Clericus, M.A., pseud.*] 603–604
Hibernicus 3668
Hiffernan, Paul 885; 2907; 3900; 4077 [*ed.*]
— See also Philo-Technicus Miso-Mimides 2794–2796
Hill, *Mr.* 2002
Hill, Aaron 681, 683 *note*, 721; 2033; 4075 [*ed.*]
Hill, Benson Earle 3034
Hill, *Dr.* [*later Sir*] John 174; 683; 1146, 1147; 2868; 3878
Hill, *Mrs.* P. 3035
Hill, *Sir* Richard 1685
— See also Gentleman of the University of Oxford 407
Hill, *Rev.* Rowland 422, 430, 437, 441, 453
Hillington, E. H. 4401 [*ed.*]
Hippisley, John, *Junior* [*i.e. A student of Oxford, pseud.*] 3711
Hitchcock, Robert 1709
Hodder, George 938
Hodson, Henrietta 3037
Hodson, James Shirley [*i.e. An old stager, pseud.*] 730; 2176
Hodson, William 3717
Hogarth, George 2082
Hogarth, John 3284
Hogg, Wentworth 813 [*ed.*]
Holbrook, Ann Catherine 3039, 3040

Holcroft, Thomas 2808, 3041; 4100, 4101 *note*
Hollingshead, John 230; 955; 1107; 1424, 1492; 3046
Holloway, Laura C. 3370
Holman, Joseph George 1182
Holmes, R. B. 498
Holtum, J. 3048
Hone, William 1003; 3485 *note*
Hook, Theodore Edward 3174 [*ed.*]; 3933
Hoole, John 3656
Hopkins, Albert Allis 786
Hopkins, Charles 314
Horatio 3691
Horne, Richard Hengist 3342 [*ed.*]
Horneck, Anthony 379
Horner, *Rev. Mr.* 2608
Hotten, John Camden 3468 *note*
Hough, Peter 3049
Houlton, Robert 1364
Hounsell, Bernard 4321 [*ed.*]
Houston, James 3050
Howard, Cecil 2498 [*joint author*]; 4244 [*ed.*]
Howard, Frederick, *Earl of Carlisle* 789
Howard, Henry 2856
Howe, J. B. 3051
Hubard, Willcocks 715 *note*
Hubert, Philip G. 773
Hudibras the younger 553.1
Hudson, William Henry 669
Hughes, Charles 1136; 3834 [*ed.*]
Hughes, Frederick 2279
Hugman, John, *junior* 474
Hull, Thomas 1547
Hum, Humphrey 1406
Hume, Sophia [*i.e. S.H.*] 413
Humphreys, R. 2672 [*ed.*]
Hunt, James Henry Leigh 3768, 3805; 4157 [*ed.*], 4159 [*ed.*]
Hurn, William 563
Husk, W. H. 3579 [*ed.*]
Hutchings, William 1696, 1698
Hutton, Laurence 2516 [*ed.*]

I., F. M. [*i.e. Frederick Maitland Innes*] 1977
Idler, An 1563
Ignotus [*pseud. of John Chater*] 415
Impartial Hand, An [*pseud. of Samuel Johnson*] 3832
— Observer, An 2470
Independent An 457
Ingleby, Clement Mansfield 1044
Inglis, Ralston 1848
Innes, Frederick Maitland [*i.e. F.M.I.*] 1977
Intimate Acquaintance, An 3618
Ireland, John 3025 [*ed.*]
Ireland, Samuel 3939, 3942–3944,
Ireland, William Henry 3940, 3945–3949
Ireson, *Brother* Frank 1061

Littleton, R. H. 3282

Littlewood, William Edensor 632

Lloyd, Evan 2908

Lloyd, Robert 689; 2304; 2869

Lloyds, F. 783

Lobb, Theophilus 400

Lockman, John 385 [*translator*]; 1453; 2052

Lockwood, E. 4308 [*ed.*]

Lodge, Thomas 253

Logan, William Hugh 1849 [*ed.*]; 1983; 2689 [*joint editor*], 3272; 4462 [*ed.*]

— See also Spitfire, Peregrine 1978–1982

Longbow, *Signor* 1237

Longinus [*pseud. of Thomas Sheridan*] 2889 *note*

Lonsdale, Mark 1511

Lord —— 1384

Louther, Hal 1491

Love, James 3240

Lover of Harmony, A 3844

— of Truth 2505

Loveridge, G. A. 1493

Lowe, Robert William 1; 856 [*ed.*]; 2295 [*ed.*]; 2458, 2564 [*ed.*]; 3062 [*joint author*]; 3774 [*joint editor*], 3805–3806 [*joint editor*]

Lowndes, W. 41

Loyd, Rev. *See* Lloyd, Robert

Lucas, Charles [*i.e. A Freeman/A. F., barber and citizen, pseuds.*] 1737, 1744

Lumley, Benjamin 1450; 3244

Lun, *Junior* [*pseud. of Henry Woodward?*] 2590

Lund, Thomas William May 4006

Lunn, Henry C. 2087

Luntley, John 3614 [*ed.*]

Luppino, T. 1460 *note* [*joint author*]

Lyddal, David 714

Lyne, Augustus Adolphus 649

Lynn, [Richard A.] Neville 760; 970; 2195 [*ed.*]

M——, *Capt.* 3114

M., A. 1559

M., E. 2003

M., E. H. [*i.e. Elizabeth Harriett Mair*] 3543

M[c] D., J 600

M., G. [*joint author*] 906

M., H. 1980 *note*

M., H. D. [*i.e. Henry Downes Miles*] 1523

M., J. 3868

Macaroni, A. [*pseud. of —. Taylor?*] 2327

M'; Mc: *names beginning with the prefix M' or Mc are arranged as if written Mac*

Macarthy, Eugene 210; 541

Macauley, Elizabeth Wright 3245–3252

Macchetta, Blanche Roosevelt Tucker 2095

McCready, William 1649

McCulla, V. 458

M'Debit, John [*pseud.*] 1888

M'Dermot, Martin 3723

McDonald, Andrew 2340

MacDonald, *Rev.* John 600, 606

McGee, T. B. 1713

MacHumbug, Leonard [*pseud. of Leonard McNally?*] 1806

Mackintosh, Matthew [*i.e. An Old Stager, pseud.*] 3253

Macklin, Charles 1789; 2829, 2831, 3261; 3918 *note*

— See also Citizen of the World, A 3262

Mackney, E. W. 3271

MacLaughlin, Emily 759

MacLaurin, John [*Lord Dreghorn*] 1871, 1876, 1894, 1901 *note*

McLoughlin, Charles 1789

McMoral, Archibald 2768

McNally, Leonard. See MacHumbug, Leonard 1806

— See also Plunder 2929

M'Nicoll, David 537, 543

Macready, William, *the elder* 1649

Macready, William Charles 1412

Mad Bull, A 1290

— Tom [*pseud. of — Sowerby*] 1291

Madan, Rev. Martin [*i.e. Anti-Profanus, pseud.*] 2780

— See also Minister of the Church of Christ, A 2776

Maddison, Robert 1151

Magnum Bonum, Alexander [*i.e. Alexander Webster*] 1866, 1890

Maidment, James 1983 [*joint editor*]; 2689 [*joint author*], 3272 *note*

Mair, Elizabeth Harriett. See M., E. H. 3543

Maitland, J. A. Fuller- 2100

Major, John 1189

Malkin, Benjamin Heath 3743

Mallet, William 2640

Malone, Edmond [Edmund] 993; 3955

Man of the World, A 572

Manager of the Theatre 1860

Manchester Layman, A 629

Mangin, *Rev.* Edward 1561; 3504

— See also X.Y.Z. 1553

Manners, Nicholas 431

Mansel, Robert 485, 508

Manton, H. 1574

Mapleson, James Henry 3301

Mara, Samuel Delaval 1634–1647

Marriott, William 1012

Marshall, Frank Albert [*i.e. An Irvingite, pseud.*] 3074

Marshall, Thomas 2239

Marston, *Dr.* John Westland 1695; 2255

Martin, H. 3196

Martin, *Sir* Theodore 2740; 3787; 4462 [*ed.*]

Marvel, Sedgley 1445

Marx, W. P. 1091

Mason, Thomas Monck 1487

Mason, William 3982

Massinger, Philip 4 [*joint author*]; 990

Mathews, *Mrs.* Anne 2238; 3303.1, 3307, 3309

Mathews, Charles, *the elder* 3312

Mathews, Charles James *the younger* 115 [*ed.*]

Mathews, John 3315

Mathias, Thomas James 1472; 3483; 3741

— See also Junior, Mr. Owen [*pseud.*] 3964; 3966

Matthews, Brander 3799 [*ed.*]

Maurel, Victor 2097

Maurice, David Samson [*joint author*] 1118

Maxfield, C. W. 4505 [*ed.*]

Mayall, John Edwin 2242 [*illustrator*]

Mayer, Marcus L. 3790

Mayhew, Edward 814

Maynard, Walter [*pseud. of Thomas Willert Beale*] 2427, 2428

Mc: *Names beginning with the prefix Mc are arranged as if written Mac*

Mears, William 13–18

Medley, Mat. [*pseud. of Anthony Aston*] 2394

Megson, William Broadley [*i.e. Trim, pseud.*] 3636

Melmoth, Courtney [*pseud. of Samuel Jackson Pratt*] 2920

Melmoth, William 348

Member of the Church of England, A 555

— of the Club 1683

— of the Company of Players, A 3255

Mercator 555

Merion, Charles 650

Merlin, *The Countess de* 3297

Merrick, *Dr.* 2054

Merritt, John 2477

Meyler, William 1551; 2922

Middleton, Thomas 4 [*joint author*]

Milbourne, Luke 314 *note*

Miles, Henry Downes 1523; 2975

Miles, William Augustus 3907

Miller, David Prince 3335–3337

Miller, James 2106

Miller, John 1540

Miller, Samuel 403 *note*

Mills, Crisp [*pseud. of Christlob Mylius*] 3918

Milman, Constance Angelena [*later Lady Arbuthnot*] 2192

Milne, John 620

Mingotti, Regina 3340–3341

Minister of the Church of Christ, A [*pseud. of Rev. Martin Madan?*] 2776, 2783.1

Mr. Neither-Side 1346

Mitford, *Rev.* John [*1812*] 1002

Mitford, John [*1856*] 1028

Moculloch, Philim 3350

Moffat, *Rev.* William 404 [*joint author*]

Molloy, Joseph Fitzgerald 862.1; 1714; 3168, 3463 [*ed.*], 3662

Monney, William 907

Moore, George 975

Moore, Mark 1537

Moore, Peter 1391, 1392, 1396

Moore, Thomas 2160; 3488, 3499

— See also Little, Thomas [*pseud.*] 3148

More, Hannah 2913

Morell, Thomas 2300

Morgan, *Lady. See* Owenson, Sydney

Morgan, J. G. 469 *note*, 477 [*joint author*], 479, 480 [*joint author*]

Morgan, MacNamara 3372

Morison, John 562

Morley, Henry 3784

Morris, James 1852

Morris, Mowbray Walter 3791

Morris, *Rev.* William 528

Mortimer, Albert 517

Moscrop, Hugh 2193 [*ed.*]

Mosely, Benjamin Lewis 3352, 3357

Möser, Justus 2109

Motteaux, Peter Anthony 303

Mottley, John 28

— *See also* Jenkins, Elijah 3339

Mount Edgcumbe, Richard, *Earl of* 2073; 2155

Mountfort [Mountford], William 3345

Mozeen, Thomas 3346

Mr.: The title 'Mr.' is arranged as if written Mister.

Mudford, William 2661

Munday, Anthony [*i.e. Anglo-Phile Eutheo, pseud.*] 255

Munden, Thomas Shepherd 3348

Munro, Thomas [*i.e. Oxoniensis, pseud.*] 898

Murphy, Arthur 2305, 2306; 2942

Murray, Alma 3356

Murray, Lindley 486; *addenda*

Murray, W. H. 1984; 3366

Mursell, Arthur 655

Mylius, Christlob [*i.e. Crisp Mills, pseud.*] 3918

Myrtle, Marmaduke [*pseud. of Thomas Dermody*] 2350

Naldi, Guiseppi 1115

Nantz, Frederic Coleman 574

Nash, George 3724

Nathan, Isaac 3294

Navarro, *Madame de. See* Anderson, Mary

Neither-Side, *Mr.* 1346

Nettle, Humphrey [*pseud. of William Jackson*] 2807

Neville, Henry 763 [*joint author*]; 946

Neville, Thomas 3983

New Renter, A 1386

Newton, Henry Chance 968

Newton, Wilson 4299 [*joint editor*]

Niblett, F. Drummond 3082

Nichols, J. B. 2651 [*ed.*]

Nichols, John 4069

Nicholson, John 3997

Nick-All, J.* 1433

Nipclose, *Sir* Nicholas [*pseud. of Francis Gentleman*] 2325

No-Body, Nicholas 3516

Non-Juror, A 3859

Norman, *Mr.* 1717

Northbrooke, John 243

Northcott, Richard 2062

Norton, Theodore 570; 3166

Nosworthy, Louisa [*i.e. A Lady Amateur Actress of Manchester, pseud.*] 618

O., R. N. [*i.e. Robert Nugent Owenson*] 1822

O—, *Mrs.* S— 371

O., S. [*i.e. Sydney Owenson*] 1819

O.P., An 1255

O.P. Amateur, An 1301

O'Blaney, Murdoch 2880

O'Blunder, Mrs. Sharp-Set [*pseud. of Mrs. Elizabeth Franchett*] 2653

O'Bryan, Daniel 3645

Observer, An 587

Octogenarian, An 3507

Octogenarian Actor, An [*pseud. of John Frederick Brent*] 2522

O'Foggerty, Paddy 1199

Ogilvie, Geo. 1855

O'Keeffe, John 3373

Old Actor, An 2512.1

— Amateur, An [*i.e. Earl of Mount Edgcumbe*] 2073

— Boy, An [*pseud. of Edward Bellasis*] 2171, 2175

— Comedian, An 2923

— Croney, An 2702

— Man of the Town, An 2881

— Playgoer, An [*1875*] 1419

— — [*pseud. of Major General Samuel Parlby, 1850*] 930

— — [*pseud. of Peter Hanley, 1883*] 962

— Stager, An [*pseud. of James Shirley Hodson, 1851, 1881*] 730; 2176

— — [*pseud. of Matthew Mackintosh, 1866*] 3253

— —, The [*1884*] 2182

Oldmixon, John 325

— *See also* Wilson, Charles 2642

Oldys, William 829 [*joint author*]

Oliphant, *Mrs.* Margaret 3509

Oliver, *Rev.* George 1013

One of His Majesty's Servants 3323

— of the Proprietors 3276

— of the Public [*pseud. of Frederick Guest Tomlins*] 212

— that Whistles in the Wood 1560

— who Dares 1254

— who Knows All About It 2823

O'Queer, Simon 1893

Oracle, *Sir* [*pseud. of William Robertson?*] 4500 [*ed.*], 4503 [*ed.*]

Ordish, Thomas Fairman 1109

O'Reilly, Robert Bray 1464

O'Rorke, J. 1843 [*joint author*]

Orton, *Rev.* Job 423

Ottley, Henry 2742

Otway, *Mr.* 220

Oulton, Walley Chamberlain 37 [*ed.*]; 843, 844; 2215; 3961

Owen, *Mr., junior, see* Junior, Owen

Owen, Charles 355 *note*

Owenson, Robert Nugent [*i.e. O., R. N.*] 1822

Owenson, Sydney [*afterwards Lady Morgan*] 1819

Oxberry, *Mrs.* Catherine 4139 [*joint author*]

Oxberry, William 4139 [*joint author*]

Oxberry, William Henry 919 [*joint author*]; 2229, 2240, 2275; 4184 [*ed.*]

Oxoniensis [*pseud. of T. Munro*] 898

P., A. 2780 *note*

P., I 557

P., J. 3149, 3157

P., R. 1454

Pack, James 3392

Padwell, Peter 3905

Paget, Alfred Henry 1048, 1071

Paget, William 3393

Painter, A 766

Palmer, Edwin P. 4271 [*ed.*]

Palmer, John 186; 699 [*ed.*]

Panglos, Peter, *ed.* [*1807*] 2664

Pangloss, Peter [*1805*] 2481

Paragraph, Peter 2792

Park, A. J. 2127 [*joint author*]; 2198 [*joint editor*]

Parke, Walter 2199

Parke, William Thomas 2078

Parker, Edward 3912

Parker, George 3398, 3399

Parkes, Joseph 556

Parkinson, Richard 3296

Parlby, *Major-General* Samuel [*i.e. An old playgoer, pseud. 1850*] 930

Parry, Edward Abbott 3270

Parsons, Samuel 3402

Partington, C. F. 1524

Partridge, Simon 3678

Pascoe, Charles Eyre 2252; 4244 [*ed.*]

Pasquin, A., Anthony [*pseud.*] 2346

W., Mr., of Edinburgh 2654
W., A. [i.e. A spectator] 4064
W., B. W. 936.1
W., C. 906 [joint author]
W., H. [i.e. Edward Purdon] 2865
W., J. [i.e. Shem, pseud.] 4503 note [ed.]
W., J. F. [i.e. J. F. White] 3634
W., P. 357
W., S. 1793
W——e, W——m, a[dvoca]te 1875
Waddington, I. 4343 [ed.]
Waddington, J. 4352 [ed.]
Wag, Walter 1401
Wagner, Leopold 739, 772, 819; 2120; 3612
Wait, William Piguenit 564
Waldron, Francis Godolphin 825 [ed.], 848; 996, 997; 1674; 3953; 4091 [joint editor]
Walker, Charles Clement 1076
Walker, Joseph Cooper 1710
Walker, Rev. V. 634
Walkley, Arthur Bingham 3802
Wallace, Lady Eglantine 4058
Wallace, Ellen 3275
Wallace, John 2128, 2129
Wallett, William Frederick 3614
Wallis, Dorothy 976
Walwyn, B. 3719
Wappineer, A 4011
Ward, Adolphus William 1049
Ward, Edward 1509
Ward, Valentine 531
Ware, Samuel 792
Warnecke, Joach. 2109
Warner, George Frederic 56
Warner, Mrs. Mary Amelia 1516
Warner, Richard 2884
Waters, Edmund 1474 [ed.], 1475, 1482
Watkins, Ben William ["B.W.W."] 936.1
Watkins, John 3494
Watson, James [i.e. A Townsman, pseud.] 1615; 4385
Weatherly, Frederic E. 233 [joint author]
Weaver, John 2105
Webb, F. [i.e. Philalethes, pseud.] 3958
Webster, Mr. [pseud. of Dr. Francis Reynardson] 3736
Webster, Alexander. See Magnum Bonum, Alexander
Webster, Benjamin 929 [ed.]
Webster, Rev. George Edis 592
Weddell, Mrs. 4060
Wedderburn, Alexander 1899
Weeks, James Eyre 682
Wells, Mrs. Mary. See Sumbel, Mrs. Mary Wells
Well-Wisher, A 387

Wemyss, Francis Courtney 3623
Werenfels, Samuel 392
West, James 3624–3627
West, Joshua 1365
Westmacott, Charles Malloy [i.e. Bernard Blackmantle, pseud.] 2761
Wewitzer, Ralph 45; 3629, 3630
Whackum Smackum 2309
Whalley, Thomas Sedgwick 3522
Wheatley, Henry Benjamin 1068; 2995 [ed.], 3000
Whincop, Thomas 28
Whip, Spur, Lash, & Co. 4467 [eds.]
Whitbread, Samuel 1369 [ed.], 1393
White, G. 1188
White, J. F. [i.e. W., J. F.] 3634
White, James 3956
White, W. 1112
Whitefield, Rev. George 2776 note
Whitehead, Charles 2968 [ed.]
Whitehead, Paul 1336 [headnote]
— See also Scriblerius Tertius [pseud.] 875 note
Whittington, G. D. 1001
Whyte, Edward Athenry 1804
Whyte, Frederic 983 [translator]; 2268
Whyte, Samuel 1803, 1804
Wightwick, George 3635
Wilde, Professor [i.e. A. H. Elworthy] 4242
Wilkes, Thomas 882
Wilkinson, Robert 1084 [joint author]
Wilkinson, Tate 3637–3641
Wilks, Robert 1321
Wilks, Thomas Egerton 578
Willan, James Nathaniel 3085
Willett, Edward 2442
Williams, David 2897
Williams, Henry Llewellyn 2386
Williams, J. M. 4103 [ed.]
Williams, James 232 [introduction]
Williams, John [i.e. Anthony Pasquin, pseud.] 2332–2335, 2347; 2420, 2703
Williams, John Ambrose 3202
Williams, Michael 1102
Williamson, David 3440 [ed.]
Willis, Richard, Bishop of Winchester 316
Wills, Freeman [later Freeman Wills Croft] 3648
Wilmot 2743
Wilson, Charles [pseud. of John Oldmixon?] 2642
Wilson, F. A. 1409
Wilson, Frank 3359
Wilson, George 1705
Wilson, H. Schütz 3475; 4005
Wilson, John 1749

Wilson, Mrs. Margaret Cornwall Bar[r]on- 2360; 3227 [ed.], 3330
Wilson, T. Walter 4244 [illustrator]
Wilson, William 2024, 2025
Winstanley, Eliza 3649
Winston, James [i.e. A Theatric[al] Amateur, pseud.] 1538, 1539
Wisgast, Wilfrid [pseud. of George Sexton] 4215 [ed.]
Witherspoon, John 402, 404
Witt. Criticism 3868
Wizard, Philomath 1388
Wodrow, Ernest A. E. 804
Wolcot, John [i.e. Peter Pindar, pseud.?] 3739
Wolfe, Francis R. 1715
Wood, Mrs. Henry 2116 [joint author]
Wooddeson, William Fane 3777
Woodward, George Moutard 2484; 3952
Woodward, Henry 3671
— See also Lun Junior [pseud. of Henry Woodward?] 2590 note
Woodward, Jos. 333 note; 1503 note
Woty, William 881, 889; 2310
Wright, James 822; 2558 note
Wright, John 635
Wright, William Aldis 3184 [ed.]
Wrighten, Mrs. Mary 3682
Wronghead, Paul 4076 [ed.]
Wroughton, Richard 183
Wyatt, Benjamin 1367, 1377, 1390
Wyatt, George 795
Wyatt, John [i.e. A Friend to Consistency, pseud.] 3954
Wyndham, Percy 3324

X.Y.Z. [i.e. Rev. Edward Mangin?] 1553

Y., B. 1345
Y., G. 1652
Y.Z. 2866
Yate, W. 602
Yates, Edmund Hodgson 3309 [ed.], 3685–3688
Yeats, W. B. 4323 [ed.]
Yorick [pseud. of Sir Henry Irving?] 3064
Young, —. [i.e. Simplex, pseud.] 2803
Young, Archibald 806
Young, Julian Charles 3689, 3690 note
Young Lady, A 1731
Young, Mary Julia 2657
— See also Lady A 2341
Young, Thomas 3527
Younger, Joseph [i.e. Smoke'em, pseud.] 1568

Z., A. 449

SHORT TITLE INDEX

Arrangement of titles follows, with a few exceptions, the Filing Rules for the dictionary catalogs of the Library *of Congress, 1956 edition.*

Title headings: works with titles headed by brief phrases (e.g. Covent Garden Theatre, By permission of . . . etc.) are filed under title heading, not under main title, except for statements of price or edition which are ignored.

Subsequent editions: Only the item number of the first edition is noted, except where there is any substantial change in title.

Periodicals: periodicals with identical titles are filed chronologically according to date, irrespective of subtitle. Periodicals precede books with identical titles. Subtitles are normally excluded, except in the case of identically titled periodicals where all known variations are noted.

Public office, Bow Street Tuesday, March 5th, 1839. £100 reward. [*1839*] 3609

Public office, Bow-Street. Whereas great riot and disturbances have taken place at Covent Garden Theatre [*1809*] 1269

Public undeceived, The 2683

Published by request — An address upon the claims of the drama 609

Pulpit and the stage, The [*by Dixon (1879?*)] 640

Pulpit and the stage, The. Four lectures [*by Ham (1878)*] 630

Pulpit justified, and the theatre condemned, The 583

Punch and Judy 2109.1

Punch and puppets 2118.1

Punch's address to the public 1930

Punch's petition to Mr. S——n 1747

Punch's real history 2109.4

Pursuit after happiness 2914

Queen Elizabeth, Croydon, and the drama 1080

Queen Street ghost, The 2000

Queens of song 2241

Queries addressed to the town 1931

Queries to be answered by the manager of Drury-Lane Theatre 1341

Queries upon Queries 1342

Questions on the art of acting 755

Quick's whim 3435

Quid pro quo, A 1664

Quin's jests 3439

Quiz album for 1883 4500

Quizziology of the British drama, The 927

Race, The 2315 *note*

Random recollections [*by Ganthony (1898)*] 984

Random recollections of an old actor [*by Belton. 1880*] 2443

Random recollections of an old playgoer, The [*by Flynn 1890*] 1718

Random recollections of the stage [*by an old playgoer, i.e. Hanley, (1883)*] 962

Random records 2633

Random scenes from the life of a Manchester green-coated school-boy 1621

Rape of Joseph, The 2760

Rational enquiry concerning the operation of the stage, A 537

Rational Rosciad, The 884

Reader, or reciter, The 705

Real friends of Kean and the drama, The 3154

Real Macbeth, The 3084

Reappearance of Miss Foote 2765

Reason versus passion 1254

Reasons for the repeal or amendment of the laws affecting theatres 226

Reasons of Mr. Joseph Hains the player's conversion, The 3016

Reasons why David Garrick, Esq; should not appear on the stage 2866

Rebellion; or, all in the wrong, The 1270

Rebuilding Drury-Lane Theatre 1369

Recantation and confession of Doctor Kenrick, L.L.D., The 2907

Recollections and reflections of J. R. Planché, The 3424

Recollections and wanderings of Paul Bedford 2430

Recollections of an actor 2691

Recollections of Ayr theatricals from 1809 1852

Recollections of Fred Leslie 3224

Recollections of the Italian Opera 2081

Recollections of the life of John O'Keeffe 3373

Recollections of the mess-table and the stage 2663

Recollections of the past 3543

Recollections on the scenic effects of Covent Garden Theatre 1307

Recollections political, literary, dramatic and miscellaneous of the last half century 934

Record in suspension and interdict John Henry Alexander 2012

Record of a girlhood 3179

Records of later life 3181

Records of my life 920

Records of the Dundee stage 1853

Reed's cheap edition 3146, 3151

Reflections: by Mrs. E. B., comedian 2493

Reflections of a gentleman in the country 1743

Reflections, of a moral and political tendency 1323

Reflections on a favourite amusement 362

Reflections on Mangora 3990

Reflections on several of Mr. Dryden's plays 4025

Reflections on the innocence and usefulness of the stage 420

Reflections on the principal characters in the Provoked Husband 3865

Reflections on the stage, and Mr. Collyer's defence of the Short View 325

Reflections upon declamation 831

Reflections upon reading the tragedy of Hecuba 4061

Reflections upon reflections 4062

Reflections upon theatrical expression in tragedy 688

Reformer admonished, The 558

Refutation of the "Apology for actors", A 272

Regulation of music halls, The 2121

Regulations instituted of good order in the Theatre Royal, Drury Lane 1403

Regulations to be observed by the company of the Theatre-Royal, Edinburgh 1976

Reid's London entertainment guide 4281

Reinforcement of the reasons, A 383

Rejected addresses, The 1387

Rejected passages in the unlicensed tragedy of Alasco 4031

Relation of public amusements, The 609

Relations of the drama to real life, The 3734

Relative value of the acted and the unacted drama, The 3725

Reluctant appeal of Mrs. R. Jackson, The 3101

Remarkable adventures of Reuben Rambler 1606

Remarkable trial of the Queen of Quavers, The 2065

Remarks, occasioned by the perusal of a pamphlet 536

Remarks on a play, call'd *The Conscious Lovers* 4047

Remarks on an article inserted in the papers of the Shakespeare society 1027

Remarks on an historical play, called, The fall of Mortimer 3892

Remarks on Miss Mitford's tragedy of *Rienzi* 3986

Remarks on Mr. Colman's preface 3192

Remarks on Mr. John Kemble's performance of Hamlet and Richard the Third 3196

Remarks on Mr. Johnson's company 1679

Remarks on Mr. Lee's letter to Mr. Sheridan 1769

Remarks on Mr. Mason's Elfrida 3983

Remarks on Mr. Rowe's Tragedy of the Lady Jane Gray 3752

Remarks on the character of Richard the Third 3193

Remarks on the Italian opera in Edinburgh 603

Remarks on the Memoirs of Tate Wilkinson 431

Remarks on the morality of dramatic compositions 607

Remarks on the new tragedy, call'd the Roman father 4064

Remarks on the present state of the English drama 933

— [1849]/And playgoers' companion 4200

Theatrical monitor, The 4080

Theatrical monopoly 1358

Theatrical museum, The Appendix

Theatrical note-book, The 4332

Theatrical notes 3803

Theatrical observer, The [periodical] [Glasgow 1820] 4475

— [1821–76] 4126

— [Dublin 1821–22]/The original theatrical observer 4430

— [Dublin 1821–23]/Nolan's Theatrical observer 4431

— [Norwich 1827] 4408 note

Theatrical Paul Pry 4195.1

Theatrical pocket book, A 45

Theatrical poems 910

Theatrical portrait, The 3523

Theatrical portraits [ca. 1780] 2329

Theatrical portraits, epigramatically delineated [by A Macaroni 1774] 2327

Theatrical portraits; with other poems [by Van Dyk 1822] 2357

Theatrical programme, The [periodical] [1849]/And entr'acte/And playgoers' companion 4200

— [1873] 4234

— [1884–6]/A weekly newspaper and guide to theatres/A weekly guide to theatres 4259

Theatrical public guide, The 4320

Theatrical record, The 4461

Theatrical recorder, The 4100

Theatrical records: or, an account of English dramatic authors 29

Theatrical register, The [periodical] [York 1788]/Containing candid and impartial strictures 4418

— [1838]/And general amusement guide 4174

Theatrical register; or, complete list of every performance at the different theatres for the year 1769, The [1770] 1081

Theatrical remembrancer, The 36

Theatrical repertory, The 4095

Theatrical review, The [periodical] [1763]/Or annals of the drama 4079

— [1807] 4101

— [1849–50]/And author's miscellany; a monthly journal of the stage [subtitle varies] 4201

Theatrical review: being remarks on favourite performers, The [1787] 2339

Theatrical review: for the year 1757, The [1758] 3755

Theatrical review; or, new companion to the play-house, The [by a society of gentlemen 1772] 3762

Theatrical rod!, The 4162

Theatrical sketches, drawn from life 2235

Theatrical speaker, The 712

Theatrical spectator 4127

Theatrical speculum, The and musical review 4459

Theatrical squabbles 2514

Theatrical tattler, The 4336

Theatrical taxation 1277

Theatrical tears 1822

Theatrical tickler 4409

Theatrical times, The [periodical] [1846–49]/A weekly magazine of Thespian biography 4188

— [1883–84]/A journal devoted to amateur & professional news 4261

Theatrical trip for a wager !, A 3429

Theatrical visitor, The 4485

Theatrical world, The [periodical] [ed. Caverly 1881–1882]/An international journal of the dramatic and musical profession 4253

— [ed. Archer 1894–98] 4306

Theatricals and tableaux vivants for amateurs 2178

Theatricals. Dramatic and musical items 4301

Theatricals, 45 years ago 3635

Theatrum illustratum 1084

Theatrum redivivum 282

Theatrum triumphans 283

"Their majesties' servants" 854

Theophilus Cibber, to David Garrick, Esq. 2617

Thespiad, The [1809] 2352

Thespiad: a poem in answer to the author, The [1804] 1823

Thespiad, The. By the author of All the Talents [by Barrett 1816] 2355

Thespian, The [periodical] [Liverpool 1821] 4360

— [Bristol 1823] 4347

Thespian and dramatic record, The 4211

Thespian censor, The 4446

Thespian critique, The 4445

Thespian dictionary; or, dramatic biography of the eighteenth century, The [1802] 42

Thespian dictionary; or dramatic biography of the present age, The [1805] 43

Thespian magazine, The 4088

Thespian mirror, The 1608

Thespian oracle, The 701

Thespian papers, The 970

Thespian preceptor, The 717

Thespian review, The 4388

Thespian sentinel, The 4142

Thespian telegraph, The 4092

Thespis on tryal 670

Thespis: or, a critical examination into the merits of all the principal performers belonging to Covent-Garden Theatre 2321

Thespis: or, a critical examination into the merits of all the principal

performers belonging to Drury-Lane Theatre 2318

Thespis to Apollo 1806

3d July 1811 1370

Third theatre. The argument of Randle Jackson, Esq. 195

Third theatre. We trust that there can be but one opinion 198

Thirty-five years of a dramatic author's life 2756

Thirty years at the play 3801

Thirty years passed among the players of England and America see Appendix

This, and every evening 1203

This day is published, Broad Hints at Retirement 1264

This is the house that Jack built 1237

Thistle, The 4482

Thomas Betterton 2458

Thoughts on Familiar Epistles 1820

Thoughts on the cause of discontent in Foote's prologue 2796

Thoughts on the entertainments of the stage 426

Thoughts on the late disturbance at the Theatre-Royal, Newcastle 1629

Thoughts on the theatre 591

Thoughts upon the present condition of the stage 789

Three celebrated plays of that excellent poet Ben Jonson, The 23

Three letters by T. H. Lacy 514

Three original letters to a friend in the country 2881

Three plays: with a preface, including dramatic observations 3721

Three poems: I. Siddons 3528

Tim Tell-Truth on the state and influence of the acting drama 538

To all maiors, sheriffs, justices 151.1

To be sold. A very unique collection of original letters 131

To David Garrick, Esq; the petition of I 2868

To diabebouloumenon 1322

To Edmund Kean, Esq. 3134

To George Colman, Esq. 1438

To His Majesty's Worshipful Justices of the Peace 161

To John Philip Kemble, Esq. 3201

To Miss Kelly 3173

To Mr. Junius Brutus Booth 2505

To opera and theatrical managers 112

To Philo-Thespis. Acrostick 1669

To R. W. Elliston, Esq. on his becoming lessee 1402

To Rivers 1666

To the editor of the Bath theatrical review 1554, 1555

To the editor of the "Observer" 1667

INDEX OF PLACES OF PUBLICATION

Excludes London. Semi-colons between item numbers denote change in subject grouping (e.g. books on the morality of the stage will be found within the number sequence 243–679; theatre arts within the sequence 680–819; periodicals within the sequence 4068–4506, etc. (See Table of Contents.)

2745, 2766–2767, 2781, 2797–2803, 2839, 2911, 2998, 3050, 3062, 3064, 3086, 3161, 3212, 3240, 3263, 3272, 3366–3367, 3421–3422, 3471, 3530, 3535, 3543, 3560, 3614, 3691; 3713, 3742, 3747, 3765, 3770, 3927, 3931, 3974; 4443–4473, 4495

Glasgow 401–403, 421, 601, 603–604, 610–611, 677; 859, 932, 941; 1848, 1971, 2000–2020; 2061; 2447, 2459, 2472–2473, 2575, 2579, 2597–2598, 2755, 3003, 3050, 3062, 3064, 3253, 3335, 3471, 3565, 3623; 3714; 4472, 4474–4505

Paisley 591, 617; 2003; 4506

Stirling 608; 3557–3558